Managing
Attention
Deficit
Hyperactivity
Disorder
in Children

Managing Attention Deficit Hyperactivity Disorder in Children

A Guide for Practitioners

Second Edition

Sam Goldstein, Ph.D.
Michael Goldstein, M.D.

CONTRIBUTIONS BY

Clare B. Jones, Ph.D.
Lauren Braswell, Ph.D.
Susan Sheridan, Ph.D.

John Wiley & Sons, Inc.
New York • Chichester • Weinheim • Brisbane • Singapore • Toronto

This book is printed on acid-free paper. ∞

Copyright © 1998 by John Wiley & Sons, Inc. All rights reserved.

Published simultaneously in Canada.

This publication is designed to provide accurate and authoritative information in regard to the subject matter covered. It is sold with the understanding that the publisher is not engaged in rendering professional services. If legal, accounting, medical, psychological or any other expert assistance is required, the services of a competent professional person should be sought.

Library of Congress Cataloging-in-Publication Data:

Goldstein, Sam, 1952–
    Managing attention deficit hyperactivity disorder in children : a
guide for practitioners / by Sam Goldstein, Michael Goldstein :
contributions by Clare B. Jones, Lauren Braswell, Susan Sheridan.—
2nd ed.
      p.   cm.
    Rev. ed. of: Managing attention disorders in children / Sam
Goldstein, Michael Goldstein. ©1990.
    Includes bibliographical references and index.
    ISBN 0-471-12158-4 (cloth : alk. paper)
    1. Attention-deficit hyperactivity disorder. I. Goldstein,
Michael, 1945– . II. Jones, Clare B. III. Braswell, Lauren.
IV. Sheridan, Susan M. V. Goldstein, Sam, 1952– Managing
attention disorders in children. VI. Title.
    [DNLM: 1. Attention Deficit Disorder with Hyperactivity—therapy.
WS 350.8.A8 G624m 1998]
RJ506.H9G652   1998
618.92′8589—dc21
DNLM/DLC
for Library of Congress   97-36626

Printed in the United States of America.

10 9 8 7 6 5 4 3 2 1

For Janet, Allyson, and Ryan.

To the memories of my father-in-law, Lawrence Kirsh, from whom I learned that one can never work too hard, and Dr. Dennis Cantwell, whose life exemplified that motto.

S. G.

For my wife Barbara and my children Rachel, Elizabeth, and Adam.

M. G.

Of course, you can argue with the proposition that all we are is . . . genes and environment. You can insist that there's . . . something more. But if you try to visualize the form this something would take, or articulate it clearly, you will find the task impossible, for any force that is not in the genes or the environment is outside of physical reality as we perceive it. It's beyond scientific discourse . . . this doesn't mean it doesn't exist.

—Robert Wright

Children do not learn by sitting passively in their seats listening to the teacher, anymore than they learn to swim by sitting in rows on a wharf watching grown-up swimmers in the water.

—Pulaski

I paid attention to everything but the teachers.

—Woody Allen

Contributors

Susan M. Sheridan, Ph.D.
University of Utah
Salt Lake City, Utah

Lauren Braswell, Ph.D.
Bloomington, Minnesota

Clare Jones, Ph.D.
Developmental Learning Associates
Phoenix, Arizona

Michael Gordon, Ph.D.
SUNY Health Science Center
Syracuse, New York 13210

Foreword

Revisions of a standard text always provide opportunities for reflection. Since the original publication of *Managing Attention Disorders in Children,* how much progress have we made in the field of ADHD? Do we have a better grasp of the disorder's underlying nature? Are our diagnostic methods more reliable or valid? How far have we come in establishing treatment programs that are effective, safe, and cost-efficient? Are we better able to target which children will likely benefit from a specific therapeutic approach? How far have we moved beyond suppositions based on clinical experience to facts based on good science?

When you read this comprehensive review of the ADHD arena, you will undoubtedly be impressed by how much this field has evolved and by the sheer volume of research at our disposal. But, inevitably, you will also note that much has indeed stayed the same. Our diagnostic methods and strategies have been reasonably consistent over time. And, despite all the empirical studies, critically important topics have gone largely ignored, especially in the areas of educational methods, family functioning, and adult variants of the disorder.

What are the major changes in the field since the first edition of this fine book? The most prominent development is our increased appreciation of ADHD's neurobiological underpinnings. With the advent of more refined neuroimaging techniques, we are developing a much clearer picture of the brain's role. Studies in molecular genetics have also confirmed that ADHD is a family affair; indeed, this behavioral disorder rivals hair color in its inheritability. Consequently, discussions of etiology more often veer away from highlighting environmental factors as predominating.

Alongside this greater appreciation of biology's contributions lies a deeper understanding of ADHD's place within the general matrix of mental health disorders. Not long ago, most researchers and clinicians talked about ADHD as if it existed in an orbit of its own, far away from the pull of other psychopathologies. Now we realize that comorbidity is far more the rule than the exception. From what I can observe, practitioners more commonly adopt an integrative view in which ADHD is one component within a constellation of other factors. The benefit is that treatment programs are more likely to be tailored to a child's panorama of needs rather than to the presence or absence of one symptom cluster.

At the conceptual level, two ideas have taken a firmer hold: The first concerns the dimensional nature of this disorder. Nowadays we are more apt to view ADHD as a trait gone awry than as a unitary disease entity that emerges like diabetes or cancer. Conceptualizing ADHD as a point along a continuum of human characteristics, in my opinion, has had a positive influence on the field, especially on diagnostic practice. Why? Because, as practitioners, we are less prone to assume that we can divine the presence of ADHD the way one might, for example, detect pregnancy. As a result, we've developed a healthier respect for inherent limitations in our quest for diagnostic precision, and we are thus forced to address the real potential for overdiagnosis, under-diagnosis, and misdiagnosis.

Second, our field is refocusing on behavioral disinhibition as the driving force behind the manifestation of ADHD symptoms. Thanks to new theories and ample research, we have come to realize that what separates ADHD children from other children (normal or otherwise) is rooted more in poor self-control than in impaired attention per se. We have also developed a much finer appreciation for how severe impulsiveness can throw a youngster off the many paths that normally lead to reasonable adjustment. In fact, the relative incapacity to delay is emerging as the major culprit behind the broad mosaic of an ADHD child's deficits.

Although theory and diagnosis have made discernible advances over the past ten years, I am not sure the same can be said for treatment. We certainly have not witnessed the emergence of new and dramatically more powerful psychosocial interventions. If anything, we have become more circumspect about touting the potential benefits of non-medical strategies. As a field, we also seem more comfortable acknowledging that pharmacotherapy, when handled well, represents the most likely source of relief for those who suffer from this disorder.

To any observer of our field, the most visible change has been in our recognition that ADHD symptoms often persist into adulthood. Compelling evidence that ADHD tends not to disappear by puberty has fueled an explosion of interest in adult forms of the disorder. Perhaps by the next revision of this book, scientific research will replace the barrage of clinical speculation that currently runs rampant.

Having now offered these broad conclusions and sweeping generalizations, I would simply like to congratulate the Drs. Goldstein on their Herculean efforts to integrate research findings with practical suggestions. Given the enormous scientific literature and the sprawl of clinical strategies, they have demonstrated a remarkable level of energy and talent in producing a significant work.

MICHAEL GORDON, PH.D.
SUNY Health Science Center

Syracuse, New York

Preface

Changes in juvenile crime since 1995, including a doubling of the homicide rate, a doubling of the number of homicides committed with guns, and a doubling of the arrest rate of non-Whites for drug offenses followed a period of relative stability in these rates (Blumstein, 1995). Although the juvenile drug industry, particularly the use of crack cocaine, has been suggested as in part contributing to these factors, it is likely that many other elements play a contributing role. On Friday, February 17, 1995, a fourteen-year-old boy and his schoolmate allegedly shot and killed the boy's mother in an ambush as she walked into the house. The boys were quickly arrested by authorities. It was believed they had plotted to kill this woman because her son was dissatisfied with his restrictions. She died from several shotgun blasts. In the aftermath, it was learned that her son was frequently teased, abused, and aggressed against at school. It was also subsequently learned that this young man had a history of attention deficit hyperactivity disorder (ADHD).

In the preface to the first edition of this volume, we cited Keith Conners's observation that ADHD appears to be a disorder marked by contradictions, uncertainty, the unexpected, and the bizarre. It is a disorder that over the past eighty years has been referred to by at least thirty descriptive terms. In 1990, we noted that despite an increasing volume of research literature, scientists and clinicians were still in disagreement about both the specific cause of ADHD and the best course of treatment. The field, we wrote, "continues to be plagued by marked differences of opinion as to the cause, definition, evaluation and treatment" (p. vii). In 1993, Helsel and Fremer suggested that the great confusion that existed in the field of ADHD was likely due to the absence of a general theory to explain the disorder. These authors suggested that "without a theory to pull together these facts, there is little hope that they will have any practical utility" (p. 44). As Whalen (1990) noted, thousands of articles to that date had been published, and there appeared to be a trend toward more. Research interests ranged across the spectrum, including cause, symptom description, comorbid conditions, etiology, and treatment. Recent publications have noted the thousands upon thousands of studies directly addressing ADHD as well as additional thousands in which ADHD is cited or included (Resnick & McEvoy, 1994). In fact, our personal observation over the past year suggests that peer-reviewed articles directly dealing with ADHD are being published at a rate of twenty to thirty each month; there is even a new journal devoted to the topic (*Journal of Attention Disorders*).

As we discuss in the opening chapter, problems with attention, including descriptions of impetuousness and extreme fixation, were perhaps first described in the Bible but clearly described as reflecting human temperamental variations by the 1500s (Pico della Mirandola, 1930). Among the more humorous suggestions is that the English marionettes Punch and Judy and the Italian marionette Punchinello may be based on descriptions of impulsive and hyperactive children (Accardo & Whitman, 1991).

Yet, for every two steps forward in increasing our understanding and ability to help children with ADHD in many arenas, we take one step backward. Despite growing acceptance that the disorder exists worldwide, ADHD continues to be conceptualized by scholars as a "North American illness." Arguments ensue not when descriptions of the disorder are provided, but when etiology is discussed. That is, there is consensus among the world's scholars and clinicians that some children present as impulsive, hyperactive, and inattentive and do not respond consistently to consequences. Yet from that point forward, the intellectual debate heats up. Italian psychiatry suggests that the origin of attention deficit is traced to mother-child relationships, sometimes linked with mental illness of the mother. It is hypothesized through psychoanalytic models that children with ADHD do not progress beyond "a depressive phase and maintain schizophrenic type mental mechanisms" (Polacco, Casella, & Condini, 1992, p. 15). In Great Britain, where inroads have been made in accepting that ADHD represents a biological disorder rather than an environmentally caused problem, the latter position is still held by the majority. A recent BBC program about these children, though providing fairly accurate information, was titled *Little Monsters.* In a 1994 survey, it was estimated that the use of stimulant medication among children in the United Kingdom was at .0003%. Nearly 45% of pediatricians polled felt sleep disturbance was necessary for a diagnosis of attention deficit, 80% to 85% felt that hyperactivity was almost always necessary, and 70% to 80% felt impulsivity was necessary. The majority used behavior modification as a primary source of treatment; 15% of pediatricians had never used stimulants, 70% had no children under their care receiving stimulant medication, and only 1% had more than twenty children receiving stimulants (Kewley, Facer, & Scott, 1994). The resistance primarily among the European countries to accepting ADHD and developing a consensus definition at times is difficult to understand; we hope that the publication of this text will play a part in improving the situation.

There is no doubt that in the United States, great progress in understanding, evaluating, and treating ADHD has been made much more quickly. Converging lines of evidence have changed the focus of this disorder from inattentiveness to a failure to inhibit or delay behavioral responding consistent with impulsivity (Barkley, 1994; Trommer, Hoeppner, & Zecker, 1991; Van der Meere & Sergeant, 1988). Data have also suggested that right frontal aspects of brain functioning are implicated in the disorder (Zametkin et al., 1990). Assessment has begun to focus on obtaining data in natural settings, although the use of computerized measures to evaluate laboratory analogues of real-life behavior has continued to gain popularity. The first edition of this text noted these assessment tools and what was at that time their emerging use in the diagnostic process. Paper-and-pencil tasks were also reviewed in depth. This edition, however, based on multiple sources of research data, looks more closely at the importance of history and observation and spends less time on the value of laboratory measures in making the diagnosis of ADHD.

On the treatment front, significant gains have been made in the recognition of behavior management and educational and medical interventions. In 1989, the first comprehensive statement on ADHD specifically directed at educators was published suggesting that children with ADHD are eligible for and should receive supportive services in school based on their diagnosis (Parker, 1989). Subsequently, ADHD was determined to be a handicapping condition under the Individuals with Disability Education Act or under Section 504 of the Americans with Disabilities Act. The National Education Goals 2000: Educate America Act (1993) emphasized the importance of partnerships between parents and schools to promote children's social, emotional, and academic growth. The U.S. Department of Education (1994) has reiterated the importance of parents playing an active role in their children's education, including the education of children with specific disabilities.

On the medical front, although stimulants continue to be the treatment of choice for ADHD, a number of alternative classes of medications have been researched; some have yielded promising results, and others, such as clonidine, increasingly find their way into the clinical treatment of children with ADHD. Many other classes of substances are in the process of being researched, including the novel use of nicotine patch for treatment of adult ADHD. Alternative treatments, including the use of EEG biofeedback, to treat ADHD have gained popularity in some circles. For this reason, this text has added a chapter covering controversial treatments, defined herein as treatments proposed or marketed beyond their proven worth.

Perhaps one of the most dramatic steps forward in the field has been the increasing interest over the past ten years in the treatment of adult ADHD and the recognition that symptoms of ADHD may have developed as evolutionary adaptations extending throughout the lifespan (Hartmann, 1993; Jensen, Mrazek, Knapp, Steinberg, Pfeffer, Schowalter, & Shapiro, 1997). The first author has published a text specifically devoted to the subject of adult ADHD (S. Goldstein, 1997b). Nonetheless, well-controlled adult research represents only a small part of the research literature on ADHD. The number of trade texts published on the disorder concerning adults likely outnumbers texts for clinicians at this time by a ratio of 10 to 1. Clinicians, however, are well aware that although medications may be effective for adults with ADHD, the childhood treatment model simply may not work effectively for them; adults with ADHD are more than just larger bodies with the same problems.

The past two decades have brought rapid and widespread changes in the conceptualization of children's circumstances and the nature of childhood. It is still unclear, however, how the numerous social, emotional, and related environmental factors children are exposed to impact their current and future lives. This has forced researchers and clinicians alike in the field of ADHD to face a hard reality: symptom relief is not synonymous with long-term outcome. That is, the field has well demonstrated that combinations of medication, education, parent training, and general behavior management are effective for relieving symptoms of ADHD; however, in most studies, they do not appear to alter the life course for these children: treated and untreated, a similar percentage progresses to more serious adolescent and adult problems. Researchers and clinicians have begun to recognize that factors that predict good life outcome for all children are even more important in predicting good outcome for children with any type of behavioral, emotional, or developmental risk, including ADHD. We have come to recognize that symptoms of ADHD act as a catalyst. Place these children in a protective, nurturing environment, and although they may cause problems, no one would call them the "twentieth-century equivalent of the devil." However, place a child with ADHD in a chaotic, high-risk setting, and those qualities of ADHD act catalytically to further worsen that child's outcome. Thus, we argue in this text that successful treatment of ADHD requires a balance between symptom relief and building in protective factors that enhance resilience, defined as the capacity to recover from stress and lead children to successful transition into adulthood. Children with ADHD are at higher risk for developing long-lasting problems affecting social relationships, academics, and adult life as well as psychiatric symptoms (Brooks, 1994). Increasingly, it is recognized that factors within families are critical to building in resilience. Physical or emotional separation from parents leads to a lack of securely based attachment and may further contribute to the negative outcomes children with ADHD experience (Heinicke, 1995). Two issues, poverty and domestic violence, are worth mentioning briefly in this preface to make the point that treatment for ADHD alone in the absence of other protective factors is not enough.

Nearly 20% of children in the United States now live in poverty. In 1960, the rate was nearly 27%; by the end of the decade, poverty had dropped to 14%; then began to increase in the 1970s, intensifying during the recession of the 1980s. U.S. poverty rates are about twice as high as in most other industrialized nations (Danziger & Danziger, 1993).

Poverty very clearly affects children's development. Problems related to low birth weight, infant mortality, contagious diseases, and childhood injury and death are greater in poor families (Klerman, 1991). Poor children are at risk for developmental delays and poor school achievement. Even in the absence of ADHD they tend to have lower average levels of school-related skills than nonpoor children. Their progress in school is slower and more subject to termination from drop out (Ramey & Campbell, 1991). They have relatively higher rates of social, emotional, and behavioral problems, including anxiety, social withdrawal, aggression, delinquency, lack of self-esteem and self-efficacy, and psychological distress (McLloyd & Wilson, 1991). By the adolescent years, these problems impinge on the larger society in the form of juvenile crime, early pregnancy, and school drop out (Garbarino, 1992). It is important to note that although many children raised in poverty are at risk for problems, not all succumb. Thus, although poverty is a risk factor complicated by higher rates of other negative elements in poverty-level homes, some children manage to overcome adversity.

It has been estimated that 25% to 30% of American women are beaten at least once in the course of intimate relationships (Pagelow, 1984). Nationwide surveys have demonstrated that nearly one-eighth of husbands in the United States commit one or more acts of physical violence against their wives each year, and one-fifth to one-third of all women are assaulted by a partner or ex-partner during their lifetime (Strauss & Gelles, 1990). In many communities, over half the calls for police assistance are the result of domestic disturbances. How much of this violence occurs in the presence of children is unknown. However, it has been estimated that at least 3.3 million children witness physical and verbal spousal abuse each year, including behaviors ranging from insults and aggression to fatal assaults with guns and knives (Jaffee, Wolfe, & Wilson, 1990). In homes where domestic violence has occurred, children are physically abused and neglected at a rate fifteen times higher than the national average (Massachusetts Coalition of Battered Women Service Groups, 1995). Several studies have found that in 60% to 75% of families where a woman is battered, children are also battered (Bowker,

1988). Relatively little research is focused on the effects of domestic violence on children's emotions, behavior, and development (Zuckerman, Augustyn, Groves, & Parker, 1995). However, there have recently been studies to suggest that young children exposed to domestic violence are more likely to exhibit emotional distress, immature behavior, and somatic complaints and in fact regress in toileting and language skills (Bell, 1995; Osofsky & Feinichel, 1994; Pynoos, 1993). Posttraumatic stress symptoms have been reported in children exposed to domestic violence (Osofsky, Cohen, & Drell, 1995), and among school-age children a greater frequency of externalizing as well as internalizing behavioral problems in comparison to children from nonviolent families (Bell, 1995; Bell & Jenkins, 1991; Margolin, 1995). Overall, it has been suggested that the general functioning, attitude, social competence, and school performance of children exposed to domestic violence is negatively affected (Jaffee, Wolfe, Wilson, & Zak, 1986). By the adolescent years, exposure to family violence may be yet another precipitating factor leading children toward delinquent and conduct-disordered problems (Bell & Jenkins, 1991; Pynoos, 1993).

Again, however, it is important to reiterate that not all children exposed to violence in the home progress to serious problems. We believe research has demonstrated that treatment for problems that may arise as the result of environmental risk in themselves are insufficient to insulate children from negative life outcome. In this text, we take a "balanced approach." We advocate that children with ADHD need to be identified at early ages and their symptoms treated through a combination of medication and educational and behavioral interventions. However, we agree with Brooks (1994) that if one has to "swim in a larger sea of dysfunction," one needs "larger islands of competence" (p. 552). We suggest that there must be a balance between treatments to relieve symptoms of ADHD and affording children with ADHD the opportunity to build islands of competence by providing them with protective factors related to school, friends, and family. We argue that what is good for all children is critical in the developing lives of children with ADHD.

Like its predecessor, the second edition of this text is directed to practitioners faced with the task of evaluation, guidance, and management of ADHD in children. As the field has grown and expanded, so too has this text. It is our intention to offer the practitioner a comprehensive volume providing a research-based understanding of ADHD, a model for assessment, and, most important, clear, well-defined guidelines for multidisciplinary treatment. In a number of other texts (S. Goldstein, 1995, 1997; Goldstein & Goldstein, 1990; Ingersoll & Goldstein, 1993), we have, with colleagues, made a conscientious effort to distinguish science from nonscience and to distinguish nonsense from either of these. We continue to believe that well-controlled research is necessary if practitioners are going to be able to make reasoned and reasonable decisions concerning the children entrusted to their care. We have come to view this text as a work in progress; even with its publication, researchers continue to generate information that we add to our knowledge base and incorporate into our clinical care. It is our hope and intent that this volume plays an important role in what we believe to be the most common yet complex disorder across the life span.

SAM GOLDSTEIN, PH.D.
MICHAEL GOLDSTEIN, M.D.

Acknowledgments

We wish to thank our colleagues Lauren Braswell, Clare Jones, and Susan Sheridan for their scholarly and thoughtful contributions to this text.

This marks the seventh text by either or both of us to which Sarah Cheminant has contributed her efficient management and tracking of our research library as well as her thorough indexes, and Kathleen Gardner has contributed her editorial, organizational, management, and secretarial skills. Their faithful efforts allow us to focus on crafting the text rather than managing what is our largest clinical volume.

S. G.
M. G.

Contents

Part One

BACKGROUND AND ETIOLOGY

Chapter 1

INTRODUCTION AND HISTORY

Over the past fifty years, the childhood cognitive and behavioral problems categorized as disorders of attention, impulsivity, and hyperactivity have presented a clinical challenge for the practitioner. This symptom constellation referred to as Attention Deficit Disorder or Attention Deficit Hyperactivity Disorder or ADHD (APA, 1994) has become one of the most widely researched areas in childhood and adolescence, with an increasing emphasis throughout the adult life span. This literature has been described as "oceanic in breadth if not always so in depth" (Munoz-Mallan & Casteel, 1989, p. 699). For over thirty years, problems arising from this constellation of symptoms have constituted the most chronic childhood behavior disorder (P. Wender, 1975) and the largest single source of referrals to mental health centers (Barkley, 1981a). It has been suggested that children with ADHD may comprise as much as 40% of referrals to child guidance clinics (Barkley, 1990a). In clinic-referred settings, males outnumber females 6 to 1. In epidemiological or community-based studies, the ratio is 3 to 1 (Barkley, 1990a). The higher clinic ratio for males has been suggested as a function of the greater prevalence of other disruptive problems such as oppositional defiance and conduct disorder in boys with ADHD (Breen & Barkley, 1988).

The cluster of problems defining ADHD constitutes one of the most complex disorders of childhood. Even now, as clinicians worldwide utilize the diagnostic symptoms of inattention, hyperactivity, and impulsivity as a hallmark for the diagnosis, researchers and clinicians alike recognize that for the majority of affected children, impulsiveness represents the core deficit. Problems with impulsivity affect children's interactions with all areas of their environment and result in their inability to meet situational demands in an age-appropriate fashion (Routh, 1978). Children with ADHD typically experience difficulty with home, school, and community behavior involving peer interaction, academic achievement, general behavior, and emotional adjustment. They are frequently enigmatic to their parents and teachers. Their uneven, unpredictable behavior is a function of knowing what to do but not always doing it. Clearly, their problems result from inconsistent performance rather than inefficient learning. This almost magicianlike quality of behavior—now you see it, now you don't—adds additional stress for parents and teachers and has led to the erroneous belief that these are problems of motivation and desire rather than neurologically based disabilities.

ADHD problems typically cause significant and pervasive impairment in a child's day-to-day interaction with the environment. The familial, social, and academic demands placed upon children are primarily determined by the adults in their lives. Restless, impulsive, or inattentive adults can modify their lives so as to minimize the negative impact of these problems; this may be the primary reason for the long delay in recognizing that for many individuals these qualities of childhood continue into adult-hood. Unfortunately, children cannot modify their environments and may not be as effective in using compensatory strategies. It is also now recognized that symptoms of ADHD have a significant impact on a child's emerging personality and cognitive skills. Although it was once suggested that the majority of children outgrow the core symptoms associated with attention deficit (Gittelman, Mannuzza, Shenker, & Bonagura, 1985; Weiss & Hechtman, 1986), even as early as 1979 Bellak suggested that these may represent lifelong problems. Recent research very clearly reflects the significant and pervasive impact symptoms of ADHD have on the majority of affected children as they enter their adult years (for review, see S. Goldstein, 1997a). It is now accepted that years of ineffective interaction with the environment and an inability to meet the expectations of one's surroundings result in a long history of negative inter-action with others. This in turn becomes a major force on the child's emerging person-ality (P. Wender, 1979). A child experiencing years of negative feedback, negative reinforcement, and an inability to meet the reasonable demands of family, friends, and teachers will certainly be affected for life. It has been well recognized that the daily, even small successes children experience significantly contribute to their resilience and capacity to deal with life stress (Werner, 1994); for children with ADHD, such successes may be few and far between. Practitioners today must not only be concerned with the core symptoms of this disorder and their impact on childhood but with the sig-nificant, secondary impact these problems have on children's current and future lives as well as on their family members.

THE NATURE OF ADHD

Through the mid-1980s many children affected with ADHD went unreferred, undiag-nosed, and untreated. Their problems were suggested as reflecting poor motivation, in-effective parenting, or simple disobedience. The rate of referral for these problems has increased, as reflected in the dramatic increase in the use of stimulant medications for the treatment of ADHD symptoms (Safer, Zito, & Fine, 1996). Some have suggested that perhaps the pendulum has swung in the other direction, resulting in inappropriate diagnosis and treatment for ADHD in children whose inattentive or impulsive problems result from other disruptive or nondisruptive disorders (M. Gordon, 1996). Nonethe-less, despite increasing recognition of potential misdiagnosis, the trend continues. By the time a child is referred, the practitioner is frequently presented with a complex set of problems that are often affected by a variety of social and nonsocial factors. Evalu-ation is complicated by the fact that there continues to be no critical diagnostic test for ADHD. This fact is not the result of lack of effort on the part of clinicians but reflects the complex interaction of ADHD symptoms with environmental factors.

There are few exclusionary developmental criteria and no unequivocal, positive de-velopmental markers for the diagnosis of ADHD (Conners, 1975a). ADHD appears to be distinct from other disorders of childhood because it is the intensity and persistence and the clustering of symptoms rather than the presence or absence of symptoms that confirms the diagnosis (Ross & Ross, 1982). In many ways, ADHD reflects an exag-geration of what is normal behavior. Either too much (e.g., fidgeting) or not enough (e.g., lack of impulse control or attention) of what adults expect in certain settings results in complaints of problematic behavior. Finally, we are able to recognize that ADHD is not an age-limited disorder. The majority, if not all, children with ADHD continue to experience some degree of symptomatic problem into adulthood, with likely as many as one-third to a half experiencing a lifetime set of ADHD problems (Biederman, Faraone, Spencer, & Wilens, 1993; Biederman, Milberger, Faraone, Guite, & Warbourton, 1994) and a very high rate of comorbid psychiatric disorders. The prevalence of ADHD in the adult population is estimated at approximately 4% (Murphy & Barkley, 1996).

Our understanding of ADHD has been marked by contradictions, uncertainty, the unexpected, and at times the bizarre (Ross & Ross, 1982). Perhaps because complaints of inattention, impulsiveness, restlessness, and general noncompliance are the most common made by parents, the popularity of ADHD as an explanation for children's problems has increased dramatically over the past ten years. Nonetheless, symptoms of ADHD do not represent a new phenomenon. Over the past 100 years this cluster of problems has been referred to by a multitude of descriptive terms. In the very early 1900s, the disorder was referred to as a defect in moral control or Still's disease (Still, 1902). Such terms as postencephalitic disorder, hyperkinesis, minimal brain damage, minimal brain dysfunction, hyperkinetic reaction of childhood, attention deficit disorder with and without hyperactivity, and attention deficit hyperactivity disorder are the most familiar to the practitioner. There continues to be disagreement in terminology. Recent literature has argued that perhaps ADHD would be best labeled a reward system dysfunction (Haenlein & Caul, 1987), self-regulatory disorder (Kirby & Grimley, 1986), or a learning disability (McGee & Share, 1988). More recently, the work of Russell Barkley and others has led to an increasing consensus that the core deficit for the majority of children receiving the diagnosis of combined ADHD may be faulty inhibition. In fact, it may be that when the *DSM-V* appears in the future, the combined type of ADHD may be reconceptualized as an impulse disorder.

ADHD is a disorder that confronts many practitioners, including physicians, psychologists, educators, social workers, speech pathologists, physical therapists, and, in increasing numbers, attorneys. The last group have found themselves representing parents attempting to advocate for their children, primarily in educational settings but increasingly with adults in vocational and legal settings (for review, see Latham & Latham, 1995). For years, each discipline worked in general isolation, developing its own set of definitions, ideas for assessment, and interventions. This has created and continues to create problems in communication among disciplines. First, the laboratory definition of attention is clearly very different from the clinical definition. Second, a psychologist's definition of appropriate attention may be very different from an educator's. Problems persist even within the field of mental health, where there are marked differences of opinion as to the cause, definition, evaluation, and best course of treatment for ADHD. Even practitioners with diverse backgrounds and opinions will agree that in every classroom there are some children for whom sticking to classroom activities, managing their impulses, and controlling the movement of their bodies is problematic. Controversy usually centers around the cause of this problem and then, not surprisingly, the solution.

The definition of ADHD is not immune from this controversy. Despite an increasing and enormous volume of research literature (Resnick & McEvoy, 1994), the precise definition of ADHD continues to be debated. In fact, many clinicians are embracing the concept of ADHD as an impulse disorder and focusing their evaluative search for symptoms primarily in this area. Differing views of the disorder, not surprisingly, causes inconsistent identification of ADHD in various research studies and even clinical settings. This makes it difficult if not impossible to compare the outcomes of these studies (Rie, 1980). This problem is particularly evident each time the American Psychiatric Association modifies the *DSM* criteria for the clinical diagnosis of ADHD. For the interested reader, Appendix A contains a sample of literature reflecting the trend in research articles concerning subjects, measures, findings, and conclusions for ADHD.

A HISTORICAL OVERVIEW

Early Citations: The Quest for Cause

St. John the Baptist provides what may be the earliest report of any symptom traditionally related to ADHD. Luke 1:41 cites John describing fetal hyperactivity as "the babe leapt in her womb." There are allusions in many of the great, early civilizations to these childhood problems. The Greek physician Galen was reported to prescribe opium for restless, colicky infants (Goodman & Gilman, 1975). In 1845, Hans Hoffman wrote "The Story of Fidgety Philip" (Papazian, 1995):

Let me see if Phillip can
Be a little gentleman;
Let me see, if he is able
To sit still for once at table;
Thus Papa bade Phil behave;
And Mamma look'd very grave.
But fidgety Phil,
He still won't sit still;
He wriggles,
And giggles,
And then, I declare,
Swings backwards and forwards
And tilts up his chair,
Just like my rocking horse;—
"Philip! I am getting cross!"

See the naughty, restless child
Growing still more rude and wild,
Till his chair falls over quite.
Philip screams with all his might,
Catches at the cloth, but then
That makes matters worse again.
Down upon the ground they fall,
Glasses, plates, knives, forks and all.

How Mamma did fret and frown,
When she saw them tumbling down!
And Papa made such a face!
Philip is in sad disgrace.

Where is Philip, where is he?
Fairly cover'd up, you see!
Cloth and all are lying on him;
He has pull'd down all upon him.
What a terrible to-do!
Dishes, glasses, snapt in two!
Here a knife, and there a fork!
Philip, this is cruel work.
Table all so bare, and ah!
Poor Papa, and poor Mamma
Look quite cross, and wonder how
They shall make their dinner now.

In this poem, the hyperactive, impulsive symptoms that today are recognized as the most debilitating of ADHD symptoms are very accurately described along with their consequences. This poem also sets the tone for these problems as stemming from naughtiness. Thus, it is not surprising that in 1902 George F. Still described Still's disease, a problem he characterized as resulting from a defect in moral control, which he defined as "the control of action and conformity with the idea of the good of all" (p. 1008). Still noted that this problem resulted in the child's inability to internalize rules and limits, as well as in a pattern of restless, inattentive, and overaroused behavior. Picking up on the prevailing thought developed in the 1890s that inattentive, restless, and overaroused behavior exhibited by brain-injured individuals he suggested that these children had experienced brain injury that had caused some type of brain damage or dysfunction, Still associated these defects in moral control with a broad impairment in intellect. He suggested that the general aim of behavioral excess in these children was self-gratification. However, Still was extremely insightful, noting that this pattern of behavior could have resulted not only from injury, but from heredity or environmental experience. He observed that the disorder occurred more frequently in males than in females, something that he believed did not occur by chance. He was also quite pessimistic, believing that these children could not be helped and should be institutionalized at an early age.

In 1917 and 1918, following a world outbreak of encephalitis, health professionals observed that there was a group of children physically recovered from the encephalitis but presenting a pattern of restless, inattentive, impulsive, easily overaroused, and hyperactive behavior not exhibited before their illness (Hohman, 1922). It was thought that this pattern of behavior resulted from some type of brain injury caused by the disease process and was described as postencephalitic disorder (L. Bender, 1942). Bender's description of the disorder suggested that the site of damage was in the brain stem.

Kahn and Cohen (1934) inferred a common causality to these problems based on the observations of similar symptomatology across groups of affected individuals. These authors speculated that the surplus of inner impulsion or organic drivenness was the consequence of damage to the brain stem. They described individuals whose hyper-kinesis was secondary to known signs of brain stem dysfunction.

From 1930 through the 1940s, behavior disorders with excessive motor activity as a primary symptom continued to be strongly associated with the hypothesis of brain damage or dysfunction. Charles Bradley, at the Emma Pendleton Bradley Home in Providence, Rhode Island, initiated the first of a series of studies that eventually spanned forty years and greatly influenced the field of ADHD. Bradley and colleagues used dextroamphetamine to treat children with syndromes of cerebral dysfunction or organic brain syndrome (Bradley, 1937). These children had been diagnosed with behavioral symptoms attributed either to encephalopathy or to difficulties at birth. Bradley documented improvements in a variety of tasks in 60% to 75% of these chil-dren (Bradley, 1937, 1950; Bradley & Bowen, 1940, 1941). He noted the lack of rela-tionship among specific diagnosis, level of intellectual functioning, and improvement in general functioning in the classroom. In 1937, Bradley attributed improvement in the changed emotional attitude of these children toward their academic tasks to the drug treatment.

At about the same time, Molitch and Eccles (1937) investigated the effects of Ben-zedrine on intelligence scores in children. These authors too noted that although intelli-gence did not improve, general behavior, compliance, and learning appeared to improve.

World War II afforded researchers the opportunity to study a wide variety of war wounds, including trauma to the head by various means (K. Goldstein, 1942). It was discovered that injury to any part of the brain frequently resulted in a pattern of inat-tentive, restless, impulsive, and overaroused behavior. This research supported the notion that children with this pattern of problems were victims of some form of brain damage or dysfunction. At the same time, Strauss and his colleagues (Strauss & Kephart, 1947; Strauss & Lehtinen, 1947) hypothesized that the core problem for these children was distractibility. Strauss believed that if distractions were kept to a minimum, these children would function much better (Strauss & Kephart, 1955). This led to the introduction of the minimal stimulation classroom in which teachers wore drab colors, the room remained undecorated, and windows were frosted; a special cur-riculum was also developed. The research literature, however, has never supported this type of intervention as significantly benefiting distractible, impulsive, or inattentive children (Sarasone, 1949).

Laufer and Denhoff (1957), a psychiatrist and a pediatrician working at the same facility as Bradley, are credited with the first behavioral description of the hyperac-tivity syndrome, although Rosenfeld and Bradley (1948) first described the syndrome with an identified cause nine years earlier. Bradley defined the primary characteris-tics of hyperactive syndrome as involving short attention span, dyscalculia, mood labil-ity, hyperactivity, impulsiveness, and poor memory. Rosenfeld and Bradley (1948) attributed these symptoms to the effects of asphyxiant illness in infancy or the seque-lae of anoxia or hypoxia at birth. They also thought that later-occuring illnesses, such as pneumonia, could precipitate this change in brain function. It was their impression that these problems reflected nonspecific dysfunction of the central nervous system.

Laufer (1979) and Laufer and Denhoff (1957) delineated a disorder of hyperkinetic, impulse problems characterized by hyperactivity. Motor development in these children was suggested as advanced. Short attention span, poor concentration, variability of behavior, behavioral impulsiveness, and inability to delay gratification were considered characteristic symptoms of the disorder. In addition, irritability, low frustration tolerance, fits of anger, explosiveness, and poor school performance were also characteristic descriptors. These authors suggested that the disorder could be observed in infancy or early childhood and that it was male dominated. Interestingly, these authors also suggested that disrupted interaction between these infants and their caretakers likely precipitated the emotional problems these children experienced throughout their childhood and in later life.

The 1950s saw a growing use of psychotropic medications. Classes of medications were developed that allowed approximately four-fifths of psychiatrically institutionalized individuals to function in society. Along with this revolution came a renewed interest in the use of medications for children, specifically the use of stimulants for children with attention and related problems. Laufer and Denhoff's (1957) tripartite set of hyperactive, inattentive, and impulsive symptoms was an early target of medication trials.

ADHD AS A CULTURAL PHENOMENON

Some researchers argue that problems with inattention, hyperactivity, and impulsivity are the result of cultural phenomena (J. Block, 1977), pointing to various cultures and subcultures that exhibit a minimal degree of these childhood problems. Yet this point of view appears to be changing with the acceptance of ADHD as a cross-cultural disorder (Sandberg, 1996; Swanson, 1997). But culture is only one ingredient, for ADHD very clearly reflects a biopsychosocial problem. It is a disorder in which the severity of the child's problems results from the interaction of temperamental traits and the demands placed upon the child by the environment. An inattentive, impulsive child living in a nontechnological culture may not gather as much food or catch as many fish as others but may not have significant difficulty meeting other demands of the culture. One hundred years ago in the United States, a child with a similar set of problems struggling at school would have been asked to leave and would be sent out to work at an early age. In fact, this child's impulsive qualities may have driven him or her to success in the work world. In today's culture, however, there is an increasing emphasis on the importance at a very early age of controlling impulses, sitting still, paying attention, and finishing tasks. Children compromised in their ability to do so, even if they do not experience any other developmental, emotional, or behavioral problem, are unable to effectively integrate into and meet the expectations of our educational system.

Ideus (1994) has argued that although cultures make a difference in terms of the expectations and systems for children, there are very clear similarities in the behavior of children with ADHD symptomatically across cultures. In 1992, Mann, Ikeda, Mueller, and Takahshi examined the degree to which mental health experts in four countries differed in their ratings of hyperactive, disruptive behaviors; they found more similarities than differences. Interestingly, in China, ADHD was popularized in the early 1980s through newspaper reports (Tao, 1992); this author suggests that based on collaborative work, epidemiologic studies find an incidence of from 1% to 13%. The stereotypical belief that Asian children are not hyperactive or disruptive appears to be contradicted. This author notes, however, that attitudes toward these behaviors clearly vary across cultures. In the Mann et al. study (1992), Chinese parents are reported as strongly wanting their children to be quiet, obedient, and orderly. Those who are hyperactive or disruptive are considered culturally unacceptable. Chinese and Indonesian practitioners provided significantly higher scores for severity of hyperactive-disruptive behaviors than did Japanese or American practitioners in response to videotaped vignettes of four 8-year-old boys participating in individual and group activities. Although it is clear that perception of problems varied across cultures, all practitioners were able to recognize the disruptive nature of the observed children's problems. A large-scale study in Great Britain in 1989 (Gray & Sime) found that the most commonly reported pupil problems related to impulsivity (talking out, poor problem solving), hyperactivity (out of seat, disrupting others), and inattention (poorly completed school work). Whether these complaints would be considered indicative of ADHD again may be a cultural phenomenon. For a number of years, the predominant school of thought in Great Britain has argued that symptoms of ADHD are a reflection of conduct disorder (Sandberg, Rutter, & Taylor, 1978), although it is important to note that one of these authors, based on research with British children, has acknowledged the presence of a hyperactive disorder (E. Taylor, 1986). After years of debate, the British Psychological Society (1996) has finally acknowledged the validity of the disorder. Because of this delay in recognition and likely because of differences in diagnostic criteria, it is not surprising that a higher percentage of conduct disorder has been diagnosed in Great Britain than in the United States, balanced by a lower diagnosis rate for ADHD or hyperactivity. In the United States, on the other hand, over the past fifteen years the trend has been to view the majority of impulsive, hyperactive, and inattentive symptoms as reflecting ADHD, and thus a higher percentage of children are diagnosed with the disorder.

It has also been argued that as the tempo of our society increases there is a greater incidence of ADHD (McNamara, 1972). Normative data obtained for the revised and third editions of the Wechsler Intelligence Scale for Children, however, do not support this hypothesis (Spring, Yellin, & Greenberg, 1976; Wechsler, 1974, 1989). In fact, it is suggested that due to children's early exposure to the media, their capacity for sustained attention at younger ages has increased rather than decreased. A more likely explanation for the increase in rate of diagnosis reflects greater community, professional, and parental awareness of the symptoms of ADHD, leading to more children being referred, correctly identified, and offered treatment (Goldstein, 1995a; Lambert, Sandoval, & Sassone, 1978).

CONTROVERSY AND MISDIAGNOSIS

Not surprisingly, in our market economy, as a particular problem becomes popular, controversy and opinion concerning that problem as well as a diversity of solutions surface. Goodman and Poillion (1992) reviewed forty-eight articles and books about ADHD written by leading authors. They report that sixty-nine characteristics and thirty-eight causes for ADHD are noted, evidencing no clear-cut pattern for identifying the condition and little agreement for what causes ADHD. Their list of characteristics

Table 1–1.   Characteristics of Attention Deficit Disorder by frequency cited

Domain	Characteristics of ADD	Count	% of Total
A	Short attention span	32	82.05
H	Hyperactive	29	74.36
I	Impulsive	28	71.79
A	Distractible	20	51.28
I	Fails to follow through	15	38.46
P	Poor muscle coordination	10	25.64
S	Poor conduct	09	23.08
A	Poor concentration	09	23.08
P	Early onset of symptoms	09	23.08
I	Greater need of supervision	08	20.51
I	Doesn't wait turn	07	17.95
A	Disorganized	06	15.38
A	Difficulty following directions	05	12.82
A	Constantly beginning task	05	12.82
I	Engages in risky play	05	12.82
S	Demands attention	05	12.82
H	Climbs on things excessively	04	10.26
H	Excessive talking	04	10.26
H	Fidgets with hands/feet	04	10.26
I	Can't delay gratification	04	10.26
S	Low frustration level	04	10.26
C	Academic difficulty	03	7.69
A	Loses materials	03	7.69
C	Poor auditory processing	03	7.69
A	Short-term memory	03	7.69
H	Movements during sleep	03	7.69
A	Difficulty following rules	03	7.69
P	Immaturity	03	7.69
S	Lack of compliance	03	7.69
S	Poor social skills	03	7.69
T	Aggressive	03	7.69
S	Emotional problems	03	7.69
S	Low self-esteem	03	7.69
T	Seems depressed	03	7.69
A	Daydreams	02	5.13
A	Inefficient attention	02	5.13
C	Cognitive immaturity	02	5.13
C	Visual motor difficulty	02	5.13
I	Accident-prone	02	5.13
H	Doesn't remain in seat	02	5.13
A	Perseverates	02	5.13
I	Blurts out answers to questions	02	5.13
S	Lies easily	02	5.13
I	Poor foresight and planning	02	5.13
S	Greater degree of questioning adults	02	5.13

(continued)

Table 1–1.   *(continued)*

Domain	Characteristics of ADD	Count	% of Total
S	Short-lived friendships	02	5.13
T	Irritable	02	5.13
T	Negative attitude	02	5.13
T	Stubborn	02	5.13
P	> Six-month delay	02	5.13
A	Dissociation	01	2.56
A	Extremely organized	01	2.56
C	Figure-background pathology	01	2.56
A	Forgetfulness	01	2.56
C	No significant academic difficulty	01	2.56
C	Perceptual deficits	01	2.56
C	Poor reader	01	2.56
C	Underachiever	01	2.56
C	Creative	01	2.56
C	Intelligent	01	2.56
P	Language delay	01	2.56
C	Lower mean IQ	01	2.56
D	Comes from small family	01	2.56
P	Poor bladder control	01	2.56
I	Interrupts others	01	2.56
I	Poor judgment	01	2.56
H	Has difficulty playing quietly	01	2.56
S	Insistent on having own way	01	2.56
T	Meek; doesn't speak out	01	2.56

Source: Goodman, G., & Poillion, M. J. (1992). ADD: Acronym for any dysfunction or difficulty. *Journal of Special Education, 26,* 44–45. Used with permission.

A = attention; C = cognition/academic; D = demographic; H = hyperactivity; I = impulsivity; P = physical/developmental; S = social emotional; T = temperament

and causes appears in Tables 1–1 and 1–2. Goodman and Poillion conclude that research is problematic because there is disagreement on what defines the population to study. They also expressed concern that clinicians are turning to ADHD as a generic explanation for a wide range of children's problems and that children identified as having ADHD "will fall victim to the ineffective cycles and spirals in America's educational system" (p. 54).

Given the data generated by Goodman and Poillion, it is not surprising that numerous authors are troubled by the contradictory data and the confusion regarding the best diagnostic process and treatment for this population (Kelly & Aylward, 1992; Sabatino & Vance, 1994). In some studies, simply being referred to an ADHD clinic results in a very high probability of receiving a diagnosis. Edwards (1996) reported on consecutive referrals to an ADHD clinic, reporting that fifty-one of the sixty children received a diagnosis of ADHD. However, Sabatino and Vance (1994) evaluated seventy-five 5- to 17-year-old children with diagnoses of ADHD because of their unsatisfactory response to medication treatment or educational intervention. Nearly one-third of these children were rediagnosed with other disruptive or nondisruptive

Table 1–2.   Causes of Attention Deficit Disorder by frequency cited

Domain	Causes	Count	% of Total
O	Genetics	12	48
B	Perinatal/prenatal problems	09	36
O	Neurodevelopmental immaturity	07	28
O	Brain abnormalities	06	24
E	Diet; additives	06	24
O	Biochemistry	05	20
O	Inborn temperamental predisposition	05	20
B	Low birth weight	05	20
E	Toxicity (lead, toxic waste)	04	16
P	Psycho/social relationships	04	16
I	Maturation delay	03	12
E	Allergies	03	12
O	Brain damage	02	8
E	Learned behavior	02	8
O	Muscular tension	02	8
0	Underlying central defect in self-regulation	02	8
P	Anxiety	01	4
I	Auditory figure-ground deficit	01	4
B	Blood incompatibility (ABO-Rh)	01	4
E	Classroom teacher techniques	01	4
P	Conduct disorders	01	4
I	Educational deficits	01	4
P	Frustration	01	4
E	Ill-fitting underwear	01	4
I	Immature language development	01	4
O	Lateralization	01	4
P	Low self-image	01	4
O	Meningitis	01	4
P	Personal space needs	01	4
E	Physical environment (hot room)	01	4
O	Physiological basis	01	4
E	Radiation leak from TV	01	4
E	Reaction to sedatives	01	4
O	Tactile defensiveness	01	4
I	Tactile/kinesthetic ground deficit	01	4
E	Task difficulty and situational factors	01	4
E	Vitamin deficiencies	01	4
E	Worms or fleas	01	4

Source: Goodman, G., & Poillion, M. J. (1992). ADD: Acronym for any dysfunction or difficulty. *Journal of Special Education, 26,* 52.

O = organic; I = intellectual; P = psychological/behavioral; E = environmental; B = birth complications disorders as the primary explanation for their symptoms. Sabatino and Vance argue that many of the symptoms of ADHD share common ground with other mental illnesses, as well as learning disabilities. Jiron, Sherrill, and Chiodo (1995) add to this literature and line of thought by reviewing multiple charts of children referred for ADHD and then subsequently referred to a specialty clinic due to failure to respond to standard ADHD treatments. Seventy-five percent of these children were found to experience other disorders, ranging from postconcussion, depression, adjustment problems, and learning disability. These disorders were considered to be the primary contributors to this population's impulsive, inattentive symptoms. Interestingly, among this group none of the children were diagnosed with anxiety disorders. In contrast, Cotugno (1993) evaluated ninety-two children with a previous diagnosis of ADHD. After a more comprehensive assessment, only 22% of the sample were provided with a primary diagnosis of ADHD, and 37% received a secondary diagnosis of ADHD. A substantial number were diagnosed instead with primary anxiety and mood disorders.

The controversy, diversity, and, at times, confusion concerning various aspects of ADHD in part may be the result of a tradition to view this disorder as a unitary phenomenon with a single cause. Voeller (1991) suggests that rather than viewing ADHD as a single behavioral abnormality with associated comorbidities, it may be better to conceptualize ADHD as a "cluster of different behavioral deficits, each with a specific neuro-substrate of varying severity, occurring in variable constellations, and sharing a common response to psychostimulants" (p. 54).

There is no doubt, however, that as a cluster of symptomatic problems, ADHD likely represents a disorder distinct from others of childhood and likely of adulthood. For example, in a clinic setting, a segregation analysis was applied to a sample of 257 6- to 17-year-old boys and 800 of their first-degree relatives to determine if genetic factors were involved in ADHD (Biederman, Faraone, Milberger, Jetton, et al., 1996). One hundred and forty of the boys were diagnosed with ADHD. The familial distribution of *DSM-III-R* ADHD was consistent with the effects of a single major gene. Major factorial, polygenetic, nonfamilial environmental and cultural transmission hypotheses were all rejected as explanations for this distinct cluster of symptoms. This group of authors has also demonstrated that though there may be an overlap of some ADHD symptoms with other psychiatric disorders, even when taking into account these other disorders, ADHD as a distinct cluster of symptomatic problems remains (Biederman, Faraone, Milberger, Jetton, et al., 1996). Numerous additional studies support this position. Accardo, Blondis, and Whitman (1990) evaluated 614 children referred for inattentive problems. Sixty-eight percent were diagnosed with attention deficit disorder. These children had higher full-scale IQs and parental educational levels. They also had a higher incidence of specific learning disabilities. The absence of hyperactivity in a subgroup of those with ADHD further exaggerated their differences with learning disability from the normal group. Interestingly, cognitive limitations, severe parental psychopathology, and child neglect and abuse were significantly higher in the group without attention deficit. The two groups did not differ in the incidence of parental or child depressive symptomatology, motor problems, language disorders, conduct disorders, or psychosomatic complaints. In this population, there was also no difference in the incidence of conduct and oppositional disorders between the groups with and without attention disorder. Further, anxiety was more common among the referred children who did not have attention disorder. The data did not support a significant role for depression in the misdiagnosis of attention deficit. These authors suggest a diagnostic conundrum among children referred for possible attention deficit. The comorbidity of other disruptive and nondisruptive symptoms may not allow for accurate differential diagnosis. In fact, as noted earlier, symptoms of ADHD are likely demonstrated by children with a variety of disruptive and nondisruptive disorders.

In regard to etiology, Fragile X, Turner's syndrome, Tourette's Disorder, neurofibromatosis, glucose-6-phosphate-dehydrogenase deficiency, sickle cell anemia, phenylketonuria, Noonan's syndrome, and Williams syndrome are all chromosomal or genetic abnormalities in which attentional problems have been reported (Hagerman, 1991). Toxins resulting in disorders such as fetal alcohol syndrome, cocaine exposure in utero, lead and vapor abuse, perinatal complications, and medical problems such as hypothyroidism, encephalitis, even radiation therapy secondary to leukemia have all been reported as responsible for creating inattentive and impulsive problems.

The second greatest controversy currently associated with ADHD likely lies in the area of intervention. Psychosocial treatments such as cognitive training, once considered promising in directly reducing ADHD symptoms, now are recognized as at best offering valuable intervention for adjunctive problems related to ADHD, most importantly issues of self-esteem and motivation (Abikoff, 1991; DuPaul & Eckert, 1994; Ingersoll & Goldstein, 1993). The greatest volume of literature on ADHD is likely in the investigation of the benefits of psychostimulants and related medications directly on symptoms of ADHD. A very large, diverse, and scientifically rigorous literature has consistently demonstrated the benefits of psychostimulants for ADHD symptoms (for review, see Greenhill & Osman 1991). Nonetheless, although it is presently recognized that stimulants offer excellent short-term symptomatic relief for ADHD symptoms, they have not been demonstrated in the long run to significantly alter the life course for those with ADHD. Although common sense would dictate that if each day of one's life was better, the sum total of one's life would be better, this finding has not been reported on a long-term basis for the ADHD population. The life outcome for children with ADHD taking medication versus those who do not take medication does not appear to be markedly different (for review, see S. Goldstein, 1997b). However, saying that the data have not been generated is not the same as concluding that the hypothesis is flawed. On the other hand, the biopsychosocial nature of ADHD makes it reasonable to conclude that it is the environment more than the direct treatments for ADHD that predict life outcome and course for affected individuals. It has been increasingly recognized that the very factors that affect life outcome for all individuals are equally powerful in affecting life outcome for children with ADHD. Symptoms of ADHD are increasingly viewed as catalysts; that is, leave them alone or place them in a good context and they may not represent a significant risk factor; place them in a child living in a dysfunctional family exposed to a poor school environment or other life stresses, and ADHD likely represents a significant risk factor.

ADHD AS A BIOPSYCHOSOCIAL DISORDER

As Carey (1988) notes, whether one's theoretical orientation of attention deficit represents a neurobehavioral phenomenon, a lack of fit between individual and environment, or in fact a matter of cognitive style is of minor importance when structuring intervention. It is likely that all three approaches must be considered in the intervention process. Recognizing that this is a biopsychosocial disorder affecting individuals differently but remaining throughout their life span shifts practitioners' focus from attempting to search for a cure to developing a balance between management and reduction of immediate symptom problems and the building in of resilience factors, increasing the likelihood of positive long-term adult outcome. As Barkley (1990b) suggests, practitioners working with children with ADHD must develop "prosthetic environments." It is clear that there is not a one-to-one relationship between any specific risk factor and future life outcome, but there is a positive relationship for a variety of biopsychosocial factors and life outcome for ADHD, beginning with perinatal factors that have been demonstrated to impact later development (Gray, Dean, Strom, Wheeler, & Brockley, 1989), early parent-child interaction and attachment (Marshall, Longwell, Goldstein, & Swanson, 1990), socioeconomic factors (Campbell, Breaux, Ewing, & Szumowski, 1986a), and educational experiences (Entwisle, 1990).

In 1995, Teeter and Semrud-Clikeman thoroughly reviewed the research literature on ADHD and proposed a transactional model involving neurobiological, neurophysiological, neuropsychological, cognitive, and behavioral data to understand, evaluate, and treat ADHD (see Figure 1–1). This model proposes that the development and maturation of the central nervous system is affected by genetic, temperamental, and pre- and neonatal environmental factors. It is also hypothesized that there is a bidirectional relationship between cortical and subcortical regions of the brain affecting neuromechanisms of attention, inhibition, and motor activity. This ultimately affects the intellectual and perceptual capacities of the child. Home, school, and social environments also interact in meaningful ways in the expression of ADHD symptoms.

Not surprisingly, as interest in the subject of ADHD increases among clinicians, a parallel interest is mirrored in the public. For some, ADHD has become the "codependency of the 90s." That is, ADHD is jokingly referred to as the explanation for people's everyday mistakes. Parents are overheard asking their children if they have ADHD when the children make mistakes. In some circles, ADHD is offered as an explanation for all human foibles, whereas in others it is offered as a set of qualities to be celebrated. The disorder has created controversy from the Food and Drug Administration to the Drug Enforcement Agency. It has generated multiple lay articles with rigorous reporters consistently demonstrating the reality of the phenomenon and the benefits of mainstream treatment (Bloch, Cole, & Willwerth, 1994; Leutwyler, 1996). Kohn (1989) in the *Atlantic Monthly* reviews the literature and raises questions about the meaning of the diagnosis and the ramifications for our society. S. Goldstein (1997b) in the *F.B.I. Law Enforcement Journal* discusses the difference between the perceived relationship and the actual scientifically demonstrated relationship of symptoms of ADHD to criminal behavior. Aleman (1991) in the *Congressional Research Service Report* for Congress reviews current issues related to ADHD for legislatures.

In the clinical arena, the concepts of etiology, definition, and evaluation continue to evolve, with a general consensus concerning the primary benefits of medications, behavior management, and, as Bob Brooks (1994) has noted, "building islands of competence" (p. 546). Medical, allied health, and mental health journals have all published review articles and, in many cases, devoted entire issues to a discussion of the subject for their readers (Barkley, 1991a, 1991b; Biederman, 1991; Cantwell, 1984;

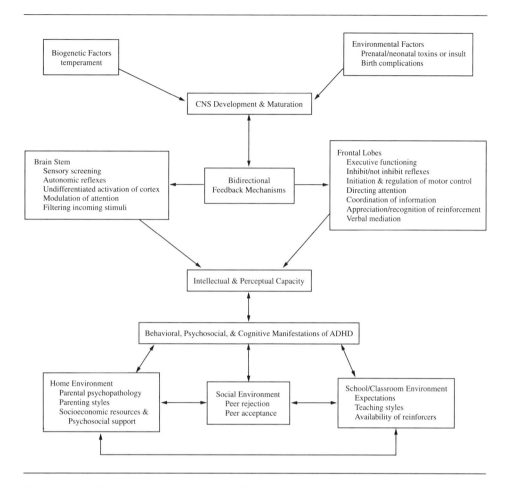

Figure 1–1.   Transactional model for ADHD

Source: Reprinted from Teeter, P. A., & Semrud-Clikeman, M. Integrating neurobiological, psychosocial, and behavioral paradigms: A transactional model for the study of ADHD. Copyright 1995. *Archives
of Clinical Neuropsychology, 10,* 443. With kind permission from Elsevier Science, Ltd. The Boulevard
Langford Lane, Kidlington OX5 16B, UK.

S. Goldstein, 1995). The consensus among these practitioners is that the core symptoms of ADHD affect a significant minority of our population, but for affected individuals, represent a poor fit between society's expectations and these individuals'
abilities to meet those expectations. The phenomenon is distinct from other disorders
of childhood and adulthood, and can be reliably evaluated and effectively treated. Finally, with the recognition that affected individuals with ADHD as adults place a high
financial cost on society, it is likely that practitioners will continue at an increasing
rate to be asked to evaluate, manage, and successfully alter for the better the lives of
individuals with ADHD. As Barkley (1991a) has noted, treatment for ADHD must
and will continue to be multidisciplinary, multimodal, and, in light of continuing cultural trends and societal expectations, likely maintained throughout the affected individual's life span.

A Disorder of Inattention

By the 1970s, however, research strongly began suggesting that the core problem was not excessive activity but inattention (Douglas & Peters, 1979). This led to a major shift in the focus of research, diagnosis, and treatment. Yet some have continued to conceptualize ADHD as part of a larger or expanded Strauss syndrome (Capute, 1991). This author suggests that the neurobehavioral cluster described by Strauss in the 1930s is in fact the best description of ADHD. It is suggested that advances in neuroscience will lead to a better understanding of neurotransmitter and neuroarchitectural damage. This will likely return the science to the use of terms such as minimal brain damage or dysfunction (Capute, 1991).

Through the 1980s, the idea that symptoms of impulsiveness and hyperactivity, but primarily inattention, were biologically based and caused myriad developmental and later life problems became more popular. Research in the field of ADHD increased at nearly an exponential rate. As with any popular topic, increased interest led to increased controversy. Critics blamed parents, schools, and the society at large for the increase in ADHD symptoms. The rate of diagnosis of the disorder was equally accelerated, with some clinicians suggesting that a child with any problem could receive a diagnosis of ADHD. Even as early as the late 1950s, when teachers were asked to identify hyperactive children in their classroom, they named more than half the males and almost half the females (LaPouse & Monk, 1958). Other studies cited incidence rates as high as 20% (Yanow, 1973). Most recently, Boyle et al. (1996) demonstrated that given different thresholds, the incidence of ADHD in a childhood population will vary, with prevalence as high as 39% for parent report and 25% for educator report to as low as 1.5% for parent report and 4% for educator report. The rate of medication treatment for the disorder has also increased dramatically, especially since the publication of the first edition of this text in 1990. Once again, some argue that the increase in treatment reflects a panacea, that medicines are being used as an excuse for not providing appropriate education and parent training; others praise the benefits of identification and treatment leading to improvement in children's lives.

The benefits of this controversy appear to outweigh the liabilities. We have become much more sophisticated as practitioners. We now ask a series of questions seeking both consistency in problems among various settings and consensus by a number of raters—including parents, teachers, and community-based professionals—concerning the severity of these problems. Professional groups have offered their members sets of guidelines to balance sensitivity and specificity in making the diagnosis of ADHD. The most widely used set of criteria was offered by the American Academy of Child and Adolescent Psychiatry in 1997. The interested reader can find these practice parameters in Appendix B.

Practitioners now seek to determine a statistical difference between the level of the identified child's behavioral problems and that of a child of the same gender. There has also been a movement to consider gender in the process of symptom assessment (Barkley, 1996c; M. Gordon, 1996). When more stringent criteria are met, the incidence rate of ADHD drops to a more reasonable 1% to 6%. This was recognized as early as 1978 (Lambert et al.). It also appears that a higher incidence of ADHD, as well as other adjustment and developmental problems in children, occurs in lower socioeconomic families. This is not surprising given findings that a percentage of ADHD children become ADHD adults, have families, do not integrate well into society, fall to the lower socioeconomic strata, and cluster in certain neighborhoods (for review, see Goldstein, 1997a).

The association of symptoms of ADHD with other childhood disorders or as a distinct disorder with a set of symptoms, clinical course, and outcome data unique to the diagnosis has encouraged much research over the past fifteen years. The Isle of Wight survey undertaken in the mid-1960s has provided twenty-five years of child epidemiologic data (Rutter, 1989b). The data suggest that correlates of pervasive hyperactivity differed from those of situational hyperactivity and that pervasive hyperactivity showed a strong association with cognitive impairment. Pervasive hyperactivity in association with other forms of disturbance carried a poor prognosis for the persistence of psychiatric disorders, especially conduct disorder (Barkley, 1988a). On the average, research studies have suggested that ADHD is approximately five to nine times more prevalent in males than females (for review, see Ross & Ross, 1982). Studies by Taylor (1989), Offord, Boyle, Szatmari, et al. (1987), and Chen, Wang, and Yang (1985) have provided confirmatory data of the marked male predominance for this diagnosis and the increase in rate of diagnosis when adverse psychosocial variables are added. Despite continued controversy, a distinct syndrome comprised of set pervasive hyperactivity, impulsivity, and inattention remains popular. Onset is seen as early as the infant years, with symptoms varying but continuing throughout the life span (Hart, Lahey, Loeber, Applegate, & Frick, 1995; Milberger, Biederman, Faraone, & Murphy, 1995).

It has recently been proposed that when males and females are compared to same-gender normative groups and controls are present for symptoms of hyperactivity and antisocial behavior, there is likely an equal or near equal occurrence of ADHD in both males and females (McGee, Williams, & Silva, 1987). Studies suggest that females with this pattern of behavior may present with more mood, affect, and emotion problems and with less difficulty with aggression (Ackerman, Dykman, & Oglesby, 1983; Kashani, Chapel, & Ellis, 1979). Others suggest that ADHD females present with greater cognitive and language function impairments (Berry, Shaywitz, & Shaywitz, 1985). Overall, however, among clinic-referred males and females, the rate of ADHD symptoms is generally equivalent.

Through the 1980s and 1990s, the concept of ADHD as a lifetime disorder potentially affecting all areas of an individual's functioning and possibly resulting in discrimination of those with ADHD became increasingly popular. Parker (1989) describes but one of hundreds of conflicts between parents and school districts under Section 504 of the Rehabilitation Act (1973) for students to receive supplementary services at school when symptoms of ADHD impair their ability to perform up to their capabilities in the school setting. At the other end of the educational continuum, Banks, Guyer, and Guyer (1995) describe studies of medical school students and physicians struggling as the result of ADHD or related symptoms.

Despite the fact that the *DSM-III-R* combined the diagnoses of attention disorder with and without hyperactivity into a single ADHD diagnosis (APA, 1987), a volume of literature has been generated to suggest that these are very different disorders in children (Edelbrock, Costello, & Kessler, 1984; Lahey, Schaughency, Hynd, Carlson, & Nieves, 1987; Porrino et al., 1983). Researchers have suggested that children experiencing attention problems without concomitant hyperactivity may present twice as frequently in epidemiological studies as those with the hyperactive-impulsive component in addition to their inattention (Lahey, Schaughency, Strauss, & Frame, 1984).

A higher percentage of hyperactive, attention-disordered children are referred to mental health clinics because of the cluster of aversive problems they present. In comparison to ADHD children without hyperactivity, children with attention and hyperactivity problems present as more aggressive, unpopular, and guiltless; they also have greater difficulty with conduct (King & Young, 1982; Pelham, Atkins, Murphy, & White, 1981a). The inattentive child without hyperactivity is more frequently described as shy, socially withdrawn, moderately unpopular, and poor at sports (Lahey, Schaughency, Frame, & Strauss, 1985; Lahey et al., 1984). Intelligence testing has yielded significantly lower full-scale IQ scores and lower verbal IQ scores for the hyperactive in comparison to the nonhyperactive inattentive child (Carlson, Lahey, & Neeper, 1986). Studies have consistently found that both groups have a higher incidence of depressive behavior, poor school performance, and poor self-concept relative to their same-age peers (Lahey et al., 1984). Further, children with inattention and hyperactive-impulsive problems have been reported as scoring eight to ten points higher on the Conners questionnaire Hyperkinesis Index than those experiencing only attention difficulties (R. Brown, 1985). The Hyperkinesis Index in general has been found to be not particularly sensitive to nondisruptive, inattentive symptoms. More recent research to be reviewed in the next chapter has provided evidence that inattentive children have a very different disorder than inattentive, hyperactive-impulsive children, with a different set of symptoms and problems, later risk, and comorbid difficulties. Although with its definition of inattentive, hyperactive-impulsive, and combined types of ADHD the *DSM-IV* has returned clinicians and researchers to what is believed to be the correct clinical road, it is likely that future editions of the *DSM* will segregate the disorders even further.

ADHD AS A DISORDER OF IMPULSIVITY

The change in focus to impulsivity as the core problem and significant cause of serious consequences for the majority of children with ADHD has not come easily. The public has finally accepted the concept of attention deficit. In fact, inattentiveness problems as a cause of life difficulties have become well accepted by the community. The preponderance of the research literature in the past ten years, however, suggests that in laboratory settings the problem is not that these children cannot pay attention, but that they do not pay attention as effectively as others. Their inconsistent attention occurs in repetitive, effortful situations and appears to be primarily a function of poor impulse control. Converging lines of evidence including laboratory tests, measures of physiological functioning, and neuroimaging studies increasingly support disinhibition as a core deficit in ADHD (Barkley, 1997c; Quay, 1997).

As we prepare to enter the twenty-first century, researchers and increasingly clinicians have come to accept the fact that the preponderance of current research literature and the reconceptualization of thousands of past studies places the source of most problems for children with ADHD squarely on the child's limited capacity for self-control leading to poor attention to cues, need for repetitive learning trials for educational and behavioral success, and a tendency to learn from and act upon experience inconsistently, ineffectively, and inefficiently.

SUMMARY

Descriptions of inattentive, impulsive, and hyperactive behavior in childhood appear in texts as old as the Bible. It is likely that these qualities of human temperament interact with demands of society and culture to result in some children greatly struggling to meet expectations and developmental tasks placed before them. Although the field of ADHD is still filled with much controversy, the blizzard of well-controlled scientific research has dramatically increased available knowledge in the field, which subsequently continues to exert impact on diagnostic nomenclature, assessment, and treatment.

Chapter 2

TOWARD A WORKING DEFINITION OF ADHD

As researchers and clinicians recognize that the core deficit for many of the children diagnosed as ADHD is in fact impulsiveness, not inattention, perception of the disorder changes. With these changes comes a significant shift in focus to definition, assessment, life course, and even etiology. As is characteristic for any scientific phenomenon that is extensively and at times minutely studied, the more data generated, the more questions asked. Before examining and proposing a set of definitions for the symptomatic and related terms used throughout this text, a brief presentation concerning critically related issues is relevant. It is essential for clinicians to possess a firm grasp of these issues, such as those related to categorical versus dimensional models of pathology, behavioral versus biological etiologies, and relationship of current symptoms to long-term outcome as well as to developmental course. Familiarity with these issues allows for a flexible, reasoned approach in the diagnostic process, an approach tempered by placing symptoms of ADHD within the broader context of environmental, biological, and statistical phenomena.

RELEVANT ISSUES

The Diagnostic Process and Its Relationship to Symptom Definition

Ideally, symptom definition should lead logically to symptom identification as part of the clinical process of assessment. Unfortunately, in the field of ADHD this process has been anything but simple and direct. Although other categories of disruptive behavior, such as those related to conduct disorder or even oppositional defiance, may be easy to identify and define, symptoms of ADHD even after definition may be difficult to evaluate. This is especially true as symptoms of ADHD overlap with many other childhood disorders. Thus, a definition must not only include a description of the behavior to be evaluated, but some diagnostic process to discriminate the cause or etiology of that behavior. Despite the field's best efforts, as will be discussed shortly, even once the theoretical aspects of a concept such as attention or impulse control are agreed upon, the operational definition and subsequent methods by which the symptom is to be evaluated are far from consensus in the research and clinical fields. Barkley (1982) found in over 200 studies of hyperactivity that less than a third set any diagnostic criteria at all and those were mostly below acceptable levels. Nonetheless, some clear themes have emerged over the past thirty years in the diagnostic process of ADHD, two of which have become quite popular. The first is based on the use of normative scores, which allows definition to statistically lead to diagnosis. The second is more qualitatively based, reflecting a process of diagnosis based on clinical intuition as the symptoms are viewed through the eyes of the evaluator. Each will be discussed in depth in the evaluative chapters.

Disruptive versus Nondisruptive Childhood Disorders

It will be helpful for a moment to digress and provide a brief overview of the conceptual system in which ADHD finds itself. From a commonsense perspective, children's emotional, behavioral, and developmental disorders are defined not by cause or etiology but by the impact they have principally upon the adults in their lives. Thus, children can exhibit problems that annoy or disrupt adults, which are referred to as externalizing. They may also exhibit a second set of problems that make adults worry about them but are nondisruptive; these are referred to as internalizing. ADHD represents a mild externalizing disorder. Within a larger framework, it is considered mild because there is a threshold of impact that children cross in which the goal of their behavior is purposely to annoy or create conflict with adults. This pattern of behavior, which is diagnostically referred to as oppositional defiance, leaves no doubt in the adult's mind that the behavior is purposeful. In fact, it is the *apparent* purposefulness of ADHD symptoms that likely misleads many adults to accuse children with ADHD of behaving in noncompliant ways. This accusation and the subsequent punishing response on the part of adults may actually precipitate the onset of increasingly resistant, purposely noncompliant behavior characterized as oppositional defiance. Thus, adults' very efforts to deal with the incompetent problems of ADHD behaviors may actually foster increasing noncompliant problems characteristic of oppositional defiance.

There is a second disruptive threshold children cross in which their behavior may not only be purposeful but designed to hurt others or violate society's rules and limits. This limited list of delinquent behaviors is referred to as conduct disorder. Thus, within this continuum, it is easy to understand why symptoms of ADHD are considered mildly disruptive, those of oppositional defiance, reflecting purposeful misbehavior, are considered moderately disruptive, and those of delinquency with the aggressive intent to hurt are considered significantly disruptive to adults.

In contrast, nondisruptive problems appear to fall on a number of spots on a continuum. Those related to emotional distress characteristic of depression and anxiety appear significantly overlapping. In children and younger adolescents, they may represent a unitary phenomenon of emotional distress. As the research reflects, anxious children are often unhappy. Unhappy children often worry. Problems related to development such as those of language, motor skills, and learning are also considered nondisruptive. The first author frequently explains this model to parents by describing a depressed child with a reading delay as one who would not annoy nearby adults on a bus but whose condition would worry his or her parents. In contrast, sitting next to a restless child threatening to steal your wallet or actually accomplishing that task is disturbing to adults. When parents are called about the disruptive actions of their children, the parents are frequently angry and disturbed as well.

With this model in mind, the catalytic nature of ADHD symptoms is understood. That is, these symptoms may increase vulnerability so that under certain environmental circumstances children with ADHD will progress to greater problems with other disruptive and nondisruptive disorders.

Categorical versus Dimensional Models

The diagnostic systems in place today (*DSM-IV* and *ICD-10*) are categorical models. That is, they present an all-or-nothing phenomenon. They are polythetic such that to receive a diagnosis a child must manifest a minimum threshold of presenting symptoms; one symptom short and the diagnosis is not provided. However, on a dimensional basis, it is assumed that everyone exhibits these symptoms from a minimal to a maximal degree. On a dimensional basis, having all but one symptom necessary to receive a categorical diagnosis makes one quite different from others. Ellis (1985) suggested that a dimensional model predicts a complete and unbroken gradient for a particular skill or symptom, such as impulsivity, ranging in those individuals that are only minimally impulsive to those that may be mildly, moderately, or more significantly impulsive. The dimensional model does not suggest that there are no heterogonic differences among mildly, moderately, and more severely affected individuals but that the differences among these individuals represent differences in severity of a homogeneous concept.

Fergusson and Horwood (1995) report a consistent and generally linear relationship between symptom severity and outcome risk. Dimensionally scored symptoms appear to be better predictors of outcome than measures based on a categorical classification. In a birth cohort of 935 New Zealand children assessed at 15 years of age, diagnoses of disruptive disorders were made based on *DSM-III-R* criteria. Children were evaluated on a continuous variable ranging from none to severe in regard to symptoms. At 16 years of age, the cohort was reassessed on a series of outcome measures, including substance abuse, juvenile offenses, and school drop out. This comparison demonstrated evidence of continuous and generally linear dose-response functions between symptom severity and outcome risks. Dimensionally scored variables were consistently better predictors of outcome than measures based on a categorical classification. Clearly, the disruptive behaviors possess dimensional properties. These authors argue that although the *DSM* categorical criteria have value in the short run, they are not particularly effective in the long run in regard to predicting future outcome.

The exclusive use of categorical criteria may result in measurement error with less than optimal predictive validity. In a population of 114 9-year-olds, categorical and dimensional approaches to diagnosis were attempted in making the diagnosis of attention deficit disorder with hyperactivity (Shekim, Cantwell, Kashani, & Beck, 1986). The Diagnostic Schedule for parents was used for the categorical approach, and the Child Behavior Checklist was used for the dimensional approach. Categorically, fourteen of the subjects were diagnosed with ADHD. Of these, two were diagnosed by the Child Behavior Checklist. These authors concluded that a combination of categorical and dimensional approaches to diagnosis offers a better perspective than a single categorical or dimensional cutoff score.

Categorical diagnoses allow the identification of a constellation of covarying behaviors that can be used to predict the relative success of a possible intervention, the risk for concurrent or future behavioral problems, and possible controlling variables (Barlow, 1981). Categorical definitions also allow standardization of the diagnostic system used by many professionals across a large geographic area. Categorical systems, however, have their limitations. Most important, the psychometric properties (reliability and validity) of many of the diagnostic criteria, including those for ADHD, are not well established (Gresham & Gansle, 1992). One must also possess a working knowledge of child development to understand how to apply and conceptualize symptoms at different ages. Characteristic symptoms of ADHD appear to diminish in presentation and severity as children grow older. Research with the *DSM-III-R* suggests that although these criteria required nine of fourteen symptoms in children, this threshold for diagnosis resulted in overinclusion of affected younger children and underinclusion of affected adolescents. In fact, recent research data suggest that into the adult years, the number of symptoms necessary to set an individual apart from others categorically in regard to inattentive and hyperactive-impulsive problems continues to diminish into the fifth decade (Murphy & Barkley, 1996b).

Kinsbourne (1977) was the first to suggest that temperament (those qualities that children bring to the world likely as the result of the interaction of genetics and biological function) falls on a continuum of characteristics such as impulsivity and hyperactivity. Thus, children receiving a diagnosis of ADHD represent the extreme of the temperamental continuum. During the 1970s, there was increasing support for the notion of hyperactivity, on a dimensional basis, reflecting delayed maturation. The hyperactive child was viewed as abnormal in rate of acquisition of certain skills. The notion of hyperactivity as a developmental delay was supported by soft sign and related biological research. Nonetheless, it is important to note that differences among children continued to be nonspecific on a case-by-case basis.

Immediate Symptoms versus Long-Term Outcome

Parents bringing their children for assessment often have a list of immediate symptoms or problems in need of relief. For the disruptive disorders, this list is usually prioritized based on those behaviors that are most annoying to the adults in the child's life. Unfortunately, a list of immediate symptoms may not be synonymous with a list of long-term symptoms that may be most predictive of future life problems. At times, the behaviors and related problems that most annoy adults may have limited predictive validity. For example, adults often focus an inordinate amount of attention on the quality of young children's handwriting, yet in future life, handwriting appears to predict very little. In contrast, in regard to the ADHD treatment Ritalin®, there appears to be minimal data to suggest that taking Ritalin® alone alters future life outcome; as a symptom reliever, however, there is more than sufficient data to suggest that it has a significant impact on daily behavior. The implication that the diagnostic symptoms and severity used to diagnose ADHD may not necessarily constitute the ideal list of risk factors contributing to future outcome must be seriously considered by the practitioner. These factors, however, must be evaluated as part of the diagnostic process and in treatment planning.

Shaffer and Greenhill (1979) suggested that attention deficit does not represent a clear-cut syndrome. They noted that assessment instruments available at the time were unable to reliably discriminate between normals and hyperactives. They also speculated that stimulants were nonspecific and simply enhanced general performance. This is a speculation that is consistent with Bradley's (1937) original comments concerning the benefits of stimulants. These authors suggested that the diagnosis of what was then termed hyperactivity did not allow consistent predictions about later outcome in life.

Differential Diagnosis

The research literature very consistently demonstrates that approximately one-fifth of our childhood population, independent of geography or culture, experiences some type of emotional, behavioral, or developmental problem that compromises their ability to meet the demands of their immediate environment (Costello, 1989b). Approximate prevalence rates from five different studies are presented in Table 2–1. The question remains whether evaluators should be urged to begin with the general and work toward the specific. That is, is there a distinct set of symptoms, behaviors, or problems that effectively distinguishes and identifies this 20% of the population in contrast to the other 80%? Further, the question must be asked as to whether, after defining and identifying the 20% and offering them assistance, there is any value in more specifically

Table 2–1. Prevalence rates of DSM-III diagnoses in nonclinic samples

	J. Anderson et al., 1987	Bird et al., 1988	Velez et al., 1989	Costello et al., 1984	Offord, Boyle, Szatmari et al., 1987
Informants Sample	Child (I) Parent (C) Teacher (C) N = 782 Age 11	Child (I) Parent (I) N = 777 Age 4–16	Child (I) Parent (I) N = 776 Age 11–20	Child (I) Parent (I) N = 789 Age 7–11	Parent (C) Teacher (C) Child (C) N = 2,679 Age 4–16
Attention deficit disorder (w/wo hyperactivity)	6.7%	9.9%	4.3%	2.2%	6.2%
Oppositional disorder	5.7	9.5	6.6	6.6	N/A
Conduct disorders (all types)	3.4	1.5	5.4	2.6	5.5
Separation anxiety	3.5	4.7	5.4	4.1	
Overanxious disorder	2.9	N/A	2.7	4.6	9.9*
Simple phobia	2.4	2.3	N/A	9.2	
Depression, dysthymia	1.8	5.9	1.7[†]	2.0	
Functional enuresis	N/A	4.7	N/A	4.4	N/A
One or more diagnoses	17.6	18.0 ± 3.4	17.7	22.0 ± 3.4	18.1

Source: Costello, E. J. (1989b). Developments in Child Psychiatric Epidemiology. Special Section. *Journal of the American Academy of Child and Adolescent Psychiatry, 28,* 836–841. Used with permission.

* "Emotional disorder"
[†] Major depression
(I) = Interview; (C) = Checklist.

"pigeonholing" and labeling the problems of subgroups of these children. It would appear that at the very least there is benefit in defining their problems as disruptive or nondisruptive (Quay, 1979). It would also appear that at the very least there is value in identifying certain target behaviors (e.g., unprovoked aggression before age 10) as having strong predictive power for children's future lives and determining the urgency with which intervention and treatment must be considered.

In an excellent review comparing and contrasting the *DSM-III-R* and *ICD-10* proposed draft criteria for ADHD, Barkley (1990a) described the variability of ADHD symptoms across settings and the parameters that appear to reflect this variability. This problem was considered to have impact on symptom instability and thus diagnostic criteria. Barkley also raised questions as to whether ADHD actually reflected a clinical syndrome. On one level, it is clear that symptoms of ADHD are highly interrelated, with factor analytic and standardization data from numerous childhood questionnaires reflecting this phenomenon. However, more problematic is the question of whether the defining features of ADHD discriminate children with this disorder from other psychiatric disturbances (Biederman, Newcorn, & Sprich, 1991). The evidence here is conflicting and less compelling given the overlap of ADHD symptoms with other childhood disorders (Reeves, Werry, Elkind, & Zametkin, 1987; Werry, Elkind, & Reeves, 1987).

Behavioral versus Biological Differences

Although the argument over behavioral versus biological differences may speak to etiology as opposed to symptom presentation, the behavioral position implies that definition of specific symptoms must take into account the context in which those symptoms are presented. Data are emerging suggesting that the severity of symptom complaints, and, for that matter, symptom presentation, can vary significantly within the same child suffering from ADHD based on the setting and the adults they deal with. The definitional process, if not the diagnostic process, must take into account this larger context. Arguing that ADHD is a biological disorder and that symptoms are consistent, unremitting, and unwavering in severity across situations ignores the obvious. Insisting that these are biologically based problems, though likely accurate, has in fact created more conflict than consensus in the field of ADHD. Professionals of varying backgrounds, fields, and opinions agree that a group of children in our society demonstrate impulsive, hyperactive, and inattentive symptoms. As discussed earlier, often the source of the disagreement is the cause of these problems, and it is over this issue that responses ranging from the absurd (e.g., ADHD caused by ultraviolet lights, too much sugar, or faulty brain waves) to the obvious (e.g., ADHD is a powerfully genetically determined disorder) conflict.

Situational Variability

The sustained attention of children with ADHD has been suggested as highly interactive with and clearly influenced by environmental factors (Zentall, 1984). The primary issue here concerns the difference in setting demands and thus symptom presentation between home and school. Some researchers and clinicians have argued that ADHD symptoms must manifest themselves in a scholastic setting for the diagnosis to be made. Others recognize the difference between settings, including differences within the teacher and the parent populations, that may account for minimal or maximal differences in symptomatic complaints and severity of complaints between settings.

Executive versus Secretarial Skills

Efficient functioning in the environment requires a set of processing or secretarial skills (e.g., rote memory, motor skills, attention). These skills require efficiency rather than thinking per se. Some consider ADHD a disorder of rote skill problems: inefficient attention or impulse control leads to faulty behavior. Yet, there has always been a fairly strong movement arguing that ADHD represents a problem of executive, conceptual, or higher-order thinking ability. Thus, the quest to demonstrate that ADHD children experience executive problems (e.g., comprehension, reasoning, judgment) has been vigorous. The literature, however, has not consistently supported executive deficits as causative problems in and of themselves but rather as likely problems that occur from rote skill deficits related to poor impulse control (Barkley & Grodzinsky, 1994).

Developmental Course

The available literature concerning the developmental course of children with ADHD will be reviewed in depth in Chapter 4. As a diagnostic issue, however, it clearly has relevance. As noted, some symptoms may be more salient at different ages. Number or severity of symptoms may also be more significant depending on the child's age. There is clearly a developmental trajectory for ADHD symptoms. For example, Holt and Lehman (1995) evaluated the relationship between children's awareness and their use of strategies for self-control. Spontaneous use of temptation-inhibited strategies increased between ages 4 and 6 and remained high when evaluated again at age 8. Four-year-olds demonstrated the most distractible behavior. All of the children had some understanding of the negative impact of distraction on task completion. When given specific strategy choices, 4-year-olds were more likely to choose a strategy focusing on rewards, whereas 6- and 8-year-olds were more likely to select a task-facilitated strategy. Thus, growing children's behavior becomes increasingly governed by internal or habit-related phenomena and less by external consequences. Knowledge of strategies is more highly correlated with process than with performance.

Sensitivity versus Specificity

There is a popular saying suggesting that if one's only tool is a hammer, every problem in the world appears to be a nail. For a behaviorally defined disorder such as ADHD, so easily influenced by a myriad of factors well beyond those few reviewed here, it is not surprising that questions arise concerning the issue of sensitivity (making the diagnosis so general that it includes 50% of the population; everyone with ADHD is identified, but so too are an excess number of false positives) in contrast to specificity (identifying a very small group of children, all of whom clearly have the disorder, but also identifying too many false negatives). For the time being, the system of diagnosis for ADHD is based on behavior. Too liberal an interpretation results in seemingly every child having the disorder, too conservative fails to identify children in need. Therefore, the integration of diagnostic information in a clinical way represents an extremely important issue in regard to sensitivity versus specificity. Practitioners must be aware of this problem and seek to develop a system that provides a balance between too liberal and too conservative errors.

Many practitioners do not routinely consider these issues but certainly confront them on a daily basis. Awareness of and consideration for these issues in conceptualizing ADHD during the diagnostic process and in fact during monitoring of treatment will ensure more accurate diagnosis and, ultimately, more effective treatment.

WHAT IS ATTENTION?

The brain possesses limited capacity for simultaneous information processing. It relies on a complex process to narrow the scope and focus of information to be processed and assimilated. Attention is a generic term used to designate a group of hypothetical mechanisms that collectively serve an important function for the organism (Mesulam, 1985). Over the past century, beginning with James (1890), researchers have identified attentional processes as essential prerequisites for higher cognitive functions. Although attention as a term used to describe diagnosis may be very different from attention as a laboratory or environmental phenomenon, it is of value for the practitioner to understand the historical perception, research, and relationship of various definitions of attention to the clinical disorder.

Blondis, Snow, Stein, and Roizen (1991) suggest a model of attentional processes beginning neonatally and progressing through development at age 10. During the first year of life, infants develop greater internal control over eye, hand, and body movements. As their capacity for attention becomes less stimulus-bound, by 3 months of age they develop the ability to make decisions about what to attend to (Olson, 1976). They then move into an exploratory stage of attention. The toddler and later preschooler operate on a level that is very much guided by the external environment (Wright & Vliestra, 1975). By 5 years of age children begin to perceive stimuli systematically (Abravanel, 1968). Wright and Vliestra (1975) suggest four levels of mature attention. At a mature level, impulsive, rapid responding eventually develops into goal-directed and task-oriented behavior. At a causative level, salient reinforcement as a primary motivation for behavior is eventually abandoned for a more logical process. At a task level, divergent and imaginative thinking develop. Finally, from a time perspective, greater efficiency in the use of time develops. Hagen and Hale (1973) suggest that maturation allows the organism the capability of ignoring stimuli of little use in an effort to facilitate problem solving. By middle childhood, most children can selectively attend to stimuli of their choice.

There is now no clear or universal consensus, operational definition, or construct for attention (Mostovsky, 1970). Posner and Snyder (1975) described attention as a complex field of study; however, some have argued that attentional skills can be operationally and statistically defined (Gordon & McClure, 1983). As Barkley (1997a) noted, there has been a trend to borrow increasingly from models in other areas of science and technology to guide model building in the area of attention deficit. This has led to an increasing awareness of the lines of convergence among different literatures. There is growing recognition that attention as defined in laboratory measures or animal research is often very different from that being measured in children and adults described as inattentive. These qualities may also be even more distinct from attention as a process in the real world.

Although many utilize the term attention as a homogeneous skill, there may be a number of distinct aspects to the attentional process. Skinner (1953) defined attention as a functional relationship between stimulus and response: attention is not a thing, entity, or mental function but a description of a set of relations between stimuli or events and responses to them. Gibson and Radner (1979) defined attention as "perceiving in relation to a goal internally or externally motivated" (p. 2). Titchener (1924) described attention as a pattern of consciousness arranged into focus and margin, foreground and background, center and periphery: what is focused on is attended to and clear; what is in the margin is obscure.

Posner (1987) discusses the concept of automatic activation versus conscious strategies in determining attentional performance. Fuster (1989) provides a concept of inhibition of interference in his neuropsychological model of executive function related to attention. All of these theories appear to be extensions of James's (1890) characterization of attention as bimodal, being either passive—reflexive, nonvoluntary, and effortless—or active and voluntary. For James, sustained attention defined the latter and was dependent on repeated redirection of effort to the focus of attention and resistance to coexisting attractions.

Picano, Klusman, Hornbestel, and Moulton (1992) report three factors of attention. The first accounts for 35% of the variance and appears to involve skills related to visual motor scanning and shifting abilities. The capacity to divide attention appears to be key to this task. The second factor accounts for 16% of the variance and appears to reflect immediate attention and conceptual tracking consistent with the ability to repeat digits forward and in reverse. The third factor accounts for 13.5% of the variance and appears to reflect sustained, effortful processing consistent with distractibility tasks. This breakdown in attentional skills is similar to factors reported by others (Shum, MacFarland, & Bain, 1990).

Attention as an executive function has gained popularity. Sustained mental effort and self-regulation in addition to skills such as planning, execution, and maintenance are considered measures of executive function (Daigneault, Braun, & Whitaker, 1992). This methodological approach to defining attention is similar to that of Mirskey, Anthony, Duncan, Ahearn, and Kellam (1991). These authors developed a neuropsychological model of attention, defining four basic concepts involving the ability to focus, execute, sustain or code, and shift. Eight traditional assessment measures of attention were used in a factor analytic study to arrive at this model. Interestingly, over 50% of the tests used by Mirsky et al. (1991), were similar to those used by Daigneault et al. (1992), yet each group felt they were measuring a different construct.

Sohlberg and Mateer (1992) describe a somewhat similar model of attention based on their work with the traumatic brain-impaired population. They note problems in sustained attention relating to duration and consistency, selective attention, and divided attention. They also suggest a clinical model of attention, including characteristics of focusing, sustaining, selecting, alternating, and dividing attention. The last reflects simultaneously tracking two sources of information. These authors then propose a series of hypothetical activities and exercises that might improve these skills. Although they provide single case examples, definitive research supporting the model or remediation of problems has not been generated. At one time this model was thought to have significant relevance for the ADHD population, but in general it appears to better apply to those with traumatic injury, especially in light of the increasing recognition that ADHD is a disorder of poor impulse control rather than faulty attention.

E. Taylor (1980) suggested that the statistically weak correlations among various tests of attention suggest there may be distinct and different aspects of attentional skills. This model, though once suggested as the most efficient means for understanding attention deficit (Goldstein & Goldstein, 1990), is not without problems. However, a brief review of a topology of attention is valuable.

A child presenting with difficulty completing two simultaneous tasks, such as listening to the teacher and taking notes, would appear to have a problem with divided attention; this child struggles to shift between tasks simultaneously and repeatedly. A child described by a teacher as often daydreaming and preoccupied with other activities instead of the task at hand might be considered to have a problem with focused attention; this child lacks the ability to become invested in the task at hand. A child easily distracted by extraneous events such as minor noises in the classroom would be considered to have a problem with selective attention; this child has difficulty prioritizing what is most important to pay attention to and has been traditionally described as distractible. A child unable to remain on task for a sufficient amount of time to satisfactorily complete the task may be considered to have a problem with sustained attention or persistence. Increasingly, however, it is recognized that it is a child's inability to invest in the task because of its repetitive, effortful, uninteresting, and low reinforcing value rather than difficulty with selective attention that is responsible for the child's problems. Finally, a child unable to perform such tasks as listening for the next spelling word presented by the teacher during a test would be considered to have a problem with vigilance or readiness to respond; this task requires the ability to delay immediate gratification.

There may be anatomical bases for different aspects of attention (Posner, 1987). In studies measuring the ability of head-injured individuals to pay attention, it has been demonstrated that these attentional skills may not be equally impaired as the result of head trauma (Van Zomeren & Brouwer, 1987). In children experiencing ADHD, a similar level of variability in attentional skills is often observed. However, as our diagnostic focus moves away from the concept of attention and toward the concept of impulsivity as the core deficit in ADHD, this model of attentional types provides less benefit in defining ADHD for assessment and treatment.

A number of skills that have traditionally been discussed within the context of ADHD must also be defined. Impulsivity is best defined operationally as an inability to separate experience from response. Thus, minimal time is spent thinking about what has happened, considering alternatives, and formulating a plan of action. Reflection is the opposite of this process. Because problems with impulsiveness have been characterized as representing the core deficit for ADHD, an indepth discussion of impulsivity and current concepts follows at a later point in this chapter.

For the purposes of this text, hyperactivity refers to excessive bodily movement, ranging from restless and incessant fidgeting while seated, to frantic, seemingly purposeless racing around on the playground. Overarousal is used to describe a responsive pattern of emotional behavior, either positive or negative, that is inappropriate in the speed at which it occurs and excessive in the frequency of its occurrence. It is quite likely that this overaroused state, which many ADHD children frequently experience, may well be precipitated by their impulsiveness.

DEFINING ADHD

There is growing consensus that ADHD represents a problem of faulty performance rather than faulty input: it is not so much that this population does not know what to do, but that they do not consistently do what they know. It is a problem of inconsistency rather than inability (Goldstein & Goldstein, 1992). Even in terms of adaptive skills, this pattern of difference between possessing a skill and using it efficiently has been well defined (Stein, Szumowski, Blondis, & Roizen, 1995).

It is important for the practitioner to possess a working understanding of the *DSM-IV* diagnostic criteria for ADHD, a practical definition of the manner in which the symptoms impact the individual's functioning, and a diagnostic strategy. The practical definition is based on an original model proposed by Goldstein and Goldstein (1990). The current *DSM-IV* definition and its relationship to previous *DSM* definitions will also be discussed. Finally, a strategy to facilitate the diagnostic process will be offered.

DeFilippis (1979) summarized the results of the then available factor analytic studies and suggested that several behavioral characteristics of hyperactive children clustered together. Rutter (1989a) reemphasized that brain dysfunction is linked nonspecifically to a variety of psychiatric disturbances and that the link between such phenomena as birth complications and ADHD is insubstantial. Sanberg et al. (1978) suggested that distinguishing ADHD symptoms from those of other psychiatric disorders is difficult and not always consistent. Some researchers argue that the traditional disease model is not relevant in the definition of attention disorder (Ellis, 1985). They suggest that attention deficit is more like obesity or intelligence: individuals differ not in having or not having the traits but, as noted earlier, in the degree of manifestation. Guevremont, DuPaul, and Barkley (1993) have suggested that attention deficit symptoms are multidimensional rather than unitary. However, the research is imprecise in suggesting which dimensions represent the most distinguishing deficits of the disorder. As noted, frequency and severity of symptoms fluctuate across settings, activities, and caregivers (Tarver-Behring, Barkley, & Karlsson, 1985; Zentall, 1984).

Based on structured interviews, Faraone, Biederman, Sprich-Buckminster, Chen, and Tsuang (1993) developed a definition and set of attention deficit diagnostic algorithms that was more efficient than others in discriminating children with ADD from controls based on a *DSM-III* definition. The algorithms appear in Table 2–2. The authors note

Table 2–2.   Optimal Quality Receiver Operating Code diagnostic algorithm for ADD

At least one item from each of Clusters 1, 2, and 3 must be positive to make a diagnosis

Cluster 1
  Speaks out in class.
  Leaves table before through eating.
  Is always on the go, as if driven by a motor.
  Leaves seat at school.
  Has trouble waiting for turn in line.

Cluster 2
  Rushes into things and gets hurt or in trouble.
  Has difficulty finishing work.
  Can't concentrate if there is noise or people.
  Has trouble concentrating on school work.
  Often runs around, even in the house.
  Climbs on things not meant for climbing.

Cluster 3
  Has difficulty sitting still.
  Often fidgets when seated.
  Usually falls behind in class.

Source: Faraone, S. V., Biederman, J., Sprich-Buckminster, S., Chen, W., & Tsuang, M. T. (1993). Efficiency of diagnostic criteria for attention deficit disorder: Towards an empirical approach to designing and validating diagnostic algorithms. *Journal of the American Academy of Child and Adolescent Psychiatry, 32,* 166–174. Used with permission.

that comorbidity with attention deficit makes this system less efficient, suggesting, for example, that many inattentive symptoms might be attributable to antisocial behavior. However, in comparison to purely inattentive children, the conduct disorder group had higher rates of all symptoms. Thus, the relationship between conduct disorder and symptoms of attention deficit appeared nonspecific compared to normal controls. The ADD-only children had significantly and substantially higher rates of all ADD symptoms. These authors suggested that ADD children with comorbid conduct, major depression, or anxiety disorders have more symptoms of ADD than ADD children who have none of these disorders. Thus, ADD children with comorbid conditions are more discriminable from psychiatric and normal controls than ADD children without comorbid problems. The ability of ADD symptoms to discriminate ADD cases with major depression or anxiety from psychiatric controls is still good.

The issue of definition must also take into account informants. Bird, Gould, and Staghezza (1993) suggest that parent information correlates most strongly with clinical diagnosis of disorders in which symptoms are externally observable. Thus, ADHD ideally fits this model. In contrast, the information provided by children, though not unimportant, is more relevant for internalizing disorders. Practical diagnostic strategy would therefore need to more strongly take into account observers' reports of behavior for ADHD than reports of affected individuals.

In some circumstances, definition may be more accurately assessed through evaluation of the impact certain qualities of ADHD have on daily functioning. (This issue will be discussed in greater depth in the next chapter.) A recent study provides an illustrative example. Tannock, Purvis, and Schachar (1993) evaluated the narrative abilities in 7- to 11-year-old boys with ADHD and a group matched for age and IQ using a story retelling task. The two groups did not differ in their ability to comprehend and extract the main ideas from the stories but did differ in narrative production. The children with ADHD provided less information overall and their stories were more poorly organized and less cohesive and contained more inaccuracies. This phenomenon is also reported clinically and is very consistently demonstrated in the written language skills of ADHD children (Mather & Roberts, 1996). Thus, it could be that a diagnostic strategy for ADHD should include at the very least a list of skills and life problems directly impacted by ADHD symptoms. Having the symptoms but not having the negative impact would in fact preclude the diagnosis according to current *DSM-IV* criteria.

DSM-III-R Definition

The third, third revised, and fourth editions of the *Diagnostic and Statistical Manual* of the American Psychiatric Association (APA, 1980, 1987, 1994) differ on specific core symptoms and the arrangement of symptoms, but in general they are quite consistent. All three diagnostic categories agree that there are two core sets of symptoms containing inattentive-disorganized qualities and hyperactive-impulsive qualities. In *DSM-III,* these were arranged in three separate areas, with hyperactivity and impulsivity separated. *DSM-III-R* grouped these symptoms together. *DSM-IV* divides them into two core dimensions, which is consistent with most current research literature.

The *Diagnostic and Statistical Manual* issued a revised third edition in 1987 (APA, 1987); this superseded the second edition, published in 1980. The definition of ADHD represented important descriptive and conceptual changes and therefore is worth review prior to discussion of the current *DSM-IV* definition.

This disorder was originally referred to in the second edition of the *DSM* as Hyperkinetic Reaction of Childhood (APA, 1968). The third edition greatly expanded the definition and retitled the disorder Attention Deficit Disorder. It included attention disorders with and without hyperactivity as well as a residual category for individuals presenting some symptoms of the disorder currently but whose history clearly demonstrated a period when the full disorder was exhibited. This was considered a diagnosis for late adolescence and possibly even adulthood.

Despite strong research suggesting a distinction between attention-disordered children with and without hyperactivity (Lahey, Schaughency, Hynd, Carlson, & Nieves, 1987), the authors of *DSM-III-R,* based on their field studies, chose to collapse the diagnostic criteria into a single diagnostic entity, Attention Deficit Hyperactivity Disorder. The diagnostic criteria contained fourteen items reflecting those related to activity level (fidgeting, difficulty remaining seated), those reflecting impulsivity (engaging in physical risk-taking behavior and shifting from one task to another), as well as those thought to reflect inattention (easily distracted, trouble sustaining attention). Part of the rationale was based on the *DSM-III-R* authors' conclusion that a diagnosis of attention deficit without hyperactivity "is hardly ever made" (APA, 1987, p. 411). Epidemiological studies, however, did not support this conclusion (Cantwell & Baker, 1985). Critics of the *DSM-III-R* noted that the manual did not provide details or results of the field studies (Rutter, 1988), studies these authors claimed did not meet the standards of "solid scientific study" (Cantwell & Baker, 1988, p. 527). The new criteria appeared "hastily derived" and "largely untested" (Werry, 1988, p. 139). In fact, the diagnostic criteria for the three disruptive disorders, although agreed upon based on results of field studies, must be questioned based on the reliance upon clinically referred children in contrast to an epidemiologic screen (Spitzer, Davies, & Barkley, 1990). Cantwell and Baker (1988) also suggested that the criteria for ADHD were poorly selected and did not appear to fit within the clinical impressions of practitioners. Shaywitz and Shaywitz (1988) concluded that there was no empirical evidence to suggest that the revised diagnostic criteria were superior to those offered in *DSM-III*.

There is a volume of literature suggesting that ADHD with and without hyperactivity are very different disorders in children (Edelbrock et al., 1984; Lahey et al., 1987). Researchers have suggested that children experiencing attention problems without concomitant hyperactivity may present twice as frequently in epidemiological studies as attention-disordered hyperactive children (Lahey et al., 1984). Bauermeister, Alegria, Bird, Rubio-Stipec, and Canino (1992) generated *DSM-III-R* data very clearly distinguishing on a factorial basis, differences between teacher-rated descriptors of inattention and hyperactive-impulsive symptoms. Factor scores appear in Table 2–3. Others

Table 2–3.   Factor loadings for teacher-rated descriptors of ADHD and inattention symptoms

Items*	Inattention Factor	Hyperactivity-Impulsivity Factor
Constantly moves body or parts (hands, feet, etc.) (1)	0.29	0.61
Can't sit still, restless, or hyperactive (2)	0.11	0.83
Easily distracted (3)	0.73	0.35
Impulsive or acts without thinking (5)	0.22	0.74
Difficulty following instructions (6)	0.73	0.31
Can't concentrate, can't pay attention for long (7)	0.77	0.27
Fails to finish things (8)	0.74	0.29
Talks too much (10)	0.11	0.81
Interrupts class (11)	0.17	0.84
Stares blankly (12)	0.77	0.02
Gets hurt a lot, accident-prone (14)	0.09	0.42
Gets tired too much	0.45	0.41
Lazy	0.76	0.30
Confused or seems to be in a fog	0.75	0.21
Apathetic and lacks motivation	0.77	0.23
Underactive, slow moving, or lacks energy	0.76	0.18
Shows lack of persistence	0.78	0.24

Source: Bauermeister, J. J., Alegria, M., Bird, H. R., Rubio-Stipec, M., & Canino, G. (1992). Are attentional-hyperactivity deficits unidimensional or multi-dimensional syndromes? Empirical findings from a community survey. *Journal of the American Academy of Child and Adolescent Psychiatry, 31,* 423–431. Used with permission.

*Numbers in parentheses identify the corresponding *DSM-III-R* symptom.

have suggested quantitative differences, such as EEG patterns, may also distinguish the inattentive from the hyperactive-impulsive type of ADHD (Kuperman, Johnson, Arndt, Lindgren, & Wolraich, 1996). However, practitioners should be cautioned that even these authors suggest that at this time, the diagnostic promise of these tools is not supported by the research literature. This issue will be discussed further in Chapter 9.

The higher percentage of hyperactive ADHD children referred to mental health clinics is likely due to the cluster of aversive problems they present. As previously discussed, they have been suggested to have greater difficulty with conduct (King & Young, 1982; Pelham et al., 1981a). (See Chapter 1.) Behavioral comparisons have demonstrated that children with ADD with hyperactivity exhibit more conduct disorder problems (Edelbrock et al., 1984; Hynd, Lorys, et al., 1991; King & Young, 1982; Lahey et al., 1987), are more impulsive (Hynd, Lorys, et al.; Lahey et al., 1987), and are less anxious (Lahey et al., 1984, 1987) than ADD children without hyperactivity. ADD children without hyperactivity are reported as being more shy and socially withdrawn (Lahey et al., 1984), and ADD children with hyperactivity are reported as more unpopular (Lahey et al., 1994) and less socially competent (Cantwell & Baker, 1992; Hynd, Lorys, et al., 1991). ADD children without hyperactivity have a slower cognitive tempo (Lahey et al., 1985, 1987) and a higher comorbidity of learning disabilities (Hynd, Alison, et al., 1991). Neuropsychological studies have also reported this pattern of slower cognitive tempo and greater learning problems (Goodyear & Hynd, 1992). It has yet to be determined, however, whether these statistically significant group differences can be meaningfully translated into useful clinical criteria. Finally, of great importance is the congruence of research during periods in which significant differences existed in the diagnostic symptoms, processes, and criteria. Although there is significant overlap, for example, between the *DSM-III* ADD with hyperactivity and the *DSM-IV* ADHD combined type, these are not operationally identical and do not allow for a continuous train of research and theory projectively across studies over the past thirty years.

Healey, Newcorn, Halperin, and Wolf (1993) found a similar two-factor solution for both *DSM-III* and *DSM-III-R* attention disorder diagnoses. The factors consisted of items believed to reflect inattention as well as those reflective of hyperactivity-impulsivity. These factors were further evaluated against results of a cognitive test battery to ascertain whether objective external validation could be demonstrated. The hyperactivity-impulsivity factor was related to continuous performance test measures of response inhibition, and the inattentive and disorganization factor was related to measures of attention and efficiency of visual processing.

The relationship between *DSM-III* criteria for ADD and the *DSM-III-R* criteria for ADHD was evaluated in seventy-two inner-city elementary-school-age children using parent and teacher ratings (Newcorn et al., 1994). Each child was assessed using a psychometric test battery evaluating cognitive function, attention, and activity level. Teacher ratings identified more children as *DSM-III-R* ADHD than *DSM-III* ADD. Among these ADHD children, those who also met the ADD criteria missed more targets on a continuous performance task (CPT) and were more overactive than controls. They also had a greater likelihood of being rated as ADHD by parents. Children rated as meeting criteria for *DSM-III-R* ADHD but not *DSM-III* ADD were not substantially different from controls on teacher ratings of overactivity, CPT performance, or parent ratings of symptoms. This certainly raises questions regarding the nature and severity of the pathology in this group. Thus, these authors found more children identified as the diagnosis changed, suggesting a greater latitude (sensitivity) in the diagnostic process. The authors recommended that symptoms be reported in multiple situations or confirmed by objective measures as a prerequisite for the *DSM-III-R* ADHD diagnosis.

Goldstein and Goldstein (1990) agreed with Cantwell and Baker's (1988) conclusions. Ten of the fourteen criteria in part A of the *DSM-III-R* ADHD diagnosis appeared to relate to hyperactivity, impulsivity, or behavior problems. Since eight of the fourteen criteria had to be met, it was theoretically possible for a child to be considered ADHD and not present with even one of the four critical criteria relating to problems with attention. Thus, this could be a diagnosis of impulsivity and hyperactivity rather than inattention.

The *DSM-III-R,* however, was not without its supporters. August and Garfinkel (1993) discussed five central issues regarding the classification of ADHD in an epidemiologically derived sample of primary school children. This was an effort to deal with the issue of the clinic-referred field study sample. The monothetic only scheme of *DSM-III* differed from the polythetic scheme of *DSM-III-R* by having a higher frequency of comorbid conduct disorder. The pervasive model was too restrictive, identifying only the most severely disruptive or conduct-disordered children. Raising the minimal threshold above eight symptoms, the *DSM-III-R* missed less disruptive children who nevertheless exhibited significant functional impairment. There was, however, minimal support for the independence of a syndrome of Attention Deficit Disorder without Hyperactivity based on the analysis of these authors. They also noted the almost too common comorbidity of diagnosis in the ADHD population, with most frequent comorbid diagnoses of conduct disorder, oppositional defiance, and anxiety disorder.

A sample of 232 fourth-grade children was assessed utilizing a checklist for *DSM-III-R* ADHD (Gallucci et al., 1993). In this population, nearly 40% had eight or more *DSM-III-R* symptoms. These children received frequent scores for these symptoms from their teachers. An additional 7% did not meet this threshold but had a total score of sixteen or more on the scale and were considered possible cases. Spitzer et al. (1990) suggested that the sensitivity for the ADHD cutoff score of eight out of fourteen symptoms diminished significantly with age, implying that at least for these criteria some developmental framework was necessary. Six of fourteen symptoms were suggested as sensitive for age 13 and older, with possibly eleven of fourteen symptoms necessary for children under age 5. As noted, the number of symptoms that appear to categorically set ADHD individuals apart from others appears to diminish with increasing age (Barkley & Murphy, 1993).

Despite complaints, the *DSM-III-R* criteria for ADHD represented an attempt to improve the operational definition of diagnostic behaviors. The revised criteria noted that the child had to present with onset of symptoms before age 7, experience the disturbance for at least six months, not experience a pervasive developmental disorder, and not have problems primarily stemming from retardation, schizophrenia, or severe emotional or behavioral problems. It is important to note that a coexisting diagnosis of ADHD can be made for these populations if the relevant symptoms are excessive, even in light of these other disorders. The suggestion was also made in these criteria to consider a diagnosis of mood disorder before making the diagnosis of ADHD. The

DSM-III-R definition also included general criteria for severity ratings of mild, moderate, and severe.

Additionally, the authors of the *DSM-III-R* included the category of Undifferentiated Attention Deficit Disorder, described as a diagnosis "for disturbances in which the predominant feature is the persistence of developmentally inappropriate and marked inattention that is not a symptom of another disorder such as retardation or a disorganized, chaotic environment" (APA, 1987, p. 96). This category represents a bridge between the categorical and dimensional systems.

Barkley (1990b) argued that a number of changes needed to be made with the *DSM-III-R* symptoms as the *DSM-IV* was developed. In addition to a return to the distinction of hyperactive-impulsive versus inattentive diagnostic considerations, it was suggested that dimension or symptom lists within criteria be established with cutoff scores and rewording of items to apply to different levels of development and gender. At that time, Barkley also suggested that the diagnosis, which appeared primarily based on history and observed behavior, should be augmented with objective tests of vigilance and impulsivity or at the very least the direct, systematic inclusion of coded observations of behavior in laboratory or real-life settings.

Although the *DSM-III-R* provided the first thorough description of behavioral problems children with ADHD present, it did not resolve the need for practitioners to understand the impact that development and life experience have on children's behavior as well as the importance of gathering information from a wide variety of sources by a wide variety of means. Without such a model, the isolated use of a categorical diagnostic system such as the *DSM*'s results in an overinclusion of children with possibly a wide variety of problems. In fact, it can be argued that the *DSM-III-R* and subsequent *DSM-IV* symptom lists represent good general lists of the most common problems that set 20% of our childhood population apart from the remaining 80% who do not experience significant life problems. Thus, symptoms of ADHD may be a good place to start as a screener but an inadequate point to end the diagnostic process. Otherwise, it is likely that children with a wide variety of emotional, developmental, and behavioral problems would be inappropriately diagnosed as ADHD. Satin, Winsberg, Monetti, Sverd, and Ross (1985), in a study screening 6- to 9-year-old boys in the general population, found 24% met the *DSM-III* ADD criteria when these criteria were the only questions asked. Ostrom and Jenson (1988) reinterpreted data from this study and suggested that over 16% of this population would have met the *DSM-III-R* ADHD criteria as well.

At one time it appeared excessively liberal to make age 7 the cutoff for the onset of symptoms when the majority of children in North America enter school at age 5. It is a well-researched phenomenon that children with unidentified learning problems or other emotional difficulties entering the school system cannot meet academic demands, and in response to the stress placed upon them may develop a pattern of inattentive, impulsive, and restless behavior (Cunningham & Barkley, 1978a). However, more recently it has been argued that even up to age 12, the later onset of ADHD symptoms may not represent a cause other than ADHD but rather represent the compensatory strengths of a particular child capable of coping with ADHD symptoms as the result of other abilities (e.g., high intelligence, good environment). Nonetheless, it is important for the practitioner to recognize that the majority of children diagnosed with

ADHD, especially the 80% to 90% with the combined type of ADHD, present a clear pattern of problems before entering an organized school program (Barkley, 1981a) and to begin the diagnostic process with a careful developmental and social history.

DSM-IV Definition

The *DSM-IV* diagnostic criteria (APA, 1994) made an effort to move forward and correct for the mistaken course that ADHD represents a unipolar disorder. The field studies for the ADHD diagnosis were more comprehensive and better structured. The *DSM-IV* criteria appear in Table 2–4.

The age of onset criteria as prior to age 7 for the diagnosis of ADHD first appeared in the third edition of the diagnostic manual in 1980. Unfortunately, it along with the other definitive criteria were not based on empirical trial. Yet since that time, the 7-year age of onset criteria has become a mainstay in the diagnostic nomenclature for ADHD. The 7-year-old criteria was placed in the *DSM-IV* prior to the analysis of this aspect of the field trial data. Recently, the validity of the age of onset criterion was examined in a clinic sample of 380 youth, ages 4 through 17 years receiving diagnoses of ADHD (Applegate et al., 1997). Although all children who subsequently receive the diagnosis of ADHD, combined or hyperactive-impulsive type, met the onset of at least one symptom for age 7 years, 50% of those with the inattentive type did not. Eighteen percent of those having the combined type, 2% of those having the hyperactive-impulsive type, and 43% of those having the inattentive type had their onset of impairment after 7 years of age. Comparisons of those subjects having an age of onset after 7 years with those before 7 years yielded no significant differences in the nature of their comorbid disorders nor in the degree of impairment as assessed by various means. Further, requiring impairment prior to 7 years of age appeared to reduce the accuracy of identification of currently impaired cases of ADHD and reduced agreement with clinicians' judgment. In light of these new data, practitioners are cautioned to not discard a diagnosis of ADHD simply if a child does not meet the age of onset criteria but meets all the other criteria currently. Practitioners are urged to carefully examine history and consider a more liberal age cutoff of 12 years.

In the field trial studies, a number of interesting phenomena emerged. Of the 276 children diagnosed with ADHD, 55% had the combined type, 27% the inattentive type, and 18% the hyperactive-inattentive type. Less than half of the ADHD hyperactive-impulsive type (44%) received that diagnosis when *DSM-III* criteria for ADD with hyperactivity were used. These two diagnoses, therefore, only partially overlapped. The hyperactive-impulsive group had fewer symptoms of inattention than children in the combined group. They also had fewer symptoms of hyperactive-impulsive problems, suggesting that this represents a less severe variant of the disorder. Despite that fact, clinicians making the diagnoses overwhelmingly asserted that the hyperactive-impulsive group should receive a diagnosis of ADHD and rated these children as having the same level of overall impairment as the combined group.

The hyperactive-impulsive group contained 20% females, the combined group 12%, and the inattentive group 27%. This last number represents clinicians' perceptions over the years that females more often demonstrate the inattentive type of ADHD.

Table 2–4.   *DSM-IV* **criteria for Attention-Deficit/Hyperactivity Disorder**

The guidelines for a diagnosis of ADHD outlined in the *Diagnostic and Statistical Manual of Mental Disorders* (4th edition, 1994) are as follows:

A. Either (1) or (2):

    (1) Six or more of the following symptoms of *inattention* have persisted for at least 6 months to a degree that is maladaptive and inconsistent with developmental level:

        Inattention

        a. Often fails to give close attention to details or makes careless mistakes in school-work, work, or other activities.

        b. Often has difficulty sustaining attention in tasks or play activities.

        c. Often does not seem to listen when spoken to directly.

        d. Often does not follow through on instructions and fails to finish schoolwork, chores, or duties in the workplace (not due to oppositional behavior or failure to understand instructions).

        e. Often has difficulties organizing tasks and activities.

        f. Often avoids, dislikes, or is reluctant to engage in tasks that require sustained mental effort (such as schoolwork or homework).

        g. Often loses things necessary for tasks or activities (e.g., toys, school assignments, pencils, books, or tools).

        h. Is often easily distracted by extraneous stimuli.

        i. Is often forgetful in daily activities.

    (2) Six (or more) of the following symptoms of *hyperactivity-impulsivity* have persisted for at least 6 months to a degree that is maladaptive and inconsistent with developmental level:

        Hyperactivity

        a. Often fidgets with hands or feet or squirms in seat.

        b. Often leaves seat in classroom or in other situations in which remaining seated is expected.

        c. Often runs about or climbs excessively in situations in which it is inappropriate (in adolescents or adults, may be limited to subjective feelings of restlessness).

        d. Often has difficulty playing or engaging in leisure activities quietly.

        e. Is often "on the go" or often acts as if "driven by a motor."

        f. Often talks excessively.

        Impulsivity

        g. Often blurts out answers before questions have been completed.

        h. Often has difficulty awaiting turn.

        i. Often interrupts or intrudes on others (e.g., butts into conversations or games).

B. Some hyperactive-impulsive or inattentive symptoms that caused impairment were present before age 7 years.

C. Some impairment from the symptoms is present in two or more settings (e.g., at school [or work] and at home).

D. There must be clear evidence of clinically significant impairment in social, academic, or occupational functioning.

E. The symptoms do not occur exclusively during the course of a Pervasive Developmental Disorder, Schizophrenia, or other Psychotic Disorder and are not better accounted for by another mental disorder (e.g., Mood Disorder, Anxiety Disorder, Dissociative Disorder, or a Personality Disorder).

Table 2–4.   *(continued)*

Types

Attention-Deficit/Hyperactivity Disorder, Combined Types: if both Criteria A1 and A2 are met for the past 6 months.

Attention-Deficit/Hyperactivity Disorder, Predominantly Inattentive Type: if Criterion A1 is met but Criterion A2 is not met for the past 6 months.

Attention-Deficit/Hyperactivity Disorder, Predominantly Hyperactive-Impulsive Type: if Criterion A2 is met but Criterion A1 is not met for the past 6 months.

Coding note: For individuals (especially adolescents and adults) who currently have symptoms that no longer meet full criteria, "In Partial Remission" should be specified.

Attention-Deficit/Hyperactivity Disorder Not Otherwise Specified
This category is for disorders with prominent symptoms of inattention or hyperactivity-impulsivity that do not meet criteria for Attention-Deficit/Hyperactivity Disorder.

Source: American Psychiatric Association (1994). Reprinted with permission of the *Diagnostic and statistical manual of mental disorders* (4th ed. rev.). Washington, DC: Author. Copyright © 1994, American Psychiatric Association.

This overrepresentation has not been well explained by any theoretical model (Silverthorn, Frick, Kuper, & Ott, 1996), nor has it been understood why preliminary research suggests that females with ADHD may be less likely to demonstrate executive function deficits than males with ADHD (Seidman et al., 1997).

In the field studies, the hyperactive-impulsive population was younger. Seventy-six percent were between the ages of 4 and 6 years. In contrast, the average age was 8.5 for the combined group and nearly 10 years of age for the inattentive group. Clinicians agreed that among this group of hyperactive-impulsive children, it was likely most would receive a combined diagnosis by school age. Further, the late age for the diagnosis of the inattentive group is not surprising given the lack of disruptiveness of their symptoms.

Surprisingly, the hyperactive-impulsive group had fewer disruptive symptoms of oppositional defiance or conduct disorder than the combined group, and the combined group was similar to the inattentive group in other disruptive disorders. The hyperactive-impulsive group demonstrated academic difficulty similar to the control group. The hyperactive-impulsive children had a similar level of peer problems as the inattentive group and were less impaired than the combined group. Finally, the hyperactive-impulsive children and those in the combined group demonstrated the same frequency of accidents, which was higher than the accident rate for the clinic controls. It is important to note that the inattentive subtype must have six or more of the inattentive symptoms but can have as many as five of the hyperactive-impulsive symptoms. The opposite is also true for the hyperactive-impulsive subtype.

Since the publication of the *DSM-IV,* a number of comparative diagnostic studies have been completed. In general, it has been suggested that the change from *DSM-III-R* to *DSM-IV* has resulted in minimal changes in case identification among clinically referred children (Biederman et al., 1997). In 1996, Morgan, Hynd, Riccio, and Hall examined a population of children who had received attention deficit diagnoses utilizing *DSM-III* and *DSM-III-R* with a retrospective diagnostic protocol utilizing *DSM-IV.* Fifty-six children were evaluated. The *DSM-III-R* ADHD diagnosis did not correspond with any *DSM-IV* subtype. Children with the *DSM-IV* combined type had more externalizing codiagnoses; their parents also reported more externalizing, delinquent, and aggressive behaviors for them. Children with a predominantly *DSM-IV* inattentive type were more likely to have a history of math learning disability. Results supported a multidimensional conceptualization of ADHD. There appears to be a close correspondence between *DSM-III* ADD without hyperactivity and *DSM-IV* inattentive type, as well as between *DSM-III* with hyperactivity and *DSM-IV* combined type.

Paternite, Loney, and Roberts (1996) generated evidence for the validity of ADHD, including the inattentive and combined subtypes, on measures of impairment and mother-, father-, and teacher-rated disruptive symptoms as well as observed playroom behavior. Few differences were obtained on measures of family context and age-corrected indices of cognitive or attentional laboratory functioning. Supplementary analyses of boys with ADHD combined type subgrouped based on the presence or absence of oppositional defiant disorder and conduct disorder appeared to highlight the role of diagnostic comorbidity as well as some of the dysfunctions that are typically misattributed to ADHD. For example, in this study, reported differences among the ADHD subtypes in regard to aggressive symptoms appeared to be the result of comorbity with other disruptive disorders. Seventy-nine percent of the combined type and 78% of the hyperactive-impulsive males were comorbid for either oppositional defiant disorder or conduct disorder. In contrast, only 29% of the inattentive type were comorbid for either of the disruptive diagnoses.

Baumgaertel, Wolraich, and Dietrich (1995) compared teacher-reported prevalence rates using *DSM-IV, DSM-III-R,* and *DSM-III* criteria within the same population of elementary-school-age children. Teacher ratings were obtained for over 1,000 children in five rural and five urban public schools in Germany. The overall prevalence for attention problems increased from 9.6% for *DSM-III* to 17.8% for *DSM-IV*. The increase is primarily due to new cases identified as the inattentive type of ADHD and, to a lesser extent, the hyperactive-impulsive type. Inattention in any subtype was associated with academic problems. Perceived behavioral problems were associated with more than 80% of the cases in the hyperactive-impulsive type. *DSM-IV* ADHD subtypes showed significant behavioral, academic, and demographic differences. Application of *DSM-IV* criteria increased ADHD prevalence rates by 64% and identified the majority of children in school with academic and/or behavioral dysfunction. These data were interpreted as suggesting a significant heterogeneity among the subtypes, implying that many children with non-ADHD problems screen into these subtypes and will require further evaluation to ensure appropriate management. These authors note that a distribution of *DSM-IV* subtypes in this study differed greatly from that of McBurnett, Lahey, and Pfiffner's (1993) field trial. In the German group, 60% of children met the criteria for the inattentive type and almost 30% met those for the hyperactive-impulsive type. In the McBurnett et al. study, the ADHD group demonstrated 65% with the combined type and 15% of the other two numbers that were not significantly different from the Lahey et al. report (1994). Baumgaertel et al. (1995) suggest that this difference may be due to the referred nature, that is, the clinic basis of the population versus their epidemiologic sample.

In an epidemiologic study of all kindergarten through fifth-grade children, nearly 8,000 in a Tennessee county school district, Wolraich, Hannah, Pinnock, Baumgaertel, and Brown (1996) had teachers complete questionnaires rating all students for *DSM-III-R* and *DSM-IV* symptoms of disruptive behavior disorders. Prevalence rates were 7.3% meeting the *DSM-III-R* criteria and 11.4% meeting the *DSM-IV* criteria. This latter group included 5.4% of the total population with the inattentive type, 2.4% with the hyperactive-impulsive type, and 3.6% with the combined type. Epidemiologically, this profile appeared more similar to the clinic-referred populations in the *DSM-IV* field studies than the German sample. In this study, factor analyses identified five factors: oppositional defiance/conduct, inattention, hyperactivity-impulsivity, anxiety-depression, and stealing-truancy. The rates of problems differed most between the inattentive and hyperactive types, with 40% versus 80% experiencing behavior problems and 75% versus 23% with academic problems. Fifteen percent versus 40% had a previous ADHD diagnosis and 21% versus 32% had previous use of stimulants. *DSM-IV* criteria appeared to increase the prevalence of the disorder compared to *DSM-III-R* rates. However, it also appeared to characterize the heterogeneity of the disorder. Consistent with findings from other studies, the combined type had a lower percentage of academic (73%) than behavioral (92%) problems. These comorbidity results are similar to those found in the German sample. These authors, too, note that this diagnostic subtype appears most similar to the *DSM-III* ADD with hyperactivity and reflects the most common conception of the child with ADHD. This group also had the highest rates of all comorbid conditions, the most impaired problems, and the worst prognoses. The authors were surprised to note that even among the combined group, 40% had been identified, yet 60% had not been identified with ADHD. The authors concluded that the *DSM-IV* criteria are likely to increase the prevalence of ADHD in comparison to *DSM-III-R* because of the creation of two new subtypes. Descriptively, the inattentive type was characterized by academic problems with fewer behavioral problems and a higher female-to-male ratio. The hyperactive-impulsive group appeared characterized by behavioral problems with few cases having academic problems and low rates of anxiety and depressive symptoms. Finally, the combined type had both characteristics and appears close to the original *DSM-III* ADD with hyperactivity. A powerful argument is made that there has been a large group of children with ADHD who go undiagnosed and untreated. The dramatic increases in the use of stimulants over the past five years (Safer et al., 1996) appears to clearly reflect the increased rate of diagnosis. Although more children are being diagnosed, it is likely that the numbers of children being diagnosed are slowly approximating that percentage of the population identified in epidemiologic studies as suffering from the disorder. It should be noted that even when the slightly different criteria defined through the ninth edition of the *International Classification of Diseases* for Hyperkinetic Disorder is utilized for assessment, the prevalence rate is approximately 1% to 2% (Taylor, Sandberg, Thorley, & Giles, 1991).

Finally, a number of researchers have demonstrated the validity of the current diagnostic conceptualization for ADHD utilizing a variety of clinical and laboratory measures. Such research has included a full battery of neuropsychological tests (Brand, Das-Smaal, & DeJonge, 1996; Halperin et al., 1993), reversal and memory tasks (O'Neill & Douglas, 1996), and neurological evaluation (Luk, Leung, & Yuen, 1991).

The general consistency in symptom, comorbid, and related findings among these large, well-controlled clinic and epidemiologic studies certainly suggests that the conceptualization of ADHD has become more refined. Nonetheless, the *DSM-IV* criteria continue to focus excessively on inattention as the core problem, limiting the scope of the impact of impulsivity as the core deficit. Change takes time. Sandwiched between researchers and clinicians, the authors of the diagnostic manuals move slowly through a process involving much time and politics. Anastopoulos, Barkley, and Shelton (1994), however, note that the continued focus on inattention perpetuates a number of major misconceptions, including that the inattentive type of ADHD represents a subtype of the combined type. Research increasingly suggests that it does not. More likely, the inattentive type represents a distinct disorder primarily reflecting difficulty attending to repetitive, effortful tasks and distinct problems with disorganization. The problems that this group experiences may very well be the result of faulty skills as opposed to inconsistent or inadequate use of possessed skills. For the time being, however, the inattentive type is still considered part of a larger cluster of attention disorder diagnoses. Ironically, though these children are not disturbing or disruptive to the adults in their lives, their disorder continues to be defined along the disruptive continuum.

As additional field studies are undertaken in the ongoing process of evolving diagnostic systems and in preparation for *DSM-V,* a number of questions will be asked and, we hope, addressed. Among these questions are those distinguishing the meaning and relationship of the combined, hyperactive-impulsive, and inattentive subtypes. As noted by others, it is likely that the hyperactive-impulsive type represents the early developmental stage of the combined type and that the two fall on a single continuum (Barkley, 1995a). Barkley goes so far as to raise the question of whether inattention should even be required to make the diagnosis of the combined type of ADHD. Among additional questions raised and yet to be answered concerning the evolution of the ADHD diagnosis are:

- Age-related symptom issues.
- Diagnostic symptoms for children under age 5 as well as adults.
- Age of onset and its meaning.
- Lower-age boundary at which a diagnosis should not be made.
- Adjustment of diagnostic criteria based on gender.
- The need for demonstration of symptoms in at least two or three environments.

The degree of agreement between parents and teachers concerning children's behavior is modest but not extensive (Achenbach, McConaughy, & Howell, 1987). The use of this criteria sets an artificial upper limit on the extent to which parents and teachers are going to agree on the severity of ADHD symptoms. As Barkley (1995a) notes, insisting on agreement may reduce the applicability of the diagnosis unfairly for some children simply as the result of differences between parent and teacher opinions or, for that matter, parent and teacher styles or home and school environments.

The Practical Definition

The practical definition was first proposed by Goldstein and Goldstein in 1990 as a commonsense means of facilitating adults' ability to see the world through the eyes of children with this set of core problems. It was suggested that this definition also would facilitate the practitioner's ability to understand this group of children and assist parents and teachers in understanding the children they live with and educate. Understanding ADHD is the first and most crucial step in making change. This practical definition represents an effort to translate the volume of research findings and clinical symptoms of ADHD into a framework to understand the everyday lives of these children, a logical framework from which to evaluate and understand the seemingly illogical pattern of behavior this group of children exhibits. It also facilitates understanding of this group of children's inability to respond to more traditional treatment interventions. The commonsense definition of Goldstein and Goldstein was based in part on the hypotheses of Douglas and Peters (1979) and Douglas (1985). These authors suggested that children with attention deficit experience a constitutional predisposition to experience problems with attention, effort, inhibitory control, and poorly modulated arousal and have a need to seek stimulation.

The original definition contained four components, each of which was considered equally important, as each was believed to exert equal impact on the child. The current conceptualization of this definition now contains five components, with the first, impulsivity, being the major contributing force in shaping the other four components. The five components will be briefly presented next, followed by a lengthier discussion of the current research literature concerning each:

1. *Impulsivity.* ADHD children have difficulty thinking before they act. They know what to do but don't do what they know. They have difficulty weighing the consequences of their actions before acting and do not reasonably consider the consequences of their past behavior. Their difficulty following rule-governed behavior (Barkley, 1981a) appears to result directly from their inability to separate experience from response, thought from emotion, and action from reaction. Although they may be well aware of a rule and able to explain it, in their environment they are unable to control their actions and to think before they act. This results in impetuous, unthinking behavior and children who seemingly do not appear to learn from their experiences. In actuality, they have learned from their experiences but have difficulty acting efficiently upon that knowledge. Frequently, they are repeat offenders. They appear to require more parental and teacher supervision. They frustrate parents and teachers with their seeming inability to benefit from experience. One parent described his frustration this way: twenty-nine times he had asked his child not to get into his tools; the child did so a thirtieth time. This child was able to explain what had been requested but his immediate need for gratification was overwhelmed by his limited capacity for self-control. Frequently, parent and teacher perspectives of this problem label the behavior purposeful, noncaring, and oppositional, which does not accurately describe what is taking place and often leads to punitive, ineffective interventions.

2. *Inattention.* ADHD children have difficulty remaining on task and focusing attention in comparison to non-ADHD children of similar chronological age (APA, 1994). It has been suggested that as children get older, they become more efficient in their ability to sustain attention, with 2-year-olds capable of sustaining

attention on the average for barely a few minutes and 5-year-olds able to sustain attention for much longer periods (Caul, 1985). From that point on, children's attention span continues to increase with age. By first grade we expect children to be able to sit and work for a half hour at a time. It is increasingly recognized, however, that the capacity to attend is intrinsically tied to multiple environmental factors. Thus, the measurement of attention as a unitary phenomenon has not provided much in the conceptualization and understanding of, as well as the assessment and intervention for, ADHD. At one time, it was also suspected that distractibility was the core problem (Strauss & Kephart, 1955). We are now aware that distractibility represents a minimal part of the ADHD child's problem. It is the inability to invest in the task rather than distractions that is primarily responsible for off-task behavior. From an attention perspective, it has been increasingly recognized that repetitive, effortful, uninteresting, and unchosen tasks are the most difficult ones for children with ADHD. Not surprisingly, these characteristics define the most difficult tasks for everyone to engage in. This reinforces an important point: ADHD represents an exaggeration, on a dimensional basis, of normal problems, such as too much fidgeting at the dinner table or an inadequate investment in tasks that must be completed. On a dimensional basis, these children represent the extreme of what adults expect. Increasingly, it is recognized that this impulsiveness results in children's inability to sustain attention under these circumstances.

3. *Hyperactivity and Overarousal.* Children with ADHD tend to be excessively restless, overactive, and easily aroused emotionally. Their difficulty in controlling bodily movements is especially noted in situations in which they are required to sit still or stay put for long periods of time. They are quicker to become aroused. Whether happy or sad, the speed and intensity with which they move to the extreme of their emotions is much greater than that of their same-age peers. This problem very clearly reflects their impulsive inability to separate thought from emotion. This pattern of behavior frequently frustrates parents because soon after becoming extremely upset, the child has forgotten the upsetting event and moves on to something else. Parents, however, continue to be agitated by these events and cannot understand why the child no longer seems to be bothered. This child is then accused of lacking guilt. As one parent has aptly put it, children with ADHD wear their emotions on their sleeves.

4. *Difficulty with Gratification.* As the result of impulsivity, children with ADHD require immediate, frequent, predictable, and meaningful rewards. They appear to demonstrate less sensitivity to changing parameters of reinforcement rate which may be secondary to problems sustaining attention and/or faulty inhibition (Kollins, Lane, & Shapiro, 1997). Once again, they are at excess or exaggeration in comparison to normal children in regard to these variables. For these reasons, they experience greater difficulty working toward a long-term goal. They frequently require brief, repeated payoffs rather than a single long-term reward. They also do not appear to respond to rewards in a manner similar to other children (Haenlein & Caul, 1987). Rewards do not appear to be effective in changing their behavior on a long-term basis. Frequently, once the reward and the accompanying structure of the behavior-change program is

removed, the ADHD child regresses and again exhibits behavior that was the target of change. Parents then perceive this child as manipulative, accusing him or her of blackmail or extortion. It has been recognized that due to impulsiveness, children with ADHD appear to require more trials to consistently demonstrate mastery over their behavior. Thus, it is not that they don't learn what to do as quickly as others, it is that they do not exhibit those behaviors as effectively. Problems result from missing the cue necessary to self-direct the behavior. Thus, they arrive at a street corner, forget that the corner is a cue to look both ways, and, despite the fact that they understand traffic safety, blindly walk out into the street. Because of their impulsiveness, their behavior remains consequentially bound. However, it also appears that given a sufficient number of trials and opportunities for generalization, their behavior, that is, the capacity to do consistently what one knows, is shaped in a way similar to that of unaffected children. For children with ADHD in regard to consequences and behavior development, the issue is not so much behavior modification as behavior management. The provision of a sufficient number of supervised, structured, and reinforced trials for everything from simple toothbrushing behavior to social skills development is essential.

It also appears that this group of children receives significantly more negative reinforcement than others. That is, instead of learning to work to earn good consequences or having their mistakes shaped by punishment, the majority of their interactions with adults are shaped by the child's efforts to avoid aversive consequences. Because of these children's impulsivity and inconsistency, adults frequently place great pressure on them. The child responds not to complete the task but to gain relief from the adult's aversive attention. Negative reinforcement appears to offer a plausible explanation for the diverse problems children with ADHD present, ranging from completing homework and not turning it in (homework is completed so Mom will stop screaming, not to earn a grade) to the lack of development of seemingly responsible behavior (e.g., if you are always acting to avoid an aversive consequence, you learn to wait for the threat of an aversive consequence before doing what has to be done, whether it is chores, schoolwork, or appropriate behavior toward others). In many ways, children with ADHD are cursed with negative reinforcement. In our efforts to help them, we actually increase their helplessness. It is important to keep in mind that they like rewards and they do not like punishments. However, over time it is the avoidance of aversive consequences rather than the earning of positive consequences by which their behavior is shaped. They learn to respond to demands placed on them by the environment, principally adults in the environment, when an aversive stimulus is removed contingent upon performance rather than for the promise of a future reward.

5. *Emotions and Locus of Control.* To the original four components of this definition this fifth component is added. Due to their impulsiveness and emotional overarousal, children with ADHD are often on a roller-coaster ride of emotions throughout their childhood. When they are happy, they are so happy that people tell them to calm down. When they are unhappy, they are so unhappy that people tell them to calm down. They learn that emotions are not to be valued but,

instead, often lead to trouble. The combination of these qualities, feedback when received for emotionality, lack of ability to develop the skills necessary to control emotions, and the disruption in relationships these qualities cause exerts a significant impact on children's emerging sense of self, locus of control, and likely subsequent personality. It has been argued that children with ADHD appear more prone to develop an external locus of control, projecting blame onto others and being unwilling to recognize and accept the role they play in their behavior. They appear more vulnerable to developing certain personality problems, especially those related to antisocial difficulties, likely in part because of these qualities combining with certain life experiences. They may also be more prone to depression due to the lack of balance between successful and unsuccessful experiences on a daily basis. It is important for practitioners to recognize this emotional impact, not just because it is important for today but because the quality of children's emotional lives very powerfully shapes their adult outcome.

CLINICAL AND PRACTICAL ISSUES TOWARD AN UNDERSTANDING OF THE ECOLOGY OF ADHD

Since publication in 1990 of the first edition of this text, the concepts of impulsiveness, attention, motivation and consequences, emotional control, and situational issues relative to aspects of ADHD have been critically and in some cases extensively examined. There has also been a trend to seek out and incorporate theories, concepts, and research literature from diverse fields with the aim of better understanding and creating a working model of the daily behavior and cognitive processes underlying the behavior of ADHD children and adolescents. This section reviews literature relevant to these issues.

Impulsivity

The concept of impulsivity as causing problems of the human condition is not new. The Greek physician, Hippocrates (460–377 B.C.) wrote about impulsive anger. The impulsive act of Lot's wife in the book of *Genesis* turning to look back at the destruction of Sodom resulted in her losing her life. In 1890, James defined impulses as ephemeral thoughts usually tied to forceful urges. The popular perception of an impulsive person is someone who acts with some degree of frequency on impulsive or unplanned thoughts that others either do not have or have but do not act on (Goslin, 1969). Whereas impulse often refers to thoughts, impulsivity refers to a constellation of repeated behaviors that are somehow related to these thoughts (Stanford & Barratt, 1992). Although this appears to represent a consensus view, further definition of impulsivity has not resulted in a more detailed delineation (Parker, Bagby, & Webster, 1993). Impulsivity has been described as a number of overlapping and somewhat contradictory definitions, including human behavior without adequate thought (Smith, 1952), behavior with no thought whatsoever (English, 1928), action of instinct without recourse to ego restraint (Demont, 1933), swift action of mind without forethought or conscious judgment (Hinslie & Shatzky, 1940), and the absence of reflection between an environmental stimulus and an individual's response (Doob, 1990). Although many dictionaries define impulsivity as acting with little thought concerning future action, impulse is also described by the dictionary as an impelling or driving forward with sudden force (Webster & Jackson, 1997).

As Eysenck and Eysenck (1985) note, an impulsive act can either be viewed positively as reflecting an inclination toward adventure or negatively as associated with actions that get oneself into trouble. Some researchers have suggested a tri-dimensional model of impulsivity involving motor, cognitive, and poor planning components (Barratt, 1985). Dickman (1990) differentiates between dysfunctional impulsivity and functional impulsivity. The difference is measured in outcome. One leads to problems, the other solutions.

Thus, it appears that four clusters of behavior are relevant to the term of impulsivity, including:

1. Acting without control, inhibition restraint, or suppression;
2. Acting without thinking, reflection, or consideration;
3. Acting without foresight, adequate planning, or regard for consequences; or
4. Acting with a sense of immediacy and spontaneity.

For an indepth review of impulsivity as a historical and contemporary issue, readers are referred to McCown and DeSimone (1993). Interested readers are referred to McCown, Johnson, and Shure (1993) for an indepth discussion of impulsivity and its hypothesized impact upon human behavior.

Interest in inhibition and its relationship to voluntary control has been a line of research with a wide variety of populations (Hasher & Zaks, 1988; Logan, Cowan, & Davis, 1984; Tipper, 1985). It has been argued that poor delay of gratification secondary to limited control of inhibition may be a risk factor for developing externalizing disorders and that the ability to delay gratification is linked to multiple adaptive tendencies in early adolescence (Krueger, Caspi, Moffitt, & White, 1996). Thus, it is not surprising that researchers began to take a look at the role impulsiveness may play in symptom presentation, severity, and comorbid problems for children with ADHD. Multiple measures have been developed to evaluate impulsivity, including self-report, personality scales, reaction time, and time perception measures. As with laboratory measures for ADHD, many of these measures do not intercorrelate very highly (Parker, Bagby, & Webster, 1997).

Oosterland and Sergeant (1996) have demonstrated that ADHD children as well as children with aggression demonstrate poor inhibitory control and slower inhibitory processes. Impulsive individuals additionally have been found to overestimate the passage of time (Gerbing, Ahadi, & Patton, 1987; van den Broek, Bradshaw, & Szabadi, 1992) take more risks and persist in the face of increasing punishment and lack of reward (Newman & Wallace, 1993) and are willing to trade accuracy for speed leading to disinhibition at the motor output stage and failure to temporarily withhold activated responses, especially when reinforcement is available (Leung & Connolly, 1997). Thus, ADHD is likely not a primary disturbance of attention. Barkley (1993, 1997c), based in part on a model developed by Bronowski (1977), developed a theoretical model of ADHD suggesting that the primary problem component in ADHD is one of disinhibition or poor delay of response rather than inattention. Citing Bronowski's model, Barkley notes that impulsive individuals have difficulty with prolongation, separation of affect, internalization, and reconstitution. Bronowski's conceptualization of each of these issues is briefly described below. Impulsive children will have difficulty with:

- *Prolongation.* This reflects the ability to hold in one's mind an event that has just happened and to sustain this mental representation over time. This process allows the individual to respond to a new event by considering past events in a series. Impulsivity results in disruption in this process. Children with ADHD learn from their experiences but have difficulty acting on that knowledge because they do not delay acting until consequences are considered. They do not work well with delayed consequences, and they don't return to an interrupted activity.
- *Separation of Affect.* Inhibition allows an individual to separate thought from feeling. Without this capacity, an individual will tend to respond to an experience without considering the emotional or cognitive components. As educator Rick Lavoie has noted, impulsive children demonstrate OTM-OTM: on the mind, out the mouth.
- *Internalization.* Disinhibited individuals are less adept at communicating rules to themselves and to others. They are less able to use rules they possess to control and direct their own behavior.
- *Reconstitution.* The ability to break down information into smaller parts and to manipulate and recombine these parts into entirely new ideas defines reconstitution. Impulsive individuals do not engage in this behavior successfully. They struggle to analyze and synthesize all relevant information available. Thus, their problem-solving skills appear limited.

These mental activities allow individuals to develop self-control and direct behavior toward the future, allow consideration of consequences, and, most important, allow for adaptation and problem solving. Based on an extensive review of the research, M. Gordon (1995a) reports that it is not inattention that is consistently demonstrated in laboratory experiments with this group of children but rather impulsivity. Impulsivity consistently distinguishes the group with ADHD from other psychiatric disorders. Gordon suggests that clinicians focus on impulsivity and the problems caused by being impulsive rather than inattention during the evaluative process.

Reardon and Naglieri (1992) found significant differences on measures of planning, attention, and follow-through between ADHD and normal children, with the ADHD children earning significantly lower scores. These authors concluded that their results reflected the decreased cognitive competency of children with ADHD, suggesting that they were unable to attend to relevant stimulus information. Their greatest difficulty appears to be formulating and monitoring plans and strategies while inhibiting impulsive responding. Others have concluded that children with reading disability may be delayed in the development of processing skills required for efficient planning and problem solving but that strategic planning behavior was not responsible for this impairment, as suggested in those with ADHD (Condor, Anderson, & Saling, 1995). These authors argue that the delay in information-processing skills may affect time and practice required by children with learning disability to become familiar with and execute tasks, a problem different from faulty inhibition observed in children with ADHD. Van der Meere, van Baal, and Sergeant (1989) have demonstrated that task inefficiency in learning-disabled children is caused by an impairment in divided attention involving memory and decision processes. Children with ADHD, however, do not demonstrate that level of problem but are delayed in motor-decision processing. This process links perception to action, suggesting difficulty handling decisions, rules, and reasoning, likely a function of impulsive responding (Sergeant & van der Meere, 1988; van der Meere & Sergeant, 1987, 1988a, 1988b, 1988c).

It appears that problems with attention in ADHD are the by-product of impulsiveness or poor response inhibition. As Barkley (1994) notes, inefficiency in this arena leads to:

- Difficulty fixing on and sustaining mental images or messages that relate to external events so that you can act or not act upon them;
- Problems referencing the past in relation to those events;
- Difficulty imagining hypothetical futures that might result from those events;
- Problems establishing goals and plans of action to implement them;
- Difficulty avoiding reacting to stimuli likely to interfere with goal-directed behavior;
- Poor utilization of internal speech in the service of self-regulation and goal-directed behavior;
- Inefficient regulation of affect and motivation or response to situational demands;
- Problems separating affect from information or feelings from facts;
- Difficulty analyzing and synthesizing information.

Barkley suggests that "ADHD represents a profound disturbance in self-regulation and organization of behavior across time" (1994, p. vii). It is likely that these functions are subserved by the prefrontal regions of the human brain (Fuster, 1989).

ADHD, then, is a disorder that affects children's ability to organize behavior over time and meet demands for present and future performance. Thus, to understand the disorder, one has to go where it lives. Over a longer period of time, laboratory tests may measure some aspects of the problem, but because it is a problem of inconsistency as opposed to inability, a disorder that results not from lack of information but rather from not doing what one knows, it is not always captured or accurately reflected in brief, laboratory observations or, for that matter, reports of parents and teachers misfocused on the inconsistent aspects of the disorder as reflecting noncompliance.

Given this model of a core inhibition deficit, ADHD represents a problem that occurs at the point of performance. It is a problem that results from being capable of learning from experience but incapable of acting efficiently on that learning at the point of performance (Ingersoll & Goldstein, 1993). It is thus a disorder of inadequate response inhibition: a problem of performance, not of skill; of inconsistency rather than inability. As such, it impacts children across their daily lives, especially in regard to repetitive, effortful, uninteresting activities such as those frequently required at school or home. As Barkley (1994) notes, "if ADHD is to be captured it must be captured in its lair" (p. ix). It must be observed on a daily basis over relatively long periods of time; thus, history, parent reports, and naturalistic observations are the best ways of capturing these qualities.

Considering ADHD as a disorder of poor impulse control, it can be hypothesized that the greater the time between an intervention designed to alter behavior and the point of performance at which the intervention taught must be used, the less effective the intervention is likely to be (Ingersoll & Goldstein, 1993). This may explain the lack of effectiveness of cognitive training in modifying the behavior of children with ADHD. Cognitive training often takes place in an analogue or laboratory setting. Skills are learned at some distance from the point of performance: real life. In contrast, treatments that take place in the natural setting, such as behavioral intervention, environmental modification, and medication, in part fulfill the criterion of intervention at the point of performance.

Due to their impulsiveness, children with ADHD often display difficulty on tasks requiring complex problem-solving strategies and organization. Again, this is not because they lack the ability to utilize these skills but because they don't utilize efficiently the skills they possess (Tant & Douglas, 1982). This characteristic may reflect insufficient effort or inefficient use of strategies (Voelker, Carter, Sprague, Gadowski, & Lachar, 1989). Deficits hypothesized as poor executive functioning for children with ADHD in fact may be a function of this problem as opposed to reflecting frontal lobe or true reasoning difficulties (Barkley, Grodzinsky, & DuPaul, 1992). However, as noted, tests of frontal lobe functioning have been inconsistent in their ability to discriminate children with ADHD. Thus, the inefficient, impulsive, and poorly organized strategies of some children with ADHD on frontal lobe tasks reported by Zentall (1988) and others may result as much from lack of interest in the task, not picking up cues to decide which skills to utilize, and inefficient strategic thinking as from lack of ability. Further, Zentall and Meyer (1987) have argued that the impulsive errors made by children with ADHD appear normalized in higher stimulation, active response conditions. They suggest that excessive activity and attraction to novel stimuli is characteristic of children with ADHD and can be channeled in appropriate instrumental, motor, and attention responses.

Reader, Harris, Schuerholz, and Denckla (1994) evaluated bright children with ADHD on a battery of tasks considered sensitive to executive functioning. These children performed below average on a number of these tasks. Significant intra-individual discrepancies were found for a selected pair of content-matched tests that differed in executive function task demands. Pennington's theory (Pennington, Groisser, & Welsh, 1993) of a double disassociation of ADHD and reading disability was tested by examining the executive function performance of ADHD children with and without reading disorder. No significant differences were found on any of the executive measures. The authors concluded that ADHD children appear at risk for executive function problems and that executive tests appeared only moderately correlated with IQ. Thus, some other variable may explain their relatively weaker performance on certain executive test measures such as the Wisconsin Card Sort.

Rothbart (1989a) proposed a useful distinction between passive and active inhibition. Passive inhibition involves anxiety, shyness, fearfulness, and inhibition to the unfamiliar (Kagan, 1989). In contrast, the active inhibition system reflects effortful impulse control, denotes more active processes of inhibition, effortful or willful control of actions, and self-regulation capable of regulating both approach and avoidance (Rothbart, 1989b), and reflects the capacity for active, voluntary inhibition and for oral modulation of conduct. This can be described as inhibitory control or the opposite of impulsivity (Rothbart, Derryberry, & Posner, 1994). It is exactly this process that may explain the report in some studies that children with ADHD who are also anxious appear more capable of managing their impulsivity (Pliszka, 1989). Passive inhibition may dampen impulsivity.

Emerging self-regulation integrates input from several developing systems, including cognitive functions such as memory and language (Kopp, 1982) and the developing attentional mechanisms (Rothbart et al., 1994). Parent-child factors, including qualities of attachment (Londerville & Main, 1981) and parental control (Maccoby, 1980; Olson, Bates, & Bayles, 1990), are also found to be contributors to the growth of inhibitory and impulse control in children. Inhibitory control is by all accounts a late-developing skill.

Low impulsiveness correlates with resistance to temptation (Milich & Kramer, 1984). As Walter Mischel and his colleagues demonstrated many years ago, children capable of resisting temptation appear to fare better throughout their childhood and adolescence (Mischel, Shoda, & Rodriguez, 1989). The ability to delay gratification has been considered a function of ego control and ego resilience (Rothbart & Ahadi, 1994). Block, Block, and Keyes (1988) found longitudinally that at preschool age, low ego control and low ego resilience predicted behavior indicative of low internalization resulting in drug abuse in adolescents. Rothbart and Ahadi (1994) have postulated and generated a line of research to suggest a link between children's inhibitory control and their development of several dimensions of morality.

In 1995, Eisenberg et al. provided research-based support of the view that individual differences in emotionality and various modes of self-regulation are important in the development of social competence. These authors noted that social competence is likely a two-way street, with experience shaping behavior and vice versa. The authors suggest that children who are uninhibited, a trait they perceive to be partly biologically driven, have more difficulty dealing in their social environment, which then in part shapes their social behavior. Other temperament theories have suggested that self-regulation and emotional reactivity are the two major dimensions of temperament and that these components jointly influence behavior (Fox, 1989). Eisenberg et al. also reported that children's sociable behavior, including popularity and low social insecurity, was associated with adults' reports of children's emotional control and self-regulation in the academic setting. However, this profile was seldom predicted by the reports of adults in the home setting. Many of the correlations between parent-reported problem behavior and measures of emotionality or regulation were found to be stronger for boys than girls, especially for father reports. The weaker link between these factors in the home setting is not surprising given the often complex nature of family relationships. These authors suggested that fathers may be particularly attuned to the misbehavior of their sons and more tolerant of their female offspring.

A diverse literature lends strong support for impulsiveness as an important if not the core deficit for children with ADHD. Kochanska, Murray, Jacques, Koneig, and Vandegeest (1996) evaluated inhibitory control as a quality of temperament in children under 4 years of age. Comprehensive behavioral batteries were utilized to measure inhibitory control at the toddler and preschool ages. Individual children's performances were significantly correlated across both assessments, indicating stable, individual differences. Girls, interestingly, surpassed boys in the quality of their performance at both ages. Children's internalization was observed while they were alone with prohibited objects, performing a mundane chore, and playing games, on occasion cheating, being induced to violate standards of conduct; assessment was by maternal report. Inhibitory control was significantly associated with internalization, both contemporaneously and as a predictor in the longitudinal sense. Thus, the impact of faulty impulse control may have significant consequence in a number of developmental arenas. These authors also argue that the development of conscience and internalization appear to be central goals for effective socialization.

Hyperactives and controls have not been found to differ significantly with respect to task efficiency when distractions are provided (van der Meere & Sergeant, 1988). In this study, the hyperactive group made more effort and their responding was more variable. The difference in error percentages was in part associated with the difference in intelligence level. Thus, it may be that variability in responding at times may be due to less optimal abilities, not distractibility. It may also be that variability in responding is the result of impulsiveness. These authors also suggested that pervasive hyperactives in comparison to situational hyperactives may have more difficulty with variable responding, a finding reported by others. Campbell, Endman, and Bernfeld (1977) first suggested that children with hyperactivity may actually benefit from extraneous distraction. They hypothesized that test inefficiency for the hyperactives might reflect a less optimal energetic state of performance and that these children were in need of more stimulation to bring them to a level at which they could respond similarly to other children. This hypothetical line of thinking has been researched and well documented (Zentall, 1975; Zentall & Zentall, 1983; Zentall, Zentall, & Barrick, 1978).

Scholnick (1995) reviews an extensive literature, nearly 11,000 references, concerning the development and implementation of planning. Planning requires an internal process of problem solving that precedes the external strategic action; requires the capacity to inhibit actions while thinking through the best ways to obtain goals; and involves multiple stages, each of which is critical in designing, choosing, and following through with a problem-solving approach, regardless of the nature of the task (Scholnick, 1995). Planning is described as involving thinking about how to act beforehand to achieve goals effectively and efficiently. Clearly, this process requires selective inhibition or impulse control. Planning relies on working memory to construct an anticipatory plan and monitor its execution; such a process requires prolongation, self-directed speech, and reconstitution at the very least. For example, children unable to anticipate future consequences of action or to reflect while acting are likely to be accident-prone. Adept planners make fast computations and think ahead several steps through the use of working memory. This skillful allocation of resources requires attention divided simultaneously between active construction and utilization of a plan. Scholnick suggests that planning performance is also influenced by long-term memory, motivation, personal attributes, and belief about personal capacities. Despite this large volume of research, it is still likely that the complex interaction of impulse control, planning, and daily effectiveness in meeting life's goals is only now beginning to be understood. For impulsive children, faulty planning may pervade all aspects of their lives, from relationships with peers and family members to the capacity to learn. The frequent clinical observation that children with ADHD appear inefficient in completing learning tasks is consistent with this model, suggesting that working memory is used inefficiently as the result of the inability to quickly and accurately develop a plan or learn a strategy and utilize that strategy efficiently. Evidence also suggests that intact, self-regulatory abilities underlie efficacy at reading and mathematics (Schwean, Kowachuk, Quinn, & Saklofske, 1991). This processing deficit may, in fact, explain the beyond-chance overlap between ADHD and learning disability.

Zentall, Harper, and Stormont-Spurgin (1993) investigated whether deficits in organization could be documented in 6- to 14-year-olds with ADHD across sources of informants (i.e., teachers, parents, and children) using a measure of both time and object organization. Specific deficits in the organization of events and objects were found for youth with ADHD relative to the control group. Lack of efficient organization appears consistently tied to lack of effective strategic thinking.

Based on a long series of studies, Virginia Douglas and her colleagues (Amin, Douglas, Mendelson, & Dufresene, 1993) have hypothesized that information-processing deficits associated with ADHD implicated it as a self-regulatory dysfunction. These researchers have suggested that children with ADHD may demonstrate a stronger pattern of type A behavior characterized by more problems with impatience and aggression. An examination of the cognitive style of children with ADHD (Sonuga-Barke, Hulberg, & Hall, 1994) consistently demonstrated that children identified as ADHD behaved more impulsively than a control group on computerized instruments. The ADHD group responded more quickly and made more mistakes. If the number of mistakes was not an issue, the ADHD group completed the task more quickly; when the length of time between each trial was fixed, the ADHD group could not complete the test more quickly. However, they still made more mistakes before identifying the correct target. Once again, this appears to reflect problems with poor impulse control leading to inefficient planning and, in this case, inability to benefit from a level of repeated experience helpful to others.

The inability to benefit from experience has been thoroughly examined. Sergeant and van der Meere (1988) examined how children with a diagnosis of attention deficit corrected errors on a display/memory-search task. The subjects with attention deficit were able to correct errors, but they differed from controls in how they adjusted to the speed of processing on a trial after they had committed an error. Controls worked faster in responding after an error when cognitive load was small; however, when cognitive load was high (e.g., a difficult task), the previous error resulted in their taking considerable time to ensure that the next response was correct. Thus, they responded to difficulty and a mistake with reflection. In contrast, after an error, subjects with attention deficit had no response adjustment and continued to maintain a constant fast rate of processing and responding.

It has been argued that due to their impulsiveness and faulty problem-solving skills, children with ADHD likely require more supervision, cues to develop strategies, and a greater number of trials and consistent consequences to learn to use those strategies efficiently. Schachar and Logan (1990) and Schachar, Tannock, and Logan

(1993) investigated the process by which children with ADHD develop inhibitory control. Consistently, children diagnosed with ADHD demonstrated deficient inhibitory control. Those children with ADHD who were described as having pervasive problems across situations had greater inhibitory control problems than those whose problems were situational (i.e., either home or school). Both of these groups had more problems than normals or children with other psychiatric problems.

Children with ADHD have also been reported as having difficulty estimating loudness and time, demonstrating a tendency to overestimate consistent with lack of inhibition (Lucker, Geffner, & Koch, 1996). Their knowledge of safety also does not appear to be different from normal subjects'; rather it is their inability to stop, think, and do what they know that leads children with ADHD to have greater problems with safety and potential injury (Mori & Peterson, 1995). In this study of elementary-school-age children evaluated by their teachers, both ADHD and normal subjects displayed comparable safety and prevention knowledge. The authors suggested that there is no apparent deficit of knowledge of safety or accident prevention to account for greater risk of injury in boys rated high on activity and impulsivity.

Impulsiveness and its impact on social relations has also been extensively studied. Most recently, Halperin et al. (1995) examined whether children who initiate physical altercations are more impulsive than other children as measured by a continuous performance task. Over 100 7- to 13-year-olds were diagnosed with *DSM-III-R* criteria and divided according to whether they demonstrated a persistent pattern of initiating physical altercations. Those who initiated fights were impulsive irrespective of whether the diagnosis of ADHD was present. A diagnosis of ADHD, however, was associated with the greatest reports of impulsivity. Oppositional defiant disorder and conduct disorder diagnoses were not associated with laboratory-measured impulsivity. These authors suggest that an underlying impulsive quality or perhaps personality trait may significantly contribute to the life outcome of children with disruptive behavior disorders.

Finally, the factors that may impact impulsivity both positively and negatively have been well researched. For example, Zentall and Dywer (1989) evaluated the impact of nonrelevant color stimulation as a means of increasing attention to task. Inattentive and normal second- and third-grade children were administered a black and white form of a matching/reflection task and one month later a colorized version, or the same in reverse order. The addition of nonrelevant color to this task normalized the response pattern of those with ADHD. Group differences were observed only in the black and white, traditional form of this task. The children with attention deficit also responded with more time on task when presented colored rather than black and white stimuli relative to controls. The authors suggest that a lack of stimulation results in children with ADHD not crossing a stimulus threshold that might act as a cue trigger or remind the children to utilize strategies they possess. Zentall and colleague (Zentall & Zentall, 1983) have hypothesized that children with ADHD satiate to stimuli faster than normals, especially when exposed to repetitive stimuli. Under these reduced stimulation conditions, children with ADHD will exhibit a sensation-seeking activity and premature task responses to novel stimulation. The effects of color stimulation may be similar to those of stimulant medication in reducing impulsive responding. According to these authors, impulsivity represents an inability to tolerate low levels of stimulation during delays as well as an inability to systematically deploy attention.

Inattention

It has long been recognized that children described as hyperactive are not necessarily inattentive or distractible (Douglas, 1983). Although it was argued by some that such failures were due to distractor stimuli external to the stimulus array (Rosenthal & Allen, 1978), multiple researchers have well documented that inattentive and distractible children are not *always* inattentive and distractible. The first edition of this text focused heavily on the theoretical framework of attention, suggesting a potential diagnostic and treatment benefit in assessing various types of attentional skills. In a practical sense, it may still be of value to distinguish children in a classroom struggling with divided versus sustained attention or vigilance versus focused attention. Research and clinical interest in the subtypes of attention have diminished parallel to the increasing interest in impulsivity as the core deficit of ADHD. Nonetheless, a brief review of the recent clinical literature dealing with attentional skills is still of value for the practitioner. Attention continues to be a multidimensional concept, likely impacted by physiological, cognitive, emotional, and behavioral variables. The interest in attention as a primary phenomenon of ADHD in contrast to impulsivity continues to be a focus of interest for the nonhyperactive or inattentive children with ADHD. Weinberg and Brumback (1992) suggest that the inattentive type of ADHD actually represents a disorder of vigilance. According to these authors, this group of children has difficulty with readiness to respond. As a result, they do not sustain attention; they avoid repetitive activities; and they may be restless, but they also demonstrate a "remarkably kind and caring temperament" (p. 720). Unfortunately, these authors can offer only single case reports to support this theory.

Goldstein and Goldstein (1990) hypothesized that attention deficit may be a disorder of faulty selective attention. That is, this group of children experience difficulty deciding what is most important to pay attention to and investing in that particular stimulus. In 1971, Broadbent suggested that selective attention enables the individual to make the best of a limited capacity. To protect the system from being overloaded, Broadbent postulated, selective attention acts as a filter allowing a specific focus in the face of multiple stimuli. Though an attractive concept, it appears to have more anecdotal than scientific support.

Van der Meere and Sergeant (1988) suggest that sustained attention may represent the core deficit for children with attention deficit. Deficits of attention are conceived of as deficits of controlled information processing. Two types of deficits of sustained attention are distinguished: perceptual sensitivity and perceptual criterion. These two deficits are linked to a model of human performance connecting controlled processes to the energetic pools of arousal and activation. Perceptual sensitivity deficits reflect arousal deficiencies, especially when observed in the early aspects of a task. Perceptual criterion deficits are associated with the activation pull and the response criterion. Despite clear evidence of perceptual deficiency in children with attention deficit to a greater extent than in controls, research by these authors has failed to support the hypothesis of a sustained attention deficit in children with attention disorder. Instead, what is demonstrated is that this group of children suffers from a perceptual sensitivity deficit (Parasuraman, 1994). A decline in performance noted in children with attention deficit in comparison to controls appears to result from the fact that this phenomenon is related to impulsivity. Deficits in performance over time, that is, sustained attention deficits, have been less clearly proven in laboratory experiments with the ADHD population. It is likely that output-related processes account for task inefficiency in children with attention deficit.

In 1976, Flynn and Rapoport suggested that hyperactive children are less likely to be perceived by teachers as distinctive and disruptive in open classrooms than in traditional classrooms, despite the fact that in both, observers reported similar levels of problems. Baldwin (1976) found that hyperactives and nonhyperactives did not differ in length of attention span or the number of stimuli to which they attended. Their difference was in focus of attention, with the hyperactives more likely focused on nonacademic tasks. In 1972, Douglas suggested that hyperactive children were not inattentive but rather were paying attention to something other than that which the teacher was directing the class to attend to.

Pearson, Lane, and Swanson (1991) suggested that patterns of errors made by children with diagnoses of attention deficit were the result of difficulty with divided attention. However, this problem appeared to be more a function of inefficient strategy than inability. Differences between the inattentive and the normal subjects on a dichotic listening task suggested that the auditory reorientation skills of the inattentive children were developmentally immature. Although the normals were temporarily distracted by the switch in focus from one ear to the other, they eventually reoriented to the cued ear. In contrast, the inattentive children when distracted did not reorient very well. Once again, this problem can be tied as much to lack of an effective plan as to lack of attention.

Russell and D'Hollosy (1992) suggested that at least among children with a history of traumatic brain injury the strength of memory recall was directly related to the strength of attention. Subjects appear to best remember information they had consistently attended to. In contrast to the work of Zentall, in this series of studies, variables such as mode of presentation and color did not result in significant performance differences. However, Higgenbotham and Bartling (1993) demonstrated that on repetitive, auditory, visual, and combined distraction tasks children with attention deficit performed more poorly in the middle and end but not at the beginning of a short-term recall task than did the normal subjects. Both groups demonstrated a decrement in performance on the short-term recall task from the beginning to the middle to the end of the task. It is important to note that the decrement in performance directly attributable to specific sensory distractions was relatively small and statistically nonsignificant in comparison with decreases in performance attributable to increasing proactive interference and increasing difficulty of the task. The volume of research is now sufficient to suggest that distractibility is a minor variable in the big picture of problems experienced by children with ADHD. It is their lack of investment in the task or lack of ability to be motivated by payoffs for completing the task that leads them to leave the task and seek other, more interesting activities. There are some lines of research, however, to suggest that distractibility may be modality-specific as a construct. Auditory distractions may impact cognitive functions, and visual distractions may correlate more highly with classroom ratings of children's behavior by teachers (Bedi, Halperin, & Sharma, 1993).

Leung and Connolly (1994) used a visual search task in 7- to 8-year-olds with a diagnosis of ADHD and compared them to children with conduct disorder and controls. None of the three groups demonstrated a performance decrement over time that was significantly different from any of the others. This lends further support for the conclusion that short attention span, at least based on a specific laboratory measure, does not reflect the core deficit of children with attention deficit, or those with conduct disorder, for that matter.

Inattention may also be a by-product of impaired cognitive flexibility. Schwartz et al. (1990) evaluated sixty-three school-age children performing a shifting-set task as a measure of cognitive flexibility. The children were divided into two groups based on teacher ratings of attention deficit symptoms and their performance on a computerized measure. The computerized measure or shift-set task involved instructing children to respond on a computer differentially to stimuli as the task proceeded. Children who met criteria for ADHD did not necessarily exhibit impairments in cognitive flexibility; only those with demonstrated impairments in sustained attention showed impaired ability to shift set. Thus, the symptom of inattention but not necessarily the presence of the full-syndrome, categorical diagnosis of ADHD appeared to be related to impaired cognitive flexibility.

There is also a consistent literature attesting to the impact problems with vigilance have on academic achievement (Levy & Hobbes, 1989; Zentall, 1990). In general, those with ADHD are reported to differ from those with learning problems and normals as the result of faulty vigilance. Problems with attention to repetitive stimuli and short-term working memory are hypothesized as reflecting core deficits for this population. The relationship of ADHD and learning disability will be discussed in greater depth in Chapter 3.

Hypotheses related to a sustained attention deficit in ADHD children, based on assessment measures utilized, has not been consistent in proving this phenomenon as the explanation for problems. Although a number of reasons are offered to explain this phenomenon, efforts at correcting these problems continue to reflect limited support for a sustained attention deficit in children with ADHD (Seidel & Joschko, 1991).

The cognitive processing of children with ADHD has also been thoroughly examined (Ott & Lyman, 1993). In a series of studies, Milich and Lorch (1994) examined attention and comprehension of children with ADHD. In the first study, subjects' parents kept a five-day TV-viewing log. Subjects were then given a fifteen-minute presentation of an educational program as well as some toys with which they could play. In study 2, subjects were shown comparable segments of the same program. In study 3, subjects viewed three different programs with no break. Finally, in study 4, subjects were shown two twenty-three-minute segments with toys present during one and absent during the other. Results demonstrated that children with ADHD can sustain attention for relatively as long and at the same level as that of controls, but that differences exist between the ADHD and control groups in terms of story comprehension and recall. Once again, the impact of strategy on learning that appears to be mediated, at least in part, by impulse control is implicated as the core deficit for ADHD. The preponderance of literature does not support that children with ADHD have a global attentional incapacity. Their inattention appears to be a product of other processes, principally those related to poor impulse control (Schachar & Logan, 1990).

Difficulty with Gratification

The need for immediate, frequent, salient, and predictable reinforcers, the inability to benefit efficiently from consequences, and the need for repeated trials to modify behavior are all characteristic of children with ADHD. All of these factors appear related to motivation and the degree to which consequences are able to modify behavior. Again, although it is increasingly recognized that this pattern of difficulty, ostensibly the need for more immediate gratification, likely results from limited capacity for self-control, a brief review of current issues in regard to consequences and ADHD is relevant. An understanding of task variables concerning the structure of the task, but more important, concerning the payoff for successful task completion, likely is the most critical step in connecting assessment to intervention.

Solanto (1990) suggested that inattentive, hyperactive, and impulsive symptoms may cumulatively result as a consequence of reduced sensitivity to reinforcement. Twenty children with attention problems and a group of controls, 4.5 to 11 years of age, were evaluated on a delayed-response task, a measure of impulsiveness under conditions of positive reinforcement and punishment in the form of response cost. Response cost—the opportunity to lose what has been earned—has been found to be particularly effective in managing and modifying the behavior of children with ADHD (Pfiffner & O'Leary, 1987; Pfiffner, O'Leary, Rosen, & Sanderson, 1985; Rosen, O'Leary, Joyce, Conway, & Pfiffner, 1984). Each of these contingencies improved performance compared to baseline but did not differ significantly from each other. Neither contingency affected the groups differently, thus failing to provide support for a reward system dysfunction or differential response to reinforcement as the underlying core deficit for ADHD. Though not significant, response-cost contingencies were slightly better than reinforcement for both groups, with normals performing better than the ADHD group.

A number of variables related to consequences, including consequence schedule and saliency, clearly impact the behavior of children with ADHD. (These issues will be reviewed in depth in Chapter 13.) Sonuga-Barke, Taylor, Sembi, and Smith (1992) evaluated a sample of preadolescent boys in their choice of small or immediate rewards over large delayed rewards under different economic constraints and delayed conditions. Both groups of normal and inattentive boys were equally efficient at earning points under most conditions. However, the inattentive group exhibited a maladaptive preference for the small reward when it was provided immediately. Results appeared to support the hypothesis that children with ADHD are more concerned about reducing delay between task and consequence than maximizing reward amount.

Douglas and Parry (1994) evaluated the effects of reward schedule in a population of children with ADHD. Schedules of reward varied from a payoff for every response to a payoff for every third response to extinction. Children with ADHD pulled harder on the lever than controls during extinction and at the lowest partial schedule, providing evidence that they responded with greater frustration than normals when expected rewards failed to appear. Groups did not differ on attentional measures in the one-to-one reward schedule. Partial schedules appeared to have an alerting or motivating effect on normals so that they responded more quickly and consistently. In contrast, it had just the opposite effect on the ADHD group, resulting in greater impulsivity and frustration.

In 1986, Mark Rapport and colleagues examined the differential effects of frustration on a population of children with attention deficit and controls (Rapport, Tucker, DuPaul, Merlo, & Stone, 1986). The groups were prematched for age, grade, and classroom placement. All subjects completed a series of arithmetic problems to earn toy rewards. Subjects were presented with two choices of delay conditions in a randomly assigned, counterbalanced sequence. In the first condition, a free choice conflict situation involved a long passive or short active reward delay, in the second, a short active delay. Results demonstrated a significantly greater proportion of the children with attention deficit chose to complete problems for an immediate reward compared to their normal control counterparts. Group differences were no longer apparent in the short active delay trial. These authors suggest that frustration tolerance and related factors such as cognitive and attentional style contribute to the behavioral problems children with ADHD manifest.

Hill, Olympia, and Angerbuer (1991) assessed seven reinforcement dimensions (parents, friends, teachers, games, television, toys, and candy) for a group of boys with ADHD and a group of controls. The groups did not differ in their stated preference for reward type. Both groups preferred parents most frequently, followed by friends. Toys and candy, interestingly, were preferred least. At least in relation to reward preference, children with ADHD appear similar to those without the diagnosis. Most important, however, is the report from this study that family attention in the form of interactions with parents is perceived as valuable by both affected and unaffected children.

The relationship of emotion to consequences has also been extensively examined. Becker, Doane, and Wexler (1993) assessed hemispheric functioning in adolescents with ADHD and response to positively toned emotional stimuli. The ADHD group demonstrated lower right ear advantage scores when presented with stimulus pairs containing positive words than when presented with pairs containing neutral words. In comparison, the non-ADHD clinical group and the control group had higher right ear scores under positive emotional conditions than under neutral conditions. These authors suggested that the abnormal response to positive emotional tone supported a reward system dysfunction hypothesis for ADHD. In response to this literature, Cantwell (1993) noted that the population studied was a group of adolescents whose problems were severe enough in regard to comorbid conditions to require hospitalization. Nonetheless, he noted that at least in this population, the reward system dysfunction, either the result of biological predisposition or environmental experience, appeared in part to contribute to the performance of these adolescents.

Hyperactivity and Overarousal

Although hyperactivity as a symptom may best locate children receiving the combined diagnosis of ADHD (Halperin, Matier, Bedi, Sharma, & Newcorn, 1992) and is the one symptom of the disorder that appears to improve rather dramatically as children age (Weiss & Hechtman, 1979, 1986, 1993), it is an increasingly less important symptom to researchers, though it maintains a consistent level of annoyance for parents seeking help. For our purposes, the term overarousal is used to define difficulty modulating both one's body in time and space as well as one's emotions. The latter problem has already been briefly touched upon. It is likely that both problems are related to the core deficit of impulsiveness, yet there continues to be a fairly powerful body of research suggesting that careful observation and assessment of physical activity is valuable in identifying children with ADHD. However, as can be seen from the following few studies, the amount of equipment and control required to obtain accurate measures often precludes the assessment of hyperactive behavior in all but anecdotal or historical ways. Although Henker and Whalen (1989) suggest that hyperactivity is a problem in the eye of the beholder, it likely can be objectively and reliably discerned in its frequency, amplitude, and pattern of body movements.

Based on an extensive review of the literature, Reichenbach, Halperin, Sharma, and Newcorn (1992a) had a group of children with ADHD and a group of normal boys wear actigraphs in a pouch on a belt around their waist. The actigraph measured activity level during the course of the day. The ADHD group was evaluated under two conditions, once while receiving stimulants and a second time while receiving placebos. The actigraph was found to have good test-retest reliability and generated measures that correlated directly with parent and teacher ratings of hyperactivity. The instrument also demonstrated the improvement toward the norm observed in the ADHD group during active stimulant treatment. Halperin and colleagues (Halperin, Matier, Bedi, Sharma, & Newcorn, 1991; Halperin et al., 1993) have demonstrated that the assessment of motoric activity during a continuous performance task can be an effective means of quantifying hyperactivity. In the 1992 study, ADHD and non-ADHD clinical groups had poorer attention than controls. Children with ADHD demonstrated greater impulsivity than normal children. Activity levels, however, were higher in children with ADHD than in the non-ADHD or normal controls. Teicher, Ito, Glod, and Barber (1996) comment that although actigraphs provide objective and valuable data, it is not entirely clear what is meant by suggesting that children with ADHD produce greater activity counts. It is unclear whether they move more often, more rapidly, or with greater vigor. Although actigraphs in natural settings are valuable, they simply do not provide that level of data.

Tryon (1993) argued that activity is a well-documented aspect of temperament and suggested that it was relevant to both normal and abnormal behavior. Based on a review of the literature, Tryon demonstrated that motor excesses have been documented as a significant phenomenon in externalizing disorders of childhood and therefore are clinically relevant. Tryon argues that the contemporary views concerning the minor importance or irrelevance of hyperactivity to ADHD may be due to invalid analogue activity assessment procedures. Content-valid behavioral assessments are reported as demonstrating that children diagnosed with ADHD are pervasively hyperactive. Tryon hypothesizes that motor excess is significantly tied to the developmental course of attention deficit and predicts adolescent outcome and parent-child interaction.

Finally, in 1996, Teicher et al. attempted to more objectively measure hyperactivity during a continuous performance task. These authors compared eighteen approximately 9-year-old boys with diagnoses of ADHD to eleven control children. The boys were recorded using an infrared motion analysis system, tracking position of the head, shoulder, back, and elbow while subjects completed the task. The ADHD boys moved their heads over twice as often as the normals, moved over three times as far, and covered nearly four times greater area. They responded more slowly and with greater variability on the task. Complexity of head movement and variability in response latency significantly correlated with teacher ratings of the boys' behavior. The authors concluded that the relative inability of ADHD boys to sit still can be objectively verified and that their fidgeting appears to consist mostly of frequent, larger amplitude, whole body movements.

Emotions and Locus of Control

In the emerging adult literature concerning the life course of individuals with ADHD, a number of hypotheses have developed and are in the process of being tested concerning the impact ADHD may have on emerging personality. Questions have been raised as to whether ADHD increases the risk of developing antisocial, borderline, or impulsive personality disorders. Disagreements have ensued concerning the comorbidity of ADHD with certain psychiatric conditions as well (e.g., bipolar disorder). Of greater importance, because ADHD is a lifetime problem, is understanding the general manner in which symptoms of ADHD shape emerging personality and emotional development. Clearly, it is who ADHD children become as adults rather than what symptoms they present that is of long-term importance to the clinician.

Although many authors have noted the emotional and self-esteem weaknesses in children with ADHD, it has been difficult to translate these weaknesses into operationally defined phenomena (S. Goldstein, 1997a). It has been a surprise to many that when measured, children with ADHD view themselves as just as competent as unimpaired children in terms of global self-worth and success in the social domain (Hoza, Pelham, Milich, Pillow, & McBride, 1993). This phenomenon may be best explained by the work of Dweck and Leggett (1988). These authors suggest that children with learning goals want to improve their ability even at the risk of encountering failure. Children with performance goals, on the other hand, are more concerned with proving their ability and avoiding looking bad at all costs. Children with this pattern appear to view difficult tasks as a threat to their self-esteem. One characteristic of helpless children when confronting difficult tasks is to boast about their success in other activities, presumably to bolster their self-image. A characteristic of impulsive children is to ineffectively assess their environment before beginning a task and potentially overestimate their chances of success. Thus, the inflated self-presentations put forth by children with ADHD may well reflect their impulsivity but also indicates that they are operating toward performance goals in which they try to look good and avoid appearing incompetent. When presented with difficult tasks, these children may offer enhanced estimates of their abilities to mask their feelings of inadequacy. Further, because they are impulsive, they may not accurately assess their performance and thus, after a task is completed, continue to overstate their success. Thus, until they become well aware of their inadequacies, children with ADHD may actually be excessively optimistic.

Rotter (1966) refers to locus of control as an individual's perception of environmental control. Externally oriented individuals perceive the occurrence of positive and negative events as independent of personal control; internally oriented individuals perceive their actions as contingently related to the occurrence of these events. It has been suggested that those with an internal locus of control are better adjusted (Searcy & Hawkins-Searcy, 1979). Linn and Hodge (1982) also reported that children with attention problems are more externally oriented. However, Elliott (1996) provides conflicting evidence suggesting that among a group of 9- to 16-year-olds there was little relationship between disruptive behavior and locus of control. It has been demonstrated that children with an internal locus of control are more competent at problem solving than children with an external locus of control (Adalbjarnardottir, 1995).

It is not surprising, however, given the lives of children with ADHD, that they appear to have a high risk of developing an external locus of control. Tarnowski and Nay (1989) administered the Nowicki-Strickland Locus of Control Scale (Nowicki & Strickland, 1973) to a group of boys with diagnoses of attention deficit, learning disability, a combination, or no diagnosis. All of the clinical groups differed significantly from normally achieving children on this locus of control measure. The attention deficit–learning-disabled group demonstrated the strongest external locus of control, with the normals representing the least external locus. This pattern is consistent with the results of others (Rogers & Saklofske, 1985). It is likely that children struggling daily to meet the demands of their environment without the opportunity to understand the process of their struggles or to receive insulating support are more prone to begin seeing their world as controlling them rather than having the capacity to control their world.

A DIAGNOSTIC STRATEGY FOR ADHD

Over the past twenty years, a number of practitioners (e.g., Barkley, 1981a, 1990a; Cantwell & Carlson, 1978; Goldstein & Goldstein, 1990) and even a pharmaceutical company (CIBA, 1974) have recommended a multicomponent approach to the evaluation, identification, and treatment of children with attention deficit. Although at one time, limited evaluative components such as obtaining a history and teacher rating as the primary means of making a diagnosis were suggested (Sleator, 1982), the multicomponent assessment process has been embraced by the clinical community.

In the original edition of this text, rather than prescribing the components of the evaluative process, the authors advocated a working definition based on their earlier work, describing the type of data necessary to make the diagnosis of ADHD (Goldstein & Goldstein, 1985, 1990). It was suggested that data concerning the child's emotional, cognitive, and behavioral functioning, intellect, achievement, social relations, family life, and medical status were all essential in seeing the world through the eyes of the child with ADHD. Because children with this problem appeared to demonstrate the greatest degree of comorbidity of additional disorders (for review, see Chapter 4), a multicomponent, multisetting, multidata assessment was critical.

The authors continue to believe that gathering a variety of data by a variety of means from a variety of sources is essential in making the ADHD diagnosis. The essence of this need is not so much in the diagnosis of ADHD but in developing an understanding of non-ADHD clinical and life factors that have been clearly implicated as impacting the life course, treatment response, and ultimate adult outcome for children affected with ADHD (for review, see S. Goldstein, 1997a).

The diagnostic strategy allows the practitioner to make the diagnosis of ADHD as well as examine comorbid issues with a high degree of confidence. As noted in 1990, this process is not offered as a scientific analogue, but rather as a clinical tool. The authors believe that it affords the practitioner the capacity to balance sensitivity with specificity in the clinical arena. Practitioners may wish to adapt or modify this strategy, utilizing various questionnaires or assessment procedures, keeping in mind issues of positive and negative predictive power, while carefully integrating clinical experience. Chapter 9 will offer a framework for utilizing this diagnostic strategy. In Chapter 10, case examples will be provided to illustrate the complexity of making the diagnosis of ADHD in the face of comorbid issues. This will firmly illustrate the need for multiple diagnostic criteria.

In making the diagnosis of ADHD, it is suggested that the following criteria be considered:

1. DSM-IV *Diagnostic Criteria.* Because at this time the *DSM-IV* offers the most utilized and best researched North American definition we possess, it is important for the child to meet one of the three criteria: primarily inattentive type, primarily hyperactive-impulsive type, or combined. We suggest that the diagnosis of not otherwise specified be used cautiously in children and adolescents.

2. *Elevated Rating Scales.* Rating scales do not diagnose: they describe behavior in an organized, statistical fashion. The most popular and commonly used scales specifically designed to measure ADHD symptoms are the Conners parents' and teachers' questionnaires (Conners, 1969). Since the publication of the first edition of this text, a number of additional questionnaires have been developed. These will be reviewed in Chapters 7 and 8. Increasingly, general adjustment questionnaires such as the Child Behavior Checklist (Achenbach, 1978), the Personality Inventory for Children (Wirt, Lacher, Klinedinst, & Seat, 1977), and the Behavioral Assessment System for Children (BASC) (Reynolds & Kamphus, 1992) have been utilized because they provide a thorough behavioral profile. These questionnaires also contain well-structured attention symptom scales. In the working definition, the child must be *at or beyond a minimum of one and a half standard deviations difference in a negative direction* on at least one of these questionnaires in comparison to children of the same chronological age and gender. This criterion should be met by *two independent raters,* usually parent and teacher. A working knowledge of the differences between these questionnaires is essential, especially if the administration of multiple questionnaires results in a pattern of seemingly different problems.

3. *Objective Measures.* As Ostrom and Jenson (1988) noted, the assessment of ADHD has rarely involved direct measures of attention. Over the past ten years, there has been increasing interest in utilizing computer technology to measure sustained attention and impulse control. Chapter 9 will discuss a number of norm-referenced measures ranging from simple paper-and-pencil assessment tasks to computer-based instruments that have been hypothesized as sensitive to the mistakes made by children with ADHD. These tasks emphasize performance rather than process. That is, tasks measuring brainwaves, metabolites in the blood stream, and so on, are not considered objective measures of ADHD due to their limited scientific support. The original edition of this text emphasized that

children with ADHD routinely demonstrate difficulty on a selection of tasks measuring various attentional skills. Given the increasing focus of ADHD as a disorder of poor inhibition, at the very least it would be reasonable to consider problems on measures of impulse control rather than just attention. However, a growing volume of literature has demonstrated that group differences do not easily translate into individual differences in clinic settings. Objective measures provide useful supportive data and may in fact represent diagnostically important distinctions among children receiving diagnoses of ADHD (Gordon & Aylward, 1995). As Zarski, Cook, West, and O'Keefe (1987) note, it is difficult to demonstrate significant differences between children with ADHD and normals on a variety of assessment procedures.

In the working definition, children with ADHD may but do not have to demonstrate problems on measures of impulsiveness. It is also important to note that these measures are not as effective in discriminating the primarily inattentive group from normals.

4. *Situational Problems.* Children with ADHD have been found to have problems of varying severity in at least half of all home and school situations (Barkley, 1981a; Breen, 1986). Zentall (1995) suggests that children with ADHD likely exhibit their greatest problems in the classroom. Gordon, Mammen, DiNiro, and Mettelman (1988) found that 72% of a population of children referred for problems of attention and impulsivity presented with a consensus between parents and teachers concerning the severity of these problems. These authors suggest that children referred for situational attention problems by only parent or teacher may have very different reasons for and kinds of problems than those for whom there is a consensus. It appears that parents, teachers, physicians, and psychologists view hyperactivity, distractibility, impulsivity, short attention span, and difficulty remaining on tasks requiring sustained effort as the primary traits of children receiving a diagnosis of ADHD (Poillion, 1991). The inclusion of situational data allows the evaluator to assess the impact on daily living of the child's symptoms. Zarski et al. (1987), based on their review of the data over ten years ago, emphasized that the most efficient means of identifying children with ADHD is to focus on direct observational methods in the classroom and playground.

It is important to note that although correlations for individual symptoms between parent and teacher raters may be at best low to moderate, studies suggest that there is at least a 90% probability that teacher report will result in a positive diagnosis of ADHD given a positive parent diagnosis. There is also a very high probability that in clinically referred children, a diagnosis of ADHD based on parent report is corroborated by teacher report. As previously discussed, the issue of difference between specific symptoms versus the issue of consensus about "the problem" is not surprising in light of differences between home and school environments.

The issue of diagnostic setting must also be considered. Epstein, Shaywitz, Shaywitz, and Woolston (1991) attempted to determine whether children given a diagnosis of ADHD in mental health settings differed from those diagnosed by physicians. Results suggested that referral bias does exist and that children referred to mental health settings differ from those referred to physicians. Thus, even before they walk in the door, these two groups of children are different. The authors suggest that ADHD will be represented by those referred primarily for attentional deficits and learning problems in the physician's office, whereas those entering mental health settings are referred for hyperactivity and aggression at a higher rate. This referral bias may in fact result in very different diagnoses and clinical perceptions of what defines the every day situational problems of the prototypical child with ADHD.

5. *Differential Diagnosis.* In the past ten years, this component has taken on increasing importance. The practitioner must obtain sufficient history, behavior, and assessment data not only to understand, but to rule in or out the contribution of medical problems, learning problems or language disorders, auditory processing disability, specific intellectual deficits, and other disruptive and nondisruptive disorders of childhood as contributing to the presentation and severity of ADHD symptoms as well as to develop insight into the daily life of the target child. That is, based on the differential diagnosis process, clinicians must seek not only to provide appropriate diagnoses but to see the world through the eyes of the children whom they set out to help.

PREVALENCE

A discussion of prevalence of ADHD has been reserved until this point to allow the practitioner to become familiar with the diagnostic nomenclature and process. As practitioners have become more sophisticated, a wider range of precise questions evaluating consistency in problems among various settings and consensus by a number of raters concerning the severity of problems increases the accuracy of diagnosis. Not surprisingly, when *DSM* symptoms are used epidemiologically, they may identify children with ADHD but also those with comorbid and other problems, in some studies finding an incidence rate of ADHD of nearly 15%. However, when a more careful analysis is conducted, the rate of attention deficit over the past twenty years consistently drops to a more reasonable 1% to 6% (Lambert et al., 1978). As discussed, it also appears that a higher incidence of ADHD as well as other childhood developmental, behavioral, and emotional problems occurs in lower socioeconomic families. This makes sense when one considers that a percentage of ADHD children become ADHD adults and fall to the lower socioeconomic strata. A variety of additional life variables certainly affect prevalence as well. For example, based on a review of the data generated by the Collaborative Perinatal Project, Molina (1990) found that among children born between 1959 and 1965, 10% of those adopted or living with foster families were hyperactive compared to only 4.5% of the entire group. Riccio, Gonzalez, and Hynd (1994) evaluated a large population of children using parent and teacher ratings. The incidence of pure ADHD with no other psychopathology was only 15% for a sample of students rated by special education teachers but ranged from nearly 12% for parent ratings only to 35% for teacher ratings only for a group of children referred to a specialty clinic for psychiatric problems. The quality of differences in children referred to clinic settings versus those identified by public school education programs results in different prevalence rates. Further, prevalence rates for ADHD were also found to vary depending on the diagnostic perspective employed by the clinician, a point made earlier in the discussion of differences in the populations and subsequent clinical perspectives of physicians versus mental health professionals.

It is important for the practitioner to recognize that to some extent the issue of prevalence is artificially determined. ADHD is defined by observable behavior, not by a blood test or brain wave analysis. Thus, the issue is not black and white nor specifically categorical, but rather dimensional. The prevalence or incidence of ADHD varies depending upon the stringency of the diagnostic process and criteria. What is important for the practitioner to recognize is that a significant minority of children, due to their impulsive qualities, are compromised in their ability to meet the environmental expectations placed upon them by the adults in their lives.

Very clearly, the stability of externalizing disorders over time and their resistance to intervention in comparison to the nondisruptive internalizing disorders would suggest consistency in prevalence, longitudinally and prospectively. Bhatia, Nigam, Bohra, and Malik (1991) evaluated 1,000 children 3 through 12 years of age in a pediatric outpatient clinic over a three-and-a-half-year period. One hundred and twelve were found to have ADHD. Prevalence increased with age from 5% in the population of 3- to 4-year-olds to nearly 20% in 11- to 12-year-olds. There were four times as many males as females with the hyperactive type of attention deficit. The disorder was most common in firstborn children and in children from lower socioeconomic strata. The hyperactive, inattentive group had a higher rate of complications during pregnancy and delivery relative to the comparison group. Delayed development, temper tantrums, enuresis, tics, broken homes, persistent parental discord, and psychiatric illness in parents were all more common among the hyperactive attention-disordered group than the controls.

As noted, the issue of prevalence varies as the clinical and psychiatric descriptions of the disorder vary. Utilizing *DSM-III* criteria in a large sample of adolescents, McGee, Feehan, et al. (1990) found that the prevalence rate for attention deficit disorder appeared to be approximately 2%. The authors suggested that into the adolescent years, children with ADD either persist with a full disorder, persist with specific attention and impulse problems, or recover. The authors hypothesized that the second alternative was the most common. In this population, attention deficit overlapped with anxiety and conduct problems but did not overlap with depression (see Figure 2–1).

McGee, Williams, and Feehan (1992) suggested that the persistence between age 11 and age 15 in diagnoses is accompanied by an increased prevalence. Disorders at age 11 demonstrated a moderate level of persistence into the adolescent years. However, new disorders also appear. Some variables such as poor social competence, a history of problems, and family disadvantage may have their greatest influence on the onset rather than the course of a specific disorder such as ADHD. The authors also suggest that early intervention may offer long-term benefit beyond the immediate amelioration of presenting symptoms. In this longitudinal study, the diagnosis of ADHD was consistent between ages 11 and 15, with internalizing symptoms of anxiety and depression increasing the most.

Prevalence is also a function of age of onset. McGee et al. (1992) evaluated the onset of behavior problems in a group of children identified as having attention deficit

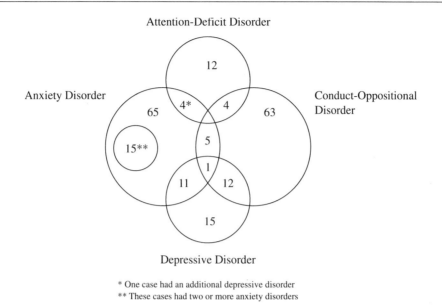

Attention-Deficit Disorder

Anxiety Disorder

Conduct-Oppositional
Disorder

Depressive Disorder

* One case had an additional depressive disorder
** These cases had two or more anxiety disorders

**Figure 2–1.   Overlap among the four major domains of disorder at age 15: attention
deficit, anxiety, conduct-oppositional, and depressive disorders**

Source: McGee, R., Feehan, M. Williams, S., Partridge, F., Silva, P. A., & Kelly, J. (1990). *DSM-III* disorders in a large sample of adolescents. *Journal of the American Academy of Child and Adolescent Psychiatry, 29,* 611–619. Used with permission.

disorder. Onset occurred during the preschool years, by the first year of schooling, or
by the end of the second year of school. Onset was strongly related to informant source
at age 11, a pattern of comorbidity of disorder at age 11, and developmental language,
perceptual motor, and IQ measures. Onset by the first year of schooling was particularly related to poor reading skills. By age 15, nearly three-quarters of those with onset
of problems before age 6 had one or more additional psychiatric disorders. The groups
that were identified early on demonstrated a consistent pattern of cognitive deficits,
perceptual motor skill weaknesses, marked family disadvantage, and lower intellect.
They also demonstrated higher comorbidity, particularly conduct disorder, and poor
outcome into adolescence. The issue of life course in predicting outcome will be discussed further in Chapter 4.

There appears to be little doubt that prevalence increased as diagnostic criteria
changed. Whether this reflects a loosening in the criteria or in fact reflects the development of a system that allows for more accurate diagnosis is unclear. Lahey et al.
(1990), when comparing *DSM-III-R* and *DSM-III* attention deficit criteria, found that
the revised criteria identified 14% more children than the original criteria. In a two-
stage design, over 3,800 children were screened by Lavigne et al. (1996); 510 received
complete evaluations. Prevalence of behavior problems was 8.3%. The probable occurrence of any Axis I *DSM-III-R* disorder was 21.4%, with 9% presenting as severe. Demographic correlates, older age, minority status, male sex, low socioeconomic status,
absent father, and small family size contributed to outcome greater than *DSM-III-R*

diagnoses. Maternal and family characteristics were generally not significant. Child correlates included activity level, timidity, persistence, and IQ. Overall prevalence of disorder rates in younger children was consistent with that in older children. The rate of ADHD in this population was 2%, with nearly twice as many males as females. Very few of these children demonstrated ADHD in the absence of comorbid problems. When severity of ADHD was noted, eighteen times as many boys as girls experienced severe ADHD, whereas the mild rate was approximately 2 to 1. The issue of gender and its relationship to the ADHD diagnosis will be reviewed further in Chapter 4.

In a six-year predictive validity study, Towe and Frame (1991) demonstrated a consistent though different course for the inattentive versus hyperactive-impulsive ADHD types. The hyperactive group demonstrated the expected pattern of conduct, peer, and to some extent internalizing problems across the six-year period. The nonhyperactive group demonstrated fewer conduct problems, were socially isolated, and in fact had more internalizing problems over time. Of significance here is the earlier point that, prevalence rates aside, it would appear that unlike internalizing disorders that may vary in their course and severity, the same children with ADHD are seen longitudinally, suggesting that the prevalence rate at any given moment is equivalent to the lifetime prevalence rate. Over an eight-year follow-up, Fischer, Barkley, Fletcher, and Smallish (1993) noted a slight decline in severity of ratings across time, but the group defined as hyperactive always remained more deviant than controls at follow-up. They also differed most on teacher report and self-report ratings.

Francis (1993) estimated the prevalence of ADHD among nearly 500 elementary-school-age children utilizing a variety of teacher-completed questionnaires. Depending on the questionnaire evaluated, prevalence for ADHD ranged from 7.4% to 9.6%. Interestingly, teachers identified children with ADHD as appropriate candidates for ADHD assessment 100% of the time, while expressing discouragement with the progress of these students approximately 75% of the time.

In 1983, Trites and LaPrade used a measure derived from a factor analysis of the Conners Teacher's Rating Scale (Conners, 1969) and identified 5.7% of a sample of nearly 10,000 children with symptoms of hyperactivity. Controlling for the presence of conduct disorder, the prevalence of pure attention deficit dropped to approximately 2%. In a study of nearly 500 children evaluated as outpatients at a children's hospital, 15% received a diagnosis of ADD based on a comprehensive assessment (McDowell & Rappaport, 1992). It is important to note, however, that in this population, comorbidity included 30% with learning disability, 19% with additional behavioral problems, 7% with motor skill problems, and 7% with family problems. Twenty-five percent of this population was reported as experiencing soft neurological signs. The issue of comorbidity will be reviewed shortly. Once again, these data reflect the difficulty in defining prevalence when one chooses to go beyond a simple screening utilizing *DSM* criteria.

Cantwell and Baker (1989) evaluated the stability of childhood psychiatric diagnoses over a four-year period. There was a high degree of stability for the diagnoses of autism, oppositional disorder, and ADHD. Eighty percent of those with the ADHD diagnosis still had the same diagnosis four to five years later. Of this group, only one had developed conduct disorder. The authors suggest that this argues for the relative independence of attention deficit and conduct disorders. However, it is also important to note that at the follow-up point, this group of children still had not entered their adolescent years, a time in which the majority of conduct disorders are diagnosed.

In light of the data presented, practitioners should be aware that they are likely to identify more children with ADHD when a single diagnostic criterion (e.g., a checklist) is utilized, when cutoff points for determining confirmation of the diagnosis on related instruments (e.g., laboratory tests) are modified, and when comorbid problems are not carefully considered as contributing to symptom presentation. However, the practitioner should keep in mind that even when utilizing the diagnostic strategies suggested, ADHD represents the most common disorder they are likely to face.

THE QUESTION OF SUBTYPES

In 1978, Rutter suggested that for a syndrome to be useful it must predict something other than what was used to define the group in the first place. Suggesting that as a syndrome ADHD predicts poor attention span, poor impulse control, and hyperactivity does not make a particularly useful diagnosis. These behaviors are obvious. The value lies in the relationship between these behaviors and predicting future outcome. Taylor, Everitt, et al. (1986) further suggested that the hyperactive syndrome was a useful conceptualization because this population of children frequently had weaker intellectual development, higher frequencies of sensorimotor incoordination, a greater number of developmental disorders, a more compromised adolescent outcome, and better response to methylphenidate than normal children. Within the larger syndrome, there has been research and a clinical quest over the past fifty years to determine if a specific subtype might speak to more or less risk of future problems or respond differently to treatment. Although subtype analysis has attempted to evaluate ADHD based on its occurrence, pervasively or in a specific situation, comorbidly with other disruptive and nondisruptive disorders, and occurring with and without the hyperactive-impulsive component, it is the last component that has been of greatest interest and yielded the greatest volume of data. These data suggest that children with simple inattention are very different from those with full-syndrome ADHD in their presentation, developmental course, and life outcome. Driscoll and Zecker (1991) reviewed the literature and found that significant differences exist between the inattentive and hyperactive subtypes. This suggests that a single diagnostic category obscured important distinctions between these two groups of children. Yet, during the same period, Dykman and Ackerman (1991) and Livingston, Dykman, and Ackerman (1990) suggested that laboratory measures may be statistically associated with diagnoses made by observer ratings but they do not yield clear separations of ADHD subgroups. These authors suggested three basic types of children with attention deficit: those with attention deficit alone, those with attention deficit and hyperactivity, and those with attention deficit, hyperactivity, and aggression. These authors followed up on their conceptualization of three types of ADHD by suggesting in 1993 (Dykman & Ackerman) that attention deficit children with hyperactive-impulsive and aggressive symptoms appeared to be at greatest risk for other disruptive disorders, whereas purely inattentive children appeared to demonstrate more symptoms of anxiety and depressed mood. Interestingly, teacher and parent ratings appeared more sensitive than laboratory measures in differentiating subtypes.

Bauermeister, Alegria, Bird, Rubio-Stipec, and Canino (1992) factor analyzed teacher ratings of ADHD symptoms in a community sample of 600 6- to 16-year-olds. Two factors were generated: inattention-disorganization and hyperactivity-impulsivity. Five clusters of symptom profiles were obtained: high in hyperactivity-impulsivity and moderately high in attention problems; demonstrated attention problems but minimal hyperactive-impulsive problems; demonstrated high problems scores in both; normal pattern; and adaptive pattern, in which children presented as exceptionally low in these problems. The first group appears very similar in outcome to the combined type of ADHD, the second to the primarily inattentive type, and the third to the hyperactive-impulsive type consistent with the *DSM-IV* categorization. In this study's subsample of 170 children, 88% of the variance was accounted for by these five subtypes.

In a population of forty-three children diagnosed with attention deficit disorder with hyperactivity and twenty-two children diagnosed with attention deficit disorder without hyperactivity, Hynd, Nieves, Connor, and Stone (1989) reported significant differences from clinical controls on speed and efficiency of cognitive processing. The hyperactive group performed significantly more slowly and variably than controls on several of the speeded classification tasks. However, the inattentive group was not distinguished on any measure. In 1991, Hynd, Lorys, Semrud-Clikeman, Huettner, and Lahey suggested that the inattentive group appeared to demonstrate an increased risk for academic deficits in comparison to the hyperactive-impulsive group. It has been hypothesized that attention-regulatory mechanisms possibly associated with anterior-posterior processes in the brain may be responsible for this deficit. Lorys, Hynd, and Lahey (1990) were unable to provide much support for a behavioral distinction between attention deficit with and without hyperactivity. They suggested an alternative conceptualization reflecting deficient right hemisphere processes in the hyperactive group that lead to behavioral as opposed to academic deficits. In this study of 100 clinic-referred children, full-scale IQ correlated significantly with neuropsychological measures. Measures of serial learning, memory, and visual orientation did not distinguish the normals from either type of attention deficit. In 1992, Hern and Hynd utilized a sensorimotor soft sign battery with limited cognitive involvement to determine differences in motor and sensory functioning between children with and without hyperactive problems. No differences were found between the hyperactives and normals. However, the hyperactive children with attention deficit exhibited more soft signs than the normal group at all ages and more than the attention deficit without hyperactivity above 96 months of age.

Frank and Ben-Nun (1988) compared twenty-one children with hyperactive ADD and eleven with the inattentive type of ADD. Parent and teacher ratings, written teacher reports, school psychological reports, and pediatric neurology clinic data were used to provide classifications. Comparison between groups indicated that the hyperactives showed significantly greater abnormality on a variety of neurological measures, including abnormal finger-sequencing movements, dyskinesia, choreiform movements, and abnormal hopping, ball handling, and tandem gait. In comparison to the inattentives, the hyperactives were also more likely to have had perinatal or neonatal abnormality (50% versus 12%). Although no differences in likelihood of having a normal medical history, family history of ADD, or delayed speech or motor development emerged between the groups, both groups demonstrated significantly poorer performance in comparison to control children on measures of visual perception, visual and auditory sequencing, visual sequential memory, reading, and writing. The hyperactives showed significantly greater abnormalities in visual perception, visual sequential memory, and writing performance. This study also found a trend for the inattentive group to experience greater internalizing problems than the hyperactive group. Both groups of children were reported as less popular with their peers. The hyperactives were reported as more rejected, the inattentives as more neglected. Although Edelbrock et al. (1984) suggested that the inattentive group might be more likely to fail a grade than the hyperactive group, this was not reflected in this population. Finally, these authors propose what continues to be a popular hypothesis: that the true difference between the hyperactive and inattentive groups does not lie in specific skill weaknesses but rather in the impact impulsivity has on neuropsychological tasks considered to be sensitive to frontal lobe functioning.

Barkley, Grodzinksy, et al. (1992) reviewed the inconsistencies of twenty-two neuropsychological studies of frontal lobe functions in children with attention disorder. Some measures presumed to assess frontal lobe dysfunction were not reliably sensitive to the deficits occurring in either the inattentive or hyperactive type of attention deficit. The comorbidity of other disorders with attention deficit was suggested as a confounding factor. Based on these data, as well as a separate study comparing hyperactive and inattentive children with attention deficits on a number of neuropsychological tasks, it was concluded that existing findings suggested a problem with perceptual motor speed and processing in the inattentive but not the hyperactive group.

Seidman, Biederman, and Faraone (1995) suggest that ADHD children with a family history of the disorder are most impaired irrespective of other variables. They suggest that neuropsychological test performance in ADHD is significantly affected by family status and presence of learning disabilities. The similarity of findings between ADHD children with and without comorbid psychiatric disorders suggests that the neuropsychological impairments these children exhibit are associated with ADHD. When family history is partialed out, differences in test measures (such as the ability to screen out a distracting stimulus), academic tasks, and memory measures remain.

Conners (1995) has suggested two subtypes of ADHD. The first reflects children with poor automatic attention associated with poor performance on visual and language processing tasks. The second relates to voluntary attention associated with poor performance on tasks requiring sustained effort. Conners suggests that children with ADHD possessing poor voluntary attention relative to automatic attention have impaired performance on all visual processing and sustained attention tasks. It is his hypothesis that decision-making processes are more affected lexically by automatic attention and that deficits in either left or right hemisphere are associated with impairment in language and sustained attention.

Using a multimeasure and multi-informant set of procedures, Gordon, Mettelman, Smith, and Irwin (1989) demonstrated that measures designed to assess attention generally tend to agree regarding a child's status as normal or abnormal. Thus, agreement on a child's status is not source-dependent, suggesting that there is more consistency among parents, teachers, and laboratory measures than is usually thought.

These authors also noted an over 50% overlap of aggression with ADHD. The aggressive ADHD children are more likely to come from families with a history of marital problems, separation, or divorce.

In a sample of over 1,000 children, August and Garfinkel (1989) defined cognitive and behavioral forms of ADHD. They describe the behavioral subtype as including 80% of those identified and characterized by distinct clinical phenomenology of attention, impulsivity, and hyperactivity problems. These children fell on a continuum of severity, with the most severe showing behavioral features nearly indistinguishable from conduct disorder. Children with the behavioral subtype of ADHD did not exhibit specific skill deficits on neuropsychological tests characteristic of reading-disabled children. A second, less prevalent type of cognitive ADHD constituted approximately 20% of their study population. In this study, August and Garfinkel identified nearly 9% with significant behavioral problems: 2.3% were inattentive and overactive, 3% were inattentive and overactive, and 3.6% had problems with conduct only. In this study, the reading-disabled subgroup differed from controls on tests of vocabulary, word decoding, and sequential memory but not on tests of abstract and conceptual reasoning. Thus, most reading disorders likely reflect phonological as opposed to comprehension problems. Skill deficits that are expressive of low intelligence may be of particular value in understanding the academic problems of some reading-disabled children but not others. The behavioral ADHD subtype overall showed grade-appropriate academic achievement, adequate verbal abilities, intact memory, good conceptual skills, and few differences compared to normals on laboratory measures. The more severe in this group demonstrated more deviant levels of impulsivity and overactivity as well as aggressive, undersocialized behavior. Although they demonstrated weaknesses in short-term memory, they were not reading disabled. This group experienced severe academic underachievement along with inattentive, impulsive, and, to some extent, overactive symptoms. Children with the cognitive subtype exhibited information-processing deficits involving inadequate encoding and retrieval of linguistic information characteristic of reading disability. Other researchers have suggested that although the antisocial problems of children with ADHD are etiologically distinct, there is likely a continuum of antisocial problems that ADHD children experience that increases the severity of their illness as the level of family risk factors increases (Biederman, Faraone, Keenan, & Tsuang, 1991).

Based on a clinic-referred sample of 116 children with a diagnosis of ADHD, de-Quiros, Kinsbourne, Palmer, and Roufo (1994) divided the sample into three subgroups: those with inattentive, impulsive, and hyperactive problems (60); those with inattentive and impulsive problems (26); and those with just inattentive problems (30). The three groups were found to be similar in mean age, gender ratio, prevalence and pattern of associated learning disabilities, family history of psychopathology, and probability of favorable response to methylphenidate. The inattentive group exhibited fewer internalizing problems. A group that was hyperactive and impulsive but not inattentive was also found. These authors suggested that the diagnostic criteria for ADHD should be based on inattentive items and then subdivided into the concurrent presence or absence of impulsivity, then further subdivided with respect to hyperactivity. The concept of a cognitive versus behavioral subtype of ADHD has also been supported by the work of Halperin, Newcorn, Sharma, and Healey (1990). These authors demonstrated that children with ADHD who scored poorly on measures of attentional skills were cognitively impaired, whereas those who met the behavioral diagnosis for ADHD but did not score poorly on attention or laboratory measures had more conduct problems.

Lahey and Carlson (1992) report that children with inattentive type ADHD exhibit fewer problems with impulsivity, overactivity, aggression, noncompliance, and peer rejection. As Barkley, DuPaul, and McMurray (1990) have demonstrated, children with ADD with hyperactivity or the combined type are more likely to receive a diagnosis of another disruptive disorder such as oppositional defiance or conduct disorder. They are more likely to be placed in special education classrooms, to be suspended, and to have received psychotherapeutic intervention. As these authors also note, because the combined type dominates the research literature, little is known about the long-term outcome of children with the primarily inattentive type of attention deficit.

As noted earlier, the issue of prevalence is a function of diagnostic criteria. Morgan et al. (1996) retrospectively report that only two children would have been assigned to a hyperactive-impulsive group in their follow-up study. The paucity of children in this group was suggested as a result of not being identified in the original cohort. In contrast to Lahey et al. (1984), the Morgan study did not reveal greater internalizing symptoms in the inattentive ADD population. This finding is in agreement with Cantwell and Baker (1992), who found no significant differences in affective or anxiety disorder diagnoses for attention deficit with or without hyperactivity. The hyperactive-impulsive type, however, was found to have a much greater rate of externalizing diagnoses than the inattentive type. Reid, Maag, and Vasa, (1994) collected demographic data, disability categories, placement, academic achievement, and educational treatment of children diagnosed with ADHD in a general school population of over 14,000 students. One hundred and thirty-six were identified with ADHD; over half of these were receiving special education services. Comorbidly, forty were identified with a behavior disorder, twenty-two as learning disabled, seven as mildly retarded, one had another health impairment, and one was orthopedically handicapped. The most common special education placement for these students was in the general education classroom with resource support (50 students). Over 90% of the ADHD students were receiving medication. Interestingly, in this sample of ADHD children, 90% were Caucasian versus 87% in the normal population; 3% were Native American with ADHD versus 1.4% in the normal population; 5% with ADHD were African American, consistent with the normal population; none were Hispanic, compared to 2.4% in the normal population; 1.5% with ADHD were Asian American or Pacific Islander compared to 3% in the normal population. In terms of grade level of the children diagnosed with ADHD, most were in second and third grade (19.9% and 26%, respectively). ADHD was fairly evenly distributed among the other grades, with the lowest percentages noted in first and sixth grade (13.2% for each).

What, then, is the reader to make of this seemingly conflicting data? In 1992, Cantwell and Baker, based on a review of available research as well as analysis of their longitudinal population, concluded that there were some very real and significant differences between the hyperactive and inattentive type of children with attention deficit disorder. Their comparisons appear in Table 2–5.

The current *DSM-IV* distinction of the combined versus inattentive types of ADHD has significant meaning for the practitioner. The inattentive group appears to represent a very different population in terms of their presenting symptoms, comorbidities,

Table 2–5.   Differences between ADD with hyperactivity and ADD without hyperactivity in the literature

	Differences Reported	References
ADHD core symptoms	Increased impulsivity in ADDH	Berry et al., 1985; Lahey et al., 1985, 1987; Pelham et al., 1981
	Increased distractibility in ADDH	Lahey et al., 1985
Conduct symptoms	Increased aggression, antisocial behavior, and total conduct symptoms in ADDH	Barkley et al., 1990; Edelbrock et al., 1984; King & Young, 1982; Lahey et al., 1987; Pelham et al., 1981
Emotional symptoms	Increased anxiety and internalizing codiagnoses in ADDWO	Lahey et al., 1984, 1987
Social relations	Increased peer rejection and unpopularity in ADDH	Barkley et al., 1990; Edelbrock et al., 1984; Lahey et al., 1984
	Increased social withdrawal in ADDWO (especially in girls)	Edelbrock et al., 1984; Pelham et al., 1981
Learning and cognition	Increased "sluggish" tempo and drowsiness in ADDWO	Lahey et al., 1985, 1987
	Increased LD in ADDWO	Edelbrock et al., 1984
	More off-task behaviors in ADDH	Barkley et al., 1990; Sergeant & Scholten, 1985
	More sloppiness in ADDH	Lahey et al., 1985
Medical	More fine motor problems in ADDH	Berry et al., 1985
	More perinatal problems and neurological symptoms in ADDH	Frank & Ben-Nun, 1988
	Different prolactin levels with methylphenidate treatment	Shaywitz et al., 1986
Family history	Increased familial substance abuse, antisocial disorder, and hyperactivity in ADDH; increased anxiety and LD in ADDWO	Barkley et al., 1990
Course and treatment	More school suspension, individual and family therapy in ADDH; more drug nonresponders in ADDWO	
	Older age at referral in ADDWO	Lahey et al., 1987

Source: Cantwell, D. P., & Baker, L. (1992). Attention deficit disorder with and without hyperactivity: A review and comparison of matched groups. *Journal of the American Academy of Child and Adolescent Psychiatry, 31,* 432–438. Used with permission.

developmental course, and future life outcome. They appear to be significantly less negatively impacted than the combined group. Although these two groups may be distinguished by their performance on certain assessment measures, their distinction lies in behavior observed in real-life settings. At the present time, this appears to best characterize differences between these two groups, far beyond that obtained by comparison of laboratory measures or related risk factors. This discussion has not included the primarily hyperactive-impulsive group, as the available data suggest that the practitioner need be aware that this group of children is often in the preschool or early school-age range. Over time, the majority of these children demonstrate the criteria necessary for the combined diagnosis.

It is reasonable for the practitioner to conclude that the available literature supports a distinct difference between the inattentive and combined types of ADHD based on current *DSM-IV* diagnostic criteria. Given the history and the evolution of the ADHD diagnosis, it is also important for the practitioner to recognize that little is known about the essential characteristics of the inattentive type and nearly nothing is known about long-term prognosis (Lahey & Carlson, 1991; Schaughency & Hynd, 1989). ADHD as it stands is a multidimensional disorder with at least two distinct subtypes. It is also quite likely that as these two subtypes diverge, future diagnostic nomenclature will consider the combined type to be an impulse disorder, moving the inattentive type off the disruptive continuum and onto the nondisruptive continuum alongside specific learning disabilities.

SUMMARY

This chapter facilitates the clinician's ability to develop a working definition of ADHD, taking into account laboratory and clinical research. It also offers a means of seeing the world through the eyes of children with ADHD, which enhances the diagnostic process as well as facilitates the practitioner's ability to help parents and teachers understand the nature of the disorder and its impact on children's lives. This chapter also reviews a number of basic issues essential for the practitioner to understand the history of *DSM* diagnoses, offers a diagnostic strategy, and discusses issues of prevalence and validity of subtypes.

Chapter 3

LIFE SPAN AND COMORBID ISSUES

Although the cluster of symptoms and problems children with ADHD present can be grouped homogeneously, each child's presentation is unique. Thus, children with ADHD at similar developmental stages and ages are very different from each other in their behavior and development. It is therefore important for the practitioner to understand the manner by which a similar problem or behavior presents differently at different maturational levels and within different individuals. For example, the thrashing, temperamental infant may develop into the frantic, overactive preschooler, then become the impulsive-hyperactive school-age child who may not be able to stay seated or remain on task, then become the restless, fidgety adolescent, and then, finally, the pacing, overenergetic adult (Ross & Ross, 1982). Further, two temperamentally difficult infants may create and be perceived as experiencing very different problems based on the temperamental qualities of their parents and home environment. It is also important for the practitioner to keep in mind that behavior easily overlooked at one age may not be well tolerated at another age. The 4-year-old preschooler unable to pay attention or sit during a group activity may be described casually by the teacher as immature but in a less structured preschool setting, not be identified as a significant problem. By 6 years of age, a similar level of inattentive or restless behavior is often described by the first-grade teacher as a significant impediment in the classroom.

As Leichtman (1993) aptly describes, the core symptoms of ADHD, principally impulsivity, shape a child's emerging personality and in a linear way affect life outcome. Impulsive qualities also shape parent-child attachment, the views children develop about themselves and their world, their ability to develop empathy, the development of positive self-esteem, age-appropriate values, learning and organizational strategies, and social skills, and the ability to develop the self-perception that one belongs within a family structure.

As noted, biological, psychological, and social risk and protective factors are often complex and at times difficult to interpret. Grizenko and Pawliuk (1994) evaluated risk and protective factors in a group of fifty 9-year-olds with disruptive problems and fifty controls. Risk factors for the development of additional life problems included the co-occurrence of learning difficulties, severe hyperactivity, perinatal complications, school failure, and a history of maternal depression. Protective factors included the child's ability to express feelings appropriately, develop coping strategies for stress, and have a good relationship with family members other than parents, such as grandparents.

Prior to examining the impact of ADHD symptoms throughout the child and adolescent life span in Chapter 4, a number of specific family and comorbid conditions that present across all life span stages will be reviewed.

CONDITIONS ACROSS ALL LIFE-SPAN STAGES

Gender

Gender differences in the diagnostic nomenclature and developmental course have been of increasing interest. A recent National Institute of Mental Health conference on sexual differences in ADHD noted the need for increased research in this area (Arnold, 1996). A number of studies in the past ten years, however, have addressed this issue. Gender differences in primary and secondary symptomatology in fifty-one boys and twenty girls, ages 5 to 13 years, referred consecutively to an outpatient clinic for ADHD were evaluated by Brown, Madan-Swain, and Baldwin (1991). A battery of psychometric tests, demographic information, and the Child Behavior Checklist were utilized. Females were more frequently retained in school and evidenced greater impairment on spatial memory tasks. Moreover, there was a tendency for females to be older at the time of referral for ADHD symptoms. With increasing age, females evidenced more severity across a wider array of measures, including problems with cognitive functioning, poor academic achievement, and more problems with peers. In a population of sixty children, Breen and Altepeter (1990) evaluated situational behavior based on gender. Their results did not support gender differences in children identified as ADHD in regard to situational problems. Males and females with ADHD presented their caregivers with similar degrees of behavior-management difficulty and similar situations resulting in parent-child conflict. The total number of problems in unsupervised settings such as recess, lunch, and in the hallway were somewhat greater for the males than females.

Nussbaum, Grant, Roman, Poole, and Bigler (1990) evaluated the performance of thirty-five males and thirty-five females with ADHD on a variety of structured diagnostic tests, including selected subtests from the Halstead Reitan Neuropsychological Battery. Subjects were age-matched and analysis was performed on five groups of cognitive variables (verbal, visual-spatial, motoric, sensory, and attention). In contrast to pilot study findings of Seidman et al. (1997), these analyses revealed no substantial differences between males and females. The authors suggested that differences between males and females in the prevalence of ADHD is not due to gender differences in the neurological substrates of the disorder itself. However, when Gordon and Mettelman (1994) compared males to females based on their clinic-referred population, females with ADHD tended to have lower verbal IQs, fewer abnormal scores on laboratory measures of impulsiveness, and patterns of scores on rating scales indicating fewer externalizing problems. To be referred, the authors suggested, females likely demonstrated fewer behavior problems but greater cognitive deficits. Gender differences persisted even when both groups reached criteria for the ADHD diagnosis. Gordon and Mettelman raised the possibility that ADHD does indeed manifest itself uniquely in females as compared to males. Seidman et al. suggest that these differences are independent of psychiatric comorbidity, hypothesizing that neuropsychological and behavioral deficits observed in females with ADHD are not due to comorbid psychiatric conditions.

Breen (1989) examined the extent to which females with ADHD differed from males and normals. Teacher ratings of child psychopathology, clinic observations, and measures of attention span, impulse control, achievement, intelligence, and memory were used to assess the three groups. Males with ADHD were viewed as more deviant than normal females. Females and males with ADHD presented similar academic and behavior profiles. All three groups performed virtually the same on an instrument measuring sustained attention and impulse control. McGee and Feehan (1991) questioned the evidence relating to gender differences in the prevalence of ADHD. They suggested that females may be underrecognized because they are not as disruptive. Their assessment of the literature at the time did not support any significant differences in the pattern of developmental, attention, or background correlates between males and females with ADHD. However, these authors suggested that gender-specific norms and diagnostic criteria should be considered in identifying females with ADHD due to the fact that they are not as disruptive as males. This issue continues to be debated (Barkley, 1996c; M. Gordon, 1996).

Most recently, meta-analytic procedures combined data across eighteen studies dealing with gender differences in ADHD to detect trends within the combined data (Gaub & Carlson, 1997). The authors noted that conclusions were complicated by these studies' dissimilar subject selection processes, measures used, findings, and conclusions. A subset of studies revealed no gender differences between males and females with ADHD in impulsivity, academic performance, or social functioning. Other studies demonstrated significant differences in areas such as level of intellectual impairment as well as ratings of internalizing and externalizing behavior. The authors argued that differences or lack of differences between males and females with ADHD should be interpreted cautiously because few data are available for the many variables studied and because populations were limited to clinic-referred samples. The meta-analytic review revealed little variability across studies and no significant gender differences in the areas of impulsivity, basic academic performance, social skills, peer status, fine motor ability, parent education, and diagnostic history. Further, little variability was demonstrated across studies in IQ, hyperactivity, and externalizing diagnoses, with females displaying slightly greater levels of intellectual impairment and lower levels of externalizing behavior and hyperactivity. Among nonreferred children identified with ADHD, lower rates of inattention, internalizing behavior, peer aggression, and peer dislike occurred for girls than boys. In clinic-referred and identified populations, boys and girls appeared similarly impaired.

These authors also reported differences between *DSM-III* and *DSM-III-R* as diagnostic processes. With *DSM-III,* boys demonstrated higher levels of peer aggression and inattention. When the *DSM-III-R* diagnosis was used, no gender differences were noted in aggression or levels of inattention. Although males and females with ADHD were found to be significantly more aggressive with peers and their same-sex counterparts, males with ADHD demonstrated relatively more aggression toward peers when compared to males without ADHD than did females. Females with ADHD were relatively more impaired in socioeconomic status than males. Males referred for treatment of ADHD were representative of the population of males with ADHD in prevalence of internalizing behavioral problems, whereas referred females with ADHD appeared to comprise the most severely internalizing group of the general population of females with ADHD. Practitioners need to be cautioned from drawing hasty conclusions about this issue. Available data result in more questions being asked than answered, due to differences in confounding variables. An appreciation of gender differences and gender

Table 3–1.   Effect size and homogeneity indices and probabilities for the meta-analysis of ADHD boys versus ADHD girl

Area of Functioning/Variable	No. of Studies	Effect Size (d)	Effect Size (p)	Homogeneity (X^2)[a]	Homogeneity (p)[a]	Interpretation
Primary symptoms						
Hyperactivity	9	0.158	.000***	9.45	.305	Boys more hyperactive
Inattention	5	0.193	.000***	9.84	.042**	Mod explored: RS*** & DS**
Impulsivity-[behavior]	3	0.033	.259	1.05	.599	No significant difference
Intelligence						
Full Scale IQ	6	−0.366	.002***	5.41	.368	Girls have lower FSIQs
Verbal IQ	3	−0.494	.002***	1.66	.439	Girls have lower VIQs
Performance IQ	3	−0.357	.018**	1.19	.558	Girls have lower PIQs
Academic						
Global	1	0.064	.427	—	—	No significant difference
Mathematics	3	−0.084	.307	3.04	.217	No significant difference
Reading	3	0.111	.275	2.34	.310	No significant difference
Spelling	1	0.144	.721	—	—	No significant difference
Language	2	−0.097	.265	15.75	.000**	Mod: non explored due to small N
Comorbid conditions						
Conduct disorder	3	0.138	.003***	0.83	.667	More boys with comorbid CD
Other externalizing	12	0.168	.031**	7.26	.778	Boys have more externalizing behavior
Internalizing	10	0.099	.016**	19.19	.023**	Mod explored: RS**
Social Functioning						
Global social skills	3	−0.003	.493	0.12	.943	No significant difference
Peer liking	2	0.155	.241	0.53	.475	No significant difference
Peer disliking	5	0.101	.239	18.19	.002***	Possible moderator: RS** & DS***
Peer aggression	4	0.348	.007***	7.33	.061	Boys more aggressive, Mod explored: RS** & DS**
Motor Skills						
Fine motor	1	−0.386	.165	—	—	No significant difference
Family						
Education–mother	3	−0.237	.130	0.59	.750	No significant difference
Education–father	2	0.036	.418	1.36	.241	No significant difference
Martial satisfaction	6	0.045	.358	12.03	.034**	Mod explored: none significant
Psychopathology	5	−0.082	.281	7.93	.093	No significant difference
Parental depression	1	−0.362	.163	—	—	No significant difference
Socioeconomic status	3	−0.241	.069*	5.91	.051*	Mod explored: non significant

Source: Gaub, M., & Carlson, C. L. (1997). Gender differences in ADHD: A meta-analysis and critical review. *Journal of the American Academy of Child and Adolescent Psychiatry, 36,* 1036–1045. Used with permission.

Note: Positive effect sizes indicate more impairment among males; negative effect sizes indicate more impairment among females; ADHD = attention-deficit hyperactivity disorder; Mod = moderate variable; RS = referral source; DS = diagnostic system; FSIQ = Full Scale IQ; VIQ = Verbal IQ; PIQ = Performance IQ; CD = conduct disorder.

[a] Significance indicates rejection of the homogeneity hypothesis.

[b] Impulsivity from behavioral measures only (no Matching Familiar Figures Test or Continuous Performance Test data).

*p < .10; **p < .05; ***pp. .01.

issues in general should be kept in mind during assessment and treatment. A summary of Gaub and Carlson's statistical findings appears in Table 3–1.

Intelligence

Three questions are frequently asked regarding the relationship between intelligence and ADHD: Does the ADHD population represent a normal distribution in terms of intellectual skills? Are there characteristics unique to children with ADHD demonstrating superior or better intellectual abilities? Are there similar or different characteristics of ADHD in those demonstrating deficient intellectual abilities?

Barkley (1995b) suggests that ADHD likely has a unidirectional affect on intelligence in two ways: first, to a smaller degree, in the acquisition of intellectual skills; second, to a larger degree, in the application of skills, that is, making effective or efficient use of skills possessed. Empirically, research studies have found a link between IQ and ADHD (Hinshaw, Morrison, Carte, & Cornsweet, 1987; McGee, Williams, & Silva, 1984), as well as a link between IQ and behavior problems (Sonuga-Barke, Lamparelli, Stevenson, Thompson, & Henry, 1994). Rates of hyperactive-impulsive behavior and measures of intelligence appear to have a negative association. In contrast, association between ratings of conduct problems and intelligence are often much smaller, in some cases nonsignificant. When hyperactive-impulsive behavior is controlled (Hinshaw et al.; Lynam, Moffitt, & Strouthamer-Loeber, 1993; Sonuga-Barke et al.), the relationship among verbal IQ, achievement, and disruptive behavior appears to be relatively specific to the hyperactive-impulsive element observed in disruptive behavior disorders (Hinshaw, 1992a, 1992b). When efforts are not made to control for IQ, samples of ADHD children do differ significantly from controls, particularly in lower verbal intelligence (Barkley & Cunningham, 1979; Barkley, Karlsson, & Pollard, 1985; McGee et al., 1992; Moffitt, 1990; van der Meere & Sergeant, 1988a). It has been suggested that this difference is consistent with a theoretical model of ADHD as a disorder of poor impulse control (Barkley, 1995a). Measures of sustained attention and inhibition are associated to a small but significant degree with measures of IQ (Schonfeld, Shaffer, & Barmack, 1989). Matching ADHD subjects with controls and statistically controlling for IQ differences appears to reduce or eliminate the effects of ADHD on intelligence. Group differences in verbal IQ should not be viewed as an artifact of group selection nor as a source of error to be statistically removed. These differences may in fact reflect real differences in these two populations (Werry et al., 1987). The preponderance of the data suggests, however, that less than 10% of the variance in verbal IQ is accounted for by ADHD.

In contrast, the impact ADHD has on the efficient use of intellectual skills is likely greater. This phenomenon, however, is nearly impossible to evaluate given the idiosyncratic differences in children and their responses to differing environmental circumstances. Thus, the practitioner is on firm ground when concluding that children with ADHD demonstrate a generally normal distribution of intellectual skills. However, due to their impulsivity, assessment at any given moment may yield underestimates of their intellectual abilities, particularly on tasks requiring inhibition. (The potential benefits in using intellectual measures to directly assess symptoms of ADHD as well as assess and answer broader developmental questions concerning children with

ADHD will be addressed in depth in Chapter 9.) Attention problems are reported as quite common in the intellectually handicapped population, with 10% to 20% reported as exhibiting inappropriate degrees of hyperactivity, inattention, and impulsivity, warranting the diagnosis of ADHD (Bregman, 1991). This author also reports that nearly 5% of the intellectually handicapped population at that time were prescribed stimulant medication. Given the broad neurological etiology leading to common symptoms of hyperactivity, inattention, and impulsivity, a higher incidence in this population is not surprising. Fee, Matson, and Benavidez (1994) evaluated teacher reports in four groups of children. The first group experienced ADHD with normal IQ; the second, ADHD with low IQ; the third, low IQ without ADHD; and the fourth was a normal control group. No significant behavioral differences were reported by teachers between the normal IQ ADHD and the intellectually handicapped ADHD groups. The intellectually handicapped subjects in general were found to be more anxious than their normal peers, and children with ADHD with normal IQs were rated higher than the other groups in disruptive social behavior.

It has been suggested anecdotally that children with ADHD tend to fall inordinately at the higher end of the intellectual distribution. However, well-controlled research has not been generated to demonstrate that this is the case. It has also been suggested that ADHD, specifically impulsivity, may reflect some form of dysfunctional creativity. Hallowell and Ratey (1994) suggest that creativity is impulsivity gone right. Viewing impulsivity as a potentially positive symptom attribute of ADHD may be a means of influencing the general public's view of the disorder as beneficial; however, impulsivity has been demonstrated scientifically to be a liability in most situations. There is no scientific data to suggest that children with ADHD are more creative. Their impulsivity may result in their being quicker to offer suggestions and ideas, and in some circumstances, this may result in adults perceiving them as more creative. Shaw (1992) completed a discriminant analysis with bright children experiencing ADHD. This author found that left-sided laterality—the ability to effectively use incidentally acquired information—stimulation seeking, and the use of imagery and problem solving in a creativity task discriminated these children from the norm. The authors suggested a hypothetical model to explain the functioning of intelligent, creative children with ADHD. However, it was not suggested that children with ADHD as a group are more creative than any other children. Shaw and Brown (1990) suggested that children with ADHD may attend to different aspects in their environment, resulting in their gathering and using more diverse information. These authors also found that the intelligent ADHD group demonstrated better figural creativity than others, suggesting a strength in nonverbal abilities. Finally, Shaw and Brown (1990) assessed nearly 100 sixth- and seventh-graders demonstrating symptoms of ADHD and having IQs above the 84th percentile on a range of tasks, including cognitive abilities, verbal and figural aspects of problem solving, and creativity. The children with ADHD demonstrated more mixed laterality and allergies, used more diverse nonverbal and poorly focused information, and showed higher figural creativity than did high IQ subjects without attention problems.

Cramond (1994) argues that there is an overlap between behavioral characteristics of creativity and ADHD. This author suggests that higher creativity scores, sensation seeking, and use of imagery are common descriptors of creative individuals. These, according to this author, are also shown to be descriptors of ADHD. The author argues that a popular behavior-management intervention for ADHD, that of structuring the learning environment, may have a negative impact on a creative child. However, no data are provided to support this hypothesis.

The preponderance of the data argues for practitioners to view intellectual processes as generally independent from ADHD. Although children with ADHD may perform inconsistently or deficiently on measures of intellectual skill, practitioners should not assume that deficiencies in intellect or, for that matter, inconsistencies in intellectual performance are diagnostic of ADHD. However, as will be discussed in Chapter 9, intelligence can be considered a protective factor. For some individuals, it can serve as an equalizer. Bright people may be more capable of responding to certain treatments and more readily able to develop coping strategies and insight into their problems.

Language

Language has been considered the window to the mind (Beitchman & Inglis, 1991). The bidirectional relationship of language development and impulsivity has been questioned but not thoroughly evaluated. Richman, Stevenson, and Graham (1982) suggested that speech and language disorders are strong predictors of poor psychiatric and educational outcome. M. Gordon (1991) strongly emphasizes the links between language and behavior. This author suggests that these limits may be the result of constitutional and temperamental factors of the child interacting with psychosocial factors. Strong argument suggests a powerful relationship between the ability to develop competent language and to learn self-control.

Articulation problems have been well demonstrated to present a low risk for long-term language-related difficulties. In contrast, receptive and expressive language delays have been consistently demonstrated to contribute to academic delays (Beitchman, Wilson, Brownlie, Walters, & Lancee, 1996). Receptive and expressive language impairments in early childhood, 5 years of age, are associated with the greatest risk at follow-up at 12.5 years. Early auditory comprehension problems appear to be a specific risk factor as well for the development of later aggressive and hyperactive symptoms (Beitchman, Wilson, Browlie, Walters, & Lancee, 1996).

Baker and Cantwell (1992) extensively reviewed the literature on speech/language disorders in children with ADHD and presented their original data in a group of sixty-five children with attention deficit and current speech and language disorders. They found a consistent pattern of elevated rates of speech/language disorders in individuals with ADHD and elevated rates of ADHD in persons with speech/language disorders. There also appear to be differences in verbal interactions between children with ADHD and normal children. Children with ADHD and speech/language disorder are a heterogeneous group linguistically, with impairments ranging from mild to severe. The authors suggest that some types of speech/language disorder found in children with attention deficit may be related to other factors such as age, gender, or comorbid psychiatric condition. For the practitioner, the implication of these data suggests that history taking should focus on linguistic milestones such as babbling, response to sounds, first words, first sentences, and rate of language development. Educational difficulties related to language deficits could include repetition, wandering off topic, difficulty remembering verbal instructions, problems fluently telling an organized story, and often seeming to be confused.

Cohen, Davine, Horodezky, Lipsett, and Isaacson (1993) evaluated 399 children routinely screened with a battery of language tests as well as parent and teacher questionnaires. In 288 children referred solely for psychiatric problems, 35% had a language impairment that had not been previously suspected. These children had more subtle language impairments than did the 111 children referred with previously identified language impairments. Groups of children with unsuspected and previously identified language impairments demonstrated symptoms associated with ADHD. Children with unsuspected language impairments demonstrated more serious externalizing behavioral problems. The authors suggest that it is uncertain whether ADHD and language impairment combined are attributable to common antecedents or whether there is a direct causal link. Regarding the latter, arguments can be made in both directions, suggesting that children who do not comprehend or remember instructions are prone to be described as inattentive and restless (Felton, Wood, Brown, Campbell, & Harter, 1987). When children are not attending, they are less likely to develop language normally. When they are impulsive, they are also less likely to learn from experience. It is important to note that a high percentage of children with receptive language impairment occurs in mixed samples of psychiatrically disturbed children (Cohen, Davine, & Meloche-Kelly, 1989).

In a population of 242 children ages 8.5 to 12.5 years with learning disability, Gibbs and Cooper (1989) evaluated the prevalence of speech and language problems. They reported 96% with at least one type of problem. In this group, 90% had a language deficit, 23% an articulation deficit, 12% a voice disorder, 1% a fluency disorder, 7.5% a hearing deficit, and 15% were suffering from a middle ear infection. Obviously, some children experienced more than one type of speech and language problem. Interestingly, only 6% were receiving services for speech problems.

A majority of children with language disorders also experience problems learning to read. Much of the language and ADHD research has focused on reading achievement as a measure of competent language functioning. Casey, Rourke, and Del Dotto (1996) demonstrated that 17% of a population of nearly 100 children with ADHD exhibited an auditory-linguistic processing deficiency. These authors suggested that a weakness in this area combined with inattentiveness fueled delayed academic achievement. These authors also suggested that ADHD with or without hyperactivity did not appear to be discriminated by the evaluation of academic skills.

As early as 1970, Rutter, Tizard, and Whitmore suggested that either problem behavior leads to reading difficulties, reading difficulty produces behavior problems, both are produced by some unknown third factor, or all three hypotheses can operate simultaneously. There is no doubt that classroom behavior is in part dependent on a variety of factors, including ethnicity (Dunkin & Doenau, 1985) and social background (Kahl, 1985), gender (Bank, 1985) as well as cognitive and affective characteristics (Debus, 1985; Sinclair, 1985). A number of correlational studies have found a strong, direct association between complaints of inattention and reading difficulties in general student populations, as well as in those identified as learning disabled (Dykman & Ackerman, 1991; Jorm, Share, Matthews, & MacLean, 1986; Levy, Horn, & Dalglish,

1987; McGee, Williams, Moffitt, & Anderson, 1989; McGee et al., 1987; Stevenson, Richman, & Graham, 1985). In fact, McGee and Share (1988) estimated that 80% of their sample of 11-year-old children identified with ADHD also experienced problems with reading and writing skills. However, the direction and magnitude of the effect of relationship was not clear.

Rowe and Rowe (1992a, 1992b) evaluated the relationship between inattentiveness in the classroom and reading achievement. In a sample of 5,000 students 5 to 14 years old drawn from a normal school population, these authors demonstrated that regardless of family socioeconomic status, age, and gender, students' inattentiveness had a strong negative effect on their achievement as well as on their attitudes toward reading and reading activity at home. The findings suggested strong reciprocal effects, with inattentive behavior leading to reduced achievement, reading achievement being mediated by attitude, and limited reading activity at home leading to increased inattentiveness in the classroom. In this study, the authors suggested that given the mutuality of learning outcomes and behavior there is a clear need to focus strategies in both the home and school domains simultaneously. This is a view echoed by Merrell (1990), who noted that although low socioeconomic status is associated with aggressive behavior in children, low socioeconomic status is not associated with the core symptoms of inattention and hyperactivity, a finding mirrored by others (Loney & Milich, 1982). Although socioeconomic status had a negative influence on inattentiveness, students' attitudes toward reading, reading activity at home, and reading achievement, the effects were small and generally insignificant. Reading activity at home, however, did have an impact on reading achievement, suggesting the importance of reading at home as a major influence affecting student achievement (Rowe, 1991). This also speaks to the important and significant impact families have on their children's school behavior and performance, an issue discussed in greater depth in the following section. Nonetheless, it is important to mention that it has been estimated that approximately 75% of the co-occurrence in some learning problems such as spelling disability and attention deficit may be the result of a shared genetic influence (Stevenson, Pennington, Gilger, DeFries, & Gillis, 1993).

Are the language skills of impulsive children delayed because they don't practice or attend to their environment effectively, or are these children impulsive because they lack efficient linguistic capacity necessary to develop appropriate inhibitory control? McRae and Vickar (1991) followed a population of thirty-eight children for nearly four years with a history of speech delay. Half of this group had poor articulation skills. These problems, however, were not related to their level of language or achievement problems. The authors suggested that articulation deficits are developmentally related with good prognosis. In a follow-up correspondence with the authors, McRae (Personal Communication, November 20, 1991) noted that all children in this population appear to have a high rate of disruptive behavioral problems. In the follow-up, over 90% of the behavioral problems improved as the quality of language skills improved. The relationship between developmental language disorders and emotional problems was investigated in ninety-eight 8-year-olds by Benasich, Curtiss, and Tallal (1993). At 4 years of age and then again at 8, the language-impaired children received higher behavior problem scores and were more likely to score in the clinical range than were control children. Neither the degree of early language impairment nor the amount of language improvement predicted behavioral and emotional status. Language-impaired children with the largest drop in IQ between 4 and 8 years of age received the highest behavior problem scores. No significant comorbid relationship was observed between language impairment and ADHD. These authors suggested that the enhanced incidence of behavior problems in this population likely is more related to lower intellectual skills than to linguistic deficits or ADHD symptoms per se. However, the powerful impact language delay may have on behavior can also be indirect. Paul and James (1990) evaluated groups of 2-year-olds in terms of parent perceptions of their development and behavior. Parent perception appeared to reflect parents' ability to interact optimally with their toddlers regardless of whether parents perceived behavioral problems secondary to language deficit or as an independent temperamental quality. Parents in this study tended to see toddlers with slow language growth as more active, inattentive, and difficult to manage than their normally speaking peers. These qualities will be discussed further when issues related to family functioning are reviewed, due to the long-term impact they have on the developing parent-child relationship.

The private speech of children with learning disability and ADHD was evaluated by Berk and Landau (1993). Results of this study found that learning-disabled children used more task-irrelevant private speech than controls. This effect was especially pronounced for the population with learning disability and ADHD.

Finally, Donahue, Cole, and Hartas (1994) and Shepherd, Broilier, and Dandro (1994) have convincingly demonstrated that regardless of the direction of effect, the play, social, and behavioral skills of language-impaired children are deficient relative to their same-age unaffected peers and are likely to increase the vulnerability for this population to receive comorbid diagnoses of other disruptive behavioral problems such as ADHD. Giddan (1991) suggests that speech pathologists be aware of the high incidence of behavioral and emotional problems in children with speech and language difficulties. It is advisable for the practitioner to heed this suggestion as well.

Learning Disability

DuPaul and Stoner (1994) reviewed seventeen studies attempting to determine the percentage of children with ADHD also experiencing learning disabilities. Averaging across studies, approximately one out of every three children with ADHD was found to have a specific learning disability. As Barkley (1990a) notes, the prevalence of learning disabilities among normal controls is much lower than the lowest estimates approximately 20% for ADHD (Semrud-Clikeman et al., 1992).

In a sample of studies evaluating the overlap of attention deficit with learning disabilities, nearly 40% demonstrated symptoms of ADHD. These ranged from a low of 18% to a high of 36% (Barkley, 1990a). Differences in these percentages are likely due to differences in the criteria used to define learning disabilities. Higher incidence is found when briefer measures (e.g., a simple cutoff questionnaire) are used, and lower when more stringent criteria are applied. Although a number of authors (Casey et al., 1996; Lahey & Carlson, 1992) suggest otherwise, others hold that children with the inattentive type of ADHD likely experience more specific learning disabilities than those with the hyperactive-impulsive type. Over ten years ago, Felton et al. (1987) suggested that the attentional problems of children with learning disabilities may be caused by or related to a different set of factors than those leading to attentional problems without reading difficulties.

As with language impairment, the direction of relationship between learning disability and attention deficit symptoms has been repeatedly questioned and thoroughly examined. Cantwell and Baker (1992) suggest that the relationship between ADHD and learning disability occurs beyond a chance level. In their studies, children with learning disability also demonstrate increased rates of other psychiatric disorders such as disruptive problems, mood disorders, and anxiety disorders. There is a clear relationship between language delay and learning disability, with estimates suggesting that the majority of children with language disorders subsequently develop learning disability (for review, see S. Goldstein, 1994). Part of the dilemma in examining the relationship between ADHD and learning disabilities relates to the lack of clearly defined subtypes within each disorder (Riccio, Gonzales, et al., 1994). In fact, some authors have argued that the most common learning disability—poor reading—simply represents the low end of a normal continuum rather than a specific developmental disorder (Shaywitz, Fletcher, Holahan, & Shaywitz, 1992). Yet, a number of years later, these same authors concluded that ADHD and learning disability represented two distinct problems (Shaywitz, Fletcher, & Shaywitz, 1995). These authors wrote that learning disability "represents a disorder of cognitive functioning. In contrast, ADHD is defined by the child's behavior as perceived by the child's parents and teachers; ADHD thus refers to a disorder affecting primarily the behavioral domain" (p. 55). Still others argue that both ADHD and learning disability possess very strong cognitive bases (Stolzenberg & Cherkes-Julkowski, 1991). These authors have asserted that among children with ADHD, those not receiving medication are found to be weakest relative to their ability to read, decode, calculate, and use verbal working memory. They assert that medication is associated with improved academic performance, a finding that has been reported by others (Badian, 1983). These authors suggest that language-based learning disability represents a pattern of phonological proficiency problems, and advocate that there is a smaller group of attention-based learning-disabled children whose delays in academic achievement result from faulty attentional processes. At one time, it was hypothesized that ADHD represented a form of learning disability. However, a review of the literature by Roberts and Pennington (1996) led to the conclusion that deficits in voluntary motor inhibition in ADHD, not deficits in verbal working memory, appeared to be responsible for academic performance problems. When working memory is described as containing components related to a visuospatial sketch pad or phonological loop and a central executive, children with ADHD have not been reported to have significant working memory deficits (Baddeley, 1992). More current conceptualization suggests that although these disorders are distinct, they do interact (Murphy & Hicks-Stewart, 1991). These authors propose an interactional perspective, arguing that independent or not, each disorder represents a different set of hurdles and problems for children that must be responded to and worked with by the adults in their lives.

As a large body of literature has reported, learning-disabled and hyperactive children differ in many domains from normal controls but not necessarily from each other. Chelune, Ferguson, Koon, and Dickey (1986) suggested that executive function tasks reflecting frontal lobe functioning may differentiate children with ADHD from controls or those with other developmental problems, such as learning disability. Keough

(1971) found that children with what were then referred to as attention problems may experience a specific neurological dysfunction, suggesting that excessive motor activity and impulsivity interfered with learning. However, among the learning-disabled, ADHD, and combined groups, minimal differences often are reported (Dykman, Ackerman, Holcomb, & Boudreau, 1983). It is reasonable to conclude that psychophysiological similarities outweigh differences. It is likely that laboratory measures may never objectively define behaviorally based disorders; thus, statistical groupings formed on the basis of laboratory measures may never validate categorizations made based on observation of behavior in the real-life setting.

Denckla (1996a) argues that the use of the terms attention and learning in cognitive neuroscience differs from their clinical use. In neuroscience, processes such as intention, working memory, and executive function are emphasized. As discussed, research suggests that neither attention nor long-term memory are the critical cognitive correlates of ADHD, or learning disability for that matter. However, when encoding processes are considered a function of working memory, children with learning and attention problems are identified as deficient. Sieel and Ryan (1989) find a significant growth in working memory capacity as a function of age. Reading-disabled children demonstrated significantly lower working memory scores; arithmetic-disabled children had significantly lower scores on a working memory counting task; and the attention-disordered group had similar scores to the normals, except at the youngest age level on a working memory sentence task. Furthermore, intention and inhibition appear to be particularly impaired in children with ADHD. These children exhibit broader deficits in executive function, which may underlie a basic problem of impulse control. Findings from cognitive neuroscience offer explanations of the neuroanatomical and neurophysiological underpinnings of learning problems and the frequent comorbidity of learning disability and ADHD.

Denckla's (1996a) review of the literature appears to support Barkley's perception that "what looks like an attention deficit is primarily an intention deficit with prominent developmental failures as the first component of intention, namely inhibition" (p. 117). In this model, intention is defined as initiating a movement, sustaining a movement or posture, and inhibiting extraneous, off-task movements while engaged in a task or shifting from one movement to another.

When learning is considered a function of acquisition, consolidation, storage, and retrieval, children with ADHD appear to have deficits in the process of acquisition, due to their deficient use of proactive strategies when engaged in learning tasks. This analysis is consistent with the work of Barkley, Grodzinsky, et al. (1992). In self-paced learning tasks, children with ADHD tend to spend less time looking at or even manipulating the components of what is to be remembered (for review, see Barkley, 1994). Under verbal learning conditions, for example, children with ADHD may ultimately obtain normal scores but fail to apply the strategy of organizing and reorganizing as they learn. Thus, their performance is inconsistent from trial to trial for both verbal and visual tasks. For example, when asked to copy a complex figure, they have poor recall, not because the reproduction was erroneous but because the approach to completing the task was disorganized and the memory system was overloaded with bits of information not encoded within an orderly frame of reference (Grodzinsky & Diamond, 1992). This phenomenon may explain why so many children with ADHD appear to know a subject the night before a test but perform poorly within the demanding framework of timed recall. Thus, children with ADHD appear to possess a production deficit (Denckla, 1996a): they may be learning but underachieving because they do not produce within the constraints defined by families and schools. Denckla suggests that this explains why children without learning disability but who have ADHD tend to be good incidental learners but poor academic learners. They effortlessly and nonstrategically acquire, consolidate, store, and retrieve whatever happens to be experienced naturally; their natural, phonological, and general language skills are normal; they may effortlessly learn to read more or less the way most children learn to talk. However, they may underachieve on a daily basis and experience academic deterioration as they move into the greater demands of advanced grades due to their lack of planning and organizational skills. Felton et al. (1987), in a sample of 8- to 12-year-olds with reading disability in comparison to those with attention deficit or normals, found that deficits in learning and memory for recently acquired information occurs as a function of attention deficit rather than reading disability. Deficits in naming are specific to reading disability rather than attention deficit. These authors concluded that attention deficit is a major source of additional and separate cognitive problems for reading-disabled children.

As noted, learning disability and ADHD both have been associated with deficits in working memory. Coupled with inhibition, working memory is currently held to be the most essential element of executive function, which in turn has been linked to the diagnosis of ADHD (Pennington, Bennett, McLeer, & Roberts, 1996). If there is no inhibition allowing delay between stimulus and response, there can be no working memory. However, what is held in working memory must possess some content. Under a construct of working memory, the child with ADHD may experience problems very similar to those of the child with LD. "As the child with uncomplicated ADHD (free of oppositional defiant or conduct symptoms) grows older, s/he may be less overtly hyperactive or impulsive and may appear more and more similar to the child with LD. Conversely, as rules are rehearsed and stored in long-term memory, the learning (language) disabled child who looks like a child with ADHD, may settle down and look more purely LD. In this developmental fashion, ADHD and LD express the overlap between them" (Denckla, 1996a, pp. 118–119).

Semrud-Clikeman et al. (1992) report comorbidity as high as 90% between ADHD and learning disability in some studies. These authors hypothesize that inconsistencies in criteria used to define learning disability are responsible for the wide variation in these statistics. Children with ADHD, with learning problems, and normal controls of both sexes were compared. Using a liberal definition of learning disability, significant differences were found among the groups: 38% of the ADHD group had academic problems, and 43% of the children with academic difficulty met the criteria for learning disability, as did 8% of the normals. More modest rates were found when more stringent methods of assessment were used, the most stringent criteria yielding 3%, 2%, and 0%, respectively. Arithmetically based learning disability appeared to be equally identified by both stringent methods. The liberal definition overidentified children in all three groups.

Elliason and Richmond (1988) evaluated the performance of ninety learning-disabled children on two measures of behavior and attentional skills. They used the revised Behavior Problem Checklist (Quay & Peterson, 1987), a parent-completed questionnaire, and a continuous performance test (CPT). As a group, the learning-disabled subjects exceeded normative standards in every measure of both behavioral scales. However, when the data were examined individually, approximately 30% of the children accounted for the majority of behavioral problems. The most common difficulties were in attention, cognitive processing, anxiety, and hyperactivity. Thus, it is clear that learning-disabled children experience more problems than others, but nearly 70% of the sample evidence no or only mild difficulties. Although the majority demonstrated a mixed or generalized pattern, the most common problem involved attention deficits and hyperactivity. Interestingly, none of this population of children had been diagnosed with attention deficit. CPT omission errors were negatively related to reading comprehension scores; as omission errors increased, reading grade level decreased. A high rate of omission errors could reflect poor attention, faulty memory, low risk-taking, or a lack of efficient processing, and these could all be implicated in reading disability. Fifty-five percent of the learning-disabled group were most likely to display a pattern of high omission–low commission scores. Swanson (1983) suggested that this phenomenon may be attributed to a memory problem or lack of active use of strategies. This author demonstrated that omission errors on vigilance tasks were more common for learning-disabled students, whereas commission errors reflecting impulsivity were more common for those with attentional problems.

In a sample of 182 clinic-referred children with ADHD, three behavioral subgroups were identified using teacher ratings (Dykman & Ackerman, 1991); 40% had ADHD with hyperactivity, 30% had ADHD with hyperactivity and aggression, and 30% had ADHD without hyperactivity or aggression. Over half the sample were poor readers, with eighty-two of these children meeting a discrepancy diagnosis for reading disability. More boys than girls (9 to 1) met the reading-disability criteria, whereas the ratio of males to females for the whole sample was 5 to 1. Boys who did not meet the criteria for reading disability had significantly higher IQs than those who did, but subgroups with and without reading disability still differed significantly on word reading and spelling scores, even when intelligence was controlled for. Both groups with and without reading disability could be differentiated from a control group on laboratory measures of sustained attention and impulse control. Interestingly, methylphenidate benefited all the groups in regard to ADHD symptoms whether or not they had reading disability. Data related to improvements in learning of ADHD children with reading disability, suggesting that the impact on pharmacologically reducing ADHD symptoms accelerates the learning rate for this population, are reviewed in Chapter 12.

Richards, Samuels, Turnure, and Ysseldyke (1990) evaluated thirty elementary students with learning disabilities and twenty controls. The learning-disabled subjects made more errors than controls on a CPT measure when letter distractors were adjacent to the target letter but not when they were distant, but they made more correct responses than controls when facilitating letters were adjacent to the target, suggesting that students with a learning disability are less able to narrow the focus of their attention. Longer response times by students with learning disabilities indicated they possess slower information-processing skills than controls. Regrouping students according to teacher ratings for attentional symptoms yielded the customary impulsive set on the CPT and more errors on the selective attention task; however, no differences were then found in response times. These authors concluded that children with learning disability demonstrate CPT deficits because they process information more slowly than normals. This likely would lead to a low processing speed score on a CPT task such as the Conners (1994). Those with attentional problems, however, appeared to possess a more complex pattern of difficulty, primarily characterized by impulsiveness. Thus, learning-disabled students may be inattentive, but students with ADHD are impulsive.

P. Robins (1992) evaluated a group of children with ADHD, those with learning disability, and those with the combined problems. A standardized battery of neuropsychological tests was administered. Multiple discriminant function analyses on the behavioral and neuropsychological tests demonstrated that one variant made clear-cut discriminations among and between each of the three groups: the construct of self-regulation relating to task accuracy, planning, and speed of responding differentiated the three groups, whereas sustained attention did not. These results further support the validity of ADHD as a diagnostic entity apart from learning disabilities and suggest that poor self-regulation and inhibition of behavior is the hallmark of ADHD.

Stanford and Hynd (1994) compared parent and teacher behavior ratings for ADHD and learning-disabled 5- to 16-year-olds. Overall, the ADHD inattentive type subjects more closely resembled the learning-disabled population behaviorally than the ADHD hyperactive-impulsive group. Specific behavioral symptoms were also demonstrated in both ADHD subtypes that were not manifested to the same degree by the learning-disabled subjects. Parents and teachers viewed subjects with hyperactive-impulsive ADHD as more disruptive than those in the other two groups, who were described as more underactive and shy as well as daydreaming more often in comparison to the hyperactive-impulsive group. These data must be considered in light of a larger body of data suggesting that teacher ratings of school behavior reflect a general trend for boys identified as behavioral problems to exhibit more nonphysical aggression and more noncompliance than the learning-disabled population in general (Sprafkin & Gadow, 1987). In this study, the learning-disabled males had higher rates of physical and nonphysical aggression and immature behavior than the learning-disabled females. Correlations among teacher ratings were modest but consistent.

Ackerman, Dykman, and Gardner (1990) report that children with ADHD and reading difficulty make significantly more errors than normally reading children with ADHD on simple auditory tests of phonological sensitivity. It has been suggested that among poor readers, those with slight delays do not differ from the ADHD group on three key measures: simple auditory phonological sensitivity, continuous naming speed, and running memory span. The single best predictor of word list reading level was nonsense-word list reading level, which was explained by the same set of variables that explained real-word reading. Severity of attentional problems has not been demonstrated to be related to reading skill. In contrast, the dyslexic group does differ significantly from the ADHD group (Dykman & Ackerman, 1993).

Pennington et al. (1993) evaluated reading problems in ADHD involving phonological processes and executive functions. Children with reading problems only and those with reading problems plus ADHD were significantly impaired compared with both the control and the ADHD-only groups on a phonological-processing composite score but performed normally on executive function tasks. The ADHD-only group had an opposite profile and was significantly different from both reading-disabled groups and from controls on the executive function composite score. These authors argue that there is a double disassociation between the reading-disabled-only and the ADHD-only groups. The comorbid group resembled a reading-disabled group consistent only with the hypothesis that their ADHD symptoms may be secondary to their reading disability. The authors also noted that the results suggest a distinction between phonological processes and executive function as an explanation for the comorbidity of the two disorders. Hypothetically, children with mild congenital language deficits associated with reading disability suffer in the environment and then develop ADHD-type behaviors.

The role of metacognition in executive processes in mediating the use of study skills in learning-disabled, ADHD, and normal subjects was evaluated by O'Neill and Douglas (1991). Those with ADHD did not differ from normals on an immediate recall of a story task or in recall following a study period; the reading-disabled group demonstrated inferior recall in both conditions. Study skills of those with ADHD were worse than those of normals on all measures. The reading-disabled group demonstrated less time spent studying, expended less effort, and employed more superficial strategies; however, their poor strategies did not reflect a lack of metacognitive awareness. These authors argued that motivational variables likely modulate strategy use in ADHD and impact children's ability to verbally process information. Again, impulsivity is implicated as a core deficit of ADHD.

August and Garfinkel (1990) suggest that children with ADHD and learning disabilities are doubly handicapped. These authors report that children with reading disability have difficulty with automatic processing tasks (rapid letter identification, naming objects, etc.). Children with ADHD were found to display normal automatic processing skills but were deficient on tasks requiring sustained effort and effortful processing, especially the memorization of rote sequential material. Children with both disabilities displayed weaknesses on both sets of tasks. These weaknesses have also been hypothesized to explain arithmetic problems in children with ADHD as well as those with reading disability (Ackerman, Anhalt, & Dykman, 1986). It is theorized by these authors that incompetence in mathematics for the ADHD and reading-disabled populations may be rooted in failure to memorize basic numerical skills. For the ADHD group, this may result from weakness in rote sequential memory; for the reading-disabled group, this may result from a weakness in automaticity in quickly identifying numerical stimuli.

Narhi and Ahonen (1995) compared groups of reading-disabled, reading-disabled plus ADHD, pure ADHD, and controls on a measure of rapid naming and executive functions. According to the phenotypic hypothesis (Pennington et al., 1993), the comorbid group should demonstrate cognitive deficits similar to those found in pure reading-disabled children but not show deficits characteristic of children with ADHD. The executive function tasks, however, failed to differentiate these clinical groups from each other, demonstrating that children with ADHD are not particularly poor on measures of executive function. These authors concluded that the performance of the comorbid group on rapid naming was impaired to a degree similar to the purely reading-disabled children. Problems in reading acquisition of children in the comorbid group appeared to be due to factors found in pure reading-disabled children and not explainable by attention deficits.

Rapid automatized naming is frequently used to identify learning disability because it is a deficit reported consistently in reading-disabled children. Torgersen and Wagner (1992) strongly suggest that deficits in phonological processing may underlie rapid naming problems and are primarily responsible for reading disabilities. Deficiency in naming speed may contribute to the variance in reading independent of phonological awareness. This may reflect inadequacy in a precise timing mechanism necessary to the development of visual codes and to the integration of these codes with phonological codes. Further, deficits in any speed may be predictive of later reading skills. Naming deficits together with poor reading skills persist through the life span.

Felton and Wood (1989) provided data from a cross-sectional study of school-referred children, a test-retest study of subtypes of reading disability, and a study of 485 first-graders. The data focused on specifying the cognitive deficits associated with reading difficulties and on separating cognitive and attentional deficits. The cognitive deficits associated with difficulty in reading were consistent across all three samples, developmental levels, and definitions and subtypes of reading disabilities. With IQ, age, and gender controlled for, those with reading weaknesses were significantly impaired on measures of naming and phonological awareness. The effects of attentional deficits were more variable and complex but were clearly separate from the reading disability effects.

Fergusson and Horwood (1992) provided a model for estimating possible reciprocal relationships between ADHD and reading achievement. These authors developed their model based on a longitudinal study of over 1,200 children in New Zealand. Interestingly, their results suggested that attentional skills influenced ultimate reading level, but that reading achievement did not appear to influence teacher reports of attentional capacity.

Elbert (1993) evaluated the occurrence and severity of reading, spelling, and written language impairments in 115 6- to 12-year-old children referred for ADHD. The group with hyperactive-impulsive problems demonstrated significantly poorer word-attack skills. However, the group with and the group without hyperactive-impulsive problems did not significantly differ from each other on other reading and written language measures. Age and gender were not found to interact in severity of problems.

Ninety-two 7- to 12-year-old boys with ADHD as well as those with ADHD and aggression were compared to a normal sample for timed performance accuracy of computer-generated math (Sentle & Smith, 1993). Response time differences documented between disordered and nondisordered groups and between diagnostic groups were not explained by the group differences that were also observed in behavior or motor response speed. Results suggested that speed of addition may be a marker of academic and social dysfunction. The prevalence of developmental dyscalculia was found to be 6.5% in a population of school-aged children (Gross-Tsur, Manor, & Shalev, 1996). Over a quarter of these children also demonstrated ADHD symptoms; 17% received a diagnosis of dyslexia as well. These authors suggest that the association between developmental dyscalculia and ADHD may be highlighted by the fact that in one of the clinical classifications of dyscalculia, the larger subgroup was reported as an attention-sequential group (Badian, 1983).

Finally, clinicians consistently report that children with ADHD eventually fall behind in school in subjects requiring practice for proficiency. These include nonphonetic spelling, math facts versus conceptual knowledge, and execution of written language versus ideas. Restasp (1994) finds that children with ADHD make more errors on visual-motor skill tasks and obtain lower scores on most written language tasks, a phenomenon found even among those who do not appear delayed in basic academic achievement.

There has been a debate in the literature as to the relationship between ADHD and auditory processing problems, much akin to the question of the relationship of general learning disability to ADHD. Auditory processing skills include the ability to focus on and understand an auditory message in the presence of distractors, raising the etiology question of ADHD. The majority of early research suggesting that auditory processing problems may actually reflect a subtype of ADHD was poorly conducted and does not allow for generalizable findings (Riccio & Hynd, 1993). Riccio, Vaughn, Morgan, Hall, and Hynd (1995) found normal auditory processing skills in a group of children with ADHD. Auditory processing deficits have been described as responsible for causing problems similar to those children with the inattentive type of ADHD appear to experience in a classroom setting. These authors found a small subgroup with difficulty processing auditory information in addition to their ADHD. This was consistent with previous studies indicating some but not necessarily a beyond-chance overlap of ADHD and auditory processing problems (Riccio & Hynd, 1993). These findings do, however, suggest that the practitioner consider the need for comprehensive evaluation of auditory and linguistic processes in children referred for ADHD. This issue will be addressed and guidelines provided in Chapter 10. Interested readers are referred to Cleveland (1997) for an in-depth discussion of central auditory processing disorders and ADHD.

The preponderance of the data regarding the etiological and symptomatic relationship of ADHD and learning disability suggests that it is reasonable for clinicians to at least screen academic achievement in all children referred for the disorder. There is a high probability that a significant minority of children with ADHD will experience deficits in achievement that may be contributed to by the combination of ADHD and other specific skill deficits. The preponderance of the available data suggests that the majority of children experiencing a learning disability do so as the result of deficits in language and, to a lesser extent, visual skills not due to symptoms of ADHD. It is reasonable for the practitioner to conceive of symptoms of ADHD as catalytic, negatively impacting and interacting with already weak academic acquisition skills to result in delayed achievement. In the later adolescent years, it is reasonable to conclude that the majority of children with ADHD, even in the absence of weak developmental skills, will demonstrate delays and/or inconsistencies in written language skills, spelling, and mathematics performance.

Family

The powerful impact family issues have on children's current and future functioning has been increasingly recognized in the research literature (Aylward, 1992; Katz, 1997; Werner & Smith, 1992). Family issues include parental psychiatric status, family socioeconomic status, geographic location, parental vocation, and even number of siblings. It is beyond the scope of this text to present a comprehensive overview of the family literature. Issues related to family functioning and their impact on ADHD, however, will be summarized in this section. These topics relate to environmental risk, a multidimensional concept that includes caregiver-child interaction, activities that foster development, disciplinary techniques, family social climate, family beliefs, values, and attitudes, parental psychiatric status, physical properties of the environment, and organization and availability of play materials.

Bradley, Caldwell, and Rock (1989) collaboratively evaluated 900 children in six cities to determine the relationship between environmental and developmental factors. Socioeconomic status was not consistently related to quality of home environment, or developmental status for that matter, during the three-year follow-up. However, factors related to parental responsivity to the child, acceptance of the child, and parent involvement and stimulation were more consistently related to later developmental status.

Children from middle socioeconomic families living in overly crowded and noisy homes with little private space generally perform less well on cognitive tasks, for example, than do similar-social-class peers from less crowded homes (Gottfried & Gottfried, 1984). Those children with structure and organization in the home have better outcome regardless of socioeconomic status (Bradley & Caldwell, 1984; Escalona, 1987). Provision of appropriate play material is associated with higher performance on tests of mental abilities; the association becomes stronger with increasing age (Bradley & Caldwell, 1984). Pre-academic activities are related to better subsequent language and reading development (Gottfried & Gottfried, 1984; Escalona, 1987). Birth order has also been found to be influential, with firstborn children performing best on developmental tasks during their first years of life (Sigman, Cohen, & Beckwith, 1981).

It is important for the practitioner to develop an appreciation for the significant impact the environment has on the ultimate phenotypic expression of a genotypic disorder such as ADHD. Bradley et al. (1989) assessed home environments of forty-two children during infancy and middle childhood. Higher scores on environment were related to higher achievement and better classroom behavior at 10 to 11 years of age. Three models of environmental action were delineated: in the first, a primacy effect resulted in early environmental stimulation leading to later success; in the second, current environmental influences over time led to success; in the third, the stability or continuity of the environment over time led to success. All three models predicted outcome, but the strongest influence came from the contemporary environmental model, in which experiences closer to the time of measurement of outcome was most influential (for review, see Aylward, 1992). This author suggests that relationships between biological and environmental risks are complex. A number of different models yield support based on available research; in general, however, biological and environmental factors interact with varying outcomes depending on a variety of medical/biological, environmental/psychosocial, and behavioral/developmental factors. Protective factors in one area can work to balance risk factors in another. A parsimonious model suggests that children are constantly reorganizing and self-righting. The data support a continuum of caretaking causality (Sameroff & Chandler, 1985), suggesting that a positive environment powerfully enhances children's resiliency.

Frick and Lahey (1991) provide a review of the available evidence to suggest that multiple environmental factors, particularly those that take place within the home, result in behaviors similar to those displayed in children with ADHD. These factors can also exacerbate or reduce the severity of behaviors associated with the disorder. Based on findings of an ongoing longitudinal study, Frick (1994) suggests that there is an association of ADHD and conduct disorder with different family variables and that these disorders appear to be transmitted across generations. Frick also notes that greater dysfunction is observed in families whose children demonstrate greater behavioral problems.

A variety of parent, child, and setting variables can interact beginning at a very early age; the report and prevalencies of resultant problems, however, can vary based on a myriad of issues (Belsky, Woodworth, & Crnic, 1996). These authors demonstrate that problems occur fairly early on for children, with most identified during the second year in life. Offord, Boyle, Racine, Szatmari, Fleming, Sanford, and Lipman (1996) suggest that the prevalence and pattern of correlates of individual disorders differ in important ways by informant. Teacher-identified conduct disorder and hyperactivity in males and females exceed the rates of parent-identified disorders. Some variables are more powerful than others. A parent's being arrested is a significant correlate of parent-identified conduct disorder in offspring but not so for teacher- or youth-identified conduct problems. Low income is strongly related to teacher-identified conduct disorder but not to parent-identified conduct disorder. In the case of conduct disorder, family dysfunction has a strong independent relationship. Family dysfunction and a failed grade appeared to correlate highly with hyperactivity. The relationship between chronic medical illness and childhood hyperactivity is significantly higher in younger than in older children. Low income, family dysfunction, male gender, and chronic medical illness have an independent positive association with hyperactivity. In contrast, urban residence and family dysfunction were more related to an emotional disorder.

What is the practitioner to make of these data? Clearly, a myriad of family issues impact complaints of childhood behavior. Because the practitioner is initially faced with complaints of behavior reported by others, principally parents, it is important to develop an understanding of the impact that family and related functioning have on childhood behavior and reports of problems. In 1990, Fischer provided a thorough review of the then available studies concerning the stress of parenting a child with ADHD, defining four clear lines of research. First, studies demonstrated increased stress reported by parents of children with attention deficit in general. Second, studies of parental psychopathology found that for some parents such disturbances, independent of the child's pathology, appear to reflect a genetic substrait for the same unrelated disorders. Third, ADHD appeared to be associated with increased marital discord. Fourth, research regarding parent-child interaction patterns suggest that the child-to-adult direction of effect is more powerful than the reverse.

Gillberg, Carlstrom, and Rasmussen (1983) found that mothers of 7-year-old hyperactive children had sought treatment for personal psychopathology in the previous year much more often than mothers of normal control children. Maternal help-seeking was mediated by the child's age. Mothers of hyperactive children sought help only slightly more than mothers of normal children during the first years of the child's life but three to four times more often during the seventh year. Studies using the Parenting Stress Index (Abidin, 1983) found that mothers of hyperactive children report markedly higher levels of stress than parents of normal children. Sibling interactions were also found to contribute to feelings of stress in mothers of hyperactive children.

Hyperactive males and females are quite similar in the nature of their psychopathology; they do not appear to differ in the degree of parenting stress associated with their care (Breen & Barkley, 1988; Mash & Johnston, 1983a, 1983b).

The hypothesis of a familial association between childhood hyperactivity and specific adult psychopathology has been supported by numerous studies. Befera and Barkley (1985) report that twice as many psychiatric disorders are found in the nuclear families of hyperactives and extended relatives as compared to those of normal children. Additional studies finding similar prevalence differences include Cantwell (1972), Morrison and Stewart (1971, 1973a), Biederman, Faraone, Keenan, Knee, and Tsuang (1990), Biederman, Faraone, Keenan, and Tsuang (1991), and Biederman, Faraone, Spencer, et al. (1993). In these studies, a significantly higher prevalence of sociopathy and alcoholism in biological fathers and hysteria and depression in biological mothers was reported when compared with adoptive and control parents. Studies by Cadoret, Cunningham, Loftus, and Edwards (1975) and Cadoret and Gath (1980) note that significantly more adoptive children whose parents had psychopathology had been treated for hyperactivity. A number also reflect the increased risk for psychiatric problems among relatives.

A significant correlation between marital discord and deviant childhood behavior, especially in males, has also been consistently reported in the literature (Emery & O'Leary, 1982). The direction of the effect is unclear, with some authors arguing that marital discord leads to behavioral disturbance in children (O'Leary, Emery, & Porter, 1981) and others suggesting that disruptive child behavior is more likely to lead to marital dysfunction (Befera & Barkley, 1985). Barkley, Fischer, Edelbrock, and Smallish (1990) report three times as many mothers of hyperactives had separated or been divorced from the children's biological fathers as mothers of nonhyperactives.

Numerous studies have also demonstrated that when interactions occur between parents and ADHD children in free play settings, these interactions are relatively similar to those that occur between normal children and their parents. However, when parents are instructed to give their children tasks to accomplish, ADHD children are less compliant to parental demands and more oppositional. Their parents provide more commands and directives, are more negative and reprimanding, and are less responsive to their children's social initiatives than parents of normal children (Barkley, 1985, 1988c; Befera & Barkley, 1985; Campbell, 1975; Mash & Johnston, 1982; Tallmage & Barkley, 1983; Tarver-Behring et al., 1985).

Conduct disorder has been associated with high levels of parent-child dysfunction and a high exposure to adverse psychosocial factors (Schachar & Wachsmuth, 1991). Attention deficit, in contrast, has not been associated with as severe a degree of parent-child dysfunction but has been associated with moderate levels of adversity (particularly prolonged parent-child separation). The group with ADHD and conduct disorder was associated with both dysfunctional parent-child relationships and at least moderate life adversity.

The impact of ethnicity on parent report and childhood behavior has been only minimally examined. For example, in contrast to thousands of articles on ADHD, only sixteen were found to deal specifically with African American youth (Samuel et al., 1997). Brooks-Gunn, Klebanov, and Duncan (1996) evaluated ethnicity differences in 5-year-olds with a history of low birth weight. Although the African American children's

IQ scores were one standard deviation lower than the Euro-Americans, adjustment for ethnic differences and poverty reduced the difference by 52%. Adjustments for maternal education and female head of household did not reduce the ethnic difference further. However, differences in home environment reduced the ethnic differential by an additional 28%. Adjustments for economic and social differences in the lives of ethnically different children all but eliminates differences in IQ scores. Steinberg, Dornbusch, and Brown (1992) lend support to this conclusion. Among ethnically different high school students, they find that the absence of peer support for achievement and a tendency toward authoritarian parenting undermine potential school success. In this study, among Asian American students, peer support for academic excellence was found to offset the negative consequence of authoritarian parenting. The Hispanic youth in this study suffered from a combination of parental authoritarianism and low peer support leading to poor academic performance. In contrast, the European American youngsters tended to come from families with authoritative parenting and to have peer support for achievement. It is likely that any ethnic differences reported in the occurrence of ADHD or symptoms of ADHD are, as these studies demonstrate, related to environmental factors and not genetic differences in the expression of the disorder.

In a study of resilience and vulnerability among preschool children, Tscheann, Kaiser, Chesney, Alkon, and Boyce (1996) found that children with more difficult temperaments in high-conflict families had the highest degree of internalizing and externalizing behavioral problems, as observed by their teachers. In contrast, children with easy temperaments in similar dysfunctional settings had fewer such problems. Temperament appears to be involved in both protective and vulnerability processes: difficult temperament appears to operate as a vulnerability factor for internalizing and externalizing behavioral problems and observed aggression; easy temperament appears to function as a protective mechanism for these risk factors. The question has been raised as to whether this profile is obtained only in clinic-referred populations. In response, an epidemiologic study completed by Szatmari, Boyle, and Offord (1993) classified children as having problems with attention if they fell in the top 10% of the distribution of problems from any informant. There was evidence for familial aggregation of these problems. The degree of familial aggregation varied according to certain family characteristics. Overall, however, this study lent strong evidence to the fact that there is a general trend of similarity of complaints and problems in clinic as in epidemiologic samples.

Socioeconomic Status

Radal, Milgrom, Cauce, and Manci (1994) evaluated nearly 900 5- to 11-year-old children from low-income families. Poverty was identified as a general risk factor for mental distress in children. Based on the use of a parent-completed questionnaire, approximately 2% of this population scored in the clinical range for attention problems.

Using census data, Coulton, Korbin, Su, and Chow (1995) found that variation in rates of officially reported child maltreatment was related to structural determinants; community social organization, including economic and family resources; residential instability; household and age structure; as well as geographic proximity of neighborhoods to concentrated poverty. Child maltreatment rates were found to be intercorrelated with other indicators of breakdown in community and social organization.

Children living in neighborhoods characterized by poverty, excessive numbers of children per adult resident, population turnover, and a concentration of female-headed households appeared to be at highest risk for maltreatment. The authors' analysis suggests that child maltreatment is but one manifestation of this community-social organization. Its occurrence is related to some of the same underlying macrosocial conditions that foster other urban problems. It is important to note that these authors suggested that poverty is not linked inevitably to child maltreatment, but the connection has been repeatedly documented. It is unclear how domestic violence leads to psychopathology; the bottom line, however, appears to be that when there is extreme marital discord, aggression by either parent toward the child often follows, and elevated undifferentiated symptoms of psychopathology in the child are likely to result. Psychological problems children under these circumstances develop are likely to be debilitating and chronic.

Taylor, Schachar, Thorley, and Wieselberg (1986) report that antisocial behavior but not hyperactivity is associated with low socioeconomic status. Family adversity, they suggest, is not uniquely linked to ADHD but may be associated with behavioral problems in general, especially the more serious combination of ADHD and conduct disorder. Among young children identified with attention deficit symptoms and a non-problem comparison group followed from age 2, Campbell et al. (1986a) found that socioeconomic status contributed to the prediction of childhood activity and aggression concurrently at ages 2 and 3. At age 6, however, socioeconomic condition continued to contribute to prediction of hyperactivity but not aggression. Other variables found to predict over time included family stress and the quality of parent-child interactions.

Parents

In a review of the literature, Miller (1995) suggested multiple determinants, including characteristics of the target age and gender, characteristics of the judges–mothers versus fathers—and characteristics of the behavior explained all contribute to parents' attribution of their children's behavior. The evidence argues that parents form attributions for their children's behavior and that these attributions vary in predictable although not perfectly consistent ways across judges, targets, and outcome. Further, although of less certainty, attributions affect parents' behavior and subsequently children's development. Camp (1996) points out that by school age, maternal hostile and controlling attitudes have been directly related to behavior problems in children, particularly aggressive behavior. As Dicks and Grusec (1995) suggest, the attributions parents make for their children's behavior is a major determinant of their emotional response to that behavior. Negative behaviors are especially upsetting to parents when they judge them to be of internal origin and reflect something about the child, not just the immediate environment; thus, parents see those types of problems as stable and not simply a one-time occurrence, likely to recur and controllable by the child. They are attributed to something the child should have been able to avoid. By the same token, positive behaviors will be rewarding to parents to the extent that these behaviors are perceived as possessing the attributes of internality, stability, and controllability. Additional variables then come into play, such as age of the child and situation. A misdeed that is attributed to lack of appropriate knowledge will elicit a different parental response than a misdeed that is believed to result from laziness or selfishness. Mood is also an issue: mothers in an angry mood tend to be more upset by misdeeds and to advocate a sterner response to them. Child-rearing ideologies also play a role: as Goodnow and Collins (1990) suggest, parents' ideas are woven into the overall fabric of parental thought, behavior, and child-rearing practices. The relationship of parent attitude and belief to parent behavior will be discussed in Chapter 16, where practitioners will be offered a model to evaluate and modify parent attributions and beliefs.

In 1989, Borden and Brown examined the attributional effects of combining medication with cognitive behavior therapy in the treatment of children with ADHD. Thirty children with ADHD received a twenty-two-session cognitive training program focusing on self-control. Children were also randomly assigned to receive methylphenidate, placebo, or no pill. Participation in the pill groups influenced parent attributions. Although child measures did not reveal significant effects, group means were directly similar to those of the parents. Parents in the no-pill group believed more strongly that their children were capable of solving their own problems; the pill groups more strongly believed that solutions would result from external and uncontrollable factors. The motivational effects of combining medication with cognitive therapy or other behavior-change techniques argued for the continued use of more than just medicine to treat ADHD. These findings are important in reflecting that parent cognitions are in fact communicated to children in the form of attributions and expectancies (Parsons, Adler, & Kaczala, 1982). These authors strongly argue that changes in parental beliefs in the long run greatly influence children's beliefs. They suggested that, in this society, people believe that if medication is needed in their treatment, attempting to take personal control over their problems is futile. This attitude may be particularly detrimental when the adjunctive treatment involves self-management or requires a high level of motivation. Further, although parent-child influence is clearly bidirectional, the asymmetry of the relationship may predict greater influence from parent to child regarding parent attributions and expectations (Maccoby & Martin, 1983).

The relationship of parental psychiatric history to severity of parental complaints and subsequent treatment outcome has been evaluated in some depth. Fergusson and Lynskey (1993) studied a large birth cohort longitudinally and found a consistent and statistically significant association over a five-year period between maternal history of depression and teacher report of behavior. However, associations between maternal concurrent depressive symptoms and child behavior were generally nonsignificant when the effects of maternal history of depression were controlled. For this sample, the association between maternal depressive symptoms and externalizing behavior in early offspring during adolescence arose largely from the effects of common contextual factors, principally social disadvantage and marital instability. Both of these factors are thought to influence maternal psychiatric symptomatology as well as independently impact rates of childhood behavior problems.

Gabel and Shindledecker (1992) reviewed the records of hospital-treated 4- to 18-year-old youth to determine whether gender-specific features exist in behavioral characteristics of children of substance-abusing parents. There was a trend for sons of these parents to have more conduct disorder diagnoses in association with severe aggressive/destructive behavior. In contrast, daughters of substance-abusing parents were generally more likely to have a diagnosis of ADHD, aggression, and conduct disorder problems than were daughters of non-substance-abusing parents.

Fathers' self-ratings of psychopathology across a full range of symptoms have been found to be consistently related to their ratings of hyperactive behavior in their sons (Gordon, Mettelman, & Irwin, 1994). Paternal levels of depression, phobia, and somatic complaints were the dimensions most closely tied to fathers' ratings of anxiety and hyperactivity symptoms in offspring. Interestingly, in this study, maternal self-ratings of psychiatric symptoms were largely unrelated to the ratings of the child's externalizing behavior. Most striking was a large number of significant correlations between paternal psychopathology and ratings of the offspring by teachers. The relationship between parent self-ratings and teacher ratings of the offspring was stronger for fathers than for mothers. The authors concluded that these data suggested that fathers' level of psychiatric symptoms, especially paranoia, should be carefully considered when practitioners review parent-completed behavior problem checklists and when histories are conducted. These authors also raise questions concerning the extent to which male offspring reflect paternal characteristics within the classroom setting. The mechanism of transmission, however, is unknown.

Schachar and Wachsmuth (1991) studied five groups of 7- to 11-year-olds with a variety of ADHD and comorbid problems. These groups were differentiated by a family history of parental psychopathology or childhood hyperactivity. In the groups with children experiencing combined ADHD and conduct disorder, conduct disorder, or an emotionally distressing disorder, all had significantly higher rates of parental psychopathology than the pure ADHD and normal groups, for which the rates were similar. Significantly more boys in the ADHD, conduct disorder, and combined groups had family histories of parental childhood hyperactivity than boys in the emotionally disordered groups. These authors suggest that pervasive hyperactivity is no more closely associated than situational hyperactivity with parental psychopathology. In this study, parents of children with conduct disorder reported the same high rate of hyperactivity in childhood as did parents of hyperactive children. A childhood history of hyperactivity in at least one parent distinguished the externalizing syndromes from the internalizing syndromes or no disorder.

Although mothers of children with ADHD have been extensively studied, fathers have been less often studied. Available research suggests that fathers of children with attention deficit and conduct disorder are more likely to have a history of aggression, arrest, and imprisonment (Lahey, Piacentini, et al., 1988), with their children similarly exhibiting the greatest amount of physical aggression and other serious law-breaking behavior (Walker, Lahey, Hynd, & Frame, 1987). Once again, however, it appears that the comorbidity of conduct disorder with ADHD accounts for these differences and that fathers of children with pure ADHD likely do not behave in ways much different from fathers of normal children. Frick, Lahey, Christ, Loeber, and Green (1991) found that mothers, fathers, and other biological relatives of children with ADHD were significantly more likely to have a history of childhood ADHD but not problems of antisocial behavior or substance use in childhood. ADHD with or without hyperactivity was similarly associated with a family history of ADHD. However, fathers of children with conduct disorder were more likely to have a childhood history of either conduct disorder or substance abuse. It is important to note that, as with other studies, these results do not remain as powerful after controlling for demographic variables. Nonetheless, the results of studies such as these provide support for the independence of ADHD and conduct disorder as clinical syndromes, especially in regard to parental variables.

Phares and Compas (1992) note, however, that conclusions concerning the relationship of fathers to family functioning or dysfunctioning for that matter, cannot be made as strongly as conclusions related to mothers. The authors suggest that fathers have not been researched as frequently due to practical issues related to participant recruitment, base rate differences, and research assumptions. Phares and Compas found that between 1984 and 1991, 48% of studies they reviewed exclusively involved mothers, whereas only 1% of the studies exclusively involved fathers.

Although the literature suggests that parents of children with ADHD recognize early on that their children may be different in poorly defined or generic ways, the age of onset by parental report for ADHD, conduct disorder, and oppositional defiance does not appear to vary. There is a moderate degree of stability in maternal recall, with school-related symptoms demonstrating the least amount of change (Green, Loeber, & Lahey, 1991). The mean age for parent report of excessive disruptive behavioral problems is 4 years. Sullivan, Kelso, and Stewart (1990), however, report a trend toward age of onset by report of 6 years in children with pure conduct disorder.

Mother-son, father-son, and mother-father-son interactions in families of hyperactive and normal 6- to 12-year-olds were observed by Buhrmester, Camparo, Christensen, and Gonzalez (1992). There was more frequent coercion in families with hyperactive boys, especially when mothers and sons interacted in a dyadic setting. The mother-son agronomy carried over to the triadic context, where fathers exhibited a rescue-coercion pattern of behavior. Fathers increased whereas mothers decreased their demands of sons in triads over dyads, and both fathers and sons became more aversive toward each other in the triads than in dyads. This pattern was not clearly evident in the interactions of families with normal children. Boys in both groups of families behaved more negatively toward mothers than toward fathers in dyadic interactions. Compared with fathers, mothers made more demands and were more emotionally expressive to their sons.

Finally, parents' locus of control and their capacity of empowerment speaks to how quickly they seek help for their problems and how effectively they benefit from help that is provided (Scheel & Rieckmann-James, 1996). These factors certainly impact family cohesion. Lewis (1992) suggests that parents of boys with primarily the inattentive type of ADHD report the highest level of family functioning. Those with ADHD plus hyperactive-impulsive problems and those who have aggression as well report more extremes in family functioning and less cohesion. This is a critical issue for the practitioner, as the family not only represents the setting in which treatment takes place but parents represent practitioners' primary treatment agents. An underestimate of family cohesion or parental sense of empowerment likely will result in appropriate treatments failing.

Siblings

Sibling temperament has been reported to be moderated by the associations of parent-child relationship quality and family problem-solving behavior (Brody, Stoneman, & Gauger, 1996). The links between mother and older child relationship quality, father and older child relationship quality, and sibling relationship quality were moderated by the older sibling's temperament. The younger and older siblings' temperaments moderated the associations between the quality of the father–younger sibling and sibling relationships. The association between family problem-solving behavior and sibling relationship quality was not, however, modified or moderated by sibling temperament. These types of studies go beyond the main effect models and begin to specify the ways in which family relationships transact with childhood temperament to create variations in sibling relationship quality. Difficult child temperament does appear to moderate the effects of parent-child relationships and family problem-solving behaviors on the development of sibling relationships. As Rutter (1985) proposed, protective factors such as a positive child-parent relationship and a harmonious family problem-solving manner may moderate the impact of a temperamentally difficult child on family members.

Discipline

In a sample of approximately 2,300 14- to 18-year-olds, families were classified into one of four parenting styles: authoritative, authoritarian, indulgent, and neglectful (Steinberg, Lamborn, Darling, Mounts, & Dornbusch, 1994). The first year and again a year later, identified subjects completed a battery of standardized instruments, tapping psychosocial development, school achievement, internalized distress, and behavior problems. Differences in adjustment associated with variations in parenting style were demonstrated to either maintain or increase over time. The benefits of authoritative parenting were largely in the maintenance of previously high levels of adjustment. The deleterious consequences of neglectful parenting continued to accumulate. As Maccoby and Martin (1983) demonstrated in their review of the literature, parental warmth, inductive discipline, and nonpunitive punishment practices combined with consistency in child rearing characteristic of the authoritative parenting model are all associated with positive outcomes in children. Children raised in authoritative homes score higher than their peers from authoritarian (firm but one-sided and punitive), indulgent (child runs the show), or neglectful homes on a wide range of measures of competence, achievement, social development, self-perception, and mental health. Authoritative families also report fewer disruptive behavioral problems in their children (Dornbusch, Ritter, Lieberman, Roberts, & Fraleigh, 1987; Steinberg, Elmen, & Mounts, 1989; Steinberg, Mounts, Lamborn, & Dornbusch, 1991). Lamborn, Mounts, Steinberg, and Dornbusch (1991) provided strong evidence that differences in adolescent outcome did not vary as a function of age, gender, ethnicity, or family background. Interestingly, studies have suggested that adolescents, not parents, are more accurate in their objective assessments of family life (Schwartz, Barton-Henry, & Pruzinsky, 1985). These authors concluded that the combination of parental aloofness and disciplinary laxity appeared universally harmful to adolescents. The combination of responsiveness and demandingness in an authoritative model carries many benefits and few disadvantages for adolescents from different walks of life. Figures 3–1, 3–2, 3–3, and 3–4 contain outcome data for school orientation, delinquency, somatic symptoms, and academic competence for the four population groups.

For practitioners, the assessment of parenting style is critically important as a foundation for understanding history and as a conduit to effective family intervention. The assessment of parenting styles will be discussed further in Chapter 8.

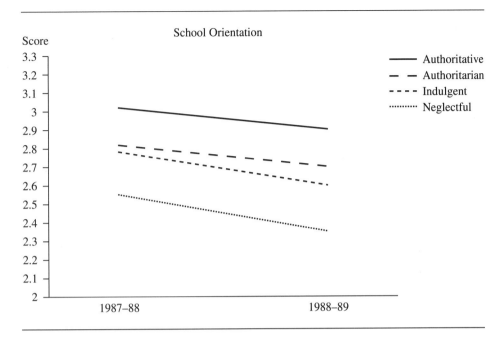

Figure 3–1.   Changes in adolescent school orientation as a function of parenting style

Source: Schwartz, J., Barton-Henry, M., & Pruzinsky, T. (1985). Assessing child-rearing behaviors: A comparison of ratings made by mother, father, child, and sibling on the CRPBI. *Child Development, 56,* 462–479. Used with permission of the Society for Research in Child Development, Ann Arbor, MI.

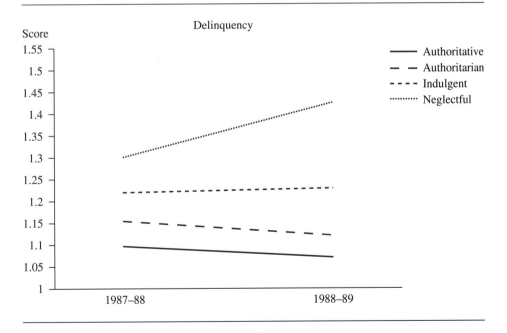

Figure 3–2.   Changes in adolescent delinquency as a function of parenting style

Source: Schwartz, J., Barton-Henry, M., & Pruzinsky, T. (1985). Assessing child-rearing behaviors: A comparison of ratings made by mother, father, child, and sibling on the CRPBI. *Child Development, 56,* 462–479. Used with permission of the Society for Research in Child Development, Ann Arbor, MI.

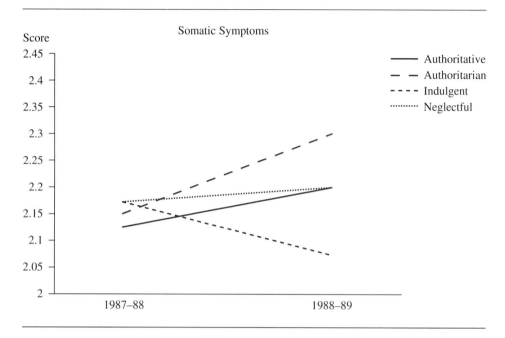

Figure 3–3.   Changes in adolescent somatic symptoms as a function of parenting style
Source: Schwartz, J., Barton-Henry, M., & Pruzinsky, T. (1985). Assessing child-rearing behaviors: A comparison of ratings made by mother, father, child, and sibling on the CRPBI. *Child Development, 56,* 462–479. Used with permission of the Society for Research in Child Development, Ann Arbor, MI.

Although it is well recognized that parenting style affects discipline practice and subsequent parental complaints, the data argue strongly that there is a bidirectional influence between parent and child (Danforth, Barkley, & Stokes, 1991). There appears to be a coercive, negative reinforcement process between parent and child; left unchecked, this pattern of negative reinforcement tends to escalate. More negative mother-child interactions and more noncompliance are reported in the interactions of parents of children with ADHD than those of normals. However, although they may receive complaints of being more noncompliant than the normals, the ADHD group rarely are reported as being more defiant or purposefully misbehaving (Gomez & Sanson, 1994). For practitioners, the implication is to carefully screen and listen for the comorbidity or presence of conduct problems, as it is quite likely that this issue is responsible for increased disciplinary problems and often leads parents down dysfunctional disciplinary roads.

In a longitudinal study (Lee & Bates, 1985), 100 normal children were assessed at 6 months of age using a maternal temperament questionnaire. From the analysis emerged a factor referred to as difficultness, comprising items concerning mother's perception of the child's moodiness, fussiness, amount of crying, and emotional intensity. These complaints powerfully predicted problem behavior at ages 2 and 3; the same predictions held at ages 5, 8, and 10 years of age (Bates, 1991). This population of children also had a higher subsequent rate of diagnoses of ADHD than the remainder of the population. Anderson, Lytton, and Romney (1986) demonstrated that differences in

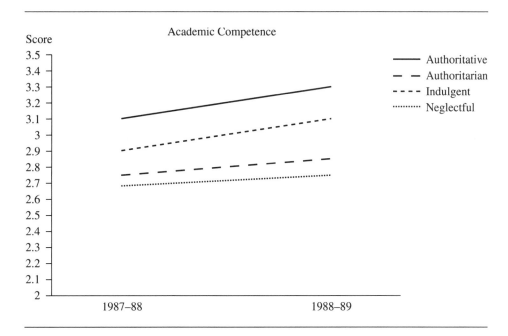

Figure 3–4.   Changes in adolescent academic competence as a function of parenting style

Source: Schwartz, J., Barton-Henry, M., & Pruzinsky, T. (1985). Assessing child-rearing behaviors: A comparison of ratings made by mother, father, child, and sibling on the CRPBI. *Child Development, 56,* 462–479. Used with permission of the Society for Research in Child Development, Ann Arbor, MI.

mother negativity and child compliance depend primarily on which group the child belongs to (normal or problem) and not as powerfully on whether mothers perceive their children as normal or abnormal. These authors argue that aversive interactions between parents and children appear to be primarily driven and controlled for by the child rather than by the parent. This is a pattern that has been repeatedly emphasized in the research literature (for review, see F. Gardner, 1992).

In an interesting variation of parent-child studies, Beck, Young, and Tarnowski (1990) evaluated children rated as being hyperactive pervasively, situationally, or not at all; children's global abilities and social skills abilities were also assessed. Mothers of pervasively hyperactive males reported significantly more overall stress in their relationship with their child and perceived their child as displaying more behavioral problems compared to mothers of situational hyperactive or nonhyperactive children. Mothers of pervasive hyperactive males also rated themselves as more depressed, less competent, more restrictive, and more frustrated compared to control mothers. Compared to mothers of control children, mothers of children with situational hyperactivity indicated that their sons displayed more behavior problems; these mothers also reported more maternal stress. Normal controls were rated as overall more socially skilled than situationally hyperactive males. These authors suggested that there is an interpersonal heterogeneity of children with ADHD and that some children with ADHD may appear socially inept, others aggressive, and others may display intrusive and bothersome behavior. Some children with ADHD appear to have relatively low social impact and can be best characterized as isolated or neglected by their peers, whereas others demonstrate high-impact behavior problems typifying actively rejected children (Pelham & Bender, 1982; Pelham & Milich, 1984). Beck et al. (1990) suggest that when dealing with children with ADHD, parents' perceptions of their children's activity level and behavioral disturbance are critical characteristics warranting close assessment and intervention strategies to ameliorate the stress of the parent-child relationship. This finding is also supported by Barkley's (1988a) assertion that pervasively hyperactive children are more likely to display aggressive and deviant behaviors. Further, children who display these characteristics at home and school appear to impact their environment much more negatively than those who display ADHD symptoms in one or the other situation.

Williams and Forehand (1984) evaluated fifty-six clinic-referred children for behavioral problems. They found that behavior immediately preceding child compliance or noncompliance typically was the best predictor of the child's behavior. Furthermore, the antecedents for child compliance and noncompliance differed from maternal antecedents to type of command served as the best predictor of child compliance or noncompliance. For child antecedents, compliance was best predicted by compliance, and noncompliance was best predicted by noncompliance. A beta command (unclear command) by parent was the best predictor for childhood noncompliance. However, when this phenomenon was partialed out, parent alpha commands (clear commands) did not best predict compliance or noncompliance in the child. As Patterson (1979) asserted, maternal commands and maternal disapproval are frequent antecedent behaviors leading to child negative behavior. Although negative reinforcement may be operating with alpha commands as well, in that the parents' command is a negative or aversive consequence, in this case the command is clear and direct and the child has a better opportunity to respond. For the practitioner, a knowledge of command type and commands utilized by parents is critical in the history and intervention process.

Van den Boom (1994) found that infants whose mothers were provided with support and assistance in managing their children's temperament over a three-month period were significantly more responsive, stimulating, visually attentive, and controlling of their infant's behavior than the untreated mothers. Intervention infants also had higher scores than controls on sociability, self-soothing, and exploration and cried less. The quality of exploration improved in intervention infants engaged in cognitively sophisticated kinds of exploration more than in controls. At 12 months of age, significantly more intervention group dyads were securely attached than control group dyads. This intervention was focused on enhancing maternal sensitivity and responding to their children. Mothers were assisted to adjust their behavior to the infant's unique cues. These authors argued that having an irritable, temperamentally difficult infant resulted in a negative cycle of interaction becoming apparent in at least the fifth month of life. As children mature, mother-child interactions in the group with ADHD are characterized by less positive affect, more conflict, and less appropriate directiveness (Campbell, Breaux, Ewing, Szumowski, & Pierce, 1986b). Although many of these variables may be related to socioeconomic status, even when this factor is controlled, mothers' ability to redirect their children is critical in shaping compliance and the mother-child relationship (diverting the child's attention away from an ongoing activity to an alternative activity). Campbell et al. (1986b) suggest that a family's socioeconomic status and observed maternal behavior at intake, but not level of stress, predicted continued hyperactivity and aggression a number of years later. Both variables continued to predict hyperactivity three years later, although only maternal behavior when the child was 3 was found to be a predictor of the child's aggression at age 6.

Barkley (1985) suggested that hyperactive boys are more negative and less compliant with their mothers, and their mothers are more directive and negative with them. Tallmage and Barkley (1983) reported a similar effect for fathers. Consistent with previous research, hyperactive boys were generally less compliant and their parents more directive than were boys and parents in the nonproblem parent-child dyads. These differences were most pronounced in structured tasks as opposed to free play, although both fathers and mothers increased their directiveness in the task situation. The hyperactive boys also increased their negative and competing behaviors in response to commands from their mothers. Tarver-Behring et al. (1985) found that hyperactive boys were less likely to respond to their mothers and more likely to engage in competing behaviors than their nonhyperactive brothers during free play; they were also found to be less compliant during the testing situation. Such differences are consistent with the diagnosis of ADHD. Interestingly, no differences were found by these authors in the behavior of mothers toward their hyperactive and nonhyperactive sons. As noted, Befera and Barkley (1985) did not find significant effects for either group inclusion or gender in a free play setting. During testing situations, however, hyperactive boys and girls were less compliant and engaged in more competing behaviors. They were also more negative than normal children. Barkley et al. (1985) subsequently found several main effects for group but not age. The boys with attention deficit were more likely to play independently of their mothers than normal boys. The mothers of attention deficit boys were found to initiate more peer interactions, give more commands, and be less responsive to their sons' initiations than were mothers of normal boys. During the task situation, the boys with attention problems were less compliant with maternal commands, less able to sustain their compliance off-task more often, and more negative with their mothers compared to the normals. The mothers of the attention-disordered boys gave more commands, were less likely to respond positively to their sons' compliance, and were more likely to respond with more control to off-task behavior. They also initiated further interactions than did mothers of the normals. Older boys in both groups were able to sustain their compliance to commands better than younger boys. Mothers of older boys gave fewer commands, responded with less control to compliance, and spent more time passively observing the boys than did the mothers of the younger boys.

Hartsough and Lambert (1982) found that parents of boys identified as hyperactive by parents, teachers, and physicians used both rational/social control and physical discipline more frequently than did parents of nonproblem children. These parents also used rational/social control discipline more frequently than parents of children identified with other problems. Constitutional factors, home environment, and parent-child interactions contributed significantly to the likelihood that a child would be identified as hyperactive (Lambert & Hartsough, 1984).

Following this line of research, Jacobvitz and Sroufe (1987) found that two early caregiver variables coupled with the constitutional variable of motor maturity assessed at 7 and 10 days of age differentiated between children identified in kinder-garten by teacher ratings as hyperactive and their nonhyperactive peers. Maternal in-terference, or the extent to which mothers disrupted the baby's ongoing activity rather than adapting her interactions to the baby's, at 6 months and maternal overstimulation at 42 months distinguished between the two groups. In another longitudinal study, Olson et al. (1990) investigated predictors of impulsivity at age 6 from a sample of children identified through published birth notices and recruited when subjects neared 6 months of age. High rates of positive verbal interaction at age 2 were associ-ated with good performance on an index of the ability to delay gratification and di-rect task orientation. Nonrestrictive, clear, consistent, and nonpunitive discipline at age 2 related to high scores on a composite index of impulse control for boys but not girls at age 6. Highly secure mother-infant attachment relationships correlated with positive performance on measures of impulse control, delay of gratification, and task orientation for boys but not girls. Girls who were most highly task-oriented and com-pliant at age 6 experienced high maternal responsiveness and intellectual stimulation at ages 13 and 24 months. Responsive, cognitively stimulating parent-child interac-tions in the second year have been found to predict laboratory indices of impulsivity at age 6. Nonresponsive, intrusive discipline may play a role in the development of be-havioral difficulties such as those seen in ADHD. Westerman (1990) suggests that maternal responsiveness is related to child compliance. Nonetheless, there is also data (Mash & Johnston, 1983a) to strongly suggest that parental behavior is at least in a significant part a response to child behavior. With ADHD, it appears that the coercive nature of the child's behavior is likely more powerful in shaping the adult than vice versa. Nonetheless, it is important for practitioners to recognize that there is a fairly strong belief among some developmental psychologists that impulsivity is more pow-erfully shaped by discipline, parenting style, and parent-child relationship than by bi-ology and temperament.

Abuse

In an excellent review article, Cicchetti and Toth (1995) provide a transactional model for understanding the manner in which environmental forces, caregiver characteris-tics, and childhood characteristics interact and influence each other to impact chil-dren's response to abuse and neglect. In this model, ADHD is considered an enduring vulnerability factor due to its biological basis and the fact that it creates, at the very least, transient challenges for families involving discipline, daily behavior, and school problems.

Different forms of abuse in the home have been suggested as being highly interre-lated (McCloskey, Figueredo, & Koss, 1995). Children of battered women appear to be at risk to be abused. Domestic violence appears to predict children's general psycho-pathology, but there appears to be little evidence for the presence of specific types of disorders as the result of family dysfunction. Mothers experiencing conjunctival vio-lence are more likely to have mental health problems; their mental health, however, does not mediate their children's response to conflict. However, there appears to be less sibling and parental warmth in families marked by aggression, although when it is present, family social support fails to buffer these children. The general pattern of re-sults appears consistent across respondents.

The question of ADHD or specific symptoms as cause or consequence of familial childhood abuse has not been well studied. Anecdotally, it has been suggested that children with ADHD, due to their impulsive-hyperactive behavior, in vulnerable environments, may be more prone to fare worse because they garner more negative attention from the adults in their lives. Some suggestion has been made longitudinally that easy temperament is an insulating factor in the face of other life stresses (Werner, 1994). However, the data have not been particularly powerful in assessing or ascribing the relationship of ADHD to abuse and neglect. Livingston, Lawson, and Jones (1993) evaluated forty-one children who were either physically or sexually abused by a parent. Conduct disorder was predicted by male gender and increasing age regardless of the type of parental abuse. Posttraumatic stress disorder was predicted by a number of stressors other than abuse, but not sexual abuse versus physical abuse. Predictors of somatization, psychotic symptoms, suicidal ideation, and separation anxiety were also identified. Gender, age, and stressors other than abuse were suggested as contributing to the prediction of psychiatric disorders in abused children. However, the relationship of abuse to specific symptoms or symptom profiles was not clear in this study. Interestingly, physical abuse, violence in the home, and a history of attention deficit disorder did not predict conduct disorder in this group of children. Thirteen children in this population presented with ADHD. It was unclear whether the symptoms of ADHD preceded or followed the abusive history. All but one had been sexually abused: all three females and nine of ten males.

McLeer, Callaghan, Henry, and Wallen (1994) compared sexually abused and nonabused children in a psychiatric outpatient clinic matched by age, gender, race, and socioeconomic status. The two groups did not differ significantly in the number of diagnoses, and in both groups ADHD was the most frequent diagnosis. The prevalence of posttraumatic stress disorder among the sexually abused children, however, was significantly greater. There were no significant differences for other diagnostic categories. ADHD presented in twelve of twenty-six sexually abused children and seven of twenty-three nonabused clinic-referred children. In contrast, posttraumatic stress was diagnosed in eleven of the abused but only two of the nonabused, and conduct disorder was diagnosed in seven of the abused but only one of the nonabused clinic-referred children.

In a sample of ninety-five children ages 4 through 16, Merry and Andrews (1994) gathered parent, teacher, and child data twelve months after disclosure of sexual abuse. Oppositional defiant disorder was diagnosed in 20%, 18% demonstrated posttraumatic stress disorder, 30% had some type of anxiety disorder, 12% had depressive disorder, and ADHD was diagnosed in 13%. Boys had a higher rate of diagnoses than girls. Abuse and social variables did not predict diagnoses; however, mental status did have a correlation, especially regarding the depressive and anxiety disorders diagnoses.

Retrospectively, two studies compared the abuse histories and home environments of adult males (20–32 years of age) referred for ADHD with their non-ADHD siblings (Whitmore, Kramer, & Knutson, 1993). In the first study, fourteen subjects and their brothers did not differ in their reporting of physical punishment, discipline, parental rejection, or positive parental contact, nor did they differ in their recollections of general atmosphere in their home environment. In the second study, the findings were generally replicated in a second group of individuals. Neither the degree of hyperactive symptoms, the degree of aggressive symptoms, nor the interactions of the two was associated with the amount of physical punishment reported retrospectively. According to the authors, these data challenge the "ADHD child as the scapegoat or target" (p. 364) hypothesis that has been popular in the ADHD literature.

Divorce

Parental divorce has been found to have a moderate, long-term negative impact on adult mental health, even controlling for economic status, children's emotional problems, and school performance preceding marital dissolution (Chase-Lansdell, Cherlen, & Kiernan, 1995). Only a minority of children, however, develop serious mental health problems in response to parental divorce. This subgroup, however, is seriously affected, producing a large proportional increase in the young adult population requiring clinical intervention. Clearly, those at risk for other life problems prior to divorce fare the worst; thus, it might be hypothesized that children with ADHD will fare poorly in the face of divorce. Fergusson, Horwood, and Lynskey (1994a) collected data during a fifteen-year longitudinal study of nearly 1,000 children with respect to exposure to parental separation during childhood. These data were compared to measures of adolescent psychopathology and problem behaviors at age 15. Children exposed to parental separation during childhood demonstrated elevated risks for a range of adolescent problems, including substance abuse or dependence, conduct or oppositional disorders, mood and anxiety disorders, and early onset of sexual activity. However, adjustment for confounding factors explained a large amount of the increased risk for adolescent disorder; after adjustment, the odds ratio between exposure to parental separation and adolescent outcome was fairly small. Males and females responded to parental separation in a similar fashion. Thus, much of the association of divorce to childhood problems appears confounded and the result of social and contextual factors often present in the child's family prior to separation. Given that ADHD is a powerfully biologically driven disorder, it is likely that it precedes the onset of oppositional defiance and conduct disorder in a population of divorced children.

Brown and Pacini (1989) reported that a higher percentage of parents of children with ADHD had been separated or divorced than in the normal population. In this study, parents of children with ADHD viewed their families as having lower levels of interpersonal relationships than did the control groups; more depressive symptoms were reported by parents; and these parents perceived their family environments as less supportive and more stressful than the normals and, in fact, than families with children experiencing other emotional, developmental, or behavioral problems. Thus, the higher frequency of divorce in families raising children with ADHD may in fact be contributed to by the stress of the ADHD child's behavior. It is unlikely, however, that this factor alone is responsible for familial dissolution. When parents of boys who are aggressive, hyperactive, or both were compared with parents of normal children, parental separation and single parenting was found to be associated primarily with childhood aggression (McGee et al., 1984). Werry, Reeves, and Elkind (1987) concluded that there was no clear pattern associating a broken home and a childhood diagnosis of attention deficit. Other studies, however, have not reported much in the way of a significant difference in marital functioning as the result of raising a child with ADHD (Breen & Barkley, 1988; Reeves et al., 1987). Breen and Barkley (1988) found that only the parents of the clinic-referred control group experience significantly more marital distress than the normal control group. In this study, the parents of males with attention deficit, females with attention deficit, and a mixed diagnostic group of clinic-referred control females and normal control females were studied. It is important to note that researchers have found an association between marital discord and general behavioral problems in boys (Emery, 1982). Hechtman (1981) has suggested that the emotional climate of the homes of hyperactive children is more negative. Others have suggested that families of hyperactives have poor interpersonal relationships (Moos & Moos, 1981). Cunningham, Benness, and Siegel (1988), however, failed to find significant differences between families of children with attention deficit and normal controls in interpersonal relations. Finally, Taylor, Schachar et al. (1986) found that antisocial behavior but not hyperactivity or attention deficit was associated with impaired family relations. The pattern that emerges is that negative family circumstances are likely related to externalizing problems in general but not uniquely associated with symptoms of ADHD.

Siblings

Over a four-year period, it has been reported that the risk of psychiatric problems in siblings of children receiving diagnoses of ADHD is significantly higher than in a normal population (Faraone, Biederman, Mennin, Gershon, & Tsuang, 1996). These authors suggest that siblings of children receiving diagnoses of ADHD are themselves at higher risk, and so practitioners should routinely consider at least inquiring about them during history-taking sessions. Anecdotally, it has also been suggested that when older children experience ADHD they are more likely to torment younger siblings, whereas when younger siblings have ADHD they are more likely to bother and disrupt the older sibling; in either case, a coercive pattern of aggressive interaction usually does not develop. The practitioner should keep in mind that the relationship between children diagnosed with ADHD and birth order has not been consistently demonstrated (Ebben, 1996).

Adoption

It is estimated that approximately 2% of the child population under the age of 18 in the United States has been adopted by nonrelatives. However, 10% to 15% of children in psychiatric treatment facilities are adopted (Brodzinsky, 1993). Adopted children are referred for psychological evaluation and treatment two to five times as frequently as their nonadopted peers worldwide (Grotevant & McRoy, 1990; McRoy, Grotevant, & Zurcher, 1988). A higher incidence of referrals of adopted children to mental health settings may result from inherited factors, overreaction of adopted parents, economic advantages of adoptive parents, or the likelihood that the adopted child will cause the family stress and be identified as the source of that stress (Warren, 1992).

In clinical settings, adopted children are much more likely to exhibit externalizing behaviors, including aggression and antisocial acts (Brinich, 1980; Offord, Aponte, & Cross, 1969). There have also been reports of a higher incidence of borderline personality (Simon & Senturia, 1966), eating disorders (Holden, 1991), substance abuse (Holden, 1991), learning disabilities (Silver, 1989), and, not surprisingly, ADHD (Dickson, Heffron, & Parker, 1990). The incidence of ADHD among adopted populations has been hypothesized as two to ten times more likely to occur. Large epidemiologic figures, however, have never been gathered. At this time, there is no available data to suggest that adopted children with ADHD pose a unique set of problems in regard to their behavior, adjustment, sense of identity, or future outcome. It has been suggested that for adopted children, the middle through adolescent years require a greater degree of reflection than others concerning the meaning of adoption, the reasons for birth parents' decision to relinquish, coping with anger, perceived abandonment, and so on (Brodzinsky, 1993; Brodzinsky, Singer, & Braff, 1984). For the practitioner, the issue of adoption for children with ADHD may play a significant role in conceptualizing a child's current problems and treatment; for others, it may be a minor issue. If in fact there is a relationship, it is likely that the emotional distress caused by adoption issues fuels ADHD symptoms rather than causing the disorder to present.

Parent ratings of temperament in infancy and childhood clearly yield evidence for genetic influence in twin studies but not in adoption studies. When parents of adoptive and nonadoptive siblings are evaluated, significant genetic influences emerge for both teacher and tester ratings of activity, for tester ratings of sociability, and for teacher ratings of emotionality (Schmitz, Saudino, Plormin, Fulker, & de Fries, 1996). Except for teacher ratings of attention span, evidence of shared family environment was nonsignificant. Thus, shared environment may play some but not necessarily a significant part in this problem. In this study, attention span demonstrated no significant genetic influence, either for teacher or tester ratings. Interestingly, attention span was one component of impulsivity that was initially included as part of the emotionality-activity-sociability-impulsivity (EASI) temperament theory of Buss and Ploman (1975). However, a decade later, these authors concluded that although evidence for the inheritability of emotionality, activity, and sociability had strengthened during the previous years, the picture had become no clearer for impulsivity. They thus dropped the *I* from their EASI model (Buss & Ploman, 1984). According to these authors, present studies supported this decision; they argue that, genetic factors aside, shared environmental influences are a powerful contributor to childhood behavior.

Physical Illness

Although symptoms of depression have been reported as occurring with greater frequency in children suffering from medical illness than in the normal population, this has not been the case for ADHD. Gortmaker, Walker, Weitzman, and Sobel (1990) evaluated 12,000 4- to 17-year-olds with chronic physical conditions. They noted that this population was at risk independent of other sociodemographic variables for increased problems related to depression, anxiety, peer conflict, and social withdrawal. Symptoms of hyperactivity and inattentiveness were not found to significantly correlate.

COMORBIDITY OF PSYCHOLOGICAL CONDITIONS

Five competing hypotheses exist for the causal basis of the development of comorbidity (Pennington et al., 1993): disorder A causes B; disorder B causes A; a third unknown factor C causes both; C causes both disorders in an etiologic subtype, but the two disorders are otherwise etiologically independent; or there is no causal basis for the observed association; rather, it is an artifact.

It appears that the greatest comorbidity with other childhood disorders occurs for the ADHD population. Thus, the evaluation and treatment of children with ADHD actually reflects the broader perspective of the evaluation and treatment of children with a wide range of co-occurring emotional, behavioral, and developmental problems. As Seidman, Benedict, et al. (1995) noted, ADHD coexists with other disorders at a rate well beyond chance. In fact, as discussed earlier, ADHD reflecting qualities of impulsiveness likely acts as a catalyst, increasing risk for developing other problems, especially in the face of additional risk factors (e.g., family, developmental, educational).

The comorbidity issues primarily facing practitioners are focused in three areas: (1) the additional presence of other disruptive, oppositional, and conduct disorders; (2) the additional presence of a specific developmental disorder resulting in a learning disability; and (3) the presence of internalizing problems related to emotional distress, particularly depression or anxiety. Practitioners must ask two questions: Do sufficient symptoms exist to provide a comorbid diagnosis? What impact does this additional diagnosis have on the severity or, for that matter, actual presence of ADHD or apparent symptoms of ADHD secondary to this additional diagnosis? This issue will be addressed further in Chapter 10.

An important initial question to be answered is whether inattention, impulsivity, and hyperactivity are diagnostic-specific to ADHD. Halperin, Matier, et al. (1991) compared children with ADHD, non-ADHD children experiencing neuropsychiatric problems, and normal controls on measures of inattention, impulsivity, and hyperactivity. Both clinical groups were inattentive relative to normals but were indistinguishable from each other. However, the ADHD group was more active than both the non-ADHD and normals. These latter two groups did not differ from each other. Inattention was hypothesized as a nonspecific symptom of child psychiatric disorders. However, the authors suggested that ADHD, as noted earlier, could be uniquely characterized by overactivity. The ADHD group had significantly more comorbid diagnoses than the non-ADHD group. This group consisted of children with other disruptive disorders, anxiety, and depressive problems. Figure 3–5 contains comparative data for these three groups. The commonality of inattentive complaints across childhood diagnostic categories and the frequent lack of association of inattentive and hyperactive complaints have been reported by others (Dienske, de Jonge, & Sanders-Woudstra, 1985).

In 1993, Fee and Matson, based on the work of Gardner and Cole (1988), offered a number of hypothetical models to explain the development and maintenance of ADHD and the subsequent development of depression and conduct disorder in this population. From a practical perspective, this model offers the practitioner a logical framework for understanding the real-world events that appear to precipitate comorbid problems in children with ADHD (see Figures 3–6, 3–7, and 3–8).

Fee and Matson (1993) posit that certain events instigate or increase the probability that ADHD will be diagnosed. These include individual characteristics such as intellectual functioning, biological predisposition, and the physical and psychosocial environments. Events in the school or home then either strengthen or decrease the behavioral symptoms of ADHD. Once ADHD is diagnosed, the risk for depression is increased as the result of social problems, school failure, and possible side effects of

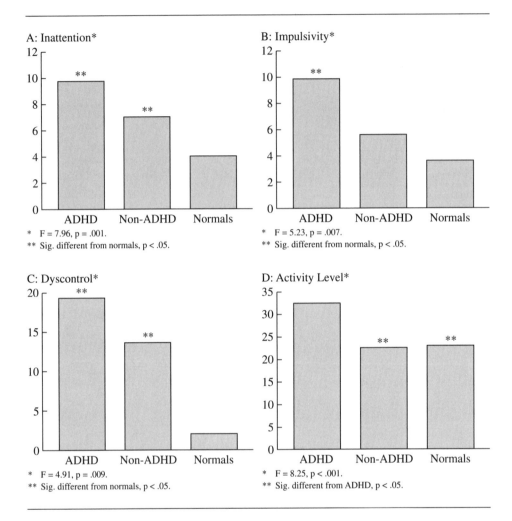

A: Inattention*

* F = 7.96, p = .001.
** Sig. different from normals, p < .05.

B: Impulsivity*

* F = 5.23, p = .007.
** Sig. different from normals, p < .05.

C: Dyscontrol*

* F = 4.91, p = .009.
** Sig. different from normals, p < .05.

D: Activity Level*

* F = 8.25, p < .001.
** Sig. different from ADHD, p < .05.

Figure 3–5.   Comparison of ADHD patients, non-ADHD patients, and normal controls on objective measures of inattention, impulsivity, dyscontrol, and activity level

Source: Halperin, J. M., Matier, K., Bedi, G., Sharma, V., and Newcorn, J. H. (1991). Specificity of inattention, impulsivity and hyperactivity for the diagnosis of attention deficit hyperactivity disorder. *Journal of the American Academy of Child and Adolescent Psychiatry, 31,* 190–196. Used with permission.

medication. The risk for conduct disorder is increased by school and social problems as well as the presentation of antisocial role models, which has been demonstrated as a critical risk factor.

Epidemiologically, it has been repeatedly demonstrated that although incidence rates vary depending on source of data collected, approximately one out of five children experiences a categorical psychiatric problem based on parent or child interview data (Costello, 1989a). In the Costello study of children ages 7 to 11 years in primary-care pediatric clinics, 2% met the criteria for ADHD with hyperactivity and .2% for

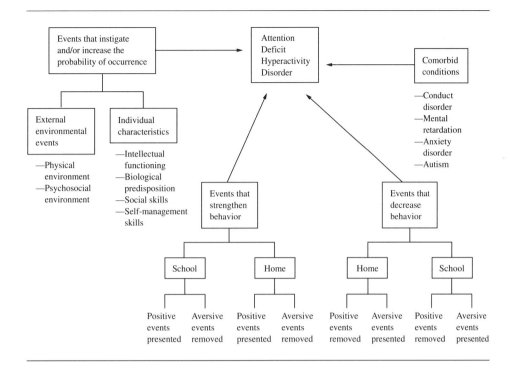

Figure 3–6.   Model for the development and maintenance of ADHD

Source: Fee, V. E., & Matson, J. L. (1993). Past development and future trends. In J. L. Matson (Ed.), *Handbook of Hyperactivity in Children.* Copyright 1993. Allyn and Bacon. Reprinted/adapted by permission.

ADHD without hyperactivity. A number of stressors in the child's life appeared to have a direct relationship with reports and incidence of all psychiatric problems.

Bird, Gould, Yager, Staghezza, and Canino (1989) generated information from an epidemiologic study concerning the comorbidity of four major diagnostic domains: ADHD, conduct and oppositional problems, depression, and anxiety disorders. A high level of comorbidity was found among the four domains. In general, the patterns of comorbidity were not affected by whether the data were put together by a clinician or by means of a computer algorithm scoring a structured interview. The patterns were also not affected in any major way by who the informants were in the diagnostic process. Minor differences were found in certain comorbidity patterns depending on gender and age. However, these were generally not significant. Comorbidity, however, was associated with greater impairment in daily life and greater utilization of mental health services.

McConaughy and Skiba (1993) generated research findings demonstrating a comorbidity of externalizing problems related to aggression and delinquency, and internalizing problems related to anxiety, depression, somatic complaints, and withdrawal and attention problems. High comorbidity rates were reported for the *DSM* diagnoses of conduct disorder with oppositional disorders, affective disorders, anxiety disorders, and attention deficit disorders. High comorbidity was also found for paired

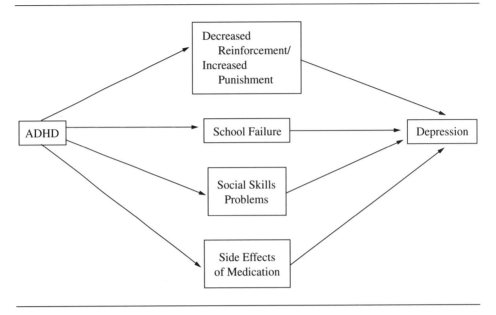

Figure 3–7. Model for the development of depression in ADHD children

Source: Fee, V. E., & Matson, J. L. (1993). Past development and future trends. In J. L. Matson (Ed.), *Handbook of Hyperactivity in Children.* Copyright 1993. Allyn and Bacon. Reprinted/adapted by permission.

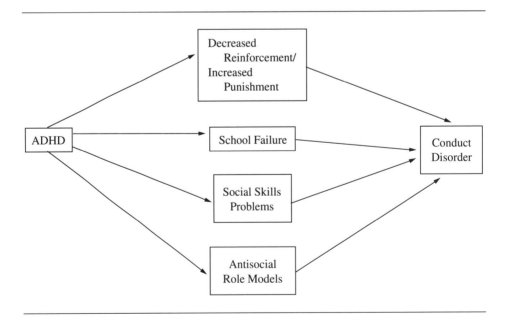

Figure 3–8. Model for the development of conduct disorder in ADHD children

Source: Fee, V. E., & Matson, J. L. (1993). Past development and future trends. In J. L. Matson (Ed.), *Handbook of Hyperactivity in Children.* Copyright 1993. Allyn and Bacon. Reprinted/adapted by permission.

combinations of aggressive behavior, delinquent behavior, and anxious/depressed and attention problem syndromes.

In New Zealand, 1,000 children were evaluated epidemiologically for *DSM* symptoms (Fergusson, Horwood, & Lynskey, 1993). Regardless of method used to make the diagnosis, nearly one-quarter of the population demonstrated at least one *DSM-III-R* diagnosis. Rates of disorders were higher for females (33%) than for males (23%). The difference was largely owing to higher rates of anxiety and mood disorders among the females. There were strong tendencies for disruptive behaviors and substance use disorders to cluster together. There were more diffuse tendencies for anxiety and mood disorders to be comorbid with each other and with other disorders. In this study, 2.8% met diagnostic criteria for ADHD by self-report; by maternal report, 3% met the criteria.

In a review of empirical studies, Biederman, Newcorn, et al. (1991) attempted to explain the comorbidity of ADHD with other disorders. The authors suggested that the literature supports considerable comorbidity of ADHD with conduct disorder, oppositional defiant disorder, mood disorders, anxiety disorders, learning disabilities, and other disorders such as mental retardation, Tourette's Disorder, and borderline personality disorder. Subgroups of children with ADHD might be delineated on the basis of the disorder's comorbidity with other disorders. A subgroup may have differing risk factors, clinical courses, and pharmacological response. However, firm data to support these hypotheses have yet to be generated. Nonetheless, it is likely the comorbid problems that children with ADHD present that are of greatest importance in predicting life outcome for children with ADHD. As we have hypothesized, the qualities of ADHD act as a catalyst: leave them alone, and they may not be terribly aversive; mix them with negative life events or risk factors, and they appear to catalytically worsen those events and the impact they have on children's current and future functioning.

In 1991, Shaywitz and Shaywitz suggested that comorbidity is a critical issue for ADHD. They suggested that the distinction of ADHD with the other disruptive disorders was blurred in early investigations by problems with referral bias. More recent studies, as interpreted by these authors, suggest that the antecedents, clinical characteristics, and prognosis for children with ADHD alone versus those with ADHD and a second disruptive disorder are quite different; the latter appear to fair far worse.

In a community sample of over 15,000 14- to 18-year-old adolescents, Lewinsohn, Rhode, and Seeley (1994) compared six clinical outcome measures with four major psychiatric disorders (depression, anxiety, substance abuse, and disruptive behaviors). The impact of comorbidity was strongest for academic problems, mental health treatment utilization, and past suicide attempts; intermediate on measures of role, function, and conflict with parents, and nonsignificant on physical symptoms. The greatest incremental impact of comorbidity was on anxiety disorders; the least was on substance abuse. Substance use and disruptive behavior were more common in males, depression and anxiety in females. The effect of comorbidity was not due to psychopathology. Limitations and number of diagnosed subjects did not allow a more fine-grained analysis of comorbidity with conduct disorder versus ADHD. The authors conclude, as others have, that there is a high rate of comorbidity in adolescents referred to clinical practice.

Finally, Steingard, Biederman, Doyle, and Sprich-Buckminster (1992) evaluated comorbidity in the association between parental reports and a structured diagnostic interview in making the diagnosis of attention deficit disorder in children. Interview-defined children with ADHD scored significantly worse on all comorbidity scales in comparison to parent-reported ADHD children and normal subjects. These findings were accounted for by the subgroup of children with ADHD who presented comorbid difficulties. Practitioners should keep in mind that current data suggest that children with the combined type of ADHD are more likely to receive a diagnosis of oppositional defiant disorder and conduct disorder than normal children or those experiencing in-attentive type ADHD. The combined ADHD group also demonstrates significantly higher parent and teacher ratings for externalizing problems. Finally, children in the two clinical ADHD groups did not appear to differ in internalizing disorders. Thus, al-though it is clear that there is significant comorbidity between the combined type of ADHD and other disruptive disorders, the corollary, that is, that the inattentive type of ADHD increases the risk for internalizing disorders such as depression or anxiety, does not appear to hold true.

Oppositional Defiant Disorder and Conduct Disorder

The greatest comorbidity for ADHD appears to be with the other disruptive disorders, oppositional defiant disorder (ODD) and conduct disorder (CD). Comorbidity may in fact reflect the differentiation of what begins as a unitary pattern of disruptive symp-toms. Bauermeister (1992) generated factor analytic data suggesting that at 4 to 5 years of age, disruptive symptoms appear to fall on a single dimension. In clinic-referred populations, the comorbidity between ADHD and CD has been reported as high as 50%, with an incidence of 30% to 50% reported in epidemiologic or commu-nity samples (Szatmari, Boyle, & Offord, 1989). Children with ADHD and comorbid ODD or CD exhibit greater frequencies of antisocial behavior such as lying, stealing, and fighting than those with ADHD who do not develop the second disruptive comor-bid disorder (Barkley, 1990a). It has also been suggested that this combined group is at greatest risk for peer rejection. These children may be neglected due to their lack of social skills and rejected due to their aggressive behavior. Common sense dictates that the comorbid group is going to require more intensive and continuous service delivery. The comorbid group also holds the greatest risk for later life problems. In fact, it is likely the co-occurrence of CD with ADHD that speaks to the significant adult prob-lems a subgroup of those with ADHD appear to develop. As Edelbrock noted in 1989 and research subsequently substantiated, more predictive of outcome than severity of ADHD symptoms is the development in ADHD children of oppositional and aggressive behaviors. Environmental consequences, including parent psychopathology, marital discord, ineffective parenting, parent aggressiveness, and antisocial parent behavior, are better predictors of life outcome for children with ADHD than the ADHD diagno-sis per se. In fact, these factors become highly stable over time and are resistant to change. Data also suggest that the comorbid conditions presenting before age 10 have a much worse prognosis than if the second disruptive behavior disorder develops after age 10 (McGee & Share, 1988). This is not surprising, as externalizing disorders have been found to be markedly stable over at least an eight-year period (Verhulst & van der Ende, 1995).

When factor scores are defined by the use of unit weights, the intercorrelation be-tween hyperactive symptoms and conduct disorder factors is high (Blouin, Conners,

Seidel, & Blouin, 1989). On the other hand, the use of factor score coefficiency to define factors produces uncorrelated factors, supporting the concept that symptoms of attention deficit or hyperactivity and conduct disorder are independent dimensions. However, these represent different statistical means by which factor scores are generated. The first method applies unit weights to the raw scores for items with factor loadings above .3; the second provides factor scores' coefficiency rather than unit weights. The intercorrelation among factors calculated by these two techniques yields different outcomes. Whether hyperactive items load on a conduct disorder factor depends on whether factor loadings or factor score coefficients are examined. This issue holds more than passing importance, as these authors suggest that the inability of other researchers to generate a distinct difference between the more moderate and severe disruptive disorders and ADHD is a function of methodological artifact rather than lack of true difference between these two problems. Yet, practitioners need to be aware that although ADHD, CD, and ODD may lie on a continuum (August, Stewart, & Holmes, 1983), aggression appears to be a defining variable for some with ODD and most with CD. However, aggression is not a characteristic diagnostic description of the impulsive process problems of children with ADHD.

After a careful review of the literature, Loeber, Lahey, and Thomas (1991) suggest that CD and ODD are strongly and developmentally related but clearly different. Factor analyses indicate that distinct covarying groups of ODD and CD symptoms can be identified but that certain symptoms relate to both disorders, particularly mild aggression and lying. Age of onset for ODD is earlier than for most CD symptoms. Nearly all youth with CD have a history of ODD, but not all ODD cases progress to CD. Interestingly, children with ODD demonstrate the same forms of parental psychopathology and family adversity but to a lesser degree than for CD. The early age of onset of some CD symptoms, specifically fighting, bullying, lying, and vandalism, suggests that some youth with CD show nearly contemporaneous onset of ODD and CD. However, the more serious symptoms of CD, such as vandalism, running away, truancy, shoplifting, breaking and entering, rape, and assault, appear to emerge at a much later age than ODD symptoms. Biederman, Faraone, Milberger, Jetton, et al. (1996) generated data suggesting two types of ODD, which appear to have different correlates, course, and outcome: one type appeared prodromal for CD, the other subsyndromal to CD and not likely to progress into CD in later years. Not surprisingly, the higher-risk form of ODD was characterized by a stronger profile of negative, provocative, spiteful, and vindictive behavior. It is important for the practitioner to recognize that diagnoses of ODD and CD are based exclusively on historical report and the observation of a pattern of disruptive behavior. It may be hypothesized that impulsivity as a process does in fact make some children and adolescents in the face of other risk factors prone to develop ODD and CD as a product of their impulsivity.

Fergusson, Horwood, and Lynskey (1994b) demonstrated a distinct but highly different constellation of behavioral domains from those corresponding to ODD, overt CD (aggression and violence), covert CD (theft and dishonesty), and ADHD. Results of second-order factor analyses suggested that these dimensions reflected two generally higher-order factors, with the first factor reflecting the extent to which the individual displayed behavioral symptoms of ODD and ADHD, and the second reflecting the extent to which the individual expressed antisocial, CD behaviors. The authors suggested that the results confirmed and supported the diagnostic classification for the disruptive disorders continuum. They concluded that although ODD and ADHD were correlated, they also appeared to have a very different set of developmental consequences, with early ODD in the absence of ADHD being associated with increased risk of later antisocial behavior but not with increased risk of academic failure. By the same token, early ADHD in the absence of ODD has been associated with increased risk of academic failure but not with future antisocial behavior (Fergusson, Horwood, & Lynskey, 1993). As Fergusson, Horwood, and Lloyd (1991) noted, measures of ADHD were factorially distinct from, although highly correlated with, other aspects of disruptive behavior.

The development of other disruptive problems leading from ADHD can best be understood based on Edelbrock's (1989) model of the development of four stages of aggressive behavior in children. First, children are oppositional by arguing, demanding attention, and being disobedient; impulsivity very clearly acts as a catalyst in this process. In the second stage, cruelty, lying, cheating, and greater peer problems are reported. In the third stage, destruction of property, attacking others, and theft are added to the first set of problems. Finally, in the fourth stage, more significant antisocial patterns develop, including vandalism, running away, truancy, fire setting, and substance abuse. It has also been suggested that the connection between CD and adult psychopathology reflects a specific pattern of symptomatic problems, particularly the demonstration of callous and unemotional patterns of behavior in childhood (Christian, Frick, Hill, Tyler, & Frazer, 1996). Further, Vitello and Stoff (1997) suggest that subtypes of aggressive behavior may be relevant in not only diagnosis and prognosis but treatment as well. These researchers, using a meta-analysis, identified two forms of aggression in children: predominently a pattern of impulsive-hostile affective aggression, which can be distinguished from a pattern of predominently controlled-instrumental predatory aggression. The former is defined as overt aggression, often undercontrolled and unplanned, the latter as planned, goal-oriented aggression. The authors note that the undercontrolled, unplanned, angry aggression appears to correlate best with levels of impulsivity. This article appears to further reinforce the existing line of research suggesting that among children with ADHD, it is more often their quantity and quality of impulsiveness that predicts risk for the development of antisocial behavior. This model may be of great value to the practitioner as efforts are made to assess risk that a particular child with ADHD may be developing or progress to more serious problems of CD.

In a large population of preadolescent children, Anderson, Williams, McGee, and Silva (1989) found that ADHD and CD frequently co-occurred but could be distinguished from each other. The authors noted, however, that the distinction was often complicated by the frequent comorbidity of these two disorders with other disorders. There was a clear trend for lower intelligence to be associated with a higher prevalence for all disorders. Low normal IQ was associated with increased prevalence of all disorders. The relationship was strongest for multiple disorders and attention deficit than for anxiety or pure CD. Socioeconomic factors of poverty, poor parenting, lack of educational encouragement, and social rejection appeared to be the most important causes of mild intellectual delay and of conduct problems. As others have noted, these two factors appeared to underlie both low IQ and increased psychiatric problems (Corbett, 1985).

In the Anderson et al. study (1989), 80% of the children with the ADHD diagnosis had one or more learning problems, and 62% had a reading disability sufficiently severe to leave them two years or more behind their peers in reading achievement. The relationship among aggressive behavior, CD, and poor reading has been described by others (Behar & Stewart, 1984). In the Anderson et al. sample, however, this relationship was not particularly strong when a single diagnosis of CD was considered separately from the nonaggressive, oppositional children. It was a major problem, however, for the children who experienced ADHD plus CD. In this study, the group with multiple disorders became increasingly more disliked over time. Neither the pure ADHD nor the conduct/oppositional group, which included aggressive children, was most disliked or solitary in their social interactions.

In this study, anxious depressed children, children with ADHD, and those with multiple disorders demonstrated low self-esteem, whereas those with oppositionality and conduct problems reported a level of self-esteem indistinguishable from that of children with no disorder. This may reflect an antisocial trend. Anxious and depressed children in particular demonstrated a marked drop in self-esteem overall in comparison to others. In contrast to other findings, between-group differences remained, even when family disadvantage and gender were controlled for.

In 1992, Pelham, Gnagy, Greenslade, and Milich collected teacher ratings for *DSM-III-R* diagnostic criteria in a population of nearly 1,000 children in kindergarten through eighth grade. Factor analysis demonstrated three disruptive factors: the first reflected ODD and several CD symptoms; the second contained primarily inattentive symptoms; and the third contained impulsive-hyperactive symptoms. Conditional probability analyses revealed that several hallmark symptoms of ADHD had poor predictive power, whereas combinations of symptoms from the ADHD factors had good predictive power. Combinations of oppositional defiant symptoms also had high predictive power (see Table 3–2). These authors suggest that ADHD symptoms clearly split into two factors, those of inattention and those reflecting hyperactivity and impulsivity, consistent with the findings of Lahey, Pelham, Schaughency, et al. (1988). Only 16% of the ADHD group also demonstrated CD symptoms. Figure 3–9 provides a visual analysis of the diagnostic disruptive overlap in this population.

Waldman and Lilienfeld (1991) examined the diagnostic efficacy of symptoms of ODD and ADHD in making a differential diagnosis, using four conditional probability indices: positive predictive power, negative predictive power, sensitivity, and specificity. ADHD symptoms were as useful as ODD symptoms as exclusion criteria for ODD, and ODD symptoms were nearly as effective as ADHD symptoms as inclusion criteria for ADHD. Although a number of symptoms appear to be useful as both inclusion and exclusion criteria for their respective disorders, these findings clearly illustrate the symptomatic differences between ADHD and ODD.

Based on an extensive review of the literature, Offord and Bennett (1994) suggested that conduct problems in childhood predicted the same increased rates of psychiatric disorders overall in males and females but that the patterns were different. For externalizing disorders, the prediction is stronger in men, and for internalizing disorders, the prediction in stronger in women. In the intervention domain, the literature provides limited evidence of the effectiveness of secondary prevention of CD. The authors write that this makes for a compelling argument in favor of an increased

Table 3–2.   Factor analysis for teacher ratings of the symptoms of the disruptive behavior disorders in a normative sample

Symptom	Factor 1 Oppositional/ Defiant	Factor 2 Inattention	Factor 3 Impulsivity/ Overactivity
ADHD items			
Fidgets with hands or feet or squirms in seat	0.20	<u>0.59</u>	<u>0.55</u>
Has difficulty remaining seated	0.17	<u>0.41</u>	<u>0.72</u>
Is easily distracted	0.22	<u>0.73</u>	<u>0.45</u>
Has difficulty awaiting turn	<u>0.44</u>	0.31	<u>0.66</u>
Blurts out answers before questions completed	0.36	0.28	<u>0.73</u>
Difficulty following through on instructions from others	0.26	<u>0.80</u>	0.21
Difficulty sustaining attention in tasks or play	0.18	<u>0.78</u>	0.34
Shifts from one uncompleted activity to another	0.26	<u>0.73</u>	0.28
Difficulty playing quietly	0.38	0.32	<u>0.68</u>
Often talks excessively	0.28	0.30	<u>0.77</u>
Interrupts or intrudes on others	<u>0.49</u>	0.35	<u>0.65</u>
Does not seem to listen to what is being said	0.34	<u>0.75</u>	0.24
Often loses things necessary for tasks or activities	0.24	<u>0.74</u>	0.19
Often engages in dangerous activities without considering consequences	<u>0.56</u>	<u>0.40</u>	<u>0.41</u>
ODD items			
Often loses temper	<u>0.84</u>	0.16	0.30
Argues with adults	<u>0.82</u>	0.25	0.27
Actively defies or refuses adult requests or rules	<u>0.81</u>	0.28	0.17
Deliberately does things that annoy others	<u>0.70</u>	0.29	<u>0.41</u>
Blames others for own mistakes	<u>0.68</u>	0.30	0.39
Touchy or easily annoyed by others	<u>0.76</u>	0.30	0.31
Angry and resentful	<u>0.82</u>	0.27	0.20
Spiteful or vindictive	<u>0.86</u>	0.12	0.21
CD items			
Often lies	<u>0.73</u>	0.27	0.15
Initiates physical fights	<u>0.77</u>	0.13	0.20

Source: Pelham, W. E., Gnagy, E., Greenslade, K. E., & Milich, R. (1992). Teacher ratings of *DSM-III-R* symptoms for the disruptive behavior disorders. *Journal of the American Academy of Child and Adolescent Psychiatry, 31,* 210–218. Used with permission.

Note: ADHD = attention-deficit hyperactivity disorder; ODD = oppositional-defiant disorder; CD = conduct disorder. Items with fewer than 5% of cases reported as having the symptom and items with more than 60% "Don't Know" responses were excluded from the analysis. Loadings that were greater than or equal to 0.40 are underlined.

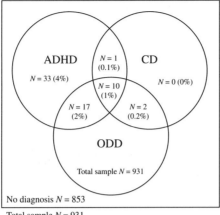

Figure 3–9. **The number of boys meeting diagnostic criteria for ADHD, ODD, and CD diagnoses as defined by the number of symptoms required in *DSM-III-R* and endorsed as "Very Much" on the Disruptive Behavior Disorders Rating Scale**

Source: Pelham, W. E., Gnagy, E., Greenslade, K. E., & Milich, R. (1992). Teacher ratings of *DSM-III-R* symptoms for the disruptive behavior disorders. *Journal of the American Academy of Child and Adolescent Psychiatry, 31,* 210–218. Used with permission.

emphasis on primary prevention of CD. The practitioner thus is required to understand the risk factors that likely contribute to the onset of CD in children receiving a diagnosis of ADHD.

In a population of over 12,000 New Zealand children evaluated by three sources at three ages (8, 10, and 12 years), Fergusson and Horwood (1993) concluded that reports of childhood behavior derived from a specific source at a given time were of limited validity as measures of predicting future behavior. These authors suggested that reports of children's behavior derived from the same source over time were subject to errors of measurement. There was evidence of strong correlation among CD, ODD, and ADHD but weaker correlations between externalizing behaviors and anxiety/withdrawal. These authors concluded that CD, ODD, ADHD, and anxiety/withdrawal emerged as having very high stability across measurement periods, a finding reported by others (Bauermeister, 1992). In this same population, Fergusson, Horwood, et al. (1993) evaluated the relationship among disruptive disorders, juvenile offending, and academic achievement. Early CD behaviors acted as a precursor of future offending patterns, but these behaviors were unrelated to later school performance when the correlation between CD and ADHD was taken into account. Early attentional and cognitive problems were related to future school performance but were unrelated to the development of antisocial behaviors when the correlations between CD and cognitive attentional variables were taken into account. These findings imply a strong and highly specific continuity between early conduct problems and later social maladjustment, as well as between early attention and cognitive problems and later achievement. These developmental progressions are highly correlated by virtue of the strong correlation that exists between early symptoms of ADHD and CD. These authors suggest that among children with similar levels of measured IQ, future academic performance varies with the child's level of attention deficit: children with similar IQ but low attention deficit scores tend to perform better than children with high attention deficit scores. These authors further suggest that attention deficit may act to impede the rate of learning acquisition.

Defiance ratings independent of hyperactivity were obtained by Satterfield, Swanson, Schell, and Lee (1994) in two groups of ADHD boys. Official arrest data obtained on all subjects nine years later were used as the outcome measure. Boys with ADHD with high defiance ratings had significantly higher felony offender rates than did boys with low ratings. However, the ADHD boys with low ratings had significantly higher felony offender rates than did normal control boys. Minor antisocial features in ADHD boys, such as defiance, signaled an increased risk for later serious antisocial behavior. However, the absence of defiance in ADHD boys does not necessarily suggest that these boys are not at risk for later life problems. In a four-year, longitudinal, prospective study, Lahey, Loeber, Hart, and Frick (1995) found that in 171 boys given a diagnosis of CD, approximately half met the diagnostic criteria a year later. However, nearly 90% met the criteria for CD at least once during the next three years. The number of symptoms fluctuated above and below the diagnostic threshold from year to year but remained relatively high. Lower socioeconomic status, parent antisocial behavior, and ADHD were significant correlates with CD in year 1, but the interaction of parent antisocial personality disorder and the boys' verbal intelligence predicted the persistence of CD symptoms over time. Only boys without a parent with personality disorder and with above-average verbal intelligence clearly improved.

Among younger children, school-based situational and pervasive hyperactivity appeared to be the most consistent risks for developing a comorbid disorder (MacArdle, O'Brien, & Kolvin, 1995). According to these authors, hyperactivity was virtually a prerequisite for a diagnosis of CD. Among older children, pervasive hyperactivity had greater comorbidity with other psychiatric disorders than situational hyperactivity. Furthermore, pervasive hyperactivity had the strongest predictive links to the development of CD.

Abikoff and Klein (1992) argue for the importance of distinguishing between referred and nonreferred samples when considering treatment and comorbidity issues. The efficacy of psychosocial and pharmacological treatments of ADHD and CD are reviewed by these authors, as are the few studies of psychostimulant medication used in the comorbid population. The authors suggest that ADHD and CD share a common dysfunction that maximizes interpersonal conflict and in turn facilitates the development of aggressive behavior, especially when the child is placed in an aggressive environment. Interestingly, these authors also hypothesize that impulsivity likely represents a core problem for both diagnoses. Keller et al. (1992) followed the onset and recovery of disruptive disorders in a population of children diagnosed with either of the three disruptive disorders; 33% of the children demonstrated two disruptive disorders, and one received a diagnosis for all three. The mean duration of ADHD was 8 years; in contrast, the mean duration of ODD was 4.5 years, with CD representing a mean duration of 3 years. Thus, one hypothesis to explain this trend suggests that the strong biological underpinnings of ADHD result in the longevity of the diagnosis, whereas the environmental impact of the more serious CD shortens the diagnosis, especially in the face of intervention. Total life estimates suggested that 14% of the children would not have recovered from any of the disorders fifteen years after their onset. Rates of recurrence were also high following recovery from each of these disorders. It is important to note, however, that this was a retrospective study. The three disorders, however, at least by history, had a very early age of onset and chronic course consistent with other studies (Gittelman et al., 1985). The persistence of CD into adulthood was reflected by a diagnosis of antisocial behavior in a significant subgroup of this population (Kelso & Stewart, 1986; Satterfield, Hoppe, & Schell, 1982). Attention deficit and depression also appear to aggregate in these families (Biederman, Munir, Knee, et al., 1986; Biederman et al., 1987).

Using a retrospective chart review, diagnoses of ADHD and CD, combined diagnoses were made by O'Brien et al. (1992). These authors compared these groups on measures of cognitive and academic functioning as well as a continuous performance computerized measure. The groups did not differ in age or IQ, but the attention deficit and the combined groups missed significantly more targets on the continuous performance test and performed significantly poorer on measures of academic achievement than did the pure CD group. However, poor continuous performance was not accounted for by learning problems. In this clinically referred patient group, these findings are consistent with dimensional and epidemiologic studies suggesting that ADHD may be a cognitively based disorder, whereas children with CD are characterized by behavioral symptoms with few cognitive and learning deficits.

Age and gender have been found to be the primary influences on the patterns of comorbidity in children with CD (Loeber & Keenan, 1994). The risk of CD in females appears to be lower than in males. Females with CD appear to be at greater risk to develop internalizing problems, and males demonstrate a more consistent history of ADHD. CD has been found to be related to heightened aggression and violent behavior, with severity of conduct problems in the home contributing directly to the degree of deviant behavior reported in a hospitalized psychiatric setting (Kolko, 1993). In this study, ADHD was related to parent reports of inattention or hyperactivity and to in-hospital measures of inattention, hyperactivity, antisocial behaviors, poor self-control, and a number of seclusions and reinforcement fines. Home and hospital measures of aggression, depression, and suicide attempts were significantly correlated in this psychiatrically impaired population.

It has been hypothesized that oppositional defiant problems represent the early common precursor for CD. In fact, some have suggested that ODD represents only a mild form of CD. In a population of 177 boys, Frick, Lahey, Loeber, et al. (1991) factor analyzed parent and teacher responses to a structured psychiatric interview. Their results yielded two dimensions of disruptive behavioral difficulty similar to the distinction between ODD and CD. However, some symptoms often associated with CD, specifically bullying and violation of major rules, consistently loaded on the factor composed of ODD symptoms. The *DSM-III-R* symptoms of fighting and lying had approximately equal loading on both factors. Cluster analysis derived from summing items with unique loadings on the two factors yielded three profiles: deviance on only the ODD factor, deviance on both, and deviance on neither. Interestingly, a distinct cluster of children with elevations only on the CD factor did not emerge in this population.

In a population of 100 inpatient children 7 to 12 years of age, Soltys, Kashani, Dandoy, and Vaidya (1992) found eight subjects with ADHD alone, eight with CD alone, eighteen with ODD, sixteen with ADHD and CD, and twenty-one with ADHD and ODD. A clinical control group of twenty-nine subjects had no disruptive behavioral problems. Subjects with ADHD and one of the other disruptive diagnoses exhibited a greater degree of psychopathology than did the other subjects. Subjects with CD and ODD were more similar than different, again suggesting the continuum of pathology between these diagnostic classifications.

Reeves et al. (1987) found that attention deficit with a second disruptive disorder differed from attention deficit alone. The group with the combined diagnoses had a higher occurrence of severe adverse family backgrounds and were functioning worse socially. These groups resembled each other more than they differed in gender, age of onset, presentation, frequency of perinatal insult, psychosocial stress, and impairment in cognition and achievement. However, only 5% of the population of children in this group had CD plus ODD without concomitant attention deficit, whereas 36% of this population had ADHD alone.

In 1995, Schachar and Tannock undertook one of the most rigorous and well-thought-out comorbidity studies to test four hypotheses to explain the comorbidity of ADHD and CD. Different patterns of cognitive developmental risk and psychosocial factors were characterized. As a part of this study, the authors reviewed and summarized previous research comparing attention deficit and CD. A summary of their review appears in Table 3–3.

In 1979, L. Robins suggested that the overall social adjustment of parents is a contributing factor to the severity of childhood problems. When social class is controlled, parents of delinquents appear less educated, make less use of available mental health services and demonstrate less ability to obtain and hold a job than parents of nondelinquents. These factors suggest that overall, this group of parents of delinquents may not be as well adjusted or cope as well when effectively parenting their children. It is likely that a child or adolescent with ADHD would not fare as well with such parents. These results appear to support the distinctiveness of ADHD and CD as well as the hypothesis that the group with the comorbid condition represents a hybrid of the purer ADHD and CD conditions.

Academic underachievment was studied in a clinic-referred population of 177 males with diagnoses of ADHD and/or CD by Frick, Kamphaus, et al. (1991). The discrepancy model was used while controlling for regression and age effects. Academic underachievement was associated with both ADHD and CD when the disorders were examined individually. When examined in multivaried, logic model analysis, the apparent relation between CD and academic underachievement was found to be due to its comorbidity with ADHD. When boys with ADHD were divided into those with attention deficits only and those with co-occurring hyperactivity, findings did not support the hypothesis that the association with academic underachievement was stronger for attention deficit without co-occurring hyperactivity. A study in 1993 by Semrud-Clikeman, Hynd, Lorys, and Lahey exemplifies research generating cognitive or achievement data reflecting differences in skills between children with ADHD and those with CD. The revised Wechsler was administered to a group of pure ADHD, a group of ADHD with co-occurring CD, and controls. Contrary to expectations, the

Table 3–3.   Summary of studies comparing ADHD, CD, and ADHD + CD on cognitive measures

Study	Sample	Groups Compared	Measures	Results
Chee et al., 1989	87 boys, 7–11 yr., clinic sample	ADHD, ADHD + CD, CD, LD, NC	CPT	ADHD but not ADHD + CD or CD deficient in sustained attention
Daugherty et al., 1993	55 boys & girls, 9–14 yr., community sample	ADHD, CD, ADHD + CD, ANX, NC	Stop signal paradigm, door-opening task	No differences in inhibitory control No differences in response perseveration
Daugherty & Quay, 1991	814 boys & girls, 8–14 yr., community sample	ADHD, CD, ADHD + CD, ANX, NC	Door-opening task	CD = ADHD + CD > NC, ANX; CD not different form ADHD
Halperin et al., 1990	85 boys & girls, 6–12 yr., community sample	ADHD, CD, ADHD + CD, NC	CPT MFFT	ADHD more inattentive, ADHD + CD more impulsive, no differences among groups
Klorman et al., 1988	63 boys & girls, 6–12 yr., clinic sample	ADHD, ADHD + CD	CPT	No group differences
Koriath et al., 1985	117 boys & girls, 4–13 yr., clinic sample	ADHD, CD, ADHD + CD	CPT & MFFT	CPT hits & false alarms did not discriminate among groups; ADHD, ADHD + CD had shorter MFFT latencies than CD
Loney & Milich, 1982	37 boys, 6–12 yr., clinic sample	ADHD, CD, ADHD + CD, PC	MFFT	No differences in latency; ADHD + CD made more errors than CD, PC
Matier et al., 1992	38 boys & girls, 6–12 yr., clinic sample	ADHD, ADHD + CD, NC	CPT	No group differences in attention but ADHD + CD group more impulsive than ADHD, NC
Moffitt & Henry, 1989	850 boys & girls, 13 yr., community sample	CD*, ADHD, ADHD + CD*, NC	Wisconsin, WISC-R, Meyers Trail Making Test, Rey-Osterreith, Rey Auditory, Verbal Learning Test	ADHD + CD > ADHD, CD, NC
Sandberg et al., 1978	68 boys, 5–11 yr., clinic sample	ADHD, CD	MFFT	ADHD faster than CD
Schachar et al., 1988	114 boys, 7–11 yr., clinic sample	ADHD, CD, ADHD + CD, ANX, LD, NC	CPT	No difference in attaining attention
Schachar & Logan, 1990a	70 boys, 7–11 yr., clinic sample	ADHD, ADHD + CD, CD, ANX, LD, NC	Stop signal paradigm	ADHD but not ADHD + CD or CD deficient in inhibitory control
Schachar & Logan, 1990b	42 boys, 6–12 yr., clinic sample	ADHD, ADHD + CD, NC	Dual task	No differences in attentional capacity
Shapiro & Garfinkel, 1986	315 boys & girls, 7–12 yr., community sample	ADHD, CD, ADHD + CD	CPT	No group differences
Szatmari et al., 1990	177 boys & girls, 6–12 yr., clinic sample	ADHD, CD, ADHD + CD, ANX	Language, visual-perceptual, visual-motor	No group differences between ADHD, CD; ADHD + CD more impaired than ANX
Werry et al., 1987	95 boys & girls, 5–13 yr., clinic sample	ADHD, ADHD + CD, ANX, NC	MFFT, CPT	No differences among groups once age, sex, and IQ controlled

Source: Schachar, R., & Tannock, R. (1995). A test of four hypotheses for the comorbidity of attention-deficit hyperactivity disorder and conduct disorder. *Journal of the American Academy of Child and Adolescent Psychiatry, 34,* 639–648. Used with permission.

Note: ADHD = attention-deficit hyperactivity disorder; CD = conduct disorder; ADHD + CD = comorbid ADHD plus CD; CPT = continuous performance task; MFFT = matching familiar figures task; ANX = anxiety disorder; LD = learning disability; NC = controls without psychiatric disorder; PC = psychiatric controls; CD* = delinquents.

freedom from distractibility factor did not significantly discriminate between the pure co-occurring and control groups. Verbal comprehension and perceptual organization factors significantly distinguished between those with and without CD but not between controls and those with ADHD. The combined group on the revised Wechsler differed from subjects with internalizing disorders, supporting that they represent a distinct diagnostic group.

In light of this large volume of data, it is reasonable for the practitioner to conclude that ODD and CD may occur at beyond-chance level with ADHD but that these reflect different disorders with different courses, impacts, symptoms, and comorbid issues. It is important for the practitioner to recognize that ODD and CD are likely the most common co-occurring diagnoses with ADHD. As will be discussed in Chapter 10, the practitioner should consider ODD and CD to be disorders that often present slightly later during the developmental period, but in the case of ODD, may present at very early ages in parallel with symptoms of ADHD.

Depressive Disorders

The beyond-chance relationship between ADHD and the emotionally distressing childhood disorders of anxiety and depression makes these disorders more than of just passing interest to the practitioner. In children, however, it is difficult at times to separate symptoms of depression and anxiety, in that they appear to represent a common underlying thread of emotional distress (Achenbach & Edelbrock, 1991). For our review, each disorder will be discussed separately. Of increasing interest in the depressive disorders has been the role of ADHD as a precursor or risk factor for, as well as a differential diagnostic issue with, manic depression or bipolar disorder.

Epidemiologically, the overlap between ADHD and depression occurs at a beyond-chance level, with some studies suggesting nearly 30% (McClelland, Rubert, Reichler, & Sylvester, 1989), and continuing into the adult years (Eyestone & Howell, 1994). Based on a longitudinal study, Rey (1994) reports a strong co-occurrence between depression and ADHD. Comorbidity between depression and CD was not higher than expected for any psychiatric disorder, but comorbidity between ADHD and oppositional disorder was higher than expected and was comparable to that between CD and oppositional disorder. Interestingly, co-occurrence of depression with other disorders did not increase the likelihood of comorbid CD. Prevalence rates for ADHD were significantly greater in offspring of parents with depression and panic disorders based on parent report, and in children of depressed parents by consensus report. Consistently higher rates of ADHD were reported by children, parents, and in consensus diagnosis when anxiety or depression was present.

Measures, including parent, teacher, and child ratings of depression, appear to suggest that the combined type of ADHD demonstrates significantly more symptoms of depression, anxiety, and internalizing behaviors in general when compared to the inattentive type and controls (Cody, Hynd, & Hall, 1996). These findings do not support Cantwell and Baker's (1992) conclusions that symptoms of depression differentiated ADD with hyperactivity from ADD without hyperactivity. Cody et al. are more indicative of current research suggesting that depressive symptomatology is exhibited in children with externalizing behavioral problems. The authors also offer evidence for a link between depression and impulsivity to frontal lobe functioning (Schaughency & Hynd, 1989).

Child Behavior Checklist findings provide a very different profile, at least for adolescents with histories of depression, ADHD, or the combined disorders (Biederman, Faraone, Mick, Moore, & Lelon, 1996). As with the combined CD and ADHD, the combined depression and ADHD group appeared to demonstrate symptomatic profiles

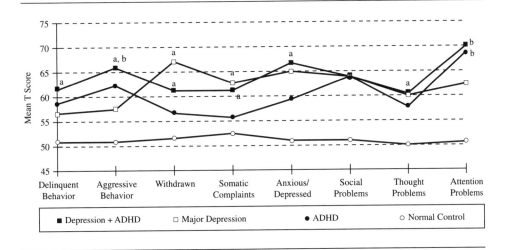

Figure 3–10. Child behavior checklist clinical scale findings. All analyses were adjusted by sex, age, and paternal marital status; all scales were significantly lower in normal controls when compared with all three psychopathological groups

Source: Biederman, J., Faraone, S., Mick, E., & Lelon, E. (1995). Psychiatric comorbidity among referred juveniles with major depression: Fact or artifact? *Journal of the American Academy of Child and Adolescent Psychiatry, 34,* 579–590. Used with permission.

[a] $p \leq .05$ versus ADHD; [b] $< .05$ versus major depression. ADHD = attention-deficit hyperactivity disorder.

consistent with the hybrid profile of pure ADHD and depressed populations (see Figure 3–10).

Biederman, Faraone, Mick, and Lelon (1995) questioned the psychiatric comorbidity among referred juveniles with major depression. In a sample of 424 children and adolescents consecutively referred to a psychiatric facility, nearly 40% were identified with a depressive disorder. They had a history of chronic course and severe psychosocial dysfunction; they also demonstrated a high rate of CD, anxiety disorder, and ADHD. Seventy-four percent with severe major depression and 77% with mild major depression received a diagnosis of ADHD, compared to 74% of the psychiatric controls and none of the normal controls. The authors hypothesized that major depression was more likely the outcome rather than the cause of co-occurring disorders based on the analysis of age of symptom onset. It is important for the practitioner to understand the overlapping symptomatology of major depression. Table 3–4 contains Biederman, Faraone, et al.'s (1995) comparison of the two depressive groups.

In 1988, Jensen, Burke, and Garfinkel evaluated twelve boys with major depressive disorder, twelve with attention deficit disorder, and eleven normal controls between the ages of 8 and 18 years. Subjects and their parents were administered a battery of tests. Children with major depression scored significantly higher than controls on the parent questionnaire, indicating a higher than normal rate of externalizing behavioral symptoms for major depressive disorder. Item analysis with a child-completed questionnaire revealed that children with major depression positively endorsed criteria suggesting poor impulse control and stress intolerance

Table 3–4.   Overlapping symptomatology of major depression

	Severe Major Depression	Mild Major Depression
Diagnosis of major depression after correcting for overlap with ADHD	(*n* = 66)	(*n* = 70)
Subtraction method	70	61
Proportion method	97	86
Diagnosis of major depression after correcting for overlap with ODD	(*n* = 66)	(*n* = 70)
Subtraction method	89	83
Proportion method	89	83
Diagnosis of ADHD after correcting for overlap with major depression	(*n* = 49)	(*n* = 54)
Subtraction method	78	76
Proportion method	86	85
Diagnosis of ODD after correcting for overlap with major depression	(*n* = 48)	(*n* = 33)
Subtraction method	77	61
Proportion method	89	91

Source: Biederman, J., Faraone, S., Mick, E., & Lelon, E. (1995). Psychiatric comorbidity among referred juveniles with major depression: Fact or artifact? *Journal of the American Academy of Child and Adolescent Psychiatry, 34,* 579–590. Used with permission.

Note: Values are percentages. ADHD = attention-deficit hyperactivity disorder; ODD = oppositional defiant disorder.

significantly more often than the other two groups. The authors concluded that children with pure major depressive disorder did not possess features of attention deficit but may demonstrate oppositional defiant symptoms. They also concluded that children with attention deficit may be prone to self-report a higher rate of dysthymic or minor depressive symptoms.

On a case-by-case basis, it has been suggested that there is a genetic relationship between depressive and anxiety disorders that likely does not exist for ADHD (Cohen & Biederman, 1988). Rosenthal (1995) reports the case of a 9-year-old girl with winter seasonal affective disorder, a form of depression, delayed sleep onset syndrome, and ADHD. Despite medication and light treatment therapy, all three disorders persisted over a three-year period.

The frequency of ADHD was assessed in twenty adolescents with *DSM-III-R* bipolar disorder diagnoses hospitalized for an acute manic episode (West, Strakowski, Sax, McElroy, & Keck, 1995); 65% of this population also met the *DSM-III-R* criteria for ADHD. Patients with both disorders were more likely to be Caucasian, male, and have a history of mixed rather than pure mania. Patients with ADHD also had a higher mean total on the Mania Rating Scale and lower serum thyroxine concentrations than patients with bipolar disorder alone. In a group of fourteen adolescents hospitalized with histories of mania, West, McElroy, Strakowski, Keck, and McConville (1994) found that 57% had previously met the criteria for ADHD. The authors of both studies suggest that a prior history of ADHD or ADHD symptoms are common in adolescents hospitalized for mania. Individuals with both disorders may have more severe manic symptoms than patients with mania alone. Although these findings may have important implications, especially in making pharmacologic treatment decisions, they do not suggest that ADHD and bipolar or manic disorder possess more than a correlational relationship.

Rates of childhood behavior and attention problems, psychopathology, and social and occupational impairment in young adulthood were reported as higher in a bipolar risk group than a normal group but not higher than in the nonbipolar combined risk group (Carlson & Weintraub, 1993). Thus, the unique relationship between childhood problems and young adult mood disorder was found only in the bipolar risk group. Nevertheless, those who develop bipolar disorder appear to include a significant minority with histories of externalizing disorders, including ADHD (Akiskal et al., 1985; Casat, 1982; Endicott et al., 1985; Koehler-Troy, Strober, & Malenbaum, 1986). In the majority of these studies, a positive family history of bipolar disorder appears to be the major variable contributing to the reformulation of the young adults' problems as consistent with bipolar disorder. Approximately 30% of the bipolar risk subjects had a history of attention problems versus 16% of the controls. However, the presence of attentional problems in childhood is also significantly related to young adult psychopathology of other types, with 27% of the at-risk group demonstrating attention problems as well. Carlson and Weintraub (1993) is consistent with West et al. (1994, 1995), concluding that mild to moderate attention and behavior problems occur significantly more frequently among the bipolar risk and combined risk offspring as compared to normal controls. The nature of the relationship between childhood behavior and attention problems and later psychopathology varies by risk status with the bipolar risk group, affective symptomatology related to early behavior, and attention problems. It is also important to note, however, that nonaffective symptomatology, including substance abuse and impaired social and occupational competence, were also significant predictors. The implication appears to be that externalizing symptoms in those who do not have a bipolar parent are different. Risk for psychiatric symptomatology in young adulthood is increased, but risk for mood disorder per se is not.

The familial association of ADHD and bipolar disorder among the first-degree relatives of children with comorbid ADHD and bipolar disorder was evaluated in a series of studies by Wozniak and colleagues (Wozniak, Biederman, Kiely, Ablon, Faraone, Mundy, & Mennin, 1995; Wozniak, Biederman, Mundy, Mennin, & Faraone, 1995). Forty-six first-degree relatives of referred children under the age of 12 who met the criteria for mania were studied. There appeared to be high rates of comorbidity between bipolar disorder and ADHD in children and high rates of both bipolar disorder and ADHD in first-degree relatives. ADHD and bipolar disorder cosegregated among the relatives of children with bipolar disorder. According to these authors, these findings were consistent with other work, suggesting strong family genetic evidence for the validity of bipolar disorder and ADHD when they exist comorbidly. The authors suggest that the comorbid condition represents a distinct nosological entity. It is interesting that in this series of studies, 94% of the population of children with a manic diagnosis also met the criteria for ADHD; the authors point out, however, that three of the seven criteria for bipolar disorder are shared with ADHD (distractibility, physical agitation, and talkativeness).

Biederman, Faraone, Mick, Wozniak, et al. (1996) suggested that children with ADHD are at increased risk for developing bipolar disorder. In this study, bipolar was diagnosed in 11% of ADHD children at baseline and an additional 12% four years later. The comorbid children demonstrated higher rates of additional psychopathology, psychiatric hospitalization, and severely impaired psychosocial functioning in comparison to other children with ADHD. The clinical picture of bipolarity reported was mostly irritable and mixed. These children also had a much more severe symptomatic picture than the nonaffected ADHD group. Recently, it has been suggested that ADHD comorbid with bipolar disorder is familially distinct from other forms of ADHD and may represent the unique variant of childhood onset bipolar disorder (Faraone, Biederman, Mennan, Wozniak, & Spencer, 1997). The Harvard group has also suggested a higher incidence of mania in children with pervasive developmental disorder as well (Wozniak et al., 1997).

Butler, Arredondo, and McCloskey (1995) found high rates of bipolar disorder (22%) in a hospitalized sample of ADHD patients. West, McElroy, et al. (1995) reported that 57% of adolescents with bipolar disorder also had ADHD. These authors suggest that the prominent factor for mania in this group is severe irritability rather than euphoria. This is consistent with other reports suggesting that manic episodes in young children are seldom characterized by euphoria (Carlson, 1983). They note that these children with bipolar disorder and ADHD appear to have "affective storms." Their irritability is severe and associated with violence. This group of children may demonstrate ADHD symptoms but, in fact, their symptoms may be the result of mood disorder and not ADHD. These findings, plus those demonstrating that ADHD and bipolar disorder cosegregate in families, suggest that ADHD in children with bipolar disorder are familiarly distinct from other ADHD children and may have what others have termed childhood-onset bipolar disorder (Strober, 1992; Todd, Neuman, Geller, Fox, & Hickok, 1993).

What, then, is the practitioner to make of these data? Children with manic depressive illness have been reported as demonstrating markedly different patterns on the Personality Inventory for Children from those with ADHD (Nieman & DeLong, 1987). The manic group demonstrated a high rate of aggression as well as being severely maladjusted from an early age, a finding reported by others (Hassanyeh & Davidson, 1980). The manic-depressive group also tends to have a longstanding history of depression (Coll & Bland, 1979) and are frequently delinquent and antisocial in their behavior (Puig-Antich, 1980). Good (1978) has suggested that the primary sign for mania may be aggression and hostility rather than elation, euphoria, or cheerfulness, although it is suspected that hostility and aggression emerge only when a manic individual's activities are thwarted. Others have noted that manic-depressive disorder is frequently characterized by hyperaggressive activities (Sheard, 1971; Tupin, 1972). However, the lack of specificity in diagnostic instruments utilized may lead to the apparent overlap between ADHD and bipolar disorder (Butler et al., 1995). In general, very little is known about the onset and course of bipolar disorder in childhood (Nottelmann & Jensen, 1995). Younes, DeLong, Nieman, and Rosner (1986) suggested that manic-depressive symptoms in children included cycling of mood, activity, and aggressivity; difficulty concentrating; distractibility; short attention span; restlessness; irritability; low frustration threshold; impulsiveness; unpredictable behavior; and aggression. It almost appears that the diagnostic description of ADHD is subsumed within the manic-depressive description. However, these authors also noted symptoms that are clearly distinct from ADHD in the bipolar-disordered children, including sadistic acts, extreme jealousy, manic behavior, flight of ideas, grandiosity, depressive symptoms, neurovegetative signs such as periods of catatonia, and symptoms of explosive behavior. Ratey (1991) suggests that a distinction in acuteness of onset and extreme behavior may facilitate the practitioner's ability, based on a history, to discriminate ADHD from manic-depressive problems. Tomasson and Kuperman (1990) suggest that an acute onset of symptoms, psychomotor retardation, and a family history of bipolar disorder in three successive generations present the practitioner with the most efficient means of distinguishing bipolarity from ADHD or diagnosing the comorbid conditions. Further, Winokur, Coryell, Endicott, and Akiskal (1993) suggested that adults with histories of bipolar disorder are more likely to have demonstrated traits of hyperactivity as children than unipolar depressed patients. These authors also found that alcoholism is more frequently found in the families of bipolar patients.

It has been suggested that ADHD and substance use disorder present with physical restlessness, racing thoughts, distractibility, and mood instability, and that they rarely occur together, although when they do, the possible relationship of substance abuse to the ADHD diagnosis must be investigated. Cococres, Patel, Gold, and Pottash (1987) suggest that individuals abusing a substance such as cocaine will behave periodically in impulsive, euphoric ways and demonstrate excessive psychomotor activity, possibly resulting in their being diagnosed with the comorbid ADHD condition.

Anxiety

Perrin and Last (1996) argue that ADHD and anxiety tend to run in families but are independently transmitted disorders. These authors note that male children of anxious mothers appear at increased risk for a diagnosis of ADHD, a finding similar to those in other studies (Sylvester, Hyde, & Reichsler, 1987; Weissman, Gershorn, & Kidd, 1984). Although Biederman, Faraone, Keenan, Steingard, and Tsuang (1991) and Biederman, Faraone, Keenan, and Benjamin (1992) suggest that anxiety disorders are more prevalent in families of ADHD subjects than in families of normal controls, the Perrin and Last study provides only partial support for this hypothesis. In contrast, family members of anxiety-disordered subjects show no increased risk for ADHD. Further, anxiety disorders are more prevalent than ADHD in both nonreferred adults (15%, Regier, Burke, & Burke, 1990) and children (8%–21%, Anderson, Williams, McGee, & Silva, 1987; Kashani et al., 1987; Kashani & Orvaschel, 1988). Anxiety disorders are also more prevalent among adult women (Regier et al., 1990) but show roughly equal gender distribution during youth (Anderson et al., 1987; Bird et al., 1988). Anxiety is often more commonly associated with depression than behavior disorders (Last, Perrin, Hersen, & Kazdin, 1992; Werry, Reeves, et al., 1987). Roughly one-third of referred and nonreferred youth with ADHD have been found to have a life-time history of anxiety disorder (Anderson et al.; Biederman, Faraone, Spencer, et al., 1993; Biederman, Newcorn, et al., 1991; Bird et al.; Lahey, Pelham, Schaughency, et al., 1988; Last et al., 1992; Pliszka, 1989; Woolston et al., 1989). It has also been reported that individuals with ADHD and anxiety tend to be less impulsive, more sluggish on memory tasks, less responsive to methylphenidate, and experience fewer disturbances of conduct than their pure ADHD counterparts (Faraone, Biederman, Lehman, & Spencer, 1993; Pliszka, 1989; Zahn, Abate, Little, & Wender, 1975).

In a population of seventy-three admissions to an outpatient anxiety disorders clinic, the most common primary diagnosis, 33%, was separation anxiety (Last, Strauss, & Francis, 1987); overanxious disorder was diagnosed 15% of the time, social phobia for school 15%, and major depression 15%. Children with a primary diagnosis of separation anxiety disorder were most likely to receive a concurrent diagnosis of overanxious disorder. Interestingly, attention deficit disorder in this group of children primarily referred for anxiety problems was diagnosed in only two of the subjects, representing a comorbidity rate of approximately 3%. In contrast, Livingston et al. (1990) found that about 40% of clinic-referred children with ADHD met concurrent criteria for an anxiety or mood disorder. Last, Hersen, Kazdin, Orvaschel, and Perrin (1991) assessed lifetime psychiatric illness in first- and second-degree relatives of ninety-four children with anxiety disorder. Significantly higher rates of anxiety disorders were found in first-degree relatives, particularly males, of children with anxiety disorder compared to relatives with ADHD and the control group. There were no significant findings for anxiety disorders among second-degree relatives. An increased risk of panic disorder was found in relatives of children with panic disorder or overanxious disorder. This finding is in contrast to Biederman, Faraone, Keenan, Steingard, and Tsuang's (1991) population, in which, among first-degree relatives of children with ADHD, 30% were reported as meeting diagnostic criteria for some type of anxiety disorder. Relatives of ADHD children had an increased risk of ADHD themselves. Relatives of ADHD children without anxiety had an increase of anxiety disorders compared with controls, but the relatives of ADHD children with anxiety showed an even higher prevalence of anxiety disorders.

Pliszka (1992) evaluated 107 preadolescent children who met the criteria for ADHD; the population was subdivided into those with and without a comorbid anxiety disorder. The two groups were then compared with each other and with a control group in terms of teacher ratings, behavioral observations during an academic task, and continuous performance on a computerized measure. The results suggested that children with the comorbid diagnosis are less impulsive and more hyperactive than those with ADHD alone, although they remain more impaired than controls. Pliszka also suggested a trend for the comorbid ADHD/anxiety group to show fewer CD symptoms than the pure ADHD group. As Pliszka (1989) noted, children with comorbid ADHD and anxiety appear less likely to be diagnosed with CD than those with ADHD alone. They are, however, equally likely to develop ODD.

Woolston et al. (1989) evaluated thirty-five psychiatrically hospitalized children drawn from a population of admissions to a university hospital child psychiatry inpatient service. Children ranged in age from 4 to 14 years. The prevalence of comorbid

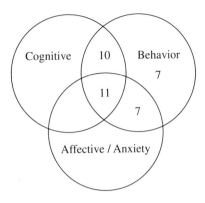

Figure 3-11.   Overlap of *DSM-III-R* diagnoses

Source: Woolston, J. L., Rosenthal, S. L., Riddle, M. A., Sparrow, S. S., Cicchetti, D., and Zimmerman, L. D. (1989). Childhood comorbidity of anxiety/affective disorders and behavior disorders. *Journal of the American Academy of Child and Adolescent Psychiatry, 28,* 707–713. Used with permission.

behavior and anxiety disorders exceeded 50% of the sample (see Figure 3–11). Children with comorbidity were similar to children with behavioral-only diagnoses in terms of demographic and cognitive characteristics but differed in terms of adaptive functioning and maladaptive behaviors. Fifty-one percent of children received at least one behavioral diagnosis and at least one affective or anxiety diagnosis as well. In this study, children with comorbid disorders were not necessarily more impaired; in fact, differences indicated that the comorbid group exhibited more age-appropriate skills in daily living. The authors hypothesized that anxious children may temper their disruptive behavior by inhibition related to their anxiety. Interestingly, both groups of children had poor general functioning on adaptive behavior. On the Child Behavior Checklist, the internalizing and externalizing domains did not distinguish the behavioral from the behavioral-plus-anxiety groups, but the internalizing and externalizing domains of the Vineland Adaptive Questionnaire (Sparrow, Balla, & Cicchetti, 1984) did support different patterns for these children. All the children had higher externalizing domain scores, but the behavioral group tended to have more externalizing behavior and less internalizing behavior. The two groups did not differ in academic areas. In summary, the differences between the two groups appeared in a display of maladaptive functioning and in some areas of adaptive behavior. In this study, CD, ODD, and ADHD were combined in their description as behavioral diagnoses. These authors also evaluated the overlap of ADHD with a developmental disorder and borderline intellectual functioning (see Figure 3–12). In this population of children, there was a significant number experiencing comorbid developmental or intellectual problems and ADHD.

Jensen, Shervette, Xenakis, and Richters (1993) evaluated forty-seven children with ADHD, a group of controls, and those with other psychiatric problems. Both

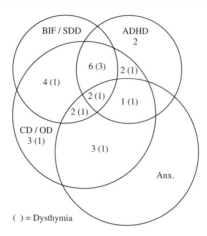

Figure 3–12.   Overlap of diagnostic domains

Source: Woolston, J. L., Rosenthal, S. L., Riddle, M. A., Sparrow, S. S., Cicchetti, D., and Zimmerman, L. D. (1989). Childhood comorbidity of anxiety/affective disorders and behavior disorders. *Journal of the American Academy of Child and Adolescent Psychiatry, 28,* 707–713. Used with permission.

BIF/SDD =   ; ADHD + attention-deficit hyperactivity disorder; CD = conduct disorder; Anx. =

clinic groups reported significantly more anxiety than the normal subjects. Subjects with ADHD had more externalizing behavioral symptoms than subjects in the general psychiatric group. However, subjects with ADHD were indistinguishable from subjects with other psychiatric diagnoses on self- or parent reported emotionally distressing symptoms. Subjects with ADHD plus a comorbid anxiety or depressive disorder had higher levels of coexisting life stress and their parents reported more symptoms of depression than did subjects who had the ADHD-only diagnosis. Recently, based on a careful review of the available data, Jensen, Martin, and Cantwell (1997) suggested that the comorbidity of ADHD and aggression and the comorbidity of ADHD and anxiety might well represent significant subtypes of ADHD and are worthy of future study. The ADHD/Aggressive subtype appears characterized by early age of onset, greater male to female ratio, and decreased likelihood of eventual remission. The latter appeared characterized by decreased impulsivity and severity of other associated disruptive problems.

As discussed earlier, the practitioner's first concern is misdiagnosing another disorder as ADHD, second is missing comorbid diagnoses in a population of children with ADHD. Problems with anxiety appear to occur at a significant but certainly lower rate than problems related to depression and other disruptive disorders in the ADHD population. Anxiety problems likely will create more difficulty for diagnosis. As Desgranges, Desgranges, and Karsky (1995) note, the increasing popularity of ADHD has resulted in more children with a variety of problems presenting for ADHD assessment in clinic settings. These authors reviewed 375 patient records; of 119 cases requesting ADHD assessment, only 45 were confirmed by diagnosis. In the remaining cases, problems related to anxiety, substance abuse, and tic disorders were suggested as contributing to ADHD-like behaviors.

Obsessive-Compulsive Disorder

Although technically an anxiety disorder, the atypical presentation of obsessive-compulsive disorder (OCD) has captured the public's imagination. Hanna (1994) provides a thorough overview of this disorder. Mean onset for this population is between 7 and 13 years of age for males and 11 and 16 years of age for females. A ratio of 3 males to 2 females is consistently reported in the literature. Concerns about contamination, harm to self or others, and symmetry were the greatest obsessions, with washing, checking, repeating, arranging, ordering, touching, and counting being the greatest compulsions. On the Child Behavior Checklist, this group had a mean of one-and-a-half standard deviations above the average for most behavioral scales. For the attention problem scale, however, five (four males and one female) out of a total of thirty-one or approximately 15% of subjects evaluated with obsessive-compulsive disorder also received a diagnosis of ADHD.

Zohar, Ratzoni, Pauls, Apter, Bleich, Kron, Rappaport, Weizman, & Cohen (1992) evaluated a sample of consecutive 16- to 17-year-olds inducted into the Israeli Army. They were screened for obsessive-compulsive disorder, Tourette's, multiple tics, and ADHD. Using *DSM-III-R* criteria, 3.6% of the population was found to have OCD, 3.9% ADHD, 1.8% multiple tics, and 1.6% Tourette's. For ADHD, Tourette's, and multiple tic disorders but not for OCD, there was a significantly higher prevalence of males than females. Among the subjects with OCD, there was an elevation of Tourette's, transient tics, and multiple tics relative to the general population. A significant group of those with Tourette's also met the criteria for ADHD.

Posttraumatic Stress Disorder

Four comorbid cases of ADHD and posttraumatic stress disorder in 5- to 12-year-old children were described by Cuffe, McCullough, and Pumariega (1994). The authors suggest that children with ADHD may possibly be at higher risk for trauma due to their impulsivity and high risk-taking behavior as well as the fact that they may have parents with a genetic predisposition for impulse control problems of their own. The authors also offer a hyperarousal hypothesis suggesting that hyperarousal is induced by severe trauma and manifested by hypervigilance and poor concentration impairing attention. This then creates an ADHD-like syndrome. Of these four cases, it was not possible to determine the exact onset of ADHD symptoms. However, it was hypothesized that the ADHD preceded the posttraumatic stress disorder diagnosis.

Suicide

The most significant risk factors associated with suicide are major depression, bipolar disorder, substance abuse, and CD. The majority of depressed suicide victims have a history of primary affective disorder (Brent et al., 1993). ADHD was not found to be a specific risk factor for suicide completers in comparison to controls. Lewinsohn, Gotlieb, and Seeley (1995), based on their longitudinal study, suggested that the risk factors specific to major depression were stress, poor emotional control, physical symptoms, disease, history of suicide attempts, and past diagnosis of depression or anxiety. A diagnosis of ADHD was not found to a specific risk factor for depression or suicide in this population.

Substance Abuse

Lewinsohn et al. (1995) report that risk factors specific to substance abuse are tobacco use, academic difficulty, and a past episode of substance abuse. Schuckit, Sweeney, and Huey (1987) evaluated young adult sons of alcoholic fathers and normal controls. Findings of this study did not indicate an elevated risk for attention deficit disorder in the sons of alcoholics.

Kaminer (1992) suggests that the development of CD and antisocial personality disorder represents an avoidable first step in the path to psychoactive substance use disorder. However, this author notes that some investigators of adult substance abuse do not subscribe to this opinion, and others give considerable weight to the self-medication theory of substance abuse in ADHD. Kaminer suggests that, based on the available data, limited conclusions can be drawn concerning the relationship of ADHD to late adolescent or adult substance abuse.

Brook, Whiteman, Cohen, Shapiro, and Balka (1995) suggest that personality traits of unconventionality, impulsivity, low ego integration, and aggression against peers are powerful longitudinal predictors of late adolescent and young adult substance abuse. These authors also suggest that certain factors decreased the risk of abuse, including developing good anger control, adequate school achievement, low aggression against others, compliance, responsibility, and low rebelliousness. ADHD as a cluster of symptomatic behaviors was not directly implicated. In contrast, Schubiner, Tzelepis, and Isaacson (1995) summarize the available literature suggesting an association between ADHD and substance abuse; though the literature is limited, these authors suggest that future studies should make a more concerted effort to evaluate the prevalence of the ADHD diagnosis in individuals presenting with a history of substance abuse. These authors described three adult patients with histories of ADHD who were able to remain abstinent from substance abuse for two to three years after being treated with psychostimulants.

In a large longitudinal study, Fergusson, Lynskey, and Horwood (1993) evaluated the early onset of cannabis use by age 15 years to assess the relationship among conduct problems, ADHD, and substance abuse. Although conduct problems during middle childhood were significantly associated with later substance abuse, there was no association between early ADHD and substance abuse when the association between conduct problems and ADHD was taken into account. These authors estimated that subjects who show tendencies toward CD in middle childhood were over two times more likely to engage in early substance abuse than were children not prone to conduct problems, even when a range of factors, including family social background, parent separation, and parental conflict, was taken into account. The authors concluded that early CD behaviors were a specific risk factor for substance abuse but not necessarily symptoms of ADHD. This was especially demonstrated when social and contextual factors associated with both early conduct problems and later substance abuse were considered.

In a population of 6- to 17-year-old boys with ADHD compared to a control group followed for four years into midadolescence, information on cigarette smoking was obtained in a standardized manner. ADHD appeared to be a significant predictor of cigarette smoking and follow-up into midadolescence. ADHD was also associated with early initiation of cigarette smoking, a finding that has been reported by others (Horner & Scheive, 1997). The association was maintained even after socioeconomic status, IQ, and psychiatric comorbidity were controlled for. In addition, among children with ADHD, there was a significant positive association between cigarette smoking and conduct disorder, major depression, and anxiety disorder. The authors hypothesize that some children with ADHD who smoke do so in an effort to self-medicate, as nicotine has been shown to modulate dopaminergic pathways. This finding is consistent with Pomerleau, Downey, Stelson, and Pomerleau's (1995) demonstrating that adults with ADHD find it extremely difficult to quit smoking.

In the Milberger, Biederman, Faraone, Murphy, and Tsuang (1994) study, 10% of the control population were smokers, similar to observations in other epidemiologic surveys (Massachusetts Medical Society, 1995). Milberger et al. (1994) reported cigarette smoking in 10% of adolescents with ADHD without comorbid disorders, 21% in those with one comorbid disorder, 35% in those with two comorbid disorders, and 40% when ADHD and three other disorders (depression, anxiety, and conduct) were present. These data lend further evidence to the report of Carroll and Rounsaville (1993) suggesting that poor substance abuse treatment outcome can be expected for subjects with untreated ADHD. Based on their findings, these authors strongly urge those treating ADHD substance abusers to carefully screen for ADHD.

Using assessments from multiple domains, Biederman et al. (1997) examined 140 children and adolescents between 6 and 17 years of age at baseline and four years later. Drug and alcohol abuse in this group were compared to a sample of normals. No differences between the groups were detected in the rate of alcohol or drug abuse or dependence or in the rates of abuse of individual substances: ADHD and controls had a 15% rate of psychoactive substance use disorders. Conduct and bipolar disorders predicted substance use disorders independent of ADHD status. A family history of substance dependence and antisocial disorders was associated with psychoactive substance use disorder in controls but, interestingly, less clearly so in ADHD subjects. The family history of ADHD was not associated with risk for psychoactive substance use disorder. The authors concluded that adolescents with and without ADHD had a similar risk for substance use disorder, which appeared to be mediated by conduct disorder and bipolar disorder. They further concluded that because the risk for substance use disorder had been shown to be elevated in adults with ADHD when compared with controls, a sharp increase in psychoactive substance use disorders is to be expected in grown-up ADHD children during the transition from adolescence into adulthood. It is important to note that among the methodological limitations of this study was that treatment was not controlled for. Many of the subjects in the clinic sample were receiving some form of treatment during the follow-up period. The authors suggested, however, that it was unlikely that treatment effects accounted for the results.

It has been suggested that adolescents with a combination of CD, substance use disorder, and ADHD experience a more virulent illness with a worse prognosis for the persistence of antisocial traits and substance abuse than do youth with conduct disorder and substance use without combined ADHD (Crowley & Riggs, 1995). Additionally, it has been suggested that ADHD is a much more treatable illness than substance abuse, and therefore the treatment of substance abusers with ADHD may enhance effective utilization of treatment for substance abuse (Thompson, Riggs, Mikulich, & Crowley, 1996). It is important for practitioners to keep in mind that some authors have suggested the validity of subtyping CD on the basis of the presence of coexisting substance use disorder. CD patients without a coexisting substance use disorder have been reported as more likely to have ADHD (Grilo, Becker, Fehon, & Edell, 1996). However, others have suggested that individuals with ADHD are more likely to have CD symptoms, earlier age of CD onset, more substance dependence diagnoses, and more comorbid depression and anxiety (Thompson et al., 1996).

Based on his research population, Comings (1994) suggests that the genes responsible for Tourette's and ADHD may be identical and may also play a role in the development of drug abuse or dependence.

Tourette's Disorder

In a family history study of 130 Tourette's patients, over 1,800 relatives and a population of controls were evaluated by Comings and Comings (1990). The frequency of ADHD and learning disorders was significantly increased in the relatives of the Tourette's children. Other than tics, the data suggest that ADHD is the most common behavioral disorder in children with Tourette's and is more common than the Tourette symptom of coprolalia. These authors reported that ADHD was present in approximately half of all Tourette's cases. It has also been reported that the relatives of children with Tourette's present with a high rate of comorbid Tourette's and ADHD (Knell & Comings, 1993).

Dykens, Leckman, Riddle, Hardin, Schwartz, and Cohen (1990) assessed the intellectual academic and adaptive strengths and weaknesses of thirty medication-free children ages 7 to 14 years with Tourette's Disorder. A battery of standardized psychoeducational and adaptive measures was utilized. Results found significant weaknesses in mental and written arithmetic and relative strengths in reading achievement and abstract logical thinking. Socialization skills emerged as a significant weakness in adaptive functioning. Comparisons between nineteen children with Tourette's with ADHD and eleven without yielded similar profiles of strengths and weaknesses in both groups in all areas assessed, but significantly lower performance IQs in the Tourette's subjects with ADHD. Children with Tourette's have been reported as having fewer executive function impairments and better perceptual organization scores than those with ADHD alone or with the combined disorders (Harris et al., 1995). Deficiencies in choice reaction time and consistency of timed responses appear to be common in all three groups, but children with Tourette's only appear to have relatively less impairment in executive function than those with ADHD only.

Autism

In a sample of forty children with the diagnosis of autistic spectrum disorder, DeLong (1994) reports that thirty-two were described as distractible and inattentive. Garretson, Fein, and Waterhouse (1990) found that autistic children's difficulties in sustaining attention appear to be attributable in part to developmental delay and in part to motivational contingencies. This is in contrast to the hypothetical underlying deficit for children with ADHD reflecting an inability to sustain attention or manage impulses. Children with high-functioning autism have also been reported as having a high co-occurrence with right hemisphere syndrome. Assessment of children with right hemisphere syndrome often yields reports of attentional problems (Voeller, 1986). Chapter 10 will discuss a number of differential issues practitioners need to consider if high-functioning autism, Asperger's disorder, or right hemisphere syndrome are suspected.

COMORBID MEDICAL CONDITIONS

Thyroid

Thyroid dysfunction has been suggested as a cause of ADHD symptoms in a small minority of children (Hauser et al., 1993). This etiology will be discussed in Chapter 5. West, Sax, Keck, Strakowski, and McElroy (1995) found differences in thyroid functioning in adolescents with bipolar disorder with and without ADHD. These authors suggested that those with ADHD may reflect a longer duration or greater severity of illness in comparison to those without ADHD.

Williams Syndrome

Tomc, Williamson, and Pauli (1991) provide anecdotal data suggesting that children with Williams syndrome, a genetic disorder characterized by a number of physical abnormalities including a heart condition and lowered intellect, demonstrate a high incidence of high activity level, poor ability to fit routines, more negative mood, less persistence, greater distractibility, and a lower emotional threshold. The authors suggests that this increases the likelihood that they may receive a comorbid diagnosis of ADHD. No studies are available assessing the prevalence of ADHD in this population of children or their response to stimulant treatment.

Asthma

The risk for asthma does not meaningfully differ between ADHD and control children (Biederman, Milberger, Faraone, Guite, & Warbourton, 1994). Relatives of children with ADHD, with and without asthma, were at significantly greater risk for ADHD in comparison to relatives of normal controls. In contrast, the risk for asthma was significantly elevated only among relatives of children with ADHD plus asthma. The authors conclude that symptoms of ADHD should not be dismissed out of hand as being a consequence of asthma.

Deafness

Kelly, Forney, Parker-Fisher, and Jones (1993b) discuss the impact of ADHD symptoms on the behavior and performance of children who are deaf or hard of hearing. Based on a review of the literature and analysis of data collected at a state residential school for the deaf, the prevalence of ADHD was reported to be similar to that reported in hearing children. However, the authors noted that some subgroups of deaf children, such as those with acquired hearing loss, appeared at greater risk for being described as inattentive, impulsive, distractible, and hyperactive. In a study of 238 students attending a school for the deaf, sixty-four students with hereditary-based deafness received significantly better ratings on parent and teacher symptom questionnaires than seventy-five students with acquired deafness. Thirty-eight percent of those with acquired deafness were rated below the 20th percentile on a standardized questionnaire; only 14% of students with hereditary deafness were rated this way. Ratings of attention span for students with hearing loss attending a residential school did not differ overall from normative data. The subgroup of children with acquired sensory neurodeficit appear to be at increased risk for attentional problems, possibly the result of a cause equal to that impacting their hearing (Kelly et al., 1990).

Hagerman and Falkenstein (1987) report that in children with ADHD there is a strong correlation between the frequency of episodes of otitis media with effusion and the degree and severity of ADHD. These children may experience intermittent periods of hearing loss. A number of studies have indicated some statistically significant but unclear relationships among intermittent conductive hearing loss, attentional problems, and learning disabilities (Addesman, Altshuler, Lipkin, & Walce, 1990; Oberklaid, Harris, & Keir, 1989; Wright et al., 1988).

Neurofibromatosis

Based on a review of the literature, Anderson (1992) suggests that ADHD is reported quite frequently in children with type 1 neurofibromatosis, a finding supported by others (Wadsby, Lindehammar, & Eeg-Olofsson, 1989). A single case study is offered as supporting evidence by Anderson.

Schizophrenia

Although the relationship between schizophrenia and ADHD appears obscure, at least one respected clinician has suggested that some relationship exists (Bellak, 1992, 1994). The relationship, however, is hypothetical, with no data generated other than anecdotal reports to substantiate the link. Schmidt and Freidson (1990) report a single case study of the onset of schizophrenia after puberty in a male treated and followed for ADHD.

Atypical outcome can occur, resulting in a seeming relationship between any two phenomena. Thus, it is not surprising that single case studies have been reported of children treated and followed for ADHD after puberty developing disorders as diverse as schizophrenia or recurrent major affective illness (Schmidt & Freidson, 1990). It is important to note that these authors suggest that such an outcome is highly atypical and rare. There do not appear to be any reliable biological or behavioral markers other than the occurrence of these types of disorders in first-degree relatives that would predict increased risk for these disorders in the ADHD population.

Encopresis and Enuresis

The prevalence of encopresis is estimated to be 1% to 3% in school-age children (Hatch, 1988). Some studies have reported a higher rate of enuresis though not encopresis in children with ADHD (Biederman, Faraone, Knee, & Munir, 1990). The etiological connection between the two disorders is not well understood. Though it has been suggested that encopretic children may have a higher rate of ADHD, data have been inconclusive (Levine, 1982). It has been suggested by others that encopresis occurs beyond a chance level in children with ADHD (Boone, 1992). Responses to Child Behavior Checklist questionnaires were analyzed by Johnston and Wright (1993) to estimate the prevalence of ADHD in a group of children with encopresis. Overall, 23% of children with encopresis had significantly elevated hyperactive subscale scores. The prevalence was estimated to be tenfold greater than expected in the normal population and was similar in gender and across age group. The association between reported attentional problems and encopresis may have significance for theories regarding etiology and for practical treatment strategies. Enuresis, however, has not been found to increase the risk of psychopathology in children with or without ADHD (Biederman, Santangelo, et al., 1995). Enuresis was not found to be associated with psychosocial adversity or developmental immaturity. However, it was found to be associated with increased risk for learning disability, impaired intellectual functioning, and impaired school achievement in normal control children, but surprisingly, not in children with ADHD. The same pattern of findings was obtained after stratifying children with enuresis by primary versus secondary and by nocturnal versus diurnal subtypes.

Based on their findings, Johnston and Wright (1993) conclude that there is a subset of children whose poor task persistence, poor prioritization, poor reinforcability, and deficient self-monitoring skills predispose them first to stool retention and then to encopresis. These authors also suggest that typical reinforcement programs used to treat encopresis are less effective for children with ADHD due to their impulsivity.

Central Auditory Processing Disorders

An ad hoc committee of the American Speech/Language Association in 1992 broadly defined central auditory processing deficits as deficits in the processing of audible signals that cannot be attributed to impaired peripheral hearing sensitivity or to intellectual impairments, but to "limitations in the ongoing transmission, analysis, organization, transformation, elaboration, storage retrieval and use of information contained in audible signals" (p. 2). This report also suggested that central auditory processing deficits may yield distractibility and inattentiveness.

The ability to discriminate words in verbal repetition and picture pointing was evaluated in two groups of children with and without ADHD (Geffner, Jay, & Koch, 1996). Subjects were asked to discriminate words presented in quiet or with a variety of background distractions. Results demonstrated no differences between the verbal repetition and the picture pointing response modes and the quiet speech discrimination condition. However, significant differences between the two groups were found in speech discrimination and the noise conditions. Those with ADHD performed more poorly than the comparisons in the noise conditions, especially in the verbal response mode task. Differential effects for the type of noise were found for comparison subjects but not for those with ADHD. Whether these findings are a function of poor inhibition or actually represent neuropsychological differences in these two groups of children has yet to be determined.

Riccio, Hynd, Cohen, Hall, and Molt (1994) explored the incidence of ADHD in a group of thirty children who met the diagnostic criteria for central auditory processing disorder. Their results indicated that although the incidence rate of ADHD was nearly 50% in this sample, significantly exceeding that found in the normal population, not all children with auditory processing problems demonstrated behavior consistent with ADHD. There was a low incidence of any other behavioral disorders in this sample as well. In contrast, it was found that the sample as a whole demonstrated impaired language abilities. No significant differences emerged across cognitive, auditory, or language measures. Ludlow, Cudahy, Bassich, and Brown (1983) found that hyperactive boys performed significantly worse on signal detection tasks than normals, suggesting deficits in temporal processing. Gascon, Johnson, and Burd (1986) found a high concordance between teacher reports of attention deficit symptoms and central auditory deficits. In this study, central auditory testing was extremely sensitive to the effects of medication. Due to this fact, these authors raised the question of whether central auditory processing and ADHD were in fact separate disorders, a question raised by other researchers as well (Burd & Fisher, 1986). Of interest are additional reports by Keith and Engineer (1991) and Keith, Rudy, Donahue, and Katbamna (1989) suggesting a similar connection. Interestingly, the senior author in both of those articles has recently published a simple test of auditory attention (Keith, 1994) advertised to diagnose ADHD and discriminate it from the comorbid central auditory processing condition. Differential questions facing practitioners when the presentation of central auditory processing deficits is possible will be discussed further in Chapter 10.

Fragile X

Fragile X syndrome is a genetic condition, cited as the most common inherited form of mental retardation (Hagerman & Sobesky, 1989). It is also associated with attentional problems, hyperactivity, autism, and general behavioral problems (Hagerman, Amiri, & Cronister, 1991). Fragile X has been reported as occurring in approximately 50% of the sons of a carrier mother (Hagerman & Sobesky, 1989). The prevalence of Fragile X has been estimated to be approximately 1 per 1,000 males, well below the incidence of ADHD (Sherman, 1991). Carrier fathers and grandfathers of individuals with Fragile X have been found to score significantly higher than control groups on an adult ADHD self-rating scale (Dorn, Mazzocco, & Hagerman, 1994). Borghgraef, Fryns, and van den Berghe (1990) and Bregman, Leckman, and Ort (1988) reported severe attentional problems in samples of males and females with Fragile X.

Hagerman et al. (1991) suggest that in addition to short attention span and hyperactivity, practitioners should take note of individuals who appear tactilely defensive, demonstrate self-stimulatory behavior such as hand flapping, or exhibit poor eye contact, perseverative speech, large or prominent ears, or a simian crease as possibly experiencing Fragile X. In these cases, a referral should be made to a geneticist to assist in the differential diagnostic process. (The interested reader is referred to Hagerman et al., 1991)

Sleep Problems

Sleep disturbance has not been listed as a symptom of ADHD since the *DSM-III-R* in 1987. Ball and Koloian (1996) report greater parent-perceived sleep problems in children with ADHD than in normal controls, a finding reported by others (Pelham, Greenslade, & Cunningham, 1990). These authors suggest that children with ADHD are less willing to go to bed, more often afraid of the dark, up more often during the night, have fewer hours of total sleep, and are more difficult to wake in the morning. Laboratory polysonogram studies have found few or no differences, however, in the sleep architecture of children with ADHD in comparison to normals (Palm, Persson, Elmqvist, & Blennow, 1992). There have been reports of increased nighttime wakening and difficulty falling asleep in children with ADHD (Sierra & Kales, 1990). Only Edwards (1996) provides data soliciting children's views of their sleep problems. It appears that parents and children are in general agreement concerning sleep difficulty. The most commonly reported sleep disturbance by children is difficulty waking up in the morning. Despite these preliminary data, D. Taylor, Szatmari, Boyle, and Offord (1996) report, an accurate clinical assessment of somatic symptoms must include parent and child report because parent report alone may not be valid.

Eating Disorders

There are no reported studies specifically relating eating disorders and ADHD. Rydell, Dahlik, and Sundelin (1995) report that children who are choosy eaters appear to have modestly elevated levels of externalizing hyperactive and internalizing behaviors. Children who are choosy eaters with a history of refusal to eat in infancy or preschool age also had more pronounced behavioral problems than other choosy eaters.

Primary Disorder of Vigilance

Over the past twenty years, Weinberg and colleagues have suggested that some children with ADHD actually experience a primary disorder of vigilance. Weinberg (1986) describes this as a familial condition affecting the states of wakefulness, watchfulness, and arousal, somewhat akin to a sleep disorder. The author suggested that this disorder is different from attention deficit without hyperactivity and hypothesized that it is manifested by inappropriate sleepiness, restlessness, and difficulty attending to certain boring tasks. Some experimental but primarily anecdotal data are provided to substantiate this hypothesis. Weinberg and Brumback (1992) have also hypothesized that a significant group of children given a diagnosis of ADHD may in fact experience depression or bipolar disorder.

SUMMARY

This chapter laid an important educational foundation for the practitioner in regard to comorbid psychiatric, developmental, behavioral, and medical conditions in ADHD, and reviewed the extensive literature concerning family issues and variables impacting the functioning and outcome for children. It is essential that the practitioner must thoroughly understand these data, as years of research clearly demonstrate that comorbid conditions and the environment of the child with ADHD represent powerful factors impacting treatment success and ultimately life outcome.

Chapter 4

DEVELOPMENTAL COURSE

To effectively and efficiently apply diagnostic criteria for ADHD, practitioners must be well versed in child development in general and in the ways factors in child development shape, interact with, and influence symptoms of ADHD and children's general health and welfare. With the foundations provided in the previous chapters concerning history, definition, and a number of what have been referred to as life span factors (e.g., intelligence as a factor that influences individuals throughout their lives), this chapter will provide the practitioner with an indepth review of the research concerning ADHD at different developmental stages. Practitioners will also be offered guidelines and issues to consider as children of different ages are evaluated and worked with.

INFANTS

Turecki (1989) popularized the term "the difficult child." He described an infant whose "innate difficult temperament makes him/her hard to raise for his/her particular family" (p. 141). Turecki suggested that difficult infants demonstrated high activity levels, were easily distracted, had a high intensity of reaction, were unpredictable in fitting routines, were negatively persistent, had a low sensory threshold, withdrew to initial new situations, did not adapt well over time, and generally had a negative mood. During their years of research on childhood temperament, Thomas and Chess (1977) and others (Carey, 1970) have described a pattern of temperamental or innate qualities children bring to the world. These qualities affect their ability to accommodate and meet the environment's expectations and play a role in determining the manner in which the environment responds to the child. Approximately 10% of the population studied have been described as having a difficult temperament (Thomas & Chess, 1977). These children tend to withdraw in a negative manner from new stimulation, have problems with changes in routine, tend to present with significantly greater negative as opposed to positive mood and have fairly intense reactions to events in their environment, and demonstrate a low frustration threshold and a high intensity of reaction. As many as 70% of this difficult infant population have been reported as developing problems at school. In a related study, Persson-Blennow and McNeil (1988) found less statistically significant individual stability for children evaluated as being of difficult temperament at 1 or 2 to 6 years of age. These authors also concluded, however, that an infant's temperament can change over several years, and thus temperament alone must be used cautiously in assessing a child's risk for further problems. In a study of slightly older temperamental children, 3-year-olds were identified using the criteria of negative mood and intense reactions and followed for five years. At that point, all were experiencing school-related problems (Terestman, 1980).

In a retrospective study, Wasserman, Diblasio, Bond, Young, and Colletti (1990) associated parent ratings of temperament in infancy to school-age behavior problems in 129 children. Low socioeconomic status, ratings of temperamental difficulty, and perceptions of temperamental difficulty at 4 months of age were associated with increased parental ratings of behavior problems at 6 years of age. Teacher-reported problems were associated only with low socioeconomic status. Clearly, child factors and parent attitudes about what constitutes typical infant behavior contribute to longitudinal outcome. The overall contribution of perceived infant temperamental difficulty in predicting behavior problems at school is small, with the association largely accounted for by females. The fact that parents perceive their infants as more difficult than other infants reflects a variety of factors that may contribute to subsequent behavior problems, including the child's temperament as well as parent assumptions, attributes, and ability to deal effectively with the child. Interestingly, in this study there was no long-term association between any single behavioral item and outcome. Certainly, difficult infancy impacts attachment. Concordance between attachment as measured in infancy and at 6 years of age was 82% in a population studied by Wartner, Grossmann, Fremmer-Bomvik, and Suess (1994). When observed in preschool at ages 5 and 6, children who were classified as securely attached at age 6 were more competent in their play quality and conflict resolution; they showed fewer behavior problems and attributed less hostility in a social perception picture test compared to the insecurely attached children. Children who were classified as disorganized at age 6 were found almost as often in the incompetent preschool behavior groups as children who were avoidantly attached, independent of fitting an alternative attachment pattern. Disorganization at age 6 is considered to be a reflection of insecure attachment. It would appear that from the end of the first year onward, attachment is increasingly established as a stable pattern with predictable correlates. In this low-risk sample of forty children with no definable psychiatric problems, a disorganized attachment status was associated with psychopathology, thus the conclusion that it suggested an insecure attachment. This finding in Germany replicated the work of others, including Erickson, Sroufe, and Edgeland (1995) in the United States.

Difficult infants have been referred to as children at risk (Ross & Ross, 1982), primarily because their problems are nonspecific in predicting the type of difficulty they may experience in later childhood. Children in this population may develop learning problems, behavioral excesses, difficulty with socialization, attention disorder, or other psychiatric problems. Many experience a combination of these problems.

Infants at risk typically present with very high activity levels. They are difficult even for experienced mothers to manage. They may be restless and overactive in their sleep patterns and present a significant challenge during routine care activities such as dressing or bathing. These are children parents describe as rolling off the bed or changing table in a split second. Lehtonen, Korhonen, and Korvenranta (1994) completed a prospective study of fifty-nine colicky infants and fifty-eight matched controls. Infant temperament was evaluated at ages 3 and 12 months and sleeping patterns at 8 and 12 months. At 3 months of age, mothers regarded colicky infants as more intense in their reactions, less persistent, more distractible, and more negative in mood. At 12 months of age, mothers regarded 23% of the colicky infants as more difficult than average compared to 5% of controls. The mothers regarded their colicky infants as more active and less persistent. Interestingly, a temperamental scale designed for toddlers showed no difference between the groups in any area of temperament, and no significant differences were found for sleep patterns. The discrepancy between infants' actual temperament and mothers' general perception of temperament may reflect the influence of infant colic on the mother-infant relationship. Thus, multiple biological, interpersonal, and environmental factors may combine to impact parents' perceptions and subsequently children's behavior.

Research studies additionally suggest that some of these difficult infants have a very different pattern of crying. Most infants cry at a sound wave frequency somewhere between 400 and 450 cycles per second. Among the at risk group, the cry may be somewhere between 650 and 800 cycles per second (Wolff, 1969). Parents describe this child as presenting with a high-pitched monotonic cry or scream. One parent described the problem as the static or whine of a car radio, another as analogous to a broken alarm clock. The parent was never sure what was distressing the child, when the child would be set off, or how to stop the child's crying once it began. During history sessions, parents frequently describe these children as experiencing excessive colic from the day they were brought home from the hospital. Careful questioning often reveals that the problem is one of excessive irritability and not necessarily colic. Colic does not begin at birth and is frequently routine, occurring at similar times during the day.

Sleep studies suggest that the at-risk population of infants presents with a pattern of sleep similar to premature infants. The pattern is characterized by a 3 to 1 ratio between rapid eye movement sleep (REM) and nonrapid eye movement sleep (Ross & Ross, 1982). REM sleep is characterized by irregular patterns of respiration and heartbeat. In older individuals, REM sleep is often described as dream sleep. It is uncertain what the purpose of this pattern of sleep is for infants. These infants at risk also present with extremely irregular patterns of sleep (Campbell, Szumowski, Ewing, Gluck, & Breaux, 1982). It is difficult for them to establish a sleep routine. They may wake repeatedly or suddenly, startle themselves, and cry (Nichamin, 1972). This pattern of different sleep may continue throughout childhood for this population of children (Luisada, 1969). At one time, sleep-related problems were considered part of the diagnostic criteria for attention disorder (APA, 1980).

At-risk infants are also frequently described as obstinate, picky, and obstructive feeders (Ross & Ross, 1982). They often have difficulty nursing and making the transition from bottle to regular foods. There is also an unexplained higher incidence of allergy to formula in this group.

Longitudinal studies have suggested that the interaction of a number of variables, including perinatal distress and low socioeconomic status, contributes to a wide range of childhood behavioral abnormalities (Werner & Smith, 1977). In an interesting study of medical problems present in ADD children, Hartsough and Lambert (1985) found that a significant degree of pre- and perinatal medical factors discriminated between a group of ADD and control children. Mothers of ADD children had a significantly higher incidence of poor maternal health during pregnancy, toxemia or eclampsia, postmaturity, and longer labor. A significantly higher percentage of the ADD children were the product of their mothers' first pregnancy. These mothers also tended to be younger than the mothers of the control children. As infants, in comparison to the control group, the ADD children were significantly different in experiencing four or more serious accidents, delays in achieving bowel control, and speech problems. It is certainly possible, however, that other moderator variables or problems contribute to some of these issues. For example, a recent large-scale longitudinal study has suggested that trips to the emergency room may be characteristic of children with ADHD as the result of the comorbidity with conduct disorder and that, in fact, conduct disorder contributes primarily to emergency room visits, not ADHD. A summary of Hartsough and Lambert's research appears in Table 4–1.

Infants with low birth weight or other medical problems have been reported to present at higher risk for developing early symptoms of ADHD in some studies (Li, Sauve, & Creighton, 1990; Robson & Pederson, 1997) but not in others (Callaghan, Byrnes, Harvey, Mohay, Rogers, & Tudehope, 1996). Follow-up assessments were made by Li et al. (1990) in a perinatal program for children with birth weights below 1,500 grams or those requiring ventilation or experiencing seizures in the neonatal period. Among the children who demonstrated delayed development, no significant differences were found with controls on school-age cognitive, language, visual-motor, work completion, or behavioral measures. Significant correlations between perinatal and demographic variables on school-age measures were found. A sizable number of high-risk children as the result of their neonatal experiences were shown to have signs of school-related problems. Specifically, the two groups of children were not described on parent and teacher questionnaires as different in their activity level or attention span; however, neonatal seizures were significantly correlated with teacher ratings of distractibility and hyperactivity, and neonatal neurologic signs with hyperactivity. Total days of ventilation was significantly negatively correlated with parent ratings of activity level; that is, the more days ventilated, the higher the child's activity level. Maternal and paternal ages were also significantly correlated with parents' ratings of activity level; older parents describe their children as less active. These authors also noted that language development in biologically at-risk children appears susceptible to the compensatory effect of competent caregiving, supportive transitional models, and appropriate interventions. Robson and Pederson (1997) studied a population of eighty-five children participating in a prospective study of the consequence of low birth weight. All of these children were born weighing 2,500 grams or less. Assessment at 5.5 years of age found that infant developmental status, in combination with the quality of the child's environment during childhood, was predictive of individual differences on reported measures of attention. These findings appear to have clinical implications for the early identification of low birth weight children at risk for ADHD. Within this group of children, risk factors for a subsequent diagnosis of ADHD include characteristics of the child as well as characteristics of the environment. It is important for the practitioner to keep in mind that the sample studied was of a group of medically high-risk, early, low birth weight children. However, as others have noted, quality of parenting has been clearly implicated in developmental status in infants (Xeanah, Boris, & Larrieu, 1997). Other authors too have reported a correlation between neonatal and infant medical problems and distractibility and hyperactivity (Calame, Fawer, & Claeys, 1986; Hunt, Tooley, & Harvin, 1982).

The commonsense conclusions we drew in the first edition of this text concerning the impact at-risk infants have on their environment still holds. It is easily observed

Table 4–1.   Medical problems present in ADD and control children

Variable	ADD	Control	X^2
Pre/Perinatal Factors	%	%	
1. Poor maternal health during pregnancy	26.4	16.2	6.45**
2. Young mother (under 20 at birth of child)	16.3	6.7	9.58**
3. At least one previous miscarriage	21.1	24.4	NS
4. First pregnancy for mother	42.7	32.8	4.34*
5. Rh factor incompatibility	14.9	12.4	NS
6. Prematurity (8 months or earlier)	7.9	5.4	NS
7. Postmaturity (10 months or later)	7.9	1.5	8.44**
8. Long labor (13 hours or more)	24.8	15.7	5.04**
9. Toxemia or eclampsia during pregnancy	7.8	2.5	5.23**
10. Fetal distress during labor or birth	16.9	8.0	7.07**
11. Abnormal delivery	26.6	20.2	NS
12. Low birth weight (under 6 lbs.)	12.2	7.8	NS
13. Presence of congenital problems	22.1	13.2	5.50*
14. Problems in establishing routines during infancy (eating, sleeping, etc.)	54.6	31.7	24.00**
15. Health problems during infancy	50.9	29.2	22.19**
Developmental Milestones			
16. Delay in sitting up	.4	0	NS
17. Delay in crawling	6.5	1.6	5.05*
18. Delay in walking	1.5	.5	NS
19. Delay in talking	9.6	3.7	4.76*
20. Delay in bladder control	7.4	4.5	NS
21. Delay in bowel control	10.1	4.5	4.18*
Childhood Illness and Accidents			
22. Presence of chronic health problems	39.1	24.8	10.47**
23. One or more acute illnesses or diseases in childhood	78.0	79.0	NS
24. Four or more serious accidents	15.6	4.8	9.73**
25. More than one surgery during childhood	27.3	19.5	NS
Childhood Health Status			
26. Poor general health	8.9	2.4	7.79**
27. Poor hearing	11.1	7.6	NS
28. Poor vision	21.6	13.4	4.86*
29. Poor coordination	52.3	34.9	13.92**
30. Speech problems	26.6	14.8	9.27**

Source: Hartsough, C. S., & Lambert, N. M. (1985). Medical factors in hyperactive and normal children. *American Journal of Orthopsychiatry, 55,* 190–201. Copyright 1985 by the American Orthopsychiatric Association, Inc. Reprinted by permission.

*p < .05.
**p < .01.
X^2 = Chi Squared

that this pattern of problems, especially in a first child, will have a significant negative impact on the relationship parents develop with their child. New parents may feel guilty due to their inability to calm or comfort this child; this may result in overly permissive or solicitous behavior. Other parents may feel angry and either consciously or unconsciously reject their child or perceive the child as damaged goods. One parent, after a miserable first week, went so far as to contact the hospital to make certain she had in fact brought home the right child. In 1974, D. W. Winnicott wrote that most mothers are good enough for most children. An infant at risk presents a challenge to even the best and most competent parents. In response to a difficult infant, many parents become frustrated, angry, irritated, or anxious. These responses will have a negative impact on the type of relationship the child and parent are able to develop with each other. An impaired parent-child relationship will certainly have an effect on the child's future development. Disharmony in the early mother-child relationship of children later diagnosed with behavioral problems consistent with ADHD has been observed in longitudinal studies (Battle & Lacy, 1972). On top of these problems there is the potential for negative or inappropriate parenting. Mothers of young children with ADHD have also self-reported experiencing a higher level of stress in parenting and feelings of lower self-esteem. Mash and Johnston (1983b) reported that the greater the level of these two variables, the more inaccurate were mothers' perception of their child's problem. Additionally, the hereditary nature of ADHD frequently results in impulsive, easily overaroused parents bearing offspring with similar problems. This unfortunate pairing of similar temperament in parents and child places the at-risk infant in even greater jeopardy of beginning a long chain of negative interactions with the environment. These additional factors cannot help but have a cumulative negative impact on the child's development and personality. As Emmy Werner eloquently described in 1994, over time almost every mild to moderate biological risk can be mediated by life experience. Thus, for many children with early signs of ADHD, the lack of support their parents receive as well as the lack of an active effort to build in protective factors may set the stage for a cascade of behavioral, developmental, and emotional problems to come.

PRESCHOOLERS

The overactive, temperamental infant frequently becomes the hyperactive, noncompliant preschooler (Barkley, 1978, 1990a). Yet the identification of ADHD in preschool children is extremely complex. Although the *DSM-IV* guidelines provide a ceiling of age 7 when the symptoms must have been observed, they do not provide a lower limit or cutoff under which the diagnosis should be made with caution. However, it is important for practitioners to recognize that when focused attention is defined as the time the child spends engaged with a specific object, there is a 98% increase in time spent engaged in focused attention between 2.5 and 3.5 years of age (Ruff & Lawson, 1990). In 1985, Campbell cautioned that the practitioner must draw the line between the 3-year-old presenting with age-appropriate behavior that may be typically vigorous and unrestrained, and a child presenting a pattern of overactivity, impulsivity, and inattention that is clinically significant. As S. Campbell (1985) notes:

Preschoolers, who are learning about the world and how to master its complexities, are expected to exhibit boundless energy, to attend readily to the new and novel, and to demonstrate unrestrained enthusiasm and exuberance. When, therefore, does a shift in activity and interest signify curiosity and exploration and when does it reflect a too rapid change in focus and an inadequate investment of attention? When does excitable and impatient behavior indicate an age-appropriate need for external support and limit setting and when does it suggest a failure to internalize standards necessary for the development of self-control? (p. 407)

The practitioner must be aware that symptoms of ADHD may reflect an exaggeration of age-appropriate behavior in toddlers.

The erratic nature of ADHD symptoms and their variability as a function of situation makes the practitioner's job with preschoolers that much more difficult (Whalen & Henker, 1980). ADHD is a disorder in which the severity of the presenting problems results from an interaction of the child with the demands made upon the child by the environment: it is the adults in the child's environment who determine the severity of the problem. A multitude of environmental variables can influence a preschool child's behavior. "The child who is an absolute terror in preschool may be relatively restrained when alone with his mother; another hyperactive child may function well in the peer group, but run wild in the supermarket where the temptation to sample everything in sight overwhelms his limited capacity for self-control" (S. Campbell, 1985, p. 408). Environmental factors to which parents significantly contribute, as opposed to biological factors, have been found to be the best predictors of young children's sustained attention (Schneider & Hans, 1996). These authors argue that external factors may play a more important role in regulating attention than previously thought. Children's behavior continues to be evaluated based on the impact it has on the adults in the lives of children; differences among adults lead to differences in reports of problems. The perceived unpredictability of the ADHD child's behavior is extremely frustrating for parents. Perplexed parents are frequently unable to understand the causes of the child's behavior. It is at this age that they begin what becomes an almost Quixote-like quest: to find the insidious cause of this behavior, in the erroneous belief that identifying the cause will lead to an eradication of the problem.

S. Campbell (1985) further points out that "differences in knowledge attribution and tolerance levels influence how the child's behavior is construed and whether typical behavior is defined by parents as problematic or problematic behavior is seen acceptable" (p. 408). Preschoolers basically exhibit two types of problems: those that annoy adults and those that worry them. Referrals of preschoolers are frequently influenced by the nuisance value of the child's behavior. Therefore, children with nondisruptive problems at preschool age are rarely referred unless they are significantly developmentally delayed. But because the nuisance value of the child's behavior is in part interpreted by parents, it is not uncommon for the practitioner to see extremely distressed parents concerned about a child temperamentally not much more difficult than average; the child is a challenge to those parents because of their rigid, unrealistic expectations. Conversely, it is also common to see parents perplexed not by the child's abnormal behavior but by the negative response expressed by nonfamilial adults in the child's life; frequently in those situations, multiple family members experience

ADHD: nothing happens on time or with any organization, so the fact that this child presents in a similar manner is not at all distressing to that family. Finally, some parents with fairly normal temperament and expectations bring very disruptive, hyperactive preschoolers in for assistance because this child is extremely disruptive to the family, even in the face of normal expectations.

Additionally, despite the increasing and large volume of literature in the field of ADHD, the majority of research does not focus on children under age 6. S. Campbell (1985) notes a similar pattern is reflected in referrals for ADHD. Parents concerned about ADHD problems in preschoolers are still frequently advised that these problems are transient and will be outgrown. Although it is well recognized that some preschool problems do in fact represent transient phases, this has been erroneously interpreted and generalized so that symptoms observed in preschoolers are dismissed by many practitioners as having little prognostic significance (L. Robins, 1979). With the increasing community awareness and knowledge of ADHD, parents are less willing to accept this explanation. Research data suggest that ignoring these signs, especially in the later preschool years, results in the loss of valuable treatment time (Cohen, Sullivan, Minde, Novak, & Helwig, 1981). Studies also suggest that 60% to 70% of children later diagnosed as ADHD were identifiable as the result of their disruptive behaviors during their preschool years (Barkley, 1981b).

Thomas, Byrne, Offord, and Boyle (1991) epidemiologically followed a large population of 4- and 5-year-old Canadian children. They noted a low incidence of parent-reported behavioral problems. Of the eighteen symptoms that were reported significantly more frequently for males, most related to disruptive behavior. No significant relationship was found between negative life events and significant behavioral problems. There was, however, a significant relationship subsequently between high scores for behavioral problems and negative family life events in the 6- to 11-year-old group. This study provides strong empirical evidence of hyperactive behavior in nearly one in ten child preschoolers in a community-based sample. Again, the issue of complex variables contributing to a single behavior is not well understood or agreed upon. Compared to preschoolers with attention deficit problems, for example, preschoolers with attention deficit plus aggression had families with more restrictive fathers, siblings who retaliated aggressively, and mothers who reported more physical aggression directed to their partners and more verbal aggression received (Stormont-Spurgin & Zentall, 1995). Negative, inconsistent parental behavior and high levels of family adversity have been associated with the emergence of problems in preschool years and in fact predict their persistence into school age (S. Campbell, 1995). Greater severity of peer problems also appears to predict greater risk for later childhood behavioral problems.

As discussed, a higher percentage of preschoolers with ADHD present with speech and language problems than in the normal population (L. Baker & Cantwell, 1987). It has also been repeatedly observed that children experiencing language problems are at significantly greater risk to develop a wide range of behavioral problems (Cantwell & Baker, 1977; Cantwell, Baker, & Mattison, 1981; Cohen et al., 1989). Ornoy, Uriel, and Tennenbaum (1993) suggested that delayed speech development may be one of the earliest clinical indicators of risk to receive an ADHD diagnosis. Beitchman (1987) hypothesized that there may be a specific subgroup of language-delayed hyperactive preschoolers. Love and Thompson (1988), in a study of 116 preschool children referred for behavioral problems, found that fifty-six out of seventy-five children diagnosed as having a language disorder also met the diagnostic criteria for an attention deficit disorder. These authors also found that fifty-six out of eighty-five children diagnosed initially as experiencing attention deficit disorder experienced a language disorder. Finally, the risk of psychiatric disorder, especially ADHD, has been suggested as being greatest among children with general linguistic impairment as opposed to those experiencing specific problems with articulation or comprehension (Beitchman, Hood, Rochon, & Peterson, 1989).

Preschool children with ADHD with speech and language problems typically present difficulty in three areas (Ross & Ross, 1982). First, they have difficulty with covert speech: they do not appear to develop the capacity to carry on an internal conversation, to reason, and to solve problems. It is unclear if this is a result of their impulsivity or if their lack of internal conversation contributes to the observation of impulsivity. Second, they have problems with overt speech: they do not develop effective communication skills and tend to impulsively act without thinking and without talking. Finally, these children typically have difficulty changing from a tactile means of dealing with the world to a visual means (Funk & Ruppert, 1984). Infants learning about the world prior to the acquisition of significant language and the ability to provide verbal labels must touch, feel, and taste things as a means of gaining information. Once effective language is established, words can take the place of tactile, sensory input. Typically, ADHD preschoolers continue to need to touch and feel things and people as a means of gaining sensory input from their environment. They often do so in an impulsive way, which further contributes to their problems. O'Callaghan, Williams, Anderson, Bor, and Najaman (1996) examined the relative predictive importance of adverse biological events and social disadvantage in young children with mildly abnormal or borderline language comprehension. Social disadvantages were strongly associated with both moderately abnormal and borderline language comprehension, although measures of biological risk were of limited importance in both mildly abnormal and borderline language comprehension groups. Thus, in this study, none of the common and readily measurable risk factors similar to those gathered by Hartsough and Lambert (1985) were associated with children's performance on a Picture Vocabulary Test. The risk of mild impairment was greatest in children whose mothers were more likely to be younger, less educated, and less economically advantaged, and had two or more children. The risk was less for older, well-educated mothers. Thus, biological adversity for this factor is only weakly associated with outcome. This study generally supports the conclusions of Sameroff and Chandler (1985) that social disadvantage and psychological factors are major determinants of development in children.

Preschoolers with ADHD are frequently impulsive, noncompliant, and fearless. The small group experiencing the inattentive type of ADHD often go undiagnosed during these years. In contrast, the combined and hyperactive-impulsive groups present with a combination of boundless energy and poor judgment. They experience more accidental poisoning and trips to the emergency room (Stewart, Thatch, & Freidin, 1970). The irregularity of their behavior creates a marked degree of family stress. Often, neither the threat of punishment nor the promise of reward has an impact on the child's behavior. Parents frequently misinterpret the child's repeated inability to benefit from intervention as purposeful rather than the result of impulsive, nonthinking behavior. This negatively impacts the child's capacity to move from behavior bound by external consequences to being internally directed.

During the preschool period, most children are developing basic foundational social skills. Preschoolers with ADHD frequently do not; although they have not developed well-set, negative patterns of social interaction, they are simply unable to integrate effectively with their peers. Only one out of five normal children experiences social problems during the preschool years (Campbell & Cluss, 1982), yet these authors found that inattentive and hyperactive children demonstrated a disproportionate rate of aggressive interactions with their peers. In 1992, Alessandri reported that in a group of 4- to 5-year-olds, those with symptoms of ADHD engaged in less overall play and greater functional or sensorimotor play. They also engaged in more transitional behavior and were less competent, attentive, and cooperative with peers during group activities. Again, as will be discussed repeatedly throughout this text, multiple developmental and environmental variables often interact with symptoms of ADHD to impact outcome. For example, children with communication disorders have been found to engage in fewer positive social interactions and converse with peers less often during nonplay activities (Gurainick, Connor, Hammond, Gottman, & Kinnish, 1996). These children were also less successful in their social bids and appeared to be less directed with their peers. Nonetheless, these children with delayed language were able to sustain group play, minimize conflict, join ongoing activities, and respond appropriately to social bids of others. These latter skills are often reported to be inefficient in preschoolers with ADHD symptoms.

Silverman and Ragusa (1992) conducted a short-term longitudinal study to determine whether self-regulation in 4-year-olds could be predicted from child and maternal measures obtained when children were 24 months of age. Criterion behaviors assessed at 4 years were very similar to symptoms of ADHD. At the 24-month child measures, maternal ratings of the child's impulsivity and attention span plus an objective measure of the ability to delay gratification were the most effective predictors. Maternal negativity predicted the criterion behaviors and maternal child-rearing attitudes were also effective predictors, even after controlling for the child's emotionality as a possible determinant of maternal attitudes. These results support the multifaceted contributions to children's behavior, but also that parental behavior exerts a significant impact on children's behavior.

Campbell, Ewing, Breaux, and Szumowski (1986) conducted a follow-up study of parent-referred 3-year-olds with early signs of hyperactivity and other externalizing behaviors and same-age controls. Results from maternal reports, cognitive and laboratory assessments, and teacher-report measures combined with classroom observations indicated that approximately half of the problem children have adjustment difficulties at home, at school, and with peers. One-third of these children met the criteria for attention deficit disorder. Maternal reports, teacher questionnaires, and observational measures discriminated between the normal and affected groups. However, differences were accounted for primarily by subjects who demonstrated persistent problems. Although laboratory measures obtained at three years did not differentiate improved subjects from those who continued to have problems, maternal ratings of initial symptom severity did discriminate.

Atkins, Vetere, and Grayson (1995) evaluated temperament as a predictor of whether children have sleep problems. Environmental factors were controlled in this study by the selection of toddlers with and without sleep problems from very similar environments. Results found a significant difference in the temperament profiles of children with and without sleep problems: children with reported sleep problems were more likely to obtain a more difficult report of temperament.

Finally, in 1990, Solanto suggested that medication treatment ameliorates the original attentional deficits but is not sufficient to remediate the skills gap and negative emotional sequelae of ADHD in later-age children. Thus, it is suggested that children with ADHD identified and treated early, preferably in their toddler ages, are less likely to manifest a discrepancy between IQ and achievement, to experience emotional difficulties and fall out as the result of their impulsivity, and in general fare better than those whose treatment began at a later age. Although an attractive belief, it has not been borne out by the clinical research. McGee, Feehan, et al. (1990) have demonstrated that a group of children identified with ADHD symptoms during their preschool years tended to have more severe symptoms, more adverse social factors, and, despite intervention, tended to fare worse into their later childhood and adolescent years.

In summary, it appears that there is a group of infants whose behavior reflects a lack fit in regard to qualities of temperament that may make them much more difficult to parent. The cause-and-effect relationship of children's temperament impacting parents or environmental factors, including parents' style and temperament impacting the developing behavior of their infants, is still not well understood. The practitioner is cautioned to utilize a bidirectional approach, accepting the fact that the behavior and temperament of each family member influences others. The practitioner is also reminded that a significant percentage of children receiving a diagnosis of ADHD are described by their parents, even during the infancy years, as being more difficult than siblings.

MIDDLE CHILDHOOD

By school age, the child with ADHD begins to venture out into the community and no longer has the family to act as a buffer. Behavior once dismissed as immature is no longer tolerated or accepted. ADHD symptoms clearly follow children longitudinally. Reports on the five-year diagnostic and symptom outcome of nearly 100 2- to 6-year-old children who attended a therapeutic preschool found that ADHD was one of the two most likely diagnoses to continue at follow-up; the other was developmental delay. Given that both problems have strong biological underpinnings, this continuity of diagnoses is not surprising. Within the home setting, the child with ADHD is a negative force, the inconsistency in the child's behavior escalating family stress. The child with ADHD is typically perceived by his or her siblings as the source of family problems; thus, a pattern of negative reinforcement intensifies. Frequently, children with ADHD are described as beginning but never completing tasks at home. This results in parents acting as negative reinforcers, bringing the child back to task and leaving once the task is begun. The parents' attention to the child's off-task behavior acts as an aversive consequence that is then removed when the child returns to task. This operationally defines negative reinforcement. Children with ADHD tend to receive very high doses of negative versus positive reinforcement or even punishment. Children with ADHD then become victims of their temperament, which makes it difficult for them to persist on task, and victims of their learning history, which reinforces them for beginning but not completing tasks.

Practitioners should be aware that at least among clinic-referred children with ADHD, hyperactive-impulsive symptoms have been reported to decline through age 12, but inattentive symptoms do not (Hart et al., 1995). The rate of decline in hyperactive-impulsive symptoms has been reported as independent of the amount and type of treatment received. As others have noted, the earlier age of diagnosis for ADHD appears to be more predictive in suggesting later conduct problems, especially among children whose ADHD symptoms remain constant over a four-year period.

The myriad problem symptoms ADHD causes during the childhood years has yet to be completely defined or well understood. For example, Gayton, Bailey, Wagner, and Hardesty (1986) suggested that children with ADHD were accident-prone, a finding substantiated by Pless, Taylor, and Arsenault (1995) in a study of 5- to 15-year-old children presenting in emergency rooms. Utilizing a compendium of evaluative procedures, these authors found statistical differences in mean scores on a continuous performance test for these accident victims in comparison to a set of normal controls. The authors argue that these data offer subjective evidence of vigilance deficits and problems with attention in children with injuries compared to controls. It is important to note, however, that although efforts were made to control for sociodemographic and clinical measures, the rate of conduct and behavioral problems was not controlled for. As discussed earlier, at least one longitudinal study has suggested that symptoms of conduct disorder are more predictive of trips to the emergency room than ADHD.

Problems of impulsiveness leading to inattention and overactivity progress to a myriad of difficulties within school settings. As DuPaul and Stoner (1994) note, a struggle with independent seatwork, consistent school performance, deficient study skills, poor test performance, disorganized notebooks, desks, and reports, and lack of attention to lectures and group discussions are all frequently reported for children with ADHD. These children disrupt the classroom, though often in nonpurposeful ways. They may call out, anger easily, or express their frustration in other overt, maladaptive ways. As in the home setting, a pattern of negative reinforcement develops at school. In the school setting, teachers' negative reinforcement leads to a focus on misbehavior rather than on termination of the behavior. This further disrupts the classroom by having a disinhibitory effect on other children for whom the competing task of schoolwork is only slightly more attractive than watching the child with ADHD (Ross & Ross, 1982).

Over twenty years ago, it was demonstrated that children with ADHD qualities exhibit lower rates of on-task behavior during instruction and independent work periods than those of their peers (Abikoff, Gittelman-Klein, & Klein, 1977). As a consequence, they may have fewer opportunities to respond to academic material and complete fewer independent assignments than their classmates (Pfiffner & Barkley, 1990). Even if they do not experience specific learning disabilities, by high school, as will be discussed, they slowly fall behind in academic tasks requiring practice for proficiency

(Cantwell & Baker, 1991). In the absence of a specific learning disability, children with ADHD often experience problems with nonphonetic spelling, math facts, and the execution of written language. Regarding the latter, they may possess good ideas but exhibit poor grammar, punctuation, and sentence structure.

Faraone, Biederman, Lehman, and Spencer (1993) evaluated the intellectual and school performance of children with ADHD and their siblings. The children with ADHD were more likely to have learning disabilities, repeat grades, be placed in special classes, and receive academic tutoring. Their performance was weaker than siblings on measures of intelligence. Comorbid disorders, however, appeared to be responsible for the lower IQ scores. Intellectual impairment was also increased among siblings of children with ADHD, providing converging evidence that ADHD is familial.

As discussed in Chapter 3, some have argued that children with ADHD are intellectually less competent than their same-age peers (Palkes & Stewart, 1972). The majority of the data, however, suggest it is lack of efficient use of intellect rather than lack of intellect that is the problem. The experienced practitioner is well aware that the interpretation of normative tests must be based on an understanding of the child's approach to those tests. Typically, children with ADHD present with a normal range of intellectual skills; weak performances on specific tasks result from the impact of impulsivity on test taking rather than an innate lack of intellect (Ross & Ross, 1982). Researchers accurately concluded over twenty years ago that children with ADHD present with a range of intellectual skills similar to that in the normal population (Prinz & Loney, 1974). The more intelligent child with ADHD often manages to survive the elementary school years and may not be referred for ADHD problems. This child's superior intellect allows him or her to compensate for an inability to remain on task; this child may not work very long, but time spent on task results in completed, frequently correct work. In junior high school, however, even the intelligent child with ADHD cannot consistently keep up with the demands of education; it is frequently during these years that intelligent children with ADHD are identified due to problems with their school performance.

In a nonreferred sample of eighty-nine children with a mean age of 9 who had been retained during their academic careers, there was a high frequency of abnormal scores on an index of sustained attention in comparison to controls who had never repeated a grade (Gordon et al., 1994). In a second sample of 200 6- to 11-year-olds who had been referred for evaluation of ADHD, eighty-five with a history of grade retention had significantly lower scores than nonretained subjects on a similar measure of sustained attention. Using a multi-informant, multimethod assessment procedure, Gordon et al. demonstrated that referred and nonreferred children who had been retained perform more poorly on a CPT than those who had never failed a grade. Retained youngsters tended to have a lower score on the index most related to sustained attention rather than impulsiveness. In the ADHD subgroup, nonretained youngsters had higher IQ scores than retained children. However, IQ was not correlated with performance on the CPT. IQ alone did not adequately explain increased retention, as the mean was still low, within the average range. Retained children for both groups tended to come from poor families; as such, economic status was suggested as playing a role in academic achievement. The authors concluded that the ability to pay attention as measured by a CPT is significantly involved in overall academic success. The data argue that certain process deficits such as managing impulsiveness and attention, rather than specific academic skills deficits, may be at the root of academic delays and subsequent grade retention.

As briefly discussed in Chapter 3, early research suggested that children with ADHD underachieve academically in elementary school relative to their same-age peers (Cantwell & Satterfield, 1978; Minde et al., 1971) and experience a higher incidence of learning disabilities (Lambert & Sandoval, 1980; Silver, 1981). In 1976, Safer and Allen estimated problems with hyperactivity in 80% of the learning-disabled population. Holborow and Berry (1986) estimated 41% of a learning-disabled population exhibited symptoms of attention deficit. Yet Halperin, Gittelman, Klein, and Rudel (1984) found that only 9% of a sample of 241 children with attention deficit had a reading disability. In 1986, Shaywitz and Shaywitz suggested that during the elementary school years, a majority of children with ADHD achieve as well as the normative population. They followed 445 children from kindergarten through third grade: 11% of the children with attention deficit were classified as learning disabled in either reading or arithmetic; conversely, 33% of the learning-disabled group satisfied the diagnostic criteria for attention deficit. These authors concluded that although the majority of children with attention deficit do not experience a specific learning disability, the small percentage of children with attention deficit who are learning disabled constitute a significant group in the learning-disabled population. Shaywitz and Shaywitz concluded that although the overlap between learning disability and attention deficit is real, it is not reasonable to believe that all or even the majority of children with attention deficit have a learning disability. They further concluded that although many investigations indicated a relationship between learning disabilities and attention deficit, the nature of the relationship is not well defined, and that these are two separate disorders, one not necessarily predicting the other. For the purposes of this text, children with a learning disability are considered to experience one or more specific cognitive deficits that impair their ability to learn. Non-learning-disabled children with ADHD described as underachieving have the capacity and potential to learn but may not do so because of the cumulative impact of impulsivity. The daily classroom performance of children with ADHD therefore may not reflect their capabilities or actual skill attainments. Thus, it is reasonable for the practitioner to assume that although there is a higher incidence of learning disabilities among children with ADHD than in the normal population, not all inattentive children present with learning problems (Cantwell & Satterfield, 1978). Conversely, the majority of learning-disabled children do not experience ADHD. By the later school years, however, the cumulative impact of the child's temperamental quality and an inability to complete tasks cannot help but have a negative effect on academic achievement. Meichenbaum and Goodman (1969) suggested in fact that this pattern may begin in the first few years of school. They reported that impulsive kindergartners performed more poorly than reflective kindergartners on a range of basic cognitive skills. Achenbach (1975) defined associative responders as children who tend to impulsively free-associate on intellectual and achievement tasks. He hypothesized that these children perform more poorly at school because of their inability to develop effective reasoning skills and begin demonstrating a slow but cumulative decrease in intellectual development and achievement. Eventually, the lack of efficiency in these skills as well as a lack of practice in effectively utilizing whatever skills have been acquired further impair intellectual and academic achievement.

In the elementary classroom setting, children with ADHD are typically described as daydreaming. Careful observation suggests that these children are not daydreaming but simply interested in tasks other than what the teacher is focusing on (Douglas, 1972). Their inability to invest in the task at hand due to their impulsivity results in the engagement of significantly more nonproductive activity during work and free time than their same-age peers. Their uneven, unpredictable pattern of behavior and work completion is equally distressing to the classroom teacher. A child with ADHD may complete a task one day but be unable to complete a similar task the next day; the resulting interpretation is that the child can do it and simply needs to try harder. For children with ADHD, this misinterpretation frequently results in increased pressure, usually in the form of negative reinforcement by the teacher on the child. The teacher's inability to recognize that impulsivity leads to inconsistent performance results in a marked degree of frustration for both teacher and child when tasks are not completed.

Inattentive children are well aware of their classroom, home, and social inabilities (Glow & Glow, 1980). By 5 years of age, most children develop the capacity to recognize that attention to a task is important for task success (Flavell, Green, & Flavell, 1995). Thus, it is not surprising that children with ADHD report an awareness of more problems than their peers in the realms of general behavior and school and social interactions (Hoza et al., 1993). There also appears to be a trend for children with ADHD to display more external attributions of positive and negative achievements over time. Thus, when most children become more internal with age (they recognize that they have control over their behavior), children with ADHD appear to become more external, especially for negative events (the perception that they have little control over their destiny; Borden, Brown, Jenkins, & Clingerman, 1987). Milich & Okazaki (1991) studied learned helplessness in a group of boys with ADHD. They tended to give up on tasks quicker than normal controls, were more frustrated by tasks than controls, and therefore completed fewer tasks. The authors suggested that children with ADHD did not become mastery-oriented and, over time, in the face of a frustrating task, learned to give up quicker. Nonetheless, there are conflicting data concerning the long-term impact ADHD has on children's self-awareness and perceptions of self. Boys with ADHD have been found to view themselves as no worse than others on self-perceived competence and global self-worth (Hoza et al.). Tarnowski and Nay (1989) suggest that locus of control scores, although demonstrating a heightened external locus for children with learning disability, were not significantly different from normal controls for a group of children with attention deficit disorder. Thus, there appear to be sufficient data to suggest that children with ADHD, although they may be ever-optimistic, due to their heightened frustration and frequent failure they may be at greater risk to develop low self-esteem and specifically an external locus of control leading to weaker task mastery.

Sociometric studies point to children with ADHD as rarely being chosen by peers as best friends, partners in activities, or seatmates. Studies in which children with no previous knowledge of each other were placed together for play periods resulted in the majority of children after the play period nominating the child with attention deficit as the child they did not want to play with again (Pelham & Milich, 1984).

Children with ADHD have been reported to receive the poorest teacher ratings for academic competence on the Child Behavior Checklist among clinic-referred children (McConaughy, Achenbach, & Gent, 1988). Barkley, DuPaul, et al. (1990) reported that children with ADHD had a 1 in 3 risk of being retained at least one grade before reaching high school. As in families, the child with ADHD has a coercive effect on teacher behavior. S. Campbell, Endman, and Bernfeld (1977) found that the overall rates of negative teacher-child interactions involving normal students were higher in classrooms that contained children with attention deficit. Teachers have also been found to be more intense and controlling in their interactions with attention deficit males than with other male students (Whalen, Henker, & Dotemoto, 1981). Abikoff, Courtney, Pelham, and Koplewicz (1993) suggest that teacher bias toward children with ADHD is unidirectional in nature. Teachers tend to rate hyperactive behaviors accurately when the child behaves like a child with ADHD; however, ratings of hyperactivity in children with ADHD were spuriously inflated when children were more disruptive and oppositional. Teachers rated oppositional and conduct problems accurately regardless of the presence of hyperactive behavior. Thus, as has been previously discussed, symptoms of ADHD may be catalytic in many ways, but at least in this particular study, disruptive behaviors may also be catalytic in certain circumstances in inflating complaints of ADHD symptoms.

Sanson, Smart, Prior, and Oberklaid (1993) evaluated groups of 8-year-olds with hyperactivity, aggression, or both. Variables of temperament, behavior, school performance, socioeconomic status, and life stress were evaluated. The two aggressive groups, particularly the hyperactive-aggressive group, were more difficult in temperament, had more behavioral problems from infancy, and had less optimal environments. In contrast, the pure hyperactive group showed more problems than did the comparison control group only from 3 to 4 years of age forward. All three clinical groups had poor academic performance in comparison to controls. These findings appear to be consistent with a transactional model of development in which aggression with or without hyperactivity emerges when difficulty in infancy interacts with a stressed environment. Hyperactivity, when unassociated with aggression, may emerge later from poor self-regulation when faced with societal, especially school, demands. The pattern of group differences found suggests that risk indicators for specific patterns of later maladjustment may well be identifiable, allowing for early intervention.

Children with ADHD compared to normals display higher frequencies of talking (Whalen, Henker, Collins, Finck, & Dotemoto, 1979), negative verbal and nonverbal behavior (Pelham & Bender, 1982), problem behaviors (Whalen, Henker, Collins, McAuliffe, & Vaux, 1979), aggression (Campbell & Paulauskas, 1979), and difficulty adapting to situational demands (Whalen, Henker, Collins, McAuliffe, et al., 1979). From a temporal perspective, sequences in behavior suggest that children with ADHD show a greater tendency to engage in social withdrawal following aggression and a pattern of limited interaction characterized by less reciprocal verbal interaction than normal children at play (Clark, Cheyne, Cunningham, & Siegel, 1988). Melnick and Hinshaw (1996) investigated social goals and behavior in a small-group peer-interaction task that elicited goals of competition, cooperation, and having fun; the association between children's social goals and their overall peer acceptance was also measured. In their self-reports, ADHD high-aggressive boys prioritized trouble seeking and fun at the expense of rules to a greater extent than did both ADHD low-aggressive and comparison boys. Observers judged ADHD high-aggressive boys as seeking attention more strongly and fairness less strongly than the other two groups. As Stein, Szumowski et al. (1995) have demonstrated, children with ADHD may choose less than desirable social goals not due to a lack of adaptive skill, but due to impulsivity. The actions of male children with ADHD appear to exert negative catalytic social effects on the behaviors of even normal children when settings require mutual problem solving and interdependent goal attainment (Granger, Whalen, Henker, & Cantwell, 1996). Further, Waldman (1996) reports that aggressive boys are characterized by a hostile social perceptual bias but not a general social perceptual deficit. Aggression appears to be linked to specific and relevant rather than global and general patterns of perceiving environmental cues. Hostile boys tend to respond aggressively following nonhostile behaviors. In this study, at least, when efforts were made to control attention and impulse qualities, the aggressive boys' tendency to respond aggressively following nonhostile interactions remained constant. As M. Atkins (1985) suggested, appropriate treatment goals and interventions cannot be developed unless global aspects of a child's functioning and an understanding of the impact of the environment in which the child lives are developed.

As discussed in Chapter 3, children with ADHD demonstrate a variety of linguistic weaknesses that likely contribute to their cognitive and subsequent academic development. They exhibit a higher incidence of dysfluent behavior (e.g., misarticulations), as well as disorganized speech on tasks requiring verbal explanation (Hamlett, Pellegrini, & Conners, 1987; Zentall, 1985). Moffitt and Silva (1988) suggest that deficits in verbal functioning may be chronic and more likely to present in adolescents, not necessarily with ADHD, but with a history of severe aggressive or antisocial problems.

Berk and Potts (1991) compared the development of spontaneous private speech and its relationship to self-control in boys with ADHD 6 to 12 years of age. They were observed in classrooms while engaged in math seatwork. The children with ADHD engaged in more externalized self-guiding and less inaudible internalized speech than the normals. These findings suggested that children with ADHD had a special need for learning environments that permit them to use spontaneous private speech actively and freely instead of programs that require children to model, rehearse, and internalize an adult's self-instructional statements. Medication that ameliorates ADHD supplemented by behavioral interventions addressing disruptive behavior is suggested as the most promising route for promoting inner speech, task-facilitating behavior, and focused attention for children with ADHD. In 1993, Berk and Landau found that children with learning disability used more task-irrelevant private speech than normal controls, an effect that was especially pronounced for the comorbid learning-disabled, attention deficit group. Use of private speech was setting- and task-specific.

The records of ninety-nine children ages 9 to 11 years referred to a school problems clinic were examined by Sandler et al. (1989). Thirty-two of this group were identified with attentional problems and a second group were identified without attentional problems. The groups did not differ in age, gender, socioeconomic status, IQ, or achievement ratings. In ratings of social problems, children with attention problems had a higher prevalence than children without attention problems: nearly 50% of the attention problem group, in comparison to only 20% of the nonattention problem group. The severity of those social problems was also higher among children with ADHD. Males in general had greater social problems than females. Among children with ADHD, proficiencies in each of two verbal fluency tasks, sentence formulation and category naming, were positively related to social problems over and above the severity of ADHD. Among children without attention deficit, eye-hand coordination was negatively related to social problems; neither measures of attention nor the verbal fluency items were related to social problems in this group. Social problems often, but not invariably, accompany ADHD. Impulsive children with strong verbal fluency may be prone to excessive talking, peer alienation, and then social failure.

In a follow-up study, Sandler, Hooper, Watson, and Coleman (1993) again grouped children based on teacher reports of inattention versus those of learning disorders and other school problems. The children with attentional deficits had greater peer problems; cognitive and attention problems were related to peer problems over and above the effects of hyperactivity. Among children with attentional difficulty, proficiency in tasks of verbal fluency was significantly predictive of peer problems: the more competent these children were verbally, the less successful they were socially.

Humphries, Koltun, Malone, and Roberts (1994) asked teachers to evaluate the language functioning of ninety-five males, 6 to 14 years of age, identified as having attention problems, learning disability, or average achievement. The three groups did not differ significantly in their frequency of articulation problems. Significantly more boys with attention problems were rated as having pragmatic difficulty than the other two groups. These boys were also viewed as having a higher frequency of receptive/expressive language problems than were the average-achieving boys but not compared with learning-disabled boys. The learning-disabled and inattentive males did not differ in their ratings for pragmatic problems. However, more learning-disabled and inattentive males were perceived as having receptive/expressive language problems. The average incidence of all types of language problems was highest for the attentional problem males at 42% with poor pragmatics, representing their most frequently rated language deficit. In this group, pragmatic difficulties appeared to be characterized by greater problems maintaining versus initiating conversation compared with the other two groups. This difficulty was positively associated with teacher ratings of impulsivity in these males. It has also been suggested that the deficiencies of children with ADHD are consistent with higher order executive function deficits while the deficiencies of children with reading disability are consistent with deficits in the basic semantics of language processing (Purvis & Tannock, 1997).

Finally, Gottschalk (1984) evaluated speech samples of boys with ADHD and normals. The boys with ADHD had significantly higher mean scores than the normals for cognitive impairment, social alienation–personal disorganization, and total depression. On the eight depression subscales, boys with ADHD had significantly elevated scores on hopelessness, self-accusation (a cluster comprised of shame, guilt, and inward hostility), and psychomotor retardation. These authors suggest that based on analysis of the speech of children with ADHD, the disorder may be associated with cognitive impairment, increased general psychiatric morbidity, and depression.

Zentall (1988) suggested that setting and task conditions have an impact on the behavior and performance of children with ADHD. Children with attention problems were more spontaneously talkative than their classmates during transitions and nonverbal tasks but were less talkative when they were asked to tell stories. These findings and those attributable to the story comparison were interpreted in line with an optimal stimulation theory, suggesting that minimal stimulation input (delays and nonelicited conditions) precipitates excessive verbal activity from children with attention deficit. Production deficiencies, on the other hand, are specific to the type of stimulus input to be processed. Stories requiring organization and planning without the external structure or salience of visual cues produced production deficiencies. Ironically, then, children with ADHD talk too much when they are not supposed to and not enough when they need to.

DuPaul and Stoner (1994) suggest a number of reasons why children with ADHD have a higher rate of academic problems. These include academic skills problems contributing to ADHD, ADHD leading to delayed academic achievement, and some unspecified third variable leading to both ADHD and academic problems. It is also important to note that much of the research in ADHD and academic problems does not clearly delineate between skills deficits causing learning disability and performance decrements as the cumulative impact of ADHD symptoms. In a normative public school sample, Coie, Dodge, and Coppotelli (1982) found that disruptive and aggressive behaviors, even when they occurred at what were considered subclinical levels, were associated with problematic social adjustment in elementary-school-age children.

In a national sample of over 7,000 children, below-average attentiveness was associated with significantly lower performance on tests of intelligence (specifically, measures of vocabulary and visual reasoning) and on tests of achievement (specifically, word reading and arithmetic problem solving; Nelson & Ellenberg, 1979a). In this study, hyperactivity was associated with differences in cognitive development and aggressivity in males but not in females. Hyperactivity, however, was associated with lower performance on measures of visual problem solving.

Nussbaum, Grant, Roman, Poole, and Bigler (1990) suggest that the majority of variance in test performance for children with attention deficit is accounted for by a negative association among age, full-scale IQ, and academic differences, and a positive correlation between age and scores on social withdrawal and poor communication. These results suggest that older children with ADHD are more likely than younger children to experience academic and social or emotional difficulties. In this study, 41% of the population met the discrepancy criteria for learning disabilities. However, the younger child with attention deficit was less likely to be diagnosed with learning disabilities than the older child when a discrepancy formula was used. In this sample, there was a significant relationship between age and poor math performance, social withdrawal, and poor communication skills. Gillberg, Matousek, Petersen, and Rasmussen (1984) suggest that perceptual motor weaknesses represent a problem independent of ADHD.

Douglas and Benezra (1990) report that poor performance on memory tasks requiring organization, deliberate rehearsal strategies, sustained strategic effort, and careful consideration of response alternatives is characteristic of children with ADHD. In contrast, children with learning problems without ADHD demonstrate a more global pattern of language or verbal processing deficits. Males with ADHD have been reported as less likely than others to benefit from metamemory knowledge when strategy is less salient and involves effortful reorganization of stimuli (Voelker et al., 1989). It is likely the impulsive qualities of the ADHD group that results in this problem. Problem solving is only in part reliant on memory strategy; however, it is considered an executive, cognitive task. As previously discussed, there is debate concerning whether children with ADHD demonstrate executive skill deficits or their impulsivity exerts a negative impact on their ability to make efficient use of the executive skills they possess. In comparison to normals, children with ADHD demonstrate weaker memory and poorer executive process regarding instructions and strategies and have greater difficulty communicating strategies and task information (Hamlett et al., 1987).

The impact of ADHD on academic performance has been questioned in regard to actual skills deficit versus inefficient use of skills. Data support the conclusion that the more pervasive ADHD symptoms are (e.g., occurring across situation), the more impact they have on verbal IQ and reading difficulties (Boudreault et al., 1988). Zentall and Ferkis (1993) suggest that the mathematical achievement of youth with ADHD is lower than their peers'. Cognitive ability, including memory and reading, contribute to the comprehension skills needed to eliminate extraneous information, handle multiple operations, and transform verbal information within problems (Zentall & Meyer, 1987). Slow computation affects problem solving by increasing attentional load. When IQ and reading skills are controlled, true math deficits are specific to mathematical concepts and problem types. The authors suggest that given the symptomatic problems of children with ADHD, attentional cues, novel instructions, and the opportunity to actively participate while learning are all necessary for children with ADHD. Further, the format and content of various teaching approaches appear to be factors that affect the attending behaviors of children with ADHD during learning tasks (Ford, Poe, & Cox, 1993).

As part of an ongoing series of studies, Zentall and colleagues (Zentall & Smith, 1992) have attempted to determine whether children with ADHD as a group have certain preferences in learning style. In this particular study, the preference for stimulation was evaluated. Overall, children with ADHD and normals report optimal learning conditions with greater social interaction and movement. Older children in both the ADHD and normal groups prefer more background auditory and visual stimulation than younger children. More severely disordered children also reported preferences for more background auditory stimulation during math fact tasks and story problems. The computer was most often selected for practicing math facts, and hard copy materials were selected for problem-solving tasks. The authors suggested that an analysis of individual response preferences can provide even more precise information of optimal learning conditions for specific children.

Higher rates of impulsivity have been associated with more conflict with peers and higher rates of disruptive behavior disorders (Halperin et al., 1995). Socially, children with ADHD are described as immature and incompetent. Even their best efforts frequently fail. They may struggle to initiate and maintain friendships with their classmates (Guevremont, 1990). Peer rejection and neglect are common for this group. Guevremont suggests that disturbed peer relationships in this group are due to inattentive and impulsive behaviors disrupting social performance. In the ADHD nonimpulsive group, however, disturbed relationships may occur as much from errors of omission (not understanding social graces) as those of commission (aggression). Children with ADHD may lack basic social skills or possess skills but not use them efficiently because of their impulsivity. The former more often occurs in the nonhyperactive group; the majority of those with hyperactivity-impulsivity demonstrate the latter. Social skills deficits result in a pattern of high-incidence, low-impact behaviors. These children may be incompetent in their ability to join an ongoing conversation or take turns. The group of inattentive but not impulsive children are not terribly aversive, but these qualities result in these children being less popular and not sought out socially. On the other hand, the majority of impulsive children with ADHD present with a pattern of low-incidence, high-impact behaviors. These are frequently aggressive behaviors that may not occur with great frequency but result in the child with ADHD being more rejected and disliked by others (Pelham & Milich, 1984).

Perceived conflicts in friendships have been reported to be associated with multiple forms of school maladjustment in males, including high levels of school loneliness and avoidance and lower levels of school liking and engagement (Ladd, Kochenderfer, & Coleman, 1996). For both males and females, validation and perceived support from classmates predict improvement in children's school attitudes. These authors suggest that their findings are consistent with the hypothesis that the relational features of children's classroom friendships yield psychological benefits or liabilities that in turn affect their general adjustment and development.

Aggression has been a popular topic of study in children with ADHD (Melnick & Hinshaw, 1996; Waldman, 1996). The aggressive group with ADHD exhibit higher rates of nonpurposeful and hostile aggression in comparison to controls (Atkins & Stoff, 1993). Children described as aggressive or shy by teachers are also likely to be rated as having poor concentration and later disruptive problems (for review see Yoshikawa, 1994). Anthony, Mirsky, Ahearn, Kellam, & Eaton (1988) suggest that shy children described as having trouble concentrating experience significant difficulty on sustained detection tasks. In contrast, children identified as impaired in concentration and abnormally aggressive were reported as performing poorly on sustained inhibition measures. The latter reflects impulse control. In a playroom setting, Buitelaar, Swinkles, DiVries, van der Gaag, and van Hoof (1994) found that hyperactive children were characterized particularly by squirming and changing seats. There were weaker contemporal contingencies between their behavior and conversational speech of the experimenter than for the nonhyperactive children.

The development of aggressive behaviors between 2 and 8 years of age was studied in a sample of children with aggressive behavior selected from 2,400 infants participating in a longitudinal study (Kingston & Prior, 1995). The children were divided into four groups: those with stable aggressive behavior, those with transient aggression, those with aggression after age 5, and a comparison group of nonaggressive children. Children with stable aggressive behavior were characterized by difficult temperament, hostile sibling interactions, maternal perception of the child as difficult, and harsher child-rearing practices. Children whose early aggression decreased over time and those who became aggressive only after entering school could not be reliably classified by selected family members. Teacher ratings of temperament factors of task orientation and reactivity, as well as ability ratings, correctly classified 74% of the children whose aggression began at school age.

Children with persistent aggressive behavior differed from those who improved, predominantly in terms of symptom severity. Problems with aggression can be identified in early development, and a significant percentage of aggressive children are at risk for continuing social and scholastic problems. This overall pattern is consistent with Patterson, Reid, and Dishion's (1992) theory of a cascade model in the development of aggressive and antisocial behavior in children. In the earliest stage of this model, a combination of child temperament with parental response factors sets the scene for the continuation of the cascade in which development of cycles of coercive family processes escalate. As children grow older, these patterns are continued and reinforced in wider environments through peer rejection, poor academic performance, low self-esteem, and later association with similarly deviant peers. Temperament plays a key role in contributing to this problem. Disruptive children, especially those who are aggressive, can be identified at very early ages, and this behavior persists into the school years and almost certainly beyond (White, Moffitt, Earles, Robins, & Silva, 1990).

Rebok, Hawkins, Krener, Mayer, and Kellam (1996) investigated the moderating effect concentration problems have on the impact of a classroom-based preventive intervention directed at aggressive and shy behaviors in an epidemiologically defined sample of a 1,000 urban first-grade children. Concentration problems, aggressive behavior, and general behavior were assessed by a structured teacher interview in the fall and spring of first grade. Children with the highest ratings of concentration problems in the fall had the highest levels of teacher-identified aggression problems in the spring. The intervention reduced aggressive and shy behavior in children regardless of fall concentration levels. Males but not females in the intervention condition with high concentration problems also had higher levels of spring aggression than those without such problems. However, they also showed the greatest reductions in aggressive behavior from fall to spring. These results suggest that aggressive behavior is modifiable in children with concentration problems and provides further evidence of the etiological significance of concentration problems in the development of maladaptive behavior. Improving classroom concentration may maximize intervention for the prevention of aggressive behavior (Barrish, Saunders, & Wolfe, 1969). At least among males, concentration problems make an independent contribution to the impact of intervention. In the Rebok et al. (1996) study, early concentration problems led to aggressive and shy behavior and poor achievement in both genders and to depression in females.

An indepth review of the socialization process, a careful analysis of the problems ADHD children experience, and an intervention model will be presented in Chapter 14. However, a brief discussion of social problems in ADHD is warranted here. To understand why learning-disabled boys with ADHD were so unpopular, data on physical attractiveness were gathered by Bickett and Milich (1990). Erhardt and Hinshaw (1994) also evaluated the influence of naturalistic social behaviors and nonbehavioral variables on the development of peer status in unfamiliar ADHD boys and normals. Physical attractiveness, motor competence, intelligence, and academic achievement constituted the nonbehavioral variables; social behaviors included noncompliance, aggression, poor social actions, and isolation. From the first day, the boys with ADHD displayed clear differences in their social behavior. The children with ADHD were overwhelmingly rejected. Prosocial behavior independently predicted friendship ratings during the first week; the magnitude of the prediction, however, was small. In contrast, boys' aggression or noncompliance strongly predicted negative nominations, even with nonbehavioral factors. Group status, ADHD versus comparison, and other social behaviors were controlled statistically. Some authors have argued that social difficulties are increasingly viewed as central to the psychopathology of ADHD (Hinshaw, Heller, & McHale, 1992). Social rejection of children with ADHD appears to develop after only brief periods of peer exposure. Findings of these authors as well as Bickett and Milich (1990) suggest that rejection of children with ADHD stems from excesses in aggressive, noncompliant, and disruptive behavior rather from deficiencies in prosocial behavior. This fits the explanation for the social problems of children with ADHD as rooted in impulsivity: they know what to do but don't often do what they know. Also noteworthy for the Erhardt and Hinshaw (1994) study was the fact that in all of the predictions, nonsignificant contributions were made by the nonbehavioral variables of intelligence, academic achievement, physical attractiveness, and motor competence. Although aggression occurred infrequently, in under 6% of the ADHD sample and 3% overall, it made a substantial independent contribution to the predictions of both friendship ratings and negative peer nominations. Although verbal and physical aggression made significant contributions, those made by physical aggression were large in magnitude and independent of the influence of verbal aggression. Noncompliant behaviors, those that disrupted ongoing activities, violated rules, or annoyed others without being aggressive, occurred far more frequently than did aggression but made similar contributions to the predictions of peer acceptance or rejection. These children were rated as less popular by their peers. Situational demands as well as judgments of physical attractiveness appeared to play a role in accounting for these differences. Children appear to form opinions about other children very quickly. Children with ADHD may have most difficulty in situations requiring that they initiate and structure interactions as well as attend and listen carefully to their partner; physical attractiveness may further insulate or contribute to risk in this group of children.

Hubbard and Newcomb (1991) found that ADHD-normal play dyads engaged in more solitary play and less associative play than normal dyads. Subsequent analyses of play patterns revealed that the ADHD-normals had problems in their progress to developing a plan to play, in sustaining associative play, and in avoiding withdrawal after rough-and-tumble play. The ADHD-normal dyads also differed in the quality of verbal interaction, as evidenced in their lower levels of verbal reciprocity and affective expression. Even when the children with ADHD received stimulant medication, the ADHD-normal dyads were not as successful as the normal-normal dyads in their initial encounters. The preponderance of the evidence suggests that rejection by peers continues for children with ADHD even when they receive psychostimulant medication (Pelham & Bender, 1982); in other words, the peer status of medicated children with ADHD is not raised to the level of normal children (Whalen et al., 1989). Even when medication-related improvements are reported, these changes occur in social behavior as opposed to sociometric status. The change also appears to vary depending on the social context in which the behavior is assessed (Whalen, Henker, Swanson, et al., 1987).

Wheeler and Carlson (1994) compared the social functioning of children with ADHD inattentive type in comparison to those with ADHD hyperactive-impulsive type. These authors emphasized aggression, anxiety, impulsivity, social processing, and communication as additional independent variables that impact the social success of children with ADHD. Further, these variables may make certain ADHD symptoms (e.g., impulsivity) more likely to contribute to poor social outcome. Swain and Zentall

(1990) compared the behavior of liked and disliked children with ADHD in high- and low-structured play settings. For the most part, differences observed did not depend on setting or gender comparisons. Children with ADHD were more active, talkative, and physically off-task than their peers. They also made fewer positive social statements. Disliked children with attention deficit made more negative statements with accompanying negative physical interactions. When playing with disliked inattentive children, normal partners became more negative and active, were less talkative and cooperative, and engaged in more solitary play than when playing with a normal child. Normal children more frequently directed positive verbalization to their normal partners and less frequently ignored their initiations than they did with ADHD partners. The authors conclude that although the data demonstrate important qualitative dimensions for treatment targets, it may be difficult to teach disliked children with ADHD to make their actions and verbalizations task-relevant. The authors also suggest that a primary target for practitioners is to train disliked boys with ADHD to engage in positive rough play and males and females with ADHD to make positive verbal statements and requests.

Using a model of social competence, Moore, Hughes, and Robinson (1992) evaluated the social-information-processing abilities of five groups of males classified as hyperactive, rejected, accepted, nonhyperactive/rejected, or nonhyperactive/accepted. Peer nomination procedures were used to determine sociometric status for these 350 third- and fourth-grade boys. Hyperactive/rejected males demonstrated a unique constellation of social-information-processing deficits relative to nonhyperactive subjects. Nonhyperactive/rejected subjects contributed more attributional errors relative to the other groups of subjects; in addition, hyperactive/rejected subjects exhibited excessive encoding and cue utilization deficiencies compared to subjects in the remaining four groups. Not surprisingly, children with ADHD tend to be intrusive, boisterous, annoying, and generally aversive to peers and others. They are not particularly responsive to using problem-solving strategies in conflict situations (Landau & Moore, 1991).

Social skill's deficits or low rates of positive interpersonal behavior correlate with peer acceptance but not necessarily with peer rejection. Factors that determine peer liking may be different from those that determine peer dislike (Hartup, 1983). Negative behavior such as aggression typically correlates strongly with peer rejection but less strongly and less consistently with peer acceptance (Bierman, 1986). King and Young (1982) report that ratings of hyperactivity and aggression contributed only common variance to the prediction of sociometric ratings, suggesting that these two problems may be associated with peer relations only through an underlying common dimension of externalizing behavior. In this study, teacher ratings of inattention and passivity are strongly predictive of poor peer acceptance. However, complaints of hyperactivity appeared to have a distinct influence on children's peer relations, similar to that of aggression. The authors also noted that some problems of ADHD, such as inattention and passivity, may have an impact on peer neglect distinct from peer problems fostered by aggression.

The relationship among emotional expressiveness, empathy, and prosocial behaviors was assessed by Roberts and Strayer (1996). In populations of 5-, 9-, and 13-year-olds, a variety of measures were used to assess these three skill areas. Emotional expressiveness, insight, and role taking were strong predictors of empathy. Empathy in males, in turn, was a strong predictor of prosocial behavior. In contrast, females' empathy was related to prosocial behavior but not cooperation with peers. Impulsivity was hypothesized to negatively affect all three areas, increasing the risk of social problems for those children.

Flicek (1992) evaluated the social status of boys with learning and attention problems in second through sixth grade. The results indicated that serious problems with peer rejection, peer popularity, and social behavior were strongly related to the combined occurrence of ADHD and a learning disability. The connections were weaker in the groups of children experiencing either disorder alone.

The middle childhood years are when most children with ADHD are referred and subsequently diagnosed and treatments attempted. Current review of the literature suggests that practitioners need to be cognizant of the myriad impacts symptoms of ADHD have on children's functioning and mastery at this age, as well as the additional, co-occurring problems that may also impact and lead to similar negative outcomes at home, at school, and in the community. The diagnostic process must be sensitive to these data. In light of the present data, lack of treatment success following diagnosis during these years may be due to lack of attention to comorbid problems and lack of understanding of treatment benefits and failures.

ADOLESCENCE

Recent research has supported a diagnostic continuity in the features familiality and patterns of comorbidity in children and adolescents receiving diagnoses of ADHD (Biederman, Faraone, Taylor, Sienna, Williamson, & Fine, 1997). However, over the past twenty years, research in the field of adolescent mental health has increasingly focused on assessing the impact of early childhood factors on adolescent outcome not just diagnostic continuity. Thus, the focus has been as much on how problems or protective factors in young children contribute to symptom maintenance and development in adolescence as on measuring adolescent adjustment. Development in adolescence is considered continuous but transitional; for most, changes occur slowly and gradually without dramatic variability. Childhood problems related to the individual (e.g., impulsivity and ability to delay gratification, inability to self-regulate emotions, low harm-avoidance, need for stimulation, low frustration-tolerance, predisposition toward aggressive behavior, low aptitude or intelligence, and deviant peers), the family (e.g., economic deprivation, health problems, poor parental supervision, family conflict, low parent involvement, high rates of violence, alcoholism) and the school (academic failure, low aspirations and goals, peer rejection, ineffective monitoring and management of students, poor adaptation to school, poor attendance) are hypothesized as most likely leading to abnormal adolescent problems, including antisocial behavior (Weiner, 1990; for review, see Gregg, 1996). Weiner suggests that, for the most part, adolescents are emotionally stable, do not necessarily experience high rates of psychiatric problems, and do not rebel against their families or society in large numbers. Contrary to popular belief, they also are not necessarily high risk takers and do not perceive themselves as more invulnerable when comparing themselves to other people than do adults (Quadrel, Fischoff, & Davis, 1993).

Normal adolescence may not reflect a terrible period of turmoil, as once thought (Nicholi, 1978). Successful passage through these years is typically based on good achievement academically, socially, or in an extracurricular activity such as athletics. Children with histories of ADHD as well as those with other psychiatric disorders have increased risk of not succeeding in these areas. Even the athletic adolescent with ADHD may have difficulty remaining on a team—not due to lack of competence, but to an inability to show up on time for practice and closely follow the coach's instructions.

A recent issue of the *Journal of the American Academy of Child and Adolescent Psychiatry* published three studies assessing the present and future risk of children with ADHD developing more severe problems during their adolescent years (Biederman, Faraone, Milberger, Jetton, et al., 1996; MacDonald & Achenbach, 1996; E. Taylor, Chadwick, Heptinstall, & Danckarets, 1996). Each of these studies represents small parts of long-term projects from three well-respected research groups, two in the United States and a third (E. Taylor et al., 1996) in Great Britain. Two utilized dimensional systems for assessment of problems, and the third utilized a categorical system (Biederman, Faraone, Milberger, Jetton, et al., 1996). Biederman et al. examined 140 children with ADHD and 120 normal controls at baseline and four years later during early adolescence; 65% of the ADHD children had comorbid ODD and 22% had CD. Among those with ODD, 32% had comorbid CD. All but one child with CD also had ODD that preceded the onset of CD by several years. The group with all three diagnoses, not surprisingly, had more severe symptoms and a wider range of symptoms than either of the other groups. ODD without CD at baseline assessment in childhood did not increase the risk for CD at the four-year follow-up by midadolescence. Further, the ADHD-only children, though they had slightly greater risk of developing major depression, bipolar, and anxiety disorders than controls, had less risk than those with the combined diagnoses.

E. Taylor et al. (1996) completed a follow-up study of a large community survey of 6- to 7-year-olds identified by parent and teacher ratings as demonstrating pervasive hyperactivity, conduct problems, a mixture of both, or neither. The children were later investigated at ages 16 to 18 years. The authors concluded that hyperactivity was a risk factor for later development, even allowing for the coexistence of conduct problems. These authors concluded that the sequelae of hyperactivity included much greater risk of other psychiatric disorders, persisting hyperactivity, violence and other antisocial behaviors, as well as peer problems. They concluded that there is likely a developmental pathway through which hyperactivity raises the probability of impaired social development, leading to additional psychiatric disorders independent of the existence of conduct problems.

MacDonald and Achenbach (1996) tested the extent to which attention problems and the continuation of early comorbid conduct problems accounted for poor outcome scores on the Child Behavior Checklist and related measures three and six years after initial assessment. A sample representative of the United States was assessed three times over six years. Children deviant in both attention and conduct problems scored significantly higher on behavior problems at outcome than did those deviant in only attention or conduct problems. After controlling for initial conduct problems, initial attention problems made little unique contribution to later conduct problems. Predictive patterns were similar across gender and age groups.

MacDonald and Achenbach conclude that "children who present with attention problems without conduct problems have a relatively low risk of developing severe and persistent antisocial behavior, at least through age twenty-two years" (p. 1237). E. Taylor et al. conclude that pervasive hyperactivity is a "risk factor for later development, even allowing for the co-existence of conduct problems" (p. 1225). Biederman, Faraone, Milberger, Jetton, et al. provide support to suggest that although ADHD in itself may be a risk factor for later disruptive problems, it is the comorbidity of ODD and CD that incurs the greatest outcome risk. As these and studies to be reviewed below strongly suggest, practitioners need to be aware that it is the combination of ADHD with the early onset of ODD progressing to CD that most powerfully contributes to the myriad adolescent problems a small group of children with ADHD eventually experience. The incidence of comorbid psychiatric disorders at follow-up in the Biederman et al. study appears in Figure 4–1.

In a six-year longitudinal study of children 4 through 11 years of age, three groups were selected based on parent behavioral ratings at two-year intervals (Ferdinand &

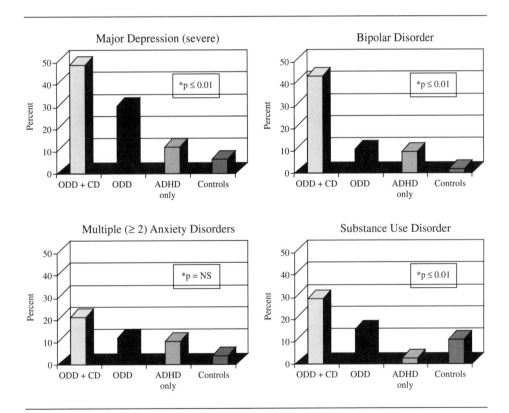

Figure 4–1.   Incidence of comorbid psychiatric disorders at follow-up

Source: Biederman, J., Faraone, S. V., Milberger, S., Jetton, J. G., Chen, L., Mick, E., Ross, W., Greene, R. W., & Russell, R. L. (1996). Is childhood oppositional defiant disorder a precursor to adolescent conduct disorder? Findings from a four-year follow-up study of children with ADHD. *Journal of the American Academy of Child and Adolescent Psychiatry, 35,* 1193–1204. Used with permission.

ODD = oppositional defiant disorder; CD = conduct disorder; ADHD = attention-deficit hyperactivity disorder. * Omnibus tests include ADHD subjects only.

Verhulst, 1994). These were groups of children whose symptoms persisted, decreased, or increased. The majority of children whose overall level of psychopathology persisted over time obtained lifetime *DSM-III-R* diagnoses classified as externalizing, including ADHD, ODD, and CD. The majority of children with the overall level of psychopathology decreasing obtained lifetime diagnoses classified as internalizing, including anxiety, major depression, and dysthymia. Children with initial behavioral scores in the normal range whose problem scores increased received lifetime diagnoses that were neither predominantly externalizing nor internalizing. This study appears to demonstrate that the majority of disordered children with the poorest outcome demonstrate aggressive, antisocial, or other disruptive behaviors during the early childhood years, whereas disordered children whose functioning improved over time have problems reflecting internalizing difficulty. Although this study is somewhat in contrast with these authors' earlier reports (Verhulst & van der Ende, 1993), they are consistent with data reflecting that disruptive disorders have the longest diagnostic presence during the child and adolescent years (Campbell & Ewing, 1990; Loeber, 1982; Moffitt, 1990). In the Verhulst and van der Ende (1993) study of children initially scoring deviant on behavioral checklists, 33% were still deviant six years later. Interestingly, continuity of problems was similar for both internalizing and externalizing difficulties; that is children whose problems were initially internalizing continued to have internalizing problems, and likewise for children with externalizing problems.

In a four-year follow-up of a community sample of children ages 4 to 12, family dysfunction and social problems significantly predicted the persistence of one or more psychiatric disorders four years later (Offord et al., 1992). Low income predicted one or more psychiatric disorders among children free of disorders four years earlier. Children initially with ADHD were likely to have attention or conduct problems four years later; the rate of conduct disorder with ADHD was dramatically higher in children who had originally presented with attentional problems than in normals. Approximately four of ten children with attention deficit in 1983 had one or more disorders at ages 8 to 16. In nearly 85% of cases, these children were classified as having attention problems at follow-up; 40% of the attention-disordered children had one or more psychiatric disorders four years later. These data strongly argue that one of the factors predicting persistence of a disorder is the disorder itself. The authors hypothesize that the strength of a relationship between risk and disorder is much reduced in longitudinal analyses compared to cross-sectional analyses. In cross-sectional analyses, chronic and thus severe cases of the disorder are included, where the relationship between disorder and correlate will be especially strong. Cross-sectional analyses also include those cases where the disorder has led to the presence of the correlate. When these two factors are removed, as they are in longitudinal work, the relationship between risk factor and disorder is consistently weakened. Further, the mechanism by which low income has its effect in predicting psychiatric disorders is not clear. However, the data argue strongly that conduct disorder has a very poor outcome, with a significant group of children with conduct disorder retaining the diagnosis into their adolescent years.

Most recently, Ferdinand, Verhulst, and Wiznitzer (1995) confirmed their earlier work (Ferdinand & Verhulst, 1994) and evaluated the four-year course of behavioral and emotional problems from adolescence into young adulthood. Almost 40% of the adolescents who were classified initially were still deviant four years later. There was no significant difference in the continuity of internalizing versus externalizing problems; all types or problems tended to persist to a similar degree. This held true for symptoms of ADHD as well.

In a mixed race, longitudinal sample of 104 14-year-old males, the relative power of aggression, low peer acceptance, and race in predicting a broad range of adolescent outcome and behavior was evaluated by Lochman and Wayland (1994). Outcome was evaluated through self-report and peer, teacher, and independent observer ratings. Preadolescent levels of aggression were predictive of males' subsequent adolescent involvement with illicit substances and delinquent activity. Aggression and low peer acceptance served as predictors of teacher, peer, and independent observer ratings of externalizing and internalizing problems at follow-up. The results also indicated that peer ratings of social acceptance and aggressive behavior operate differently across different racial groups. It also appears that aggressive and socially disliked males are at risk for engaging in a progressive series of behaviors that increase their engagement in contranormal behavior. The moderating effects of race may be due to biases in elementary-school-peer ratings and mixed race samples. They may also represent actual differences in how risk markers operate with males of different racial status; these authors suggested that race, at least in this sample of Caucasians and African Americans, is an important moderating variable on how risk factors operate. Early childhood aggression, for example, was found to have a direct impact on African American males' subsequent levels of depression and anxiety, whereas aggressive Caucasian males did not display this level of internalized distress. In contrast, early dislike by male peers served as a predictor of self-esteem difficulties for Caucasian but not African American males.

Twenty years ago, alcohol abuse was reported as higher in populations of children with histories of attention problems (Blouin, Bornstein, & Trites, 1978). Parental substance abuse, low socioeconomic status, and oppositional child behavior have been found to be key factors in male progression in the adolescent years to conduct disorder (Loeber, Green, & Keenan, 1995). Physical fighting, although not a symptom of oppositional defiant disorder, is suggested by these authors as a progressive risk factor and should be targeted in preventive interventions. The authors suggest that ADHD is implicated in the early onset of conduct disorder under age 10 but not in later-onset conduct disorder. The longitudinal relationship between conduct problems and attention deficit suggested that for outcome risks such as alcohol, tobacco, and illicit drug use, it is early conduct disorder problems that more powerfully predict later substance abuse, either in the presence or absence of ADHD (Lynskey & Fergusson, 1995). Yet, other authors have suggested that aggression, inattention, hyperactivity, and impulsivity represent a single, superordinate risk factor. In this study of 183 10- to 12-year-old boys with or without a family history of substance abuse, these four factors appeared to combine to provide best prediction of risk. The greater the family history of these four factors, the more risk for substance abuse (Martin, Earleywine, Blackson, & Vanyukov, 1994). Milin, Halikas, Meller, and Morse (1991) found that 91% of a group of adolescent juvenile offenders experienced conduct disorder, present in both substance-abusing and non-substance-abusing offenders. Higher rates of ADHD and aggressive conduct disorder were present in those offenders who abused drugs and alcohol (over 50%); 39% of the substance abusers versus 14% of the non-substance-abusing offenders demonstrated comorbid psychiatric diagnoses when conduct and oppositional disorders were partialed out. Interestingly, only 23% of all abusers had a history of ADHD, whereas 58% had a history of oppositional defiance and 68% had a history of aggressive conduct disorder.

It seems clear that myriad symptoms and problems beyond those defining ADHD, as well as environmental and experiential issues, combine to contribute to adolescent outcome. It was initially suggested that many of the primary symptoms of ADHD diminished in intensity during the adolescent years (Weiss & Hechtman, 1979). Nonetheless, even twenty years ago, a careful review of related research indicated that adolescents with ADHD continued to experience significant problems (Ackerman, Dykman, & Peters, 1977; R. T. Brown & Borden, 1986; Huessy, Metoyer, & Townsend, 1973; Mendelson, Johnson, & Stewart, 1971; Milich & Loney, 1979; Thorley, 1984; Weiss, Minde, Werry, Douglas, & Nemeth, 1971). In some studies, 20% (Sassone, Lambert, & Sandoval, 1982) to 60% (Satterfield et al., 1982) were involved in antisocial behavior when the normal occurrence was reported as 3% to 4%. Loney (1986) pointed out that the high prevalence of antisocial problems may reflect the initial comorbidity of attention deficit with conduct disorder. In other studies, 35% with ADHD were suspended from school at least once, when the normal occurrence was reported as 8% to 10% (Ackerman et al., 1977). Finally, it has been found that by the adolescent years, four-fifths of those with ADHD are behind one or more years in at least one basic academic subject (Cantwell & Satterfied, 1978; Loney, Kramer, & Milich, 1981). These early studies consistently suggested that symptoms of ADHD as well as the secondary problems resulting from ADHD persist, intensify, and become increasingly complex during the adolescent years.

E. Wender (1995) has suggested that the typical behavioral manifestations of ADHD during adolescence are somewhat different from the *DSM-IV* criteria. Wender's description is presented in Table 4–2. This author argues that feelings of restlessness, interruption during conversation, academic underachievement, immaturity, low frustration tolerance, and disobedience are characteristic symptoms of ADHD during the adolescent years.

Early studies suggested that a significant proportion of adolescents with ADHD may also present symptoms of depression (Cantwell, 1979) as well as problems maintaining social contact (Waddell, 1984). Adolescents with ADHD were reported as lacking confidence and experiencing greater feelings of helplessness relative to their peers, consistent with our earlier discussion of locus of control (Battle & Lacy, 1972). Given their long history of lack of success and not meeting the expectations of the environment, this is not a surprising pattern. Zagar, Arbit, Hughes, Busell, and Busch (1989) in a sample of almost 2,000 adjudicated delinquents with an average age of 14 years reported that 9% met the criteria for attention deficit disorder with hyperactivity, and 46% met the diagnostic criteria for attention deficit without hyperactivity. The hyperactive adolescents also demonstrated greater scholastic delays than the nonhyperactive group.

Among the most often-cited outcome studies for ADHD is the series of articles published by Barkley and colleagues as the result of a longitudinal study of a group of

Table 4–2.   Typical manifestations of ADHD during adolescence

Fidgety behavior and feelings of restlessness
Interrupting and intruding
By talk and actions

Academic underachievement due to:

   Failure to finish work
   Disorganization
   Failing to sustain attention
   Not listening or following directions

Immaturity:

   Excessive "fooling around"
   Inappropriate silliness
   Overreaction to teasing or normal peer interactions

May see:

   Talking back
   Frequent fighting
   Disobedience
   Low frustration tolerance

Source: Wender, E. H. (1995). Attention-deficit hyperactivity disorders in adolescence. *Journal of Developmental and Behavioral Pediatrics, 16,* 192–195. Used with permission.

nearly 100 children with symptoms of ADHD and a group of normal controls followed over sixteen years through their childhood and adolescent years into adulthood (Barkley, Anastopoulos, Guevremont, & Fletcher, 1992; Barkley, Fischer, Edelbrock, & Smallish, 1990, 1991; Fischer et al., 1990, 1993). Nearly 80% of those identified as having attention deficit disorder initially received a diagnosis of ADHD eight years later; 60% had either oppositional defiant disorder, conduct disorder, or both at the eight-year outcome assessment. Rates of antisocial acts were considerably higher among the attention deficit than normal groups, as were cigarette and marijuana use and negative academic outcome. The presence of conduct disorder accounted for much, though not all, of the negative outcome. Family status of those with ADHD was much less stable over time than in the normal subjects. Based on these results, Barkley, Fisher, Edelbrock, and Smallish (1990) suggested that the use of three antisocial symptoms listed in the *DSM-III-R* and consistent with the *DSM-IV* may be too restrictive in identifying conduct disorder in teenagers. Using a normal sample to calculate the cutoff that would place an adolescent at two standard deviations above the mean for delinquent behavior, these authors concluded that two of the thirteen criteria were sufficient. When this cutoff was applied, the number of those with ADHD meeting or exceeding the cutoff was 60%. Although the rate of antisocial outcome in this group was somewhat higher than in other studies, it is still fair to conclude that a significant minority of those with ADHD over time experience a progression to more serious disruptive problems. Although the rate among clinic-referred populations is higher, it is still significant among epidemiologic populations. Further, the group that began with ADHD and progressed to more serious conduct problems have a three times greater chance of failing a grade or being suspended and an eight times greater chance of being expelled or dropping out in comparison to the pure ADHD group. However, much of this outcome again appears to be contributed to by the development of conduct disorder. This was also true for substance abuse and exclusively true for expulsion from school, in which the pure ADHD group did not exhibit an expulsion rate different from normals. In general, it appears fair to conclude that children with ADHD, due to either their core symptoms or the development of other disorders, are at substantially higher risk for negative outcomes in psychiatric, social, legal, academic, and family functioning domains than normals. Again, differences in findings among studies likely result from a lack of control for risk and protective variables that contribute to resilience.

In their follow-up (Fischer et al., 1990), those with ADHD demonstrated impaired academic achievement, impaired attention and impulse control, and greater off-task, restless, and vocal behavior during an academic task compared to normal subjects. A limited set of frontal lobe measures administered did not differentiate these two groups, including the use of the Wisconsin Card Sort. Age did not interact with group membership. However, several measures demonstrated age-related declines in problems in both groups. Those with ADHD appeared to remain chronically impaired in academic achievement, inattention, and behavioral disinhibition well into their late adolescent years, and academic achievement declined over time. Differences from normal controls were most likely to be apparent when those with ADHD were administered tasks long enough to endure potential for boredom and when adult supervision was not immediately present to provide a discriminative stimulus to remain on task. Fischer et al. concluded that children with ADHD do demonstrate a developmental or maturational lag because these children do not appear to "catch up." Barkley, Fischer, et al. (1991) reported that those with ADHD continue to have more conduct and learning problems and exhibit more hyperactive, inattentive, and impulsive behaviors than controls. They were rated by their mothers as having more numerous and intense family conflicts. Mother–ADHD adolescent interactions displayed more negative and controlling behaviors and fewer positive and facilitating behaviors toward each other than in normal dyads. Interaction patterns were significantly related to patterns observed eight years earlier. Mothers of those with ADHD reported more personal psychological distress than other mothers. The presence of ODD accounted for much of the difference between those with ADHD and normals on interaction measures, ratings of home conflict, and, interestingly, ratings of maternal psychological distress. Barkley, Grodzinsky, et al. (1992) further studied the population, dividing those with ADHD into groups with and without oppositional defiance. Parents reported that both ADHD groups had more topics on which there was conflict and more angry conflicts at home than controls. The adolescents with ADHD and oppositional defiance reported many more conflicts, endorsed more extreme and unreasonable beliefs about their parent-teen relations, and demonstrated greater negative interactions during a neutral discussion. Mothers of these comorbid teens demonstrated a greater negative interaction during a neutral discussion, more extreme and unreasonable beliefs about their parenting relations, greater personal distress, and less satisfaction in their marriage.

Finally, within this population, Fischer (1990) reported that adolescent academic skills were related to childhood cognitive and academic competence, whereas school conduct was predicted by other variables, including early family stress. Duration of mental health treatment received often was negatively related to outcome, apparently serving as a marker variable for severity of disturbance in the child. Childhood hyper-activity-impulsivity and paternal antisocial acts were associated with later opposi-tional defiant behaviors. However, of the oppositional symptoms, only child defiance is perhaps indicative of a more severe type of oppositional defiant disorder: predicted later arrests. Emotional problems in this adolescent group were predicted by more special educational enrollment. Adolescent social competence was associated with parental personal competence, whereas maternal mental health status and outcome was related to variables unassociated with child adjustment. The authors suggest that although limited amount of variance in outcome was explained by the factors studied, the findings strongly argue that promoting family and parental competence as well as assessing and treating defiance and aggression in the preadolescent years stands the best chance of improving adolescent and subsequent adult outcome for children with ADHD. The authors concluded that by understanding childhood risk factors and pre-dicting developmental paths and outcomes, practitioners can be more effective advo-cates. Fischer (1990) writes that this knowledge

> (1) allows clinicians to better evaluate the type and extent of additional risks individual cases may be subject to when presenting for clinical assessment and management, (2) provide significant information needed in determining the nature and degree of treatments that may be brought to bear in such cases, (3) permits the counseling of par-ents of these children with realistic appraisals of what may lie in store for their children (and them) over time, (4) initiates the development of theoretical models as to the mech-anisms that may lead to these adverse (or successful) outcomes, and (5) provides for the possible testing of competing developmental causal models of these outcomes. (p. 324)

This series of studies makes a strong argument that family factors play a significant role in the adolescent and subsequent adult outcome of those with ADHD (for review, see S. Goldstein, 1996). Moffitt (1990) followed 435 boys from birth into their adoles-cent years. Correlates for delinquency included childhood antisocial behavior prob-lems, low verbal intelligence, reading difficulty, and family adversity. The boys with attention deficit and delinquency consistently fared worse on assessments of family adversity, verbal intelligence, and reading than nondisordered delinquent and pure at-tention deficit males. Their antisocial behavior began before school age and escalated at school entry, persisting into the adolescent years. The pure attention deficit group had normal family functioning, intelligence, and reading scores; they demonstrated only mild antisocial behavior in middle childhood. The delinquent-only boys showed no early risk from family, intelligence, or reading deficit and remained relatively free of conduct problems until the initiated delinquency at age 13. Persistence of criminal offending beyond adolescence was predicted to be quite powerful for the attention deficit plus delinquent males; often, this group developed antisocial personality.

Moffitt (1990) also noted that in a significant group of the pure ADHD cases, home and family conditions were actually slightly more favorable than those in the normal group. It is important to note that in this study, the pure delinquency group comprised 73% of all delinquents. It is unclear why this group suddenly develops antisocial behav-ior. The attention deficit plus delinquency group represented about half of all the atten-tion deficit subjects and one-quarter of the total delinquents. This group demonstrated no other negative developmental features. They began life with significant motor skill deficits and had the greatest level of family adversity; by age 5, they demonstrated stable, intellectual deficits and more problems with health. Parents of this group of children were four times more likely to have sought help for their son than any other group. Moffitt suggests that strong verbal skills, in good family circumstances, may help overcome the risk for delinquency associated with ADHD. Finally, in this longitudinal study, the most striking increase in antisocial behavior for the attention deficit group occurred between ages 5 and 7; school entry and reading failure coincided temporally with this exacerbation of antisocial behavior. It may be that differences in family environment make for significant differences in prognosis for children with ADHD.

Pelham (1991) suggests that adolescents with ADHD are more likely to abuse alcohol and other substances and when they do, are more likely to have serious problems than other adolescents. Based on Pelham's research, fathers of boys with ADHD are more likely to have alcohol problems than fathers in society as a whole. Pelham suggests that perhaps 50% of males with ADHD themselves develop problems with alcohol. He also suggests that adults with alcohol problems often have symptoms characteristic of ADHD. Pelham observed that when parents are given alcohol and then interact with their ADHD children, they tend to pay less attention to the child, give more commands, engage in more irrelevant talk, and generally increase the amount of physical contact. These effects are larger in fathers than mothers. However, both mothers and fathers while intoxicated appear to give less appropriate attention to their child: mothers increase their attempts to control the child, and fathers decrease their attempts. Thus, alcohol consumption in fathers results in more tolerance of the child and parental withdrawal, whereas in mothers it results in more interaction and conflict.

Hovens, Cantwell, and Kiriakos (1994) found in an inpatient setting that 85% of substance abusers versus 65% of non-substance-abusers demonstrated psychiatric comorbidity. Substance abusers had a higher incidence of dysthymia, major depression, social phobia, and a loose grouping of other diagnoses in which ODD, CD, and ADHD prevailed. Overanxious disorder was predominant among female and conduct disorder among male substance abusers. Psychopathology preceded or coincided with substance abuse except for major depression. No correlation between the severity and type of substance abuse and the number and degree of varying coexisting psychopathologies was found. Psychopathology in parents and siblings of substance abusers was similar to that of non-substance-abusers.

The literature has clearly demonstrated the comorbidity of CD and substance abuse (Bukstein, Brent, & Kaminer, 1989; Greenbaum, Prange, Friedman, & Silver, 1991). CD was diagnosed more frequently and ODD less frequently in a group of substance abusing, hospitalized patients (Grilo et al., 1995). Anxiety disorders were diagnosed less frequently in the substance abuse group, and borderline personality more frequently. There appears to be a higher rate of other psychiatric disorders in substance abusers; specifically, 29% of this group compared to 33% of the hospitalized non-substance-abusers had a history of ADHD. At least among adolescents considered for inpatient psychiatric care, ADHD is not a significant predictive factor for substance abuse (only 34%). In contrast, CD predicted substance abuse in 75% of the population.

In one of the most recent comprehensive outcome studies, Wilson and Marcotte (1995) followed a group of males and females 14 to 18 years old with a history of ADHD versus a group with other neurodevelopmental disorders. The groups were then subdivided based on the presence of CD. There were no significant gender differences in this population. The ADHD group had significantly lower academic performance and poor social, emotional, and adaptive functioning in comparison to the clinical controls. Cases with CD had significantly lower academic performance, greater externalizing behaviors and emotional difficulties, and lower adaptive functioning than cases without CD. Cases with CD fared far worse than clinical controls, and self-report measures of behavior, socialization skills, and alcohol and substance abuse were more negative. Although ADHD clearly is a risk factor for later adolescent problems, once again it appears that the presence of CD is the more powerful of the two in moderating outcome. Although Wilson and Marcotte concluded that their study lends further support to the hypothesis that "individuals with childhood diagnosis of ADD are at high risk for psychosocial, educational and adaptive problems in adolescence" (p. 584), in the absence of CD this risk appears to be minimal. This study is significant in that a group of clinical rather than normal controls was utilized, and still those with ADHD fared worse. Also, only 38% of the group continued to meet the criteria for ADHD, lower than the 43% reported by Lambert, Hartsough, Sassone, and Sandoval (1987) and significantly lower than the 80% reported by Barkley, Fischer, et al. (1990). Not surprising, the adolescents in this study reported fewer behavioral and psychological problems than their parents reported about them; however, this should not be interpreted as suggesting that adolescents with histories of ADHD are unaware of their problems. Schaughency, McGee, Raja, Feehan, and Silva (1994) found that adolescent self-reported attention difficulties at age 15 were clinically significant markers of adjustment difficulties for males and females. Self-reported attention problems at age 15 were associated with continued symptoms at age 18, adjustment difficulties, and adverse outcome. Thus, adolescents with ADHD may in fact be able to accurately report their symptoms and problems. It is likely that practitioners will encounter more difficulty with honest reporting in those adolescents experiencing more severe disruptive problems: the conduct-disordered group may underreport symptoms, where those with more severe internalizing symptoms, including depression, may amplify their symptoms as the result of strong feelings of helplessness.

Forehand, Wierson, Frame, and Kempton (1991) specifically evaluated the prevalence of ADHD in a group of incarcerated male adolescent delinquents; 75% of the group met the diagnostic symptom presentation for CD, whereas only 25% met the criteria for combined CD and ADHD. The results indicated that the combined group were arrested at an earlier age and had more total arrests than those in the former group; however, they did not have more criminal charges against them. The authors concluded that ADHD appeared to have an additive influence on the development and persistence of juvenile delinquency. Halikas, Meller, Morse, and Lyttle (1990) examined the role of attention deficit and conduct disorder symptoms and their role in substance abuse. Conduct disorder symptoms, specifically aggression but not ADHD, predicted substance abuse. These authors argue that the relationship of ADHD to substance abuse appears to be confounded by concurrent symptoms of aggression evident in a significant group of adolescents with ADHD. Finally, Gabel and Shindledecker (1992) hammer a final nail in the hypothetical coffin of ADHD as a primary cause of substance abuse based on their evaluation of hospitalized adolescents with severe aggressive problems. In this group of 348, 11% had received a diagnosis of ADHD, whereas CD was diagnosed in 81% and depression in 62%. Severe aggression correlated directly with parent history of substance abuse and the diagnosis of CD, but demonstrated only a weak link to ADHD.

Other authors have urged caution that practitioners not be misled by these studies into believing that most ADHD boys are not defiant or that ADHD males are not at risk for serious antisocial behavior such as arrests in later life (Satterfield, Swanson, Schell, & Lee, 1994). These authors predicted teenage arrests based on measures of childhood defiance in a population of ADHD males. Defiance ratings that were independent of hyperactivity were obtained on eighty-one drug-treated males with ADHD, fifty multimodality treated ADHD males, and eighty-eight normal controls. Official arrest data obtained on all subjects nine years later were used as an outcome measure. Subjects with ADHD with high defiance ratings had significantly higher felony offender rates than did subjects with low ratings. However, the subjects with ADHD with low ratings had significantly higher felony offender rates than did normal controls. The presence of minor antisocial features in young males with ADHD should be considered a risk factor indicating an increased probability that a particular child may progress to more serious adolescent conduct problems.

Researchers have also begun to examine outcome measures other than additional psychiatric conditions, delinquency, and substance abuse. For example, Barkley, Guevremont, Anastopoulos, DuPaul, and Shelton (1993) evaluated driving risks over a five-year period in adolescents with histories of ADHD. In general, these adolescents use less sound driving habits and had greater driving-related negative outcomes in all categories surveyed. They were more likely than controls to have had auto crashes, more crashes, more bodily injury associated with crashes, and to be at fault for more crashes than controls. They were also more likely to have received traffic citations and more citations than controls, particularly for speeding. The group of adolescents with ADHD with greatest comorbid disruptive disorders, particularly CD, appeared at the highest risk for deficient driving skills and habits and negative driving-related outcome.

Based on a series of longitudinal studies, Christopher Gillberg and colleagues (Gillberg, Gillberg, & Groth, 1989; Hellgren, Gillberg, Gillberg, & Enerskog, 1993) evaluated accidents and motor control in children with histories of attention deficit symptoms. Over a long-term basis into adolescence, more than two-thirds of children identified with attention problems no longer had clearly detectible motor problems by age 13, but they still had significantly prolonged complex reaction times. These authors also noted continuation of mild coordination problems and clumsiness, as well as an increased incidence of substance abuse and accidents in the attention deficit population. Further, Nada-Raja et al. (1997) report in a sample of over 900 adolescents followed longitudinally, that symptoms of ADHD and CD were strongly associated with driving offenses. Females with ADHD had significantly more driving offenses and accidents compared with those with other disorders or no disorder. Practitioners should be cautioned that at-risk driving behavior cannot be entirely attributed to symptoms of

ADHD. Again, the development of moderate to severe disruptive disorders best predicts a host of environmental consequences, including automobile accidents, substance abuse, and trips to the emergency room.

Hinshaw (1992a) reviewed the literature dealing with learning disability, ADHD, and outcome in the adolescent years. He noted that externalizing behaviors, particularly ADHD, often overlap with various indices of academic underachievement during childhood. By adolescence, delinquency is also clearly associated with school failure. The link between behavior and learning problems often appears before formal schooling, and the development of comorbid delinquent problems appears to predict a negative course. Hinshaw suggested that early intervention is necessary to avert the chronic onset of problems these children experience. Summaries of controlled treatment investigations with youngsters who show these combined problems are rare, and when they are available, such studies present a host of methodological and practical problems. Nonetheless, common sense, based on available data, dictate that there is a need for practitioners to intervene early to break a cycle of school failure and the subsequent development of externalizing disruptive behavior in young children. The early presentation of the combination of these two appears to markedly compromise adolescent outcome.

Pfeffer and colleagues (Pfeffer et al., 1991) conducted a 6- to 8-year follow-up of 106 preadolescent and young adolescent inpatients and 100 preadolescent and young adolescent nonpatients for risk of suicide. Adolescents who attempted suicide in the follow-up period were seven times more likely to have had a mood disorder during the follow-up period than those who did not attempt suicide. ADHD was reported in 31% of these subjects; however, CD was reported at a higher rate than ADHD, and depression and anxiety problems appeared to contribute the greatest risk. A review of these contributing factors appears in Table 4–3.

Zentall, Smith, Lee, and Wieczorek (1994) found that adolescents with ADHD had significantly lower problem-solving scores in specific math concepts and slower computational performance than normals. Poor performance as well as poor knowledge of math facts also co-occurred with greater activity level. Those with ADHD were observed more frequently to be looking away from the task, physically active, and vocalizing.

Zentall, Falkenberg, and Smith (1985) suggested that adolescents with histories of attention problems perform better on high-stimulation than on low-stimulation tasks. This was the reverse of the performance pattern of controls. These authors propose an optimal stimulation theory, that adolescents with histories of attention deficit are less tolerant of lower levels of arousal than normals and should derive greater gains from stimulation added to repetitive tasks. Shaw and Giambra (1993) suggested that task-unrelated thoughts occur more frequently than in normals in adolescents and young adults with histories of ADHD. In boring tasks, the ADHD individuals demonstrated higher levels of nonconscious processing and poor inhibitory control; these factors produced greater frequency of spontaneous, intrusive thoughts. Giambra (1989) suggested that task-unrelated thoughts are produced in an inverse relationship with age. Although this does not offer much in the way of diagnostic utility for practitioners, the implication for intervention is clear. Adolescents with histories of ADHD need to talk, move, question, interact with, and be stimulated by their environment, especially in school

Table 4–3. Psychiatric disorders among 133 subjects at initial assessment and during the follow-up period

Psychiatric Disorder	Assessment		Follow-up Period		Z	P
	N	%	N	%		
Any disorder	111	83.5	110	82.7	0.0	NS
Mood disorder	42	31.6	63	47.4	2.5	0.01
Major depressive	17	12.8	32	24.1	2.2	0.03
Dysthymic	25	18.8	34	25.6	1.2	NS
Bipolar	0	0.0	2	1.5	—	—
Disruptive disorder	54	40.6	77	57.9	5.1	0.0001
Attention deficit hyperactive	12	9.0	42	31.6	4.4	0.0001
Conduct	37	27.8	58	43.6	2.6	0.01
Oppositional defiant	12	9.0	23	17.3	1.8	NS
Schizophrenic disorder	11	8.3	8	6.0	0.5	NS
Anxiety disorder	27	20.3	56	42.1	3.7	0.0001
Separation anxiety	6	4.5	35	26.3	4.8	0.0001
Substance abuse disorder*	0	0.0	35	26.3	—	—
Alcohol abuse	0	0.0	25	18.8	—	—
Substance abuse	0	0.0	25	18.8	—	—
Other disorder	27	20.3	25	18.8	0.2	NS
Developmental disorder	41	30.8	15	11.3	3.7	0.0001

Source: Pfeffer, C. R., Klerman, G. L., Hurt, S. W., Lesser, M., Peskin, J. R., & Seifker, C. A. (1991). Suicidal children grown up: Demographic and clinical risk factors for adolescent suicide attempts. *Journal of the American Academy of Child and Adolescent Psychiatry, 30,* 609–616. Used with permission.

*Comparison of substance abuse disorders is not applicable, as no subject had such disorders initially.

settings, to be successful. It has been demonstrated that parent ratings of temperament, specifically impulsivity, hyperactivity, and inattention, account for approximately 25% to 30% of the variance in teacher ratings of classroom behavior (Guerin, Gottfried, Oliver, & Thomas, 1994). In contrast, parent ratings of temperament accounted for only 5% to 10% of the variance in academic achievement when IQ was controlled for, and 10% of the variance in self-concept and student-teacher relationships.

Bar-Joseph, Mester, and Rothenberg (1995) report on a group of young adolescents first diagnosed with ADHD. These authors urge practitioners to consider that psychological stressors related to life events and daily environment are likely to push some children with more severe dimensional qualities into meeting the categorical diagnosis of ADHD. Finally, Wilson and Marcotte (1995) suggest, based on adolescent outcome data, that length of treatment for ADHD, specifically the use of psychostimulants, does not appear to significantly alter adolescent outcome.

Adolescents with ADHD present a significant challenge for the practitioner. As the number of environmental and psychosocial stressors increases (e.g., low socioeconomic status, family psychiatric history), and number of comorbid diagnoses increases (e.g., CD, depression, learning disability), the practitioner is faced with a tidal wave of problems that may overwhelm not only the adolescent with ADHD but his or her family and the best efforts of practitioners. Adolescents newly diagnosed with ADHD and comorbid problems are at even greater risk, as their patterns of interaction with the environment are frequently well entrenched and reinforced; these adolescents are often unwilling to accept responsibility for their problems and resistant to treatment. Increasingly, work with adolescents experiencing ADHD has focused on helping the adolescent accept his or her problems and become an active rather than passive participant in the treatment process (Goldstein, 1989b). It continues to be the case that the initial treatment hurdle with adolescents experiencing histories of ADHD is to convince them to be active, responsible partners in the assessment and treatment process.

PREDICTING CHILD AND ADOLESCENT OUTCOME

In 1990, Goldstein and Goldstein suggested that the toughest question the practitioner will face from parents is not "What's wrong with my child?" but "How will these problems affect my child when she grows up?" and "What kind of an adult will he be?" Over the past ten years, it has become increasingly apparent to clinicians that the list of ADHD symptoms that most concern parents may not coincide well with the list of risk or insulating factors that predict future life outcome. Symptom relief is not necessarily synonymous with improving long-term outcome. Increasingly, practitioners have been directed to help parents understand that the armamentara of behavior management and medication are the two interventions with proven effectiveness for ADHD and have well demonstrated their benefits in reducing symptoms. However, these treatments have not necessarily demonstrated their benefits in altering the life course for children with ADHD. It has become increasingly recognized that what predicts life course for all children likely is also equal if not more powerful in predicting the life course for children facing life stress.

Practitioners have been directed to help parents recognize that they must develop a set of interventions to relieve ADHD symptoms but also, because of the increased risk of future problems their child faces, to develop a set of resilience or insulating interventions to increase the likelihood of positive adult outcome. Many of these insulators appear powerfully related to the quality of parent-child relations and the daily functioning of families. (These issues will be reviewed in depth in Chapter 15.) Clinicians are increasingly aware that children with ADHD followed over multiple-year periods, even those receiving multiple interventions, may not have better future adjustment than children receiving no intervention or a single intervention in light of other factors such as serious medical illness and family problems that may compromise even the best ADHD treatments. A child with ADHD receiving appropriate treatment but living in a family with an untreated depressed mother and an abusive alcoholic father, for example, is not likely to benefit very much from the ADHD treatments in the long run. This is not to argue that multidisciplinary intervention for ADHD is not beneficial. In fact, in 1981 Satterfield, Satterfield, and Cantwell clearly demonstrated that multidisciplinary intervention for attention deficit over a three-year period resulted in better behavioral and related outcomes than receiving no intervention or, for that matter, a single intervention. A multidisciplinary program of intervention provides assistance to the child and family for home, school, social, and psychological problems. Chapter 11 will provide an overview of and rationale for the successes and failures in the current research dealing with multidisciplinary treatment for ADHD.

Increasingly, the adult literature suggests that the majority of children with ADHD grow up to become adults with a significant number of ADHD symptoms. Personalities have clearly been affected. In most cases, these individuals do not achieve as well based on estimates of their intellect or family history. The years of ADHD problems take their toll on adult outcome. (The interested reader is referred to S. Goldstein, 1997a).

In the first edition of this text, we reviewed a number of general variables that, at least in some way appeared to impact adult outcome for children with ADHD. Since then, the process of predicting outcome has become more complex. The more we know about children, their successes and failures, their families, their cognitive abilities, behavior, and adult outcome, the more complex becomes the process of deciding which factors actually provide support, resilience, and insulation. We believe the factors reviewed in the first edition of this text are still of value for the practitioner and thus worthy of a second visit. We will also provide summaries of longitudinal, prospective studies in ADHD and discuss related literature that has attempted to predict life outcome for children in general, as these predictors may be independent of a specific type of childhood problem. As we noted ten years ago and have emphasized in this edition, intellectual ability, learning problems, level of aggression, peer rejection, family stability, parenting, and sibling relationships represent the best predictive variables for children with ADHD.

Intelligence

It is accepted that more intelligent individuals make a better adjustment to adult life, attain higher vocational status, and, as a group, are better adjusted emotionally. Children with ADHD with higher intellect may at younger ages use their intellectual skills to compensate; thus, they may not be identified until later ages, especially if they are not particularly hyperactive, because they appear to fare better than their counterparts with average or below average intelligence.

Socioeconomic Status (SES)

Lower SES families have a higher incidence of poor medical and nutritional care for their offspring, tend to be less educated concerning appropriate child rearing, and are more likely to experience psychiatric problems. Higher SES parents are more likely to seek and follow through with treatment. Additionally, children from higher SES families as adults tend to obtain a level of status similar to or better than their families. Because a percentage of children with ADHD have parents with similar problems, many of these families tend to fall to a lower socioeconomic stratum, thereby providing further negative impact on adult outcome for their children. In 1979, Trites found that as many as one out of every four children in lower socioeconomic areas of Ottowa, Canada, presented significant symptoms of attention deficit. It has also been suggested that low SES parents are more inconsistent in their parenting than are high

SES parents (Paternite, Loney, & Langhorne, 1976). Lower SES parents are more likely to have difficulty setting appropriate consequences for behavior and may use excessively aggressive punishments. Lower SES has also been found to correlate with childhood aggression (Paternite & Loney, 1980).

Socialization

In all likelihood, the best single predictor of adequate emotional adjustment in adulthood is the ability to develop and maintain positive social contacts and friendships in childhood (Milich & Landau, 1981). Children with ADHD with a positive social interaction frequently cope better with their disorder and the daily frustrations of home and school.

Activity Level

It has now been well documented that the hyperactive-impulsive qualities of ADHD place children at much greater risk than the inattentive symptoms. At least one study has suggested that there is an inverse relationship between the degree of hyperactive-impulsive behavior in elementary school and academic achievement in high school: more problems in elementary school lead to an increased risk that high school achievement will be negatively effected (Loney et al., 1981). In the first edition of this text, we hypothesized that the hyperactive-impulsive symptoms may well be a general marker of the severity of ADHD. Current research supports this. Children with more severe ADHD problems can be expected to have greater achievement and behavior problems in later school years.

Ability to Delay Rewards

Based on a comprehensive review of the literature, Mischel et al. (1989) suggested that children who are more competent at delaying rewards tend to develop into adolescents who perform better on tests of intelligence, have greater success resisting temptation that may result in problems, demonstrate more appropriate social skills, and have higher achievement strivings. With ADHD increasingly viewed as a disorder of poor impulse control, the findings of these researchers takes on greater significance. Children competent at spontaneously developing effective strategies to delay gratification and inhibit impulsive responding have also been reported as less aggressive than children matched for similar problems who are unable to generate or master these strategies (Rodriguez, Shoda, Mischel, & Wright, 1989).

Aggression

At one time aggression was considered a secondary symptom of attention deficit. However, it is now well recognized as more closely related to the interaction of impulsive behavior, parenting style, and socioeconomic status (Conners & Wells, 1986). One of the best single predictors of antisocial behavior and poorly adjusted emotional status in adolescence is a history of aggressive behavior in younger childhood (Loney,

1980a). It appears that once a child develops a pattern of aggressive behavior it is extremely difficult to extinguish. As a society, we tend to deal with aggressive behavior aggressively; it is therefore not surprising that in our attempts to extinguish aggressive behavior in children, we may in fact be reinforcing this pattern of behavior.

It has been well established that aggression is an independent variable that may or may not occur with ADHD but tends to occur more frequently if hyperactive-impulsive symptoms are present (Loney & Milich, 1981). Shapiro and Garfinkel (1986) found a prevalence rate in a nonreferred elementary school population of 2.3% for inattentive, hyperactive symptoms, 3.6% for aggressive and oppositional symptoms, and 3% for both sets of symptoms. Concentration problems, impulsivity, and excessive motor behavior were associated with all groups of children. The Conners Teacher's Rating Scale was the only assessment tool that differentiated the three groups. Other measures alone, including a child interview and attentional test battery or school performance, could not validate the diagnostic distinction.

Over the past twenty years, the elementary-school-age child with ADHD combined with a pattern of aggressive behavior has had a poor prognosis for appropriate adjustment in adolescence and beyond (August, Stewart, & Holmes, 1983; Loney et al., 1981). In 1989, August and Garfinkel reported that approximately two-thirds of children with ADHD present a comorbid externalizing diagnosis; of this group, approximately half appeared to have marked problems with aggression and to be at greater risk for mixed substance abuse and antisocial behavior into adulthood. As discussed earlier, the practitioner must be alert to this problem and intensively work to extinguish aggressive behavior, ideally before the child with ADHD enters junior high school. Studies also suggest that interventions that relieve symptoms of ADHD are typically not effective or long term in reducing aggressive behavior. Aggression must be dealt with as an independent problem of childhood (M. Stewart, 1980).

Family Mental Health

Families with multiple generations of ADHD as well as more serious psychiatric problems tend to be extremely difficult to deal with in treatment. These multiproblem families are often unhappy with the behavior of their ADHD child, but they frequently lack skills, persistence, and the ability to stick with a practitioner and a treatment program. A history of psychiatric problems in a family increases the likelihood that the ADHD child will present with a similar or related set of problems as an adult (Weiss et al., 1971).

PREDICTING YOUNG ADULT OUTCOME

In 1992, Lie reviewed the literature on follow-up studies with children with ADHD. Specifically, the hypothesis that ADHD is a precursor to criminality and abusive substances was evaluated. This author noted that many clinicians confused ADHD with CD, leading to methodological problems. Nonetheless, despite methodological shortcomings, the available studies suggested that about one-third of subjects with ADHD retained the full-syndrome diagnosis into early adulthood. Subjects with ADHD with comorbid problems related to low intellectual skills, more serious psychiatric problems such as psychosis, or cerebral dysfunction usually had a poor prognosis. Lie suggests that ADHD may be an exacerbating factor in the rate of delinquency and law breaking. Conduct problems and not ADHD appeared to predict poor outcome. In 1990a, Barkley suggested that as children with ADHD progress into their teenage years, the absolute frequency and intensity of their symptoms decline. Nonetheless, at least 70% to 80% continue to exhibit significant deficits, inattention, and impulsivity relative to their age-mates during their adolescent years (Barkley, Fischer, et al., 1990). Of the prospective studies through 25 years of age, over 50% of children with ADHD continue to evidence symptoms of the disorder into adulthood, especially in the ability to sustain attention and inhibit impulsive responding (Barkley, Fischer, et al.; Gittelman et al., 1985; Weiss & Hechtman, 1993). Barkley, Fischer, et al. report that nearly 33% of these adults will have dropped out of high school and only 5% complete a university program, compared to over 40% of the control group. Nearly 25% of this population progress through CD and develop a chronic pattern of antisocial behavior, including interpersonal difficulties, occupational instability, and substance abuse. Interestingly, Barkley (1990a) also reported that approximately 33% of children with ADHD followed into adulthood appear to be relatively well-adjusted and demonstrate minimal symptoms.

In 1991, Klein and Mannuzza suggested that although dysfunction in individuals with ADHD is markedly reduced in adulthood, the pattern of outcome remains unchanged. Except for failure to document cognitive deficits for a significant group of those with ADHD, adulthood is characterized by the development of increased risk for antisocial personality and alcohol substance use disorders, which are associated with criminality. There appeared to be little existing information to suggest the difference in outcome between males and females. Efforts to consistently demonstrate which ADHD-related variables best predicted good or poor outcome to that point had been unsuccessful. In a recent report, Mannuzza, Klein, Bessler, Malloy, and Hynes (1997) noted that into young adulthood those with ADHD completed significantly less formal schooling than controls, had lower ranking occupational positions yet fewer than one in ten was unemployed. The rate of unemployment did not distinguish those with ADHD from controls. Further, the hypothesis that individuals with ADHD preferentially select self-employment in adulthood did not appear valid based upon this longitudinal set of data. After reviewing the available literature, Klein and Mannuzza (1991) concluded, "if one considers the findings from the existing analyses, even including those that inflate the predictability of childhood measures, a relatively poor job is done at predicting the outcome of hyperactive children" (p. 386). Overall, however, studies suggest that children with ADHD who develop more comorbid problems have worse outcome. Earlier studies did not efficiently identify comorbidity, making it difficult to tease out the impact on outcome of ADHD versus other disorders. As numerous authors have noted, the association between one outcome measure and childhood predictor is not strong. Some variables have been found to predict, but again, strength of prediction is better when variables are combined; these include IQ, socioeconomic status, emotional instability, aggressivity, and parental mental health (Hechtman, Weiss, Perlman, & Amsel, 1984). However, when better statistical controls are applied to these early studies, no significant predictors remain (Mannuzza, Gittelman-Klein, Konig, & Giampino, 1989).

In a prospective follow-up study of 103 males diagnosed at ages 6 to 12 as having attention deficit disorder with hyperactivity, official arrest records were evaluated at 16 to 22 years of age (Mannuzza, Gittelman-Klein, & Konig, 1989). Significantly more of the attention deficit group than controls had been arrested (39% versus 20%), convicted (28% versus 11%), and incarcerated (9% versus 1%). The presence of an antisocial conduct disorder in young adulthood almost completely accounted for the increased risk for criminal activities in children with attention deficit, whether or not it was accompanied by a substance use disorder. Continuing attention deficit at follow-up by itself was not associated with arrest history. These findings were interpreted by the authors as supporting the view that ADHD in childhood is a risk factor for criminality but that the relationship is exclusively mediated by the development of an antisocial disorder in late adolescence and early adulthood. A second follow-up study by this group (Mannuzza et al., 1991) demonstrated higher rates of attention deficit, antisocial, and drug abuse disorders in the attention deficit than in the control group. As in the previous study, more children with histories of ADHD than controls were given an adult diagnosis of ADHD (43% versus 4%), antisocial disorder (72% versus 8%), and drug use disorder (10% versus 1%). The absolute rates of these disorders were comparable for corresponding groups across studies. Mannuzza, Klein, Bessler, and Malloy (1993) evaluated educational, occupational, and psychiatric outcome for nearly 100 males with a history of attention deficit disorder in their midtwenties in comparison to a population of normal controls. Those with ADHD histories completed fewer years of formal schooling than controls, but 90% were gainfully employed; their jobs, however, were of lower occupational ranking. Those with a history of attention deficit were over seven times more likely than controls to have an antisocial personality disorder in adulthood or a drug abuse problem.

Mannuzza, Gittelman-Klein, and Addalli (1991) evaluated the psychiatric outcome of fifty boys with a history of attention deficit compared to their unaffected brothers and a group of controls at ages 16 to 23 years. Siblings provided built-in control for potential confounding factors such as social class and parental psychopathology. Blind assessments at follow-up demonstrated that significantly more boys with ADHD (30%) than siblings (6%) and controls (10%) had multiple *DSM-III* diagnoses. Boys with a history of ADHD had a more severe form of antisocial disorder than their siblings. The increased risk for multiple and more pervasive disorders in young adulthood in this population of boys with attention deficit appears not to be attributed to childhood factors shared with siblings but rather due to the unique experience of being impulsive and inattentive throughout one's childhood. In this study, 42% at follow-up demonstrated some attention deficit symptom; over 50% demonstrated antisocial, conduct-disordered symptoms; and 20% experienced alcohol and non-alcohol substance abuse. Within the group of those with ADHD demonstrating the antisocial and conduct-disordered symptoms, 100% had been suspended or expelled from school, had routinely violated rules, and had been repeatedly truant; 50% had vandalized; nearly 80% had been arrested and 30% incarcerated; 80% had been caught for breaking and entering; 93% were reported as persistent liars; and 100% were reported by their caregivers as disobedient. In this group, the brothers behaved worse than brothers of the pure ADHD group, but in general, the conduct-disordered ADHD siblings and controls looked very similar in their problems, although the ADHD population were described more often as disobeying teachers and persistently lying to a significant degree.

A population of 6- to 17-year-old Caucasian, non-Hispanic boys with and without ADHD were followed for four years; 85% of the population met the ADHD diagnosis four years later (Biederman, Faraone, Milberger, Curtiss, et al., 1996). Of those who remitted, half did so in childhood, the other half in adolescence. Predictors of persistence were a family history of ADHD, psychosocial adversity, and comorbidity with conduct, mood, or anxiety disorders. The authors suggest that the majority of children with ADHD continue to present the disorder into adolescence. For a minority of children, ADHD appears to be a transient disorder that remits early on. Familiality, adversity, and psychiatric comorbidity appear to be clinically relevant, useful predictors of who is at risk to persist. These findings are consistent with those of others, including Gittelman et al. (1985), Hart, Lahey, Loeber, Applegate, and Frick (1995), and Lambert et al. (1987). Further, Seidman, Biederman, and Faraone (1995) demonstrated that familial ADHD children are more neuropsychologically impaired than other children with ADHD. Family indices of psychosocial adversity assessed using exposure to parental psychopathology and parental conflict also predict worse outcome for ADHD children (Biederman, Milberger, & Faraone, 1995; Seidman et al., 1995). These authors note that early remittors demonstrate a baseline, phenotypic picture of ADHD that was not markedly different from persistent or late remittors. Taylor et al. (1991) found that 37% of 6- to 7-year-old boys were hyperactive nine months after being diagnosed. Hart et al. (1995) reported a number of children who showed a relatively rapid improvement in symptoms after their initial assessment. Again, reduced comorbidity with CD appears to be one of the best and most significant predictors for the ADHD population in regard to good or poor outcome.

Barkley, Anastopoulos, Guevremont, and Fletcher (1991) generated behavioral, adjustment, academic function, and treatment utilization data over time in a group of ADHD adolescents. Parent ratings included a Child Behavior Checklist and Conners questionnaires. Teacher ratings included the Child Behavior Checklist. Self-report measures included the Child Behavior Checklist Youth Self-Report, Reynolds' Adolescent Depression Scale, Adolescent Stressful Life Event Scale, and a locus of control scale. Psychological tests included the Peabody Picture Vocabulary Test, Wide Range Achievement Test, Matching Familiar Figures Test, Gordon Diagnostic Test protocol, and a selective reminding task. The ADHD group displayed significant impairments on objectively assessed attention, impulsivity, and overactivity as well as on academic achievement, social competence, and behavioral adjustment. They demonstrated a higher risk for comorbid antisocial disorders and school maladjustment. The data also argued that as a disorder, ADHD in adolescence presents in a pattern very similar to that in younger childhood. More teenagers with ADHD had a history of ODD (68%) and CD (39%) and were rated as more impaired in social competence, behavioral and emotional adjustment, and school performance by parents and teachers than were controls. The youth with ADHD, however, rated themselves as better adjusted than did their parents and teachers, differing from controls only in depressive symptoms and admission of antisocial acts. Although this could be attributed to lying on their part, as previously noted it also may be that their impulsivity results in their overestimating their functionality and underestimating their history of problems. Barkley, Anastopoulos, et al. (1991) also noted poorer performance in verbal learning and vigilance tasks and more symptoms of ADHD behavior during a math test as distinguishing the ADHD from control teenagers. These authors suggested that in this type of research, lost subjects may actually reflect individuals with less severe symptoms, subsequently leaving only the more severe subjects to be followed. Table 4–4 contains an interesting comparison of demographic and initial subject characteristics of the ADHD and control groups.

In related fields, authors have examined numerous variables that predict life outcome for children. The work of Werner (1994) and McGee and colleagues (McGee, Williams, & Feehan, 1992) exemplifies the diverse and creative ways this issue has been approached. Of importance for the practitioner is an understanding of the relationship between inborn biological risk consistent with the genetic underpinnings of ADHD, environmental risks, and developmental outcome.

Buchsbaum et al. (1985) screened 400 college men using a continuous performance computer task. The individuals in the best and worst 5% of performance were compared through multiple measures of psychiatric disturbance, cognition, and psychophysiologic functioning. The group with the poorest performance had a higher incidence of symptoms of hyperactivity in childhood and as adults; however, they had no higher incidence of other psychopathology as assessed through interview and self-report measures. The cognitive differences between lower and upper groups, including differences on measures of intellectual ability, reaction time, even evoked potentials, appear to substantiate the difference. The authors concluded that attentional problems appeared more closely linked to the childhood disorder of hyperactivity than to more serious psychiatric disturbances.

Table 4–4. Demographic and initial subject characteristics by group

Measure	ADHD (N = 84)		Control (N = 77)		t	p<*
	$\overline{X}$	SD	$\overline{X}$	SD		
Adolescent age (yrs)	14.1	1.4	14.3	1.9	−1.11	—
Adolescent IQ (PPVT-R)	103.3	15.5	107.8	15.4	−1.82	—
Mother age (yrs)	40.4	5.6	41.1	5.1	−0.85	—
Mother education (yrs)	13.7	2.4	14.4	2.1	−1.84	—
Mother socioeconomic status	45.7	24.9	52.6	24.3	−1.77	—
Father age (yrs)	42.0	5.9	43.6	5.9	−1.66	—
Father education (yrs)	14.2	2.9	14.8	2.8	−1.22	—
Father socioeconomic status	54.7	23.1	59.4	23.3	−1.23	—
Number of ADHD symptoms	10.2	1.9	0.9	1.5	34.82	0.0001
Onset of ADHD symptoms (yrs)	4.1	2.0	7.0	1.4	−10.56	0.0001
CBCL Hyperactive Scale	78.9	8.6	56.4	2.9	22.66	0.0001

Source: Barkley, R. A., Anastopoulos, A. D., Guevremont, D. C., & Fletcher, K. E. (1991). Adolescents with ADHD: Patterns of behavioral adjustment, academic functioning and treatment utilization. *Journal of the American Academy of Child and Adolescent Psychiatry, 30,* 752–761. Used with permission.

Note: ADHD = attention deficit hyperactivity disorder; PPVT-R = Peabody Picture Vocabulary Test–Revised; CBCL = Child Behavior Checklist (Parent Report); Socioeconomic status was determined by the Hollingshead Two-Factor Index of Social Position.

*p < indicates the probability value for the t-test (two-tailed) between groups if p < 0.05.
$\overline{X}$ = Chi Squared
SD = Standard Deviation

Teacher ratings of behavior at age 13 with respect to concentration and hyperactivity problems were analyzed in relation to alcohol problems and violent offending from 15 to 26 years of age for 540 males (Klinteberg, Anderson, Magnusson, & Stattin, 1993). Hyperactive behavior in childhood was found to be significantly related to subsequent alcohol problems as well as later violent offending. Two significant types were found. One indicated that high hyperactive childhood behaviors closely linked later alcohol problems and violent offending in the same individuals. The other type supported the frequently observed co-occurrence of a pattern of low hyperactive behavior in childhood with no subsequent alcohol problems or violent offending. Given current trends in perception of the ADHD diagnosis, it is likely that the former describes the combined type of ADHD, and the later describes only the inattentive type.

Biederman and colleagues (Biederman, Faraone, Knee, et al., 1990) examined the validity of retrospective diagnosis of ADHD in nonreferred relatives of children with ADHD by evaluating the association between ADHD and antisocial disorders. Nonreferred individuals with ADHD had a significant increased risk for a spectrum of antisocial problems consisting of oppositionality, conduct disorder, and antisocial personality disorder. Risk was calculated to be threefold higher in twenty-four nonreferred adults with ADHD than in fifty-one non-ADHD relatives and fourteenfold higher than in relatives of twenty normal controls. Increased psychopathology and a high rate of enuresis was found in the nonreferred adults with histories of ADHD. The authors concluded that the symptom profile for this nonreferred population was similar to those who had been referred and treated in childhood.

Aylward (1992) suggests that when a biological risk is severe, the influence of the environment is minimized. Environmental and genetic factors are assumed to be the underlying cause of, for example, low intelligence because biological factors cannot be identified. Negative components in the environment may have synergistic or additive effects on vulnerable children. This is consistent with the hypothesis of Goldstein and Goldstein (1990) suggesting that characteristics of ADHD are catalytic. In the face of other adversity, they increase risk of poor outcome.

Kurzweil (1992) followed forty children from 7 to 14 years of age with a developmental reading disorder. IQ was suggested as a possible good predictor of recovery potential. Forty percent of the subjects were reading appropriately at follow-up. Improvement in recovery was significantly related to parents' educational status, especially IQ and not to gender of the subject or to having a speech articulation problem or to ADHD. The association among parental, psychological, and behavioral control in childhood problems and outcome appears fairly strong (Barber, Olsen, & Shagle, 1994). In a sample of nearly 500 fifth-, eighth-, and tenth-graders, psychological control was defined as patterns of family interaction that intrude upon or impede the child's individuation process or the relative degree of psychological distance a child experiences from parents and family. Behavioral control was defined as family interaction that is disengaged, provides insufficient parental regulation of the child's behavior, and lacks rules and restrictions. It was demonstrated that psychological control was more predictive of adolescent internalized problems and behavioral control was more predictive of externalizing problems. Again, the complexity of variables seemingly as simple as parenting style has made it more difficult to understand the impact parents have on children. Based on the work of Barber et al. (1994), a child with

ADHD in a setting in which behavioral control is primarily utilized would likely experience an exacerbation of problems. This is likely also true for children coming from neglectful and abusive settings.

Though not ADHD research per se, Friedman et al. (1995a, 1995b) suggest that a characteristic trait consistent with impulsivity was one of the most significant childhood personality characteristics predictive of reduced life expectancy by all causes of death. This group reported on the follow-up study of an original sample of highly intelligent children, half of whom at the time of research were in their seventies and half of whom were deceased. In this group, individuals placed in the lowest quartile of the sample on this characteristic of impulsivity (referred to as conscientiousness) lived an average of two to four years less than those who did not. All causes of death were at greater risk, not just accidents. These authors also suggested that divorce was an independent variable. In this population, children who were impulsive and had divorced parents had an average reduction in life of seven years relative to children who were impulsive and whose parents were not divorced.

However, behavioral precursors to accidents and physical impairment have been more closely tied to noncompliance in childhood than to impulsivity specifically (Pulkkinen, 1995). This author collected data at ages 8, 14, and 27 years on nearly 300 males and females. The results demonstrated that 44% of the men and 14% of the women had been in at least one accident by age 27. Accidents and subsequent impairment were most frequent among individuals whose behavior had been characterized by low emotional and behavioral control. In adulthood, heavy drinking increased the risk of accidents. Aggression and conduct problems were the most significant precursors to male impairment, although subgroups of men who had accidents but were not aggressive or antisocial were found. The predictions of accidents and impairments were less accurate for females than for males.

In a sample of over 800 unselected subjects, behavioral styles and temperament at age 3 were studied to assess their link to personality traits at age 18 (Caspi & Silva, 1995). As young adults, those who were undercontrolled at age 3 consistent with the impulsive description of ADHD scored high on measures of impulsivity, danger seeking, aggression, and interpersonal alienation. In contrast, children who were rated as inhibited at age 3 scored low on measures of impulsivity, danger seeking, aggression, and social potency. Interestingly, competent children scored high on impulsivity. Well-adjusted children continued to exhibit normal behavior. The confident children, though similar in some ways to the undercontrolled children, did not demonstrate all of the other negative variables characteristic of this problem group; they were more often described as zealous in their approach to life.

Longitudinal reports from parents, teachers, and self were tested as predictors for later reports of academic problems, school behavior problems, receipt of mental health services, suicidal behavior, police contact, substance abuse, and the sum of these six signs into young adulthood (Achenbach, Howell, McConaughy, & Stanger, 1995). The predictors accounted for a large percentage of the variance in most signs and predicted fairly accurately which members of the case-controlled samples would manifest specific signs. The six signs were weakly related to each other. The delinquent behavior and attention problem syndromes plus stressful experiences predicted the most signs. Specifically, a clinically significant score on the attention problem scale predicted academic problems, school behavior problems, and the receipt of mental health services in females. The delinquent behavior syndrome predicted more signs than any other, and attention problems predicted the second largest number of signs. These findings are consistent with those of others, such as a large Dutch sample (Verhulst, Koot, & van der Ende, 1994). In 1995, Achenbach et al. followed their sample into young adulthood. The young adult syndrome they designated as irresponsible was predicted by the adolescent attention problem syndrome. These authors suggest that the adult inattentive type of attention deficit disorder may be best characterized as irresponsibility. Attention problems were associated with more diverse problems among females than males. A new syndrome in young adults not previously observed on the Child Behavior Checklist sample was designated as showing off and an adult aggressive behavior syndrome were both predicted by the adolescent aggressive behavior syndrome. This appeared to indicate a developmental transition away from overt aggression among some aggressive youth but not others. These authors suggest that when asked to evaluate adults for ADHD, practitioners need to look beyond the disruptiveness associated with childhood ADHD. Problems related to irresponsibility such as being fired from a job, problems making decisions, and low self-confidence may be more pathonomic for adults with ADHD then at earlier ages, whereas overactivity or overt impulsivity per se may not be found in the adult syndrome. The authors also suggest that the attention problem syndrome in adolescence predicts a broad spectrum of problems among adults differing in females and males; this argues for gender-specific diagnostic cutoff points for ADHD.

In an epidemiologic study, Cohen, Cohen, Kasen, and Velez (1993) and Cohen, Cohen, and Brook (1993) examined age-specific prevalence for overanxious disorder, separation anxiety, major depressive disorder, ADHD, CD, ODD, alcohol abuse, and marijuana abuse in a general population sample ages 10 to 20 years. Age and gender patterns for several disorders suggest developmental-stage-associated risks. These include oppositional disorder in both genders and conduct disorder and major depression in girls. Major depression demonstrated a pattern suggestive of a role for the onset of puberty. The prevalence of one or more disorders did not differ by age or gender; however, the pattern of specific diagnoses varied greatly by both age and gender. There were substantial levels of diagnostic persistence over the two-and-a-half-year study period for all diagnoses except major depression. With few exceptions, persistence was roughly equivalent for age and gender subtypes.

Rubin, Xinyin, McDougal, Bowker, and McKinnon (1995) in the Waterloo Longitudinal Project demonstrated that aggression is the best predictor of adolescent delinquent activity. Social competence predicts security in the peer group, with social withdrawal at a young age contributing to the prediction of adolescent loneliness, insecurity, and negative self-regard. In a thorough review of risk factors, Brier (1995) suggests that temperamental qualities including high activity level, impersistence, distractibility, and limited attention span lead to childhood noncompliance, undercontrol, and impulsivity. Brier suggests that an association among temperament, school failure, and delinquency has clearly been established based on the existing literature. Although Brier concludes that "temperamental attributes of hyperactivity, distractibility, rigidity and impulsivity" (p. 273) may be strong correlates for school failure and delinquency, comorbid factors are not well addressed, once again leading to the possibility of erroneous associations made between ADHD and outcome. Brier, however, comments that aggression appears to be the precipitating factor connecting these behavioral symptoms with poor life outcome.

SUMMARY

This chapter provided an indepth review and analysis of symptom profiles and impact of ADHD throughout the child and adolescent periods. The complex interaction of ADHD symptoms with a variety of biological, familial, environmental, and experiential factors makes the job of diagnosis one that must be approached with patience and tenacity. Knowing that a child meets the diagnostic criteria for ADHD in the absence of understanding the presence and/or severity of these other factors will likely significantly negatively impact treatment success. We believe that these developmental data argue strongly that adolescent and young adult outcome for youth with ADHD are best predicted by understanding the interaction of ADHD symptoms with these other variables.

Chapter 5

ETIOLOGY

Commonly suspected causes of ADHD have included toxins, developmental impairments, diet, injury, ineffective parenting, and heredity. It has been suggested that these potential causes affect brain functioning, thus ADHD can also be considered a disorder of brain function. This chapter will review brain function and suspected causes of ADHD to provide an academic and medical framework for understanding this disorder.

BRAIN INJURY

In the early twentieth century, the cluster of symptoms now called ADHD was hypothesized to relate to brain trauma (Still, 1902). This theory gained wide acceptance, and a range of behavioral and cognitive problems were diagnosed in children and adults who had suffered encephalitis. Most children with these symptoms, however, did not have definite brain injury (Bond & Partridge, 1926; Ebaugh, 1923; Hohman, 1922). The concept of minimal brain dysfunction (MBD) emerged and was applied to a large group of children who had MBD symptoms but did not have obvious neurological signs of injury. This concept was based on the theory that a lesser degree of injury could cause observed behavioral changes without other signs of brain injury (Knobolc & Pasamanick, 1959). The overwhelming majority of children with ADHD symptoms could then be considered victims of a minimal degree of brain injury and their ADHD symptoms the result of mishaps in pregnancy, labor, or delivery or of later illness or injury. Most families with children manifesting attention deficit symptoms could point to one difficulty or another, during or after the pregnancy, as the cause of the child's problem. As a result, the theory that mishaps of pregnancy, labor, or delivery or other brain injury was the major cause of attention deficit symptoms was widely held through the 1950s.

Thinking was refined in the 1970s. Routh (1978) reported that there was little evidence to support the view that brain damage was a major cause of attention deficit. Other studies found that only a very small percentage of children with histories of attention deficit also had histories suggesting brain injury (Stewart & Olds, 1973). Major studies did not find a significant relationship between severe perinatal stress and later adjustment (Werner et al., 1968).

One of the largest pregnancy studies, cited in Neson and Ellenberg, 1979a, 1979b, the Collaborative Perinatal Project of the National Institute of Neurological and Communicative Disorders and Strokes, was a multicenter, cooperative effort studying the outcome of 55,000 pregnancies. All aspects of pregnancy, labor, and delivery were recorded, and psychological, neurological, and medical follow-up examinations were carried on during the development of the child. At birth, every child was evaluated for movement, tone, color, respiratory effort, and heart rate. The results of this evaluation when totaled was the Apgar score, which is a measure of the health of the baby at birth. K. Nelson and Ellenberg (1979) reported a study correlating the Apgar scores and long-term neurological follow-up for this large group of children. They found no correlation between symptoms of attention deficit and Apgar scores. Large numbers of children with severe difficulty at the time of birth developed no attention deficit symptoms, and some children without difficult delivery developed severe symptoms of attention deficit. The observation of large numbers of children in the Collaborative Perinatal Project demonstrated that in an individual instance, a history of difficulty with delivery alone would not be sufficient to establish birth injury as the cause of ADHD.

The theory that some children develop ADHD and other mild developmental problems as the result of brain injury has regained some scientific support. Delaney-Black et al. (1989) followed forty-nine children born with a high red blood cell count and hyperviscosity (poor blood flow as the result of excessive red blood cells, possibly causing damaged blood vessels in the brain). At 7 years of age, this group of children was found to have lower spelling and arithmetic achievement as measured on the Wide Range Achievement Test than similar children who had not had a high red blood cell count and hyperviscosity at birth. The authors concluded that the lower achievement scores were the result of the hyperviscosity. Hartsough and Lambert (1985) analyzed prenatal, perinatal, and developmental factors for groups of ADD and normal children. A significantly higher incidence of fetal postmaturity, toxemia, and eclampsia during the pregnancy and long labor occurred in the ADD group. The authors concluded, however, that these "medical variables have minor etiological significance as compared to other factors in the generation of hyperactivity" (p. 200).

Other studies do suggest a link between ADHD in some children and pregnancy, delivery and infancy complications (PDIC). Sprich-Buckminster, Biederman, Milberger, Faraone, and Lehman (1993) compared the birth histories in normal and ADD children (ADD, $N = 73$). They found that ADD children with a positive family history of ADHD or PDIC did not differ from the normal population. However, PDIC were more common in children with other comorbid psychiatric problems in addition to ADD and nonfamilial ADD. This relatively small study suggests that PDIC may have relevance as etiological factors for an ADD child who has other comorbid psychiatric diagnoses or in whom no family history of ADD is present.

Chandola, Robling, Peters, Melville-Thomas, and McGuffin (1993) looked at 129 referrals for hyperactivity in children ages 3 to 6 years and compared these children to the 24,656 members of a geographically defined 3-year birth cohort. They concluded that a six-factor model, including social class, maternal age, antipartum hemorrhage, length of labor (2nd stage), one minute Apgar, and gender, had some predictive value for determining children referred for hyperactivity. However, as this was a study looking at referrals rather than diagnosis, the significance of these results was uncertain.

There have been several studies showing that premature and low birth weight infants are at higher risk for developmental and behavioral problems. One study of preterm children in Rotterdam (birth weight less than 1,500 grams, gestational age less than 36 weeks, N =114) found that by 3.5 years they exhibited more depressed behavior and more internalizing problems by parent report. Cognition-influenced behavior suggested that attention problems might be linked directly to brain damage via cognitive impairments. Neither findings in neonatal cerebral ultrasound nor neurologic exam in this study predicted behavioral outcome. A study of a cohort of thirty boys weighing below the 2nd percentile (1,560 to 2,495 grams) suggested some correlation between features of attention deficit disorder and extent to which birth weight deviated from normal. However, this study combined absolute birth weight and weight relatively low for gestational age and studied only thirty children. They also concluded that even very small babies are likely to develop unscathed with good postnatal, social, and family care. It has been postulated that subcortical injury due to germinal matrix hemorrhage is the mechanism of brain injury in premature infants (Nass & Ross, 1991).

Extremely low birth weight (ELBW) children, who weigh less than 1,000 grams at birth, may be a more definable risk for ADHD. One group of 143 ELBW infants evaluated at 3 to 5 years of age was significantly disadvantaged on every measure tested (Saigal, Szatmari, & Rosenbaum, 1991). Even when a group is considered neurologically "normal," as were sixty-eight ELBW children reported by Saigal et al. (1991), ADHD and more "subtle handicaps" are uncovered. A group of eighty-two of ninety survivors of 500 to 1,000 gram birth weight found that at 5 years of age, 16% had attention deficit disorder compared with 6.9% of controls. Conduct disorder and "emotional disorder" were not increased. The authors concluded that ELBW was a specific risk factor for ADDH (Szatmari, Saigal, Rosenbaum, Campbell, & King, 1990). Those who survive are at high risk for neurobehavioral dysfunction and poor school performance. The lower the birth weight, the higher the likelihood of problems. Sixty-eight surviving children with birth weights under 750 grams were compared with sixty-five children weighing 750 to 1,499 grams and sixty-one children born at term. The smallest babies had poorer social skills and adaptive behavior and more behavioral and attentional problems than either of the other two groups (Hack et al., 1994).

The possibility that some children suffer ADHD as the result of perinatal injury has been supported in a single photon emission-computed tomography (SPECT) blood flow study (Lou, Henriksen, & Bruhn, 1984). When radioactive xenon gas is inhaled, radioactivity is emitted from the brain proportional to the blood flowing through the region. Thirteen children were studied with this technique; eleven had been diagnosed as ADD. The authors found a consistent pattern of decreased blood flow in the basal ganglia and in the border zone or space between major arterial distributions within the brain. Treatment with methylphenidate increased the perfusion to these areas, as well as improving ADD symptoms as judged by clinical observation. The authors suggested that the data presented supported the hypothesis that early hypoxic ischemic brain injury may be involved in a substantial percentage of patients with attention deficit.

This study of brain blood flow shows a physiological difference between children with attention deficit and normal children. In addition, it demonstrates a change in blood flow related to clinical improvement with medication. The small number of children and the fact that no standard diagnostic criteria were used, however, make any conclusions drawn from this study preliminary and tentative. In addition, there is no evidence presented to show that the variation in blood flow has a direct relationship to early hypoxic ischemic brain injury. Nevertheless, this blood flow study adds to the large body of information demonstrating that children with attention deficit symptoms are physiologically different from other children.

REFINED SUGAR

Refined sugar has been suggested as a cause of attention deficit, often as a result of uncontrolled or anecdotal reports. These accounts are difficult to interpret. For example, a parent who experienced considerable difficulty with her 8-year-old son after an extended birthday party reported long hours of stimulation by a large group of friends and then a sleepless night. She concluded, however, that her son must be sensitive to sugar because he had a piece of chocolate cake during the party. Other variables such as the sleeplessness and excitement of the party may have been more important to the subsequent difficulty with behavior than the chocolate cake, but without a carefully controlled environment it is difficult to be certain. Higher plasma epinephrine level response to a glucose tolerance test in children compared to adults prompted T. Jones et al. (1995), to conclude that enhanced adrenal medullary response to modest reduction in plasma glucose concentration may contribute to adverse behavioral and cognitive effects after sugar is ingested by healthy children. After hypoglycemia, cognitive symptoms recovered more slowly than physical symptoms (Puczynski, Puczynski, Reich, Kaspar, & Emanuele, 1990), suggesting that control for low blood glucose may be needed to determine whether diet is a cause of ADHD symptoms.

A group of carefully controlled studies have been completed (see also, a review by Milich, Wolraich, & Lindgren, 1986). Twenty-one boys, selected because they were reported by their parents to respond adversely to sugar, were studied by Behar, Rapoport, Adams, Berg, and Cornblath (1984). A placebo blind challenge with sugar drinks revealed the possibly surprising result of a slight but significant decrease in observed motor activity three hours after the sugar challenge. Two additional studies of sucrose ingestion and behavior in hyperactive boys were presented by Wolraich, Milich, Stumbo, and Schultz (1985) and a third by Milich and Pelham (1986). Careful dietary control with 1.75 gram/kg of sucrose or placebo (aspartame in equivalent sweetness) was presented. The results of all three studies revealed no difference in the boys' performance on the challenge days.

Would a greater effect from the sugar have been seen if the boys had been allowed to use any amount of sugar they wanted? Kaplan, Wamboldt, and Barnhardt (1986) allowed children to select any amount of sweetened breakfast they desired. On some days, they were given aspartame sweetener and on others, sucrose. Conners rating questionnaires were used to evaluate behavior. In addition, some children received methylphenidate and others did not. The authors believed the study had additional significance because the children could use any amount of sugar they desired. Under these conditions, differences of behavior produced by methylphenidate were apparent, but no differences in behavior caused by aspartame versus sucrose.

Changes in the CPT performance suggesting decreased attention were seen in seventeen subjects with ADHD studied by Wender and Solanto (1991). No changes were observed in aggressive behavior either with the placebo, sugar, or aspartame groups.

The authors were skeptical as to whether the change observed in CPT performance would be clinically significant.

In a carefully controlled double-blind study of twenty-five normal preschool and twenty-three school-age children described by their parents as sensitive to sugar, Wolraich et al. (1994) concluded that even when intake of sucrose or aspartame exceeded typical levels, neither dietary sucrose nor aspartame affected children's behavior or cognitive function. A meta-analysis by Wolraich et al. showed that controlled studies were as likely to find that sugar improves behavior as worsens it.

These studies provide evidence that dietary sugar does not cause ADHD symptoms to worsen in groups of children. Although it is impossible to prove that sugar *never* worsens behavior in any child, carefully controlled studies fail to demonstrate that sugar ingestion by children is a significant contributor to the problem of attention deficit.

Feingold Diet

In relation to ADHD, other foods or food additives have received possibly even wider interest than sugar. Feingold (1974) hypothesized from anecdotal observations that ingestion of certain commonly occurring foods and additives had a toxic, not allergic, effect and contributed to behavioral deterioration. He was concerned about artificial colors and a group of food constituents called "natural salicylates," which are compounds chemically related to salicylic acid found in many fruits and other common foods. Feingold postulated that the elimination of these from the diet would produce substantial improvements in behavior. Again, to support this, he cited anecdotal evidence. To eliminate these substances, a complex dietary restriction was required; many foods commonly eaten by and readily available to children would be prohibited by such a diet.

Studies of artificial colors and other additives were conducted by Conners (1980). He first placed children on a controlled diet free of certain additives. During this time, he evaluated their behavior with the Conners Parent's Questionnaire to determine the severity of symptoms. He next reintroduced the possibly offending substances in a double-blind manner. Every day the children received a cookie; some days it contained a full day's supply of food additives, and some days it contained none of these substances. In this way, neither subjects nor examiners knew whether the children had received the additives. Conners' first observations suggested that there was a substantial improvement in symptoms when the diet was undertaken. This information could be used by advocates of the diet program. However, when the offending substances were reintroduced, there was no clear deterioration of behavior. This would suggest that the improvement seen on the diet was unrelated to the specific dietary exclusion. As a result of this group of studies, it was concluded that there is no clear evidence implicating artificial salicylates or food additives as a substantial cause for attention deficit.

Some studies, however, suggest that food additives may play a role in attention deficit. Swanson and Kinsbourne (1980) found that 85% of a group of twenty medication-responder hyperactive children experienced adverse effects after ingestion of food dye in a double-blind crossover study. Egger, Carter, Graham, Gumley, and Soothill (1985) found that after ingestion of a combination of dyes and preservatives, 79% of twenty-eight children referred for suspected food-based behavior problems suffered behavioral deterioration. Lester and Fishbein (1988) suggest several reasons for the earliest studies producing false negative results: first, the dosage of dyes may have been too low in studies conducted before 1980; second, the combination of preservatives found in normal diets but not in test situations may be needed to produce behavioral symptoms; and third, artificial flavors, which outnumber dyes, may also be important precipitants of behavior change. Seventy-three percent of nineteen children responded favorably to a multiple elimination diet and showed deterioration on challenge days (Boris & Mandel, 1994). The deterioration from single food challenges in this study was not as great as the improvement on multiple eliminations. The authors suggest that this is an indication that multiple eliminations are stronger than single challenges. They also noted that atopic children had a significantly higher response rate to the elimination diet.

A study of preschool-age boys further supports the hypothesis that diets eliminating multiple offending agents are effective at improving behavior (Kaplan, McNicol, Conte, & Moghadam, 1989). Twenty-four hyperactive preschool boys were studied. All foods were provided by the investigators. They eliminated not only artificial colors and flavors but also chocolate, monosodium glutamate, preservatives, caffeine, and any substances that families reported might affect their specific child; the diet was also low in simple sugars and was even milk-free if the family reported a history of possible problems with cow's milk. Based on Conners Parent's Questionnaires, more than half of the children were reported to improve on the diet but not on the placebo. In addition, halitosis, night awakenings, and sleep latency, or time to sleep onset, were improved. The authors believed their diet had a stronger effect than previous challenge studies because they eliminated many offending agents.

A "few foods" elimination diet helped fifty-nine of seventy-eight children in an open trial (C. Carter et al., 1993). A double-blind study of these children using disguised additives showed a significant reversal of behavior with the food challenges as evidenced by Conners Parent's Questionnaires, the Matching Familiar Figures Test, and psychologists' behavioral observations. No changes on a Paired Associate Learning Test were seen. A dose response effect (the higher dose produced a longer effect) to tartrazine at six dosage levels was found when Rowe and Rowe (1994) studied a group of fifty children selected from 800 diagnosed with ADDH according to *DSM-III* criteria placed on a six-week open synthetic-food-coloring-free diet.

Although some (Kaplan et al., 1989) have suggested that overall nutrient intake may affect behavior, others (Cromer, Tarnowski, Stein, Harton, & Thornton, 1990) found no behavioral changes when a government-supplied breakfast was substituted for a low-calorie meal. Several studies have probed the question of complex interactions between foods. Conners has suggested that a sugar load following a carbohydrate breakfast produces negative learning effects, whereas a sugar load following a high-protein breakfast produces positive learning effects (Conners, 1990). The relationship between overall nutrition and sugar lends a new twist to the old controversy about the effect of diet on behavior.

The studies above raise significant questions as to whether food additives may provoke hyperactive responses in some children. Although it is clear that dietary sugar is not an important factor for hyperactivity, the role of additives in aggravating ADHD behavior and the appropriate place for elimination diets and the treatment of ADHD will require standardization of treatment and replication of the above results.

In 1986, when E. Wender wrote her review of food additives, the conclusions were clear: only one study suggested a significant effect of food additives. Subsequently, however, a number of additional studies have reexamined the question. The new approach looks at the combination of many substances and studies children on diets so restricted that all their food must be supplied by the examiner. Only further research will determine if this approach has any relevance to the daily lives of most ADHD children.

FETAL EXPOSURE TO DRUGS AND ALCOHOL

Alcohol and other substances consumed by the mother during pregnancy are transferred through the placenta to the fetus. What effect does this have on long-term behavior? One hundred and fifty-eight children suffering from fetal alcohol syndrome were studied by Steinhausen, Williams, and Spohr (1993). Structured interviews, behavior checklists for parents and teachers, and intelligence tests found an excess of psychopathology with a wide variety of psychiatric syndromes presumably due to the alcohol exposure. Hyperkinetic disorders, emotional disorders, sleep disorders, and abnormal habits and stereotypes persisted over time. Nanson and Hiscock (1990) compared twenty children with fetal alcohol syndrome or fetal alcohol effect with twenty age-matched ADD and normal controls. In time, it was learned that alcohol-effected children were significantly more impaired intellectually. Attention deficits and behavior problems were similar to those of ADD children. They concluded that prenatal alcohol exposure and postnatal environmental disruption contributed to the problems with hyperactivity and attention. This study of 512 children whose mothers reported midpregnancy alcohol consumption showed that the younger children who scored poorly on tests of vigilance continued to fare poorly into adolescents at age 14. It has even been suggested that a fetal alcohol effect subtype of ADHD might be appropriate (O'Malley, 1994).

Children exposed prenatally to amphetamines, cocaine, and heroin have also demonstrated attention deficits. A study from Holland (van Baar & de Graff, 1994) evaluated the longitudinal development of children whose mothers used combinations of cocaine, heroin, and methadone during pregnancy; these children showed delays in cognitive functioning at preschool age. In a study of forty prenatally exposed children referred for psychiatric evaluation, Sumner, Mandoki, and Matthews-Ferrari (1993) found that children had better results if intervention was begun at an earlier age. The extent of amphetamine exposure during fetal life correlated with psychometric tests, aggressive behavior, adjustment, and general assessment, indicating a worse outcome for children who had a greater exposure to amphetamine during fetal life (Billing, Ericksson, Jonsson, Steneroth, & Zetterstrom, 1994). Alcoholic parents' lifestyle interacts with the central nervous system (CNS) insult produced by prenatal alcohol to produce problems with hyperactivity and attention (Nanson & Hiscock, 1990). When Brown, Coles, Smith, and Platzman (1991) studied sixty-eight ADHD children with poor-functioning alcoholic parents as well as prenatal exposure to alcohol, they discovered that improving postnatal parental alcoholism improved the child's behavior. They concluded that the ADHD seen in children of alcoholics results from the environment after birth as well as the fetal alcohol exposure.

Cocaine-exposed infants were retested at one to two days of age by Napiorkowski et al. (1996). While alcohol may have contributed synergistic effects, drug-exposed babies showed increased tone and motor activity, more jerky movements, startles, tremors, back arching, and signs of central nervous system and visual stress than unexposed infants. Poorer visual and auditory following were also seen.

In another study comparing 251 infants at 2 and 17 days of age found a dose response curve between cocaine exposure and regulation of arousal at 17 days of age (Tronick, Frank, Cabral, Mirochnick, & Zuckerman, 1996).

Genetic influences may be as important as alcohol exposure. (Compelling evidence for a genetic influence on many children with ADHD is presented later in this chapter.) Harman and Morton (1993) concluded from a study of eighty children that those who were both dyslexic and alcoholic had similar family histories to twenty control dyslexic children who had no history of prenatal exposure to drugs; 98% of the chemically dependent parents had dyslexia and/or ADD. A common link between genetic predisposition for drug dependence and ADHD was suggested by Comings (1994), who concluded after studying fifty-eight ADHD patients, thirty-five of their relatives, and fifty controls that the genes responsible for tuberous sclerosis and ADHD also seemed to play an important role in drug abuse and dependence. Griffith, Azuma, and Chasnoff (1994) concluded that generalizations about the fate of drug-exposed children must await additional research.

The studies available to date inspire substantial concern that drug and alcohol exposure represents a risk factor for the development of ADHD. However, we are not able to determine at this point how much of the risk is due to the inheritance transferred from parents who suffer from both ADHD and drug abuse, how much is the result of the chaotic environment into which these children are often born, and how much is due directly to the toxic effect of the drug or alcohol exposure.

THYROID DISORDERS

Some children with thyroid disorders show hyperactive behavior. Hauser et al. (1993) studied families afflicted with generalized resistance to thyroid hormone (GRTH). They found a close association between the inherited GRTH and ADHD symptoms and concluded that the study identified a linkage between ADHD and this genetic abnormality. The linkage could be due to lack of thyroid hormone effect causing ADHD or the close proximity of the resistance of the GRTH gene to a gene that causes ADHD. An accompanying editorial (Hauser et al.) emphasized the association of thyroid abnormality with ADHD and suggested that the routine evaluation of children with ADHD be expanded to include assessment of thyroid function. However, subsequent studies failed to demonstrate thyroid abnormality in children with ADHD (Elia, Gulotta, Rose, Marin, & Rapoport, 1994; Preuss et al., 1994). However, it has been suggested that analysis of thyroid-stimulating hormones concentrations (TT3 and

TT4), may provide a physiological basis for the dichotomy between symptoms of inattention and hyperactivity (Hauser, Soler, Brucker-Davis, & Weintraub, 1997). These authors noted that although thyroid-stimulating hormone concentrations were not significantly correlated between subjects with resistance to thyroid hormone and their unaffected family members within the cohort group, when symptoms of *DSM-IV* criteria were used, there was a positive correlation between TT3 and TT4 concentrations and symptoms of hyperactivity/impulsivity. Based on the evidence, thyroid disorders are not a significant cause of ADHD.

OTHER ENDOCRINE DISORDERS AND TOXINS

Other associations between endocrine disorders and ADHD include a single report linking low cholesterol levels with aggressive behavior (Virkkunen & Penttinen, 1984). Another single study suggested a link between cortisol and ADHD. Kaneko, Hoshino, Hashimoto, and Okano, 1993 studied saliva cortisol and found an abnormal diurnal rhythm and nonsuppression on a dexamethasone suppression test in ADHD subjects. A relationship between testosterone and observed aggression, and cortisol and emotional disorders in a group of disruptive children was suggested by Scerbo and Kolko (1994).

The association between amino acid abnormalities and ADHD was reported in phenylketonuria by Braverman (1989). Children with ADD were found to have significantly lower levels of phenylalanine, tyramine, tryptophane, histidine, and isoleucine by Bornstein, Baker, Carroll, and King (1990).

The question of candida yeast as a cause of ADHD has been raised but never established (Crook, 1985). Serum carnosinase deficiency has been suggested as a cause of ADHD (M. Cohen, 1985), as has cadmium toxicity as shown by hair analysis (Steward-Pinkham, 1989). A case report suggested a link between serum and hair zinc levels and ADHD (McGee, Williams, Anderson, & McKenzie-Parnell, 1990).

An evaluation of children following strep infections found the production of antineural antibodies in many children after beta hemolytic strep infections, leading the authors to suggest a possible linkage between strep infections and ADHD (Kiessling, Marcotte, & Culpepper, 1993).

LEAD

Lead is a trace element that has no known use in the human body. Ingested flakes of lead paint can poison the energy production within brain cells; as the brain becomes more and more swollen, general brain function decreases and thinking becomes confused. Convulsions can occur, and swelling can progress to brain injury and death (Byers, 1959).

Can lead intoxication too mild to produce brain swelling and convulsions cause attention deficit symptoms? De la Burde and Choate (1975) presented a collaborative study of sixty-seven 7-year-old children. These children had a history of eating plaster and paint when they were between 1 and 3 years of age. At that time, their qualitative urinary coproporphyrin tests were positive (suggesting lead poisoning), and they had elevated blood lead levels (.04 mg/dl and above) and/or radiological findings suggesting lead poisoning but no clinical symptoms. At age 7 their performance on a series of psychological tests was compared with those of seventy children of the same age and socioeconomic background who did not have significant exposure to lead. Lead-exposed children had deficits in global IQ and associative abilities, in visual and fine motor coordination, and in behavior. School failure resulting from learning and behavior problems was more frequent in the lead-exposed than in the control group. The question remained, however, whether the children had problems as a result of lead or had ingested lead as a result of abnormal behavior.

The relationship between lead level and IQ in a group of children exposed to lead in the environment was studied by Landrigan et al. (1975). Forty-six symptom-free children, aged 3 to 15, with blood lead concentrations of 40 to 68 (mean 48 mcg/100 ml.) and seventy-eight ethnically and socioeconomically similar controls with levels less than 40 (mean 27) were compared. All the children lived within 6.6 kilometers of a large lead-emitting smelter. "Testing with Wechsler Intelligence Scales for school children and preschool children showed age-adjusted performance IQ to be significantly decreased in the group with higher lead levels (mean scores WISC or WPPSI: 95 versus 103). Children in the lead group also had significant slowing in a finger-wrist tapping test" (p. 708). Full-scale IQ, verbal IQ, and hyperactivity ratings were unchanged by lead exposure. This study suggests that for this group of children living in a high-lead environment, higher blood lead levels are associated with lower-performance IQ.

Exposure also has been associated with increased risk for antisocial and delinquent behavior. Needleman, Riess, Tobin, Biesecker, and Greenhouse (1996) used K-X-ray spectroscopy of the tibia to determine lead exposure. They discovered that high bone lead levels were associated with an increased risk of exceeding the critical score for attention, aggression, and delinquency problems. Kahn, Kelly, and Walker (1995), however, found no correlation between elevated blood lead and ADHD. In a study of forty-three children, only one had an elevated blood level.

Possibly the most influential study of lead was reported by Needleman et al. (1979). The authors studied 3,329 children attending first and second grades in two Massachusetts towns, Chelsea and Summerville. Voluntary collection of shed teeth was obtained in 70% of the children. The 10% of the children with the highest concentration of dentine lead and the 10% with the lowest were chosen for analysis. Four or five years earlier, blood readings had been taken in twenty-three children with high lead levels and fifty-eight with low lead levels. When lead levels in shed teeth were compared with earlier determinations, there was a significant correlation between previous blood lead levels of the high-tooth-lead and low-tooth-lead groups. The blood lead level of both groups was well within normal limits. When IQ was evaluated, a strong correlation was seen between full-scale WISC-R IQ and lead level. The low-lead group had an IQ score over four points higher than the high-lead group. Significant correlation was also seen with three measures of auditory and verbal processing on attentional performance and with most items of a teacher's behavioral rating.

These findings suggest that there may be a group of children with attention deficit, behavior, or developmental symptoms that at least in part are the result of lead exposure. How much of the behavior and learning problems is caused by other differences in the two groups (such as genetic influences evidenced by poor parental education in the high-lead group) or by sample bias (higher percentage of males than females in the high-lead group) is yet to be determined. The significant correlation between blood and dentine lead levels on the one hand and full-scale IQ, verbal and auditory processing reaction time, and behavioral ratings on the other suggests that lead may be a significant contributor to ADHD symptoms.

It is difficult to know what should be done as a result of these studies. Long-term longitudinal studies continue to investigate the relationship among lead level, cognitive development, and behavior (Wyngaarden, 1988). There is no evidence that treatment for lead poisoning would improve the performance of the children with the higher dentine lead levels. In addition, there was substantial performance overlap between the two groups. Finding slightly above average lead level in either blood or teeth could not be used to help diagnose ADHD. Without understanding how these children came to acquire higher lead levels, one cannot judge which public health measures would be effective in preventing the problem. Nevertheless, there is a disturbing suggestion of a relationship between lead ingestion and learning and attentional problems. There may be some children in whom lead is a contributing factor to attention deficit.

ALLERGY

Allergies cause a wide range of symptoms, including stomach pain, diarrhea, runny nose, wheezing, and sleeplessness, to mention only a few. But what about hyperactivity? ADHD behavior was more common in eighty-one atopic children (eczema, hayfever, and asthma) than in seventy-one age- and gender-matched controls (Roth, Beyreiss, Schlenzka, & Beyer, 1991). In a review of the literature, Marhsall (1989) suggested that a small subgroup of ADHD children may be provoked by allergies. Children with eczema severe enough to warrant treatment at a dermatology clinic may constitute a special group. However, the higher incidence of depression and other emotional disorders in children suffering from chronic illness may be a nonspecific secondary feature of the chronic illness. In 1,037 children studied, the development of allergic symptoms was not associated with increased incidence of ADHD (McGee, Stanton, & Sears, 1993).

Children who are symptomatic from allergy, eczema, or asthma may have ADHD symptoms due to medications used to treat the allergies, nonspecific effect of chronic illness, or coincidental occurrence of the two disorders in the same child. Available information, however, does not support the concept that ADHD symptoms may be the result of an allergic reaction that produces no other symptoms.

Does treatment for asthma improve or worsen ADHD? Two studies have suggested that theophylline used for treatment of asthma does not affect ADHD behavior. When children in a double-blind crossover study were given either theophylline or placebo, neither parents nor children could accurately guess the child's medication condition (L. Rappaport et al., 1989): there was no correlation between medication and behavior. The second study (Bender & Milgrom, 1992) found that parental beliefs that theophylline caused behavioral change were not consistent with their direct observations, which showed no correlate between taking theophylline and deterioration of behavior.

ADHD SECONDARY TO MEDICAL PROBLEMS

Some children exhibit ADHD symptoms as a result of unrelated medical illness (P. Wender, 1987). Possibly, the term ADHD should not be applied to the inattentive, distractible, variable, and impulsive behaviors observed in children with certain medical illnesses. Cantwell and Baker (1987) reviewed the "diagnostic processes in making the differential diagnosis of hyperactivity" (p. 159). They presented the view that the primary care physician will be able to conduct an initial evaluation and make an active differential diagnosis. They separated clinical psychiatric disorders, developmental disorders, physical and neurological disorders, and psychosocial and environmental factors from birth weight various forms of pre-, peri-, and postnatal difficulties (e.g., very difficult deliveries, asphyxia, and maternal infection during pregnancy), movement disorders (e.g., Sydenham's chorea), hyperthyroidism, infection with pinworms, and sleep apnea. Cantwell and Baker argue that the diagnosis of ADHD is not appropriate to characterize the impulsive, inattentive, and distractible behavior seen in children with these medical conditions.

Discovery of a medical disorder associated with ADHD may result in a definitive treatment eliminating the ADHD symptoms, modifying factors that aggravate ADHD behavior, or simply producing additional knowledge about the background of the behavior. Although there is much speculation about the role of various medical and environmental problems, it is only rarely that uncovering a medical problem results in successful elimination of ADHD symptoms.

Otitis Media

An association between otitis media (ear infection) and hyperactivity was reported by Hagerman and Falkenstein (1987). Ninety-four percent of a group of children with a *DSM-III* diagnosis of ADD with hyperactivity had a history of three or more ear infections, whereas only 50% of nonhyperactive school-failure children used as controls had three or more infections. Of the hyperactive group, 69% had a previous history of more than ten infections, whereas only 20% of the nonhyperactive group had more than ten infections. Further support for the hyperactivity–ear infection link came from another retrospective study (Addesman et al., 1990). Children seen in a child development clinic with ADD-H had, by parent report, significantly more complaints of earaches during the preceding three months and significantly more infections during the preceding year. Other studies, however, have shown no relationship between otitis media and behavioral outcome. Black and Sonnenschein (1993), studying thirty-one inner-city children, found that language-developmental status was unrelated to a history of otitis media. Arcia and Roberts (1993) studied seventy children prospectively, determining the presence of otitis media by examination rather than basing the diagnosis on parents' recollection; they found no significant association between otitis media and effusion during the first three years of life and two measures of attention (psychologist ratings and CPT performance). Initial reports of increased incidence of ear infections in ADHD children raised concern that ADHD might be an additional sequelae of otitis media. Prospective studies, however, have suggested that otitis media carefully diagnosed does not predispose to ADHD. It is possible that although a screaming child is not more likely to develop otitis, he or she may be more likely to have it diagnosed.

Anemia

Early studies of teenage males found a correlation between anemia and personality disturbance, conduct problems, feelings of inadequacy, and immaturity (Webb & Oski, 1973, 1974). Lassitude, ability to concentrate, and mood were improved by treating iron-deficiency anemia in a double-blind crossover study of fifty-nine 16- and 17-year-old girls (Oski & Rosenstein, 1992). Additional studies are needed to determine how much of the ADHD seen in children and adolescents can be helped by treating iron-deficiency anemia.

Seizure Disorders (Epilepsy) and Medication for Their Treatment

Children with epilepsy show significant differences in motor speed, impulsivity, and inattention when compared with normal children (W. Mitchell, Chavez, Zhou, & Guzman, 1988). Whether epilepsy itself causes ADHD, or an underlying brain injury causes both epileptic seizures and ADHD, remains unanswered. Goulden and Shinnar (1988) reported that the behavior disorders seen in mentally retarded children or children with cerebral palsy are unrelated to the presence or severity of seizures, suggesting that the high incidence of behavior disorder in this population is a reflection of the underlying brain injury. Generalized absence epilepsy (previously called petit mal) produces spells of staring and inattention during a seizure; this condition must be diagnosed and treated differently from ADHD. (Additional information concerning this disorder is presented in Chapter 6.) A rare form of subclinical seizure activity entitled continuous spike waves during slow wave sleep (CSWS) because of the EEG findings, has been reported to cause symptoms similar to those of ADHD (Perez, Davidoff, Despland, & Deonna, 1993).

Medications used to treat epilepsy may cause some ADHD symptoms in some children. In one study (Pellock et al., 1988), thirty children changed from phenobarbital or diphenylhydantoin to carbamazepine showed significant improvement in color naming, finger oscillation, continuous performance time, reaction time, digit vigilance, and Conners Parent's Questionnaire total score.

Not all studies, however, have shown an effect of medication on behavior. For example, W. Mitchell et al. (1988) found no difference, including on the Conners questionnaires, between children taking antiepileptic drugs and those who were drug-free in a group of 110 children with epilepsy compared to 152 normal controls. In addition, performance on a microcomputer-based video game showed no change with varying levels of medication, including phenobarbital and carbamazepine (Tegretol®).

Fragile X Syndrome

A genetic deficit known as Fragile X syndrome has been associated with ADHD. A fragile site on Q27 of the X chromosome gives this syndrome its name. Clinical symptoms include large ears and testes in males; most children with Fragile X are mentally retarded. Hagerman, Kemper, and Hudson (1985) report four boys who were not retarded but had learning disabilities and attentional problems associated with Fragile X syndrome. Their report points to a group of children whose learning disabilities and attentional problems apparently result from a definable genetic defect; the abnormal chromosome is the presumed cause of the learning and attention problems seen in these four children. Because chromosome studies are ordinarily not performed on most children with attention deficit, it is difficult to be certain how common this syndrome is. Individuals with Fragile X manifest a variable clinical phenotype that includes distinctive facial features, macro-orchidism, cognitive and language impairments, and impressive prevalence of attention deficit disorder and infantile autism (Biederman et al., 1987; Bregman, Dykens, Watson, & Ort, 1987). Presence of unusual features (ears and testes) in a child with ADHD might warrant evaluation by chromosome studies to determine whether Fragile X is present. Although some improvement in genetic counseling might be possible if the Fragile X was discovered, at this point not enough is known about the children with ADHD and Fragile X to comment on changes in treatment or expectation of outcome for this group.

ADHD SECONDARY TO NONMEDICAL PROBLEMS

It has been suggested that attention deficit symptoms are the result of difficulty with learning (Cunningham & Barkley, 1978a; McGee & Share, 1988). Attention-deficient children function better if their academic tests are not challenging, and demonstrate increasing difficulty as task-complexity increases (Whalen et al., 1978). They perform better on self-paced tasks than when required to work at a pace set by others (Henker & Whalen, 1980). The inattentive child functions best when frustration is kept to a minimum (Battle & Lacy, 1972). It follows that the successful treatment of learning difficulties may result in resolution of the ADHD symptoms. Reinforcement contingent on academic productivity has been shown to increase the quality and quantity of academic output in disruptive children (McGee & Share, 1988). This body of research provides evidence that there may be a subgroup of learning-disabled children who develop ADHD symptoms as the result of school frustration.

Other behavioral problems of childhood, such as depressive and oppositional disorders, as well as other cognitive problems involving memory, achievement, language, auditory processing, and general intelligence, can produce symptoms similar to ADHD (see discussion in Chapter 4).

HEREDITY

The majority of children with learning and attention problems are found to have none of the specific etiologies mentioned above. A positive family history of ADHD symptoms, however, is a common finding. In many children, a close family member has had symptoms of attention deficit in childhood. Hyperactivity is present in the parents of hyperactive children four times more often than those of controls (Biederman et al., 1986; Cantwell, 1972; Morrison & Stewart, 1971).

The genetic contribution to ADHD has been postulated by a number of authors (Hechtman, 1993; Rutter et al., 1990; Stevenson, 1992). The underlying mechanism genetically has recently been suggested to be associated with a single dopamine transporter gene (Cook, Stein, & Krasowski, 1995) as well as with variation in the D4 receptor gene (LaHoste, Swanson, & Wigal, 1996). It has also been suggested by some that the trait locus for reading disability on chromosome 6 identified by Cardon et al. (1994, 1995) may also be a locus for ADHD (Warren et al., 1995). Recent studies linking polymorphisms in the dopaminergic system to ADHD (Comings, Wu, & Chiu, 1996) and the dopamine D4 receptor polymorphisms to dimensional aspects of impulsivity (Benjamin et al., 1996; Ebstein, Novick, & Umansky, 1996) suggest polymorphisms identified to date do not account for all of the relevant heritable variation in ADHD. The findings of Sherman, Iacono, and McGue (1997) suggest that future molecular genetic studies of ADHD may yield more information of ADHD as a disorder composed of two quantitatively, continuously distributed dimensions—inattention and hyperactivity/impulsivity—rather than a homogenous categorical disorder.

Eaves, Silberg, and Hewitt (1993) note two complimentary approaches to the genetic analysis of ADHD. The first, a dimensional approach, involves the study of a normal range of activity and assumes that ADHD is at one end of the continuum of a specific trait. The second categorical approach is based upon studying children of families who meet diagnostic criteria and assumes that ADHD is a discreet disorder (Faraone, Biederman, Chen, & Krifcher, 1992). It is important for practitioners to recognize that dimensional approaches have been found to better predict life outcome (Fergusson & Horwood, 1995).

Twin studies often help differentiate genetic and environmental factors. Monozygotic (identical) twins have identical genetics, as they originate from the same fertilized egg; dizygotic (fraternal or nonidentical) twins differ from each other genetically, as they arise from separate eggs fertilized by different sperm. Monozygotic twins raised in different environments (adopted by different sets of parents) will develop similar genetically determined characteristics. Willerman (1973) studied ninety-three sets of twin girls. If one identical twin was hyperactive, the other was more likely to be hyperactive; very few of the genetically different, dizygotic twins were both hyperactive. This finding suggests a strong element of heredity, at least in this group of twin girls. Gilger, Pennington, and DeFries (1992) found similar although nonsignificant enhanced concordance in monozygotic versus dizygotic twins.

Among trait approaches, Willerman (1973) found heritability of scores on an activity questionnaire to be 0.77 for a sample of 54 monozygotic and 39 dizygotic twin pairs. However, Goodman and Stevenson (1989) reported a heritability estimate of greater than one in a sample of 285 twin pairs. This finding appeared to be due to an extremely low dizygotic correlation. Corresponding dizygotic correlations for fathers but not mothers compared with teacher reports of behavior were much higher, resulting in heritability estimates from 0.48 to 0.68. A subsequent twin study by Thaper, Hervas, and McGuffin (1995) using the same three activity items confirmed the low dizygotic correlation in maternal ratings and suggested the role of reciprocal interactions in which twins interact with each other to be different or mother's exaggerate differences between their dizygotic twins. The low dizygotic correlations may, however, be unique to these specific questions about activity level. Edelbrock, Rende, Plowman, and Thompson (1995) reported correlations predominantly from mothers' of .86 for monozygotic twins and .29 for dizygotic twins giving a heritability estimate of 0.66. Zahn-Waxler, Schmitz, Fulker, Robinson, and Ende (1996) obtained a very similar estimate. However, somewhat lower heritability values were obtained from fathers' and teachers' ratings and the correlation between raters was low.

From a categorical or diagnostic approach, Goodman and Stevenson (1989) demonstrated a proband-wise concordance rate of 51% in 39 monozygotic twin pairs and 30% in 54 dizygotic twin pairs yielding a heritability estimate of 0.64. De Fries and Fulker (1985, 1988), utilizing a statistical regression method developed by Gillis, Gilger, Pennington, and De Fries (1992), estimated the heritability of ADHD as 0.91 plus or minus 0.36 for twins participating in a research project.

Studies of ADHD families have added to our knowledge of the disorder. Despite the complexity of ADHD, the hypothesis that it is caused by a single gene has been supported by some family studies. Faraone, Biederman, Chen, and Krifcher (1992) found that segregation analysis suggested a single gene hypothesis best fit their group of 257 ADHD boys and 808 of their relatives. The GRTH genetic linkage studies also suggest a single gene for ADHD. Dominant inheritance was suggested by Deutsch, Matthysse, Swanson, and Farkas (1990) as a result of a study of minor physical anomalies present in forty-eight ADHD boys and eighty-two first-degree relatives. Genetic studies suggest ADHD is different from learning disability and CD (Faraone, Biederman, Keenan, & Tsuang, 1991; Frick, Lahey, Christ, et al., 1991). When ADHD is combined with CD or ODD, offspring are more likely to have those disorders than if only one of the problems is present (Faraone et al.).

Additional evidence for a familial pattern of transmission of ADHD was found from a study of parental psychopathology in children with CD and ADHD (Lahey, Pelham, Schaughency, Atkins, et al., 1988). When CD and ADHD occurred together, markedly more aggression and illegal activity in both fathers and children was seen. Attention deficit is more common in the fathers and uncles of attention-disordered children than in the relatives of children without attention disorder (Cantwell, 1972, 1975; Morrison & Stewart, 1971; M. Stewart, DeBlois, & Cummings, 1980). Inattentive symptoms are not more common in the nonbiological relatives of attention-disordered children adopted and raised by biologically unrelated families (Cantwell, 1975; Morrison & Stewart, 1973a).

The issue of phenotypic definition as indicated by the variation in estimates of siblings' risk is 53%, 25%, or 17% depending upon whether the behavior is defined as hyperactivity, attention deficit disorder or ADHD. This speaks to the complexity of relating phenotype to genotype (Biederman, Faraone, Keenan, & Benjamin, 1992; Biederman, Faraone, Keenan, Knee, & Tsuang, 1990; Faraone, Biederman, Chen, & Krifcher, 1992; Safer, 1973). Levy, Hay, McStephen, Wood, and Waldman (1997), based upon a cohort of 1,938 families with twins and siblings, ages four through twelve years recruited from the Australian National Health and Medical Research Council Twin Registry, reported that ADHD is best viewed as the extreme of behavior that varies genetically throughout the entire population rather than as a disorder with discreet determinants. In this study, as with others, heritability estimates for monozygotic versus dizygotic twins were significantly higher. As Levy et al. note, ADHD has an exceptionally high heritability compared with other behavioral disorders. These authors reported that 82% of monozygotic twins and 38% of dizygotic twins met an eight-symptom ADHD cutoff for proband concordance.

Heredity appears to represent the most common identifiable cause of ADHD (Stevenson, 1994). However, the disorder represents a complex interaction of genetics and experience (for review, see Rutter, 1997). From an experiential perspective, the nonshared environment likely plays a more significant role than the shared environment (Pike & Plomin, 1996) in the presentation of behavioral disorders such as ADHD (van den Oord & Rowe, 1997). However, some researchers have suggested that shared environment may well contain some genetic effects from conditions shared by parents and their children. Genetic effects on the environment by individuals living in that environment may increase rather than decrease across development (Elkins, McGue, & Iacono, 1997).

BRAIN DYSFUNCTION AS THE CAUSE OF ADHD

We will now examine the brain neurochemical and structural basis for ADHD behavior. Dopamine and norepinephrine are chemicals that help to transmit information from one brain cell to another; an animal model and other metabolic studies that support this theory are presented below. Right hemisphere and frontal lobe dysfunction are also considered. Studies showing abnormality in the size and function of deep frontal lobe structures are presented as an anatomical correlation with ADHD. Large networks involving frontal, parietal, and cingulate structure as the basis for ADHD are discussed. Finally, a brain model integrating these concepts is suggested.

Animal Model

Animal studies give important clues to the cause of some illnesses observed in humans. If an animal equivalent or animal model of illness is discovered, the cause of the animal illness may be similar to that of humans. The more features seen in the animal illness that correspond to the human disorder, the better are the insights of cause and treatment learned from the animal model.

An animal model of attention deficit based on dopamine has been developed by S. Shaywitz et al. (1982). An infant rat is administered a chemical that seeks out and selectively destroys dopamine nerve endings. The chemical (6 hydroxydopamine) is administered into the spinal fluid at the base of the skull. Rapid and permanent reduction of brain dopamine to concentrations of 10% to 25% of that in controls is produced. Other brain chemicals, notably norepinephrine and serotonin, remain unaffected.

As the rats develop, they go through a period of time while immature during which they demonstrate increased activity and increased difficulty learning. As they mature, the hyperactivity resolves, but they continue to have difficulty with certain types of learning tasks. The hyperactivity and learning problems seen in the dopamine-depleted rat pups improved with amphetamine (B. Shaywitz, Yager, & Klopper, 1976) and methylphenidate (B. Shaywitz, Klopper, & Gordon, 1978), and exacerbation of the hyperactivity was produced by administration of phenobarbital (B. Shaywitz & Pearson, 1978). The rat pups also had difficulty with a novel environment (B. Shaywitz, Gordon, Klopper, & Zelterman, 1977). Environmental manipulation (being raised with normal littermates) was shown to improve motor activity in the avoidance performance of these rats as well (Pearson et al., 1980).

In the animal model, increased activity and difficulty with certain kinds of learning are produced not by damage to any specific location of the brain but by damage to the nerve endings that deliver dopamine in their locations throughout the entire brain. This lends substantial support to the concept that a dysfunction of dopamine-containing neurons is the underlying structural defect that results in the clinical syndrome of attention deficit.

Metabolic Studies on Human Subjects

Chemicals such as dopamine flow from the brain to the cerebrospinal fluid (CSF) that surrounds the brain. CSF reflects chemical change within the brain. Changes in dopamine metabolism, as measured in spinal fluid, were found in children with MBD (Shaywitz, Cohen, & Bowers, 1977). The presence of changes in dopamine rather than serotonin metabolites raised the suspicion that dopamine was the principal system involved with the chemical changes of attention deficit.

Homovanillic acid (HVA) is a dopamine metabolite; 5-hydroxyindoleacetic acid (HIAA) is a metabolite of serotonin. Shetty and Chase (1976) studied HVA and HIAA levels in spinal fluid of twenty-three children aged 2 to 13 years. They found that the base levels of the dopamine and serotonin metabolites (HVA and HIAA) were identical, but that the level of the dopamine metabolite (HVA) was substantially reduced by dextroamphetamine treatment and that the amount of HVA correlated closely with the degree of clinical improvement. These results support the view that an alteration in central dopamine-mediated synaptic function may occur in children manifesting the hyperactive syndrome.

Chemical metabolites or breakdown products of brain chemicals are found excreted in urine. Changes in chemical composition of this readily available substance may reflect changes in brain chemical composition. Shekim et al. (1987) found subtle correlations between dopamine metabolites secreted in urine of hyperactive children and various behavioral and academic qualities.

Other studies, however, have suggested the importance of the noradrenalin system and the interconnection of the noradrenalin and dopamine system in controlling behavior (for review, see Shekim, Dekirmenjian, & Chapel, 1977). To explain some of the conflicting reports, a mechanism of feedback inhibition of norepinephrine- and dopamine-containing neurons has been proposed (Raskin, Shaywitz, Shaywitz, Anderson, & Cohen, 1984). Medications such as clonidine, which have been effective in treating attention deficit symptoms in some children, also act to decrease the release of norepinephrine (Bunney & Aghajanian, 1976; Huang & Maas, 1981; Stark & Montel, 1973).

Using the prolactin response to the fenfluramine challenge as a measure of serotonergic function, Halperin et al. (1997) found that aggressive boys with a parental history of aggressive behavior have a significantly lower prolactin response than aggressive boys without a parental history of aggression. They concluded there was an association between parental aggressive behavior and lower serotonergic function in aggressive boys with ADHD. The significance of this association remains for further investigation.

Attempts to show that ADHD is the result of a change in dopamine, noradrenalin, or serotonin may suffer from oversimplification. The interconnection of dopamine, noradrenalin, and serotonin systems raises the possibility that a change in the function of the dopamine system may be reflected as decreased or increased performance of a different chemical system, such as the noradrenalin or serotonin system. To understand this, consider the hypothetical change in dopamine in hyperactive children. Say that ADHD children are found to have a lower level of dopamine in the brain. At first, this might seem to imply that dopamine is responsible for ADHD; however, a possible alternative explanation is that dopamine changes were a reaction to the ADHD. In other words, another system, such as the noradrenalin system, would be responsible for the ADHD, and in response to the noradrenalin change, dopamine metabolism would change. In this hypothetical example, the change in dopamine metabolism would represent a secondary response of the brain in an attempt to compensate for the primary change.

Data presented on the interaction of dopamine and norepinephrine remind us that these systems are complex and that simple measurements of increased and decreased levels do not suffice to explain the workings of the catecholamine systems. Nevertheless, the finding that metabolism of these chemicals is changed in children with attention deficit symptoms and that these chemical systems are changed by medications that improve the symptoms of attention deficit lead to the important conclusion that the chemical systems that have their nerve-cell bodies in brain stem nuclei are important factors in ADHD.

The Frontal Lobe

Injury to the right cerebral hemisphere in adults produces a syndrome of neglect of the left side, spatial discrimination difficulties, and other characteristics. Developmental right-hemisphere-deficit syndrome is characterized by ten-point disparity between WISC-R verbal and performance IQ, weakness on picture completion and object assembly subtests, impaired design copying, low math computation, and reading comprehension one grade below oral word recognition (Sunder, DeMarco, Fruitiger, & Levey, 1988). Of twenty children studied, 75% were also described as apraxic (poor fine motor skills), and 75% had attention deficits that did not respond well to a trial of medication; 75% also had significant social and emotional difficulties beyond hyperactivity. Further evaluation of this collection of symptoms may prove useful in defining a group that can be expected to be unresponsive to medication.

Abnormal scores on the Boder test of reading-spelling patterns was diagnostically helpful; 80% with poor scores fell into the right-hemisphere-deficit syndrome in one study. Others have found that cancellation tasks suggest right-hemisphere dysfunction in ADHD children (Voeller & Heilman, 1988). ADHD children were found to have significantly more difficulty with right hemisphere functions of motor impersistence, sustaining movement, tongue protrusion, lateral gaze, and central fixation (Voeller & Heilman, 1988).

There is significant evidence, however, that not all attentional processes reside in the right hemisphere. Mesial frontal lobe and neostriatal lesions have produced behavioral abnormalities in an animal (Iversen, 1977; verFaellie & Heilman, 1987), but similar lesions have not been found in children with ADHD. Amobarbital injected directly into the right or left carotid arteries produces sedation of either the right or left hemisphere and is used to determine whether surgical removal of one temporal lobe will produce language and memory defects. This technique allowed Huh, Meador, Loring, Lee, and Brooks (1989) to study the attentional effects of anesthetizing one hemisphere. They found substantial inattention using hand-button response to quasi-random strobe flash. When the stimulus was presented to the nonanesthetized hemisphere, the hand controlled by the nonanesthetized hemisphere responded. They found substantial alterations of attention when *either* hemisphere was sedated. Although they agreed that previous studies have shown right hemisphere dominance for spatial and tactile attention, they believed their studies supported the theory that the left hemisphere contains motor engrams necessary for elaborating skilled, purposeful movement. Proposing bilateral frontal involvement in attention, they suggested that right intracarotid amobarbital produced failure in sensory scanning and subsequent release of motor inhibition, whereas left intracarotid amobarbital would interfere primarily with the executive mechanisms of motor attention required to perform the task. This theory explains evidence of inattention with either right or left frontal dysfunction.

Understanding the cause of attention deficit from the point of view of the brain as a neurological organ has interested many researchers. Early concepts such as underarousal and overarousal (Ross & Ross, 1982) were discarded after attempts to find the physiological basis for overarousal and underarousal met with limited success. The frontal lobe dysfunction model was summarized by Conners and Wells (1986). Levine (1987) proposed an understanding of attention deficit as a dysfunction of multiple control systems, including vocal, sensory, associative, appetitive, social, motoric, behavioral, communicative, and affective control. Levine reviewed different etiologies affecting a variety of the control systems and viewed as essential understanding the symptoms as well as the treatment related to these control symptoms. Zametkin and Rapoport (1987), in a comprehensive review concerning the neurobiology of ADHD, observed that the large number of efficacious drugs do not support any single neurotransmitter defect hypothesis (see Table 5–1).

Lack of inhibition of responses may affect apparently unrelated behaviors, including prolonging the events in the mind, separating feelings from facts, self-directed speech, and breaking apart and recombining events. These functions permit self-control as well as directing future behavior. Barkley (1993) presents ADHD as the result of inability to inhibit immediate response and believes that this single dysfunction lies at the heart of ADHD behavior. As these executive functions are believed to derive from the prefrontal cortex, Barkley's approach can be seen as building on the frontal lobe theory and the concept of ADHD as an executive dysfunction.

Functional imaging, the ability to see brain activity, commonly using magnetic resonance imaging (MRI) or positron-emission tomography (PET) techniques, has increased our understanding that multiple areas of the brain engage synergistically. Spatial attention requires a network of neurons in frontal lobe to explore, parietal lobe to sense, and cingulate gagrus to develop the motivation (Gittelman et al., 1996; Mesulam, 1990). ADHD can be seen as the dysfunction of a similar network.

Network theories of ADHD also suggest frontal striatal or posterior parietal lesions. Networks are postulated for selective attention and vigilance. The selective attention network deals with engagement and disengagement and orientation of attention and is a connection among the parietal lobules, thalamus, and midbrain. Executive attention is postulated to be a function of the anterior cingulate and basal ganglia, which

Table 5–1. Neuroanatomical hypothesis of dysfunction in Attention Deficit Disorder with hyperactivity

Investigator	Hypothesis	Test
Laufer & Denhoff, 1957	Diencephalic dysfunction (thalamus, hypothalamus)	HA have lower photometrazol seizure
Knobel et al., 1959	Cortical "overfunctioning"	
Satterfield & Dawson, 1971	Decreased levels of reticular activating system excitation	
Wender, 1971, 1972	Decreased sensitivity in limbic areas of positive reinforcement (medial forebrain bundle: hypothalamus; NE)	Multiple medication trials
Conners et al., 1964	Lack of "cortical inhibitory capacity"	
Dykman et al., 1971	Defect in forebrain inhibitory system over ventral formulation + diencephalon	
Hunt et al., 1985	Locus coerulens dysfunction (hypersensitive alphapostsynaptic receptor)	Clonidine growth hormone response
Lou et al., 1984	Central frontal lobes, anterolateral, posterolateral Caudate region	Cerebral blood flow
Gorenstein & Newman, 1980	Dysfunction of medial septum, hippocampus orbito-frontal cortex	Animal lesion studies
Porrino et al., 1984	Nucleus acumbens	Animal studies, 2-D-C studies with low-dose stimulants
Mattes, 1980	Frontal lobe	Speculation
Gualtieri & Hicks, 1985	Frontal lobe	Speculation
Arnold et al., 1977	Nigrostriatal tract	Amphetamine Rx
Chelune et al., 1986	Frontal lobe	Neuropsychiatric testing

Source: Zametkin, A. J. & Rapoport, J. L. (1987). Neurobiology of attention deficit disorder with hyperactivity: Where have we come in 50 years? Copyright 1987 by the *Journal of the American Academy of Child and Adolescent Psychiatry, 26,* 676–686. Used with permission.

detects and brings into awareness. A vigilance network has been postulated for the right frontal lobe with a purpose of maintaining attention (Posner & Petersen, 1990; Posner & Raichle (1994).

The concept of networks is important because it implies that different parts of the brain function simultaneously and synergistically to produce results. Injury or abnormality in any of the network stations will produce symptoms (Mesulam, 1990). Further evidence for the basal ganglia and frontal lobe to participate in developing and sustaining attention comes from many sources. The development of the right anterior cingulate region is proportional to the development of attention in children (Casey, Giedd, Vauss, Vaituzis, & Rapoport, 1992). Duplication of aspects of ADHD with frontal or caudate lesions has been noted (Heilman, Voeller, & Nadeau, 1991; Voeller, 1991). In animal studies (monkeys), MPTP, a chemical that depletes frontal and striatal dopamine and norepinephrine, was shown to produce delayed response, frustration, need for redirection, restlessness, and fidgetiness believed similar to ADHD symptoms (Roeltgen & Schneider, 1991). Decreased striatal perfusion in ADD children partly reversed with methylphenidate is a further suggestion of a striatal contribution to ADHD (Lou, Henriksen, Bruhn, Borner, & Nielsen, 1989).

The results of positron emission tomography studies have been difficult to interpret (Ernst, Cohen, Liebenauer, Jons, & Zametkin, 1997). A low brain metabolism in pre-frontal and cingulate regions as well as right thalamus, caudate and hippocampus was uncovered in adults with a history of ADHD (Zametkin et al., 1990). Further studies, however, suggested that only a few statistically significant differences in regional glucose utilization between ADHD boys and control boys were seen (Ernst et al., 1994; Zametkin, Liebenauer, & Fitzgerald, et al., 1993). An additional study with PET, however, showed decreased glucose utilization in different areas, including the left frontal lobe, thalamus, right temporal lobe, and right hippocampus, as well as different patterns with methylphenidate or Dexedrine (Matochik et al., 1994). Although the authors concluded that these studies suggest glucose utilization was changed throughout the brain, the inconsistent findings raised a question as to the essential nature of a particular glucose utilization pattern in ADHD. In girls, however, reduced glucose metabolic rates were highly suggestive. Further studies (Ernst et al., 1997), however, failed to reproduce the lower global metabolic rate in girls, but suggested functional interactions between sex and brain development. The authors recommended that sexual maturation should be controlled in future regional metabolic glucose studies. Regional abnormalities of glucose metabolism demonstrated by PET studies have been widely publicized and have appeared to show a fundamental biologic difference between ADHD and normal subjects have left doubts as to the significance of these findings.

MRI is a sensitive tool for evaluating brain structure. Several MRI studies of brains of ADHD children show asymmetries and unusual findings; unfortunately, findings are not consistent across studies. Reversal of the normal left-to-right asymmetry in the caudate was seen in one study (Hynd, Hern, Novey, & Eliopulos, 1993); a symmetric caudate volumes with the right larger than left in the normal population was seen in another study (Castellanos, Giedd, Eckburg, et al., 1994). Further support for a right hemisphere basal ganglia/frontal lobe abnormality in ADHD is supplied by the quantitative magnetic resonance imaging study of Castellanos et al. (1996). Fifty-seven boys with ADHD and 55 healthy matched controls, age 5 to 18 years, were compared examing 12 subcortical regions. Total cerebral volume was smaller for the ADHD boys. Loss of normal right left asymmetry in the caudate and the smaller right globus pallidus, right anterior frontal and cerebellar regions were seen. In addition there was reversal of the normal lateral ventricular asymmetry. The authors concluded that the ADHD theory which hypothesizes a dysfunction of the right sided prefrontal striatal system was supported by these measures. A smaller total brain volume was reported in one study (Hynd, Semrud-Clikeman, et al., 1991), but another found no difference between ADHD and controls (Hynd et al., 1990). Morphological studies of the corpus callosum, the main pathway for connections between the hemispheres, have also resulted in different conclusions. Two parts of the corpus callosum, the genu and splenium, were found to be smaller in ADHD subjects in two studies (Hynd, Semrud-Clikeman, et al.; Semrud-Clikeman et al., 1994), but another part of the corpus callosum, the rostral section, was found abnormal in another study (Giedd et al., 1994). In another MRI study, Filipek et al. (1997) found that ADHD children had a small left total caudate and caudate head, representing reversed asymmetry, decreased right frontal region, decreased bilateral anterior inferior region, and decreased bilateral retrocallosal region. There was a correlation between findings and lack of medication responsiveness, with the small symmetric caudate and the smallest left anterior superior region seen in nonresponders. Quantitative evaluation of basal ganglia structures in ADHD boys (10) and girls with both Tourette's syndrome and ADHD (16) compared to normal boys (11) matched for age, concluded that small globus pallidus volume especially on the left is associated with ADHD (Aylward et al., 1996). Many studies have found unusual asymmetries or other abnormalities in the front basal ganglia, or the corpus callosum, but these results have not been consistent across studies. Nevertheless, when taken as a whole, one suspects a dysfunction of the frontal striatal system is likely important in the development of ADHD symptoms. It should not be surprising that the search for structural abnormality underlying ADHD has been elusive, as consistent structural abnormality underlying mental retardation and learning disabilities as well as schizophrenia, depression, and other disorders has also remained elusive.

A BRAIN MODEL OF ADHD

The model that will be presented may help to explain some of the conflicting information concerning experimental work on attention deficit and the mechanism of drug action.

Within the cerebral hemispheres, information from primary senses, such as vision, smell, and hearing, and somatosensory information is converted into electrical impulses that are sent to specific areas of the cerebral cortex. There is a primary area for sensory information for each of the senses: the occipital region for visual information; the temporal region for hearing and sound; the parietal, postcentral region for touch; and the inferior frontal lobes for the sense of smell. Injury to these areas produces a specific set of symptoms involving inability to utilize these primary sensory modalities.

Other areas of the cerebral hemispheres involve translating primary sensory input into symbolic function or preparing a response. These association areas are usually adjacent to the primary sensory or motor areas and lie in the parietal-occipital, frontal, and temporal-parietal region. Some of these association areas, when injured, prevent the codification and understanding of primary sensory information. For example, the inability to understand words written on the page is the result of an injury to the association area in the parietal-occipital region.

The brain stem includes midbrain, pons, medulla, caudate, putamen, globus pallidus, and thalamus. Among other things, some brain stem nerve cells have regulatory function. For example, the hypothalamic hunger and satiety centers do not affect the ability to chew or swallow but do regulate interest in acquiring and ingesting food. Other brain stem centers regulate tiredness and wakefulness, temperature, heart rate, blood pressure, sensitivity to pain, and many other functions.

Other groups of cells make certain chemicals, including dopamine, noradrenalin, and serotonin. They then distribute these chemicals through axons to all other areas of the brain. Dopamine is transferred from the substantia nigra of the midbrain, noradrenalin from the locus ceruleus of the pons in the brain stem, and serotonin from neurons located in the raphe nuclei in the medulla. For example, dopamine travels to the basal ganglia; disruptions in dopamine pathways result in the clinical symptoms of Parkinson's disease, including stiffness and decreased movement. It is possible to improve the functioning of this dopamine system with a medication, L-dopa, which is converted into dopamine by nerve cells, improves the symptoms of Parkinson's disease.

Attention and concentration is not an all-or-nothing phenomenon. There are situations when one would be appropriately inattentive. For example, a person walking on a lonely and deserted city street would react to the rustling of paper a few feet away by looking in the direction of the rustling paper; in different circumstances, for example when sitting in a classroom, a person would try to concentrate on the teacher and inhibit responding to the same rustling of paper. Most students are able to adjust their attention and concentration ability so that they can be less inhibited in certain situations and yet remain focused in other situations.

The attention system that allows this change of inhibition and subsequent concentration and distractibility does not represent a single group of neurons or a single microscopic, anatomical location. It projects to all areas of the brain and modulates a change in state from intense concentration to easy distractibility in normal subjects. When it is functioning well, a child will be able to pay attention to the teacher at one time and at a different time be sensitive to distractions. A short time later, this child might he pitching in a baseball game, where it is necessary to concentrate on both the batter and the catcher, as well as to listen for distractions such as a player stealing second base. The attention system allows the normal subject to change concentration and attention as necessary across a wide spectrum, from intense concentration to a high degree of sensitivity to outside distractions.

The attention system may coordinate several groups of nerve cells, possibly dopamine, noradrenalin, and serotonin cells. Additional limbic, right hemisphere, and frontal cells are most likely part of this system. It need not have a single microscopic physical location to be a functional coordinating system. It most likely utilizes the dopamine neurons, whose cell bodies lie in the brain stem, but may also utilize other brain stem neurons, including noradrenalin neurons, whose cell bodies lie in the locus ceruleus, or the serotonin neurons, whose cell bodies lie in the midline raphe nuclei of the medulla. The projections of these neurons to all areas of the brain is important for a regulatory system, the purpose of which is to modulate whole brain activity.

This model may help in understanding some of the complex and conflicting information concerning attention and concentration and the symptoms of ADHD. Figure 5–1 represents a diagram of the brain, indicating a brainstem center and its communication with other areas of the brain. Attention and concentration is variable in

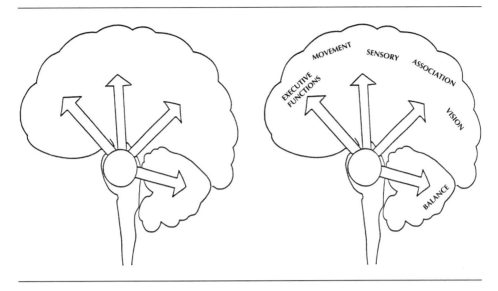

Figure 5–1.   Brain stem center and its communication with other areas of the brain

normal subjects; a wide range of possible levels of concentration and activity is needed. A normal subject must be able to act quickly without deliberation in emergency situations and yet restrain the impulse to act in other situations. A brain stem attention modulating system projecting to the many areas of the brain involved in the attention network could inhibit impulsive activity in some situations and facilitate it in others. A normal child must be able to sit quietly in a classroom at one time and run explosively on a playing field at another. The brain stem center projections to motor areas, both basal ganglia and cortex, would allow this kind of change by inhibiting motor activity and restlessness at one time, but releasing it at another. This model of brain function would suggest that changes in normal attention, concentration, motor activity, restlessness, and impulsive behavior can be viewed as resulting from different "settings" of the attention center.

The attention system must communicate with all areas of the brain because changes in motor activity, restlessness, and concentration involve all areas of the brain. The presence of dopamine, noradrenalin, and serotonin nerve cell bodies grouped in brain stem nuclei projecting to all areas of the brain would be compatible with this function. The large body of biochemical information suggesting that injury to dopamine neurons produces attention deficit is consistent with the attention center utilizing the dopamine system to effect changes in state of the entire brain. The attention center may utilize noradrenalin and serotonin as well as dopamine.

Connections among the brain stem, frontal parietal and limbic systems, and right hemisphere neurons also give and receive input. In this way, data suggesting that other chemical systems, such as noradrenalin and serotonin, and other anatomic locations, such as the frontal lobes or right hemisphere, are involved are consistent with the attention-center concept.

The clinical disorder of ADHD can be seen as a dysfunction of the attention system. A disorder in the mechanism for setting the level of the system would produce situations where the subject was always set on a high or low degree of concentration, a high or low degree of restlessness and impulsivity, or a high or low degree of motor activity. A system working ineffectively might produce responses that were variable and unpredictable; a poorly functioning center might sometimes produce an appropriate and sometimes an inappropriate level of concentration, restlessness, motor activity, or impulsivity.

In addition to the regulatory neurons, the functioning of the attention system requires an intact delivery system to transfer the message to other parts of the brain and receptors to receive these messages. The messages might be sent out appropriately from the brain stem through dopamine or noradrenalin neurons, but if the dopamine nerve endings located throughout the brain are not functioning, the system will be ineffective. There might be difficulty with synthesis of the proper amounts of the neurotransmitter or with the receptors in various parts of the brain. Dysfunctions of the target frontal or network neurons would also produce similar symptoms. The attention system consists of multiple parts, including a central core of nerve cell bodies, axons projecting to all areas of the brain, and nerve endings that act through chemical neurotransmitters and receptors throughout the brain to respond to the messages delivered by the neurotransmitters. A breakdown in any of these parts would produce symptoms of poor functioning of the system.

This model can be used to understand various kinds of data concerning attention deficit symptoms. Treatments that improve the functioning of the nerve cell bodies, axons, nerve endings, neurotransmitters, or receptors would result in improvement of the system. Injury to dopamine nerve endings by 6-hydroxydopamine in rat pups produces symptoms of distractibility and hyperkinetic behavior (Shaywitz, Hunt, Jatlow, Cohen, Young, Pierce, Anderson, & Shaywitz, 1982). Low blood flow to the basal ganglia (Lou, Henriksen, & Bruhn, 1984) or low glucose utilization of the frontal lobe (Zametkin et al., 1990), even right hemispheric dysfunction (Voeller, 1986) can be seen as the result of dysfunction of this system, resulting in decreased activity in the frontal lobes. From the point of view of the attention system, the destruction of the dopamine nerve endings would mean that messages sent by the nerve cell bodies in the brain stem would have no effect because the neurotransmitter would never be released. Methylphenidate, amphetamine, and other chemical agents that improve ADHD symptoms could act to improve the functioning of the nerve cell bodies in the brain stem or the release of neurotransmitter in the nerve endings to improve sensitivity of the postsynaptic receptors. The high degree of variability of ADHD symptoms could be seen as a variability in effectiveness of the attention system. The complex system of nerve cell bodies, axons, nerve endings, and postsynaptic receptors can be seen as working well at some times and working poorly at others, either for day-to-day or situation-to-situation variability.

The attention system model allows us to understand why treatment of attention disorders usually does not help learning disabilities. Learning disabilities can be seen as dysfunctions of cerebral cortical function as opposed to poor function of the brain stem regulatory centers. Chemical agents such as methylphenidate or amphetamine, which improve the attention system, would not improve the function of cortical neurons.

The attention system regulates a child's ability to concentrate on reading, whereas the cerebral cortical centers would determine the child's reading comprehension. Improving the attention center might improve a child's interest in reading or receptivity to reading, which may secondarily improve reading skill. The attention system concept explains why ADHD is a separate problem from a learning disability and why medications that improve attentional skills may have little direct affect on learning.

SUMMARY

This chapter presented two ways to view the cause of ADHD: as the result of environmental factors, and as the result of brain dysfunction. Some commonly suspected factors have been disproven by scientific research; for example, despite intense efforts to demonstrate the effect of sugar on behavior, well-controlled studies have consistently failed to show that dietary sugar is a significant cause of ADHD behavior. The Feingold hypothesis that food additives and natural salicylates cause ADHD symptoms has also been subjected to scientific study; food additives and not other ingested substances have usually not been shown to have a significant effect on the behavior of groups of ADHD children. Birth injury, as reflected in Apgar scores, does not correlate with subsequent development of ADHD.

Some factors associated with ADHD symptoms, such as iron-deficiency anemia as well as other medical illnesses, can cause a secondary decrease in brain function and an increase in ADHD symptoms. Evidence suggests ADHD children are more likely to have suffered frequent ear infections in infancy. Medications such as phenobarbital have been implicated. A group of provocative studies on the relationship between lead ingestion and ADHD are troublesome. Although they seem to show that there is some correlation between lead and behavior, the frequency and severity of this problem and the means of correcting it still need to be studied.

Data suggesting a correlation between learning and behavior problems and early medical problems such as hyperviscosity, fetal postmaturity, toxemia and eclampsia during pregnancy, and low blood flow were presented. Children with Fragile X chromosomal defect appear to have a high incidence of ADHD in addition to mental retardation. Children with encephalitis may develop ADHD symptoms. This group was possibly the first to stimulate scientific thinking concerning brain injury as the cause of ADHD symptoms. Taken as a group, however, all these causes account for only a small number of the children who suffer from ADHD.

Studies of heredity suggest that at least one component of the cause of ADHD is inheritance. Studies show a fourfold increase in ADHD in the fathers of ADHD boys. If one identical twin develops ADHD, the other carries a significantly increased risk of developing ADHD.

Considering the brain as a body organ, the cause of ADHD can be viewed in terms of organ dysfunction. Studies from human and animal subjects suggest that chemical pathways utilizing dopamine neurons that originate within brain stem nuclei help to modulate inhibition and attention. Other studies suggest right hemisphere, frontal lobe, basal ganglia, or attention network dysfunction. The attention system can be considered to consist of a brain stem center composed of dopamine, serotonin and noradrenalin neurons that project to many areas of the brain, including basal ganglia and frontal lobe. This system adjusts the sensitivity of the brain to stimuli and regulates the degree of activity, attention, and concentration as well as the degree of impulsivity. ADHD children are unable to appropriately modify their degree of attention and impulsive actions; from this point of view, the cause of ADHD is the dysfunction of this attention system.

Part Two

MULTIDISCIPLINARY ASSESSMENT OF ATTENTION DISORDERS

Chapter 6 ·───────────────────────────

MEDICAL EVALUATION

It often appears that no two observers agree on the role of the physician in the evaluation and care of children with ADHD. This chapter will help the physician and non-physician practitioner develop an understanding of the basis for the medical diagnostic evaluation.

THE PHYSICIAN'S DILEMMA

When the patient or physician expects a few simple questions to suffice for an adequate history, a brief examination or a few laboratory tests to suffice for adequate testing, and a simple prescription to be an adequate treatment, both the physician and family may find understanding and treating children with ADHD more difficult than expected. The complexity of information required to make the diagnosis and develop medication and nonmedication treatment options is greater for ADHD than for most medical illnesses. For example, diagnosis and treatment planning for a child brought to see the physician because of fever and ear pain may require only a few minutes of questioning concerning history and a few minutes of examination to determine the cause of the symptoms to be a middle-ear infection. If that same child were to see the same physician for evaluation of school difficulty, the diagnostic process would be more complex.

When a child comes to the physician with a fever and possible ear infection, the physician performs tests, including an ear examination, possibly a white blood count, and temperature measurement, as well as inquiring about a history of ear pain and other symptoms. The physician then makes the determination as to whether an ear infection exists. The prescribed treatment, possibly involving decongestants and antibiotics, can be written out on one or two sheets of a prescription pad. Parents are instructed on fulfilling the prescribed treatment, which may involve administering a set number of medication tablets for a specified period of time and observing for improvement in symptoms. A follow-up exam to recheck for the ear infection is usually sufficient to see the resolution of the problem. In a brief period of time, the physician is able to take an appropriate history, perform needed diagnostic studies with his or her own hands, prescribe the simple and effective treatment, and explain both the disease process and the treatment to the family. This process may be appropriately completed in its entirety in fifteen minutes. The patient, the family, and the physician all may feel comfortable that a proper evaluation and treatment of the problem has been accomplished.

Attention deficit does not fit into this mode of medical evaluation and treatment. The information required to make a diagnosis cannot be obtained simply as a result of a brief conversation between the physician and a parent or the physician and the child. Important information is often obtained from parents, teachers, siblings, and others. Diagnostic tests are often not simple to order, perform, or interpret; the diagnostic testing must be based on history and other ancillary information, and interpretation of these studies requires discussion with the family and often teachers and other persons as well.

A demonstration of these principles is reflected in a study by Brunquell, Russman, and Lerer (1988). These authors examined mental status testing by child neurologists in children with learning disorders. In a survey of 128 child neurologists, mental status testing was divided into six categories: fundamental processes, language, memory, constructional ability, higher cortical functions, and related cortical functions. The authors found a progressive decline in testing frequency with increasing complexity of mental status category. They concluded that higher and related cortical functions are tested significantly less often than other categories of mental status function in children with learning problems and that the diagnosis ascribed to a child with learning problems is based on findings other than those provided by the mental status exam.

In children with suspected ADHD, the physician's direct observations may be misleading. Two anecdotes will be helpful in illustrating this point. A child who was functioning well in school and at home without symptoms of ADHD became quite restless when the doctor was delayed by an emergency. After sitting in the waiting room for two hours anticipating the possibility of receiving a shot, the 8-year-old became anxious, hyperkinetic, and impulsive. Even though the child was there for a routine examination and immunization visit, the physician watching the usually orderly examining room rapidly deteriorate commented to the mother, "Don't you know your child is hyperactive?"

Other situations may also lead to an incorrect conclusion. A child with a severe ADHD problem became acutely anxious when the white-coated physician entered the room. The child's eyes widened and his heart raced as he sat on the exam table in fear of the physician. After ten minutes of listening to the mother's description of the severe ADHD symptoms and observing the child frozen to the table, the physician remarked, "He seems all right to me; you must have the problem, not him."

After experiences such as these, the physician may adopt one of two extreme positions. He or she may decide to prescribe medication such as Ritalin on a "trial" basis for all children with the complaint of learning or behavior problems, saying to the parent, "Your child is having difficulty in school? Try this medication." Another response to the frustration of dealing with ADHD could be a physician who refuses to participate in diagnosis or treatment of ADHD, telling the family, "Your child is having difficulty in school? There is nothing I can do. I am a physician, not a teacher." Neither approach is likely to prove satisfactory. The first approach exposes children to possibly unnecessary medication and overlooks the importance of nonmedication interventions; the second overlooks an enormously effective treatment modality: medication intervention.

The nonmedical practitioner, such as the teacher, psychologist, or other therapist, also needs to understand the role of medical evaluation in the diagnosis and treatment of children with ADHD. Understanding which questions medical evaluation can answer will lead to improved and more effective treatment of the ADHD child by decreasing the frustration often experienced by nonmedical practitioners who are also working with the child. Physicians with appropriate training and expertise may choose to expand their role beyond what is described here as the medical evaluation. A physician may choose to undertake every aspect of the diagnosis and treatment of ADHD children. Or, a physician may choose to work with one or more nonmedical practitioners, such as a psychologist or educational specialist, to accomplish the other aspects of the evaluation. The physician, along with the patient, parents, siblings, and others such as teachers, psychologists, social workers, speech therapists, and educational specialists, can work together in an interdisciplinary team. The physician also can increase his or her effectiveness by understanding what role the medical evaluation plays in the evaluation and treatment of ADHD. Understanding what the physician can and should do and understanding the questions the physician can and should answer will improve the effectiveness of the other members of the team as well.

THE ROLE OF THE PHYSICIAN IN THE DIAGNOSTIC EVALUATION

The role of the physician in the diagnostic evaluation of children suspected of having ADHD can be described through answers to four questions.

1. Does the child's history or examination suggest the etiology of an underlying medically remediable problem contributing to the ADHD symptoms?
2. Are any medical diagnostic tests needed to determine the presence or absence of a remediable medical problem contributing to the ADHD symptoms?
3. What do the physical and neurological exams demonstrate?
4. Are any medical problems apparent from the history or exam that would indicate an increased risk from medication intervention?

This approach allows the parent and the referring clinician or nonmedical participant in the multidisciplinary team to understand the role of the medical evaluation of children with suspected ADHD. The greater understanding the nonmedical practitioner and parent have of the role of the medical evaluation, the more appropriate will be their expectations. The more clearly the medical practitioner understands the role of the medical evaluation of the child with ADHD, the more reasonable will be the medical practitioner's expectations and the more effective his or her participation in the evaluation.

Medically Remediable Problems

There are many advantages in the use of a syndrome name to describe a collection of clinical symptoms; one of the disadvantages, however, is the potential to overlook disorders that have alternate treatments. Weinberg and Brumback (1992) and Weinberg and Emslie (1991) emphasized this point to the extent of describing ADHD as a "myth" insofar as the use of a syndrome diagnosis encourages diagnostic complacency and allows overlooking other treatable disorders. Denckla (1992) also emphasized that a syndrome diagnosis such as ADHD is likely to include several different entities. Those charged with the diagnosis of behavior disorders in children must be vigilant to this pitfall. There may be some controversy as to whether the symptoms of behavior disorder that occur as the result of medical illness should be a separate diagnostic categorization from ADHD (Cantwell & Baker, 1987; P. Wender, 1987); nevertheless, medical evaluation is needed to be certain that the behavioral symptoms observed are not the result of a treatable medical illness. Cantwell and Baker (1987) discuss specific illnesses that can cause abnormal behavior, including Sydenham's chorea, hyperthyroidism, infection with pinworms, and sleep apnea. Essentially all medical illnesses have the potential to cause some ADHD symptoms; it is most uncommon, however, for the behavioral manifestations of medical illness to be the major symptoms. As a result, it is not likely that medical evaluation of a child who otherwise appears healthy to family and school personnel will uncover a specific medical etiology for the behavior problem. Some medical factors have been shown to be associated with ADHD. These include a history of fetal postmaturity, long labor, maternal toxemia, encephalitis or other brain injury, frequent ear infections, and subclinical lead poisoning. However, a history of ADHD in other family members is often the only cause found. Although some of these causes of ADHD are not remediable, thorough evaluation for these identifiable factors is an important part of the evaluation for a medical cause of ADHD.

The routine medical evaluation includes a history of the presenting problem; a past history with information about the pregnancy, labor, and delivery and the child's development; and a review of systems. During the review of systems, the physician should ask about symptoms of disease occurring in organ systems such as the central nervous system, gastrointestinal system, genitourinary system, cardiovascular system, hematopoietic system, and skin. A review of the family history for medical as well as psychosocial problems should also be included. The family physician or pediatrician who has been familiar with the child for some time may be able to accomplish this evaluation for medical causes of behavioral abnormality quickly and simply. The ease of this evaluation for the medical practitioner and the likelihood of its being negative do not diminish its importance (American Academy of Pediatrics, 1987). The medical history should contain the results of completed and up-to-date tests of vision and hearing.

Medication needed for treatment of other disorders may produce behavioral change as a side effect. Phenobarbital and diphenylhydantoin, which are anticonvulsants used to treat generalized tonic/clonic seizures as well as partial complex seizures, have been implicated as a cause of ADHD symptoms (Pellock et al., 1988). A child taking phenobarbital who is also having difficulty with ADHD symptoms must be carefully evaluated. The decision to discontinue the phenobarbital or diphenylhydantoin, change to an alternate anticonvulsant, or proceed with evaluation and treatment of ADHD symptoms without changing the medications must be based on medical evaluation of the need for the anticonvulsant, alternatives, and previous response to medications. Other medications (see Chapter 5), especially those that produce sleepiness, may cause some ADHD symptoms. If the child is taking any medication on a regular basis, it must be determined whether this medication is contributing to the ADHD symptoms.

Medical evaluation must also determine the child's growth pattern. The child's present height and weight are documented and history of growth pattern obtained, and baseline measures of blood pressure and heart rate and signs or symptoms of cardiovascular disease are documented.

Medical Diagnostic Studies

Medical diagnostic studies are often undertaken to determine whether a medical illness is present. An important part of the medical evaluation for ADHD is the determination of the need for medical diagnostic studies. Clinical evaluation alone may not be sufficient to exclude medical illnesses as the underlying cause of ADHD symptoms. The need for medical diagnostic testing to uncover a possible remediable disorder causing the behavior symptoms is the second determination made by the medical evaluation.

EEG

The electroencephalogram (EEG) can help establish the diagnosis of epilepsy as the remediable cause of ADHD symptoms. An EEG is obtained by placing wires on the skin over the brain and measuring the voltage differences between them. Changes in voltage occurring over time are plotted on paper; the voltage measurement produce a pattern of electrical change. Many patients with epilepsy have a characteristic pattern of abnormality on the EEG, and problems such as brain tumor, abscess, subdural or other intracranial hemorrhage, and metabolic abnormalities also produce changes in the characteristic pattern of the EEG recording. However, other diagnostic studies have essentially replaced the EEG in the diagnosis of all disorders except epilepsy.

Primary generalized absence epilepsy, which was called petit mal seizures in the past, is characterized by clinical symptoms of brief episodes of abrupt inattention often associated with eye fluttering and sometimes with jerky movements of the hands or additional body movements. The appearance of a child and his EEG before and during a generalized absence seizure is represented in Figure 6–1. These seizures may occur frequently during the day; clinically observed spells lasting a few seconds may occur four to five times an hour. The sudden loss of attention resulting from generalized absence seizures is often associated with eye blinking. These symptoms are rarely confused with ADHD. When a child with ADHD has unusual sudden episodes of inattentiveness or when a child with previously diagnosed generalized absence seizures has inattentive episodes with eye blinking or other movements, the possibility of epilepsy may be raised as the cause of the inattentive episodes. Primary generalized absence seizures are spells that are associated with a characteristic three-cycle-per-second spike-wave pattern on the EEG. When the characteristic pattern of generalized absence epilepsy is seen on the EEG along with appropriate clinical symptoms, the clinical diagnosis of absence epilepsy can be established. Most children with ADHD symptoms do not have paroxysmal episodes of loss of attention and eye blinking. However, some children seen for evaluation of possible ADHD have staring spells as a major symptom. If the possibility of primary generalized absence seizures remains after evaluation, including history and exam, an EEG can be obtained to help differentiate ADHD from generalized absence epilepsy.

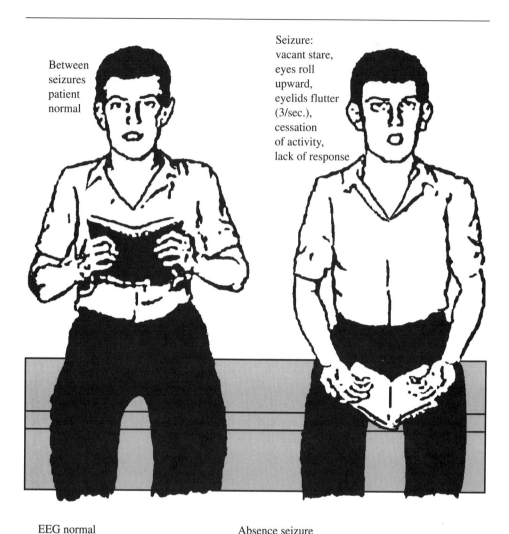

Between seizures patient normal

Seizure: vacant stare, eyes roll upward, eyelids flutter (3/sec.), cessation of activity, lack of response

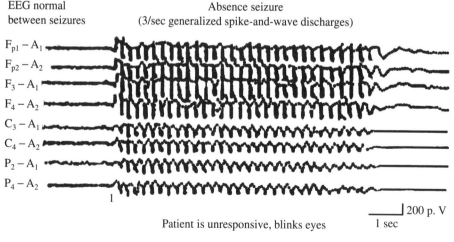

EEG normal between seizures

Absence seizure
(3/sec generalized spike-and-wave discharges)

$F_{p1} - A_1$
$F_{p2} - A_2$
$F_3 - A_1$
$F_4 - A_2$
$C_3 - A_1$
$C_4 - A_2$
$P_2 - A_1$
$P_4 - A_2$

1

Patient is unresponsive, blinks eyes

200 p. V

1 sec

Figure 6–1.   EEG before and during generalized absence seizure

From *CIBA Collection of Medical Illustrations* by Frank H. Netter, M.D. All rights reserved. Copyright 1986 by CIBA-GEIGY Corporation. Used by permission of the publisher.

EEG and ADHD Symptoms   As discussed above, the EEG may be helpful in diagnosing children whose paroxysmal staring spells raise the possibility of seizures. EEG studies of children from Japan, China, and Korea found that children with similar diagnoses had patterns that differed from normal (Matsura, Okubo, Toru, & Kojima, 1993). The EEG has also been proposed to help define subclassifications of children with attention disorder (Miller & Kraft, 1992).

The EEG has been studied to determine its ability to diagnose learning and behavior problems. There have been several attempts to judge the effectiveness of medication using an EEG (Epstein, Lasgna, Conners, & Rodriguez, 1968; Satterfield, Cantwell, Saul, Lesser, & Podosin, 1973; Shekim, Dekirmenjian, Chapel, Javaid, & Davis, 1979; Steinberg, Troshinsky, & Steinberg, 1971). A report by Halperin, Gittelman, Katz, and Struve (1986) is representative of these studies. The authors rated a group of eighty children with ADD defined by clinical exam and Conners rating scales. Baseline- as well as placebo-controlled trials of drug adjustment were used to determine the usefulness of EEG recordings. No relationship was found between EEG abnormalities and the severity of symptoms or responsiveness to methylphenidate treatment. Caresia et al. (1984) studied EEG recordings and power spectral analysis to predict responders to pemoline. They found that the power spectrum of the EEG was not helpful in predicting the outcome of trials of pemoline in children. However, they found what they described as a paradoxical calming effect of pemoline on the EEG of adult patients who would eventually show a clinical response to pemoline.

Studies of EEG and various behavioral conditions have shown a number of abnormalities in many children who have ADHD and other behavioral symptoms. However, the nonspecific nature of the abnormality and the finding that similar abnormalities are seen in some asymptomatic children result in the conclusion that an EEG cannot be used to help make the diagnosis of ADHD: a negative EEG will not exclude ADHD, and changes in the EEG do not determine whether ADHD is improving, worsening, or responding to medications. Although the EEG is a helpful test in determining the presence or absence of epilepsy as a cause of sudden spells of inattention, most children with ADHD symptoms do not have the clinical features that suggest absence epilepsy. EEG testing, therefore, is needed for only a small percentage of children suspected of having ADHD.

The American Academy of Neurology and the American Clinical Neurophysiology Society in a re-evaluation of digital EEG, quantitative EEG, and EEG brain mapping, note that neurophysiological studies of children with ADHD, learning and attention have shown neurophysiological responses that differentiate these from normal children (Nuwer, 1997). They wrote that while the relationship between a patient's EEG pattern and outcome of therapy have been proposed, controls of verification have not been accomplished. They conclude that diagnostic tests, including EEG brain mapping have not been proven useful in establishing the diagnosis or treatment plan for individual children. This report raised questions on the basis of inappropriate spectrum of patients for whom the diagnostic tests would be applied in clinical practice, lack of evidence that outcome was changed by diagnostic testing and lack of evidence that treatment plans were predicated on such testing. They concluded that there was no evidence that patients were better off for having had these tests performed.

Topographic EEG Mapping   The EEG can be recorded as a topographic picture of the head that in some respects resembles the slices seen on computed tomography (CT) or MRI images. That dyslexia could be diagnosed by this process has been suggested by Duffy, Denckla, Bartels, Sandini, and Kiessling (1980). Among a group of dyslexic readers, a significant decrease in the amplitude of the P300 wave using topographic mapping was reported by Trommer, Bernstein, Rosenberg, and Armstrong (1988). However, these authors concluded that the topographic mapping of evoked potentials alone was not sufficient for diagnosis of dyslexia. EEG mapping has also been suggested as a potentially useful diagnostic tool for ADHD (Senf, 1988). Although these reports are positive and optimistic, the technique of EEG mapping has not been widely enough studied to be considered more than experimental. A review of brain mapping and other electrophysiological studies by the American Academy of Neurology (Nuwer, 1997) has found that evidence is lacking for the usefulness of brain mapping or other quantitative EEG testing in the diagnosis and treatment of children with ADHD.

Evoked Potentials and Remediable Medical Etiology   Visual or auditory evoked potentials begin with a visual event such as the flashing of a particular pattern on a TV screen or an auditory event such as a click or sound. These events produce a very slight change in the pattern of the EEG, which occurs in all normal subjects. The change associated with the visual or auditory event is visually too small to be seen in the routine. If the click or pattern is repeated a second time, the two recordings will have the same click response pattern, but the EEG pattern unrelated to the click will change randomly. If repeated EEG tracings are averaged, eventually the ordinary EEG signal becomes a flat line. The repeated visual or auditory stimulus (click) produces a repetitive signal that becomes relatively larger as the signals are averaged. Evoked-potential testing may show a characteristic pattern for some types of brain tumors, multiple sclerosis, and other disorders. Ordinarily, these disorders would not be within the differential diagnosis of children presenting with behavior and learning problems, and standard evoked-potential testing usually is not part of the evaluation of possible medical causes for ADHD symptoms.

Some studies, however, have found evoked potentials helpful in the diagnosis and follow-up of children with ADHD and other behavioral symptoms. Klorman, Salzman, Borgstedt, and Dainer (1981) reported on the late positive component of the evoked potential performed during a CPT involving letter ordering. In this report, evoked potentials were studied in relation to methylphenidate. In comparison with normal children, subjects diagnosed with attention deficit had lower amplitude of the late component (P300); the children treated with methylphenidate then had an enhancement of this depressed component.

Comparison of evoked potentials of nineteen learning-disordered and nineteen normally achieving children showed a difference in late positive components of evoked potential in relation to "critical stimuli" in the task (Dainer et al., 1981). Prichep, Sutton, and Hakerm (1976) and Klorman, Salzman, Pass, Borgstedt, and Dainer (1979) showed that during tasks requiring focused attention, hyperkinetic children with learning problems exhibited smaller evoked response than did normal children. Satterfield, Schell, and Backs (1987) studied auditory evoked response potentials and EEG recordings from childhood through adolescence in a longitudinal study of thirty-four nondelinquent normals, twenty-five nondelinquent hyperactives, and nine delinquent hyperactives. The results showed abnormal maturational changes in the nondelinquent hyperactive subjects and were more likely to be normal in the delinquent hyperactive subjects.

Logan, Farrell, Malone, and Taylor (1988) studied P300 response on the event-related potential using an oddball paradigm to determine whether this test could be used to predict medication response. Twelve out of fourteen children with ADHD responded to medication according to psychological measures and behavioral observations. These twelve also responded with P300 increase in amplitude and more clearly delineated P300 response. They concluded "that the use of visual evoked response appears to be an effective and perhaps a more objective method for evaluation of stimulant medication effect in patients with Attention deficit disorder. It also appears to be sufficiently sensitive to predict optimal medication dosage in patients who respond favorably to stimulant drug therapy" (p. 72). Another explanation, however, is that because attention is required for a normal P300 response, the response of P300 to medication is the secondary result of the child's improved concentration and attention rather than a measure of the underlying process.

Event-related potentials have been shown to differentiate groups of children in several studies (Harter, Anllo-Vento, Wood, & Schroeder, 1988; Harter, Diering, & Wood, 1988; Klorman, 1991; Lubar, Mann, Gross, & Shively, 1992; Robaey, Breton, Dugas, & Renault, 1992; Satterfield, Schell, Nicholas, Satterfield, 1990). Other studies of evoked potentials have shown no correlation with the diagnosis and treatment of ADHD. Conners and Wells (1986) find the results of a number of studies difficult to correlate with otherwise known theories of attention deficit. Evoked potentials were evaluated in relation to attention and reading retardation by Lovrich and Stamm (1983). As the subjects counted signals in one ear, event-related potentials were recorded. Different wave forms were noted with children who were reading-retarded. Evoked potentials related to attention, however, appeared to be normal in comparison with controls.

To achieve an evoked potential response in ADHD children, authors often utilize unique clinical situations and unique experimental designs. There is wide variability from one laboratory to another. Evoked-response information suggests a physiological basis to the behavior abnormalities that are the ADHD syndrome. However, we concur with the American Academy of Neurology assessment that the value of evoked potential studies in the diagnosis and treatment of children with ADHD is at present unproven.

CT and MRI

CT and MRI provide a picture of the structure of the brain. CT employs a thin beam of X-ray. After passing through the patient, the X-ray beam not absorbed is measured by an electronic sensor. In ordinary X-ray, the beam not absorbed by the patient is recorded directly on X-ray film. In CT, the pattern of X-ray absorption measured by the electronic sensor is converted by a computer into a picture, or slice. This allows direct information about the brain structure to be obtained. Conditions that result in an alteration of the X-ray density within the brain produce an abnormal appearance on the CT scan. Tumor, hydrocephalus, abscess, hemorrhage, and malformations of the brain are particularly well visualized by CT.

MRI produces images of brain structure displayed in slices that have some similarities with CT. MRI, however, utilizes the radio waves emitted by molecules within the body in response to a radio frequency pulse in a strong magnetic field. Although the advent of CT scanning resulted in a revolution of improved imaging of the brain, within fifteen years of the introduction of CT, MRI had replaced it for many applications. MRI produces more detailed pictures of brain anatomy, allowing a diagnosis of some abnormalities that cannot be seen as well on CT. MRI, however, is more expensive, it cannot be used in the presence of electronic pacemakers, and does not visualize calcium well. In situations where these features are important, CT may be preferable to MRI.

On occasion, a child evaluated for ADHD will have signs or symptoms suggesting a disorder such as hydrocephalus, brain tumor, hemorrhage, or abscess that requires specific medical or surgical treatment. A CT or MRI scan may be needed to uncover this problem so that appropriate surgical or medical intervention can be undertaken. The medical evaluation outlined earlier should include evaluation of the history and physical findings to determine whether a CT or MRI scan is needed to diagnose a medically or surgically remediable disorder.

CT, MRI, and Other Neuroimaging and ADHD Symptoms   Studies using CT scans have been disappointing in the search for a medical test that can diagnose ADHD. A report by Thompson, Ross, and Horwitz (1980) and an additional study reported by Denckla, LeMay, and Chapman (1985) found that even in children with minor neurological abnormality, the CT images were not helpful in making the diagnosis or following the progress of behavioral symptoms. Harcherik, Cohen et al. (1985) studied CT scans in subjects with ADHD as well as other psychiatric syndromes and measured ventricular volume and brain density by quantitative computer-based methods. There were no significant differences between neuropsychiatric patients and medical control patients in total ventricular volume, right-left ventricular volume ratios, ventricular asymmetries, ventricle-brain ratios, or brain density.

Although CT studies in ADHD children have been disappointing, there has been a suggestion that groups of children with similar problems may be differentiated by CT scans. Hier, LeMay, Rosenberger, and Perlo (1978) studied the CT brain scans of twenty-four dyslexics between the ages of 14 and 47 and found an increased incidence of reversal of the usual posterior hemispheral asymmetry than is present in the majority of normal individuals. This brain asymmetry reversal serves as evidence that a group of children with dyslexia are physically different from those without dyslexia. Although this asymmetry differentiated a group of dyslexic children, in individual children this finding may not be present, and it may be present in many normal children. As a result, even in this group, the reversal of brain asymmetry seen on CT scans could not be used to diagnose the problem in an individual child or predict the outcome of intervention. Other studies have shown no asymmetries (Lorys-Vernon, Hynd, Lyytinen, & Hern, 1993; Shaywitz, Shaywitz, Byrne, Cohen, & Rothman, 1983). Insular length was found to be bilaterally smaller in ADHD children. PET and SPECT studies have been suggested as helpful in the diagnosis of ADHD based only on anecdotal evidence. Although neuroimaging studies suggest subtle differences in the brains of children with ADHD and lend support to the hypotheses that structural differences do exist in the brains of individuals with ADHD, these data remain experimental and at this time should not be used by practitioners as part of the diagnostic process. T. Heaton and Bigler (1991) recommend the use of neuroimaging studies in connection with research on ADHD only.

A CT or MRI scan is indicated for a child with ADHD symptoms only when other signs or symptoms are present to suggest a condition that would call for such diagnostic studies in children without inattention and hyperactive symptoms (Behar, Rapoport, Berg, et al., 1984).

Other Medical Diagnostic Testing

We agree with the point of view expressed by Rapin (1995) that medical diagnostic tests should be reserved for specific indications. Blood tests and other common medical tests are sometimes needed for children suspected of having ADHD. For example, if symptoms such as heat intolerance, smooth/moist skin, rapid pulse, and tremor are noted, blood studies to measure the thyroid status of the child may be needed. Pallor, poor dietary ingestion of iron, or other suggestion of anemia may lead the medical practitioner to obtain a blood count to determine the presence of anemia. Other findings in the history or exam may suggest the need to obtain a blood chemistry evaluation to check on the status of glucose metabolism, sodium or potassium balance, liver function, or kidney function. Exercise intolerance by history or the findings of a heart murmur, cyanosis, or other findings suggesting cardiovascular abnormality may prompt the medical practitioner to obtain a chest X-ray or electrocardiogram to further evaluate cardiac status. Blood studies to rule out mononucleosis or other chronic infection, appropriate testing to determine the presence of pinworms, and a sinus X-ray to determine the presence of sinusitis are just a few more of the medical diagnostic tests used to uncover common medical problems that could indirectly be responsible for behavior abnormality. Usually, the history and exam are sufficient to exclude the illnesses mentioned above, and these additional diagnostic tests are rarely needed.

Physical and Neurological Exam: Soft Signs and Minor Physical Anomalies

Can a diagnosis of ADHD be made on physical exam? Mikkelsen, Brown, Minichiello, Millican, and Rapoport (1982) credit L. Bender (1956) as being one of the first to introduce the term "soft signs." McMahon and Greenberg (1977) credit Larsen (1964) and Werry et al. (1972) for linking soft neurological signs with hyperactivity and showing that hyperactive subjects display these signs with greater frequency.

Soft Signs

There are several factors contributing to the controversy and confusion over the presence and value of abnormalities on physical examination in ADHD children. Two different groups of soft signs are described by Mikkelsen et al. (1982). The first group of soft signs, such as clumsiness, overflow, and speed of movements, may be reliably reproduced from one day to the next and one examiner to the next but are considered "soft" because they are not clearly associated with a dysfunction in a specific area of the brain. These signs might also be called nonlocalizing neurological abnormality.

The second group includes traditional neurological signs such as reflex or tone asymmetries, but of mild degree or poor reliability and reproducibility. The combination of right-side weakness, increased reflexes, Babinski's sign, and increased tone in the right arm and leg would be considered "hard" neurological signs and suggest a specific area of brain dysfunction. A normal child may have a slightly increased deep-tendon reflex, a slight degree of increased tone, or a mild degree of incoordination in one arm. These asymmetries might vary from one day to the next so that an increase in the right-biceps reflex on one day might be followed by an increase in the left-biceps reflex on the next day. These minor asymmetries would be considered of uncertain significance because of their uncertain reliability and reproducibility. In a child with a minor degree of increased reflexes and tone in the right arm and leg and decreased strength, there would be a much lower likelihood of uncovering a specific abnormality within the left hemisphere. These signs, then, are considered soft because of the unreliability, variability, and minor degree of the abnormality.

Different studies have chosen different signs to evaluate. For example, McMahon and Greenberg (1977) chose to study three signs. One was posturing of the upper extremities by flexion at the elbows and hyperextension at the wrists when a subject was asked to walk ten paces on his or her heels. The second was posturing of the upper extremities with extension of the elbows and palmar flexion of the wrists when the subject was asked to walk ten paces on tiptoe. The third was dysrhythmic or dysynchronous movements or posturing of the hands or fingers when a subject alternately supinated and pronated the forearms. McMahon and Greenberg's study found that there was a high degree of variability of response within individuals and no evidence of interaction between treatment and subject responses. They concluded that "the value of these signs for purposes of diagnosis or assessment of therapy is doubtful" (p. 584). They further concluded that "these observations raised serious doubt whether testing for these soft neurological signs has any justification in a clinical setting" (p. 587).

Halperin and Gittelman (1986) used a 130-item test for soft signs (Clements & Peters, 1962) to study a group of eighty children with ADD as defined by clinical exam and Conners rating scales. In a placebo-controlled trial of medication, soft signs of the group of responders were not different from those of the group who did not respond to medication. The authors concluded that "in view of the findings that these neurological measures are not related to either treatment responsivity nor the severity of behavioral disorder, the need for a determination of neurological status prior to the initiation of stimulant treatment in hyperactive children seems unwarranted unless the presence of specific neurological disorder is suspected" (p. 824). Sleator, Ullmann, and von Neumann (1982) propose that a physician can make the diagnosis of hyperactivity based on an interview with the parents and the teacher questionnaire. They argue against the use of complex diagnostic instruments and suggest that most psychiatric and neurological examinations of the child are of little value in the evaluation for inattention and hyperactivity.

Denckla and Rudel (1978) assessed scores for timed right- and left-sided performance on eight different movements, overflow movements, and other changes such as "sticky turns." They found that overflow movements differentiated hyperactive boys from control boys at all ages. The authors concluded that these associated (overflow) movements appear to be the stigmata of deficient motor inhibition/control, which has been suggested as being central to the hyperactive syndrome. Denckla, Rudel, Chapman, and Krieger (1985) used six motor tasks, measuring time to do the task as well as observations of overflow. Using these signs, a group of children with dyslexia but no ADD symptoms was differentiated from a group of children with dyslexia who, although they had not been screened for ADD, showed signs of ADD as well as dyslexia. Figure 6–2 from Denckla, Rudel, et al. (1985) illustrates in graphic terms the separation of the discriminant scores of the groups of hyperactive dyslexic boys screened for ADD and those not screened. One can also see the overlap between the groups. Denckla and Rudel devised a detailed neurological examination recommended for children with ADD as well as other possible behavior disorders. The neurological abnormalities were then called "subtle signs," and the exam that had been used by Mikkelsen et al. (1982), among others, was revised. Unreliable or seldom scored signs have been dropped, and some signs not used previously have been added. This revision has the potential advantage of standardizing the soft signs, now called the subtle signs, exam (presuming that other authors will adopt this exam). The change in exam, however, has the disadvantage of making it even more difficult to compare studies that utilize the new exam with older studies that employed a different exam. Subsequently, however, Vitiello, Ricciuti, Stoff, Behar, and Denckla (1989) found that some classic subtle signs such as overflow and dysrhythmias showed unsatisfactory test-retest reliability at two weeks. Practice effect was evidenced in the graphathesia test. The authors advocated use of continuous items such as time needed to perform twenty consecutive movements.

The value of neurological examination for prediction of medication response in ADHD children is supported by Urion (1988) in a preliminary report. Three groups of

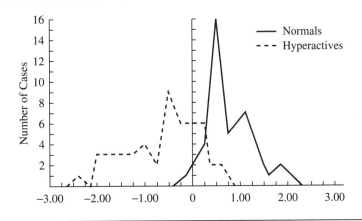

Figure 6–2. Discriminant function scores

Source: From Denckla, M. B., & Rudel, R. G. Anomalies of motor development in hyperactive boys. Copyright 1978 by the American Neurological Association. Reprinted with permission of Lippencort-Raven Publishers.

fifty children with the diagnosis of ADHD based on *DSM-III-R* criteria, including Conners Parent's and Teacher's Questionnaire scores in excess of 15 (mean = 18), were studied. The group that had essentially no abnormalities on classic and extended neurological examination responded well to methylphenidate. Of these fifty children, forty-three responded favorably, as defined by a Conners parent and teacher hyperkinesis score that decreased at least seven points and parental and school impressions of improved attention. But the remaining 100 children had difficulties on at least ten of twelve measures of the Denckla Timed Motor Performance Tasks or performed poorly on the Rey Osterrieth Complex Figure Test. Despite meeting the criteria for the *DSM-III-R* diagnosis of ADHD, only eighteen of these children responded positively to methylphenidate. This preliminary result supports use of the extended neurological exam to help predict medication response. The overall response rate of 41% for all 150 children in this study is quite low; it is not clear why this group of children had such a low response rate. In addition, the 18% response rate of the group with the abnormal extended neurological exam is lower than the response rate found for placebo in most studies. Considering these unusual features, one must be hesitant to draw conclusions about other groups based on this study.

Additional arguments in favor of using soft signs suggest that they can be helpful in predicting behavioral outcome (Hadders-Algra & Touwen, 1992; Hellgren, Gillberg, Gillbert, & Enerskog, 1993; Soorani-Lunsing, Hadders-Algra, Loinga, Huisjes, & Touwen, 1993) correlating with impulsivity (Vitiello, Stoff, Atkins, & Mahoney, 1990) when they are present with a persistent psychiatric disorder characterized by anxiety and withdrawal (Shaffer et al., 1985). Inadequacies of balance and coordination and difficulty with execution of fine motor initiative movement when assessed in childhood were not found to correlate with adult outcomes (Hall & Kramer, 1995).

The findings of Denckla (1985) and others showing that certain soft signs can distinguish groups of ADD from normal or dyslexic children are important. These studies demonstrate a physical difference that distinguished children with learning and attention problems. There is now evidence that a group defined by clinical and psychological testing is physically as well as behaviorally different from other children. The body of work on soft signs has great significance in our understanding that there is a physical basis for learning and attention problems.

In a review of forty-five studies of the relationship of neurological soft signs and hyperactivity, Reeves and Werry (1987) relate the difficulty of drawing conclusions to the variability of signs described. They believe that the majority of studies have found an increased number of soft signs in hyperactive as compared to normal children. However, they state that soft signs have yet to demonstrate any clear clinical utility in hyperactivity (ADD).

It is recommended that some tests of coordination be performed as part of the search for signs of an underlying, medically remediable neurological disorder. Observations for nonspecific or nonlocalized neurological abnormalities are listed below. Remember: younger children have more of these signs than older children.

1. *Eye Movements.* Ask the child to follow an object such as the examiner's finger through full horizontal and vertical range of movement. Watch the smoothness of pursuit movements. Some ADHD children will lose concentration during the

exam and look at the wall or other objects in the room momentarily and then look back at the examiner's finger. These lapses of attention are readily apparent and may provide an insight into the child's variable focus of attention.

2. *Finger Sequencing.* Ask the child to sequentially touch the second, third, fourth and then fifth fingers to the thumb and repeat the sequence several times. Watch for slowness and overflow of movements to other parts of the body, including the other hand, legs, tongue, face, arms, and shoulders. It often appears that the ADHD child has difficulty focusing and directing effort to one part of the body.

3. *Tandem Gait.* Ask the child to walk with one foot placed directly in front of the other. Watch to see how the child translates verbal direction into physical activity. Many ADHD children require repeated demonstration because they cannot observe or listen to the examiner or they impulsively start a task before directions are completed.

4. *Choreiform Movements.* Ask the child to hold arms outstretched with palms facing forward and eyes closed. Watch to see whether the fingers wiggle in piano playing movements (chorea). Watch to see whether other parts of the body, such as the tongue, legs, and trunk, begin to wiggle.

Several more formal and quantitative soft sign exams are available. One of the most comprehensive is the Physical and Neurological Examination for Soft Signs (PANESS; the reader is referred to Guy, 1976, pp. 383, 406, for this exam).

Is the soft signs exam useful in determining the presence or absence of attention and learning problems? The American Academy of Pediatrics (1987) recommended a physical, neurological, and neuromaturational examination, without specifying what exam should be done or how this information might be used. Studies that show statistically significant differences between groups of children based on soft signs also include the findings that many children with a normal soft signs exam have learning and attention problems and many children with an abnormal soft signs exam do not have attention deficit (Denckla, 1985). For this reason, soft signs alone cannot be used to rule out or diagnose attention deficit. If a random sampling of children is tested, more will have soft signs than have attention deficit; therefore, a child with a positive soft signs examination may have either normal attention skills or ADHD. The presence of soft signs may be of interest but cannot be used to establish the diagnosis. Furthermore, other studies have shown that the change of soft signs is not an adequate indicator of medication response. Follow-up soft signs examination cannot be used to determine the success or failure of treatment. It is important to understand that the concept of soft signs has been useful in adding to our research knowledge and understanding of ADHD and has indicated that there is a biological and physical basis for attention deficit. A soft signs exam, however, cannot be used either to establish or rule out the diagnosis of attention deficit and cannot be used to determine the effectiveness of treatment.

Minor Physical Anomalies and ADHD

Can minor physical anomalies (MPA) such as narrow or widely separated eyes, low-set ears, abnormal position of facial features, shape or space between fingers or toes, and unusual creases in the palm indicate ADHD? Some reports suggest that MPA can be associated with ADHD symptoms. Pomeroy, Sprafkin, and Gadow (1988) reviewed studies of normal populations, including more than 1,500 children in ten studies; there were 933 newborns included in the studies reviewed. These studies found that the group of children within the normal population scoring highest for MPA also had abnormal behavior. The children with high anomaly scores had inability to delay gratification, oppositionalism, and perseveration. They also had high teacher ratings of hyperactivity for boys, peer nomination of "mean-noisy" for boys and girls, sleep problems, and parental reports of hyperactive-impulsive behavior at 2 years. In boys, high anomaly scores correlated with distractibility, gross motor incoordination, hyperactivity, and restlessness. Some studies, however, found no correlation with severity of hyperactivity.

Pomeroy et al. (1988) studied a group of 193 children with Down syndrome (trisomy 21) and compared them to 154 mentally retarded children without Down syndrome. Despite the much higher incidence of minor congenital anomalies in the Down syndrome group, the incidence of conduct disorder (10%) was the same in both samples, and the hyperkinetic syndrome was only slightly more common in the Down syndrome group (9% versus 7%) Pomeroy et al. concluded from this data that even in this grossly deviant group of children with known chromosomal abnormality and high prevalence of MPA, the manifestation of psychiatric and behavioral disturbance was nonuniversal, diagnostically nonspecific, and probably a factor of mental retardation and not the Down syndrome.

Correlation between MPA (dysmorphology) and ADD led Deutsch, Matthysse, Swanson, and Farkas (1990) to look for genetic linkages between the minor congenital anomalies and attention disorder. They found that ADD subjects had first-degree relatives with dysmorphic features and that non-ADD relatives also had more dysgenic features than controls. When subjected to a linkage test, an autosomal dominant inheritance for both ADD and minor congenital anomalies best fit the available data. They suggested that a common pathway to the development of congenital anomalies in ADD may exist in the dominant genetic form. Other authors (Accardo, Tomazic, & Morrow, 1991), however, found no correlation between minor malformation scores and hyperactivity or attention disorders.

A study of 100 emotionally disturbed children by Pomeroy et al. (1988) concluded that higher MPA scores were found at a frequency greater than expected in a random population. The clinical features of the children with higher MPA scores were inattention, speech delay, and clumsiness. Their findings do not support the measurement of MPA as a routine procedure for identifying children at risk because many other straightforward historical, developmental, and performance measures help define these children's educational and clinical needs.

The search for congenital anomalies, as illustrated in Table 6–1, is part of the general physical examination. Eyes that are too close together or too far apart, ears that lie too low on the skull, abnormal finger or palm creases, and abnormal distance between the first and second toes are associated with certain genetic defects. Most children, however, who have minor anomalies do not have a specific genetic abnormality. Some children with minor congenital abnormalities may have ADHD. However, like the soft signs exam, the diagnosis of learning or attention problems can neither be made nor excluded on the basis of presence or absence of minor congenital anomalies.

Table 6–1.   Minor physical anomalies and neurologic status in hyperactive boys

Anomaly	Scoring Weights
Head	
Head circumference	
> 1.5 S.D.	2
1 >< 1.5 S.D.	1
"Electric" hair	
Very fine hair that won't comb down	2
Fine hair that is soon awry after combing	1
Two or more whorls	0
Eyes	
Epicanthus	
Where upper and lower lids join at the nose, point of union is:	
deeply covered	2
partly covered	1
Hypertelorism	
Approximate distance between tear ducts:	
> 1.5 S.D.	2
1.25 to 1.5 S.D.	1
Ears	
Low-set	
Bottom of ears in line with:	
mouth (or lower)	2
area between mouth and nose	1
Adherent lobes	
Lower edges of ear extend:	
upward and back toward crown of head	−2
straight back toward rear of neck	1
Malformed	1
Asymmetrical	1
Soft and pliable	0
Mouth	
High palate	
Roof of mouth steepled	2
Roof of mouth moderately high	1
Furrowed tongue	1
Smooth-rough spots on tongue	0
Hands	
Fifth finger	
Markedly curved inward toward other fingers	2
Slightly curved inward toward other fingers	1
Single transverse palmar crease	1
Index finger longer than middle finger	1
Foot	
Third toe	
Definitely longer than second toe	2
Appears equal in length to second toe	1
Partial syndactility of two middle toes	1
Gap between first and second toe (approximately ¼ inch)	1

Source: Quinn, P. O., & Rapoport, J. L. Minor physical anomalies and neurologic status in hyperactive boys. Copyright 1974 by *Pediatrics.* Reproduced by permission of *Pediatrics.*

Contraindication to Medication Intervention

The fourth aspect of the medical evaluation involves evaluation for medication intervention. (The decision whether to undertake medication intervention, and if so, which medication to use at which dosages, treatment schedule, and reevaluation program, is the subject of Chapter 13 in this volume.) The initial medical evaluation should obtain information concerning possible contraindications to medication intervention. Medical history should include inquiry into possible previous episodes of overanxious or psychotic behavior, as these may be exaggerated by some medications used for the treatment of ADHD symptoms. History of abnormal movements and/or multiple habit spasms or tics, especially with vocalization, would raise caution concerning the use of stimulant medication because of the possibility of exaggerating symptoms of Tourette's syndrome. Poor dietary history might suggest concern for the possible anorexic effects of medication. A history of previous treatments, especially medications, such as stimulants, tranquilizers, or antidepressants, should be obtained; a history of medication for other illnesses is needed to determine if these might interact with medication for ADHD. Ability and willingness of the family to participate in nonmedication intervention programs and follow through with reevaluation programs will contribute to reducing the risk of medication intervention. Finally, findings on exam that might include increased risk of medication include the age of the patient, cardiovascular status (e.g., pulse rate, blood pressure), presence of psychosis, and overanxiousness or tenseness.

SUMMARY

The physician's role includes directing the search for remediable medical causes of ADHD, participating in the multidisciplinary diagnostic evaluation, and, when medication is indicated, supervising the medication intervention program. Medical evaluation includes:

1. Searching for a medically remediable cause for ADHD symptoms such as hyperthyroidism, pinworms, sleep apnea, iron-deficiency anemia, and medications such as phenobarbital. Disorders correlated directly with ADHD but not remediable include perinatal factors, previous ear infection, brain injury or encephalitis, previous lead poisoning, and, most commonly, those due to heredity.

2. Determining the need for medical diagnostic testing, which ranges from a blood count to an MRI scan. Each test is helpful to exclude specific medical illness that can occasionally masquerade as ADHD. These tests do not help make or confirm the diagnosis of ADHD, and unless specific indications of other disorders are present, these tests are usually not needed.

3. Conducting an appropriate physical and neurological examination. Research studies using examinations for anomalies and soft signs have given us valuable information suggesting that there is a physiological basis to the cluster of clinical symptoms constituting ADHD. These findings are less helpful than other tests for the diagnosis or exclusion of ADHD because these findings are often

present in normal children and often absent in children with ADHD. A limited soft signs exam as presented is recommended.

4. Establishing baselines to determine any contraindication to medication intervention and to serve as a comparison at subsequent reevaluation. Although the decision to use medication is part of medication treatment rather than diagnostic evaluation, gathering information on risks of possible medication intervention is part of the physician's initial diagnostic evaluation. A family medical and social history may contain clues to psychosis or Tourette's syndrome; other family members may have had positive or negative response to medications for ADHD; and the family may have a good or poor history of following through with treatment programs. The child's medical history may show symptoms such as previous reactions to medications, psychosis, growth problems, or cardiovascular problems suggesting increased medication risk. During physical exam, clues to increased medication risk may be found, including the child's age; abnormalities of height, weight, or blood pressure; signs of tics, psychosis, or depression; and abnormalities suggesting disorders of other organ systems.

Ensuring that the patient, family, teacher, psychologist, social worker, and other school/community nonmedical personnel understand what medical evaluation can and cannot accomplish will lead to more effective utilization of medical services. The medical practitioner must also understand what the medical evaluation can accomplish: medical evaluation is only one part of the multidisciplinary evaluation for ADHD; additional qualitative or quantitative information by direct observation as well as reports from other observers such as parents and teachers will be needed to establish the diagnosis of ADHD. This additional information can be obtained by the medical practitioners who performed the medical evaluation if they have appropriate training and expertise. In a multidisciplinary team, nonmedical practitioners may perform the other parts of the evaluation.

Chapter 7 —————————————————————————

EVALUATION OF SCHOOL FUNCTIONING

Children with ADHD present an unpredictable variety of school problems. For a significant percentage, problems observed in the preschool setting have a high incidence of progression to school-age problems (Campbell et al., 1977; Schleifer et al., 1975). A review of the available literature suggests that measures of attention, activity, and vocalization in the classroom consistently distinguish children with ADHD from comparison groups of children (Platzman et al., 1992). These authors identified ninety-four articles published between 1967 and 1991 focusing on school-based ADHD-associated symptoms. The activity category was described as problems with global activity, gross motor movement, minor movements, disruptive motor movements, and solitary activity. The vocalization category was divided into excessive quantity and negative quality. The attention category consisted of off-task behavior or repeated changes in activities. An interpersonal set of characteristics, including initiation of negative interaction, initiation of positive interaction, solicitation of attention, positive response, and negative response, were also found on a fairly consistent basis to distinguish children with ADHD from others in school settings.

At a secondary-school level and likely into post-high-school education, continued problems of ADHD combine increasingly with a history of negative experience to exert a cumulative negative impact on behavior, achievement, emotions, and self-esteem. Especially for adolescents, a careful school history concerning experiences in the early grades as well as the progression of problems must be patiently documented by the practitioner.

Barkley (1981a) argues that certain environmental conditions may reinforce and maintain symptoms of ADHD. Factors such as deficient reinforcement arrangements, escape or avoidance learning, and goodness of fit between environmental demands and the child's capacity each serve to maintain or in fact increase the severity of ADHD-related problems. Further, Barkley proposed a motivational deficit for children with ADHD, suggesting that their need for immediate, frequent, predictable, and salient reinforcers at a longer exposure schedule rather than lack of ability to be motivated may reflect one of the core problems. It is also important for the practitioner to recognize that escape or avoidance learning is mediated by negative reinforcement, a powerful factor shaping the lives of children with ADHD.

A number of issues related to children and their teachers are worth reviewing. Lewit and Baker (1995), in a thorough overview of the readiness literature, describe differences between characteristics that parents and those that teachers believe are important as children enter school. Among the most important variables for parents are the ability to take turns and share, sit still, pay attention, use pencils or paintbrushes, know letters of the alphabet, and count to twenty; yet these were among teachers' lowest-rated variables. Teachers highly rated a child's physical well-being, ability to communicate his or her needs, an enthusiastic approach to new activities, and the ability to follow directions, to not disrupt the classroom, and to be sensitive to the needs of others. Figure 7–1 provides the comparison between parent and teacher ratings. Despite this line of research, there continues to be a lack of consensus as to what defines readiness for school. There is no doubt, however, that over the past twenty years, the threshold for school readiness in regard to early academic achievement has increased. Kindergartners are routinely screened for readiness skills that at one time were considered to reflect readiness for first grade. Interestingly, ratings related to compliance, a problem often reported by teachers for children with ADHD, appear to play a role in parents' and teachers' views reflecting a lack of school readiness.

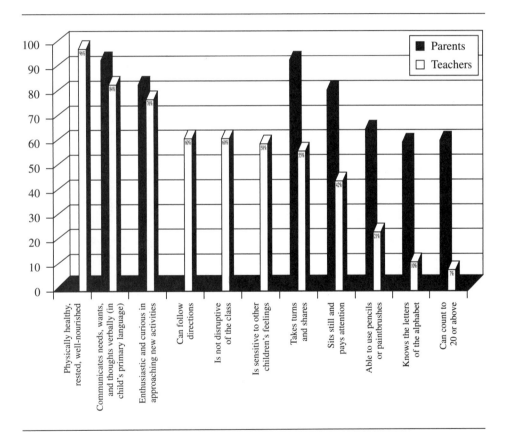

Figure 7–1.   Percentage of preschoolers' parents and kindergarten teachers who rate specific characteristics as either "essential" or "very important" to being ready to start kindergarten, 1993

Sources: U.S. Department of Education, *Readiness for kindergarten: Parent and teacher beliefs.* Statistics in brief, NCES 93-257. Washington, DC: National Center for Education Statistics, Office of Educational Research and Improvement, 1993; National Center for Education Statistics, *Public school kindergarten teachers' views on children's readiness for school.* Statistical analysis report. Washington, DC, U.S. Department of Education, 1993. Used with permission.

Granger, Whalen, and Henker (1993) evaluated the role of adult's social cognition in mediating judgments of ADHD children's behavior. Two videotapes of target boys with ADHD playing a group game with two peers were shown to 288 education undergraduates. Each target boy was taking either methylphenidate or placebo, and the excerpts were presented in random fashion. Adults were then asked to evaluate the quality of the target child's interactions. The observers combined their perceptions of the two behavior samples and formed a composite impression. Thus, even though it was clear that in one situation the target child's behavior was better than in the other, there appeared to be a tendency to combine both reports, making the medication report slightly less positive and the nonmedication report more positive. The authors concluded that adult ratings are powerfully shaped by multiple experiences rather than single experiences. As has been demonstrated (Abikoff, Courtney, Pelham, & Koplewicz, 1993), an increased pattern of negative experience often leads to a negative halo effect, resulting in a worsening in teacher ratings compared to classroom behavior. Thus, it is not surprising that, independent of their actual achievement, children with ADHD have been reported to receive the poorest teacher ratings of academic competence (McConaughy et al., 1988).

Teachers must be helped to see that although understanding the symptoms of ADHD is critical in understanding the how and why of child behavior in the classroom, emphasis must be on behaviors that teachers can measure, observe, and interact with directly. Symptoms of ADHD can be modified through basic behavior management; to do so requires an effective teacher, someone willing to focus on academic goals, carefully select instructional materials, structure and plan learning activities, involve students in the learning process, closely monitor student progress, and provide frequent feedback on progress and accomplishments (Goldstein & Goldstein, 1990). Such teachers are capable of organizing and maintaining the classroom learning environment to maximize time spent engaged in productive activity and minimize time lost during transitions or for disruptions requiring disciplinary actions. Teachers capable of managing a classroom effectively are more likely to find success as they educate children with ADHD and less likely to complain as loudly or as frequently as teachers experiencing problems managing everyday occurrences in classrooms. Further, practitioners should also be aware that misbehaving students are responded to differently by even the most effective teachers. Teachers tend to allow less time for these students to answer, often negatively reinforce their behavior, criticize them more frequently, praise them less, pay attention to them less in a positive way, call on them less frequently, demand less from them, and in some situations seat them as far away from themselves as possible (Brophy & Good, 1974). Further, most teachers do not recognize the subtle differences in their interactions with these students or the effect of these disparities in the classroom. Thus, one of the goals for practitioners when gathering school-based data concerning ADHD is to make certain to develop at least a rudimentary relationship with the teachers providing behavioral reports as well as the means with which they deal with students day in and day out.

Thus, a variety of teacher factors influences and shapes teacher behavior toward children, which then plays a significant role in shaping and determining teacher levels of complaints. One study examining teacher behavior toward prosocial and inappropriate behavior in children classified as behaviorally disordered found that teacher-child interactions varied: some teachers provided a significant number of commands followed by student compliance, with positive consequences for prosocial behavior rarely occurring (Shores et al., 1994). Despite a careful analysis of antecedent and subsequent social stimuli of student's aversive behavior, no significant reason other than a long history of negative teacher-child interactions could be identified for this pattern. Low rates of teacher delivery of positive consequences have been reported in other studies (Gable, Hendrickson, Shores, & Young, 1983; Walker & Buckley, 1973; M. White, 1975). Interestingly, teachers in segregated classrooms are nearly three times more likely to use positive consequences with their students than teachers in integrated classrooms. Thus, from a reinforcement perspective, children with more severe ADHD symptoms may actually be better off in smaller, segregated classrooms. In integrated classrooms, teachers appear to rely on other systems, such as token reinforcers rather than positive social consequences, to manage difficult child behavior; they appear to take appropriate behavior for granted and therefore provide low rates of positive reinforcement even when the ADHD child is behaving appropriately.

Further, individual teachers differ significantly in their overall use of commands (Strain, Lambert, Kerr, Stagg, & Lenkner, 1993). However, in this study, teachers did not differentially respond to high- versus low-rated children in regard to behavioral adjustment. Children rated as well adjusted were more likely to comply with commands than children rated as poorly adjusted. Although the overall level of positive social consequences was extremely low, there was some indication that well-adjusted children were more likely to receive positive feedback for compliance than poorly adjusted children, a phenomenon that is the opposite of what needs to happen and may in fact maintain low rates of compliance. Strain et al. (1993) additionally found that poor-compliance children receive significantly more positive feedback than high-compliance children for noncompliance! Teachers gave negative feedback for noncompliance at an equal level to both groups of children. Although repeated teacher commands following noncompliance were equal across groups, poor-compliance children were exposed to significantly higher levels of repeated commands following compliance than were high-rated youngsters.

As the diagnosis of ADHD has focused increasingly on developing a symptom list and empirically determining symptom severity to increase reliability, the predictive validity of ADHD for educational impairment has increased (McBurnett et al., 1993). The educational setting particularly lends itself to the type of multidata assessment consistently reported as essential in the evaluation of ADHD (M. Atkins & Pelham, 1991; Barkley, 1988a; Barkley, DuPaul, et al., 1990). Atkins and Pelham note that teacher rating measures, direct observation in the classroom and playground, peer ratings, including sociometric measures, and academic performance are all essential in the ADHD diagnostic process. Sociometrics has been suggested as an optimal means of gaining an understanding of how children function and relate to each other without causing a negative impact in the classroom (Bell-Dolan, Foster, & Sikoria, 1989). In fact, classroom settings may be the optimal place to approach the diagnosis of ADHD, some clinicians suggest that school impairment must be an essential component if the diagnosis is to be made (Ullmann, Sleator, & Sprague, 1985a). The value of school-based diagnosis has spread to non-English-speaking countries (Bauermeister, Berrios, Jimenez, & Acevedo, 1990).

A MODEL FOR SCHOOL-BASED ASSESSMENT

Since the first edition of this text, in which we proposed a general model for assessment, numerous authors have described such models. Most of these have not been empirically tested but hold much face validity. August, Ostrander, and Bloomquist (1992) used a multistage identification process in an epidemiological screening method for diagnosis to identify ADHD in nearly 1,500 students in grades 1 through 4. The procedure involved teacher and parent endorsements of symptoms as well as a diagnostic interview. Children diagnosed with ADHD exhibited more impairment on measures of behavior, academics, and social adjustment and were more likely to have a coexisting disruptive disorder than were children without ADHD.

Burnley (1993) suggested that a team approach to school-based assessment of ADHD is essential for appropriately identifying children with the disorder. A four-step team approach was presented: (1) the preliminary assessment; (2) the follow-up meeting; (3) the development of strategies; (4) follow-up. Burnley noted that careful data collection by school personnel was essential if recommendations were to be made to parents to seek medical assessment. A number of authors have described indepth rating scales, observational systems, and to some extent clinical tests for educators to utilize as part of the diagnostic process (Blondis, Accardo, & Snow, 1989; McKinnery, Montague, & Hocutt, 1993). These authors emphasize the importance of using these assessment processes not just to make the diagnosis of ADHD but to consider differential diagnostic issues, especially to avoid what is perceived in the literature as the easy risk of false positive diagnoses.

Not surprisingly, researchers have increasingly focused on the assessment component of ADHD in school settings. DuPaul (1992) suggests that evaluators ask themselves the following five basic questions:

1. Does the child exhibit a significant number of ADHD symptoms?
2. Are the symptoms exhibited at a frequency that is greater than presented by other children?
3. At what age did these symptoms begin, and do they occur across situations?
4. Is functioning at home, school, or with peers significantly impaired?
5. Are there other factors such as learning disability or emotional problems that could account for occurrence or severity of ADHD symptoms?

DuPaul emphasized that the goals of evaluation are to establish the child's diagnostic status and then to translate assessment data into a potentially successful intervention plan. Screening is a critical component, not just because it may prevent the escalation to more serious problems, as noted by DuPaul and Stoner (1994), but because screening for problems offers an essential component of teacher support. It has also been suggested as helping to avoid teacher burnout (Horner, Albin, & O'Neill, 1991). A screening system for behavioral problems such as that developed by Walker and Severson (1988) can usefully meet this need.

DuPaul (1992) suggests a five-stage system to evaluate ADHD in the schools, utilizing a model of decision making proposed by Salvia and Ysseldyke (1991). Figure 7–2 is an overview of this school-based assessment model.

Teacher complaint of inattention, impulsivity, and/or overactivity

STAGE I
SCREENING
Teacher ratings of ADHD symptoms

STAGE II
MULTIMETHOD ASSESSMENT OF ADHD
Parent and teacher interviews
Reviews of school records
Parent and teacher rating scales
Observations of classroom behavior
Academic performance data
Quality of desk organization

STAGE III
INTERPRETATION OF RESULTS
Number of ADHD symptoms
Deviance from age and gender norms
Age of onset and chronicity
Pervasiveness across situations
Degree of functional impairment
Other disorders ruled out

STAGE IV
DEVELOP TREATMENT PLAN
Based on:
Severity of ADHD symptoms
Functional analysis of behavior
Presence of associated disorders
Response to prior treatment
Community-based resources

Figure 7–2.   Four stages of the school-based assessment of ADHD
Source: DuPaul, G. J. (1992). Adapted from the five stages of the school-based assessment of Attention-Deficit Hyperactivity Disorder. *School Psychology Quarterly, 7,* 60–74. Used with permission.

G. Martin (1993) describes the importance of assessment with attention on differential diagnosis, including a focus on the presence of persistent problems related to inattention and impulsivity, a careful developmental history, ratings of school as well as home behavior, the assessment of behaviors across situations, test results, and an integration of data focusing on differential diagnosis.

It is important for the practitioner to recognize that from a situational perspective, teachers may overidentify children with potential ADHD (August, Realmuto, Crosby, & MacDonald, 1995). Utilizing teachers as first-line screeners completing a Conners checklist, these authors epidemiologically identified 9% of a school-age population as at risk for a diagnosis of disruptive problems. Adding parent ratings of behavior as a second screening narrowed the risk group to 5.5% and identified more severely and pervasively maladjusted children. The third and final gating employed a rating scale of perceived family discipline practices, a variable that is suggested as mediating the progress of oppositional defiant problems to conduct disorder. This three-stage procedure resulted in a substantial reduction in the number of high-risk children identified to approximately .6%. This group demonstrated the highest levels of inattention, hyperactivity, aggression, and conduct problems as rated by parents and teachers and likely represents 20% or fewer of children with ADHD, a group identified by other researchers as experiencing multiple comorbid problems in the greatest risk of progression to later-life psychiatric problems (Biederman, Faraone, Spencer, et al., 1993).

It is of importance to note that teacher ratings of *DSM* symptoms for disruptive behavior have been found to load into three factors: one reflects oppositional defiance and some symptoms of conduct disorder; a second, ADHD symptoms primarily of the inattentive type; and a third, ADHD symptoms primarily of the impulsive/overactive type (Pelham, Gnagy, et al., 1992). Combinations of symptoms from the two ADHD factors and combinations of ODD symptoms had good predictive power. Thus, it may appear that teachers are more accurate at reporting ADHD than CD symptoms. This is consistent with the findings of others, suggesting that measures of attention and activity are associated with poor cognitive performance, whereas measures of defiance are not (E. Taylor, Schachar, et al., 1986). In contrast, these authors note that defiance scales and not hyperactivity scales are associated with impaired family relationships and adverse social factors.

Parental history, report cards, and yearly group achievement tests are the best sources for piecing together a child's academic history. In the early grades, it is often a child's restless, fidgeting, or hyperactive behavior that is most apparent to the classroom teacher; thus, it is not surprising that the greatest percentage of ADHD combined type children are identified in the lower grades. The inattentive child with ADHD may be misidentified early on as poorly motivated or learning impaired. Work incompletion is a common, nondisruptive complaint made by classroom teachers. Many teachers report an apparent lack of congruence between the child's observed capabilities or achievement test scores and daily classroom performance.

Given the demands and structure of our educational system, it is not surprising that symptoms of ADHD often set the stage for multiple problems in the classroom. School data concerning the child's behavior, work completion, achievement, and social interaction are an integral part of the assessment process. Because teachers spend significantly more structured and unstructured time with children than nearly any other adult in the child's life, their observations can provide a rich source of data helping the practitioner understand the nature of the child's behavior and the impact that behavior has on daily classroom functioning. As noted, it has been suggested that a diagnosis of ADHD should not be made for a child capable of functioning effectively in the school system (Ullmann et al., 1985b).

It is important to obtain a description of the child's behavior in various school situations because it is uncommon for a child with ADHD to experience equal difficulty across all school activities and situational contexts. Obtaining behavioral/situational data helps the practitioner gain an understanding of possible compensatory strategies the child or system may use to improve functioning in some situations. This type of data also allows the practitioner to develop an understanding of the classroom environment and specific teacher factors that may minimize or escalate the child's problems. Barkley (1990a) reports that practitioners also need to be aware that observer reports vary based on a number of factors, including the observer's sharing of a common understanding of the attribute or behavior to be rated with the practitioner. Further, based on situation or setting, teachers may be less accurate in identifying and describing classroom problem behavior. For example, Landau and Milich (1988) suggest that in large-group settings, teachers are accurate in discriminating symptoms of attention deficit from those related to aggression; however, during small-group seatwork or independent seatwork, teachers' ability to discriminate accurately may be equivocal.

It is also essential for the practitioner to obtain a description of the child's social and problem-solving skills as they relate to various settings, as it is not uncommon for children with ADHD to function well with a single playmate but to struggle in a group setting. Further, as noted, greater severity of impulsive-hyperactive symptoms appears to coincide with more complaints of social rejection, whereas children presenting the inattentive pattern of ADHD symptoms are more often neglected socially.

Finally, the practitioner must obtain data on the child's academic achievement and estimates of the child's classroom performance on a daily basis. Frequently, children with ADHD possess better academic skills than they can demonstrate in classroom activities. As they progress into higher grades, as noted, they may increasingly experience problems with academic tasks requiring practice for proficiency, including nonphonetic spelling, math facts, and the execution of written language. This pattern of adequate achievement but poor performance is not surprising given the fact that lack of task persistence may result in performance levels falling below capability. The behavioral description and achievement and social skills data are especially important in the evaluation of the context of situations in which these problems occur. Situational data provide a measure of the impact or effect these factors have on the child's daily school functioning. Further, an analysis of antecedents and consequences in a variety of settings helps the practitioner bridge the span between assessment and intervention. In fact, focus on situations in which the child is not described as a problem, a task the child can complete, or activities the child enjoys is essential, as it provides insight for intervention.

As alluded to earlier, attention and related problems are often inferred as explanations for children's misbehavior, noncompliance, and inadequate work in the classroom. Such problems, however, could be caused by myriad other difficulties, including lack of interest, depression, anxiety, inappropriate reinforcement, and cognitive or learning impairments (Shaffer & Schonfeld, 1984). Figure 7–3 contains an overview of the type of school data the practitioner must collect, as well as a sample of specific methods and instruments to facilitate this process. The remainder of this chapter is devoted to a review of these methods and instruments and a discussion of confirmatory data necessary to make the diagnosis of ADHD.

TEACHER-REPORT QUESTIONNAIRES: QUANTITATIVE MEASURES

Practitioners should consider the reliability, validity, standardization, age range, and effects (e.g., repetitive completion of questionnaires, halo, negative response bias) for

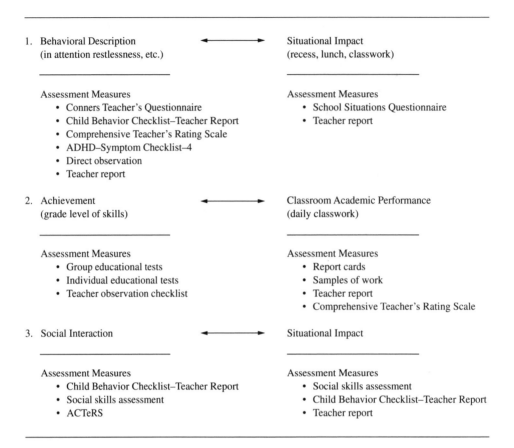

1. Behavioral Description ←————————→ Situational Impact
   (in attention restlessness, etc.)   (recess, lunch, classwork)

   Assessment Measures
   • Conners Teacher's Questionnaire
   • Child Behavior Checklist–Teacher Report
   • Comprehensive Teacher's Rating Scale
   • ADHD–Symptom Checklist–4
   • Direct observation
   • Teacher report

   Assessment Measures
   • School Situations Questionnaire
   • Teacher report

2. Achievement ←————————→ Classroom Academic Performance
   (grade level of skills)   (daily classwork)

   Assessment Measures
   • Group educational tests
   • Individual educational tests
   • Teacher observation checklist

   Assessment Measures
   • Report cards
   • Samples of work
   • Teacher report
   • Comprehensive Teacher's Rating Scale

3. Social Interaction ←————————→ Situational Impact

   Assessment Measures
   • Child Behavior Checklist–Teacher Report
   • Social skills assessment
   • ACTeRS

   Assessment Measures
   • Social skills assessment
   • Child Behavior Checklist–Teacher Report
   • Teacher report

Figure 7–3.　A model for the evaluation of school functioning

Source: Used with permission.

any questionnaires utilized. Clinicians must also be aware of the design and the appropriate use of the questionnaire, utility from a cost perspective, as well as level of difficulty and time required for completion. Blondis, Accardo, and Snow (1991) found that most questionnaires completed by parents are at a fourth- to fifth-grade level, and teacher questionnaires range from a sixth- to eleventh-grade level. It is also important for practitioners to keep in mind that questionnaires do not diagnose: they describe behavior in a standardized format, ranging from simple laundry lists to empirically derived factors. As Blondis et al. (1989) note, questionnaire data alone in the absence of other sources of information are insufficient for diagnostic sensitivity.

Factor analysis of teacher-report questionnaires has yielded a number of generalizable findings. First, teachers can discriminate based on behavioral report between ADHD combined type and ADHD inattentive type (R. T. Brown, 1985). An analysis of the intercorrelations of teacher ratings of the classroom behavior of 158 children with ADHD yielded three factors: emotional lability/conduct, temperament, and attention/concentration. Brown (1985) suggested that, in part, these factors corresponded to the *DSM-III* childhood diagnostic classification system. Bauermeister (1992) compared factor analyses of teacher ratings of ADHD and oppositional defiant symptoms in children 4 through 13 years of age. In a population of over 1,300 children referred for psychoeducational services, a younger cohort yielded factors consistent with ADHD and oppositional defiant symptoms, and an older cohort yielded symptoms consistent with hyperactivity-impulsivity, inattention-distractibility, and oppositional defiance. Further, correlations between parents and teachers, although low for individual symptoms, are fairly high (77%) when thresholds for meeting diagnostic criteria are used as dependent measures (Biederman, Faraone, Milberger, & Doyle, 1993). In clinically referred children, at least these authors suggested a clinical diagnosis of ADHD based on parent report and history is likely to be corroborated by teacher report.

As discussed earlier, teacher reports of behavior and thus responses to questionnaires can be impacted by a number of variables. Of critical importance is the child's level of disruptive, confrontive behavior with the teacher, teacher personality, teaching style, and classroom expectations in shaping the severity of teacher symptom reports. Teacher ratings of certain behavioral problems, such as aggression and hyperactivity, significantly change from kindergarten through the first few grades as teachers change their management styles (Vitazro, Tremblay, & Gagnon, 1995). Although it could be hypothesized that changes in teacher style are a function of changes in children's behavior, parent reports of ADHD children in the home setting do not change particularly dramatically during these years. The transition from kindergarten through the first few grades of school parallels a change from learning to read to reading to learn, an increased need for autonomy, independence, responsibility, and an increased ability to function as a member of a group. Thus, as teacher expectations change, even though the behavior of children with ADHD may remain the same, the severity of teacher complaints increases. As noted earlier, the severity of complaints is a function not solely of the child's behavior but of teacher expectations and the impact that behavior has on the classroom setting. Finally, it has been suggested that these questionnaires are appropriate for children with specific developmental problems, such as hearing impairment (D. Kelly et al., 1990).

Conners Teacher's Rating Scale

The original thirty-nine-item Conners Teacher's Rating Scale (Conners, 1969, 1970, 1973) was revised and shortened to twenty-eight items (Conners, 1982, 1989a; Goyette, Conners, & Ulrich, 1978). The shortened rating scale contains many of the characteristics of the original scale. A sample appears in Figure 7–4. Items that did not load in previous factor analytic studies were omitted, and similar or redundant items were combined into single items (Ross & Ross, 1982). Trites, Blouin, and Laprade (1982) conducted a factor analysis of the Conners Teacher's Rating Scale using a stratified sample of nearly 1,000 schoolchildren. Their research suggested that a primary hyperkinesis factor was present and that the use of the Conners Teacher's Rating Scale as an assessment tool for ADHD is a valid procedure. In 1987, Conners revised the data and provided standard scores for the teacher's rating scale for children from ages 4 through 12 years.

The Conners Teacher's Rating Scale continues to be the most widely used questionnaire for academic reports of symptoms related to ADHD. It is a simple questionnaire for classroom teachers to complete. Each item is scored on a four-point Likert scale according to the following ratings of severity: not at all (score = 0); just a little

Not at All	Just a Little	Pretty Much	Very Much	CTRS-28
0	1	2	3	1. Restless in the "squirmy" sense
0	1	2	3	2. Makes inapproprate noises when s/he shouldn't
0	1	2	3	3. Demands must be set immediately
0	1	2	3	4. Acts "smart" (impudent or sassy)
0	1	2	3	5. Temper outbursts and unpredictable behavior
0	1	2	3	6. Overly sensitive to criticism

Figure 7–4.   Sample items from Conners Teacher's Scale by C. K. Conners

Source: Conner's Teacher Rating Scales—Revised (S) by C. Keith Conners. Copyright, 1997 by Multi-Health Systems, Inc., 908 Niagara Falls Blvd., North Tonawanda, NY 14120-2060, (800) 456-3003. All rights reserved

(score = 1); pretty much (score = 2); and very much (score = 3). The twenty-eight items were originally analyzed to yield three factors referred to as conduct problems, hyperactivity, and inattentive-passive. The scale can also be scored for a ten-item Hyperkinesis Index containing the ten items Conners included in an abbreviated parent-teacher questionnaire (Conners, 1973).

The Hyperkinesis Index is considered a sensitive measure of ADHD problems in the classroom, as well as an excellent measure of a child's response to treatment interventions, specifically medication. Items on the Hyperkinesis Index include descriptors referring to restlessness, temper outbursts, unpredictable behavior, distractibility, poor attention span, excitability, impulsivity, failing to finish things, and being easily frustrated in efforts. The Hyperkinesis Index is computed by adding the scores of the ten critical items, dividing by ten, and comparing the child's score to factor norms (Goyette et al., 1978). Although Conners held the copyright for this questionnaire and the parent form, he allowed the scale to be reproduced without cost and widely used until the late 1980s. At that time, the scale was redesigned, a scoring sheet and proto-col were constructed, and an administration manual written.

Conners (1997) has once again restandardized the teacher and parent scales, issuing them in a revised form. These new forms have included closely worded versions of *DSM-IV* ADHD symptoms but maintain the dimensional questionnaire format. Multi-ple additional scales are provided making this an excellent general use questionnaire for school settings. The restandardization contains one of the largest and best repre-sentative samples for questionnaires of this type. The teacher versions consist of both long and short forms. The long form contains fifty-nine items and includes subscales of the *DSM* symptoms and ADHD index as well as scales reflecting oppositional, cog-nitive, hyperactivity, anxious-shy, perfectionistic, and social problems. The teacher short form contains twenty-eight items and screens for four scales: oppositional and cognitive problems, hyperactivity, and ADHD index. The ADHD index contains what has been described as the best set of items for distinguishing children with ADHD from nonclinical children. This index may be helpful in a screening process. (The scale is available from Multi-Health Systems, Inc., 908 Niagara Falls Blvd., North Tona-wanda, New York, 14120.)

Moehle and Fitzhugh-Bell (1989) provided a factor analysis of the Conners Teacher's Rating Scale with brain-injured and learning-disabled children. There was a similar general pattern for both groups, with the distractibility factor being the highest and the hyperkinesis factor with introversion being the lowest. Twenty-five percent of the learning-disabled group were 1.5 standard deviations above the mean on the clini-cal factor for conduct problems, whereas only 17% of the brain-injured group fell above this range. As with other factor analytic studies of the Conners, this study too generated four main factors. Table 7–1 provides a comparison of factor analytic results comparing Moehle and Fitzhugh-Bell with three other studies. Table 7–2 provides Moehle and Fitzhugh-Bell's factor scores for the two populations. Table 7–3 provides percentages of groups above the 1.5 standard deviation and clinical cutoff.

Efforts have been made to assess the validity of applying the Conners Teacher's Rating Scale to populations of mild mentally handicapped children. It has been con-cluded that for all but the most extreme cases, children should be compared to a same-age sample as opposed to adjusting for developmental level. Pearson and Aman (1994) report negative correlations between chronological age and severity of hyperactive symptoms. These authors suggest that their results provide very weak support for in-cluding mental age when judgment is made about the severity of hyperactive and re-lated symptoms in children. Das and Melnyk (1989) developed a questionnaire for attentional deficits without reference to hyperactive behavior observed in the class-room with a group of mildly mentally handicapped children (mean IQ = approximately 71): 33% of subjects were above the 1.5 cutoff on the Conners scale. The two sets of ratings correlated strongly when checklist items were grouped under one factor; 70% of the variance was explained. Thus, practitioners should not be surprised that a sig-nificantly higher percentage of intellectually handicapped children may cross clin-ical threshold for inattentive complaints even independent of hyperactive-impulsive symptoms.

Although in previous years the cutoff score for the Hyperkinesis Index of 1.5 was considered to reflect a threshold for ADHD symptoms, age by sex normative data have

Table 7–1. Comparison of factor analytic results across studies

Factor	Moehle & Fitzhugh-Bell (1989)	Conners (1969)	Cohen & Hynd (1986)	Trites et al., (1982)
Factor 1	Conduct Disorder	Conduct Disorder	Conduct Disorder	Hyperactive
Number of items	15	17	17	17
Variance	28%	36%	34%	36%
Factor 2	Hyperkinesis	Inattentive-Passive	ADD Hyperactive	Conduct Disorder
Number of items	5	6	11	13
Variance	8%	16%	10%	11%
Factor 3	Distractibility	Tension-Anxiety	Anxiety-Passivity	Emotional
Number of items	4	8	7	8
Variance	7%	12%	6%	6%
Factor 4	Dependent-Depressed	Hyperactive	Depression	Anxious-Passive
Number of items	4	8	4	6
Variance	5%	20%	6%	6%
Factor 5	Dyssocial	Sociability		Asocial
Number of items	3	4	N/A	5
Variance	4%	14%		3%
Factor 6	Introvert			Inattention
Number of items	3			4
Variance	3%			3%

Source: Moehle, K. A., & Fitzhugh-Bell, K. B. (1989). Factor analysis of the Conners Teacher Rating Scale with brain-damaged and learning-disabled children. *Psychology in the Schools, 26,* 113–124.

Table 7–2. Factor scores for the current sample

Factor	Brain-Damaged (n = 112)	Learning-Disabled (n = 172)	Total Sample (N = 284)
1.	.91 (.63)	1.03 (.70)	.91 (1.06)
2.	1.17 (.73)	1.28 (.73)	1.24 (.73)
3.	1.54 (.79)	1.74 (.76)	1.66 (.78)
4.	1.13 (.70)	1.03 (.67)	1.07 (.68)
5.	.40 (.57)	.68 (.81)	.57 (.74)
6.	.86 (.64)	.89 (.59)	.88 (.61)

Source: Moehle, K. A., & Fitzhugh-Bell, K. B. (1989). Factor analysis of the Conners Teacher Rating Scale with brain-damaged and learning-disabled children. *Psychology in the Schools, 26,* 113–124. Used with permission of the publisher.
Note: Factor scores were calculated by adding item ratings and dividing by the number of items in each factor. Scores presented are means, with standard deviations in parentheses.

Table 7–3.   Percents of groups above clinical cutoff points

	Total Sample ($N = 284$)	Learning-Disabled ($n = 172$)	Brain-Damaged ($n = 112$)
Conduct Disorder	22	25	17
Hyperkinesis	36	40	31
Distractibility	66	70	60
Dependent-Depressed	29	28	31
Dyssocial	14	18	6
Introversion	16	16	16

Source: Moehle, K. A., & Fitzhugh-Bell, K. B. (1989). Factor analysis of the Conners Teacher Rating Scale with brain-damaged and learning-disabled children. *Psychology in the Schools, 26,* 113–124.

Note: The convention of regarding a score of 1.5 or above on a factor as clinically significant (Sprague, et al., 1974) was used to determine cutoff points.

demonstrated that this is an inefficient application of this measure. For example, females typically obtained lower scores than males, and the mean of the Hyperkinesis Index decreases with age; in one normative sample, a score of approximately 1.8 male 3- to 5-year-olds is only one standard deviation above the mean, but for a 15- to 17-year-old male sample, a score of 1.3 is two standard deviations above. Thus, an arbitrary cutoff score of 1.5 would result in false positives for younger children and false negatives for adolescents (Goyette et al., 1978). Based on a comparison of the child's score with the age by sex normative data, the practitioner can make a statistically relevant comparison of the child's attentional skills to a normative sample. Although some practitioners have suggested that the cutoff of 1.5 standard deviations above the mean is valid (Barkley, 1990a), a cutoff closer to 2 standard deviations above the mean is more conservative and could be considered a significant indicator of symptoms consistent with the diagnosis of ADHD.

As noted in the first edition of this text and based on subsequent data, the practitioner must be aware that the original Hyperkinesis Index may not be a good indicator of symptomatic problems for the ADHD-IN population. T. Brown (1995) reported that children with ADHD and concomitant hyperactive-impulsive problems are rated approximately 0.8 to 1.0 higher on the Hyperkinesis Index than children experiencing ADHD without hyperactive-impulsive behavior. The revised edition, however, has added two additional items to the Hyperkinesis Index, now referred to as the Global Index, and there has been an effort to clarify symptom descriptors to make certain respondents are able to make a distinction between purposeful and nonpurposeful behavior. For example, teachers are asked to rate whether the child is experiencing difficulty following through on instructions and failing to finish schoolwork, but they are cautioned to make certain that this problem is not the result of oppositional behavior or failure to understand instructions. The practitioner must also be aware that noncompliant children who are not necessarily inattentive may also receive elevated ratings on the Hyperkinesis Index due simply to their resistant behavior.

Loney and Milich (1981) modified the Conners Teacher's Rating Scale to a ten-item scale, with five items tapping inattention-overactivity and five tapping aggression. It has been suggested that this measure can be used to identify children with ADHD, children with aggressive problems, and children experiencing both sets of symptoms (Langhorne & Loney, 1979). Pelham, Milich, Murphy, and Murphy (1989) obtained ratings on this questionnaire referred to as the IOWA Conners Teacher's Rating Scale for 293 males and 315 females from kindergarten through fifth grade in two elementary schools. Mean, standard deviations, and suggested cutoff scores were reported by grade and gender for this sample on the inattention-overactivity and aggression (oppositional defiant) subscales. Significant grade and gender effects produced lower mean scores for older children and females.

Regarding practice effects, Brandon, Kehle, Jenson, and Clark (1990) did not find that repeated completions of the Conners Teacher's Questionnaire led to significant trends in either worsening or improvement of symptom complaints. Nonetheless, practitioners are cautioned concerning issues related to regression to the mean when repeated similar measures are obtained from teachers. In fact, some advocate the completion of a second baseline questionnaire following assessment and diagnosis but prior to medication trials because of this concern (Barkley, 1990a).

Finally, J. D. Parker, Sitarenios, and Conners (1996) provided a factor analytic study of the abbreviated Conners Teacher's Rating Scale. This scale contains only the ten items from the Hyperkinesis Index. The factor structure for the ten-item parent and teacher scales were examined with a sample of over 2,000 parents and nearly 1,800 teachers. The two scales were found to have identical two-factor structures: a restless-impulsive dimension and an emotional lability dimension. As in previous research with this instrument, males demonstrated higher scores or more problems than females. Thus, as noted, because it taps a restless-impulsive dimension, the Hyperkinesis Index is likely a better measure of the combined type versus the inattentive type of ADHD.

ADD-H Comprehensive Teacher Rating Scale

In response to statistical and definitional criticism of the Conners Teacher's Rating Scale, Ullmann, Sleator, and Sprague (1985a) developed the ADD-H Comprehensive Teacher's Rating Scale (ACTeRS). A sample of the scale appears in Figure 7–5. The items on the ACTeRS are scored on a five-point Likert scale with "almost never" equaling a score of 1 and "almost always" equaling 5. Two of the categories (attention and social skills) are worded positively, and higher scores reflect more appropriate behavior; the remaining two categories (hyperactivity and oppositional behavior) are worded negatively, a higher score indicating less desirable behavior. Normative data were originally collected for elementary school children ranging from kindergarten through fifth grade and then expanded into junior high school. Initial normative data for the ACTeRS were based on over 1,300 students. The restandardization included nearly 500 students in grades 6, 7, and 8. The ACTeRS was recently restandardized on over 2,300 males and females from kindergarten through eighth grade (Ullmann, Sleator, & Sprague, 1991, 1997). Correlations among factors for the restandardization demonstrate a very strong relationship between the attention and social skills factors, as well as the hyperactivity and oppositional factors. Once again, validity of these four factors was supported, and the latter relationship is consistent with the hypothesis that hyperactive-impulsive problems appear to precipitate risk and be associated with more severe disruptive behavior. Factor loadings for each of the items and correlations among factors appear in Table 7–4.

	Almost Never				Almost Always
ATTENTION					
1. Works well independently.	1	2	3	4	5
2. Persists with task for reasonable amount of time.	1	2	3	4	5
HYPERACTIVITY					
7. Extremely overactive (out of seat, "on the go").	1	2	3	4	5
8. Overreacts.	1	2	3	4	5
SOCIAL SKILLS					
12. Behaves positively with peer/classmates.	1	2	3	4	5
13. Verbal communication clear and "connected."	1	2	3	4	5
OPPOSITIONAL					
19. Tries to get others into trouble.	1	2	3	4	5
20. Starts fighting over nothing.	1	2	3	4	5

Figure 7–5.   Sample questions from ACTeRS, the ADD-H: Comprehensive Teacher's Rating Scale, by R. K. Ullmann, E. K. Sleator, & R. L. Sprague

Source: Copyright 1986, 1988, 1991 by MetriTech, Inc. Used with permission of the copyright holder. Permission has been granted for this publication only and does not extend to reproductions made from the publication.

A sample of male normative data is provided in Figure 7–6. The items are arranged in the scoring protocol such that scores equating to lower percentiles are equivalent to impairment. According to Ullmann et al. (1985), scoring at the 10th percentile or below reflects significant problems, and children scoring between the 10th and 20th percentile are considered to be impaired. Among the value of the ACTeRS is its separation of ratings for attention and hyperactivity versus social skills and oppositional behavior. The original research addition of this questionnaire also asked teachers to evaluate the child's integration and acceptance within the classroom and the amount of additional teacher time the child required. Unfortunately, these items were eliminated from the subsequent revisions. (The ACTeRS is now available in a Spanish format and is available from MetriTech, Inc., 111 North Market Street, Champaign, Illinois 61820.)

ADHD Symptom Checklist–4

In 1982, Sprafkin, Loney, and Gadow, utilizing the *DSM-III* criteria developed the SLUG Checklist. The checklist contained symptoms of disruptive behavior ranging from hyperactivity to conduct disorder. The authors subsequently expanded and developed their questionnaire into the Stony Brook Child Symptom Inventory–3 and 3R (Gadow & Sprafkin, 1994). The most current version in this genesis is the ADHD Symptom Checklist–4 (ADHD-SC4). The instrument was designed as a screening tool to evaluate mild and moderate symptoms of the disruptive disorders ADHD and Oppositional Defiance. Items in the ADHD-SC4 are based upon the *DSM-IV* diagnostic criteria. The items on this checklist are either identical or very similar to respective

Table 7–4.   Factor loadings and factor intercorrelations of ACTeRS items for restandardization sample

Factor Loadings (Pattern Values)				
	I	II	III	IV
Attention				
Works well independently	.89	−.05	.01	.05
Persists with task for reasonable amount of time	.86	−.03	.02	.07
Completes assigned task satisfactorily with little additional assistance	.93	.04	−.01	.02
Follows simple directions accurately	.94	−.01	.01	−.00
Follows a sequence of instructions	.90	−.03	−.03	−.03
Functions well in the classroom	.80	−.01	−.11	.08
Hyperactivity				
Extremely overactive (out of seat, "on the go")	.00	−.87	−.00	.04
Overreacts	−.01	−.68	−.05	.24
Fidgety (hands always busy)	−.00	−.97	−.03	−.10
Impulsive (acts or talks without thinking)	.02	−.81	−.00	.10
Restless (squirms in seat)	.05	−.95	.02	−.06
Social Skills				
Behaves positively with peers/classmates	.02	.08	.68	−.25
Verbal communication clear and "connected"	−.20	.02	.70	.09
Nonverbal communication accurate	−.15	.05	.74	.12
Follows group norms and social rules	−.03	.17	.63	−.20
Cites general rule when criticizing ("We aren't supposed to do that")	.03	.03	.67	−.03
Skillful at making new friends	.09	−.04	.89	−.04
Approaches situations confidently	−.25	−.08	.68	.08
Oppositional				
Tries to get others into trouble	−.06	.17	.02	−.70
Starts fights over nothing	−.03	.06	.04	−.82
Makes malicious fun of people	−.04	.04	−.04	−.89
Defies authority	−.09	.07	.05	−.71
Picks on others	−.03	−.03	−.01	−.95
Mean and cruel to other children	.02	−.07	.05	−.89

Correlations Among the Factors				
	Attention	Hyperactivity	Social Skills	Oppositional
I Attention	1.00	.46	.78	.38
II Hyperactivity	.46	1.00	.40	.66
III Social Skills	.78	.40	1.00	.44
IV Oppositional	.38	.66	.44	1.00

Source: ACTeRS, the ADD-H: Comprehensive Teacher's Rating Scale, by Ullmann, R. K., Sleator, E. K., Sprague, R. L. Copyright 1988, 1991, 1997 by MetriTech, Inc., Champaign, IL. Used with permission of the copyright holder. Permission has been granted for this publication only and does not extend to reproductions made from the publication.

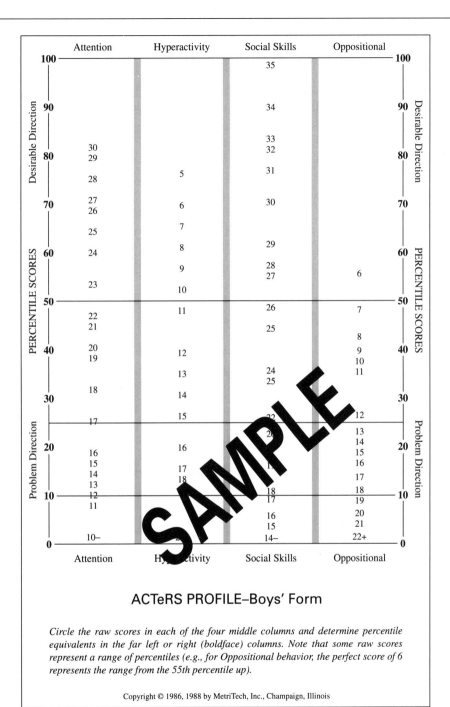

ACTeRS PROFILE–Boys' Form

Circle the raw scores in each of the four middle columns and determine percentile equivalents in the far left or right (boldface) columns. Note that some raw scores represent a range of percentiles (e.g., for Oppositional behavior, the perfect score of 6 represents the range from the 55th percentile up).

Figure 7–6.   ACTeRS Profile–Boys Form from the ADD-H: Comprehensive Teacher's Rating Scale, by R. K. Ullmann, E. K. Sleator, & R. L. Sprague

items also appearing on the Early Childhood Inventory–4 (Sprafkin & Gadow, 1996), the Child Symptom Inventory–4 (Gadow & Sprafkin, 1994) and the Adolescent Symptom Profile–4 (Gadow & Sprafkin, 1995). The ADHD-SC4 also contains a measure of peer aggression as well as measures of mood, behavior and physical complaints that may develop during stimulant treatment. The ADHD-SC4 is available in both teacher and parent versions. The versions are highly similar allowing for global as well as symptom-by-symptom comparison across settings. Individual items can be scored in two different ways. The screening cutoff score method allows the practitioner to determine whether or not the symptom occurs often enough to warrant concern. The total number of symptoms rated as being of concern for a specific disorder can then be compared with a symptom criterion score. The symptom severity score method consists of the minimum number of symptoms necessary for the diagnosis of a specific disorder. This method allows the practitioner to determine whether further evaluation is necessary. This method requires items to be rated on a Likert system. Scores are then summed to generate a symptom severity score for each category that can then be compared to a normative sample.

The ADHD-SC4 possesses acceptable reliability and validity data and is a good measure for assessing ADHD and Oppositional Defiant Disorder in school and home settings. The categorical scores for each of the two primary sets of symptoms assessed correspond well with the comparable scales from commonly used dimensional measures such as the Child Behavior Checklist. Thus, the instrument possesses good concurrent validity and adequate sensitivity. (These questionnaires can be ordered from Checkmate Plus, Ltd., P.O. Box 696, Stony Brook, NY 11790-0696.)

Child Behavior Checklist–Teacher Rating Form

This 113-item questionnaire, with two pages provided for recording teacher observations of the child's academic progress and overall functioning within the classroom, has become the standard in child research. It was originally developed in 1978 by Thomas Achenbach at the University of Connecticut as a parent-report measure. Edelbrock and Achenbach (1984) constructed a parallel form to obtain teacher ratings of many of the same problems rated by parents. Due to the fact that parents and teachers rate somewhat different items and observe children in different contexts, Achenbach (1984) suggested that it was not necessary for teachers and parents to agree in their ratings of similar children.

The Child Behavior Checklist was restandardized in 1991. Clinical cutoffs were adjusted, taking into account cross-informant ratings. It has been suggested that this pattern may in fact reduce the severity of an individual rater's observations, leading to the suggestion that a clinical cutoff of 1.5 standard deviations (approximately 93rd percentile) should be considered indicative of an ADHD profile.

Teachers should have interacted with the child or adolescent on a daily basis for approximately two months before completing this questionnaire. A sample of the Child Behavior Checklist–Teacher's Report Form appears in Figure 7–7. Parts I through IX consist of questions concerning a child's overall academic and classroom performance. The 113 items that comprise part XII are divided into eight or nine behavioral scales, depending on the child's age and sex. These scales deal with specific,

	—for office use only—
	IDENTIFICATION #

CHILD BEHAVIOR CHECKLIST–TEACHER'S REPORT FORM

PUPIL'S AGE	PUPIL'S SEX □ Boy □ Girl	RACE	PUPIL'S NAME
GRADE	THIS FORM FILLED OUT BY □ Teacher (name) ———————		
DATE	□ Counselor (name) ——————— □ Other (specify) ——————— name:		SCHOOL

PARENTS' TYPE OF WORK (Please be specific—for example, auto mechanic, high school teacher, homemaker, laborer, lathe operator, shoe salesman, army sergeant.)

FATHER'S   MOTHER'S
TYPE OF WORK ————————————————   TYPE OF WORK ————————————————

I.   How long have you known this pupil?

II.   How well do you know him/her?   □ Very Well   □ Moderately Well   □ Not Well

III.   How much time does he/she spend in your class per week?

IV.   What kind of class is it? (Please be specific, e.g., regular 5th grade, 7th grade math, etc.)

V.   Has he/she ever been referred for special class placement, services, or tutoring?
           □ No   □ Don't Know   □ Yes—what kind and when?

VI.   Has he/she ever repeated a grade?
           □ No   □ Don't Know   □ Yes—grade and reason

VII. Current school performance—list academic subjects and check appropriate column:

Academic subject	1. Far below grade	2. Somewhat below grade	3. At grade level	4. Somewhat above grade	5. Far above grade
1. _____	□	□	□	□	□
2. _____	□	□	□	□	□
3. _____	□	□	□	□	□
4. _____	□	□	□	□	□
5. _____	□	□	□	□	□
6. _____	□	□	□	□	□

(continued)

Figure 7–7.   Teacher report form

Source: From T. M. Achenbach. Copyright 1991. Printed with permission of the author and publisher.

VIII. Compared to typical pupils of the same age:	1. Much less	2. Somewhat less	3. Slightly less	4. About average	5. Slightly more	6. Somewhat more	7. Much more
1. How hard is he/she working?	☐	☐	☐	☐	☐	☐	☐
2. How appropriately is he/she behaving?	☐	☐	☐	☐	☐	☐	☐
3. How much is he/she learning?	☐	☐	☐	☐	☐	☐	☐
4. How happy is he/she?	☐	☐	☐	☐	☐	☐	☐

IX.   Most recent achievement test scores (if available):

Name of test	Subject	Date	Percentile or grade level obtained

X.   IQ, readiness, or aptitude tests (if available):

Name of test	Date	IQ or equivalent scores

XI.   Please feel free to write any comments about this pupil's work, behavior, or potential, using extra pages if necessary

_____
_____
_____
_____
_____
_____
_____
_____
_____
_____
_____
_____
_____
_____
_____
_____
_____
_____
_____
_____
_____
_____

Figure 7–7.   *(Continued)*

XII. Below is a list of items that describe pupils. For each item than describes the pupil now or within the past 2 months, please circle the 2 if the item is very true or often true of the pupil. Circle the 1 if the item is somewhat or sometimes true of the pupil. If the item is not true of the pupil, circle the 0. Please answer all items as well as you can, even if some do not seem to apply to this pupil.

0 = Not True (as far as you know)	1 = Somewhat or Sometimes True	2 = Very True or Often True

0 1 2   1. Acts too young for his/her age

0 1 2   2. Hums or makes other odd noises in class

0 1 2   3. Argues a lot

0 1 2   4. Fails to finish things he/she starts

0 1 2   5. Behaves like opposite sex

0 1 2   6. Defiant, talks back to staff

0 1 2   7. Bragging, boasting

0 1 2   8. Can't concentrate, can't pay attention for long

0 1 2   9. Can't get his/her mind off certain thoughts;
           obsessions (describe): ——————

0 1 2   10. Can't sit still, restless, or hyperactive

0 1 2   11. Clings to adults or too dependent

0 1 2   12. Complains of loneliness

0 1 2   13. Confused or seems to be in a fog

0 1 2   14. Cries a lot

0 1 2   15. Fidgets

0 1 2   16. Cruelty, bullying, or meanness to others

0 1 2   17. Daydreams or gets lost in his/her thoughts

0 1 2   18. Deliberately harms self or attempts suicide

0 1 2   19. Demands a lot of attention

0 1 2   20. Destroys his/her own things

0 1 2   21. Destroys property belonging to others

0 1 2   22. Difficulty following directions

0 1 2   23. Disobedient at school

0 1 2   24. Disturbs other pupils

0 1 2   25. Doesn't get along with other pupils

0 1 2   26. Doesn't seem to feel guilty after misbehaving

0 1 2   27. Easily jealous

0 1 2   28. Eats or drinks things that are not food
           (describe): ——————

0 1 2   29. Fears certain animals, situations, or places
           other than school (describe): ——————

0 1 2   30. Fears going to school

0 1 2   31. Fears he/she might think or do something bad

0 1 2   32. Feels he/she has to be perfect

0 1 2   33. Feels or complains that no one loves him/her

0 1 2   34. Feels others are out to get him/her

0 1 2   35. Feels worthless or inferior

0 1 2   36. Gets hurt a lot, accident-prone

0 1 2   37. Gets in many fights

0 1 2   38. Gets teased a lot

0 1 2   39. Hangs around with others who get in trouble

0 1 2   40. Hears things that aren't there (describe):
           ——————

0 1 2   41. Impulsive or acts without thinking

0 1 2   42. Likes to be alone

0 1 2   43. Lying or cheating

0 1 2   44. Bites fingernails

0 1 2   45. Nervous, high-strung, or tense

0 1 2   46. Nervous movements or twitching (describe):
           ——————

0 1 2   47. Overconforms to rules

0 1 2   48. Not liked by other pupils

0 1 2   49. Has difficulty learning

0 1 2   50. Too fearful or anxious

0 1 2   51. Feels dizzy

0 1 2   52. Feels too guilty

0 1 2   53. Talks out of turn

0 1 2   54. Overtired

0 1 2   55. Overweight

          56. Physical problems without known medical cause:

0 1 2   a. Aches or pains

0 1 2   b. Headaches

0 1 2   c. Nausea, feels sick

0 1 2   d. Problems with eyes (describe): ————

0 1 2   e. Rashes or other skin problems

0 1 2   f. Stomachaches or cramps

0 1 2   g. Vomiting, throwing up

0 1 2   h. Other (describe): ——————

(continued)

Figure 7–7.   *(Continued)*

0 = Not True	1 = Somewhat or Sometimes True	2 = Very True or Often True

0 1 2   57. Physically attacks people

0 1 2   58. Picks nose, skin, or other parts of body
(describe): _____

0 1 2   59. Sleeps in class

0 1 2   60. Apathetic or unmotivated

0 1 2   61. Poor school work

0 1 2   62. Poorly coordinated or clumsy

0 1 2   63. Prefers being with older children

0 1 2   64. Prefers being with younger children

0 1 2   65. Refuses to talk

0 1 2   66. Repeats certain acts over and over;
compulsions (describe): _____

0 1 2   67. Disrupts class discipline

0 1 2   68. Screams a lot

0 1 2   69. Secretive, keeps things to self

0 1 2   70. Sees things that aren't there (describe):

0 1 2   71. Self-conscious or easily embarrassed

0 1 2   72. Messy work

0 1 2   73. Behaves irresponsibly (describe): _____

0 1 2   74. Showing off or clowning

0 1 2   75. Shy or timid

0 1 2   76. Explosive and unpredictable behavior

0 1 2   77. Demands must be met immediately, easily
frustrated

0 1 2   78. Inattentive, easily distracted

0 1 2   79. Speech problem (describe): _____

0 1 2   80. Stares blankly

0 1 2   81. Feels hurt when criticized

0 1 2   82. Steals

0 1 2   83. Stores up things he/she doesn't need (describe): _____

0 1 2   84. Strange behavior (describe): _____

0 1 2   85. Strange ideas (describe): _____

0 1 2   86. Stubborn, sullen, or irritable

0 1 2   87. Sudden changes in mood or feelings

0 1 2   88. Sulks a lot

0 1 2   89. Suspicious

0 1 2   90. Swearing or obscene language

0 1 2   91. Talks about killing self

0 1 2   92. Underachieving, not working up to potential

0 1 2   93. Talks too much

0 1 2   94. Teases a lot

0 1 2   95. Temper tantrums or hot temper

0 1 2   96. Seems preoccupied with sex

0 1 2   97. Threatens people

0 1 2   98. Tardy to school or class

0 1 2   99. Too concerned with neatness or cleanliness

0 1 2   100. Fails to carry out assigned tasks

0 1 2   101. Truancy or unexplained absence

0 1 2   102. Underactive, slow moving, or lacks energy

0 1 2   103. Unhappy, sad, or depressed

0 1 2   104. Unusually loud

0 1 2   105. Uses alcohol or drugs (describe): _____

0 1 2   106. Overly anxious to please

0 1 2   107. Dislikes school

0 1 2   108. Is afraid of making mistakes

0 1 2   109. Whining

0 1 2   110. Unclean personal appearance

0 1 2   111. Withdrawn, doesn't get involved with others

0 1 2   112. Worrying

113. Please write in any problems the pupil has
that were not listed above:

0 1 2   _____

0 1 2   _____

0 1 2   _____

Figure 7–7. *(Continued)*

empirically derived childhood categories. Achenbach (1996) recently reported a strong relationship between these empirically derived scales and the categorical diagnostic system of *DSM-IV*. Scales on the teacher-report form include withdrawn, somatic complaints, anxious/depressed, social problems, thought problems, attention problems, delinquent behavior, and aggressive behavior.

The 113 items on part XII are rated as 0 (not true), 1 (somewhat or sometimes true), or 2 (very true or often true). The score for each scale is obtained by summing the points for those items loading on each. The scores are plotted on profile sheets using percentiles or standard scores based on the normative sample. A computer scoring system also provides diagnostic probabilities.

Normative data were first obtained in 1978 on disturbed 6- to 11-year-old males (Achenbach, 1978). Separated profiles have been standardized for each gender at ages 6 through 11 and 12 through 16 years. Age-graded normative data is essential, because the prevalence and severity of many behaviors associated with ADHD decline with age (Achenbach & Edelbrock, 1981). Scoring profiles also provide standard scores based on normative samples for teacher ratings of academic performance, adaptive behavior, and behavior problems. Behavioral problem scales are organized as either internalizing (e.g., anxiety, social withdrawal) or externalizing (e.g., aggressive, delinquent). Summary internalizing, externalizing, and total problem scores can also be computed. Figure 7–8 contains a sample profile sheet for males.

E. Kirby and Horne (1986) suggested that the original hyperactivity and aggression scales on this checklist appear fairly similar in profile for a population of children with ADHD versus a population of children with aggression. Background information about the two groups, however, was very different. The aggressive children were more likely to come from chaotic homes, where physical punishment was employed and aggression was modeled. Additionally, Edelbrock et al. (1984) found that boys presenting with attention deficit without hyperactivity obtained higher scores on the inattentive scale, and boys experiencing attention disorder with hyperactivity scored high on this scale as well as on nervous-overactive scale.

To better define the relationship between *DSM-IV* categories and empirically derived patterns of children's behavior, Achenbach (1996) factor analyzed the Teacher Rating Form–Attention Problems Scale. The Teacher Scale was chosen because the twenty items provided more opportunity to identify subsets of co-occurring symptoms than the parent form. Principal factor/variable mixed analyses were conducted in over 2,800 clinically referred children. Items such as fails to finish things, difficulty learning, poor schoolwork, and failure to carry out assigned tasks loaded on an inattention factor; acting too young, being restless, and hyperactive or impulsive loaded on a hyperactivity-impulsivity factor; can't concentrate, difficulty following directions, messy work, and inattentive were associated with both factors (see Table 7–5). Achenbach suggests that the strong association of the four attention-impairment items with both of the other factors indicates that these items reflect a central core of the empirically based Attention Problem Syndrome. Achenbach further suggests that clinicians consider summing these two subsets separately by adding the ten inattentive items in the four co-occurring items and generating one score, while adding the six hyperactive-impulsive items with the four co-occurring attention items and generating a second score. Ninety-fifth percentile cutoff points for these scores by gender and age

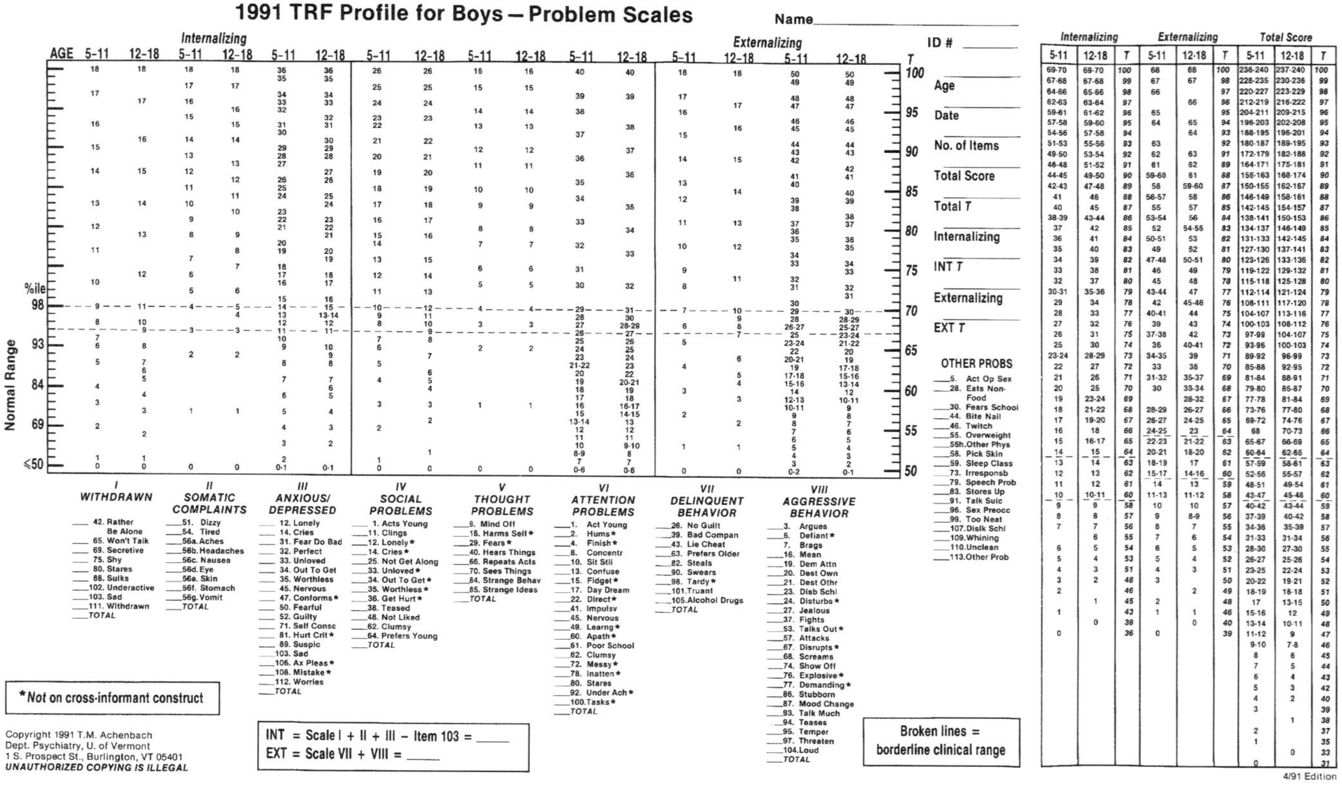

Figure 7-8. Teacher-reported behavior problems for boys

From T. M. Achenbach, 1991. *Teacher's Report Form.* Copyright 1991. Printed with permission of the author and publisher.

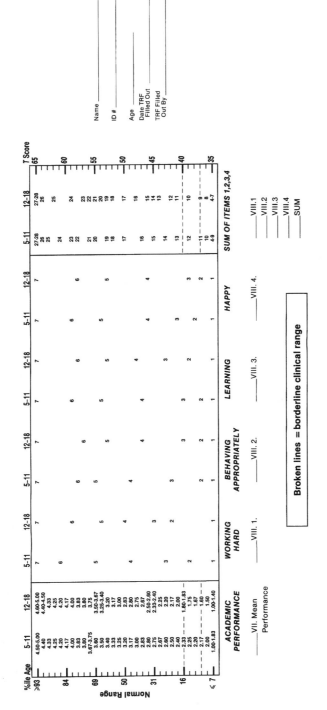

Figure 7-8. (Continued)

Table 7–5.   Inattention and hyperactivity-impulsivity items on the TRF attention problems scale

Inattention Items	Hyperactivity-Impulsivity Items
4. Fails to finish things he/she starts	1. Acts too young for his/her age
13. Confused or seems to be lost in a fog	2. Hums or makes other odd noises in class
17. Daydreams or gets lost in his/her thoughts	10. Can't sit still, restless, or hyperactive
49. Has difficulty learning	15. Fidgets
60. Apathetic or unmotivated	41. Impulsive or acts without thinking
61. Poor school work	45. Nervous, high-strung, or tense
62. Poorly coordinated or clumsy	
80. Stares blankly	
92. Underachieving, not working up to potential	
100. Fails to carry out assigned tasks	

Core Items Associated with Both Subsets
8. Can't concentrate, can't pay attention for long
22. Difficulty following directions
72. Messy work
78. Inattentive, easily distracted

Source: Achenbach, T. M. (1996). Subtyping ADHD: A request for suggestions about relating empirically based assessment to *DSM-IV. The ADHD Report, 4,* 5–9. Used with permission.

are provided in Table 7–6. (The teacher and parent forms of the Child Behavior Checklist are available from University Associates in Psychiatry, 1 South Prospect Street, Burlington, Vermont 05401.)

Attention Deficit Disorders Evaluation Scale

McCarney (1989) developed the Attention Deficit Disorders Evaluation Scale (ADDES) through field testing nearly 5,000 students in grades kindergarten through 12. Demographic characteristics of the standardization sample represented national percentages of gender, residence, race, geographic area, and occupation of parents. The school version consists of sixty items, the home version forty-six items. A prereferral attention deficit checklist accompanies the scale. McCarney suggested that each item on this scale was associated with one of the three characteristics of *DSM-III-R* for ADHD: inattention, impulsivity, and hyperactivity. Each item on this questionnaire is rated on a five-point scale from 0 for not engaging in the behavior to 4 for engaging in the behavior several times per hour. The questionnaire yields scores on three scales, which are then converted to percentiles.

Although normatively structured, the lack of factor analysis raised the question of the validity of three separate but equal ADHD scales. Therefore, it is not surprising that in the absence of reliability and validity, Addesman (1991) suggested that clinicians should be cautious in interpreting the results of this questionnaire. In response to emerging data reflecting a two-factor explanation for ADHD symptoms, McCarney

Table 7–6.   Judging deviance on combinations of inattention and hyperactivity-impulsivity items with the four core items

Computing Subtest Scores

Inattention	Hyperactivity-Impulsivity
1. Sum the scores of 1 and 2, obtained on TRF items 4, 13, 17, 49, 60, 61, 62, 80, 92, 100	1. Sum the scores of 1 and 2 obtained on TRF items 1, 2, 10, 15, 41, 45

2. To each of the above subsets, add the scores of 1 and 2 obtained on TRF items 8, 22, 72, and 78.

	95th Percentile Cutpoints[a] for the Above Scores			
	Boys' Ages		Girls' Ages	
	5–11	12–18	5–11	12–18
Inattention	19	21	16	15
Hyperactivity-Impulsivity	15	14	10	9

Source: Achenbach, T. M. (1996). Subtyping ADHD: A request for suggestions about relating empirically based assessment to *DSM-IV. The ADHD Report, 4,* 5–9. Used with permission.

[a] Scores that reach these cutpoints are in the top 5% of the TRF national normative sample of 1,391 pupils who were not receiving mental health services or special remedial classes (Achenbach, 1991b).

(1996) restandardized the questionnaire to parallel current theory. The current questionnaire yields scores on two factors: inattention and hyperactivity-impulsivity (McCarney, 1996). The Attention Deficit Disorders Evaluation Scale has become increasingly popular for use in educational settings. (It is available from Hawthorne Educational Services, 800 Gray Oak Dr., Columbia, MO 65201, 1-800-542-1673.)

ADHD Rating Scale

DuPaul (1991a) developed the ADHD Rating Scale as part of ongoing research. The scale and normative data are available with permission to reproduce as part of the package of forms edited by Barkley (1991c). DuPaul obtained data from parents and teachers for 623 girls and 594 boys ages 6 to 12 years and collected criterion measures (e.g., direct observations of classroom behavior, academic achievement scores) on a smaller subsample. The ADHD Rating Scale was found to be highly reliable with adequate criterion-related validity. It was also found to be internally consistent, stable across time, and related to criterion measures of classroom performance. Further, strong differences between males and females were evident with respect to the frequency of ADHD symptoms. A sample of this questionnaire appears in Figure 7–9.

Childhood Attention Problems Questionnaire

The Childhood Attention Problems Questionnaire (CAP) was developed by Craig Edelbrock and cited in Barkley (1990a). Edelbrock developed this assessment instrument primarily for evaluating drug effects. Items that tapped the dimensions of inattention

---

Child's Name ————————————————— Age ———— Grade ————

Completed by ————————————————————————

Circle the number in the one column which best describes the child.

	Not at All	Just a Little	Pretty Much	Very Much
1. Often fidgets or squirms in seat.	0	1	2	3
2. Has difficulty remaining seated.	0	1	2	3
3. Is easily distracted.	0	1	2	3
4. Has difficulty awaiting turn in groups.	0	1	2	3
5. Often blurts out answers to questions.	0	1	2	3
6. Has difficulty following instructions.	0	1	2	3
7. Has difficulty sustaining attention to tasks.	0	1	2	3
8. Often shifts from one uncompleted activity to another.	0	1	2	3
9. Has difficulty playing quietly.	0	1	2	3
10. Often talks excessively.	0	1	2	3
11. Often interrupts or intrudes on others.	0	1	2	3
12. Often does not seem to listen.	0	1	2	3
13. Often loses things necessary for tasks.	0	1	2	3
14. Often engages in physically dangerous activities without considering consequences.	0	1	2	3

Figure 7–9. The ADHD Rating Scale

Source: DuPaul, G. J. (1991). Parent and teacher ratings of ADHD symptoms: Psychometric properties in a community-based sample. *Journal of Clinical Psychology, 20,* 245–253. Used with permission of the author.

and overactivity were selected from the teacher-report Child Behavior Checklist. A twelve-item scale was developed. Normative data were obtained from 1,100 children, ranging in age from 6 to 16 years. The questionnaire has been found to be sensitive to stimulant drug effects (Barkley, McMurray, Edelbrock, & Robbins, 1989). At one time, it was suggested that this questionnaire might also be useful in discriminating between the inattentive and combined types of ADHD. The questionnaire and normative data are available in a package of forms edited by Barkley (1990c).

Academic Performance Rating Scale

The Academic Performance Rating Scale was developed by DuPaul, Rapport, and Perriello (1991) using a standardization sample of nearly 500 6- to 12-year-olds. Factor analysis yields three factors. All subscales were found to be internally consistent, possessing good test-retest reliability. The total score on this questionnaire was found to discriminate accurately between children with and without classroom performance problems. This questionnaire and normative data are available as part of a reproducible packet edited by Barkley (1990c).

TEACHER-REPORT QUESTIONNAIRES: QUALITATIVE MEASURES

Teacher Observation Checklist

The Teacher Observation Checklist (Figure 7–10) was developed by S. Goldstein (1988b) as a brief teacher-response questionnaire to provide supplemental data absent from many of the quantitative checklists. When used in conjunction with quantitative measures, the Teacher Observation Checklist provides additional descriptive data concerning a child's classroom functioning. The questionnaire was principally designed for elementary and junior high school students. Normative data have not been collected on this questionnaire.

Social Skills Assessment

A number of questionnaires have been developed to directly and quantitatively assess social skills; two are the Social Skills Rating System (Gresham & Elliott, 1990) and the Walker-McConnell Scale of Social Competence and School Adjustment (H. Walker & McConnell, 1988). The Social Skills Assessment Teacher Form (Goldstein, 1988a) was developed to provide a qualitative description of a child's social interaction with classmates (see Figure 7–11). The questionnaire was generated to assess a range of disruptive and nondisruptive social problems. Normative data have not been collected. This questionnaire may be particularly useful in identifying targets for social skills remediation.

School Situations Questionnaires

The School Situations Questionnaire (Figure 7–12) was developed by Barkley (1997b) as a means of evaluating the impact of a child's behavioral and related problems in specific school situations. Information from this questionnaire allows the practitioner to make the important connection between symptoms of ADHD and the impact they have in a variety of school situations. This form additionally enables the practitioner to develop an understanding of the child's compensatory skills, which in specific situations may reduce the negative impact of ADHD and related behavioral problems. The School Situations Questionnaire also allows the practitioner to develop an understanding of teacher behaviors that, in specific situations, may minimize the negative impact of the child's ADHD symptoms. Barkley's original School Situations Questionnaire appears best suited for elementary age; it was reduced to fewer items by Goldstein and Goldstein (1990) and suggested for use with adolescents (see Figure 7–13). Barkley developed this questionnaire primarily to provide the practitioner with qualitative information. From his research, Barkley (1997b) noted that children with ADHD present with problems in at least 50% of the most frequently encountered school situations. Breen (1986), based on a sample of almost 600 children, developed normative

TEACHER OBSERVATION CHECKLIST

Name _____   Date _____

Teacher _____   Grade _____

Please check the phrase that best describes this student.

1. *SELF-CONCEPT*

- ☐ Appears to feel inadequate, self-critical
- ☐ Appears to have mild feelings of inadequacy
- ☐ Appears self-confident in most situations
- ☐ Confident in all areas, good concept of ability
- ☐ Over-confident, unrealistic

2. *MOTIVATION*

- ☐ Low interest, never initiates activity
- ☐ Little interest, limited and narrow
- ☐ Some enthusiasm
- ☐ Above-average, initiates some
- ☐ Enthusiastic interest

3. *ADAPTABILITY TO NEW SITUATIONS*

- ☐ Dependent, lost in new situations
- ☐ Difficult adjustment as a rule
- ☐ Usually adapts
- ☐ Adapts easily, confident in new areas
- ☐ Excellent adaptation

4. *ATTENTION-SEEKING*

- ☐ Constantly seeking attention
- ☐ Often seeks attention
- ☐ Moderately seeks attention
- ☐ Usually does not seek extra attention
- ☐ Does not seek extra attention

5. *APPROACH TO A PROBLEM*

- ☐ Slovenly, unorganized
- ☐ Inexact, careless
- ☐ Moderately careful
- ☐ Consistent and logical
- ☐ Precise, organized approach

6. *LISTENING TO INSTRUCTIONS*

- ☐ Unable to follow instructions; always confused
- ☐ Usually follows simple instructions but often needs individual help
- ☐ Follows instructions that are familiar and not complex
- ☐ Remembers and follows extended instructions
- ☐ Usually skillful in remembering and following instructions

7. *LEARNING RATE*

- ☐ Learns very slowly
- ☐ Learns slowly
- ☐ Learns at an average rate
- ☐ Learns at above-average rate
- ☐ Learns quickly

8. *WORK RATE*

- ☐ Works very slowly
- ☐ Works slowly
- ☐ Works at an average rate
- ☐ Works at above-average rate
- ☐ Works quickly

9. *FRUSTRATION-TOLERANCE*

- ☐ Gives up easily, cries
- ☐ Shows some ability to tolerate frustration
- ☐ Average degree of tolerance
- ☐ Above-average degree of tolerance
- ☐ Perseveres, handles frustration well

Figure 7–10.   Teacher observation checklist

Source: By S. Goldstein. 1988b. Used with the author's permission.

10. *COOPERATION*

☐ Continually disrupts classroom; poor impulse control
☐ Frequently demands attention; often speaks out of turn
☐ Waits turn; average for age and grade
☐ Above average; cooperates well
☐ Excellent ability; cooperates without adult encouragement

11. *VOCABULARY*

☐ Always uses immature, poor vocabulary
☐ Limited vocabulary, primarily simple nouns; few precise, descriptive words
☐ Adequate vocabulary for age and grade
☐ Above-average vocabulary; uses numerous precise, descriptive words
☐ High-level vocabulary; always uses precise words; conveys abstractions

12. *LANGUAGE USAGE*

☐ Always uses incomplete sentences with grammatical errors
☐ Frequently uses incomplete sentences; numerous grammatical errors
☐ Uses correct grammar; few errors in the use of prepositions, etc.
☐ Above-average oral language; rarely makes grammatical errors
☐ Always speaks in grammatically correct sentences

13. *FINE MOTOR COORDINATION*

☐ Considerable difficulty using a pencil, cutting, tying
☐ Below average skills in writing; poor finger dexterity
☐ Average fine motor skills
☐ Above-average ability to draw, print, or do cursive writing
☐ Excellent ability in drawing, coloring, cutting, and writing

14. *GROSS MOTOR COORDINATION*

☐ Very poorly coordinated; clumsy
☐ Below average; awkward
☐ Average for age
☐ Above average; does well in motor activities
☐ Excels in coordination; graceful

15. *VISUAL PERCEPTION*

☐ Much difficulty with reversals, directionality, and illegible writing
☐ Below-average written work and copying skills
☐ Average visual perception of written material
☐ Above-average printing or writing
☐ Excellent, well-organized, clearly legible written assignments

16. *ACHIEVEMENT*

	Reading	Mathematics
Very poor	☐	☐
Below average	☐	☐
Average	☐	☐
Above average	☐	☐
Exceptional	☐	☐

Figure 7–10.   *(Continued)*

SOCIAL SKILLS ASSESSMENT
(Teacher Form)

Student's Name _____ **Date** _____

Individual Completing This Form _____ **Grade** _____

Description: Please check any statements which you feel describe this student in interaction with peers. If parts of these statements apply to this student, please qualify your response by specifically underlining those parts.

Not True	Sometimes True	Frequently True	This Student:
____	____	____	appears socially isolated. A large proportion of school time is spent in solitary activities. Isolation appears to result from the student's withdrawal as opposed to rejection by classmates.
____	____	____	interacts less with classmates due to shyness or timidity.
____	____	____	appears anxious in interactions with classmates and adults.
____	____	____	spends less time involved in activities with classmates due to a lack of social skills and/or appropriate social judgment.
____	____	____	appears to have fewer friends than most due to negative, bossy, or annoying behaviors that alienate classmates.
____	____	____	appears to spend less time with classmates due to awkward or bizarre behavior.
____	____	____	disturbs classmates by teasing, provoking, fighting, or interrupting.
____	____	____	will openly strike back with angry behavior if teased by classmates.
____	____	____	is argumentative with adults and classmates. This student must have the last word in verbal exchange.
____	____	____	displays physical aggression toward objects or persons.
____	____	____	will use coercive tactics to force the submission of classmates. This student will manipulate or threaten.
____	____	____	speaks to others in an impatient or cranky tone of voice.
____	____	____	will say uncomplimentary things to others, including engaging in name calling, ridicule, or verbal derogation.
____	____	____	will respond when a classmate initiates conversation.
____	____	____	engages in long conversation.
____	____	____	will share laughter with classmates.
____	____	____	will spontaneously contribute during a group discussion.
____	____	____	will volunteer in class and freely take a leadership role.
____	____	____	will spontaneously work with classmates during classroom activities.
____	____	____	will verbally initiate with classmates.

Additional Comments: _____
_____
_____
_____
_____

Figure 7–11.   Social skills assessment

Source: By S. Goldstein. 1988a. Used with the author's permission.

SCHOOL SITUATIONS QUESTIONNAIRE

Child's Name _____ **Date** _____

Name of person completing this form _____

Instructions: Does this child present any problems with compliance to instructions, commands, or rules for you in any of these situations? If so, please circle the word Yes and then circle a number beside that situation that describes how severe the problem is for you. If this child is not a problem in a situation, circle No and go on to the next situation on the form.

| | | | If yes, how severe? | | |
Situation	Yes/No		Mild		Severe
When arriving at school	Yes	No	1 2 3 4 5 6 7 8 9
During individual desk work	Yes	No	1 2 3 4 5 6 7 8 9
During small group activities	Yes	No	1 2 3 4 5 6 7 8 9
During free playtime in class	Yes	No	1 2 3 4 5 6 7 8 9
During lectures to the class	Yes	No	1 2 3 4 5 6 7 8 9
At recess	Yes	No	1 2 3 4 5 6 7 8 9
At lunch	Yes	No	1 2 3 4 5 6 7 8 9
In the hallways	Yes	No	1 2 3 4 5 6 7 8 9
In the bathroom	Yes	No	1 2 3 4 5 6 7 8 9
On field trips	Yes	No	1 2 3 4 5 6 7 8 9
During special assemblies	Yes	No	1 2 3 4 5 6 7 8 9
On the bus	Yes	No	1 2 3 4 5 6 7 8 9

Figure 7–12.   School situations questionnaire

Source: From Russell A. Barkley's *Defiant Children, 2E* (1997b), p. 178. New York: Guilford Press. Copyright 1997. The Guilford Press. Reprinted with permission.

data for the School Situations Questionnaire for children ranging in age from 6 to 11 years. These data are presented in Table 7–7. Subsequently, Altepeter and Breen (1989) generated additional data; however, these data were not stratified to population demographics, were drawn from a limited geographic area, and underrepresented minorities. Nonetheless, interrelated reliability and moderate but significant correlations with Conners factors were reported. In 1992, Altepeter and Breen conducted further factor analysis from data on 163 clinic-referred children 5 to 12 years of age. Three factors emerged for the School Situations Questionnaire: unsupervised settings, task performance, and special events; factors were similar to those derived from nonreferred children. These factors significantly discriminated children with attention deficit disorder with hyperactivity from nonreferred children. The revised version of this questionnaire appears in the material published by Barkley (1990c). DuPaul and Barkley (1992) evaluated the psychometric properties of the Revised Home Situations Questionnaire with a population of nearly 1,000 6- to 12-year-old children. The questionnaire was found to possess adequate levels of internal consistency, test-retest reliability, and construct validity. The instrument also shared considerable variance with

ADOLESCENT SCHOOL SITUATIONS QUESTIONNAIRE

Name of Adolescent _____

Name of person completing this form _____

Does this adolescent present problems for you in any of these situations? If so, indicate their severity and a brief description if possible.

Situation	Yes/No (Circle One)		If yes, how severe? (Circle One) Mild Severe
During individual task work	Yes	No	1 2 3 4 5 6 7 8 9
During small-group activities	Yes	No	1 2 3 4 5 6 7 8 9
During free time in class	Yes	No	1 2 3 4 5 6 7 8 9
During lectures to class	Yes	No	1 2 3 4 5 6 7 8 9
During lunch	Yes	No	1 2 3 4 5 6 7 8 9
While in the hallways	Yes	No	1 2 3 4 5 6 7 8 9
While in the bathroom	Yes	No	1 2 3 4 5 6 7 8 9
During special assemblies	Yes	No	1 2 3 4 5 6 7 8 9
While on the bus	Yes	No	1 2 3 4 5 6 7 8 9

Figure 7–13.   Adolescent school situations questionnaire

Source: Reduced by S. Goldstein (1987a) from the original *School Situations Questionnaire* by R. A. Barkley (1981a) and copyright by Guilford Publications. Modified and reprinted with permission of the author and publisher.

criterion measures such as parent and teacher behavior ratings, direct observations of classroom on-task behavior, and productivity on academic tasks.

Clinicians should be aware that between settings (i.e., school and home), severity of problems may actually be worsened by communication between parent and teacher. Costello, Loeber, and Stouthamer-Loeber (1991) suggest that when sources of information are independent of parents' and teachers' judgment, no differences are found

Table 7–7.   Norms for the elementary school situations questionnaire

Age	n	#Problem Settings	Mean Severity
Boys:			
6–8	170	2.4 (3.3)*	1.5 (2.0)
9–11	123	2.8 (3.2)	1.9 (2.1)
Girls:			
6–8	180	1.0 (2.0)	0.8 (1.5)
9–11	126	1.3 (2.1)	0.8 (1.2)

Source: Breen, M. J. Normative data on the Home Situations and School Situations Questionnaires. Copyright, 1986. *ADD/H Newsletter.* Used with permission of the publisher.

These entries are means with standard deviations in parentheses.

between the severity of situational problems reported between settings. As communication between informants increased, agreement in symptom complaints increased, suggesting that informants may have been biased toward agreement.

Finally, Reeve, Spressard, Walker, Welch, and Wright (1994) suggest that practitioners ask questions about differences in behavior and performance between seatwork and group activities, morning and afternoon, and academic versus nonacademic tasks.

Additional Teacher-Report Questionnaires

A number of comprehensive, school-based assessment programs have been developed that include components containing teacher questionnaires. L. Brown and Hammill (1990) have authored the second edition of the Behavior Rating Profile, an instrument that examines a child's behavior in a variety of settings. This profile provides a highly standardized, norm-referenced, validated system for analyzing and summarizing childhood behavior. The profile consists of six different instruments, five of which are rating scales for home, school, and peer behavior, teacher and parent assessment, and a sociogram. The teacher scale offers normative data from grades 1 through 12 and can be used without the other scales. The profile's summary score compares the target student with a normative sample for general behavior problems primarily of a disruptive nature.

Reynolds and Kamphus (1992) have authored the Behavior Assessment System for Children. Like the Behavior Rating Profile, the Behavior Assessment System presents a comprehensive overview of a child's behavior, incorporating teacher, parent, and self-report, a developmental history, and even an observational system for directly recording behavior in the classroom. This system provides summary scores for externalizing problems, including aggression, hyperactivity, and conduct difficulty, as well as internalizing problems of anxiety, depression, somaticization, inattention, learning difficulty, social withdrawal, and general adaptive skills. The questionnaire also offers an overall behavioral symptom index for the teacher form. This questionnaire lends itself to use with other comprehensive measures such as the Child Behavior Checklist, and assesses symptoms consistent with the *DSM* nomenclature for normative samples for comparison: general, female, male, and clinical.

There are other questionnaires practitioners may find useful. Prinz, Conner, and Wilson (1981) developed a Daily Behavior Checklist to differentiate between hyperactive and aggressive problems within school settings. As discussed, the overlap between ADHD symptoms and behaviors and oppositional or aggressive behaviors, especially within school settings, creates a diagnostic thorn for the practitioner. This checklist provides operational descriptions along with criteria for the assessment of purposeful versus nonpurposeful behavior. For noncompliant children, problems usually occur as the result of premeditation or wrong thinking. For children with ADHD, aggressive problems may occur as the result of impulsivity or not thinking. The child with purposeful disruptive behavior is typically angry and often vengeful in his or her acts.

Kendall and Wilcox (1979) developed a thirty-three item, self-control rating scale, primarily relating to issues of self-control and impulsivity. The scale appears sensitive to classroom behavioral problems and, given the specificity of scale items, can be useful in identifying specific target behaviors for treatment intervention.

In 1971, Davids developed a seven-characteristics rating scale to be completed by either parents or teachers. The scale covers school performance and symptoms of what was then referred to as hyperactivity. Each item is rated on a six-point scale comparing the target child to other children. Although the scale has been a subject of research and may be sensitive to drug effects (Denhoff, Davids, & Hawkins, 1971), it has found only limited clinical use.

The Springs Hyperactivity Rating Scale is a thirty-three-item scale used to obtain ratings of children's behavior in the classroom (Spring, Blundin, Greenberg, & Yellin, 1977). Teachers rate items organized into eleven categories on a one-to-five Likert scale. Normative data were collected for males and females in kindergarten through fourth grade. At the time, children referred to as hyperactive scored higher in the categories containing items dealing with restlessness, distractibility, and impulsivity. This scale, too, has not found much clinical utility but may be of value for classroom research for younger children.

L. Behar (1977) developed a preschool behavior questionnaire that is one of the few behavior rating scales specifically designed for young children ages 3 to 6 in school settings. The scale is comprised of thirty items; teachers respond to each on a three-point Likert scale. The questionnaire can also be scored for three factor-based scales, reflecting aggression, anxiety, and hyperactivity. S. Campbell et al. (1982) demonstrated that this questionnaire can be used clinically to identify toddlers at risk for hyperactivity in preschool settings.

The Homework Problem Checklist (Anesko, Schoiock, Ramirez, & Levine, 1987) provides a qualitative set of data regarding the frequency of various problems children experience related to homework (e.g., denies having homework, loses it, fails to finish it or turn it in). Although completed by parents, this questionnaire provides an organized way for clinicians to address homework issues.

SUGGESTED COMBINATION OF QUESTIONNAIRES

In situations in which teachers have a limited amount of time, it is suggested that at the very least, each of the child's teachers complete the Child Behavior Checklist. Because of its empirical basis and close relationship to the *DSM* diagnostic classification, this questionnaire provides a reasonably quick overview and allows for an analysis of a variety of disruptive and nondisruptive symptoms. It is strongly recommended, however, that teachers also complete either the Conners, ACTeRS, ADHD-SC4, or ADDES as a specific measure of ADHD symptoms. Additionally, the Teacher Observation Checklist, Social Skills, and Situational Problems questionnaires each adds components of slightly different data.

In secondary school settings, it is frequently beneficial to obtain ratings by all of the adolescent's teachers. This affords the practitioner the opportunity to assess patterns of consistency or discrepancy in the adolescent's problems throughout the school day. Additionally, classes in which the adolescent with ADHD would be expected to have more problems (e.g., due to academic load) can be contrasted with those in which less difficulty would be expected if ADHD was the primary problem (e.g., physical education, shop). The examination of behavior between classes frequently provides the practitioner with useful data in making a distinction between symptoms of ADHD and symptoms of purposeful noncompliance. It is also not uncommon for children and adolescents with ADHD to function significantly better in classes allowing movement and interaction with learning materials as well as those requiring a reduced cognitive load or need for sustained attention.

OBSERVATION IN EDUCATIONAL SETTINGS

It is strongly recommended that the practitioner obtain observational data of a child's behavior in the school environment. Platzman et al. (1992) reviewed thirty-nine empirical studies in which direct observational methods were used to assess children in whom ADHD had been diagnosed. Classroom studies distinguished ADHD children from comparison groups better than laboratory studies. Measures that most consistently distinguished children with ADHD from comparison groups included those of attention, activity, and vocalization. Barkley (1990a) suggested that for females, off-task behavior may be the best behavior to observe when ADHD is suspected in the classroom.

Direct observation can also provide the practitioner insight into myriad social and nonsocial factors that may elicit problem behavior. For one thing, the antecedent and consequent events can be observed. The School Situations Questionnaire can assist the practitioner in choosing an appropriate classroom or related school situation to observe. The practitioner may choose to observe either a single behavior or multiple behaviors; in either case, each behavior must be operationally defined. Further, the practitioner must determine the type of behavioral report that will best address referral and assessment questions.

The practitioner may wish to determine the frequency of a particular behavior during a rating period, the duration of that behavior, or simply whether the behavior occurs at least once in a given interval. For example, if the target child's behavior is being out of seat: in some situations, the number of times the child gets out of seat would be important; in others, the amount of time the child spends out of seat would be more critical; in a third situation, the progression and time of occurrence for out of seat behavior would be of interest. In the last case, for example, the child may remain seated during the first fifteen minutes of a half-hour work period but be out of seat repeatedly during the final fifteen minutes. These are important distinctions when structuring an intervention plan. Special educators and school psychologists are often helpful in collecting observational data for the community-based practitioner.

Specific normative data for classroom observation are often unavailable, as the majority of practitioners do not have the time to obtain normative data on behaviors to be observed. Also, it is often difficult to obtain normative data because a specific classroom's level of acceptable behavior, such as talking or being out of one's seat, varies depending upon a particular teacher's expectations and tolerance. Rhode, Jenson, and Reavis (1992) offer a practical behavioral observation system allowing the observer to watch the target student and a student behaving appropriately at the same time. This fairly simple but unscientific method of comparison involves simultaneously gathering data on another child in the classroom whom the teacher views as average in regard to the behavior to be observed (Deno, 1980). This generates comparative data allowing for some standard, as normative data concerning children's behavior in the classroom is usually not available from class to class. This system observes talking out, out of seat behavior, lack of activity, noncompliance, and quality of teacher interaction (see Figure 7–14).

As discussed, a number of assessment systems such as the Behavioral Assessment System for Children include observational components. Whalen et al. (1981) suggest that it is helpful to also observe teacher behaviors, including prompts, reprimands, and feedback. The coding system developed by Saudargas and Creed (1980) incorporates observation of teacher behavior as well. This type of time-sampling dual-behavior assessment allows for a better understanding of the antecedents and consequences of student and teacher behavior (reduce negative attention or provide reinforcement) and can easily be generated from these types of observations.

Although observation is essential, practitioners need to be aware that their presence in the classroom may affect student and teacher behavior (Johnson & Bolstead, 1973). These authors report that observation in the classroom may have a negative effect, especially if the observer is conspicuous, if students are uncertain as to the purpose of the observer's presence, or if the observer actually interacts with students in the classroom. Saudargas and Fellers (1986) suggest that observers enter the classroom quietly and quickly. They should proceed to an observation area, collect data, and exit without interacting with anyone in the classroom. The observer should ignore any approach by students and avoid any verbal or nonverbal response to the behaviors in the classroom. The observer should also not stare at the target student for long periods. In a pre-observation interview, teachers should be directed to explain the observer's presence in general ways, such as "This person is here to observe a typical class in our school." The observer should not be directly introduced to the class.

It is infrequent in the typical school evaluation for suspected ADHD that the practitioner needs to obtain classroom observational data coding all possible behaviors exhibited by a child during observation. All-encompassing observation systems are frequently complex, requiring multiple operational definitions and indepth coding manuals for utilization. For example, the Stoneybrook Code (Abikoff et al., 1977) contains fourteen observable behaviors; the Classroom Observation System (Whalen et al., 1978) contains twenty-one behaviors to be rated. As with simple rating systems, these more complex systems require the collection of local normative data to draw conclusions concerning normal versus abnormal behavior.

Additional classroom rating systems include those developed by Bergan and Kratochwill (1990); M. Atkins, Pelham, and Licht (1985); Blunden, Spring, and Greenberg (1974); and Vincent, Williams, Harris, and Duval (1981). Barkley (1990a) developed an ADHD behavior coding system. In this system, the child or adolescent is observed during performance of independent academic work in an isolated setting. Behaviors observed include off-task, fidgeting, vocalizing, playing with objects, and being out of seat.

The Code for Observing Social Activity (Sprafkin, Grayson, Gadow, Nolan, & Paolicelli, 1986) may be helpful in developing a better understanding of specific social behaviors resulting in rejection or neglect by peers. Research with this instrument and others reflects that the rates of positive social behavior for children with ADHD may

Behavioral observation of a student is possibly one of the most accurate and valid of all the suggested assessment measures. In effect, behavioral observation is a collecting of a sample of the problem behavior in the setting in which it occurs. No recall from memory or judgment as to its severity is needed with behavioral observations. If the behavior occurs, it is simply recorded. However, difficulties with behavioral observation occur when observation systems are complicated and time consuming. In addition, few classroom observation systems have been standardized on groups of children and allow normative comparisons between students.

One simple behavioral observation approach that does allow normative comparisons is the **response discrepancy observation method.** The system is called response discrepancy because it allows a behavior discrepancy (difference) comparison between a target student (suspected Tough Kid) and the classroom peers. We suggest a teacher use the observation form given How to Box 1-3.

This observation form is based on observing the on- and off-task behavior of a referred target student. The observer should be familiar with the on-task and off-task behavior codes listed on the bottom of the form. The basic class activity for a particular observation should be filled in (e.g., teacher directed whole class, teacher directed small group, independent seat work) plus the additional information on the form.

The actual observations are based on ten-second intervals (each box in the center of the form represents ten seconds) with 90 of these intervals included in the 15-minute observation period on which this form is based. The top interval box is for the referred target student and the bottom interval box is for a randomly selected, same-sex peer. For each ten-second interval, the target student is observed along with a randomly selected, same-sex peer. If the target student is on-task for the entire ten-second interval, then an on-task code (i.e., a dot) is recorded. However, if the target student is off-task, the appropriate off-task code is recorded in the interval box. Only one off-task behavior is recorded for each ten-second box. If more off-task behaviors occur, they are ignored until the next ten-second interval. The same recording process occurs for the same-sex peer during the same ten-second interval for each box.

At the end of the 15-minute observation sample, a record of on- and off-task behavior is collected for the referred target student. The actual on-task percentage can be easily calculated for the 15-minute observation sample with the following equation: divide the number of on-task intervals by the total number of on- and off-task intervals, then multiply by 100. This equals the actual on-task percentage. Formula:

$$\frac{\text{\# of on-task intervals}}{\text{\# of on-task} + \text{off-task intervals}} \times 100 = \underline{\quad}\% \text{ on-task}$$

In addition, a micro-norm or sample for on- and off-task behavior has been simultaneously collected on the same-sex peers in the classroom and can be similarly calculated. This allows a comparison between our suspected Tough Kid and his/her peers. If our student is on-task 60% or less of the time and the peer's average is on-task 85% or more of the time, we know we have a distractible student. However, if both the suspected Tough Kid and the peer average for on-task behavior is below 60%, the problem may be a more general classroom management problem.

(continued)

Figure 7–14.   Behavior observation form

Source: From Rhode, G., Jenson, W. R., & Reavis, H. K. (1992). *The Tough Kid Book: Practical Classroom Management Strategies.* Longmont, CO: Sopris West. Used with permission of the authors.

Target Student _____ **M/F** ___ **Grade** _____ **Date** _____

School _____ **Teacher** _____

Observer _____

Class Activity _____

Position ☐ Teacher directed ☐ Teacher directed ☐ Independent
whole class small group work session

Directions: Ten-second interval. Observe each student *once;* then record data. This is a partial interval recording. If possible, collect full 15 minutes under teacher directed or independent condition. If not, put a slash when classroom condition changes. *Classmates observed must be the same sex as the target student.*

						1					2					3		
Target																		
Student*																		

*Classmates of same sex

						4					5					6		
Target																		
Student*																		

*Classmates of same sex

						7					8					9		
Target																		
Student*																		

*Classmates of same sex

						10					11					12		
Target																		
Student*																		

*Classmates of same sex

						13					14					15		
Target																		
Student*																		

*Classmates of same sex

Note: To observe class, begin with the first same-sex student in row 1. Record each subsequent same-sex student in following intervals. Data reflect an average of classroom behavior. *Skip unobservable students.*

ON-TASK CODES: Eye contact with teacher or task and performing the requested task.

OFF-TASK CODES:

  T = *Talking Out/Noise:* Inappropriate verbalization or making sounds with object, mouth, or body.
  O = *Out of Seat:* Student fully or partially out of assigned seat without teacher permission.
  I = *Inactive:* Student not engaged with assigned task and passively waiting, sitting, etc.
  N = *Noncompliance:* Breaking a classroom rule or not following teacher directions within 15 seconds.
  P = *Playing with Object:* Manipulating objects without teacher permission.
  + = *Positive Teacher Interaction:* One-on-one positive comment, smiling, touching, or gesture.
  − = *Negative Teacher Interaction:* One-on-one reprimand, implementing negative consequence, or negative gesture.

Figure 7–14. *(Continued)*

Table 7–8.   Operational definitions of behaviors in the TOAD system

1. Talking Out: Spoken words, either friendly, neutral, or negative in content, directed at either the teacher without first obtaining permission to speak or unsolicited at classmates during inappropriate times or during work periods.

2. Out of Seat: The child is not supporting his weight with the chair. Upon knees does not count as out of seat behavior.

3. Attention Problem: The child is not attending either to independent work or to a group activity. The child is therefore engaged in an activity other than that which has been directed and is clearly different from what the other children are doing at the time. This includes the child not following teacher directions.

4. Disruption: The child's actions result in consequences that appear to be interrupting other children's work. These behaviors might include noises or physical contact. They may be intentional or unintentional.

Source: TOAD System. From *Managing Attention Disorders in Children: A Guide for Practitioners* by S. Goldstein & M. Goldstein, 1990. New York: John Wiley & Sons, Inc. Used with permission.

not be different from normal counterparts but that these children may insert a high rate of aggressive or negative behaviors (Guevremont, 1990; Pelham & Bender, 1982).

The *T*ime on task, *O*ut of seat *A*ttention to task *D*isruptive (TOAD) System (Goldstein & Goldstein, 1990) is a simple four-behaviors observational model that can be adapted easily to any classroom setting or school situation. The TOAD System allows the practitioner to collect interval data on four classroom behaviors demonstrated as problematic for children with ADHD: talking out, out of seat, attention problems, and disruption. The data are usually observed in fifteen-second intervals, and all four behaviors are observed simultaneously. If a behavior occurs within the fifteen-second interval, whether once or more, a single notation is made for the interval period. Table 7–8 contains suggested operational definitions for the four behaviors. Figure 7–15 presents a sample coding sheet for the TOAD system.

Once the observation has been completed, the practitioner totals the number of affirmative observations in each category and divides this by the total number of observation points to obtain a percentage of negative behavior for each category. This is a "bad" observational system; thus, the lower the percentage, the more impaired the child. For example, if the child was observed for 100 intervals and was marked affirmatively for talking out in fifty of those intervals, talking out behavior would be 50%. This is considered a high percentage, as the majority of children, especially during work time, rarely talk out of turn in class. If the TOAD system is used in one setting extensively, it may be beneficial for the practitioner to collect normative data within that setting. This observational system may also lend itself to providing baseline and follow-up during medication trials within the school setting.

COMMUNICATING WITH TEACHERS

During the course of the school year, teachers may spend as much if not more structured and unstructured time with a child than any other adult in his or her life. Once

CHILD: _____   DATE: _____

TEACHER: _____   TIME BEGIN: _____ TIME END: _____

ACTIVITY: _____   LOCATION: _____

OBSERVER: _____   INTERVAL: ☐ 15 seconds   ☐ 30 seconds

                                                                   ☐ 45 seconds   ☐ 60 seconds

Interval	T	O	A	D		Interval	T	O	A	D		Interval	T	O	A	D		Interval	T	O	A	D
1.						33.						65.						97.				
32.						64.						96.						128.				

Figure 7–15. TOAD System

Source: From *Managing Attention Disorders in Children: A Guide for Practitioners* by S. Goldstein and M. Goldstein. 1990. New York: John Wiley & Sons, Inc. Used with permission.

observational and questionnaire data have been obtained, it is often helpful for the practitioner to speak directly with a classroom teacher. This will allow for clarification of the teacher's comments and response and will assist in the interpretation of observational data.

Prior to communicating with the teacher, it is suggested that the practitioner carefully review teacher responses to questionnaires and make note of extreme responses as well as those that appear inconsistent; teachers can then be asked to clarify and expand on these particular responses. It is frequently helpful to attempt to identify social and nonsocial factors that may elicit difficulty within the school setting. It is also important to seek out the positive, including activities a child enjoys, a task the child can complete, and settings in which the child appears to function similarly to others. It is important for the practitioner to keep in mind that although questionnaires are helpful in obtaining data, they often do not provide much insight into the chain of events that precipitate problems; in some situations, on the other hand, observational data can facilitate insight. However, observations are often conducted for brief periods of time. In complex situations, it may also be helpful, if the teacher has the time, to request that the teacher complete a brief diary of the child's behavior during a week's time.

The practitioner's first goal in an interview with the teacher is to establish rapport so that the teacher perceives the practitioner as a potentially helpful resource. Next, the interview should identify not only target behaviors but the antecedent and consequent conditions under which those behaviors present, focusing on student and teacher behaviors. During problem-identification interviews, it is important to assess teacher motivation as well (Forehand & McMahon, 1981). By identifying teachers who may be poorly motivated or willing to go only so far in their involvement with students' behavior, the practitioner can avoid setting teachers up for failure, which will perpetuate or escalate the child's problems.

The interview also allows the practitioner to briefly explain the model for approaching, evaluating, and intervening in the problem. The practitioner should attempt to determine if teachers are passive participants, contributors, or the direct cause of the problem that is causing distress. As Rhode et al. (1992) point out, children exhibiting behavioral problems in the classroom often do not respond to usual authority and become even more difficult when teachers attempt appropriate interventions. The difference between these students and others is their excesses: their problems are more frequent or more severe. When speaking with teachers, practitioners can identify these students by their high degree of noncompliance, argumentative behavior, and rule breaking.

As part of the teacher interview, the practitioner must learn how the teacher is presently dealing with the problem behavior. Teacher methods of commands, directing students, and other efforts to obtain compliance are all critical in determining severity of classroom problems (Barkley, 1987a; Clark, 1986; D. Morgan & Jenson, 1988; Patterson & Forgatch, 1988; Phelan, 1985). Kratochwill, Elliott, and Rotto (1990) offer an outline for a problem-analysis-and-identification interview practitioners can utilize with teachers to identify specifics of behaviors, setting issues, antecedents, consequences, existing means of dealing with the problem, and a system for data collection. Table 7–9 provides an outline for their model.

Table 7–9.   Problem-identification interview

Behavior Specification

Definition: The consultant should elicit behavioral descriptions of client functioning. Focus is on specific behaviors of the child in terms that can be understood by an independent behavior. Provide as many examples of the behavior problem as possible (e.g., What does Cathy do?).

    a. Specify behavior:

    b. Specify examples of the problem behavior:

    c. Which behavior causes the most difficulty? (i.e., prioritize the problems from most to least severe):

Behavior Setting

Definition: A precise description of the settings in which the problem behaviors occur (e.g., Where does John do this?).

    a. Specify examples of where the behavior occurs:

    b. Specify priorities (i.e., Which setting is causing the most difficulty?):

Identify Antecedents

Definition: Events that precede the child's behavior. Provide information regarding what happens immediately before the problem behavior occurs (e.g., What happens right before Kristy hits other children?).

Sequential Conditions Analysis

Definition: Situational events occurring when the behavior occurs. Environmental conditions in operation when the problem behavior occurs. For example, time of day or day of week when the problem behavior typically occurs. Sequential conditions are also defined as the pattern or trend of antecedent and/or consequent conditions across a series of occasions (e.g., What is happening when the behavior occurs?).

Identify Consequent Conditions

Definition: Events that occur immediately following the client behavior (e.g., What happens after the problem behavior has occurred?).

Behavior Strength

Definition: Indicate how often (frequency) or how long (duration) the behavior occurs. Behavior strength refers to the level or incidence of the behavior that is to be focused on. The question format used for each particular behavior strength will depend upon the specific type of behavior problem (e.g., How often does Shelly have tantrums? or How long do Brett's tantrums last?).

    a. Frequency of behavior:

    b. Duration of behavior:

Tentative Definition of Goal-Question

Definition: Appropriate or acceptable level of the behavior (e.g., How frequently could Matthew leave his seat without causing problems?).

Assets Questions

Definition: Strengths, abilities, or other positive features of the child (e.g., What does Steve do well?).

Table 7–9.   *(continued)*

Approach to Teaching or Existing Procedures

   Definition: Procedures or rules in force which are external to the child and to the behavior (e.g., How long are Sue and other students doing seat work problems?).

Data Collection Procedures

   Definition: Specify the target responses to record. This recording should include the kind of measure, what is to be recorded, and how to record. Specific details of data recording should be emphasized.

Date to Begin Data Collection

   Definition: Procedural details of when to begin collecting baseline data.

Source: Kratochwill, T. R., Elliott, S. N., & Rotto, P. C. (1990). *Best Practices in School Psychology.* Copyright ©1990 by the National Association of School Psychologists. Reprinted by permission of the publisher.

ADDITIONAL SCHOOL DATA

The majority of parents save their children's report cards. As noted, report cards can often provide a chronology of history; they provide the practitioner with an invaluable time line of the child's functioning as he or she has progressed through school. It is not uncommon for parents to be uncertain when problems began and specifically which problems came first; report cards are often helpful in providing this pattern of data. Report cards are also useful in developing a general overview of the child's classroom performance because they typically reflect the quality of daily work completion as opposed to acquired knowledge or academic achievement.

   All schoolchildren complete a battery of achievement tests, usually on an annual or alternate-year basis. The most common batteries are the California Achievement Tests, Stanford Achievement Tests, Iowa Test of Basic Skills, and the Metropolitan Achievement Test. These are often fairly extensive batteries, providing an indepth analysis of the child's skills and local and national normative comparisons. However, the practitioner must keep in mind that these tests are administered on a group basis, requiring a lengthy amount of completion time. Often, they are as much a measure of the child's lack of task persistence as a measure of achievement. Nevertheless, group tests provide valuable data that allow the practitioner to compare the child's achievement with daily school performance.

   Despite advances, it is still the case that the majority of children with ADHD in the absence of significant behavioral or educational problems are not referred for special education assessment. Thus, individually administered tests of academic skills are often not available to the practitioner. When such data are available, they should be reviewed. Assessment instruments include the Woodcock-Johnson Psychoeducational Battery–Revised (Woodcock & Johnson, 1987), Woodcock Reading Mastery Tests–Revised (Woodcock, 1987), Peabody Individual Achievement Test (Dunn & Markwardt, 1970), Key Math Diagnostic Inventory (Connoloy, Nachtman, & Pritchett, 1976), Test of Written Language 3 (Hammill & Larsen, 1996), Gray Oral Reading Test–3rd Edition (Wiederholt & Bryant, 1992), and Test of Reading Comprehension–3rd Edition (V. L.

Brown, Hammill, & Wiederholt, 1995). These tests can provide accurate, indepth measures of a child's level of academic achievement. Although many children with ADHD present with some degree of achievement difficulty (Holborow & Berry, 1986), it is the practitioner's job initially to rule out learning problems as the primary etiological factor contributing to the child's ADHD symptoms. A clinical evaluation protocol described in Chapter 9 will offer an overview and suggest approaches for this differential diagnostic process.

Data Necessary for Confirming ADHD at School

It is important for practitioners to keep in mind that observation and test behavior often correlate and are in agreement for most children receiving diagnoses of ADHD. When they are not, however, it does not necessarily mean that ADHD is not present; then, clinically meaningful information may be obtained based on an analysis of different setting and symptoms (Gordon, DiNiro, & Mettelman, 1989).

In making the diagnosis of ADHD within the school setting, it is recommended that a child fall below the 10th percentile on the ACTeRS or ADDES or is above the 95th percentile in comparison to same-sex and age-normative groups for the Conners Global Index on the Conners Scale, ADHD-SC4 or the Attention Scale on the Child Behavior Checklist. It is additionally suggested that these problems cause the child difficulty in at least 50% of school situations. The collection of additional social, cognitive, academic, and situational data assists the practitioner in making a differential diagnosis (e.g., attention problems secondary to learning disability). This process also allows the practitioner to define the unique aspects of each child's strengths and weaknesses within the school setting, a critical process in facilitating the development of an effective treatment plan. Once it is established that a child shares sufficient characteristics with children receiving a diagnosis of ADHD, the practitioner is urged to also consider qualities that the child shares with all students, as well as those qualities that are unique to a particular child.

SUMMARY

This chapter provided a model for the collection of school data involving the definition and clarification of situational behaviors, social skills, scholastic achievement, and classroom performance. Teacher-report questionnaires, direct observation, and interview are invaluable in the collection of behavioral and social data from a variety of situations. Individual and group achievement tests as well as report cards provide essential educational data. Teacher observations and reports elicited through a direct interview provide data concerning the child's classroom performance and insight into the social and nonsocial factors and antecedent and consequent factors that contribute to the child's school functioning.

Chapter 8 ――――――――――――――――――――――

EVALUATING ADHD IN THE HOME

The data argue strongly that the majority of children receiving diagnoses of ADHD present clinically significant symptoms early in life. Historically, the child's behavior within the home and community has been an essential component of the practitioner's evaluation. The home evaluation typically involves collecting data about the child's behavioral and developmental history, as well as current behavior, social functioning, and achievement. Parents are essential to the diagnostic process; their observations, anecdotes, and impressions often serve as cornerstones in the evaluation. Children with ADHD have been consistently found to exhibit more impairment on measures of behavioral, academic, and social adjustment and more likely to have co-existing disruptive behavior disorders than non-ADHD children based on parent endorsements of symptoms and diagnostic interview (August et al., 1992). Although concerns have been raised in the past about parental accuracy, caregiver estimates of children's development suggest that practitioners should pay close attention to their concerns and observations (E. Harris, 1994). Diamond (1993) found parents to be accurate in identifying developmental problems in their young children. Children whose parents reported specific concerns were significantly more likely to be referred for follow-up evaluation than were other children. Only approximately 30% of parents who expressed specific concerns about their children's cognitive development had children whose screening scores fell within the normal range. Further, among this problem population, children referred for further assessment had higher levels of activity.

Mulhern, Dworkin, and Bernstein (1994) characterized parental concerns in the areas of inattention, impulsivity, and overactivity. In 92% of the subjects, significant school-related problems were diagnosed and 38% received a diagnosis of ADHD in this retrospective comparison study of nearly 250 children ages 4 through 15 years. Parental concern for one or more major symptoms of ADHD identified almost all children who received a diagnosis of ADHD. However, a number of additional children were identified without the diagnosis. Thus, focusing on one symptom may lead to good sensitivity but poor specificity. Concerns for impulsivity and overactivity were specific but not sensitive; concerns for inattentiveness had the best balance between sensitivity and specificity. Positive predictive value was moderate for all categories and concerns. These findings support the importance of eliciting parents' concerns for their children's school performance and of performing comprehensive assessment to identify the underlying characteristic and symptoms of ADHD. Parental concern reflected problems but did not necessarily predict an ADHD diagnosis at outcome.

One of the major questions facing practitioners is the accuracy of parental reports about their children's behavior. Although the research is limited, the majority of studies suggest that parents are in fact accurate reporters. On the negative side, Seifer, Sameroff, Barrett, and Krafchuk (1994) compared mothers' reports of their infants' behavior with observers' ratings. Although week-to-week correlations were moderate, aggregates of the eight observations had higher reliability for both observers and others. Mother reports were tied to observation sessions by having mothers rate their infants during the same period of observation. A questionnaire that mirrored this scoring system was used for observation. There was little evidence of mother-observer correspondence. These authors suggest that the literature that utilizes mother report as the sole basis of describing child behavior and temperament should be questioned. They concluded that "mothers are a poor source of information about their infants' behavioral style" (p. 1489). In contrast, Faraone, Biederman, and Milberger (1995) note that with some exceptions, maternal reports of children's psychopathology provide reliable and accurate means of assessment. In general, maternally derived diagnoses are less accurate for internalizing compared to externalizing disorders. Specificity in this one-year recall of psychiatric diagnoses was high for all diagnoses, suggesting that mothers were not biased in reporting symptoms that had not occurred. Reliability and accuracy were excellent for ADHD symptoms in this population of clinic-referred ADHD and normal control children. Further, S. Green, Loeber, and Lahey (1991) note a moderate degree of stability over a one-year period, with school-related symptoms showing the least amount of change. These authors suggest that the age of onset reported by mothers as the starting point of the ADHD child's noticeable symptoms is valid. The majority of accurate reports have been completed with mothers, and the available data suggest that parents are accurate reporters of their children's behavior.

It is the clinician's job to provide a framework of concrete, operationally defined behaviors and markers to assist parents in organizing their thoughts and reporting about their children's behavior. However, it is critical for the clinician to recognize that parental characteristics can exert an influence on parental report of child behavior. In general, the more adverse the characteristics, the more likely they are to influence behavior. Sanger, MacLean, and Van Slyke (1992) evaluated a sample of 110 children 2 to 12 years of age referred to a pediatric clinic for a variety of common behavioral concerns. Maternal psychological distress and marital adjustment were significantly correlated with mothers' ratings of children's behavior. Maternal psychological distress also accounted for a significant amount of the variance in maternal child behavior ratings over and above that accounted for by fathers' ratings of the same behaviors. Given the covariance of maternal characteristics with reports of childhood behavior problems, Sanger et al. (1992) concluded that parental reports of childhood behavior should be evaluated within an understanding of the overall family context. This finding is also reinforced by the work of Cohen and Bromet (1992), suggesting that there is a complex relationship among maternal, familial, and childhood variables in determining how loudly parents complain about their children's problems.

D. Arnold, O'Leary, Wolff, and Acker (1993) note that numerous aspects of parenting play roles in the socialization of children. A number of discipline strategies are among those clearly implicated in the development and maintenance of children's disruptive behavioral problems. For example, inconsistent, harsh, and excessively lax parenting discipline has been found to correlate with the development of delinquency and aggression (McCord, McCord, & Howard, 1961). Observational studies of parenting style suggest that mothers who are harsh or too permissive in the use of discipline tend to have children who either are noncompliant or aggressive (Baumrind, 1968). Inconsistent use of commands, enforcement, and demonstration of affection during behavioral problems has been associated with the degree of resistance and noncompliance displayed by young children (Kuczynski, Kochanska, Radke-Yarrow, & Girnius-Brown, 1987). Children referred for psychological problems in comparison to nonreferred children in general tend to behave in aggressive, antisocial, and noncompliant ways. Their parents often engage in lengthy and intensive coercive interchanges with them. Over time, their parents become increasingly more inconsistent in their response to the child's behavior (Patterson, 1976a). Inadvertently, parents in these situations are likely to reinforce oppositional behavior with attention, softening of commands, or coaxing (Patterson & Fleishman, 1979).

In a large epidemiologic population, Fergusson and Lynskey (1993) reported a tendency for increasing maternal depression to be associated with a tendency for mothers to overreport child behavior problems. These authors also noted that in this population of 12- and 13-year-old children, there was evidence of small but significant associations between maternal depression and disruptive behavioral problems, including ADHD and CD.

The practitioner may also wish to use the parent interview/history session as an opportunity to provide parents with an understanding of the current conceptualization of and related problems experienced by children with ADHD. The interview/history session is usually the practitioner's first lengthy interaction with the child's parents. It also affords the practitioner the opportunity to develop hypotheses about the parents' skills and abilities and the role they may play in the child's problems. For the practitioner, the parent interview/history session is both an information-gathering and an information-giving session. Barkley (1991a) points out that the parent interview serves several purposes, including establishing rapport between the practitioner and parents, providing a source of descriptive information about the child and family, revealing the parents' view of problems, allowing the practitioner to narrow the focus of the evaluation, assisting the parents to develop an understanding of the child's problems, and beginning the diagnostic process. Clinicians should seek to create a problem-solving atmosphere, push for details with specific examples, encourage parents to offer their own theories, carefully evaluate for comorbid symptoms, draw no hasty conclusions, and seek clarification, as words chosen by one person may have different meaning for others (Gordon, 1995a); for example, one person may describe another as careful, and a third may describe that individual as slow.

Norm-referenced questionnaires allow the practitioner to obtain an assessment of the child's functioning within the home and community in comparison to a normative group. For children with histories of multiple behavioral and developmental problems, the home evaluation may also involve in-depth assessment of parents' skills and their ability to manage child behavior effectively. The home evaluation may include direct observations of the parent and child interacting, either in the home or in the practitioner's office. As with the school assessment, it is essential for the practitioner to relate behavioral problems to specific situations in which they occur. It is also important for the practitioner to form etiological hypotheses of the contributions that temperament, family dynamics, parenting skills, and developmental problems such as language disability make toward the ADHD child's behavior.

Appendix 2 contains the Childhood History Form for Attention Disorder–Revised (S. Goldstein & Goldstein, 1993). This form was developed to gather developmental, behavioral, social, and academic history with an emphasis on ADHD-related problems. It represents a restructuring and modification of a number of generic history forms. This original questionnaire (S. Goldstein & Goldstein, 1985) was based on a questionnaire developed by R. Gardner (1979). It can be used as a general framework to conduct the parent interview. Data from parent questionnaires can be integrated at appropriate points into the history-taking session.

THE PARENT INTERVIEW/HISTORY SESSION

Guevremont et al. (1993) suggest that the history session cover five broad dimensions: (1) details of referral concerns; (2) medical and developmental history; (3) school and educational background; (4) family history and psychosocial functioning; and (5) psychiatric history and current status of the child. Parents should be questioned about symptoms, frequency of symptoms, development of symptoms, and related behavior as well as situational occurrences. Questions should routinely be asked concerning family risk for marital disharmony, depression, and alcohol abuse. These have all been suggested as problems more frequently occurring in families of children with ADHD; they have also been found to influence parent reports (Befera & Barkley, 1985; Biederman, Faraone, Keenan, & Benjamin, 1992). The comorbid psychopathology in parents of children with ADHD should not be taken lightly. Biederman, Munir, Knee, Armentano, Autor, Waternaux, and Tsuang (1987) found that nearly a third of mothers of children with ADHD had a history of depression. As previously discussed, a high rate of antisocial patterns of behavior has been reported in fathers of children with the combined type of ADHD, especially those who progress to comorbid CD (Lahey, Piacentini, et al., 1988).

The parenting interview/history session should begin with an overview of parents' perceptions concerning their child's problems; the first question asked is "Why are you here?" It is helpful for the practitioner to suggest to parents in advance that they make a list of specific questions they would like addressed as part of the evaluation. This initial discussion of referral concerns often leads to a general discussion of parents' history, specifically directed at determining if parents experienced similar problems when younger. Data should be gathered on extended family members, especially nieces and nephews. It is suggested that the practitioner determine whether siblings of the referred child are currently having or have at some time experienced similar problems.

The history proceeds through pregnancy, infancy, toddler, preschool, and school-age periods. At each point, the examiner is seeking to identify data related to the development, occurrence, and progression of ADHD and related problems. For this reason, it is essential for the practitioner to possess a thorough understanding of the developmental course and specific developmental problems children with ADHD experience at various ages. The practitioner must be able to develop a chronology for the occurrence of problems and their progression. Frequently, problems with ADHD begin benignly, reflecting atypical temperament (e.g., difficulty with sleep patterns) but very quickly progress in severity as the result of environmental response (e.g., parents' efforts to get the child to bed). Practitioners must seek to identify and differentiate environmental factors. When evaluating an adolescent, this problem of differential diagnosis is especially complex. Frequently, the ADHD adolescent's symptoms may be overshadowed by secondary emotional and disruptive behavioral problems. With younger children, the problem is also complex but for different reasons: there is often very little data concerning the child's behavior away from parents or family members. The practitioner then must rely heavily on parental report, increasing the likelihood of misinterpreting a parent-child interaction problem as a temperamentally based disorder.

It is suggested that the practitioner elicit and clarify disciplinary methods parents have used to manage their children's behavior. In their efforts to extinguish an aversive behavior, parents may inadvertently reinforce that or an additional behavior. Practitioners can identify this coercive pattern of negative reinforcement in which parents pay attention exactly to that behavior they wish to extinguish, and remove their attention when the child stops the behavior, further reinforcing the probability that the behavior will reoccur in the near future. It is also critically important for the practitioner to discriminate childhood behavior that results from purposeful noncompliance from that resulting from incompetence. It may be helpful to suggest to parents that children purposefully misbehave usually for one of four reasons: (1) to gain attention; (2) to seek revenge; (3) as a sign of frustration and giving up; (4) in an effort to control situations. It may also be helpful to determine if parents view their children's behavior as internal or external, stable or unstable, or controllable or uncontrollable from within the child. From an attributional perspective, parents viewing symptoms of ADHD as internal within the child and stable and uncontrollable by environmental or consequential manipulation are less likely to acknowledge their role in the maintenance or improvement of their children's behavior.

Bloomquist (1996) describes ten areas that appear critically related to symptom severity and treatment success for children with ADHD. It is recommended the practitioner discuss each of these with parents and pursue any in greater depth if problems are suggested. These include: (1) parenting stress; (2) parent thoughts about themselves and their children; (3) parental involvement with the child; (4) the child's involvement with other family members; (5) general areas of disobedience; (6) the child's social relations; (7) the child's ability to solve problems; (8) the child's ability to manage anger; (9) the child's academic problems; (10) the child's low self-esteem or emotional problems. Problems in any of these areas may exacerbate symptoms of ADHD and may create additional hurdles to successful intervention. Many of these are problems in themselves that must be addressed in conjunction with treatment for ADHD. It is important for the practitioner to maintain a correlational rather than causational model; that is, it is not necessarily the case that these problems worsen ADHD or that ADHD causes these problems because they co-occur at a greater-than-chance level.

Typically, there are differences in disciplinary methods reported between mothers and fathers. Thus, the practitioner should attempt to engage parents in a conversation concerning the child's positive attributes and specifically what each parent likes about the child. Parents struggling to speak positively about their child will in all likelihood experience greater difficulty following through with treatment recommendations because the necessary foundation for positive parent-child interaction is not present. Practitioners will have little difficulty identifying these parents. Asking them to complete a parental attribution questionnaire (see Chapter 13) often helps elicit maladaptive thoughts parents may have about themselves and their children (e.g., this is a bad child, I can do nothing to help him). Parents with a positive attachment and appropriate attribution will describe their child's ADHD problems as nonpurposeful and make an effort to convince the practitioner that theirs is a loving, caring, nice child despite his or her problems. Conversely, parents who are angry, unhappy, poorly bonded, or hold strong negative attributions will struggle to speak positively about their child. The strength of the ties that bind parents to children must at the very least be qualitatively assessed by the practitioner. These bonds form the foundation for treatment. Weak bonds must be addressed in many cases prior to treatment initiation. This issue will be discussed further in the treatment chapters.

It is also recommended that the practitioner identify the basic parenting style within the home. Steinberg et al. (1994) summarize the available literature and describe the four basic types of parenting style: authoritative, characterized by parental warmth, inductive discipline, nonpunitive punishment, and consistency in child rearing; indulgent, characterized as overly permissive, difficulty setting limits, and often reversed family hierarchy; authoritarian, characterized by limited warmth, punitive punishment, and one-sided discipline; and neglectful and abusive, characterized by disrespect of the child's basic needs, physical aggression and discipline, disregard for the child's welfare, and limited involvement in the child's life. Steinberg et al. provide the results of a two-year study with 1,000 families. The data consistently demonstrated that for a variety of variables—delinquency, academic competence, even physical symptoms— the authoritative parenting model was the best, whereas the neglectful and abusive model was generally the worst.

As part of the history session, the practitioner should determine any previous treatment, both self-help (e.g., parents reading a book or attending a parenting class) and professional. It is also helpful for the practitioner to identify the specific problem or problems that most motivate parents to seek help. Parents who do not perceive the child as having significant difficulty but are following through with recommendations for evaluation because of complaints by the school or community may be only minimally motivated to comply with treatment recommendations. As part of the evaluation, these data can be used by the practitioner to determine prognosis.

Some practitioners suggest that children or adolescents be present during the parent history session, but the liabilities of this model outweigh the benefits. Although it is recommended that children and parents be seen together at some point, the child's or adolescent's presence during a history session is a distraction. It often does not allow parents of younger children to speak at length; parents may be reticent to speak their mind in front of adolescents. It is important, however, to involve the adolescent being evaluated for ADHD with his parents during the initial contact for the history session. During this time, a brief discussion concerning the reasons for evaluation, especially focusing on the adolescent's reasons, can begin paving the way to help the adolescent be an active participant in the evaluative and ultimately the treatment process.

At the close of the history session, clinicians should summarize with a brief overview of the child's behavior and history, placing the child's behavior within the basic internalizing (depression, anxiety, learning disability) and externalizing (ADHD, ODD, and CD) format. Problems should be briefly reviewed, the situations in which they occur should be presented, and the severity of problems in comparison to the experiences of other children should be offered as an opinion by the practitioner. Summarizing may also help parents understand the practitioner's recommendations, which at that point may range from suggesting the child be followed over the coming few months, offering parents the opportunity to participate in a parenting class, or making general suggestions for further assessment; in some extreme cases, psychiatric hospitalization may be recommended. A sample summary statement by a practitioner for John, an 11-year-old fifth grader, follows:

> Based on what we have discussed today, it appears that very early in his life you were aware that in many ways John was different from his siblings. As an infant, he had problems fitting routines, was often irritable, restless, and experienced difficulty nursing. As soon as he was mobile, John was constantly into things. It appeared that very early on he had difficulty benefiting from his experiences and you became exasperated in your attempts to discipline John and alter his behavior. This, as you describe, has clearly had an effect on your relationship with him, and has affected his role as a family member. In preschool, John was restless, inattentive, and overactive. You anticipated that he would have problems in kindergarten and your perceptions were correct. His academic career has been marked by complaints of poor work completion, apparent lack of motivation, restlessness, inattention, and behavioral problems, which in many cases, appear nonpurposeful. Although he appears to value social contact, John appears incompetent socially and has had more difficulty maintaining friendships. Within the home setting, John creates more problems than his siblings and has in fact been identified by his siblings as the family problem. All of these experiences have affected his self-esteem, and over the past year you have observed an increasing pattern of helplessness and an unwillingness to attempt challenging activities. It is positive to note that John is not presenting as seriously depressed. He sleeps and eats well. He has not had serious medical problems, and the majority of time he appears to be a happy child from whom you are able to derive pleasure. It is also positive to note that despite his difficulty with work completion, individually administered achievement tests at school suggest he is not learning disabled. His problems appear to relate to faulty performance. John knows what to do but does not do what he knows. His behavior is often inconsistent as opposed to noncompliant. We have discussed the core symptoms of ADHD, and it certainly appears that John's history strongly raises the possibility that he experiences this disorder. His increasing pattern of resistance at home suggests that, possibly as the result of frustration, he has become more noncompliant as well. Finally, our discussion suggests that his self-esteem may not be as strong as you would like. It may therefore be beneficial for us to pursue further evaluation, obtain additional school data, and administer brief psychometric testing to clearly identify and understand John's problems and design a treatment plan to help him function more effectively.

OBSERVATION OF PARENT-CHILD INTERACTION

Rarely does the practitioner have the time or the opportunity to directly observe the child functioning within the home. Additionally, children with ADHD respond well in new or novel situations, so the practitioner's visit to the home may not allow observation of typical ADHD problems. It is also unusual for the practitioner to directly observe parents and children interacting on structured tasks during evaluation; most practitioners have neither the facility nor the behavior observation system in place to conduct such interactional evaluations.

Because parents frequently do not have the opportunity to watch their child function at length in a structured situation, some practitioners allow parents to observe parts of the evaluation through a one-way mirror or sit directly in the testing room. In the latter situation, parents are directed to be passive participants and simply observe the child. At times, the parents' presence affords the practitioner the opportunity to observe parents' ability to sit still and attend for up to an hour as well as to gain insight concerning the manner in which the child chooses to interact with each parent in such a setting. For children under 5, parents are routinely allowed to participate directly in the evaluation. Between the ages of 5 and 10, the child may be asked if he or she would like parents present during parts of the evaluation. Most children feel more comfortable with their parents initially participating, especially if they are meeting the practitioner for the first time.

Allowing parents to observe the evaluation not only involves them intimately in the evaluation process but helps them during feedback sessions to understand the test data and gain insight into the child's behavior. If the child has not been present during the parent history session, then having a parent participate in part of the evaluative session is frequently helpful in engaging the parent and child in a discussion of their perceptions of current problems. The practitioner must be aware that adolescents attempting to establish a sense of identity separate from their families typically prefer to be evaluated in private. However, adolescents aware of their problems and actively seeking help will value the opportunity to participate with their parents during the disposition session when a practitioner's impressions are discussed and recommendations for intervention are made. A. Robin and Foster (1989) offer a set of forms to be completed by parents and adolescent as a precursor to identifying family styles of communication and problem solving, cognitive distortions, and family structure.

Although direct laboratory observation may be beneficial, it is clear that quantitative observation in the natural setting is by far preferred. Barkley (1981a) believes strongly that when direct observation of the parent and child is feasible, it should be an integral part of the evaluation. A number of clinical analogue observational procedures have been developed (Barkley, 1990a; M. Roberts, 1979). Barkley designed a playroom setting for a clinic furnished like a den or living room. He developed multiple tasks in which the parent is sequentially directed to engage the child. Activities generally revolve around compliance, beginning with simple tasks such as standing up and progressing to more complex tasks such as directing the child to complete math problems or build a house out of Lego blocks. The use of such procedures is not widespread and continues to be problematic based on available time and space. It is important to note, however, that these types of laboratory measures have also been found to be sensitive for discriminating ADHD from normal children (Breen, 1989) and sensitive to stimulant drug dose effects (Barkley, Fischer, Newby, & Breen, 1988).

Because adolescents typically resist a playroom-type setting or task, Barkley (1981a) recommends that a parent and adolescent engage in a discussion of topics, ranging from the adolescent's compliance in the home setting for completing chores and homework to the adolescent's use of free time, favorite music, and friends.

PARENT-REPORT QUESTIONNAIRES

Parent rating scales or questionnaires are designed to provide a standardized format for obtaining a differential picture of parents' perceptions of their children. Although when originally developed, these questionnaires were little more than laundry lists, eventually they were normatively based and, more recently, factor analytically structured. The current norm-rated factor analyzed questionnaires allow for comparison of a parents' report of problems with those of parents of normative groups. Such questionnaires have played an increasingly important role as part of the intake and assessment process, as well as for reassessment to evaluate treatment effects and follow-up (Achenbach, 1996). These questionnaires play an important role in the evaluative process when integrated with other sources of data such as teachers' observation, psychometric evaluation, and clinical interview.

Symptoms of ADHD appear to lend themselves particularly well to the use of parent rating scales. Dimensions of impulsivity, inattention, and hyperactivity are measured on these instruments consistent with the *DSM* categorical system (Lambert & Hartsough, 1987). For example, utilizing the Conners Parent's Rating Scale, Child Behavior Checklist, and Self-Control Rating Scale (Kendall & Wilcox, 1979), Zelko (1991) studied three groups of boys. The Conners was the best single predictor of group membership child behavior because it includes internalizing scales and a scale for social competence yielding improved overall group classification. However, the Conners frequently misclassified psychiatric controls. Thus, a combination of single-dimension and multidimension rating scales offer the practitioner the best option. As discussed earlier in this chapter, children's behavior is a function of tolerance and response to the environment as much as the child's self-control; practitioners should keep in mind that parents' psychiatric status, ongoing marital conflict, or simply unrealistic expectations can and often do impact parent responses to questionnaires. Thus, it is strongly recommended that after questionnaires are scored, practitioners spend time reviewing them with parents.

Conners Parent's Rating Scale

Developed by C. Keith Conners, the Parent's Rating Scale is the most widely used rating scale of parental opinion concerning ADHD (Barkley, 1981a; S. Goldstein, 1997a). The original ninety-three-item parent questionnaire (Conners, 1970) was revised and shortened to forty-eight items (Conners, 1982). Like the Teacher's Rating Scale, the shortened Parent's Rating Scale retains most of the important characteristics of the original scale. Factor analysis of the forty-eight-item scale yielded factors in the areas of conduct problems, learning problems, psychosomatic problems, impulsivity-hyperactivity, and anxiety. As with the teacher's rating scale, a Hyperkinesis Index was also obtained. Cohen (1988) replicated the factor analytic work of Goyette et al. (1978); results indicated that rather than presenting as a discreet factor, attention problems clustered with hyperactivity to form a single attention deficit disorder/hyperactivity factor. The factor structure of the Conners was correlated with the Revised Behavior Problem Checklist; results suggested that children diagnosed with ADHD do not demonstrate the same behavioral profile as children diagnosed with emotional handicaps.

The Parent's Rating Scale is simple for parents to complete. The forty-eight items are scored on a four-point scale with the following ratings: not at all (score = 0); just a little (score = 1); pretty much (score = 2); and very much (score = 3). Of the forty-eight items in the Parent's Rating Scale, ten are used to compute the Hyperkinesis Index; these include descriptors of excitability, impulsivity, excessive crying, restlessness, failing to finish things, distractibility, inattention, being frustrated in efforts, disturbing other children, and wide or drastic mood changes. The Hyperkinesis Index is a sensitive measure of ADHD behavior within the home, especially for children with the combined type. Anecdotal reports suggest that the index may not be as sensitive for the inattentive type of ADHD (S. Goldstein, 1997b). The Hyperkinesis Index has also been found sensitive to response to treatment intervention, specifically medication. The Hyperkinesis Index is computed by adding the scores of the ten critical items, and dividing by ten; the child's score is then compared to factor norms originally developed by Goyette et al. (1978) and recently revised by Conners (1997). Like the Teacher's Rating Scale, the Parent's Rating Scale is copyrighted and can no longer be reproduced.

Many research studies on the Parent's Scale utilized the Hyperkinesis Index cutoff score of 1.5, considered to reflect significant problems with symptoms of attention disorder. Age by sex-normative data generated from parental responses to the parent's questionnaire have demonstrated that this is an inefficient application of the Hyperkinesis Index. Based on a comparison of the child's score with the sex by age-normative data, the practitioner can make a statistically relevant comparison of the child's symptoms to a normative sample. A cutoff score of at least 1.5 to 2 standard deviations higher than the mean should be considered to reflect significant symptoms of ADHD in the home. On the average, females generally have lower hyperkinesis indices than males. Overall, the Hyperkinesis Index score decreases with age. For 3- to 5-year-old females, for example, the mean plus two standard deviations cutoff is approximately 2.1, whereas the mean plus two standard deviations for the 15- to 17-year-old female group is approximately 1.1 (Goyette et al., 1978).

Conners (1997) has restandardized and reissued the Parent's Rating Scale. The scale was restandardized to parallel the *DSM-IV,* to provide a large normative sample, and to include standardization data for the adolescent self-report scales. Efforts were also made to clarify items so that parent responses might best reflect symptoms of ADHD versus problems causing similar behavior such as those related to oppositional defiance or learning disability. Both long- and short-form scales were standardized. The long form contains eighty items, which results in fourteen subscales: those related to *DSM-IV* symptoms, an ADHD index, and scales measuring oppositional problems, cognitive problems, hyperactivity, anxiety, perfectionism, social problems, and psychosomatic symptoms. The Hyperkinesis Index is now referred to as the Conners Global Index. The short form contains twenty-seven items loading on four scales: oppositional, cognitive problems, hyperactivity, and ADHD index. A sample of items appears in Figure 8–1. (The Conners Parent's Rating Scale is available from Multi-Health Systems, 65 Overlea Blvd., #21, Toronto, Canada, M4N IPI 800-456-3003.)

Child Behavior Checklist–Parent Form

This questionnaire was designed to record behavioral problems and competencies of children ages 2 through 16 as observed by parents or adult caretakers. The form was

Child's Name: _____ **Gender:** M   F

Birthdate: _____ **Age:** _____ **School Grade:** _____

Parent's Name: _____ **Today's Date:** _____

Instructions: Below are a number of common problems that children have. Please rate each item according to your child's behavior in the last month. For each item, ask yourself, "How much of a problem has this been in the last month?", and circle the best answer for each one. If no, not at all, seldom, or very infrequently, you would circle 0. If very much true, or it occurs very often or frequently, you would circle 3. You would circle 1 or 2 for ratings in between. Please respond to each item.

	Not True at All (Never, Seldom)	Just a Little (Occasionally)	Pretty Much True (Often, Quite a Bit)	Very Much True (Very Often, Very Frequent)
1. Inattentive, easily distracted	0	1	2	3
2. Angry and resentful	0	1	2	3
3. Difficulty doing or completing homework	0	1	2	3
4. Is always "on the go" or acts as if driven by a motor	0	1	2	3
5. Short attention span	0	1	2	3
6. Argues with adults	0	1	2	3

Figure 8–1.   Conners' Parent Rating Scale–Revised (S)

Source: By C. Keith Conners. Reproduced with permission from Multi-Health Systems, Inc, 908 Niagara Falls Blvd., North Tonawanda, New York, 14120-2060, 1-800-456-3003.

originally developed by Thomas M. Achenbach (1978). In 1984, Achenbach completed a revision of the scoring profile; a second revision with adjustments in scales utilizing a cross-informant system was published in 1991.

The Child Behavior Checklist contains 113 items in which possible behavioral descriptors for a child are rated as 0 (not true); 1 (somewhat or sometimes true); or 2 (very true or often true). The Child Behavior Checklist also contains two pages of questions concerning the child's social activities and social interaction. Information from these two pages yields scores for social competency scales. Parents are asked to rate their child's behavior as it occurred over the previous six months. The scoring profile has separate normative data for each sex, at ages 4 to 5, 6 to 11, and 12 to 16 years. A shorter, alternative questionnaire and slightly different scales are provided for each sex at ages 2 to 3. A sample of the Child Behavior Checklist scoring profile appears in Figure 8–2.

Achenbach and Edelbrock (1983) developed names for the behavioral scales to summarize the items that comprise each scale. They note, however, that the scales are not directly equivalent to clinical diagnoses: "A high score on a behavior problem scale should never be the sole basis for conferring a diagnostic label" (p. 18). The practitioner should be aware that the items on the Achenbach scales were generated through

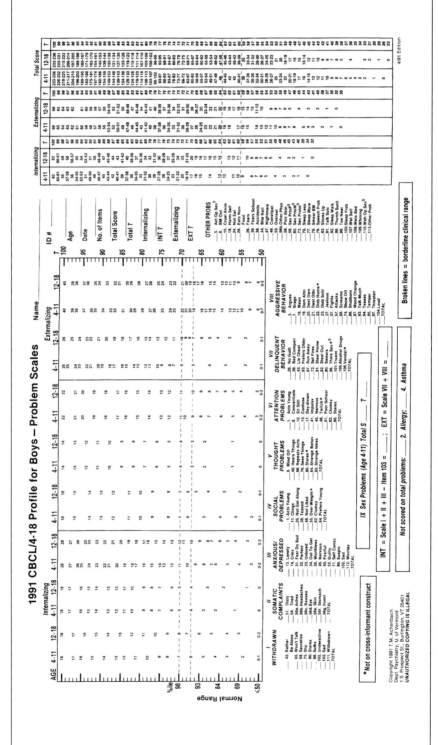

Figure 8–2. Child Behavior Profile for Boys

From T. M. Achenbach, *Parent Form.* Copyright 1991. Used by permission of the author and the publisher.

1991 CBCL Profile for Boys – Competence Scales

Figure 8–2. (Continued)

factor analysis. Titles of the scales were arbitrarily determined by the authors. Although the current version of this questionnaire contains an inattentive factor, Achenbach (1996) recently reanalyzed the data from this factor and generated two distinct factors with four overlapping symptoms consistent with the categorical *DSM* model of clusters of inattentive and hyperactive-impulsive problems.

In their taxonomy of profile patterns, Achenbach and Edelbrock (1983) present a pattern for attention-disordered children of various ages generally characterized by elevated externalizing scales. It has been difficult to provide a clear-cut profile for children experiencing attention problems as particularly distinct from those with other disruptive disorders. This is not surprising, as this population of children frequently presents a heterogeneous group of additional behavioral difficulties. Many children receiving a diagnosis of ADHD have secondary developmental and conduct problems in addition to their ADHD. Barkley (1981a) collected data on the Child Behavior Checklist from parents of sixty boys identified as hyperactive; the group profile obtained by Barkley appears in Figure 8–3. E. Kirby and Grimley (1986) also obtained a typical profile for children in their ADD sample. Both studies concurred with Achenbach and Edelbrock's results in finding that this population of children scored high on externalizing scales.

In the original Child Behavior Checklist, children with attention deficit also presented difficulty on the social withdrawal and obsessive-compulsive scales. This appeared to be an artifact of items on these scales including difficulty with daydreaming,

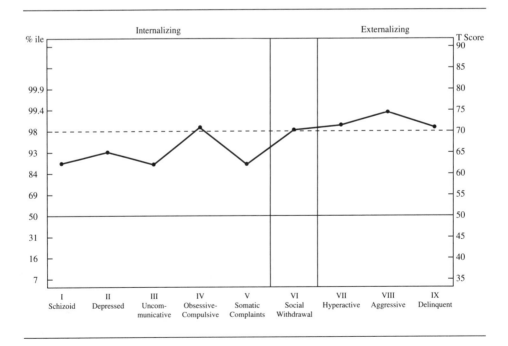

Figure 8–3.   Profile for 60 hyperactive boys on the Achenbach child behavior checklist–parent form

Source: From R. Barkley, *Hyperactive Children* (p. 26). Copyright 1981a by Guilford Press. Reprinted with permission.

talking excessively, perseverating on thoughts or ideas, having a difficult time sleeping, and at times odd or different behavior. Scores on the hyperactive scale were also found to correlate significantly with high symptom scores for attention deficit based on a child assessment interview (Hodges, Kline, Stern, Cytryn, & McKnew, 1982).

In a population of children with ADHD, the parent-completed Child Behavior Checklist, attention problem scale had the highest discriminating power for ADHD (Chen, Faraone, Biederman, & Tsuang, 1994). Adding other scales from this questionnaire did not increase accuracy. Findings suggest the attention problems scale can serve as a quick and useful screening instrument not only to identify cases likely to meet diagnostic criteria for ADHD in clinical settings but also to identify cases of ADHD among the siblings of children with the disorder. Excellent convergence was found between the Child Behavior Checklist, attention problem scale and a diagnosis of ADHD by Biederman, Faraone, Doyle, and Lehman (1993). In a sample of 6- to 17-year-old males, the strength of association between each Child Behavior Checklist scale and a structured interview was derived. These authors also found convergence between the delinquent behavior scales and a diagnosis of conduct disorder, as well as between the anxiety/depression scale and a diagnosis of anxiety disorder.

Comprehensive Teacher's Rating Scale: Parent Form

Ullmann, Sleator, and Sprague (1996, 1997) took the original teacher-developed questionnaire and collected parent ratings of nearly 900 children, half of whom received diagnoses of ADHD. The ACTeRS parent form contains twenty-five items rated on a five-point scale with response categories ranging from "almost never" to "almost always." The items load onto five factors: attention, hyperactivity, social skills, oppositional behavior, and early childhood. The factors are reported to have high internal consistency, test-retest reliability, and good interrater agreement.

ADHD Symptom Checklist–4

As discussed in the previous chapter, the ADHD-SC4 provides standardized data for parents' observations of both ADHD and oppositional defiant symptoms. Relevant research concerning this disorder with parents and concordance rates between parents and teachers were discussed in Chapter 7.

Attention Deficit Disorders Evaluation Scale

The Attention Deficit Disorders Evaluation Scale (ADDES) (McCarney, 1989) was developed through field testing in kindergarten through grade 12 with a standardized scale of nearly 5,000 students. Demographic characteristics of the standardization sample represented national percentiles of gender, residence, race, geographic area, and occupation of parents. The home version contained forty-six items. A prereferral attention deficit checklist accompanied the scale. The original scale contained three subscales: inattentive, impulsive, and hyperactive. Each item on the ADDES is rated on a five-point scale: 0 (does not engage in the behavior); 1 (one to several times per month); 2 (one to several times per week); 3 (one to several times per day); 4 (one to several times per hour). Three types of scores are obtained: raw scores for individual items, subscale standard scores, and percentiles. McCarney (1996), in response to factor analytic data, revised the questionnaire to contain two subscales consistent with the *DSM-IV* categorical system, inattentiveness and hyperactive-impulsive.

Brown Attention Deficit Disorder Scales

T. E. Brown (1995) reports that although most descriptive symptoms of ADHD focus on overt behaviors, the most problematic symptoms are internal, influencing cognition and affect. In response, he developed the Brown Attention Deficit Disorder Scales (Brown, 1995). This self-report measure can be used in an interview format instead and is appropriate for adolescents and adults. Normative data continues to be collected for children (T. Brown, personal communication). Symptoms are grouped into five clusters: (1) difficulty activating and organizing work; (2) problems sustaining attention and concentration; (3) problems sustaining energy and effort; (4) low emotional threshold, including irritability and depressed mood; (5) poor working memory characterized by excessive forgetfulness. (The Brown Questionnaire can be obtained from The Psychological Corporation, 7500 Old Oak Blvd., Cleveland, Ohio 44130, 800-211-8378.)

Home Situations Questionnaire

This questionnaire (Figure 8–4) was developed by Russell Barkley (1981a) and revised by DuPaul and Barkley (1992) as a means of assessing the impact of the child's ADHD symptoms on home and community-based situations. Like the School Situations Questionnaire, this form allows the practitioner to make the important connection between the child's difficulties and the specific situations in which those difficulties cause problems. This form is invaluable during the history session as the practitioner attempts to understand the approaches that parents use to manage children's behavior in various situations and settings. Barkley developed this questionnaire to provide the practitioner with qualitative as opposed to quantitative data. Barkley noted that most children with attention deficit disorder present with problems of at least moderate severity in at least 50% of most home situations. Breen (1986) developed normative data for the Home Situations Questionnaire for children ranging in age from 4 to 11 years. Altepeter and Breen (1989) generated additional normative data finding good interrater reliability between mothers and fathers. Comparisons of the Home Situations Questionnaire with the Revised Conners Questionnaire provided moderate but significant correlations on a number of Conners factors. It is important to note, however, that among the limitations of these data are the fact that normative samples were not stratified to approximate population demographics, likely underrepresenting minorities and geographic distribution. The normative data collected by Altepeter and Breen appear in Table 8–1.

Breen and Altepeter (1990) examined the protocols of two separate groups of thirty 6- to 11-year-old children with ADHD on the Home Situations Questionnaire. Protocols were investigated across individual items and factorial dimensions. Situational variability and behavior was not found to be sensitive to gender differences in children

HOME SITUATIONS QUESTIONNAIRE

Child's Name _____ **Date** _____

Person Completing This Form _____
( ) Mother   ( ) Father   ( ) Foster Parent

Instructions: Does your child present any problems with compliance to instructions, commands, or rules for you in any of these situations? If so, please circle the word Yes and then circle a number beside that situation that describes how severe the problem is for you. If your child is not a problem in a situation, circle No and go on to the next situation on the form.

Situation	Yes/No (Circle One)		If yes, how severe? (Circle One) Mild Severe
While playing alone	Yes	No	1 2 3 4 5 6 7 8 9
While playing with other children	Yes	No	1 2 3 4 5 6 7 8 9
At mealtimes	Yes	No	1 2 3 4 5 6 7 8 9
Getting dressed	Yes	No	1 2 3 4 5 6 7 8 9
Washing and bathing	Yes	No	1 2 3 4 5 6 7 8 9
While you are on the telephone	Yes	No	1 2 3 4 5 6 7 8 9
While watching television	Yes	No	1 2 3 4 5 6 7 8 9
When visitors are in your home	Yes	No	1 2 3 4 5 6 7 8 9
When you are visiting someone's home	Yes	No	1 2 3 4 5 6 7 8 9
When in public places (restaurants, stores, church, etc.)	Yes	No	1 2 3 4 5 6 7 8 9
When father is home	Yes	No	1 2 3 4 5 6 7 8 9
When asked to do chores	Yes	No	1 2 3 4 5 6 7 8 9
When asked to do homework	Yes	No	1 2 3 4 5 6 7 8 9
At bedtime	Yes	No	1 2 3 4 5 6 7 8 9
While in the car	Yes	No	1 2 3 4 5 6 7 8 9
When with a babysitter	Yes	No	1 2 3 4 5 6 7 8 9

Figure 8–4. Home Situations Questionnaire

Source: From Russell A. Barkley's *Defiant Children, 2E* (1997b), p. 177. New York: Guilford. Copyright 1997. The Guilford Press. Reprinted with permission.

with ADHD. Altepeter and Breen (1992) expanded on the factor analysis of this questionnaire, reporting four consistent factors: (1) nonfamily transactions; (2) custodial transactions; (3) task performance transactions; and (4) isolated play. These four factors discriminated children receiving a diagnosis of ADHD from a control sample. Finally, DuPaul and Barkley (1992), in their revised version of the Home Situations Questionnaire, reported that the questionnaire possessed adequate levels of internal consistency, test-retest reliability, and construct validity. The situational questionnaire was also reported to share considerable variance with parent behavior ratings. Boys displayed more severe attention problems across a wider number of settings than girls.

Table 8–1. **Means, standard deviations, and significant cut-off points for the number of problem situations and mean severity for the home and school situations questionnaire**

Age	n	Number of Problem Settings	Mean Severity
		Home Situations Questionnaire	
Boys:			
4–5	162	3.15 (2.79) (9)[*]	1.65 (1.40) (4)
6–8	203	4.13 (3.36) (11)	1.98 (1.36) (5)
9–11	139	3.54 (3.19) (10)	1.97 (1.54) (5)
Girls:			
4–5	146	2.16 (2.60) (7)	1.25 (1.42) (4)
6–8	202	3.40 (3.47) (10)	1.60 (1.54) (5)
9–11	142	2.66 (3.24) (9)	1.55 (1.45) (5)
		School Situations Questionnaire	
Boys:			
6–8	169	2.41 (3.25) (9)	1.51 (1.96) (5)
9–11	124	2.77 (3.16) (9)	1.86 (2.09) (6)
Girls:			
6–8	180	.95 (2.00) (5)	.77 (1.52) (4)
9–11	126	1.24 (2.11) (5)	.84 (1.24) (3)

Source: Altepeter, T. S. & Breen, M. J. (1989). The Home Situations Questionnaire (HSQ) and the School Situations Questionnaire (SSQ): Normative data and an evaluation of psychometric properties. *Journal of Psychoeducational Assessment, 7,* 312–322.

[*] In order of presentation: mean, standard deviation, and significant cutoff.

A significant percentage of children with ADHD experience difficulty when playing with others, at meals, when parents are on the telephone, when visitors are in the home, when visiting others, when accompany parents in public places, when asked to do chores at home, and when going to bed (Barkley, 1981a); they are least likely to experience problems when playing alone. This is consistent because they have no one to disagree with and, as long as they can find something to interest them or multiple tasks to engage in that do not threaten their own safety, they can frequently occupy themselves. Barkley (1981a) suggests that if problems occur in specific home situations, the examiner should question parents concerning what it is about the child's behavior that disturbs them, how they respond, what the child does next, how often the problem occurs, and how the problem is finally dealt with.

Social Skills Assessment

The Social Skills Assessment (S. Goldstein, 1988a) was developed to assist the practitioner in gaining descriptive data about the child's social behavior along a continuum of withdrawn to disruptive patterns (see Figure 8–5). As with the teacher Social Skills Assessment, this form is used qualitatively and normative data have not been collected by the author. Discussing responses on this questionnaire with parents

SOCIAL SKILLS ASSESSMENT
(Parent Form)

Name _____ **Date** _____

Individual Completing This Form _____
( ) Mother   ( ) Father   ( ) Foster Parent

Description: Please check any statements which you feel describe your child or adolescent. Please make note if there are differences in your child's behavior with siblings or peers.

Not True	Sometimes True	Frequently True	My Child:
____	____	____	appears socially isolated. For example, he or she spends a large proportion of time engaged in solitary activities, and may be judged independent and capable of taking care of himself/herself.
____	____	____	interacts less with friends, appearing shy and timid. My child can be described as somewhat overanxious with others.
____	____	____	spends less time involved in activities with other children due to a lack of social skills and/or appropriate social judgment.
____	____	____	appears to have fewer friends than other children due to negative, bossy, or annoying behaviors that "turn off" others.
____	____	____	spends less time with friends than most due to awkward or bizarre behaviors.
____	____	____	distrubs others: teases, provokes, fights, interrupts others.
____	____	____	openly strikes back with angry behavior to the teasing of others.
____	____	____	can be argumentative and must have the last word in verbal exchanges.
____	____	____	displays physical aggression toward objects or persons.
____	____	____	will manipulate or threaten peers.
____	____	____	speaks to others in an impatient or cranky tone of voice; says uncomplimentary or unpleasant things to others. For example may engage in name calling or ridicule.
____	____	____	will respond when other children initiate conversation.
____	____	____	will engage in long conversations.
____	____	____	will share laughter with friends.
____	____	____	will spontaneously contribute to a family discussion.
____	____	____	can take a leadership role at home.
____	____	____	will work with family members on projects.
____	____	____	can verbally initiate with family members.

Additional Comments: _____

_____
_____
_____

Figure 8–5.   Social skills assessment–parent form

Source: From S. Goldstein. (1988a). Social Skills Assessment Questionnaire. Printed with permission of the author.

during the history session is helpful. This questionnaire may also be useful to determine specific treatment targets for the development of deficient social skills.

Additional Parent-Report Questionnaires

Numerous questionnaires have been developed in part to assess impulsive, inattentive, and hyperactive symptoms. Practitioners may find some of these helpful. A number may be difficult to obtain. The Werry Weiss-Peters Activity Scale (Werry, 1968) presents seven behavioral categories, five of which relate to situations in the home (doing homework, playing, sleeping, etc.) and two areas of activity in situations outside of the home (behavior at school and in the community). Ross and Ross (1982) suggest that this scale is a measure of inappropriate activity rather than of total activity; it is therefore useful in the assessment of the hyperactive components of ADHD. The scale was shortened by Routh, Schroeder, and O'Tauma (1974). Normative data have been collected for children ranging in age from 3 to 9 years.

The Personality Inventory for Children (Wirt et al., 1977) contains a reasonably good hyperactivity scale. This questionnaire is considered to be the childhood equivalent of the Minnesota Multiphasic Personality Inventory. The Inventory is completed by parents based on observation of their children. Six hundred true/false items on the Inventory yield fourteen clinical subscale scores and two validity subscale scores. A shortened form has been developed. Normative data have been collected for children ranging in age from 3 to 16 years. The hyperactivity subscale is comprised of thirty-six items. The Personality Inventory for Children has proven to be a difficult questionnaire for parents with literacy problems; however, when a child presents a complex or confusing pattern of behavioral problems, it may be helpful in assisting with differential diagnosis. Voelker, Lachar, and Gadowski (1983) collected data suggesting that the Personality Inventory for Children may be useful in predicting response to stimulant treatment as well. Nieman and DeLong (1987) reported that the Personality Inventory for Children correctly identified 100% of subjects with mania versus ADHD.

S. Shaywitz (1987) and S. Shaywitz, Schell, Shaywitz, and Towle (1986) offer an alternative, thorough, though primarily research-based tool for assessing children's development and behavior, the Yale Children's Inventory. The Inventory consists of eleven narrow-band and two broad-band scales—behavioral and cognitive. The attention scale overlaps with both broad domains, consistent with the current conceptualization of ADHD. Shaywitz et al. (1986) demonstrated that subscales of attention, hyperactivity, and impulsivity correlated with children receiving diagnoses of ADHD.

In a large epidemiologic sample, Boyle, Offord, Hofmann, and Catlin (1987) demonstrated that parent ratings of conduct disorder, hyperactivity, and somatization showed good agreement with psychiatric diagnoses on the Ontario Child Health Study Questionnaire. Boyle, Offord, Racine, and Fleming (1993) evaluated a revised form of this questionnaire among a population of youth 6 to 16 years of age. The questionnaire was found to possess adequate psychometric properties and appeared to provide an efficient means to obtain measurements of childhood psychiatric disorders, including ADHD.

With preschoolers, assessing temperament as distinct from behavior that has been primarily shaped and influenced by the environment is also helpful for gaining insight into the child's behavior. Temperament questionnaires developed by A. Thomas and Chess (1977) and Carey (1970) have been norm-referenced and are useful as part of a clinical assessment. The practitioner is cautioned, however, not to arbitrarily assume that patterns of behavior generated on the basis of these questionnaires are primarily or solely a function of temperament versus environmental experience. The practitioner is also cautioned that the older the child, the more likely it is that the environment has played a role in shaping behavior.

The Childhood Autism Rating Scale (Schopler, Reichler, & Renner, 1988) and the Autism Behavior Checklist (Krug, Arrick, & Almond, 1978) may be particularly useful when questions of autism arise. Adaptive behavior scales such as the Vineland (Sparrow, Balla, & Cicchietti, 1984) or the American Association of Mental Deficiency Adaptive Behavior Scales (Lambert, Windmiller, Tharinger, & Cole, 1981) have not been sufficiently researched with ADHD to aid in assessing adaptive functioning for this population. In general, as noted, problems for children with ADHD result not so much from lack of ability but inconsistent use of skills the child possesses.

Parent Log

During the parent interview/history session, it is often readily apparent to the practitioner when the child's parents may be inadvertently contributing to their children's problems. Confronting parents in these situations often increases tension rather than insight. In these situations, it may be beneficial to request parents to maintain a log or diary covering two or three of the most problematic behaviors and the situations in which they occur. A parent data sheet can be constructed simply. It is suggested that the behavior to be observed be operationally defined at the top of the sheet; the sheet can then be divided into four columns for the date, time, parent's action, and child's response. It is important for the practitioner to assist parents in operationally defining problems and to help them understand that the time spent collecting these data is useful, not only for the diagnostic process but also for developing a treatment plan. The practitioner's ability to help parents understand the critical connections between assessment and treatment is important. Parents can be encouraged to attempt a number of different interventions and to evaluate their impact as well by monitoring their child's responses. It is suggested that initially parents track only one behavior; as they become more proficient in data collection, two or three behavioral problems and responses to intervention can be tracked simultaneously. This system leads nicely to continuity between assessment and intervention.

Parenting Style Interview

Among the variables that influence discipline outcome are those related to timing of commands (Aronfreed & Reber, 1965), intensity (Parke, 1969), and consistency (Sawin & Parke, 1979a). Timing (Abramowitz & O'Leary, 1990), length (Abramowitz, O'Leary, & Futtersak, 1988), loudness (O'Leary, Kaufman, Kass, & Drabman, 1970), and consistency (Acker & O'Leary, 1988; Pfiffner, O'Leary, Rosen, & Sanderson, 1985) have been found to influence the effectiveness of reprimands on children's behavior. Modifying these variables with clear, firm, consistent, and appropriate consequences has been demonstrated to result in a reduction in noncompliant, aggressive behavior (Forehand, Wells, & Griest, 1980). Practitioners should be aware that high rates of early discipline challenges to parents appear to contribute to an early emergence of stable patterns of ineffective interactions between parents and children, focused primarily on disciplinary problems (Power & Chapieski, 1986).

If the practitioner suspects that parental expectations, interactional style, or general behavior plays a significant role in the development and maintenance of the ADHD child's problems, it may be beneficial to conduct a separate interview concerning parenting style. Data gathered during such an interview can prove invaluable in helping parents understand the role they may play in their child's behavioral difficulty and in making them more effective facilitators of behavioral change in their child. The purpose of the interview is not only to gain practical data concerning parent problem-solving skills but to develop an understanding of the parents' philosophy and perceptions of parenting.

It may be beneficial to begin the interview by asking the parents whether they have some particular philosophy about how children should be raised. Parents often find that a challenging question, but after a few moments of thought, their answers may be quite revealing about the manner in which they interact with their children. The extreme responses may range from the view that children should be seen and not heard, to the view that children should be allowed to do whatever they want because these are the formative years and discipline may stifle their future creativity.

Frequently, parents are not aware of the impact their behavior has on their children's personality development and future behavior. In many cases, parents inadequately describe their own behavior and, more important, the reasons that motivated their behavior. The goal of this type of interview is to gather information about parenting style. Determining whether parental style is good or bad is not the issue. Instead, the practitioner attempts to understand parental style and the way it shapes the child's behavior.

Through experience, the authors have identified ten parenting variables that appear to underlie and affect the manner in which parents interact with their children. The best way to obtain information concerning these underlying parent variables is to provide parents with examples of hypothetical problem situations and interpret their responses. Each variable will be defined and an illustrative problem situation that the practitioner can use to gain information about the variable will be provided. For each sample situation, a number of multiple-choice responses are offered, but it is suggested that hypothetical situations be presented without these responses. If parents have difficulty generating a response, multiple-choice alternatives can be helpful in providing them with a structure for responding.

Variable 1: Consistency

Consistency is a critical parenting behavior. Research has found that children can tolerate a variety of adult behavior so long as that behavior is predictable. Children have greater difficulty tolerating inconsistency. If children are dealt with inconsistently by their parents, they will have a difficult time dealing effectively with people in other areas of their lives, including adults and children at school and personal friends. Because of the unpredictability of their behavior, ADHD children are at significant risk to be dealt with inconsistently by even the most competent parents. The combination of an ADHD child and an inconsistent parent frequently leads to significant behavioral problems. It is important for the practitioner to develop some understanding of the parent's behavior as it relates to consistency. A sample situation for a young child follows:

> Assume the rule in your house is that toys must be put away when young children are finished playing with them. Your child is slow to put away his toys and you must leave the house with your child. You would:
> a. Quickly help the child clean up.
> b. Allow the child to clean up later when you return.
> c. Wait until the child is done, no matter how long the child takes.
> d. Punish the child by taking the toys away and then leave.
> e. Put all the toys away yourself.

The rigidly consistent parent will wait until the child is completed, no matter how long it takes. The inconsistent parent will put the toys away without the child's help. The flexibly consistent parent will assist the child but insist the toys be put away before leaving.

Variable 2: Passivity/Democracy/Autocracy

Parents usually deal with their children in one of three manners: they may be democratic, making decisions with the child's input; autocratic, making decisions without the child's input; or passive, allowing the child to make decisions alone. Both autocratic and passive parents often encounter great difficulty with their children's adjustment. Autocratic parents often end up in significant power struggles with their ADHD children. The ADHD child is frequently unable to meet the autocratic parent's demands; over time, a significant pattern of oppositional, resistant behavior develops as the child repeatedly fails and is punished. Alternatively, some parents of ADHD children become passive over time and set minimal limits rather than engage in repeated conflicts with the child; although the passive parent avoids conflict, in the long run, passivity does not help the child develop an internal sense of responsibility and maturity. Autocratic parents make decisions for the child; passive parents play little or no role; democratic parents provide input and work cooperatively with the child to reach the decisions. A sample question for an adolescent follows.

> Your teenager has the opportunity to choose between two summer jobs with very different responsibilities but similar salary. You are aware of the choices she faces. You:
> a. Say nothing, allowing her to choose.
> b. Insist on discussing it with her, citing pros and cons, but allowing her to choose.
> c. Make the decision for her based on your greater experience.
> d. Strongly recommend one choice, allowing her to have the final say.
> e. Offer to discuss it with her but allow her to choose.

Variable 3: Conformity

From infancy, parents subtly or directly teach their children to think for themselves or to routinely behave in the manner expected by others. In the extreme, completely conforming children have difficulty thinking for themselves. Many parents, especially those stressing conformity, may pressure the ADHD child to "fit in" and meet the expectations of others. These children, who are temperamentally nonconforming, often experience difficulty following the rules and limits. Additionally, because of their inability to meet the expectations of others and their repeated failures, ADHD children may become excessively nonconforming as a means of coping with their environment. The combination of a rigidly conforming parent and an ADHD child may lead to an exponential increase of problems. A sample question for a preschool child follows.

> At snack time in kindergarten, milk is routinely served with cookies. Your child complains that he does not like milk and he does not want to drink it at school. You then:
>
> a. Insist that he must drink milk at school like everyone else.
> b. Discuss it with him in an attempt to reach a compromise for him to drink at least some of the milk.
> c. Restrict cookies at school unless he drinks milk.
> d. Discuss alternatives with the child and then present them to the teacher, attempting to reach a compromise.
> e. Tell the child he does not have to drink the milk, should have his cookie, and send a note stating so to his teacher.

Insisting the child must drink milk at school like everyone else fosters blind conformity to society's rules and limits. At the other extreme, allowing the child to avoid the milk issue altogether may foster too much nonconformity.

Variable 4: Self-Esteem

Many factors influence the way children feel about themselves. These include the manner in which they are parented and the success they have with friends and teachers. Because children do not often think about or evaluate themselves, they usually respond in a manner that reflects how they have been dealt with by others. Without realizing it, many parents of ADHD children subtly undermine and sabotage their children's self-esteem. Inability to meet parental demands causes the ADHD child to receive a significant amount of negative feedback related to competence and worth, typically characterized by comments such as Quit it, Stop it, Cut it out, Don't do that, Can't you do anything right? A sample question for an elementary-school-age child follows:

> Your child experiences the loss of a close friend. She expresses concern to you that she won't be able to make another close friend ever again. You:
>
> a. Discuss what she may have done to lose that friend.
> b. Reassure her that friends are easy to make.
> c. Discuss with her how she made and kept that friendship, emphasizing her worth as a person.
> d. Point out that she has other friends.
> e. Do nothing, she will get over it.

Allowing the child to understand the role she may play in friendships and realistically praising her past successes while building her self-confidence and motivation for future social contacts is an important self-esteem builder.

Variable 5: Responsibility

ADHD children have great difficulty developing an internal sense of responsibility because of their skill deficits and repeated failures. They frequently remain externally controlled. As children grow, we hope that they will internalize control and learn to deal appropriately with society, not because they have to, but because they want to. The development of responsibility is often a sore point for many parents of ADHD children. A sample question for an adolescent follows:

> Your son agrees to fill in for a friend at work on a Saturday. At the last minute, he is invited to go water skiing. Water skiing is a very special event. He is uncertain what he should do and wants your recommendation. You:
>
> a. Tell him he must work.
> b. Tell him to go skiing.
> c. Encourage him to find someone else to fill in at work.
> d. Tell him to go skiing if he can get a friend to work.
> e. Review all of the alternatives and allow him to make the decision.

Fostering responsibility requires parents to help their ADHD children develop a sense of obligation to themselves and to others. Telling the child what to do does not foster responsibility. Providing alternatives for children and being supportive of their choices but allowing them to experience the natural consequences of these choices certainly fosters responsible behavior. The practitioner must be aware, however, that ADHD children may require specific educational training to ameliorate their incompetencies in addition to experiencing natural consequences for their actions. More information will be provided concerning this point in the intervention chapters.

Variable 6: Gender Stereotypes

The emphasis on gender stereotypes in our society is not surprising. Research has indicated that even as young as 2 years of age, children are bombarded with messages to behave in ways consistent with and expected for their gender. ADHD males are often excused for their behavior problems with "He is just a boy." However, gender stereotypes and stereotypic behavior often impede children in many situations. A sample question for an elementary-school-age child follows:

> Your daughter comes home and wants to join the local Little League baseball team. She is a fairly athletic child. You:
>
> a. Tell her baseball is only for boys and end the discussion.
> b. Offer her an alternative activity such as volleyball.
> c. Discuss the pros and cons with her and let her make the decision.
> d. Take her right down and sign her up.
> e. Seek out an all-girl baseball team.

It has been suggested that children faced with fewer gender stereotypes have better potential to succeed socially and academically. The ability to combine what have been typically defined as male and female characteristics has been found to be a positive personality trait. It is beneficial to avoid teaching children gender-stereotypic behavior.

Variable 7: Emotions

Many adults have difficulty dealing with and expressing their feelings. It is not surprising, therefore, that many children have the same problem. Researchers suggest that individuals unable to express their feelings and emotions appropriately are at increased risk for psychological stress and physical responses such as ulcers. ADHD children, who typically express their emotions quickly and intensely, may constantly receive messages to repress rather than control their feelings and emotional reactions. A sample question for a preschool child follows:

Your child's grandparent passes away: You:
a. Show no emotion in front of the child.
b. Discuss your feelings with the child.
c. Openly display grief and anguish in front of the child.
d. Act as if nothing happened in front of the child.
e. Display your emotions and discuss them with the child.

Variable 8: Problem Solving

To deal effectively with the world it is important for children to recognize a problem, define it, review alternatives, and make appropriate decisions. Effective problem solving is important in all areas of our lives. Their impulsive, inattentive nature makes ADHD children typically poor problem solvers. Often, parents do not realize that the manner in which they deal with their own problems can have a positive or negative effect on the development of the child's problem-solving behavior. A parent modeling effective problem solving increases the chances of even an ADHD child becoming a more effective problem solver. A sample question for an elementary-school-age child follows.

Your child comes home with a social studies project. You:
a. Tell her to work on it whenever she wants to, as long as it gets done by the deadline.
b. Sit down and plan out a work schedule for the child to complete the project in small parts.
c. Assist the child in determining a work schedule.
d. Threaten restrictions if the work isn't completed by the deadline.
e. Tell the child to get started and check on her progress periodically.

Variable 9: Reward

Most parents have at least a superficial awareness that behavior that is reinforced or rewarded is strengthened and will be exhibited at a later time. But parents are often unaware of the subtle reinforcement and rewards they provide for many behaviors their children exhibit. With ADHD children, it is fairly common for a pattern of negative reinforcement to develop between parents and child. Parents do not recognize the complexity of this type of behavior. Sample questions dealing with positive reinforcement for an adolescent and negative reinforcement for a latency-age child are provided.

Your teenage daughter, generally a good student, comes home with an A− average on her final report card. You are pleased and you:
a. Send her on a trip for the summer.
b. Take her on a limited clothing/shopping trip.

   c. Do nothing except tell her what a good job she has done and to keep up the good work.

   d. Give her a few choices of rewards to choose from.

   e. Extend her curfew by one hour.

You send your 8-year-old son into his room to get dressed. Ten minutes later you check on him, and although he had begun to prepare his clothes, he did not begin dressing but had begun looking at a favorite book. You:

   a. Tell him to get started again, watch to see that he does, and then leave.

   b. Tell him to get started again and walk out.

   c. Threaten to restrict television that evening if he does not finish dressing immediately and walk out.

   d. Tell him to start dressing again and stay there until he completes the task.

   e. Say nothing to him but just walk out.

A discussion of rewards must focus on the parent's ability to choose appropriate rewards and use them effectively. Some parents fail to acknowledge significant achievement; others overreward for minor accomplishments. With ADHD children, it is especially important to review the issue of negative reinforcement with parents, helping them understand that pattern of behavior and the role they may play in reinforcing their child for beginning but not completing tasks. Guidelines for dealing with negative reinforcement problems will be reviewed in the intervention chapters.

Variable 10: Punishment

Parents usually attempt to develop good behavior in their children by first offering rewards. When this fails, they resort in a reactionary manner to their second choice, punishment. Punishment requires the occurrence of an aversive consequence following a particular behavior. Punishment can be an effective intervention, but it must be appropriate and followed by giving the child the opportunity first to learn and then to exhibit the appropriate alternative behavior. Frequently, ADHD children are punished for nonpurposeful behavior that results from incompetence. Punishing the child without affording the opportunity to learn more appropriate behavior often leads to a spiral of failed punishments in an attempt to change the child's behavior. A sample question for a preschool child follows:

Your child continues to hit his sister after a positively stated direction to stop. You:

   a. Warn him again.

   b. Send him to his room, telling him he can come out when he can behave himself.

   c. Spank him.

   d. Time him out for one minute and then allow him to continue playing with his sibling.

   e. Immediately restrict a privilege such as watching television later in the evening.

The final part of the parenting style interview may consist of providing the parents with typical child behavior problems and assessing their general strategy and capacity to respond. For example, R. Gardner (1982b) provides a set of sixteen typical child behavior problems as part of a maternal discipline interview.

Table 8–2.　Items that load greater than .35 on each factor and their factor loadings

---

Laxness

.72	When I say my child can't do something, I let my child do it anyway.	I stick to what I said.
.71	If my child gets upset, I back down and give in.	I stick to what I said.
.70	When my child does something I don't like, I often let it go.	I do something about it every time it happens.
.66	When I give a fair threat or warning, I often don't carry it out.	I always do what I said.
.66	When my child won't do what I ask, I often let it go or end up doing it myself.	I take some other action.
.60	If saying no doesn't work, I offer my child something nice so he/she will behave.	I take some other kind of action.
.57	I coax or beg my child to stop.	I firmly tell my child to stop.
.57	I let my child do whatever he or she wants.	I set limits on what my child can do.
.44	I threaten to do things that I know I won't actually do.	I only threaten things I am sure I can carry out.
.41	If my child misbehaves and then acts sorry, I let it go that time.	I handle the problem like I usually would.
.40	When we're not at home, I let my child get away with a lot more.	I handle my child the same way.

Overreactivity

.77	I get so frustrated or angry that my child can see I'm upset.	I handle it without getting upset.
.74	Things build up and I do things I don't mean to.	Things don't get out of hand.
.66	I raise my voice or yell.	I speak to my child calmly.
.62	I spank, grab, slap, or hit my child most of the time..	Never or rarely.
.58	I often hold a grudge.	Things get back to normal quickly.
.57	When I'm upset or under stress, I'm on my child's back.	I am no more picky than usual.
.53	I insult my child, say mean things, or call my child names most of the time.	Never or rarely.
.52	I usually get into a long argument with my child.	I do not get into an argument.
.47	I give my child a long lecture.	I keep my talks short and to the point.
.43	I almost always use bad language or curse.	I rarely use bad language.

Table 8–2.   *(continued)*

Verbosity

.66 I make my child tell me why he/she did it.	I say no or take some other action.
.61 I say a lot.	I say very little.
.61 If saying no doesn't work right away, I keep talking and try to get through to my child.	I take some other kind of action.
.47 I threaten to do things that I know I won't actually do.	I only threaten things I am sure I can carry out.
.37 If my child talks back or complains when I handle a problem, I give a talk about not complaining.	I ignore the complaining and stick to what I said.
.35 I give my child a long lecture.	I keep my talks short and to the point.
.35 I give my child several reminders or warnings.	I use only one reminder or warning.

Items not on a specific factor

— I do something about it later.	I do something right away.
— I can't ignore my child's pestering.	I can ignore the pestering.
— When my child is out of my sight, I often don't know what my child is doing.	I always have a good idea of what my child is doing.
— When I handle a problem, I tell my child I'm sorry about it.	I don't tell my child I'm sorry.

Source: Arnold, D. S., O'Leary, S. G., Wolff, L. S., & Acker, M. M. (1993). The parenting scale: A measure of dysfunctional parenting in discipline situations. *Psychological Assessment, 5,* 137–144. Copyright 1993 by the American Psychological Association. Reprinted with permission.

Note: On the actual scale, the choices are preceded by a leader that makes it clear that the question refers to discipline encounters such as "When my child misbehaves . . ." Also, the items are not grouped by factor, and the dysfunctional strategy appears on the right side as often as the left.

D. Arnold et al. (1993) have designed a structured interview to identify specific parent behaviors. Although data are still preliminary, the questionnaire qualitatively and to some extent quantitatively can be a very effective tool in understanding parent disciplinary practices, an essential component in the behavior management of children with ADHD. The scale exhibits adequate reliability and internal consistency. It yields three strong factors: laxness (e.g., When I say my child can't do something, I let my child do it anyway), overreactivity (e.g., I get so frustrated and angry that my child can see I am upset), and verbosity (e.g., I give my child long lectures). Table 8–2 contains the factor loadings and items as well as suggestions for effective strategies for this questionnaire. The questionnaire appears in Appendix 3.

CONFIRMING THE DIAGNOSIS OF ADHD AT HOME

Since the original publication of this text in 1990, a number of studies have been generated reflecting the strength and importance of parent-based diagnosis of ADHD. For example, Biederman, Keenan, and Faraone (1990) examined the probability of obtaining a confirmatory diagnosis of ADHD by a teacher in forty-three 4- to 17-year-old children meeting the *DSM-III* criteria for attention deficit disorder. Parents and teachers independently completed an assessment process. Although correlations for individual symptoms were low to moderate, there was a 90% probability that the teacher report would result in a positive diagnosis given a positive parental diagnosis. This suggests a very high probability that in clinically referred children, a clinical diagnosis of ADHD based on parent report is likely.to be corroborated by teachers. These data are also important in recognizing that although specific symptoms may not always be corroborated, the sum total of symptoms usually fits a consistent pattern between settings. In a follow-up study, Biederman, Faraone, Milberger, et al. (1993) utilized the revised *DSM-III* symptoms, finding correlation between parent and teacher reports for individual symptoms to be low to moderate as noted, but there was nearly an 80% probability that the teacher report will result in a positive diagnosis given a positive parent diagnosis. As Kolko (1993) noted, the pattern becomes even more complex when co-morbid diagnoses are added. In this study of hospitalized children with ADHD and CD, the diagnosis of ADHD was related to parent reports of heightened inattention and hyperactivity, and CD was related to heightened aggression and conduct problems at home.

In making the diagnosis of ADHD in the home setting, it is recommended that the child present as approximately 1.5 to 2 standard deviations higher than the same-gender and normative group for the Conners Global Index on the Conners Parent's Rating Scale, the attention problems scale on the Child Behavior Checklist (Anastopoulos, 1993), or similar questionnaire. Practitioners should keep in mind that this threshold may not be met for children with the inattentive type of ADHD. It is additionally recommended that problems secondary to ADHD symptoms should be reported in at least 50% of home and community situations. Once again, this number may be fewer for those with the inattentive type. The majority of children with ADHD also experience chronic problems with ADHD symptoms from infancy. These problems are recognized before the child enters an organized school setting. A careful collection of behavioral data referenced to a variety of specific situations and an analysis of parenting style as well as an understanding of comorbid symptoms assist the practitioner in making a differential diagnosis between ADHD and other disruptive and nondisruptive childhood disorders.

SUMMARY

This chapter provided a model for the collection of data within the home, facilitating the practitioner's ability to define and clarify situational behavior, developmental history, parenting style, and severity of current problems. Parent-report questionnaires, direct observation, and interview are invaluable in the collection of data. The practitioner's ability to integrate and find consensus among the child's developmental and behavioral history, current symptoms, and questionnaires is essential in making the diagnosis of ADHD, as well as addressing comorbid and differential diagnostic issues.

Chapter 9

CLINICAL ASSESSMENT

Researchers and clinicians have questioned the ecological validity of laboratory tests to identify, define, and determine the severity of symptoms of ADHD (Barkley, 1991a; Barkley & Grodzinsky, 1994). As ADHD is a disorder defined by behavior in the real world, it is not surprising that laboratory measures frequently fall short in defining and identifying symptoms of the disorder in comparison to naturalistic observation, history, and organized report in the form of questionnaires. Nonetheless, practitioners take comfort in supplementing their clinical impressions with laboratory-generated objective scores (DuPaul, Guevremont, & Barkley, 1991). It is increasingly accepted, however, that these scores do not make the diagnosis of ADHD but may be helpful in the process of differential diagnosis (e.g., when is impulsivity a function of ADHD versus other disorders?) as well as the process of differentiating severity or related prognosis in a group of individuals with ADHD (M. Gordon, 1995a; S. Hall, Halperin, Schwartz, & Newcorn, 1997). However, as Barkley (1991a) cautions, based on a review of the evidence of the relationship between laboratory methods of assessing ADHD and measures of the same constructs in a natural setting, ecological validity of most methods is low to moderate with some proving unsatisfactory. Only a few tasks demonstrate acceptable degrees of ecological validity, and these require improvement. Based on this study and review, Barkley argues for greater reliance on assessment of target behaviors in natural settings with a combination of several promising tasks and analogue methods offered in a laboratory assessment over a longer period of time than customary and, if possible, averaged across repeated administrations.

The development of a norm-referenced psychometric assessment battery specifically designed for ADHD has been an elusive goal of researchers and practitioners. Children and adolescents with ADHD have been found to perform poorly on a select battery of neuropsychological tests. The impairments measured are not a function of referral bias. However, research is still needed to test the hypotheses that these dysfunctions hold diagnostic and prognostic significance (Seidman, Biederman, Faraone, & Weber, 1997; Seidman, Biederman, Weber, Monuteaux, & Faraone, 1997). The first edition of this text attempted to contribute to that end by providing a hypothetical model with problems related to vigilance, impulsivity, sustained focus, and selective and divided attention. In the past nine years, however, efforts to further develop this model or other similar models have met with limited success. As first suggested by Barkley (1981a), psychometric or laboratory tests as part of the ADHD assessment battery are likely unnecessary. Thus, a basic premise of the first edition of this text, that symptoms of ADHD must be observed on standardized norm-referenced assessment instruments, has been dropped in favor of a more realistic, rational view consistent with current research (S. Goldstein, 1994).

Halperin (1991) provides an overview of hypothesized types of attention and reviews efforts to evaluate those based on a variety of measures. It is suggested that continuous performance tests (CPTs) are likely the most efficient means of differentiating inattentive from normally attentive children. However, Halperin notes that children inattentive on CPTs may have cognitive or learning problems, whereas those who appear attentive despite environmental complaints may experience behavioral or conduct problems. Thus, not all children described by parents and teachers as inattentive manifest deficits on laboratory measures of attention.

It is important to note, however, that structured psychometric testing affords the practitioner the opportunity to interact with the child in a well-defined situation. This adds further qualitative data concerning the nature of the child's behavior. A clinical or school psychologist is best qualified to administer psychometric instruments. The majority of instruments demonstrating some capacity to identify and differentiate symptoms of ADHD are fairly simple to administer; interpretation of test scores, however, is a more complex process. This problem is complicated by the fact that most research evaluating the potential discriminative power of tests for ADHD focus on sensitivity and specificity issues. That is, groups of children (e.g., normal versus ADHD) are evaluated on specific tests and significant differences are searched for (Barkley & Grodzinsky, 1994; Saklofske & Schwean, 1993). However, the fact that a test may be sensitive for identifying an already diagnosed group of ADHD children does not speak to its positive predictive power (ability to differentiate children as ADHD versus not ADHD when the entire group is presented as inattentive). This issue is relevant to clinical practice, where children come for evaluation not with diagnoses but with symptoms requiring diagnoses. Positive predictive power, the probability that the child has ADHD given an abnormal test score, must be distinguished from negative predictive power, the probability that the child does not have the disorder given a normal score on the test (Elwood, 1993). As Barkley (1996b) notes, these are important statistics in the process of differential diagnosis, given that clinicians do not initially know whether a child has ADHD. This is the key question to be answered. The value of an assessment instrument for clinicians is its positive and negative predictive power; most researchers, however, report on sensitivity and specificity. When predictability is examined, few if any clinical laboratory instruments meet necessary criteria to strongly suggest their utility in the diagnosis of ADHD.

The distinction between sensitivity/specificity and positive/negative predictive power cannot be overemphasized. For example, in a sample of sixty children with ADHD, J. Golden (1996) found that twenty-three received discrepant scores on two Wechsler subtests: The digit span subtest score was one standard deviation lower than the vocabulary subtest score. In this population, a CPT had positive predictive outcome of only 57% and negative predictive outcome of 43%. The authors concluded that the subtest discrepancy as well as the CPT appeared to be poor predictors of an ADHD diagnosis but may in fact represent significance in groups of already diagnosed ADHD children.

This chapter will provide an overview concerning research in the use of clinical or laboratory assessment instruments as part of the ADHD diagnostic battery. Suggestions for observing the child's behavior during the evaluation and making inferences concerning motivation and emotional status will also be described. Clinical instruments currently in use in the diagnostic process will be reviewed with accompanying research data provided. The chapter will also provide an overview for assessing personality and emotional functioning, conducting a clinical interview, and using clinical data effectively as part of the diagnostic process.

THE COMPLEXITIES OF ASSESSMENT

Clinical assessment is directed at generating hypotheses to guide intervention rather than to provide just a diagnostic label (Grimley, 1993). Given the complexities of ADHD symptoms and the high rate of comorbidity, practitioners must consider a multidimensional set of data in making the diagnosis, including data generated during clinical assessment. As noted, clinical assessment may provide as much value in regard to direct observation as in test scores generated. For example, differences in body activity between a group of ADHD children and controls have been found to be significant: the hyperactives looked away from the task more frequently than controls (Alberts & van der Meere, 1992). Assessment for ADHD first must consider not only symptoms of ADHD but differential diagnosis and coexisting behavioral, learning, or emotional problems (Guevremont, DuPaul, & Barkley, 1990). Some ADHD symptoms occur in a wide variety of childhood disorders, including those related to anxiety, depression, family dysfunction, physical and sexual abuse, intellectual handicap, and language disorders (Haake, 1991). Thus, as M. Gordon (1995a) notes, "ADHD symptoms rarely occur in isolation and . . . they are by no means unique to ADHD" (p. 1). Some have even gone so far as to suggest that ADHD represents symptoms of "elusive entities and . . . mistaken identities" (Levine, 1992, p. 449).

Mis- or overdiagnosis of ADHD may be inevitable because there is no uniform assessment protocol. ADHD occurs at a higher rate with other disorders, but practitioners are left to make individual judgments of severity and abnormality. Diagnosis hinges heavily on reports and opinions of others, and practitioners may be too quick to assume all symptoms of inattention, impulsivity, and hyperactivity reflect ADHD (M. Gordon, 1995b). Gordon also notes that the same social forces that lead to a legitimate increase in the identification of ADHD may also be promoting overidentification.

The comorbidity issue and the lack of specificity that many tests have in discriminating ADHD from other disorders cannot be overemphasized. For example, Aylward, Verhulst, and Bell (1993) compared a battery of rating scales, computerized tasks, and psychometric assessment in a population of children referred for school and learning problems. For all subjects, a nine-factor solution accounted for 66% of the variance. This was reduced to five factors accounting for 48% of the variance, including a variety of measures; each factor contained four to six variables. Significant group differences were found for the rating scales and computerized assessment factors between ADHD and non-ADHD subjects. However, the authors urged caution in that the majority of the instruments administered did not discriminate between the two groups. Compromised scores, they suggested, may be due to a variety of causes and so score profiles rather than single scores should be focused on during the diagnostic process.

Further, instruments routinely used in the clinical assessment, such as the Matching Familiar Figures Test and Gordon Diagnostic System, have been found to share little variance with parent and teacher reports on several behavior rating scales used to identify ADHD. Clinic test scores alone or in combination resulted in classification decisions that frequently disagreed with the diagnosis of ADHD based on parent interview and behavior rating scales (DuPaul, Anastopoulos, Shelton, Guevremont, & Metevia, 1992). Further, Szatmari et al. (1990) report that neuropsychological tests appear to distinguish ADHD children from those with pure anxiety or affective disorders. However, they may not as efficiently distinguish ADHD from other disruptive disorders. These authors conclude that neuropsychological tests are more strongly associated with externalizing than internalizing diagnoses. Further, they appear to correlate with psychiatric symptoms at school but not at home. Edelsohn, Ialongo, Werthamer-Larrson, Crockett, and Kellam (1992) found that self-reports of depression were significantly correlated to level of academic achievement, peer relations, and, interestingly, teacher reports of attention/concentration in the classroom. Stein, Weiss, and Refetoff (1995) demonstrated that children with resistance to thyroid hormone, although they demonstrate symptoms of ADHD, also displayed lower nonverbal intelligence and academic achievement when compared to children with ADHD only. This phenomenon presents even into the adult years, for which some researches have reported severity of depression as covarying positively with an endorsement for ADHD symptoms currently and in retrospect (Wyejartz, Bair, Besyner, Hawks, & Seidenberg, 1996).

Reichenbach, Halperin, Sharma, and Newcorn (1992b) examined the relationship between activity level as measured using a solid state actigraph, attention with a CPT, and behavioral ratings in daily life. Their results suggested that objectively assessed activity level and attention are independent of each other when age is controlled for; both, however, are found to be related to teacher ratings of inattention and hyperactivity. Massman, Nussbaum, and Bigler (1988) report that ADHD symptoms exert a deleterious effect on laboratory test performance relative to same-age peers as age increases. Thus, in a group of children under age 8 there was no significant association between parent report and neuropsychological test data. Yet from age 9 forward there was a significant negative correlation between Child Behavior Checklist hyperactivity scores and a number of neuropsychological measures. Risser and Bowers (1993) found that although children with ADHD demonstrate differences from normals on a variety of neuropsychological measures, when medication was provided the performance of these children did not dramatically or significantly improve. Even variables not often considered, such as wave length of color may have an impact on test performance. Williams, Littell, Reinosos, and Greve (1994) administered the Wisconsin Card Sort to a group of ADHD and normal children. The test was administered in four color conditions: blue, red, gray, and white. Short wave length stimuli (blue and gray) appeared to enhance attention and thus led to better performance in both subject groups. The authors hypothesized that color of a stimulus will affect processing in the brain's dorsal neurostream, which is believed to mediate key attentional operations.

Ecological validity has also been referred to as concurrent or predictive validity (Anastasi, 1976). This reflects the degree to which the results of a particular task, such as a CPT given in a laboratory, reflect the actual problems of an ADHD child in a classroom doing academic work. This is a significantly different question than asking whether a laboratory measure captures the fundamental behavioral deficit believed to be present in ADHD. It is also important to note that laboratory measures need not be ecologically valid to be useful in research but must be ecologically valid to be useful as clinical tools. These issues have led some researchers to develop tasks of attention related to everyday activities (Robertson, Ward, Ridgeway, & Nimmo-Smith, 1996).

Thus, it is not surprising that Barkley (1991a) argues that although laboratory measures can be helpful, standardized behavior ratings and behavioral observations in classroom settings are essential in the evaluation of ADHD. In fact, this author argues that when results conflict with laboratory measures from those obtained from parent and teacher behavior ratings, history, and observations in natural settings, laboratory results should "probably be disregarded in favor of these more ecologically valid sources" (Barkley, 1991a, p. 173).

A FRAMEWORK FOR CLINICAL ASSESSMENT

It has been hypothesized that the heterogeneity of problems related to ADHD makes it worthwhile to evaluate distinct aspects of attention. This in part was a basic premise of the first edition of this text. Mesulam (1985) notes that there is an advantage and practical value in assessing the various components of attention separately. Assessment of attention skills provides a backdrop against which other skills are measured. For example, hypothesized cognitive impairments resulting from assessment of an inattentive, impulsive child are certainly suspect. It may be that a particular aspect of attention exerts greater influence on a particular type of cognitive task (e.g., divided attention as essential for taking notes from the blackboard). Though a noble endeavor, efforts at delineating, evaluating, and subsequently relating types of attentional skill (e.g., sustained, divided) to specific problems in ADHD or, for that matter, subtypes of ADHD have met with limited success (S. Goldstein, 1994). Thus, efforts to develop batteries of ADHD measures to assess attentional skills have for the most part been discontinued. Nonetheless, there is a strong market for specific measures suggested as "key" diagnostic tools in evaluating ADHD; these clinical tools will be reviewed in this chapter. The majority, however, as critics noted over twenty years ago, focus on reliability often at the expense of validity (Werry, 1978). Also important to note is that the qualitative inferences made by practitioners during assessment may be more valuable than psychometric measures, structured tasks, or interviews. The clinical evaluation for ADHD must include a qualitative assessment by the examiner of the child's capacity to initiate, sustain, and be vigilant on the tasks presented. In some situations, it may be helpful to obtain information concerning the child's or adolescent's insight into his or her problems; a structured self-report questionnaire or an incomplete-sentences task in addition to the clinical interview can prove helpful in obtaining this type of information.

It is not the intent of this chapter to provide a broad outline of psychological or psychometric testing. Psychometric tests presented and discussed are offered because they are frequently utilized by practitioners when questions concerning ADHD are raised diagnostically. Often, ADHD questions are not the only ones being raised during structured assessment; such tasks, therefore, frequently must be integrated into an overall evaluation. A complete psychometric or psychological battery for a child or adolescent would include the administration of standardized intelligence tests such as the Wechsler Intelligence Scale for Children–Third Edition (1974); measures of motor, perceptual, and academic skills; and an in-depth assessment of the child's personality.

Because of the pervasive, multisetting nature of problems related to ADHD and the significant rate of comorbidity with other childhood disorders, assessment for ADHD involves a thorough emotional, developmental, medical, and behavioral evaluation. The comprehensive evaluation should collect data concerning the child's behavior at home, with friends, and at school; academic and intellectual achievement; medical status; and emotional development. It is during the history-taking and subsequent face-to-face assessment process that this information is correlated and integrated with clinical measures. Barkley (1991a) recommends that assessment for ADHD include the use of standardized behavior rating scales, review of laboratory measures when available, and observations in the classroom and clinic. As noted, in the past, laboratory or clinical measures were advocated as an essential component of the ADHD evaluation (for review, see Goldstein & Goldstein, 1990; Barkley, 1990a); however, the ecological validity of these instruments continues to be questioned. Many have played a declining role in the assessment of ADHD but an increasing role in the assessment of comorbid problems children with ADHD may experience. Yet, some instruments have gained popularity in ADHD assessments.

Numerous authors have suggested frameworks for evaluation. Achenbach (1985) described a multiaxial system for evaluating children, including domains of parent report, teacher report, cognitive assessment, physical assessment, and direct observation. Multiple assessment techniques are typically suggested for the comprehensive evaluation of children with ADHD (DuPaul, 1992; Schaughency & Rothlind, 1991). Schools are excellent places to identify and evaluate children with ADHD for a number of reasons, including that problems with attention and behavioral control are among the most common complaints teachers offer. Schools offer a natural setting to observe children in both special education and disability. Federal and state legislation require educational settings to identify, evaluate, and work with troubled children. In the latter case, although the debate rages concerning which children should receive special education versus which should receive 504 ADA (Americans with Disabilities Act) accommodations, there is consensus that ADHD children are entitled to receive assistance at school if their ability to complete school tasks is compromised (Hakola, 1992). It is important for practitioners to keep in mind that classroom settings, off-task behavior, excessive motor activity, and negative vocalization have been the most visible manifestations of ADHD (DuPaul, Guevremont, & Barkley, 1992).

Gordon (1995b) suggests a framework specifically for organizing clinical assessment data regarding ADHD. This author discusses six factors: (1) impulsiveness; (2) age of onset of symptoms; (3) chronicity of symptoms; (4) severity of symptoms; (5) pervasiveness of symptoms; (6) and intentionality, which must be met before diagnosis of ADHD is made. Direct interviews with teachers and adults as well as other forms of face-to-face assessment with the child are necessary, depending on specific problems identified during the history-taking session (Goldstein & Goldstein, 1990).

Barkley (1994) suggests that if ADHD primarily reflects problems responding, inhibiting, and managing impulses, this population of children will have trouble with separation of affect, prolongation, internalization of language, and weak reconstitution. These skills would be expected to begin maturing at different ages, reach maturity at different points, and have different life trajectories. There are significant increases in executive function as sensitivity to feedback, problem solving, concept formation, and response inhibition improve between 7 and 12 years of age (Levin & Culhane, 1991). Memory strategy, planning, problem-solving, and hypothesis-seeking skills improve between 9 and 12 and again between 13 and 15. Organized strategic and planful behavior, however, can be detected in children as young as 6 years of age (Passler, Isaac, & Hynd, 1995; Welsh, Pennington, & Groisser, 1991). More complex, planful behavior and hypothesis-testing skills mature by 10 years; verbal fluency, motor sequencing, and complex planning abilities, however, do not reach adult-level performances until well after 12 years of age. Grodzinsky and Diamond (1992) have found a stable pattern of delay between 6- and 8- and again between 9- and 11-year-old children with ADHD versus normals on measures of response inhibition, verbal fluency, problem solving, and response planning.

DuPaul and Ervin (1996) suggest a functional assessment model for ADHD. These authors posit that the reinforcing functions of specific responses should be identified as a means of making a more direct connection among behavior, intervention strategy, and subsequent behavioral change. The most likely function for inattentive behavior is the avoidance or escape of effortful tasks; secondary goals could be to gain teacher or peer attention, access a tangible object, or seek stimulation. Thus, practitioners should consider as part of the assessment process whether the child's behavior is directed at gaining attention from peers; if so, an intervention strategy might be to structure a system in which peers ignore behavior, or make attention from peers contingent on alternative behaviors. If a student's goal is to avoid or escape an effortful task, the task itself or the payoff for completing the task can be altered to increase motivation and effort.

Clinical batteries for ADHD have been proposed, discussed, and in some cases evaluated. Considerations in the selection and use of assessment techniques should result in a best-estimate diagnosis (Schaughency & Rothlind, 1991). At this time, however, there is no precise battery or specific test that has been found to be more valid, accurate, or reliable than obtaining a careful history and evaluating for comorbid diagnoses. Efforts at comparing and contrasting various assessment methods routinely lead authors to conclude that multiple methods should be utilized in the assessment of ADHD (Cohen, Becker, & Campbell, 1990; Cohen, Riccio, & Gonzalez, 1994). The first set of authors, for example, did not find clinical measures such as the freedom from distractibility factor of the Revised Wechsler Intelligence Scale for Children to enhance the diagnostic process of ADHD; in fact, these authors found a weak relationship of this factor with performance anxiety. Cohen et al. (1994) further suggested there may in fact be a difference in prevalence rates based on assessment procedures and setting of evaluation (clinic versus school).

ASSESSMENT OF ATTENTION VERSUS ADHD

Historically, the term attention has meant different things to different professionals. Laboratory measures of attention may not correlate with clinical symptoms of ADHD. Issues related to construct validity (e.g., which constructs account for variance in test performance) are a key for measuring psychological processes such as attention and correlating them to real-life behavior. However, little construct validation and research have been completed with laboratory assessment instruments directed at evaluating ADHD. Assessment devices used to measure attention, memory, and even executive function often overlap, yet they are suggested as measuring different skills based on the particular theoretical perspective of the investigator. This tendency by researchers and clinicians to provide more construct validity than is present has been referred to as the "bootstraps effect": if the task appears to measure something, the construct becomes valid solely by lifting itself up by the bootstraps of the criterion. This appears to be the case for laboratory measures suggested as valid in the assessment of ADHD.

Based on a factor analysis of a large number of studies, Schmidt, Trueblood, Merwin, and Durham (1994) concluded that clinical measures possess significant limitations for the assessment of attentional processes. The authors noted that most tests are not theoretically based on any particular model or component of a model. In 1990, Lorys et al. questioned whether neurocognitive clinical measures differentiate children with different types of ADHD; a battery of neurocognitive measures could not do so successfully. Korkman and Peltomaa (1991), using factor analysis, examined two groups of children with ADHD-type symptoms, including poor impulse control and difficulty with sustained and selected attention. Children with these weaknesses six months later, based on teacher reports, had a higher frequency of attention problems in the classroom. Braun, Kundert, Hess, and May (1992) developed a comprehensive attention battery that was reported as predicting 86% of cases of hyperactive and non-hyperactive children with ADHD. The two clinical groups shared deficits in three out of four elements related to attention, sustained effort, and shifting, focusing on, and executing tasks. The authors suggested that both groups have related neurocognitive disorders. Differences in attentional processing between the two clinical groups were found only on the encode element under the condition of increased demands for speed of processing. The hyperactive group manifested more overt behavior problems than the nonhyperactive group; the hyperactive group also were more often retained and placed in special education. Hynd, Lorys, Semrud-Clikeman, Nieves, et al. (1991) examined whether children diagnosed with attention deficit with or without hyperactivity could be distinguished on a cognitive, academic, rapid naming, and behavioral set of measures. No significant differences in cognitive ability were noted between groups. Significant underachievement was found in the subjects diagnosed without the hyperactive component, particularly in math achievement; these children were slower on rapid naming tasks as well. Interestingly, 60% of the nonhyperactive group experienced a developmental reading or arithmetic disorder, whereas none in the hyperactive group received such a codiagnosis. However, 40% of the hyperactive ADD subjects had a codiagnosis of CD. As reviewed in an earlier section of this text, questions have been raised related to underlying neuropsychological processes of ADHD versus reading and other learning disorders. It is generally agreed, as McGee et al. (1989) reported, that children with learning disability, in contrast to those with ADHD, are more likely to have deficits in memory and verbal skills.

Based on a review of twenty-one behavioral studies and ten neuropsychological studies, Goodyear and Hynd (1992) suggested that in comparison to children with hyperactivity, children with ADHD without hyperactivity may have deficits in automatic processing similar to children with learning disabilities. No other significant conclusions could be drawn. Practitioners should not assume tests or observations of "attention" in laboratory settings are predictive of or correlate well with observed reports of attention (e.g., task persistence) in the environment.

AN OVERVIEW OF LABORATORY ASSESSMENT RESEARCH IN ADHD

Over the past ten years, much research has been completed on individual or groups of assessment measures that may be sensitive to differentiating children with ADHD from children with other disorders and that may be clinically useful and manageable. Because children with ADHD usually perform similarly to their peers on traditionally administered laboratory measures, reports of daily classroom and home behavior and a review of history are more effective means of identifying and distinguishing this population (Barkley, DuPaul, et al., 1990). In fact, M. Rapport (1987a) suggests that the completion and accuracy rates of assigned work are an effective way of identifying ADHD children in the classroom. Further, M. Atkins et al. (1985) suggest that the organization of a child's desk in terms of neatness and availability of items necessary in the class may be as valid a measure for identifying children at risk for a diagnosis of ADHD as any laboratory test. As Katz, Wood, and Auchenbach (1994) report, the utility of the more common neuropsychological measures of attention/concentration do not adequately differentiate individuals with ADHD from those with other psychiatric disorders or controls. This conclusion has been made by others (Crinella, Teixeira, Wigal, & Yu, 1994). This group reported no significant differences in cluster composition between children with ADHD and children with ADHD plus behavioral disorders on a battery of laboratory measures.

This section reviews and acquaints the practitioner with the breadth and scope of research efforts in the area of laboratory assessment for symptoms of ADHD. In contrast to the first edition of this text, these measures are not advocated nor recommended as essential components of the ADHD evaluation. However, if they are utilized as part of the assessment processor in the evaluation of other comorbid conditions, it is valuable for the practitioner to be aware of research conducted with these tools or batteries, specifically those that focus on symptoms of ADHD.

Over the past forty years, researchers have diligently attempted to develop laboratory tasks that could measure specific components of attention or inhibition (Rosenthal & Allen, 1978). For example, tasks involving either immediate or prolonged attention by the child to visual stimuli presented on a screen yield data suggesting that inattentive children make more errors that go uncorrected (Douglas, 1972). The most sensitive of these measures is the CPT developed by Rosvold, Mirsky, Sarason, Bransome, and Beck (1956). This test was originally designed to be a measure of brain injury and was originally used with a population of individuals experiencing petit mal epilepsy. However, based on nearly thirty years of research, the auditory and visual components of this test have been suggested as sensitive measures of vigilance, sustained attention, and reflective capability.

Although some tasks may discriminate children with ADHD from normals on a group basis, utility of these measures on an individual clinical basis has yet to be clearly documented. Significant correlations between observational self-report measures, such as parent and teacher ratings, and scores on a variety of tests, such as continuous performance instruments, have not been consistently demonstrated (Halperin, Sharma, Greenblatt, & Schwartz, 1991; Lovejoy & Rasmussen, 1990), nor have paper-and-pencil tasks correlated well with parent report (Barkley, 1991a; Milich & Kramer, 1984). When the effects of age, gender, and receptive vocabulary skills are partialed out on these types of tasks, they have failed to discriminate between children with ADHD, CD, anxiety, and normals (Werry, Elkind, et al., 1987) Even when significant correlations are obtained, they tend to be of low magnitude (below .5). Thus, the results of clinic- or laboratory-based tasks account for minimal variance in explaining the behavior of children with ADHD.

As a preview to this section, the ecological validity of a number of laboratory or clinical measures is briefly presented:

- CPT scores for omission and commission have been found to correlate statistically with a number of errors on some paper-and-pencil tasks. Modest correlations have been found between CPT scores and direct observation of ADHD behavior in the classroom. Omission scores appear to correlate modestly with behavioral categories on the Gordon Diagnostic System. CPT performance has been found to be sensitive to stimulant medication but not always reliably so (Barkley, 1978; Barkley, DuPaul, & McMurray, 1991; Barkley et al., 1988; Swanson & Kinsbourne, 1979). CPT scores, particularly commission scores, may have moderate ecological validity as assessed by parent and teacher ratings of inattention and overactivity. The practitioner must question whether the CPT is necessary in the primary diagnosis of ADHD if similar information can be gleaned by obtaining history and parent and teacher ratings.

- Performance on cancellation tasks, such as the Children's Checking Task (J. Margolis, 1972), suggests that children with ADHD differ from normals on omission and commission errors (Aman & Turbott, 1986; R. T. Brown, 1982). They may not differ, however, from other clinical groups (Keough & Margolis, 1976). This type of measure may also be sensitive to the benefits of stimulant medication (Charles, Schain, Zelniker, & Guthrie, 1979).

- Correlations of the Matching Familiar Figures Test with parent and teacher ratings of ADHD have been low to moderate but become nonsignificant when age and intelligence are partialed out (Brown & Wynne, 1982; Fuhrman & Kendall, 1986; Milich & Kramer, 1984). Milich and Kramer suggest that the ecological validity of the Matching Familiar Figures Test as a measure of impulsivity in ADHD children appears weak.

- The Draw-a-Line Slowly Test has been used to measure impulsivity but has not been found to discriminate children with ADHD from normals or other clinical groups once age and IQ are controlled for (deHaas & Young, 1984; Werry, Elkind, et al., 1987).

- The Cookie Delay Test developed by Campbell et al. (1982), based on a model developed by M. Golden, Montare, and Bridger (1977), has found young children with ADHD to be significantly more impulsive than others. Rapport, Tucker, et al. (1986) provided a similar delay of gratification procedure that involved much longer time delays; 94% of the ADHD subjects, as compared to 31% of the controls, chose the immediate over the delayed task. This issue has significance for the practitioner, as consequences are designed in a behavior-change program. This will be discussed in depth in the intervention chapters.

- The ecological validity of movement or activity level devices, such as actimeters, stabilimetric cushions, or activity chairs, is similarly poor (Schulman & Reisman, 1959; W. Tryon, 1984). The actimeter can discriminate ADHD from normal children (Luk, 1985; Tryon, 1984) but not in all cases (Barkley, DuPaul, et al., 1990; Koriath, Gualtieri, Van Bourgondien, Quade, & Werry, 1985). Unfortunately, these measurements have not correlated well with parent ratings of hyperactivity (Barkley & Ullman, 1975; Ullman, Barkley, & Brown, 1978). There may be an exception when actimeter measures are taken over longer periods of time, but they may then correlate better with parent and teacher behavioral reports (Stevens, Kupst, Suran, & Schulman, 1978).

- Analogue observations of ADHD yield encouraging associations between observations in the laboratory analogue settings and naturalistic reports beginning with the work of Hutt, Hutt, and Ounsted (1963), in which the floor of a clinical playroom is divided into grids using tape. A number of studies with similar methodology have demonstrated that children with ADHD display more grid crossings, more toy changes, and shorter durations of play with toys during free play than do normal children (S. Campbell et al., 1982; L. Pope, 1970; Routh & Schroeder, 1976; Touwen & Kalverboer, 1973). Yet again, some studies have not found differences between the ADHD groups and others (Barkley & Ullman, 1975; Koriath et al., 1985). Barkley (1977b) found similar effects in reducing the number of grid changes and toy changes but not for mean duration of toy play. A few studies that have attempted to correlate free play with parent ratings of hyperactivity have yielded nonsignificant results (Barkley & Ullman, 1975; Ullman et al., 1978). When children with ADHD are asked to complete directed tasks with parents in analogue settings, they appear to have more difficulty than in free play situations with parents.

- Analogue measures that evaluate out of seat, off-task, vocalization, and attention shifts during free play in restricted play settings have yielded more promising findings (Milich, 1984; Milich, Loney, & Roberts, 1986). These findings have correlated significantly with parent and teacher ratings of hyperactivity. Studies comparing ADHD, normal, and clinic control groups have found significant differences among the ADHD group, the ADHD group with aggression, the purely aggressive children, and normals (Milich, Loney, & Landau, 1982; M. A. Roberts, 1990). Barkley et al. (1989) placed children in a playroom setting with a shelf full of toys and asked them to sit at a small table and complete a written math task at or below their grade level for fifteen minutes. They were told to not leave their seat or touch the toys. They were then observed. This procedure discriminated the ADHD from normal children but was inconsistent in discriminating ADHD from other clinical groups when behavior such as off-task, out of seat, vocalization, fidgeting, and playing with objects was evaluated (Barkley, DuPaul, & McMurray, 1990;

Breen, 1989). Barkley (1991a) provides a summary of these and other measures (see Table 9–1).

Douglas (1988) suggests that basic information-processing capabilities of children with ADHD are intact; thus, they frequently perform adequately when exerting minimal effort, almost independent of the task. It is when more effort is required that they experience problems. Based on a thorough review of the research literature, Douglas listed tasks on which deficits have been found and those on which deficits have not been found for populations of children with ADHD (see Tables 9–2 and 9–3). Thus, the examiner is more likely to find a qualitative pattern of performance for ADHD children in which they perform reasonably well as tasks begin, but as task complexity increases, which is characteristic of most clinical measures, children with ADHD appear to drop off in their performance more quickly than their abilities would predict.

Cherkes-Julkowski, Stolzenberg, and Siegal (1991) suggest that the dropoff in performance for ADHD children is a function of inability to control focus of attention. These authors found that when prompts are provided during testing, children with ADHD perform significantly better. In a study evaluating children with ADHD with and without medication compared to learning-disabled children and a group of normal

Table 9–1.   A summary of the evidence for the ecological validity of commonly used laboratory and analogue assessments of ADHD[a]

Measures	Group Differences from		Related to Other Laboratory or Analogue Measures	Sensitive to Experimental Manipulations	Related to Ratings Observations in Home/School
	Normal	Clinical			
Attention					
Reaction time tasks	Yes	Yes	Yes (.70)	Yes	No
Continuous performance tasks	Yes	No	Yes (.25–.35)	Inconsistent	Yes (.21–.51)
Children's checking task	Yes	No	Yes (.25–.73)	Yes	?
Impulsivity					
Matching familiar figures	Inconsistent	No	Yes (.25–.75)	Inconsistent	Yes (.21–.53)
Differential Reinforcement of Learning (DRL) Tasks	Yes	?	?	No	Yes (.33–.58)
Draw-a-line-slowly	No	No	No	No	Yes (.30)
Delay of gratification	Yes	?	Yes (.74)	?	?
Activity					
Actometer	Yes	?	Yes (.17–.53)	Yes	Yes (.17–.65)
Stabilimetric cushion	Yes	Yes	?	Yes	No
Analogue Behavior Observations					
Free play in lab playroom	Yes	No	Yes (.42–.88)	Yes	No
Restricted play in playroom	Yes	Yes	Yes (.42–.88)	Yes	No
Restricted academic setting	Yes	Yes	Yes (.17–.47)	Yes	Yes (.17–.60)

Source: Barkley R. A. (1991a). The ecological validity of laboratory and analogue assessment methods of ADHD symptoms. *Journal of Abnormal Child Psychology, 19,* 149–178. Reprinted with permission.

[a]ADHD = attention deficit–hyperactivity disorder. The column headed Group Differences indicates whether evidence exists that the results on the measure have been significantly different between ADHD and normal groups or ADHD and other clinical control groups. Within the table, the term Inconsistent means that the evidence has been inconsistent in establishing this issue. A ? indicates that no evidence could be found to address this issue. Correlation coefficients which appear in parentheses only indicate the magnitude of the relationship and not the direction of the relationship (positive or negative).

Table 9–2.   Tasks on which deficits have been found

Monitoring tasks and automated reaction time tasks:
   Deploying continuous, careful and sustained attention to ongoing stimuli
   Inhibiting responses to inappropriate stimuli
   Inhibiting responses at inappropriate times

Perceptual search tasks:
   Conducting an organized, exhaustive, intensive and focused search of task stimuli
   Ignoring irrelevant stimuli
   Inhibiting responses to irrelevant stimuli

Logical search tasks:
   Clarifying task demands
   Generating and evaluating possible problem-solving strategies
   Generating and evaluating possible solutions
   Inhibiting premature, inadequate responses

Memory tasks:
   Processing task stimuli adequately
   Generating and applying effective rehearsal strategies
   Generating and applying effective retrieval strategies

Motor control and perceptual motor tasks:
   Guiding, controlling movement
   Inhibiting inappropriate movement
   Carrying out a careful perceptual analysis of complex figures
   Drawing accurate reproduction of complex figures

Source: Douglas, V. I. (1988). Cognitive deficits in children with attention deficit disorder with hyper-activity. In L. M. Bloomingdale & J. Sergeant (Eds.). *Attention deficit disorder: Criteria, cognition and intervention.* A book supplement to the *Journal of Child Psychology and Psychiatry,* no. 5. New York: Pergamon Press.

controls, the greatest gains for prompts were observed in the unmedicated group with ADHD. However, practitioners should be cautioned that prompts, especially on measures designed to evaluate response inhibition, may actually test the ability of the child to follow directions rather than to inhibit. Practitioners should also keep in mind that there are data to suggest that level of reinforcement during test performance may have an impact on scores. Devers, Bradley-Johnson, and Johnson (1994) found that improvement in verbal IQ scores of twelve points accrued when token reinforcers followed immediately for correct responses. The impact of praise on test performance has not been systematically evaluated. Draeger, Prior, and Sanson (1986) reported more deterioration in ADHD children's performance on a CPT than in controls when the examiner left the room. These authors suggest that even examiner presence acts to mitigate test performance. It may be that some children who perform poorly on test measures under these circumstances have an application rather than an ability deficit.

Continuous Performance Tasks

The introduction of computer technology has allowed myriad CPTs to be developed. Newer tasks require response inhibition rather than initiation. In 1957, Mackworth

Table 9–3. Memory tasks on which deficits were not found[a]

Verbal memory tasks:

    Digits forward

    Digits backward

    Letters forward

    Letters ordered alphabetically

    Consonant trigrams (after filled and unfilled delay intervals)

    Word lists (12 words)

    Paired associates for related word pairs (including 45-minute delayed recall)

    Story recall[b]

Nonverbal memory tasks:

    Block series forward

    Block series backward

    Recurring figures (geometric and nonsense figures)

    Recall of visual positions along a straight line (after filled and unfilled delay intervals)

    Recall of spatial locations[c]

Source: Douglas, V. I. (1988). Cognitive deficits in children with attention deficit disorder with hyperactivity. In L. M. Bloomingdale & J. Sergeant (Eds.). *Attention deficit disorder: Criteria, cognition and intervention.* A book supplement to the *Journal of Child Psychology and Psychiatry,* no. 5. New York: Pergamon Press.

[a] Except where stated below, data are from Benezra (1980) and Benezra & Douglas (in preparation).

[b] Data from O'Neill (in preparation) and O'Neill & Douglas (in preparation).

[c] Data from Shue (in preparation) and Shue & Douglas (in preparation).

first used the CPT specifically to study sustained attention. It has also been used with other populations (for an in-depth review, see Pasuraman, 1994). It is beyond the scope of this text to review the CPT literature in great depth, but we have provided a relevant review. The interested reader is referred to a concise outline by Conners (1994) and an ongoing database compiled by Gordon (1988).

M. Gordon (1993a) developed a portable apparatus, the Gordon Diagnostic System, using a CPT. Garfinkel and Klee (1983) developed a CPT as part of an attentional battery. This battery also included a computerized progressive maze task and a task of sequential organization. Shapiro and Garfinkel (1986) found this attentional battery to discriminate between a nonreferred population and children experiencing attention problems. The battery, however, was not able to discriminate between a group of children with attention problems and a second group experiencing specific conduct problems. Goldberg and Konstantareas (1981) developed the Operant Vigilance Task, which requires the child to push a button that initially presents a stimulus picture of a clown; the child must then push another button if the clown is missing a nose. Children with attention problems were slower to respond and made more errors of commission when the stimulus was intact. Trommer, Hoeppner, Lorber, and Armstrong (1988) utilized a go–no-go paradigm: the child is asked to respond to five go signals with one tap and five no-go signals with two taps. The stimulus is presented at twenty-five-second intervals. In this study, the investigators evaluated the paradigm as a diagnostic procedure. Children with attentional problems without hyperactivity made the most errors of omission and commission initially but also demonstrated the greatest improvement over time; children with ADD with hyperactivity made less progress when compared to nonhyperactive ADD children and a control group.

Reaction-time tasks have also been used as measures of attention (Douglas & Peters, 1979). The delayed-reaction timed task has specifically been used to study the sustained attention and poor inhibitory control of children with ADHD (Cohen, Douglas, & Morgenstern, 1971; Douglas, 1985). This task consists of a warning signal and interval, and a reaction signal and a response. The child receives a warning signal, a delay period follows, and then a reaction signal; the child is expected to make some response to the reaction signal. Differences between ADHD and non-ADHD children have been demonstrated relating to specificity of warning signal and response to noncontingent partial reward.

Choice-reaction timed tasks have also been used with ADHD (Sergeant & Scholten, 1983). Choice-reaction timed tasks are modified versions of delayed-reaction timed tasks. The child is first presented with a target and then instructed to make the quickest response possible; the task then begins with a presentation of stimuli followed by a warning signal, usually a tone. Following a very brief delay period, an imperative signal is given. The child is asked to respond yes or no by a pair of microswitches and to not respond if the answer is neither yes or no. This measure appeared to differentiate children with ADHD from non-ADHD children on a group basis. Dependent variables included a reaction time and error rates. Conners (1994) expanded and modified his CPT, developing a go–no-go paradigm focusing on measuring inhibition rather than initiation. As many of these CPTs have been developed and marketed, their actual diagnostic utility may become lost in a flurry of marketing strategy. In fact, even the developers of these instruments have debated the other's operation and clinical utility (Conners, 1996; Greenberg, 1996) or marketed the advantages of one CPT against another (M. Gordon, 1997).

Approximately one-third of children with a *DSM-III-R* diagnosis of ADHD are not detected by presently available CPT measures. Children with ADHD classified as abnormal on the CPT, however, have also been found to score below those classified as normal on other measures, such as abstract reasoning, logical problem solving, simple verbal reasoning, nonverbal problem solving, and simple arithmetic skills (for review, see Conners, 1994). The CPT, therefore, may offer a measure of more than just the capacity to inhibit impulsive responding and sustain attention. It can, therefore, provide false negatives and positives. Further, researchers have argued that there is no compelling evidence for a sustained attention deficit in ADHD (Corkum & Siegel, 1993). In fact, many of the initiation CPTs (in which the child must inhibit responding the majority of the time and respond only when the target appears) may have good positive predictive power in identifying individuals with ADHD. Problems with their negative predictive power, however, have made these tasks inefficient in general. If a child passes the test, no conclusions can be drawn. The Conners CPT requires response inhibition; that is, one must respond continuously as noted and inhibit responding when the target appears. This task may be a measure consistent with more recent theories of ADHD involving problems with response inhibition. It may also prove to be a more efficient measure in avoiding problems related to negative predictive power.

Variable parameters for CPTs have included the total number of stimuli presented, test duration, stimulus duration, and interstimulus interval (for review, see Goldstein, 1997). The technical aspects of CPTs have been examined carefully. Corkum and Siegel (1993) report that stimulus type complexity, duration rate, and sensory modality as well as overall test length all appeared to influence to some degree results obtained on CPTs. Further, Conners, March, Fiore, and Butcher (1993) demonstrated that variations in interstimulus intervals greatly determine the extent of errors on a CPT and the nature of the effects of stimulant drugs on CPT performance for children with ADHD. Shorter, interstimulus intervals of up to two seconds resulted in faster presentation rates and were much less likely to evoke error responses than longer rates of two to four seconds. Shorter rates did not demonstrate any deleterious effects of high doses of stimulant medication, whereas longer rates demonstrated a decrease in sensitivity of these doses. Posner (1987) reported that slower event rates led to poor motor preparation and alertness, whereas faster event rates led to declines in arousal. As van der Meere, Vreeling, and Sergeant (1992) noted, manipulation of event rates induces a strategy effect; therefore, differences among studies using CPTs may not reflect a process effect but a strategy difference as a function of task variables. Schachar et al. (1993) have used a stop-signal paradigm in a reaction-time task to create a priming effect directing the subject to respond at each trial. Such priming has been hypothesized as increasing the sensitivity of the task to measure impulsivity when target signals appear. Such a paradigm may be more sensitive to identifying impulsive children as well as the dose effects of stimulant medication.

The variability in performance based on manipulation of task variables has led to alternative explanations concerning the processes that underlie poor performance on CPTs. Warren (1984) notes that decline in perceptual sensitivity with time on task is the classic index of a failure in sustained attention. The two vigilant measures typically assessed in CPTs are perceptual sensitivity (d-prime) and response bias (beta). False positives have traditionally been a measure of sustained attention; however, false positives can also be the result of either poor perceptual sensitivity or response bias. No conclusion can be drawn solely on the basis of a false positive rate. False negatives, that is, failures to detect a target, may have more validity as an index of failure of attention. Fisk and Schneider (1981) offered an alternative approach to sustained attention, suggesting that it reflects a decline in controlled processing over time. As Halperin, Matier, Bedi, Sharma, & Newcorn (1992) note, false positives cannot be considered measures of impulsivity without the inspection of response latency. T. J. Power (1992) has also demonstrated that contextual factors play a role in CPT performance. For example, children with ADHD having relatively high levels of aggression appear to demonstrate a significant decline in d-prime scores when the examiner is absent, but those with relatively low levels of aggression do not. Thus, children with ADHD without other disruptive disorders can complete computerized tasks alone. Those with comorbid problems, such as ODD or CD, will likely decline in their performance if the examiner leaves due to their behavior and personality factors, not due to ADHD problems.

Populations of preschoolers (Weissberg, Ruff, & Lawson, 1990), latency-age children (Seidel & Joschko, 1991), adolescents (Fischer, Newby, & Gordon, 1995), and adults (Holdnack, Noberg, Arnold, Gur, & Gur, 1995) have all been evaluated utilizing a variety of CPT paradigms. It has been suggested that there is a direct relationship between CPT performance and maternal alcohol consumption in children from birth through late adolescence (Streissguth, Bookstein, Sampson, & Barr, 1995). In most studies on group bases, children with ADHD, when other variables are held constant, often perform more poorly than controls. Their performance on CPTs is reported as correlated with teacher ratings of school performance (Seidel & Joschko, 1991), subtests of the Wechsler Intelligence Scale–Revised (Seidel & Joschko, 1991), and measures of behavior (Lassiter, D'Amato, Raggio, & Whitten, 1994; O'Brien et al., 1992; Rasmussen, Colligan, & Suman, 1995), achievement (J. Campbell, D'Amato, Roggio, & Stephens, 1991; Halperin, 1991; B. Johnson, 1995), academic readiness (Edley & Knopf, 1987), and psychomotor speed (Holdnack et al., 1995). Children with ADHD appear to be uniquely affected on CPT measures, with less accurate performance at the fastest and slowest stimulus display. However, when the effects of time on task are controlled for, the ADHD group appears to have its greatest problems with the slower rate of stimulus presentation (Chee, Logan, Schachar, & Lindsay, 1989).

It is important, however, to be aware that children with ADHD and normal controls respond to motivation similarly. The influence of rewards is seen in the normalization of the ADHD group under the reward condition (Corkum, Schachar, & Siegel, 1996). In this study, children with ADHD were considered to display a sustained attention deficit based on poor CPT performance and a differential vigilance decrement over time. The deficit does not appear to be a function of motivational issues, but rather is related to poor sustained attention.

The CPT has been effective in identifying children described as impulsive and inattentive. It has also been reported as sensitive to improvements observed with drug treatment (Conners, Eisenberg, & Barcai, 1967; Corkum et al., 1996). Although CPTs are designed to measure sustained attention, studies demonstrate they may not always measure attention alone. Thus, it is not surprising that some studies do not find a consistent decline in performance over time (Schachar, Logan, Wachsmuth, & Chajczyk, 1988). As H. L. Swanson (1993) reported, the performance decline for some children with ADHD may not result from changes in target detection but may indicate that while completing a boring task, some children become less efficient as they become less strict in deciding whether a signal is a target. However, their ability to detect the target, that is, their ability to sustain attention, does not deteriorate.

Keith (1994) suggests that an auditory CPT may be useful in discriminating ADHD children from controls. However, a comparison study of children with central auditory processing deficits with and without ADHD suggested limited potential for the use of this instrument in the differential diagnosis of ADHD (Riccio, Cohen, Hynd, & Keith, 1994, unpublished manuscript).

Future developments with computerized measures may include chronometric tests as well as electrophysiological methods. It has been suggested that CPTs combined with these may allow for fine-grained differential diagnosis (Conners, 1994). Computerized measures appear to have a valid role in confirming the diagnosis of ADHD, if nothing else (Gordon, 1993b). This author suggests that good performance on the Gordon Diagnostic System, despite data strongly suggestive of ADHD, may not only prompt the practitioner to look further for environmentally based factors as contributing to the child's problems but may serve in a differential diagnostic capacity. Gordon (1993b) further reports that based on a survey of Gordon CPT users, only a minority of practitioners rely solely on CPT data for the diagnosis of ADHD. Many practitioners reported that differences between CPT performance and clinical data in their view reflects relevant information concerning the patient rather than test error. Finally, it has been suggested that "use of the Gordon Diagnostic System (a computerized CPT) also appears to enhance the clinician's ability to convince parents and teachers that the diagnosis is credible" (Gordon, 1993b, p. 5). Gordon and Aylward (1995) suggest that because children diagnosed with ADHD demonstrate clear deficits in their ability to manage a situation that requires delay and a sense of time, it is these impairments that contribute to failure to perform effectively on the Gordon Delay Task.

Conners Continuous Performance Test

The Conners CPT measures omission and commission errors as well as reaction time. The task requires the child, adolescent, or adult to respond continuously for fourteen minutes as single letters are exposed to the screen for brief periods of time with varying intervals between them. The individual must inhibit responding when the target (an X) appears. A person with ADHD may respond slowly to a target, which produces an omission error often followed by a commission error (Conners & Rothchild, 1968). This instrument allows for multiple variations, making it extremely attractive to researchers. Ultimately this form of CPT—requiring inhibition of response as a measure of the ability to manage impulsivity—may prove to be effective in operationally defining impulsivity, the hypothesized central quality of those with ADHD.

Tests of Variables of Attention (TOVA)

The TOVA is a twenty-five-minute CPT (Greenberg & Crosby, 1992). It is non-language-based and sets a repetitive task in which individuals are asked to watch for a designated target and ignore nontargets. The individual is to respond when a small square appears inside instead of above a larger square. The TOVA, like the Conners CPT, offers normative data through adulthood (Greenberg & Crosby, 1992). It measures omissions, commissions, correct response time, and anticipatory errors. The length of the task is thought to make it more sensitive to ADHD-related problems. The TOVA has also been suggested as an effective way to monitor response to methylphenidate (Greenberg & Waldman, 1991).

Intermediate Test of Auditory and Visual Attention

Sandford (1994) has developed an integrated thirteen-minute auditory and visual performance test designed to combine visual and auditory measures of attention and impulse control with normative data provided for 5 to 55 years of age. The computerized printout offers a fairly complex analysis evaluating aspects of sustained attention and impulse control.

Gordon Diagnostic System (GDS)

The GDS is a portable, electronic device designed to assess deficits in impulse control and inattention (M. Gordon, 1988). The instrument was developed for use in the diagnosis of ADHD and has been increasingly employed as a neuropsychological assessment tool as well. At this time, it is the most widely utilized CPT in clinical practice and research studies. Three types of tasks are administered: delay, vigilance, and distractibility. The first measures the ability to refrain from responding in a self-paced setting. The individual must time responses to earn a maximum number of points; a premature response does not earn a point. The second task assesses how well an individual maintains self-control in situations requiring sustained attention. This is a standard CPT in which the individual must respond whenever the target (the number 9) immediately follows the cue (the number 1). The third task is similar to the second but includes distraction; single-digit numbers flash alternately on either side of the spot the individual must observe and respond to. An auditory version of the GDS has recently been introduced. Although questions have been raised as to its added diagnostic benefits, at least one study has suggested that the auditory GDS tasks may be more difficult than the visual tasks (D. Baker, Taylor, & Leyva, 1995). Lewis and Greenberg (1995) suggested that the auditory version of the GDS provided a different profile in terms of longer response latency and fewer total correct stimulus identifications on the vigilance subtest but not the distractibility subtest in an ADHD group. These authors suggest that auditory and visual CPT measures are not comparable, but that it is premature to state the differences between what each purports to measure versus what it may actually be measuring. Although normative data were available initially only through 16 years of age, a number of researchers have now generated normative data for younger adults and the elderly. The GDS has been reported to differentiate accurately between children experiencing ADHD and those classified in school settings as reading-disabled, overanxious, or unimpaired (Gordon & McClure, 1983). It has also been suggested that the delay task of the GDS may be a good measure of current theories of ADHD representing problems with faulty inhibition.

Numerous studies have suggested that scores on the three GDS tasks on a group basis may correlate with a variety of behavioral, academic, and cognitive measures (Aylward, Verhulst, & Bell, 1990; Grant, Ilai, Nussbaum, & Bigler, 1990; Timmermans & Christensen, 1991). However, not all research findings have consistently demonstrated the clinical utility of the GDS in differential diagnosis (Wherry, Paal, Jolly, & Adam, 1993).

Wechsler Intelligence Scale for Children

Perhaps no other single instrument secondary to the CPTs has been touted to be as effective in facilitating the diagnosis of ADHD as the revised and third editions of the Wechsler Intelligence Scale for Children (Wechsler, 1974, 1989). In fact, data have been generated to suggest diagnostic differences within subtypes of ADHD (C. Carlson et al., 1986). These authors reported that children with ADHD combined type versus inattentive type demonstrated differences in intellectual performance, with the combined type demonstrating lower verbal IQ scores. Both groups performed more poorly than controls on spelling and reading tasks. Subtests of the Wechsler have been suggested as measures of vigilance and concentration (R. Gardner, 1979), efficient mental tracking (Lezak, 1983), and divided attention (Van Zomeren, 1981). A. Kaufman (1979) suggested that on the revised Wechsler, the coding, arithmetic, and digit span subtests factored into an index he referred to as freedom from distractibility. Kaufman suggested that the freedom from distractibility factor should be at least three points below the verbal and performance factors, and that factor scores should be not excessively different from each other, as it would be suspected that such a pattern might reflect learning disability. Sattler (1988) suggested that the arithmetic, coding, information, and digit span subtests on the revised Wechsler comprised the (ACID) profile, which may be of benefit in identifying learning disability. The ACID profile is reported as being exhibited in just over 11% of a sample of children with ADHD and thus may not be particularly helpful in the diagnostic process (Wechsler, 1989). The freedom from distractibility factor has not been found to correlate well with observation or parent or teacher reports (Cohen et al., 1990). However, other authors have suggested that specific subtests from the revised Wechsler may be sensitive to discriminating ADHD children from those with other disorders as well as controls (Bowers et al., 1992; Lufi, Cohen, & Parrish-Plass, 1990). The latter group of authors discussed the Wechsler deterioration index, a method that compares subtests of vocabulary, information, object assembly, and picture completion to digit span, similarities, coding, and block design. The former tests are considered "hold tests," thought to be insensitive to deterioration in the face of brain injury or insult. This index classified 59% of children with ADHD and 86% of the non-ADHD group correctly. The authors suggested that in populations of children, this index may represent a developmental rather than a deterioration phenomenon. Finally, Semrud-Clikeman et al. (1993) found that although verbal comprehension and perceptual organization factors distinguish between children with and without CD, these factors did not distinguish between children with ADHD and a control group.

Given interest in the freedom from distractibility factor on the revised Wechsler, it is not surprising that the third edition of the Wechsler has spurred continued research in use of subtest analysis to identify ADHD. The Wechsler third edition (WISC-III) manual (Wechsler, 1989) cites a sample of sixty-eight children with ADHD between 7 and 16 years of age, balanced for ethnic background. The sample had low mean scores on the processing speed and freedom from distractibility factors. The ACID composite was two-thirds of a standard deviation below average. However, these differences were not of sufficient size to provide any type of clinical utility. Anastopolous, Spisto, and Maher (1994) found that the freedom from distractibility factor index score was significantly lower than either the verbal comprehension or perceptual organization factor scores for a group of children with ADHD. Group-level correlation analyses also revealed significant associations between a freedom from distractibility factor and teacher ratings of inattention. Nevertheless, when analyzed on an individual level, the freedom from distractibility factor was not significantly lower than the verbal comprehension or perceptual organization factors for a substantial number of children, and thus the task lacks positive predictive power. However, on a group basis, children with ADHD demonstrated lower freedom from distractibility and processing speed indices in comparison to verbal comprehension and perceptual organization index scores, a pattern that differs from the standardization group (Prifitera & Dersh, 1993). Similar results have been reported by Schwean, Saklofske, Yackulic, and Quinn (1993); these authors reported that children with ADHD scored significantly lower than the standardization group on the freedom from distractibility and processing speed indices.

Mealer, Morgan, and Luscomb (1996) examined differences in patterns of cognitive functioning using the WISC-III. Twenty boys with ADHD and twenty clinic controls were compared. The ADHD group demonstrated significantly lower scores on the WISC-III freedom from distractibility index (94.2 versus 104.7). Discriminant analysis correctly classified 75% of the ADHD group. At a subtest level, the ADHD group scored significantly lower than the non-ADHD group on digit span and symbol search subtests. Differences approached significance on arithmetic and block design subtests. The authors suggest that examination of the pattern of subtest results on the Wechsler can provide specific information concerning cognitive deficits; they "stress, however, that these measures should not be used for diagnosis of ADHD but rather as supplementary to diagnoses" (p. 143). Molter (1995) suggested that the difference between the verbal comprehension and freedom from distractibility indices may actually reflect problems related to auditory processing or memory rather than ADHD. Finally, it is reasonable for the practitioner to heed the advice offered by Anastopolous, Spisto, and Maher (1993), that practitioners not rely heavily on WISC-III factors in ruling in or out the diagnosis of ADHD.

Kaufman Assessment Battery for Children

Given Kaufman's factor analytic work with the Wechsler and a relationship to the diagnosis of ADHD, it is not surprising that the Kaufman Assessment Battery for Children has been looked at as potentially helpful in the diagnostic process (A. Kaufman & Kaufman, 1983). The Kaufman Assessment Battery for Children has been designed to assess cognitive processes, including sequential and simultaneous processing as well as achievement in nonverbal abilities. It has been suggested that children with ADHD experience greater problems with sequential than simultaneous tasks (Carter, Zelko, Oas, & Waltonen, 1990). However, this finding has not been consistently reported, and analysis of subtest scores contributing to this sequential versus simultaneous processing difference has suggested that it may be the hand movement or the word order subtests that contribute the majority of variance in creating this difference. Carter et al. (1990) suggested that the hand movement subtest is particularly suited to differentiate ADHD because it requires integrated functioning of multiple sensory modalities and motor systems, processing of auditory information, visual inspection, and coordinated fine motor movements. However, even these authors raised concern that the Kaufman not be used as a primary measure to diagnose ADHD.

Woodcock Johnson Psychoeducational Battery–Revised

Only one preliminary study has been completed with the Woodcock Johnson Psychoeducational Battery–Revised with ADHD children (Harvey & Chernouskas, 1995). These authors suggest that children with ADHD in comparison to a normative group score poorly on tasks of punctuation and capitalization in comparison to spelling and usage; writing fluency in comparison to writing samples; processing speed and fluid reasoning in comparison to comprehension, knowledge, and oral language scores. Thus Harvey and Chernouskas (1995) provide preliminary evidence that children with ADHD may present a distinctive pattern of scores on the Woodcock Johnson. This ADHD group specifically had weaknesses in basic writing skills, writing fluency, and of processing speed. The third edition of the Woodcock Johnson is currently in preparation. Efforts are underway to provide further data and analyses with populations of children with ADHD (N. Mather, personal communication). These findings are consistent with what has been anecdotally reported for children with ADHD as they progress through school. In the absence of specific learning disabilities, they often experience problems in tasks that require "practice for proficiency" (Goldstein, 1992) and often experience problems with the visual memory aspects of spelling, attention to detail when completing mathematics, and the execution aspects of written language.

Memory Measures

Questions have been raised as to whether faulty acquisition due to poor attention and impulse control or faulty retention related to forgetting is characteristic of children with ADHD (Cahn & Marcotte, 1995). Weingartner et al. (1980) suggested that children with ADHD perform more poorly than normals on tests of free recall. These authors attributed the impaired performance of deficiencies in organizing material in meaningful ways to facilitate retrieval. Hamlett, Pellegrini, and Conners (1987) reported that children with ADHD did not differ on a card-sorting task in their ability to sort the cards but were significantly impaired in their recall of the task and their ability to communicate effectively strategies necessary for carrying out the task. Thus, it was suggested that strategic rather than memory problems accounted for faulty performance. The children with ADHD retained as much information as they processed initially; it was lack of acquisition rather than forgetting that was responsible for their poor performance.

Clearly, components of memory are required for successful performance on a number of the Kaufman and Wechsler subtests. Specific weaknesses in memory skills have been reported to exist for children with ADHD. Children with ADHD perform poorly on memory tasks involving rote information (Adams, Robins, & Sheslow, 1991; Duish, Adams, Sheslow, Robins, & Luerssen, 1996). However, memory performance has not consistently discriminated children with ADHD from those with other disruptive disorders (Moffitt & Silva, 1988).

Among specific memory batteries, the Wide Range Assessment of Memory and Learning (WRAML) (Adams & Sheslow, 1990) has been most often cited as beneficial in the diagnosis of ADHD. Based on factor analysis of the WRAML subtests, Haut, Haut, Callahan, and Franzen (1992) reported an attention factor composed of the digit span, sentence memory, number/letter, and finger/windows tasks. This factorial analysis has been confirmed by others as well (Phelps, 1995). Hooper, Linz, Tramontana, and Stein (1992) divided two groups of children based on their performance on a CPT. The groups did not differ on any demographic variables but differed on intelligence. Controlling for intelligence demonstrated that the group with lower CPT performance performed significantly worse on the WRAML screening index and picture memory subtest. The verbal learning subtest approached significance in the expected direction, but the groups did not differ on the design memory or story memory subtests. These authors discussed the utility of using the WRAML screening index in the assessment of attention problems or ADHD in children.

Mealer et al. (1996) utilized the WRAML to compare performance in a group of twenty boys with ADHD and twenty clinic-referred controls. These authors hypothesized that children with ADHD would be expected to have difficulty with memory "due to the tremendous dependence of short term memory on attentional skills" (p. 135). Utilizing a model based on Shiffrin and Atkinson (1969), they hypothesized that attention is a gateway to the sensory register, which then controls access to short-term and in turn long-term storage of memory information. The results demonstrated that the ADHD group scored significantly lower on the general memory index (89.1 versus 103.2), visual memory index (87.1 versus 98.1), and learning index (91.8 versus 106.5). Discriminant analysis correctly classified 65% of the ADHD group. Regarding subtest difference, the finger windows and verbal learning subtests demonstrated significant differences between the two groups. Differences approached significance on the sound symbol and visual learning subtests. The authors found the results consistent with expectations based on the Shiffrin and Atkinson model of memory storage. A substantially lower general memory index for the ADHD group as well as discrepancies within that group between full-scale IQ and general memory index, a finding reported by others (Brown, personal communication), suggest particular problems at a stage of processing in which information must enter a sensory register and proceed to short-term memory.

Practitioners should keep in mind that research with the WRAML has been limited, and at least one study (Tobin & Selby, 1995) has reported no significant differences among ADHD, learning-disabled, and combined groups based on age, gender, or intelligence.

Paired associate learning tasks, however, have been demonstrated in laboratory settings to discriminate ADHD from control children. The child is typically presented with pairs of words, letters, or symbols; he or she learns the pair and then must respond when the initial stimulus is presented. Numbers of lists and lengths of lists vary in different versions of these tasks (Douglas, Barr, O'Neil, & Britton, 1986; Stephens, Pelham, & Skinner, 1984). Some investigators continue the task until the child's recall is perfect. However, children who can apply metamemory strategies such as mnemonics will perform well on paired associate learning tasks. Results of investigations of children with ADHD with and without stimulant medication on this instrument have varied, although they at least support that stimulants are indirectly responsible for improved performance (J. Swanson & Kinsbourne, 1979). J. Swanson, Sandman, Deutsch, and Baren (1983) hypothesized that a paired associate learning task may be sensitive to whether a child is experiencing decreased learning due to stimulant overdosage. However, Rapport, Loo, and Denney (1995) suggest that paired associate learning tasks have poor negative but good positive predictive power in regard to methylphenidate response in classroom settings. Several computerized and noncomputerized versions of paired associate learning tasks are available (Denman, 1984; J. Swanson, 1985).

Paper-and-Pencil Measures

Kuehne (1985) reported that the Porteus Mazes Test significantly discriminated between inattentive and normal children. Paper-and-pencil tasks represent one of the simplest instruments utilized to purportedly measure reflective strategy and inhibition. For example, the Symbol Digit Modalities Test (A. Smith, 1973), a code-copying task, has been suggested as measuring new learning, visual scanning, perception, visual shifting, and information processing as well as graphomotor speed.

Visual tracking tasks such as the Trail Making Test (Reitan, 1958, 1987) have been suggested as able to distinguish ADHD from normal controls. Chelune, Ferguson, Koon, and Dickey (1986) demonstrated that children with ADHD had more difficulty on Part B of the Trail Making Test than normal controls. There are normative data and a simpler version designed for children 9 through 15 years of age, a parallel version for older adolescents and adults, and a younger children's version (Reitan, 1987). On Part A, the child is required to sequentially connect dots in numerical order; on Part B, the child must not only connect dots in numerical order but also track the alphabet in order, creating an alternating sequence of numbers and letters. Both parts of this test require persistence. Part B may also be a good measure of focused and divided attention. Mesulam (1985) considers the Trail Making Test a good measure of response inhibition and vulnerability to interference. Normative data for the Trail Making Test have been extensively collected (Fromm-Auch & Yeudall, 1983). These tasks have also been reported as sensitive measures of flexible thinking, new learning capacity, and visual-motor speed.

The Bender Visual Motor Gestalt Test have been suggested as beneficial in the diagnosis of ADHD. Despite significant interrater reliability utilizing the Koppitz scoring system, no significant agreement has been reported in subscores or in diagnoses made (Svensson & Hill, 1990).

More recently, children's capacity to reproduce a complex figure has been evaluated as beneficial in the diagnosis of ADHD. Chan et al. (1995) reported that children with ADHD perform more poorly than controls when copying the Rey Osterreoth Figure. These authors suggested that children with ADHD experience greater problems with attention to detail, accuracy, and neatness, and tended to expand the size of the figure. They hypothesize that these problems may relate to faulty executive functioning. In general, they reported that the performance of children with ADHD was more characteristic of younger, normal children. The lack of accuracy of reproduction of this figure by ADHD children has been reported by others (Sadeh, Ariel, & Inbar, 1996). Finally, Seidman, Benedict, et al. (1995), in a group of sixty-five boys with ADHD 6 to 17 years of age, found that those with ADHD with learning disability performed significantly more poorly than ADHD children without learning disability, whereas psychiatric comorbidity and family history had no effect. The authors suggested that their results reflected developmental analysis consistent with organizational difficulties associated with ADHD.

The Cancellation of Rapidly Recurring Target Figures Test was originally developed by Rudel, Denckla, and Broman (1978) as part of a research project to differentiate reading and learning disorders in children. The diamond and 592 subtests are simple and appear to be good measures of visual persistence. Successful performance on these tasks also requires a certain degree of reflection, visual discrimination, and, as always, motivation. The diamond subtest (Figure 9–1) requires the child to locate and mark all of the diamond figures placed randomly among an array of 140 geometric forms. The total amount of time the child takes to complete the task and the number of errors, including omissions and commissions (marking a nondiamond), are recorded. The 592 task (Figure 9–2) requires the child to scan an array of 143 three-digit numbers all beginning with the number 5 and having second digits of 6 or 9. The child is instructed to place a line through only the 592 sequence. Completion time as well as combined omission and commission errors are obtained. Normative data, though limited, provide the practitioner with a general feel for the quality of children's performance with maturation (see Table 9–4). Of interest for the practitioner is the observation of the child during the task. By the age of 6, most children are fairly well organized, beginning in the upper left corner and proceeding either vertically or horizontally. Most children will also check their answers because the instructions urge the child to find all the target stimuli and to make certain that all the items are found

Figure 9–1.   Cancellation of Rapidly Recurring Target Figures Test–Diamond Form

Source: From R. Rudel, M. Denckla, & M. Broman, Rapid Silent Response to Repeated Target Symbols by Dyslexic and Non-Dyslexic Children. Copyright 1978, *Brain and Language.* Used with permission of the publisher.

				592					
569	562	598	561	591	564	563	591	569	561
564	561	592	599	562	594	591	562	598	592
599	593	563	564	591	598	562	564	569	599
563	599	594	569	561	591	592	599	592	564
561	564	591	562	599	599	561	569	598	594
594	592	563	569	594	564	594	599	561	563
569	562	569	599	598	563	591	564	599	592
563	592	561	563	591	561	569	598	562	569
562	591	594	564	592	563	599	592	599	591
598	561	592	599	562	594	564	562	563	598
564	563	599	598	594	569	592	561	599	562
598	592	569	591	564	562	594	598	594	591
561	563	564	562	592	598	563	592	564	562
569	591	598	594	561	569	591	594	561	563

Figure 9–2.   Cancellation of Rapidly Recurring Target Figures Test–592

Source: From R. Rudel, M. Denckla, & M. Broman, Rapid Silent Response to Repeated Target Symbols by Dyslexic and Non-Dyslexic Children. Copyright 1978, *Brain and Language*. Used with permission of the publisher.

Table 9–4.   Cancellation of rapidly recurring target figures–normative data

	DIAMOND				
	Total Errors			Time (Seconds)	
Age	Mean	S.D.		Mean	S.D.
4–5	12	(4)		—	—
6–7	5	(3)		103.43	(46.30)
8–9	4	(3)		66.26	(21.63)
10–11	3	(3)		70.10	(24.55)
12–13	2	(3)		40.90	(8.88)

	592				
	Total Errors			Time (Seconds)	
Age	Mean	S.D.		Mean	S.D.
4–5	13	(4)		—	—
6–7	6	(3)		200.76	(81.51)
8–9	2	(2)		116.00	(33.71)
10–11	2	(2)		90.70	(24.66)
12–13	2	(2)		67.13	(15.76)

Source: From R. Rudel, M. Denckla, & M. Broman. Rapid Silent Response to Repeated Target Symbols by Dyslexic and Non-Dyslexic Children. Copyright 1978. *Brain and Language*. Used by permission of the publisher.

before stopping. It has been suggested that some children will have difficulty accurately assessing task demands and may perceive the diamond subtest as very simple; in response, they will not carefully scan the stimulus items, which results in more errors of omission. On the 592 subtest, however, children recognize the task complexity, exert more effort, and so perform competently. It has been the authors' observation that children with ADHD often use a random search strategy and do not check their performance. The child with ADHD, primarily inattentive type, may remain on task a significantly long period of time, utilize an ineffective approach, and make many errors of omission.

R. Gardner, Gardner, Caemmerer, and Broman (1979) developed a measure of motor steadiness by modifying an instrument originally designed by Knights (1966). The child is required to insert a stylus into a somewhat larger hole and hold it there as steadily as possible. Contact duration of the stylus with the hole's perimeter is electronically recorded. R. Gardner (1979) suggested that the steadiness test is a good measure of motor persistence, resting tremors, and choreiform movements, but it may also be a measure of hyperactivity and difficulty with task persistence. Gardner hypothesizes that motor impersistence, resting tremors, and choreiform movements are relatively uncommon in children with ADHD. Therefore, he considers the steadiness tester a measure of drive from within, suggesting that steadiness problems reflect a lack of task persistence. An alternative theory has suggested that kinesthetic input can phase information about relative body position, direction and extent of movements, speed velocity, and the force of contraction generated in muscles (Laszlo, 1990). Whitmont and Clark (1996) reported that children with ADHD perform relatively poorly in comparison to normals on tasks of kinesthetic and fine motor skills. The authors suggested that it is likely that children with ADHD pay relatively little attention to proprio receptive signals. This, then, is responsible for their poor performance on tasks such as the steadiness tester. Motor persistence has not been a major focus in the evaluation of ADHD, nor has it been demonstrated to discriminate ADHD children from others. For practitioners interested in motor persistence, however, the task may be useful and normative data are available (R. Gardner, 1979).

Finally, Restasp (1994) reported that children with ADHD made more errors on measures of visual-motor skill and had lower scores on most writing tasks. It is important for the practitioner to keep in mind that children with ADHD, due to their lack of attention to detail, may perform poorly on tests of written language.

Complex Visual and Auditory Tasks

Despite a large body of research beginning over twenty-five years ago (Cohen, Weiss, & Minde, 1972; Douglas, 1972, 1974) demonstrating that lack of sustained attention rather than distractibility reflects a basic problem for children with ADHD, interest has continued in tasks of distractibility as means of identifying children with ADHD. These tasks have been suggested as sensitive to distractibility, divided attention, and inhibition.

Color distraction tasks (Santostefano & Paley, 1964; Stroop, 1935) assess the child's ability to name items or colors when the stimuli are interfered with by distracting cues. The Stroop is a novel task that has been reported as measuring the ability to

maintain set and avoid distractions. The child is first asked to read as quickly as possible 100 color words (red, blue, green) printed in black and white and arranged in random sequence; this establishes a response tendency. Then a second response tendency
to name colors is developed by having the child read 100 colored dots (red, blue,
green). In the third or distraction condition, the child is presented with 100 color
words, each of which is printed in a color other than the one spelled by the letters; for
example, the word *green* is printed in red ink. The time to complete this third task as
well as errors are recorded. Comalli, Wapner, and Werner (1962) developed normative
data for children and adults. Trennery, Crosson, DeBoe, and Leber (1989) recently
published a new two-part version of this test. Douglas (1972) reported that children
with attention problems made more errors of commission that went uncorrected. When
the inattentive group was receiving stimulant medication, the difference between them
and the normals did not measure as statistically significant. Lavoie and Charlebois
(1994) used a more recent version of the Stroop to screen sixteen disruptive boys with
ADHD compared to sixteen disruptive boys without ADHD and a group of 12-year-old
boys. The ADHD group was significantly distinct in having a lower score in comparison with the other two groups. This group also showed more hesitations on the Color
Word Cards than did the combined group. However, the practitioner should be cautioned: as with many of these instruments, conflicting research findings are reported.
Lufi, Cohen, and Parrish-Plass (1990) report that the Stroop may help differentiate
children with ADHD from emotionally disturbed children. Interestingly, although the
ADHD children's performance was the least efficient, it was not statistically different
from the emotionally disturbed population.

Likely the most widely researched and clinically used of these complex tasks is the
Matching Familiar Figures Test (Kagan, Rosman, Day, Albert, & Phillips, 1964). This
test was designed specifically as a measure of reflection and impulsivity (Kagan,
1964). A number of alternative forms have been developed, and normative data have
been collected for children and adults. Kagan's original task consists of twelve items;
each contains a stimulus picture of an object and six similar pictures, only one of
which matches the stimulus picture exactly (see Figure 9–3). The child selects a response and is allowed to continue responding until a correct choice has been made. The
child's time from stimulus exposure to the initial response is recorded along with
the number of errors per item. Messer (1976) collected extensive normative data on the
Matching Familiar Figures Test and found that impulsive children present short reaction times and make many errors; reflective children have longer reaction times and
make fewer errors; some children respond quickly and are accurate; others take a long
time to respond but are inaccurate. It has been suggested that this last response style
may characteristically be consistent with the approach utilized by the inattentive
group with ADHD. These children struggle with attention, organization, and efficient
approach to tasks but are not necessarily impulsive. Although the Matching Familiar
Figures Test has its critics (Berry & Cook, 1980; Egeland & Weinberg, 1976), there
are data suggesting that children with ADHD are more disorganized, respond quicker,
and make more matching errors on this task than normal children (Klee, 1990;
Kuehne, 1985). The latter study reported strong correlations of the Matching Familiar
Figures Test with other measures of ADHD, suggesting that performance on this task
significantly differentiated ADHD children from non-ADHD clinic controls. However,

Figure 9–3.   Matching Familiar Figures Test
Source: From J. Kagan, *The Matching Familiar Figures Test.* Copyright 1964. Used by permission of the author.

not all studies have supported this finding. S. Stoner and Glynn (1987) did not find a significant difference on the Matching Familiar Figures Test when intelligence was controlled for in a group of ADHD and control children.

The Children's Embedded Figures Test (Karp & Konstadt, 1971) and the visual closure subtest of the Illinois Test of Psycholinguistic Abilities represent another class of tests reported to be sensitive to sustained attention and organizational skill. Stoner and Glynn (1987) report a significant main effect for these instruments between ADHD and control children. These authors suggest that children with ADHD are field-dependent, which accounts for their difficulty in locating embedded figures in a stimulus array. These tests overall require the child to locate stimulus items hidden in a larger visual field; they also require adequate visual/perceptive skills. E. Kirby and Grimley

(1986) report that the Children's Embedded Figures Test is a sensitive discriminator between inattentive and normal children.

Finally, J. Snow (1990) conducted three studies of mental rotation tasks with children utilizing a task involving the rotation of letters, words, objects, and figures. This task appears to focus on visual integrative functions. In the third study, twenty normal, twenty ADHD, and twenty neurologically dysfunctional children were compared. Normal subjects demonstrated higher performance than ADHD and neurologically dysfunctional children. This task, however, did not discriminate between the two clinical groups.

Frontal Lobe Measures

Frontal lobe measures are often collectively referred to as measures of executive function; they appear to reflect a collection of constructs that have in common what they are not rather than what they are (Denckla, 1996b). Frontal lobe measures are fundamental resources that are separable from specific cognitive content domains such as language or visual-spatial functioning; thus, they may be catalytic. Strong executive function skills may help a child compensate for weak linguistic or visual-spatial skills; the latter may compound learning problems (E. Harris et al., 1995; Reader et al., 1994). The finding of frontal lobe or executive function deficits in children with ADHD has been inconsistent (Denckla, 1996b). This author concludes that executive function appears to be a factor not accounted for by intelligence; in studies finding executive dysfunction in ADHD, the finding is likely confounded as the result of the linguistic content-relation factors and the construct validity of measures proposed as sensitive to executive dysfunction. Studies containing more ADHD children with linguistic weaknesses would therefore not surprisingly find a greater relationship between ADHD and executive dysfunction.

As reported in earlier chapters, deficits in frontal lobe functioning have not been consistently demonstrated for ADHD children in their performance on hypothesized frontal lobe tests. Among the most popular instruments has been the Wisconsin Card Sorting Test (R. Heaton, 1981). Riccio, Hall, Morgan, and Hund (1995) suggest a moderate relationship between cognitive ability and the performance on the Wisconsin Card Sort. Greve et al. (1993) reported that 91% of the variance in the Wisconsin Card Sort was accounted for by two factors: the first reflects problem solving and accounts for 70% of the variance; the second is consistent with inefficiency.

Chelune, Ferguson, Koon, and Dickey (1986) initially suggested that executive function tasks suggestive of frontal lobe functioning such as the Wisconsin Card Sort may differentiate children with ADHD from controls on the Wisconsin perseverative errors. Boucugnani and Jones (1989) also found ADHD children to be deficient on this task. This finding has been supported by others as well, suggesting a relationship between problem solving and attentional skills on the Wisconsin (Greve, Williams, Haas, Littell, & Reinoso, 1996). Perseverative error scores relative to controls appeared to be the most sensitive measure on the Wisconsin Card Sort. The authors suggest that perseveration reflects the child's inability to use information provided by the examiner and to alter the classification principle. Instead, the child continues to sort the cards according to a previously reinforced category. Caufield and Rattan (1996) have suggested that errors on the Wisconsin are consistent with a theory of ADHD as a problem reflecting poor inhibitory control.

Consistent with E. Sullivan et al. (1993), Greve et al. (1993, 1996) suggest that the first factor reflects executive function, specifically problem solving. The second may in fact be a measure of sustained attention. However, correlations with parent ratings of behavior have generally not been reported. Teacher ratings of attention problems were found in this study to be correlated with a number of variables on the Wisconsin Card Sort, and teacher ratings of learning problems were found to correlate with a cognitive index obtained on the Wisconsin. Inattention, however, was not found to be correlated with failure to maintain set. Hyperactivity was also not found to be correlated with any Wisconsin Card Sort variable. Significant correlations emerged only when the hyperactivity and inattentive components were measured separately. These authors suggested that individuals with ADHD have difficulty shifting set, which in turn is associated with frontal lobe dysfunction. Perseverative responses and errors were found to be significantly correlated with the inattentive subscale of both parent and teacher questionnaires.

Although instruments such as the Wisconsin appear to have quite a bit of face validity in the assessment of ADHD, there are too many variables that can affect performance, thereby making these tools inefficient in the evaluation of ADHD. For example, D. Martin, Oren, and Boone (1990) reported that depressed individuals demonstrated increased perseverations, failure to maintain set, and decreased conceptual level response. Greve et al. (1996) demonstrated that color overlays influenced perseveration and efficient sorting; these authors suggested that color affects performance and that wave length manipulation may have an effect on attention and neurosystem influence for individuals with ADHD (Heilman et al., 1991). Greve et al. cautioned, however, that lack of a group main effect casts doubt on this conclusion.

Single measures as well as batteries of tasks reported to measure frontal lobe functioning in children with ADHD have not consistently discriminated these children from controls (Loge, Staton, & Beatty, 1990; Weynandt, 1995). Koziol and Stout (1992), utilizing a verbal fluency measure, reported that children with ADHD performed significantly lower than expected and lower than control children in their ability to quickly generate words beginning with similar letters. These authors suggested that their findings supported the hypothesis that frontal lobe dysfunction is involved in ADHD, and that this task may be clinically useful in a diagnostic screening for ADHD.

Finally, Barkley, Grodzinsky, et al. (1992) emphasize the lack of ability of frontal lobe functions to differentiate ADHD. They report that the totality of the existing findings suggest a problem with perceptual motor speed and processing, which presents only in the inattentive type of ADHD. However, Mariani and Barkley (1997) have suggested that poor behavioral inhibition and faulty sustained attention may in fact contribute to executive function deficits.

Projective Instruments

Many of the most popular personality assessment or projective instruments have been examined in the evaluation of ADHD. These include the Rorschach Ink Blots, Thematic Apperception Test, and storytelling techniques. Bartel and Solanto (1995) and

Cotugno (1995) suggest that quantitative differences in a structured scoring system as well as qualitative differences demonstrate distinctions in ADHD from normal controls and other clinical populations on the Rorschach. Cotugno suggests that those with ADHD demonstrate more feelings of isolation and discomfort, less social involvement, more avoidance of decision making, and more independence. The author suggests that although this test may not be considered a diagnostic tool in the evaluation of ADHD, it may have ramifications in understanding the secondary personality and life issues for children with ADHD.

Constantino, Collin-Malgady, Malgady, and Perez (1991) used the Tell Me A Story Apperception Test (Constantino, Malgady, & Rogler, 1988) to assess ADHD, arguing that this instrument afforded direct observation of subjects' behavior and an objective system for scoring omission of stimulus details. No consistent findings were reported. The authors suggest that if "the projective approach to ADHD assessment is to prove useful, further confirmation is needed that attention deficit is being assessed and not other cognitive or dynamic factors correlated with performance" (p. 87).

Brain Wave Analysis

As discussed in Chapter 5, the theory underlying abnormal EEGs as discriminative of ADHD versus other childhood problems is consistent with what is known about low levels of arousal and frontal brain areas in individuals with ADHD (Lou et al., 1984; Zametkin et al., 1990). It has also been suggested that some children with ADHD produce more theta and fewer beta waves, particularly in frontal regions (C. Mann, Lubar, Zimmerman, & Muenchen, 1990; Satterfield, Schell, Nicholas, & Backs, 1988). However, not all studies have found EEG abnormalities in children with ADHD to have distinct diagnostic utility (Halperin et al., 1986).

The use of EEG measurements as diagnostic tools for ADHD has been touted based on limited research data (Lubar, 1991). Proponents of these measures as diagnostic tools often cite clinical experience, anecdotal data, case examples, and patient testimonials in lieu of scientific evidence (Othmer, 1993). However, there is even less well-controlled research than for many of the other instruments reviewed in this section to suggest that the EEG assessment and other neurometric techniques should be considered by the practitioner as part of the ADHD assessment protocol. Based on extensive reviews of the literature, Levy (1994) and Cantor (1990) conclude that these techniques have not been able to distinguish between children with ADHD and those with other psychiatric disorders. Culbert, Kajander, and Reaney (1996) note that although interest in EEG as a diagnostic tool has been great, "the literature to support its efficacy suffers from many methodological flaws. This is an area in which clinical practice has outpaced clear scientific evidence of efficacy" (p. 346).

Neuropsychological Batteries

Neuropsychological batteries have been demonstrated to provide valuable information that differs from data obtained from single measures or intelligence tests (Kupke & Lewis, 1985). Thus, it is not surprising that efforts have been undertaken to determine if such batteries can be effective in the diagnostic process for ADHD.

Unfortunately, these batteries, as with single tests or small groups of tests, have not been found to distinguish ADHD children from normal controls or other clinical groups (Barkley, Grodzinsky, et al., 1992). Although subtests on some neuropsychological batteries have been suggested as beneficial in the diagnosis of ADHD, the limited research available does not allow practitioners to utilize these tests in the diagnosis of ADHD with any great confidence. These studies have included batteries of arbitrary tests (Gorenstein, Mamamoto, & Sandy, 1989; Grodzinsky & Diamond, 1992), the Luria Nebraska Neuropsychological Battery–Children's Revision (Schaughency, Lahey, Hynd, Stone, Piacentini, & Frick, 1989), and computerized batteries (Arcia, Ornstein, & Otto, 1991).

Mariani and Barkley (1997) compared thirty-four preschool-age males with ADHD to thirty community-comparison males without any type of disruptive behavioral problem on a battery of neuropsychological measures. Males with ADHD performed more poorly than controls on two of four dimensional measures: motor control and working memory-persistence. Motor tasks included those related to speed and coordination as well as visual-spatial construction; memory tasks focused on simple verbal, spatial, and short-term memory. No differences were found on tasks related to verbal learning or factual knowledge. The authors suggested that early deficits in motor control and working memory may be an inherent part of ADHD and a comorbid risk for subsequent academic achievement problems. The authors concluded that their data supported ADHD as a problem involving deficits in executive function, likely contributed to by poor behavioral inhibition and faulty sustained attention.

The majority of research-based assessment instruments for ADHD have been designed for and used with children 6 to 12 years of age. Assessment of preschool children with suspected ADHD more often focuses on observation of the child and parent report. Campbell et al. (1982) observed inattentive 2- and 3-year-olds shifting activity more readily at a free play setting and exhibiting problems with restlessness, out of seat, and off-task behavior in structured situations when reflection and sustained attention were required. With adolescents, a careful history is often the most valuable component of the assessment process.

Many tasks have demonstrated sensitivity and specificity on a group basis in discriminating ADHD from other disorders. However, none of these tasks has been consistent and found always to discriminate; none has been able to meet the litmus test of consistent positive and negative predictive power. Thus, as these tasks have transitioned into clinical practice, their reported benefits and utility often exceed the available research literature. Many practitioners utilize these tasks because they have face validity; that is, on the surface, they make sense and in the practitioner's eyes are of assistance in making the ADHD diagnosis. Experienced practitioners, however, have learned that in many cases it is not necessarily the task or the score but rather their observation of the child's approach to the task that provides valuable data in attempting to see the world through the eyes of the child being assessed. For the present, it would appear that the majority of these instruments, although valuable in cognitive, behavioral, emotional, and academic assessment, should be considered adjunctive tools in the diagnostic process specifically for ADHD. If any tests are to be utilized as part of the primary ADHD battery, the CPTs appear to offer the greatest potential in providing valuable data concerning the laboratory behavior of children with ADHD.

BEHAVIORAL OBSERVATION DURING ASSESSMENT

It is important for the practitioner to qualitatively evaluate the child's or adolescent's behavior from the moment of meeting until the close of the evaluation. A number of forms designed to organize the practitioner's observations during assessment are available. S. Goldstein and Goldstein (1985) have developed and revised a simple one-page form to meet this need. It appears in Figure 9–4.

It is important to observe the child's initial response to meeting in the waiting room or classroom. The child's ability to separate from parent or the setting and accompany the practitioner to the testing room is also important. The child's physical size and appearance should be noted. The majority of children with ADHD without additional psychiatric problems experience little difficulty separating from their parents or classroom and accompanying the practitioner into the testing room.

The practitioner should observe the child's ability to make appropriate eye contact as well as initiate and maintain conversation. Even in a one-to-one setting, many ADHD children have difficulty focusing on a practitioner and frequently look around the room even as they respond to questions. General observation of the child's receptive language skills, voice quality, expressive syntax, and articulation is also suggested.

The practitioner must note if the child presents as excessively anxious or unhappy. At times, it is difficult to distinguish excessive mobility and restlessness, which are characteristic of most children with ADHD, from signs of anxiety. When questioned, however, anxious children will usually openly acknowledge that they are feeling uncomfortable; the ADHD child frequently denies these feelings. These subjective data are important in making the distinction between anxiety and inattention. Further, anxious children often engage in behaviors characteristic of anxiety, such as hand wringing, whereas children with ADHD engage in behaviors such as wiping the desk with their arms, kicking the desk, and fidgeting excessively in their seats. Some children are overly concerned about their performance; others lack emotion and appear quite constricted. Some children are extremely labile, jumping from one extreme of emotion to another. Typically, children with ADHD do not experience significant problems with these emotional characteristics; thus, problems in these areas are often signs of additional emotional disturbance.

The practitioner must note if the child is alert. Based on the mental status assessment (Strub & Black, 1977), being alert refers to the child's ability to remain awake. The practitioner must also note if the child is able to pay attention for short periods of time sufficient to follow task instructions. Observations of sustained attention, also referred to as concentration or vigilance, must also be made. The majority of psychometric assessment instruments take only a few minutes each to complete, and many children with ADHD can remain on task for a sufficient amount of time to complete them.

The practitioner must note if the child is cooperative. Some children are passively resistant, agreeing with the examiner but dawdling and not completing tasks; others are openly defiant, refusing to comply. These behaviors are not diagnostic of ADHD. When they are exhibited, they should be considered indices that the child may experience other problems along with ADHD or in fact may not be experiencing ADHD. Practitioners should keep in mind that the lack of task persistence for most ADHD

GOLDSTEIN BEHAVIORAL OBSERVATION CHECKLIST

Name _____   Age _____   Date _____

Size _____
Appearance _____
Separation and Waiting Room _____
Eye Contact _____
Speech and Language: Receptive _____
    Expressive syntax _____
    Expressive articulation _____
    Maintains conversation _____
    Initiates conversation _____
Expression: Anxious _____ Sad _____
    Miserable _____ Unhappy _____
    Calm _____
    Concerned about performance _____
    Lack of affect _____ Labile _____
    Other _____
Emotional Stability _____
Tearfulness _____
Alert _____
Attention _____
Concentration _____
Cooperation _____
Attempt _____
Motivation _____
Maturity _____
Persistence: Normal _____
    Needs occasional prompting _____
    Needs continuous examiner praise and
    encouragement _____
    Inconsistent effort _____
Preoccupation with topics of:
    Anxiety _____
    Depressive _____
    Aggressive _____
Muscular tension: Clinching jaw _____
    Sitting stiffly in chair _____
    Gripping table or chair _____
    Gripping hands together _____
    Other _____
Habitual mannerisms: Tics _____
    Rocking _____
    Twisting hair _____
    Facial mannerisms _____
    Sucking _____
    Flapping arms _____

Activity: Underactive, little spontaneous
    movement _____
    Normal _____
    Tendency to increased activity _____
    Markedly overactive relative to
    situation _____
    Extremely overactive, tempo of
    activity increases _____
Fidgetiness: Normal _____
    Occasional squirming or wriggling ____
    Marked fidgetiness _____
Distractibility: Not distracted _____
    Occasionally distracted _____
    Easily distracted _____
    Seeks distraction _____
Orientation to purpose of testing _____
Self-Confidence: Extremely confident _____
    Overly confident _____
    Moderately confident _____
    Inclined to distrust abilities _____
    Very insecure _____
Comprehension _____
Orientation to testing _____
Relationship with examiner _____
Emotional responsiveness to examiner _____
Smiling: Smiles appropriately _____
    Smiles only occasionally _____
    No or very little smiling _____
Final adjustment _____
Thought processes: Logical _____
Focused _____
Relevant _____

Notes:

Figure 9–4. Goldstein Behavior Checklist

Source: From S. Goldstein & M. Goldstein, *The Multi-Disciplinary Evaluation and Treatment of Attention Deficit Disorders in Children: Symposium Handbook.* Copyright 1985 by Neurology, Learning and Behavior Center. Used with permission of the publisher.

children results not only from their temperament but from their experience over time: some children learn to avoid tasks actively. It is important for the practitioner to observe whether the child is actively seeking distractions as a means of avoiding tasks.

Practitioners should observe the child's degree of muscular tension, habitual mannerisms, and activity level, distinguishing between restless fidgeting while remaining seated and excessive activity that results in the child's being out of seat and moving about the room excessively. W. Tryon (1993; G. Tryon, 1997) suggests that an activity monitor be used to offer an objective measure of activity level. W. Tryon and Pinto (1994) demonstrated that the device correlated well with teacher reports of severity of hyperactive behavior in the classroom. Perrino, Rapoport, Behar, Ismond, and Bunney (1983) suggested that such a device is sensitive to medication changes as well. Practitioners, however, should keep in mind that clinic or laboratory-based observations of activity level have not been found to differ from those reported by parents and teachers (Tripp & Luk, 1997).

It is beneficial to obtain some observation of the child's level of self-confidence. As has been discussed, children with ADHD may be initially overconfident and, at the conclusion of tasks, inflate their perception of performance. At times, it is difficult for practitioners to determine whether a child's tendency to give up quickly as task complexity increases results from impulsive frustration or feelings of helplessness. Frequently, direct questioning of the child will help make this distinction. Parent and teacher questionnaires are also of assistance in interpreting observable behavior as stemming from anxiety, helplessness, or ADHD.

It is helpful to determine how well-oriented the child is to the purpose of the evaluation. Some children present with very poor orientation but will accept an explanation of the need for assessment; others will deny a need for assessment, even in the face of problems at home and school. The child's ability to relate to the practitioner is observed by whether the child smiles and how well the child progresses emotionally through the evaluation. Assessment of the child's thought processes determines whether they are logical, focused on the tasks at hand, and relevant to the examiner's questions. Overall observation of the child's final adjustment and orientation during the close of the evaluation should also be made.

IMPACT OF ADHD ON OVERALL TEST PERFORMANCE

The practitioner inexperienced in evaluating children with ADHD may draw inaccurate or erroneous conclusions about the child's skills and abilities based on test performance. As task complexity increases, the low frustration threshold and impulsivity of these children tend to take over. They may begin tasks with lower effort and thus fall below the threshold of effort required for successful performance quicker than other children (van der Meere & Sergeant, 1988c). To avoid such problems, it is strongly recommended that the practitioner test the child's limits routinely when psychometric assessments are administered. This is especially important if there is a question of learning disability. It is not uncommon during limit testing to determine that the child with ADHD knows more information, can locate more missing items, can sequent cards or puzzle pieces more efficiently, and has better social judgment than is revealed during standardized test administration. Although the improved performance cannot be counted when tests are scored, the data are certainly important in helping the practitioner understand that the assessment obtained is an underestimate of the child's potential. In such situations, an accurate assessment of the ADHD child's capabilities may be impossible.

MEASUREMENT OF ACADEMIC SKILLS

Frequently, academic and achievement information can be obtained through group or individual assessments administered at school. Because there is a likelihood that the older ADHD child will experience some degree of academic deficiency, it is beneficial for the practitioner to obtain a measure of the child's academic skills. If in-depth data are not available and deficiencies are suspected, the child's word reading, comprehension, spelling, written language, and arithmetic capabilities should be screened as time permits. An in-depth battery such as the Woodcock-Johnson Psychoeducational Assessment Battery–Revised (Woodcock, 1989) is recommended. This instrument offers by far the most thorough, well-developed assessment of academic skills. Normative data are available from childhood through adulthood. Subtest analysis often reveals patterns consistent with verbal or visual rote or conceptual weaknesses. Achievement tests such as the Woodcock Reading Mastery Tests–Revised (Woodcock, 1987) offer a shorter, skill-based reading assessment. The Wide Range Achievement Test III (Wilkenson, 1993) can generate observations of conceptual versus rote sequential mathematic abilities, phonetic versus visual memory deficits in spelling, and phonetic versus visual memory aspects of single-word reading. The story writing subtest from the Test of Written Language III (Hammill & Larsen, 1996) can be used to observe differences in written thematic maturity, vocabulary, capacity to organize ideas, grammar, punctuation, and oral execution. Oral reading subtests from the Gilmore (Gilmore & Gilmore, 1968), the Gray Oral Reading Test–3rd Edition (Wiederholt & Bryant, 1992), and the Test of Reading Comprehension–3rd Edition (V. Brown et al., 1995) allow the practitioner to assess reading capacity, specifically ability to read in context, rate of reading, and simple comprehension.

Overall, administration of academic instruments allow the practitioner to draw conclusions not only about the child's quantitative skills (e.g., grade levels) but about distinctions in reading, writing, and mathematical abilities, as described. The practitioner should keep in mind that a key goal is to distinguish between what the child knows and what he or she is capable of doing consistently. DuPaul and Stoner (1994) suggest that children with ADHD should perform at least 1.5 standard deviations below the mean on reported measures of academic performance in the classroom before learning disability is suspected.

ASSESSMENT OF PERSONALITY AND EMOTIONAL ADJUSTMENT

In response to their increased problems dealing successfully with the environment, children with ADHD present an increased risk for the development of helplessness,

depression, poor self-esteem, a variety of personality problems, and general oppositionality. As part of the evaluation for ADHD, it is recommended that the practitioner
obtain at least a general overview of the ADHD child's self-awareness, emotional adjustment, and coping and problem-solving skills. The child's behavior can accurately
be reported by parents and teachers; however, to understand how the child feels, the
practitioner must take the time to conduct a clinical interview. A number of self-report
and interview measures are available for this part of the evaluation.

Self-Report Measures

Achenbach and Edelbrock (1983) have developed a parallel form of the Revised Child
Behavior Profile designed to be completed by children 11 through 18 years of age. The
youth self-report contains normative data and requires at least a fifth-grade reading
level to be completed. Qualitative assessment of the adolescent's response is often
helpful because questions deal with peer relations, community activities, fears, emotional problems, and perceived attentional difficulty.

A. Robin and van der May (1996) reported on the internal consistency and concurrent validity of the ADD/H Adolescent Self-Report Scale (Conners & Wells, 1985).
ADHD adolescents reported significantly more problems than controls on all eleven
scales, including core symptoms of ADHD as well as negative emotions, family problems, anger, self-esteem, and peer relations. This instrument, developed specifically
for ADHD, may be particularly beneficial when assessing adolescents. Gittelman
(1985) has also developed a self-evaluation ADHD report for teenagers. This report
has twenty-seven items and uses a four-point Likert response scale similar to the Conners questionnaires.

Additional instruments that may have utility in the clinical assessment include
the Diagnostic Interview for Children and Adolescents (Herjanic & Reich, 1982) and
the Social Adjustment Inventory for children and adolescents (Biederman, Faraone, &
Chen, 1993); the latter is a semistructured interview schedule that assesses adaptive
functioning.

The Children's Depression Inventory (Kovacs, 1983, 1996) is a self-report measure
requiring the child to check one of three descriptors in each item that best character-
izes the child over a two-week period. Normative data are available. Borden et al.
(1987) report that children with ADHD in comparison to a normal control group acknowledge significantly more depressive symptoms. These authors also found that in
comparison to normal children, children with ADHD demonstrated more external attribution for both positive and negative experiences. The Reynolds Adolescent Depression Scale (W. Reynolds, 1987) as well as the Reynolds Child Depression Scale
(W. Reynolds, 1989) are also practical and efficient means of gaining self-report data
concerning depressive symptoms. The Revised Children's Manifest Anxiety Scale
(C. Reynolds & Richmond, 1985) is useful in assessing perceived level of emotional
distress. These instruments may prove helpful in developing an understanding of the
youth's awareness of the severity of his or her problems and the level of contact with
his or her feelings. Practitioners are cautioned, however, that at least in regard to the
Children's Depression Inventory, the task may not discriminate children with major
depression from those with conduct disorders (Woodside, Brownstone, & Fisman,

1987). Further, Perrin and Last (1992) suggested that the Revised Children's Manifest Anxiety Scale differentiates children with ADHD from normal controls but does not consistently differentiate ADHD children from those with anxiety disorder. Thus, many of these self-report measures may have excellent predictive power in separating children with problems from those without, but may not be particularly useful in providing data for differential diagnosis (Hodges & Craighead, 1990; Wendel, Nelson, Politano, Mayhal, & Finch, 1988).

Piers and Harris (1984) have recently revised the Piers Harris Self-Concept Scale, subtitled The Way I Feel About Myself. It was developed as a brief self-report measure to evaluate self-concept in children and adolescents. Many consider it a measure of self-esteem. The eighty-item true/false questionnaire is designed to evaluate children's conscious feelings about themselves. Item content includes questions about behavior, school status, physical appearance, anxiety, popularity, and happiness. The instrument can be used with children as young as 8 years of age. The practitioner must be cautious, however, as children may provide overly positive profiles, especially if their responses are impulsive.

In-depth self-report measures such as the Minnesota Multiphasic Personality Inventory (Hathaway & McKinley, 1989) and the Millon Adolescent Clinical Inventory (Millon, Green, & Meagher, 1982) offer comprehensive, actuarially based overviews of acute psychiatric status and personality function. These instruments can be extremely valuable during the differential diagnostic process. As of this date, however, no subtypes of these instruments have been found to be specifically indicative of adolescent ADHD. The Millon, however, does address the issue of whether a profile reflects an individual prone to impulsive behavior.

Clinical Interview

Barkley (1981a) writes that it is important to pay close attention to the child's style and quality of responses during an interview. Practitioners should keep in mind that as interviews are usually not highly stimulating or interesting for children with ADHD, this time during the assessment may be particularly revealing, reflecting the child's lack of inhibitory control (Barkley, 1990a). Children with ADHD frequently respond impulsively, thus revealing their immediate feelings but not necessarily their ability to respond accurately to questions. Although the reliability and validity of self-report data provided by children with ADHD have not been demonstrated, self-report does provide qualitative information concerning the child's thoughts at the moment (LaGreca, 1990); thus, observation of the child's ability to interact in a semistructured clinical interview is an essential component of the evaluation.

The practitioner should keep in mind that data obtained during a clinical interview have been suggested as the best means of differentiating between ADHD and bipolar disorder (American Academy of Child and Adolescent Psychiatry, 1997). ADHD reflects a chronic, persistent disorder beginning before age 7 and possibly evolving into more serious disruptive problems. In contrast, bipolar disorder is described as episodic, with onset after age 12, a disorder that affects regulation "characterized by abnormal mood and mental excitement, usually presenting as a marked change in the youth's baseline functioning" (p. 142).

E. Kirby and Grimley (1986) suggest that when interviewing children, the focus should be on (1) the child's perception of the problem; (2) the child's attributional style; (3) the child's awareness of attention variables; and (4) the child's view of treatment. Landau, Milich, and Widiger (1991), based on standardized interviews with seventy-six 6- to 12-year-old clinic-referred boys, examined which self-reported symptoms were the most efficient predictors of the ADHD diagnosis; they found that the ultimate predictors of the diagnosis were not those symptoms typically considered hallmarks of the disorder. It is important to recognize that, at least in this study, no symptom was found to be an efficient exclusion criterion for the diagnosis. Thus, the interview provides valuable data on the child's personality and view of life and on self-awareness of behavior. Very structured interviews have been found in some settings to correlate well with parent and teacher reports (Aronen, Noam, & Weinstein, 1993). Schaughency et al. (1994) found that adolescent self-reported attention difficulties were clinically significant markers of adjustment problems. Most important, self-reported attention problems at 15 years of age were associated with continued symptoms at age 18, adjustment difficulties, and increased adverse outcomes.

Children with ADHD may demonstrate inflated self-perception, which serves an adaptive functioning, allowing them to preserve their self-respect even when things are not going well. They may offer high ratings of self-esteem in peer relationships or deny problems in these areas, not because they are oppositional, but because their self-ratings are based on faulty attribution. Thus, their self-reports may be misleading and should be examined closely. Self-ratings following a challenging or difficult experience may be more indicative of the true level of self-esteem or feelings of competence in children with ADHD (Milich & Diner, 1995).

Some children enjoy a verbal presentation by the practitioner, in which the practitioner begins a sentence and the child must complete it with the first thing that comes to mind. This activity can be a useful icebreaker. Other children respond more openly and personally if the sentence-completion task is administered toward the end of the assessment. The practitioner needs to be aware that children with limited intellectual skills or language problems may find an open-ended task such as this extremely difficult. Adolescents are usually provided with a written incomplete-sentences form and asked to write their responses; Figure 9–5 contains a sample set of incomplete sentences. Rotter (1950) developed an incomplete-sentence form specifically for adolescents. Information concerning self-image, family relations, motivation, outlook concerning school, and adult relations can be obtained. Although there is no profile of responses characteristic of ADHD, the practitioner can draw inferences concerning the child's or adolescent's view of the world based on his or her responses.

In lieu of incomplete sentences, some practitioners find storytelling cards a useful icebreaker. Photographs or line drawings depicting children engaged in various home, social, and school activities can be helpful in eliciting information concerning the child's social perception and problem-solving skills. Children are asked to tell stories about the pictures or place themselves in the situation and explain how they would respond. With young children, the Plenk Story Telling Test (Plenk, 1975) or the Children's Apperception Test (Bellak & Bellak, 1968) can be used to elicit a wide variety of information. The Roberts Apperception Test (G. Roberts, 1982) provides a wide variety of real-life stimulus pictures. Although lacking in ambiguity, which is the basis

Name _____ Age _____ Date _____

I like _____

I dislike _____

When I go to bed _____

My mother _____

Working is _____

School _____

Most boys _____

When I am mad _____

Fighting _____

I want to know _____

My father _____

Most girls _____

I would like to forget _____

I wish my mother _____

My friends _____

When I grow up _____

My parents _____

I cannot _____

At home _____

My teacher _____

I need _____

I am afraid _____

My family _____

I wish my father _____

My looks _____

Grown-ups _____

I worry _____

I like people who _____

When I cannot have my way _____

Babies are lucky because _____

Nobody likes children who _____

If I had a gun _____

Sometimes I make believe _____

Even the best parents may forget _____

Children are usually certain that _____

If only people knew how much _____

There would be fewer divorces if _____

The worst thing that could happen to a family is _____

The best kinds of homes are the ones that _____

Figure 9–5.   Incomplete sentences

Source: From S. Goldstein, *Incomplete Sentences.* Copyright 1987. Used with permission of the author.

for some projective tests, the Roberts Apperception Test is often quite revealing of a child's limited social perception and poor problem or conflict resolution skills.

It is suggested that the clinical interview begin with fairly general novel questions designed to increase the child's interest in the interview process. Children can be asked what they would wish for if they had three wishes. Children with ADHD typically respond impulsively, their wishes not well thought out, which is often true for many of their answers during the clinical interview. Children can then be asked who they would like to take and what single object they would take to a deserted island. Responses to this question are quite revealing. Older children typically choose a friend, but it is not uncharacteristic for a child experiencing significant family or social problems to choose a pet, despite the fact that the question asks for a person. One child experiencing significant social and family problems responded that he would not take anyone because no one would want to go with him; this is an extremely revealing response concerning the child's feelings about himself and others.

Other questions include what kind of an animal the children would like to be, what one thing they would like to change about themselves, what person they might like to be for a day, and what they like to do best. Novel questions include what a fly might say if it followed the child around all day, and what the walls of the child's house would say about the child and her family if walls could talk. It is often useful to elicit data concerning the child's self-image by asking what the child feels he or she is best at or does better than other children; children experiencing problems with self-image may have difficulty suggesting something they do better than others. Brief discussions of emotions might begin by asking children whether they feel they are as happy as others and what makes them feel happy; if they are ever sad and what makes them sad; if they become angry and why. It may also be helpful to ask children to name specific things they like and do not like about themselves. Children with ADHD who are aware of their struggles may respond by naming a specific ADHD symptom, such as "hyperness."

A discussion of friends is an integral part of the clinical interview. It is suggested that children be asked initially if they have a best friend and then the relationship between the child and the best friend explored in terms of what they like about each other and their favorite activities. It is helpful to ask whether children feel they have as many friends as others and if not, why not. Children can be asked if they are satisfied with their friends and if they feel friends at home and at school are different and why. Because of their lack of insight and impulsiveness, it is not uncommon for children with ADHD to recognize difficulty with friends but lack understanding of the impact their behavior has on others, which results in socialization problems.

A discussion of school can follow, initially asking children to identify their favorite and least favorite aspects; for children experiencing school problems, characteristic answers concerning favorite aspects include recess, lunch, final bell of the day, physical education, and vacations. When asked about his least favorite aspect of school, one ADHD child impulsively but insightfully noted "sitting still." Children can also be asked if they are as smart as other children and if not, why not, as well as whether they learn as well as other children. Questions specific to ADHD problems include asking children if they have difficulty finishing work, whether the teacher frequently tells them they are not listening, whether they have difficulty playing with one friend or activity for a long period of time, whether they have problems waiting their turn, whether they have difficulty staying seated, and whether they perceive that they have more energy than other children.

For the practitioner desiring a more in-depth interview specifically focused on attentional issues, E. Kirby and Grimley (1986) developed a sixteen-item child interview form based on the *DSM-III* ADD diagnostic criteria. P. Miller and Bigi (1979) developed an even longer structured interview designed to assess a child's understanding of the concept of paying attention.

The interview can then proceed with a discussion of the home and family relations, asking children what they like and do not like about each parent, the best and worst thing that has happened to them in the family, and questions about relationships with siblings. Given recent trends in child depression and suicide, it is also recommended that the practitioner broach the question of death, asking children if they have thought about death and specifically if they have thought about killing themselves. If the practitioner questions the adequacy of the child's reality testing, further questions concerning the child's experience of auditory or visual hallucinations may prove fruitful. Initially, children can be asked if they ever hear or see things that other people cannot; clarification can proceed if the child responds affirmatively.

Children with pragmatic or semantic language problems, especially those with high-functioning autism or Asperger's disorder, may respond atypically to examiner's questions, not because they are out of touch with reality but because they struggle to communicate their thoughts and feelings efficiently and tend to perceive their environment somewhat atypically. Guevremont (1993) suggests that when clinicians suspect these problems and at least some atypical symptoms are present, ADHD symptoms should be considered secondary to pervasive developmental disorder.

CLINICAL CRITERIA FOR CONFIRMING ADHD

At this time, the diagnosis of ADHD is based on a child's exhibiting a certain pattern of behavior over time, in different settings, and with sufficient severity. None of these issues is directly addressed through the clinical or laboratory-based evaluation as part of the diagnostic process. Although Douglas and Peters (1979) reported accurately that impairment in inhibition and sustained attention are the hallmarks of ADHD, there are minimal data to confirm that what is measured in a laboratory is an accurate representation of what is observed in the real world. At the present, the *DSM-IV* diagnostic protocol for ADHD consists of real-world symptoms and behaviors. Although it may be rare that a child with environmentally reported ADHD symptoms will perform successfully on many clinical tasks, these instruments must be considered at best adjunctive in the ADHD diagnostic process. Thus, it is difficult to fault practitioners who do not devote time to them. It is also difficult to fault practitioners who choose to administer some of these tasks because they believe they provide differential diagnostic data concerning subtypes of ADHD or, for that matter, the myriad comorbid problems ADHD children are known to experience. It is valid for practitioners to rely on such instruments, particularly a CPT, to provide additional data in the diagnostic process so long as they are not using these tools as the litmus test to confirm or disconfirm the diagnosis of ADHD. Psychometric tests assist the skilled practitioner in making the distinction between the child who may have skills but chooses not to use them and the child with ADHD. Chapter 10 will provide a structured model to facilitate this process and make other diagnostic distinctions.

SUMMARY

This chapter provided a review of the dramatically expanded literature in the use of laboratory, clinical, and related measures as part of and adjunct to the diagnosis of ADHD and comorbid conditions. Models for behavioral observation, self-report, and clinical interview were presented. These procedures assist the practitioner to draw conclusions concerning the child's cognitive, academic, and emotional functioning, as well as offer adjunctive data regarding ADHD symptoms. Given the combination of psychometric instruments and interview techniques recommended, a psychologist is the ideal practitioner to obtain these types of data in the ADHD evaluative process.

Chapter 10

MAKING THE DIAGNOSIS OF ADHD

The previous chapters have presented models and specific methods for collecting data essential to make the diagnosis of ADHD. This chapter provides a framework to organize and interpret that data. The practitioner must be aware that no single score or observation that confirms or rules out the presence of ADHD. Additionally, collection of in-depth data facilitates the practitioner's ability to deal with the critical issue of false positives. As discussed in earlier chapters, symptoms of impulsivity and inattention are often characteristic of ADHD but are also associated with other emotional, behavioral, developmental, and adjustment problems of children and adolescents. Careful review and integration of all collected data using the five components of this working definition provides the framework for a logical etiology and helps to avoid the occurrence of false positives. Conversely, concerns about a false negative diagnosis constitute a less significant issue; it would be rare for the presentation of multiple impulse and attention problems to be overlooked because most practitioners almost automatically consider these symptoms of ADHD.

Figure 10–1 contains an overview of the diagnostic strategy integrated into a checklist format. The current format initially developed in 1989 (Goldstein & Goldstein,

---

   I. *DSM-IV* Diagnostic Criteria for ADHD

____ A. Inattentive type (6 of 9 symptoms)

____ B. Inattentive-impulsive type (6 of 9 symptoms)

____ C. Combined type (if both of the above are met, check only this one)

____ D. Not otherwise specified (subthreshold number of symptoms, but they have significant impact on daily life)

  II. Rating Scales

____ A. Home

      ____ Conners

      ____ Child Behavior Checklist

      ____ Attention Deficit Disorders Evaluation Scale

      ____ Comprehensive Rating Scale–Parents

      ____ ADHD-SC4

(continued)

Figure 10–1. ADHD Diagnostic Checklist

Source: Adjusted from S. Goldstein, *ADHD Diagnostic Checklist.* Copyright 1989a. Used with the author's permission.

___ B. School

    ___ Conners

    ___ Child Behavior Checklist

    ___ Attention Deficit Disorders Evaluation Scale

    ___ Comprehensive Rating Scale–Teachers

III. Objective Data

___ A. Impulse Problems

___ B. Attention Problems

    ___ Initiating

    ___ Sustaining

    ___ Vigilant

    ___ Dividing

    ___ Organizing

IV. Situation Problems

___ A. Home

___ B. School

___ C. Community

  V. Differential Diagnosis

___ A. Disruptive Problems

    ___ Oppositional Defiant Disorder

    ___ Conduct Disorder

___ B. Nondisruptive Problems

    ___ Depression

    ___ Dysthymia

    ___ Manic-Depressive Disorder

    ___ Anxiety Disorders

___ C. Tourette's

___ D. Life Adjustment Problems

    ___ Family

    ___ School

    ___ Medical

___ E. Learning/Developmental Problems

    ___ Language difficulty

    ___ Auditory processing dysfunction

    ___ Memory problems

    ___ Specific cognitive deficits

    ___ Achievement problems

    ___ General intellectual deficits

Figure 10–1. *(Continued)*

1990) has been adjusted to reflect changes in the diagnostic nomenclature as well as conceptual changes in the core symptoms and assessment process for ADHD. Components of the diagnostic strategy include the *DSM-IV* diagnostic criteria for ADHD, home and school data, objective clinical data, the assessment of situational problems, and, most important, the consideration of differential diagnosis as contributing to ADHD symptoms. The checklist is designed as a tool to be used by the practitioner to integrate data. It is not a statistical tool and there is no absolute minimum or maximum number of variables that must be present or absent for the diagnosis of ADHD to be made. However, in the majority of situations in which the diagnosis of ADHD is made, most criteria point to ADHD as a core or comorbid problem for the child being evaluated. Each section of the ADHD diagnostic checklist will be reviewed, with an extended presentation concerning the issue of differential diagnosis. In Chapter 11, an expanded section of new case studies will illustrate the manner in which data are collected and integrated. Given the increasing presentation of ADHD comorbid with other disorders, the majority of cases presented will include various types of compounding problems. This will assist the practitioner in understanding the complexity of ADHD and its interactions with other disorders of childhood and adolescence.

I. *DSM-IV* DIAGNOSTIC CRITERIA FOR ADHD

The current *DSM-IV* criteria are well defined. The practitioner should qualitatively review history as well as parent and teacher questionnaires to determine if symptom criteria are met.

A categorical diagnosis may not be similar to or provide data on a dimensional basis. Fergusson and Horwood (1995) report consistent and generally linear relationships between symptom severity and outcome risk. Dimensionally scored variables were considerably better predictors of outcome, however, than measures based on categorical classification. Thus, the *DSM-IV* diagnostic criteria certainly have value in the short run, but they may not be as effective in the long run in regard to treatment planning and prediction of future problems as dimensionally derived criteria.

Because problems with attention, impulse control, and hyperactivity constitute the most frequent complaints of parents and teachers, not all children with these symptoms suffer from ADHD. Children with language, socialization, cognitive, and other behavioral difficulties that are the result of life experience of atypical development also exhibit attention-related problems. In fact, especially among young children with histories of language problem, complaints of inattention, hyperactivity, and impulsivity appear to be the rule rather than the exception. It has been hypothesized that although some of these children experience both disorders (ADHD and Language Disorders), many experience ADHD symptoms secondary to frustration (Goldstein & Hinerrman, 1988).

II. RATING SCALES

Recommended rating scales were reviewed and discussed in Chapters 7 and 8. These represent the authors' favorite scales because of their utility and psychometric properties.

The practitioner will likely find general adjustment scales such as the Child Behavior Checklist or Personality Inventory for Children extremely useful in providing a general description of the child's functioning in relation to others. In settings or situations in which time is limited, it is recommended that parents at least complete the Child Behavior Checklist as a general overview and one additional questionnaire specifically pulling for symptoms of ADHD, such as the Conners, ADHD-SC4, ADDES, or Comprehensive Rating Scale. School data should include the Child Behavior Checklist as a general overview and at least one specific rating scale for attention. The practitioner must keep in mind that noncompliant, oppositional, or conduct-disordered children will frequently present with elevated attention and overarousal problems on all of these questionnaires. The revised editions of the Child Behavior Checklist and Conners have attempted to control for this issue by separating out specific inattentive problems from those related to more overt noncompliance and aggression.

Parent-teacher symptom agreement on questionnaires has been found to be generally low (Offord et al., 1996). The pattern of associated features of disorders such as ADHD varies markedly between parent-identified and teacher-identified problems. Combining informants has the disadvantage of masking the distinctive patterns of associated features noted in informant-specific disorders such as ADHD. It is suggested that practitioners in part consider ADHD an informant-specific phenomenon. As noted, severity of the child's symptoms is critically related to multiple environmental factors. Thus, differences in symptom report and severity between settings should be considered valuable diagnostic information.

III. OBJECTIVE DATA

Chapter 9 extensively reviewed assessment instruments with a focus on those seemingly sensitive to various symptoms of ADHD. However, as discussed, although some of these instruments meet acceptable sensitivity and specificity criteria, their positive and negative predictive powers are generally much weaker. However, it is reasonable to conclude that children with ADHD usually do not perform well on these types of tests. As M. Gordon (1995b) noted, among children receiving the diagnosis of ADHD, those performing relatively better on some of these measures may in fact reflect a different diagnostic subgroup, one with fewer comorbid problems or possibly better prognosis.

In the 1990 edition of this text, we suggested that it was essential that the child demonstrate difficulty on at least a selection of attentional tasks in order to make the diagnosis of ADHD, especially as the primary condition. We suggested that in fact tasks sensitive to sustained, divided, and selective attention could be differentiated. Current research, however, does not support this as a valid, clinical hypothesis. Rather, we believe, as discussed, that objective data are valuable though not essential in making the diagnosis of ADHD. These measures provide the clinician with laboratory data of the child's inability to sustain attention and inhibit impulsive responding. As discussed, the CPTs utilizing computer technology have demonstrated the most promising utility as part of the diagnostic process. It is strongly recommended that objective data be collected; when findings are present, they likely strengthen the hypothesis that this is a child with ADHD. When absent in the face of the home and school data suggesting

ADHD, they may be a signpost to examine potential comorbid problems leading to symptom presentation.

IV. SITUATIONAL PROBLEMS

It is uncharacteristic for children with ADHD to exhibit severe problems in one situation but be relatively free of problems in other situations. However, the number and severity of problems a child exhibits is frequently determined by the demands placed upon the child by the environment; as discussed in earlier chapters, it is common for children with ADHD to experience more problems in one situation than another, as reflected in differing parent and teacher complaints. In fact, researchers have suggested that situation-specific symptoms may be a more accurate way of defining childhood disorders (Offord et al., 1996).

Frequently, children with ADHD have more difficulty in school than at home when school is more demanding and restrictive. On the other hand, especially among younger children, some demonstrate minor problems at school but have difficulty at home due to their inability to meet parental expectations. The working definition requires consistent observation of problems in at least 50% of common situations in the home, school, and community; the problems do not have to be identical. The practitioner may wish to use Breen's data (see Chapters 7 and 8) to make statistical comparisons to a normative sample concerning the severity of situational problems; though these data are a number of years old, they are still valid.

Interpretation of the actual number and severity of situational problems within the home must be based on the practitioner's assessment of parents' expectations and disciplinary style. At one extreme, the overly rigid, unrealistic parent may report a significant number of situational problems for a child with fairly mild attention and impulse difficulty. At the other extreme, the unstructured, possibly ADHD parent may report very little difficulty with a severe ADHD child because the parent, due to his or her own temperamental problems, is quite indulgent and makes little effort to structure or set limits. There are also parents that naturally or intuitively are able to understand the ADHD child's incompetencies and adapt their expectations and parenting style to meet the child's abilities. Frequently, these parents will acknowledge the severity of their child's problems but report few situational difficulties given the manner in which they manage the child. Often, asking parents to compare the child to siblings or same-age peers reveals that the parents understand the degree of their child's disabilities but have restructured their expectations and strategies to reduce the severity of problem behavior.

Recently generated research suggests that in regard to adolescent psychopathology there are clear advantages for clinicians to obtain a consensus opinion across multiple situations involving multiple raters, especially for externalizing disorders (Cantwell, Lewinsohn, Rhode, & Seeley, 1997). In this study involving 14- to 18-year-olds, excellent agreement between parents and adolescent self-report was found for CD; good agreement was found for separation anxiety disorder, ADHD, ODD, and substance abuse/dependence. Interestingly, poor agreement was found for the internalizing disorders, including major depression, dysthymia, most anxiety disorders, and bipolar disorder. Thus, if practitioners are interested in searching only for disruptive disorders, it may not be necessary to talk to the adolescent; but for ascertaining the occurrence of or risk for internalizing disorders, practitioners must elicit self-report information from the adolescent.

S. Campbell (1993) suggests that understanding the developmental and family context in which children's behavior occurs can be significantly helpful in the diagnostic process. Campbell writes that it is important to consider the severity, frequency, and exact nature of problem behaviors, the constellation of co-occurring problems, and their chronicity. It is also important to consider whether problems are apparent across different settings and with different caregivers.

V. DIFFERENTIAL DIAGNOSIS

Given the very high comorbidity of problems ADHD children experience, it is essential to screen for symptoms consistent with these comorbid problems in the history and questionnaire data.

Disruptive Problems

Oppositional Defiant Disorder

It is not surprising that a large percentage of children with ADHD develop a pattern of oppositional behavior. Their behavior frequently does not meet the expectations of the adults in their lives; thus, they are prone to receive a great deal of negative feedback concerning the inadequacy or inappropriateness of their behavior. This feedback is often in the form of punishment or negative reinforcement, neither leading to improvement. Eventually, this pattern of feedback leads to frustration and an attitude on the part of the child to oppose or push back. Often, parents initially perceive much of their child's behavior as stemming from purposeful opposition; closer scrutiny frequently reveals that for most children with ADHD, this behavior results from inability to conform rather than planned opposition. It would be rare that a child placed in such a position would not develop some pattern of oppositional attitude or behavior. Over time, poor fit between the child's competencies and parental expectations leads to further inappropriate parental demands and escalating punishment. The result is an angry, frustrated child who may become negative, provocative, and oppositional with parents and other authority figures.

Temperamentally, some children are more difficult to manage: children with a strong need to control are more likely to engage in power struggles with authority figures and to develop a repertoire of oppositional behaviors. Thus, not all children with ADHD develop oppositional defiance; as discussed in earlier chapters, however, the overlap in clinic-referred populations is usually over 50%. It is likely that for the majority of children with ADHD, their impulsivity precedes the development of their oppositionality. Thus, a pattern of preexisting oppositionality is not a condition for these children but likely develops over time as a result of the unique aspects of the ADHD child's interactions with the environment.

Symptoms of ODD include negative, provocative, spiteful, and vindictive behavior as well as a general pattern of purposeful noncompliance, anger, and projection of blame that exceeds the behavior of most children. A number of these criteria are frequent descriptions of children with ADHD; further, because many adults misinterpret the ADHD child's problems as resulting from purposeful misbehavior, they may report that a number of these other criteria have been met. A careful review of the child's history will often yield an etiology strongly suggesting that attention and impulse problems preceded and represent a significant cause of the child's oppositional behavior. Thus, it is not surprising that in this group of children, when stimulants are effective, the majority of oppositional defiant symptoms fade away. It is also important to recognize that it is rare for a child with ODD only to present sufficient behavioral, situational, and objective data to meet the criteria for ADHD.

Conduct Disorder

It is not surprising that there is a significant overlap in the presentation of ADHD and CD, as discussed in Chapter 3. Even ten years ago, S. Shapiro and Garfinkel (1986) determined the prevalence of CD combined with ADHD as 3% in an epidemiologic population. Symptoms of CD include significant aggression, theft, cruelty, sexual activity, destruction of property, and truancy.

As with ODD, some of the milder CD symptoms are frequently seen in children with ADHD. Their impulsivity may lead them to steal, lie, or engage in other impulsive behaviors such as initiating physical fights when frustrated. Although the diagnostic system is polythetic, it is important to recognize that meeting three of the milder symptoms for CD is very different from meeting three of the more significant symptoms. Again, because the nonthinking, impulsive, and nonpurposeful behavior of many children with ADHD is often perceived by adults as planned, it would be easy for a number of their behaviors to be misinterpreted. The seriously conduct-disordered child or adolescent is destructive and aggressive; they herald malicious forethought consistently when they engage in activities designed to hurt others for their own gain.

As with ODD, it is important for the practitioner to recognize that, especially in clinic-referred samples, at least 30% and possibly as many as 50% of children with ADHD will progress to CD. As discussed in earlier chapters, ADHD operates as a catalyst with environmental factors, principally those related to family, fueling the development of CD. Careful history often reveals that for the majority these children, ADHD symptoms preceded CD. Practitioners must be sensitive to those children demonstrating ADHD symptoms and CD before age 10, as this likely presents a more severe variant or hybrid of the combined disorder with a much worse prognosis.

Although researchers have agreed that it is difficult to generate laboratory test scores to differentiate CD from ADHD, behaviorally these disorders are very different (Hinshaw, 1987). Milich, Whidiger, and Landau (1987) suggested that in the environment, certain behaviors are more valuable as inclusionary, others as exclusionary diagnostic criteria, and some behaviors can be used both ways. For example, the presence of stealing strongly suggests CD, and its absence strongly suggests that CD is not present. Lying and suspension from school, however, are not distinguishing factors and occur frequently in CD as well as in ADHD. Not lying, however, appears to be an efficient symptom for ruling out CD. In this study, if the child did not lie it was highly unlikely that he was having serious conduct problems. Similar observation was made for setting fires. The authors point out that the absence of symptoms such as "doesn't listen," "acts without thinking," and "easily distracted" was useful in excluding the CD diagnosis. (For an in-depth review of disruptive disorders in children, the reader is referred to Goldstein, 1995.)

Although some authors suggest that measures of intellectual and academic skills help differentiate CD from ADHD (O'Brien et al., 1992; Semrud-Clikeman et al., 1993), others have not consistently found these measures to discriminate (Abramowitz, Lieberwitz, Hollander, & Fazzini, 1994). CD is defined by measurable, observable behavior over time, but laboratory tests offer a far less efficient means of identification of ADHD. Differential diagnosis between ADHD and CD using these tests is an insufficiently developed field to be of help to the practitioner. Practitioners are advised (Luiselli, 1991) that the assessment of disruptive problems should be targeted at understanding motivational determinants; these are clearly different for children with CD versus those with ADHD.

Nondisruptive Problems

Depression

As first noted by Weiss, Minde, Werry, Douglas, and Nemeth (1971) and Stanton and Brumback (1981) and discussed in earlier chapters, symptoms of ADHD have been reported in as many as 60% of depressed children. Complaints of sadness, helpless feelings, and poor self-image in children with ADHD are consistently reported by practitioners. However others (Jensen et al., 1988) have found that depression symptoms are commonly noted in children with ADHD, but the reverse is not as common. These authors went so far as to suggest that the more impulsive symptoms of ADHD, when they occur in the absence of inattention, may actually reflect problems with depression. The administration of depression rating scales and questions related to depression during the clinical interview and history should be considered routine parts of the assessment.

A diagnosis of *DSM-IV* major depression must include five of nine symptoms present during a two-week period representing a change in previous functioning. These are important differentiating criteria for the practitioner to consider. The majority of problems the ADHD child experiences are chronic and persistent; on this basis alone, most ADHD children will not be considered to experience a single-episode major depressive disorder unless there is an acute change in their presentation. Also, using these criteria, it would be rare for the majority of children with ADHD to present with recurrent major depression, as the primary criterion for this disorder involves two or more major depressive episodes, each separated by at least two months or more of usual functioning, whereas the majority of children with ADHD present chronic problems. Characteristic symptoms of ADHD that overlap with depression include sleep problems, irritability, hyperactivity, impulsivity, and difficulty with concentration. For a diagnosis of depression, at least one of the symptomatic problems must be depressed mood or loss of interest or pleasure. Symptoms of depression include depressed mood most of the day every day, diminished interest or pleasure in most activities, a decrease in appetite and weight loss or weight gain, insomnia or hypersomnia nearly every day, physical agitation or retardation nearly every day, fatigue or loss of energy nearly ever day, feelings of worthlessness or guilt nearly ever day, a diminished ability to think or concentrate or indecisiveness every day, and recurrent thoughts of death or suicidal ideation.

Dysthymia

This represents what many consider to be a milder, more chronic form of depression. Symptoms of low self-esteem, lack of confidence, feelings of inadequacy, pessimism, and hopelessness are all symptomatic descriptions of dysthymia. Because an individual has to meet only three symptoms, it would not be surprising for practitioners to determine that a significant minority of children with ADHD also experience minor dysthymia. Symptoms must be present for at least one year in children and adolescents and reflect depressed mood or irritability for most of the day and occurring more days than not. During depressed periods, additional symptoms include generalized loss of interest in pleasurable activities, social withdrawal, chronic fatigue, feelings of guilt or brooding, subjective feelings of irritability or anger, decreased activity or productivity, and difficulty with concentration, memory, or decisiveness. (For an in-depth review of depressive disorders in children, the reader is referred to S. Goldstein, 1995; Stark, 1990; and Compas, Ley, and Grant, 1993.)

The *DSM-III-R* noted that in children and adolescents, ADHD could be a predisposing factor for dysthymia. Dysthymia is also often observed to begin with a clear onset and a chronic course. However, the practitioner should be cautioned that the diagnosis is further complicated by the fact that dysthymic children may exhibit confrontive, negative behavior toward others and be poorly motivated and inattentive at school.

Manic-Depressive Disorder

Bipolar disorder or manic-depressive illness may occur in children at a much higher rate than previously thought (Wozniak & Biederman, 1994). Differentially, the practitioner should consider the possibility of manic-depressive illness when the referred child demonstrates wide mood swings for no apparent reason, lengthy periods of unhappiness followed by periods of elation, and extremely intense, angry tantrums that may go on for long periods. Family history is also essential in considering the diagnosis of manic-depressive illness, as more often than not, one parent has experienced a pattern of bipolar disorder diagnosed or undiagnosed. Practitioners should keep in mind that bipolar disorder is episodic, usually has its onset after age 12, and reflects problems with affect regulation, involving abnormal mood and mental excitement reflecting a marked change from baseline functioning (AACAP, 1991).

Based on a review of the literature, it has been suggested that there is a subgroup of children with ADHD who have prodromal bipolar disorder (Glasser, 1995). Adult bipolar patients as a group report a higher than expected rate of ADHD symptoms in childhood. Parents in which bipolarity exists also appear to have a higher rate of children with ADHD symptoms. Grigoroiu-Serbanescu et al. (1989) report that 21% of their sample of children with bipolar parents had ADD with hyperactivity, compared to 7% in the control group. Kestenbaum (1979) found that 38% of high-risk children of bipolar parents had learning problems with depressed mood, 15% with behavioral problems, and 8% were hyperactive. Wozniak, Biederman, Kiely, et al. (1995) argue that the picture of ADHD in manic children is much more severe, with greater symptoms and aggressivity. Nieman and DeLong (1987) suggest that the Personality Inventory for Children is successful in differentiating mania from childhood ADHD. This instrument correctly identified 100% of the subjects with mania, whereas 20% of the subjects with ADD with hyperactivity were incorrectly classified as manic-depressed.

Those with manic-depressive illness all had a significant family history of affective disorder and a high rate of aggression and, as reported by others, were severely maladjusted from an early age (Hassanyeh & Davidson, 1980). As Puig-Antich (1980) has reported, these children also appear to be frequently delinquent and antisocial as they enter their adolescent years. In fact, Good (1978) suggested that the primary sign for mania in childhood is aggressive, hostile behavior rather than elation, euphoria, or cheerfulness. Hostility and aggression may emerge only when a manic individual's activities are thwarted (Sheard, 1971; Tupin, 1972). Brent et al. (1988) reported that adolescents who completed suicide had higher rates of bipolar disorder with comorbid ADHD than did a group of adolescents who attempted suicide. It is important to note that in children with mania and those with ADHD, similar scores are often reported on the Conners parent and teacher rating Hyperkinesis Indices (Fristad, Weller, & Weller, 1982). However, a mania rating scale (Fristad et al., 1982) has been found to discriminate between the two groups. As Milberger et al. (1994) have noted, one can retain the diagnostic status for both mania and ADHD after removing overlapping symptoms. The significant comorbidity between ADHD and mania, even after adjusting for the fact that some symptoms are shared by the two disorders, points to the need for caution in making the two diagnoses when symptoms of each are present. It is likely that some children with mania have ADHD and children with ADHD have a higher risk to develop mania than others.

Anxiety Disorders

Worrisome thoughts and fears generally referred to as anxiety appear to be common in childhood. These thoughts and fears change and diminish in severity and occurrence as children grow older. Thus, the practitioner must evaluate the possibility of anxiety from a developmental perspective. Symptoms of childhood anxiety often manifest across a number of dimensions involving physical, behavioral, and cognitive components (Lang, 1968). Physical or physiological components are generally considered to reflect activity in the autonomic nervous system which, among its other roles, is responsible for regulation of internal body functions. Symptoms of perspiration, stomach pain, and trembling can be suggestive of anxiety (Barrios & Hartmann, 1988; Strauss, 1988). Anxious children have also been reported as being cognitively inefficient in managing their worries; they may be anxious because they lack the cognitive skills to deal with a particular situation and so manage anxious responses inefficiently (Kendall, Stark, & Adam, 1990). The *DSM-IV* criteria contain separation anxiety disorder as a distinct entity of childhood, but the diagnosis of generalized anxiety in children is now found along with the adult criteria. Among the anxiety disorders clinicians need to inquire about during history and assessment are separation anxiety, avoidant disorder, obsessive-compulsive disorder, panic disorder, posttraumatic stress disorder, and simple phobias. It is beyond the scope of this text to review the diagnostic criteria for each of these. (The interested reader is referred to S. Goldstein, 1995, for an indepth discussion of each of these disorders as they present in childhood.)

ADHD and posttraumatic stress disorder are frequently reported among children exposed to traumatic stressors (K. Fletcher, 1994). Prevalence of ADHD among traumatized children has been suggested to be between 20% and 43% (Earls, Smith, Reich, & Jung, 1988; Famularo, Kinsherff, & Fenton, 1992; Zamvil, Wechsler, Frank, & Docherty, 1991). It may be difficult for the practitioner to determine if symptoms of

ADHD arise secondarily as the result of posttraumatic stress disorder due to abuse, especially when the abuse is of a protractive nature. Famularo et al. (1992) have gone so far as to suggest that temperamentally difficult children may actually provoke abuse in high-risk situations.

Life Adjustment Problems

The practitioner should always keep in mind that hyperactive, inattentive, and impulsive symptoms are the most common in childhood and can in fact be driven by stress. Significant changes in family functioning, a geographic move, attendance in a new school, divorce, loss of a family member, or medical problems represent significant life issues; when they significantly impact and effect a change in a child's life, they can subsequently cause changes in children's behavior. For the practitioner, the key is to determine the child's functioning prior to the onset of the specific stressor. Practitioners should be cautioned that it may be difficult to provide differential diagnoses for young children experiencing significant early life stressors, when ADHD may represent a pattern of symptoms secondary to life stress rather than a problem of temperament. In such a situation, the practitioner must keep in mind that etiology is not required in the diagnosis of ADHD. If symptoms are met, the child should be provided with a diagnosis; however, the child's current problems and the treatment plan are certainly impacted by this pattern of early life history.

There are multiple adjustment disorders listed in the *DSM-IV*. Their primary feature reflects a maladaptive reaction to an identifiable psychosocial stressor or stressors that occur within three months after the onset of the stressor and persist. The diagnostic criteria include impairment in school functioning, social activities, and relationships with others. Symptoms can vary but are in excess of what is normal and expected. The disturbance must not be one instance of a pattern of overreaction to stress. Diagnostic criteria for an adjustment disorder also indicate that the disturbance usually does not meet the criteria for any specific mental disorder. Adjustment diagnoses can include those with anxious or depressed mood, disturbance of conduct, physical complaints, withdrawal, academic inhibition, or emotional factors.

In response to the stress of school, many children with ADHD develop a repertoire of mixed emotional symptoms. Frequently, these problems are not strong enough in presentation or severity to warrant diagnoses of depression, anxiety, opposition, or conduct disorders but appear to meet the diagnosis of an adjustment disorder if ADHD is considered a factor that must be adjusted to. The *DSM-IV* criteria note that in some cases, so long as the stressor is present it would not be surprising for the individual to experience chronic problems of maladjustment. For many children with ADHD, adjustment problems are frequently cyclical and do not actually represent a single instance in a pattern of overreaction to stress. More accurately, these problems represent the number of forces acting upon the child and the child's ability to meet the demands of the environment. Summer brings fewer demands, and thus many children with ADHD function better then. They begin school and after a number of months of failure, demonstrate increasing emotional difficulty. Once school ends, they again have a period of relative freedom and decreased demands; in response, their emotional difficulties diminish.

By definition, adjustment disorders do not present a pattern of chronic disability. It is therefore rare for a child experiencing only adjustment problems to present a history of ADHD on a long-term basis. As with many other disorders of childhood, children with ADHD experiencing adjustment disorders stemming from a specific stressor, such as death in the family or a move to a new home, usually present with a preexisting pattern of ADHD symptoms. The adjustment difficulties arise from the new demands placed upon the child and the child's inability to meet those demands.

Among medical factors associated with ADHD, the most common appears to be head trauma; as such, there is a strong likelihood that practitioners will be faced with children presenting ADHD symptoms as a consequence of head injury. Although it has been suggested that children with mild head injury presenting in mental health centers do not experience symptoms any different from children without head injury, nonetheless, they still present (Max & Dunisch, 1997). It has been observed that children with mild attention and arousal problems are at risk to develop a full-blown pattern of difficulty with these behaviors following head trauma. It is important for the practitioner to rule out the contribution of a specific neurological trauma in the development of the ADHD child's problems. If trauma appears to be the source of attention and arousal problems, the practitioner must make additional effort to provide a well-documented overview of attentional skills, situations, and problems. Frequently, children with ADHD-related problems stemming from head trauma present a checkerboard pattern of attention difficulty, in which certain attentional skills are not affected and others are significantly impaired. For many head-injured children, problems with speed of information processing and concept formation contribute to inattentiveness. Often, this population of traumatically induced ADHD exhibits significantly high levels of over-arousal and behavioral problems; such children are often an enigma to their parents and teachers. For such children, a careful evaluation is essential to define problems and facilitate treatment planning.

As explained in Chapter 5, the practitioner, with input from the child's physician, must make certain that ADHD symptoms are not primarily caused by a specific physical or neurological abnormality. It is rare for such a problem to be the cause of ADHD. Nonetheless, a thorough medical evaluation is important to allow the physician to rule out these potential contributing factors. A variety of medical conditions can also affect cognitive performance; for example, children with epilepsy have been reported to demonstrate a nonspecific profile of weaknesses on neuropsychological tests (Aldenkamp, Alpherts, Dekker, & Overweg, 1990).

Behavioral and emotional disturbances have also been described at length in the visually impaired (D. Warren, 1984). In some literature, these children have been described as hypoactive and passive, mimicking ADHD inattentive type. In the case of those who have had parenting problems, visually impaired children have been described in contrast as hyperactive and disruptive (Jan, Freeman, & Scott, 1977). Schnittjer and Hirshoren (1981) identified three aspects of behavior among 104 visually impaired residential school students: conduct problems characterized by aggression; personality problems involving anxious, withdrawn behavior; and immaturity involving short attention span and distractibility. These authors hypothesized that the attentional problems were secondary to other behavioral difficulties. Heinze, Helsel, Matson, and Kapperman (1987) examined seventy-five visually impaired children and young adults from 9 to 22 years of age in a day school and residential setting. Elevated scores of aggression, delinquency, hyperactivity, hostility, and withdrawn behavior were noted on four standardized checklists. However, the overall profile did not appear to differ significantly from a comparison with a nonvisually impaired population. (A thorough review of ADHD in regard to visual as well as hearing impairments can be found in Ultmann & Kelly, 1991.)

Learning/Developmental Problems

Language Difficulty

Research by L. Baker and Cantwell (1987) suggests that as children with significant speech and language problems mature, a significant percentage, as high as one-third, appear at risk to develop patterns of inattention and overarousal. Many of these children develop this pattern of behavior in response to the stress and frustration that arises as a result of their difficulty communicating.

The emergence of complex language skills coincides with a child's improvement in self-control. As verbal abilities improve, children are able to more effectively process information and express their needs: language becomes a substitute for action. When language development is abnormal, the development of behavioral control is potentially disrupted. Many parents and clinicians do not understand the connection between language development and a child's behavioral self-control. Children with language impairments are frequently placed in situations where their ability to respond appropriately is compromised, not because of a lack of motivation or an attention deficit but because of specific language disability. When parents and teachers inadvertently continue to pressure the language-disordered child to conform behaviorally, a chronic pattern of behavioral, attention, and arousal-level problems may develop. Parental frustration over the child's inability to follow directions may lead to anger and exaggerate the language-impaired child's level of frustration, which leads to characteristic temper tantrums.

In the preschool years, more subtle and complex language impairments frequently go unrecognized by parents and many professionals. Frequently, the child's misbehavior ends up being the focus of treatment, resulting in interventions directed at symptomatic behavior rather than the underlying cause of that behavior. As the public's awareness of overarousal and attention problems in children increases, it is likely that the practitioner will be asked to evaluate a young child by a parent who believes that the source of the child's overarousal and attention problems stems from ADHD. Even behaviorally disordered children with clear-cut histories of speech and language problems are frequently thought to be "hyperactive" without any consideration that their behavioral problems might arise from language disability. The errant focus on the source of the child's problems precipitates a frustrating cycle of interventions that may be misdirected. It is important for practitioners to recognize that delayed or deviant language development can lead to a wide range of behavioral problems, including symptoms mimicking ADHD.

Differential diagnosis for both young and older language-impaired children is difficult. When preschool children experience both language and attention difficulty, the practitioner may be unable to clearly determine which disability came first. With these preschoolers, it is judicious to initially assume, unless the history strongly suggests otherwise, that a significant component of the child's attention and overarousal difficulty stems from specific language impairments. For such children, the focus and intervention must initially be language-based, providing professional remediation and parent training. Such children must be monitored closely as they enter school. Many 2- and 3-year-olds with significant language problems accompanied by serious temper outbursts improve significantly in behavior when an appropriate course of language intervention is provided.

With school-age children, language-processing impairments are significantly more subtle and may be difficult for the practitioner to detect. The frustrated language-impaired child presenting symptoms of attention deficit is frequently not significantly hyperactive. Although, based on parent or teacher ratings, the child may receive elevated attention deficit scores, he or she usually performs well on objective measures of attention. Characteristically, these children present as significantly weaker on tasks of auditory and verbal attention, as opposed to tasks of visual or perceptual attention. Their verbal subtest scores on the Wechsler are frequently lower than their performance scores.

As children mature, those with pragmatic disorders may appear increasingly more inattentive. Pragmatics refers to grammatical factors that govern the choice of utterances in particular settings (Crystal, 1987); such skills include appropriate use of eye contact, turn taking in conversation, topic maintenance and change, intonation and loudness of voice, and the use of facial expressions and gestures. Given this description, it is not surprising that, due to their impulsiveness, children with ADHD may be at greater risk for or appear to experience a higher incidence of pragmatic disorders. Speech pathologists routinely measure pragmatic skills as part of a comprehensive assessment. Practitioners are also increasingly developing materials to improve pragmatic abilities, including those that directly address remediation (E. Johnston, Weinrich, & Johnson, 1984). If the practitioner suspects problems with pragmatics or semantics, a thorough speech and language evaluation should be considered.

Auditory Processing Dysfunction

Efficient operation of the auditory system involves not only adequate acuity and the collection of auditory information but the efficient capacity to transmit, decode, and integrate signals received along the aural pathway. Impairment in the auditory processing system can result in poor auditory attending skills, deficits in discrimination, limitations in auditory memory and retrieval, and delays in receptive and expressive language development. An overlap in symptoms of ADHD inattentive type and central auditory processing problems has been found (Moss & Sheifele, 1994). These authors suggest that children with the inattentive type of ADHD should routinely be screened for central auditory processing problems.

In a home or classroom setting, children with specific auditory processing dysfunctions related to attention and memory may appear to present many of the same symptoms as the attention-disordered child without hyperactivity. These children rarely become overemotional and are not terribly impulsive. Other family members may experience similar disorders. These children usually have normal hearing acuity but poor auditory association, retention, closure, discrimination, and recall. They may or may not have more observable speech and language disorders, such as articulation difficulty.

Memory Problems

Norman (1969), in his excellent text on memory and attention, notes that all paths of human processing lead to memory. Attention is the initial step in the process. Children with attentional problems will not process as much information and therefore will not have the opportunity to store and recall that information. Attention-disordered children may then appear to have memory deficits. Conversely, children with memory disorders but intact capacity to pay attention may, based on their poor recall, be accused of faulty attentional skills. Differential diagnosis can be a difficult process.

Memory, much like attention, is an extremely complex process that is used in all of our interactions with the environment. Psychology has not yet developed a widely accepted, comprehensive model of memory processes and specific types of memory skills. We make a rough distinction between auditory and visual memory, as well as between immediate, short-term, and long-term memory. Memory is frequently inferred by a child's performance on a variety of auditory, visual, and motor tasks. Children with memory difficulty, but not attention problems, will present with lower scores on attention-related behavior checklists and minimal situational problems. They usually perform well on tasks of persistence, sustained attention, and divided attention. For example, on tasks such as the Detroit Auditory and Visual Attention Span Tests, the child with impaired memory will consistently recall just so many stimulus items and consistently demonstrate the ability to recall the first few and last few items in each presentation; this reflects a serial position learning effect. Conversely, the ADHD child will be very inconsistent in performance, for example, demonstrating the ability to recall a sequence of five stimulus items one moment, but only two or three the next moment. In objectively making the differential diagnosis from memory problems, the Wide Range Assessment of Memory and Learning (W. Adams & Sheslow, 1990) and the Test of Memory and Learning (C. Reynolds & Bigler, 1994) can be utilized.

Achievement Problems

The *DSM-IV* lists a group of four academic skills disorders: reading disorder, mathematics disorder, disorder of written expression, and learning disorder not otherwise specified (APA, 1994). All four qualified as reflecting standardized test data presenting substantially below what is expected based on age, intellect, and age-appropriate education. The disturbance must interfere with the child's academic achievement. If the individual experiences a sensory deficit, the learning disability must not exceed that which would be predicted based on the sensory deficit. The *DSM-IV* also contains a developmental coordination disorder diagnosis, reflecting weak larger fine motor skills that interfere with academic achievement or activities of daily living.

When examining underlying skills that contribute to academic achievement, it is helpful for the practitioner to possess a basic model. Two broad groups of causes for learning disabilities appear to exist:

1. Those that involve auditory/verbal processes resulting in reading disorders and other language-based learning problems.
2. Those that involve visual and motor (nonverbal) processes resulting in poor handwriting difficulty with mathematics and deficits in certain social skills.

Table 10–1 contains a model for conceptualizing these skills in a two-by-two grid that examines auditory and visual skills on rote (simple) and conceptual (complex) levels. Table 10–2 provides descriptions of these processes and sample behaviors. Some children struggle to master basic foundational academic skills due to auditory, visual, or automatic-rote problems. Other children are capable of learning to read, but when the curriculum begins to accelerate in second grade and they must read to learn, they struggle due to conceptual weaknesses. The former may be related to language, memory, and auditory processing problems; the latter may be related to more specific cognitive deficits, as reviewed. (The interested reader is referred to S. Goldstein, 1995; Ingersoll & Goldstein, 1993; and Goldstein & Mather, 1998, for an in-depth review of this model.)

Language-based learning disabilities represent the majority of children presenting with problems in school settings. The visual-motor and nonverbal learning disabilities are less often represented, with estimates of 1% to 10% of children referred for learning problems (Pennington, 1991; Rourke, 1989). This type of learning disability is at

Table 10–1. Categories of academic skills

	AUDITORY/VERBAL				VISUAL/MOTOR			
C O N C E P T U A L	Verbal Conceptual				Visual/Nonverbal Conceptual			
R O T E / A U T O M A T I C	Auditory Motor	Auditory Perceptual	Rote Auditory/ Sequential Memory	Rote and Association Memory and Retrieval	Letter Perception	Spatial Organization and Nonverbal Integration	Rote Visual/ Sequential Memory and Retrieval	Motor Sequencing/ Fine Motor Control

Source: Ingalls, S. Copyright 1991 by the Neurology, Learning and Behavior Center. Used with permission.

Table 10–2. Levels of processing related to learning disability/disability characteristics

	Auditory/Verbal	Visual/Motor
C O N C E P T U A L	—language semantics—word meaning, definition, vocabulary —listening comprehension—understanding and memory of overall ideas —reading comprehension—understanding and memory of overall ideas —specificity and variety of verbal concepts for oral or written expression —verbal reasoning and logic	—social insight and reasoning—understand strategies of games, jokes, motives of others, social conventions, tact —math concepts—use of 0 in +, −, ×; place value, money equivalences, missing elements, etc. —inferential reading comprehension, drawing conclusions —understanding relationship of historical events across time; understanding science concepts —structuring ideas hierarchically; outlining skills —generalization abilities —integrating material into a well-organized report
A U T O M A T I C	—early speech—naming objects —auditory processing—clear enunciation of speech, pronouncing sounds/syllables in correct order —name colors —recall birthdate, phone number, address, etc. —say alphabet and other lists (days, months) in order —easily select and sequence words with proper grammatical structure for oral or written expression —auditory "dyslexia"—discriminate sounds, esp. vowels, auditorily blend sounds to words, distinguish words that sound alike, e.g. mine/mind —labeling and retrieval reading disorder—perceives aud. and vis. okay but continually mislabels letters sounds, common syllables sight words (b/d, her/here) —poor phonic spelling —poor listening/reading comprehension due to poor short-term memory, especially for rote facts —labeling and retrieval math disorder—trouble counting sequentially, mislabels numbers (16/60), poor memory for number facts and sequences of steps for computation (e.g., long division) —recall names, dates, and historical facts —learn and retain new science terminology	—assembling puzzles and building with construction toy —social perception and awareness of environment —time sense—doesn't ask, "Is this the last recess?" —remembers and executes correct sequence for tying shoes —easily negotiates stairs, climbs on play equipment, learns athletic skills, and rides bike —can execute daily living skills such as pouring without spilling, spreading a sandwich, dressing self correctly —using the correct sequence of strokes to form manuscript or cursive letters —eye-hand coordination for drawing, assembling art project, and handwriting —directional stability for top/bottom & left/right tracking —copy from board accurately —visual "dyslexia"—confused when viewing visual symbols, poor visual discrimination, reversals/inversions/transpositions due to poor directionality, may not recognize the shape or form of a word that has been seen many times before, i.e., "word-blind" —spelling—poor visual memory for the non-phonetic elements of words

Source: Ingalls, S. I. Copyright 1991 by the Neurology, Learning and Behavior Center. Used with permission.

times referred to as reflecting a right hemisphere deficit. This group of children frequently experience problems with spelling, dysgraphia, graphomotor problems, and a somewhat slow, passive cognitive tempo (Gross-Tsur, Shalev, Manor, & Amir, 1995). Children with visual-motor learning disabilities, not surprisingly, are often described as poorly coordinated for large and fine motor skills and possess sloppy handwriting; the latter is a complaint often echoed by parents and teachers of children with ADHD. Due to their lack of organizational and follow-through skills, they may also be described by teachers and parents as passively inattentive. Although they may possess well-developed rote verbal memory ability, they experience a great deal of difficulty adapting to new or complex situations. These children often experience difficulty with handwriting, mathematics (not due to difficulty learning basic math facts or reversals, but due to problems conceptually understanding math processes), social skills deficits, and internalizing emotional problems (Weintraub & Mesulam, 1983). Children with Tourette's Disorder have been suggested as experiencing a nonverbal learning disability. Brookshire, Butler, Ewing-Cobbs, and Fletcher (1994) reported that children with Tourette's demonstrate poor performance on visual-motor and written arithmetic tasks with better word-reading and spelling skills.

General Intellectual Deficits

Because attention is a complex process in the brain, it is not surprising that children with intellectual deficits experience attention-related problems. The more intellectually impaired a child is, the more likely it is that the entire brain is dysfunctional and the greater difficulty there will be with related skills such as attention span. For this population, difficulty with attention is a symptom of faulty intelligence. Such children will present with elevated scores on attention-sensitive behavior checklists, multiple situational problems, and difficulty on objective measures of attention and reflection, and may, on a superficial level, meet the *DSM-IV* diagnostic criteria for ADHD. The majority of these children, however, do not experience primary attention deficit. When their behavior and test performance is compared to their mental age, they do not present with problems significantly different from other intellectually handicapped children. However, there are some intellectually handicapped children who, even when this comparative adjustment is made, continue to appear to have attention and overarousal problems that are significantly greater than other children of their chronological age and cognitive skills. This small population of intellectually handicapped children may be experiencing significant attention problems relative to their overall cognitive abilities. Although treatment for the attention difficulty must be approached with caution, this population of children may benefit from stimulant medications and behavior management to improve on task behavior.

For the practitioner, differential diagnosis of intellectual deficit versus ADHD is based on a careful history, which may demonstrate a long-standing pattern of developmental delays present before the observation or onset of attention- and arousal-related problems. Considering the child's mental age also assists in making the differential diagnosis.

MAKING THE DIAGNOSIS OF ADHD

The risk of false diagnosis is minimized when a systematic approach is utilized. The two biggest problems facing the practitioner in making the diagnosis of ADHD occur when it is difficult to clearly rule out alternative etiologies and when the data do not consistently suggest ADHD. Because ADHD is a common disorder of childhood, it is more likely than not that the majority of children experiencing emotional, learning, or cognitive problems with concomitant symptoms of ADHD have presented with foundational attention and impulse problems prior to or in conjunction with these other difficulties. As discussed, it is not uncommon for children with ADHD over time to be at great risk to develop other disruptive disorders in the face of frustration and certain environmental variables. Further, children with ADHD have a higher lifetime risk for depression and anxiety and a higher occurrence of learning disability than unaffected children. Case studies to follow will describe not only these coexisting problems but other less frequently encountered problems that are reported to occur with a diagnosis of ADHD. Practitioners should keep in mind that for more cases than not, the issue will not be whether a child's symptoms reflect ADHD or another disorder, but whether the child's symptoms reflect ADHD *and* another disorder.

The practitioner is cautioned that the diagnostic checklist is meant as an organizational tool, not a normative or score-based checklist upon which to *make the diagnosis of ADHD.* Practitioners, not checklists, make diagnoses. Use of this checklist, however, provides the practitioner with a solid framework to consider the diagnosis of ADHD in childhood and adolescence.

Werry (1993) suggests that the term diagnosis is used in different ways but usually implies a process of defining what problems present so as to allow the application of professional knowledge. Although there are critics of the accuracy of the diagnostic process for ADHD (Prior & Sanson, 1986), there is much evidence that at least moderate reliability across diagnosticians can be obtained in regard to the ADHD diagnosis (J. Anderson et al., 1987; Horn, Wagner, & Ialongo, 1989; Lahey, Pelham, Schaughency, et al., 1988; Reeves et al., 1987). Practitioners should keep in mind that the diagnosis of ADHD, based on the premises and model under which the diagnostic nomenclature was developed, must be made first and foremost on clinical symptomatology and historical grounds (Werry, 1993). As discussed, information from checklists and behavioral observations offer valuable data; this can also be said of clinical and laboratory measures. But in the end, "it is up to the diagnostician to decide which data are relevant, how to weigh them and how to aggregate them into a final judgment" (Werry, 1993, p. 143).

A number of authors have suggested the sequence of questions practitioners must ask themselves as data are evaluated in the diagnostic process. A sampling of these are presented below. Practitioners may find one or some particularly useful. It is recommended that at least one set of these questions be considered as part of the diagnostic process.

DuPaul and Stoner (1994) suggest that clinicians must ask themselves the following five questions:

1. Does this child exhibit a significant number of behavioral symptoms based on parent and teacher report?
2. Does the child exhibit symptoms frequently, that is, greater than demonstrated by children of the same gender and age?
3. At what age does the child begin evidencing these symptoms, and are they chronic or acute, presenting in one or more situations?
4. How does this child fare socially?
5. Do other problems related to emotions or development possibly account for ADHD symptoms?

M. Gordon (1995) suggests six questions practitioners should ask:

1. Is there clear evidence of an impulsive style as well as symptoms of inattention and hyperactivity?
2. Is there evidence these symptoms significantly interfere with the child's functioning at home and at school?
3. Did these symptoms have an early onset?
4. Have the symptoms been enduring and consistent in the child's presentation across time and situation?
5. What evidence is there that these problems are not solely the consequence of other psychiatric or developmental difficulties?
6. Is there evidence these symptoms are joined by other problems?

M. Gordon (1995) also cautions practitioners that diagnosis is not just an intellectual exercise: it determines the logic that will underlie treatment. Gordon also notes that all diagnostic decisions inevitably involve a mixture of clinical and objective judgments. He cautions that diagnostic errors are caused by insufficient data gathering and a neither/nor rather than integrative decision-making process. Finally, Gordon notes that the competence of the diagnostician is based more on quality of thinking than on quantity of degrees.

Schaughency and Rothlind (1991) review the available literature on assessment of ADHD and suggest four key questions that must be asked by practitioners:

1. Does the child meet the *DSM* criteria?
2. Are there alternative explanations for the symptoms?
3. Are the symptoms developmentally inappropriate?
4. Do the symptoms impair the child's functioning?

These authors offer a framework of methods and assessment tools to answer these questions; their suggestions appear in Table 10–3.

S. Goldstein (1994) suggests a diagnostic decision tree utilizing the following questions:

1. Does this child exhibit thoughts, feelings, affect, physical symptoms, or behaviors that are different in type or frequency than expected for the child's age and developmental level?
2. Can these behaviors be dichotomized into those that are disruptive versus those that are nondisruptive?
3. Do these problems fall best into a less commonly occurring childhood disorder (e.g., autism)?
4. Within each of the disruptive and nondisruptive groups, do these problems fall primarily into one *DSM-IV* diagnostic category?
5. Are there sufficient symptoms within a specific diagnostic category to warrant a diagnosis?
6. How do the various symptoms interact?
7. How do the various diagnoses interact?
8. What explanations are available to explain this child's presentation?

THE WRITTEN REPORT

It is essential for the practitioner to organize, present, and summarize all of the data collected in the process of evaluation. The depth and format of the written report are matters of individual preference, but the report should include a summary of the developmental history; analysis of parent and teacher questionnaires; presentation and interpretation of available objective data, including an interview with the child; a synthesis of the accumulated data in the diagnostic impression; and recommendations. For

Table 10–3. The multi-method assessment of ADHD

Assessment Question	Method	Possible Device/Tests
1. Does this child meet the DSM-III-R diagnostic criteria for ADHD?	Structured diagnostic interview with multiple informants	Diagnostic Interview for Children and Adolescents (DICA/DICAP)
		Diagnostic Interview Schedule for Children (DISC/DISCAP)
		Schedule for Affective Disorders and Schizophrenia for Children (K-SADS)
		Interview Schedule for Children (ISC)
		Child Assessment Schedule (CAS)
2. Does an alternative diagnosis or conceptualization account for his/her difficulties (Differential Diagnosis)?	Structured diagnostic interview Other tests as appropriate (e.g., IQ, Achievement) Information on developmental course and onset	Same as 1 Tests of cognitive ability, norm-referenced achievement tests, curriculum-based assessment, tests of adaptive behavior Developmental history
3. Does this child display these behaviors to a developmentally inappropriate extent (for children with Mental Retardation, compared to developmental level)?	Behavior rating scales with multiple informants	Child Behavior Checklist (CBC) Comprehensive Behavior Rating Scale for Children (CBRSC) Revised Behavior Problems Checklist (RBPC) Conners Parent and Child Rating Scales (PRS/TRS)
4. Do these behaviors impair the child's functioning in the school, in social relations, and/or in the home?	Behavior rating scales with multiple informants Sociometrics Archival data—referrals, grades, classroom performance, etc.	Same as 3 See Hops & Lewin (1984)

Source: Schaughency, E. A., & Rothlind, J. (1991). Assessment and classification of attention deficit hyperactivity disorders. *School Psychology Review, 20,* 187–202. Copyright 1991 by the National Association of School Psychologists. Reprinted by permission of the publisher.

some practitioners, this results in a report of two to three pages; for others, the report can be ten pages or more. Although longer reports may not be read carefully by other practitioners, for those who do read them the data presented often facilitate insight into the child's history and functioning and the process by which the practitioner drew diagnostic conclusions and made recommendations. Regardless of the length of the report, it is this document that the practitioner uses to explain and transmit his or her impressions to parents, teachers, and other professionals. It is this document that will remain as a record of the evaluation and a standard against which to compare the child's future functioning. Increasingly, it is this document that is used by schools, higher education, and even federal agencies to make critical decisions in children's and adolescents' lives.

Some practitioners provide lengthy treatment recommendations. Often, these recommendations, due to their specificity, may be unwanted by other professionals or teachers; for example, classroom recommendations that do not fit within a particular teacher's style and classroom structure stand little chance of being implemented. It is recommended that the practitioner, unless very familiar with the receiver of treatment recommendations, provide general recommendations concerning the basic treatment model. These focus on improving the child's interest in completing required tasks, as well as his or her motivation through consequences for completing tasks that cannot be made more interesting or less repetitive. These interventions are then implemented through manipulation of environmental factors. Such interventions include a structured environment with clear rules and consequences for following or breaking them, use of response cost, greater one-on-one learning opportunities, and a reduction in length of assignments. Recommendation of texts or programs encompassing this model offer a better resource than a brief list of suggested interventions.

The practitioner should communicate to parents and other professionals a willingness to provide specific assistance if that assistance is requested and if the practitioner is given an understanding of the system in which recommendations will be implemented.

It is recommended that parents be provided with a copy of the evaluation report. Practitioners must be willing to share with parents the majority of information and impressions they relay to other professionals. Additionally, in some situations, parents may wish to have certain information deleted from the evaluation report before granting permission for it to be released to schools or other community agencies.

Latham and Latham (1995) suggest that when assessments are to be used for legal purposes, such as to advocate for services under the Individuals for Disability Education or Americans with Disabilities Acts, written reports should clearly delineate that diagnoses are based on history, interview, testing, and clinical observations. The written assessment should state whether the impairment substantially limits one or more of the individual's major life activities, including thinking, concentrating, and interacting with others. Documentation should be supported by citations to authoritative sources, specifically *DSM-IV* or the *International Classification of Diseases*. Latham and Latham (1995) note that a document designed to provide legal support for diagnosis differs from a document designed to provide structure for an intervention program. (The reader interested in structuring assessment reports for legal purposes is referred to Latham & Latham, 1995.)

EXPLAINING THE DIAGNOSIS AND TREATMENT RECOMMENDATIONS TO PARENTS

Making the diagnosis is a critical part of the evaluation. Helping parents understand the specific problems their child is experiencing and the implications of the diagnosis is even more important, because this provides a critical link between diagnosis and intervention. Helping parents see the world through the eyes of their child and understand the reasons for and causes of the child's difficulties facilitates the process of beginning treatment. It allows parents to play an active role and helps them make appropriate treatment decisions for their child.

Unless parents are helped to be active participants, even the best diagnoses may not yield compliance with recommendations for treatment. If parents, educators, physicians, and therapists do not understand the diagnostic process, the means by which the diagnosis was determined, and the reasons certain treatment recommendations should be followed, compliance will likely be decreased. Because ADHD is a disorder that cannot be cured and must be managed throughout the child's life span, it is important to reiterate that first, parents must understand the disorder. Practitioners must spend sufficient time with the child's parents summarizing the collected data, highlighting consistencies and inconsistencies within the data, defining the means by which the diagnosis was made, identifying the behavioral characteristics of the diagnosis, and explaining the rationale for treatment and recommendations. Practitioners should also focus on what is right; that is, they should spend a reasonable amount of time discussing the child's assets. It is through their assets that human beings learn to manage their liabilities. Practitioners must recognize that the best predictors of outcome for a child with ADHD lie within the child's social frame of reference rather than within the child himself or herself. Parents must be helped to recognize that the most powerful predictors of positive adult outcome for children with ADHD include parents who are competent, develop a warm relationship with their child, are available, take an interest in the child's education, bolster the child's self-worth, and meet the child's physical needs. Parents should not be provided with guilt as a motivator, but rather with an understanding that as long as the balance between stressful life events and surrounding protective factors is favorable, children with ADHD stand a significantly better chance of entering adulthood successfully. Parents' ability to see the world through their child's eyes exerts a significant impact on their daily interactions with the child.

The practitioner may find it helpful to explain test data to parents by placing the child in specific situations and explaining how the child's weaknesses, impulsivity, or other skill problems compromise his or her ability to function in and meet the demands of that setting. *A day in the life of your child* is often a helpful way of explaining this to parents. For descriptive purposes, the hypothetical example of Allen will be presented below. The example describes the impact Allen's disabilities are having on his ability to function at school.

> The assessment data have revealed that Allen is extremely intelligent and was able to initially use his intelligence to compensate for his inattention and lack of persistence in kindergarten. He began having increasing problems in first and second grade.

The assessment data we collected suggest that Allen has difficulty with vigilance, which means he has trouble waiting or being ready for the teacher to present important information. He also has trouble with selective attention and even after a task is presented, he may have difficulty selecting this task as important and settling down to work. He also has problems with persistence and does not stick to tasks until they are completed. We have also discovered that he has difficulty effectively manipulating a pencil. Even when he pays attention and knows what to do and gets down to task, it is harder for him to write his work on the paper neatly and efficiently. During a spelling test, for example, even when he is paying attention to the teacher, knows what word is to be spelled, and how to spell the word, it takes him longer to get it written down on the paper. By that time, the teacher may have gone to another word or Allen may become frustrated and not finish spelling the word correctly. These problems appear related to his impulsivity. In a situation where choices must be made, he tends to choose the path that is going to involve the least effort and the choice that initially seems most attractive. He does not stop and use his intelligence to carefully consider each choice and make the best choice.

Socially, Allen's inability to plan, difficulty compromising, and inability to stop and think about the consequences that his behavior may have upon his peers have resulted in delayed development of social skills and, over time, social isolation. A pattern of negative reinforcement has resulted in Allen's not only having difficulty remaining on task due to his temperament but also being reinforced for beginning tasks but not for completing them. Given these attention and arousal-level problems, it is not surprising that despite adequate intellect and ability to learn, Allen is experiencing significant difficulty fitting into the school setting.

Such a description not only helps parents understand the extent and nature of their child's problems, but ties those problems to specific situations, which then allows the practitioner to describe a model for intervention and specific strategies that may be of benefit.

In many cases, it may appear to parents that ADHD is a diagnosis of exclusion (Hurley, 1994). Therefore, practitioners must take the time to help parents understand the diagnosis and its ramifications. This issue will be discussed further in Chapter 16.

SUMMARY

This chapter synthesized and integrated a model for collecting data and considering important factors for making the diagnosis of ADHD as well as comorbid problems. The practitioner is directed to use a multifaceted diagnostic procedure, including *DSM-IV* criteria, data from behavioral and situational questionnaires, and objective assessment. It is important for the practitioner to consider emotional, developmental, cognitive, and medical factors as alternative or contributing causes to ADHD symptoms. The ADHD diagnostic checklist is provided to summarize and facilitate the diagnostic process. A series of diagnostic questions and gates is recommended, due to the complexity of ADHD symptoms, the occurrence of many of these behavioral problems as the result of other disorders of childhood, the co-occurrence of other disorders with ADHD, and the likelihood that the use of a single data point will result in a high number of false positive diagnoses.

Chapter 11

DEALING WITH THE DATA:
CASE STUDIES

The most helpful approach for understanding the complexity of ADHD and comorbid problems, integrating the data, making the diagnosis, developing a treatment plan, and assessing progress is through case studies. Specific cases follow describing children with ADHD, ADHD and comorbid problems, as well as problems that masquerade as ADHD. The greatest risk practitioners face today is making the diagnosis of ADHD based on a narrow theoretical scope, limited review of the data presented, or an inappropriate emphasis on specific elements of historical, behavioral, or test data to the exclusion of other relevant data.

D. M.—ADHD COMBINED TYPE

D. M., a 12½ year-old male seventh-grader, was referred due to a history of inattentive and organizational problems. One of D. M.'s siblings had been diagnosed with ADHD. Neither of D. M.'s parents, both college graduates and one a physician, reported a history or family history of ADHD symptoms. D. M. was described as curious and into things as a toddler. By 3 years of age, he became more difficult behaviorally. A year earlier, a pediatrician's diagnosis of ADHD resulted in a brief trial of Ritalin, which appeared beneficial but was discontinued when the summer began. D. M. was described as a very pleasant child by his parents despite his difficulty responding consistently to consequences, impulsivity, disorganization, and inattentiveness.

Parent responses to questionnaires placed D. M. in the borderline clinical range for attentional problems. On the Conners questionnaire for the Hyperkinesis Index, parent responses placed D. M. in the worst 2% without medicine and in the average range with improvements noted last year when medicine was initiated. Within the home setting, D. M. was noted to have mild to moderate problems across most situations. Teacher questionnaires were based on D. M.'s presentation without medication; he was noted as being inattentive and restless in most classes. A review of group achievement data placed D. M. in the average range, with excellent mathematic skills.

During the assessment, D. M. related well to the examiner. He was emotionally stable and motivated to perform. His work style was occasionally inconsistent. D. M.'s performance on the Wechsler Intelligence Scale yielded a verbal IQ of 115, performance IQ of 95, and full-scale IQ of 106. Clearly, D. M. possessed much better verbal than nonverbal skills. However, his performance on nonverbal tasks was hampered by his impulsivity and difficulty with strategy. The quality of his performance did not appear to reflect perceptual weakness as much as impulsivity. On the memory battery, this pattern was further exemplified, with D. M. demonstrating very poor strategic learning skills. In contrast, his performance on the Peabody Picture Vocabulary Test, a measure of receptive vocabulary, was at the 82nd percentile, while his performance on the Test of Non-Verbal Intelligence, a reasoning task with figures, was at the 70th percentile. On both of these measures, the examiner provided firm limits and structure before D. M. was allowed to respond. D. M.'s performance on the Conners computerized measure reflected difficulty sustaining attention and managing impulses. Academic screening placed D. M. in the high average range. D. M. was a fluid, efficient reader; although at times he read too quickly, his comprehension was well above his grade placement. His pattern of impulsivity resulted in his not being particularly efficient on tasks requiring planning and reflection.

D. M.'s responses to depression and anxiety questionnaires yielded scores within the normal range. During the clinical interview, D. M. was responsive and open with the examiner. He appeared aware of his attentional and impulse problems. He presented as someone with a moderate level of sensitivity to the needs of others and reported a reasonable degree of satisfaction with himself and personal well-being.

D. M.'s history and current functioning appeared consistent for the combined type of ADHD. Rating scales completed at home and school were consistent for this profile, with very few comorbid symptoms reported. Objective data also reflected this pattern. For D. M., idiosyncratically impulsivity appeared to exert a significant negative impact on his performance of tasks requiring reflection and planning. Problems were noted situationally within the home and school. In Scouts, D. M. was also described as impulsive. From a differential diagnostic perspective, D. M. did not demonstrate other symptoms of disruptive or nondisruptive problems. His family was supportive and stable. From a developmental perspective, it was determined that weak test scores in light of above-average academic achievement appeared to be a function of impulsiveness rather than reflecting a developmentally based learning disability.

D. M.'s physician reinitiated the stimulant medication, and significant improvements were reported by parents and teachers. D. M. met briefly with a counselor and was provided with a number of resources concerning attention problems in adolescents. The goal was to increase D. M.'s active participation in the treatment process. D. M.'s parents were provided with additional resources concerning ADHD in adolescents. It was also recommended that D. M. participate in a creative writing class the following summer. D. M.'s educational team was provided with a copy of the assessment as well as additional resources concerning classroom strategies for adolescents with ADHD. It was recommended as well that D. M. be closely monitored as he made the transition to high school.

G. T.—ADHD COMBINED TYPE

G. T., a $9\frac{1}{2}$ year-old male fourth-grader, was referred due to a history of impulsive and reported inattentive problems. G. T.'s family history was positive for similar problems in his father. His mother reported a lifetime history of mood disorders. Two nephews on her side of the family had received diagnoses of ADHD.

G. T.'s early developmental milestones were reached within normal limits. However, he continued to be nocturnally enuretic. He also had a history of recurrent otitis media.

G. T.'s home behavior was described as hyperactive, impulsive, and inattentive. He enjoyed Scouts and completed Scout activities without prompts or support. G. T.'s parents had developed a fairly strong pattern of negative reinforcement as a means of managing his behavior within the home setting. G. T.'s entrance to school was followed by immediate complaints of restless and hyperactive behavior. G. T.'s grades were adequate because he didn't experience specific learning problems. However, each year teachers commented about his problems completing work without significant prompts and support.

Questionnaires completed by G. T.'s parents placed him above the 95th percentile for the attention problems scale and above the 98th percentile on the Conners Hyperkinesis Index. A pervasive and consistent set of mild to moderate home situation problems were noted. Socially, G. T. was described as happy-go-lucky but impulsive. Questionnaires completed by G. T.'s teachers noted that he learned quickly but worked slowly. G. T. was described as disruptive in the classroom in nonpurposeful ways. Teacher ratings placed G. T. below the 10th percentile for attention span and below the 5th percentile for hyperactivity on the Comprehensive Teacher's Rating Scale. He was described as rarely working well independently and being rather overreactive, impulsive, and restless. Although G. T. was described as having social problems, his teacher noted that he did not appear mean nor cruel.

Interestingly, group achievement tests completed when G. T. was in kindergarten placed him, based on national percentiles, at the 99th percentile for prereading skills, 88th percentile for mathematics, 82nd percentile for general knowledge, and at the 95th percentile in the overall battery. Subsequent testing in second grade yielded above-average scores but not in the top 20th percentile.

G. T. presented as a child of normal size and appearance. He was emotionally stable. With feedback and structure, he demonstrated good ability to adjust his mildly impulsive work style. Though slightly fidgety, he was not hyperactive during the two-hour assessment.

On the Wechsler, G. T. obtained a verbal comprehension factor at the 82nd percentile and perceptual organization factor at the 63rd percentile. Careless, impulsive errors appeared to result in the lower perceptual organization score. G. T.'s verbal reasoning skills were exceptionally good. His visual-motor skills were rated as above average. On the Conners continuous performance test he demonstrated a pattern of inconsistency, resulting in an abnormal score.

In a clinical interview, G. T. was open and responsive to the examiner. He described a normal range of emotions. He did not acknowledge specific symptoms reflecting anxiety nor unhappiness. G. T. appeared to have a reasonable understanding of the problems he experienced at school, explaining to the examiner that he may not be as smart as other people because "I don't stop and think."

Diagnostically, G. T.'s history, behavior, and current symptoms appeared consistent with the combined diagnosis of ADHD. The decline in G. T.'s achievement scores did not appear to be explained by specific developmental weaknesses consistent with learning disability. A brief screening of G. T.'s word-reading skills yielded a score at the 90th percentile, suggesting that as he progressed through school, the majority of achievement grades likely reflected his effort at the time rather than his true achievement. G. T.'s parents were directed to a parent training program for children with ADHD; they were also provided with additional parenting resources. G. T.'s educational team structured a 504 plan centering on a response-cost daily reinforcement system. G. T. was also provided with additional information concerning impulsiveness in children. He participated in a university-based research program designed to improve problem-solving and conflict resolution skills for impulsive children. Finally, G. T.'s physician, upon review of the assessment and with the consent of G. T.'s parents, initiated a trial of stimulant medication. Over a three-month period, marked improvements in G. T.'s school, home, and interpersonal behavior were reported.

R. S.—ADHD COMBINED AND OPPOSITIONAL DEFIANT DISORDER

R. S. was an 8½ year-old male entering third grade. He was referred due to a history of inattentive behavior and an escalating problem of social and school performance problems. R. S. was an only child. There appeared to be some history of impulsive behavior on his mother's side of the family. Both parents were college graduates.

R. S. was described as an extremely busy, active toddler. His medical history reflected frequent otitis media, until his tonsils and adenoids were removed at 6 years of age. In kindergarten, although R. S. appeared to keep up academically, he had difficulty completing work independently and sticking with group activities. He was attending a private school program with a small classroom, which afforded the teacher more time to provide assistance. His teacher noted that he had "lots of energy." Within the home setting, R. S. was described as fidgety, restless, and impulsive. Over the past year, he had become increasingly more noncompliant, including not responding appropriately to disciplinary interventions. Rewards were reported as not particularly effective in modifying R. S.'s behavior.

Behavioral checklists completed by R. S.'s parents placed him in the clinically significant range for attention problems and delinquent and aggressive behavior. In addition to his inattentiveness, R. S. was described as lacking guilt, being argumentative, disobedient, and stubborn, and having temper outbursts. To assist the family, R. S.'s physician had attempted a brief trial of stimulant medication prior to the end of the second-grade school year. R. S.'s parents completed the Conners questionnaire, reporting on R. S. with and without stimulant medication. On the Hyperkinesis Index, his score was in the clinically significant range without medicine but, based on parent report, on the weekends with medicine he dropped into the normal range. Situationally, R. S. was described as having problems in the home and community settings.

R. S.'s second-grade teacher also reflected the improvements at the end of the school year when stimulant medication was added. She noted that despite his impulse and inattentive problems, R. S. was a pleasant child and was not particularly disruptive in the classroom. Even without stimulant medication, he was able to work independently, but the quality of his work often reflected his impulsiveness. R. S.'s teacher clearly liked him, describing him as a bright child with "an excellent range of ideas."

During assessment, R. S. was pleasant and cooperative. He had been provided with a single 10 mg. dose of Ritalin approximately one and a half hours before the start of the two-hour assessment. Although his affect was a bit flat, he was neither anxious nor emotionally labile. R. S. related well to the examiner.

R. S.'s performance on the Wechsler Intelligence Scale yielded a full-scale IQ at the 98th percentile. Interestingly, despite 95th percentile or above cluster factor scores, R. S.'s freedom from distractibility factor was only at the 61st percentile. Clearly, R. S. was functioning in the superior range intellectually. Performance on a number of memory tasks reflected his inconsistent approach to strategies as tasks began but generally good memory skills over time. His performance on the Conners computerized measure was completed approximately three hours after R. S. received his morning dose of medication. Even with medication, R. S.'s performance on this task was somewhat inconsistent, demonstrating problems in changing response speed depending on the length of time between stimulus items. Academic screening suggested generally intact, though certainly below his level of intellect, academic skills. R. S.'s weakest skills, not surprisingly, were on early academic tasks requiring practice for proficiency. He was a good phonetic but poor sight-memory speller, had good conceptual math skills but made careless errors, and demonstrated good ideas when writing but poor execution.

R. S.'s responses during the clinical interview and to structured self-report measures did not reflect any atypical emotional patterns.

R. S. very clearly met the ADHD combined type diagnosis. Rating scales from home and school consistently reflected impulse and attention problems, with improvements noted with the short-term trial of a stimulant medication. The disruptive behaviors reported on parent but not teacher questionnaires appeared to reflect a pattern of increasing demands and R. S.'s inability to meet those demands within the home setting. Objective case data, even that obtained while R. S. was receiving stimulant medication, consistently reflected his impulsive tendencies. Situationally, problems were noted within the home and school. From a differential diagnostic perspective, R. S. had developed some oppositional symptoms, which appeared at the time of assessment to cross the threshold for a diagnosis of ODD. The pattern, however, appeared tied to R. S.'s impulsiveness and his parents' increasing negative efforts to force his compliance. From a developmental perspective, his academic skills, though above average, were not commensurate with his intellect, reflecting weaknesses consistent with lack of practice.

R. S.'s physician continued his stimulant medication as he began third grade. His adjustment and performance in third grade were exceptionally good. R. S.'s parents were provided with additional resources and strategies concerning behavior management for impulsivity in the home. His third-grade teacher was provided with additional strategies to involve him intellectually in the classroom. Finally, given R. S.'s rote academic weaknesses, it was suggested that in the following summer he become involved in a creative writing program.

S. G.—ADHD HYPERACTIVE-IMPULSIVE TYPE, LANGUAGE-BASED LEARNING DISABILITY, AND OPPOSITIONAL DEFIANT DISORDER

S. G., a 14-year-old female entering ninth grade, was seen for reevaluation. She had been initially evaluated at 9 years of age. At the time of the original assessment, she was found to be functioning in the low-average range intellectually, with a significant language-based learning disability. Her academic achievement was delayed. Her self-confidence and emotional adjustment were weak. Questions were raised about inattentiveness secondary to her learning disability or as a primary symptom suggestive of ADHD. It was recommended that S. G. be followed and worked with prior to considering additional diagnoses.

S. G.s family lived in a rural area. Though she continued to struggle at school, no further assessment was sought or requested. At the time of reevaluation, S. G. was referred due to an escalation of problems in her last year in junior high school.

S. G.'s siblings and family history were not indicative of learning or developmental problems. Over the previous four years, S. G. had continued to act in impulsive, disorganized ways. As the demands of school had increased, S. G. had become increasingly more noncompliant and had become involved with "a rough group of friends." She was described at home as defiant, provocative, and oppositional with her parents.

Parent questionnaires placed S. G. in the significant range for anxiety, depression, attention problems, and delinquent and aggressive behavior. Her profile was similar to that observed in previous years but reflected an escalation in disruptive and depressive symptoms. Situationally, S. G. was described as having a wide range of problems in the home, community, and school. Questionnaires completed by S. G.'s teachers consistently reflected poor attention span, hyperactivity, poor social skills, and, in at least half of her classes, defiance of authority. Teachers noted S. G.'s difficulty working independently; a number raised questions about her capabilities to complete required work in class.

Two years earlier, S. G.'s educational team had completed a reevaluation in school as part of her special education placement. S. G. had continued to be served as a learning-disabled student with speech and language problems. Her performance on the Wechsler Intelligence Scale yielded a full-scale IQ of 88. Academic assessment yielded scores between the 5th and 10th percentiles. Her performance on a language battery placed S. G.'s language skills at only the 5th percentile for adolescents of her chronological age.

S. G. was neatly dressed and well groomed. Her behavior was pleasant and appropriate with the examiner. S. G.'s performance on the Conners computerized measure reflected her impulsive style: she made a large number of commission and omission errors and demonstrated poor perceptual sensitivity. Her self-report on the ADHD behavior checklist placed her at the 98th percentile for complaints of inattentiveness, 75th percentile for hyperactive complaints, and the 95th percentile combined in comparison to a late adolescent–young adult population. In contrast, S. G.'s responses to anxiety and depression questionnaires placed her within the normal range.

During the interview, S. G. denied excessive feelings of depression or worry. She reported wanting to have a well-paying job but was uncertain about a specific vocational activity. She agreed that it had been difficult for her to stick to schoolwork and that she often did not understand the work requested of her at school. Clearly, S. G.'s personality and behavior had been shaped by her impulsivity. Her personality profile was consistent with adolescents who may be pleasant with casual acquaintances but, with those whom they have a more intense and enduring relationship, are often likely to be testy, irritable, and manipulative.

S. G.'s history and current functioning, taking into account her developmental problems, appeared consistent for a diagnosis of ADHD hyperactive-impulsive type. Although she met a number of the inattentive symptoms, the total number was below the six-symptom threshold. Clearly, over the years it was S. G.'s impulsivity that caused her primary problems. Her rating scale data at home and at school consistently reflected this pattern, as well as an escalating pattern of additional disruptive behavior. Objective data also reflected S. G.'s problems with poor impulse control. Situationally, S. G. clearly demonstrated problems in many home and school settings. From a differential diagnostic perspective, S. G.'s oppositionality had increased to the point where a diagnosis of ODD appeared warranted. She clearly did not experience nondisruptive problems. From a developmental perspective, S. G. continued to experience a fairly severe language disorder. Her rote language for label storage and retrieval as well as her sequential memory for short- and long-term information continued to be considerably weaker than her semantic language skills. S. G. continued to experience an auditory/verbal and visual/spatial sequential pattern of deficits; these impaired her academic development severely.

The examiner recommended that S. G.'s academic team closely monitor her progress and consider intensive support as she entered high school. S. G. was referred to her physician for a trial of stimulant medication. She was a motivated participant and interested in the trial. A trial of short-acting Ritalin yielded a significant improvement in S. G.'s classroom behavior. It was also recommended that S. G. work with a counselor to learn more effective assertive skills. Her parents were provided with a number of resources for parents of adolescents experiencing developmental and behavioral problems. Finally, it was recommended that S. G. be evaluated in depth during her junior year of high school, and plans were made to facilitate her post–high school vocational transition.

D. S.—ADHD COMBINED TYPE, OPPOSITIONAL DEFIANT DISORDER, AND VISUAL-PERCEPTUAL LEARNING DISABILITY

D. S., a 10-year-old male third-grader, was referred due to a history of impulsive and inattentive problems. His parents were also increasingly concerned about his oppositional behavior. There did not appear to be any history of attentional, learning, or oppositional problems in D. S.'s siblings or parents. D. S. was described as having a difficult toddler period reflecting a low emotional threshold and frequent temper outbursts; D. S. started school a year late for this reason. His teachers noted that he appeared to be falling behind academically and was inattentive and increasingly noncompliant, a pattern reported by parents at home as well. D. S.'s parents noted that they could "be on his case all the time."

Parent responses to questionnaires placed D. S. in the borderline clinical range for attention problems on the Child Behavior Checklist but in the clinical range on the Hyperkinesis Index on the Conners questionnaire. D. S. was described as distractible, inattentive, excitable, and restless. Situational problems were noted in the home and community. Teacher questionnaires noted that D. S.'s work was inexact and careless. He was described as below average in reading and very poor in math achievement. He was in the significant range for attention and hyperactive problems. Socially, D. S. was described as anxious in his interactions with others, and his behavior often resulted in others rejecting him because of his impulsive, disruptive interactions. D. S.'s past report cards indicated problems with work completion, inattention, and responsibility for work.

D. S.'s interaction with the examiner was appropriate. He lacked continuity of effort and perseverance as he worked. He was willing to attempt most tasks. He was slightly fidgety.

D. S.'s performance on the Wechsler Intelligence Scale placed him at the 18th percentile intellectually. Verbal abilities (30th percentile) were somewhat better than nonverbal skills (10th percentile). D. S.'s persistent trial-and-error approach without any attempt at strategy resulted in his lower performance subtest scores. He recalled meaningful verbal information quite well but was inconsistent in his ability to recall rote verbal information. His fine motor speed and coordination were quite poor. His reproductions of complex designs and handwriting were also quite poor, reflecting an approximate three-year delay in visual-motor-perceptive ability.

On the Conners computerized measure, D. S. was inconsistent and made a large number of omission errors. His performance was strongly indicative of inattentive and impulsive problems.

D. S.'s money skills were good, but his time-telling skills were poor. Academically, his word-reading skills were average. He utilized an almost exclusively phonetic approach to reading and spelling. His visual memory for phonetically different words was poor. His comprehension was limited when he read only by his poor decoding skills. His written story reflected poor written language skills despite reasonably good ideas.

D. S.'s responses to structured self-report measures and during the interview did not appear to reflect any significant signs of emotional problems. The quality of his responses and his insight reflected his history of impulsivity. He also appeared relatively well aware of his current problems and in response, had adopted a somewhat oppositional stance.

D. S.'s history and functioning appeared consistent for the combined type of ADHD. Home and school rating scales also consistently reflected ADHD problems. D. S.'s ability to work academically up to his potential and slight patterns of oppositionality combined with the escalating pattern of disruptive behavior at home. His presentation crossed the threshold for the diagnosis of ODD. Given D. S.'s struggles, it was not surprising that his self-esteem appeared somewhat weak. Objective data consistently reflected D. S.'s impulsive problems, as well as visual-perceptive weaknesses. Problems were noted across home and school situations. From a differential diagnostic perspective, oppositional defiant symptoms clearly followed rather than preceded symptoms of ADHD. D. S. was aware of his struggles but clearly was not depressed or excessively anxious. Visual-perceptive weaknesses further impaired D. S.'s ability to perform in school.

Based on the assessment, D. S.'s physician initiated a trial of stimulant medication, and a very positive response was noted during the following months in school. D. S.'s parents were provided with additional strategies to manage ADHD and oppositional defiant problems in the home setting. He initiated work with a counselor on a short-term basis to help him understand his strengths and weaknesses. D. S. continued his work with an academic tutor, focusing on strengthening his written language and math skills and his organizational and study skills. Consultation with an occupational therapist was also recommended to determine if exercises to improve visual-perceptive and fine motor abilities were warranted.

G. F.—ADHD COMBINED TYPE, OPPOSITIONAL DEFIANT DISORDER, ROTE LEARNING DISABILITY, AND EMOTIONAL DISTRESS

G. F., a 7-year-old male first-grader, was referred by his physician due to a history of impulsive, hyperactive, and oppositional behavior. G. F.'s parents had separated two and half years prior. G. F. had a good relationship with each parent. His mother had remarried. G. F. was often noncompliant and verbally abusive with his stepfather. Two older siblings had not experienced school or behavior problems.

From an early age, G. F. had been impulsive and hyperactive. His moods had cycled frequently. His medical history was uncomplicated. He had chronic problems settling down to sleep at night. Developmental milestones were reached within normal limits. G. F. had become increasingly oppositional at his mother's home. Parent responses to questionnaires placed G. F. in a clinically significant range for attention problems and delinquent and aggressive behavior. G. F. was consistently described by parents as impulsive, hyperactive, and inattentive. He demonstrated a range of situational problems. Socially, he was usually rejected rather than being neglected. He was noted as teasing, provoking, fighting, interrupting, and being argumentative and aggressive with others. Questionnaires completed by his educational team reported that G. F. appeared to have low academic self-confidence. Teachers too described his impulsive, inattentive, and hyperactive behavior. Past intellectual assessment placed G. F. in the average range with average academic skills. He had been classified at school as experiencing a behavior disorder and was receiving consultation and counseling with the school psychologist.

G. F. was somewhat controlling and passively resistant during assessment. Nonetheless, he worked with the examiner and did not demonstrate excessive behavioral problems. During a discussion of his family, G. F. became teary and distressed at his parents' divorce, expressing a desire for them to remarry.

Assessment data reflected G. F.'s average intellectual skills. His conceptual memory appeared quite a bit better than his rote memory abilities. He appeared to experience difficulty integrating multisensory information when learning. He was extremely impulsive, inconsistent, and somewhat noncompliant on a computerized measure of attention. His rate of reading appeared extremely slow, with poor sight-word recognition and inconsistent phonetics. Verbally and nonverbally on a conceptual level, he appeared quite bright. His impulsive temperament resulted in his not acting or performing at a level that he was capable of. He also experienced mild rote memory problems, especially for short-term memory. The quality of his speech and pronunciation of short vowels suggested that he experienced some type of auditory discrimination difficulty as well. He also was noted to have mild reversals and directionality problems beyond what would be expected for his age.

G. F.'s responses to self-report and anxiety and depression measures yielded scores within the normal range. Nonetheless, G. F. acknowledged getting mad easily at home and feeling that people did not like him. During the clinical interview, his primary focus was on expressing his anger concerning treatment by his parents and his unhappiness with their separation.

G. F.'s history and functioning met the combined type of ADHD diagnosis. Parent and teacher rating scales were consistent for ADHD, oppositionality, and some level of emotional distress. Objective data consistently reflected G. F.'s impulsive, at times noncompliant behavior. Situational data reflected a fairly consistent pattern of problems, with greater behavioral difficulty noted in his mother's rather than father's home or at school. From a differential diagnostic perspective, G. F. demonstrated a pattern of symptoms consistent with ODD. Although he was not depressed or anxious, he clearly was quite a bit more emotionally distressed, reflecting life adjustment issues secondary to family problems. From a developmental perspective, he demonstrated good verbal conceptual abilities but weaker rote verbal memory skills. These weaknesses appeared to have slightly delayed his academic achievement.

G. F.'s physician initiated a trial of stimulant medication, and a very positive response was reported at home and at school. His parents worked with a parent trainer and structured a consistent set of rules and consequences within each home setting. G. F.'s response to this was moderate. In his mother's home, he could be resistant enough to anger her and thus distract her from following through consistently. Consultation with G. F.'s educational team resulted in the development of a daily school report sent home, which was beneficial in providing his parents with daily feedback. G. F. also participated in individual academic tutorial after school, focusing on developing his phonetic skills and number fact knowledge. Finally, G. F. was seen in individual counseling to explore his feelings about parental separation and anger as well as teach him more assertive coping skills. For approximately a year, this combination of treatment yielded improvements, but continued behavioral problems were reported. After an approximate three-month period of not seeing a counselor, G. F.'s mother called. It appeared he had entered a major depressive episode, was refusing to get out of bed, was not eating, and appeared extremely morose and tearful. He was subsequently seen and a diagnosis of major depression was made. Due to the severity of his behavioral presentation, G. F.'s physician added a low-dose serotonin antidepressant. G. F. was seen in crisis counseling. After a month, his functioning had improved to baseline. Of significance, however, is the fact that after all of the interventions and time spent, G. F.'s mother and stepfather continued to be very angry at him, creating an atmosphere of emotional tension in the home regardless of G. F.'s behavior.

B. M.—ADHD COMBINED TYPE, OPPOSITIONAL DEFIANT DISORDER, POSTTRAUMATIC STRESS DISORDER, AND WEAK VERBAL SKILLS

B. M., an 11½ year-old female fifth-grader, was referred due to a history of school performance problems and an increasing pattern of delinquent behavior. B. M.'s life history was extremely complex. Her parents had never married. She was living at home with her mother, maternal grandfather, stepgrandmother, and 14-year-old half sister. She rarely saw her father. The family history on both sides was positive for depression, alcoholism, ADHD, and learning disability. At 5 years of age, B. M. was repeatedly molested by an adult male living in her apartment complex; the male subsequently was prosecuted and sentenced to prison. B. M. worked with a counselor for six months. In fourth grade, B. M. accused a 15-year-old brother of a friend of raping her; charges were not filed, and it was never clear what took place between B. M. and this person. B. M. was seen in counseling for four months at that time. The counselor described her as a chronic liar.

B. M.'s mother noted that she had done well in school until fifth grade, when she began having increasing academic and behavioral problems. In the home setting, she was described as hyperactive, impulsive, inattentive, and oppositional.

Parent questionnaires reflected clinically significant problems related to the social, thought, attention, delinquent, and aggressive behavior scales. B. M. was consistently described as impulsive, hyperactive, and inattentive. Situational problems were noted at home, and increasing problems noted in the community. B. M. had been caught stealing. Parent response to the parenting stress index yielded significant scores for general family stress and a very stressful relationship between B. M. and her mother.

A review of B. M.'s report cards revealed problems with poor self-discipline, impulsivity, and inattention beginning in kindergarten and continuing through fifth grade. Academically, however, teachers did not complain that B. M. appeared delayed. Questionnaires completed by B. M.'s teachers reflected consistent problems with inattention, hyperactivity, impulsivity, poor social skills, and an escalating pattern of defiant behavior with authority.

A review of school data, including a school psychology assessment, yielded conclusions that B. M. likely experienced an attention deficit disorder and increasing oppositional problems.

During assessment, B. M. appeared to lack confidence, but with support was willing to persist. She was occasionally fidgety and inclined to distrust her abilities. Intellectual assessment yielded a Wechsler verbal IQ of 90, performance IQ of 91, and full-scale IQ of 90. Memory skills reflected a fairly consistent pattern, with better conceptual than rote memory abilities. B. M. rarely utilized strategies as she attempted to learn new information. Receptive vocabulary was weak. Her performance on the computerized measure of attention reflected inattentiveness and impulsivity. Academically, B. M. appeared to be in the low-average range for reading and spelling but average in arithmetic. She read for accuracy a grade below her placement, relying on sight recognition and context to read. She tended to make insertion or omission errors. Her comprehension was at a level with her reading accuracy.

B. M.'s responses to self-report questionnaires suggested a significant degree of self-reported anxiety and a moderate degree of depressive complaints. She noted that she worried frequently and often felt nervous. She described somatic symptoms related to depression, including difficulty falling asleep, feeling fatigued, and not having much appetite. From an emerging personality perspective, it was clear that B. M.'s behavior was typified by variable and unpredictable moods, resentful irritability, impulsivity, and feelings of being cheated, misunderstood, and unappreciated. B. M.'s moods appeared unpredictable and impulsive. She appeared to lack skills to deal with frustration. She appeared extremely concerned about who she was and how others regarded her.

From an early age, B. M. had demonstrated symptoms consistent with the combined type of ADHD. Although she experienced an emotional trauma at age 5, the history suggested that she was a temperamentally difficult child prior to that time. Parent and teacher rating scales reflected not only problems with ADHD but symptoms related to oppositionality, increasing conduct difficulty, weak verbal skills, and emotional distress. Discussion with B. M.'s mother concerning her history suggested that she may well have experienced a period of symptoms consistent with posttraumatic stress disorder at a young age. It was clear that she did not meet the categorical diagnosis for posttraumatic stress at this time, but that her behavioral problems had escalated dramatically at age 5 for reasons attributed to sexual abuse. During the interview, B. M. also discussed recurrent thoughts of suicide. Her presentation appeared consistent for young adolescents experiencing dysthymia. Life adjustment issues reflected stress within the family and a long history of her having difficulty developing firm attachments and relationships to important adults in her life. From a developmental perspective, B. M. demonstrated average achievement and intellect. However, her slightly weaker verbal skills appeared responsible for her slightly below-average academic achievement. B. M. had traveled a long distance for evaluation; she was referred to a local counselor. It was suggested that although B. M. would not be a compliant counselee, she was in need of developing a therapeutic relationship, at least to deal with increasing conflicts within the home setting. B. M.'s physician was asked to review the assessment and consider stimulant medication as part of her treatment plan. B. M.'s educational team was provided with a copy of the current assessment. It was recommended that she be placed in a mentoring program for sixth grade and closely monitored as she entered junior high school the following year. B. M.'s mother was carefully counseled that the combination of B. M.'s emotional distress, ADHD, and increasing oppositionality at her age placed her at significant risk for developing more severe symptoms related to depression and delinquency.

A. S.—ADHD COMBINED TYPE, OPPOSITIONAL DEFIANT DISORDER, AND RIGHT HEMISPHERE WEAKNESSES

A. S., a 12½ year-old male seventh-grader, was referred by his physician due to a long history of multiple disruptive problems, apparent learning disability, and concerns about increasing emotional distress. A. S. was the second of three children. A younger sibling died at 7 months of age from Sudden Infant Death Syndrome. An older brother had a history of ADHD. ADHD also appeared prevalent in the childhood histories of both parents. Further, A. S.'s parents frequently disagreed on the best means of parenting their children.

As a toddler, A. S. was extremely active, easily distracted, and did not adjust to change well. He had difficulty settling down to sleep and sleeping through the night. Given a diagnosis of ADHD in second grade, A. S. was provided with a trial of stimulant medication, which led to reported improvements at home and at school.

Medication was discontinued two years later due to parental concerns that A. S. did not appear to be growing.

A. S. had a history of late-developing large and fine motor skills. He was described as uncoordinated. His handwriting was noted as poor. Problems in school presented in kindergarten, and by second grade A. S. was placed for a number of hours per day in a resource room due to disruptive behavioral problems. In junior high school, A. S. participated in a number of resource classes for academic support but otherwise was not receiving any additional assistance. He was reported to have a number of friends but was frequently controlling in social situations. At home, he was described as impulsive, inattentive, and continuing to be disruptive. His parents noted that he had a good imagination, was enthusiastic for activities he enjoyed, and had a "heart of gold."

Of interest was the fact that A. S. had been evaluated due to disruptive behavior as a preschooler. At that time, on an intellectual measure, he scored at the 97th percentile. He subsequently participated for a year in a therapeutic preschool program for children with disruptive behavioral problems. A psychiatric assessment when A. S. was 8 years of age yielded diagnostic impressions of ADHD, ODD, and concerns of bipolar affective disorder.

Questionnaires completed by A. S.'s parents placed him above the 98th percentile for the attention problems scale and at the 95th percentile of the social problems and delinquent and aggressive behavior scales. A. S. was also above the 98th percentile on the Hyperkinesis Index. He was described as failing to finish things, distractible, inattentive, excitable, impulsive, and restless. Multiple situation problems were also noted. Socially, A. S.'s parents described him as argumentative, negative, and bossy.

Teacher questionnaires noted A. S.'s difficulty completing work, following instructions, and controlling his impulses in all but two classes. In these two classes, math and history, A. S. was not described as a disruptive problem. Interestingly, he reported enjoying both of these classes. A. S.'s principal described him as extremely disruptive with authority. A. S. continued to be classified as behavior-disordered. His individual education plan noted that he had two resource periods. He had been referred multiple times during the school year for disruptive, noncompliant behavior.

A. S. presented as a slim, tall adolescent. He was cooperative, though his affect was somewhat flat. His work style was impulsive. At times he lacked continuity of effort and perseverance. With prompting, he was willing to exert reasonable effort on all tasks.

A. S. performed intellectually at the 19th percentile, with 32nd percentile verbal skills but only 14th percentile nonverbal skills. He struggled on visual-perceptive abstract tasks such as block design and object assembly subtests. He appeared to be a somewhat concrete problem solver, rarely generating sufficient strategies as he worked. On the Test of Non-Verbal Intelligence, his performance was below the 2nd percentile. A memory battery yielded a similar patter of relatively stronger verbal and weaker nonverbal skills. A. S.'s reproduction of the Rey Osterrieth Figure reflected a piecemeal approach; he had significant difficulty effectively integrating all parts of the figure. On the Conners continuance performance test, A. S. gave slower responses; as the evaluation progressed, he made a number of omission errors, was inconsistent, and demonstrated a change in response speed. Performance was consistent with adolescents described as impulsive and inattentive.

A. S.'s academic skills were noted by average word reading but below-average ability to read within context. He demonstrated poor spelling for the visual aspects of nonphonetic spelling and weak academic skills. He continued to have trouble efficiently telling time.

A. S.'s self-report measures did not suggest a significant degree of depression or anxiety. On the Millon, his profile was consistent with a group of adolescents exhibiting a history of impulsive behavior and resentful attitudes. Consistent with his increasing oppositional behavior, his response profile was consistent for adolescents strongly insecure about their self-worth and quick to take a defensive posture to counteract perceived humiliation. Adolescents with this profile consistent with A. S.'s behavior appear to be reinforced in their rebellious, defiant, and suspicious attitudes when punishment is provided. Tough, arrogant, and brash behavior is used to avoid responsibility as well as dampen unhappiness.

Diagnostically, A. S. demonstrated a long history and present symptoms consistent with a combined diagnosis of ADHD. Problems were noted across situations. From a young age, he had also demonstrated a pattern of provocative, annoying, spiteful, and vindictive behavior consistent with a diagnosis of ODD and placing him at risk for progression to more serious delinquent problems. A. S.'s pattern of intellectual and academic skills appeared consistent for adolescents with a history of relatively weaker right hemisphere skills, reflecting poor nonphonetic spelling, difficulty with mathematics achievement, and weak visual perception and processing skills. The examiner also raised concern that although A. S. denied depressive thoughts, his pattern of low emotional threshold, irritability, and escalating behavioral difficulties combined with the pattern of right hemisphere weakness strongly indicated his risk for developing a depressive disorder.

A. S.'s parents were provided with resources concerning negotiation and problem solving for parents and adolescents. A. S. was recommended for therapy and further psychiatric consultation concerning the possible benefits of medications. Unfortunately, he was unwilling to consider either intervention. He and his parents were referred to a family therapist to work out a set of guidelines for home problems. A. S.'s academic team was provided with a copy of the assessment and agreed to provide A. S. additional resources and support at home as well as attempt to locate activities at school that he enjoyed and that might increase his motivation toward academic activities. A. S. was also unwilling to consider additional academic tutorial to improve his basic academic skills.

D. G.—ADHD COMBINED TYPE AND
NEUROFIBROMATOSIS TYPE I

D. G., a 6-year-old male preschooler, was referred by his speech pathologist, who had been treating him for a phonological disorder. The pathologist noted that D. G. was extremely impulsive. When he was able to reflect, his phonological skills improved dramatically. Concerns were raised about his general behavior and pre-academic development.

D. G. was the youngest of four children; 16-year-old fraternal twins had not experienced developmental or behavioral problems, but a 12-year-old brother had received a diagnosis of ADHD. D. G.'s father had a childhood history of ADHD symptoms.

Despite an uncomplicated pregnancy and planned cesarean section, D. G.'s delivery was somewhat complicated. Questions were raised about placenta deterioration and fluid buildup around D. G.'s heart.

As a toddler, D. G. was described as wild. At 2 years of age, café-au-lait spots were diagnosed as Neurofibromatosis Type I. D. G. had a history of early-morning nausea, vomiting, and negative mood. He was nocturnally enuretic, had trouble settling down to sleep, and was an extremely restless sleeper.

D. G. began a private kindergarten but was extremely impulsive and disruptive and was removed after a few weeks. In the home, D. G. was described as impulsive, demonstrating poor self-control, with frequent temper outbursts and hyperactivity. He was described as stubborn, argumentative, defiant, and quick to anger.

Parent questionnaires placed D. G. above the 98th percentile on the Child Behavior Checklist for the scales of somatic complaints, attention problems, and aggressive behavior. He was above the 98th percentile on the Hyperkinesis Index. Situational problems were described as moderate in most settings. D. G.'s mother noted that her greatest concern was his increasing difficulty dealing with frustration, his anger toward others, and "his hyperactivity makes learning situations and home situations difficult."

During assessment, D. G. was rather controlling in the waiting room, insisting that the examiner wait until he finished reading a book before coming into the assessment. D. G. maintained and initiated conversation. He was unintelligible approximately 50% of the time. His syntax was poor. Nonetheless, D. G. loved to talk. He jumped from one topic to another. The quality of his vocabulary reflected age-level or better intellectual skills.

D. G.'s performance on the Wechsler Intelligence Scale yielded a verbal IQ at the 45th percentile but nonverbal IQ at the 4th percentile. He demonstrated reasonably good vocabulary and comprehension skills but very poor visual-perceptive skills; this pattern is consistent for children experiencing Type I Neurofibromatosis. They often experience delays in visual-perceptual abilities, attention, and organizational skills.

D. G.'s pre-academic skills appeared below the 1st percentile for his age. His play skills, with support, were near age-appropriate. Nonetheless, it was clear that D. G. was extremely impulsive and controlling.

D. G.'s developmental weaknesses were consistent with Neurofibromatosis. However, because he clearly met the combined criteria for ADHD, the second diagnosis was provided as well. D. G. also demonstrated a history of phonological weaknesses impacting articulation, and a strong controlling personality, which, combined with his impulsiveness, often led to disruptive, noncompliant problems.

D. G. continued in speech therapy with good progress noted. A trial of stimulant medication resulted in significant improvements in general behavior. He also began working with a pre-academic coach and entered kindergarten successfully. It was recommended that D. G. be closely followed due to the risk that the Neurofibromatosis could also impact later-developing conceptual skills.

L. J.—ADHD COMBINED TYPE, DEVELOPING ANTISOCIAL PERSONALITY

L. J., a 19-year-old male, had dropped out of school in the eleventh grade and was employed as a glass installer. He was asked to come to assessment by his parents with the hope that evaluation would motivate L. J. to return to school. L. J.'s family history was noted only by ADHD in a number of cousins. L. J. had a long history of difficulty, beginning in kindergarten, with inattentive behavior resulting in poor work completion. A review of his report cards reflected teacher comments of competent academics but poor follow-through. Teachers repeatedly described his short attention span, daydreaming, and difficulty applying himself. L. J. was described as having a large group of friends. He stopped attending church with the family a year earlier. He was reported as smoking tobacco and experimenting with alcohol and marijuana. L. J. and his girlfriend had had a child six months earlier; however, they were not living together nor were there any plans for them to be married. L. J. was providing financial support for the child. His parents were quite religious and distressed at his rejection of his religious values.

L. J.'s parents were asked to complete questionnaires describing L. J. as he functioned during his adolescent years. Their responses were consistent for difficulty with disruptive behavior, including delinquency and ADHD. He was described as distractible, inattentive, impulsive, and failing to finish things. Nonetheless, he was not noted as creating significant behavioral problems at home. L. J.'s responses to a young adult ADHD checklist was consistent for self-reports of difficulty with sustained attention, organization, and close attention to details, but not for complaints of impulsivity.

A review of L. J.'s academic group achievement testing was surprising. In eleventh grade, just prior to dropping out, L. J. was at the 92nd percentile for reading, 81st percentile for mathematics, 77th percentile for science, 73rd percentile for social science, and an overall academic battery placed him at the 78th percentile. He had completed a general adult testing battery a year prior, on which his skills measured at well above average. In contrast, his grade-point averages in junior high school and high school began in the C range and then showed a decline in performance and increase in failures.

L. J. presented as a well-groomed young adult. He had long hair, two small earrings in his left ear, and wore a baseball cap. He related well to the examiner. His thoughts were logical, focused, and relevant.

L. J.'s performance on an adult intelligence scale yielded a verbal IQ of 113, performance IQ of 114, and full-scale IQ of 114. Additional memory, verbal, and nonverbal measures placed him between the 75th and 90th percentiles. His performance on a computerized measure reflected slight problems with inhibiting impulsive responding. Self-report measures did not reflect complaints of anxiety or depression. During the interview, L. J. expressed his frustration about finding a direction in life. He also reported wanting to move out of his parents' home because of their different views concerning his friends and behavior. From a personality perspective, L. J.'s responses to the adult Millon and interview suggested someone who was unsentimental, independent of others, viewed obligations as not a high priority, felt rather superior, and would likely lack deep feelings of loyalty toward others. On an actuarial basis, the profile appeared most consistent with individuals experiencing an antisocial personality disorder.

Although L. J. had never been evaluated, his history and current functioning was consistent at the very least for the inattentive type of ADHD. A review of his history and reports of others resulted in the examiner's deciding the combined diagnosis was appropriate. Home rating scales were consistent for a history of ADHD and, to some extent, oppositional problems. Objective data reflected L. J.'s excellent intellect but continued difficulties with impulse control. From a differential diagnostic perspective, L. J. was extremely intelligent and advanced in his academic achievement despite long histories of poor school performance. He was neither depressed nor suffering from an anxiety disorder. The quality of his personality, however, suggested an emerging pattern of antisocial personality.

Because L. J.'s participation in the evaluation was at the request of his parents, it was not surprising that he did not return for a disposition visit nor take any other action after discussing the evaluation with his parents.

N. B.—ADHD COMBINED TYPE AND MILD MENTAL RETARDATION

N. B., a 6-year-old male, was referred by his physician due to questions concerning the differential diagnosis between symptoms of ADHD and delayed development.

N. B. was an only child. His parents denied a family history of developmental or behavioral problems. Pregnancy, labor, and delivery had been unremarkable. N. B. presented as a normal infant, though slightly difficult to comfort. As a toddler, he was somewhat active and did not pay attention well. He suffered from Rubella at 3 years of age. His development had been slow. He appeared to understand more language than he could spontaneously produce. His articulation was limited. Toilet training was delayed. N. B.'s parents thought he understood toileting skills but was resistant to toileting. He soiled on a daily basis, and he was nocturnally enuretic. N. B.'s large motor skills were described as good but fine motor skills poor. He had participated in a developmental preschool program beginning at 3 years of age. At the time of assessment, he was placed in a self-contained developmental kindergarten. N. B. was described as having poor attention span and being somewhat impulsive and quick to frustrate. His parents expressed their increasing frustration that what they initially thought was to be a brief developmental delay was quickly becoming a more pervasive pattern of slower development. They expressed concern as to whether N. B. would ever "catch up."

Parent responses placed N. B. at above the 98th percentile for the scales of attention and social problems and above the 95th percentile for aggressive behavior. He was described as being stubborn and having moods that changed quickly. He appeared above the 85th percentile on the Hyperkinesis Index. Situationally, problems of a mild to moderate degree were noted in most home and community situations. Socially, N. B. was described as rather awkward and at best engaging in parallel play. Parent responses to a developmental profile placed N. B. overall at an early 3-year-old level.

N. B.'s educational team provided copies of past testing and his educational plan. He was receiving one hour a week of communication therapy and two and a half hours per week of physical therapy in addition to the special kindergarten program. Assessment data placed N. B.'s pre-academic skills at a 36-month level. On the Stanford-Binet

Intelligence Scale, N. B. obtained a verbal reasoning score of 57, abstract reasoning score of 76, and test composite of 55 (mean = 100; s.d. = 15).

Teacher questionnaires placed N. B. above the 95th percentile on the Hyperkinesis Index. Situational problems were working independently and in small-group activities. N. B. was described as having difficulty understanding instructions and following through with tasks. This behavior was noted as being erratic, flighty, and at times scattered.

N. B. presented as markedly younger than his chronological age. Eye contact was appropriate. He chose to separate from his parents and accompany the examiner. His parents noted that N. B. attended speech therapy by himself and had been told this was going to be like a speech therapy visit.

N. B. was unintelligible approximately 30% to 50% of the time. He did not initiate conversation easily. He was generally calm but his concentration was limited, requiring significant support and encouragement from the examiner. He demonstrated no significant habitual mannerisms. He lacked continuity of effort and perseverance. It was difficult, however, to ascertain his level of logic, focus, or relevance and thought processes.

The Wechsler Intelligence Scale was administered as a structured set of tasks. N. B. obtained a verbal IQ of 47, performance IQ of 54, and full-scale IQ of 46. It was clear that his poor language skills exerted a negative impact on Wechsler performance. On the Peabody Picture Vocabulary Test, his performance was at a 2.5-year-old level. He held a pencil with a rather loose five-finger grip. Performance on the Developmental Test of Visual-Motor Integration yielded a 3.5- to 4-year-old level of visual-perceptive skills. N. B.'s play was also consistent for a 3- to 4-year-old. His behavior could be goal-directed; however, he did not appear to clearly understand how to stay engaged in goal-directed play. He was comfortable with the examiner at his developmental level.

Multiple sources of data consistently reflected N. B.'s delayed and slowly progressing pattern of general development. He also demonstrated symptoms consistent with the combined type of ADHD. However, provisional diagnosis was made given the very clear and at times difficult to discriminate interaction between N. B.'s attention and impulse control and marked developmental problems. It was clear, however, that he was not a disruptive behavior problem as the result of defiance but rather lack of self-control and developmental delay.

With the support of N. B.'s educational team, a trial of stimulant medication was initiated; and marked improvements were noted in his general behavior in preschool. N. B.'s parents were provided with additional resources. The educational team recommitted their efforts to work with N. B. By the close of the school year, his level of developmental delay resulted in referral to a self-contained program for children with intellectual handicaps.

S. P.—ADHD COMBINED TYPE, ROTE LEARNING DISABILITY, AND ANXIETY

S. P., a 7½ year-old second-grade male, was referred by his parochial education team due to a history of inattentive behavior and delayed reading skills. S. P.'s brother had achieved quite well in school. The family history was significant for attention deficit and anxiety. As a toddler, S. P. was described as extremely active, not handling changes well, having a low frustration threshold, but also being shy and hesitant with new people. Previous diagnoses of ADHD had resulted in a trial of stimulant medication, which was discontinued due to nausea, and a trial of Welbutrin, which was discontinued due to a severe allergic reaction. A recent trial of a second stimulant, Dexedrine, resulted in significant rebound irritability and emotional lability.

S. P.'s parents noted that he had required significant help at school from kindergarten forward. He was described as rejected by peers because he frequently lost his temper. In the home, he often had tantrums but at times also appeared quite anxious.

Parent responses to questionnaires placed S. P. in the clinically significant range on the Child Behavior Checklist for anxiety, depression, attention problems, and aggressive behavior. Even with medication, on the Conners, S. P.'s Hyperkinesis Index appeared above the 98th percentile. He was described as impulsive, inattentive, and hyperactive. Nonetheless, improvements were noted with a reduction in symptoms when stimulant medication was administered. Situationally, S. P. demonstrated problems in the home and community. Socially, he was described as lacking in social skills and experiencing "all emotions more deeply" than others.

Questionnaires completed by S. P.'s teacher noted improvements when he received stimulant medication. They also reflected his difficulty completing schoolwork and low self-esteem. S. P. was rated as below the 5th percentile on teacher questionnaires for attention span, hyperactivity, social skills, and oppositional behavior. He was described as not accepted nor in demand with other students, and as being overactive and noncompliant.

During assessment, S. P. appeared mildly anxious and gave up quickly. His affect was somewhat flat. He was clearly unhappy when asked to do academic-related tasks. His nails appeared mildly bitten. He had a tendency to pull at his lips or fingers or twirl his hair.

Intellectual assessment on the Wechsler placed S. P. in the average range. His verbal comprehension factor, however, was at the 50th percentile in contrast to a 91st percentile perceptual organization factor. S. P.'s perceptual skills appeared significantly better than his verbal abilities. Weaknesses in rote, verbal, and conceptual skills were noted. On the Test of Non-Verbal Intelligence, a reasoning task with figures, he performed at the 94th percentile, reflecting his excellent visual-perceptive ability. On a memory battery, his overall memory index was at the 75th percentile, with relatively weaker rote memory problems, both visual and verbal. A qualitative assessment of S. P.'s knowledge of rote verbal information reflected his inability to cite his address, birthday, or months of the year or days of the week in sequence. His performance on the Conners continuous performance test reflected problems with inattentiveness and impulsivity.

Academically, S. P. struggled with time and money knowledge. He experienced problems with mirror-image letter reversals. Academic screening reflected his poor attention to detail and limited comprehension as the result of poor decoding skills. His written story was very poorly structured.

During the clinical interview, S. P. acknowledged that learning "new stuff" was difficult. He reported liking school but was clearly rather negative about his academic abilities. No reports of excessive anxiety were made on a self-report measure or during the clinical interview.

From a diagnostic perspective, S. P.'s history and functioning were consistent for the combined type of ADHD. Home and school rating scales consistently reflected this profile. However, rating scales at home also reflected additional disruptive problems and symptoms consistent with emotional distress. Additional disruptive problems were also reported by S. P.'s teacher. Objective data were consistent for a rote and conceptual verbal-based learning disability, as well as problems with inattention and impulsivity. Situational complaints were consistent across home, school, and community. From a differential diagnostic perspective, although S. P.'s behavior could be somewhat difficult, he clearly did not cross the threshold for oppositional defiance. Although questions were raised about anxiety, data were insufficient during the assessment to suggest that S. P.'s problems were secondary to anxiety. The family was supportive and involved. From a developmental perspective, S. P.'s struggles at school appeared to be exacerbated by the combination of his ADHD symptoms and a rote language-based learning disability.

Stimulant medication was retitrated by S. P.'s physician, and a very positive response was reported at home and at school. Nonetheless, problems with rebound irritability continued. S. P.'s parents were provided with additional resources concerning behavior management for ADHD children in the home. S. P. worked with an academic tutor in close conjunction with his educational team and made excellent progress. Finally, he was seen in counseling to provide additional diagnostic data concerning his emotional adjustment and self-perceptions. Over the course of a year, it was clear that anxiety played a significant role in S. P.'s functioning. Efforts focused at teaching him cognitive strategies to manage anxious, worrisome thoughts yielded improvements in his daily functioning, despite continued anxious symptoms. S. P.'s physician structured a plan to gather additional data over a six-month period, and referral to a child psychiatrist was considered to evaluate the potential benefits of an anti-anxiety medication as part of S. P.'s treatment plan.

D. F.—ADHD COMBINED TYPE AND
PSEUDO-LEARNING DISABILITIES

D. F., a 13-year-old male seventh-grader, was referred due to a history of impulsive, inattentive behavior. D. F. was the second of two children. His older sister had not experienced academic or attentional problems. D. F.'s mother recalled being a daydreamer as a child. As a toddler, D. F. did not "sit for very long unless fatigued." He would wander off in public places. He rarely wanted to stay in his stroller. He demonstrated a high activity level and "always had to be told many times before he paid attention." As a toddler, he would throw tantrums if he did not get his way.

D. F. demonstrated no history of developmental or academic weaknesses. He was reported to be on grade level academically; in fact, he was taking an advanced math class. Nonetheless, he did not take notes or record assignments and often forgot to turn in homework. Teachers had consistently described his lack of work completion and disorganization throughout his school career. A number of teachers noted that D. F. was the class clown.

In the home, D. F. fidgeted and was easily distracted. He had trouble following through with instructions and did not attend well to repetitive, effortful activities. His behavior appeared consequentially bound; he worked well for immediate reinforcers. D. F. enjoyed a number of activities, was a talented pianist, and played on a competition soccer team. His parents noted that he had a good sense of humor.

Parent responses placed D. F. at the 95th percentile for the attention problems scale. He was at the 85th percentile on the Hyperkinesis Index. Problems were noted with routine home activities as well as completing homework; his parents reported that "every night is a battle."

D. F.'s group achievement tests had consistently placed him at or above the 80th percentile in reading, above average in math concepts, but lower than average in math computation. His report cards consistently noted teacher complaints of inattentiveness, poor self-control, and difficulty completing school work. Questionnaires completed by three of D. F.'s classroom teachers noted his varying quality of schoolwork, problems working independently, and impulsivity.

D. F. presented as well groomed. He wore corrective lenses. He related well to the examiner. His work style was impulsive and reflected poor problem-solving skills. When prompted, he was often able to perform more competently.

On the Wechsler Intelligence Scale, D. F. obtained a verbal IQ of 119 and performance IQ of 100. He demonstrated excellent verbal reasoning and comprehension skills. Careless attention to detail appeared to be responsible for his average nonverbal Wechsler performance. His performances on story memory and verbal learning task were consistent for rote memory problems but also consistent for poor strategy on verbal learning and difficulty with spontaneous recall on story memory. Measures of visual-perceptive ability yielded scores above average. D. F.'s performance on the Conners computerized measure reflected typically fast-responding omission errors, inconsistency, and poor perceptual sensitivity. The overall performance was consistent with complaints of impulsivity and inattention. A brief screening of D. F.'s academic skills placed him well above the average, with reading comprehension skills a number of years beyond his current grade placement.

D. F.'s responses to self-report measures did not suggest a pattern of anxiety or depression. He was quick to project the source of problems onto others, noting that teachers gave too much work. Nonetheless, he acknowledged that it was difficult for him to stick to schoolwork and remember to turn in completed work.

From a diagnostic perspective, D. F. demonstrated symptoms and history consistent with the combined type of ADHD. Although he also demonstrated rote memory weaknesses, his level of academic achievement as well as observation during test performance reflected problems with impulsiveness rather than learning disability as responsible for weaker scores. D. F. demonstrated a history of gifted verbal reasoning and comprehension skills.

D. F.'s physician initiated a trial of stimulant medication, and positive response was noted at home and at school. D. F. participated in brief educational-based counseling. He recognized, but more important, accepted that impulsivity was the frequent source of his problems. He also participated in ongoing coaching. During the course of a year, his school performance improved to near straight-A average. Teachers also reported on a change in D. F.'s attitude and general functioning in the classroom. D. F. and his parents additionally participated in a number of family therapy sessions to develop a consistent system at home to communicate and resolve differences.

J. J.—ADHD COMBINED TYPE AND RIGHT HEMISPHERE LEARNING DISABILITY

J. J., a 9½ year-old fourth-grade female, was referred due to a history of inconsistent school performance and attention and socialization problems. J. J. had a number of older siblings with histories of learning disability. Her father also had a history of learning disability despite the fact that he attended college and was a successful businessman.

J. J.'s toddler history was not significant. She was nocturnally enuretic until 6 years of age. She was described as uncoordinated with poor handwriting. Academically, J. J. was described as being weakest in mathematics and handwriting. Teachers have been concerned that she was somewhat slow academically; questions were raised about her attention span and increasing problems as the demands of school increased. J. J. was also described as somewhat neglected socially, often not caring about social interaction. In the home, she appeared very routine-oriented but was not described as rigid or ritualistic or as a discipline problem. Her parents noted that she appeared quite kind and thoughtful.

Parent responses to questionnaires placed J. J. in the clinically significant range for social and attention problems. She was not noted as particularly excitable, impulsive, or restless. Mild situational problems were noted. Socially, J. J. was described as often isolated. Teacher questionnaires noted that she could be impulsive in the classroom. She was described as having poor visual-perceptive fine and large motor skills but being an exceptional reader. One teacher described her as "inattentive-spacey-slow-unprepared—either too focused or not focused at all." Teacher questionnaires reflected J. J.'s inattentiveness, restlessness, and social isolation. She was not described as disruptive. Another teacher noted that J. J. appeared "perfectly content living in her own little world."

A review of assessment data generated when J. J. was in first grade yielded a Wechsler verbal IQ of 106, performance of 72, and full-scale of 88. She was competent in word reading but below average in spelling and arithmetic. She was described as inconsistent in her schoolwork.

J. J. presented quite normally, although the topics of her conversations during testing were often mildly irrelevant. Her conversation at times was immature. She appeared inclined to distrust her abilities. No odd mannerisms were presented. Her thoughts, though logical, appeared mildly unfocused.

J. J.'s performance on the third edition of the Wechsler Intelligence Scale yielded results similar to that obtained in previous years. She obtained a verbal IQ of 110, performance IQ of 70, and full-scale IQ of 89. Tasks requiring fairly pure visual-perceptive skills were among J. J.'s weakest. Her performance on the memory battery reflected a very poor learning index due to her inability to master the visual-learning task. Her verbal memory skills appeared better than her visual memory skills. Her fine motor speed and coordination were inconsistent. Ocular dominance, though reflecting right eye preference, was also a difficult task for J. J. Her ability to reproduce simple designs was in the 5th percentile. Her performance on the Gordon Diagnostic System reflected borderline to abnormal scores on the delay and vigilance tasks, consistent with an impulsive approach.

Academically, J. J. possessed excellent word-reading and spelling skills, but only 4th percentile arithmetic skills. She read for accuracy above her grade placement but her comprehension was two grades below. Her written story, though containing a large number of words, reflected good ideas but very poor organization. A clinical interview did not yield data suggesting that J. J. was experiencing any type of emotional problem. The quality of her responses suggested that she appeared to often struggle to make sense of her world, read and interpret social cues, and reason and understand when to respond and how to respond appropriately.

J. J.'s history and current functioning was consistent for the combined type ADHD diagnosis. Rating scales from home and school consistently reflected problems with ADHD and socialization. Objective test data, though reflecting attentional problems, most strongly reflected a clear and consistent pattern of right hemisphere weakness. Situationally, J. J. was reported as having problems at home and at school. From a differential diagnostic perspective, it was clear that she did not experience other serious disruptive or nondisruptive disorders. Developmentally, however, her pattern of right hemisphere weakness spoke to good rote-learning abilities, especially verbal skills, but very poor nonverbal abilities. Problems with writing, including difficulty with fine motor skills and spatial alignment, as well as marked weaknesses with mathematics, were consistent for right hemisphere weakness. J. J.'s social difficulties also appeared consistent for children with right hemisphere weakness. Careful review of the data suggested that J. J.'s right hemisphere weaknesses were further compounded by her history of impulsive and inattentive behavior; the combination of those two sets of symptoms made life perplexing and difficult for her. Her difficulty socially tracking combined with her disinhibition resulted in marked problems guiding and directing her own behavior appropriately. It was clear that linguistically, J. J. was quite intelligent but struggled to make effective use of her intellectual skills.

A trial of stimulant medication was suggested by J. J.'s physician on review of the assessment. The trial resulted in significant improvements in her on-task behavior and compliance at home. J. J.'s parents were provided with additional resources concerning behavior management for children with right hemisphere problems as well as ADHD. Her teachers were provided with additional resources as well. It was also suggested that in later school years, J. J. take only as much mathematics as absolutely required for graduation. Consultation with an occupational therapist resulted in a set of recommendations to improve J. J.'s motor skills. She was also directed to an academic coach, focusing on strengthening nonverbal academic abilities. Finally, given J. J.'s lack of awareness and the changes in social skills required in the coming years, it was recommended that she work with a counselor on a per need basis to provide her with a therapeutic resource and teach her more effective interpersonal skills.

J. K.—GIFTED INTELLECT, ADHD COMBINED TYPE, RISK OF INTERNALIZING DISORDERS

J. K., a 10½ year-old female fifth-grader, was referred by her pediatrician after years of complaints of underachievement at school. A number of J. K.'s older siblings had received diagnoses of ADHD. Her father, a helicopter pilot, reported being a poor student in school. Her mother recalled being inattentive and having a short temper as a child.

J. K.'s developmental history was consistent for difficult temperament from an early age, including a pattern of impulsivity, hyperactivity, and difficulty attending to routine, repetitive activities. At school, J. K.'s teachers each year described her as quite bright, academically accomplished, but seemingly disinterested in completing schoolwork. In the home, J. K. was described as "delightful when she chooses to be." She worked exceptionally well on the computer. She enjoyed chemistry experiments with her father. Nonetheless, she was rather disorganized, verbally impulsive, had a difficult time keeping track of her possessions, and, as she approached adolescence and in response to increased parental pressure to mature, was becoming increasingly more negative, provocative, and oppositional when requests were made within the home.

Parent checklists placed J. K. above the 85th percentile on the attention problems scale of the Child Behavior Checklist and above the 98th percentile on the Conners Hyperkinesis Index. She was described as possessing good social skills but, as the result of her impulsivity, often not using those skills effectively. Teacher questionnaires described J. K. as enthusiastic and interested but disorganized and inattentive. Because she was able to complete most classwork, she was not described as having significant problems functioning in the classroom relative to classwork. Nonetheless, she was described as extremely overactive, fidgety, impulsive, and restless, placing her below the 5th percentile on the hyperactivity and social skills scales of the Comprehensive Teacher's Rating Scale.

Group achievement test data completed in fourth grade placed J. K. at the 99th percentile for total mathematics, 92nd percentile for total language, and 84th percentile for total reading. Her science score was at the 95th percentile, with an overall battery at the 96th percentile.

J. K. presented as a child appearing more mature than her age. She was well groomed and quite pleasant with the examiner. At times, there was a somewhat hurried or pressured quality to her speech. She often apologized or was negative about her skills whenever mistakes were made. It was not difficult to establish a working relationship with her despite the fact that she was rather impulsive and often required prompting from the examiner.

J. K. performed well above the 99th percentile on the Wechsler, with exceptional verbal reasoning, vocabulary, comprehension, and visual-perceptive skills. On memory tasks, J. K.'s performance was characteristic of inattentive children. Her immediate recall of a story was below average; yet when questioned about the story, it was clear that she processed and retained all of the information. Her verbal learning score reflected a slow start with a quick acceleration. On a computerized measure, J. K.'s response style reflected a somewhat impulsive profile. However, her scores were not particularly abnormal. Following completion of the tests, J. K. commented that she had to "concentrate" to keep from making mistakes.

During the clinical interview, despite the fact that there had not been previous complaints of anxiety, J. K. noted that she frequently worries that her work is inadequate, that people may not like her, and that life isn't fair. She complained about peers being bossy and adults expecting "too much." It was clear that J. K. had a lot more on her mind than she was willing or had taken the time to tell anyone else.

J. K.'s history and current functioning were consistent for the combined type of ADHD. Her gifted intellect often allowed her to compensate for impulse problems. Nonetheless, as the demands of school increased, J. K. experienced increasing problems meeting those demands. Clearly, her intellectual and academic skills were in the gifted range.

J. K. appeared well aware of her problems and in fact experienced significantly more negative thoughts about herself than others were aware of. She was referred to a child therapist and a number of sessions were spent further exploring her anxious thoughts. J. K. was then provided with a cognitive model to manage anxiety. She applied and was accepted to a gifted and talented curriculum at her school. A trial of stimulant medication resulted in improvement in class work and a reduction in complaints of problems in the home.

A. S.—ADHD COMBINED TYPE, HIGH INTELLIGENCE, AND SLIGHT ANXIETY

A. S., a nearly 12-year-old male, was completing sixth grade when referred for increasingly negative behavior and poor work completion. There did not appear to be any family history in A. S.'s siblings or parents for inattentive or school problems.

A. S.'s parents recalled that although he paid attention well as a young child, he did not pay attention to things that were "chosen for him." His medical history was unremarkable. He was described as a restless sleeper from early childhood. His parents recalled that since toddlerhood, he "doesn't seem to listen." They reported that intellectually and academically he was average. A. S. was described as having a period of time between 3 and 4 years of age when he would change his clothes eight to ten times per day. Despite his age, he continued to favor a security blanket, which he would manipulate, and suck his thumb while watching television.

Parent responses to questionnaires placed A. S. within the normal range. He was in the borderline clinical range for attention problems. His behavior was described as often inconsistent. He could be impatient. His parents noted that as he had matured he had developed an increasingly "sarcastic sense of humor" and a "bad attitude."

A review of A. S.'s report cards from the private school he attended noted, beginning in first grade, comments by teachers of inconsistent completion of assignments and problems using time efficiently and demonstrating self-control. A. S.'s third-grade teacher noted that "basic skills are not usually his topic of interest." His sixth-grade teachers noted that although he was "informed and thoughtful," he appeared to lack organization and was easily distracted, and he became increasingly more morose as the school year progressed.

During the assessment, A. S. appeared mildly anxious. His verbal skills were excellent. His self-confidence as task became more difficult appeared to decline quickly.

On the Wechsler Intelligence Scale, A. S. performed in the gifted range, with 99th percentile verbal skills but only 68th percentile nonverbal or performance skills. His somewhat slow, at times impulsive work style resulted in lower performance on the coding, object assembly, and symbol search subtests. A. S.'s performance on memory tasks reflected good general comprehension but an inconsistent approach to memorization. His reproduction of a complex figure resulted in an average score but was haphazardly reduced. The overall profile test data appeared to reflect a mild right hemisphere weakness. A. S.'s performance on the Conners computerized measure reflected problems sustaining attention and inhibiting impulsive responding.

A. S.'s responses to depression and anxiety questionnaires appeared to primarily reflect more worrisome and anxious rather than unhappy and depressed thoughts and feelings. During the clinical interview, he was responsive to the examiner. His thoughts reflected that he possessed reasonably good awareness of his current life problems and was quite frustrated and worried about his future.

A. S.'s history and current functioning met the threshold for the inattentive symptoms of ADHD and nearly met the hyperactive-impulsive threshold. Nonetheless, the combined diagnosis was made. It was hypothesized that his strong intellectual skills often allowed him to minimize the negative impact of his hyperactivity. Rating scales at home and school consistently reflected his problems with inattention, impulsivity, and restlessness. Parent and school scales also reflected an escalating pattern of worry in response to life stress. Objective data consistently reflected A. S.'s problems managing impulsivity, strong verbal intellectual skills, and slightly weaker nonverbal skills. A review of A. S.'s group achievement testing was consistent for this profile, reflecting his relatively weaker math and written language in comparison to his excellent reading skills. A. S. was described as having a fairly consistent pattern of situational problems at home and at school. Differential diagnosis reflected the onset of mild anxiety as consistent with an adjustment reaction to life stress. Though at times oppositional, A. S. did not meet the diagnostic criteria for any other disruptive disorder. From a developmental perspective, he appeared to experience mild right hemisphere weaknesses, but overall his academic skills and achievement were well above average.

A. S.'s physician initiated a trial of stimulant medication. The last three months of his sixth-grade year showed marked improvements in A. S.'s classroom functioning as well as his ability to complete homework and get along with family members. He was also involved in short-term counseling, focusing on increasing his sense of responsibility and awareness of life problems and motivating him to be an active participant in determining his future. A. S. responded very well to this short-term model and became his own best ally. Counseling also further explored A. S.'s feelings of anxiety and worry, teaching him a number of coping strategies, which he used effectively to combat worrisome thoughts. A. S. was also involved in a study skills class, and his parents were provided with additional resources concerning parenting adolescents. Finally, A. S. was closely followed as he successfully entered seventh grade.

A. B.—ADHD COMBINED TYPE, HIGH INTELLIGENCE, AND ANXIETY

A. B., an 8½ year-old female third-grader, was referred due to an increasing pattern of academic difficulty and emotional distress. She was referred to a psychiatrist on a crisis basis, and diagnoses of generalized anxiety disorder and combined type ADHD were made based on history and presenting symptoms. A trial of a serotonin-based medicine was initiated, and a slight improvement was noted in A. B.'s functioning. Further assessment was recommended by the psychiatrist to determine if A. B. was experiencing a learning disability or might benefit from counseling.

A. B.'s family history was significant for depression and anxiety on both sides of her parents' family. In the home, A. B. was described as having always been rather impulsive, inattentive, and hyperactive. Her parents had never sought further assessment for this problem, as it did not create marked situational difficulties in their home. Teachers had commented during the first few grades about A. B.'s inattentiveness; however, she was not a significant disruptive problem in the classroom.

During assessment, A. B. appeared to lack confidence. She frequently commented that tasks were too difficult or that she was not competent to complete them. Concentration was poor. As tasks became more difficult, she often commented that she did not want to continue working or disliked the task.

Questionnaires completed by A. B.'s parents reflected problems with impulsivity, hyperactivity, and inattention as well as signs of emotional distress related to anxiety and depression. Teacher questionnaires reflected a pattern of mild to moderate disruptive behavior and increasing concerns about A. B.'s social isolation and seeming unhappiness at school.

On a Wechsler Intelligence Scale, A. B. clearly demonstrated that she was quite bright, obtaining a verbal IQ of 119, performance IQ of 119, and full-scale IQ of 121. Despite her complaints, it was clear that A. B. was quite competent intellectually. Her performance on memory tasks resulted in well above average scores as well. A computerized measure was obtained, during which she made a large number of commission errors, had difficulty sustaining attention, and demonstrated poor perceptual sensitivity. This task was completed while A. B. was receiving the serotonin medication. Academic screening suggested that her skills were average but certainly not at a level commensurate with her intellectual abilities. Weaknesses were in rote rather than conceptual academic skills. She reflected poor visual memory for spelling, poor math facts, and difficulty with execution in written language.

A. B.'s self-reports on anxiety and depressive questionnaires appeared to reflect problems primarily related to worry rather than unhappiness. During the interview, although she was quite negative about herself and school, her discussions focused on her concerns that she was not good enough, smart enough, or attractive enough.

From a diagnostic perspective, A. B. was extremely interesting. Her history and functioning were consistent for the combined type of ADHD. Parent and teacher rating scales consistently reflected her inattentive, impulsive, and hyperactive symptoms. Parent rating scales reflected a recent increasing onset of anxious symptoms well. Objective data consistently reflected A. B.'s impulsivity. From a situational perspective, problems were noted in the home and at school. Differential diagnosis was complicated by symptoms of emotional distress that appeared more consistent with generalized anxiety than depression. Nonetheless, certain depressive qualities, including a sense of helplessness, were noted in A. B.'s functioning. From a developmental perspective, she was extremely bright. Her academic achievement, on a conceptual level, was consistent with her intellect. On a rote level, her problems were consistent for children with histories of impulsivity. There were no data to suggest that she experienced a specific learning disability.

A. B.'s psychiatrist was provided with a copy of the assessment, and a low-dose trial of stimulant medication was added to A. B.'s serotonin medicine, after which, a very positive response was noted in her behavior at home and at school. Consultation with the educational team resulted in a daily school note sent home, and efforts were made to more actively involve her in classroom activities. A. B.'s parents were provided with additional strategies for behavior management; they also worked individually with a parent trainer. Finally, A. B. was placed in short-term counseling, teaching her skills to cope with anxious thinking.

B. C.—SUPERIOR INTELLIGENCE, ADHD COMBINED TYPE, AND ANXIETY

B. C., an 8½ year-old female third-grader, was referred by her pediatrician due to a reported history of anxiety. A number of differential diagnostic questions were asked concerning anxiety versus ADHD.

B. C. is the second of three children. An elder sister had a history of mild anxiety. A 5-year-old sister had a history of stubborn temperamental behavior. B. C.'s mother had a history of anxiety for which she had been treated a number of times with anti-anxiety medicines and counseling. B. C.'s father's family had a history of a number of cousins receiving diagnoses of ADHD.

B. C.'s mother recalled that her infancy was unremarkable. However, as a toddler, she seemed "distracted by her own misery." She appeared somewhat intense in her emotions and often appeared unhappy. A trial of Paxil the previous year appeared to result in improvements in anxiety symptoms but was discontinued due to parental concerns of long-term side effects. Intellectually, B. C.'s parents described her as "very good at some things and poor at others."

B. C. had been evaluated at 6 years of age and provided with a diagnosis of anxiety. She was seen in psychotherapy for a year, with minimal changes in daily behavior. Subsequent consultation by a general psychiatrist yielded no specific diagnoses and a number of trials of medication. A trial of Imipramine appeared to reduce anxiety and improve attention span but caused skin problems. A trial of Trazodone caused sleep difficulty. A trial of Zoloft appeared somewhat beneficial, but there were a number of unwanted side effects. A trial of Dexedrine resulted in improved symptoms but was discontinued due to decreased appetite.

In the home, B. C. was described as talking excessively and having a low frustration tolerance. She lost her temper several times per day. She appeared impulsive and when frustrated would respond in an exaggerated, often anxious fashion.

Parental responses to questionnaires placed B. C. above the 98th percentile on the anxious/depressed, attention problems, and delinquent behavior scales. On the Hyperkinesis Index, she was at approximately the 50th percentile. B. C. was described as excitable and easily frustrated but not necessarily inattentive. Numerous situational problems were observed at home.

Past in-school assessment noted B. C.'s above-average intellectual abilities but relatively weaker reading achievement scores. Her classroom teacher described her as impulsive but not necessarily inattentive. She was described as having average academic skills. She appeared above the 98th percentile on the Hyperkinesis Index of the Conners questionnaire. Only mild problems, however, were noted during individual task work, small-group activities, free time, class lectures, and recess. B. C. was described as socially awkward. Her teacher noted that she appeared to not understand the "give and take of social relations."

B. C. presented as an attractive, well-groomed child. She made numerous self-deprecatory statements during the assessment process. She was concerned about the quality of her performance and would often apologize. She appeared mildly anxious. As the evaluation progressed, rather than become more secure, she appeared to become increasingly more uncertain about the quality of her performance.

On the Wechsler, B. C. obtained a verbal IQ at the 95th percentile, performance IQ at the 87th percentile, and full-scale IQ at the 94th percentile. Her verbal reasoning and comprehension skills were in the top 2%. Her performance on the memory battery yielded well above average conceptual memory skills but average to low average rote memory skills. Although B. C. experienced mild problems on two different computerized assessment measures, upon observation, her problems appeared to be more the result of her anxiety rather than lack of capacity to inhibit impulses or pay attention. Due to her concerns about the quality of her performance on the computerized measures, B. C. became somewhat overwhelmed.

Brief academic assessment placed B. C. within the average range. There was, however, an inconsistent quality to her spelling and word-reading skills. During limit testing, it was clear that her academic abilities were better than she could spontaneously generate. Anxiety appeared to be the most likely explanation for decreased performance. When reading in context, B. C. read mid-fifth-grade level with comprehension at a fourth-grade level.

B. C.'s responses to the Children's Depression Inventory and manifest anxiety scale placed her above the 99th percentile for both self-report measures. She reported feeling unhappy, frequently worrying, feeling disliked, lonely, upset, sad, bored, and worried. She reported being excessively fearful, concerned what others may think or say about her, and worried that people may dislike her.

B. C.'s responses during the clinical interview were consistent for anxious children, perceiving herself as less adequate than others, worrying more, and anticipating future failure and stress.

From a diagnostic perspective, although B. C.'s presentation and history were consistent for the combined type of ADHD, a diagnosis was made only provisionally, given the extent to which anxiety appeared to impact her daily behavior and functioning. Her history and presentation appeared consistent with a generalized anxiety diagnosis. Although she performed somewhat more weakly on a rote memory task, this pattern appeared also to be explained by anxiety.

B. C. was referred for cognitively based therapy to help her gain greater insight into her anxious thinking and learn more assertive thinking skills. Her parents were provided with additional resources concerning anxiety and participated in the training program as well. Over a three-month period, B. C. made marked improvements in her general behavior. However, as she was taught to track her anxiety levels, it became clear that she cycled somewhat through greater and lesser periods of anxiety for no specific etiological reason. B. C. entered a new, smaller private school where she received significant support from her teachers. She integrated quite well in this new educational setting. Closer observation by teachers strongly suggested that even when anxiety was taken into account, B. C. appeared to demonstrate symptoms consistent with the combined type of ADHD. Due to parental concerns about medications and B. C.'s success with therapy and educational support, no further medication trials were attempted. B. C.'s parents were also provided with a number of additional parenting strategies to utilize in the home.

K. M.—ADHD INATTENTIVE TYPE AND NONVERBAL LEARNING DISABILITY

K. M., a 10½ year-old female fourth-grader, was referred due to a history of inattentive behavior and slow academic achievement. Family history was not suggestive of learning disabilities nor were there any significant risk factors in the family structure. K. M. demonstrated a history of delayed speech development. In first grade, due to inattentive behavior, a diagnosis of ADHD was provided. A brief trial of stimulant medication did not yield benefits. She was nocturnally enuretic until 5 years of age.

K. M. was described as a very pleasant child. She was noted as having a few friends but in general being socially isolated. Her parents described her as an enthusiastic child, quite positive about most things.

Parent responses to questionnaires placed K. M. in the clinically significant range for social and attention problems. Moderate difficulties were consistently noted with inattention, restlessness, and impulsivity. Despite these problems, she was not described as creating significant situational problems at home or in the community.

K. M.'s classroom teacher described her as having low academic self-confidence and poor work completion. Nonetheless, she was not described as disruptive in the classroom and appeared to get along fairly well with other students. On the playground, at times, she could be a loner. Nonetheless, she was described as keeping busy, even when she was playing alone.

A review of educational records reflected K. M.'s average language skills but slightly below-average academic abilities. Her weakest area appeared in the conceptual area of mathematics.

K. M. was very pleasant and cooperative with the examiner. She demonstrated a mild degree of performance anxiety. She tended to fidget somewhat and could be easily distracted.

K. M.'s performance on the Wechsler yielded a verbal IQ of 100, performance IQ of 83, and full-scale IQ of 92. Her verbal abilities were clearly better than her nonverbal skills. She demonstrated fairly strong verbal reasoning abilities. On a number of tasks, her impulsive style and inconsistency lowered performance. In contrast, she struggled to perceive perceptual relationships on the block design and object assembly subtests. Her performance on a memory battery yielded a verbal memory score of 106, visual memory score of 81, learning score of 74, and general memory index of 84. In contrast to intellect, K. M. clearly experienced memory problems. The pattern was consistent with her intellectual performance, reflecting much better verbal than nonverbal memory skills. Her learning curves were somewhat flat, demonstrating good initial performance but poor strategic learning. K. M.'s visual-motor skills were rated as low average. Her performance on a computerized measure reflected a large number of commission and omission errors, as well as inconsistency suggestive of ADHD. A screening of her academic skills reflected good reading skills but a relative weakness in mathematics ability for both rote and conceptual math skills. She appeared to experience visual-spatial problems; this affected her decoding slightly but mostly affected visual organization. She did not appear to understand mathematics on a conceptual level.

K. M.'s self-reports suggested slightly more anxious, worrisome thinking than others. She reported difficulty worrying frequently, being fearful, and being concerned that people at school felt she was not performing well. During the interview, she was cooperative and pleasant. Her comments reflected some degree of impulsivity.

Although K. M. demonstrated some impulsive qualities, from a diagnostic perspective, her symptom profile met the ADHD inattentive type but did not meet sufficient criteria to make the combined type diagnosis. Rating scales reflected her inattention and disorganization at home and at school. They were also consistent for some degree of social isolation, often characteristic of children with nonverbal learning disability. Objective data reflected K. M.'s inconsistent attentional skills. Situational data demonstrated a fairly similar pattern of problems at home and at school. From a severity perspective, problems were rated as fairly mild, primarily due to the fact that her overall environment offered a significant degree of protective factors. From a differential diagnostic perspective, developmental issues appeared paramount for consideration. On a verbal conceptual level, K. M. appeared to function at least in the average range. Her nonverbal conceptual skills were weaker. She appeared to experience visual-spatial problems, which was affecting her academics, especially mathematics and ability to organize written language. Although she reported somewhat more anxious thoughts than others, this appeared to be the logical consequence of her struggles and did not meet criteria for an anxiety disorder diagnosis.

K. M.'s teachers were provided with additional insight and information concerning her learning problems. Efforts were made to more actively involve her socially in the classroom. She also began working with an academic tutor. K. M.'s parents were provided with additional resources concerning parenting children with nonverbal learning disabilities. It was recommended that K. M. be provided with additional support for developing written language skills and closely monitored as she prepared to make the transition into junior high school. After consultation with K. M.'s physician, it was decided to attempt nonmedical interventions over at least a six- to twelve-month period before considering a trial of stimulant medication. K. M. also began intermittent work with a counselor to build her academic self-esteem and avert the development of increasing feelings of helplessness.

T. L.—ADHD INATTENTIVE TYPE

T. L., a 12-year-old male sixth-grader, had been diagnosed two years previously with oppositional defiant disorder. It was the evaluator's impression that T. L.'s oppositionality was passive rather than aggressive. Questions were raised at that time of the possibility that T. L. also experienced ADHD. He was referred as the result of an escalating pattern of defiant and oppositional behavior at home.

T. L. was the eldest of his parents' two children. His parents were in the process of separating but were still living together. Their fourteen-year marriage had been extremely difficult from the beginning. T. L. had been exposed to a significant degree of conflict between his parents. Neither parent was able to set limits. Each attempted to create an alliance with T. L. against the other parent.

Questionnaires completed by his parents were significant for delinquent and aggressive behavior. Problems with impulsivity were reported as of recent onset. Problems of disorganization and inattention were described as long-term and chronic. T. L. was also described as having difficulty socially due to his strong, controlling behavior.

Questionnaires completed by his teacher noted that during the past year, his motivation appeared limited and his work completion was poor. He appeared disinterested in school. He was described as inattentive but not hyperactive. He was noted as being somewhat shy and quiet socially. A review of school-completed test data placed T. L. intellectually in the high end of the average range, with a verbal IQ of 112, performance IQ of 100, and full-scale IQ of 107. Further assessment reflected T. L.'s average memory skills but stronger conceptual than rote memory abilities. His inconsistent motivation during testing raised questions as to the accuracy of test results. Academic testing reflected his slightly weak, rote academic skills. However, he was not significantly behind academically.

T. L.'s self-report on depression and anxiety scales did not yield significantly escalated scores. During the interview, it was clear that he was extremely egocentric and controlling. His primary focus of problems concerned conflicts between his parents and the manner in which that resulted in difficulty for him and his sister. He appeared somewhat narcissistic and indifferent to others when describing friends and teachers.

Though impulsive, T. L. did not demonstrate a history of sufficient symptoms to cross the hyperactive-impulsive threshold. He had demonstrated long-standing symptoms sufficient for the inattentive type of ADHD. Rating scales were also consistent for this pattern, as well as an escalating profile of aggressive oppositionality. Teacher reports reflected a passive pattern of oppositionality and complaints of inattentiveness. Objective data were difficult to interpret given T. L.'s lack of motivation and inconsistent performance. Data collected during the assessment and from the school, however, suggested that T. L. was bright and likely did not experience a specific learning disability. His situational problems had become increasingly more pervasive. At home, he had struggled to successfully make the transition into junior high school. From a differential diagnostic perspective, it appeared that T. L. was experiencing life adjustment problems as the result of a long history of ongoing and escalating family conflict. There were insufficient symptoms to warrant a diagnosis of depression or anxiety. He was not demonstrating delinquent behavior but had become increasingly more angry and defiant with adults, principally his parents.

T. L.'s physician initiated a trial of stimulant medication, which parent and teacher reports suggested improved T. L.'s home and classroom behavior. He also began individual psychotherapy, spending his time venting his anger about his parents and their behavior. Efforts at working with his parents resulted in small gains but larger setbacks. T. L.'s behavior at home became increasingly more disruptive. His mother moved out, and T. L.'s behavior problems continued to escalate, including becoming openly noncompliant and staying out late at night. T. L. was subsequently sent to live with an aunt nearby. His father discontinued treatment.

W. M.—ADHD INATTENTIVE TYPE AND RIGHT HEMISPHERE LEARNING DISABILITY

W. M., a 9-year-old male fourth-grader, was referred due to attentional problems as well as concerns with comprehension. W. M. was an only child. His parents, though divorced, were on amicable terms. There appeared to be some history of learning disability and attentional problems on both sides of the family. Nonetheless, both parents were college graduates.

W. M. experienced separation anxiety from his mother through 5 years of age; the problem gradually diminished but was noted even in first grade. As a toddler, W. M. appeared extremely fearful and did not adjust to new situations well. He reached developmental milestones without significant problems. He was reported as being on grade-level academically despite his problems with inattentiveness. At school, he struggled increasingly as academic tasks became more complex. His parents described him as frequently appearing younger and more immature than his classmates. They reported that he had recently commented, "You just don't get it, I don't understand things. I didn't when I was four in kindergarten, first, second, and third grade."

Parent responses to behavioral questionnaires placed W. M. in the clinically significant range for attention problems. He was not described as particularly impulsive or hyperactive. Only mild situational problems were noted. He was described as doing reasonably well socially.

Questionnaires completed by W. M.'s teacher noted that he was easily distracted but not disruptive. He struggled to understand and follow instructions consistently. He was reported as being below average in reading achievement.

During assessment, W. M. demonstrated age-appropriate behavior. He did not easily initiate conversation but would respond. He demonstrated a mild lateral lisp. He appeared slightly anxious but not excessively so. He was generally competent in his skills.

W. M.'s performance on the Wechsler Intelligence Scale yielded a verbal IQ of 113, performance IQ of 87, and full-scale IQ of 101. His verbal comprehension factor was 30 points higher than his perceptual organization factor. His fund of information, verbal reasoning, and comprehension scales appeared exceptional. In contrast, he was overwhelmed by the block design and object assembly subtests. His performance on the memory battery yielded memory scores consistent with his intellectual abilities. However, the marked discrepancy between verbal and visual skills observed on intellectual measures was not observed on the memory battery. Visual-motor skills were at the 40th percentile. A measure of visual perception suggested well above average perceptual skills, reflecting faulty performance as indicative of poor motor skills. His performance on the Conners computerized measure reflected a change in response speed and consistency depending on the length of time between stimulus letters. The profile appeared more consistent with weak perceptual sensitivity than inattentiveness.

Academic assessment placed W. M. in the average range. His ability to read in context was better than single-word reading. He tended to make visually based minor mistakes as he read aloud. His overall approach to academics appeared more verbally than visually based.

W. M.'s responses to self-report questionnaires and his reports during the interview reflected his awareness of school problems but did not reflect any marked symptoms of emotional distress.

Diagnostically, W. M.'s history and current functioning met the criteria for the inattentive type of ADHD. Rating scales consistently reflected this pattern at home and at school. As discussed in earlier chapters, children with the inattentive type of ADHD often score in the borderline or subclinical range on questionnaires considered sensitive to the combined type ADHD diagnosis. This pattern is also evident in W. M.'s more mild situational difficulties. Objective data were also consistent with inattentive rather than impulsive problems. From a differential diagnostic perspective, W. M.'s excellent verbal abilities were contrasted by his rote right hemisphere weaknesses involving visual-motor skills, principally output skills. His weak reading skills appeared to be visually based. His written language abilities, not surprisingly, represented his greatest weakness. The examiner also raised concerns about W. M.'s awareness of his problems and increasing frustration in the face of school struggles.

W. M. was referred to an academic tutor. His teachers were provided with additional resources concerning the nature of his skills weaknesses and suggestions to provide support in the coming school year. A text concerning learning problems in children, specifically written for young adolescents, was provided to W. M. and his parents to avert the onset of further self-esteem problems. W. M. was seen intermittently by a counselor to help him focus on his intellectual assets. Given his good intellect, combined with the fact that he did not experience impulsive problems, W. M. was referred to a study and organizational skills class. It was also recommended that he be closely followed as he made the transition into junior high school. Based on the data provided, W. M.'s physician decided to utilize a nonmedicine approach and follow W. M. closely over the coming years.

P. K.—ADHD INATTENTIVE TYPE, HIGH IQ, GENERALIZED ANXIETY, AND MILD ROTE LEARNING DISABILITIES

P. K., a $14\frac{1}{2}$ year-old ninth-grade male, had a history of poor school performance. He was referred upon entering high school due to his apparent disinterest in completing schoolwork. The family history included the difficult divorce of P. K.'s parents when he was 9 years old and his inconsistent relationship with his father. There appeared to be a history on both sides of the family of depression and alcoholism.

P. K. was described as not listening well from a young age. Nonetheless, he was not reported as experiencing significant behavioral, developmental, or emotional problems during his elementary school years. He appeared to be somewhat self-critical but did reasonably well socially. In the home, he could be funny, creative, and positive but also inconsistent and struggling to complete tasks. At 9 years of age, he was evaluated and worked with a psychologist for emotional reactions to divorce issues. Assessment at that time placed him intellectually at the 86th percentile. His problems were described by the evaluator as "one of motivation, not ability."

Questionnaires completed by P. K.'s mother and stepfather, with whom he had a fairly good relationship, were consistent for inattentive but not hyperactive or impulsive problems. There were no significant complaints of situational difficulty except those related to chores and homework. P. K. was described as socially slightly uninvolved.

A review of group achievement tests placed P. K. during his early elementary school years as well above average with a slow decline in achievement into the average range through eighth grade. Questionnaires completed by teachers placed him in the average range in most classes. Teachers, however, noted that he frequently required help and had some difficulty working independently.

P. K. presented as slightly overweight. He was mild to moderately anxious, frequently apologizing due to what he perceived as the inadequacy of his test performance. On the Wechsler Intelligence Scale he performed at the 90th percentile intellectually with a fairly well-balanced profile of skills. Weakest performance were on tasks relating to rote memory. Subsequent administration of the memory assessment battery reflected good conceptual memory but relatively weaker rote memory, principally in the verbal area. P. K.'s learning scores were in the superior range. He appeared to learn exceptionally well with repeated practice. His anxiety level may have further impaired his immediate memory. P. K.'s performance on the Conners computerized measure reflected an atypical pattern consistent with inattentiveness. Academically, P. K. presented in the above-average range. No definable skill weaknesses were observed. His mild rote memory weaknesses did not appear to have exerted a significant negative impact on his achievement.

P. K.'s responses to a depression questionnaire yielded a score in the average range. In contrast, his responses on an anxiety questionnaire were reflective of slightly more anxious and worrisome thoughts than others. During the clinician interview, P. K.'s responses reflected his level of intellect as well as his excessive worry, dependency, and insecurity. He appeared to experience early adolescence as socially painful. He viewed school activities as less than satisfying and was quite concerned about his future educational and vocational abilities.

P. K.'s history and functioning appeared consistent with the inattentive type of ADHD. Home and school rating scales, though not excessive, were suggestive of this profile, especially qualitative descriptions made by parents and teachers. Objective test data also appeared consistent for inattentive symptoms. Situationally, P. K. did not experience a significant pattern of problems, except when organization, rote memory, and attentional skills were required. From a differential diagnostic perspective, he did not experience disruptive symptoms. He demonstrated symptoms of anxiety, which appeared subthreshold for a generalized anxiety diagnosis but certainly were sufficient to likely further impair his daily functioning. His emerging personality appeared rather dependent and noncompetitive and lacking in initiative.

It was strongly recommended to P. K. and his parents that he consider individual counseling. After attending a number of brief counseling visits, P. K. withdrew from counseling; this was not surprising, given his resistance and anxiety to accepting more responsibility for himself and his life. P. K.'s physician suggested an initial trial of stimulant medication, which over a short period, was reported as beneficial by P. K.'s teachers as well as by P. K., who reported that the medicine increased his ability to sit down and complete homework. P. K.'s mother was provided with additional resources concerning adolescent family problems. It was also suggested that his father be apprised of his son's condition and that efforts be made to improve P. K.'s relationship with his father.

N. R.—ADHD INATTENTIVE TYPE, LANGUAGE DISORDER, ANXIETY, AND DEPRESSION

N. R., a 14-year-old male ninth-grader, was referred by his physician due to an extended history of poor school performance. N. R.'s parents had separated when he was 8 years old. His father had been home infrequently during the marriage and had had minimal involvement with N. R. or his sibling. Following the divorce, he was jailed for thirty days for nonpayment of child support. N. R.'s mother noted that N. R. frequently commented that he hated his father.

N. R. had an unremarkable infant, toddler, and preschool history. His life was further complicated by the fact that after the divorce, his father stopped making payments on the family home as ordered. The home was foreclosed and N. R., his mother, and his sibling had to move. During this period, N. R.'s paternal grandmother died unexpectedly, resulting in a period of major depression for his mother. During this period as well, N. R.'s father would repeatedly appear unannounced at the family home and a number of times was physically violent with N. R.'s mother.

A trial of Ritalin following a physician diagnosis of ADHD was attempted in second grade. The medicine appeared to sedate N. R. and was discontinued. N. R.'s behavior at home was not problematic. He enjoyed snowboarding and skateboarding. At school, he had a long history of teacher observations that he appeared "in outer space."

Parent questionnaires placed N. R. at the 85th percentile on the attention problems scale of the Achenbach but only the 73rd percentile for the Hyperkinesis Index of the Conners. However, he was at the 90th percentile for the inattentive scale of this instrument. Testing completed when N. R. was in second grade yielded a Wechsler IQ score at approximately the 82nd percentile. Academic testing placed N. R. in the average range.

Questionnaires completed by N. R.'s high school teachers consistently reflected his problems working independently, persisting on task, following directions, and completing assignments. There were no complaints of hyperactivity or oppositional behaviors. Socially, N. R. was described as isolated and often uninvolved with peers.

During assessment, N. R. presented as an adolescent of average size and appearance. He initiated and responded to conversation. However, he experienced word-finding problems. There were often long silences before he responded to questions. He also appeared mildly anxious.

A pattern on the Wechsler was similar to that observed a number of years earlier, with N. R. performing at the 98th percentile perceptually but at the 45th percentile verbally. He demonstrated an exceptional pattern of visual-perceptual skills but only average verbal abilities. A similar pattern was observed in a relative weakness in verbal versus visual memory. A computerized measure of attention placed N. R. at a level consistent with adolescents reported as inattentive and impulsive. Academic testing was quite interesting, reflecting fluid reading skills but limited comprehension.

N. R. appeared to experience fairly significant mixed receptive-expressive language disorder. Comprehension appeared to be his primary deficit. It was noted that adolescents with this pattern often are described by parents and teachers as seeming not to hear, being confused, and not paying attention. Long silences appeared to be the result of N. R.'s attempts to think about and decide how to respond to what he had heard or been asked.

N. R.'s responses to the anxiety and depression scales placed him in the top 5% for anxious and hopeless thoughts. He reported feeling hopeless, worrying excessively, and being a nervous person. He echoed these concerns during the clinical interview. His responses to the adolescent Millon were similar to an adolescent sample fostering fairly strong feelings of helplessness, anxiety, and dependency. He expressed considerable concern over feeling confused if not lost in his life. He appeared to find little to admire in either what he achieved or in himself as a person.

N. R.'s history and symptoms appeared consistent for the inattentive type of ADHD. His problems appeared to be compounded by a pattern of developmental weakness consistent with a language-based learning disorder, mild symptoms of anxiety, and moderate symptoms of depression. Regarding the last, diagnoses of the not otherwise specified anxiety disorder and a mild major depressive episode were made.

N. R. was referred for further language and auditory processing evaluations, which better defined areas of weakness and resulted in his participation in language therapy. Efforts were made at school to provide him with an academic coach and to locate areas at school that he enjoyed and found motivating. A number of study and organizational resources were also suggested. N. R. agreed to participate in cognitive therapy and was referred for psychiatric consultation to determine if a specific type or combination of psychotropic medications might be of benefit.

C. H.—PSEUDO-ADHD: DEPRESSION

C. H., a 10-year-old fifth-grader, was referred by his physician. In the previous year, he had demonstrated an increasing pattern of emotionally distressing symptoms, as well as the onset of multiple episodes of daytime encopresis. C. H. appeared sad, had trouble concentrating, and there was a decline in his schoolwork. He was lethargic, had gained weight, and had become socially isolated.

C. H.'s siblings had not experienced developmental or behavioral problems. There was a history of depression on the mother's side of the family, including the fact that she had been treated for depression and her grandfather evidently had a history of manic-depressive disorder.

C. H.'s preschool history was not noted by particular behavioral, developmental, or emotional problems. Efforts at treating his encopresis by the primary-care physician had resulted in a reduction of but continued episodes. C. H. was otherwise healthy.

C. H. appeared to enjoy school. In third grade, the family moved to a new home and he seemed to have increasing problems. Teachers thought he had an inferiority complex. In fourth grade, he appeared extremely stressed, at one point running away after complaining about school. His parents noted that he had a tendency to hold anger in and once every few months explode. Discipline was noted by the need for constant reminders. C. H. had always worked well for short-term rewards but not as well for long-term rewards.

Questionnaire data placed C. H. in the clinically significant range for social isolation, anxiety, depression, and attention problems. He was above the 98th percentile on the parent Conners Hyperkinesis Index. Situationally, problems were noted in the home and community. Questionnaires completed by C. H.'s teacher showed that he appeared extremely isolated. He demonstrated low frustration tolerance and did not pay attention. He seemed to not be very interested in school. He was in the clinically significant range for inattention, hyperactivity, and social problems. In general, he was neglected rather than rejected.

During assessment, C. H. did not appear particularly invested in success. His affect was rather flat. He rarely made conversation. He often required prompting during testing. He smiled only occasionally. He frequently made negative statements or would give up as tasks became more difficult.

Assessment data placed C. H. at the 84th percentile for nonverbal skills but only the 19th percentile for verbal skills on the third edition of the Wechsler Intelligence Scale. Despite a 91st percentile perceptual organization factor, his freedom from distractibility factor was at the 25th percentile, with a processing speed factor at the 18th percentile. Receptive vocabulary on the Peabody Picture Vocabulary Test was at the 21st percentile and performance on the Test of Non-Verbal Intelligence at the 61st percentile. A memory battery yielded consistently low scores, with a learning index at the 14th percentile and a general memory index at the 5th percentile. On the computerized Conners, C. H. performed well, yielding no signs of difficulty with inattention or impulsiveness.

Academically, C. H.'s performance was in the average range. His comprehension when reading appeared lower than his decoding skills. He demonstrated good sight-decoding ability and phonetic use. He read single words better than in context. He spelled phonetically. He made careless, impulsive errors mathematically.

C. H.'s responses were at the 86th percentile on the Children's Depression Scale, reflecting an increase in negative or helpless thoughts. His responses on the Piers Harris Self-Concept Scale yielded very low scores. His responses on the Manifest Anxiety Scale were at the 84th percentile, reflecting slightly more anxious and worrisome thoughts.

During the clinical interview, C. H. explained that his parents loved him but did not understand him. He had difficulty talking about enjoyable activities. He noted that he did not get along well with his siblings because they irritated him. He described disliking everything about school. His presentation and behavior reflected a pattern of moody, impulsive actions. He felt misunderstood and unappreciated and thus was easily offended by trifles and quickly provoked into angrier, contrary behavior. During the interview he spoke freely of feelings of low self-esteem.

C. H.'s presentation did not meet the *DSM-IV* criteria for ADHD. Although rating scales at home and school suggested attention and impulse problems, the scales were more characteristic of symptoms related to emotional distress. Objective test data provided a consistently weaker pattern of verbal than nonverbal skills. It was unclear whether this pattern was more pronounced due to C. H.'s depression affect. Tasks sensitive to ADHD did not yield significant findings. Situationally, C. H. demonstrated a pattern of behavioral differences at home and at school. From a differential diagnostic perspective, it was clear that he had become increasingly more oppositional during the past year. However, his presentation was more consistent with a major depressive episode and encopresis. From a developmental perspective, C. H.'s weak language skills were also likely contributing to his academic struggles and behavior in the classroom.

C. H. was referred for psychotherapy, focusing on a cognitive-behavioral model for childhood depression. His parents were provided with additional depression resources. He was also placed on a compliance program for encopresis. His physician was provided with the assessment and guidelines to closely monitor C. H. over the following three months. It was suggested that if depressive symptoms escalated, antidepressant medication as part of C. H.'s treatment plan should be considered. Finally, given C. H.'s excellent drawing skills and interest in drawing, it was recommended he enroll in an art class. As his depression lifted, additional speech language and academic assessment was recommended.

T. B.—PSEUDO-ADHD AND MAJOR DEPRESSION

T. B. was a 16-year-old male eleventh-grader referred due to a history of poor school performance and a recent onset of apparent depressive symptoms. T. B.'s family history was significant for depressive episodes in a sister, brother, and one parent.

According to the family history, T. B. did not experience problems until the birth of his sister when he was 4 years old. At that time, it was suggested that his symptomatic problems related to sibling rivalry. Nonetheless, this pattern continued as T. B. matured. During the previous year, he had suddenly stopped attending school and resisted leaving the house. Over an eight-week period, T. B. appeared to return to his previous state of behavior. He discontinued the anti-depressant medicine, complaining that he did not like the way it made him feel.

T. B.'s history included a diagnosis of ADHD at 9 years of age with a brief trial of stimulant medication. His parents could not recall if the medication was beneficial. It was discontinued at the end of that school year. In the home, his parents described a history of seemingly inattentive, poorly motivated behavior, low frustration threshold, and an increasing pattern of oppositionality.

Parent questionnaires yielded scores above the 98th percentile for the withdrawn and anxious/depressed scales of the Child Behavior Checklist and a score at the 95th percentile for the attention problems scale. T. B. was also above the 98th percentile on the Hyperkinesis Index. At home he was described as failing to finish things, being easily frustrated in his efforts, distractible, inattentive, and with wide mood changes; however, he did not demonstrate an extensive pattern of situational problems. He was described as disruptive with his siblings, procrastinating, and watching too much television.

Questionnaires completed by T. B.'s teachers did not yield complaints of inattentiveness, impulsivity, or hyperactivity. In fact, only one teacher noted slight restlessness. Most teachers, however, suggested that T. B. was rather socially isolated and did not appear very competent academically but was usually able to finish his work.

T. B. presented as a well-groomed, neatly dressed, pleasant adolescent. He appeared slightly anxious, was generally calm, and persisted on all tasks. Nonetheless, he was rather quiet and rarely initiated conversation.

T. B. obtained a performance at the 90th percentile on the Wechsler. His verbal reasoning and comprehension scores were exceptionally good. His visual-perceptive skills were also above average. A slightly lower performance on some of the nonverbal tasks appeared to result from a slow style rather than a lack of cognitive efficiency. He also performed at a level commensurate with his intellect. His ability to recall stories demonstrated an accelerated verbal learning curve. His reproduction of the Rey Osterrieth Figure was approached from a configuratal basis, well planned out, and reproduced at a level commensurate with T. B.'s intellectual skills.

T. B.'s self-report on attention checklists yielded scores slightly above average for complaints of difficulty paying attention and procrastination. His responses to a self-report depression scale yielded a score at the 85th percentile. Although this score is not excessive, T. B. noted that at times he worried about school, feels lonely, sad, worried, bored, and upset. During a clinical interview, his responses were generally minimal. Although he did not speak very positively about himself he did not complain. In contrast, his responses to the Millon Adolescent Profile reflected an adolescent rather self-deprecating, feeling vulnerable and defenseless. Consistent with his history, adolescents with this profile often have a shaky self-concept and are significantly more prone to feelings of hopelessness and depressive complaints. Adolescents with this profile, because of their hypersensitivity to criticism, however, rarely complain. They often feel misunderstood and disappointed but suffer in silence.

Although there have been intermittent complaints and a previous diagnosis of ADHD, T. B.'s history, current symptoms, and their severity did not meet the criteria for any of the ADHD types.

By history and report, T. B. had experienced at least one major depressive episode. The family history for depression was consistent in suggesting a risk for future depressive episodes. T. B.'s current symptom profile was consistent with a diagnosis of dysthymia.

T. B. agreed to participate in a coping with depression therapy program. Prior to initiating the program on an individual basis, a number of therapy sessions were scheduled to build his fragile trust. His participation in the program was good. Parents and teachers reported that he had become more assertive and outgoing at home and at school. T. B. resisted suggestions of a trial of antidepressant medication. He began working with an academic coach, focusing on keeping up with classwork. He also decided that he wanted to attend college and with the assistance of a college counselor, began considering different schools.

L. P.—PSEUDO-ADHD AND PERVASIVE DEVELOPMENTAL DISORDER

L. P., a 10-year-old female, was entering fifth grade. She was referred due to inattentive and impulsive symptoms. Concerns were also raised about her general development and social skills. L. P.'s parents were divorced and she lived with her father and stepmother. Her mother had a history of substance abuse and depressive problems. There appeared to be a history of ADHD on both parents' sides of the family. L. P. had an inconsistent relationship with her mother.

L. P. was reported to have demonstrated a number of odd behaviors as a toddler. She would frequently arch her back and roll around on the floor or in the swimming pool. She would sit for hours at a time picking up sand and letting it slip through her fingers. She had a propensity to watch the same movies over and over again. She was reported as having some difficulty with eye blinking. A past trial of stimulant medication resulted in "taking the edge off" L. P.'s behavior but no significant improvements. The medicine was not being used at the time of assessment.

L. P. had come to live with her father at 6 years of age. It was his recollection that the odd behaviors and delayed development that she demonstrated may have been related to her mother's neglect. Nonetheless, L. P. continued to struggle at school and was behind academically. She was described as sweet and pleasant but "different."

L. P. had been evaluated a number of times previously. One assessment yielded a diagnosis of ADHD. Another yielded a diagnosis of oppositional defiance and specific learning disability. A third suggested that L. P.'s problems may have been related to her parents' divorce.

Parent questionnaires placed L. P. in the clinically significant range for inattentive, impulsive, anxious, depressed, and social problem behaviors. Situationally, she was noted as having problems with self-care, fitting routines, and behavior in the home and public places. She was described as having odd or atypically conversational skills.

L. P. had received special education services over the previous two years, focusing primarily on improving her math skills. Academic assessment from the school team placed her cognitive abilities at the 7th percentile, reasoning at the 1st percentile, and verbal ability at the 45th percentile. Group achievement tests placed her at the 1st percentile for math, 22nd percentile for language, 9th percentile for reading, and overall battery at the 4th percentile.

L. P. presented for two assessment sessions with fairly similar behavior. She received a low dose of stimulant medication two hours prior to the morning assessment session. Her behavior was not particularly different between sessions. Her conversational skills were often atypical. She asked numerous, irrelevant questions. She appeared mildly anxious. Her thoughts, though logical, were mildly unfocused and irrelevant based on her conversation.

On the Wechsler, L. P. obtained a full-scale IQ of 73, placing her at the 4th percentile. Her average performance on the similarities and vocabulary subtests suggested better intellectual potential. On a memory battery, her general memory score was at the 8th percentile and learning score at the 27th percentile. She was markedly weaker in visual (1st percentile) than verbal skills (27th percentile). On the Peabody Picture Vocabulary Test, she performed at the 13th percentile and at the 2nd percentile on the

Test of Non-Verbal Intelligence; on this measure, L. P. was unable to obtain even a basal. Her motor speed and coordination were below the 10th percentile. Her ability to draw simple and complex designs was also poor. A computerized measure, the Gordon Diagnostic System, was administered approximately three hours after she received her morning dose of medication; her performance was in the normal range.

Academically, L. P. struggled with her knowledge of money and time telling. She read for accuracy and context at her grade but had poor comprehension. Despite good decoding, she seemed unable to understand or integrate what she was reading. Her math skills were at the 8th percentile, reflecting adequate rote skills but poor conceptual understanding of mathematics. Her written story contained two sentences without punctuation. There was no logical thought in content or idea flow.

L. P.'s responses to a depression questionnaire yielded scores within the average range, although her responses to an anxiety questionnaire yielded scores at the 84th percentile, suggesting somewhat more worrisome thoughts or feelings. Her responses to the examiner's questions were fairly unfocused and atypical. For example, when asked about the most difficult part of growing up, she answered driving, explaining that it would be difficult to keep a car "in one lane." She noted she did not want to grow up because "it's scary." She appeared to possess reasonable awareness of her struggles, despite her atypical presentation.

L. P.'s history and current functioning met the ADHD combined type diagnosis. Her rating scales consistently reflected her impulsive and social problems as well as raising concerns about her emotional adjustment. Based on her reports, problems appeared to be more reflective of anxiety than depression. Questionnaire data completed by teachers reflected L. P.'s atypical social interaction and inattentiveness but no marked complaints. Objective test data obtained while L. P. was receiving stimulant medication did not particularly reflect marked problems with impulsiveness and inattentiveness, appearing more consistent with a pattern of nonverbal skill weaknesses. Situationally, L. P. demonstrated problems in the home and school. From a differential diagnostic perspective, although L. P.'s history appeared consistent with ADHD, the overall profile reflected a pattern of right hemisphere weakness. Further, her atypical social interaction, odd behavior, and atypical interpersonal skills suggested problems consistent with a pervasive developmental disorder. Though not meeting the full symptom presentation for Asperger's, L. P.'s profile was generally similar to that group of children. From a developmental perspective, L. P.'s relatively weaker right hemisphere skills had resulted in her good rote academics but poor comprehension, conceptualization, and concept formation. It appeared to the examiner that L. P.'s odd or atypical responses or behavior observed by others was a function of her lack of ability to process rather than manipulative efforts to avoid or misbehave.

L. P. was referred to a child psychiatrist with expertise in pervasive developmental disorder for a second opinion, and the diagnosis of high-functioning pervasive developmental disorder was confirmed. Her educational team was provided with additional resources and strategies, and she was reclassified under the school classification of autism. Plans were made to closely monitor and support L. P.'s transition into junior high school. Her parents were provided with additional resources and ideas for children and adolescents experiencing both right hemisphere and high-functioning pervasive developmental disorder. L. P.'s physician maintained her dose of stimulant medication.

She was also referred to a counselor to begin preparing her to make what was hypothesized as a difficult transition into adolescence.

M. B.—PSEUDO-ADHD AND CONCEPTUAL LANGUAGE PROBLEMS

M. B., a 10-year-old fourth-grader, was referred by his speech/language pathologist. M.D. had a history of weak conceptual language skills. He was adopted at two and a half years of age from a foreign country after having minimal interaction with adults. It was reported that he had been placed in a crib and left for long periods of time with no stimulation. He appeared slow to develop language skills and was poor in generalizing his skills. He was quite sensitive to environmental pressure and between 3 and 5 years of age would shut his eyes and sit doing nothing if he became overstimulated. For reasons unknown, M. B. was born missing his entire right leg and part of his hip. He was fitted with an artificial leg, which he used quite efficiently to walk independently. He had a history of chronic ear infections.

Throughout his school career, M. B.'s parents had provided intensive academic support. He attended a private parochial school and received academic and language services. Interpersonally, he was described as gracious and well liked but did not easily initiate. He was also described as somewhat inattentive. It was noted, however, that although he worked slowly, if left alone, he would complete tasks.

Parent responses to questionnaires placed M. B. in the clinically significant range for inattentive but not impulsive problems. He was not described as having social or situational difficulties. A review of past assessments noted M. B.'s consistently adequate rote language skills but very poor pragmatic and semantic language skills. Academically, he had been able to perform in the average to high-average range as a result of all the support he received. Nonetheless, his best scores were in rote skills and his weakest in areas of comprehension and concept formation.

Teacher questionnaire data yielded scores all within the normal range. M. B. was described as relating positively with his classmates. He appeared accepted but not often in demand for activities.

During assessment, M. B. presented as a well-groomed, quiet child. His enunciation was poor. He rarely maintained or initiated conversation. He demonstrated slight word-finding problems. His approach to tasks was inconsistent; this appeared to be more a function of lack of verbal mediation to direct his behavior than of impulsivity.

On the Wechsler Intelligence Scale, M. B. performed at the 27th percentile. Not surprisingly, he performed best on rote tasks such as general information, and his weakest performance was on tasks requiring greater conceptual skills. As tasks required greater linguistic competence and reasoning, M. B.'s weaknesses became more apparent. His performance on a memory battery yielded poor verbal memory skills (8th percentile) and low-average visual memory skills (27th percentile). M. B. learned best with repetition. His academic scores were in the average range. His comprehension was markedly weaker than his rote reading skills. His written story was very poorly integrated.

M. B.'s responses to an anxiety questionnaire suggested somewhat more worry and anxiety than others. However, when questioned further, it was clear that he did not completely understand the meaning of many of the questions asked. During a clinical interview, though his responses were brief, he denied excessive feelings of unhappiness or worry. It was clear, however, that he did not perceive himself as particularly smart or competent academically.

Although at first look, M. B. demonstrated some symptoms of ADHD, his history and functioning did not cross thresholds for either type of ADHD diagnosis. His symptoms did not warrant a not otherwise specified diagnosis either. Rating scales, though reflecting his inattentiveness, were more consistent for children with pragmatic and semantic language problems. Objective test data were also consistent with this pattern. M. B. did not have problems completing a Conners continuous performance test. Situational behavior also appeared consistent with language rather than impulse problems. From a differential diagnostic perspective, it was clear that M. B. did not experience emotional or other disruptive problems. He was in a very supportive family environment. From a developmental perspective, data were consistent with a semantic pragmatic disorder. M. B.'s functioning reflected the combined efforts of his academic team, parents, and community providers.

It was recommended that M. B. continue to receive augmentive educational and language services. Further data were collected concerning his limited social interaction and a plan was put in place to increase his social contacts, with an effort to help him develop at least one close friend as he entered his adolescent years. M. B. also developed a working relationship with a counselor. However, efforts at increasing his insight met with limited success.

J. D.—PSEUDO-ADHD AND MULTIPLE LEARNING DISABILITIES

J. D., a 4½ year-old, male was referred by his pediatrician due to concerns of slower development. J. D.'s parents both held Ph.D.s. There did not appear to be any family history of developmental problems. His medical history was unremarkable. He had reached milestones somewhat later, especially those related to language skills. He also continued to be nocturnally enuretic. He was delayed in learning rote skills, such as colors and the alphabet. His coordination was described as slightly below average. J. D.'s preschool teachers described his problems as "purely maturational." He continued to be somewhat limited in his social relations but was not disruptive. He was described by his parents as having a sweet nature.

Parent responses to questionnaires did not reflect disruptive or nondisruptive problems. On a parent developmental inventory, however, J. D.'s general development yielded a score approximately one year below his chronological age, principally the result of weaker language skills. Teacher questionnaires reflected normal preschool behavior, although he was described as being easily distracted, having problems with dysfluency and language skills, as well as not responding consistently to rewards.

During the assessment, J. D. related well to the examiner. He was mildly unintelligible but his conversational skills were reasonably good. He was attentive and willing to attempt most tasks provided. Despite requiring structure, he worked quite well with the examiner.

J. D.'s responses to the preschool Wechsler scale yielded scores within the average range. However, this average score was somewhat deceiving, as J. D.'s fund of information was in the top 2% for his age and vocabulary at the top 15%. Markedly weaker performances were noted on tasks requiring more complex pragmatics and semantics. Nonverbal skills were consistently weak. On the Gordon Diagnostic System, J. D. required prompting, but his total correct and commission scores were average for his age. With structure, he could count five objects consistently. His one-to-one correspondence broke down quickly. He could count to fifteen. He could recognize sets of two without counting but struggled with early basic math concepts. His ability to recognize letters was inconsistent. On the Test of Early Reading Ability he performed at a 3-year-10-month level. During play, he tended to be somewhat undirected. However, over time the theme of this play was appropriate for a 4-year-old, as were his interactions with the examiner.

Although there were complaints of inattentiveness, J. D.'s overall presentation did not meet the criteria for ADHD. A not otherwise specified diagnosis was not considered, given the likely contribution of J. D.'s developmental weaknesses to adult observations of his behavior. Rating scales did not consistently reflect inattentive, impulsive, or hyperactive problems. Objective data were generally more consistent for a child with a pattern of semantic, pragmatic language problems and weaker visual-perceptive skills. In contrast, a number of test indices suggested that his intellectual potential was likely well above average. It was not surprising that this pattern of developmental weakness was delaying his acquisition of early academic skills as well as impacting his behavior in the home and school. From a differential diagnostic perspective, J. D. clearly did not experience any other type of disruptive or nondisruptive problem. His family and family life were quite good.

J. D. was referred to a preschool speech pathologist specializing in pragmatic semantic problems and over the course of a year made excellent progress. With support in the preschool, his acquisition of pre-academic skills increased. Efforts were made to also improve his visual-perceptive abilities and writing skills. J. D.'s social skills slowly and steadily continued to improve. He was recommended for reevaluation at the end of his kindergarten year.

G. P.—PSEUDO-ADHD, IMPULSIVE TEMPERAMENT, HIGH IQ, AND RIGHT HEMISPHERE LEARNING DISABILITY

G. P., an 11-year-old sixth-grade male, had a history of poor learning. He was also described as impulsive, though not necessarily inattentive. G. P. was adopted and no information was available concerning his biological parents. As an infant, he was often irritable and had difficulty being comforted. Developmental milestones were reached at normal limits. His motor skills were described as average but his handwriting was noted as poor. His parents commented that he understood directions but often had to have them repeated. At school, G. P. was described as having a history of doing the least amount of work possible, forgetting to complete assignments, and not handing in completed assignments. At home, his behavior was clearly impulsive, including order-ing nearly $20,000 worth of computer equipment with his father's credit card through the Internet. In contrast, his parents described him as rather sweet and kind, noting that they had a good relationship with him despite his impulsive problems.

Parent responses to questionnaires placed G. P. within the normal range. His impul-sivity resulted in intermittent but not consistent problems. His teachers did not reflect any significant complaints. They noted that he could work independently quite well, and was accepted by the other students but not often in demand for social activities. One teacher described G. P. as a quiet, thoughtful child, and another said he was "very capable when he chooses." Group achievement tests placed G. P. overall at the 44th percentile, reflecting 68th percentile reading skills but 33rd percentile math skills and 36th percentile language skills. His spelling skills were at the 70th percentile in con-trast to his 93rd percentile listening skills.

G. P. presented as a very pleasant child. He was responsive to the examiner. He ap-peared moderately confident in his skills. His work style was slightly impulsive.

G. P.'s performance on the Wechsler Intelligence Scale yielded a full-scale IQ at the 84th percentile. In contrast, his freedom from distractibility factor was at the 53rd percentile and processing speed factor at the 47th percentile. G. P.'s verbal skills ap-peared markedly better than his nonverbal or performance skills. His fund of informa-tion, verbal reasoning, vocabulary, and comprehension skills were well above average. His performance on the block design and object assembly subtests were barely average.

G. P.'s receptive vocabulary on the Peabody was at the 97th percentile. His nonver-bal reasoning skills on the Test of Non-Verbal Intelligence were at only the 50th per-centile. On a memory battery he obtained 73rd percentile verbal memory skills but only 21st percentile visual memory skills. Although he was able to learn with repeti-tion, his approach to learning tasks was rather impulsive. His performance on the Con-ners computerized measure, however, did not reflect problems. Academic screening placed G. P.'s skills in the average range. He read for accuracy well above his grade level, with comprehension at grade level. His written story reflected poor handwriting but good ideas. G. P. demonstrated some difficulty comprehending and integrating information. This appeared to be a function of his impulsive style, although it was hy-pothesized that it might also reflect a pattern of right hemisphere weakness compen-sated for by a bright child.

G. P.'s self-reports did not suggest problems with anxiety or depression. A number of his observations clearly reflected an awareness of his impulse problems.

Although G. P. had a clear history of impulsivity, his presentation and behavior did not cross the threshold for either type of ADHD diagnosis. Although the not otherwise specified diagnosis was considered, it was rejected given concerns that providing the di-agnosis might dissuade school and parents from the need to provide a strong nonmedi-cine program. Further rating scales were not consistent for ADHD problems. Objective data were more consistent for right hemisphere weakness and mild impulsivity than the full syndrome of ADHD. Situational problems also reflected this profile. From a differ-ential diagnostic perspective, G. P. did not experience disruptive or nondisruptive prob-lems. His pattern of developmental weakness, including weak fine motor skills, poor handwriting, marked difficulty with mathematics and reading comprehension despite good intellect, as well as difficulty reading the social environment, appeared consistent with mild right hemisphere learning disability.

G. P.'s teachers were apprised of his weaknesses and an effort was made to begin preparing him for the transition into junior high school. He began working with an academic tutor, specifically to improve his mathematic skills. A study skills class to improve organizational, note-taking, test-taking, and study skills was also suggested. G. P.'s parents were provided with additional resources concerning managing adolescent behavior in the family. G. P. was provided with short-term counseling to focus on his assets and increase his motivation toward school. It was recommended that he be closely monitored as he made the transition into junior high school and that if continued impulse problems were observed and disrupted G. P.'s functioning despite other efforts at intervention, his physician reconsider the possible risks versus benefits of a trial of medication as part of G. P.'s treatment plan.

J. D.—ADHD INATTENTIVE TYPE, ROTE LEARNING DISABILITY, AND PAST MAJOR DEPRESSIVE EPISODE

J. D., a 17-year-old male, was referred after dropping out of tenth grade. Six months earlier, while J. D.'s parents were on a trip to Europe, he stopped attending school and appeared to enter a major depressive episode. During that period, he reported smoking an excessive amount of marijuana. Efforts to coerce him to return to school met with no success. At the time of assessment, he had not attended school for six months and was spending his days working on his computer and visiting friends. He was not working.

The family history is noted for alcoholism, depression, and learning disability. J. D. had struggled in elementary school. A review of his report cards reflected consistent teacher complaints of inattention and disorganization. He was never described as disruptive. A number of teachers commented that he appeared to have good thinking skills but poor memory for basic academic skills.

Parent responses to questionnaires placed J. D. in a clinically significant range for socially withdrawn, anxious/depressed, and attention problem scales. His parents noted that with them, especially with his mother, he could be quite argumentative; with other adults he was very pleasant.

A review of school assessment data completed a number of years previously reflected J. D.'s average academic skills but very poor written language abilities. He had taken the ACT college entrance exams, scoring in the average range for college-bound students.

J. D. was pleasant and appropriate during the evaluation. On the Wechsler, he obtained a verbal IQ of 105, performance IQ of 108, and full-scale IQ of 107. He performed best on tasks requiring more complex conceptual skills such as similarities and comprehension, performing weakest on tasks requiring rote memory. Administration of a memory battery yielded average nonverbal memory skills but very poor verbal memory abilities, especially for rote nonmeaningful information. A qualitative review of J. D.'s academic sample reflected his good conceptual skills but poor execution of written language, spelling, and knowledge of math facts.

J. D.'s self-reports did not suggest that he was currently depressed. However, his personality style reflected an adolescent tending to be overly self-critical and self-deprecating. He appeared sensitive to the demands of others and in response had withdrawn from most adolescent activities. He reported feeling confused and uncertain about himself and his future.

J. D.'s history and functioning appeared to meet the threshold for the inattentive type of ADHD. Parent rating scales, though reflective of continued depressive behavior, did not provide sufficient data to suggest a continued major depressive episode. Objective data reflected J. D.'s rote language and visual weaknesses resulting in poor academic skills. He clearly was bright on a conceptual level. At home, J. D. was more oppositional with his mother than his father; however, in general he was not a behavior problem. Given his age, he had been allowed by his parents and the school team to withdraw from school.

On a differential basis, his depression certainly appeared to follow rather than precede reported symptoms of ADHD. The depressive episode appeared to have lifted, though risk of a second episode, given his life situation, was judged to be at least moderate. His lack of self-confidence was further impairing his ability to make important life decisions and proceed with his education.

A trial of stimulant medication was initiated. J. D. reported feeling organized and attentive. He was seen in cognitively based individual psychotherapy to further explore his thoughts and feelings and build his self-confidence. After four months, J. D. decided to enroll at the community college, taking high school equivalent courses as well as beginning his college education.

SUMMARY

This chapter presented extensive case examples to help the practitioner understand the model used in making the diagnosis of ADHD and to sensitize the practitioner to the interaction of ADHD with other disorders of childhood.

Part Three

INTERVENTION

Chapter 12

MULTIDISCIPLINARY MULTITREATMENTS FOR ADHD

The efficacy of psychological, educational, and behavioral treatments has been well established through meta-analytic review (Lipsey & Wilson, 1993). Yet, despite the proven benefits of these interventions, the majority of children and adolescents in need of such help often find it unavailable (Burns, 1991). The syndrome of ADHD symptoms, the myriad settings in which symptoms are presented, the extensive demands placed upon youth educationally and behaviorally, as well as the high incidence of comorbid problems in the ADHD population have all served as barriers in the development of a literature clearly attesting to the benefits of single or combined treatments for ADHD in all but one case—the use of medications. However, even pharmacological treatments for ADHD may not meet all criteria necessary to prove treatment effectiveness. Table 12–1 describes a set of factors practitioners should consider to determine if treatment is effective (Whalen & Henker, 1991). It is important to note that due to the chronicity, severity, cross-situational nature, and myriad symptoms of ADHD, treatment logically must be long-term and require creativity and perseverance (Rapport, 1992).

ADHD is a disorder that is managed, not cured. Thus, each of the child's specific problems, whether behavioral, cognitive, or psychological, must be identified and treated. At this time, primary symptoms of ADHD are most effectively treated with medication. Others can be treated with a combination of medication, behavior management, and skill building. The secondary by-products of living with ADHD (e.g., low self-esteem issues) can be addressed through psychotherapy. Parents and professionals must understand that with ADHD, it is rare for an effective management or treatment plan to consist of only one intervention. Further, the ADHD child, parents, siblings, teachers, and other professionals must be active participants in the treatment program. It is essential that all involved develop sensitivity to the complex and pervasive impact ADHD has on daily functioning and how it can compromise a child's ability to meet the expectations of his or her world. Treatment for ADHD must consist of a partnership among the child, family, school personnel, practitioner, and physician (Culvert, Banez, & Reiff, 1994). Logically, the assessment process should not only provide accurate diagnoses and behaviors targeted for change, but facilitate everyone's ability to see the world through the eyes of the child with ADHD. Issues related to the use of jargon, rationales for treatment, personal resources, severity of the child's problems, and available alternatives are critical in determining response to recommended treatment. Parents, teachers, and the ADHD child are all consumers. Their willingness to

Table 12–1.   Comparing and contrasting treatment modalities: an array of therapeutic "-abilities"

Applicability: What is the bandwidth or scope of problems that can be treated, and what is the developmental range of effectiveness?

Adaptability: How readily can the treatment be turned or tailored to meet particular clinical and developmental requirements?

Communicability/teachability: How readily can the basic therapeutic skills and ingredients be identified and taught?

Availability: Once the initial research and demonstration projects conclude, how readily can the treatment be provided by community practitioners under real-life conditions?

Controllability: How readily can standards of delivery be ensured across administratively, philosophically, and geographically diverse treatment settings?

Compatibility: How readily can the treatment be combined with other necessary or desirable interventions?

Durability: What is the stability or predictability of improvement during the course of treatment, and how long are treatment-generated gains maintained once treatment is discontinued?

Generalizability: How well do positive outcomes generalize beyond the treatment targets and settings? What is the range and quality of positive emanative effects?

Constrainability: How widespread and serious are the unintended side effects and undesirable emanative effects of the treatment?

Feasibility: How manageable is the sum total of temporal, psychological, economic, and other burdens imposed on the child and his significant others?

Visibility: How likely is the child to be stigmatized because of his participation in treatment?

Palatability: How good is the match between client goals, values, and proclivities and therapeutic philosophies and tactics?

Source: Whalen, C. K., & Henker, B. (1991). Therapies for hyperactive children: Comparisons, combinations and compromises. *Journal of Consulting and Clinical Psychology, 59,* 126–137. Copyright 1991 by the American Psychological Association. Reprinted with permission.

accept and follow through with recommendations is in part based on the practitioner's ability to increase their understanding and motivation. For example, Rostain, Power, and Atkins (1993) attempted to identify specific family variables that predicted receptiveness to and compliance with medication and counseling recommendations for children with ADHD. This initial effort, though it met with limited success, demonstrates a trend toward understanding that it is the consumer's view of what is recommended that is critical in determining compliance. Rostain et al. (1993) found that a history of the child's receiving medication was mildly correlated with a willingness to use medication, and a history of counseling was moderately correlated with a willingness to use medication and pursue counseling. Brown, Borden, Wynne, and Spunt (1988) demonstrated that adherence to pharmacotherapy and psychotherapy in children with ADHD was at greatest risk in low socioeconomic status families. Interestingly, in this study, compliance with medication was more of a problem than compliance with psychotherapy. In this three-month treatment study, nearly half of the group did not complete treatment.

This chapter serves as a brief introduction to the treatment chapters that follow, providing an overview of single treatments and combinations of treatments that have been reported as beneficial to children with ADHD. The chapter also presents an approach to help the practitioner motivate parents concerning the need for multiple treatments in response to the multiple problems children with ADHD experience.

SINGLE TREATMENTS

Medication

Well over a million children in the United States are believed to be taking a central nervous system stimulant, primarily methylphenidate, for ADHD (Swanson, Lerner, & Williams, 1995). This suggests a steady increase in the use of stimulant medication over the past twenty years (Safer & Krager, 1983; Sprague & Sleator, 1977). Based on global measures, 75% respond positively to the drug (DuPaul & Barkley, 1993). Methylphenidate improves attention and social interactions, increases academic productivity but not necessarily achievement, and reduces disruptive and impulsive behavior (DuPaul & Barkley, 1993). Methylphenidate has been suggested at slightly higher doses than typically administered to optimize attention and recall of complex, nonverbal information (O'Toole, Abramowitz, Morris, & Dulcan, 1997).

The continued and widespread use of medications, specifically stimulants, in the treatment of ADHD is a result of both cost efficiency and the large volume of research demonstrating significant short-term positive effects (for review, see Greenhill & Osman, 1991). However, despite their effectiveness, medications too have had their disadvantages. These include reports of a lack of effectiveness in a small but significant percentage of children (Barkley, 1977a; Rapport, DuPaul, Stoner, & Jones, 1986); unwanted side effects, including potentially irreversible problems with tics (Lowe, Cohen, Detlor, Kremenitzer, & Shaywitz, 1982); anorexia, insomnia, and irritability (Barkley, 1977a); and a lack of consistent positive impact in improving long-term academic performance, social behavior, and emotional development (for review, see S. Goldstein, 1997a). Additionally, ethical and legal questions relating to methylphenidate use have been raised, including the right of school systems to require children to take medication, alleged harm as the result of side effects, negligence in diagnosis leading to wrongful medication treatment, and constitutional questions concerning limitations on parents' right to decline medical care for their children balanced against states' interest in safeguarding children's health and welfare (Ouellette, 1991).

Medications are not found to contribute significantly to a positive outcome as children with ADHD grow into adulthood (for review, see S. Goldstein, 1997a). It has been increasingly recognized that relieving symptoms of ADHD may not equate to significantly altering the future life of this population. The combination of the limitations of medication in solving the multiple problems of the ADHD child, medication-related

Table 12–2.   Frequency and percentage of classroom strategies for children with ADHD study characteristics

Characteristics	Frequency	Percentage
Reasons for Excluding Studies		
Insufficient data to calculate meta-analysis	37	27.0
Not conducted in a school setting	14	10.2
Participants not identified as ADHD	7	5.1
Participants not school-aged	5	3.6
Absence of no-treatment control	4	2.9
Participants identified with mental retardation/ brain damage	3	2.2
Data previously published	3	2.2
No intervention conducted	1	0.8
Study met inclusion criteria	63	46.0
Year of Publication[*]		
1971–1975	4	6.3
1976–1980	12	19.0
1981–1985	13	20.6
1986–1990	15	23.8
1991–1995	19	30.2
Source of Study		
Dissertation or thesis	9	14.3
Published study	51	80.9
Unpublished study	3	4.8
Type of Intervention		
Contingency management	26	41.3
Cognitive-behavioral	29	46.0
Academic intervention	8	12.7
Experimental Design		
Between-subject design	8	12.7
Within-subject design	17	27.0
Single-subject design	38	60.3
Assignment of Participants		
Randomized	10	15.8
Nonrandomized	16	25.4
Not applicable due to use of single-subject design	37	58.7
Use of Control Group		
Yes	15	23.8
No	11	17.5
Not applicable (single-subject design)	37	58.7

Table 12–2. *(continued)*

Characteristics	Frequency	Percentage
Follow-up Assessment		
1–4 weeks	6	9.5
5–8 weeks	2	3.2
9–12 weeks	1	1.6
12 weeks	5	7.9
None	49	77.8
Reliability Assessment		
Yes	49	77.8
No	14	22.2
Treatment Integrity Assessment		
Yes	8	14.5
No	55	87.3
Social Validity Assessment		
Yes	8	14.5
No	55	87.3

Source: DuPaul, G. J. & Eckert, T. L. (1997). The effects of school-based interventions for ADHD: A meta-analysis. *School Psychology Review, 26,* 5–27. Copyright 1997 by the National Association of School Psychologist. Reprinted by permission of the publisher.

[*] All subsequent frequencies and percentages based on $n = 63$ (i.e., all studies that met inclusion criteria).

side effects, and the increasing volume of studies demonstrating moderate effectiveness of nonmedication treatments has led to interest in the clinical use of nonmedication treatments for this disorder. However, the interest in nonmedication interventions is not new; researchers and clinicians have been using nonmedication treatments and combinations of treatments for ADHD-related symptoms for nearly 100 years.

Behavioral Techniques

A recent meta-analysis of sixty-three outcome studies conducted from 1971 to 1995 (DuPaul & Eckert, 1997) has demonstrated that contingency management strategies and academic interventions are effective for children with ADHD in classroom settings. Table 12–2 contains frequency and percentage of study characteristics.

Systematic efforts to use contingency management techniques for children with ADHD initially relied on manual or electronic devices to provide contingent feedback (Doubros & Daniels, 1966; Patterson, 1964; Quay, Sprague, Werry, & McQueen, 1967). A second generation of studies utilizing behavior management sought to improve children's behavior by utilizing contingent social praise (Allen, Henke, Harris, Baer, & Reynolds, 1967), modeling (Nixon, 1969), tokens (Twardosz & Sajwaj, 1972), and home-based reinforcement systems (O'Leary, Pelham, Rosenbaum, & Price, 1976). Along the way, the initial tendency to focus on a single dimension of behavior gave way to treating broader classes of behavior. Clinicians have increasingly suggested that for children with mild symptoms of ADHD, behavioral interventions should represent the treatment of first resort. In many cases, it has been suggested that the reported failures of behavioral interventions with children experiencing ADHD result from poorly designed and controlled studies containing methodological flaws rather than actually demonstrating lack of effectiveness. For practitioners in clinical settings, it is important to make certain that behavioral treatments have been implemented as planned before deciding they are ineffective (Gresham, 1991; Peterson, Homer, & Wunderlich, 1982). Further, practitioners should be aware that in part, children and families compliant with behavioral interventions are likely to start out as less impaired than those prone to drop out of treatment (Kazdin, Mazurieck, & Siegel, 1994).

The primary focus has been on using positive reinforcement to increase task-related attention and completion of tasks at school and home (DuPaul, Stoner, Tilly, & Putnam, 1991). The effective management of consequences may increase not only motivation but the likelihood the child will know what it is he or she is required to do (Guare, 1988). Behavioral treatments for ADHD have demonstrated consistent effectiveness even in the absence of medication. Cocciarella, Wood, and Lowe (1995) provided seven latency-age ADHD children with a program to reinforce appropriate behavior and punish negative behavior. There were significant decreases over a multiweek period in reports of impulsive behavior at home and at school. The intervention also appeared to generalize somewhat. Among the components of behavior management that have been utilized and found to be particularly effective with children with ADHD has been the use of response cost. However, when using response cost, practitioners need to consider several factors, including not allowing the child to go bankrupt, introducing the number of rules or behaviors that can be consequated at one time, and avoiding having the system take on an overly negative tone (Pfiffner & O'Leary, 1987; Pfiffner, O'Leary, Rosen, & Sanderson, 1985; Rosen et al., 1984). Fiorella, Douglas, and Baker (1995) examined the effects of reward and response cost on a population of children with ADHD. Two evaluative conditions involved both reward and response cost, one response cost only, and a fourth reward only. Children with ADHD made more errors than controls on a laboratory task across all four conditions. Learning curves indicated that group differences became larger in later trials. Impaired inhibition appeared to explain this phenomenon. This problem became more evident when children were required to improve learning across trials. The combined use of reward and response cost led to the most improvement in performance for those with ADHD.

The impact of reward size has also been extensively evaluated with ADHD children. For example, in a sample of preadolescent boys with ADHD, Sonuga-Barke et al. (1992) evaluated their choice of small or immediate rewards over large or delayed rewards under different economic constraints and delayed conditions. Both groups of normal and ADHD boys were equally efficient at earning points under most conditions. The ADHD group, however, exhibited a maladaptive preference for the small reward when it was provided immediately. The authors concluded that children with ADHD were more concerned about reducing overall delay levels than in maximizing reward amount, a factor that should be kept in mind by practitioners when working with parents and educators.

Questions have also been raised as to whether providing tangible rewards for behavior change, such as completing a task or meeting a standard of quality, may result in a reduction in intrinsic interest when the task is not provided. However, an analysis of a quarter of a century of accumulated research provided little evidence that reward reduced intrinsic task interest (Eisenberger & Cameron, 1996). Interestingly, these authors' meta-analysis determined that with verbal reward, people spend more time on task following the removal of reward than prior to its introduction. Further, people report that they like tasks better after verbal or tangible reward that depended on performance quality. There has also been a focus on identifying appropriate behaviors to substitute for less desirable symptoms of ADHD. Among the more interesting controversies has been the question of whether children with ADHD are being reinforced for developing "dead boy" behavior (Lindsley, 1991); that is, "if a dead boy could do it, it wasn't behavior" (p. 457). Treatment targets such as sitting still or not calling out violate the dead boy's rule. In other words, the treatment should focus on what the child *should* do.

Parent Training

The second most widely used treatment for ADHD focuses on increasing parents' ability to manage the behavior of their children. It has long been recognized that increasing parental competence has a positive effect on children's behavior. The majority of parent training programs suggested for ADHD are based on basic learning theory principles (Barkley, 1997a; Patterson, 1974). Parents are taught techniques for manipulating the environment in an organized fashion to reduce the probability that symptoms of ADHD will lead to noncompliant behavior, while concomitantly increasing the probability of compliant behavior. In some studies, parent training programs have demonstrated fairly good short-term positive results (Graziano, 1983; Moreland, Schwebel, Beck, & Wells, 1982), but as noted, these may not be effective in precipitating long-term change for this population of children (Phillips & Ray, 1980; Gittelman-Klein et al., 1980). The importance of parent training, however, cannot be overemphasized. Barkley (1981b) suggests that children with ADHD have a more powerful coercive effect on their parents than vice versa.

Children with ADHD are more likely than learning disabled or normal children to act in noncompliant ways (Campbell, 1985). It is clear, however, that they are not likely to be as noncompliant as children experiencing oppositional defiant or conduct disorders. When observed in playroom settings, mothers of hyperactive boys give more commands, are less responsive, and respond more negatively than mothers of normal boys (Barkley & Cunningham, 1980). Although studies such as these suggest that parental behavior may cause child misbehavior, researchers have demonstrated, again in a playroom setting, that reducing children's attention, arousal, and hyperactivity problems with a treatment such as stimulant medication has a significant effect in producing more normal parent-child interactions (Humphries, Kinsbourne, & Swanson, 1978). Normalization of parental behavior was achieved specifically by the reduction of excessive negative child behaviors. As Barkley (1981a) points out, "the child's behavior exerts a great deal of control over parental responses" (p. 60).

Conners and Wells (1986) noted that a decrease in negative parent behaviors as a result of a reduction in ADHD symptoms in the child is not always accompanied by a corresponding increase in positive parent behaviors. Barkley and Cunningham (1979) and

Cunningham and Barkley (1978b) have consistently demonstrated that stimulant medication does not increase positive maternal social initiation or maternal reward for child compliance and free play. Pollard, Ward, and Barkley (1983) also demonstrated that the stimulant medication did not consistently increase the total amount of reward and social reinforcement provided by mothers during a structured task with their children. From an interactional perspective, this makes sense. The medicated child's increased compliance may result in the parent's perception of less need for negative, controlling behavior; however, parents of such children frequently have not had the opportunity to develop a repertoire of positive interactional skills. In such situations, the data suggest that parents' behavior becomes neither negative nor positive but benign. These data argue for a combination of medication and parent training to improve basic communication and interactional style between parents and their ADHD children.

Cognitive Techniques

The intuitive appeal of helping children with ADHD develop internal strategies to allow them to act as their own change agent has been seductive to researchers and clinicians alike over the past forty years (Rapport, 1988). These models represent an outgrowth of the work of Luria (1961) and have their basic premise in the fact that children with ADHD lack effective cognitive or mediational skills. These models attempt to teach such skills through a variety of techniques. For example, teaching children to accurately monitor and record their behavior is thought over time to increase self-management and task completion. Although positive results have been reported in a variety of childhood problems, as well as in some laboratory settings utilizing a population of ADHD children, the child with ADHD appears to have difficulty generalizing and using these strategies in the environment (Abikoff & Gittelman, 1985). It is hypothesized that knowing what to do is not the same as knowing when to do it (S. Goldstein, 1997a). Interventions for ADHD work best at the point of performance (Ingersoll & Goldstein, 1993). Thus, children with ADHD may master cognitive strategies in a laboratory setting but have difficulty knowing when to use those strategies in real life. This may result from either the child's impulsive, inattentive style or a history of behavioral contingencies in the environment that elicit and maintain the learned component of the ADHD child's maladaptive behavior (Abikoff, 1985; Abikoff & Gittelman, 1985).

Braswell and Kendall's (1988) summary of ten years of cognitive behavioral therapy reveals a dismal record of controlling for subject variables, assessment, and flexible study treatment length. These may be responsible for the lack of long-term benefits of cognitive behavioral therapy. However, an increasing volume of literature suggests that even when these issues are addressed, the failure of cognitive behavioral therapy to modify problems with ADHD is not simply the result of insufficient trials or inadequate efforts at generalization. As Abikoff (1991) noted, although face validity of cognitive behavioral therapy makes it appear inherently appealing, there is little empirical support for its clinical utility for children with ADHD. Cognitive training, according to Abikoff, is not competitive with the stimulants. There is no consistent data that it enhances the behavioral effects of stimulants either. Again, this is not to argue that cognitive interventions may not be beneficial for a host of problems, including comorbid disorders that can present with ADHD. For example, Morris (1993) utilized a rational emotive treatment program over a twelve-week period with a group of conduct-disordered adolescents and a second group of those with ADHD. The program consisted of lecture, discussion, and video. Findings revealed that the CD group significantly changed in all dependent variables, but no changes occurred in the ADHD group. Similar findings have been reported by others (Swenson & Kennedy, 1995).

Although the data argue strongly that cognitive interventions do not directly impact ADHD symptoms, there is an increasing volume of literature suggesting that cognitive strategies can be effective in dealing with self-esteem and related problems that develop as the result of living with ADHD and in motivating and changing perception and attitude in parents and teachers (Fehlings, Roberts, Humphries, & Dawe, 1990). On even a basic level, increasing parents' and teachers' ability to understand, anticipate, and see the world through the eyes of the ADHD child leads to a more motivated participant and ultimately a more effective change agent. It is fair to conclude, as do Whalen and Henker (1991), that cognitive behavioral therapy does not appear "as pervasive nor scientifically justified as either stimulant or behavioral treatments for ADHD. Cognitive-behavioral therapy approaches have, however, produced solid and growing enthusiasm for their use as adjuncts or even alternatives to more traditional, pharmacologic and behavioral strategies" (p. 126).

Educational Techniques

Symptoms of ADHD exert a pervasive impact on children's school performance and behavior. Thus, the increasing focus over the past ten years on developing strategies and programs to effectively educate children with ADHD is not surprising. Educational strategies and intervention for children with ADHD, however, have not been without controversy. Interestingly, the controversy has not been generated, as with other treatments, as the result of conflicting research findings but rather simply as the result of different opinions. Questions have been raised as to whether children with ADHD should be served in special education, require classroom strategies and support, or should be educated without specific accommodations (Reid, Maag, & Vasa, 1994). Although treatment research findings in educational settings do not represent a robust literature, there is sufficient data to state that classroom accommodations for children with ADHD can be beneficial for them and their educators (Fiore, Becker, & Nero, 1993).

Though there is a need to develop and study educational interventions for children with ADHD (DuPaul & Stoner, 1994), skillful teachers willing to shift focus from performance to task and recognize that ADHD is a problem of development rather than noncompliance can provide supportive environments for children with ADHD in educational settings. As Zentall (1995) notes, the educational environment for children with ADHD must take place across school settings, focus on building generalization, and allow children to talk, move, question, and actively interact with their learning environment. Such strategies are likely best centered around a classroom philosophy of brief, varied classroom experiences (C. B. Jones, 1994).

Social Skills Building

Recognition of the relationship between impulsivity and aggressive behavior has prompted strong interest in developing effective social skills programs for children with ADHD (Sheridan, 1995). Initial efforts at developing and adapting programs to improve the social interaction of children with ADHD have been refined and led to a number of programs that have developed proven research-based criteria to identify, remediate, and actually improve the social interaction of children with ADHD (Sheridan, Dee, Morgan, McCormick, & Walker, 1996). Student-mediated conflict education programs (Schrumph, Crawford, & Usadel, 1991) and collaborative student mediation projects (Cunningham, Cunningham, et al., 1995) have focused on improving ADHD interactions. In the Cunningham, Cunningham, et al. (1995) program, student mediators participated in fifteen hours of training; teams of two per playground quadrant was deployed during recess, lunch breaks, and transitions. These children interrupted emerging conflicts, introduced themselves, and asked disputants whether they were prepared to solve problems. They then explained the rules of mediation, which include listening without interrupting, keeping hands and feet to themselves, and taking responsibility for finding a solution. Such programs have been suggested as efficacious because they target conflicts among students schoolwide, mediators are present, skills transfer better and generalize, and the interventions are universal and may shift attitudes, norms, and social processes that regulate teasing, bullying, conflict, and dispute resolution.

Other Treatments

Since the publication of the first edition of this text, there has been a dramatic increase in interest in other nontraditional treatments that may be beneficial for ADHD. These have included various modifications of diet; alternative forms of therapy, including optometric visional training and sensory integration therapy; biofeedback; osteopathic treatment; and neuro-organization techniques. Although some of these treatments deserve continued research attention, for the purposes of this text, these treatments are organized under the title "controversial." They are controversial because their proponents market them with overstated claims, single-case testimonials, in some cases exorbitant fees, and a general lack of any scientific support.

MULTITREATMENT APPROACHES

Hechtman (1993) outlines the growing acceptance in use of multimodal treatment approaches for ADHD. Despite limitations in previous studies in assessing outcome of efficacy and controlling for a variety of measures, Hechtman describes the reality of conducting valid outcome multimodal research with ADHD children. Multitreatment approaches to ADHD have included various combinations of specific interventions:

- Behavioral parent training and self-control therapy (Cocciarella, Wood, & Lowe, 1995; Horn, Ialongo, Greenberg, Packard, & Smith-Winberry, 1990; Horn, Ialongo, Popovich, & Peradotto, 1987).

- Environmental variables and medication (Cooper, Wacker, Millard, Derby, & Mark, 1993).
- Medication and self-control training (Borden & Brown, 1989; Horn, Chatoor, & Conners, 1983).
- Medication and behavioral management at home and school (Abramowitz, Eckstrand, O'Leary, & Dulcan, 1992; Bugental, Whalen, & Henker, 1977; C. Carlson, Pelham, Milich, & Dixon, 1992; DuPaul & Barkley, 1993; Gittelman-Klein et al., 1980; Hall & Kataria, 1992; Pelham, Carlson, Sams, & Vallano, 1993; Pelham, Schnedler, et al., 1986; Wolraich, Drummond, Salomon, O'Brien, & Sivage, 1978).
- Medication and family therapy (Glick, 1992; Hollon & Beck, 1978).
- Medication, self-control training, teacher and parent behavioral management (Grizenko, Papineau, & Sayegh, 1993; Ialongo et al., 1993; Pelham, Schnedler, Bologna, & Contreras, 1980; Satterfield et al., 1981).

By far the greatest interest has been in the evaluation of the additive effects of medication and behavior management. Reviewing eighteen treatment studies, including combinations of medication and behavior management, Horn and Ialongo (1988) found that medication enhanced the efficacy of the behavioral and social intervention in twelve studies. Whalen and Henker (1991) reviewed additional comparative studies and concluded that they were impeded by methodological problems, limited focus, poor research design, and heterogeneity of the ADHD population, making it difficult to draw firm conclusions as to the efficacy or added benefits of stimulant treatment, behavioral intervention, and cognitive training. Yet, there appears to be an insufficient basis for determining under which circumstances and with which child characteristics (comorbid conditions, gender, family history, home environment, age, nutrition, metabolic status, etc.) do which treatments or combinations of treatments (stimulants, behavior therapy, parent training, school-based intervention) have which impacts (improvement, no change, deterioration) on which domains in child functioning (cognitive, academic, behavioral, neuropsychological, neurophysiological, peer relations, family relations) for how long (short versus long term), to what extent (effect size, normal versus pathological range), and why (processes, underlying change). A multisite, multimodal treatment National Institute of Mental Health program has been initiated over a five-year period to address these questions (Richters et al., 1995).

Researchers have also attempted to evaluate the best means of delivering multitreatment services. Clinic (Whalen & Henker, 1991), school (DuPaul & Stoner, 1994), and summer programs (Goldhaber, 1991; Pelham & Gnagy, 1995) have been studied. Summer programs have been of particular interest to clinicians. The program developed by Pelham and Gnagy (1995), begun in 1980, is an eight-week program for children 5 to 15 years of age, attending from 8 A.M. to 5 P.M. on weekdays. Participants are placed in groups of twelve and treatment implemented in teams of five clinical staff members. Children spend three hours daily in classroom sessions: one hour on academics, one on computer-assisted instruction, and one in art; the remainder of each day is spent in recreational activities. A token reinforcement point system is a major component of this program. Three hundred and sixty hours of treatment are provided in eight weeks. Although such programs have led to short-term benefits, questions remain as to their long-term efficacy.

Investigators have not systematically examined the effects on treatment outcome of educating parents concerning various aspects of ADHD, helping them to see the world through the eyes of their children, and making them effective case managers. It is our experience that the parent knowledgeable about the causes and ramifications of ADHD as well as possessing a repertoire of treatments for ADHD and activities to build in other protective factors responds better to treatment interventions. Parents able to attribute the ADHD child's problems to incompetence as opposed to purposeful noncompliance appear more motivated, less threatened, and overall less angry in their dealings with their children. It has also been suggested by Horn and Ialongo (1988) that a combination of parent-child–centered behavioral treatments has an additive effect in improving behavior, resulting in lower doses of stimulant medications being required. It has been suggested that parent cognitions are communicated to children in the form of expectancies (Parsons, Adler, & Kaczala, 1982). These authors argued strongly that changes in parental beliefs will greatly influence children's beliefs in the long run. They suggest that in our society, people believe that if medication is needed in their treatment, attempting to take personal control over their problems is futile. This attitude may be particularly detrimental when the adjunctive treatment involves self-management or requires a high level of motivation. Further, although parent-child influence is clearly bidirectional, the asymmetry of the relationship may in some cases predict greater influence from parent to child (Maccoby & Martin, 1983). Borden and Brown (1989) report that there appears to be a motivational effect from combining medication with cognitive therapy or other behavioral change techniques.

It has been repeatedly emphasized that the use of multiple treatment modalities in ADHD produces therapeutic benefit greater than the sum of each modality's contribution (for review see Goldstein, 1997). Although the best combination and methods of treatments for specific groups of children with ADHD have yet to be completely delineated, the philosophy of multimodal treatment for ADHD has been well accepted. In an excellent review of the status of multimodal treatment for ADHD in children, Horn and Ialongo (1988) make a strong case that single modality treatment other than stimulant medication has not been effective in dealing with the wide range of problems experienced by children with ADHD. Further, these authors concluded that the failure of some researchers to find positive additive effects of stimulant medication and behavioral treatments (Abikoff & Gittelman, 1985; Brown, Borden, Wynne, Schleser, & Clingerman, 1986) may result from the exclusion of either the parent or child therapeutic component. Based on our experience, the child component must include educating the child about ADHD and building in a sense of self-efficacy, self-esteem, and the willingness to participate actively in recommended treatments. Similarly, the parent-training component must include education to help parents understand cause; parents must attribute problems benignly and incorporate positive behavioral techniques and strategies. Initial studies that have included medication and this combination of parent and child intervention have consistently reported statistically positive results from treatment (Horn & Ialongo, 1988; Satterfield et al., 1981). However, Horn and colleagues subsequently have taken a more conservative stand on the additive effects of psychostimulants, parent training, and self-control therapy. In a study completed in

1991, Horn, Ialongo, Pascoe, and Greenberg found only limited support for the hypothesis that the effects of a high dose of psychostimulant medication could be achieved by combining the low dose with a behavioral intervention. In 1990, Horn et al. evaluated the separate and combined effects of behavior parent training and cognitive behavioral self-control therapy with forty-two elementary-school-age children diagnosed with ADHD. Subjects were randomly assigned to one or a combination of the two treatments. The combined treatment produced significantly more treatment responders at follow-up than either of the treatments alone in regard to parent report. No treatment, however, had a significantly greater effect on school behavior than any other treatment. This led these authors to conclude that there was only weak support for the additive effects hypothesis for nonmedication treatments, at least in regard to these two treatments. Further, no evidence of the superiority of the combined condition relative to medication alone was found. In a follow-up study, Ialongo et al. (1993) examined the effects of methylphenidate alone and in combination with behavioral parent training plus child self-control instruction. Seventy-one children with ADHD completed the treatment protocol. Mean effects were found for medication in posttest. However, there was no evidence of additive effects. Nine months after the termination of the behavioral interventions and the withdrawal of the stimulant medication, almost no evidence was found to support the hypothesis that the combined condition would produce greater maintenance of treatment gains than would medication alone.

Based on concerns that eight-week summer intervention programs do not afford sufficient opportunity for maintenance and generalization of effects after treatment, J. Swanson (1988) extended the program developed by Whalen, Henker, and Hinshaw (1985). Length of treatment was extended from eight weeks to one year and included planned generalization training on a daily basis in the classroom and on the playground. This multimodality program included direct intervention on a daily basis in the classroom, daily social skill and cognitive training sessions in small groups, interactions with parents approximately three to five hours per week, and a careful assessment in the use of medication with each child. Swanson noted that "as these interventions mature, they will require a long-term prospective follow-up of treated and untreated cases to document effectiveness" (p. 545). Other researchers have demonstrated the efficacy of multimodal day treatment programs for children with ADHD in improving general behavior, academic functioning, and self-esteem (Grizenko et al., 1993).

Although the available literature clearly reflects that the introduction of stimulant medication leads to the greatest percentage in improvement, it does not suggest that alternative or combined treatments are ineffective or should be discontinued. The mean effect size of medication has been suggested as twice as great as that of behavior modification, but behavioral interventions have demonstrated improvements in specific symptoms for children with ADHD (Pelham et al., 1993). In a case control study, Cooper et al. (1993) found that for one child, management of environmental variables improved behavior regardless of the use of medication; this was not the case for a second child. DuPaul and Barkley (1993) suggest that treatment approaches combining stimulant medication and behavior modification have been found superior for some children with ADHD. They hypothesize that the dose or strength of each of these treatments must be varied in a systematic fashion for each child to obtain a comprehensive picture of response to treatment combinations. This position has been noted by others, with studies suggesting that for some children with ADHD, a simple behavioral intervention implemented in its most intense form can achieve results comparable to those achieved with medication; for other children, medication can obviate the need for the more intense forms of behavioral intervention (A. Abramowitz et al., 1992). The incremental benefits of methylphenidate combined with reinforcement or behavior management have also been demonstrated by Pelham, Milich, and Walker (1986). Glick (1992) has suggested that medication combined with behavioral intervention may be synergistic, with behavioral intervention increasing overall compliance, including the efficient use of medication.

C. Carlson et al. (1992) found that a low dose of methylphenidate or behavior therapy produced roughly equivalent improvements in classroom behavior. The combination of behavior therapy and low-dose methylphenidate resulted in improved benefit that was nearly identical to that obtained with a slightly higher dose of methylphenidate without behavior management.

Finally, Horn and Ialongo (1988) suggested that there may be a "sleeper effect" in which the combination of behavioral interventions and medication results in improvements not usually observed or measured until long after treatment is completed. Based on parent report, Goldstein and Goldstein (1990) suggested that the combination of parent training and the child's therapy significantly reduces the severity of ADHD problems in the home. Problems at school, however, remained high. The authors theorized about which type and situational manifestation of ADHD problems might be best addressed by a particular treatment. They suggested that problems with attention span are dealt with most effectively through the use of stimulant medication. Problems with impulse control, however, were hypothesized to require medication intervention and behavioral training. Academic achievement problems were suggested as requiring all three components.

What is the practitioner to make of these data? In summary, the available data argue that stimulant treatment accounts for by far the greatest percentage of behavioral improvement in children with ADHD. Nonmedication treatments, educational modifications and behavior management for parents and teachers have been demonstrated as beneficial for most children with ADHD, adding half or fewer to the improved observations reported. Finally, issues related to child, parent, and teacher self-perceptions, knowledge of the disorder, and sense of efficacy in perceiving symptoms as capable of being changed may act catalytically to improve compliance with all interventions, including compliance with the medication. For the time being, the available research data argue strongly that medication should be considered a first-line treatment for all children and adolescents with an ADHD diagnosis; education about the disorder and modification of tasks to make them more interesting and payoffs to make them more valuable to the child with ADHD should be considered as integral parts of a multimodal treatment program.

The multimodal treatment model offers a combination of interventions that provide the promise of effective management for a wide range of problems children with ADHD experience. It is clear that the combination does not provide a cure. It has not been demonstrated that any single treatment or combination of treatments leads to significantly better outcome as individuals with ADHD move into adulthood (for review, see Goldstein, 1997a). It has been our experience, however, that over the short term, the suggested combination of treatments offers significant symptom relief and the promise of greater therapeutic progress than the use of any one treatment alone.

Implications for Parents

The ADHD child's parents must be included in each step of the evaluative process, diagnosis, and, most important, development of a treatment plan. This recommendation was strongly emphasized in the first edition of this text and since that time has become an even more important variable for ADHD children. Knowing a number of specific skills deficits causing varied and multiple problems in most if not all areas of the ADHD child's interaction with the environment facilitates parents' ability to understand the need for multiple interventions. If parents perceive problems of ADHD as stable, internal, and consistent within their children, they stand little chance of doing very much about the problem. On the other hand, if they recognize that their attitude, perception, and knowledge of ADHD can facilitate change in their children, treatment will be more effective.

The following story was related in the initial volume of this text; it is offered again with follow-up, as it will help parents understand the need for multiple treatments. It is the story of Tom, a second-grade child with a history of attention and overarousal problems. As Tom began second grade, he very much desired to succeed. His attention problems resulted in unfinished schoolwork. Impulsivity had also interfered with the development of appropriate social interaction skills. The combination of these two problems led to Tom's being identified as the family problem. In response to all of these difficulties, Tom began to develop a pattern of increasing helplessness, frustration, and angry, oppositional behavior. Out of frustration, he impulsively picked up a rock and threw it at a car as an expression of anger. Assessment by the pediatrician, based on a medical model, resulted in a diagnosis of ADHD and initiation of stimulant medication as the treatment plan. Medication was effective in assisting Tom to sit still and remain on task, which resulted in his attempting schoolwork more consistently. Unfortunately, Tom was also experiencing a learning disability, and the quality of his work did not increase significantly. Because study skills must be learned rather than ingested, his approach to his work continued to be disorganized. On the playground, Tom did not frustrate quite as easily but continued to lack effective social and problem-solving skills. At home, his siblings continued to identify him as the family problem even in situations where he was not at fault; medication had little impact on changing this pattern of family behavior. Finally, the stimulant medication allowed Tom to be somewhat more reflective and not act as impulsively; instead of picking up the first rock he saw, he could now look around for a nice large one. He was also able to delay gratification and wait until a bus came by before throwing the rock.

Tom is now in tenth grade. He has continued to receive stimulant medication with benefits. As he progressed into junior high school, he worked with an academic coach, developing effective study, organizational, note- and test-taking skills. He also continued to strengthen basic academic skills that were negatively impacted by his unwillingness to practice. Thus, he continued to work on strengthening basic math skills, nonphonetic spelling, and organization for written language. Over the years, Tom had developed a number of friendships he has been able to maintain. He is participating in a number of extracurricular activities at school, is well liked by a number of teachers, and participates in a number of out-of-school activities, including those at his church and through the Boy Scouts. At home, Tom has learned to be a "good" big brother and is no longer identified as the family problem. Tom's grades have been reasonably good and he is making plans to attend college.

One point of this story, as explained to parents, is that *pills will not substitute for skills*. Parents must also be helped to understand and accept the premise that ADHD is a disorder that is managed through multiple means.

SUMMARY

This chapter briefly reviewed the current state of single and combined treatments for ADHD in childhood. Practitioners are increasingly aware that the multiproblems, multiskills deficits that children with ADHD experience, though they may stem from faulty inhibition and related difficulties, require a well-organized treatment plan. A plan for ADHD must include treatments with demonstrated success, including medication, parent education, parent and teacher behavior management training, social skills training, and academic support. The judicious use of cognitive mediational training may also be beneficial for children and caregivers by building self-esteem, avoiding patterns of helplessness, and modifying beliefs. Although questions continue to be raised concerning the additive benefits of multiple treatments, medication consistently contributes to the most improvement. Research has demonstrated that providing an appropriate combination of treatments as needed for individual children results in improved functioning over the short term. Practitioners should keep in mind that one of the overriding themes for all ADHD treatments is a focus on enhancing the child's self-esteem (R. Brooks, 1993). This issue will be addressed further in Chapter 14. Practitioners also need to be aware that a multitreatment model has been suggested for children of various ages as well as those with ADHD experiencing other developmental risk factors (Blackman, Westervelt, Stevenson, & Welch, 1991; Desmond, Forney, Parker-Fisher, & Jones, 1993). The practitioner must assist parents to understand the need for multiple treatment modalities to deal with multifaceted problems. The following treatment chapters will provide the practitioner with in-depth information and specific recommendations concerning these treatments for ADHD.

Chapter 13

MEDICATIONS FOR ADHD

Michael Goldstein, M.D.

In the late 1980s, 700,000 children were treated with medication for ADHD. By 1995, the number had increased 2.5-fold to 1.6 million (Safer, 1995). Yet only about half of the 6% to 7% of children believed to have ADHD were being treated. Prevalence of treatment varies by insurance company: only 1.1% of the 5- to 14-year-olds enrolled at Northwest Kaiser Permanente in 1991; 2.9% for Baltimore County students ages 5 through 18 in 1993; and 3.7% for Medicaid-insured children ages 5 through 14 in 1993. Safer (1995) reports that boys are four times more likely to be treated than girls in primary grades and five times more than girls in middle school. Medication is prescribed for a smaller percentage of African Americans than Caucasians.

Prevalence of diagnoses varies with physician groups. Pediatricians diagnosed ADHD in 5.3% of elementary-school-age children, a slightly higher rate than the 4.2% diagnosed by family practitioners (Wolraich et al., 1990). Although only 73% of the children medicated would have qualified as ADHD by *DSM-III-R* criteria, 88% were treated with methylphenidate. Surprisingly, fulfilling *DSM* criteria did not affect the likelihood of treatment success; parents of 85% of the children considered medication successful whether or not children fulfilled *DSM* criteria.

Another trend in medication treatment for ADHD is the increasing number of adolescents remaining on medication. Safer and Krager (1994) report that although the proportion of high school students to all students receiving medication was only 11% in 1975, it had risen to 30% in the 1990s. For high school students, the gender gap also narrowed from a female-to-male ratio of 1 to 12 in 1981 to 1 to 6 in 1993.

This increase in medication treatment for ADHD has generated public controversy. Prevalence and variability of methylphenidate prescriptions has been used to suggest inappropriate prescriptions (Diller & Morrow, 1997), but those who have collected the data argue that the 2.5-fold increase in methylphenidate prescriptions between 1990 and 1995 does not necessarily represent inappropriate change in descriptions. Safer, Zito, and Fine (1997) chastised Diller and Morrow's letter (1997) as going "beyond the data presented in our paper." The authors urge additional research to determine effectiveness of medication treatment under usual practice conditions, long-term effectiveness, and parental satisfaction with treatment among other questions necessary to determine optimal prescription practice. In 1991, the Virginia Department of Education developed a report on methylphenidate based on a review of the scientific literature. Its reasonable conclusions about both the benefits and side effects of medication represented an attempt to balance non-evidence-based opinions and an anti-Ritalin media and lawsuit campaign (Safer & Krager, 1994). Some articles in the popular press exploring questions of medication usage presented a balanced and educational approach (Black, 1994). Articles in professional journals have also questioned the numbers of children treated with stimulant medication (Ruel & Hickey, 1992); some have concluded that stimulants are well accepted (Liu, Robin, Brenner, & Eastman, 1991), others warn of too much school support for medication (Welsch, 1974). Between 1989 and 1991, a decline in initiation of stimulant medication for hyperactive, inattentive students was seen (Safer & Krager, (1992). The media blitz and threatened lawsuits are believed responsible for the decline, which proved, however, to be only temporary.

METHYLPHENIDATE

Methylphenidate is by far the most common chemical substance used for medication intervention. Ritalin® is the brand name of methylphenidate. Population studies have shown substantial variation in methylphenidate usage from one region to another and between races. Zito, Safer, dos Reis, Magder, and Riddle (1997) reported a study of Medicaid methylphenidate prescriptions discovered a 5-fold difference in prevalence of methylphenidate prescriptions from one area of Maryland to another. They also reported that African Americans are 2.5 times less likely to receive methylphenidate than Caucasian youths. The average daily dose of methylphenidate was estimated at 18.7 plus or minus 10.4 mg for 5- to 9-year-olds and 26.8 plus or minus 14.0 mg for 10- to 14-year-olds. The gender ratio is 3.7 to 1 (m:f). On average, 2.2% of 5- to 14-year-olds were prescribed methylphenidate but this varied from 0.4% for 5-year-olds to 3.4% for 9-year-olds. Surveys of nurses in public and private schools in Baltimore County revealed that 93% of medication used to treat hyperactivity and inattention was methylphenidate (Safer & Krager, 1988). In addition, a survey mailed to 800 randomly selected members of the American Academy of Pediatrics revealed that 84% of the pediatricians responding used methylphenidate (Copeland, Wolraich, Lindgren, Milich, & Woolson, 1987). Because of the prevalent use of methylphenidate, we will consider its risks and benefits as well as alternative interventions. Other medications will then be considered.

Risks of Methylphenidate Intervention

Assessing the risks of methylphenidate is not a simple task. Side effects are often presented in long lists that are difficult to apply to an individual patient. The *Physician's Desk Reference* (*PDR,* 1997) contains contraindications, warnings, precautions, and adverse reactions for the Ritalin brand of methylphenidate (see Figure 13–1).

It is difficult to assess the risks to an individual patient from the list of reported side effects. Barkley (1988a) described "a national campaign against the labeling of children with a diagnosis of Attention-Deficit Hyperactivity Disorder and especially its treatment with stimulant medication such as Ritalin®" (p. 1). Others have agreed (Cowart, 1988a, 1988b). According to Barkley, the Church of Scientology "watch dog"

Contraindications

Marked anxiety, tension, and agitation are contraindications to Ritalin, since the drug may aggravate these symptoms. Ritalin is contraindicated also in patients known to be hypersensitive to the drug, in patients with glaucoma, and in patients with motor tics or with a family history or diagnosis of Tourette's Syndrome.

Warnings

Ritalin should not be used in children under six years, since safety and efficacy in this age group have not been established.

Sufficient data on safety and efficacy of long-term use of Ritalin in children are not yet available. Although a casual relationship has not been established, suppression of growth (i.e., weight gain, and/or height) has been reported with the long-term use of stimulants in children. Therefore, patients requiring long-term therapy should be carefully monitored. Ritalin should not be used for severe depression of either exogenous or endogenous origin. Clinical experience suggests that in psychotic children, administration of Ritalin may exacerbate symptoms of behavior disturbance and thought disorder.

Ritalin should not be used for the prevention or treatment of normal fatigue states.

There is some clinical evidence that Ritalin may lower the convulsive threshold in patients with prior history of seizures, with prior EEG abnormalities in absence of seizures, and, very rarely, in absence of history of seizures and no prior EEG evidence of seizures. Safe concomitant use of anticonvulsants and Ritalin has not been established. In the presence of seizures, the drug should be discontinued. Use cautiously in patients with hypertension. Blood pressure should be monitored at appropriate intervals in all patients taking Ritalin, especially those with hypertension. Symptoms of visual disturbances have been encountered in rate cases. Difficulties with accommodation and blurring of vision have been reported.

Drug Interactions

Ritalin may decrease the hypotensive effect of guanethidine. Use cautiously with pressor agents and MAO inhibitors.

Human pharmacologic studies have shown that Ritalin may inhibit the metabolism of coumarin anticoagulants, anticonvulsants (phenobarbital, diphenylhydantoin, primidone), phenylbutazone, and tricyclic antidepressants (imipramine, clomipramine, desipramine). Downward dosage adjustments of these drugs may be required when given concomitantly with Ritalin.

Usage in Pregnancy

Adequate animal reproduction studies to establish safe use of Ritalin during pregnancy have not been conducted. Therefore, until more information is available, Ritalin should not be prescribed for women of childbearing age unless, in the opinion of the physician, the potential benefits outweigh the possible risks.

Drug Dependence

Ritalin should be given cautiously to emotionally unstable patients, such as those with a history of drug dependence or alcoholism, because such patients may increase dosage on their own initiative.

Chronically abusive use can lead to marked tolerance and psychic dependence with varying degrees of abnormal behavior. Frank psychotic episodes can occur, especially with parenteral abuse. Careful supervision is required during drug withdrawal, since severe depression as well as the effects of chronic overactivity can be unmasked. Long term follow up may be required because of the patient's basic personality disturbances.

Figure 13–1.   Physician's Desk Reference/Ritalin

Source: From *Physician's Desk Reference,* 1997, pp. 866–867. Printed with permission of the publisher.

Committee Concerned for Human Rights put out a "set of exaggerated claims" (that) "these drugs are highly addictive, can often lead to suicide and permanent severe emotional disturbance as a common consequence, in some instances have led to murder by children treated with Ritalin®, significantly increased the risk of criminal behavior and substance abuse among children so treated, and are prescribed excessively as a strait jacket for the mind creating a zombie-like state in order to subdue children" (p. 2).

Even well-meaning school programs, the purpose of which are to decrease illicit drug use, may emphasize the risks of methylphenidate and imply that the use of stimulant medications, even for medical treatment of ADHD, is "wrong" and will produce substantial injury. An 11-year-old related to the authors that a report presented in her classroom program to discourage wrong use of drugs stated that Ritalin was harmful. Children in the class who were taking such medication were asked by the teacher to identify themselves. These children became the subject of peer pressure to stop using medication. One child responded by refusing to take her medication, which resulted in recurrence of her ADHD symptoms. She continued to refuse medication despite deterioration in her academic performance and relationships with friends.

A physician may respond to the concern over drug abuse and lists of potential side effects by rejecting medication intervention for most, if not all, ADHD children. Or a physician may respond to false exaggeration of some medication-related problems by ignoring the potential side effects and advocating medication intervention on a "trial basis" for every child with a school, social, or family problem, possibly telling the child and family that the medication "can't hurt and might help." Blanket rejection of medication overlooks an effective treatment, and unselected medication intervention results in increased risk of potentially harmful side effects. Only with an understanding of the true risks of medication can medication intervention be appropriately evaluated.

Side Effects of Placebo

There have been many studies comparing methylphenidate and placebo. A study reported in two parts (Barkley, 1989; Barkley, McMurray, Edelbrock, & Robbins, 1990) was a carefully designed, double-blind crossover study measuring the side effects of methylphenidate in comparison with placebo. Eighty-three children were entered into this study. Direct observation as well as parent and teacher questionnaires were used. Placebo was compared with 0.3 mg/kg and 0.5 mg/kg of methylphenidate. Three of the eighty-three children discontinued the study because of side effects: one child had nervous facial tic, dizziness, and headache; a second had dizziness, headache, and increased hyperactivity; and a third had excessive speech and disjointed thinking. Medication dosages were in the morning and at lunch time. Four side effects occurred statistically more often on medication than placebo: decreased appetite, insomnia, stomachaches, and headaches. Two of the side effects, decreased appetite and stomachaches, increased significantly with each increasing dose. Insomnia and headaches were more likely to occur with medication and placebo but not more likely to occur with high-dose and low-dose treatment. Decreased appetite occurred in 52% of low-dose subjects and 56% of high-dose subjects; 7% were considered severe on low dose but 13% were considered severe in the high-dose condition. Stomachaches occurred in 39% and 35% of the low- and high-dose subjects, respectively, with severe symptoms occurring in 1% and 6% in the low- and high-dose subjects, respectively. Insomnia was the most common side effect, occurring in 62% of the low-dose and 68% of the high-dose subjects, with severe symptoms occurring in 18% of both conditions. Headache was present in 26% and 21%, respectively, with severe symptoms in one low-dose subject and in 4% of the high-dose subjects. A symptom termed anxiousness occurred in 58% of the low-dose and 52% of the high-dose subjects; symptoms were severe in 9% of low-dose and 7% of high-dose subjects. In comparison with placebo, however, there was a significant decrease in anxiousness with medication, considering that 12% of children given placebo were rated as severely anxious, but only 9% in the low- and 7% in the high-dose conditions. Anxiousness was not otherwise defined. Possibly the most significant result was the high rate of symptoms reported with placebo treatment. Many of these problems were not increased by medication. As depicted in Table 13–1, parents noted irritability present in 72%, sadness in 43%, anxiousness in 58%, insomnia in 40%, and prone to crying in 49% of placebo condition children.

Teachers noted high frequency of different side effects in the placebo condition, including 30% with tics, 38% talks less, 55% anxious, 45% irritable, 68% staring, and 40% sadness (see Table 13–2).

Another carefully designed placebo-controlled crossover study of side effects of methylphenidate is notable because three daily doses were given (Ahman et al., 1993). Morning, noon, and afternoon doses of 0.3 or 0.5 mg/kg dosages were administered and compared to placebo. The higher dose decreased appetite more than the lower dose. The authors noted, however, that there was no significant dose effect for insomnia, stomachache, headache, or dizziness. Nail biting, considered a possible side effect, actually decreased with the higher dose. Daydreaming, irritability, and anxiety also decreased with medication compared with placebo, and there was no difference between low and high dose of medication. Again, baseline or placebo incidents of insomnia, decreased appetite, stomachache, and headache were quite high. In this study of 234 consecutive children, only four had side effects serious enough to warrant discontinuing medication. These included one child reported being in a "daze," having a rapid heartbeat and difficulty breathing; one reported being a "zombie"; one had stomachache, headache, decreased appetite, and insomnia; and the fourth child had decreased appetite and sleep problems.

Studies involving comparisons of medication and placebo reveal that children taking placebo also suffer a significant number of problems. Barkley (1989) studied eighty-two ADHD children taking placebo and two doses of Ritalin (0.3 and 0.5 mg/kg, twice daily). He found that side effects, including irritability, sadness, and excessive staring, were essentially the same among the placebo group as the medication group. Barkley related that "many of the purported side effects are actually pre-existing behavioral or emotional problems in an ADHD population" (p. 2). It is important to understand that many of these symptoms may be reported by patients taking medication but not be the result of medication ingestion.

Mild Side Effects

It has been clear for some time that loss of appetite and difficulty sleeping are common side effects of stimulation medication. As a result of a review of 110 studies including more than 4,200 hyperactive children, Barkley (1976) was able to conclude that the

Table 13–1.   Percentage of 82 subjects displaying each of 17 side effects of methylphenidate during each drug condition (parent ratings)[*]

Side Effect	Placebo	Low Dose (0.3 mg/kg)	High Dose (0.5 mg/kg)
Decreased appetite			
%	15	52	56
% severe	1	7	13
Insomnia			
%	40	62	68
% severe	7	18	18
Stomachaches			
%	18	39	35
% severe	0	1	6
Headaches			
%	11	26	21
% severe	0	1	4
Prone to crying			
%	49	59	54
% severe	10	16	10
Tics/nervous movements			
%	18	18	28
% severe	4	7	5
Dizziness			
%	4	10	7
% severe	0	0	1
Drowsiness			
%	18	23	20
% severe	1	2	1
Nail biting			
%	22	26	29
% severe	7	4	9
Talks less			
%	16	20	22
% severe	1	1	2
Anxiousness			
%	58	58	52
% severe	12	9	7
Disinterested in others			
%	18	18	15
% severe	0	1	2
Euphoria			
%	41	34	43
% severe	9	4	7
Irritable			
%	72	65	66
% severe	18	15	13
Nightmares			
%	20	20	21
% severe	0	0	3
Sadness			
%	43	48	41
% severe	5	6	8
Staring			
%	40	38	38
% severe	2	4	1

Source: Barkley, McMurray, Edelbrock, and Robbins (1990). Used with permission.

[*] % refers to the percentage of subjects in whom the side effect was rated 1 or higher on the scale of severity 1 to 9; % severe refers to the percentage of subjects in whom the side effect was rated 7 or higher.

Table 13–2.   **Percentage of 53 subjects displaying each of 17 side effects of methylphenidate during each drug condition (teacher ratings)[*]**

Side Effect	Placebo	Low Dose (0.3 mg/kg)	High Dose (0.5 mg/kg)
Decreased appetite			
%	17	15	21
% severe	2	2	6
Insomnia			
%	4	6	6
% severe	2	0	2
Stomachaches			
%	17	17	17
% severe	0	2	2
Headaches			
%	17	7	17
% severe	0	2	0
Prone to crying			
%	21	11	4
% severe	0	4	0
Tics/nervous movements			
%	30	25	26
% severe	11	8	4
Dizziness			
%	6	4	2
% severe	0	0	0
Drowsiness			
%	23	21	25
% severe	4	4	2
Nail biting			
%	13	13	8
% severe	2	2	4
Talks less			
%	38	42	38
% severe	4	2	7
Anxiousness			
%	55	49	42
% severe	9	6	6
Disinterested in others			
%	36	43	30
% severe	4	0	9
Euphoria			
%	45	42	40
% severe	8	8	6
Irritable			
%	45	34	25
% severe	9	7	2
Nightmares			
%	0	0	2
% severe	0	0	0
Sadness			
%	40	38	30
% severe	9	11	2
Staring			
%	68	57	57
% severe	19	11	9

Source: Barkley, McMurray, Edelbrock, and Robbins (1990). Used with permission.

[*]% refers to the percentage of subjects in whom the side effect was rated 1 or higher on the scale of severity 1 to 9; % severe refers to the percentage of subjects in whom the side effect was rated 7 or higher.

primary side effects noted for the stimulants were insomnia, anorexia or loss of appetite, weight loss, and irritability. These and other side effects were reported to be transitory and to disappear with a reduction in dosage. Another early review (Ross & Ross, 1982) agreed that "the most frequent short-term side effects of the stimulants are anorexia and insomnia, both of which are usually of short duration" (p. 190). Other mild but less common side effects include sadness, depression, fearfulness, social withdrawal, sleepiness, headaches, nail biting, stomach upset, and weight loss. These are reported to resolve spontaneously with decrease in dosage, or considered acceptable side effects in light of clinical improvement. These side effects are mild, but they occur in 20% to 50% of children treated with stimulant medication.

Serious Side Effects

Hallucinations

Seven reports of toxic psychosis associated with stimulant medications were described by Barkley (1976). Four were associated with methylphenidate and three with amphetamine. After the administration of the stimulant, symptoms of visual and tactile hallucinations occurred but subsided in each case once drug treatment had been discontinued. Bloom, Russell, Weisskopf, and Blackerby (1988) reported a methylphenidate-induced delusional disorder in a child with ADHD and concluded that "it is strongly recommended that children undergoing stimulant therapy receive careful monitoring of their behavior and emotional status" (p. 89). These reports suggest that hallucinations, though rare, can be induced by stimulant medications. Though the symptoms resolved when the medication was discontinued, the risk of toxic hallucinations must be considered when determining whether to use medication intervention.

Seizures

The *PDR* (1997, p. 866) suggests that the use of methylphenidate carries with it a risk of epileptic seizures. Adequate information is not available to allow accurate determination of the likelihood of seizures resulting from treatment of ADHD symptoms with commonly used dosages of medication or to assess what increased risk is present, if any, in children with a history of epilepsy, family history of epilepsy, or abnormal EEG. In a small study involving ten children with ADHD and controlled seizure disorder, methylphenidate 0.3 mg/kg per dose morning and noon produced improvement in ADHD symptoms without producing seizure recurrence (Feldman, Crumrine, Handen, Alvin, & Teodori, 1989). Seizures were not a reported side effect in over 2,000 cases of children with hyperkinetic symptoms treated with stimulant medications (Barkley, 1976). It is difficult for the medical practitioner and family of the child with ADHD to be certain of the risk of seizures resulting from treatment with stimulant medication. However, the available information indicates that the risk of epileptic seizures resulting from medication intervention for ADHD must be quite low.

Tourette's Syndrome

Gilles de la Tourette's syndrome is a combination of multiple motor tics and at least one vocal tic (APA, 1994). Age at onset is between 2 and 15 years, and the tics must be present for more than one year before the diagnosis can be made (APA, 1994). The peak onset of the disorder is at age 5, with onset usually between ages 4 and 9 (Mc-Daniel, 1986). Severity of the disease is variable. Vocal outbursts and coprolalia characterize some of the more severe cases. Tics, which are stereotyped repetitive movements, are different from fidgetiness; each tic movement has the same appearance as the one before, whereas each fidgety movement is a little different from the one before (Denckla, Bemporad, & MacKay, 1976; Erenberg, Cruse, & Rothmer, 1985; G. Golden, 1987).

Tics have long been known to appear in children with ADHD treated with stimulant medication. Barkley (1976) commented on several children treated with dextroamphetamine and methylphenidate who developed tics. In a study of 1,520 children treated with methylphenidate (Denckla et al., 1976), tics occurred in twenty cases, or 1.3%. Only one of the twenty developed Tourette's. Tics resolved completely when medication was withdrawn in the other nineteen. This data suggest roughly a 1% risk of the development of motor tics and a .07% risk of the development of Tourette's with methylphenidate treatment for ADHD symptoms. Pemoline (Cylert®) has also been associated with the onset of tics and Tourette's (Bachman, 1981; Mitchell & Matthews, 1980). A careful study of forty-five hyperactive boys during a double-blind, crossover treatment trial of methylphenidate and dextroamphetamine given in a wide range of dosages (Borcherding, Keysor, Rapoport, Elia, & Amass, 1990) found that 76% of the group developed abnormal movements or pervasive, compulsive behaviors. The clinical significance of these, however, was uncertain, as most resolved after a few days even though medication was continued. The authors noted that the abnormal movements generally occurred in only one of the two drugs rather than both. Medication was discontinued because of abnormal movements in only one of the forty-five children. In another study, 9% of a group of 122 children with ADHD treated with stimulant medication developed tics or dyskinesias (Lipkin, Goldstein, & Addesman, 1994); one child developed Tourette's. Age, medication dosage, and family history of tics was not related to onset of symptoms. These authors concluded that the incidence of chronic tics was 1% or less, and that personal or family history of tics, medication selection, and dosage were not related to the onset of tics or dyskinesias.

More than 50% of children with Tourette's manifest behaviors of inattention and hyperactivity (G. Golden, 1977; E. A. Shapiro, 1981). These symptoms may be more prominent than the other symptoms of Tourette's and/or may appear before the tics. As a result, many children with Tourette's have been treated with stimulant medications.

To understand the relationship of Tourette's to stimulant medication, Erenberg et al. (1985) studied 200 children with Tourette's syndrome. Of these 200 children, forty-eight had received stimulant medication at some time, nine had been treated with stimulants before the onset of the tics, but only four were still receiving stimulants when tics began. Therefore, only these four had their first symptoms of Tourette's while they were taking stimulant medications. Thirty-nine of the children had tics before their treatment with stimulant medication. Of these, eleven had worsening of tics on stimulant medication, twenty-six had no change in their tics when treated with stimulants, and two actually experienced improvement. Although uncertain whether some patients develop Tourette's only and entirely as a result of stimulant medication, Erenberg et al. (1985) stated, "We believe that exposure to stimulants causes the premature onset of GTS in patients who would have developed their symptoms spontaneously at a later age" (p. 1347). They recommended that close observation and caution is necessary when siblings of children with Tourette's are treated with stimulant medications. The authors also recommended that for patients who develop tics or whose prior tics worsen, medication should be discontinued.

The studies presented suggest that stimulant medication can bring out latent symptoms of Tourette's syndrome in children who might eventually develop these symptoms without stimulant medication. It is virtually impossible to prove that medication is never a primary cause of Tourette's. Therefore, it may be more prudent to summarize the available information by stating that stimulant medication is rarely, if ever, a primary cause of Tourette's.

Other studies found that methylphenidate does not cause Tourette's syndrome. A review of four apparent cases of methylphenidate-induced tic exacerbation suggested they were not convincingly related to the medication (Sprafkin & Gadow, 1993). This report raises the question of whether any of the observed tic exacerbations with methylphenidate are related to the medication. One report (Chandler, Branhill, Gualtieri, & Patterson, 1989) suggested that if tics do occur, treatment with Tryptophan may help to decrease their severity.

A study of monozygotic twins suggests Tourette's may be aggravated, but not caused, by methylphenidate. Price, Leckman, Pauls, Cohen, and Kidd (1986) studied six pairs of monozygotic twins in which one twin had developed Tourette's following treatment with methylphenidate and the other was untreated. All untreated twins also developed the disorder.

Children with Tourette's and ADHD often benefit from stimulant medication. Gadow, Nolan, and Sverd (1992) studied eleven prepubertal hyperactive boys with tic disorders. Methylphenidate effectively suppressed hyperactive, distractible behaviors in the classroom as well as physical aggression in the lunchroom and on the playground. In this study, methylphenidate use was associated with a decrease rather than an increase of vocal tics in the classroom and in the lunchroom. On an operationally defined minimal effective dose, only one boy experienced motor tic exacerbation. In an earlier commentary, Gadow and Sverd (1990) suggested that although there was some risk with methylphenidate, there was also potential benefit from stimulant treatment for ADHD children with comorbid tic disorders. They recommended careful evaluation of the risks and benefits to determine appropriate treatment.

Methylphenidate substantially improves behavior in some children with ADHD and comorbid chronic tic disorder. Treatment with methylphenidate (.1 to .5 mg/kg) made the probands less easily distinguished from their peers (normalization). Many children still scored in the deviant range for at least one ADHD behavior when receiving the 0.5 mg/kg dose (Nolan & Gadow, 1997).

Growth Suppression

The question of the effect of stimulant medication on height and weight was first raised by Safer, Allen, and Barr (1972) and Safer and Allen (1973). Some short-term studies (one to two years) have found mild growth suppression, but others have not. Summer growth rebound off medication was measured by Klein, Landa, Mattes, and Klein (1988) with methylphenidate treatment during two consecutive summers against matched controls who were off stimulant treatment for two consecutive summers.

Height and weight assessment suggested that there was no growth rebound after one summer and no differences in growth between those who did and those who did not take medication over the first summer. However, small but significant decrease in growth in the children who had taken medication two summers in a row was found, in comparison with those tho had been off medication for two summers.

Other studies, however, have not shown growth suppression. A study of thirty-one hyperactive adolescents treated with methylphenidate for at least six months showed no significant deviation from expected height and weight growth velocities (Vincent, Varley, & Leger, 1990). The authors suggested that adolescents were insensitive to the growth suppression effects of methylphenidate. Safer and Allen (1973) studied forty-nine children taking dextroamphetamine or methylphenidate and fourteen children used as controls. The children were compared with standard growth percentiles as published by Vaughn (1969). The twenty-nine children taking dextroamphetamine had an average loss of 20 percentile points in weight and 13 points in height over an average of 2.9 years. The twenty children on methylphenidate showed smaller losses of 6 percentile points in weight and 5 in height. The fourteen hyperactive controls not on medication showed small percentile increases during the 4.2 years that the growth was followed. Dextroamphetamine produced a statistically significant weight percentile loss that was greater than any other group. They concluded that "the long-term use of dextroamphetamine depresses growth to a significantly greater degree than does methylphenidate," and that "the greater growth suppressant effect of dextroamphetamine lies clearly in favor of the use of methylphenidate for hyperactive children" (Safer & Allen, 1973, p. 666).

Safer et al. (1972) also suggested that discontinuation of medication over the summer might allow for increased weight and height gain. Through analysis of variance, summer disuse of medication was evaluated. There was a significant increase in height without medication over the summer for the methylphenidate group but not for the dextroamphetamine group. Eliminating medication over the summer did not produce a significant weight gain for either group. The authors concluded that stimulants cause growth suppression and that this growth suppression can be ameliorated by drug holidays. The evidence for this belief, however, was very limited. Only dextroamphetamine (not methylphenidate) was found to significantly decrease height and weight growth. In addition, the significant rebound growth with methylphenidate drug holiday over the summer was not replicated in a later study (Safer & Allen, 1973).

Belief that stimulants cause long-term growth suppression has been difficult to disprove. Gross (1976) reported the growth status of 100 children followed for 5.8 years versus the 3.0 years for Safer, Allen, and Burr (1972). Sixty were treated with methylphenidate, twenty-four were given dextroamphetamine, and sixteen were given antidepressants, either imipramine or desipramine. Dosage of daily medication (34 mg methylphenidate, 16.5 mg dextroamphetamine) was higher than that used by Safer and Allen. Decreased weight percentiles were seen with both methylphenidate and dextroamphetamine for the first three years. This was consistent with Safer and Allen's work. However, as the years progressed, the rate of weight gain increased, so that at final follow-up after the seventh year there was an increase in weight of 16% for dextroamphetamine and 11% for methylphenidate. A significant increase in the weight percentile in children taking stimulants means that children treated with methylphenidate and dextroamphetamine were heavier than predicted by their weight prior to receiving medication.

The authors discussed several possible reasons why the children might have grown more than predicted, but whatever the reason, the important finding was no long-term suppression of height or weight. A child with attention-deficit symptoms treated with methylphenidate or dextroamphetamine could expect, on the average, to be in a higher percentile for height and weight after an average of 5.8 years than prior to treatment. For the first three years, however, the child would be at the same or a lower percentile. These data were not related to the duration or the dosage of treatment. It is important to note that the dosages of medications used were in the "high" group, by Safer and Allen's terminology, and children were taking medication on a daily basis without weekend or vacation holidays. Attempts to understand the metabolic basis of these changes was reported by S. Shaywitz et al. (1982). They studied release of growth hormone as measured by blood levels and found that a low dose of methylphenidate increases the release of growth hormone at two hours after the ingestion of medication.

Other long-term studies of stimulant effect on growth have demonstrated similar results. No significant changes in growth were noted when McNutt, Ballard, and Boileau (1976) studied twenty-three normal and twenty hyperactive children on daily doses of 0.67 mg/kg of methylphenidate for one year. Kalachnik, Sprague, Sleator, Cohen, and Ullmann (1982) studied twenty-six hyperactive children. Dosages of methylphenidate up to 0.8 mg/kg per day were used and predicted stature was measured at zero, one, two, and three years of therapy. No significant differences were found for any dosage at any time during the study. The authors concluded, "This study indicates that stature suppression does not occur in male children below thirteen years of age when methylphenidate is used up to 0.8 mg/kg per day for one or two years and up to 0.6 mg/kg per day for three years" (p. 593). The American Academy of Pediatrics Committee on Drugs (1987) reported, "There was fear that stimulant medications would lead to growth retardation; however, growth suppression is only minimally related to stimulant dosage. Results of a study indicate that no growth suppression occurred in doses of methylphenidate up to 0.8 mg/kg during a prolonged period" (p. 759).

Nevertheless, there appears to be a common misconception that stimulant medications can and regularly do cause growth suppression, and that discontinuation of medication over the summer will prevent the presumed growth suppression. Children treated with stimulant medications (especially dextroamphetamine) may have a transient decrease in weight and may have a period lasting two to three years of slight slowing of growth. This must be taken into consideration when deciding whether to undertake medication intervention. However, studies do not show a risk of long-term effects on height or weight. The decision to use stimulant medication intervention for ADHD symptoms should not be affected by the incorrect hypothesis that stimulant medication results in a long-term decrease in height or weight of the child.

Drug Abuse

There has been concern that medication intervention with a controlled substance such as methylphenidate could increase the likelihood of future drug abuse. Stimulant use as a recreational activity by some adolescents and young adults encourages this perception. Research has not provided a clear response to this concern. Arguing in favor of the risk of drug abuse are studies suggesting: (1) an increased likelihood that children

many studies for/against

may take more than their prescribed medication to "get high" (Goyer, Davis, & Rapoport, 1979); (2) that hyperactive adolescents, because of their histories of poor achievement and difficulty with social interaction, are at greater risk for drug abuse (Loney, 1980b); and (3) that many hyperactive children and adolescents are rewarded for taking their medication (Whalen & Henker, 1980). Jaffe (1991) reported a 16-year-old who became addicted to intranasal ingestion of methylphenidate prescribed for ADHD. It has also been suggested that some drug-seeking behaviors are actually self-medication of ADHD symptoms (Carroll & Rounsaville, 1993).

Arguing against increased risk for potential drug abuse are a number of studies, including one by Beck, Langford, MacKay, and Sum (1975). These authors compared thirty adolescents previously medicated with thirty similar nonmedicated controls. No difference in drug abuse was found. Further, it has been suggested that the stigma associated with having to take a medication on a regular basis decreased the likelihood that this population of children would be willing to take or abuse other drugs (Collins, Whalen, & Henker, 1980). Although the ADHD group of adolescents, because of their history of impulsive behavior and social failure, may be at greater risk to abuse drugs, there does not appear to be data at this time to suggest that taking stimulant medication for medical reasons increases the likelihood of drug abuse (Gittelman et al., 1985; G. Weiss & Hechtman, 1986).

Other Risks

In January 1996, notification was sent to physicians that a study in B6C3FI mice showed increase in hepatocellular adenomas (benign tumors) and, in males only, an increase in hepatoblastomas (rare malignant tumors) at a daily dose of approximately 60 mg/kg/day of methylphenidate. As this represents thirty times the maximum dose used in humans, the significance of these results is unknown. At the time, the drug manufacturer reported that the "FDA considers these findings in the aggregate to represent a weak signal of carcinogenic potential for the drug" (CIBA, 1996, p. 1). The findings were only in one organ in one species and mouse liver is known to be very sensitive for drug effects. The increased tumors were primarily benign. No decrease was found in latency of tumor appearance and no increase in mortality was associated with the tumors. The manufacturer commented that other widely used drugs generally perceived as safe were known to have stronger signals of carcinogenicity in animal studies. Liver tumors have not been reported in human patients taking methylphenidate. No action was taken by the FDA to restrict the use of methylphenidate, and it is believed that these findings do not represent a significant risk.

Obsessive-compulsive symptoms and cognitive perseveration have been reported with methylphenidate. Tannock and Schachar (1992) noted an increase in perseveration and a decrease in cognitive inflexibility in twenty-six children. Children with anxiety have been reported to have a poorer response to stimulants (Pliszka, 1990). Two cases of obsessive-compulsive symptoms resulting from stimulant treatment have been reported (Koizumi, 1985).

Increases in blood pressure have been observed (Brown & Sexson, 1989; Safer, 1992), but the authors considered the increases not to be "meaningful." No EKG abnormalities or cardiovascular injury has been attributed to standard dosages of methylphenidate in otherwise healthy children.

Chewing of medication was associated with the lower response rate, quicker and higher peak plasma level, and more intense side effects (Pleak, 1995). Rebound or ex-aggeration of ADHD symptoms following medication has also been commonly re-ported (e.g., C. Johnston, Pelham, Hoza, & Sturges, 1988), although this side effect has not been carefully studied. A single case of an association between methylphenidate and thrombocytosis or elevation of platelets has been reported (Sood, Kirkwood, & Sood, 1994).

Higher Risk Situations

Are there identifiable situations where a higher risk of side effects can be predicted? It has been suggested that younger children (under the age of 6) and children with autism, psychosis, tics, or a family history of these problems are more likely to encounter side effects. Some families have difficulty following through with instructions and non-medication intervention. If children in these situations are more likely to encounter side effects, physicians should be more reluctant to undertake medication intervention.

Children with both ADHD and a neurodevelopmental disorder were equally likely to respond to methylphenidate as thirty-six children with ADHD alone (Mayes, Crites, Bixler, Humphrey, & Mattison, 1994). Neurodevelopmental disorders such as cerebral palsy, spina bifida, mental retardation, autism, chromosome disorder, and acquired brain injury did not affect the likelihood of medication response to comorbid ADHD. The authors found that IQ and age did not affect response rate. Response rate for preschool children was 71.4%, not significantly lower than for school-age children (81.6%). But though 50.7% of children with neurodevelopmental disorders exhibited side effects, this was not significantly different from the ADHD group without these other problems. No significant increase in side effects among preschool children was found. Other studies, however, have found a higher incidence of side effects and lower incidence of positive effect among these groups.

Autistic Children

Autistic children may be at higher risk for adverse side effects. Cantwell and Baker (1987) suggested that some retarded and autistic children have symptoms similar to ADHD. However, they believe that these children, when treated with stimulant med-ication, experience a further narrowing of an already fixed narrow attention span. This was disputed by Strayhorn, Rapp, Donina, and Strain (1988), who presented a case of a 6-year-old autistic boy and concluded that negative effects on mood and tantrums seemed to be outweighed by positive effects on attention and activity, destructive be-havior, and stereotyped movements. They concluded that this result failed to support past statements that stimulants are contraindicated with autistic children.

Improvement in autistic children was also reported by Birmaher, Quintana, and Greenhill (1988). They studied methylphenidate in hyperactive autistic children ages 4 to 16. Methylphenidate was used in doses ranging from 10 to 15 mg per day. Eight of the nine children showed significant improvement on all rating scales. No major side effects or worsening of stereotyped movements was seen. These reports suggest that methylphenidate may be helpful in children with autism and ADHD. Studies on the ef-fect of stimulants on children with autism and ADHD are limited, however. One cannot be certain of the frequency or severity of side effects, or of positive effects, in this group of children.

Intellectually Handicapped Children

Intellectually handicapped children have been considered candidates for stimulant medication to improve both cognitive functioning and behavior. Early studies focusing on the effects of stimulants on cognitive functioning did not yield positive results (Cutler, Little, & Strauss, 1940). More recent research has attempted to evaluate the effects of stimulant medication on a select population of intellectually handicapped individuals who also exhibit significant symptoms of attention deficit (Helsel, Hersen, & Lubetsky, 1989). These authors report, however, an idiosyncratic response to dosage level and negative changes in social behavior resulting in increased social isolation. The authors suggest that this idiosyncratic response may reflect the difficulty in accurately differentiating attention-deficit from other problems in intellectually handicapped individuals or may simply reflect the fact that stimulants are not as beneficial, even for specific target behaviors, for this population of individuals. Mayes et al. (1994), studying a group of sixty-nine children, found a positive methylphenidate effect for children with ADHD and coexisting neurodevelopmental disorders. Although the response rate of 69% was slightly lower than that for the group with ADHD alone (88%), the difference was not significant. They also found that within the subgroup of mental retardation, no trend for a better response of higher IQ was seen.

Although Campbell's (1985) caution that the use of stimulants or other psychotropic medications with preschoolers should be considered in extreme cases with careful monitoring and close supportive work with the child's family is still true, an increasing body of literature has demonstrated the safety and efficacy in the use of stimulants with young ADHD children (Musten, Firestone, Pisterman, Bennett, & Mercer, 1997). These authors evaluated thirty-one, 4- to 6-year-olds with ADHD in a double-blind, placebo-controlled study using twice daily doses of methylphenidate. Improvements related to medication were observed on cognitive tests of attention and impulsivity, as well as parent reports. Observer's reports demonstrated improvement in the children's ability to work productively with their parents in laboratory settings. However, no changes were obtained with respect to the children's tendency to comply with parental requests. Side effects increased slightly with increasing dosage of medication but remained mild.

Studies of children with ADHD and comorbid mental retardation (MR) have shown that the ADHD behavior responds well to methylphenidate. Although response rates are good (64–75%), they may not be as high as rates for ADHD children without MR. One study showed fewer side effects, but others found severe social withdrawal and noted that tics were much more common in this population than previously reported in ADHD children without MR. Moderate to severe MR (IQ less than 45) substantially decreases the likelihood of a positive response to methylphenidate and increases the likelihood of behavior deterioration. Hyperactivity responds favorably to methylphenidate even in children with mild MR (Bregman, 1991). Improvement in irritability, anxiety, moodiness, and activity is seen (Handen, Feldman, Gosling, Breaux, & McAuliffe, 1991). Mildly retarded children with ADHD are as likely to respond to methylphenidate as those with normal IQ and ADHD. Approximately two-thirds of hyperactive children with IQ between 45 and 78 have been responders (Aman, Marks, Turbott, Wilsher, & Merry, 1991; Handen, Breaux, Gosling, Ploor, & Feldman, 1990; Handen, Breaux, Janosky, McAuliffe, Feldman, & Gosling, 1992; Handen et al., 1991; Mayes, Sanderson, Bixler, Humphrey, & Mattison, 1993). Factors that predict medication efficacy in normal children also predict response when MR is present (Handen, Janosky, McAuliffe, Breaux, & Feldman, 1994). Children in the 45 to 75 IQ group did not correlate with methylphenidate success rate (Mayes et al., 1993). Specific neurodevelopmental problems such as cerebral palsy or spina bifida also responded to methylphenidate with 69% of the thirty-six children studied by Mayes et al. Lower-functioning children (IQ less than 45) did not respond as well and were more likely to have unacceptable deterioration in behavior (Aman et al., 1991).

Does methylphenidate act as a nonspecific performance enhancement for MR children? Studies of the medication in normal children are limited. MR children without ADHD did not show improved behavior with the medication, only the abnormal ADHD behavior improved. This suggests that methylphenidate does not act as a nonspecific enhancement of performance: improvement was due to a decrease in abnormal behavior, not simply nonspecific improvements in learning, concentration, and alertness (Handen et al., 1994).

Younger Children

Younger children are sometimes considered to have a higher incidence of side effects and a lower incidence of positive response to methylphenidate. Conners (1975b) and Schleifer et al. (1975) found the effectiveness of methylphenidate relative to placebo in attention-disordered preschool children was not as dramatic, consistent, or positive as the results usually obtained with older children. Conners (1975b) did not report significant or serious side effects of methylphenidate. These data, combined with the observation of some improvement in behavior, resulted in Conners suggesting that methylphenidate may be an effective treatment for preschoolers. Schleifer et al., however, observed more significant side effects, including irritability and solitary play, leading these authors to recommend that methylphenidate should not be considered an effective treatment for preschoolers.

Dextroamphetamine improved tantrums and other behavioral measures for a 4-year-old (Speltz, Varley, Peterson, & Beilke, 1988), but there was a tendency for increased social isolation. Even more careful supervision may be needed in this age group because of subtle changes that may occur, such as increase in solitary play. The use of stimulants in children under the age of 6 has not been well studied; thus, one cannot state with certainty the likelihood of positive effects or negative side effects in this age group. Mayes et al. (1994) studied fourteen preschool children under 5 years of age and found that the response rate of 71.4% did not differ significantly from the 81.6% response rate for children 5 years and older. Further studies are needed to produce additional information for this age group.

Females

There have been few studies comparing the effect of methylphenidate on girls and boys. Pelham, Walker, Sturges, and Hoza (1989) studied the effect of .3 mg/kg methylphenidate in twelve ADD boys and twelve ADD girls and found the effects were equivalent. They concluded that methylphenidate should be as useful a treatment for ADD girls as boys.

Other Childhood Populations

Methylphenidate does not improve psychotic symptoms. Thirty-eight patients who met research diagnostic criteria for definite or probable schizophrenia or schizo-affective disorder and experiencing a first acute episode of psychosis were given intravenous methylphenidate followed by neuroleptic treatment (Jody, Lieberman, Geisler, Szymanski, & Avir, 1990); 61% of these patients exhibited psychotic symptom activation and 39% showed no change. The presence of schizophrenia or schizo-affective psychosis is thus at least a relative contraindication to the use of methylphenidate.

Although some children with anxious appearing behavior, as reported above, benefit from methylphenidate, children meeting *DSM-III-R* criteria for overanxious disorder have a higher likelihood of side effects. Pliszka (1989) studied seventy-nine children who met *DSM-III-R* criteria for ADHD, ODD, CD, and overanxious disorder. Children with the overanxious disorder had a significantly poorer response to stimulants than those without anxiety. Pliszka speculated that children with comorbid overanxious disorder may represent primary anxiety and the secondary development of inattentiveness or a different subgroup of ADHD.

Presence of anxiety and/or depression may lead to a lower incidence of positive effects of medication or a higher incidence of side effects. Of forty ADHD children, those with anxiety and/or depression had a lower response rate (DuPaul, Barkley, & McMurray, 1994). Anger and hostility were increased in another group of ADHD children treated with methylphenidate (Walker, Sprague, Sleator, & Ullmann, 1988).

Some hyperactive children with Williams syndrome respond to methylphenidate. In one study, hyperactivity was defined as > 1.5 standard deviation scores on Conners behavior checklists, Conners parent and teacher rating scales, and child behavior checklists (Bawden, MacDonald, & Shea, 1997). .5 mg/kg of methylphenidate was used per dose morning and noon. The authors concluded that two of the four children responded favorably in terms of decreased impulsivity, decreased irritability, and lower activity level.

Findings on examination can indicate higher-risk situations. Cardiovascular side effects should be considered if the initial examination suggests hypertension or other cardiovascular abnormality. Follow-up examination, including cardiovascular evaluation, is generally recommended as part of the routine reevaluation process. A child with brain injury may be at higher risk but may also benefit from medication intervention. Kelly, Sonis, Fialkov, Kazdin, and Matson (1986) present a 6-year-old girl who experienced frontal lobe damage. Her positive response to methylphenidate without side effects suggests that children with brain injury may be candidates for medication intervention without undue side effects. Further research is being conducted.

Management and Evaluation of Risks

Counseling the family concerning the short-term side effects, such as irritability, sleeplessness, anorexia, and possible disturbance of weight and height gains, may minimize the disruptiveness of these usually mild symptoms and alert the medical practitioner to a situation where the child's individual reaction is beyond that normally expected. The family should be alerted to the possibility of a hypersensitivity reaction (rash, etc.) and the possibility of developing tics or psychosis so that these symptoms can be promptly reported to the medical practitioner.

Reevaluation is an important part of the medical program to identify and minimize the risk of medication intervention; failure to obtain adequate follow-up evaluation can increase the risks. An assessment of the family's willingness and ability to participate in a follow-up evaluation program, therefore, is an important factor in determining the risk of medication intervention. If the child does not return for follow-up evaluation, side effects may continue and the child will be at increased risk for medication-related problems.

Although some practitioners may advocate medication as the initial treatment of choice for ADHD, behavioral, or nonmedication intervention is an important part of the treatment of ADHD. These interventions may be sufficient for control of ADHD symptoms; in fact, many children with ADHD symptoms will not need medication intervention if nonmedication intervention is used appropriately. The expected benefits of medication intervention cannot be adequately assessed until the effect of nonmedication intervention is known. For this reason, the assessment of expected benefits of medication usually cannot be completed until after a trial of nonmedication intervention.

An adequate evaluation, both to determine the presence or absence of ADHD and to determine the presence or absence of other risk factors, such as mental retardation, psychosis, autism, and depression, will help to assess and control medication risks. The incidence of serious problems with stimulant medications is low; even the child with an inadequate evaluation is not likely to develop a serious reaction to stimulant medication. Nevertheless, complete evaluation prior to initiation of medication intervention can screen out high-risk children and, therefore, decrease the risk for the development of serious medication-related side effects. The increased risk of incomplete evaluation must be taken into consideration when deciding whether medication intervention is appropriate.

Medication may change a child's performance on tests, may change the child's appearance and behaviors during evaluation, and may affect the parent's recollection of details. Once medication intervention has begun, it is difficult to sort out medication effects from natural course. Double-blind studies show that improvement of symptoms may be unrelated to the actual effect of medication. At times, response to medication may be used in the diagnosis, but the placebo response suggests that the response to medication alone cannot be used to diagnose or exclude ADHD.

A crisis may make prompt medication intervention as a response to an emergency: medication can be started quickly and has a rapid onset of action, so the temptation may be to begin medication intervention before completion of the diagnostic evaluation in hope of alleviating the crisis. But it is exactly in those situations where a complete evaluation before medication intervention may be most important. Treatment of ADHD with a multidisciplinary approach includes nonmedication intervention. After the crisis, it may be more difficult to piece together everything needed for a complete diagnostic evaluation. As a crisis situation may involve symptoms of ADHD in combination with other problems, the additional difficulties are often obscured by the initial response to stimulant medication. Additional assessment and lost time may result. A family's request to start medication before the evaluation may be a sign that they are not willing to undertake the complete evaluation and follow through with nonmedication interventions. The family may want to "just give him something" to alleviate the problems. The families that are the most anxious to start medication before completion of the evaluation may benefit the most from postponing medication intervention until the entire evaluation is completed and the plans for nonmedication interventions have been established.

Benefits of Methylphenidate Intervention

The dramatic effect of stimulant medication on children with ADHD was described by Conners and Wells (1986):

> Without doubt the single most striking phenomenon of hyperkinetic children is their response to stimulant drugs. The effect is both immediate and obvious. Often within the first hour after treatment a perceptible change in handwriting, talking, motility, attending, planfulness and perception may be observed. Classroom teachers may notice improvement in enrollment and academic productivity after a single dose. Parents will frequently report a marked reduction in troublesome sibling interactions, inappropriate activity, and non-compliance. Even peers can identify the calmer, more organized cooperative behavior of stimulant-treated children. (p. 97)

Stimulant medication for ADHD children has been demonstrated to lead to a dramatic reduction in negative behaviors with a concomitant increase in classroom on-task behaviors (Pelham, Bender, Caddell, Booth, & Moorer, 1985a). As the dosage of stimulant medication increased, on-task behavior increased and negative behaviors decreased. Pelham (1987) stated, "Medicated children make fewer impulsive responses to non-target stimuli, they maintain attention and miss fewer targets. These effects are most pronounced during the later portion of the task" (p. 101). Other effects include children being less likely (a) "to talk out inappropriately in class; (b) to bother peers who are working; (c) to violate classroom rules or engage in other behaviors that require teacher attention; and (d) to interact aggressively and otherwise inappropriately with peers" (p. 101).

By 1977, the progress of nearly 2,000 children treated with stimulant medications for symptoms of hyperactivity had been studied. The review by Barkley (1977a) presented data on 915 children treated with amphetamines and judged by eighteen observers in fifteen studies. On amphetamines, 74% showed improvement; 26% did not improve or were worse. In a total of fourteen studies, 77% of 866 methylphenidate-treated children improved. Two studies found a mean improvement rate of 73% in 105 children treated with pemoline. In eight studies, of 417 children given a placebo, 39% showed significant improvement. The overall average of these studies was 75% showing improvement with stimulant medications and 25% remaining unchanged or worse. Because 39% improved with placebo, Barkley concluded that future studies will have only limited value if they fail to employ a placebo condition.

It has been suggested that stimulant medication therapy alone may be the most effective form of therapy. Brown, Wynne, and Medenis (1985) studied hyperactive boys using a three-month period of cognitive training, stimulant drug therapy (methylphenidate), or the two treatments combined. They concluded that, in their study, the combined medication and cognitive therapy condition was not any more effective than medication alone.

The most widely held opinion concerning medication, however, is reflected in a study by Hinshaw, Henker, and Whalen (1984b). Based on a comparison study of methylphenidate, placebo, and cognitive-behavioral intervention investigating social behavior, these authors believe that medication is not a sufficient treatment for hyperactivity and that alternatives or adjuncts are required (APA, 1987; Hinshaw et al., 1984b). We argue that medication for children with ADHD should never be used as an isolated treatment. Proper classroom placement, physical education, programs for behavior modification, counseling, and provision of structure should be used before a trial of pharmacotherapy is attempted. This integrated approach should continue once the medication is begun.

Effect on Peer Relationships

The effect of medication is readily apparent to the child's peers. Whalen, Henker, Castro, and Granger (1987) studied the reaction of normal fourth- and sixth-grade children to videotapes of students diagnosed as hyperactive. The children easily distinguished the medication responders on the basis of a broad range of behaviors. Observed differences between the medicated hyperactive boys and normal boys were rare. The authors described their results as systematic evidence that school-age youngsters detect the effects of methylphenidate in hyperactive peers. Methylphenidate decreases controlling interactions in ADHD children and there is also a reciprocal decline in controlling behavior in peers of the ADHD children (Cunningham, Siegel, & Offord, 1991). Observations must be placebo-controlled, as placebo alone has been found to help peer interactions (Whalen, Henker, Hinshaw, Heller, & Huber-Dressler, 1991).

Adult observers felt the changes occurring with medication represented improvement. Whalen, Henker, Swanson, et al. (1987) studied dose-related medication effects on social behaviors in a "natural context." The children, as a group, were judged to have improved their social interactions as a result of methylphenidate. The authors concluded that disruptive behaviors can be reduced successfully without decreasing overall sociability using methylphenidate. Others found that a dampening affect on social behavior with reduced social engagement and increasing dysphoria may result from methylphenidate (Buhrmester, Whalen, Henker, & MacDonald, 1992). Adults judging ninety-six ADHD subjects found that children who had taken medication were identified as engaging in lower rates of aggressive, destructive, and noncompliant behaviors. Methylphenidate resulted in the ADHD children also engaging in more socially withdrawn and passive behaviors, although they engaged in more leader/planner behaviors. Medication improves some behavior problems but may increase observations of dysphoric, disengaged behavior (Granger, Whalen, & Henker, 1993). Although peer appraisals were not normalized in this study, methylphenidate (0.3–0.6 mg/kg) produced increasing nominations of twenty-five hyperactive boys as best friends, cooperative, and fun to be with (Whalen et al., 1989). Even improved attention during sports activities has been demonstrated to result from methylphenidate treatment (Pelham,

McBurnett, et al., 1990). Additional social skills research will be reviewed in Chapter 14.

Effect on Family Relationships

Relationships between inattentive children and their families have been shown to improve with medication treatment. In a study of family relationships in relation to methylphenidate, a group of thirty-five boys with ADHD and other problems was treated with methylphenidate (Schachar, Taylor, Wieselberg, Thorley, & Rutter, 1987). In the eighteen boys found to be Ritalin responders, interaction between the ADHD child and his siblings and mother demonstrated increased maternal warmth, decreased maternal criticism, greater frequency of maternal contact, and fewer negative encounters with siblings. These positive changes were not observed in the methylphenidate nonresponders. In contrast, no significant changes occurred in the frequency of paternal contact, parental ability to cope with a wide range of problems, or interparental consistency. The methylphenidate responders also did not appear to present an increased frequency of isolation within the family, as previously reported by Barkley and Cunningham (1979). The finding of increased maternal warmth and contact, increased positive encounters with siblings, and decreased maternal criticism in the families of children who responded positively to methylphenidate led the authors to conclude that families of children who respond to methylphenidate might be more amenable to other types of intervention than before this treatment.

Similar improvement in interactions between inattentive children and their mothers was reported by Barkley, Karlsson, Strzelecki, and Murphy (1984) and Barkley (1988c). In the first study, Barkley et al. (1984) found that mothers decrease their control and negative behavior toward children during high-dose conditions, which resulted in improved mother-child interactions. The effect was not related to the age of the child. Conners and Wells (1986) reported, however, that in many instances, decreased negative parenting behavior was not associated with an increase in positive parenting behaviors in a playroom setting. Barkley (1988c) reported that twenty-seven preschool ADHD children decreased their off-task and noncompliant behavior and significantly increased their rates of compliance as well as the length of sustained compliance with maternal commands while taking methylphenidate. These studies suggest that medication intervention consistently decreases negative parent behaviors and in some settings may lead to an increase in positive parent behaviors.

Effect on Self-Esteem

Intervention that includes medication has been shown to increase self-esteem for preadolescents with attention deficit. In a study of twenty-one children ages 8 to 12 diagnosed with ADHD by *DSM-III* criteria, multimodal management including 5 to 10 mg of methylphenidate used twice daily, improved general as well as academic self-esteem, as measured by the Culture-Free Self-Esteem Inventory for Children (Kelly, Cohen, Walker, Caskey, & Atkinson, 1989). Improvement was seen for the long-term (average = 16 months) follow-up group, but no significant improvement in self-esteem was seen after only one month. The authors concluded that long-term multimodal management that includes methylphenidate does appear to improve self-esteem in ADD children.

Effect on Academic Achievement

Attempts to demonstrate effects of medication intervention on learning have had difficulty separating improved performance secondary to improved attention and concentration from primary effect on learning. Nevertheless, there is general agreement that classroom behavior is improved by stimulant medication (Wallander, Schroeder, Michelli, & Gualitieri, 1987). At the most effective dose (0.6 mg/kg), Pelham, Bender, Caddell, Booth, and Moorer (1985b) found a lesser effect on reading comprehension than on arithmetic. Similar dosage schedules (Gittelman, Klein, & Feingold, 1983) showed improvement on some measures of reading without improvement on others. After reviewing over 200 reports on methylphenidate, J. Murray (1987) concluded that the attention and concentration of ADHD children seems to benefit from treatment with methylphenidate, but except for contribution of improved attentional control, schoolwork does not appear to be facilitated by the drug.

Some authors argue that methylphenidate is effective at improving reading ability. Increased output, accuracy, and efficiency and improved learning acquisition were reported by Douglas et al. (1986) for ADHD children treated with 0.3 mg/kg methylphenidate. The authors described evidence of increased effort and self-correcting behavior and concluded that previous studies may have underestimated the potential of stimulants to improve the performance of ADHD children in academic learning and cognitive tasks. An early report suggested that methylphenidate, dextroamphetamine, and pemoline treatment produced substantial improvements on a number of academic measures as well as behavioral improvement (Conners, 1972).

Methylphenidate was found effective for inattentive reading-disabled children by Richardson, Kupietz, Winsberg, Maitinsky, and Mendell (1988) and Kupietz, Winsberg, Richardson, Maitinsky, and Mendell (1988). Various dosages were studied, but the major conclusion was that methylphenidate had a positive effect on reading, which the authors believe was mediated through both the behavioral control and through a direct effect on learning ability. They concluded that successful methylphenidate treatment of behavioral symptoms of ADHD is associated with improvement in academic learning, that this effect is primarily mediated by the behavioral change itself and is likely to be strongest in the early phases of treatment, and that methylphenidate has a direct positive effect on retrieval mechanisms involved in word recognition.

One of the factors contributing to the controversy about the effect of stimulant medication on learning ability is medication dose. Is the best dose for academic improvement different from the best dose for behavior? Sprague and Sleator (1977) reported that maximal effect on learning occurred at methylphenidate doses of 0.3 mg/kg, whereas maximal effects on behavior occurred at higher dosages up to 1 mg/kg. However, other studies have found that the best dose for behavior is the same as the best dose for learning.

Ullmann and Sleator (1985) studied eighty-six children diagnosed as ADD and ADHD (diagnostic criteria not described). Using a teacher questionnaire they had previously developed, attention, hyperactivity, social skills, and oppositional behavior were evaluated on baseline, placebo, and 0.3, 0.5, and 0.8 mg/kg of methylphenidate. A linear progression of improvements in all areas was seen with increasing doses of medication. However, the improvement in attention and hyperactivity was substantially greater than for social skills and oppositional behavior, leading the authors to conclude that methylphenidate has a major effect in improving attention, that it is helpful in decreasing activity level, but that it often has only a minor effect on deficient social skills and oppositional (aggressive) behavior.

Elementary-school-age children with histories of academic achievement problems treated with medication alone demonstrated marked improvements in Scholastic Achievement Test math and reading scores (Abikoff et al., 1988). Based on this study, the authors suggested that controlled investigations of the long-term efficacy of stimulant treatment on achievement should seriously be considered. Results of this study further suggested that cognitive training and academic tutoring improves aspects of academic achievement that are not facilitated by stimulant medication treatment alone.

The effect of methylphenidate on reading grade level in ADHD children was studied by Winsberg, Maitinsky, Richardson, and Kupietz (1988). They evaluated forty-two children diagnosed by *DSM-III* criteria as displaying ADHD and a developmental reading disorder with behavioral ratings from parents and teachers and achievement test scores. Using methylphenidate doses from 0.3 to 0.7 mg/kg, a positive correlation between improved reading grade level and rating-scale improvement of ADHD symptoms was noted. Richardson, Kupietz, and Maitinsky (1987) reported similar findings that the effective treatment of inattentive and hyperactive symptoms appeared to produce dramatic improvement in reading ability. Children who demonstrated better behavioral response to Ritalin also demonstrated greater gains in reading grade level (see Figure 13–2). Because the reading grade level did not improve without improvement in rating scales of ADHD symptoms, Winsberg et al. (1988) concluded that when ADHD symptoms are effectively controlled, a positive response to reading instruction will follow. Unless children with learning difficulties are provided with effective remedial instruction, methylphenidate is not likely to have either a positive or negative effect on achievement. The effects of methylphenidate on children's cognitive functions are interactive, independent, and highly complex (Rapport & Kelly, 1991). A graphic representation of some complex interactions is presented in Table 13–3.

Measures of reading and math ability improve in some children with administration of methylphenidate, though there is disagreement about whether this represents a direct effect of methylphenidate on reading and math ability or reflects improved concentration and attention. With a few exceptions, the best dose for reading and math has been found to be the same as the best dose for behavior. Children are much less likely to experience a dramatic improvement in academic skills than in behavior. Nevertheless, there is ample experimental evidence to conclude that many ADHD children will improve their reading ability directly or indirectly as a result of stimulant medication treatment.

Tannock, Schachar, Carr, and Logan (1989) suggested that a 1.0 mg/kg dose of methylphenidate given in the morning produced effects lasting into the afternoon. They found in the same study that a 0.3 mg/kg dose, although producing equivalent effects in the morning, did not produce effects that could be discerned in the afternoon.

Medication Effect and Dosage Time Course of Medication Activity

The effect of medication varies with time after ingestion. Initially after medication is ingested, there will be a time when it is partly effective; it will then have a time of full

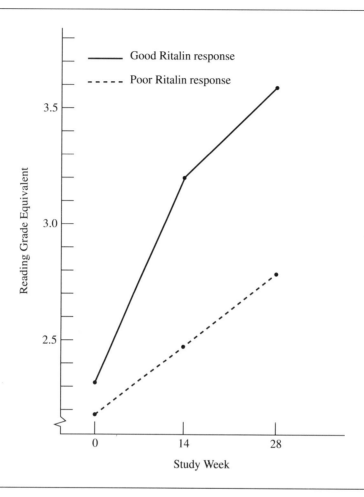

Figure 13–2.   Reading Grade Scores of Good and Poor Ritalin® Responders

Source: From E. Richardson, S. Kupietz, & S. Maitinsky. (1982). What is the role of academic intervention in the treatment of hyperactive children with reading disorders? In J. Loney (Ed.), *The Young Hyperactive Child: Answers to Questions about Diagnosis, Prognosis and Treatment.* Copyright 1987 by Haworth Press. Printed with permission from the publisher.

effectiveness. Following the period of full effectiveness, there is a period when the medication still has some effect but is decreasing in its effectiveness. At a later time, the medication will have ceased to become effective, and observed changes in behavior will not be related to the effect of medication but to the effect of the medication's dissipation or "wearing off." Finally, a return to baseline function will be seen. Observers of behavior must note the amount of time after medication ingestion so that an observed effect can be related to the time course. Medication given before a child goes to school may have its effect during the school hours. When a parent sees the child at home after school, rebound from medication rather than medication effect may be present, and the parent's observations that the child either improved or worsened while taking medication may reflect the response of the child during the withdrawal period rather than to the medication response period.

Table 13–3.   Task X dose effects on methylphenidate on children's cognitive performance

Convergent Tasks	(a)	% of Tasks Using Doses of			% of Sign Med Effects	% Comparing Low/High Conditions	Low	% Sign Between-Dose Difference	High
		1	2	3					
Stimulus equivalence	(1)	0	0	100	100	100	0	0/0	100
Matching to sample	(12)	25	67	8	83	25	0	33/0	67
Paired associates	(13)	62	15	23	85	23	0	67/0	33
Spelling	(2)	100	0	0	100	0	0	0/0	0
Picture recognition	(8)	63	25	12	50	29	0	50/50	0
Long/Short-term recall	(6)	33	67	0	50	0	0	0/0	0
Visual/perceptual	(2)	50	50	0	0	0	0	0/0	0
Stimulus identification	(6)	83	17	0	33	0	0	0/0	0
Perceptual/motor	(3)	67	33	0	33	0	0	0/0	0
Reaction time	(7)	71	29	0	100	14	0	0/0	100
Vigilance	(15)	73	20	7	80	7	0	100/0	0
Divergent Tasks	*(6)*	*33*	*33*	*34*	*33*	*33*	*0*	*0/100*	*0*

Source: Rapport, M. D., & Kelly, K. L. (1991). Psychostimulant effects on learning and cognitive function: Findings and implications for children with Attention Deficit Hyperactivity Disorder. *Clinical Psychology Review, 11,* 61–92. Used with permission.

By studying forty-eight patients' ability to learn eight successive word lists, Swanson, Kinsbourne, Roberts, and Zucker (1978) determined that the "behavioral half-life" (the time taken for a 50% decline from maximum effect) of methylphenidate was four hours, and its maximum effect was reached in two hours. The dosage of methylphenidate ranged from 5 to 20 mg with an average of 12 mg. The behavioral half-life was independent of the dosage. The authors found that increasing the maximum effective dose resulted in decreased learning performance that followed the same time course as the positive performance rather than simply extending the time of positive medication effect. It is important to understand that medication effect varies with time from ingestion. The relationship between time and effect must be understood to manage medication effectively.

Optimal Dosage

Attempts to find the best dose of stimulant medication have looked at positive effects, such as improved learning and behavior, as well as side effects, such as sleeplessness and irritability. A mg dose schedule reflects typical pediatric practice in the United States. Children's response to methylphenidate dosage manipulation has been shown to be independent of total body weight (Rapport et al., 1988). Even at the highest dose of 20 mg (0.39 to 1.10 mg/kg), no significant deterioration in behavior was observed. The Teacher's Self-Control Rating Scale used by Rapport et al. showed significant improvement when the 10 mg dose was increased to 15 or 20 mg. This careful work with a relatively small group of children strongly suggests that 15 to 20 mg of methylphenidate will improve some aspects of learning as well as behavior. A linear dose-response relationship of methylphenidate was shown in twenty ADHD children

(Rapport et al.). Selected criteria included: (1) pediatrician and psychologist diagnosis using *DSM-III* criteria; (2) maternal history showing problems in at least 50% of home situations; (3) maternal rating of 2 standard deviations above the norm for age on the Werry-Weiss Peters Activity Scale; (4) teacher rating on the Abbreviated Conners Teacher's Rating Scale above 15; and (5) absence of any gross neurological sensory or motor impairment. Assessment for medication response included the Teacher's Self-Control Rating Scale (Humphrey, 1982), measures of on-task behavior, and the Matching Familiar Figures Test. Placebo versus 5, 10, 15, and 20 mg dosages of methylphenidate was used. A linear relationship between dose and effect was uncovered, with increasing dose associated with improved effect. This is especially true between the 5 and 10 mg doses, with a significant improvement between 10 and 15 mg noted on the Teacher's Self-Control Rating Scale. Significant differences in the Matching Familiar Figures Test, however, were seen only between placebo and 15 mg or 20 mg. The 20 mg dose was significantly better than the 5 mg dose for all measures, and the 20 mg dose was significantly better than the 10 mg dose based on results from the Teacher's Self-Control Rating Scale (see Figure 13–3).

A report by Sprague and Sleator (1977) sparked a controversy that still persists. They suggested that a higher dose of methylphenidate was more effective at controlling behavior but that a lower dose was more effective at improving learning skills. They reported an improvement in arithmetic scores with methylphenidate on a 0.3 mg/kg dose, but less improvement on a 0.6 mg/kg dose. The difference was not statistically significant, but the authors suggested that an even higher dose might have shown a significant decline in arithmetic skills. Even in their study, however, reading comprehension improved only with the 0.6 mg/kg dose and not with the 0.3 mg/kg dose. Other investigators have found that within a range of 0.3 to 0.8 mg/kg, performance on both behavioral and cognitive tasks improves in a dose-related fashion (Charles, Schain, & Zelniker, 1981; Rapport, Stoner, DuPaul, Birmingham, & Tucker, 1985; Sebrechts et al., 1986). A higher dose of methylphenidate (0.8 mg/kg) was determined to optimize retention and recall of complex nonverbal information, while on the same study, impulsivity was reduced with both the low dose and high dose of methylphenidate (O'Toole, Abramowitz, Morris, & Dulcan, 1997).

Other studies have suggested a linear improvement in learning with dosage increases to 0.8 mg/kg. Pelham et al. (1985a) partly disagreed with the earlier study of Sprague and Sleator (1977). They felt that the 0.6 mg/kg dose was better for many cognitive functions and further expressed the opinion that their results suggested some beneficial effect of methylphenidate at doses as low as 0.15 mg/kg and as high as 0.6 mg/kg. Winsberg et al. (1988) reviewed several studies in which individual doses as high as 0.8 mg/kg did not produce a decrease in learning performance. They also noted that their dose of 0.7 mg/kg was not quite as high as the Sprague and Sleator dose. Improved reading, arithmetic, and spelling improved more on 0.6 mg/kg than on 0.3 mg/kg in another group of twenty-nine children with *DSM-III* ADD (Pelham et al., 1985a). Some studies of maternal-child interaction (Barkley, 1988c; Barkley et al., 1984) suggested that a higher dosage of methylphenidate is more effective. The earlier study compared high-dose to low-dose therapy and concluded that mothers decrease their control and negative behavior toward the children during the high-dose conditions. This effect was not related to age. The higher dose also helped twenty-seven

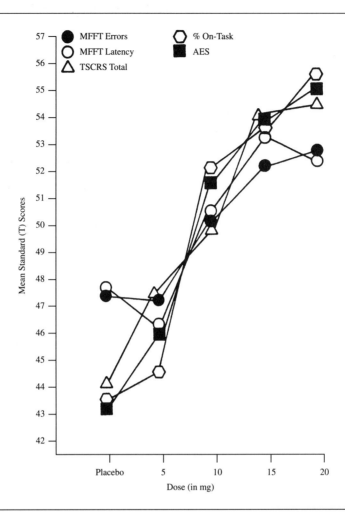

Figure 13–3.   The effect of methylphenidate dose on five performance and behavior variables

Source: From M. D. Rapport, G. Stoner, G. DuPaul, K. L. Kelly, S. B. Tucker, & T. Schoeler. (1988). Attention Deficit Disorder and methylphenidate: A multilevel analysis of dose-response effects on children's impulsivity across settings. Copyright 1988 by Williams & Wilkins. Printed with permission of the publisher.

MFFT = Matching Familiar Figures Test; TSCRS = Teacher Score Conners Rating Scale; AES = Average Error Score

preschool children with ADHD "decrease their off-task and noncompliant behavior and significantly increase their rates of compliance as well as the length of sustained compliance with maternal commands" (Barkley, 1988b, p. 336). In a review, Pelham et al. (1987) concluded that numerous studies that have administered the methylphenidate doses up to 0.75 mg/kg have found improvement on cognitive tasks.

Effect of methylphenidate on disruptive behavior is seen to improve with medication dosage from 0.15 to 0.6 mg/kg (Cantwell & Carlson, 1978; Conners & Werry, 1979). Other researchers have found similar patterns (Winsberg, Kupietz, Sverd,

Hungdung, & Young, 1982). However, Pelham et al. (1985a) pointed out that 67% of the drug effect on negative behavior was accounted for by the 0.15 mg/kg dose of methylphenidate.

While it is well accepted that some ADHD children do better than others when taking methylphenidate, defining the difficulties some children encounter with methylphenidate has presented a challenge. Cantwell and Swanson (1997) comment on the difficulty when using average performance to describe cognitive results. They note that some children have a cognitive decline when taking methylphenidate. Solanto (1997) emphasizes that no single published study has shown an actual reduction in cognitive performance with increasing dose when compared with placebo. Cantwell and Swanson (1997) agree that averaging data results in overall positive effects but again look at individual children who may show cognitive or other decline while taking one dose or another of methylphenidate and emphasize the importance of individual dosage titration rather than predetermined mg/dose or mg/kg dosage.

Taken in total, these studies demonstrate the need to closely monitor a number of variables, including schoolwork, socialization, and behavioral compliance, as methylphenidate is titrated.

Many studies have shown positive effects of methylphenidate on one or another laboratory-measured aspect of learning. Methylphenidate raised the "breaking point" above which the hyperactive child was unwilling to continue with a task (Wilkinson, Kircher, McMahon, & Sloane, 1995). Contrary to concerns expressed by other authors, Douglas, Barr, Desilets, and Sherman (1995) found methylphenidate (up to 0.9 mg/kg) has improved mental flexibility and other cognitive processes, improved persistence rather than perseveration, and did not worsen performance on tasks designed to assess divergent thinking, perseveration, ability to shift mental set, convergent thinking, problem solving, speed, and accuracy of processing.

Methylphenidate and Laboratory Measures of Learning

One of the approaches to understanding the effect of methylphenidate on learning is to compare performance on laboratory measures of learning (Solanto & Wender, 1989). A Wallach-Kogan battery that calls for cognitive flexibility or divergent thinking was used to show that methylphenidate does not decrease sustained output (Solanto & Wender, 1989). These data contradict the hypothesis that methylphenidate causes constriction of cognitive function (Milich, Licht, Murphy, & Pelham, 1989). A CPT has been used to show that medication increased correspondence between boys' self-evaluation and their performance. The boys picked medication as an explanation for their successes significantly less often than they attributed success to either effort or ability (Milich et al., 1989). Learning of trained and untrained complex figure relationships has been used to show that methylphenidate enhanced children's learning of both taught and untaught visual relationships (Vyse & Rapport, 1989). Methylphenidate improves both the rate of acquisition and accuracy in learning paired associations (Rapport, Quinn, DuPaul, Quinn, & Kelly, 1989). Methylphenidate resulted in significantly faster reaction times to tone probes and faster answers to arithmetic problems (Carlson, Pelham, Swanson, & Wagner, 1991). Although placebo was associated with a decrement in performance following attempts to solve unsolvable problems, methylphenidate prevented this deterioration in performance while working on unsolvable problems (Milich, Carlson, Pelham, & Licht, 1991). Methylphenidate-treated subjects are more likely to make external attribution for failure and internal attribution for success. Using the Stroop Color and Word Test and Wisconsin Card Sorting Test, Everett, Thomas, Cote, Levesque, and Michaud (1991) were able to show that after one year of methylphenidate and pemoline treatment, there was improvement in the functional frontal deficit. A deficit of selective attention, however, persisted. Selective and sustained attention tasks as well as other psychological and neurological measures were judged by some to show that although methylphenidate selectively alleviates attention deficits, it does not affect divided attention except for an increase in accuracy of response organization (deSonnerville, Njiokiktjien, & Bos, 1994). Improved focus and sustained attention vigilance, impulsivity, and the behavioral adaptivity to feedback were seen. The Posner Letter Matching Test and four additional measures of phonological processing suggest that methylphenidate improves nonspecific aspects of information processing (Balthazor, Wagner, & Pelham, 1991).

Methylphenidate and the Classroom

A constructed simulated classroom was used to show that the medication improved attention and decreased disruptive behavior during lectures and improved teacher ratings in the classroom (Evans & Pelham, 1991). A quasi-naturalistic classroom setting comparing quiet versus noisy conditions showed that placebo-treated hyperactive boys demonstrated lower rates of past attention and higher rates of gross motor movement, regular and negative verbalization, noise making, physical contact, social initiation, disruption, and acts that were perceived as energetic, inappropriate, or unexpected (Whalen, Henker, Collins, Finck, et al., 1979). In this setting, high ambient noise levels reduced task attention and increased the rates of many other behaviors.

Methylphenidate exerts a significant effect on classroom measures of attention and academic efficiency. DuPaul and Rapport (1993) found that methylphenidate-treated ADHD children were no longer statistically deviant from scores obtained by normal control children; 75% of these children obtained normalized levels of classroom performance without ancillary school-based interventions. In a review of eighty-four studies, Rapport and Kelly (1991) concluded that only a handful of studies were compared to cognitive performance of normal and ADHD children using stimulant medications; most of these used low doses of medication and studied only less difficult and complex tasks. Rapport and Kelly concluded nevertheless that the evidence strongly supports the contention that methylphenidate facilitates cognitive function in children with ADHD.

Evaluation of Medication Effects at School

A survey of 322 teachers in two school systems revealed some disturbing information concerning teacher knowledge and training about ADHD (Kasten, Coury, & Heron, 1992). Between 92% and 94% of teachers stated that they had too little or no inservice training about stimulants and 60% believed they had not had adequate access to specialists to help them manage their students with ADHD (Kasten et al., 1992). Ninety-six percent of regular and special education teachers stated they had received too little or no training about stimulants in their undergraduate education programs. Fifty percent of regular classroom teachers and 19% to 32% of special education teachers stated they did not know what physical and behavioral side effects might result from the use of stimulants. Over 80% of special educators and over 60% of regular educators knew that stimulants might increase concentration and decrease impulsiveness (Kasten et al.). It is apparent that part of the task of assessing the effect of stimulant medication is being certain that the classroom teachers understand the medication benefits as well as potential side effects.

Behavioral rating questionnaires have been the most widely accepted means of evaluating behavior at school to determine medication effect; the Conners questionnaires are used most often (DiTraglia, 1991), and other questionnaires are also used (Gadow & Nolan, 1993). Subjecting each child to a blind comparison of medication and placebo is inconvenient, cumbersome, and expensive; therefore, this approach to determining efficacy of medication is not widely accepted, even though it improves acceptance of medication by demonstrating to parents the efficacy or lack of efficacy of medication (Fine & Jewesson, 1989). Other methods to predict medication response have been proposed. Cerebrospinal fluid homovanillic acid levels change with medication (Castellanos, Elia, et al., 1996) but this procedure is not likely to be of clinical utility as it requires an invasive lumbar puncture. Hair zinc levels were shown by Arnold, Votolato, Kleykamp, and Baker (1990) to not correlate with clinical response. Test performance on laboratory measures have consistently been a disappointment. Aman and Turbott (1991) found little correlation between clinical change and performance tests. Buitelaar, Rutger, Swaab-Varneveld, and Kuiper (1995) found that only strong levels of response could be predicted by baseline characteristics. Mayes and Bixler (1993) and C. Johnston and Fine (1993) have suggested specific rating programs for evaluation of methylphenidate effect. Many attempts, such as that by Trommer, Hoeppner, and Zecker (1991), used laboratory testing to determine medication effect but have not demonstrated improvement over standard behavioral means such as those discussed in Chapter 6.

Are children in community settings placed on medication for genuine ADHD symptoms, and do these children really respond as they do in research studies? Surveys of Baltimore County have been used to try to answer these questions (Safer & Krager, 1989). Three-fourths of the 176 students on stimulant medication had pretreatment ratings consistent with moderate to severe hyperactivity/inattentiveness. By teacher ratings, over 90% of students evidenced at least 50% of improvement initially following stimulant treatment, and 76% of medicated students continued to show this level of improvement at the end of the school year.

Medication Dose with Age

Age also is a variable that affects medication response. The relationship between dose and response may change substantially at different ages. Whalen, Henker, Castro, et al. (1987) found that the optimal dose for younger children was more mg/kg than for older children. They measured placebo against 0.3 mg/kg and 0.6 mg/kg dosages of methylphenidate on observed playground behavior during a seven-week summer program for forty hyperactive children. Diagnosis was by referral, and clinical evaluation by the project director and Conners Questionnaire. The authors studied dose-related medication effects on social behaviors in this "natural" context. As a group, the children improved their social interactions as a result of methylphenidate. In younger children (ages 7 to 8), the higher dose was more effective than the lower dose. Other studies have not found age-related medication effect (Barkley, 1988c; Barkley et al., 1984). With additional research, we may better understand the variation of medication benefits in relation to age.

Studies suggest the effect of medication does not disappear with adolescence. Methylphenidate significantly reduced teacher and parent ratings of hyperactivity, inattention, and oppositionality in a group of forty-eight adolescents to age 18 (Klorman, Brumaghim, Fitzpatrick, & Borgstedt, 1990).

Effect of Medication and Blood Levels

Blood-level evaluation of medications such as anticonvulsants, antidepressants, and antibiotics has proven useful in adjusting these medications. Studies of methylphenidate, however, have not shown that plasma levels of this medication are likely to become part of the standard of treatment of ADHD. Winsberg, Maitinsky, Kupietz, and Richardson (1987) studied oral dose in relation to plasma levels of methylphenidate and compared dose and blood level to behavioral response. They discovered that there is both a correlation between blood levels and response and a correlation between oral dose and blood levels. One can conclude from these data that titration of oral dose is equivalent to titration by blood levels. This implies that changes in oral dose will result in proportional changes in blood level and that differences in dosage requirement reflect differences in blood-level requirement for optimal effect. Gualtieri, Hicks, Patrick, Schroeder, and Breese (1984) did not find a relationship between serum levels of methylphenidate and either side effects (see Figure 13–4) or clinical response (see Figure 13–5). Blood studies do not give additional assistance over clinical evaluation in maximizing benefits or decreasing risks of stimulant medication.

Long-Term Effects of Methylphenidate

Despite the dramatic short-term effects of methylphenidate treatment on symptoms of ADHD, it has been surprisingly difficult to demonstrate long-term effects. Riddle and Rapoport (1976) reported on a group of seventy-two hyperactive boys who had been followed for two years; they were able to follow 94% of an initial sample. Conners Questionnaires, among other measures, were used. The patient group continued to have academic difficulties, low peer status, and depressive symptoms in comparison with a control group. A group consisting of 86% of the responders who were judged to be optimally medicated was compared with a group of dropouts from drug treatment. The authors concluded that the dropouts had almost identical academic achievement and social acceptance to that of the optimally medicated group. This report suggests limited effectiveness of medication intervention on long-term outcome.

A group of twenty children treated for hyperactivity for three years or longer were subjects of a ten-year follow-up study by Hechtman, Weiss, and Perlman (1984). At an

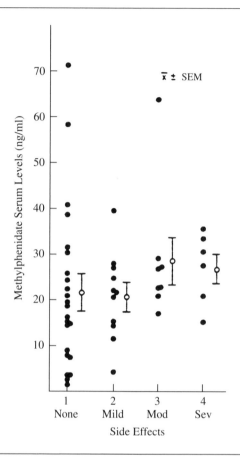

Figure 13–4. Methylphenidate serum levels and side effects

Source: From C. T. Gualtieri, R. E. Hicks, K. Patrick, S. R. Schroeder, & G. R. Breese. (1984). Used with permission.

average age of 21.8 years, these patients were compared both with hyperactives who had not been treated by Ritalin and with a control group of nonhyperactives. The treated hyperactives did not do as well as matched controls in areas such as schoolwork and personality disorders, but had fewer car accidents, a more positive view of childhood, less delinquency, and better social skills and self-esteem than untreated hyperactives. The authors concluded that stimulant treatment for hyperactive children may not eliminate educational or personality difficulties but may result in less social ostracism and more positive feelings toward themselves and others.

Other studies have not shown much more positive effect on long-term outlook. Weiss, Kurger, Danielson, and Elman (1975) presented a five-year follow-up of methylphenidate and no-treatment groups. They found that methylphenidate was helpful in making hyperactive children more manageable at home and at school but did not significantly affect the outcome after five years of treatment. Following forty-eight ADD children through adolescence in a study not controlled for comorbid CD, Wilson and Marcotte (1995) found that length of treatment with psychostimulants alone did

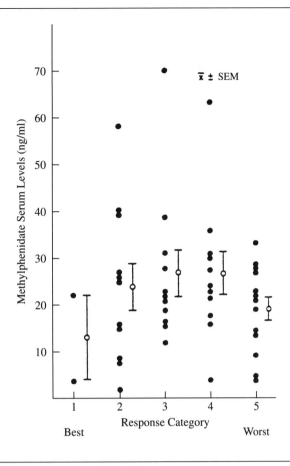

Figure 13–5.   Methylphenidate serum levels and clinical reponse
Source: From C. T. Gualtieri, R. E. Hicks, K. Patrick, S. R. Schroeder, & G. R. Breese. (1984). Used with permission.

not alter negative outcomes for the adolescents with childhood diagnosis of ADD. Cantwell and Baker (1987) suggested that those in a multidisciplinary treatment program for three years or longer did show some long-term benefits of intervention.

When evaluating the benefits of medication intervention, one must accept that, although medication intervention has many dramatic positive effects, there is little evidence to support expectation of long-term benefits.

Sustained-Release Methylphenidate

The clinical effects of methylphenidate are usually dissipated after four hours. To maintain effectiveness throughout the school day, a second dose is often needed. This exposes children to the social disadvantages as well as the potential for missed medication when taking medication at school. A sustained-release medication, which would allow a single morning dose with effectiveness throughout the school day, would therefore have a substantial advantage. A wax matrix has been used to create a sustained-release methylphenidate (Ritalin SR®). Pharmokinetically, sustained-release methylphenidate was shown to have a longer duration than regular methylphenidate in one study (Birmaher, Greenhill, Cooper, Fried, & Maminski, 1989). However, the maximum concentration measured in blood samples was not as high for the sustained-release preparation as it was for the standard methylphenidate. A study of twenty-two boys with ADD (Pelham et al., 1987) found that although effects of the sustained-release preparation were still evident eight hours after ingestion, the medication displayed several substantial disadvantages. First, the onset of action was slower than the regular methylphenidate; second, on key measures of behavior, the sustained preparation showed less efficacy at controlling disruptive behavior. Analyses of individual responsivity showed clearly that most boys responded more positively to standard methylphenidate than to the sustained-release preparation.

At least three other studies, however, did not find any significant difference between the standard preparation and the sustained-release form of methylphenidate. One studied nineteen children with ADD in a double-blind study for two weeks on each medication condition (Fitzpatrick, Klorman, Brumaghim, & Borgstedt, 1992). The second studied thirty children for two weeks with questionnaires comparing standard methylphenidate, sustained-release methylphenidate, and two other longer-acting preparations, sustained-release dextroamphetamine and pemoline (Whitehouse, Shah, & Palmer, 1980). The third study (Pelham, Greenslade, et al., 1990), of twenty-two children with ADHD using a double-blind, placebo-controlled crossover study design, also found no difference among standard or sustained-release methylphenidate, dexedrine, or pemoline: all four showed improvement in CPT measures. This effect was seen within two hours of ingestion and effects lasted for nine hours. All four medications were found to be clinically beneficial and generally equivalent. However, the authors report that dexedrine spansules and pemoline tended to produce the most consistent effects and were recommended by the treating team for ten of the fifteen children. Of the fifteen children, six were recommended to continue dexedrine spansules, four were recommended to continue with 10 mg of methylphenidate bid, four sustained-release methylphenidate, and four pemoline. Seven of the group of twenty-two were recommended to not continue with any of the medications.

Information concerning sustained-release methylphenidate is quite limited. Fewer than 100 children have been reported in trials of the medication, and trials lasted at most two weeks in duration. Not discovering a difference between two conditions is far from discovering that the two conditions are the same. One author (Pelham et al., 1987) has concluded that sustained-release methylphenidate is not as helpful at relieving ADHD symptoms as the standard preparation. It is our experience that most families, when given the option, choose to return to standard methylphenidate after a trial of sustained-release medication, even though the children must then take medication at school. Some children, however, manage quite well with the sustained-release preparation and do not have to take medication at school. Additional comparison studies of sustained-release methylphenidate, sustained-release dextroamphetamine, and pemoline compared with the standard preparations of methylphenidate and dextroamphetamine are needed. Considering the number of children for whom these medications are prescribed, the paucity of controlled comparison studies is striking.

Methylphenidate and Behavioral Intervention

Nonmedication intervention programs are discussed in Chapter 16. It has been very difficult to determine whether behavior interventions have an additive effect. Behavioral interventions do improve ADHD symptoms and are accepted as useful and recommended for most ADHD children. In mild cases, they may make medication unnecessary (Anastopoulos, DuPaul, & Barkley, 1991; Barkley & Murphy, 1991). Increasing behavioral interventions have been shown to have increasing effects (a dose-response relationship) (Abramowitz et al., 1992). Which behavioral interventions work? Some authors have recommended biofeedback as a behavioral treatment (Pelham et al., 1993; Potashkin & Beckles, 1990), but biofeedback is not widely accepted (A. Abramowitz et al., 1992). To determine the relationship between behavioral and medication interventions, the National Institutes of Mental Health undertook a collaborative multisite, multimodal treatment study of children with ADHD (Richters et al., 1995). This five-year study concerns the long-term effects of both pharmacological and psychosocial treatments, synergistic or additive effects of stimulant and psychosocial treatments, and interactions of treatment types with comorbidity pattern and socioeconomic status. Initial outcome findings should be available by the year 2000.

OTHER MEDICATION INTERVENTIONS

Methylphenidate has become the overwhelming first choice for treatment of ADHD. Between 1971 and 1987, its use in Baltimore County went from 40% to 90% of children medicated for hyperactivity (Safer & Krager, 1983, 1988). But other medications, such as antidepressants, antipsychotics, anticonvulsants, and antihypertensives, are useful in selected situations.

Amphetamine

Bradley is often credited with the first report of the effect of a stimulant medication on inattentive and hyperactive symptoms as part of a study of the amphetamine Benzedrine (Bradley, 1937). In 1950, Bradley was one of the first to compare the effect of different medications. He compared two chemically related amphetamines and decided there was no substantial difference between them.

The relationship of attention-deficit symptoms and plasma levels of amphetamine was reported by Brown, Hunt, Ebert, Bunney, and Kopin (1979). A single dose of dextroamphetamine of 0.45 mg/kg was administered. The plasma half-life was 6.8 hours, but the maximum effect occurred in one to two hours, which was the time of absorption of the dextroamphetamine. The authors speculated that this is the time of catecholamine release by medication. The time of most significant difference between placebo and amphetamine was at two hours after administration. The time of highest plasma level of d-amphetamine was at four hours. At five to six hours, no significant differences between placebo and amphetamine could be determined, but the blood level was still more than three-quarters of the maximal level. One can see from these results, presented in Figures 13–6 and 13–7, that the clinical effect of dextroamphetamine

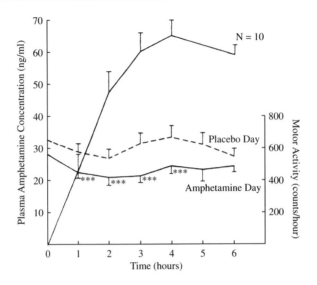

Figure 13–6.   Amphetamine blood levels and motor activity

Source: From G. L. Brown, R. D. Hunt, M. H. Ebert, W. E. Bunney, & I. J. Kopin. (1979). Plasma levels of d-amphetamine in hyperactive children. Copyright 1979 by *Psychopharmacology*. Used with permission.

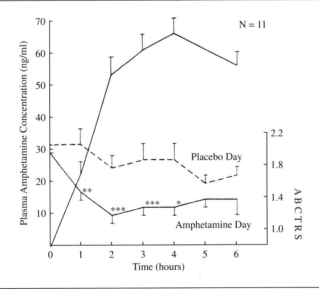

Figure 13–7.   Amphetamine blood levels and behavior

Source: From G. L. Brown, R. D. Hunt, M. H. Ebert, W. E. Bunney, & I. J. Kopin. (1979). Plasma levels of d-amphetamine in hyperactive children. Copyright 1979 by *Psychopharmacology*. Used with permission.

follows a different time course from the plasma blood level. Blood levels, therefore, cannot be used to measure clinical effect of dextroamphetamine.

Measurements in the plasma concentration of the noradrenalin metabolite MHPG following methylphenidate and amphetamine suggest some difference in the mechanism of action of these two medications. Shaywitz et al. (1988) reported results of a study of twenty-six children with ADHD. They were treated daily for eight days with either 0.25 mg/kg of dextroamphetamine, 0.5 mg/kg methylphenidate, or placebo. Significant differences in MHPG were noted with amphetamine treatment over four, five, and six hours as compared with placebo and methylphenidate. Methylphenidate did not have the same effect on plasma MHPG concentration as amphetamine. Despite the possibility that changes in peripheral metabolism unrelated to brain metabolism could also affect plasma MHPG, the authors concluded that amphetamine and methylphenidate differ in their effects on brain catecholaminergic systems. They believed that amphetamine influences brain noradrenergic mechanisms, perhaps by reducing turnover of brain norepinephrine.

Dextroamphetamine is the only stimulant approved for children between the ages of 3 and 6. The *PDR* (1997) describes Dexedrine-brand of dextroamphetamine as "not recommended" for children "under three years of age." The warning issued for methylphenidate, pemoline, and even Desoxyn (methamphetamine chemically similar to dextroamphetamine) suggests these medications should not be used for children younger than 6 years of age. A dosage schedule for dextroamphetamine is listed for children from 3 to 5 years of age but suggests the medication should not be used for children under 3 years of age. A starting daily dose of 2.5 mg is suggested with 1.5 mg increments weekly until optimal response is obtained.

Dextroamphetamine optimal dosage is often 5 to 10 mg per dose, almost half that of methylphenidate. Dextroamphetamine is available in tablets of 5 mg and spansules of 5, 10, and 15 mg. While the *PDR* (1997) relates that peak blood level of radioactive-labeled dextroamphetamine contained in the spansule was, on the average, eight to ten hours post administration as opposed to the peak blood level at two hours for regular tablets, it remains to be shown that the spansules have significant clinical advantage over the regular tablets.

In an extensive review by Barkley (1977a), studies of dextroamphetamine, methylphenidate, and pemoline were presented. No significant differences between percentage of responders or percentage of nonresponders was shown. No significant differences in the types, severity, or frequency of side effects was noted. Safer et al. (1972) suggested that growth suppression was more pronounced with dextroamphetamine than with methylphenidate. Conners, Taylor, Meo, Kurtz, and Fournier (1972) suggested that dextroamphetamine produced more "sadness" than pemoline. The growth suppression effect of dextroamphetamine, however, has been subsequently shown to remit spontaneously with time, and the depressant effects of dextroamphetamine were not considered severe nor did they require discontinuation of medication (Conners et al., 1972).

The FDA has released dextroamphetamine for treatment in children above the age of 3. Alessandri and Schramm (1991) report positive effects without side effects in a single case report of a 4-year-old boy with ADHD treated with 2.5 mg of dextroamphetamine twice a day.

The effect of dextroamphetamine on a single brain-injured child was reported by Max, Richards, and Hamdan-Allen (1995). The 14-year-old, who was described as having manic behavior, improved with dextroamphetamine increased to 25 mg per day. Unsuccessful treatment had previously been attempted with divalproex, lithium, haloperidol combination, and carbamazepine.

Comparison between Methylphenidate and Dextroamphetamine

There have been more comparison studies of methylphenidate and dextroamphetamine for treatment of ADHD symptoms than for any two other medications. Elia, Borcherding, Rapoport, and Keysor (1991) studied forty-eight children with ADHD using dexedrine, methylphenidate, and placebo in a double-blind crossover study. Only one of the forty-eight was not discharged from the study taking one of the two medications, prompting the authors to conclude that nonresponse is rare when both stimulants and a wide range of dosages are given. In a review of five comparative studies in 137 subjects, Elia et al. (1991) found dextroamphetamine and methylphenidate to be equally useful with similar side effects. Some reports showed more side effects for dextroamphetamine, but the side effects were similar and not substantially different for the two medications. As some children who do not respond to methylphenidate will respond to dextroamphetamine, and others who would be considered a responder to one medication do even better on the other, Elia and Rapoport (1991) strongly urged consideration of a trial of both stimulant medications for children with ADHD.

No Similar Effects on Normal Adults

Some concern has been raised that stimulant medications are merely "performance enhancers." Fleming, Bigelow, Weinberger, and Goldberg (1995) showed that there was no improvement in cognitive or memory function in normal, nonfatigued adults given dextroamphetamine. IV infusion of dextroamphetamine did not significantly alter brain glucose metabolism studied in eight adults with ADHD in a three-hour, eighteen-Fluoro decay-glucose (FDG) pet study (Ernst et al., 1994).

Amphetamine Combination: Adderall

A combination of salts of amphetamine, including sulfates that are absorbed quickly and saccharates that are absorbed more slowly, was originally released as a treatment for obesity and called Obetrol for obesity control. This combination of amphetamine salts has been renamed Adderall and approved by the FDA for treatment of ADHD. Each pill contains a total of 10 mg of amphetamine. Peer-reviewed literature on this medication, however, is very limited. In a retrospective review of patients with ADHD seen in a clinical practice, C. Jones (1994) compared clinical responses of Adderall and methylphenidate. The author concluded that both products were safe and effective and produced similar responses. In this study, patients who did not respond well to initial medication usually did well on the alternative. Side effects were similar, with anorexia and insomnia being the most frequent, and were found to be transitory when changes in eating and bedtime routine were followed. Whether this combination of amphetamine salts actually produces longer acting clinical effects remains to be demonstrated with clinical studies.

Pemoline

Pemoline (Cylert®) is a stimulant medication, as are dextroamphetamine and methylphenidate. One of the earliest studies to report the effectiveness of pemoline on hyperactive symptoms was reported by Conners et al. (1972), who studied eighty-one children with a diagnosis of minimal brain dysfunction based on questionnaires, CPTs, and clinical evaluation. Both pemoline and dextroamphetamine were administered on a blind basis, one morning dose of pemoline and a morning and before-lunch dose of dextroamphetamine. At the end of the eight-week treatment period, both dextroamphetamine and pemoline appeared effective in improving symptoms. Approximately 96% of the dextroamphetamine patients and 77% of the pemoline patients were rated as improved or much improved. As in other studies, approximately 30% of the placebo patients were improved but none were much improved. Teacher ratings roughly paralleled the clinician's evaluation. Both medications produced similar side effects, although the incidence of insomnia and anorexia was slightly less with pemoline than with dextroamphetamine. One important difference was the time for onset of drug effect. At two weeks and at four weeks into the therapy, there was a significant difference between the effects of pemoline and dextroamphetamine: dextroamphetamine was fully effective at the end of two weeks, but pemoline was not fully effective until six weeks. At four weeks, dextroamphetamine was still significantly more effective than pemoline. By six weeks, the difference had disappeared and both were more effective than placebo. No changes in blood pressure or liver function studies were noted in these subjects. Conners et al. (1972) showed that pemoline was effective when used only once daily (an advantage over dextroamphetamine) but was not fully effective until it had been taken daily for four to six weeks.

Other studies of pemoline demonstrated positive effects and side effects similar to other stimulants (Pelham, Swanson, Bender, & Wilson, 1980). Page, Bernstein, Janicki, and Michelli (1974) reported a multiclinic trial of pemoline that included 238 patients. Parent and teacher questionnaires, global ratings, and psychological tests as well as physical and laboratory data were evaluated at nine weeks of therapy. Side effects attributed to pemoline were insomnia and anorexia. Five of the patients had stomachache, mild depression, nausea, dizziness, headache, or drowsiness requiring discontinuation of the medication. Although side effects were more common in the pemoline group than in the placebo group, 33% of the side effects were noted in the placebo group. All observers, including physicians, parents, teachers, and psychologists, noted a significant therapeutic benefit from pemoline when compared to placebo in this double-blind multiclinic trial. The authors noted that improvement with pemoline appears to be gradual, as reported by global ratings and individual questionnaire items. Significant benefit may not be evident until the third or fourth week of drug administration. Longer follow-up times also showed significant benefits and side effects much the same as for other stimulants.

Studies have also shown improvement in the intellectual functioning of children taking pemoline. Dykman, McGrew, and Ackerman (1974) studied 216 children taking pemoline over a nine-week period. Increase in performance was observed for IQ

(WISC), reading and arithmetic Wide Range Achievement Test (WRAT), auditory perception Wepman Auditory Discrimination Test (Wepman), motor coordination involving complex left-right maneuvers (Lincoln-Oseretsky Factor II), and attention to details and organization (Draw-a-Man). The authors concluded that pemoline improves attention while decreasing distractibility and level of restlessness. Stevenson, Pelham, and Skinner (1984) studied methylphenidate and pemoline in comparison on paired-associate learning tasks and spelling tasks in hyperactive children. They studied thirty-six children ages 5.8 to 11.6 who met the *DSM-III* criteria for a diagnosis of ADD. Maximum effect on learning occurred one hour after ingestion for methylphenidate (0.3 mg/kg) and two hours after ingestion for pemoline (1.9 mg/kg). Testing took place after two weeks on medication. Significant improvement in the paired-associate learning task was seen. The authors believed that pemoline was superior to methylphenidate in some respects, especially in the paired-associate learning task. However, they felt that this finding needed to be replicated.

Similar findings of four- to eight-week delayed onset of effectiveness for pemoline when compared to methylphenidate was reported by Conners and Taylor (1980) in a study of sixty hyperactive children. Children were selected on the basis of clinical evaluation, multiple psychological tests, and parent and teacher ratings. Assessment of medication was determined on an individual basis. By the end of the treatment, approximately 88% of the pemoline and 90% of the methylphenidate groups were either improved or much improved, and 34% of the placebo group was improved. The authors related that, as in a previous study where pemoline was compared with dextroamphetamine, the clinical effect of pemoline had a slower onset, with the major positive differences not appearing until between the fourth and the eighth weeks. Both drugs produced more side effects than placebo; however, it is notable that two-thirds of the patients had side effects from placebo. When medication was discontinued, the methylphenidate group immediately regressed, whereas the placebo group did not change. The pemoline group returned to baseline over several weeks, suggesting a longer-lasting effect of pemoline than methylphenidate. Pemoline was found to be less helpful than methylphenidate, but this difference was not significant. Side effects of pemoline were considered similar to other stimulants and included anorexia and insomnia.

The finding of a high degree of variability of pemoline metabolism has been suggested as a possible explanation of rare negative reactions such as psychosis or Tourette's. A 600% interindividual variation in elimination and a 300% variation in total body clearance of pemoline was discovered by Sallee, Stiller, Perel, and Bates (1985) in a study of ten children, ages 5 to 12, diagnosed as hyperactive on the basis of Conners scores. The authors felt this finding may explain the unpredictable reactions of children to pemoline in some cases.

Possibly the greatest disadvantage of pemoline is the concern that it may cause liver failure. Prescription information for physicians in regard to Cylert includes a warning about possible hepatic dysfunction or failure. "There have been reports of hepatic dysfunction including elevated liver enzymes, hepatitis and jaundice in patients taking Cylert. The occurrence of elevated liver enzymes is not rare and these reactions appear to be reversible upon drug discontinuance. Most patients with elevated liver enzymes are asymptomatic. Although no causal relationship has been established, two hepatic-related fatalities have been reported involving patients taking Cyler." As a result, laboratory tests are recommended. "Liver function tests should be performed prior to and periodically during therapy with Cylert. The drug should be discontinued if abnormalities are revealed and confirmed by follow-up tests" (*PDR,* 1997).

Jaffe (1989) obtained the FDA 1639 forms that contained the reports of the two pemoline-related deaths cited in the *PDR* (1997). The first was a 10-year-old who died in 1977. He had hypoplasia of extrahepatic ducts and biliary cirrhosis before taking pemoline. He developed jaundice three weeks after being placed on pemoline and died of liver failure eighteen months later. The second was a 12-year-old boy who died in 1981 after taking pemoline for three years. Data were limited to very high SGOT (liver enzyme) and bilirubin, as well as a negative test for infectious hepatitis A and B. The death was attributed to a toxic hepatitis secondary to overdose. Jaffe concluded that the liver function tests should be done before beginning and periodically when using pemoline and that a history of liver disease/dysfunction should be a contraindication.

Page et al. (1974) studied 288 patients for as long as seventy-seven weeks (most more than fifty weeks) in an open trial of pemoline at a dosage of 1.91 to 2.51 mg/kg/day. Nine of the 288 patients discontinued pemoline because of elevations of SGOT and/or SGPT liver enzymes. These elevations occurred after 250 days or more of continuous pemoline therapy and were discovered during routine testing procedure. There were no clinical signs or symptoms present in any patient demonstrating enzyme elevation. Bilirubin did not rise, and there was only inconsistent sporadic elevation of alkaline phosphatase in these patients. Drug administration was discontinued when elevations were noted, and the enzyme levels returned to normal. Two patients were rechallenged with pemoline, and their serum liver enzymes rose again. The authors believed that this represents an individual delayed hypersensitivity to pemoline that is reversible on discontinuation of the medication. They reported the overall incidence of this reaction in all studies as in the range of 1% to 2%. The authors did not find the problem of liver enzyme elevation a serious one, and no deaths or permanent liver failure were reported. Nevertheless, possible liver failure and need for frequent blood tests represent a significant disadvantage and may account, in part, for the lack of popularity of pemoline.

A review of 100 cases of hepatocellular injury attributed to pemoline was undertaken by Nehra, Mullick, Ishak, and Zimmerman (1990). Only forty-three had sufficient accompanying information to permit analysis. Forty-one of the forty-three subjects were under 20 years of age and 80% were less than 12 years old. High values of blood aminotransferase levels and death from massive necrosis in one patient suggested hepatocellular injury. It was suggested that injury was a metabolic idiosyncracy rather than immunologic. Injury occurred as early as one week or as late as greater than one year after beginning the medication.

Other side effects that have been the subject of isolated case reports include a single case of a ninth-grader treated for six years with pemoline whose response changed from paradoxical calming to wakefulness, alertness, and anxiety (Waltz, 1990). An 11-year-old female suffered depression after withdrawing from pemoline (R. T. Brown, Borden, Spunt, & Medenis, 1985).

Pemoline was found to cause abnormal involuntary movements in dosage of 2 mg/kg in five of twenty subjects (Sallee, Stiller, Perel, & Everett, 1989). The effect of pemoline on a dopamine D1 receptor could be responsible for the abnormal movements.

In two studies comparing placebo, pemoline, and methylphenidate, Dykman, Mc-Grew, Harris, Peters, and Ackerman (1976) found that pemoline was less desirable than methylphenidate because of the eight- to nine-week delay in onset of full activity, an overall lower level of effectiveness compared to methylphenidate, and the finding that a smaller group of children responded better to pemoline than to methylphenidate. However, some children did respond better to pemoline.

Not all studies of pemoline have shown it to be effective on a once-a-day schedule. Collier et al. (1985) found that after six months of treatment, most children were using Cylert on a morning and noon dosage schedule. In their study, twenty-one boys and six girls ages 5 to 12, diagnosed as ADD using *DSM-III* criteria, were followed for six months on pemoline with a clinically adjusted dosage. In 70% of the children, the medication was taken twice daily at breakfast and at noon. The other 30% took their medication only at breakfast. The authors were surprised that most (70%) of the children were judged on clinical evaluation to require twice-daily dosage.

Like the reports of psychosis from methylphenidate, there has been one report of a manic episode precipitated by Cylert. Sternbach (1981) reported a case of a 20-year-old female who, within twenty-four hours of an increased dose of pemoline, was noted to be euphoric, grandiose, and hyperactive; she also had pressured speech with flight of ideas. Pemoline was discontinued, and the manic episode was treated with lithium. The author presented this report to suggest that pemoline can induce mania in susceptible individuals. The scarcity of additional similar reports indicates that this occurrence, if more than coincidental, is quite uncommon.

The effect of pemoline on growth was studied by Friedman, Carr, Elders, Ringdahal, and Roache (1981) in a group of twenty-two children treated with pemoline for ADD. The majority of children were followed for four years. At the study onset, the children ranged from age 6.5 to 11.8, with a mean age of 8.4 years. They were treated continuously for twelve months and then allowed drug vacations. Dosage of pemoline was 56 to 150 mg per day during the first year of treatment. Both weight and height growth of treated children were found to lag significantly behind expectations of standard tables at six and twelve months. However, by forty-eight months, the treated group was essentially identical to expectation for height percentile and had actually surpassed expectation for weight. These results were strikingly similar to results observed with methylphenidate-treated children (American Academy of Pediatrics Committee on Drugs Report, 1987). Pemoline-treated children may experience short-term but not long-term deficits in weight and height growth.

The relationship between pemoline and Tourette's is similar to that of other stimulants (E. Mitchell & Matthews, 1980). Bachman (1981) reported a single case of Tourette's induced by pemoline. Tics immediately developed when the medication was started, but they did not resolve when medication was discontinued two months later. Subsequently, additional tics, including humming, panting, and puppy-like sounds, developed. Improvement was seen for Tourette's after treatment with haloperidol.

Cylert is available in three dosage strengths: 18.75 mg, 37.5 mg, and 75 mg, as well as chewable 37.5 mg tablets. Cylert has a recommended starting dose of 37.5 mg per day (*PDR,* 1997). The dose should be gradually increased by 18.75 mg at one-week intervals until the desired clinical response is obtained. The effective daily dose for most patients will range from 56.25 to 75 mg. The maximum recommended daily dose is

112.5 mg. Telephone prescriptions and refills for six months are allowed. This is more convenient than methylphenidate, which can be prescribed for a maximum thirty-day supply with no refills.

Children receiving pemoline do not develop tolerance of the effect on memory-search efficiency or serum levels after three weeks of daily treatment (Sallee, Stiller, & Perel, 1992).

Tricyclic Antidepressants

Tricyclic antidepressants (TCAs) such as imipramine (Tofranil), the chemical structure of which is shown in Figure 13–8, have been shown to help ADHD symptoms. Tricyclics have been advocated by some for many years. Huessy and Wright (1970) suggested that tricyclic antidepressants were safe and effective based on clinical global impressions, objective measures of cognitive functioning, and improvement in behavioral rating scales.

In a series of articles (Biederman, Baldessarini, Wright, Keenan, & Faraone, 1993; Biederman, Baldessarini, Wright, Knee, & Harmatz, 1989a; C. Brown, Wells, Cold, & Froemming, 1990), Biederman et al. undertook a six week trial of desipramine for ADHD. A dose of 4.6 mg/kg resulted in 68% of the children very much or much improved compared with improvement in only 10% of placebo-treated subjects. Higher serum levels were associated with greater clinical improvement. Diastolic blood pressure was significantly increased. There was also a higher incidence of sinus tachycardia and EKG evidence of intraventricular conduction block in the desipramine-treated children. Of note was that presence of comorbid CD, major depression, anxiety disorder, or a family history of ADDH did not affect response to desipramine. The authors concluded that desipramine was helpful, even in complex cases with other comorbid problems.

Several studies have compared TCAs and stimulants. Twelve male subjects who met the *DSM-III* criteria for ADD were given imipramine, desipramine, and methylphenidate for a double-blind crossover study (Garfinkel, Wender, Sloman, & O'Neill, 1983). The TCAs were more useful with affective symptoms and less likely to disturb sleep than methylphenidate, but behavior ratings by teachers and child care workers

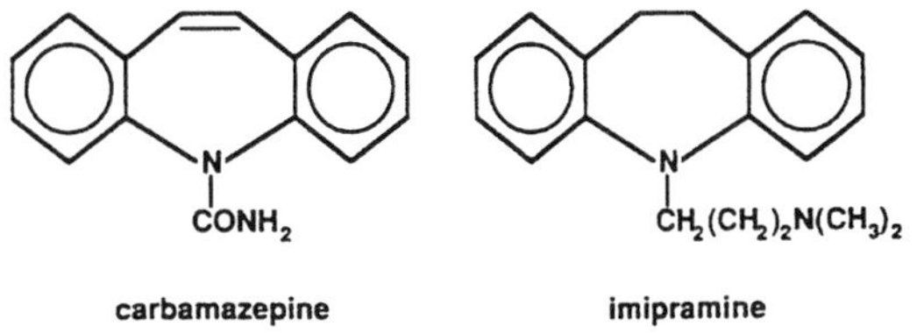

carbamazepine   imipramine

Figure 13–8.   Structural comparisons of carbamazepine and imipramine

Source: From R. R. Pleak, B. Birmaher, A. Gavrilescu, A. Abichandini, & D. T. Williams. (1988). Mania and neuropsychiatric excitation following carbamazepine. *Journal of the American Academy of Child and Adolescent Psychiatry, 27,* 500–503. Copyright 1988 by Williams & Wilkins. Printed with permission of the publisher.

indicated methylphenidate had a greater efficacy than the other drugs. They concluded that different medications could have differential effects on specific component symptoms of ADD.

Stimulant medications were also judged superior to tricyclics for the treatment of attention-deficit symptoms in a review by Pliszka (1987) of five quantitative studies of imipramine reported between 1972 and 1983. Pliszka concluded that for children who do not respond to stimulants, imipramine or a similar tricyclic might be an appropriate second choice. Children who were highly anxious or had mood disturbance might fair better with imipramine, but children with aggression might deteriorate on imipramine (Pliszka, 1987). He also concluded that lower dosage, 50 mg per day or less, or doses less than 1 mg/kg per day, had not been demonstrated to be effective. Dosages of 50 to 150 mg (3 to 5 mg/kg on a weight basis) were standard. Control for blood levels and the presence of conduct and anxiety disorders in addition to clearly defining attention-deficit criteria were recommended for future studies.

Tricyclics were again advocated as the drug of choice for ADHD symptoms by Huessy (1988). In a study reporting that 90% of patients will respond to TCAs without side effects, Huessy (1988) argued that methylphenidate should be the drug of last resort. But others have argued that the scientific literature does not support Huessy's allegation that the TCAs are equal in efficacy over the long term to the stimulants (methylphenidate, amphetamine, methamphetamine, and pemoline) (Cowart, 1988b) and that a delayed response time of several weeks is a disadvantage for most patients.

In an extensive review of the effect of antidepressants, Ambrosini, Bianchi, Rabinovich, and Elia (1993) note the lack of studies indicating efficacy of antidepressants with anxiety disorders and even affective disorders, including major depressive disorder. Although efficacy has been adequately demonstrated for treatment of ADHD and enuresis, even the initial claims of antidepressants as a treatment for panic disorder and school phobia appear to be less secure with additional evaluation (Ambrosini et al., 1993).

Side effects such as sleepiness, dryness of the mouth, and constipation are common problems with TCAs but are usually mild and rarely require change of medication. Additional symptoms such as other gastrointestinal symptoms, blurred or double vision, and other changes in mood are uncommon and usually mild in severity, rarely requiring alteration of dose or discontinuation of medication.

Weight loss had not been considered a likely side effect from TCA use, but desipramine may cause weight reduction similar to methylphenidate. Spencer, Biederman, Wright, and Danon (1992) studied deficits in growth, weight, and height in a sample of forty-five children and adolescents followed for a mean of only fourteen months. Desipramine and methylphenidate resulted in significant weight deficits. Desipramine did not result in growth deficits, but methylphenidate did. When it was suggested that the weight reduction might be due to affective symptomatology (Holt, 1992), Spencer and Biederman (1992) replied that appetite changes secondary to possible comorbid mood disorders are a possible complicating factor in judging the weight and height effects of medication.

Side effects can sometimes be minimized by beginning with a low dose (10 to 25 mg) and gradually increasing to an effective dose of 50 to 150 mg (3 to 5 mg/kg) in a single daily dose. Preskorn, Bupp, Weller, and Weller (1989) offer an alternate means of adjusting imipramine dosage to the therapeutic range based on the fact that individual blood levels are reproducible and linearly correlated with dose. These authors suggest that studies of major depression have found a therapeutic level of 125 to 250 mg/ml. The steady-state method of adjustment begins with an initial dose of 75 mg, followed by determination of the plasma blood level over a 7- to 10-day period. Using this 75 mg initial dose, only 12% of the children were found to have a high plasma level initially. The relationship between this initial 75 mg dose and the child's plasma level was then used to determine the optimal suggested dosage. This system resulted in plasma levels of imipramine and metabolites within the therapeutic range in 84% of the sample population. In the other 16%, further dosage adjustment was needed. Preskorn et al. (1989) emphasized the importance of obtaining plasma levels to be certain that imipramine is not used in too high a dose. Use of plasma levels of imipramine will serve to help prevent side effects due to therapeutic overdosage. In the absence of information that defines the therapeutic range of plasma levels for imipramine in treatment of ADHD, use of the established therapeutic range for treatment of major depressive disorder is recommended.

Cardiac Toxicity and Sudden Death in Children Treated with Tricyclic Antidepressants

In 1990, the *Medical Letter* reported the death of an 8-year-old boy with no known cardiac abnormality treated with unknown doses of desipramine for two years for ADD. It was also reported at that time that at least two other sudden deaths in children treated with desipramine were known to the manufacturer, an 8-year-old boy treated for ADD with 50 mg per day for six months and a 9-year-old boy, dosage and duration of treatment unknown. Plasma levels of the drug obtained from all three of these children were in the therapeutic or subtherapeutic range as reported by the *Medical Letter*. Riddle, Geller, and Ryan (1993) report that a twelve-and-a-half-year-old girl raised from 125 mg in a single dose to 50 mg three times a day was found unconscious in bed; subsequent resuscitative efforts were unsuccessful. Saraf, Klein, Gittelman-Klein, and Groff (1974) reported the sudden death of a 6-year-old girl receiving 15 mg/kg of desipramine in a single daily dose; three days after the dosage was increased to 250 to 300 mg a day, the child was found unresponsive two hours after going to bed.

Is imipramine, widely used for enuresis, safer than desipramine? Deaths have been reported only in children taking an extraordinarily high dose of desipramine. The mechanism of sudden death has been debated extensively (Bartels, Varley, Mitchell, & Stamm, 1991; Elliott & Popper, 1991; Riddle, Nelson, et al., 1991; Tingelstad, 1991; Walsh, Giardina, Sloan, Greenhill, & Goldfein, 1994; Waslick, 1995). Tricyclics can increase the heart rate, prolong the PR interval, increase the QRS duration with the development of right bundle branch block pattern, shorten the QT interval, increase the corrected QT (QT_C) and produce ST segment-T wave changes. More frequent premature atrial contractions and runs of supraventricular tachycardia may also be associated with tricyclics (Biederman, 1991; Tingelstad, 1991; Waslick, 1995). However, because none of the children who experienced sudden death has undergone cardiovascular and cardiac electrophysiological evaluation, the association of these potential electrocardiographic changes with the incidence of sudden death is unknown. One can only speculate which, if any, of the potential EKG changes are most serious. Some have suggested that the TCAs are too dangerous to be used commonly for treatment of ADHD (for example, see Werry, 1993). Many medications, however, that are commonly available have been associated with reported deaths.

The formula for evaluating children taking desipramine developed by Biederman (1991) is summarized as follows: Obtain a baseline ECG and initiate treatment with a single 10 or 25 mg dose (approximately 1 mg/kg), increasing every four to five days by 20% to 30%. When an effective dose or 3 mg/kg (whichever is lower) is reached, steady-state serum level medication and an ECG should be obtained. Follow-up ECG should be obtained with dose changes or every few months, if normal, on a constant dose. Desipramine would be considered unsafe if (1) PR interval greater than 200 ms; (2) QRS interval greater than 30% increase over baseline values (or greater than 120 ms); (3) blood pressure greater than 140 systolic or 90 diastolic; and (4) heart rate greater than 130 BPM at rest (FDA recommendation). Beiderman (1991) suggests that serum level below 300 mcg/ml, ECG PR interval longer than 200 ms, and QRS duration longer than 120 ms appear to be more important clinical dosage parameters. Treatment with TCAs, especially a daily dosage above 3.5 mg/kg or serum levels higher than 150 mcg/ml per mil may increase the risk of asymptomatic electrocardiographic changes, especially slight prolongation of PR interval as well as moderate increase in QRS duration. This may indicate delayed cardiac conduction or minor increments in diastolic blood pressure and heart rate (Biederman, Baldessarini, Wright, Knee, Harmatz, & Goldblatt, 1989).

Do metabolites of TCAs produce the cardiotoxicity? Multiple metabolic pathways (Oesterheld, 1996) have been proposed to determine which medications have potential for cardiotoxicity and which patients are most susceptible. Unfortunately, the hypotheses relate to complexities of enzyme metabolism that are not determinable a priority and may in fact change with other medications or foods. On the other hand, it has been proposed that the TCAs may exert cardiotoxicity by direct finding with sodium channel (Meyer et al., 1996).

TCAs are slower to act and probably somewhat less effective than stimulants for most children. Nevertheless, in children who are at higher risk for side effects with stimulant medication because of anxiety, psychosis, or tics, imipramine or a similar tricyclic may produce satisfactory symptom resolution.

Combination Methylphenidate and Desipramine

Combinations of TCAs and methylphenidate produce more side effects than when taken alone. There are, however, surprisingly few studies of children given a combination of methylphenidate and desipramine. In 1993, Pataki, Carlson, Kelly, Rapport, and Biancaniello reported that they could find no previous reports delineating the study of side effects of this combination in children (hypotension had been reported in adults). Twenty children were studied with a double-blind crossover method titrating desipramine to a final blood level between 125 and 225 mg/ml, and methylphenidate was given at 10, 15, and 20 mg twice daily for a week at each dosage. The methylphenidate was added to the desipramine. The authors discovered that nausea, dry mouth, and tremor were present in at least twice as many children on combined methylphenidate and desipramine compared with any other condition. Nausea/vomiting, headaches, other aches, refusal of food, and feeling "tired" were significantly more frequent during the combined methylphenidate plus desipramine condition when compared with either methylphenidate alone or with baseline. Significantly higher ventricular heart rate was found on combined methylphenidate plus desipramine when compared with desipramine alone, methylphenidate alone, and baseline. Prolonged pr interval occurred during desipramine alone compared with baseline. The authors concluded that side effects from combined medication appeared similar to and no more serious than those associated with desipramine alone, the increased frequency of side effects was noted.

Desipramine and methylphenidate had slightly different effects in sixteen hospitalized ADHD and mood-disordered children. Rapport, Carlson, Kelly, and Pataki (1993), used a double-blind placebo-controlled prospective crossover study, with methylphenidate at 10, 15, and 20 mg and desipramine dosage titrated clinically to the maximum effective dosage (75 mg bid/maximum dosage and a blood level of 121 to 291). The children were assessed using CPTs, the Matching Familiar Figures Test (MFFT), a paired-associate learning test (K-PAL), and a stimulus equivalence paradigm (SEP). Methylphenidate produced more improvement in vigilance (CPT) and ability to learn (K-PAL) as well as improvement in the MFFT. Additional improvement in MFFT and SEP was seen as desipramine was added to the methylphenidate, suggesting the two drugs act additively. However, desipramine did not affect vigilance and caused a slight blocking of the effect of methylphenidate on CPT performance. It significantly improved performance on K-PAL but was not as helpful as methylphenidate or the combination of medications. The most pronounced effects of desipramine occurred on MFFT performance, which the authors ascribed to behavioral inhibition and the use of visual search strategies. The overall effects of desipramine was approximately equal to that observed by methylphenidate. The authors concluded that neither drug, alone or in combination, impaired cognitive performance on the broad array of measures used. A combination of medications had the maximum effect on several measures of vigilance and learning. Only three of the fifteen children who completed the study, however, were chosen to continue on the combination of medications at the conclusion of the study.

Combinations of desipramine and methylphenidate produce modest improvement on some measures but at a cost of substantial increase in side effects. Methylphenidate may accelerate response to tricyclics in children with major depressive disorder (Ambrosini et al., 1993). In this study, ten of sixteen children responded to desipramine and methylphenidate after two weeks; side effects included dizziness and orthostatic blood pressure changes, dry mouth, increased anxiety (n = 3 for each), and hypomania in one. Methylphenidate was discontinued because of side effects in three patients. Although this study suggests that selecting depressed ADHD children for combination treatment might result in improvement in both depression and ADHD, more extensive studies are needed to determine which characteristics found in ADHD children suggest combination of medications might be helpful. Evaluation for cardiotoxicity has been advised (Spencer, Biederman, & Wilens, 1994) in children treated with combinations that include TCAs.

Multiple Drug Toxicity

It has been postulated that tricyclics such as Clomipramine might have increased toxicity if other medications such as fluoxetine are also present. Metabolism of tricyclics is substantially influenced by medications that vary as widely as ciproflaxacin, theophylline, grapefruit juice (inhibitors) and carbamazepine, caffeine, omeprazole, and cigarette smoking (inducers) (Osterheld, 1996). Combinations of medicines may therefore produce unsuspected toxicity.

Tricyclics in Children with ADHD plus Tics/Tourette's

In studies of children with chronic tic disorder and ADHD in combination, Spencer, Biederman, Kerman, Steingard, and Wilens (1993) and Spencer, Biederman, Wilens, Steingard, and Geist (1993) report substantial improvement with either nortriptyline or desipramine. Sixty-seven percent of the children given nortriptyline improved chronic tic disorder symptomatology and 92% significantly improved ADHD symptoms without major adverse effects over an average follow-up period of nineteen months. In a group of thirty-three children treated with desipramine, 82% had significant improvement in chronic tic disorder symptomatology and 80% significantly improved ADHD symptoms without major adverse effects over an average follow-up period of sixteen months. Riddle, Hardin, Cho, Woolston, and Leckman (1988), however, reported that 71% of ADHD and comorbid Tourette's children showed no improvement or worsening in tic symptoms.

Desipramine has been shown to have greater efficacy than clonidine for ADHD symptoms with comorbid tic disorders. Singer et al. (1995) studied twenty-three children with Tourette's and ADHD using a double-blind placebo-control protocol. Desipramine, 25 mg four times daily, was compared with clonidine, 0.05 mg four times daily. Improvement on every measure was significantly greater with desipramine than with clonidine. Neither drug made tics worse. Desipramine showed a significant improvement on some measures of tic severity but not on others. Clonidine did not significantly alter the tic severity on any measure. Comparative studies, which are so valuable in determining the relative efficacy of medications, are unfortunately extraordinarily rare. The only study comparing clonidine and desipramine supports the greater efficacy of desipramine to clonidine in treatment of ADHD in children with comorbid Tourette's.

Disorders comorbid with Fragile X syndrome, including enuresis in addition to ADHD, have been reported to respond to low-dose imipramine (10 mg tid to 1.5 mg/kg per day) (Hilton, Martin, Heffron, Hall, & Johnson, 1991).

Other Antidepressants

Clomipramine, a specific serotonin re-uptake inhibitor, is reported in a single case study (Wilens, Steingard, & Biederman, 1992) to improve both OCD and ADHD as well as trichotillomania (hair pulling), with improvement lasting at least six months. In a study of ten adults in whom clomipramine was rapidly discontinued, however, three (33%) suffered withdrawal reactions ranging from physiological symptoms of increased sweating and elevated temperament in one patient to rebound worsening of preexisting depression, suicidal ideation, and rebound worsening of preexisting obsessive-compulsive behavior (including homicidal threats) in two other patients. These side effects have not been reported in children (Diamond, Borison, Katz, & DeVeaugh-Geiss, 1989). A single case is reported of tardive dyskinesia in an adult taking clomipramine along with chronic dextroamphetamine (Clayton, 1995).

Nortriptyline

Nortriptyline (Pamelor®), a derivative of amitriptyline (Elavil®), has been shown to help children with chronic tic disorder and ADHD. Spencer, Biederman, Wilens, Steingard, and Geist (1993) found that 67% of the twelve male children tested had improvement in their chronic tic disorder symptomatology and 92% had significant improvement in ADHD symptoms without major adverse effects over an average follow-up period of nineteen months.

Fluoxetine

Side effects limited usefulness of fluoxetine in twelve of twenty-four children ages 8 through 16 treated for obsessive-compulsive or depressive symptoms by M. Riddle, King, et al. (1991). When a dosage of 20 to 40 mg daily was used, motor restlessness, sleep disturbance, social disinhibition, or a subjective sensation of excitation was noted in 50% of the children. Decreasing the dose by half or discontinuation of medication resulted in side effect resolution. Improvement in depression and OCD symptoms was maintained on the lower dosage. In addition, a case report of mania in a 13-year-old treated with fluoxetine, 20 mg daily, was reported by Rosenberg, Johnson, and Sahl (1992). Decreasing the dosage rather than discontinuation of medication should be considered if fluoxetine produces useful effects limited by side effects.

Fluoxetine (Prozac) is one of a group of medications that exerts its effect by inhibiting the re-uptake of serotonin into the nerve cells. Re-uptake of released serotonin may be a principal means of inactivating the chemical that transmits messages from one nerve cell to another. Unlike stimulants and TCAs, the specific serotonin re-uptake inhibitors work primarily by affecting the re-uptake of the serotonin nerve cells. The popularity of this class of medications is at least in part the result of the lower incidence of cholinergic side effects (dry mouth, constipation, stomach pain, sleepiness). Fluoxetine has been shown to improve ADHD symptoms in nearly 60% of the subjects in a study of nineteen 7- to 15-year-olds with ADHD (Barrickman, Noyes, Kuperman, & Schumacher, 1991). A 3-year-old with ADHD symptoms was reported improved on fluoxetine, 10 mg daily (S. Campbell, Tamburrino, Evans, & Franco, 1995). A limited study of fluoxetine in combination with stimulants suggests potential improvement in ADHD children nonresponsive to stimulants. Thirty-two children and adolescents studied by Gammon and Brown (1993) all showed positive therapeutic response to the addition of fluoxetine to methylphenidate; they had all been previously judged inadequate responders to methylphenidate alone. A case report of an 11-year-old with OCD and ADHD showed improvement in OCD symptoms with fluoxetine but no improvement in ADHD symptoms with fluoxetine alone or with fluoxetine in combination with dextroamphetamine; the child did respond to a combination of 20 mg fluoxetine daily in combination with 5 mg methylphenidate twice daily (Bussin & Levin, 1993).

A case report of a 3-year-old boy with ADHD, temper tantrums, and oppositional behavior, unsuccessfully treated with methylphenidate and thioridazine (Mellaril®), was successfully treated with 5 mg and subsequently 10 mg of fluoxetine daily. Venlafaxine (Effexor) has a chemical effect of specific serotonin re-uptake inhibition similar to fluoxetine. It is not surprising that an open-label study of sixteen improved ADD/ADHD symptoms, an average of 50% in a group of adult patients

(Adler, Resnick, Kunz, & Devinsky, 1995). The combination of methamphetamine and fluoxetine did not appear to be associated with significant adverse effects in a single case study by Wilson and Marcotte (1995).

Bupropion

One of the side effects reported with bupropion (Welbutrin) was aggravation of tics in children with ADHD and comorbid Tourette's; these children also had tics aggravated by methylphenidate (Spencer, Biederman, Steingard, et al., 1993). In eighteen of thirty children completing a study, significant improvement was seen with bupropion (6 mg/kg) (Casat, Pleasants, Schroeder, & Parler, 1989)

The antidepressant, bupropion hydrochloride, was tested in a preliminary study by Casat, Pleasants, and Van Wyck Fleet (1987). A group of thirty outpatient children, ages 6 to 12, was selected on the basis of *DSM-III* criteria and Conners hyperkinesis questionnaires. Improvement in clinical global impression and reduction in hyperactivity as reflected in the Conners Teacher's Questionnaire were statistically significant. Minimal side effects were noted. Further studies are needed to determine if additional antidepressants may be helpful for attention deficit as well.

Like most medications for ADHD, studies comparing Welbutrin to methylphenidate are limited, making judgments of relative efficacy difficult. In a double-blind crossover trial, Barrickman et al. (1995) concluded that both bupropion and methylphenidate were helpful and did not differ in their overall efficacy as treatments for ADHD. Further analysis of this study, however, is illustrative of the difficulties comparing efficacy of two medications. The study used only fifteen ADHD subjects, ages 7 to 17 years. Poorer response to treatment with bupropion compared to methylphenidate was seen by teachers but not parents. The clinical global improvement scores, judged by physicians, at week five showed statistically significant symptom improvement with methylphenidate. Nine of fifteen patients reported adverse reactions to bupropion, including drowsiness, fatigue, nausea, anorexia, dizziness, spaciness, anxiety, headache, and tremor, but only five of fifteen reported adverse reactions to methylphenidate, including anger, drowsiness, headache, insomnia, irritability, low mood, nausea, and stomachache. At the end of the study, when parents were given the opportunity to choose which medication they wanted to continue, ten of the fifteen chose methylphenidate, whereas only five chose bupropion.

Possibly because of the small size of this study, the fact that methylphenidate produced consistently better clinical global improvement scores, nearly half of the incidence of adverse reactions, and was chosen by parents 2 to 1 over bupropion did not reach clinical significance. The authors concluded that as the differences were not statistically significant in this small study, the two medications had similar efficacy and side effect. Technically, their conclusion that overall efficacy of the two were not different may be accurate, but data included in this study suggest that bupropion is substantially less helpful than methylphenidate. The lack of adequate comparison studies makes choosing between medication alternatives sometimes quite difficult. Comparison studies using adequate numbers are expensive and difficult to accomplish and not well supported by either industry (pharmaceutical manufacturers) or government funding sources. Nevertheless, more comparison studies are needed to help determine which medications are best for a particular patient.

Antipsychotics

Thioridazine (Mellaril), chlorpromazine (Thorazine), haloperidol (Haldol), and risperdal (Risperidone) are major tranquilizers that are commonly used to control psychotic symptoms. They produce a decrease in activity and have also been used for treatment of children with ADHD symptoms. The major side effects of stiffness, sedation, and possibly slower cognitive processing have proven a substantial disadvantage (R. Klein, 1991). They have also been implicated as causing tardive dyskinesia, a permanent movement disorder. Nevertheless, these medications have been considered effective by parents in some studies (Gittelman-Klein, Klein, Katz, Saraf, & Pollack, 1976; Werry, Aman, & Lampen, 1975), and are sometimes used in the treatment of hyperactive children (Ross & Ross, 1982). The average daily dosage of thioridazine for children ages 2 to 12 is 0.5 to 3.0 mg/kg; the dosage of haloperidol for ages 3 to 12 is 0.05 to 0.075 mg/kg. The sedation often caused by these medications, along with the risk of tardive dyskinesia, precludes the use of the major tranquilizers for most children with ADHD. However, these medications may have a role in helping to control impulsive and overactive behaviors in the rare situation when these behaviors present a danger to the child or others. Occasionally, the authors have seen these effectively used as a short-term addition to other treatments to help avoid hospitalization when overactivity or self-destructive behavior precipitates a crisis situation.

Both haloperidol and lithium were found better than placebo for sixty-one treatment-resistant hospitalized children with a diagnosis of CD, aggressive type. Haloperidol was associated with more untoward effects than lithium carbonate. For autistic children, haloperidol and behavior therapy in combination was more effective than either at facilitating the acquisition of imitative speech (Campbell et al., 1978).

A major drawback to the use of neuroleptics is tardive dyskinesia, a movement disorder often precipitated by discontinuation of neuroleptic medications. As it may persist for long periods of time and not respond to treatment, it is a serious potential side effect for treatment of ADHD with these medications. Gualtieri, Quade, Hicks, Mayo, and Schroeder (1984) found that eighteen of forty-one children, adolescents, and young adults withdrawn from chronic neuroleptic treatment developed tardive dyskinesia or other withdrawal movement disorder. Cumulative neuroleptic dose and possibly gender of the subject was associated with increased risk of withdrawal movement disorder.

Lithium

Lithium carbonate is a standard medication for bipolar disorder. Studies have suggested that symptoms of aggression and unipolar depression as well as bipolar disorder may respond to lithium carbonate treatment. Aggression may respond to lithium even in mentally retarded children. Starting doses of approximately 13 mg/kg per day are suggested with a mean steady-state blood level of 0.6 to 1.2 ml equivalence per liter. Frequent blood levels are needed. Altered cognitive processes and increased headaches are common side effects. Reversible cardiac conduction defect, polyuria, thyroid hormone changes, and weakness have also been reported (Alessi, Naylor, Ghaziuddin, & Zubieta, 1994). Frequent side effects were noted in children ages 6 years and younger with initiation of lithium treatment, increased dosage, and high serum lithium levels

(Hagino et al., 1995). Sixty percent of children ages 4 to 6 manifested central nervous system side effects, including tremor, drowsiness, ataxia, and confusion. Abdominal discomfort, nausea, vomiting, and diarrhea were also common, as were polydipsia, polyuria, secondary enuresis, and blurred vision. Cardiovascular, pulmonary, autonomic, hemotalogic, or integumental side effects were not noticed in the Hagino et al. (1995) study.

Although lithium has been used successfully to treat bipolar disorder, it has not been successful for treatment of ADHD (Greenhill, Rieder, & Wender, 1973; Whitehead & Clark, 1970). Licamele and Goldberg (1989) showed improvement in ADHD symptoms with combined treatment of lithium carbonate 300 mg bid (blood level 0.7 to 0.9 mileequivalents per ml) and methylphenidate 20 mg tid. This response had not been obtained with either treatment alone. Some subgroups of ADHD patients may respond to lithium and methylphenidate combinations. Seven children in a hospital setting with a combination of bipolar or major depressive disorder and disruptive behavior responded to a combination of lithium (600 to 1500 mg per day, blood levels between 0.7 and 1.1 mileequivalence per liter) and methylphenidate 0.3 to 0.6 mg/kg bid, with improvement in disruptive behavior (Carlson, Rapport, Kelly, & Pataki, 1992). Side effects are common with lithium treatment of children. Hagino et al. (1995) found that 60% of twenty hospitalized aggressive and/or mood-disordered children ages 4 to 6 manifested one or more side effects more commonly. Nervous system effects were commonly seen at serum levels of 0.65 to 1.37 mileequivalence per liter. Because of these side effects, lithium should be reserved for ADHD children who fail methylphenidate and for whom the diagnosis of bipolar disorder is reasonable.

Guanfacine

Guanfacine (Tenex®) is an alpha 2 noradregeneric antagonist that has been available as a hypotensive agent for more than two decades. In comparison with another alpha 2 noradrenergic agonist, clonidine, guanfacine has a longer excretion half-life (eighteen hours in adults), is less sedating, and produces less hypotension (Hunt, Arnsten, & Asbell, 1994). An open trial using thirteen outpatients with ADHD reported by Hunt et al. (1994), found mean Conners scores improved significantly. Side effects were reported as minimal. Horrigan and Barnhill (1995) also reported helpfulness of guanfacine (0.5 to 3 mg/day mode 0.5 mg bid) for fifteen boys ages 7 to 17 in a nonblinded, open-label trial. Two of the fifteen discontinued the medication, one due to clinical ineffectiveness and one due to overactivation. Chappell et al. (1995) studied boys, ages 8 to 16 years, in a four- to twenty-week trial with 1.5 mgs per day as the most common dosage. Side effects included mild increase in tiredness, headaches, and stomachaches in the first two weeks, with no patient discontinuing the medication. Although these studies demonstrate that guanfacine can improve ADHD symptoms, the relative efficacy of guanfacine and other medications for ADHD has not been determined.

In an open label study of ten children with Tourette's and ADHD ages 8 to 16, guanfacine in a final total daily dose of 1.5 mgs produced significant decrease in errors of commission on the A task of the CPT (a measure of impulsivity) and phonic tic ratings as well as self-ratings of motor tic severity (Chappell, Riddle, Scahill, Schultz,

& Leckman, 1994). Conners hyperactivity and inattention scores were improved in thirteen ADHD outpatients treated with guanfacine in a separate study (R. Hunt, Arnsten, & Asbell, 1994).

Clonidine

Clonidine (Catapres) is an alpha noradrenergic antagonist that has been helpful for ADHD children with comorbid Tourette's. The mechanism of action is believed similar to that of the stimulant medications, in that the catecholamine systems are affected. Because clonidine has been studied less extensively than methylphenidate, the frequency of side effects is not as well documented.

Clonidine has the potential advantage of administration by skin patch. R. Hunt (1987) studied ten children who met *DSM-III* criteria for ADD and who scored more than 1.5 standard deviations above the mean on the parent and teacher forms of the Conners questionnaire. These children were administered oral clonidine openly for eight weeks using the effective dosage determined in a previous study (5 mcg/kg/day). Those with a favorable response to oral clonidine were switched to transdermal clonidine administered via skin patch. They were also treated with placebo as well as low-dose (0.3 mg/kg) and high-dose (.06 mg/kg) methylphenidate for one week each in random sequence. Six children had a preferential response to clonidine and continued on that medication. Three of the nine children who received both the clonidine and methylphenidate had an overall better response to the methylphenidate and continued taking it after the study. One of the most interesting features of this report is the skin patch application of medication. The medication contained within the skin patch is slowly released through the skin; no pills are required and the patch's effectiveness is five days. Many families liked the ease of administration, and the author concluded that clonidine, especially with skin patch administration, may be the treatment of choice for a group of children with ADD.

Transdermal therapeutic system administration of clonidine (TTS or the clonidine patch) was also studied for efficacy in ADHD patients by Comings, Comings, Tacket, and Li (1990). Some improvement in symptoms was noted, along with a low incidence of side effects. Patient compliance and lack of interference with school routine were noted as positives. Comings et al. (1990) used the clonidine patch in an open-label trial without placebo control in 270 patients with Tourette's and ADHD or CD. Dosage was the TTS-1 strength utilizing one quarter patch and increasing to a maximum of two patches at a time (half patch in 50%). Local skin reaction occurred in 30% and required discontinuation of the patch in 16%. Improvement in the entire spectrum of Tourette's and ADHD symptoms, irritability, depression, phobias, obsessive-compulsive behaviors, panic attacks, and oppositional confrontive behavior was seen. Half or more of the symptoms improved in 40%; 12% showed worsening of symptoms. An extended release tablet of clonidine was specifically prepared by a pharmacist for children who were too sleepy on the tablets and had a skin reaction to the patch (Horacek, 1994). A review in the *Annals of Pharmacotherapy* (Santora & Hart, 1992) concluded that despite positive outcomes presented in studies reviewed, it was difficult to support or discount the utility of clonidine until additional studies were performed and recommended that clonidine treatment for ADHD should be limited to those cases where drug therapy is necessary and all other viable forms of treatment have been exhausted.

Clonidine may be more helpful for ADHD children with comorbid tic disorders. In a study of fifty-four ADHD children with and without comorbid tic disorder, clonidine treatment resulted in improvement in both ADHD and tic symptoms (Steingard, Biederman, Spencer, Wilens, & Gonzalez, 1993). Children with comorbid tic disorders, however, had a higher likelihood of behavioral response than children without comorbid tic disorders (96% compared to 53%).

O'Malley (1997) and Storch (1997) remarked about the paucity of controlled studies of medication combinations of children. Storch (1997) also comments on the short half-life of clonidine, suggesting that children are withdrawn from clonidine on a daily basis when they take it at night, alone. Connor and Swanson (1997) note that the average half-life of clonidine in children is 8 to 12 hours with considerable individual variability, whereas the behavioral effects are only 3 to 6 hours. Night awakening may represent a withdrawal phenomenon in children given clonidine at nights.

The deaths of three children taking a combination of methylphenidate and clonidine have raised concern about potential risk of this combination of medications. Information available from the FDA about three fatalities and one episode of hypotension was reported by Walkup (1995). The link, if any, between the combination of methylphenidate and clonidine and the tragic deaths of these youngsters was believed to be thin. One child had twice been given general anesthesia; one was on multiple other medications with suggestions of a significant overdose. Although the relationship between sudden death and clonidine-methylphenidate combination is tenuous, Walkup (1995) suggested that EKG, blood pressure, and pulse monitoring accompany combinations of clonidine and methylphenidate, as well as tapering clonidine at 0.05 mg per day when the medication is discontinued.

Anticonvulsants

A group of medications released by the FDA for the treatment of epilepsy, including sodium valprote (Depakote®), carbamazepine (Tegretol®), and clonazepam (Klonopin®), have been used for treatment of ADHD symptoms. Carbamazepine, a widely used anticonvulsant for focal and generalized epileptic seizures, has been more extensively studied for ADHD than the other anticonvulsants. Carbamazepine was associated with clinically and statistically significant decline in target symptoms of aggressiveness and explosiveness in a group of nine boys and one girl, ages 5.25 to 10.92, treated with 600 to 800 mg of the medication (Kafantaris et al., 1992).

Carbamazepine also has been considered an established treatment for mania (Small, 1990). Using a meta-analysis of ten reports involving carbamazepine treatment for behavior disorders, Silva, Munoz, and Alpert (1996) concluded that carbamazepine was significantly better than placebo for treating ADHD symptoms. Daily dosages ranged from 100 to 800 mg per day and serum blood levels fell between 4.8 and 10.4 mcg per mil (mean = 6.2). Side effects were significant. Rash occurred in 5% to 6% and sedation in 7.5% to 13.2%. The authors conclude that the evidence was "preliminary" and that carbamazepine may be an effective alternative treatment in children with features of ADHD. The combination of carbamazepine and imipramine may decrease the plasma levels of imipramine (C. Brown et al., 1990). However, no studies comparing the efficacy of carbamazepine and other medications for the treatment of ADHD have been published.

After a meta-analysis, Pliszka (1992) concluded that carbamazepine may have usefulness in a subgroup of children that show severe impulsivity, aggressiveness, and emotional instability but that this medication should be used only after stimulant and antidepressant medications have failed. Aggressive/impulsive children with a strong family history of rapid-cycling bipolar disorder might be candidates for treatment with carbamazepine, however, as it has been shown to be effective in adults with rapid-cycling bipolar disorder. Pliszka cautions against using carbamazepine as the drug of first use.

Reduction of tic symptoms was noted in a group of seven patients suffering from these and ADHD treated with clonazepam (Steingard, Goldberg, Lee, & DeMaso, 1994). The patients were studied by retrospective analysis and treated with other medication in addition to clonazepam. Other anticonvulsants, such as phenobarbital diphenylhydantoin (Dilantin) and valporate, as well as carbamazepine, produced substantial side effects ranging from impairment of mental and motor speed to impairments of memory and cross-sustained attention and concentration (C. Reynolds, 1994). Although some studies show that one of the anticonvulsant medications produces fewer side effects than another, the results of the studies taken as a whole do not favor any of them (C. Reynolds, 1994). Anticonvulsants may be helpful for some children with ADHD and other comorbid disorders, but at this time, data are too limited to be certain which patients will benefit and which will not.

Other Medications

Caffeine

Caffeine is a widely available stimulant, shown to improve reaction time in normal children (Rappaport, Jenswold, & Elkins, 1981) and enhance performance on a test of attention and a motor task (Bernstein et al., 1994). Normal children also felt less sluggish. One study (B. D. Garfinkel, Webster, & Sloman, 1975) did find a therapeutic effect from low doses of caffeine. Several well-designed, double-blind, crossover studies of children with ADHD symptoms, however, found little or no benefit from caffeine and significant side effects (Conners, 1975b; Firestone, Davey, Goodman, & Peters, 1978; Garfinkel, Webster, & Sloman, 1975; Huestis, Arnold, & Smeltzer, 1975). Despite the common perception that caffeine is safe, studies suggest significant side effects with very little benefit.

Propranolol

Propranolol (Inderal®) was helpful for 75% of a group of thirty patients with rage outbursts and aggressive behavior who were previously unsuccessfully treated by stimulants, neuroleptics, anticonvulsants, or a combination (Williams, Mehl, Yudofsky, Adams, & Roseman, 1982). This retrospective study found an average dosage to be 161 mg (50 to 1600 mg daily). Six of the thirty patients suffered somnolence and lethargy, which was reversible by lowering the dosage; four patients encountered hypotension that limited extent of dosage increases. Further studies are needed to determine the place of propranolol in the armamentarium against aggressive behavior.

Medicine for Asthma

A two-week course of oral prednisone did not change academic or behavioral ratings in a group of nineteen nonsteroid-dependent asthmatic children (Nall et al., 1992). Theophylline, however, as an anti-asthma treatment was found to aggravate ADHD in some vulnerable children (Schlieper, Alcock, Beaudry, Feldman, & Leikin, 1991).

Phenfluramine

Studies show conflicting findings concerning the effect of phenfluramine on ADHD. Aman and Kearn (1989) suggested that phenfluramine may enhance social relatedness, reduce stereotypic behavior, lessen overactivity, and improve attention span in some autistic children. The authors recognized that the results do not appear consistent across studies. Donnelly et al. (1989), studying thirty children, found no effect of phenfluramine on behavior even though dextroamphetamine produced immediate and marked improvement in disruptive, overactive behaviors in the same children.

Moclobemide

Eleven children ages 6 to 13 for whom methylphenidate treatment had to be discontinued because of side effects benefited from treatment with moclobemide. However, further studies are needed to confirm these findings and determine the usefulness of this medication (Trott, Friese, Menzel, & Nissen, 1992).

Levodopa, Deprenyl, and Bromocryptine

The suspected relationship between abnormal dopamine metabolism and ADHD has prompted researchers to try medications approved for the treatment of Parkinson's disease, a disorder with symptoms quite different from hyperactivity but also believed to be related to abnormal dopamine neurons. In fact, studies of Sinemet®, a combination of levodopa and carbidopa widely used for treatment of Parkinson's, found it to be mildly effective in the treatment of children with an attention and classroom restlessness (Langer, Rapoport, Brown, Ebert, & Bunney, 1982). However, even these authors would not recommend it for general use because of the incidence of side effects and the low level of efficacy.

Levodopa (Wood, Reimherr, & Wender, 1982), in addition to other anti-Parkinson agents such as bromocriptine (Cavanagh, Clifford, & Gregory, 1989), have been shown to improve ADD symptoms in adults. Deprenyl, a monoamine oxidase inhibitor used to treat Parkinson's disease, has been associated with a mixed outcome in different studies. Jankovic (1993) saw improvement in twenty-six of twenty-nine patients treated for ADHD.

Many other chemicals have been used to treat ADHD symptoms; none has proven as effective as the stimulants or TCAs. Several examples are presented to represent the range of substances that have been administered to children to find effective treatments for ADHD symptoms.

The beta blocker Pindolol was surprisingly equal to methylphenidate in decreasing hyperactivity and conduct problems at home and hyperactivity at school. However, the study was discontinued after thirty-two participants because of paraesthesias, intense nightmares, and hallucinations (Buitelaar, van der Gaag, Swaab-Varneveld, & Kuiper, 1996).

Gamalinic acid (Efamol) was found to work better than placebo but not as well as D-amphetamine. One study suggested that cerebellar-vestibular stabilizing anti-motion-sickness medications may be useful in treating learning disabilities, dyslexia, and ADHD.

D-phenylalanine is an essential amino acid and precursor to dopamine. Zametkin, Karoum, and Rapoport (1987) studied its effect on symptoms of inattention and hyperactivity. A group defined by parent and teacher behavioral ratings and cognitive measures was studied in a double-blind, placebo-comparison crossover study. Twenty mg/kg per day of d-phenylalanine was not associated with any improvement or deterioration in behavior.

The tetracyclic antidepressant mianserin was tested for effect on symptoms of attention deficit by Winsberg, Camp-Bruno, Vink, Timmer, and Sverd (1987). No significant improvement was seen and side effects were encountered. Promethazine was studied by Zametkin, Reeves, Webster, and Werry (1986); eight children with ADD by *DSM-III* criteria were treated with promethazine in a double-blind study. The authors concluded that there was no improvement with promethazine, although there was behavioral deterioration in four subjects that necessitated discontinuation of the drug in two cases.

Treatment of ADD children with essential fatty acids was studied by Aman, Mitchell, and Turbott (1987) and found to have no effect on behavior.

Sleep Disorders and Medication

Resistance to going to bed and fewer total hours of sleep are important sleep disturbances in children with ADHD. Sleep deprivation may worsen the clinical presentation of ADHD symptoms and sleep problems may contribute to disruptive behaviors that intensify family discord for children with ADHD (Barkley, Fischer, Edelbrock, & Smallish, 1990; Wilens & Biederman, 1992; Wilens, Biederman, & Spencer, 1994). Dahl, Pelham, and Wierson (1991) report improvement in ADD symptoms with treatment of the comorbid sleep disturbance. L. Miller and Kraft (1992) have even suggested subtypes of ADHD based on sleep evaluation. Do methylphenidate or other stimulants worsen sleep problems in ADHD children?

Although most studies find that methylphenidate produces mild sleeplessness in many children with ADHD and a severe problem for some, other studies have found no effect of stimulant medication on sleep. Kent, Blader, Koplewicz, Abikoff, and Foley (1995), studying twelve children admitted to a child psychiatric inpatient service, found no effect on sleep from an afternoon 10 or 15 mg methylphenidate dose. Sleep latency was evaluated, and the authors also found no effect on sleep of a dinnertime dose, but weight loss was apparent among 83% of the patients. The authors encouraged consideration of a third dose of methylphenidate in children whose ADHD behavior creates distress in the afternoon or evening hours. However, Tirosh, Sadeh, Munvez, and Lavie (1993) showed that even a 7:30 A.M. dose of 0.3 to 0.4 mg/kg methylphenidate produced shorter total sleep duration compared with placebo treatment.

Clonidine has been recommended for treatment of sleeplessness comorbid to ADHD. Rubinstein, Silver, and Licamele (1994) and Wilens et al. (1994) suggest an initial dose of 0.05 mg (half tablet) titrated upward from 0.05 mg increments as necessary to 0.4 mg maximum. Very young or underweight children may require lower doses (i.e., 0.025 mg, quarter tablet). Wilens et al. suggest this approach will supplement the effect of stimulant medication on the ADHD behavior. The only side effect reported in hundreds of children evaluated was daytime drowsiness.

Medications for Aggression, CD, and ADHD Combined

Aggressive behavior is one of the most troublesome symptoms associated with ADHD, and improvement of aggressive behavior is one of the most important benefits of methylphenidate treatment. Many controlled studies demonstrate a decrease in aggressive behavior with this treatment (Barkley et al., 1989; Casat, Cherek, Van Davelaar, & Pearson, 1994; Casat, Pearson, Van Davelaar, & Cherek, 1995; Gadow, Nolan, Sverd, Sprafkin, & Paolicelli, 1990; Gadow, Paolicelli, Nolan, & Schwartz, 1992; Hinshaw, Buhrmester, & Heller, 1989; Hinshaw, Henker, Whalen, Erhardt, & Dunnington, 1989; Klorman et al., 1989; Matier, Halperin, Sharma, Newcorn, & Sathaye, 1992; Pelham, Milich, Cummings, Murphy, Schaughency, & Greiner, 1991). Antisocial behaviors seen in laboratory evaluations were decreased by methylphenidate (Hinshaw et al., 1992). Aggressive ADHD children had a greater decrease in activity level and a larger incremented behavioral improvement than the nonaggressive ADHD group treated with methylphenidate (Barkley et al., 1989; Matier et al., 1992). Hinshaw, Buhrmester, et al. (1989) studied response to provocation and noted that ADHD children treated with methylphenidate (0.6 mg/kg) showed significantly enhanced self-control and decreased physical retaliation. Display of coping strategies was only marginally increased, however. Gadow et al. (1990) showed that methylphenidate suppressed non-physical aggression in the classroom and a moderate dose decreased physical and verbal aggression on the playground. Hinshaw, Buhrmester, et al. showed that 0.6 mg/kg methylphenidate in a summer research program reduced aggression to levels comparable to those of the control subjects. Gadow et al. (1992) showed that the peers of the aggressive-hyperactives treated with methylphenidate also changed their demeanor in response to the improvement in aggressivity of the hyperactive children. Matier et al. found activity level decreased only in the nonaggressive ADHD group. However, a single 5 mg dose of methylphenidate may have been too low a dose to show a response. These studies represent a substantial body of literature showing that methylphenidate reduces aggressive behavior in ADHD children.

Not all studies show improvement in aggressive behavior on all measures. A double-blind study of only six subjects found a significant reduction of aggressivity with methylphenidate measured by the adolescent antisocial behavior checklist, but improvement in the Conners Teacher's Rating Scale for hyperactivity and aggression was not significant (Kaplan, Busner, Kupietz, Wasserman, & Segal, 1990). Methylphenidate treatment of ADHD with comorbid CD results in some improvement of symptoms. It is likely, however, that it is the ADHD component rather than the CD that is improved by the stimulant medication (Lavin & Rifkin, 1993; Rifkin, 1992).

Other medications, including carbamazepine, lithium, and haldol, have been used in aggressive behaviors. Carbamazepine, an anticonvulsant, improved aggression with

CD in a pilot study, but the double-blind continuation of this study showed no significant benefit (Cueva et al., 1996). Clonidine was shown to improve aggression in seventeen children. Of note is the finding of Sanchez, Armenteros, Small, Campbell, and Adams (1994) that ten out of twenty-five conduct-disordered, aggressive children had at least some level of response to placebo. Neuroleptics, primarily haloperidol in dosages 1 to 6 mg per day, have been shown to improve the aggressiveness associated with CD (Lavin & Rifkin, 1993; Rifkin, 1992). Lithium carbonate may be helpful for a subgroup of aggressive, non-ADHD conduct-disordered children (Malone, Luebbert, Pena-Ariet, Biesecker, & Delaney, 1994; Silva, Ernst, & Campbell, 1993). Lithium has also been shown to improve symptoms of CD with fewer side effects than haloperidol (Lavin & Rifkin, 1993; Rifkin, 1992). Long-term safety and efficacy, however, of both lithium and haloperidol for treatment of symptoms of CD are unknown.

MEDICATION INTERVENTION AND THE BRAIN MODEL OF ADHD

In our discussion of the causes of ADHD (Chapter 5), we described a brain model for the attention system; the concept of an attention network that links all areas of the brain and functions to modulate attention was presented. This attention network acts on all areas of the brain to modulate a spectrum of attention from thoughtful and deliberate to quick and impulsive. On one end of the spectrum is highly focused behavior: the child is locked onto one target such as the teacher, book, or even TV screen; other factors, including extraneous noise, rattling of papers, speech, or music emanating from a different source, are suppressed, as is the impulse to respond to these extraneous distractions. On the other end of the spectrum, the child is aware of many different surrounding activities, sounds, and sights and is ready to respond to noises by running toward or away from the sounds. In some situations, the ability to respond quickly to a sharp noise, rustling activity, or extraneous speech is more important than a thoughtful analysis; impulsive activity based on quick response is sometimes needed, for example, in dangerous situations. Thoughtful, focused activity is more important in the classroom. Most normal children are able to change their behavior in many gradations along this spectrum. They can choose appropriate times for quick, impulsive actions and other times for deliberate, thoughtful responses.

Children with ADHD are not able to control their attentional network. They may be intently concentrating when they should be aware of their surroundings, and they may be too easily distracted and ready to run off when they should be focused. Medication for ADHD works to enhance the functioning of the attentional network so that children can choose when to be sensitive to outside distractions and when to focus their attention. The attention center is stimulated by these medications, with the result that the child has better control of himself or herself. The child's ability to interact in a purposeful way is greatly improved by medications (Barkley et al., 1984; Pelham, 1987; Schachar et al., 1987; Whalen, Henker, Swanson, et al., 1987).

From this point of view, attention deficit is a result of the malfunction of the system that allows the brain to discriminate situations where focused, deliberate behavior is appropriate from situations where quick, impulsive actions are needed. This model allows us to differentiate ADHD from a learning disability. An ADHD child is unable to

change as needed from focused concentration and deliberate action to impulsive action, whereas learning disability results from inappropriate processing and coordination of sensory input with memory and motor output. Medication intervention for
ADHD improves the child's ability to control and focus attention, concentration, and
activity but usually has little if any direct effect on the ability to process and coordinate sensory input, memory, and motor output.

For example, a child with ADHD may have difficulty paying attention to the book
being read, but with medication intervention may improve the ability to concentrate on
the printed words. A learning disability results from difficulty understanding or processing the words. A child with simple ADHD may appear to have difficulty reading
because of a lack of concentration; if the distractibility and inattention are corrected,
the child's reading will improve. However, if the difficulty lay in understanding the
written word and processing the information, improving the child's concentration will
not improve the ability to obtain information from written words; in this case, appropriate attention to the book is a necessary, but not a sufficient, condition. Medication
stimulates the attention network deep within the brain, but may have little effect on
the cortical ability of the brain to process information. This model may aid in the understanding of the effect of medication intervention on ADHD symptoms and the lack
of effect on learning disabilities.

Using this model also allows the practitioner to understand the nature of medication
side effects. Stimulants adjust the functioning of chemical brain systems, including
dopamine, noradrenalin, serotonin, and possibly others. These chemical systems are
involved in other functions of the brain in addition to attention and concentration.
The other systems may also be stimulated by the medication and change their level of
functioning.

For example, one can think of the child's appetite as a network parallel to the attentional network. Stimulating centers in a way that affects satiety may result in decreased interest in food. If the appetite network were more sensitive than the attention
network, the result would be anorexia at a dose that would not affect attention. If one
considers the attention network to be similar to the appetite network but, in most children, more sensitive to stimulant medications, one can understand why children will
have some decreased appetite as they improve their ADHD symptoms. The sleep network can also be sensitive to stimulant medication. Increasing the dose of medication
stimulates wakefulness and may interfere with sleep; when this occurs as an unwanted
effect of medication, it is termed a side effect. Fortunately, in most children with
ADHD, the attention network is more sensitive to the effect of stimulant medication
than other networks. In some children, however, the sleep or appetite networks appear
to be more sensitive, and in other children the attentional network appears to be unresponsive to the effects of the stimulant medication.

ALTERNATIVES TO MEDICATION

Comparisons of medication risks and benefits with alternatives depend on understanding the alternatives to medication intervention. The alternatives include nonmedication
intervention and nonintervention. There is very little evidence that medication intervention has a long-term effect on the child with ADHD symptoms, but it may have a

very dramatic effect in the short term. Many of the beneficial effects of medication can be achieved in some settings with nonmedication intervention programs. When medication is not employed, however, the results are less dramatic, do not generalize as well, and require more organization and effort on the part of the family and therapist. In addition, effective nonmedication intervention programs may not be available to all children. Nonmedication intervention programs are more costly than medication, both in terms of the financial resources required to support the therapy and in terms of personal resources required by the family.

THE DECISION TO USE MEDICATION

Practitioners should compare the risks of benefits of, and alternatives to medication before making a decision concerning medication intervention. Baseline assessment and the expected benefits of intervention with medication are compared to the expected outcome without medication intervention. If children are at higher risk for medication side effects (such as those with tics, psychosis, or a family unable to follow through with programs), this must be carefully weighed against the alternatives of nonintervention and nonmedication intervention.

The weighing of risks, benefits, and alternatives to determine appropriate intervention is a common part of medical practice. Clinical judgment of the physician must be used; involvement of the family can be important. The process of comparing risks, benefits, and alternatives brings the decision-making process concerning medication intervention for treatment of ADHD closer to the decision-making process for other medical problems.

A PRACTICAL APPROACH TO ADMINISTRATION OF METHYLPHENIDATE

The best or optimal dose and schedule of medication is the one that produces greatest benefits and fewest side effects. There are no studies that demonstrate the preferred means of determining the optimal dose or schedule of medication. This section will present some practical suggestions that may serve as a guide to the clinical use of methylphenidate when consideration of risks, benefits, and alternatives leads to the conclusion that a trial of medication intervention is warranted. Many of these suggestions are applicable to other medications as well.

A multidisciplinary team is used for evaluation of ADHD and for supervising a treatment regimen. One member of the team functions as a case manager to coordinate the gathering of information concerning the effect of medication at differing dosages and/or time schedules. This information is then communicated to the physician to allow appropriate medication adjustment.

Methylphenidate: How Often, How Much?

R. D., an 8-year-old boy with ADHD, was started on Ritalin in the morning before school. His mother felt that, rather than helping, it seemed to aggravate the symptoms.

His morning teachers, however, felt that he was dramatically better on the medication. His afternoon teacher didn't see much difference. How do these different observers reach such different conclusions? Methylphenidate reaches its greatest effect one to two hours after it is taken. The time it takes to lose half its maximum effect, or its half-life, is approximately four hours in most children. Medication taken at 7:00 A.M. will be most effective from 8:00 to 10:00 A.M. and then become less effective during the day. In this example, R. D.'s morning teacher observed him while the medication was fully effective and concluded that it was helping. His afternoon teacher observed him after the medication had lost much of its effect and saw little change. After school, his mother observed him during a period of rebound and felt that the medication was aggravating his symptoms.

This example illustrates the importance of understanding the time course of medication effect. We advocate an approach to medication adjustment that is communicated to the patient to encourage appropriate medication treatment, making adjustments along the way (Gadow & Nolan, 1993). For most children treated with methylphenidate, the pediatrician is responsible for supervising drug therapy. In this study, most parents were satisfied with their current physician and approximately half of children studied had three or more office visits per year. Teachers, however, were rarely asked to use standardized procedures to evaluate drug response, and direct contact between teacher and physician was all but nonexistent. Parents and teachers disagreed concerning drug efficacy, dosage, and the need for medication. Parents appeared to exert considerable degree of control over treatment-related decisions. Evidence for an integrated, multimodal treatment approach was lacking.

Medication begun at a very low dose (5 mg) and gradually increased, with information obtained about the child's performance at school and at home at each dosage change, allows maximum flexibility. In some children, the results are clear in only a few days. For others, it requires two weeks before the results of a medication change are clear. Initiating medication intervention with a very low dose often will allow children who are very sensitive to methylphenidate, either with a positive or negative response, to demonstrate this sensitivity. In these children, dosages that work well for other children may cause unacceptable side effects. For some children, a very low dose will produce the best response, and a higher or more frequent dose may produce fewer positive or more negative effects.

ADHD symptoms respond well to stimulant medication. However, symptoms of CD, oppositional behavior, specific learning disabilities, depression, or other problems not the result of ADHD often are not improved with stimulant medication. Symptoms of attention deficit can be separated from other symptoms by careful evaluation. It is recommended that ADHD symptoms be clearly identified and that the dosage of methylphenidate be adjusted to a level that maximizes the effect on these symptoms. Feedback on a regular basis is necessary for this determination, and reevaluation of the target symptoms is needed. Obtaining subjective and objective information from teachers and parents, as well as independent observation, is usually necessary to determine the effect of medication and the optimal dosage.

As all children do not respond to the same dose or have the same time course of medication response, arbitrarily predetermining dosage amounts is not recommended. Although it is simpler to place all medicated children on the same dose and schedule, arbitrary selection of amount and frequency of medication ingestion will result in too much or too little medication for some children. Medication adjustment, a single dose at a time, will produce more positive results and fewer side effects.

Once a single dose of medication is adjusted to optimal effect, one can determine whether a second dosage is appropriate. Methylphenidate is most effective one to two hours after it has been administered; thus, evaluation two hours after ingestion will help determine if there is substantial improvement in attention deficit symptoms. Evaluation at other times of the day is also needed: after four or five hours, the effect of medication may no longer be present; six to twelve hours after ingestion, the symptoms of attention deficit will often return to their premedication levels. For some children, the ADHD symptoms are actually worse in the period six to twelve hours after medication is administered than they were on days when no medication was administered. This is known as the rebound effect. If symptoms are troublesome at the six-hour time, whether this is caused by rebound or simply by the return to nonmedication functioning, a second dosage of methylphenidate may be helpful four hours after the initial dose.

Initiating a single morning dose of methylphenidate and following its progress through the day will allow one to separate side effects related to the presence of medication from side effects related to medication withdrawal or rebound. The second dose of medication, when required, may be administered at lunch time. When the second dose is titrated independently of the initial morning dose, the amount of methylphenidate required may be less for the second dose than for the first. Much of the clinical effect of the methylphenidate has dissipated after four hours. However, some medication effect is still present, and continuation of the medication effect with a much lower second dose may be possible. One-half to two-thirds of the morning dose may suffice for a noon dose.

By evening, the morning and most of the noon medication will have lost its effectiveness. Most children will function well in the evening, possibly as a result of the effects of medication given earlier in the day. If rebound or return of ADHD symptoms is a problem in the evening, a third dose of medication may be helpful. Individual titration allows more flexibility in determining whether a third dose is helpful and what dosage is most effective. An after-school dose given between 4:00 and 6:00 P.M. may improve ADHD symptoms in the late afternoon and evening. However, this third dose may produce difficulty falling asleep at night and decrease appetite for dinner. If difficulty falling asleep or anorexia persists, it may preclude use of a late-afternoon dose of medication. If a third dose is required, a lower dosage than the morning and possibly even lower than the noon dose may be effective. Reevaluation of the ADHD symptoms can help determine the need for and value of the third dose of medication.

The determination of the optimal dose and administration time of medication requires careful monitoring. Some children with ADHD also have other disorders, such as learning disabilities, oppositional behavior, depression, anxiety, and social skills deficits, yet the attention deficit symptoms are likely to be the only problems responsive to stimulant medication. Use of non-attention-deficit symptoms to judge the effect of medication can result in overlooking medication effectiveness or can lead to dosage adjustments that are higher than optimal. When adjustment of medication results in dosages greater than 20 mg of methylphenidate, the target symptoms that were used to adjust medication should be reevaluated. Retitration of the medication may prove helpful.

For example, a 10-year-old fifth-grade boy taking 35 mg of Ritalin three times a day was seen because of persistence of ADHD symptoms as well as restlessness, sleeplessness, and an increase in anxiety. A thorough evaluation revealed that the methylphenidate had been increased every time he had developed oppositional behavior under the mistaken belief that this was a symptom of attention deficit. When the episode of oppositional behavior subsided, it was thought to confirm the effect of the increased methylphenidate dosage, and subsequent episodes of oppositional behavior were further treated by increases in medication. Initially, the family was resistent to the idea of discontinuing the medication. After medication had been discontinued, an increase of attention deficit symptoms did occur, but a decrease in oppositional behavior, anxiety, restlessness, and sleeplessness was also seen. When the Ritalin was retitrated to a dose of 15 mg in the morning and 10 mg after lunch, inattentive, distractible, and impulsive behavior improved without the side effects of exaggeration of the restlessness, anxiety, and sleeplessness. A single dose greater than 20 mg and a total daily dose of more than 60 mg should alert the practitioner that retitration may lead to better results at a lower dosage of methylphenidate. In a group of Medicaid recipients the average daily dose of methylphenidate was 18.7 ± 10.4 mg for 5- to 9-year-olds and 26.8 ± 14.0 mg for 10- to 14-year-olds (Zito et al., 1997).

Minimizing Anorexia and Insomnia

Anorexia is a common side effect of methylphenidate. In general, it is transient and self-limited. Many children will have decreased appetite and possibly even a pound or two of weight loss over the first few weeks. Appetite and weight will usually improve shortly thereafter. If the anorexia or weight loss is particularly troublesome, there are several techniques to alleviate this problem.

Administering the morning dose after breakfast may allow increased appetite for the morning meal. Increasing the caloric content of breakfast may increase the 24-hour caloric intake. A similar approach, with the noon dose administered after lunch, can sometimes be helpful in restoring a relatively normal appetite for lunch. If an afternoon dose of methylphenidate is administered, there may be some decrease in appetite at dinner. Giving the after-school dose of medication as early as possible and having dinner as late as possible may improve appetite for the evening meal. Some children will have a return of appetite near bedtime, and some families have found that a bedtime snack will increase the 24-hour caloric input. Many children have a dosage threshold for anorexia: a dosage of 10 mg may produce little anorexia, whereas 15 mg may produce significant anorexia. Titration of medication dosage to maximize therapeutic effects and minimize side effects will be useful in this situation.

Some children will have difficulty with sleeplessness after taking methylphenidate. There are at least two reasons why this might occur. In one situation, the medication has a direct effect to stimulate wakefulness; this is often especially true if an afternoon or evening dose is used. This can be minimized by decreasing the afternoon or evening medication dosage. In some sensitive children, dosages that are so low as to barely affect the ADHD symptoms produce insomnia. Some tolerance to the sleep effects may occur, but sleeplessness may necessitate discontinuing methylphenidate and considering alternative medications.

A second explanation for sleeplessness is as a result of rebound: increase in inattention and distractibility caused by rebound will prevent these children from concentrating on falling asleep. This rebound sleeplessness may appear similar to restlessness caused by direct effect of the methylphenidate. Observation of other symptoms during the day may give a clue to the occurrence of sleeplessness as a rebound symptom. Other symptoms of ADHD may also have rebounded; as the medication wears off, an increase in inattentive and distractible behavior may be seen. Children with rebound sleeplessness may actually fall asleep more easily with increased medication. For example, if a child receiving 15 mg of Ritalin once in the morning becomes restless in the afternoon and evening and has difficulty falling asleep, a second dose of 5 to 10 mg of methylphenidate either after lunch or immediately after school may improve the symptoms of restlessness at night. In these children, the medication may help them to settle down enough to fall asleep.

Noncompliance

Noncompliance is a possible explanation of medication failure. Sleator et al. (1982) found that many children in their study disliked the medication and tried to avoid taking it. They concluded that although the physician interview provides valuable information about noncompliance, other sources of information must be used to be certain medication is being taken as directed. In a study of fifty-eight children with attention deficit involved in medication as well as nonmedication therapy, R. Brown, Borden, Wynne, Spunt, and Clingerman (1987) reported that slightly more than half of these children completed a three-month treatment protocol. They concluded that it is often difficult to determine whether failure of medication intervention is the result of noncompliance: some children become skilled at disguising their noncompliance, and families may not be aware of the problem unless the prescription does not need to be renewed at the expected time or unless carelessly discarded medication is discovered in the sink or on the floor. The practitioner must keep in mind that various forms of noncompliance can be the cause of medication failure.

Generic Formulations

Generic formulations of medications are often less expensive than brand name medications and are usually as effective. The lesser price is based on the fact that the generic manufacturer is not attempting to recover research-and-development costs incurred in an effort to bring the medication to the market place. Although the reported bioavailability of methylphenidate has been suggested as equal to Ritalin, some questions have been raised in individual patients as to whether methylphenidate is as effective as the Ritalin brand. Although it has been our experience that several children had a deterioration in effectiveness of medication when changed from Ritalin to methylphenidate, controlled comparison studies have not been performed. At this time, methylphenidate is produced by one generic manufacturer, M.D. Pharmaceuticals. It is quite likely that in the coming years a number of additional manufacturers will bring methylphenidate to the marketplace. Although it is unlikely that practitioners will encounter a child demonstrating a drop in medication effectiveness when changed from Ritalin to methylphenidate, a dramatic and sudden lack of response to the medication should trigger a question from the practitioner.

Double-Blind Clinical Evaluation

Some authors have proposed determining medication effect by double-blind placebo trials in individual children (Ottinger, Halpin, Miller, Durmain, & Hanneman, 1985). Citing results of a study of 118 children with ADD under double-blind conditions, Ullmann and Sleator (1982) advocated use of a double-blind crossover technique for all children given methylphenidate. Eighteen of the 118 children had nearly 50% improvement on the teacher rating scale for attention while taking placebo; this was essentially the same response that they had to the best dose of methylphenidate. The authors concluded that a significant group of children who appear to respond to methylphenidate may be responding to what they describe as nonspecific factors also present in the placebo trials. They urged all clinicians to use placebo trials and implied that this will allow children to have the benefits without the risks of medication.

Several questions are raised by placebo studies: What is the long-term effect of placebos? Should children who respond be continued on placebo? Should children who respond to placebo simply be eliminated from consideration of medication intervention? The American Academy of Pediatrics (1987) has not recommended routine placebo trials, as Ullmann and Sleator have advocated. It is not certain why double-blind trials have not become widespread in clinical practice; possibly, the difficulty in arranging for a placebo trial or understanding how to proceed if such a trial yields positive results has discouraged this practice. Nevertheless, some children seem to respond to medication at first, and then when the response wears off, they respond again to an increased dose. This group of children may contain some who are placebo responders. It remains to be shown that double-blind trial administration of medication in clinical practice has a lower risk or greater benefit than other means of evaluation.

Case Examples

Our first case reviews the treatment of uncomplicated ADHD with methylphenidate. The other case examples look at children with more complex problems: those who are younger or older or not hyperactive as well as those who have associated problems including sleeplessness, mental retardation, aggressive behavior, anxiety, Tourette's syndrome and obsessive-compulsive symptoms.

Case 1

Allen, an 8-year-old boy, was always described as mischievous. He released the handbrake of his parents' car when he was only 3, causing it to roll into another vehicle. In school he is always getting out of his seat, talking to other students, and disrupting the class. He seems to learn well and is liked by his peers, but he does not achieve successful grades, often forgetting to hand in his homework.

Before making a decision about medication, one needs an evaluation to determine whether ADHD is present and whether other disorders are also present. We will assume that in this case, evaluation shows ADHD to be present without comorbid disorders. Next, one must evaluate and appropriately initiate nonmedication interventions; for example, it would have been best not to leave Allen at age 3 in the car by himself. In trying to determine whether medication will be appropriate for this child, we use the basic medical model of decision making; we evaluate the risks and the alternatives to medication treatment and compare these with the expected benefits.

We will first consider the risks of treatment for Allen. Mild side effects are common with methylphenidate, but symptoms of anorexia, headache, stomachache, and sleeplessness severe enough to require stopping medication are uncommon and occur in fewer than 5%. Tics or psychosis, though rare, do require discontinuing the medication. Available evidence suggests that Tourette's, epilepsy, growth suppression, and drug addiction are probably not caused by methylphenidate.

The benefits of methylphenidate include improvement in conduct, academic efficiency, and on-task behavior. There is a dramatic improvement in Conners scores. Scores of several measures of learning and behavior respond to increasing the dosage of methylphenidate, evidenced by a dose-response curve for medication effect: the higher the dose, the greater the response, from 5 to 20 mg. The greatest improvement is seen when the dose is increased from 5 to 10 mg, but significant additional improvement is seen when the dose is increased from 15 to 20 mg as well. One of the most important benefits of methylphenidate is its effect on normalizing classroom behavior: 75% of ADHD children have enough improvement to consider their behavior normal and no other interventions are needed. Some still have problems, however: their behavior, though improved, is still below average. There is also a substantial improvement in ADHD-related aggression, a very important benefit of methylphenidate as nonmedication interventions that work primarily by environmental manipulation do not help when the child is not in the controlled environment.

Let us now assume that after weighing the risks and benefits of methylphenidate for Allen, we have decided to begin medication treatment. As the expected effect of methylphenidate will last about four hours, most children take the first dose before school and will receive the second dose of medication at school. Although many studies employ a dosage of methylphenidate based on the weight of the child, most practitioners have found that individualizing medication for a particular child will result in maximizing benefits and minimizing side effects. There are several approaches to finding the best dose; the simplest both to prescribe and to follow is a fixed regimen in the morning and at noon, increasing on a weekly basis from 5 to 10 to 15 mg. It has been our experience that some of the methylphenidate effect may persist to the afternoon and that titrating the noon dose separately will result in a lower noon dose for many children. Reported dosages range from 5 to 20 mg, but most children take dosages of 10 to 15 mg in the morning and at noon. Some researchers have recommended a placebo-controlled trial for every child taking methylphenidate; this approach, which is expensive and cumbersome, has not found wide acceptance.

We have found that some children develop rebound irritability and increased symptoms after medication effect has worn off. Sometimes adding a small dose of methylphenidate about a half hour before rebound is expected to begin helps avoid this problem.

Follow-up reevaluation is necessary. We recommend the first follow-up two to four weeks after initiating medication. Obtaining information from the school and home will be helpful in evaluating both the positive and negative effects of medication. Checklists and other methods to determine medication effect are discussed at length in Chapters 7 and 8.

If treatment has not been successful, additional evaluation is needed. Was treatment unsuccessful because of too few positive effects or too many negative effects or both? Were there not enough resources to follow through with nonmedication interventions? It is necessary first to review the diagnosis to be certain that ADHD is present, as other disorders will not respond to methylphenidate. Review of potential treatment alternatives, including other medications, nonmedication interventions, and family and school support systems is needed. If methylphenidate is helping but producing side effects, a lower dose or a different stimulant medication may be needed. Dextroamphetamine and methamphetamine have actions very similar to methylphenidate; though their side effect profiles are similar, many children who have a particular side effect with one stimulant will not have that same side effect with a different stimulant.

Often, midday dosage is inconvenient. Some children have rebound from abrupt onset and withdrawal of action. A long-acting stimulant such as Dexedrine Spansules®, Ritalin SR, Desoxyn Gradumates®, or pemoline may be helpful for these problems. Dextroamphetamine is also available in a combination of salts marketed under the brand name Adderal, which is said to have a longer duration of action. However, data about duration of action for Adderal is limited to uncontrolled studies and metabolic analyses. The efficacy of other long-acting stimulants has also not been well studied. It has been our experience that most children changed from standard preparation to sustained-release preparation prefer the standard preparation despite the inconvenience of taking medication at school.

Case 2

> Ben, a 5-year-old boy, is still not sleeping through the night. During the day he has boundless energy. He is now attending his third preschool, having been asked to leave by the other two because of disruptive yelling. The family has run out of babysitters who will stay with him.

There are three problems facing the physician making a medication decision concerning Ben. He is hyperactive, has problems sleeping, and, in addition, is younger than most children medicated for ADHD. As with all children, a careful evaluation is needed to determine which disorders are present. In young children, language delays, hearing loss, ear infections, and other medical problems can be mistaken for ADHD and will not respond to medication. Behavioral interventions should be considered for all children, especially those under 6 who may be more likely to have problems with medication. This child might benefit from a structured prebedtime program or cooling-off period, a set bedtime, and other behavioral practices. Problems with separation may contribute to difficulty with school and may also be amendable to nonmedication interventions. However, if these have failed, medication is a reasonable consideration. Methylphenidate is the gold standard for ADHD treatment and may be very effective in a preschooler, but the likelihood of unacceptable side effects is high in children under 6. All the problems commonly seen in older children, including anorexia and sleeplessness, are more common; behavioral deterioration is also possible.

The Food and Drug Administration has allowed Dexedrine for use in children 3 and older, but methylphenidate is not recommended for children under 6, though there are no data to suggest that methylphenidate has a higher incidence of side effects or a lower likelihood of success in younger children. Stimulants such as methylphenidate, dextroamphetamine, or pemoline may worsen the problem of sleeplessness present in Ben. The antidepressants thus represent the most appealing alternative to stimulant medication for this child. Imipramine and desipramine are the best-studied antidepressants in childhood. Imipramine has been widely used in children for over thirty years to treat enuresis. These medications are administered at night, as they often produce mild drowsiness. This would be an advantage for Ben, because they may also help alleviate his sleeplessness. These medications have not been as extensively studied as the stimulants, but they have been shown to be helpful for most ADHD children. They have no drug abuse potential and therefore are subject to less governmental regulation than the stimulants. Their long duration of action allows for once-a-day dosage and eliminates ups and downs and rebound effect. Imipramine is considered for Ben, because it helps sleeplessness more than desipramine.

The TCAs have several disadvantages, however, that result in their being a second choice for most children with uncomplicated ADHD. They are not as efficacious at controlling symptoms. The few comparison studies available show that methylphenidate has a greater effect on Conners questionnaire scores and other measures of ADHD symptoms. The onset of action is slower, sometimes taking two to four weeks to become fully effective. One of the principal drawbacks to the use of TCAs, however, is concern over several reported sudden deaths.

After a baseline EKG, Ben could begin imipramine 20 mg at night, increasing by 10 mg increments to 50 mg or until a positive effect is achieved. Follow-up in three to four weeks should include an EKG and follow-up questionnaires and a side effects checklist. If there is no improvement after a month, a different medication could be considered. If we decide to stop the medication, the imipramine should be tapered over two weeks to prevent withdrawal increase in sleeplessness.

An alternative to imipramine for sleeplessness is the antihypertensive medication, clonidine. For many, the occurrence of sleepiness is an undesirable side effect, but for Ben, sleepiness produced by clonidine can be viewed as a positive effect. Although this medication is used to lower blood pressure in adults, it rarely causes symptoms of low blood pressure in normal children. Treatment is usually initiated by administration of half a 0.1 mg tablet (0.05 mg) at bedtime. If this is not enough, half-tablet increases per week are reasonable. Clonidine is also available as a skin patch, which gives uniform administration without swallowing pills; patches could be considered after the dosage is established with the tablets. Based on our experience with clonidine, Ben may have unacceptable tiredness during the day, but if the imipramine fails, clonidine would be worth a try.

Case 3

Charles, a 9-year-old boy, was slow to develop. He walked at 18 months, said his first words at 19 months, and has been tested to have an IQ of 75. When challenged on the playground, he hits other children. He does better in special classes when he is alone with the teacher.

In addition to the symptoms described in this case, a careful evaluation showed inattention, distractibility, and impulsive behavior, fulfilling *DSM-IV* criteria for ADHD combined type, in addition to mild mental retardation. This case illustrates the importance of a thorough baseline evaluation. Some very active children who are globally delayed may actually have normal activity for their developmental age and not have ADHD. Aggression can also be a symptom of a problem other than ADHD, such as CD or depression. Before considering medication, one should look at nonmedication interventions. Classroom aggression may be managed by environmental manipulation, but the lack of generalization of nonmedication intervention makes improving behavior in unstructured playground situations difficult. One approach is to exclude this child from unstructured social interactions, but this would deprive him of these important experiences. Can medication help?

One of the striking discoveries about methylphenidate is its effect on aggressive activity in children with ADHD. Unfortunately, aggression related to CD is insensitive to methylphenidate, again showing the importance of evaluation before beginning medication treatment. The effect of methylphenidate on non-CD aggression is one of the recent pleasant surprises in this field. As it is difficult for nonmedication treatments to produce effects in other settings, medication is one of the few ways of helping symptoms in unstructured settings.

ADHD children with IQs of 44 to 79 respond well to medication but may have a much higher incidence of side effects.

There are alternatives when methylphenidate is unsuccessful. Antidepressants or clonidine may be helpful. The neuroleptic medications thioridazine, chlorpromazine and haloperidol, as well as Risperidone are not first-line medications for ADHD; although they decrease activity level, they produce unwanted side effects, including motor stiffness, potential for tardive dyskinesia, and a dulling of personality. Lithium has been used for aggressive behavior related to bipolar disorder but is generally not helpful for ADHD except when ADHD is combined with bipolar disorder. Anticonvulsants have been used for several decades for treatment of ADHD. Uncontrolled studies thirty to forty years ago suggested diphenylhydantoin might be helpful, but better-controlled studies suggested it is more likely to aggravate than improve behavior. Studies of carbamazepine and valproate have been promising; these medications may be worth a trial if all else fails, but are not as useful as stimulants and antidepressants.

Case 4

Debra, a 10-year-old girl, was diagnosed as having inattentive ADHD. She is not disruptive in class but often forgets to complete or hand in assignments. She has a normal IQ and learns well when tutored by her parents. She often forgets to bring assignments home. When she is tried on methylphenidate she becomes very quiet, appears depressed, bites her fingernails, and often seems quite frightened.

Here we have a girl with inattentive ADHD who developed anxiety and depression when treated with methylphenidate. A complete evaluation will be helpful in planning treatment. Counseling or psychotherapy may help for symptoms of anxiety and depression. Inattentive ADHD may respond to methylphenidate, but the likelihood of improvement is less than for hyperactive ADHD. Some children report that they do not like the way methylphenidate makes them feel; their rejection of medication was mistakenly believed due to oppositional behavior. It is worthwhile asking children about their feelings after they take the medication to try to find children who have increased anxiety due to stimulant medication. Some researchers recommend use of antidepressants for this group; there are many from which to choose. Response of symptoms of anxiety to medication treatment in ADHD children is not well studied. OCD, which is considered an anxiety disorder, has been shown to respond to the specific serotonin re-uptake inhibitors. Fluoxetine and clomipramine have been demonstrated to work for OCD; replacing these medicines in a blind fashion with desipramine resulted in relapse of OCD symptoms. Other medications reported helpful for adults with anxiety disorders have not been shown to produce long-term benefit to children with feelings of either anxiety or depression. We have found Buspirone helpful in some older children. Long-term results from anti-anxiety medications are uncertain. Propranolol, which blocks beta monoamine receptors, has been surprisingly helpful for some with panic attacks. Debra could be started on a low dose of a specific Serotonin Reuptake Inhibitor (SSRI) such as 10 mg of fluoxetine (Prozac®) or 25 mg of sertraline (Zoloft®) and the dose doubled after one or two weeks if improvement is not seen.

Case 5

James, an 11-year-old boy, had been hyperactive since the first grade. He never made friends well because he was always afraid of getting dirty. He washes his hands when no one else would consider them dirty. After being on methylphenidate for a year, he developed repetitive movements, including first, eye blinking and then shoulder shrugging. He now has started clearing his throat quite a lot.

Complete evaluation may show James to have ADHD in addition to comorbid disorders of OCD and Tourette's syndrome. Stimulant medication may be the most useful for treating the ADHD symptoms. Stimulants usually do not aggravate Tourette's, and it is our observation that most who treat patients with Tourette's regularly use methylphenidate to treat comorbid ADHD symptoms. TCAs also work well for the ADHD symptoms.

Clonidine is helpful for ADHD and Tourette's, as it does not aggravate the tics and may produce less daytime sedation in children with ADHD and Tourette's than in children with ADHD alone. There are few comparison studies, but it has been our experience that desipramine helps ADHD more and has fewer side effects than clonidine. haloperidol or pimozide is used to treat the tics, but many children with this combination of problems will not need treatment for tics if the ADHD symptoms are controlled.

Many children with these disorders are placed on multiple medications, including a stimulant and an antidepressant and even a third medication for the tics. Two basic principals of combining multiple medications, or polypharmacy, should be kept in mind. First is that side effects are additive but the benefits are not: each medicine adds all of its own side effects to the child but may add little benefit; for example, adding an antidepressant to methylphenidate will add the side effects of the antidepressant to those of the methylphenidate but will not double the benefits. The second principal is that no combination of medications has been adequately tested. There have been very few studies looking at problems or benefits of medication combinations. Some combinations are particularly dangerous: combining a monoamine oxidase inhibitor with other psychotropic medications increases the risk of a hypertensive crisis; the SSRI antidepressants change the metabolism of the TCAs, and this combination can lead to unexpectedly high concentrations of the tricyclics and their active metabolites; beta blockers used for panic attacks can precipitate asthma attacks in susceptible children. Therefore, we recommend always starting with only a single medication. When faced with symptoms that are not responding to methylphenidate or when the medication is producing unacceptable side effects, try first changing to a different stimulant such as Dexedrine or changing from the stimulant to an antidepressant. Adding a second medication may be a reasonable alternative when the first medication is working well for one set of symptoms but other symptoms are also present. For example, if a stimulant is helping ADHD symptoms but comorbid symptoms of sleeplessness, anxiety, depression, or agitation are present, adding a second medication such as a TCA or clonidine may be worthwhile.

Case 6

> Sean, a 13-year-old boy, has been successfully treated with methylphenidate since age 7. When he was 8 years old, his parents were called to school whenever they forgot his medication. Over the past year, however, Sean has done quite well at home and in social situations on days he does not take his medication.

What does the future hold for ADHD children? At one time, it was believed that all ADHD children outgrew their symptoms. Now we know they usually become less hyperactive but often continue to have problems with inattentive and impulsive behavior. How do we tell if an adolescent still needs medication? The only way is to stop the medication and see what happens. Usually there is no 10:00 A.M. call from the teacher the first day without medications; however, all too often, even when the adolescent believes everything is going well, failing grades are seen at the end of the term.

Our knowledge of adolescent and adult ADHD is limited but growing as more research is accomplished.

SUMMARY

How does one decide whether a child should be placed on medication for treatment of ADHD symptoms? We have suggested that the risks of medication and possible alternatives be compared with the benefits. Stimulant medication has a dramatic effect in improving a wide range of ADHD symptoms in 75% to 80% of ADHD children. Classroom behavior and interactions with peers improve; even interactions between mothers and children change for the better. This effect appears to be the result of improved or "stimulated" functioning of the brain center, which determines whether concentration and deliberate action or quick response is appropriate. The mild degree of loss of appetite, difficulty falling asleep, or irritability seen in many children as a result of stimulant medication can be viewed as the result of stimulation of other brain centers such as those for sleep or appetite. These side effects usually resolve spontaneously and do not detract from the overall positive results.

Although it rarely occurs, some children develop severe depression or a toxic psychosis with delusion or hallucination, and 1% of treated children develop tics as a result of medication. These symptoms usually disappear when medication is discontinued, but reports of persistent tics and Tourette's syndrome raise the possibility of permanent injury from stimulant medication as a rare occurrence in some children. Other concerns, such as permanent growth suppression, have been dispelled by studies suggesting that children treated with stimulant medications will eventually reach projected height even if medication is continued through weekends and summer vacation. An increase in the likelihood of drug addiction, criminal behavior, suicide, or other mental illness has also been proven, after study, not to be associated with stimulant treatment of ADHD in childhood.

Some factors increase the risk of side effects. Young children (below age 6) and children with anxiety, depression, psychosis, tics, or Tourette's are more likely to have side effects. Children with symptoms of disorders other than ADHD, such as learning disabilities, depression, anxiety, oppositional disorder, or aggressive behavior, are less likely to improve with medication. A careful evaluation can increase the likelihood of benefit and decrease the likelihood of side effects. History and examination can be directed to separate ADHD symptoms from others and to search for conditions that increase risk of medication intervention. Multidisciplinary nonmedication behavioral intervention programs may increase the benefit of medication.

The practitioner must keep in mind that there are both medical and nonmedical alternatives to the use of methylphenidate. These include nonmedication (behavioral) interventions as well as other medications. Although other medications have been shown to be effective in treatment of ADHD symptoms, methylphenidate remains the choice of those prescribing for most ADHD children. Pemoline has the disadvantages of a two- to four-week delay to reach maximum benefit and worrisome reports of liver function abnormalities in a few children; these may outweigh such benefits of pemoline as effectiveness in single daily dose for many children and less restrictive government regulation. Amphetamines are associated with a higher incidence of anorexia and insomnia in some studies; sadness is described in some children treated with dextroamphetamine.

Dextroamphetamine, which in the early 1970s was the most common medication used for treatment of ADHD symptoms, has been steadily declining as the medication preferred by prescribing physicians. TCAs have the advantage of a single daily administration and non-controlled-substance status. Although they often are effective, some comparative studies suggest that tricyclics are not as effective as methylphenidate in treating ADHD symptoms in most children. They have the added disadvantage of delay reaching maximum benefit (two to four weeks). However, for ADHD children with tics, depression, anxiety, or unacceptable side effects from methylphenidate, imipramine may be the best choice. Other medication, including major tranquilizers, clonidine, anticonvulsants, and antihistamines, may be helpful in some children but are not first-choice medications for most ADHD children.

By understanding the risks of medication and how to decrease them, the benefits of medication and how to increase them, and the alternatives to medication and how to use them, it is possible to make a reasoned and reasonable decision concerning medication intervention. In patients carefully selected so that the expected benefits outweigh the risks, medication intervention can be an effective addition to a nonmedication intervention program,

Chapter 14

COGNITIVE BEHAVIORAL APPROACHES AS ADJUNCTIVE TREATMENTS FOR ADHD CHILDREN AND THEIR FAMILIES

Lauren Braswell, Ph.D.

Cognitive behavioral approaches with children represent a small but growing portion of the larger literature exploring the usefulness of cognitive behavioral treatments with a variety of emotional and behavioral concerns. Cognitive behavioral therapy (CBT) has been the object of considerable study and discussion since the 1970s (Foreyt & Rathjen, 1978; Kendall & Hollon, 1979). A number of definitions of this therapeutic approach have been proposed over the years, but the definition initially offered by Kendall and Hollon (1979) defines CBT in its historical context. These authors describe the cognitive behavioral perspective as "a purposeful attempt to preserve the demonstrated effectiveness of behavior modification within a less doctrinaire context and to incorporate the cognitive activities of the client in the effort to produce therapeutic change" (Kendall & Hollon, 1979, p. 1). The intense research attention afforded cognitive behavioral approaches seems to have been the result of both the behaviorists' interest in the phenomenon of self-control (Bandura, 1969; Kanfer, 1970) and the development of cognitive learning models of psychotherapy (Beck, 1970; Ellis, 1962). Over the past two decades, CBTs of various forms have emerged as important, and often preferred, treatments for a host of difficulties manifested in adults, including depression, anxiety disorders, eating disorders, and marital discord (Freeman, Pretzer, Fleming, & Simon, 1990; Jacobson, 1987).

Since the publication of the first edition of this text, there has been a steady increase in research exploring the usefulness of CBTs with a variety of conditions presenting in childhood (Kendall, Panichelli-Mindel, & Gerow, 1995; Spence, 1994). Successful applications with children identified as depressed (Stark, Rouse, & Livingston, 1991), anxious (Kendall, 1994), and conduct-disordered (Kazdin, Siegel, & Bass, 1992) have emerged. Also, cognitive behavioral approaches have been successfully employed to treat social skills issues in child populations ranging from teacher-referred elementary students to incarcerated delinquents (Ager & Cole, 1991). Meta-analyses summarizing across diverse forms of cognitive behavioral interventions employed with equally diverse child populations indicate that this class of interventions is capable of producing meaningful improvements, particularly with children 11 and older (Durlak, Fuhrman, & Lampman, 1991). Within the context of educational research, an entire literature examining the value of cognitive behavioral approaches with specific academic concerns has also developed (Graham, Harris, & Reid, 1992; Trapani & Gettinger, 1996; Wong, 1992). Despite the variety of forms of CBT employed in these different applications, these approaches share the characteristic of focusing in some way upon the child's thoughts, beliefs, expectancies, or problem-solving processes as well as enacted behaviors.

But what does the literature say about the specific value of CBT approaches in meeting the needs of ADHD children and their families? The evolution in thinking regarding the role of CBT in the treatment of ADHD reflects, in many ways, the cycle of science. Within many fields, including mental health and education, a new approach to a given difficulty is greeted with great initial enthusiasm, the approach is widely employed, and then, with broader application, problems in the use of the method become apparent. As will be elaborated in this chapter, certain forms of CBT that seemed quite promising have not proven to be so, yet other types of CBT may play a circumscribed but useful role in adequately meeting the full treatment needs of children with ADHD and their families.

For the purpose of this chapter, three broad classes of CBT will be examined. One class or category of interventions with ADHD children is referred to as self-instruction/problem-solving training. It emphasizes the training of self-statements to be used in guiding task approach or problem solving with various types of academic and/or social problem situations. Next, cognitive restructuring approaches will be considered. This category of CBT focuses on identifying unhelpful thoughts, beliefs, or expectancies in the parent or child and then guiding the parent or child toward more useful ways of thinking. Self-management or self-regulation approaches will then be described and discussed in terms of appropriate applications with ADHD children and their families. Typically, self-regulation interventions involve the use of traditional operant principles but emphasize greater involvement of the child in the monitoring, evaluating, and reinforcing of his or her own behavior. In the final section of this chapter, discussion will focus on how an understanding of these forms of CBT might influence the process of treatment planning.

SELF-INSTRUCTIONAL/PROBLEM-SOLVING APPROACHES

As previously noted, when the first edition of this text was published, it was an open question whether or not self-instructional training/problem solving (SIT/PS) could add meaningfully to the treatment of ADHD youngsters. Problem-solving training approaches have a long history of application within both the adult and child treatment literature (D'Zurilla, 1986; Mahoney, 1977a; Spivack & Shure, 1974). Different authors' formulations of the problem-solving process have varied somewhat in their articulated stages or steps, but, generally speaking, there is similarity in the basic context of the various problem-solving formats that have been evaluated. Most approaches attempt to train the client to improve his or her capacity to engage in problem recognition and identification ("Slow down. What's the problem?"), alternative generation ("What are my choices/solutions?"), evaluation of consequences, ("What would happen with each choice?"), selection and implementation ("Now I need to do the best choice"), and evaluation of the success of the selected alternative ("How did that choice work? Should I make another choice next time?"). Self-instructional training, as initially articulated by Meichenbaum and Goodman (1971), was often presented as a more specific form of problem-solving training that provided the child with a verbal framework to guide his or her approach to a specific cognitive task. Later applications of self-instructional training addressed social as well as cognitive tasks, and the distinctions between self-instructional training and problem-solving training diminished (Braswell & Bloomquist, 1991; Kendall & Braswell, 1982).

From the perspective of face validity, it is easy to understand how training a more reflective approach to problem solving would seem like a useful strategy for children struggling with ADHD. Parents and teachers often comment that these children would do so much better if only they could stop and think a bit longer or tell themselves to slow down before responding in academic and social problem situations. Self-instructional/problem-solving approaches, buoyed by positive findings with teacher-selected samples of impulsive children (Kendall & Braswell, 1982; Reid & Borkowski, 1987; Schleser, Meyers, & Cohen, 1981) and positive patient satisfaction and program evaluation ratings (Bloomquist, August, & Garfinkel, 1989), have, in fact, received significant research attention over the past two decades. Baer and Nietzel (1991) conducted a meta-analytic review of the cognitive behavioral outcome literature with impulsive children and concluded that such interventions were associated with improvements of approximately one-third to three-quarters of a standard deviation relative to untreated controls, but the targeted groups had scores that fell close to comparison group means both before and after treatment. Thus, the severity of the behavioral concerns of these groups must be questioned. Also, as is common in such reviews, quite different therapeutic techniques were lumped together to determine an average effect size, making these findings not particularly useful for making decisions about the merits of a specific form of CBT.

In contrast to these positive reports with more mildly impaired samples, other researchers have not achieved such outcomes on either academic or social outcome measures when working with samples of children meeting full criteria for ADHD (see reviews by Abikoff, 1985, 1991; Kendall & Braswell, 1993). Although CBT may be capable of producing some positive outcomes in terms of changes on parent ratings and improvement in child self-esteem relative to interventions involving only supportive contact (Fehlings, Roberts, Humphries, & Dawe, 1991), there is little support for the view that child-focused CBT makes a meaningful contribution beyond outcomes achieved with medication and/or behavioral parent training for ADHD (Abikoff et al., 1988; R. T. Brown et al., 1986; R. T. Brown, Wynne et al., 1985). Most recently, Braswell et al. (1997) evaluated the effects of a two-year school-based child group training program that included significant parent and teacher training components with a sample of children displaying cross-setting disruptive behavior, two-thirds of whom met *DSM-III-R* criteria for ADHD. Results at posttest and one-year follow-up indicated no impact for this training relative to a control group that received parent and teacher information but no child-focused problem-solving training. Both conditions displayed improvement at immediate posttest but no meaningful long-term improvement that could be attributed to treatment.

Despite even this author's initial optimism regarding the potential for SIT/PS methods, the findings of others as well as my own more recent data force me to agree with the comment in Chapter 1 of this volume indicating that these approaches must be viewed as, at best, an intervention for adjunctive problems related to ADHD but not as an effective treatment for reducing primary symptoms. As previously observed, children with ADHD appear to need interventions that occur at the point of performance. The time interval between training and skill use in a target situation may be one factor contributing to the lack of meaningful impact of cognitive training for this population (Ingersoll & Goldstein, 1993).

Interestingly, this observation is also consistent with one of the domains in which cognitive problem-solving training seems to offer some promise or, more accurately, to perform no worse than other psychosocial interventions—that is, the arena of parent–ADHD adolescent conflict management. Barkley, Guevremont, Anastopoulos, and Fletcher (1992) compared the efficacy of structural family therapy, behavioral management training, and problem-solving/communication training modeled on the work of Robin and Foster (1989) in the treatment of ADHD adolescents and their parents. Posttest and three-month follow-up reports indicated reductions in negative communication, conflicts, and anger during conflicts, and improvement in the adolescents' school adjustment. Reductions in adolescents' symptomatology and maternal depression were noted and consumer satisfaction was high for all three approaches; however, more stringent judgment of clinically significant changes suggested that only 5% to 30% (depending on the criteria used) of the families displayed reliable improvement related to treatment. Unlike the studies cited earlier in which children were trained in individual or group contexts and then expected to use their skills with parents, teachers, and peers outside the training context, in the Barkley et al. (1992) study, the ADHD adolescents learned and practiced their problem-solving and communication skills with the very people with whom they were to employ their skills, that is, their parents. Thus, in this circumstance, intervention was not removed from at least one point of performance: the parent-child relationship.

Curiously, despite the negative findings regarding SIT/PS training for children identified by their ADHD symptomatology, such training has been found to be effective with children identified as aggressive and/or conduct-disordered (Kazdin et al., 1992; Kolko, Loar, & Sturnick, 1990; Lochman, 1992). Although these treatments included many components, cognitive problem-solving was the central strategy. These findings become even more interesting and puzzling when one notes the high rates of comorbidity for ADHD and aggressive, conduct-disordered behavior, as discussed in Chapter 4.

In conclusion, cognitive problem-solving interventions are not appropriate as a primary treatment for ADHD, although such approaches may be viable strategies for intervening with coexisting issues such as aggressive behavior and/or parent-adolescent conflict.

COGNITIVE RESTRUCTURING APPROACHES

A second type of cognitive behavioral intervention has emphasized the importance of attending to preexisting cognitions of the client and his or her family member and attempting to understand how these cognitions impact emotions and behavioral choices. Clearly, how one perceives events and explains them to oneself significantly influences how one feels and responds to perceived events. Although there is still much to clarify about the impact of parental cognitive style upon the child's cognitive style (Barrett, Rapee, Dadds, & Ryan, 1996; Brewin, Andrews, & Furnham, 1996), there is a burgeoning literature exploring the effect of both parent and child attributions on a variety of feelings and behavioral choices.

Parent and Teacher Attributional Issues

How significant adults in the lives of ADHD children think about these children is undoubtedly important. Some cognitive behaviorists tend to view the field of assessment of the parental cognitions as in its infancy (Epstein, Schlesinger, & Dryden, 1988), yet in reality, the study of parental attitudes and beliefs has a long-standing history within the psychology and child development literatures. As noted by Holden and Edwards (1989), the first review of research on parental attitudes occurred over fifty years ago (Stogdill, 1936)! Thus, an interest in the impact of parental thinking on parenting behavior and child adjustment began long before the emergence of a school of thought specifically referred to as cognitive behavioral.

This ever-expanding literature has yielded fascinating information about the interplay of cognitions, emotions, and parenting behavior. As discussed in Chapter 16, parental beliefs regarding the causes (e.g., intentional versus unintentional) and controllability of child behavior can affect the parent's emotional and disciplinary response to the child (Johnston, Patenaude, & Inman, 1992). Studies of families with non-behavior-problem children suggest that parents of these children tend to attribute negative behavior to external, situational factors, whereas families with difficult children attribute child misbehavior to factors internal to the child (Baden & Howe, 1992; Dix & Lochman, 1990). When parents perceive their child's misbehavior as more the result of dispositional factors, more intentional, and more under the child's control, they are likely to express more negative affect and attach greater importance to responding to the child's misbehavior (Dix, Ruble, Grusec, & Nixon, 1986). Although responding to the child's misbehavior may be extremely appropriate, the combination of negative emotional arousal in the parent and child-blaming attributions regarding the misbehavior is associated with the use of overreactive or harsh parenting behaviors (Smith & O'Leary, 1995).

Extending these issues specifically to the families of ADHD children, Johnston and Patenaude (1994) asked parents to share their beliefs about both the inattentive-overactive and oppositional-defiant behaviors observed in their children. Parents tended to view the child's oppositional-defiant behavior as more under the child's control, and this type of behavior elicited more negative reactions from parents. Thus, with parents of children with ADHD it also appears that parental attributions of child behavior as relatively more controllable and internal results in more negative emotional reactions. In addition, Johnston and Patenaude (1994) observed that parents who were most upset by oppositional-defiant child behaviors also reported reduced parenting satisfaction and a lower sense of parental efficacy. The observation of a reduced sense of parental efficacy echoes earlier work by Bugental and Cortez (1988). These authors found that adults who perceive that they have little control over a discipline encounter are also more likely to report greater negative affect, helplessness, and arousal in response to difficult children than adults who espouse beliefs reflecting high perceived control.

Taken as a whole, these observations point to the importance of attending to parental attributions about the causes and controllability of various child behaviors so that dysfunctional attributions, expectancies, or beliefs can be replaced with more functional viewpoints. Unrealistic or unhelpful beliefs have been associated with increased levels of parent-adolescent conflict (Roehling & Robin, 1986). Similarly, others have speculated about the role unhelpful thinking might play in exacerbating the challenges of parenting or teaching an ADHD child. Table 14–1, adapted from Braswell and Bloomquist (1991), presents several common unhelpful thoughts that parents and teachers of children with ADHD have informally shared regarding various aspects of ADHD. Being sensitive to the presence of such thinking could help the practitioner be sure to address related concerns in the context of parent groups or individual parent sessions. Although some of these unhelpful thoughts can be easily modified by straightforward educational approaches, in other circumstances it may be necessary to engage in more formal cognitive restructuring. For example, such an approach might involve helping the family consider other ways of interpreting their child's behavior or guiding them in the development of an experiment that could test the usefulness of the beliefs in question. Anastopoulos (1991) observed that the ADHD child's inconsistency of performance and situational variability of symptoms may, in particular, lead to the development of faulty beliefs in parents and teachers, such as "He's just lazy" or "She should just try harder." Misunderstandings about the assessment process and treatment options may also need to be addressed. Any practitioner working with ADHD children and their families is well aware of the host of misconceptions that may be associated with medication treatment in particular. In fact, some families' negative views regarding pharmacological treatments are so strongly held and resistant to influence by information that simple parent education approaches may not be adequate for broadening the parents' perspective. Providing such families with repeated opportunities to interact with families who hold other beliefs about treatment may, over time, yield more change in parental attitudes than direct attempts by the clinician to alter these misconceptions.

Treatments other than medication also interact with parental beliefs. Borden and Brown (1989) found that parental attributions for the symptoms of ADHD children were influenced by whether a cognitive behavioral treatment was offered alone or in combination with medication. When cognitive behavioral treatment was offered alone, parents were more likely to express the belief that their children were capable of changing their behavior. Although expectations of change can be positive, one would hope that, ideally, treatment is being presented in a manner that leads to realistic expectations for change and accurate beliefs about what is and is not controllable in a given circumstance. In essence, the clinician has the complex task of communicating the viewpoint that, although parent behavior does not cause ADHD, parental attitudes and behaviors, as well as choices of treatment, can have an impact on the child's level of functioning within parameters determined by biological factors.

Child Attributional Issues

Compared to our understanding of the role of attributional issues in parent behavior, less is known about the attributions of ADHD children and how these might influence their emotions and behavior. In the past, it was observed that relative to same-age controls,

Table 14–1.   Commonly reported problematic parent and/or teacher beliefs regarding ADHD and possible therapist responses

- This child is acting this way intentionally.

  (Alternative: Highlight the importance of not personalizing the symtoms of the ADHD child.)

- It's the parent's/teacher's fault the child is experiencing these difficulties.

  (Alternative: Emphasize the importance of engaging in constructive problem solving rather than playing the "blame game.")

- It's my fault the child is having these difficulties.

  (Alternative: Emphasize the importance of parents not playing the "blame game" with themselves, for it can diminish their capacity to be an effective resource for their child.)

- I have no control over this child. I give up.

  (Alternative: Note that the parent has total control over his or her response to the child's behavior, not total control over the child.)

- This child's furture is bleak. He/she will grow up to be irresponsible, a criminal, etc.

  (Alternative: Note that in our concern for this child's future, we need to be sure that we focus on what needs to happen to make today better rather than demoralizing ourselves worrying about what might happen.)

- This child should behave like other children. I shouldn't have to teach this child how to behave. I shouldn't have to treat this child any differently than any other child.

  (Alternative: Note that, actually, we do have to teach this child to behave, for just as children master academic content at different rates, they also vary in how able they are to "master" behavioral expectations. Just as some children have legitimate needs for additional instruction so they can learn to read, others need more behavioral supports so they can learn to display appropriate behavior.)

- This child must do well in school (or sports, or be popular, etc.) to be viewed as successful within this family.

  (Alternative: Help the parents broaden their conceptualization of what it means to be a successful human being and accept that the route to feeling worthwhile for their ADHD child may be quite different from the pathway pursued by their other children.)

- This child is "defective." We shouldn't expect too much of this child, for he/she has so many problems.

  (Alternative: Help family understand that the issue is developing *appropriate expectations* for the child at home and school, not dropping all expectations.)

- Medications are the answer for this child and that's all we need to pursue.

  (Alternative: Help the family recognize the importance of good parent education and advocacy within the child's school to be sure all the child's major treatment needs are being addressed.)

- Medications are to be avoided at all costs.

  (Alternative: Help the family recognize the positive role that medication might play in a given child's treatment plan and that the use of medication does not imply failure or inadequacy on the part of the parent.)

ADHD children have a more externalized locus of control (Linn & Hodge, 1982). More recently, however, it has been suggested that among children with psychiatric problems involving behavior and emotions, locus of control does not differ from normal children (J. Elliott, 1996). However, this author utilized a mixed sample of children.

Attributions have been of interest in terms of their relationship to response to treatment in children (Braswell, Koehler, & Kendall, 1985). Some investigators in the past have even suggested that treatments should be consistent with a child's attributional style (Bugental et al., 1977). For example, more externally oriented children might benefit most from receiving interventions such as medication and externally controlled behavior management, whereas those with more internal loci of control might benefit from approaches that place a greater emphasis on self-regulation strategies, such as those highlighted in this chapter. This consideration, however, must also take into account the fact that certain treatments have the potential to change one's degree of internality versus externality. For example, those receiving self-management-oriented treatments may increase their sense of personal control (Bugental, Collins, Collins, & Chaney, 1978).

Interestingly, this issue of how treatments interact with and/or can change one's attributional pattern has been studied in relation to the use of medication with ADHD children. In the past, concerns have been raised that medication treatment might have the negative attributional side effect of decreasing ADHD children's sense of personal control over their successes (Whalen & Henker, 1980). Fortunately, a body of research by Pelham, Milich, and colleagues speaks directly to this concern (Carlson, Pelham, Milich, & Hoza, 1993; Milich et al., 1989, 1991). The results of these studies indicate that when ADHD children are treated with stimulant medication, they exhibit more appropriate behavior and achieve greater success on study tasks. When experiencing such success, the majority of ADHD children in their samples displayed the attributional pattern exhibited by normal adults, which is to attribute positive behavior or successes to their own efforts and failure to factors external to themselves. In addition, with medication, children displayed greater persistance when confronted with difficult tasks. Among medicated subjects, even prior exposure to insolvable tasks did not result in a more "helpless," less persistent approach to subsequent tasks. In their discussion of these findings, Pelham, Murphy, et al. (1992) note, however, that though these results characterize the response of most of the children in their studies, there was a subgroup of ADHD children who did manifest a more maladaptive cognitive style of attributing success to external factors, in this case medication, and failure to factors internal to themselves. Children displaying this style also displayed greater behavioral disruption. The authors note that it is not clear whether this maladaptive style reflects the presence of a mood disorder, exposure to adults who attribute success to the medication, or some other factor. Fortunately, the findings of this body of research suggest that for the majority of ADHD children, successful treatment with medication results in children who are able to take credit for their successes and are more persistent, less helpless problem solvers.

In considering the role of attributional issues it must be noted that such concerns are rarely likely to be the primary targets of treatment for the ADHD child or his or her family. Rather, they may temporarily become the focus when an unhelpful belief or attitude seems to be interfering with the child's or family's acquisition of a particular skill or hindering effective utilization of primary treatment options.

SELF-CONTROL/SELF-REGULATION APPROACHES

A number of methods potentially suitable for use with children presenting ADHD symptomatology fall into the category of self-control or self-regulation methods. Most self-regulation approaches have a consistent set of discrete components, such as those outlined by Kanfer (1970b), including self-monitoring, self-recording, self-evaluation, and self-reinforcement. The self-monitoring phase refers to the act of noting the occurrence of a specifically defined behavior or cognitive event (e.g., on-task behavior, blurt-outs, negative self-statements). In the self-recording phase, the client makes some type of record of the observed event; depending on the event being monitored, this might involve actions as diverse as making a mark on a recording form, adjusting a wrist counter, or recording a narrative description in a special journal. The self-evaluation phase involves comparing the data the individual has observed and/or recorded against a predetermined standard, such as a treatment goal, a set of classroom rules, or a certain target percentage of on-task behavior. If the target goal is achieved, then the individual can administer a prearranged self-reinforcement, which could be anything from recording points earned or number of items correct on a special chart to selecting a tangible or activity reward. Some systems include the option for self-punishment for the occurrence of undesirable behaviors; this could include point loss within an ongoing contingency system or more unique consequences determined by the self-management plan participants.

Self-management approaches have a long history within the behavioral psychology literature and have received increasing attention in the educational literature. Carter (1993) notes that self-control/self-management approaches have great appeal for educators because these methods decrease the student's reliance on external change agents, seem to engender less student resistance than traditional external control strategies, and inherently involve the student in his or her own behavior change. Self-regulation approaches are generally viewed as most appropriate for use with children in third grade and older. Adolescents are considered excellent candidates for self-regulation approaches, given that these methods increase their responsibility in the intervention process and decrease the role of external authorities.

General reviews of the self-management literature have concluded that these methods can be useful with children manifesting a variety of academic and behavioral concerns in the school environment (Nelson, Smith, Young, & Dodd, 1991; Shapiro & Cole, 1994). More specifically, self-monitoring has been found to be equal or superior to teacher monitoring for decreasing off-task behavior and improving academic work products with difficult-to-teach, nonhandicapped elementary students (Bahr, Fuchs, Fuchs, Ferstrom, & Stecker, 1993). Both elementary and secondary learning-disabled and academically at-risk students have achieved improved on-task behavior with self-monitoring approaches (Hallahan, Lloyd, Kneedler, & Marshall, 1982; Hughes & Hendrickson, 1987; Prater, Joy, Chilman, Temple, & Miller, 1991). Improved classroom behavior has also been observed with students identified as presenting with behavior disorders (Rhode, Morgan, & Young, 1983) and/or as severely emotionally disturbed (Dunlap et al., 1995; Ninness, Ellis, Miller, Baker, & Rutherford, 1995). Graham and Harris (1989) have demonstrated improved writing skills in learning-disabled students using a self-management approach called self-regulated strategy development, and

Graham et al. (1992) summarize a range of other interesting academic outcomes that have been achieved with self-management interventions.

Within this literature, there is debate over the relative merits of training children to monitor attention-to-task versus monitoring academic productivity or performance. Both approaches appear to increase attention-to-task, but some investigators find monitoring of attention also increases productivity, although others do not (K. Harris, 1986; Lloyd, Bateman, Landrum, & Hallahan, 1989; Reid & Harris, 1993). Interestingly, Reid and Harris (1993) report that, when asked, students say they prefer graphing the number of practice trials correctly completed (monitoring performance) to monitoring attention, which some described as being intrusive and disruptive of their thinking process. These articles conclude that the preferred form of self-monitoring may depend on the specifics of the learning situation as well as the preferences of the students involved.

Although the self-management literature continues to grow and become more refined, the actual number of studies with children identified as ADHD is still quite small. Barkley, Copeland, and Sivage (1980) trained ADHD children to evaluate their own behavior in relation to posted classroom rules whenever a tone was sounded. If a child's self-evaluation matched that of an independent observer, then the child received tokens that could be exchanged for backup rewards. This approach was effective in producing improved on-task behavior and decreased disruptive behavior during seatwork in the training session but did not improve behavior during group instruction time in the training classroom or generalize to behavior in the regular education classroom.

Hinshaw and colleagues have described a self-evaluation approach they refer to as the "match game," which is suitable for use in child groups or small classroom settings (Hinshaw & Erhardt, 1991; Hinshaw, Henker, & Whalen, 1984b). This form of self-evaluation was adapted from Turkewitz, O'Leary, and Ironsmith (1975) and involves clarifying a specific behavioral criterion for reinforcement, such as waiting for others to finish before speaking or keeping one's hands off others. When implementing this procedure, the leader halts the ongoing activity of the group or class and displays a "match game" sheet that states the behavioral criterion and includes a rating system ranging from 1 (not at all good) to 5 (great). The leader then asks the children to think about how well they have executed the behavioral criterion over the designated time period and to rate themselves on the 5-point scale. The leader further explains that the leader or the group assistant will also rate each child. If the child's rating is within one point of the leader's rating, the child earns a bonus point for accurate self-evaluation. The children then each announce their rating and the reasons for their rating and the leader does the same, being careful to give detailed feedback for why a particular rating was selected. Hinshaw and Erhardt (1991) recommend that, initially, bonus points for accuracy should be awarded even if the quality of the behavior is low, because the first goal is to train accurate self-evaluation. Over time, however, the behavioral expectations can be raised by requiring that the quality of the behavior be at least acceptable before the bonus point is awarded. Standards can also be tightened by requiring the child to exactly match rather than just come close to the leader's rating. This procedure is most appropriate for use in self-contained classes, resource rooms, therapy groups, or other small-group settings. It could also be conducted by a paraprofessional working with a small number of special needs children in a mainstream classroom environment.

In an interesting application of the match game procedure, Hinshaw et al. (1984a) trained ADHD children to accurately evaluate their own social behavior (sharing, listening to adult directions, not fighting). The investigators compared the effects of such training with the impact of traditional external reinforcement in the presence and absence of conjoint medication treatment. At posttest, the group receiving both self-evaluation training and medication exhibited the most positive social behavior. The behavior of the group receiving self-evaluation only was also observed to be better than that of the external-reinforcement-only group. These findings are consistent with those of Chase and Clement (1985), who observed that the combination of psychostimulant treatment and self-reinforcement was more effective than either treatment alone in improving the academic performance of ADHD children. More recently, Ajibola and Clement (1995) attempted to correct some of the methodological weaknesses of Chase and Clement (1985) by examining the impact of more than one dose of methylphenidate and including multiple outcome measures. In this more refined and controlled evaluation, the combination of self-reinforcement for each completed response and low-dose methylphenidate was more effective in improving academic performance than either treatment alone.

One could also view correspondence training (CT; Paniagua, 1987) as a variant of self-monitoring/self-evaluation training. There are several forms of CT, but this procedure basically involves reinforcing matches between children's public statements about how they will or did behave and their actual behavior in the situation in question. Thus, it is similar to the training of accurate self-evaluation that occurs in the context of other types of self-regulation programs. In studies by Paniagua (1987) and Paniagua and Black (1990), ADHD children were able to demonstrate more improved on-task behavior and decreased disruptive behavior in response to the enactment of CT.

Another study by Hinshaw and colleagues (Hinshaw, Henker, & Whalen, 1984a) evaluated a stress inoculation approach to helping ADHD children cope with anger-inducing situations. Although this intervention involved more than just the common elements of self-management training, it placed great emphasis on training the children to monitor and recognize both external events that triggered anger responses and internal cognitive and physiological cues of anger arousal. The children were then presented with various strategies they could select to effectively cope with the provoking situation and their own reactions to the situation. The children then engaged in what Hinshaw and Melnick (1992) discussed as the most essential element of the training: reinforced practice of the selected coping skills with increasingly challenging situations. Children in this training condition displayed increases in their use of active coping responses in a provocation situation relative to children in the control condition. Half the subjects in each condition were also treated with medication, which resulted in decreased intensity of responding but did not impact the children's use of specific strategies. These results were obtained in an immediate posttest, so information about the durability or generalizability of the improved responding does not exist. The findings of Hinshaw et al. (1984b) and Hinshaw and Melnick (1992) highlight the potential of well-titrated combinations of psychosocial and pharmacological treatment to produce change in domains such as anger/frustration management. The work of Ninness et al. (1995) with severely emotionally disturbed, aggressive teens also supports the value of self-management training approaches that include creative opportunities to practice the use of aggression-control skills in real-life settings.

In light of the available research, self-management approaches must be viewed as potentially useful methods of addressing both academic and behavioral issues associated with ADHD. In addition, these approaches offer a means by which the ADHD child can become somewhat more directly involved in the science of his or her own behavior management. As long as such procedures are implemented with focused behavioral targets and realistic expectations, these methods may become the means by which ADHD children can function at the top of their biologically determined behavioral range, even in somewhat nonoptimal settings.

SUMMARY: TREATMENT PLANNING CONSIDERATIONS

Given the current status of the literature concerning children with ADHD and the cognitive behavioral approaches just reviewed, what should a practitioner consider when engaging in treatment planning? First, a child group curriculum that focuses on broad-based problem-solving and verbal self-instructional skills, such as the kind of group advocated in the first edition of this text, is not a good choice for an ADHD child. Group training that focuses on identifying one's own anger cues and learning and practicing specific strategies for successfully coping with provocation might be useful for those ADHD children whose peer relations and school adjustment are seriously impacted by their poor anger/frustration management. As will be discussed in Chapter 16, such training should offer many opportunities for reinforced practice of the newly acquired skills and include skills practice in real-life settings. Problem-solving training involving the parents and ADHD teens may be a useful strategy for reducing parent-child conflict.

Cognitive restructuring approaches are perhaps best viewed as ready adjuncts to any form of treatment when it appears that the ADHD child and/or family members are being influenced by expectations or beliefs that are not helpful for the building of a positive parent-child bond and/or are interfering with the enactment of other potentially useful treatment. Ideally, such cognitive restructuring would help parents and the child accept aspects of the situation that they cannot change, while simultaneously helping them take responsibility for what they can, in fact, control.

Self-management approaches can be valuable additions to the ADHD child's behavior management program in the classroom, particularly to the extent that the procedures fully engage the child in the process of learning to evaluate the appropriateness of his or her own behavior. As previously noted, self-regulation procedures are most appropriate for children with a mental age of approximately 8 years and older. Incorporating elements of self-management may be particularly appropriate in work with adolescent clients. In addition, self-management procedures can be useful as a means of helping parents keep track of their own attempts to enact more positive child management approaches, as illustrated in Bloomquist (1996).

Although medication and behavioral management approaches must be viewed as first-order treatments for ADHD, cognitive behavioral methods can serve as useful adjuncts in tailoring treatment plans to meet the needs of a particular child, family, and school staff.

Chapter 15

MANAGING AND EDUCATING CHILDREN WITH ADHD

Sam Goldstein, Ph.D.
Clare Jones, Ph.D.

Schools exert a significant influence on children's development (Entwisle, 1990). Beginning at age 5, children spend the largest proportion of their day at school. Their experiences at school affect them in multiple ways. The school environment has the potential to either insulate or protect children from other stressful risks in their lives; however, all things being equal, school factors in themselves contribute to life outcome for children. For example, school size is associated with school drop out: smaller schools are more protective, and so fewer children drop out (Rumberger, 1987). Dropping out is associated with low academic motivation, achievement, and commitment, which have all been linked in turn to adolescent drug use (Barnes & Welte, 1986; Coombs, Wellisch, & Fawzy, 1985; Hawkins, Catalano, & Miller, 1992). Rutter, Maughan, Mortimore, and Ouston (1979) demonstrated longitudinally that from birth through tenth grade, children vary in their behavior, attendance, school performance, success, and delinquency. These outcomes have been systematically and strongly associated with school characteristics (Zimmerman & Arunkumar, 1994).

School-based interventions have primarily employed a deficit model (Weissberg, Caplan, & Sivo, 1989), typically targeting children likely to be educationally disadvantaged, disruptive, or delinquent (Maughan, 1988). These programs stress individual behavior change rather than creating a climate or community to foster the development of appropriate behavior in everyone, including those at risk. Rutter (1987) has suggested that schools can be protective because they promote self-esteem and self-efficacy, providing opportunities for children to experience success and enabling them to develop important social and problem-solving skills. School-based supportive ties have been demonstrated to buffer children against other risk conditions in the home and out of the school environment (Brook, Nomura, & Cohen, 1989; Dubois, Felner, Brand, Adam, & Evans, 1992).

The motivational climate of schools also has an influence on children's feelings of self-efficacy and self-esteem (Maehr & Nicholls, 1980). These qualities are tied to goals related to task and performance. Task goals stress learning for learning's sake and successes measured by improvement; the focus is on the intrinsic value of learning (Nicholls, 1984). In contrast, performance goals stress demonstrating superior ability relative to others or avoiding appearing unable; the goal is decidedly competitive in nature and success is defined in terms of relative standing on some scale (e.g., test score, grade-point average). In performance goals, emphasis is on the extrinsic aspects of learning. Performance orientation necessitates that there be winners and losers, and children in these situations tend to attribute failure to lack of ability (Ames & Ames, 1984; Elliot & Dweck, 1988). It appears that the majority of North American schools operate in this fashion. Thus, it is not surprising that children with ADHD struggle at times even beyond what might be expected based on ADHD symptoms. What takes place in school for children with ADHD is critical to their success.

In contrast, children in task-focused situations are more likely to view failures as challenges, to try harder, and to develop more useful strategies. The view that mistakes are something to be learned from rather than reflecting failure is critical in developing an internal sense of self-efficacy and locus of control. Students who have an internal locus report less negative effect in response to failure; they respond with greater self-efficacy when pursuing task goals than when pursuing performance goals (Urdan, Turner, Park, & Midgley, 1992). Task-oriented schools influence perceptions of self and self-esteem (Ames, 1992). A sense of belonging enhances motivation and has also been shown to demonstrate the capacity to be an insulator against adolescent substance abuse (Hawkins et al., 1992). Thus, schools must play a protective role, not only by identifying and working with children experiencing ADHD but by offering a curriculum focused on building self-confidence and instill resilience.

The presence of knowledgeable, understanding teachers, the availability of appropriate support systems, and the opportunities for every student to engage successfully in a variety of activities are imperative. These opportunities build self-esteem, resilience, and most likely contribute to the future lives of children with ADHD. Yet, as straightforward an issue as education would appear to be for children with ADHD, controversy abounds. This should not be surprising, given that controversy follows ADHD regardless of the setting or situation in which it presents. Reid, Maag, and Vasa (1994) note, "not since the establishment of learning disability as a special education category has a condition so captivated both the professional community and the general public as has attention deficit hyperactivity disorder" (p. 198). These authors contest the validity of ADHD as a psychiatric disorder, question whether students with this disorder have educational problems that are not addressed under existing categories, challenge the reliability of estimates used to justify the need for additional services, and question whether any services offered students in school are specific to ADHD or necessitate the creation of an additional disability category. As Fiore et al. (1993) report, the research-based knowledge on ADHD is exploratory, not prescriptive, with findings yielding inconsistent conclusions. Relatively few daily educational interventions for ADHD have been systematically evaluated. Thus, it is not surprising that Reid et al. (1994) conclude that all of these factors preclude ADHD from being made a specific disability category for the schools. Further, they argue that there is a danger in implicitly allowing new categories in the absence of solid empirical knowledge. However, others have argued that children's needs should be the primary means of determining whether they qualify for assistance rather than the qualification for a diagnosis or educational placement (G. Stoner & Carey, 1992; Zirkel, 1992).

Although Reid et al. (1994) do not suggest that children with ADHD are not in need of help, their cynical stance certainly decreases the likelihood that immediate help will be forthcoming (Hakola, 1992). Nonetheless, in the past decade, ADHD has become a widely used term in school systems throughout the world. The description has been used to identify children and adolescents presenting in class as inattentive, hyperactive, and impulsive. In 1992, the U.S. Department of Education set clear guidelines necessitating that American schools identify and provide services for children with ADHD. There has been a groundswell of literature directed at educators (Bowley & Walther, 1992; Burcham, Carlson, & Milich, 1993; Busch, 1993; Buchoff, 1990; Schwean, Parkinson, Francis, & Lee, 1993), yet to this date, classroom teachers continue to receive minimum direction and instruction in working with these children in the classroom setting. This text will not substitute for the need to aggressively educate all teachers concerning ADHD but, as with the first edition, will provide practitioners with a practical means to consult with regular and special educators.

Effective interventions in educational settings will require the development and implementation of programmatic behavior and teacher support (Horner et al., 1991). DuPaul and Stoner (1994) suggest that the design, implementation, and evaluation of these interventions must be data based, driven by child advocacy, focused on attainment of clearly identified socially valid goals, thoroughly defined, implemented with integrity, and must lead to increased rates of appropriate behavior rather than just decreasing undesirable behavior. It is also important to keep in mind that student success may have different meanings for different teachers. For some, success for students with ADHD might mean reduced restlessness, fewer classroom disruptions, mastery of academic material, completion of assignments, following directions the first time, improved peer relations, and even enhanced self-esteem (Greene, 1993). The degree to which a teacher's definition of success is compatible with a student's capacity for change is critical. Practitioners are advised to make certain they understand teacher attitudes, personality, and the compatibility of teacher factors to classroom management recommendations. Practitioners should be aware of available resources within the community to refer families to. It takes skill to structurally plan collaboratively rather than unilaterally; in their unique role, practitioners may increasingly find themselves in a position not only of advocacy but of negotiation as they attempt to balance needed service with available resources.

THE PRACTITIONER AS CLASSROOM CONSULTANT

It is not surprising that children with ADHD have experienced increasing problems in our school systems over the past thirty years. Successful school performance is dependent on children's ability to persist, concentrate, and inhibit and delay gratification efficiently, and schools demand competence in these skills at earlier ages. It is essential that practitioners assist the ADHD child's teachers in understanding why this group of children will be at significant risk and often unable to meet the typical classroom demands. It is likely that in school, children with ADHD develop a host of secondary behavioral and adjustment problems in part in response to frequent and repeated failure. The model presented in this chapter is not meant as a step-by-step all-encompassing classroom management or educational system. Practitioners are referred to a number of excellent resources in this regard (C. Jones, 1991, 1994; H. Parker, 1988; Rief, 1993).

Effective management and education of the ADHD child in the classroom is a multistep process. Skillful teachers must be willing to shift focus from performance to task. They must understand the ADHD child's behaviors from the perspective of developmental impairment and be able to make the distinction between incompetent and noncompliant behavior. It is helpful for teachers to understand the causes of ADHD, its developmental course, and the common symptomatic manifestations of ADHD children in the classroom. The effects that specific behaviors, such as punishment and negative reinforcement, may have secondarily on this population of children must also be understood. Teachers must be able to identify and define problem behavior in the classroom through practical, operational, nonblaming means. Once identified, problems can be prioritized and interventions developed.

It is also important for practitioners to be mindful of teachers' beliefs, attitudes, and perceptions concerning ADHD. For example, Cornett-Ruiz and Hendricks (1993) evaluated the effects of labeling ADHD behaviors on peer and teacher judgments with thirty-nine primary education teachers. They found that teachers' first impressions and predictions of the child's future behavior were based not on the diagnostic label but on the child's behavior. Abikoff et al. (1993) found that teachers tended to exert a bias, unidirectional in nature, resulting in their inflating the severity of ADHD symptoms when they were exhibited along with oppositional defiance. In contrast, teachers rated oppositional and conduct problem behaviors accurately regardless of the presence of ADHD symptoms. Finally, Power, Hess, and Bennett (1995) found that among elementary and middle school teachers, daily school home notes were rated as a more acceptable intervention for ADHD than response-cost behavior management or stimulant medication alone; teachers rated medication as far more acceptable when used in combination with behavioral interventions than when used alone. The research also indicated that knowledge of ADHD in years of teaching experience was unrelated to ratings of acceptability. Interestingly, teachers were differentiated into several profile types with regard to their perceptions of treatment acceptability for ADHD; they are more likely to endorse recommendations for children to receive medication when behavior management interventions are also applied simultaneously. Finally, teachers generally view time-efficient, positive-consequence interventions more favorably than more time-consuming, reductive methods. Practitioners need to be aware that teachers differ markedly with regard to their perceptions of the acceptability of interventions for ADHD. Thus, they must make certain they understand teachers' beliefs about interventions as well as symptoms.

It is also important for the practitioner to be sensitive to the teacher's ability and the demands of each classroom. Some teachers are unable to make significant changes in their teaching style or may not have the time to implement more extensive interventions. It is important that the practitioner not encourage a power struggle between the child's family and the school. In some situations, placing the child with another teacher or providing out-of-school interventions is in the best interest of the child in the long term.

Given the nature of ADHD, the hallmark of intervention is to make the task interesting and the payoff valuable. As Zentall (1995) notes, the educational environment for ADHD children must be structured to allow them to talk, move, and question; such a program will allow them to start, stop, and engage in tasks in a nondisruptive fashion. Interventions can be designed to be situation-specific and implemented within the classroom or in a non-classroom setting. Interventions can then be stratified into those designed to help the child manage himself or herself and those that may alter the environment, thereby assisting the child to function more effectively.

Educators often feel alienated and misunderstood by professionals outside of the classroom or educational system. Community-based professionals often make recommendations and provide reports directly to parents concerning what should happen in the classroom without communicating with the teacher or understanding classroom variables. This creates secondary problems rather than contributing to successful intervention and the effective management of the ADHD child's problems within the classroom. As a practitioner outside of the school system and therefore an "invited guest" to the school, it is important to treat the situation with courtesy and respect. Communication can be encouraged by sending a brief letter with the teacher questionnaires during the evaluative process. It may be beneficial to ask teachers to provide input concerning specific areas of problems, current concerns, and questions they would like to see addressed in an evaluation. Once permission is obtained from parents, providing the educational team with a copy of the written evaluation or making a follow-up phone call to the classroom teacher also helps to establish a professional link with the school, setting the groundwork for future communication. For physicians, teachers' feedback and observations of the child's behavioral change in the classroom in response to medication is essential. If teachers perceive that their opinions are respected and their input is important to the process they will be advocates in the child's treatment.

Suggestions for behavior management should be made within the context of the existing classroom. Some teaching styles and personalities simply do not adapt well to certain behavioral recommendations. Making those recommendations rigidly without understanding the teacher's style and personality will result in increased problems and, in all likelihood, increased resistance from the teacher. Teachers should be invited to communicate directly with the practitioner whenever concerns are raised or help is needed. The message from the practitioner to the classroom teacher must be clear: *You are an essential part of this child's treatment team.* This is true for both special and regular educators. Frequently, the special educators within the school system act as a liaison, providing additional assistance and ideas to the classroom teacher.

Over the past ten years, educational systems have accepted and undertaken the responsibility of educating their faculty concerning definition, problems, cause, developmental course, educational issues, and intervention of ADHD in childhood. Although hands-on inservices and video satellite workshops are effective, one of the most efficient means of educating educators about ADHD continues to be practical written materials and videos (e.g., Goldstein & Goldstein, 1990b; C. Jones, 1991, 1994; H. Parker, 1988; Rief, 1993). These materials contain information that is straightforward and reasonable to implement. However, the majority of materials available to educators focuses on the elementary school years (Fiore et al., 1993). This is not surprising, as the elementary school years are the most common for diagnosis and intervention. There are, however, increasing efforts to provide secondary educators with practical, useful strategies as well (C. Jones, 1994).

Stephen Covey's (1989) axiom *Seek to understand before being understood* cannot be too strongly emphasized when dealing with ADHD in educational settings. Educators making change based on understanding are more likely to be active, motivated participants; educators lacking an understanding of strategies recommended and uncertain why these interventions will be of benefit are more likely to be passive, frequently unsuccessful agents of change.

A LOGICAL MODEL

Goldstein and Goldstein (1990) first offered a model for classroom intervention suggesting the categorization of strategies into two sets. The first set is designed to change cognitions, thoughts, and feelings, with the goal of increasing self-management in children with ADHD. The second set is designed to provide managed consequences as well as manipulate environmental factors to increase the likelihood of the child's classroom success. Zentall (1995) subsequently suggested a model emphasizing the need for children with ADHD to move, talk/question, and learn. Zentall emphasizes that a focus on antecedents directly affects learning and behavior and falls within the realm of what teachers are trained to do. This model suggests that when students are allowed to move, channel activity appropriately, talk and question actively, and are provided with novel, interesting instruction, they function better in classroom settings. (The interested reader is referred to Zentall (1995), for an expanded explanation and description of this model.)

Based in part on Zentall's suggestions, Goldstein (1994) defined three key goals for children with ADHD trying to fit into the existing educational system: to start, to stop, and to think in a manner consistent with others. As a framework for educators, these goals focus intervention on increasing the child's ability to start when everyone else starts, for both academic and nonacademic tasks; to stop when everyone else stops, including completing the product required; and to think about what the teacher is directing students to focus on. Everyone learns best when a conceptual framework is provided and understood; thus, facilitating educators' ability to develop an initial framework will encourage the reception of and ultimately the ability to successfully implement strategies offered. Also, for children with ADHD in classroom settings, making tasks interesting and payoffs valuable while allowing for opportunities for repeated trials of success are key ingredients of educational interventions.

How can an educator effectively individualize instruction for all students? For the time being, the general framework and educational system offered for children is inadequate for children with ADHD to meet their educational potential. Although it can be argued that what is good educationally for ADHD children is likely equally good for all learners, it does not appear that in the near future the educational systems of the world will be receptive to major modifications. Thus, practitioners need to facilitate teachers' receptiveness to making specific modifications for the ADHD child in the classroom regardless of age or grade, and the logical model offered must not only increase understanding but facilitate motivation. In part, motivation can be facilitated by helping educators understand that the modifications suggested will not be difficult to administer and, from a cost-benefit perspective, will be worth the effort in students' positive outcome. We suggest that practitioners incorporate the talk, move/question, learn and start, stop, think models, as these offer a transition from understanding ADHD to impacting ADHD problems in the classroom. This framework is built around making tasks more interesting and payoffs more valuable and providing an increased number of trials to success. Additionally, three concepts are critical in working with ADHD children (C. Jones, 1989):

1. ***Brevity.*** As discussed in earlier chapters, children with ADHD begin most tasks with less effort than is necessary. Although they may not decline in sustained attention more quickly than other children, the fact that they begin with less attention results in their more quickly falling below a threshold necessary to remain on task (van der Meere & Sergeant, 1988a). Thus, the axiom that attention in classroom settings is greatest in short activities is valid for children with ADHD. Frequent brief drills or lessons covering small chunks of information result in better classroom performance. As discussed in earlier chapters, children with ADHD likely require more trials to success; the brevity concept suggests that these trials be of short duration. Further, the actual pace at which tasks are presented has been found to be an instructable variable related to classroom problem behaviors (Carnine, 1976; Dunlap, Dyer, & Koegel, 1983; West & Sloan, 1986). Data collected with special and general education students show that relatively fast pacing within the capacity of the student's ability to learn is associated with fewer complaints of misbehavior in the classroom.

2. ***Variety.*** Douglas (1983) suggested that children with ADHD experience "flagging attention": as tasks are presented repeatedly, they perform with decreasing effort and motivation. Thus, in a commonsense way, children with ADHD may be quicker to perceive tasks as repetitive or uninteresting. If they require the need for repeated trials to develop the same level of competence as their peers, the challenge for the classroom educator is to present the same material in slightly different ways or different applications to maximize the child's interest in the task. Further, the availability of choice among what is to be learned is also an important variable (Dunlap, Kern-Dunlap, Clarke, & Robbins, 1991), for choice likely increases task interest and thus subsequent effort and motivation.

3. ***Structure/Routine.*** A consistent routine enhanced by a highly organized format of activities is recommended to provide a "focused environment" for children who experience difficulty investing in classroom tasks (C. Jones, 1989). Specific, daily schedules, including well-planned experiences with managed and fine transitions, are optimal for children with ADHD. Rules, expectations, and consequences should be clearly stated and specific. With this in mind, it will be obvious to the practitioner that as the number of transitions within an educational day increases, the likelihood that children with ADHD will struggle also increases. ADHD adolescents are particularly unsuited to meet the multiple transitions required during the course of their school day.

Brevity, variety, and structure should be incorporated into three basic principles paramount for intervention (C. Jones, 1994). First, practitioners must help educators understand that children with ADHD function better when a variety of materials to enhance visual, verbal, and tactile interactions is offered. The manipulation of materials makes the task more interesting and increases motivation and, when educational tasks are used in creative ways as rewards for completing other tasks, facilitates work completion to earn desired consequences.

The second principle focuses on cooperative learning activities, defined as those activities in which students work together during the learning process. Working with other students offers opportunities to model new behaviors and reinforce existing skills. All students learn best through a combination of watching others and subsequently having the opportunity to exhibit and experiment with new behaviors.

The third principle covers effective strategies, defined as conduits or frameworks in which educational information is placed. How materials are manipulated, work stations structured, ideas presented, and daily schedules determined all reflect strategic efforts to improve the classroom behavior and educational achievement of children with ADHD. Practitioners can illustrate for educators that by integrating these three principles with the concepts of brevity, variety, and routine, along with the basic philosophy of making tasks interesting and payoffs valuable, they will be prepared to offer a strategy-based model for specific students in the classroom.

One note of caution: practitioners should not overstate the success rate of research in classroom interventions for children with ADHD. A number of behavior management strategies have proven effective in modifying behavior and task performance with ADHD and other related problems in the classroom (for review, see S. Goldstein, 1995). The interventions offered in this chapter for the most part fit within the philosophical framework suggested, but many reflect the practical, time-tested, nonscience experiences of educators as opposed to meeting the rigors of double-blind scientific research. These strategies, however, should not be discarded as nonsense simply because they have not been researched in great depth. Ultimately, how well the model and the strategies offered in this chapter improve the learning, behavior, and performance of children with ADHD will need to be examined. However, with conscientious planning, careful listening, and a logical set of intervention strategies, the practitioner, as a consultant, can greatly enhance the classroom functioning of children with ADHD (S. Goldstein, 1995; C. Jones, 1994).

Teaching Styles

There is little support for the notion that a generic set of teaching skills is successful for all students in all educational situations. Few, if any, specific teacher behaviors are appropriate in all contexts. However, several patterns of behavior appear to be consistently related to learning gains for all students. Effective teachers (1) focus on academic goals, (2) carefully select instructional materials, (3) structure and plan learning activities, (4) involve students in the learning process, and (5) closely monitor student progress and provide frequent feedback concerning progress and accomplishments.

Effective teachers develop the ability to organize and maintain the classroom learning environment to maximize time spent engaged in productive activities and minimize time lost during transition periods over disruptions requiring disciplinary action. The ADHD child's tendency to disrupt classroom functioning can stress even the most effective teacher. Kounin (1970) used the term "withitness" to describe the successful classroom teacher. "Withit" teachers are organized and manage time well; they do not tolerate negative behavior, allow interruptions during class activities, socialize extensively during academic times, or engage in nonteaching behaviors to a significant degree during class time.

In regard to classroom discipline for inattentive students, Lasley (1986) suggests that effective teachers develop a workable set of rules in the classroom: (1) respond consistently and quickly to inappropriate behavior, (2) structure classroom activities to minimize disruption, and (3) respond to but do not become angry with or insult the disruptive students. Students in classrooms where these three goals were successfully implemented demonstrated greater improvements in behavior and academic work than students with similar attention problems in other classrooms. The effective classroom teacher for the ADHD student must also be well-organized, an efficient time manager, flexible, and able to handle multiple task demands. The teacher must be capable of setting realistic goals for the student with ADHD and, most important, find means to help these students achieve their goals. The skillful teacher will be able to quickly discriminate between the ADHD child's incompetent and noncompliant behavior. Interventions must be applied efficiently and consistently. The effective educator for a student with ADHD must be able to maintain an ongoing awareness of the entire classroom's activities, even when working one-on-one with the ADHD student. The effective classroom educator is able to carefully time interactions for maximum effect. Such a teacher is democratic, responsive, and understanding. The kindly, optimistic, friendly teacher will be better able to accept and meet the needs of students with ADHD.

In contrast, the autocratic teacher who is intolerant and rigid will experience difficulty with the ADHD child's frequent inability to follow directions. The aloof, distant, condescending teacher, stiff or formal in relationships with students or unable to view students as children, will experience difficulty with the ADHD child's differences. The restricted, rigid teacher able to recognize only the need for academic accomplishments, focusing only on the very good or bad, and impatient with students who do not fit expectations will have difficulty with the ADHD child. The hypercritical, faultfinding, threatening teacher will be frustrated by the ADHD child's inability to adjust and change quickly. The hopeless, pessimistic, unhappy teacher with a tendency to categorically view all misbehavior and unfinished work as the result of willful disregard will not develop a good relationship with the ADHD child. Finally, impulsive, short-tempered, disorganized teachers will experience difficulty caused by the similarity in their behavior with that of a typical ADHD child. In short, the personality qualities that make teachers good for all students will, with increased understanding and strategic suggestions, make them good teachers for students with ADHD as well.

To the extent that the practitioner is aware of these dimensions of teaching style and behavior, he or she is in a better position to determine the course of consultation. For some teachers, more time must be spent making certain they understand and are able to relabel the basis of this child's behavior. Chapter 14 offers numerous strategies to modify cognitive style and thereby increase receptivity to change for educators as well as parents. For example, the rigid, autocratic teacher must be educated about and willing to accept the ADHD child's incompetencies if that child is to succeed in that classroom; the disorganized teacher must be helped to structure and organize if the ADHD child is to be expected to complete tasks.

It is not difficult for practitioners to informally assess teacher style through parental reports concerning the teacher's past behavior, interaction with parents, written data provided by the teacher to parents, review of the teacher's written comments about the ADHD child's work and behavior, the effort the teacher exerts in providing the practitioner with needed assessment data, telephone conversations with the teacher, and the ADHD child's self-report concerning the teacher. S. Goldstein (1995) offers a comprehensive model for a structured teacher interview. It is important for the practitioner to remember that standards set by teachers often act as self-fulfilling prophecies for their students: when expectations are high, students achieve at higher levels, exhibiting fewer conduct problems. However, just as with parents, the ADHD child's off-task and inappropriate behavior has a coercive effect in shaping the teacher's behavior. It is not uncommon that, over time, poorly performing students are praised less and criticized more.

Defining Problem Behaviors in the School Setting

The practitioner can assist educators to define the ADHD child's behavioral difficulties and to specify the situations in which those difficulties manifest. The assessment process often accomplishes this task, allowing the practitioner to provide the classroom teacher with a summary of the child's problems, severity, and situational occurrences. It may also be beneficial for the practitioner to request teachers to prioritize behavioral problems of greatest concern and the situations in which they occur. Often, it is impossible for the practitioner to address simultaneously all of the ADHD child's behavioral and situational problems within the classroom. By providing the classroom teacher with relief for the most problematic behaviors and situations, the practitioner is immediately seen as a valuable ally. The reduction of one or two significant problems often makes other behavioral and academic difficulties much more bearable for the classroom teacher.

The practitioner can help teachers operationally define behavioral problems and to take baseline data before initiating intervention. Data can be collected in a number of ways: sample tally, video, observation, checklists. Some behaviors lend themselves easily to a particular form of data collection; other behaviors can be scored and observed in a number of ways, depending on the teacher's need.

A brief example will serve to demonstrate and reinforce baseline data process. To intervene with the child who repeatedly and inappropriately leaves her seat, baseline data must be collected. The teacher may be concerned with the frequency of the behavior: How many times the child leaves her seat during a half-hour lesson. A sample tally can record the number of occurrences. In other situations, the absolute number of times out-of-seat may not be as important as the amount of time spent out-of-seat; in this case, the teacher would record duration data and arrive at a time score for total number of minutes out of seat during the half-hour lesson. Finally, in some situations, neither frequency nor duration is as important as the pattern in which these behaviors occur; for example, the child may remain in her seat for the first fifteen minutes, but then be out of her seat twelve times in the last fifteen minutes of a lesson. Recording either frequency or duration data for this child would not assist understanding what is occurring in the classroom. In such a situation, interval recording is best: during a fixed interval, such as ten or fifteen seconds, the observer responds either yes or no for the target behavior. As discussed in an earlier chapter, it makes no difference whether the child is out of her seat once, twice, or for an infinite number of times during the interval. If the child is out of her seat even once, an affirmative score is given. The data are then observed on a continuum and the intervals in the progression of the child's behavior during the half-hour lesson are noted. Interval data collection is also helpful when classroom behavior and performance problems are difficult to define in terms of a beginning and ending. (The interested reader is referred to DuPaul and Stoner, 1994, and S. Goldstein, 1995, for in-depth descriptions of classroom observational systems.)

Educational Programming

Over the past thirty years, numerous programs and curricula have been suggested for ADHD but none has demonstrated magical properties in the classroom. Some advocated an open classroom to allow children with ADHD to choose whatever tasks and activities they would like to pursue. Open classrooms are often places in which children have both considerable flexibility in scheduling and more individualized instruction. Although the issue of choice may be beneficial for children with ADHD, research studies have not clearly demonstrated that the open classroom is any more beneficial for them than the traditional setting. Anecdotal reports suggest that in open classroom situations, the child with ADHD may not create as many problems for the teacher, but often very little else is accomplished.

In contrast to the open classroom, Strauss and Lehtinen (1947) hypothesized that on-task performance improves and activity level decreases when environmental stimulation is reduced. Minimally distracting environments are advocated in many special education settings through the use of individual cubicles. Again, research, though at some points promising, has not clearly demonstrated that children with ADHD benefit from being visually or auditorially isolated from the rest of the classroom.

Despite federal legislation, increased awareness, and to some extent a change in educational policy, public education continues to experience difficulty designing solutions for and meeting the needs of children with ADHD. Despite the fact that these are the most common problems of childhood, educators are forced to continue to provide programs based on available dollars and legislators' opinions, where intervention is focused almost exclusively on achievement factors. Although a valid focus, achievement level has not proven to be an effective watermark for beneficial ADHD interventions in the classroom.

The majority of children with ADHD will spend most if not all of their time in a regular classroom setting. To the extent that the practitioner can assist teachers by providing practical, commonsense interventions within the classroom, these children will benefit. Chapters in the intervention section of this text can be used to augment this chapter, including those related to the use of cognitive strategies, socialization, and behavior management. The remainder of this chapter provides strategies and suggestions for helping educators serve as effective environmental engineers. Issues related to class placement, managing consequences, the classroom environment, and curriculum adaptation will be discussed.

THE EDUCATOR AS AN ENVIRONMENTAL ENGINEER

A functional environment for students with ADHD has been described as a good learning environment for everyone (Reeve, 1994). In this regard, the role of the classroom teacher is that of an environmental engineer (Jones, 1991): the teacher creates an environment for the child's success and encourages learning within that environment. Teachers have the opportunity to provide children with ways to express their ideas and to participate socially, academically, and emotionally. Through this interactive participation, students begin to develop adaptive and independent behaviors. It is critical for classroom teachers and other educational professionals dealing with ADHD children to understand the disorder. We accept that all children learn, but we also know that they learn differently (Jones, 1991; Zentall, 1993, 1995). Therefore, the challenge for today's educational professional is to understand ADHD and its impact on children in the classroom. Further, as environmental engineers, it is their responsibility to implement interventions to allow each child to benefit from the educational experience. What takes place in school for children with ADHD is critical to their future life success.

The effectiveness of classroom-based interventions with ADHD children depends on two factors: characteristics associated with or inherent in the child and components of the treatment intervention itself (Rapport, 1989). It is important for the practitioner to consider both sets of variables separately as well as jointly. Child characteristics include:

1. Breadth and severity of behavioral dysfunction.
2. Intelligence.
3. Presence or absence of a learning disability.
4. Gender.
5. Presence of co-occurring classroom problems.
6. The time interval during which adequate treatment has not been administered (e.g., it may be more difficult to break the dysfunctional habits of a sixth-grader than of a kindergartner).

Characteristics associated with behavioral interventions effective for children with ADHD include:

1. Using nonverbal feedback to help the child focus on what he or she is supposed to be doing.
2. Limiting delays as much as possible between the child's behavior and scheduled consequences.
3. Strengthening positive and productive behavior that is incompatible with non-productive and inappropriate behavior, as opposed to focusing on the latter with the hope that the former will occur in its absence.
4. Using a mixture of positive and negative consequences.
5. Incorporating a practical feedback system that does not require a disproportionate amount of teacher time.

Rapport (1989) also suggests that there are a finite number of educational variables that have been empirically demonstrated to improve classroom functioning:

1. Limiting the number and types of distractors frequently printed on educational materials.

2. Planning short versus lengthy assignments.

3. Utilizing stimulating assignments and materials whenever possible.

4. Minimizing repetitive drill exercises and, when necessary, breaking them into smaller chunks.

5. Making efforts to determine that the child understands assignments and prompts offered.

6. The Premack Principle: Using a highly-sought behavior as reinforcement for a less desirable behavior is followed; more interesting assignments and other learning activities are located to serve as motivational incentives.

Rapport suggests that a managerial attitude, problem solving, and "dogmatic determinism" in applying these strategies are of most benefit in the classroom.

The practitioner will note that the basic philosophy underlying these six variables involves making tasks more interesting and payoffs more valuable. As the strategies listed in the following pages are discussed with teachers, it is critically important for the practitioner to periodically return to the framework within which these strategies are offered. Over time, it is hoped this will facilitate teachers' capacity to generate their own strategies, adhering to the basic philosophy of what works and does not work for children with ADHD in the classroom.

Incompetence versus Noncompliance

As outlined in earlier chapters, it is important for teachers to understand the distinction between behavior resulting from incompetence, which must be dealt with through education, and behavior resulting from noncompliance, which must be dealt with through appropriate consequences. This distinction cannot be emphasized too strongly. Incompetent behavior needs to be responded to empathetically and educationally, and noncompliant behavior must be responded to with firm, consistent consequences. The practitioner may find it helpful to use many of the techniques described in Chapter 16 for teachers. Often the teacher-student relationship is very similar to the parent-child relationship.

Placement in the Classroom

Although children vary in their ability to selectively ignore stimuli and it has been repeatedly demonstrated that the focus on distractions is intrinsically tied to investment or lack thereof in the task at hand, many teachers report that classrooms relatively free from extraneous auditory and visual stimuli are desirable (Telzrow & Speer, 1986). However, complete removal of distractions is not warranted. It is suggested that practitioners focus on helping teachers make tasks and payoffs of greater interest and value to children with ADHD rather than invest energy in creating a "bland" classroom. In fact, some evidence suggests that such efforts are counterproductive (Douglas & Peters, 1979; Zentall, 1993). Once again, it is important for practitioners to help educators understand that it is the child's inability to invest in the task that leads to off-task behavior, not the number of distractions in the environment; even in the most sterile environments, children with ADHD are prone to lose concentration (C. Jones, 1994).

There has been increasing interest in the arrangement of children's desks in the classroom, specifically preferential seating for a particular student or actually reconfiguring everyone's seating. Preferential seating in the class, away from a distracting neighbor or closer to the teacher, may increase compliance and decrease disruptive behavior. Teachers, however, should be cautioned to avoid placing the ADHD child so close to them at all times that the child's behavior is then shaped by negative reinforcement (C. Jones, 1994). This issue will be discussed in the coming pages. However, when the primary focus in the classroom is to reduce the occurrence of disruptive behaviors, rows of desks appear to be the best choice. It has been reported that among children with behavioral or learning problems, on-task behavior doubles as conditions change from desk clusters to rows. The rate of disruptions has been reported as three times higher in the desk cluster seating arrangement (Wheldall & Larn, 1987).

At times, however, seating arrangements may be more conducive to one type of problem but actually facilitate another. Liberman (1986) reports that a U-shape for desks is an effective way to enable students to imitate the strongest role model in the classroom: the teacher. Students have the benefit of physical proximity in a U-shape arrangement, as they are all within easy reach of the teacher, and the teacher appears to have more time and energy to look at each student without having to walk around, turn, or stand behind some students in the classroom. In this seating configuration, the teacher is in direct view of all students. This arrangement also increases the time that students may be able to see teaching materials, demonstrations, and so on without frontal distractions. Additional suggestions and strategies regarding various seating arrangements and classroom settings can be found in Paine, Ridicchi, Rosellini, Deutchman, and Darch (1983). Though the research upon which this text was structured was conducted nearly twenty years ago, the material continues to be eminently practical.

It has also been suggested that teachers consider room arrangements that facilitate and ensure student participation in class activities while not restricting opportunities to learn and benefit from instruction (DuPaul & Stoner, 1994). Such arrangements, however, should limit proximity to potential distractors inherent in the classroom. For example, a child with ADHD probably will not do well when seated beside a frequently used classroom activity center.

There is long standing evidence that actively planning for a positive classroom climate has a significant impact on student learning (Brophy & Good, 1974). The physical environment of classrooms affect the behavior of children and teachers. The authors suggest that teachers plan the placement and storage of materials to ensure that unnecessary distractions are minimized and access to needed and intended materials are enhanced. Disorganized students are more successful in a classroom offering orderly routines for storing materials and supplies; managing and storing materials efficiently so students can find them easily is essential. It is also suggested that in the classroom environment, teachers arrange a buddy system to enable individual children requiring special help in orienting or moving to be assisted without reliance on the teacher. Students who move frequently and have difficulty organizing their papers and materials can be provided with a clipboard on which they can mount and secure their work (Jones & Jones, 1986). The clipboard provides a tangible structure for organization and offers a sturdy format for papers.

Regarding the emotional climate of the classroom, there has been greater focus on helping teachers learn to develop skills to facilitate communication, conflict resolution, empathy, and respect for one's fellow students. (The interested reader is referred to Brooks, 1991; Mendler, 1992.)

Managing Consequences

Numerous studies have documented the efficacy of a wide range of behavior-based classroom interventions for students with ADHD (Abramowitz & O'Leary, 1991; DuPaul, 1991b). The majority of these interventions are contingency based; several, however, deal with management of antecedent behaviors. The manipulation of consequences includes contingent teacher attention, both positive and negative; classroom token economies, including reinforcement and response cost; and contingencies arranged between home and school. Time out for positive reinforcement and other reductive procedures based on reinforcement have also been utilized. Pfiffner and O'Leary (1993) note that there is a tendency in schools to manipulate consequences as a means of classroom intervention. The emphasis has been on the use of positive reinforcement along with mild forms of punishment such as response cost and time out. However, as Sulzer-Azaroff and Mayer (1991) note, there has been a shift in the emphasis toward preventing and managing behavior through antecedent manipulations and environmental arrangements: an emphasis on prevention rather than response. Further, the management of consequences has become more creative, ranging from the use of computers and related technology (Gordon, Thomason, Cooper, & Ivers, 1991) to the use of peers as tutors and consequence monitors (DuPaul & Henningson, 1993). In regard to the latter, these authors suggest that peer tutoring may be a viable adjunct or alternative to teacher-mediated behavioral interventions for ADHD. It is important to note that children often promote or maintain problem behavior in their peers rather than encourage their display of appropriate behaviors (Solomon & Whaler, 1973). Children with ADHD may find it particularly difficult to develop positive peer interactions due to a mismatch between their need for frequent and consistent reinforcement and the typical low rates of reinforcement children provide one another. The success of peer-mediated programs depends on the ability and motivation of children to learn and accurately implement them (O'Leary & O'Leary, 1977).

Positive Reinforcement

White (1975) found that in the early elementary school grades, teachers exhibit a significant degree of positive reinforcement for desired behavior; that is, when a desired behavior is exhibited, teachers frequently respond for the consequence that is likely to increase the reoccurrence of that behavior. By middle elementary school and through secondary school, however, teachers begin paying greater attention to undesirable behavior and less attention to appropriate behavior. This level of interaction results in the child's being negatively reinforced and the teacher positively reinforced. When the teacher pays attention to the undesirable behavior, it ceases in the short run but is increasingly likely to occur in the long run. This will be discussed further in the next section.

This naturally occurring pattern of teachers paying less attention to desirable behavior and more attention to undesirable behavior as children progress through school places the ADHD child at a greater disadvantage than classmates. In the first few grades, when teachers make a conscientious effort to positively reinforce their students, the ADHD child often does not receive his or her share. In the later grades, as teachers exhibit less positive reinforcement, perhaps because they feel it is not needed, the child with ADHD is at even greater risk as an increasing pattern of negative reinforcement develops between the child and teacher. The practitioner must help teachers understand that the appropriate application of positive reinforcement increases both on-task behavior and work completion. (For a thorough review, the reader is referred to S. Goldstein, 1995; Barkley, 1990a; DuPaul & Stoner, 1994; and Walker & Walker, 1991.)

If teachers are going to structure specially designed, positive reinforcement programs in the classroom, it is important that such programs begin at a level at which the child with ADHD can succeed and be positively reinforced. All too often, teachers set up wonderful behavioral programs but set criteria too high initially; the child with ADHD in this system never tastes success. The practitioner must assist educators to define problem behavior in an operational sense and to obtain a level of baseline occurrence, as previously discussed. It is suggested that at first reinforcement be provided when the child is at or slightly better than baseline. For example, if a child is out of his seat ten times during a work period, reinforcement can be provided initially if this child is out of his seat no more than eight times. As the child succeeds, the necessary criteria for reinforcement can be gradually tightened, requiring fewer out of seat behaviors during a given period of time. Such a model can also be implemented through the control of the number of reinforcers provided initially in a response-cost program.

Bushell (1973) cautions that some consequences teachers provide for children are irrelevant and neither strengthen nor weaken the behavior they follow. The teacher may feel that placing stars on a chart as a reward or providing a prize are consequences that all children will work for, but this may not be the case; some children may be motivated by these consequences, others may not. Further, children with ADHD may find these consequences salient one day but lose interest in them the next. Therefore, the fact that certain consequences follow a child's behavior may neither strengthen nor weaken the chances for that behavior to reoccur. Bushell refers to neutral consequences that are irrelevant as "noise." Practitioners must help teachers evaluate whether chosen consequences in the classroom are positively reinforcing or simply "noise." A reinforcement inventory completed jointly by the ADHD child and teacher often ensures that the former rather than the latter will occur.

Robinson, Newby, and Ganzell (1981) used a token reinforcement system for successful completion of four tasks, two involving learning to read and using vocabulary words and sentences, and two involving teaching these tasks to other students. Tokens were exchanged for access to a pinball machine or electronic game. Using a reversal design, the token intervention program resulted in a ninefold increase in the mean number of tasks completed over the baseline level and significant improvement in performance on the school district's standardized weekly reading-level exams. A reduction in disruptive behavior was also anecdotally reported. It is important to note that this reinforcement system was managed by a single teacher working with eighteen children, all of whom had received diagnoses of ADHD. (The interested reader is referred to Walker & Shea, 1991, for an in-depth model of structuring a token economy successfully in the classroom.)

Negative Reinforcement

The most powerful event in the classroom for the ADHD student is the coercive pattern of negative reinforcement that develops between students and teachers. Clark and Elliott (1988) found that negative reinforcement was rated by teachers as the most frequently used classroom intervention. However, teachers do so unwittingly, and they use this method of intervention without an understanding of its long-term ramifications. It is important to help teachers understand that the use of a negative reinforcer may help the ADHD child begin tasks but not complete them. In the classroom ADHD students frequently return to the task at hand to avoid an aversive consequence, usually the teacher's attention to the fact that the child is off-task. Once the child returns to work, the teacher's attention is diverted to others, thus negatively reinforcing the child. Work is then stopped until attention is once again paid. Thus, ADHD children in classrooms are victims of their temperament, which makes it difficult for them to complete tasks, but also victims of their learning history, which reinforces them for beginning but rarely finishing work.

There are a number of simple ways to assist teachers to deal with this problem. If the teacher uses negative reinforcement, it is important to pay attention to the ADHD student until the assignment is completed. Although this too is negative reinforcement, it teaches the child that the only way to get rid of the aversive consequence (teacher's attention) is to not just start but to complete the task at hand. As an example, the teacher may move the student's desk closer to the teacher's desk until that particular piece of work is completed.

A second alternative involves the use of differential attention, or ignoring. This involves ignoring as the negative consequence for exhibiting undesirable behavior and attention as a positive consequence for exhibiting the competing desirable behavior. This is an active process in which the teacher ignores the child engaged in an off-task activity but pays attention immediately when the child begins working. Many teachers avoid interaction with the ADHD child when he or she is on task for fear of interrupting the child's train of thought; it is important, however, to reinforce the child when he or she is working so that a pattern of working to earn positive reinforcement rather than working to avoid negative reinforcement is developed. Secondary school teachers at times complain that if they ignore the ADHD teenager during an hour class, they will never have the opportunity to pay positive attention, as the student may never exhibit positive behavior. It is important to reassure these educators that waiting, even if one has to wait until the next day, in the long run will be a more effective intervention than paying attention to off-task behavior. It is also important to remind teachers to make a distinction between off-task behavior that disrupts and off-task behavior that does not disrupt; differential attention works effectively in regard to the latter. However, when an ADHD child is off-task and disturbing a neighbor, teachers may find that negative reinforcement can stem the tide of an off-task behavior that may involve other students. It is also important for educators to understand that differential attention alone has been demonstrated to be ineffective in maintaining high rates of on-task behavior and work productivity for ADHD students (Rosen et al., 1984). In part, these authors suggest that there are many factors other than teacher attention that maintain and influence student behavior in the classroom.

Differential attention is a very powerful intervention when used appropriately. Once the strategy of ignoring inappropriate behavior is employed, it must be continued despite escalation; if not, teachers run the risk of intermittently reinforcing the negative behavior, thereby strengthening its occurrence. For example, if a teacher decides to use differential attention for a child's out-of-seat behavior but becomes sufficiently frustrated after the child is out-of-seat for ten minutes and responds by directing attention to the child, the behavior will be reinforced rather than extinguished. The ten minutes of ignoring will quickly be lost in the one incident of negative attention.

Madsen, Becker, and Thomas (1968) evaluated rules, praise, and ignoring for inappropriate behavior in two children in a normal second-grade classroom and one behavioral problem child in a kindergarten class. The results indicated that in the absence of praise, rules and ignoring were ineffective; inappropriate behavior decreased only after praise was added. D. Thomas, Becker, and Armstrong (1968) also demonstrated the importance of praise in a regular classroom; specifically, when teacher approval was withdrawn, disruptive behaviors increased.

Overall, however, the research on differential attention with hyperactive children has been inconsistent. Rosen, O'Leary, Joyce, Conway, and Pfiffner (1984) evaluated the results of praise and reprimands in maintaining appropriate social and academic behaviors in second- and third-grade children with ADHD. Children's on-task behavior and academic performance deteriorated when negative feedback was withdrawn but not when positive feedback was omitted. Students' on-task behavior remained high, even after nine days of no praise from the teacher. Acker and O'Leary (1987) have demonstrated that the use of only reprimands for behavior management without positive consequences does not lead to dramatic improvement in on-task behavior when praise is added. Dramatic deterioration in on-task behavior was observed when reprimands were subsequently withdrawn, even though the teacher was still delivering praise for appropriate behavior. As noted elsewhere, children with ADHD perform as well as normals with a continuous schedule of reinforcement but perform significantly worse when a partial schedule of reinforcement, which is typically found in classrooms, is provided (Douglas & Parry, 1983). Praise is important for the development of other attributes in human beings, such as self-esteem, school attitude, and motivation toward academics (Redd, Morris, & Martin, 1975). The corollary is also true that punishment can exert a negative impact on emotional development and self-esteem.

Differential Reinforcement

When consequences are provided for two competing behaviors, the term used to describe the process is differential reinforcement of other behavior (Sulzer-Azaroff & Mayer, 1977). The practitioner can help teachers understand that this is a very powerful intervention when used appropriately. The target behavior that is to be decreased when it occurs can be responded to with a negative consequence such as ignoring or punishment. The competing positive behavior can be praised and reinforced when it occurs. Competing behaviors include teasing and playing cooperatively, aggression and negotiation, emotional outbursts and self-control when frustrated. Differential attention is an example of a differential reinforcement procedure.

Punishment

Punishment suppresses undesirable behavior but may not extinguish it (McDaniel, 1980). Suppression may be of short duration, and in the absence of a punisher, may reoccur. Punishment can take the form of an unpleasant consequence or the loss of a pleasurable consequence following the occurrence of a target behavior; these may or may not be related to the exhibition of the inappropriate behavior. Punishment reduces the probability that the behavior that precedes it will reoccur. Punishment can be an effective way of changing behavior if the child has the capacity to act differently. Punishment is often suggested as inefficient for ADHD children, as it is frequently directed at changing symptoms of ADHD over which the child has little control. Punishment can also be a seductive intervention, as it can be reinforcing to teachers and thus overused (Neisworth & Smith, 1983).

Punishment does not provide an appropriate model of acceptable behavior and for many teachers is accompanied by emotional outbursts. Common punishments by teachers include depriving students of participation in enjoyable activities, loss of snack, verbal reprimands, and time out (Walker & Shea, 1991). If punishment is to be used effectively, students should know which behaviors will be punished and how they will be punished; then punishment should be immediate, consistent, and fair, as well as impersonal (Walker & Shea, 1991). At the same time, appropriate models for acceptable behavior need to be provided.

Reprimands

Verbal reprimands are the most common negative consequences in the classroom (M. White, 1975). An early body of literature suggested that reprimands may increase inappropriate behavior (Madsen, Becker, Thomas, Koser, & Plager, 1968). Other researchers have suggested that reprimands are essential in the classroom management of children with ADHD (Rosen et al., 1984). Abramowitz, O'Leary, and Futtersak (1988) compared the effects of short and long reprimands in an alternating treatment design. Over the course of the study, short reprimands (a brief statement) resulted in significantly lower off-task rates than long reprimands (a series of consecutive statements). Prudent reprimands that are immediate, unemotional, brief, and consistently backed up with consequences are clearly preferred to imprudent reprimands, which are delayed, loud, emotional, and not well tied to consequences. Abramowitz and O'Leary (1990) suggest that immediate reprimands result in much lower rates of off-task interactions with peers but no change in off-task behavior not involving peers. The authors hypothesize that noninteractive off-task behavior may be an avoidance response to difficult schoolwork that is affected by the timing of the teacher's reprimands. Interactive off-task behaviors may be reinforced by peer attention and modified more effectively by the timing of feedback. Acker and O'Leary (1988) suggest that consistent reprimands are clearly superior to inconsistent reprimands for minimizing calling out and other disruptive behaviors characteristic of ADHD. However, when misbehaviors followed by reprimands versus ignoring are evaluated, reprimands are not particularly effective in managing off-task behavior. Reprimanding every incidence of off-task behavior did not prove to be any more effective than reprimanding one quarter of misbehaviors. Increasing consistency in these situations does not appear to lead to significant difference (Pfiffner, O'Leary, Rosen, & Sanderson, 1985). Further, the intensity or aversiveness of the initial delivery of reprimands may be critical for children with ADHD (Futtersak, O'Leary, & Abramowitz, 1989). In this study, children were exposed to teachers who delivered either consistently strong reprimands from the outset with immediate brief and firm close proximity to the child or reprimands that increased in severity over time. Results supported the hypothesis that gradually strengthening initially weak reprimands was less effective for suppressing off-task behavior than the immediate introduction and maintenance of full-strength reprimands. Gradually increasing the strength of reprimands resulted in a greater frequency of negative feedback than initially applying full-strength reprimands. It has also been suggested that reprimands are more effective when delivered with eye contact and in close proximity to the child (Van Houten, Nau, MacKenzie-Keating, Sameoto, & Colavecchia, 1982).

Walker and Shea (1991) note that effective reprimands are specific, do not derogate the children, are provided immediately, are given with a firm voice and controlled physical demeanor, are backed up with a loss of a privilege, include a statement encouraging more appropriate behavior, and are delivered in a calm way that does not embarrass the child in the presence of others.

Response Cost

Most teachers understand response cost as a system in which students lose positive reinforcers they have earned for appropriate behavior when they exhibit inappropriate behavior. Empirical data suggest that response cost may be the most powerful means of managing consequences for children with ADHD or other disruptive behavioral problems (Rapport, Murphy, & Bailey, 1982). In a traditional model of response cost, many ADHD children may immediately go bankrupt. Alternative systems include adjusting the ratio of a number of reinforcers provided for each positive behavior versus those lost for negative behavior, as well as increasing the number of opportunities to exhibit positive behavior and receive reinforcement. A slightly altered form of response cost has been found to be quite effective with ADHD children (Rapport et al., 1982). Under this system, the child is initially provided with a maximum number of points or tokens to be earned during a school day and must work throughout the day to retain those reinforcers. It appears that impulsive children work better to keep their plates full rather than refill an empty plate. Further, possibly because they have a long history of not working well for positive reinforcement, a system in which they are provided with all of their reinforcement initially and must work to keep it may be more motivating or attractive to them. As will be discussed in Chapter 17, this method of managing consequences also applies well in the home.

Kazdin (1982) reviews a substantial body of research documenting the effectiveness of response cost in the classroom. One of the earliest studies (Rapport et al., 1982) compared response cost and stimulant medication for task-related behavior in a group of hyperactive boys. The response-cost procedure resulted in significant increases in on-task behavior and academic performance; stimulant medication, interestingly, was notably less effective. Pfiffner, O'Leary, Rosen, and Sanderson (1985) found that response cost in the form of lost recess was more effective than reprimands in maintaining on-task behavior. When response cost is compared to reward, both conditions result in a twofold increase in academic output or reduction in inappropriate classroom behavior and a corresponding increase in on-task behavior. Children often do not show a preference for either reward or response-cost procedures (Hundert, 1976; Iwata & Bailey, 1974). Children rated as hyperactive or aggressive have been found to maintain treatment gains better during fading and withdrawal of response cost than with traditional reward (Sullivan & O'Leary, 1990).

A response-cost system can be as simple as chips in a cup, marks on a chart, or marbles in a jar. A more complex means of managing response cost includes electronic devices such as the Attention Training System (M. Gordon et al., 1991; Rapport, 1987). The Attention Training System is a remote-controlled counter that sits on the student's desk. This device provides the student with a digital readout showing the number of points he or she has earned. Using a remote-control device, the classroom teacher can add or remove a point from anywhere in the classroom contingent upon the child's on- or off-task behavior. By not having to move within physical proximity of the child, the teacher avoids becoming a negative reinforcer when the child is off-task. DuPaul, Guevremont, and Barkley (1992) demonstrated the efficacy of response-cost contingencies alone and in combination with directed-rehearsal procedures for managing classroom behavior and academic productivity utilizing the Attention Training System. Response-cost contingencies led to marked improvements in task-related attention and a reduction in ADHD symptoms during work time. Interestingly, response-cost effects on academic productivity and differential effects associated with directed-rehearsal contingencies were equivalent.

Morgan and Jenson (1988) suggest that for response cost to be effective, the procedure must be used for most if not all of the classroom day. The number of students in the program must be manageable for the teacher and highly motivating consequences must be provided. If not managed effectively and well thought out, response cost can backfire and increase problem behaviors in the classroom (Burchard & Barrera, 1972).

Time Out

Time out has become the familiar abbreviated description for time out from reinforcement. Time out procedures can be as simple as requiring a child to place his or her head on a desk for a period of time or move to an isolated part of the classroom for a specific period of time. (The interested reader is referred to S. Goldstein, 1995, for an in-depth review of time out procedures in the classroom.)

The effectiveness of time out is well established. However, additional research is needed to identify specific situations, parameters, and procedures associated with success of time out for ADHD children in the classroom. Clearly, time out has a low probability of directly impacting ADHD symptoms for the better. Time out can be quite effective for noncompliance, but teachers must be helped to distinguish between noncompliant behavior that should be consequated and incompetent behavior resulting from ADHD that must be managed and about which the child must be educated. Time out is also an effective behavior deceleration technique (Brantner & Doherty, 1983).

Ethical and legal issues have also been raised concerning the use of time out in classrooms (Brantner & Doherty, 1983). One of the few studies utilizing time out with what was then referred to as hyperactive children in the classroom was a single case study by Kubany, Weiss, and Sloggett (1971) using nonexclusionary time out and group reinforcement. The procedure involved the use of a good behavior clock. Rewards were earned for a child and the class contingent upon a clock running for a specific period of time. The clock ran whenever the child was seated and working quietly, but stopped for at least fifteen seconds when the child was noisy or out of seat. The procedure resulted in a dramatic decrease in disruptive behavior.

Time out has been extensively researched and found to be effective in a variety of educational and treatment situations (Fleece, O'Brien, & Drabman, 1981; M. W. Roberts, 1988; Rutherford & Nelson, 1982). However, it can be difficult to implement, particularly in regular classrooms. Shriver and Allen (1996) offer a step-by-step system for analyzing the effectiveness of time out and making modifications using a "time out grid" (see Figure 15–1). In condition A, time out is most effective; in

	Low Reinforcement	High Reinforcement
High Reinforcement **Time-In**	**(A)** **Behavior Improvement** Intervention Problem: None	**(B)** **No Change in Behavior** Intervention Problem: Too little contrast Solution: Decrease time-out reinforcement
Low Reinforcement	**(C)** **No Change in Behavior** Intervention Problem: Too little contrast Solution: Increase time-in reinforcement	**(D)** **Behavior Deterioration** Intervention Problem: High-contrast intervention Solution: Reverse reinforcement contingencies

Figure 15–1. The time-out grid

Source: From Shriver, N. D., & Allen, K. D. (1996). The Time-Out Grid: A guide to effective discipline. *School Psychology Quarterly, 11,* 67–74. Copyright 1996. The Guilford Press. Reprinted with permission.

condition D, time out is least effective. Time out will have limited if any impact on conditions B and C. B is more likely to occur in special education classrooms where teachers are quick to respond in a negative way to off-task behavior. C is likely to occur when behavior problems are not particularly disruptive and can be ignored. D occurs when children are disruptive or defiant and available reinforcement for cooperative, prosocial, or academic behavior is minimal.

In condition D, high rates of reinforcement are often focused on disruptive behavior, which then becomes the focus of intervention. This procedure is effective if behavioral outcomes are analyzed and consequences in the classroom are completely understood. Time out should not be used in situation A as it will rarely, if ever, be effective. Time out should also be avoided if students are resistant to remaining in time out and can reliably escape from the consequence.

To make time out more effective, Shriver and Allen (1996) suggest that more than one reinforcement be provided for "time in." In addition, other studies recommend that (a) students should be separated from reinforcement; (b) time out should be short; (c) cooperation should be shaped; (d) confrontation should be avoided; (e) verbal interaction should be limited; and (f) there should always be a time contingent release (Bean & Roberts, 1981). Children warned less during time out also respond better (G. Roberts, 1982).

Consequential versus Rule-Governed Behavior

As discussed in earlier chapters, due to their inhibitory problems, children with ADHD may function quite well under appropriate external or environmental consequences but struggle to develop the internal self-monitoring skills to govern their own behavior. The latter was referred to by Barkley in 1981a as "problems following rule-governed behavior." It is important for the practitioner to help teachers understand that children with ADHD may acquire behavior at a rate similar to others but take longer to learn to self-manage that behavior in the absence of external consequences and cues. Thus, it should be expected that even when appropriate reinforcers are located, it will take the ADHD child a greater number of successful trials to transition to self-management.

In part, this speaks to the difference between behavior modification and behavior management. Teachers are repeatedly taught that if they provide consequences appropriately, within a reasonable period of time, children's behavior will be "modified." Success is usually based on the child's continuing to demonstrate the desired behavior when consequences are removed. When this model is applied to children with ADHD, interventions are often deemed failures at demonstrating the behavior without consequences. Demonstrating a behavior in the presence of consequences for the ADHD child is not synonymous with having developed self-management skills to utilize the behavior. Teachers should be encouraged to focus on behavior management; that is, success occurs if the child's behavior is modified in the presence of consequences. As consequences are removed, if the child's behavior regresses, this should not be seen as failure but rather a too quick change in the schedule of reinforcement: the child has yet to transition from consequentially managed to rule-governed behavior for that particular task.

Quality of Reinforcers

Paine et al. (1983) found that the five most frequent reinforcement ideas suggested by elementary school students were additional recess, free time in class, material reinforcers, field trips, and games in class. Intermediate-grade students more frequently favored activities that involved interaction with teachers, including acting as an assistant in grading papers, carrying on a discussion, and playing a game on a one-to-one basis. As previously discussed, reinforcers take on different value for different individuals and thus broad assumptions should not be made for all students.

It is important for the practitioner to help teachers develop a hierarchy of the behaviors they would like to see the ADHD child exhibit in the classroom. For example, in response to out-of-seat behavior, teachers may initiate a reinforcement system to increase in-seat behavior. Although the child may earn multiple reinforcers for remaining in seat, this does not guarantee that he or she will engage in constructive or appropriate behavior while remaining seated. Often, multiple reinforcers and multiple levels of reinforcement must be initiated; for example, a child can be provided with a reinforcer for sitting and a second reinforcer for working while sitting.

INTERACTIVE ISSUES

Be Positive

It is important for teachers to understand the need to tell ADHD students what they want to have happen rather than what they do not want to have happen. Although this appears to be a simple concept, it is the essence of being positive. Instead of pointing out behavior the teacher does not like, the teacher must tell the ADHD student what he or she wants to see happen instead. The emphasis on what is to be done as opposed to what is to be stopped will help the ADHD student understand the task demands and the teacher's needs. This also avoids the frequent dilemma of the child following the teacher's direction to stop a particular behavior but then engaging in a different nonproductive behavior. When teachers tell ADHD students specifically what they want to have happen and make certain the child understands, the stage is set to punish noncompliance if the student doesn't follow through.

Give Clear Directions

Compliance and task completion increase when teachers provide simple, single directions and seek feedback from the child. Researchers have found that most teachers issue a sequence of directions when guiding their students (for review, see S. Goldstein, 1995). Often teachers are unaware of the complexity of instructions they provide in the classroom. It will be beneficial for the practitioner to help teachers focus on the manner in which they provide instructions in the classroom. The ADHD child does not respond well to multiple instructions; for them, the teacher's awareness of the complexity of instructions being given often results in a simplification of instructions, leading to increased compliance by the ADHD student. Compliance in the classroom increases when the ADHD child is required to repeat directions. When group instructions are given, this intervention may be difficult to implement. It is suggested that once the group is given an instruction the teacher then approach the ADHD child and request the child to repeat the instruction even if the child has begun to comply. The teacher may approach with a reinforcer, indicating the child is doing a good job, but nevertheless, request the child to restate the direction.

State Rules

Compliance with instructions and classroom procedure increases when children are required to learn a set of rules and follow them (Paine et al., 1983). On an intermittent basis, it is suggested that teachers make certain that the ADHD child understands the rules of specific settings. For example, before sending the ADHD child out to recess, the teacher may quickly ask the child to review the rules of the playground and the kind of behavior that is expected. Although this does not guarantee a reduction in impulsive behavior, it does help the teacher understand that the child is aware of the rules but, due to impulsivity, may be unable to consistently follow them.

Teach Self-Pacing

Children with ADHD often function better if they can learn to manage their own schedule and pace work completion rather than having an imposed time table. In many classroom situations, this is not always possible. However, teaching the child with ADHD to structure work and divide larger tasks into smaller parts that can then be approached and accomplished in stages will increase task completion. In some situations, self-pacing is facilitated when the teacher provides smaller portions of work, which increases the likelihood the child will successfully complete the entire task. Whalen and Henker (1985) demonstrated that during self-paced periods, the intensity of the ADHD child's behavioral problems was lower than in situations in which the child's behavior was paced by others. Parker (1988) offers a system to develop and facilitate self-pacing in the classroom.

Provide Cues

Providing the ADHD child with external visual or auditory cues that do not directly involve teacher intervention can be beneficial in maintaining appropriate classroom behavior and fostering the completion of classwork. External self-monitored cues help the ADHD child be an active participant in behavior change. Auditory and visual cues are as effective as direct teacher monitoring (Hayes & Nelson, 1983). Providing an auditory cue, such as running a tape on which an audible variable stimulus reminds children to continue working, has been demonstrated to result in increased on-task behavior and academic performance (Blick & Test, 1987).

The success of such a system requires the student to be motivated and cooperative. The intervention often works best with older students. Studies have suggested that students who are more accurate in recording their behavior were on task more than the less accurate recorders (Hallahan & Sapona, 1983). Self-management procedures such as this have also proven effective in stimulating generalization of skills (Stokes &

Baer, 1977), a problem frequently encountered when teaching attention and reflection skills. The practitioner interested in expanding a repertoire of behavior analysis and self-recording skills in the classroom is referred to Tawney and Gast (1984). In addition, C. Jones (1994) illustrates a system of using external visual cue cards.

Structure and Minimize Transitions

ADHD children move easily from formal to informal, focused to unfocused, and structured to unstructured settings. That is, they are the last to begin but the first to stop. If the teacher allows the ADHD child a few extra minutes in the morning to unwind and be off-task, the result will likely be more difficulty getting the child to settle down and focus on task requirements. Even minor interruptions such as someone entering the classroom are often sufficient to redirect the ADHD child's attention off the task. The ADHD child may be the last child to settle down and return to work after an informal break such as recess. In team-teaching situations, they will have trouble moving from one classroom to another efficiently. Keeping such informal transitions to a minimum, providing additional structure during transitional periods, providing positive reinforcement contingent on the child's abilities to successfully complete the transition and help the ADHD child settle into a formal setting again can have a significant positive impact on the child's overall functioning in the classroom.

The issue of transitions is even more important in secondary school settings, where this problem is often among the most frequently reported by teachers. Ways to avert transition problems include minimizing the number of transitions during the day, assigning a "buddy" for the child to move from class to class with, and providing two sets of textbooks, one to be left in class and the other to be left at home (Jones, 1994).

Provide a Consistent Routine . . .

ADHD children function significantly better in a consistent setting. Varying a sequence of daily activities may confuse, decrease attention to task, and hamper work completion. The impulsive, spontaneous, randomly organized teacher may match very well with the gifted, attentive child; the ADHD child, however, will experience problems in a classroom lacking planned routine. There is research to suggest that children tend to become less cognitively efficient as the day progresses, implying that more complex problem-solving tasks should be taught in the morning and less structured activities in the afternoon (Zabar & Bowers, 1983).

. . . But Keep Things Changing

Within the consistent routine, however, the ADHD child will function significantly better when provided with multiple shortened work periods, opportunities for choice among work tasks, and enjoyable reinforcers. In regard to the latter, it is essential that practitioners help teachers understand that although children with ADHD respond to consequences, both positive and negative, in ways that are similar to other children, they require more immediate, frequent, predictable, and meaningful reinforcers than other children due to their inhibitory problems. Reinforcement provided along this schedule does not constitute extortion or blackmail but, rather, better fits the ADHD child's temperament.

Allow Nondisruptive Movement

We are now well aware that it is the impulsive, disorganized, subsequently inattentive style of the ADHD child that primarily interferes with successful classroom performance and not the child's activity level. It is important for the practitioner to help teachers focus and prioritize their goals for the ADHD child in the classroom. Most teachers will designate organization and work completion as priorities. The practitioner must guide teachers to understand that the ADHD child, even when medicated and functioning successfully in the classroom, is likely during the course of the day to exhibit a greater degree of movement in the form of restless, overactive behavior than other children. This pattern of behavior need not be a detriment if the teacher can be flexible and the child is nondisruptive, completing work, and being positively reinforced at a rate similar to other students in the classroom.

Offer Feedback

Teachers frequently observe that there appears to be a direct relationship between the amount of one-to-one instruction ADHD children receive and their compliance and task completion. It is obvious that children with ADHD function significantly better if they can be provided with immediate feedback and increased teacher attention. In some situations, moving a child's desk closer to the teacher's in an affirmative rather than punishing way will facilitate the opportunity to provide functional feedback. In other situations, teachers should have the opportunity to employ adult aides or even children from upper grades as peer tutors during independent work periods. It is also important for teachers to understand the role of both positive and negative reinforcement. Frequently, the social feedback ADHD children receive from teachers is negative and thereby contributes to the child's view of the world as a place where he or she does not often succeed and where it is necessary to comply with requests to avoid aversive consequences. Some teachers must be actively coached to provide numerous positive instructions, reinforcers, and social feedback to the ADHD child in the classroom.

Build Success

It is most important that interactions with ADHD students end successfully. Because of the pattern of negative reinforcement that ADHD students frequently elicit from teachers and the multiple failures they frequently experience, they often end up being punished without being given the opportunity to succeed. Teachers must be counseled to be certain that the ADHD student has an opportunity to try again, succeed, and be praised. Many ADHD children develop a view of the world as a place where they are unable to succeed and over time develop feelings of helplessness and poor motivation. It is important for the practitioner to help teachers develop a system to provide frequent positive reinforcement of the ADHD student's successes, no matter how minor they may be. A good rule of thumb is to help teachers note how often they reinforce all students in their classroom and make an effort to reinforce the ADHD child even more. The importance of success in predicting children's future life outcome, especially those facing adversity, cannot be overstated (E. Werner, 1994).

Prepare the ADHD Child for Changes

Unexpected or unexplained changes often precipitate significant behavioral problems in ADHD children due to their tendency to become overaroused easily and their difficulty moving from one setting to another. It is helpful to prepare the ADHD child for changes by mentioning the amount of time remaining in a work period and by taking the child aside to explain any change in routine that might occur later in the day. Time countdowns and advance warning will help the ADHD child anticipate changes and respond more appropriately.

Adjust Expectations

The practitioner must help teachers understand that the successful performance of the ADHD child in the classroom is as much the result of changes in the teacher's expectations as the provision of additional educational, behavioral, or medical interventions. Strategies and suggestions to help teachers adjust their perceptions about children with ADHD are provided in Chapter 14. Without such self-cognitive modifications, some teachers develop extensive reinforcement systems that do not take into account the ADHD child's developmental impairments. As noted earlier, the very child that a specific classroom intervention may have been designed for may not have the confidence to succeed, thus creating increased frustration for everyone involved. It is helpful for teachers to understand that in some settings, the best immediate solution for a child with a short attention span is to structure the environment so the child is not required to concentrate for long periods of time. Cognitive and behavioral interventions can then be developed to slowly increase the child's capacity to remain on task.

Use Cognitive Interventions Strategically

Although cognitive strategies do not directly impact ADHD symptoms in the classroom, as discussed in Chapter 14, they can be very effective in helping teachers understand and reattribute the basis of the child's behavior. In addition, cognitive interventions can help children with ADHD become active participants in the treatment process, develop an internal locus of control, and learn effective means of dealing with the emotional by-products of their struggles.

Use Preventive Strategies

The practitioner can help teachers anticipate potential problems and show them how to develop preventive rather than reactionary strategies. Successful classroom consultation provides teachers with skills that will solve immediate problems but can also be generalized for use with future problems. A thorough understanding of the ADHD child's skills and abilities facilitates the development of preventive intervention. Some teachers may benefit from considering the task demands placed on the ADHD child during a typical day and planning specific strategies for situations where problems are anticipated. In a preventive model, teachers can be taught to intervene by modifying the environment, such as altering the demands placed on the ADHD child or modifying the child through the use of educational opportunities to increase competence. Although preventive strategies may not totally avoid problems, the old adage that an ounce of prevention is worth a pound of cure is particularly true in regard to ADHD. Planning ahead will minimize the severity of problems and likely retard the development of secondary adjustment and related problems that result from repeated failure.

With the increased need for structure and routine, planning for the establishment of an effective climate and use of class time is critical for ADHD students. Unfortunately, teachers often spend a disproportionate amount of time planning what to teach and insufficient time considering how they will teach; for example, elementary school teachers have been found to vary significantly in the actual time they use for instruction during the course of the day, from 50% to 90% of the total time available (for review see S. Goldstein, 1995). The following are some additional planning tips:

- When presenting the daily schedule to students, use both visual and verbal cues. Consider color coding the list for easy recall and add verbal cues for additional support. Then select a student to come forward to orally repeat the plan for the class (C. Jones, 1994).
- As directions are written on the board, distinguish work by boxing or coloring it. Also, number information placed on the board and use highlighting or arrows to cue critical words (C. Jones, 1994).
- Teach students to highlight key word directions on their own worksheet or test before they begin working. This will reduce the likelihood that impulsive ADHD children will start before they clearly understand what they need to do. The practitioner should explain to teachers that when students with ADHD are required to remain on task for fixed amounts of time, they more effectively manage their impulses. It is only when they are allowed to complete tasks and move that they may begin without understanding what to do as well as move too quickly through the material (C. Jones, 1994).
- Arrange class schedules to allow specific times each day for calendar and homework recording. Students should copy homework assignments together as well as check each other to make sure information has been accurately recorded (Goldstein & Goldstein, 1990).
- Provide students with advance schedules of assignments, tests, and homework on a weekly basis. A copy of this schedule should be left in the office for parents to check when needed or if the student needs to see a copy (C. Jones, 1994).

Deal with Note-Taking Problems

It is unclear if the problems children with ADHD experience taking notes and copying from the blackboard are due to their difficulty dividing attention, impulsiveness, lack of picking up the cue that it is time to write something down, or in fact reflects weak visual-motor integration skills. What is clear is that more often than not, ADHD students experience significant problems with note taking in the classroom. In the later school years, notes must also be taken while attending to the teacher's lecture. The simplest solution to this problem is either for the teacher to prepare a set of notes and make them available to the ADHD student, or perhaps all students, or allow the ADHD student to listen intently during class and obtain a copy of a designated classmate's notes. In some situations, using a tape recorder may also be of benefit. However, it has been the authors' experience that most ADHD children simply do not make time out of school to listen to the entire lesson on tape.

Other strategies that can be effective in facilitating note-taking skills include the use of semantic feature analysis, charts, and visual maps (Bos & Vaughn, 1991). Semantic feature analysis is a prelearning activity designed to activate a student's prior knowledge of a topic as well as introduce and organize key concepts in vocabulary (for review, see Mather, 1996). Learning-disabled students have been found to make greater progress with this procedure than traditional vocabulary study strategies for learning new vocabulary and conceptual comprehension of tasks (Bos & Vaughn, 1991).

Beginning the School Year

One of the best preventive strategies is to educate a new teacher about the ADHD child's history and abilities before the first day of school. Although some parents are concerned about biasing teachers, it is our impression that the benefits of informing and working with a teacher far outweigh the liabilities of providing information about the child before he or she enters the teacher's classroom. Although parents' concerns about teacher bias are valid, silence can lead to more problems, for example, when the teacher pressures the ADHD child to conform during the first weeks of school without understanding that the child cannot do so. The practitioner should help parents understand that the teacher is a professional and part of the child's treatment team. It is beneficial for parents to meet with the ADHD child's teacher or teachers before the beginning of the school year. In a secondary school setting, it is essential for a counselor, special education teacher, or volunteer to be designated as the adolescent's "go-to person." This person should meet with the adolescent frequently, review progress in each class, assist in communicating with teachers concerning problems, and serve as a liaison between the family and school team.

It may also be beneficial for parents to allow the practitioner working with the ADHD child to speak with the teacher before school begins. The first few weeks of school are critical in determining consistent classroom routine, normative behavior, and the teacher-child relationship. The informed teacher can closely monitor the ADHD child during this time, identify and understand potential problems, and begin preventive intervention strategies when needed.

Daily Progress Reports

School home notes have been reported anecdotally as quite beneficial for children with ADHD. They require clear and accurate communication between parents and teachers, as well as teachers' ability to consistently report behavior and parents' ability to deliver consequences. Hyperactive children have been responsive to home note programs (O'Leary et al., 1976; Pelham, 1977). In fact, for the general population, home note programs targeting only academic performance have been found to result in improvements in both academic and social behavior (Witt, Hannafin, & Martens, 1983). These programs also give parents more consistent feedback about their children's daily behavior. Samples of an elementary and secondary daily report appear in Figures 15–2 and 15–3. (The interested reader is referred to Kelly, 1990.)

Daily reports have been found to be an acceptable intervention for ADHD among elementary and middle school teachers (Power et al., 1995). Teachers can design their own daily report. In middle school, it may be a simple one-page checklist carried from teacher to teacher and including boxes for checking that homework has been received, assignments completed, and daily grade results. In elementary school, it can include suggestions for homework, book reports, and long-term assignments. Teachers' input is recorded daily. The report is then sent home, initialed by parents, consequences are provided, and the report is returned to the school the next day.

Home notes have been reported to be effective whether or not they are very specific (Kelly, 1990). They have been reported to improve classroom conduct and academic performance in students of all ages, including kindergartners (Budd, Liebowitz, Riner, Mindell, & Goldfarb, 1981), elementary school children (Imber, Imber, & Rothstein, 1979), and secondary school students (Schumaker, Hovell, & Sherman, 1977). With teenagers, however, the manner of presenting the note program and the teenager's willingness to accept and participate actively in its use are critical in determining whether the intervention will be effective. It is beneficial to offer teenagers the opportunity for effective feedback, the potential advantages of the note in achieving the student's

---

Name: _____   **Date:** _____

Please rate this student in each of the following:

Completed classwork	☺	😐	☹
Followed class rules	☺	😐	☹
Got along well with others	☺	😐	☹
Used class time wisely	☺	😐	☹

Comments _____

_____

_____

_____

Figure 15–2.   Home notes

Source: From User's manual, *It's Just Attention Disorder* (videotape) by S. Goldstein and M. Goldstein. Copyright 1991, Neurology, Learning and Behavior Center, Salt Lake City, Utah. Used with permission.

Name: _____   Date: _____

Please rate this student in each of the areas listed below as to how he/she performed in school today using ratings of 5 = excellent, 4 = good, 3 = fair, 2 = poor, 1 = did not work.

	CLASS PERIODS/SUBJECTS						
	1	2	3	4	5	6	7
Participation							
Class work							
Interaction with peers: Class							
Recess							
Teacher Initials							

HOMEWORK:

COMMENTS:

Figure 15–3.   Daily student rating

Source: From User's manual, *It's Just Attention Disorder* (videotape) by S. Goldstein and M. Goldstein. Copyright 1991, Neurology, Learning and Behavior Center, Salt Lake City, Utah.

goals, and the opportunity to earn rewards for becoming more competent in school functioning. Twenty years ago, Ayllon, Garber, and Pisor (1975) found that although school-based reinforcement only modified academic and disruptive behavior in a special classroom on a short-term basis, a daily home note fortified with home rewards reduced classroom behavior problems and resulted in longer-lasting positive impact. McCain and Kelly (1993) successfully used a note intervention with an ADHD preschooler. Teachers were required to write down daily behaviors and observe skills; the note was sent home and predetermined consequences were administered by parents. In a reversal design, the authors demonstrated increased attentiveness, decreased disruptiveness, and decreased activity change during the home note condition; the effect reversed when the child was returned to baseline each time.

Based on an in-depth review of the literature, Lerner and Lowenthal (1992) suggested that teachers adopt fourteen suggestions when working with ADHD students. It is important to note that the suggestions are generic, often described as offering a shotgun approach. Although this model has been criticized (Ysseldyke, Algozzine, & Thurlow, 1992), it may be the best means of providing remedial and compensatory interventions because it reflects the continued lack of specificity in understanding the core deficits of ADHD.

1. Place the youngster in the least distracting location in the class. This may be in the front of the class, away from doors, windows, air conditioners, heaters, and high traffic areas. It may be necessary for the child to face a blank wall or be in a study carrel to enable the child to focus attention.

2. Surround the student with good role models, preferably peers that the child views as *significant others*. Encourage peer tutoring and cooperative learning.

3. Maintain a low student-teacher ratio whenever possible through the use of aides and volunteers.

4. Avoid unnecessary changes in schedules and monitor transitions, because the child with ADHD often has difficulty coping with changes. When unavoidable disruptions do occur, prepare the student as much as possible by explaining the situation and what behaviors are appropriate.

5. Maintain eye contact with the student when giving verbal instructions. Make directions clear, concise, and simple. Repeat instructions as needed in a calm voice.

6. Combine visual and tactile cues with verbal instructions; generally, multiple modalities of instruction will be more effective in maintaining attention and increasing learning.

7. Make lists that will help the student organize tasks, and have the student check them off when they are finished. Students should complete study guides when listening to presentations.

8. Adapt worksheets so that they contain less material on each page.

9. Break assignments into small chunks. Provide immediate feedback on each assignment. Allow extra time if needed for the student to finish the assignment.

10. Ensure that the student has recorded homework assignments each day before leaving school. If necessary, set up a home-school program in which the parents help the child organize and complete the homework.

11. If the child has difficulty staying in one place at school, alternate sitting with standing and activities that require moving around during the day.

12. Provide activities that require active participation, such as talking through problems or acting out the steps.

13. Use learning aides such as computers, calculators, tape recorders, and programmed learning materials. They help to structure learning and maintain interest and motivation.

14. Provide the student opportunities to demonstrate strengths at school. Set up times at which the student can assist peers.

It is also important for the practitioner to help educators understand that symptoms of ADHD can have a pervasive negative impact on progress in relation to other disorders, especially learning disability. Richardson, Kupietz, and Maitinsky (1986) demonstrated in a five-year study of reading achievement in children with learning disability and ADHD that the degree to which methylphenidate reduced the behavioral symptoms of ADHD was a crucial factor in determining a child's response to and progress in a specialized reading program.

ADAPTING THE CURRICULUM

The modification of instructional activities to promote desirable behavior and increase effective classroom performance is based on an extensive research literature (for review, see Dunlap & Kern, 1996). This framework for modification is referred to by some as diagnostic teaching. Whether for kindergarten or high school, it is in the process of adapting the curriculum for the ADHD child that diagnostic teaching differs considerably from traditional teaching. The Greek roots of the word diagnostic are "to know thoroughly." The practitioner must help classroom teachers understand not only the basic issues of ADHD but the unique qualities of each student: their strengths, their weaknesses. A flexible classroom model attempts to meet all students' needs. Flexible teachers will find making adjustments to the needs of their ADHD students no more difficult than making adjustments for any student.

The following suggestions provide a limited, clearly not exhaustive list of practical ways to modify curriculum materials. (The interested reader is also referred to Mather & Roberts, 1996; Mather, 1996; C. Jones, 1994. These texts offer a wealth of practical educational suggestions for the classroom.)

Reading

- Regular classroom assignments should be broken down into shorter assignments. Worksheets and workbooks should be divided into fragments or chunks. Students should be encouraged to work on one chunk at a time.
- Consider the use of color, as described in the coming pages.
- Teach the SQ3R technique to review content material. SQ3R stands for Scan, Question, Read, Recite, and Review. Scanning requires a survey of the material in regard to pictures, headlines, featured key words, and a summary. Questioning means turning each boldface heading and word into a question. After reading the material thoroughly, boldface type should be recited aloud, and finally, key words and questions raised from boldface titles should be reviewed.
- Students should listen to reading selections on tape prior to class discussions.
- If students are asked to read silently at their desk, a list of new words found in the reading should be written on the blackboard.

- Consider having students read together in teams, with one reading aloud while the other listens. Turns should be switched every paragraph.
- Present key vocabulary words in sentence format when they are introduced. This gives immediate meaning to an unknown word.
- Students should be allowed to select high-interest material for independent reading reports and projects. Students should also be encouraged to orally discuss what they have read and even use a tape recorder to record highlights. A system to facilitate organization of ideas, especially when written assignments will be required, should be strongly considered. Such programs can be found in Rooney (1990) and Davis, Sirotowitz, and Parker (1996).

Mathematics

- Use color codes when math symbols are changed on worksheets; for example, make plus signs in green and minus signs in red.
- Students should be encouraged to use one-inch graph paper to help with organization of columns.
- Novel strategies such as "math rap tapes" (Pace, Inc., 7803 Pickering Street, Kalamazoo, Michigan 49022; SRA Technology Training Company, 155 North Wacker Drive, Chicago, Illinois 60606) should be considered to increase interest in exerting the effort necessary to memorize math facts.
- Visual models of lessons taught should be placed on the blackboard when students are required to work independently in class.
- Mnemonic strategies should be considered to help students remember multiple steps in math problems. For example, long division has five separate steps to remember. The teacher can assist the class in creating a mnemonic acronym to **D**ivide, **M**ultiply, **S**ubtract, **C**ompare, **B**ring **D**own.
- Calculators should be offered as a means to help ADHD children check the accuracy of their work.
- Computers and interesting software should be considered for tedious math review and drill.

Written Language

- Encourage use of manipulatives when studying for spelling tests, for example, letter tiles and magnetic letters. This strategy should be alternated with recordings of words on tape, as well as making use of colorful magic markers on a white board to highlight key areas of difficulty (C. Jones, 1991).
- Teach students a simple system to work from a beginning idea, developing connecting thoughts, to completing a written project.
- Offer untimed writing assignments. However, a note of caution: written assignments should be broken into parts with periodic checks to make certain that progress is being made.

- Teachers should be encouraged to offer a grading scale for in-class written assignments that includes one grade for content, one for mechanics, and a final grade that is the average of both (C. Jones, 1994).
- Encourage the use of the computer as a compensatory strategy for both spelling and grammar problems.

Problems related to planning, organization, and final draft appear to plague ADHD students when written assignments are required. Techniques such as acquisition outlines, structured organizers, semantic maps, webs, and matrices help students recognize and focus on main ideas, sequence information, and ultimately stimulate the ability to retain information effectively and efficiently (Schumm & Strickler, 1993). A writing process approach can be particularly beneficial. Such an approach involves steps including:

1. Brainstorming.
2. Categorizing.
3. Mapping.
4. Verbalizing relationships among items.
5. Drafting.
6. Editing.
7. Revising.

An alternative adaptation utilizes a mnemonic monitoring strategy: **SH! COPS!** stands for **S**entence complete, **H**andwriting, **C**apitalization, **O**verall appearance, **P**unctuation, and **S**pelling (Mather & Jaffe, 1992).

Spelling

- Use color cues on word flashcards to identify patterns in spelling words.
- Teach students to clap out syllables while spelling.
- Use repetitive letter sets to enhance recall and add a motor component to the task.
- Teach students mnemonics within word patterns (e.g., do you see the end in friend, it comes at the end).
- Use the computer for spelling review; its highly visual format makes it appealing for practice and rehearsal.
- Allow students to take spelling tests orally or to audiotape them.
- Consider assigning two grades to written projects, one for content and one for spelling.

Test Taking

Hughes (1987) suggests helping children develop "test wiseness." Test wiseness skills are a set of cognitive abilities involving strategies that can be applied in a variety of test settings regardless of test content. Hughes suggests that test taking is a means to evaluate the possession of knowledge. However, most data suggest that test performance depends not only on how hard one studies or how much one knows but on how "test wise" one is. Davis, Sirotowitz, and Parker (1996) offer an extensive set of test-taking strategies.

Improving Attention Using Color

The effective use of color to draw attention to relevant, discriminative stimuli has been well documented (Zentall & Kruczek, 1988; Zentall, 1989, 1993). In one study, children with ADHD attended more readily to a task when color was added than did normal comparison children (Zentall, 1989). When color was added to relevant cues on a spelling task, the result was improved performance. Alternatively, there is evidence to suggest that adding additional color to early trials of a difficult task could produce performance disruption. Zentall (1989) demonstrated that when children with ADHD practiced a spelling assignment with all black letters first and then color was added, they outperformed comparison children. The converse was not found to be true. It is suggested that color be used to enhance rather than distract from tasks. Color accents add key features to repetitive tasks, perhaps increasing interest and motivation. Color cues can also be added to written work, worksheets, and study sheets. Color coding may even increase reading comprehension for students with inattentive problems (Belfiore, Grskovic, Murphy, & Zentall, 1996). These authors report that the use of color had an immediate effect on comprehension across testing assessments with boys experiencing comprehension problems as well as ADHD. In this study, color highlighting was added to silent reading tasks to improve reading comprehension. The first paragraph appeared in black and white, with subsequent paragraphs each appearing in a different color.

Teachers may find these additional tips beneficial:

- Many ADHD students do not remember assignments and related materials; color coding material may improve associations. If the student's math book is coded in blue, a blue box can be provided in which math papers are to be placed. Students may also write their math homework with a blue pencil and place a blue dot on their daily calendars when a math test is scheduled.
- Weekly vocabulary lists can be divided into groups or categories (e.g., all words about animals can be placed in one group; all words that begin with *sh* in another; all words about cars in another; etc.). Each group can then be placed on its own color card.
- Homework folders can be color coded; for example, work going home goes in a green folder, work coming back in a red folder.
- When reading a literature book that may involve remembering characters and names, characters could be color coded as they are introduced in the book by placing a removable, colorful star or dot above the character's name.
- When studying for a content test such as history, factual information can be color coded; all dates to be remembered can be placed on one color card, important places on another, and so on.

- When studying a foreign language and attempting to increase vocabulary recall, all nouns can be placed on one color card, adjectives on another, verbs on a third. Vocabulary cards can then be kept in a word box and reviewed often.

Mnemonic Strategies

Mnemonic symbols or memory devices are excellent alternatives to the typical rehearsal method of memorization. Mnemonics are used to recode, transform, or elaborate information by adding meaningful connections to seemingly unconnected information. Mnemonics may aid in coding by forming associations that do not exist naturally. There is a growing body of literature to support the use of mnemonic techniques in helping students create meaningful links between new and existing information (Carney, Levin, & Levin, 1993). Mnemonic strategies are highly appealing to children who may have difficulty either investing effort or memorizing information (C. Jones, 1994). Mastropieri and Scruggs (1991) provide data to suggest that in classroom applications, student performance on content tasks more than doubles with the application of mnemonic strategies. Mnemonic strategies involving rhythm (beat or chant), categorization or clustering (visual cues that highlight chunks of information), and association (making connections of previously learned materials) can be effective with ADHD children. Once these mnemonics become a tool for learning, students can generalize and transfer these strategies to all learning situations, becoming progressively less dependent on teachers providing strategies (C. Jones, 1994). Practitioners can suggest these additional mnemonic strategies:

- Acronyms and acrostics can be used to make lists of words to be memorized easier to recall. An acronym turns the first letter of each word to be recalled into a phrase or sentence. For example, to remember the five Great Lakes, think of *HOMES* (the first letter of each lake organized this way spells a cue word). Using acrostics, the opposite of acronyms, the sentence is constructed with the first letter of each word used to cue the retrieval of information (e.g., *my very educated mother just sent us nine pizzas* facilitates remembering the nine planets in our solar system in order).
- Help the ADHD student visualize patterns within words that can make a word easier to recall. For example, think of *end* in friend when you write the word.
- Clap out the beats or syllables in a multisyllable word. Students clap with you as you say them aloud. The beat is then repeated as students look at the word and say it silently.
- Teach the mnemonic capital letters RCRC when studying vocabulary words; this stands for **R**ead it, **C**over it, **R**ecite it, **C**heck it. The student takes each word in the list and practices using this cue.

Adolescents

Adolescents with ADHD offer a unique challenge for educators. As reviewed in Chapter 4, the increasing demands for organization to simultaneously complete multiple

Table 15–1. ADD characteristics and remedial strategies used by resource center teachers

Characteristic	Remedial Strategy
Academic	Monitor progress, assist in planning and scheduling courses; maintain communication with other teachers.
Cognitive fatigue	Provide prompts, cues, encouragement; teach metacognitive strategies.
Fine motor dysfunction	Promote use of computers, calculators; modify assignments.
Poor quality control	Encourage self-awareness and self-management.
Disorganization	Support use of acquisition outlines, structured organizers, semantic maps.
Time management problems	Foster use of daily notebook; assist in short- and long-term planning.
Performance inconsistency	Prompt student to use compensatory, self-help, self-monitoring skills.
Problem understanding standing directions	Persuade student to request assistance, clarification; oversee implementation of instructional/test modifications.
Difficulty sequencing information	Teach mnemonic devices.
Poor working memory	Advocate the use of study skills techniques; test-taking strategies.
Inconsistent attention patterns	Maintain close supervision; provide direct instruction.
Difficulty expressing needs	Coach self-advocacy skill development through role play, verbal rehearsal.
Social adjustment problems	Recommend and facilitate involvement in extracurricular activities

Source: Spinelli, C. G. (1997). Accommodating the adolescent with attention deficit disorder: The role of the resource center teacher. *Journal of Attention Disorders, 4,* 213.

tasks places additional burden on adolescent students with ADHD. Spinelli (1997) offers a summary list of remedial strategies that should be considered when working with ADHD adolescents (see Table 15–1). (The interested reader is also referred to Dendy, 1995, for additional strategies and suggestions.)

Computers

The first edition of this text devoted a significant amount of space to a discussion of the use of computers, not necessarily as aids to facilitate learning but as devices to improve attention and reduce impulsivity. In regard to the latter, computers have not met with success; in regard to the former, however, they offer a structured format of infinite variety. They fit the model of brevity, variety, and structure: video games provide brevity in the sense that they contain short sequences with a minimal of delay; the use of highly interesting software provides variety; the use of color animation and graphics may enhance attention for everyone. However, some have suggested that stimulation may actually overwhelm children with ADHD (Lathrop, 1982). At the same time, computer software and other video devices operate within a structured format. Immediate reinforcement in regard to progress in the game is provided. Dailey and Rosenberg (1994) suggest also that computers may teach self-regulation by controlling practice and providing prompts, feedback, and repetitive trials without criticism.

Increasingly, educational software is being designed to meet these criteria and anecdotally is reported as working well with ADHD children. However, research is completely lacking. Fitzgerald, Fick, and Milich (1986) compared computer-assisted instruction to traditional instruction for 9- and 10-year-olds with ADHD. When the results of each student were compared, no differences were found between the traditional instruction and the computer-based instruction for a number of spelling words learned. However, the computer method was at least as effective as a teacher method. Further, while some students were using the computer, the teacher was free to work with other students; freeing up the teacher's time may be the greatest benefit from the use of computers for children with ADHD. Computers are forgiving: they simply repeat the task until mastery is demonstrated. Software and other video activities offer self-paced activities that guide the child to develop independent work skills (Desch, 1986). Computer software that corrects mistakes immediately and operates under continuous reinforcement appears to work best for children with ADHD (Parry & Douglas, 1983).

It has been suggested that computer-assisted instruction that is self-paced and provides immediate, frequent opportunities for responding and consistent correction procedures may be quite beneficial for children with ADHD (Budoff, Thormann, & Grass, 1984). Such instruction may be stimulating and motivating at a much higher rate than typical seatwork activities. However, thus far there has not been definitive research to suggest that the computer actually enhances classroom behavior, time on task, or actual achievement for children with ADHD. However, computers have been found to increase attention to academic tasks among students diagnosed as having learning disabilities (Reith, Bahr, Polsgrove, Okolo, & Eckert, 1987). Such techniques can also be used to accomplish a variety of educational tasks, including drill and practice, tutoring, teaching problem solving, and the practice of written skills (Reith & Semmel, 1991). These authors suggest that the efficacy of computer-based instruction is dependent on a number of variables, including teacher behavior, availability of computers, the degree to which the computer is integrated with teacher-mediated instruction, and students' interest in computer activities. Thus, the conditions under which computers are used with ADHD children, rather than the computer itself, may very well determine the children's success.

Desch (1991) lists aspects of software and hardware that need to be considered when making a choice of computer-assisted instruction for children with ADHD (see Table 15–2).

Books on Tape

There are no data to suggest that books on tape will be particularly beneficial for children with ADHD. However, it can be hypothesized that the use of such instruments at

Table 15–2. **Aspects to consider when evaluating microcomputer software for children with ADHD**

Aspects of the Child	Aspects of the Software	Aspects of the Hardware
Age and developmental level	Appropriate to current curriculum	Appropriateness of the hardware for use with the desired software
Grade level		
Physical disabilities	Quality of documentation	
Learning disabilities	Availability of assistance from the company	Adaptability of hardware (alternative input and output devices available)
Visual-motor abilities		
Attentional control	Single versus integrated program	Durability and maintenance concerns
Parent's perceptions and expectations	Availability of optional input (e.g., large keyboard, touch screen, etc.)	Portability (use at home)
Availability of microcomputer at home		Personal versus shared with others
	Minimal or no sound effects	
	Control over pace of instructional presentation	Cost of equipment and maintenance
	Cost versus perceived benefits	

Source: Desch, L. W. (1991). Microcomputer software in the treatment of attention deficit hyperactivity disorder. In P. J. Accardo, T. A. Blondis, & B. Y. Whitman (Eds.), *Attention deficit disorders and hyperactivity in children.* New York: Marcel Dekker, Inc. Reprinted by courtesy of Marcel Dekker, Inc.

bedtime, in the car, or while the child is engaged in some other enjoyable activity (e.g., coloring or playing with Legos) may prove effective.

If the ADHD child also experiences a learning disability, especially one in which their limited ability to decode is impacting comprehension, books on tape may be extremely beneficial. Books on tape are available from the Recordings for the Blind/Dyslexic, a national, nonprofit organization. It provides textbooks for individuals unable to read standard print due to visual, physical, or perceptual disability. For the past four years this group has responded to the rising demand for these resources for learning-disabled students. This organization has a 7,500 master tape library, with texts ranging from upper elementary to postgraduate levels. If a text is unavailable and has not been previously taped, if deemed to fit within the scope of the collection, the text will be recorded. There are currently over thirty recording studios operated around the country by Recordings for the Blind. To register or request a packet, families should write to Recordings for the Blind/Dyslexic, 20 Rozelle Road, Princeton, New Jersey 08540. A small fee will be required from a family requesting a packet; this fee is paid only once a year, and students can continue using the master tape library throughout their collegiate and vocational career.

A wide selection of unabridged audio books are also available. These tapes can be rented for a month for a nominal fee and then returned by mail (Books on Tape, P.O. Box 7900, Newport Beach, California 92658; and Recorded Books, Box 409, Charlotte Hall, Maryland 20622). Because recorded books have become popular with a wide population, public libraries now offer a variety of books on tape for loan. In addition, books on tape are offered by many retail bookstores.

Accommodation Plans

The majority of students with ADHD do not qualify for related services under the Individuals with Disabilities Education Act (1990). Specific legalities in regard to qualification, types of services one qualifies for, and the responsibility and manner in which these services are provided continue to be debated (Reid et al., 1994; Teeter, 1991). As this text goes to press, ADHD students also do not qualify for Social Security benefits unless extenuating circumstances are present. Students with ADHD who do not experience a specific learning disability or any other type of handicapping condition under IDEA, however, may be eligible for services under Section 504 of the Individuals with Disabilities Act (IDEA; 1977), which protects all students with any disability recognized by the community, even if it is not acknowledged under IDEA. Such disabilities are defined as those related to physical and mental impairment that substantially limits one or more major life activities; one major life activity is learning in an academic environment. Although definitive guidelines have not been provided for school districts to make a determination as to when a child with ADHD requires a 504 plan, should students with ADHD experience difficulty in the classroom, a 504 plan should always be considered. Practitioners should help parents understand that Section 504 prohibits discrimination against persons with disabilities, including students and staff members, in school districts receiving federal financial assistance. Thus, to fulfill its obligation under Section 504, the school district has the responsibility to avoid discrimination in policies and practices regarding its personnel and students. (The interested reader is referred to Latham & Latham, 1994, 1997.)

A 504 plan can be individually designed to include accommodations within the regular classroom. The plan is typically in writing, describes the handicap, and states the accommodations and related services to be provided, how, and by whom. When the school team considers all relevant information, including comprehensive assessments with the parents' input as well as the input of the practitioner, they may then devise a series of accommodations to help students in the classroom. Typical accommodations that might be suggested on the written plan for students with ADHD include:

- Modified assignments.
- Breaking tasks into shorter chunks or segments.
- Assistance from professionals in the school who are familiar with ADHD.
- Consultation with classroom teachers by such professionals.
- A reduction of written or copying tasks.
- Alternative testing measures or methods, including oral testing and the opportunity to take tests in secluded settings.
- The use of compensatory tools in the classroom (e.g., calculators, computers).
- Advance notice of due dates for tests and assignments.
- Home note.
- An outline of the class discussion.
- Supplementing verbal instructions with visual information.

504 ACCOMMODATION PLAN

Name _____ Date _____

Student ID# (FST) _____ Date of Birth _____ CA _____

School _____ Teacher _____ Grade _____

1. Describe the nature of the concern: _____

_____

_____

2. Describe the basis for the determination of handicap (if any): _____

_____

_____

3. Describe how the handicap affects a major life activity: _____

_____

_____

4. The Child Study Team/Intervention Assistance Team has reviewed the files of the above named student and concludes that he/she meets the classification as a qualified handicapped individual under Section 504 of the Rehabilitation Act of 1973. In accordance with the Section 504 guidelines, the school has agreed to make reasonable accommodations and address the student's individual needs by:

PHYSICAL ARRANGEMENT OF ROOM:

____ seating student near the teacher
____ seating student near a positive role model
____ standing near the student when giving directions or presenting lessons
____ avoiding distracting stimuli (air conditioner, high traffic area, etc.)
____ increasing the distance between the desks
____ *Additional accommodations:* _____

LESSON PRESENTATION:

____ pairing students to check work	____ providing written outline
____ writing key point on the board	____ allowing student to tape record lessons
____ providing peer tutoring	____ having child review key points orally
____ providing visual aids	____ teaching through multi-sensory modes
____ providing peer notetaker	____ using computer-assisted instruction
____ making sure directions are understood	
____ including a variety of activities during each lesson	
____ breaking longer presentations into shorter segments	
____ *Additional accommodations:* _____	

(continued)

Figure 15–4.

Source: Developed by the School Board of Broward County, Florida. Used with permission.

ASSIGNMENTS/WORKSHEETS:

___ giving extra time to complete tasks   ___ using self-monitoring devices
___ simplifying complex directions   ___ reducing homework assignments
___ handing worksheets out one at a time   ___ not grading handwriting
___ reducing the reading level of the assignments
___ requiring fewer correct responses to achieve grade
___ allowing student to tape record assignments/homework
___ providing a structured routine in written form
___ providing study skills training/learning strategies
___ giving frequent short quizzes and avoiding long tests
___ shortening assignments; breaking work into smaller segments
___ allowing typewritten or computer printed assignments
___ *Additional accommodations:* _____

TEST TAKING:

___ allowing open book exams   ___ allowing extra time for exam
___ giving exam orally   ___ reading test item to student
___ giving take-home tests
___ using more objective items (fewer essay responses)
___ allowing student to give test answers on tape recorder
___ giving frequent short quizzes, not long exams
___ *Additional accommodations:* _____

ORGANIZATION:

___ providing peer assistance with organizational skills
___ assigning volunteer homework buddy
___ allowing student to have an extra set of books at home
___ sending daily/weekly progress reports home
___ developing a reward system for in-school work and homework completion
___ providing student with a homework assignment notebook
___ *Additional accommodations:* _____

BEHAVIORS:

___ praising specific behaviors   ___ allowing legitimate movement
___ using self-monitoring strategies   ___ contracting with the student
___ giving extra privileges and rewards   ___ increasing the immediacy of rewards
___ keeping classroom rules simple and clear   ___ implementing time-out procedures
___ making "prudent use" of negative consequences
___ allowing for short breaks between assignments
___ cueing student to stay on task (nonverbal signal)
___ marking student's correct answers, not his mistakes
___ implementing a classroom behavior management system
___ allowing student time out of seat to run errands, etc.
___ ignoring inappropriate behaviors not drastically outside classroom limits
___ *Additional accommodations:* _____

Figure 15–4. *(Continued)*

MEDICATION:

    Name of Physician: _____ Phone: _____

    Medication(s): _____ Schedule: _____

    _____ Schedule: _____

    Monitoring of Medication(s): _____ Daily _____ Weekly _____ As Needed Basis

    Administered by: _____

SPECIAL CONSIDERATION:

____ suggesting parenting program(s)   ____ alerting bus driver

____ monitoring student closely on field trip   ____ suggesting agency involvement

____ in-servicing teacher(s) on child's handicap   ____ providing group/individual counseling

____ providing social skills group experiences

____ developing intervention strategies for transitional periods (e.g., cafeteria, physical education, etc.)

DISCIPLINE (Check One):

☐ This student's Section 504 disability (AIDS, asthma, other) would not cause him to violate school rules.

☐ This student's Section 504 disability could cause him to violate school rules. (If second box is checked, fill out Behavior Modification Disciplinary Plan.)

Participants: (name and title)

_____   _____

_____   _____

_____   _____

_____   _____

_____   _____

Case Manager's Signature: _____

Figure 15–4.   *(Continued)*

After the team determines which accommodations can be helpful to the student, every teacher receives a copy of the accommodation plan and one remains in the student's file. Periodic meetings are scheduled by the team and a designated date scheduled to determine accountability. The purpose of these meetings is to assess whether the accommodations made a difference and are still necessary. Figure 15–4 contains a simplified, checklist format 504 plan.

In 1991, a policy memorandum issued by the Office of Special Education and Rehabilitative Services in the U.S. Department of Education expressly recognized that children with ADHD were eligible for assistance in public school settings (Davila, Williams, & MacDonald, 1991). This policy memorandum clarified a number of confusing issues concerning the rights of ADHD children within the public schools. Interested readers are referred to CHADD (499 N.W. 70th Avenue, Suite 109, Plantation, Florida 33317, 954-587-3700) to obtain a complete copy of this memorandum.

DEALING WITH NONCOMPLIANT PARENTS

One of the most frustrating aspects of evaluating and treating children with ADHD occurs with parents who experience the same cluster of temperamental problems as their child. This often precipitates an inability to follow through with what could be beneficial recommendations. Even more frustrating are parents who, for whatever reasons, either deny or choose to ignore the child's problems and are unwilling to participate to help their child. For the community-based practitioner, this often results in valuable information not being passed along to school personnel. However, this situation creates even greater problems for the practitioner in the school setting. Some parents are unresponsive to the educational team's request for increased parental support at home. In extreme situations, some parents may deny the school system the right to provide special services. In such situations, it may be beneficial for the classroom teacher to refer such parents to an outside practitioner or family physician to discuss the child's current behavioral and possible medical problems. It is important for teachers not to engage in a power struggle with parents nor to label the child's behavior as ADHD or any other diagnostic condition. The teacher's role in such situations is to describe, not diagnose. It is also important for teachers to avoid a struggle in which the school advocates for the child to be placed on medication for behavioral problems; this is an inappropriate position for the school to be in and frequently results in more anger and resentment than compliance from parents. Patience and persistence on the part of school personnel is suggested in these situations.

MANAGING MEDICATION

Chapter 13 contains an overview of methods for collecting data that physicians require to effectively manage medication. It is important for the practitioner to help teachers understand that the use of psychoactive medications with children is scientifically sound and that treatment decisions are based on changes observed in the child's behavior in an ongoing rather than a one-time evaluative process. Like the rest of the population, teachers can form distorted opinions about medications, ranging from the idea that they cause additional problems to viewing medications as a "miracle cure." The practitioner must provide classroom teachers with a realistic overview of medications and the areas of problems that can be addressed through medication intervention.

SUMMARY

Teachers play a vital role in the successful school experiences of the ADHD child. This chapter provided the practitioner with the framework to educate teachers regarding an educational model and a specific set of strategies that stem from that model for children with ADHD. It is important for the practitioner to be available and supportive to the classroom teacher. Initially, the practitioner must educate teachers concerning basic background and developmental aspects of ADHD. The practitioner must understand each teacher's style and capability before recommending classroom interventions. He or she must be certain that teachers understand the basic framework within which problems related to ADHD increase the likelihood of classroom difficulties as well as the manner in which the framework for intervention and specific strategies logically follows from an understanding of ADHD symptoms. The interventions suggested in this chapter were designed to be applied in any form of classroom structure or routine. The practitioner must be sensitive to the multiple daily demands placed on teachers and the increased pressure teachers experience when faced with educating one or more children with ADHD. As with parents, the practitioner must be supportive and maintain lines of communication with the ADHD child's teachers.

Chapter 16

SOCIAL SKILLS TRAINING FOR ADHD CHILDREN

Susan M. Sheridan, Ph.D.

The social problems of children with ADHD have been documented by several authors (Frederick & Olmi, 1994; Landau & Moore, 1991; Pelham & Bender, 1982; Whalen & Henker, 1985; Wheeler & Carlson, 1994). Perusal of the diagnostic criteria for all subgroups of ADHD clarifies the nature of the social difficulties experienced by these children. For example, among the central behavioral features of ADHD/HI (hyperactive/impulsive) and ADHD/COM (combined type) are problems with aggression, impulsivity, overactivity, noncompliance, and antisocial tendencies. Children with ADD/I demonstrate deficits in focused attention (Barkley, 1990a), are more socially withdrawn (Edelbrock et al., 1984; Lahey et al., 1984), and are more apt to display symptoms of depression and anxiety than children with ADHD/HI (Lahey et al., 1987). These correlates directly or indirectly interfere with social interactions, the formation of relationships, and the maintenance of friendships over time. Attention to this pervasive difficulty of children with ADHD is therefore essential.

WHY BE CONCERNED WITH THE SOCIAL PROBLEMS OF CHILDREN WITH ADHD?

Interestingly, although the ability to interact appropriately and effectively in social situations is among the most important aspects of one's behavioral competence (Gresham, 1988; Sheridan & Walker, in press), the social world of the child with ADHD has received attention only recently. It has been suggested that over 50% of children with ADHD have problems with interactions with peers (Pelham & Bender, 1982) and in the relationships these children have with others. Concern with the problematic social interactions of children with ADHD is relevant given their centrality, pervasiveness, durability, and recurrence (Whalen & Henker, 1985).

If left untreated, the long-term prognosis of many children with ADHD is bleak. Approximately 50% of children continue to exhibit antisocial symptoms into adulthood (Weiss & Hechtman, 1993). A fifteen-year follow-up found that on behavioral, oral response, and questionnaire tests, hyperactive individuals performed significantly worse than their matched control peers in the areas of job interviews, heterosocial interactions, and assertion. Additionally, they were found to have more problems with severe forms of antisocial behaviors, experience significantly more court appearances, and more often become involved in the selling of nonmedical drugs.

It is important to reiterate what Weiss and Hechtman (1993) emphasized regarding the long-term social outcomes of children with ADHD. Specifically, outcomes are not uniformly good or bad. Some hyperactive young adults appear to function quite adequately; some continue to show significantly more social, emotional, and impulsive problems but do not experience severe psychiatric or antisocial pathology; and some experience significant disturbance that requires psychiatric hospitalization or incarceration. According to these authors, "often not one factor affects outcome in itself, but rather the cumulative effect of a number of factors acting synergistically results in positive or negative picture in adulthood" (p. 105).

DEFINITIONAL CONSIDERATIONS

The term social skills has been defined in numerous ways. Typically, a distinction is made between *social skills* and *social competence*. Social skills are discrete, learned behaviors exhibited by an individual for the purpose of performing a task (Sheridan & Walker, in press). For example, if a child desires to play with a group of children, he or she may use the skill of "joining in." The behavior is observable, measurable, and concrete. Social competence, on the other hand, is concerned primarily with the evaluative judgments of others (Gresham, 1986). It is typically conceptualized in terms of the opinions of others as recipients of social overtures.

Sheridan and Walker (in press) presented a framework of "social skillfulness" that represents a combination of social skills and social competence. They defined social skills as "goal-directed, learned behaviors that allow one to interact and function effectively in a variety of social contexts." To be socially skillful, according to this model, a child must (a) learn a range of important social behaviors that will be necessary in a variety of situations (social skills), and (b) learn to relate in a way that is acceptable to others in a range of social situations (socially competent). In other words, children must have within their behavioral repertoire skills to use across situations, and an awareness of reciprocity within relationships and interactions (including the impact that their behaviors have on others and an ability to take the perspective of another person). They must be able to "read" social situations, have a range of alternative social responses, know what is appropriate in a particular situation, and respond in a way that others find acceptable. Implicit in this complex web of skills and knowledge is the ability to discriminate and generalize from one social situation to another. These are often difficult concepts and skills for any child to master, and they become pronounced when the child has ADHD. The specific social difficulties of children with ADHD are explored below.

THE NATURE OF SOCIAL PROBLEMS OF ADHD CHILDREN

The social problems of children with ADHD are pervasive and durable. Further, their problems are evident not only in their behaviors but also in their relationships and in the perceptions that others have of them. Campbell et al. (1977) found that elementary-aged children with hyperactivity elicit more negative feedback from their teachers, and that the presence of a hyperactive child in a classroom may influence behavioral and interactive patterns within the classroom as a whole (i.e., teachers have been found to interact more negatively with all children in the class when a child with hyperactivity is present). Peers tend to view children with ADHD as deviant and problematic (Pelham & Bender, 1982), and have described them as "noisy," "causes trouble," and "sad or unhappy" (Whalen & Henker, 1985).

Differences between children who are primarily hyperactive-impulsive and those who are primarily inattentive are described elsewhere in this book. Important social differences are also apparent, which may indicate different prognoses and treatment recommendations. The nature of social problems of children with ADHD/HI and ADHD/COM, and those of children with ADHD/I are summarized below.

ADHD/HI and ADHD/COM

The problematic social behavior patterns of children with hyperactivity are now well established (Frederick & Olmi, 1994; Whalen & Henker, 1985; Wheeler & Carlson, 1994). Hyperactive children tend to be demanding, insensitive, bothersome, disruptive, irritating, and socially busy. They are often aggressive (Loney & Milich, 1982; Stewart, Cummings, Singer, & DeBlois, 1981) and may also be the targets of aggressive behaviors of others. They demand a great deal of attention from others, with their behaviors often being more intense or forceful than the situation requires. Although children with hyperactivity generally interact at the same rates as other children (Pelham & Bender, 1982; Whalen & Henker, 1985), the quality of their interactions is often problematic. They have difficulties modulating their responses to match situational demands, they are ineffective at modifying their behaviors to adapt to different expectations, and they are inadequate at establishing or orchestrating plans for positive social interactions.

Children who demonstrate hyperactive symptoms are often actively disliked and rejected by their peer group. Exclusion from play situations places them at greater risk given that it minimizes opportunities for learning socially appropriate responses and forming positive relationships with others.

ADHD/I

Much less research exists on the social functioning of ADHD children whose symptoms are primarily related to inattention rather than hyperactivity and impulsivity. However, research continues to demonstrate that these children also have social difficulties, such as being negatively rated by their peers (Carlson, Lahey, Frame, & Walker, 1987; Carlson, Lahey, Frame, Walker, & Hynd, 1989) and engaging in fewer social interactions overall. Similar to their ADHD/HI counterparts, therefore, they may have fewer opportunities to learn appropriate social behaviors and interaction skills.

Behaviorally, children diagnosed as ADHD/I appear to demonstrate their social difficulties through anxiety, shyness, and social withdrawal (Edelbrock et al., 1984; Lahey et al., 1984; Wheeler & Carlson, 1994). They are more likely to receive a codiagnosis of anxiety or affective disorder, but even when codiagnoses are excluded, they are consistently rated as more anxious and withdrawn by their teachers (Lahey et al., 1987). Much more research is needed with this population of ADHD children, including their processing of social information, abilities to engage in successful social interactions, and status within groups (i.e., neglected or rejected) (Wheeler & Carlson, 1994).

ASSESSING SOCIAL SKILL DEFICITS

There are at least three objectives associated with social skills assessment. First, a good assessment approach will help practitioners accurately identify general and specific social difficulties that are important in situations and contexts that are meaningful to the child with ADHD. Second, assessment outcomes should lead to effective social interventions. Third, assessment procedures should be appropriate to effectively measure the outcomes of a social skills treatment program.

A standard procedure for social skills assessment is not generally recognized (Gresham & Reschly, 1988). Rather, a multisource, multisetting, multimethod model is recognized as best practice (Gresham, 1995). And, rather than focusing solely on the child's social behaviors and deficits, consideration of his or her environment is also useful in a comprehensive assessment.

The identification and definition of specific and observable social behaviors or skills provide the basis of individual social skills assessment. Informant reports (e.g., rating scales), self-reports, skill-based direct or analog observations, and child interviews are methods for assessing the child's social skillfulness. Assessment of the child also considers whether the child is lacking the critical information or behavioral ability to apply a particular skill (skill deficit), or simply does not successfully render the skill in appropriate contexts or with sufficient frequency (performance deficit).

Informant Reports

Informant reports (e.g., rating scales and behavioral checklists completed by parents, teachers, or others who know the child well) are often used for identification and classification purposes. They provide estimates of the frequency of social behaviors, appraisals of skills or performance deficits, and indications of problem areas to investigate when gathering information by interviews or direct observations. Rating scales can also provide normative information, thus providing a general developmental perspective. Sources for rating scales are typically teachers or parents. A number of rating scales are presented in Table 16–1. (Interested readers are referred to Demaray et al., 1995, for more extensive coverage of major social skills rating scales.)

Self-Reports

Self-reports provide unique information about the child's subjective interpretations of social status or skill level. They are best used to assess important cognitive events such as a child's thoughts and opinions about his or her social behaviors and relationships.

Table 16–1.   Review of common social skills checklists and rating scales

Scale	Informant	Scales	Number of Items	Scores	Ages	Psychometric Evidence
Social Skills Rating System (Gresham & Elliott, 1990)	Parent, Teacher, Student	Cooperation Assertion, Responsibility, Empathy, Self-Control; Internalizing, Externalizing, Hyperactivity (parent and teacher forms only); Academic (teacher form only)	Parent = 70 Teacher = 57 Student = 34	Standard scores; M=100; SD=15	Scales available for preschool, elementary, secondary levels	Reliability: test-retest, internal consistency, interrater. Validity: construct, content, criterion-related
Walker-McConnell Scale of Social Competence and School Adjustment (Walker & McConnell, 1988)	Teacher	School adjustment, Peer-preferred social behavior, Teacher-preferred social behavior; Empathy scale (adolescent form only)	43	Standard scores; M=100; SD=15	Scales available for children and adolescents	Reliability: test-retest, internal consistency; interrater. Validity: construct, content, criterion-related
School Social Behavior Scales (Merrell, 1993)	Teacher	Social competence; Anti-social behavior	65	Standard scores; M=100; SD=15	Grades K–12	Reliability: test-retest, internal consistency, interrater. Validity: content, criterion-related, construct
Social Behavior Assessment Inventory	Teacher	Interpersonal behaviors, environmental behaviors, task-related behaviors, self-related behaviors	135	Criterion-referenced; lacks group norms	Grades K–9	Reliability: internal consistency, interrater. Validity: content criterion-related

Very few social skills self-reports are available; the Social Skills Rating System–Self-Report form (Gresham & Elliott, 1990) is one notable exception. In general, self-reports are inherently subjective, lack criterion-related validity, and fail to predict performance on other measures (such as teacher and parent rating scales, sociometric measures, and direct observations of actual social behavior). Therefore, child self-report measures are not recommended as selection or outcome measures (Gresham, 1986). However, given the social cognitive deficits of children with ADHD, it is particularly important to include self-report measures in a comprehensive assessment.

Direct Observations

Direct observations of ADHD children's social behavior are key to understanding peer relationships; they provide information about the frequency of interactions with other children as well as the range of behaviors within the child's repertoire. La Greca and Stark (1986) provide an excellent overview of naturalistic behavioral observations. Focusing on specific skills provides information regarding the nature of the problem and directions for skill-based interventions.

Direct observation of a behavior at the time and place of its actual occurrence provides information about frequency, antecedent, consequent, and sequential conditions. When conducted with specific, operational definitions of target behaviors, it can minimize the subjectivity inherent in many forms of indirect assessment (la Greca & Stark, 1986). Likewise, it is useful for identification, analysis, and evaluation purposes. Specifically, it is conducive to repeated measurements over time, demonstrates sensitivity to treatment effects, and effectively differentiates situational specificity of behaviors.

There are many social skills observational measures available (e.g., Hops, Walker, & Greenwood, 1988; Kahn & Hoge, 1983; Rubin & Daniels-Bierness, 1983; Sheridan, 1995), however, none of these is designed specifically for use with ADHD children. Most systems focus on topographical features of social behaviors, such as rate. However, other aspects of peer interactions, such as quality of behaviors and duration of social exchanges, are generally preferable because they can provide specific information about the nature of the ADHD student's social difficulties, the importance of certain skills, and the effects of interventions on social contacts. As with other assessment methods, direct observations should occur across settings.

Analog Observations

Performance in analog situations (e.g., behavioral role plays) is another means of assessing actual behavioral skills. Analog settings for direct observations are useful when naturalistic observations are not practical. When using role play assessments, the individual conducting the assessment sets the stage for the ADHD child to demonstrate certain behaviors. For example, a hypothetical social problem may be posed to a child (e.g., being teased by a peer), who is asked to provide a response or act out what he or she would do if that situation were experienced personally. Sheridan et al. (1996) used analog role play assessments as one measure of the attainment of social skills in boys with ADHD during social skills training.

Concerns have been raised about the lack of ecological validity of analog role plays, with some studies reporting a lack of correspondence between role play assessments and behavior in the naturalistic setting and sociometric status (see Gresham, 1986 for a review). They are useful, however, in assessing low-frequency behaviors or behaviors that occur in very restricted settings (Shapiro & Kratochwill, 1988). Likewise, they are useful for assessing a child's ability to perform discrete steps that constitute an appropriate social skill (i.e., identification of a skill deficit).

Child Interviews

There are two approaches for using child interviews as an assessment tool. A nonstructured interview will provide information about the child's perceptions of strengths and weaknesses in social situations. Important directions for investigation and intervention can be brought to light by obtaining impressions about antecedent and consequent conditions related to social skills and the perceived effects of one's behavior. A structured interview can help identify specific social skills that should be targeted for intervention. In both cases, reliability and validity are difficult to document because of the diversity inherent in interview conditions (interviewer bias, interviewee response, type and situation of interview) (Sheridan & Walker, in press).

Teacher Nominations and Rankings

Teacher nominations and rankings provide a relative assessment of a child on specific social behaviors in comparison to other children. In nomination techniques, teachers are asked to list a certain number of students who demonstrate a certain behavior to the greatest or least extent compared to other classmates. Teacher ratings of popularity can reliably predict positive interactive behavior (Landau, Milich, & Whitten, 1984). They are cost and time efficient in identifying children who act out but do not provide information regarding the specific nature of a problem or determine goals for treatment.

Sociometric Techniques

Although cross-setting, multimethod, adult-based assessments are important in social skills assessment, a large portion of the peer culture is not accessible to adults, and adults' assessments may be biased by the child's academic performance or behaviors toward adults (Rubin, 1985). Sociometric methods (i.e., peer ratings or nominations) provide important information regarding the child's relative standing within his or her social group. Sociometric methods are used to obtain information on the social impact and preference (i.e., sociometric status) of a child (e.g., popular, rejected, neglected, or controversial). They are based on the assumption that the peer group is a reliable source regarding a child's social acceptability and impact. Indeed, the peer group is most often the primary recipient of the ADHD child's social overtures, and peers are most familiar with the context in which social behaviors occur.

Sociometric techniques take several forms, including peer nominations and peer ratings. Peer nominations require children to identify three to five members of their social group or class according to some criterion. Both positive nominations (e.g., "Circle the names of 3 children you like the best") and negative nominations (e.g., "Circle the names of 3 children you like the least") are used. Children who receive several positive nominations but few negative nominations are considered popular, and those who receive several negative and few positive nominations are classified as rejected. Some children are not named by anyone in the peer group; these children are considered neglected. Finally, those who receive a great deal of both positive and negative nominations are controversial. Early research by Coie, Dodge, and Coppotelli (1982) indicated that approximately 55% of the children in any classroom will be classified in one of these categories. An alternative, multidimensional nomination system, the Revised Class Play, is described by Masten, Morison, and Pelligrini (1985). In this system, children are asked to nominate classmates who fit thirty behavioral descriptors, as if they were casting a play. Standardized scores are obtained for each child across three social competence dimensions: sociable-leadership, aggressive-disruptive, and sensitive-isolative. Using this system, all students in a class receive a score.

Peer ratings consist of a list of the names of every child in the class. A three-option response (positive, neutral, negative) follows each name. Scoring involves averaging the rating of each student; a negative response is given 1 point, a neutral response given 2, and a positive response given 3. When used in conjunction with a positive nomination measure (Asher & Dodge, 1986), this method has been found to be especially reliable in identifying rejected children.

Environmental Assessment

An important consideration in social skills assessment is understanding the environment in which the social behaviors are expected to occur. Some specific objectives of assessing the environmental context include (a) determining the expectations, demands, and norms for behavior in the social environment, and (b) determining conditions within the environment that may precipitate, reinforce, or discourage specific social behaviors.

Careful assessment of the environment through observations and interviews allows for a greater understanding of common behaviors that are likely to be reinforced. Important tasks that are central to success in a particular environment, such as playing group games or cooperative activities with peers, might be identified. Various expectations, norms, and implicit and explicit rules for behavior might be uncovered. Also, by identifying the social behaviors used by children who appear to have several friends, or who are socially competent, additional intervention targets may be identified.

TREATMENT OF SOCIAL DEFICITS

There are several approaches to teaching social skills to children with ADHD, and many are combined in comprehensive programs to maximize treatment effects. Social learning procedures address the specific discrete behaviors of students and focus on teaching alternative, appropriate methods of interacting with others. Social cognitive procedures address the internal events of the ADHD child or adolescent and focus on such cognitions as attributions for social events and means-end thinking. Operant procedures focus on environmental contingencies such as antecedents and consequences of social behaviors, often attempting to manipulate such contingencies to maximize a child's use of effective social skills.

Social Learning Procedures

According to social learning theory, social behaviors are acquired through observation and reinforcement (Bandura, 1977). The most common form of social skills intervention using social learning principles in modeling.

Modeling is an effective type of social learning procedure often used in social skills training (Gresham, 1988; Wandless & Prinz, 1982). It involves the use of films, audiotapes, videotapes, or live demonstrations to depict the skills to be acquired.

Modeling is typically carried out in three steps. The first step is skill instruction. Skill instruction entails the identification of essential skill components, a discussion about the rationale for a particular social skill, and dissemination of information about skill performance. In this first step, ADHD children and adolescents are taught verbally the behavioral sequence (i.e., step-by-step process) for performing important social skills.

The second step of modeling is skill demonstration. In this step, the behavior is modeled by a social skills trainer, teacher, peer, or videotaped demonstration. The child or adolescent is instructed to observe the social behaviors and identify salient components of the performance.

The third step in modeling is skill performance. After social skills are presented and modeled, the ADHD individual is required to perform the skill through role-play procedures. It is typically best to request that the child physically act out the behaviors that have been observed (Cartledge & Milburn, 1995). Active attempts at skill performance are typically responded to with constructive feedback from social skills trainers, who instruct the child to continue role-playing until accuracy is achieved.

Research on the effects of modeling has yielded generally positive results. For example, modeling has been shown to effectively increase the amount of social interaction (O'Connor, 1969, 1972), positively affect problem-solving behavior (Debus, 1970), and improve sociometric status (Gresham & Nagle, 1980).

To learn new skills via modeling, the ADHD child must attend to and understand the most important components of the model's behaviors, retain these for future use, and demonstrate adequate motivation to perform the desired behavior. Therefore, modeling is often coupled with cognitive-based strategies and operant techniques in social skills training programs.

Cognitive Behavioral Procedures

Cognitive behavioral intervention procedures emphasize a child's internal cognitions (thoughts, self-statements) and problem-solving abilities. Two common procedures include coaching and social problem solving.

Coaching

Coaching procedures involve direct verbal instructions and discussion as the major mediums of intervention. A coach (e.g., social skills trainer, teacher, or parent) first provides the child with specific rules or steps for a behavior. The coach and child then rehearse the steps, and the coach provides feedback about the child's performance. Coaching is often paired with other social skill intervention methods (such as modeling and positive reinforcement) to maximize its effects.

The efficacy of coaching has been studied empirically, with generally favorable results (e.g., Gottman, Gonso, & Schuler, 1976; Gresham & Nagle, 1980; Ladd, 1981; Mize, 1995; Oden & Asher, 1977). For example, Oden and Asher (1977) used coaching to effectively teach participation, communication, cooperation, and peer reinforcement. The procedure resulted in increased demonstration of the target social skills and improved participants' sociometric status. Similarly, Mize (1995) coached children on specific social skills (i.e., leading, supporting, questioning, and commenting) and the underlying components of social competence (social knowledge, performance proficiency, and monitoring/self-evaluation) and found substantial improvements in both skill use and sociometric ratings.

Social Problem Solving

Social problem solving (SPS) interventions address a combination of cognitive, emotional, and behavioral factors associated with social competence. Such approaches teach children the process of solving social problems by logically evaluating interpersonal problems and considering alternative, adaptive solutions (Spivack & Shure, 1982; Weissberg, 1985). These interventions attempt to teach target students (a) that they can resolve most problematic social situations; (b) how to recognize when problems exist; (c) to generate various alternative solutions to reach social goals and to consider their consequences; (d) how to select a strategy and develop a plan of action; (e) means of carrying out the strategy competently; and (f) methods of self-monitoring behaviors, evaluating their effectiveness, and modifying plans (Weissberg, 1985). The procedures typically teach children to analyze problems by asking a series of questions, such as What is the problem?; What are my choices?; What are the consequences?; What is my best choice?; and How did I do? They are common components of several social skills curricula.

As reviewed in Chapter 13 research on cognitive-based social-problem-solving procedures has produced mixed results. Several reviewers report the overall findings from social-problem-solving interventions to be positive (e.g., Spivack & Shure, 1982; Urbain & Kendall, 1980), but others interpret the general outcomes as negative (e.g., Abikoff & Gittelman, 1985; Durlak, 1983; Kirschenbaum & Ordman, 1984). It should be noted that many of the studies investigating the efficacy of cognitive-based social-problem-solving procedures assess cognitive thoughts or ideas as the primary outcome measures, without attention to behavioral change as a function of training.

Operant Techniques

Operant techniques are those that focus on manipulation of antecedents and consequences with the intent of increasing the likelihood that ADHD students will demonstrate improved social skills in the natural environment. Antecedent events are those that precede desired social behaviors and increase their likelihood of occurrence, and consequent events are those that follow a behavior and increase future use.

Manipulation of Social Antecedents

By altering the social environment, a stage can be set for positive interactions to occur naturally. Thus, these techniques are important in promoting successful relationships in ADHD children and adolescents. Methods of manipulating antecedent events include cooperative learning and peer-initiation strategies.

Cooperative learning is a technique whereby small groups of students work together toward an academic goal. The objectives of cooperative learning are typically characterized as enhancing personal growth, peer relations, interracial relations, classroom climates, and academic achievement (Furman & Gavin, 1989). Research in each of these areas yields generally positive results. Although there are methodological flaws in some of the empirically based outcome research, cooperative learning has been found to have a positive impact on self-esteem (Blaney, Stephan, Rosenfield, Aronson,

& Sikes, 1977), interpersonal cooperation and altruism (Hertz-Lazarowitz, Sharan, & Steinberg, 1980), locus of control (Johnson, Johnson, & Scott, 1978), role-taking (Bridgeman, 1981), sociometric status (Slavin & Karweit, 1981), interracial relations (DeVries, Edwards, & Slavin, 1978; Slavin, 1983a), classroom environment (DeVries & Slavin, 1978), and student achievement (Johnson, Maruyama, Johnson, Nelson, & Skon, 1981; Sharan, 1980; Slavin, 1983b).

An important social skills intervention method involves peer-initiated contact, wherein confederate peers initiate social interactions with target children. Peers are also taught how to respond to the target child's possible responses. The research in this area has produced convincing evidence that children can foster socially interactive behavior in each other (e.g., Hendrickson, Strain, Tremblay, & Shores, 1982; Sisson, Van Hasselt, Hersen, & Strain, 1985; Strain, Kerr, & Ragland, 1979; Strain, Shores, & Timm, 1977); however, it has been used most extensively to encourage the social interactions of withdrawn children.

Manipulation of Consequences

Procedures that attempt to alter behavioral consequences generally focus on reinforcing positive social behaviors in the natural settings in which they occur. Two reinforcement techniques are common in social skills interventions: contingent social reinforcement and group contingencies.

Contingent social reinforcement is often used to increase the effective use of appropriate social behaviors in desirable situations. In contingent social reinforcement, a teacher, parent, or other significant person reinforces appropriate social behavior socially and/or concretely, with the delivery of reinforcers contingent on the child's demonstration of a desired behavior. A variety of reinforcement methods can be used to maximize interest and motivation, such as contracts, spinners, tokens, or point systems (Rhode, Jenson, & Reavis, 1992; Sheridan, 1995).

Group contingencies involve the application of consequences for behaviors of group members (e.g., classrooms) and can be applied in various ways. For example, reinforcement can be applied contingent on the behavior of selected children rather than an entire group (dependent group contingency), based on individual behavior regardless of the behavior of others (independent group contingency), or based on the collective behavior of the entire group (interdependent group contingency). These procedures have been found to be effective for teaching social skills in classrooms (Crouch, Gresham, & Wright, 1985; Gamble & Strain, 1979). Because children serve as behavior managers for themselves, group contingencies are also efficient in teacher time and effort.

GENERALIZATION OF SOCIAL SKILLS

Social skills interventions with ADHD individuals are effective only if they can demonstrate that appropriate behaviors are being used in naturally occurring, meaningful social situations. Considerations about generalization should occur early in the assessment process when selecting skills to teach. It is important that the behaviors taught in the first place have social validity (Moore, 1994). In other words, it is critical that social skills interventions produce behaviors that are empirically linked to important social outcomes (Sheridan & Walker, in press).

A number of strategies designed to promote generalization of social skills have been documented, including the train-and-hope method, modifying consequences, and training sufficient exemplars. In the train-and-hope procedure, an intervention is employed in a training setting, and generalization is examined without any active treatment. Not surprisingly, this is the least effective generalization strategy (DuPaul & Eckert, 1994). When consequences are modified in the natural setting, contingencies are put into place to alter the environmental control of social behaviors (e.g., providing social praise each time an appropriate or desired social behavior is exhibited). Finally, when sufficient exemplars are used, stimuli (e.g., significant persons, objects, or settings) that are common to the natural environment are included in training. For example, significant peers might be included in training sessions, and training may occur on the playground to increase the similarity between the training and criterion environments.

Additional means of promoting generalization are summarized in Table 16-2. Some promising and easy-to-implement strategies include teaching relevant behaviors that are likely to be maintained naturally (e.g., turn taking and sharing toys; McConnell, 1987); fading contingencies (e.g., reinforcers) to occur at a level that approximates the natural environment; training important social behaviors across multiple contexts (e.g., teaching sharing behaviors in the classroom, on the playground, and in structured groups such as Scouts); general case instruction (teaching a range of skills with instruction on the social contexts in which they are appropriate and inappropriate; Horner, McDonnell, & Bellamy, 1986); and offering booster sessions at regular intervals (Elliott & Busse, 1991). Examples of empirical studies that have effectively incorporated generalization strategies into social skills interventions include Bierman, Miller, and Stabb (1987), Foxx, Faw, and Weber (1991), Gunter, Fox, Brady, Shores, and Cavanaugh (1988), Hansen, St. Lawrence, and Christoff (1989), Lewis and Sugai (1993); Rhode et al. (1983), and Smith, Young, West, Morgan, and Rhode

Table 16–2. Examples of generalization facilitators

1. Teach behaviors that are likely to be reinforced and maintained by the others in the natural environment (e.g., prosocial behaviors).

2. Teach a variety of alternative positive social responses.

3. Make the training situation as comparable to the natural environment as possible by including stimuli (e.g., meaningful persons and settings) that are common to the natural environment.

4. Fade consequences to approximate those that occur in the natural environment.

5. Reinforce the use of positive social skills in new and appropriate situations.

6. Reinforce social goal-setting, accurate self-reports, and self-monitoring of performance.

7. Include peers in training.

Source: S. M. Sheridan. (1995). Building social skills in the classroom. In S. Goldstein (Ed.), *Understanding and managing children's behavior in the classroom: A biopsychosocial approach.* New York: Wiley.

(1988). (Interested readers are referred to Landrum and Lloyd, 1992, for a review of these and other studies.)

CURRICULA FOR SOCIAL SKILLS TRAINING

Several curricula are available focusing on social skills training with children and adolescents. Most programs can be characterized as skill-based or problem-solving approaches. Additionally, programs to prevent aggression and violence are gaining popularity recently. Although some research support exists for most programs, few have been developed or empirically validated for children with ADHD. Exceptions are *The Tough Kid Social Skills Book* (1995) and *Why Don't They Like Me?* (1998) program by Sheridan. A number of programs are reviewed briefly below.

Skill-Based Approaches

Skill-based approaches assume that ADHD children lack the basic skills to carry out social interactions effectively and focus on teaching discrete skills to get along with others. Skills such as asking for help, having a conversation, accepting praise and criticism, and giving feedback are examples of training targets in these programs. Often, direct instruction coupled with social learning and operant techniques are used to teach skills. Examples of skill-based programs include Skillstreaming, ASSET, Getting Along with Others, and ACCEPTS.

Skillstreaming

Skillstreaming (Goldstein, Sprafkin, Gershaw, & Klein, 1980; McGinnis, Goldstein, Sprafkin, & Gershaw, 1984) is a structured learning approach to teaching social skills. Components of structured learning include modeling, role-playing, performance feedback, and transfer of training. Separate programs are available for elementary students and adolescents. Skills taught in the programs include beginning social skills, advanced social skills, skills for dealing with feelings, skill alternatives to aggression, skills for dealing with stress, and planning skills. Homework assignments involving skill practice and self-monitoring of skill use are integral parts of the programs. Assessment checklists and leader instructions are included.

ASSET: A Social Skills Program for Adolescents

ASSET (Hazel, Bragg-Schumaker, Sherman, & Sheldon-Wildgen, 1981) is a skill-based program for adolescents that teaches eight specific social skills: giving positive feedback, giving negative feedback, accepting negative feedback, resisting peer pressure, problem solving, negotiating, following instructions, and conversation. Nine steps are used to teach each skill, including discussion, rationales for using the skill, modeling of the skill, and verbal and behavioral rehearsal. Homework is assigned following skill mastery, and parents are asked to evaluate their child's use of each social skill. A videotape is also available, which depicts adolescents in situations that require the use of social skills taught in the ASSET program.

Getting Along with Others: Teaching Social Effectiveness to Children

The Getting Along with Others program (Jackson, Jackson, & Monroe, 1983) was designed for elementary-aged children, and it can be modified for use with older students and mentally retarded adults in a variety of settings (regular and special classes, day care centers, group homes). It combines a number of structured teaching strategies, including positive feedback, ignore-attend-praise, teacher interaction, direct prompt, sit-and-watch, and relaxation training. The seventeen lessons that constitute the program include following directions, joining a conversation, offering to help, sharing, and problem solving. An activity period is included to allow for the practice of newly learned skills. Homework is also assigned to promote the use of skills in nontreatment settings.

The Walker Social Skills Curriculum: The ACCEPTS Program

The ACCEPTS program (Walker et al.1983) is designed for mildly and moderately handicapped and nonhandicapped students in kindergarten through grade 6. Emphasis is placed on the teaching of skills to facilitate adjustment to mainstream settings. ACCEPTS (A Curriculum for Children's Effective Peer and Teacher Skills) categorizes twenty-eight discrete skills into five major areas: classroom skills, basic interaction skills, getting along skills, making friends skills, and coping skills. The teaching approach incorporates clear definitions of each skill, use of positive and negative examples, sequencing of skills on a continuum of increasing complexity, provision for practice activities, and use of systematic correction procedures. Assessment materials for screening and placement of students and a videotape are available to enhance appropriate skill training.

Problem-Solving Approaches

Problem-solving approaches to social skills training teach students to identify social problems, generate solutions or alternatives, determine consequences, and evaluate outcomes. These programs typically utilize cognitive behavioral training techniques such as cognitive modeling; overt external guidance; faded, overt, self-guidance; and covert self-instruction. Examples of problem-solving curricula include Think Aloud and Spivack and Shure's interpersonal cognitive problem-solving program.

Think Aloud Classroom Program

The Think Aloud program (Camp & Bash, 1985) was developed to teach elementary students (grades 5 and 6) steps to solve interpersonal problems. Students are taught to ask themselves four questions: (1) What is my problem?; (2) How can I do it?; (3) Am I using my plan?; and (4) How did I do? The program was originally designed to teach aggressive boys methods of dealing with social problems.

Interpersonal Cognitive Problem Solving

Interpersonal cognitive problem solving (ICPS) focuses on how children think about and approach interpersonal problems. Attention is placed on the problem-solving process, not problem solutions per se. Most noteworthy of the programs developed using this framework is the Problem-solving Approach to Adjustment (Spivack, Platt, & Shure, 1976), which consists of lessons to teach students to generate novel and competent solutions to interpersonal dilemmas.

The primary method used to encourage children to think about social situations is called dialoguing, a verbal interaction technique designed to help students generate their own solutions to problems, rather than providing them with solutions. Six skills constitute the focal training targets: alternative solutions thinking, consequential thinking, causal thinking, interpersonal sensitivity, means-end thinking, and perspective training. Although the original program was designed for young aggressive children, it has been extended to preadolescents, adolescents, and adults.

In ICPS, there are generally three levels at which interventions can be directed: (1) knowledge of specific behavioral strategies and the context in which those strategies should be displayed; (2) the ability to convert knowledge of social strategies into skillful social behaviors in interactions with peers; and (3) the ability to evaluate one's own performance and adjust it according to environmental demands. Programs that emphasize all three areas have been found to be the most successful.

Aggression and Violence Prevention Programs

A number of programs have recently been published that focus on addressing or preventing aggression and violence. A comprehensive review of such programs is provided in Larson (1994). Many noteworthy programs that deal with issues of violence include interventions that emphasize anger control using cognitive behavioral procedures.

Anger-Control Training

Anger-control training programs are aimed at teaching aggressive youth means for decelerating anger arousal, which is believed to be an important precursor of antisocial behavior (Feindler & Ecton, 1986; Feindler & Fremouw, 1983; Novaco, 1975). Anger-control training procedures typically consist of modeling, role-playing, performance feedback, and homework.

The original anger-control intervention developed by Novaco (1975) consisted of three stages: cognitive preparation (instruction on the cognitive, physiological, and behavioral aspects of anger; its positive and negative functions; and its antecedents); skill acquisition (teaching alternative coping skills and self-instruction for use during provocations); and application training (including imaginal and role-play situations and homework to facilitate practice of coping skills and self-statements). The process of anger control is achieved by a series of self-statements that corresponds with each component of the provocation sequence, including preparing for provocation, impact and confrontation, coping with arousal, and reflecting on the provocation. Extensions of the original model emphasize cues (the physiological and kinesthetic sensations that signal anger arousal); triggers (external events and internal appraisals that serve as provocations to anger); reminders (the self-instructional statements that may serve to reduce anger arousal); reducers (additional techniques that may reduce arousal, such as relaxation techniques); and self-evaluation (self-reinforcement or self-correction strategies; Feindler & Fremouw, 1983), and an emphasis on adaptive skills for anger expression (Feindler & Ecton, 1986).

Second Step: A Violence Prevention Curriculum

The Second Step program (Committee for Children, 1992) is designed to "reduce impulsive and aggressive behavior in young children and increase their level of social competence" (p. 1). Three skills are taught via direct instruction: empathy, impulse control, and anger management. Separate curricula packages are available for preschool/kindergarten, grades 1–3, and grades 4–5. Each package consists of up to sixty lessons using photos, queries, modeling, and role-playing (puppets and a song tape are also included at the preschool level).

Social Skills Training for ADHD Children

Although several social skills curricula now exist, few have been developed or validated for children with ADHD. An exception is a two-tiered program (i.e., child and parent training) by Sheridan (1995, 1998). This combination program focuses not only on the specific skill and performance deficits of children with ADHD, but also on ways that parents can serve as social skills agents and generalization facilitators. In other words, an extensive parent training component (Why Don't They Like Me?) is added to the child training component (Tough Kid Social Skills) to maximize treatment effects and generalization. Together, these programs combine important elements of social skills training (i.e., modeling, coaching, role-playing, reinforcement, generalization programming) to address specific social difficulties encountered by ADHD children.

The Tough Kid Social Skills Program

The Tough Kid Social Skills program (Sheridan, 1995) targets children with ADHD between the ages of 8 and 12. It can be conducted in small or large groups (e.g., pull-out groups or classrooms) over a period of ten weeks. Group sessions are sixty minutes in duration and follow a similar sequence from week to week.

Three skill areas are taught in the Tough Kid Social Skills program: social entry (e.g., joining in), maintaining interactions (e.g., having a conversation), and problem solving (e.g., dealing with teasing). Each of these are taught using cognitive behavioral procedures such as discussion, modeling, role-playing, and performance feedback. In addition, this model emphasizes the development and use of personal goals, which allow group facilitators to individualize program objectives for students within each session. Specifically, along with the general skills training provided for all group members, individual targets are defined for students that address identified needs. For example, likely personal goals for students with ADHD include such behaviors as "pay attention to peers by using eye contact and responding to questions or comments," "suggest at least three positive choices to problems discussed," and "use 'I statements' when describing problems." Often, personal goals are incorporated into homework and contracts (i.e., self-monitoring and contingency programs) to maximize attention to these important behaviors outside of the treatment setting. Although research on the effects of personal goals is preliminary, it appears that they are important contributors to the overall effects of social skills training.

Several additional procedures are incorporated into the Tough Kid Social Skills program to facilitate assessment, treatment, and generalization. Assessment forms for teacher nominations, sociometric assessments, interviews (adult and child), and structured behavioral observations are included. Detailed outlines for group implementation are provided for each skill, including specific statements that can be used for instruction, discussion, demonstration, and role plays. The general structure of these sessions is depicted in Table 16–3. Generalization facilitators include goal setting, contracts, self-monitoring, and reinforcement. Importantly, generalization cues in the form of structured prompts and contingent reinforcement are encouraged for use by adults in naturalistic environments (e.g., teachers, parents).

In addition to the structured implementation outlines for conducting training sessions, reproducible forms (e.g., self-monitoring skill sheets, social skills contracts, behavior charts, home-school notes), and how-to suggestions for trainers are included in the program. Likewise, forms that solicit information about specific social situations encountered by target children are used to allow for relevant and meaningful role plays. One such form is presented in Figure 16–1.

Why Don't They Like Me? Program for Parents

In Why Don't They Like Me? Helping Your Child Make and Keep Friends (Sheridan, 1998), parents are taught various skills and strategies to allow them to be the primary treatment agent for their child. First, they are presented with techniques to teach their child social skills using procedures similar to those used by professionals (e.g., coaching, modeling, role-playing, reinforcing, goal setting). Second, step-by-step strategies that parents can use to encourage their child to use appropriate social skills in real-life situations (e.g., cueing, prompting) are included. Third, parents are taught important means to support their child's friendships by increasing social opportunities, talking openly with their child, and problem solving. A script for parents to follow with their child, how-to recommendations, recipe cards for skill training, skill checklists, and flowcharts for decision making are included to simplify the procedures. Flowcharts for talking and solving problems and reminding (cueing) are depicted in Figures 16–2 and 16–3.

The Why Don't They Like Me? program can be used in a group format or it can be self-administered. When taught in a group, leaders use discussion, modeling, role-playing, and feedback to structure the training. Importantly, the group structure allows

Table 16–3. General outline for social skills training

1. Review from previous week.
2. Skill introduction.
3. Rationale and discussion.
4. Skill instruction.
5. Skill demonstration (modeling).
6. Skill practice (role-playing).
7. Performance feedback.
8. Delivery of contingent concrete reinforcement.
9. Goal-setting/contract development (with parents).
10. Skill prompts.

Source: Excerpted and adapted from Sheridan, S. M. (1995). *The tough kid social skills book.* Longmont, CO: Sopris West. Used with permission of the author.

Student's Name _____ **Date** _____

Your Name _____

This student is involved in a social skills group where he/she is learning how to improve his/her relationships with others. We would like your help in making the group a positive experience for this student. Please take a few minutes of your time and complete the following questions. We will use this information during the group as examples and situations for the student to work through. In this way, the things we do in group should be much more meaningful for him/her. Thank you!

Describe any general concerns you have about this student's friendships and social skills. In other words, generally speaking, how does this student get along with his/her peers?

Describe at least three specific problematic situations that recently occurred between this student and other students. Be specific with your examples.

1. _____

_____

_____

_____

_____

_____

2. _____

_____

_____

_____

_____

_____

_____

3. _____

_____

_____

_____

_____

_____

_____

Figure 16–1.   Social situations for role play form
Source: From Sheridan, S. M. (1995). *The Tough Kid Social Skills Book.* Longmont, CO: Sopris West. Used with permission of the author.

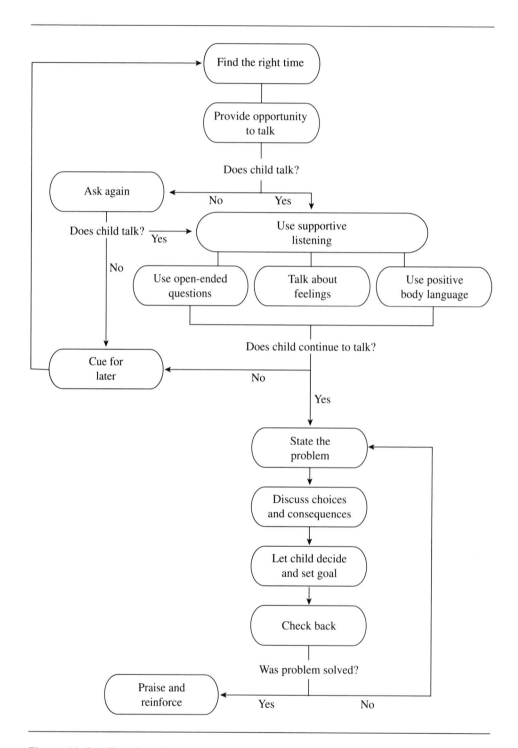

Figure 16–2.   Flowchart for talking and solving problems

Source: From Sheridan, S. M. (1998). *Why Don't They Like Me? Helping Your Child Make and Keep Friends.* Longmont, CO: Sopris West. Used with permission of the author.

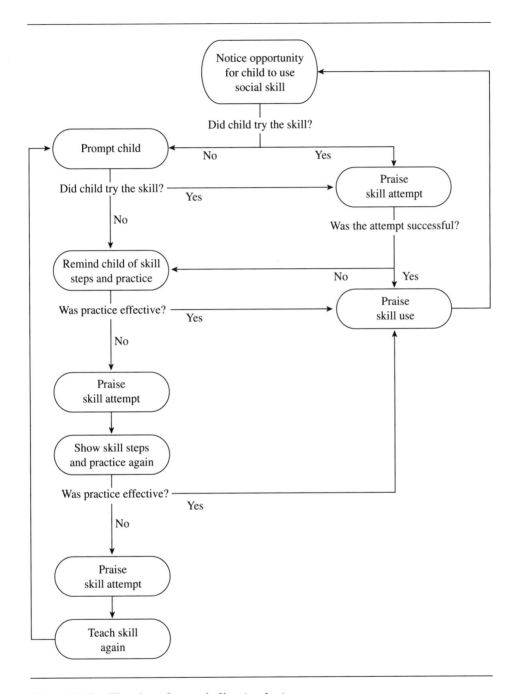

Figure 16–3.   Flowchart for reminding (cueing)

Source: From Sheridan, S. M. (1998). *Why Don't They Like Me? Helping Your Child Make and Keep Friends.* Longmont, CO: Sopris West. Used with permission of the author.

facilitators to combine elements of the child sessions with the parent program to max-imize training efficiency and efficacy. However, research to date has not investigated the differential effectiveness of the self-instructional materials versus the materials in combination with a parent group (or the additive benefits of the group model) in pro-ducing meaningful change in parents' skills as related to social skills training for chil-dren with ADHD.

Sheridan et al. (1996) described a study that tested the efficacy of the Tough Kid Social Skills and Why Don't They Like Me? programs for elementary-aged boys with ADHD. The child-based intervention comprised ten weekly sessions focusing on target skills in the areas of social entry, maintaining interactions, and solving problems. Training modalities included skill instruction, modeling, role play, homework, and re-inforcement. A parent group met separately but simultaneously with the children's group to teach parents skills to help their children with their social problems. Parents were taught the skills of debriefing/active listening, problem solving, and goal setting. A multiple baseline across behaviors design was used for child and parent subjects. Child subjects demonstrated substantial positive changes in their social initiation and maintenance skills as assessed in analog role plays. Positive changes also were noted in subjects' problem-solving skills; however, more variability in performance was noted in these behaviors during treatment. Parents' skills in debriefing, problem solving, and goal setting also improved, as demonstrated on home-based audiotape assessments. All subjects reported improvements of at least one standard deviation on self-report social skills rating scales, and parent and teacher reports also suggested general improvement for most subjects. Positive changes also were evident in some aspects of the subjects' cognitive problem-solving abilities. In general, behavioral changes were considered to be socially valid, and all parent and child subjects viewed the social skills interven-tions very positively. Some subjects generalized some skills to playground settings; however, more research is needed in this area.

SUMMARY

The social difficulties of children and adolescents with ADHD are broad. Problems with impulse control, behavioral regulation, and attributional biases—the cornerstone characteristics of ADHD—interfere with the ability to make and keep friends. Many children with ADHD are actively rejected by their peer group, and children who are both rejected and aggressive are at great risk for long-term social-behavioral problems. Therefore, professional attention must be paid to remediating the specific social skills deficits of these children and adolescents.

A number of procedures for social skills assessment, intervention, and generaliza-tion were offered in this chapter. Additionally, a brief review of various social skills curricula was provided. Comprehensive social skills training that addresses the com-plex cognitive and behavioral deficits of these children is important. Likewise, to max-imize effectiveness and increase generalization, several individuals in the child's life (e.g., parents, teachers, peers) should be included, and training should occur across multiple settings (e.g., home, school, community). This will ensure coordinated and integrated services.

Chapter 17

TEACHING PARENTS TO COPE WITH AND MANAGE ADHD CHILDREN

In general, our society believes that good parenting leads to positive parent-child inter-actions and ultimately optimal child life outcome. However, the definition of "good parenting" certainly varies by culture and observer. Differences arise not only be-tween researchers and clinicians but between parenting experts and the community. As Erikson (1963) hypothesized, children with a difficult temperament may be difficult to parent well, which sets the stage for problems with trust and forming healthy rela-tionships. Although the links among parental attitudes and knowledge of child rearing, parenting behavior, and child outcome are not always consistent, researchers have demonstrated that these elements are related beyond a chance level (Holden & Ed-wards, 1989; for review, see Benasich & Brooks-Gunn, 1996). The latter authors have demonstrated that a small but significant effect is found between maternal knowledge of child development and child outcome. They suggest that direct and indirect influ-ences are operating. As others have noted, maternal knowledge and beliefs in fact provide a mechanism for facilitating long-lasting changes in child outcome (Bronfen-brener, 1975; Freeman & Johnston, 1992; Zigler, 1992). A diagnosis of ADHD in their children has been found to facilitate parents' ability to feel better about themselves, understand their children, and feel more competent in their ability to help (Siegal, 1992).

Although it is clear that parent training for ADHD does not contribute as much to symptom relief as medication, it is important for practitioners to recognize that family characteristics, including parental psychiatric problems, capacity to cope with stress, beliefs, attitudes, and parenting style, contribute much to life outcome for children. Family characteristics and secondary symptoms associated with family functioning, such as aggressive behavior, have been demonstrated to be among the strongest pre-dictors of long-term outcome for children with ADHD (Weiss & Hechtman, 1986). Positive future outcome for all children has been associated with stable family envi-ronments, consistent discipline, positive parental expectations for their future, positive parent-child relationships, perceptions of competence perceived by parents, and low rates of parental criticism (Doberman, 1993).

Based on a comprehensive review of the literature, Yoshikawa (1994) suggested that chronic delinquency has an early age of onset and is highly stable. Programs providing early family support and education serving urban low-income families in-volving both child-focused educational components and parent-focused informa-tional training and emotional support components were suggested as the most promising method of primary prevention of early-onset chronic delinquency. Programs that last at least two years and provide high-quality educational intervention, infant day care or preschool information, and emotional support concerning development as well as child-rearing training, were suggested as the most beneficial. Given the beyond-chance relationship of ADHD to chronic delinquency and that chronic delinquency is the "worst nightmare" outcome for ADHD, these data have significant relevance for the practitioner. Evidence for the effectiveness of parent training specifically for ADHD on symptom relief is inconclusive, but this may not be because these treatments are ineffective. Instead, evidence may be lacking because research in this regard is extremely difficult, including the appropriate identification and selection of subjects, the ability to evaluate parental compliance in using the procedures at home and issues related to long-term follow-up. Nonetheless, Barkley (1987a) suggests that because the effects of clinic-based interventions have limited generalizability, training parents to implement daily interventions at home cannot but help to facilitate generalization. Even with current medications, there are down times when parents must manage the behavior of their ADHD children. Parent training can also be hypothesized to add to adults' sense of efficacy and the capacity to manage their child. Parent training has been demonstrated to reduce parenting stress and increase sense of competence (Pisterman, McGrath, Firestone, Goodman, Webster, & Mallory, 1992).

This chapter begins by providing the practitioner with the available research related to parenting children with ADHD. The initial focus will be on parents, including their levels of stress, psychiatric problems, beliefs and cognitions, as well as parenting style. Although parent training programs have been suggested as perpetuating a tone of "maternal inadequacy or hostility as the predominant stimulus for behavior difficulties in most ADHD children" (Whitman & Smith, 1991, p. 189), the preponderance of research on ADHD and child psychopathology in general does not suggest this to be the case. The chapter also briefly reviews patterns of service delivery and the research on training parents to effectively cope with and manage the behavior of their ADHD children. Finally, a model is presented to facilitate the practitioner's success in not only motivating but helping parents modify how they interact with their ADHD children. The model and suggestions for preschool through adolescence is not offered as a comprehensive parent program, but can be used in conjunction with a wide range of group or individual parent training programs developed for the general population.

It is critical for practitioners to begin with an understanding that the level of stress, marital discord, parental psychiatric problems, and family functioning issues are often quite different for families in which children with ADHD are being raised. It is also important for practitioners to keep in mind that many parents respond to a diagnosis of ADHD in their child with a grief process similar to that for losses. Such a process may include initial denial, such as refusing to accept the condition, anger or defensiveness, the projection of the problem onto the child, and finally, with support and acceptance, which is often accompanied by a sense of relief, especially when effective treatments are provided. The practitioner must begin with empathy, acceptance, and understanding, motivating parents by helping them recognize that, as D. W. Winnicott (1974) has written, "most mothers are good enough for most children." With increased understanding of attitudes and beliefs, modification in perceptions of self-efficacy and the acquisition of a number of behavioral strategies, parents can have a significant positive impact on the behavior of their ADHD children.

PARENT BELIEFS AND PERCEPTIONS

Wilson and Jennings (1996) provided a general sample of parents with a hypothetical set of symptoms of a child diagnosed with ADHD. Parents were asked to evaluate three psychosocial treatments (self-management therapy, parent training, and parent-child interaction training), a no-treatment option, and a psychostimulant treatment option. Psychosocial treatments combined with psychostimulant medication were rated significantly lower in acceptability than psychosocial treatments alone. Child self-management therapy, parent training, and parent-child interaction training were generally rated as equivalent, although parent-child interaction training revealed the highest acceptability scores. All therapies were preferred to the no-treatment option. These authors suggest that despite the increased use of stimulant medication, at least in this sample of parents, there continues to be a stigma concerning the use of the most popular and effective treatment for ADHD: medication. It may be that this problem contributes to lack of compliance with medicine (for review, see Chapter 13). It is of interest that this compliance phenomenon is also true of treatments for all children's disorders in which parents must provide the treatment and act as case managers and intermediaries between care providers and the child.

Parents' knowledge about their children's daily experiences was assessed by Crouter, McDermid, McHale, and Perry-Jenkins (1990). These authors found that although monitored boys received lower grades than did other children, their parents did not know as much about their day as others. Of significance, however, is the fact that the less well-monitored children were rated as more impaired by their parents. Scheel and Rieckmann-James (1996) suggested that problem identification of the child through a diagnosis such as ADHD may limit the scope of treatment or the probability of generalization of treatment from one context to another.

Parent empowerment and self-efficacy, defined as parents developing an internal locus of control (believing they can make a difference), appears to increase treatment outcome. Parents with a high level of self-efficacy believe they can influence their children in a positive way. Parental cognitive strategies such as reasoning and induction may be particularly beneficial for children who are highly capable of inhibitory control, whereas structured and simple directives and prohibitions may be more effective with children who are impulsive (Kochanska, 1991, 1993). Thus, this author suggests that what parents think to themselves is critical in determining how they interact with their children. The erroneous belief that logic and reason can impact poorly inhibited children creates more problems.

The role of adults' social cognition and mediating judgments of hyperactive children's medication-related behavior change was evaluated by Granger et al. (1993). Two videotape excerpts of hyperactive target boys playing a group game with two peers were shown to 288 undergraduates. Each target was taking either methylphenidate first, followed by placebo, or placebo first, followed by methylphenidate. Accumulative social evaluation of the child was assessed after the undergraduates viewed both video segments. Results indicated that observers combined their perceptions of the two behavior samples to form a composite impression using an equal-weight averaging algorithm. Even for children whose behavior improved, adults' ratings of undercontrolled behaviors continued to meet or in some cases exceed research cutoffs used to identify hyperactive children.

In a thorough review, Anastopoulos et al. (1991) evaluated stimulant medication and parent training as the two most commonly used therapies for ADHD. The authors concluded that ADHD requires multiple treatment methods, applied over long intervals if they are to produce positive impact. The authors concluded that even in the absence of stimulant medication, parent training is an effective intervention for children with ADHD.

Rostain et al. (1993) administered a questionnaire to a sample of 116 families attending an outpatient ADHD clinic. Parents' willingness to use medication or pursue counseling was not related to family factors. History of the child receiving medication was mildly correlated with parents' willingness to use medication. History of counseling was mildly correlated with parents' willingness to use medication and to pursue counseling. Mothers who viewed their families as enmeshed reported a significantly higher sense of competence than those viewing the family as connected or disengaged. The authors suggest that parental knowledge and belief about ADHD is critical in making treatment decisions and in determining the potential benefits of specific treatments.

Ninety-one parents provided reasons for compliance and noncompliance of their ADHD or non-ADHD children in six different situations (Sobol, Ashbourne, Earn, & Cunningham, 1989). Although parents use the same categories to explain the reasons for their children's compliance behavior, they use different dimensional ratings for these explanations (locus, stability, or controllability). Mothers rated attributions for noncompliance as more external than did fathers. Mothers of children with ADHD viewed the causes of their children's behavior to be more unstable than mothers of controls. Also, parents of ADHD children had lower expectations of achieving future compliance from their children than did parents of non-ADHD children. Thus, parents of ADHD children present a belief pattern reflective of their encounters with their children. That is, they perceive compliance as being a less frequently expected event, more unpredictable, more unstable, and more uncontrollable. Practitioners must keep this in mind. Mothers in this study rated the causes of their children's behavior as being more external to themselves than did fathers. Mothers also suggested the causes of noncompliance as being more unstable. Parents may use the same words to account for their children's behavior but to some extent use differential dimensional ratings for these words, suggesting the need for practitioners to carefully listen to what parents are actually saying. As Weiner (1979) noted, parents' perceptions of their children's behavior as stable, internal, and uncontrollable markedly decrease their confidence in managing and changing the behavior of their ADHD children. Koren, DeChillo, and Friesen (1992) utilized a questionnaire to measure parental sense of empowerment. Attitude, knowledge, belief, and behavior formed one dimension of parents' sense of empowerment, and the availability of supportive resources, family functioning, and the community in general formed the second dimension.

It is important for the practitioner to keep in mind that although parent and child behaviors are shaped in a bidirectional way, in many situations the child with ADHD may be much more powerful than the parent. Barkley, Anastopoulos, Guevremont, and Fletcher (1992), for example, examined groups of adolescents with ADHD alone and those with oppositional defiance and ADHD. Parents reported that both ADHD groups had more topics on which there was conflict and more angry conflicts at home than controls. However, adolescents in the combined group reported more such conflicts, endorsed more extreme and unreasonable beliefs about their parent-teen relations, and showed greater negative interactions during a neutral discussion. Mothers of the combined group teens displayed greater negative interactions during a neutral discussion, more extreme and unreasonable beliefs about their parent-teen relations, greater personal distress, and, interestingly, less satisfaction in their marriages.

Neonatal irritability has been found to be a predictor of mothers' postnatal depression (L. Murray, Stanley, Hooper, King, & Fiori-Cowley, 1996). Further, R. T. Brown, Borden, Clingerman, and Jenkins (1988) found that children with ADHD and their parents reported higher levels of depression than did controls in whom a significant relationship was found between mothers' depression and children's reports of depression. These authors suggest a "demoralization syndrome" (Carlson & Cantwell, 1980) developing as a result of repeated dysfunctional interactions and frustration between children with ADHD and their parents. Parental TV viewing habits have been strongly associated with ADHD symptoms in children. The amount of viewing itself has not been found to suffice as a diagnostic and prognostic indicator; however, parental viewing habits were correlated with an increased pattern of disruptive behavior in a small group of ADHD children.

PARENT PSYCHIATRIC STATUS

In the clinical community, there is a general perception that psychiatric status of parents exerts an influence on child behavior and functioning. In general, it is believed that the more compromised the parental psychiatric status, the more compromised the child functioning. Fischer (1990) reviewed available studies concerning the stress of parenting a child with ADHD and reported four clear lines of research. First, studies have demonstrated increased stress reported by parents of children with ADHD. Second, studies of parental psychopathology have suggested that for some parents such disturbances are independent of the child's pathology and reflect a genetic substrate for the same related disorders. For example, Daly and Fritsch (1995) reported a case study in which the mother's level of ADHD appeared to hamper her ability to consistently care for her child; treatment of the mother's ADHD with methylphenidate led to improvement in the child's care and subsequent improvement in mother-child interactions. Third, Fischer reports that ADHD is associated with increased marital discord, and fourth, research regarding parent-child interaction patterns suggest that the child-to-adult direction of effect is greater than the reverse.

Gillberg, Carlstrom, and Rasmussen (1983) found that mothers of 7-year-old hyperactive children had sought treatment for personal psychopathology in the previous year much more often than mothers of normal control children. Maternal help seeking was mediated by the child's age: mothers of hyperactive children sought help only slightly more than mothers of normal children during the first years of the child's life but three to four times as often during the seventh year. This report, however, runs somewhat counter to other research suggesting that, especially among mothers who are depressed, it is less likely they will seek help that may be routinely available (Seeley, Murray, & Cooper, 1996).

Studies using the Parenting Stress Index (Abidin, 1983) find that mothers of ADHD children report markedly higher levels of stress than parents of normal children. There also appears to be little difference between maternal and paternal reports of parenting stress (Baker, 1994); child behavior, socioeconomic status, and years of marriage have been reported to contribute more to parenting stress than gender. These studies also find that sibling interactions contribute to feelings of stress in mothers of ADHD children and that ADHD males and females are quite similar in the nature of their psychopathology and do not differ from each other in the degree of parenting stress associated with their care (Breen & Barkley, 1988; Mash & Johnston, 1983a, 1983b). The hypothesis of a familial association between childhood ADHD and specific adult psychopathology has been supported by numerous studies. Befera and Barkley (1985) report that twice as many psychiatric disorders are found in the nuclear families of children with ADHD and extended relatives as compared to normal children. Biederman, Farone, Keenan, & Benjamin (1992) report similar findings. These findings have been consistently reported from the early 1970s (Cantwell, 1972; Morrison & Stewart, 1971, 1973a). In these early studies, a significantly higher prevalence of sociopathy and alcoholism in biological fathers and hysteria and depression in biological mothers was reported when compared with adoptive and control parents. Studies by Cadoret, Cunningham, Loftus, and Edwards (1975) and Cadoret and Gath (1980) as well as more current literature note that significantly more adoptive children whose parents had psychopathology had been treated for symptoms of ADHD. A significant correlation between marital discord and deviant child behavior, especially in males, has been consistently reported in the literature (Emery & O'Leary, 1982). The direction of the effect is unclear; some authors argue that marital discord leads to behavioral disturbance in children (O'Leary et al. 1981), and others that disruptive childhood behavior is more likely to lead to marital dysfunction (Befera & Barkley, 1985). It has been reported that three times as many mothers of children with ADHD had separated or been divorced from their children's biological fathers (Barkley, Fischer, et al., 1990).

Numerous studies have demonstrated that when parent–ADHD child interactions occur in a free play setting, these interactions are relatively similar to those that occur between normal children and their parents. However, when parents are instructed to provide their children with tasks to accomplish, those with ADHD are less compliant with parent commands, and thus unable to sustain compliance and are more oppositional. Their parents are reported to provide more commands and directives to their children, are more negative and reprimanding, and are less responsive to their children's social initiatives than parents of normal children (Barkley, 1985, 1988c; Befera & Barkley, 1985; S. Campbell, 1975; S. Goldstein, 1980; Mash & Johnston, 1982; Tallmage & Barkley, 1983; Tarver-Behring et al., 1985).

Varni and Setoguchi (1993) evaluated the relationship among parental depression, anxiety, and marital discord. Higher father depression predicted higher child depression and higher anxiety. Higher father anxiety predicted higher child depression and anxiety as well as lower self-esteem. Higher marital discord predicted higher childhood depression and anxiety and lower self-esteem. Maternal anxiety and depression, in contrast to previous studies, did not predict child psychological adaptation. Of value to the practitioner is the report that providing psychiatric help to parents resulted in a positive impact on reports of child behavior. Further, Baker (1994) found that fathers of children with ADHD experience levels of parenting stress similar to those experienced by mothers; however, mothers appear to be somewhat more likely to perceive child characteristics as more stressful. Child behavior, socioeconomic status, and years of marriage contributed more to parenting stress than did parent's gender. This finding is consistent with Risser (1996). This author, however, also notes that an increased pattern of stress is characteristic not just for families raising children with ADHD but for families in which children have a whole range of neuropsychological disorders.

Brown and Pacini (1989) compared the perceptions of parents of fifty-one 6- to 12-year-old males with ADHD regarding family environment and depression with those of clinic controls and nondisabled controls. More mothers and fathers of children with ADHD reported themselves depressed than did parents of either control group. The parents of the ADHD children perceive their family environment as less supportive and more stressful than did either control group. Further, more parents in the ADHD group were divorced or separated.

Beck et al. (1990) compared the perceived stress of mothers of pervasive, hyperactive, situational hyperactive, and normal boys. The mothers of both pervasive and situational hyperactive boys reported more maternal stress than normals. When compared to mothers of controls, mothers of pervasively hyperactive boys rated themselves as more depressed, less competent, more restricted, and more frustrated. They also reported experiencing significantly more overall stress in their lives than did mothers of situationally hyperactive boys.

Marshall et al. (1990) evaluated whether parent and child affective attitudes and interactional behavior covaried with aggressive symptomatology in families raising a child with ADHD. These authors suggested that aggressiveness and a negative family climate independently determines the long-term course for children with ADHD. Children's behavior toward parents was highly correlated with their aggressiveness but not their expressed emotional status regarding their parents. Expressed emotion appeared to predict parental interactional behavior, but the degree of child aggressiveness did not.

Lewis (1992) examined cohesion and family type in families of males with ADHD. Parents of boys with the inattentive type of ADHD alone reported the highest level of family functioning. A larger percentage of parents whose children had the combined type or also were reported as aggressive reported more extremes in family functioning. Lewis-Abney (1993) reported that the combination of variables that best predicted family functioning when a child had ADHD was complex. A significant correlation between family functioning and age of the child was supported: families of older children reported poorer functioning, and parenting competence was negatively related to parental perception of the child's behavior. Older age of the child in combination with higher levels of impulsivity and hyperactivity were significant in predicting family functioning. Prinz, Myers, Holden, Tarnowski, and Roberts, (1983) first hypothesized that child aggression may be associated with marital discord in children with ADHD. However, in a population of 5- to 8-year-old males, these authors found that marital adjustment, overt hostility, and conflict tactics as reported by mothers were not significantly correlated with any measures of aggression or conduct problems. Marital discord in families with ADHD males did not explain differential rates of aggressive behavior. Marital discord was marginally related to the severity of ADHD symptoms as measured by a CPT. The authors suggested the need for caution in attempting to extend findings from a general population (e.g., undifferentiated clinic-referred children) to a specific diagnostic subgroup (e.g., ADHD children).

Lang, Pelham, Johnston, and Gelernter (1989) investigated levels of distress and alcohol consumption in adults interacting with problematic versus nonproblematic child confederates. Social drinkers were randomly assigned to interact with boys trained to enact behaviors characteristic of either normal or ADHD/CD children. Children in the ADHD/CD role produced comparably distressed moods for both male and female subjects. However, only males in the ADHD/CD child condition drank to higher blood alcohol levels. The authors suggested that their results reflect higher rates of drinking observed in fathers of ADHD/CD children, which may be partly a function of their particular response to the distress associated with interacting with such children.

A retrospective analysis of the records of 124 2- to 17-year-olds referred for symptoms of ADHD was undertaken for reports of child abuse by Heffron, Martin, Welch, and Perry (1987). Children with and without ADHD were more often physically abused than children in the general population. The period of prevalence of physical abuse in subjects with ADHD did not differ significantly from those subjects without ADHD.

Finally, in a thorough assessment of parenting stress among families of children with ADHD, Anastopoulos, Guevremont, Shelton, and DuPaul (1992) found that child and parent characteristics more than family environmental factors accounted for a substantial portion of variance in overall parenting stress. The child's oppositional defiant behavior and maternal psychopathology were especially potent predictors. The severity of the child's ADHD symptoms, the child's health status, and maternal health status also emerged as significant predictors.

From this series of studies concerning the impact of parenting stress on psychopathology, marital status, parent perception and belief, and family functioning, a number of conclusions can be drawn. First, it appears clear that the stress of daily, often less than optimal interactions with ADHD children results in parents feeling distressed and less satisfied with their parenting capacity, less-functional operations of families on a daily basis, an increase in self-reports of problems, and lower social competencies in ADHD children. These factors appear to then combine, as discussed in earlier chapters, leading to less-functional parent-child interactions, including the use of controlling, aversive, and punitive parenting behaviors; beliefs and perceptions that the behavior of ADHD children are stable, consistent, and uncontrollable by parents; and an increasing pattern of dysfunctionality as ADHD children grow up.

EFFECTIVENESS OF PARENT TRAINING FOR CHILDREN WITH ADHD

Based on a review of the literature, Newby, Fischer, and Roman (1991) suggested that to a great extent, the same types of variables found to be important in other types of psychotherapy outcome research are also important in understanding and evaluating the effectiveness of parenting training for ADHD. Careful initial assessment of the problem, determination of the appropriateness of the intervention for the family, establishment of good therapeutic rapport, and flexibility, as well as therapist variables of warmth, empathy, and the ability to deal with natural family resistance to change, are all critical in determining whether parent training is ultimately effective. Once again, the importance of parent attitudes and beliefs must be emphasized. Johnston and Behrenz (1993) found that parents of ADHD high-aggressive and ADHD low-aggressive children without conduct problems do not differ very much in their suggested strategies during discussions of parenting behavior. However, more punishing responses are elicited by conduct problems, and more proactive preventive studies are elicited by ADHD symptoms. Couples with children in both ADHD groups were less positive in discussions of all behaviors and more negative in discussing conduct problems than couples with children who had no problem. Couples with aggressive ADHD children were more negative than either the no-problem or low-aggression ADHD parents in discussing their children's ADHD symptoms.

Strayhorn and Weidman (1991) randomly assigned eighty-nine families to a minimal treatment, extensive parent training, or control group. The extensive parent-training group demonstrated significant parent-reported improvement in daily management of children's behavior. Such improvements have been reported by other researchers as well. Erhardt and Baker (1990) reported improvements in parents' confidence in their child management ability and knowledge of behavioral principles, ratings of hyperactivity, and parent-child relationships for parents receiving a ten-week child management parent training program for children with ADHD combined with a number of follow-up sessions. In 1991, these authors completed a one-year follow-up of this same population; at that time, parent ratings and child achievement test scores showed no differences between treatment and nontreatment groups. Teachers blind to interventions, however, rated experimental children as significantly superior to controls with respect to ADHD symptoms. Composite teacher ratings of behavior also significantly favored the experimental groups. Children's improvements in classroom behavior was significantly correlated with improvements parents had shown during the intervention in their behavior toward their children. These authors note that this program emphasized parental influence on the child representing a benign form of moral indoctrination and improvement in the quality of parent-child relationships; this is in contrast to some parenting programs that emphasize a contract and compliance exchange for parental reward. The extensive intervention produced significantly more improvements in parents' ratings of children's symptoms of ADHD as well as symptoms of internalizing problems. A blind measure, videotaped interaction between parents and their children, also demonstrated significantly more improvement from the experimental intervention. Both treatment groups improved with respect to parent ratings of children's oppositional symptoms. Change in parent ratings of children's behavior was correlated with the change in blind observers' ratings of parent behavior. These authors suggest that parent training "is one of the fairly small set of interventions demonstrated useful in reducing children's psychiatric symptoms in either the short run or the long run and as such should be in the repertoire of clinicians" (p. 895). Anastopoulos, Shelton, DuPaul, and Guevremont (1993) examined changes in parent functioning resulting from parent participation in the behavioral parent training program specifically designed for parents of school-age children with ADHD. Relative to wait list controls, mothers of the ADHD children who completed the nine-session parenting program showed significant posttreatment gains, which were maintained two months after treatment. There were gains in both child and parent functioning; in particular, there were parent-training-induced reductions in parenting stress and increases in parenting self-esteem, which accompanied the parent-reported improvements in the overall severity of children's ADHD symptoms.

Pisterman et al. (1989) utilized a parent training program with parents of ADHD preschoolers randomly assigned to either an immediate or delayed group parent training program. The program was specifically aimed at improving child compliance. Positive treatment effect was obtained on measures of compliance, parenting style of interaction, and management skills. These improvements were maintained at three-month follow-up. Evaluation of treatment effects on non-targeted child behaviors, however, indicated no generalization. Subsequently, Pisterman, McGrath, Firestone, Goodman, Webster, Mallory, and Goffin (1992), with a second population of ADHD preschoolers, demonstrated that a parent training program had positive effects on measures of child compliance but not on measures of attention. Parental compliance, management skills, and overall style of interaction were also positively effected. These authors suggest that if early intervention is to be comprehensive, different treatment modalities will be required to target specific deficits and problems. It is important for the practitioner to recognize that parent training for parents of children with ADHD may act prophylactically, preventing the escalating spiral of noncompliance and subsequent oppositional defiance that results from poor inhibition, but it likely will not reduce ADHD symptoms per se.

Probably the most comprehensive and well-planned parenting program for ADHD was designed by Cunningham, Bremner, and Secord-Gilbert (1993) to increase availability of service while controlling costs, reduce obstacles to participation, and improve outcome via an approach to training that reduces resistance and improves adherence. Data from three cohorts containing over 100 families of children at risk for ADHD suggested that large school-based courses maximize cost effectiveness, increase utilization, and yield significantly greater improvements (Cunningham, Bremner, & Boyle, 1995). Parents in the community group reported significantly greater improvements in behavior problems at home and better maintenance of those gains at six-month follow-up. Appendix 4 contains an overview of the Cunningham et al. parenting program.

Practitioners should keep in mind that parent satisfaction must also be taken into account when deciding how to best deliver parent training programs. Beardslee, Wright, Rothberg, Salt, and Versage (1996) found that although individual and group intervention parent training programs are of benefit, parents in individual sessions report being more satisfied. In individual settings, clinicians are better able to focus on modifying specific attitudes that may impact receptivity and ultimate follow-through of parenting recommendations.

DELIVERING PARENTING PROGRAMS

Training parents to act as behavior change agents for their children in the natural environment has been practiced for quite some time and has become extremely popular, even among unaffected children (L. Clark, 1986; Dinkmeyer & McKay, 1982; Gard & Berry, 1986; Graziano, 1977; Patterson & Forgatch, 1988; Popkin, 1986; C. D. Williams, 1959).

Teaching parents to more effectively manage the behavior of children with ADHD is but one component of a parent training program. Parents must also be taught to search and remove causative or aggravating factors in the environment, reorganize the environment to minimize problems, advocate within educational and social settings, and, finally, use medication when indicated. Grant's (1991) definition of a supportive environment consists of effective communication, avoidance of pressure, proper use of behavioral techniques, building self-esteem, and prioritizing problems.

It is critical for practitioners to help parents understand that a parenting class offers a financially affordable means of gaining new skills, including general parenting ability, problem-solving strategies, the ability to effectively understand and manage child problems, communication between parents and children, and conflict resolution skills for all family members. Curricula for parenting programs in general vary philosophically from those focusing on behavior to those with a focus on thoughts or feelings. Many traditional parenting programs may not be effective for children with ADHD due to the unique needs of this population, including the need for immediate, frequent, predictable payoffs over long periods of time, and due to a tendency to lose interest quickly with repetitive, effortful activities. However, regardless of the parenting program utilized for children with ADHD, the focus must be on strengthening parent problem-solving skills, increasing parent's ability to pay attention to positive behavior, balancing family relationships, and helping parents manage transitions, plan ahead, avoid conflicts, reduce stress in other areas of life, learn to deliver commands effectively, and deal proactively with school and community resources. Barkley (1996a) suggests that practitioners must help parents make accommodations for their ADHD children, focusing on eight key principles:

1. The use of immediate consequences.
2. The use of consequences at a greater frequency.
3. The use of meaningful consequences.
4. Starting incentives before punishments.
5. Focusing heavily on consistency.
6. Planning ahead for problem situations.
7. Keep a disability perspective, which for ADHD requires parents to recognize that they must provide consistent behavior management over long periods of time.
8. Practice acceptance and forgiveness.

Forms of parent training programs have included group or individual meetings (Arnio, 1991; Barkley, 1987, 1996, 1997; Koth, 1991), family therapy (Bernier & Siegel, 1994; Robin & Foster, 1989; Ziegler & Holden, 1988), summer programs (Goldhaber, 1991; Pelham & Hoza, 1987), and residential programs (Moretti, Holland, & Peterson, 1994). Among the more interesting efforts at reducing symptomatic problems for children through parent training is the use of marital therapy (D. Snow, 1992).

In a population of 5- to 12-year-old children with disruptive behavior, this author demonstrated that conjoint marital therapy over a twelve-week period targeting marital and parental boundaries modified parents' attitudes, which subsequently led to improvements in parent-child behavior and reports of improved behavior by teachers. Parents can also be taught a variety of relaxation techniques, which they can then utilize with their children to increase self-control and compliance (Donney & Poppen, 1989). Although this approach has intuitive appeal, as reviewed in Chapter 12, available research does not permit firm conclusions as to the sources of reported benefits, or for that matter, the potential that benefits will remain long term.

The family therapy approach to increasing parental competence is of particular interest as children enter their adolescent years. Bernier and Siegel (1994) reviewed the ecological and family system issues encountered by families raising children with ADHD. These authors argue that a systems theory framework is essential for describing the impact ADHD has on a family and for addressing family needs. They propose that family therapists are best suited to work with families raising children with ADHD because they approach treatment from a systems basis. Case studies are offered by Ziegler and Holden (1988) suggesting that the ability to categorize families as healthy, fragile, disorganized, blaming, or split allows therapists to focus on important underlying issues that may critically contribute to the success of parent training.

Barkley, Guevremont, et al. (1992) directly compared three family therapy programs for treating families with adolescents with ADHD. They assigned sixty-one 12- to 18-year-olds randomly to eight to ten sessions of behavior management training, problem-solving and communication training (Robin & Foster, 1989), or structural family therapy. Families were assessed at pre- and posttreatment and three-month follow-up. All treatments resulted in reports of significant reductions in negative communication conflicts and anger during conflicts. They also resulted in improved ratings of school adjustment, reduced internalizing and externalizing symptoms, and decreased maternal depressive symptoms. Most outcomes remained stable between posttreatment and follow-up; some continue to improve over time. Nonetheless, these authors note that despite group improvements, analyses of clinically significant change and clinical recovery within subjects showed that only 5% to 30% reliably improved from treatment, and only 5% to 20% recovered following treatment. Interestingly, the three treatments did not differ in this rate.

Newby et al. (1991) evaluated three types of parenting programs, all relying heavily on social learning principles for families with ADHD children. Such programs focus on the coercive interaction and escalation to explain children's behavior problems. Each of the programs differed on issues related to balance between informal, social reinforcement and formal behavioral reward systems as well as the exact procedures for the implementation of time out. The three programs studied were Barkley's (1987a), Patterson's (1976a), and Forehand and McMahon's (1981). A tabular comparison of these three programs appears in Table 17–1.

Barkley's program targets noncompliance. Parents are first taught the typical causes of child misbehavior, then how to attend and interact with their children appropriately, how to use time out to reduce noncompliance, and how to generalize procedures learned at home to the general community. Patterson's program begins with helping parents understand childhood behavior, then focuses on teaching parents to

Table 17–1. Basic features of three parent training programs

Program Feature	Barkley	Patterson	Forehand and McMahon
Age range	2 to 11	Up to 12	3 to 8
Training format	Parents from single family or parent	Parents from single family	Parent-child dyad
Typical number of training sessions	8 to 10	5 or more	10 or more
Assessment procedures	Interviews, parent & teacher questionnaires, observations	Parent and family interviews	Interviews, parent question-naires, clinic and home observations
Procedures emphasized for positive reinforcement	Attending to play, social response, & token systems	Formal point program, informal social feedback	Attending, social reinforcement
Punishment procedures	Time-out chair, taking away points in token system	Time out in closed room	Ignoring, time-out chair

Source: Newby, R. S., Fischer, M., & Roman, M. A. (1991). Parent training for families of children with ADHD. *School Psychology Review, 20,* 252–265. Copyright 1991 by the National Association of School Psychologists. Reprinted by permission of the publisher.

issue requests more effectively; parents are then taught punishments, specifically in the form of time out, and how to use time out in situations outside of the home. Forehand and McMahon's program begins with a more extensive overview and direct observation of the child and family. Parents are then taught how to demonstrate differential attention, compliance training, and time out. Time out is utilized in each of these programs; however, it differs regarding physical proximity of the child to the parent. All of these programs have demonstrated short-term symptomatic relief for children with ADHD (for review, see Newby et al., 1991).

A MODEL TO INCREASE PARENTAL COMPETENCE

Education

Parents must be counseled to understand that managing their ADHD child's behavior at home requires accurate knowledge of the disorder and its complications. They must be consistent, predictable, and supportive of their child in their daily interactions. As the resilience literature reviewed reflects, the best outcomes for children facing adversity are achieved through the habitual relationships they develop with their caregivers (Fonagy, Steele, Steele, Higgitt, & Target, 1994; Werner, 1994).

The first step to increase parental competence requires assisting parents to understand and accept the primary cause of the ADHD child's behavior. Many of the published materials or clinical services available to parents continue to stress the use of techniques at the expense of understanding. Practitioners too quick to focus on technique are likely to find parents with low compliance. Practitioners must help parents move beyond dependence on a handful of techniques or on a parent training model by initially assisting them in seeing the world through the eyes of their child. The philosophy and model offered in this chapter can be used with a wide range of parenting programs. Many of these are helpful for parents of ADHD children; however, success may be intermittent and short-lived unless parents develop an understanding of the ADHD child's behavior, their interaction with the child, and the long-term effects problems of ADHD are going to have on the child. Practitioners should keep in mind that parents of children with ADHD have been reported to have lower expectations of achieving future compliance from their children than parents of unaffected children (Sobol et al., 1989); thus, education can be a conduit to motivating parents of ADHD children that their effort will lead to long-term change.

The importance of seeing the world through the eyes of the ADHD child cannot be overemphasized. Adopting this perspective will assist parents in coping when the daily demands become stressful, and will encourage parents to modify their perceptions and beliefs about the sources of their children's behavior as well as their ability to manage that behavior. Simply providing parents with a number of basic behavioral techniques will not lead to long-lasting change. As a result of the nature of their temperament, ADHD children present an unending variety of problems. For example, parents must be helped to understand that punishment will be successful when it is applied appropriately for problems of noncompliance but will not succeed when it is chosen as the intervention for incompetent behavior. This will be discussed further in the next section. Parents must be urged to become educated consumers and active case managers for their children. They must understand this disorder thoroughly; because it will affect their child throughout his or her life, parents will repeatedly be placed in an advocacy position with schools and community resources. Fortunately, ADHD represents a cottage industry in regard to materials available for parents. It is beyond the scope of this text to review these materials in depth; Appendix 5 contains a list of text and video materials that have been reviewed and, in our opinion, offer generally equal benefits. It is suggested that practitioners take into account parent and family variables in choosing materials recommending only those they have read and are familiar with. A critical issue in this regard is parents' educational level. Singh (1995) suggests that many resources available for parents are written at a level beyond that of the general public. It is our belief that parents benefit from meeting on an individual basis over one or two sessions separated by approximately two or three weeks once a diagnosis is made. This affords parents individual time to interact with the practitioner, ask questions, and begin to develop an understanding of their child's problems and what they must do to become effective advocates and behavior change agents. This also affords the practitioner the opportunity to make certain that parents understand why the ADHD child experiences so much difficulty meeting the demands of his or her environment. An assessment such as this is often not available in a group setting. Once parents have developed a reasonable understanding of themselves and their child, they are then better prepared to participate in a parent training program with greater confidence and ultimately greater success.

It is also recommended that the practitioner assist parents in understanding their temperamental style. As reviewed earlier, there is a significantly greater degree of impulsive, inattentive qualities in parents of children with ADHD as well as a higher rate of comorbid psychiatric problems. The discussion of teacher style is also applicable to parents. Practitioners must take into account parental style and temperament when suggestions are made for effective management at home. Often, data generated during a parenting style interview can help the practitioner develop a better understanding not only of parents' awareness, skills, and abilities, but of their temperament and possible coexisting psychiatric problems as well. The practitioner must keep in mind that the best parenting strategies will fail if parents are unable, due to a variety of reasons, to implement them. For example, impulsive, easily overaroused parents must first be taught to master their own temperament before they can be taught strategies to master their children's temperament; such strategies will not be effective if parents are unable to control their own emotional level in the face of problems.

Incompetence versus Noncompliance

Practitioners must help parents develop the capacity to distinguish between problems that result from incompetence and those that result from noncompliance. The former must be dealt with through education and skill building, and the latter is usually quite effectively dealt with through manipulation of consequences. The majority of parents will agree that a large percentage of their ADHD child's behavior problems results from incompetence rather than purposeful noncompliance. The ADHD child's difficulty settling into a task, lack of persistence, repetitive mistakes, and tendency to become overaroused, easily frustrated, impulsive, and restless often result in a wide variety of nonpurposeful behaviors that are clearly disturbing to others. Parents must be helped to understand that over time, these behaviors result in a steady diet of "Quit it, Stop it, Cut it out, Don't do it" responses from all areas in the environment. In part, this may play a role in the development of oppositional defiance in children with ADHD. ADHD children are at significant risk to perceive their social environment as restrictively controlling and dissatisfied with their performance, which then leads to the child's becoming increasingly oppositional. By successfully distinguishing between incompetent and noncompliant behavior, parents can reduce negative feedback, increase compliance and success, and stem the tide of the development of oppositional behavioral problems, all other factors being equal.

To make certain that parents understand the distinction between incompetence and noncompliance, numerous examples tied specifically to the child in question may prove helpful. It is important for parents to understand that if they punish a child for symptoms of ADHD, there is a strong likelihood the child will be remorseful and promise to behave better. Unfortunately, the next time the child is in that situation the impulsive need for gratification will quickly overwhelm the child's limited capacity for self-control; thus, the problem will recur. Developing an understanding of this critical issue not only helps parents relabel the majority of their ADHD child's behavior but acts as a motivator in changing the way they deal with the majority of problems. Analogies are often quite helpful: parents would not punish a 5-year-old child unable to read and expect that punishment would increase reading capacity; instead, the child would be educated to develop a basic foundation of reading skills. Parents of children with ADHD must be helped to understand that punishing symptoms of ADHD alone offers little chance of changing that behavior.

Providing appropriate commands, as will be discussed in the next section, is one way of making this distinction. By building in success, offering incentives, and providing clear, consistent punishments for noncompliance, parents stand the best chance of minimizing the progression of noncompliant disruptive problems many ADHD children experience.

When dealing with noncompliance, it is best to minimize negative reinforcement and maximize positive reinforcement. Parents should be directed to gain the child's attention, be specific and direct, provide eye contact, offer a start rather than stop direction, use appropriate language, offer clear commands, not argue, and allow only one opportunity for noncompliance. The best way to deal with noncompliance is to make certain that parents have control over consequences; appropriate commands, management of rewards, and the use of response cost are all effective means to do so.

Teach Positive Direction

Once parents understand the distinction between noncompliance and incompetence and can begin to differentiate their ADHD child's behavior, the next key step is to teach positive direction. This assists parents in determining whether punishment, management, or skill building is the most appropriate intervention.

Research literature dealing with directing others has focused on alpha and beta commands. Beta commands are often unclear (e.g., Do that), whereas alpha commands are clear (e.g., Go stand by the door). Alpha and beta commands can be provided with a start or a stop direction. Start and stop beta commands are equally ineffective (e.g., Stop that or Start that). Stop alpha commands tell the child what not to do but leave a wide range of other possibilities open (e.g., Stop pushing your sister . . . so the child now kicks his sister). Start alpha commands, by which children are very clearly directed to what they should be doing, are favored. However, human nature appears to direct all of us to point out that which we don't like; when a child exhibits an aversive behavior, most parents respond by directing a child to stop doing it. The focus on what is to be stopped as opposed to what is to be started may not be an issue for most children because they spend the majority of their time meeting parental expectations. The ADHD child, however, frequently does not meet expectations and may then receive a steady diet of negative directions. This does not help the child understand what is to be done.

Consider, for example, a child with his feet on the wall. The parent directs the child by saying "Take your feet off the wall." This is a stop alpha direction: the child is not being told what to do, leaving open a range of all other behavioral possibilities. He may then take his feet off the wall and place them on the coffee table. The child has complied with the parental request but is now doing something else that is aversive and may increase parental anger. The problem escalates. The parent then directs the child to take his feet off the coffee table only to have the child place his feet on the bookcase. Anastopoulos and Barkley (1990) suggest that children with ADHD are more likely to attend to commands that are given in a straightforward, declarative manner than those delivered as a question, demand, or request. These authors also suggest that instructions are more likely to be followed when they are delivered without distractors and that compliance is enhanced by continuous supervision for the brief period after the command is offered (Barkley, 1987a).

A number of authors have provided frameworks to guide parents on providing commands. For example, M. Gordon (1990) suggests that parents make eye contact; praise the behavior, not the child; resist habitual criticism; and use the "blind man technique." In this technique, how one describes the behavior that the child just performed and what the child is to do next should be understandable to a blind man present in the room. Sheila Eyberg (personal communication) suggests that parents of young children should describe, imitate, and praise rather than command, question, or criticize. Whitman and Smith (1991) offer a three-step model in which parents are directed first to state their expectation (e.g., In our family, this is what we do, or You may not do this); then provide a statement of consequences for failure to comply, either by commission or omission (e.g., If you do this, then this will occur); then apply consequences for behavior change completed. Most children master this type of behavior management system quickly; children with ADHD, however, because their behavior is so consequentially bound as the result of their impulsivity, often do not. Parents usually respond by escalating punitive measures out of frustration. Parent training programs offer a "normal bias" suggesting that logical consequences when carefully applied will change *all* children's behavior. Programs training parent effectiveness base their models on outcomes of clear, concise communication combined with behavioral contracting; these models implicitly assume the child has the capacity to change if parents act in a certain way. This concept of normalcy underlies most parent training programs. It is critical for practitioners to help parents of ADHD children understand that what works for all children will work for their ADHD child so long as they adjust expectations by making tasks more interesting, payoffs more valuable, and allowing more trials to reach success.

It is recommended that the practitioner direct parents to practice telling their children what they want instead of what they don't want for at least a week before beginning any other intervention. Although this sounds like an easy task, it is not. Most parents will report that old habits are difficult to change; many parents find themselves focusing on what is to be stopped without considering the nature of their actions. Again, the purpose of this model is to assist parents to think about what they do and how they interact with their children rather than passively applying behavioral techniques. In some cases, parents will frustratingly report that it is easy to see what they don't want the child to do but much more difficult in that instance to decide what they want the child to do instead. A good rule is to remind parents to ask themselves "What do I want to see the child doing instead of what he is doing right now?" At the very least, the child could be directed to go to his or her room. Parents with histories of negative direction often report increased compliance when they begin telling the child what they would like to see happen.

Alpha commands can be used to help parents make the distinction between incompetence and noncompliance. If the child is directed to place his feet on the floor and does not comply within a very brief period, this has nothing to do with ADHD, but rather reflects noncompliance. It is at that point that punishment will prove beneficial in the long run and increase compliance when parental directions are given. Parents must be helped to understand that once they make a request, they must remain to see what happens. If a parent asks the child to place his feet on the floor, walks out of the room, and comes back ten minutes later and the child's feet are on the wall, the parent cannot be certain whether the child's feet on the wall now are the result of incompetence or noncompliance: the parent has no idea whether the child complied for a few minutes but was distracted and again put his feet on the wall.

The need for repeated trials to success cannot be overemphasized. Parents of ADHD children must be instructed that they serve as a control system for the child: their child is going to need more management and supervision in an appropriate, consistent, affirmative way than others. An example of an ADHD child playing in a house with a friend illustrates this process. The ADHD child becomes overly loud because he does not track the volume of his voice, just as he does not track many other variables. The parent then makes a positive direction for the child to speak in an inside voice. The child complies for a few minutes, but ten minutes later his voice is loud again. For most parents, this results in an escalation of parental intervention; by the third offense, it is a major failure on the child's part, and the child is sent to his room and the friend sent home. Parents of ADHD children, however, are counseled to make the distinction between incompetence and noncompliance: if the child is asked to lower his voice and he complies for a period of time but his voice gradually becomes louder, this is not the result of noncompliance but rather reflects ADHD. Parents are then directed to provide a supportive system so that the child is not punished for his lack of persistence. Parents must ask themselves what happens after a request is made. If the child complies, then he is making an attempt to meet parental expectations. If, over time, the child has a problem again, it is most likely the result of incompetence and therefore the child is entitled to another positive direction. In this situation, the results are a number of small successes rather than one large failure.

Rewards

Children with ADHD require more immediate, frequent, predictable, consistently applied consequences and more trials to mastery. Social (e.g., praise) and tangible (e.g., toys, treats, privileges) rewards must be provided more frequently when a child with ADHD is compliant or succeeds. The acquisition of behavior is not the issue, but the child's ability to learn to consistently act when expected behaviors are required. ADHD leads to problems not from inability but rather faulty executive management; that is, most ADHD children know how to do what is requested but have difficulty doing so when they are supposed to.

Due to their symptoms, children with ADHD receive less positive reinforcement than their siblings. Parents must work to keep a balance as well as to avoid negative reinforcement, which results only in the removal of aversive consequences when the child complies. This leads to immediate compliance but in the long run reinforces rather than discourages inappropriate behavior.

The key is to end interactions successfully. Typically, the ADHD child creates a problem, is punished, is sent to his or her room for an indeterminant period of time with no effort made for the child to return to the situation and comply with parental requests. The message must be very clear to the child that regardless of the time involved, he or she will eventually comply with parent requests. For this reason, parents are directed to utilize short punishment periods for overt noncompliance, designed to clearly give the message that the parent is dissatisfied and to quickly return the child to the problem situation, allowing an additional try at compliance.

It is important for practitioners to help parents understand that children with ADHD often choose smaller, more immediate rewards over larger, delayed rewards contingent upon task completion (Rapport, Tucker, et al., 1986). Further, children under age 10 with ADHD struggle when asked to identify reinforcers in an open-ended fashion; thus, parents must offer forced-choice reinforcers (e.g., Would you like this or that?) (Northup, Broussard, Jones, & George, 1995). Finally, both ADHD and non-ADHD children do not differ in their stated preference for reward types; both groups prefer parent time most frequently, followed by friends, and toys and candy are preferred least often. Practitioners must help parents understand that family attention is perceived as valuable to children with ADHD (Hill, Olympia, & Angerbuer, 1991).

Token economies are often an effective means of providing consistent reinforcement for ADHD children in the home. The interested reader is referred to Barkley (1996a) for a description of token economy systems for children and teens at home. This author suggests that token systems at home fail not because they are inherently ineffective for children with ADHD, but because they are poorly managed. Thus, the focus of such programs should be on their management rather than on setting up the system. In regard to management, Barkley suggests:

1. Parents should be enthusiastic.
2. A list of required activities should be kept to a reasonable length.
3. There should be an extensive list of reinforcers.
4. At least one-third of all reinforcers should be available each day.
5. Tokens should be used with 4- to 7-year-olds and points with 8-year-olds and older.
6. Inflation should be balanced with available tokens.
7. Children should be able to spend approximately two-thirds of points or tokens earned each day on a variety of privileges.
8. Bonuses should be paid for a good attitude.
9. Tokens should be traded in daily.
10. Tokens or points should be paid only for compliance to initial requests.
11. Children should be allowed to spend tokens liberally.
12. The reward-to-fine ratio should be 2:1.
13. Parents should avoid an escalating pattern of punishment.
14. Minimum quotas of points to be given away should be set each day.
15. Parents should stand fast: no follow-through, no points or tokens.
16. The system of rewards should be changed frequently.
17. Parents should always allow children to earn their way off the system through compliant behavior, but a minimum of six to eight weeks on a token system once it is initiated should be required.

Timing

Parents should pick their battles, reinforce the positive, apply immediate consequences for behaviors that cannot be ignored, and use token points with ADHD children (Blackman et al., 1991). These authors note that it is essential for parents to stay one step ahead; they should also walk a while in the child's shoes, recognizing and accepting the difficulties their children experience due to their ADHD. The practitioner must help parents understand that, in the absence of efficient timing, the benefits of appropriate consequences are diminished. Consequences, both rewards and punishments, should be provided quickly and consistently. Even in regard to punishment, immediate punishment is more effective than delayed punishment for ADHD children (Abramowitz & O'Leary, 1990).

Response Cost

The literature concerning response cost was extensively reviewed in Chapter 15. Most parents understand the use of positive reinforcement as a means of motivating children; few, however, understand the use of response cost. Parents should be helped to understand that children with ADHD work harder to keep their plate full than to fill an empty plate: if a give-and-take response-cost system is utilized, parents must make certain the child does not go bankrupt. This can be accomplished by providing a ratio of approximately three to five times the number of rewards earned for good behavior to what is lost for negative behavior (e.g., earn three points for doing something right, lose one point for doing something wrong). It may be equally effective, especially with older children and adolescents, to start with the entire payoff and then have the individual work to keep it. For example, instead of giving the child a $5.00 allowance at the end of the week when she behaves appropriately, parents may place $5.00 in nickels in a jar on a shelf that is visible to the child. So long as she behaves appropriately, the $5.00 belongs to her; for every infraction that has been clearly defined and agreed upon between parents and child, a nickel is removed from the jar.

Parents must also be helped to recognize when they act as a negative reinforcer, even during the utilization of a response-cost model. For example, children may comply when told to withdraw a point or a token, not because they are losing something, but because the parent's presence is aversive and by complying, the parent will move off. Practitioners should make certain that parents understand negative reinforcement and develop strategies to avoid being a negative reinforcer as they manage consequences for their children.

Planning

Parents must be helped to understand the forces that affect their children. They must not personalize their child's problems. When children act the way parents hope they will, it is natural for them to feel that they are being good parents. When children do not meet expectations, parents tend to judge themselves harshly. Parents must learn to respond to their children's limits in a proactive way. The practitioner should guide parents to avoid placing their children in situations that will exacerbate ADHD symptoms.

Such strategies include minimalizing stimulation, adjusting schedules and routines so they are consistent and rarely vary, and stating rules clearly and concisely. In this regard, consistent management is essential: if a rule is broken and a determination is made that this resulted from noncompliant behavior, a negative consequence should follow every time.

Punishment

Punishment is an effective way of helping children receive feedback for behavior that is to be stopped. However, it is essential that parents of children with ADHD understand that punishment alone likely will not reduce ADHD symptoms. Thus, in the management of ADHD, punishment plays a role with behaviors deemed to be directly noncompliant. Punishment is also partially appropriate if the rule is violated even as the result of an ADHD symptom; however, in this circumstance, punishment must not be provided by itself, as it will not change the child's long-term behavior. Parents should explain to the child that this is a rule everyone must follow; when it is broken, there will be a punishment. However, parents must understand that for the child with ADHD, unless a managing strategy is provided along with punishment, it is not likely that the punishment will precipitate change.

Frequently, partial loss of a privilege or possession is a more aversive punishment than complete loss. Again, children with ADHD have a long history of not obtaining positive reinforcement and losing many privileges; thus the loss of an additional privilege may have very little long-term impact. Structuring punishment so that all is not lost as the result of one infraction provides continued opportunity for the ADHD child to at least receive partial positive reinforcement. For example, if a child is ten minutes late coming home for dinner, rather than restricting the child from going out at all the next day, requiring that the child come home earlier by an equivalent or double amount of time the following day is a better intervention. Instead of taking the child's entire allowance, taking half or two-thirds leaves the child with some money but not enough to purchase all that he or she may want. The mind set is important: rather than losing everything and simply forgetting about it, the child has something as a reminder of the punished behavior. This may stimulate more reflection and increase the likelihood that the child will benefit from this punishing experience.

Care

The final axiom for practitioners to impress upon parents is the importance of taking care of themselves as well as nurturing the relationship they have with their child. Due to their greater stress, families with a child suffering from ADHD are more likely to experience even minor problems as more disruptive. It is important for parents to understand the impact their child has on other family members and to diffuse tension in a constructive manner. And because parents of ADHD children must serve as their case managers, it is important that they take care of their own issues, because they will have to be available, consistent, supportive, and healthy on a long-term basis.

Parents must recognize that due to their child's ADHD, there is greater likelihood that the relationship they develop with this child will be more strained. Many families follow the "leave the child alone" rule; that is, so long as the child is not bothering any-one, parents withdraw their attention. Yet this model, in the long run, tends to create a schism between parents and children. It is in fact when the child is doing well that par-ents should make an effort to interact, offering positive feedback and perhaps joining in the activity that is promoting the "good behavior." A better rule for parents to follow is to seek out enjoyable activities to share with their children.

Parents of children with ADHD must recognize that if they approach each day with a sense of hope, encouragement, acceptance, and honesty, they will empower them-selves and their children. If they approach each day with a sense of despair, discour-agement, anger, and blame, they will not only jeopardize their child's future but further feed their own sense of powerlessness and hopelessness.

MANAGEMENT ISSUES

Time Out

Time out is an effective intervention for children between the ages of 4 and 12 years. Many parents use time out by sending the offending children to their room, where they may watch TV or play with toys. In this model, time out serves as both a punishment to let children know their parents are dissatisfied with their actions and an instructional opportunity to quickly bring children back to the situation to comply. Time out is used for noncompliance and not as an intervention for incompetence.

When children are noncompliant, for example, refusing to take their feet off the wall and place them on the floor, they should be sent immediately to time out. It is recom-mended that the time-out chair be in the same room as the offense, preferably facing a wall or corner. The only requirement is that the child's bottom remain on the chair. Children may cry or talk to themselves, but may not play with toys or be talked to by others. The time-out period is one minute. This is such a short amount of time that even the most hyperactive ADHD children can easily comply and control themselves if they choose to do so. This brief time out also allows children to return almost immediately to the problem situation and again attempt compliance.

The purpose of time out is not to make the child feel bad or make the parent feel better. The purpose is to consistently let children know when they are being noncom-pliant and allow them to return to the situation quickly to make a second attempt at compliance. When the child has returned to the situation, the reason for time out is briefly stated by the parent and the direction is again stated. In this example, the child is directed to place his or her feet on the floor. If the child's feet remain on the floor for the next ten to fifteen seconds, the interaction is ended with a verbal positive rein-forcement by the parent. If fifteen minutes later the child's feet are on the wall, most parents escalate in their annoyance and anger. For the ADHD child, a second positive direction is given to place his or her feet on the floor. The distinction must be made between noncompliance and incompetence: if the child responds appropriately, a ver-bal reinforcer is offered; if the child again refuses, time out is initiated, again for one minute.

If children seek to pick a fight and exercise opposition and control with their par-ents, they may come out of the time out and immediately respond negatively to the repeated direction by engaging in the behavior a second time. It is easy for parents at that point to make the distinction that this is behavior that is purposeful and therefore must be punished; there is no need for a positive statement. The child is sent back to time out and one additional minute is added. In this way, even in repeated situations, time out does not turn into an all-afternoon affair. Once the child returns from time out, again the positive instruction is given and the parent waits for compliance. If the child does not comply, the interaction continues and another minute of time out is added. This is a battle the child cannot win. Eventually, the child will comply and be reinforced. Once that happens, parents may then wish to provide a cognitive explanation, indicating that the child's choice of actions is up to the child, but sooner or later he or she will comply, and it is certainly easier for everyone when the child complies sooner. Children may be told that time spent working toward compliance could be spent doing something else much more enjoyable.

When children are noncompliant to the direction to go to time out or stay in time out, parents should go to the next disciplinary step. In the case of the child either refusing to go to time out or attempting to change the subject by throwing a tantrum, parents are directed to use differential attention. This will be described further in the next section. If children get out of the chair before the minute is over, they are asked to return to the chair and instructed that if they leave the chair a second time, the clock will be started over and they will be given one spank. For younger children, a clap of the hands is often an effective accompaniment with the word *spank*. Some parents are unwilling to use a single spank, and this component is not essential; however, a spank should not be used as a threat if parents are unwilling to follow through. Some researchers have found that hyperactive children respond well to mild forms of corporal punishment (Hanf, 1978). If parents wish to use the spank, it is recommended that this be the only situation in which spanking is used so that it maintains its effectiveness as a significant intervention. Each subsequent time the child leaves the chair, one spank is given and time is started over again. Regardless of the number of times the child leaves the chair, only one spank is given each time and no penalty time other than starting the clock over is added to the time-out period.

Some parent trainers advocate restraining noncompliant children or physically dragging them to time out. This is not recommended for the ADHD population of children. One of the reasons our prisons do not successfully rehabilitate is that the majority of individuals in prison believe they are there because they were unfortunate enough to be caught, convicted, and placed behind locked doors. If children are physically restrained in a punishment, their perception of the reason for being restrained is focused on the parent's being inappropriate and unfair rather than on the fact that they have made a mistake and should accept the negative consequence as penalty. When children are voluntarily sitting in the time-out chair, they must resolve the cognitive dissonance created by that situation by telling themselves that they have done something wrong and this is their punishment. This greatly increases the likelihood that punishment will be effective in reducing noncompliant behavior.

Differential attention can be used effectively to deal with children refusing to go to or remain in time out. The practitioner must be cautioned, however, that there are some children who refuse to buy into any level of intervention. Some children will continuously escalate in their opposition until they have a major tantrum and are out of control. Such children may require a safe, padded, illuminated, ventilated time-out booth. Occasionally, if needed, parents will construct such a booth and use it as a final or last intervention if less restrictive forms of time out are not accepted by the child. In most cases, the child tests the parent's intention to use the time-out booth once or twice and then no longer escalates to the point where the booth is necessary. There are some children, however, who do not benefit from this level of intervention either. Frequently, these children are severely disturbed, and their problems are much greater than just ADHD; often, these children require psychiatric hospitalization. For additional strategies and systems of time out, the reader is referred to Phelan (1985) and Clark (1986).

Differential Attention (Ignoring)

Many parents ignore. They ignore the good, the bad, and just about everything else their children do. Parents must be helped to understand that ignoring is an active process requiring them to not pay attention to behavior they don't like but immediately to pay attention in a positive way when the child begins to exhibit more acceptable behavior. Parents must also be helped to understand that in the majority of situations, once they make a direct request of the child and the child is noncompliant, ignoring the child at that point will be an ineffective intervention. Ignoring is recommended following a direct request to follow through only when the child engages in an additional aversive behavior in an attempt to manipulate, control, or alter the situation. At that point, ignoring children provides a clear message that parents will not deal with them when they are being inappropriate or noncompliant. When the child once again gains self-control, the parent can return to the situation, reinforce the child for being in control, and again direct the child to follow through with the punishment, usually time out. This is another battle the child cannot win. Some children may repeatedly test such a situation. When that happens, parents are instructed that when the child is not compliant a third time, it is beneficial to add an additional aversive consequence, such as earlier bedtime or restriction from television. It is rare for a child to continue to be noncompliant when a second aversive consequence is introduced.

Overcorrection (Positive Practice)

If the child engages in a behavior such as slamming a door, the parent may then reply, "Doors need to be shut quietly." The child is not going through another door, so there is no opportunity to assess the issue of compliance versus incompetence. In such situations, most parents will have the child return and go through the door in an appropriate manner; when this process is repeated a number of times, it is referred to as overcorrection. Overcorrection is a good intervention for both incompetent and noncompliant behavior. Although overcorrection of a nonrelated behavior (i.e., having an autistic child stand up and sit down when he or she self-stimulates) is used as a punishment, practicing an appropriate behavior makes overcorrection an intervention for incompetence. It is helpful for the practitioner to assist parents to develop an attitude in which they approach the child in such situations with a smile and give a very clear message that this is not punishment: If we do not read well, we practice. If we do not kick a soccer ball well, we practice. If we do not close doors well, we also practice. Research suggests that behavior in which we engage repeatedly, in a similar fashion, becomes automatic. Having the child practice ten times consecutively walking through the door in an appropriate way will increase the likelihood that the next time the child goes through a door he or she will act appropriately.

Parents are directed to further explain to the child that if there is a problem the next time, it simply means there was not enough practice, and the number of practice sessions is doubled. The practicing of appropriate behavior is an excellent intervention, working well with a wide range of behaviors, including forgetting to flush the toilet, to hang up a coat, or to wash hands before dinner.

Interventions with Young Children

Because of the wide variation of what is considered normal attention and related skills in young children, it is especially important for the practitioner to make certain that the child's parents have realistic expectations for their ADHD child. The overly rigid parent with inappropriate expectations will very quickly reinforce a pattern of problematic behavior in the child, much of which will not stem from a physiological basis but from the child's inability to meet excessive demands. With younger children, it is also extremely important to rule out the possible contribution to the child's behavioral problems of other developmental impairments, especially language disability.

Pediatricians are becoming increasingly responsive in identifying and providing support to parents with difficult infants. With difficult infants and toddlers it is essential to increase parental competence by (1) providing education concerning the nature and pattern of the child's behavior; (2) helping parents understand the role they may play in reinforcing that behavior; and (3) teaching behavior management skills. Effective daily management of the difficult infant and toddler is a crucial determinant of long-term outcome. Parents approaching a difficult offspring with skills, patience, and tolerance will diffuse power struggles and prevent the development of further problems. Parents approaching a similar child with anger, irritation, anxiety, and ultimately emotional withdrawal will certainly enhance the development of secondary problems. As parents learn management skills, the practitioner must be supportive and available to help when problems arise.

One of the most frequent complaints about difficult infants is problems with sleep. Higher rates of enuresis, difficulty rising, sleep onset problems, night waking, and bedtime resistance have been reported in children with ADHD (Corkum, Beig, Tannock, & Moldofsky, 1997). However, these authors suggest that the base rates of these problems, though greater than the normal population, appear more often related to comorbid conditions occurring with ADHD (e.g., oppositional defiant disorder or anxiety disorders) than to ADHD symptomatology. Thus, the sleep problems reported for difficult infants may not necessarily represent the early precursors of ADHD. Regardless of etiology, parents must be helped to explore numerous alternatives to find a specific routine or pattern that will enhance sleep. The range of possibilities includes rocking, a monotonous noise such as a metronome, playing of a lullaby, or use of a pacifier. Some parents report that the only way they get their infant to sleep is to put the child in the car and drive around the block; interestingly, a product has been marketed that can be attached to the child's crib and provides a vibration simulating a moving automobile, along with a monotonous carlike sound.

Parents also complain about problems with restlessness during waking hours. Frequently, visual, auditory, or tactile stimulation can be effective in reducing restless behavior. Many parents have found that a pacifier reduces irritability. Although some parents feel guilty about using a pacifier, parents of difficult infants and toddlers should be supported by the practitioner in using, within reason, any intervention that works. It is recommended, however, that the use of a pacifier be gradually eliminated as the child reaches 2 years of age, because extinction of pacifier use in older toddlers is an extremely difficult and stressful process.

Parents of difficult infants must be counseled about potentially stressful activities such as bathing and changing. It is essential that both parents play an active role in the care of the child and have enough breathing space so that they do not feel overwhelmed by the child's demands. A monthly group for parents of difficult infants in which ideas are shared and a brief presentation is made by a community-based professional is often an effective and valued support.

Interventions for Adolescents

By 12 years of age, interventions that are effective with younger children very quickly lose their potency. The adolescent often reacts to time out and overcorrection with resistance. Differential attention may be an effective technique but alone is insufficient. With adolescents, it is often helpful to bring the family together to learn negotiation and contracting skills (Robin, 1979, 1981; Robin & Foster, 1989). Problem behaviors in ADHD teens also differ: in part due to their forgetfulness and impulsivity, much of the teen-parent conflict centers around schoolwork and chores. Particular attention must be paid by the practitioner to help parents accept and understand the impact ADHD symptoms have on teenagers. Robin and Foster (1989) describe the parent-adolescent conflict as verbal arguments about specific issues, disputes based on the teen's increasing independence from the family, and the family's difficulty due to poor communication. The model they propose has been found effective for ADHD due to its focus on problem definition, conflict resolution, and alternative solutions. Of interest is their focus on the cognitive misconceptions parents develop about their children (e.g., need for obedience, self-blame), as well as faulty beliefs adolescents develop about their parents (e.g., perfectionism, unfairness).

Adolescents who refuse to participate in parental interventions or who are passively resisting participants cannot be forced. It is therefore important for adolescents to feel that their opinion is important and their input will be considered in the rule- and decision-making process. Adolescents with ADHD have well-developed, often dysfunctional patterns of behavior that are habitual and may be resistant to intervention. Helping the adolescent feel comfortable, accepted, and in partial control of the treatment process will facilitate change.

It is recommended that at least a brief period of psychotherapy be considered for all ADHD adolescents to help them understand their history and current problems, assist them in beginning to think about their adult lives, and facilitate the ability to be active participants in the treatment process. It is also recommended that medications not be used as punishment; for passive and marginally involved ADHD adolescents, medication will simply provide another issue and opportunity to rebel. On the other hand, if medication is presented as a choice, to accompany willing participation in psychosocial interventions, including therapy and educational support, there is a greater likelihood of treatment progress and compliance once medication use is initiated.

Robin (1990) suggests a number of additional guidelines for parents of adolescents with ADHD:

1. Taking the time to understand normal adolescent development and how it impacts an individual with ADHD.
2. Allowing the adolescent with ADHD the opportunity to provide input and participate in the decision-making process when possible.
3. Straightening priorities so that parents can decide which are important versus unimportant issues.
4. Developing an effective problem-solving system with all family members.
5. Staying involved, setting conditions and consequences.
6. Learning effective communication skills (this should include all family members).
7. Encouraging the continued use of medication.

It is critical that all adolescents, even those with ADHD, be given the opportunity to make decisions, even if they make mistakes. It is far better for them to make mistakes at younger ages rather than have their lives managed through negative reinforcement; the latter leads to frustration and failure as they get older, when sufficient negative reinforcement simply cannot be provided by parents to keep adolescents in line. It is also strongly recommended that parents of adolescents with ADHD focus on the present rather than the past or future, separate events from people, focus on change and alternatives, and take notice of the positive.

Siblings

Anecdotal reports from parents frequently note that siblings of ADHD children have a variety of reactions. Younger siblings of the ADHD child may be afraid and intimidated, wary and self-protective. The ADHD child's behavior may cause injury or destruction of their possessions, creating increased conflict. Younger siblings with ADHD may frequently disturb and interrupt as well as disrupt the activities of their older siblings. Parents need to take into consideration the needs of all their children. Special time should be set aside for each child, and these times honored despite the possible disruptions caused by the ADHD child.

When siblings complain that the child with ADHD is being treated preferentially, parents should refocus the complaint, first by asking whether the sibling would like to be the ADHD child; the standard answer is no, which is why the sibling is complaining. The focus then should be on what each child needs rather than creating comparisons or a fairness contest. (For more information concerning sibling issues, the interested reader is referred to S. Goldstein, 1996.)

SUMMARY

This chapter reviewed the literature concerning the impact of a number of variables, including parent beliefs and perceptions, psychiatric status, and environmental and delivery factors, on the success of parent training for ADHD. The chapter provided a practical model to increase parental competence and management at home for the child with ADHD. A number of specific management issues that are critical to effective home functioning were also reviewed. Finally, additional suggestions were made for working with young children, adolescents, and siblings of the child with ADHD. Practitioners should be aware that there is a movement in the medical and mental health communities to utilize a solution-building family systems model, helping parents take an equal and active role in meeting their children's emotional, behavioral, and educational needs (Stein, 1997).

Chapter 18 ————————————————————

CONTROVERSIAL TREATMENTS

When the first edition of this text was published in 1990, the groundswell of interest in the understanding, evaluation, and management of ADHD in childhood was just beginning to crest. With the tremendous upsurge of scientific and public interest in ADHD, children and the systems designated to educate and help them have greatly benefited. On the negative side, however, a great deal of media attention, especially in the past eight years, has focused on controversial, unproven, or alternative treatments for ADHD children. As with any issue facing the general public, from gasoline additives to treatments for children's learning or behavior problems, the more attention drawn to a particular issue, the more likely it is that scientists, entrepreneurs, and others will come forward, for a variety of reasons, proposing methods to benefit the problem. Regarding ADHD, these unproven treatments move into the realm of controversy when they are unfairly, inappropriately, and at times ruthlessly marketed as proven effective. The treatments reviewed in this chapter, although proponents claim they are proven solutions, are controversial in that they have not been shown to be effective, at least not according to the standards by which the scientific community judges effectiveness.

Parents of children with ADHD and practitioners who treat them are easy prey for those who promise quick fixes or miracle cures. Parents are often desperate to obtain help for their children. Because even well-educated parents seldom possess the training or expertise to critically evaluate scientific findings concerning the effectiveness of new treatments, practitioners must be sufficiently knowledgeable and prepared to advise parents concerning these approaches. When they are not, or take a "Let's try it and see" attitude, they are acting beyond the ethical and scientific principles that have been designed to guide our actions.

In this chapter, we review a number of controversial methods that have been proposed and are actively marketed for the treatment of children with ADHD. These treatments have not as yet met scientific standards of effectiveness. Some of these approaches merit continued research; others clearly do not. Practitioners need to be informed about these treatments to help parents make wise decisions concerning the treatment of their children with ADHD.

EVALUATING NEW TREATMENTS

The scientific process by which a particular treatment is shown to be effective can be long and arduous. Each step takes time and careful planning. The process usually begins with a formulation of a hypothesis usually based on an existing body of knowledge (e.g., because counseling is beneficial for a number of childhood problems, it might also be beneficial for children with ADHD).

The second step requires the development of a protocol to evaluate the effectiveness of the proposed treatment. The treatment itself, and the way in which it will be implemented, is carefully defined (e.g., a specific set of counseling methods will be provided to a number of children with ADHD for a fixed period of time).

Researchers must also specify the means by which effectiveness of treatment will be evaluated. Issues related to factors that might impact treatment effectiveness (e.g., placebo) must be carefully thought out and planned for. Even in the best of research studies, it is impossible to control all potential mediating variables. Appropriate measurement techniques and statistical tests must meet the rigors of scientific standards. The results of these studies must be subjected to the scrutiny of one's peers, often published in journals accepting articles only after careful peer review, analysis, and revision. Finally, initial findings are not considered substantive until additional studies are conducted to reaffirm the original findings. The process can take years, but it is the only way the scientific community can make sound decisions about new treatments (G. Golden, 1991).

Specifically in regard to ADHD, we believe that effective treatments must impact the child at the point of performance (Ingersoll & Goldstein, 1993). These treatments must fit with what is already known about ADHD and have consistently and repeatedly demonstrated effectiveness across a variety of situations and settings. It is our belief that the further a treatment deviates from the point of performance, the less likely it is to benefit children with ADHD. Proven treatments, such as behavior management and medication, are active at the point of performance, that is, the point at which the child behaves or interacts with the environment. As treatments are removed from the point of performance (e.g., cognitive training, which takes place in the clinician's office), they are less likely to be beneficial. The further treatments are from the point of performance as well as from what is logically known and accepted about the disorder, the less likely they are to benefit ADHD children.

Another Path to Treatment Evaluation

There is a second path that some scientist-practitioners follow, sometimes to avoid the longer, more accepted, certainly arduous process. But this path is fraught with danger. On this path, proposed treatments often stem from concepts outside the mainstream of existing knowledge. These treatments are often instituted long before there is any research supporting their effectiveness. Often only brief, poorly designed trials involving a small number of subjects are offered as proof of the effectiveness of these treatments. Single case studies are often the major proof offered. Measurement techniques and statistical means of evaluation are usually limited. In fact, as Casti (1989) points out, this path may in fact represent pseudo science; such science consists of anachronistic thinking, a casual approach to evidence, use of spurious similarities, research by literary interpretation, refusal to revise, and, most controversial, the belief that something is true until proven false.

This treatment approach is usually publicized in texts or journals that do not require peer review. Often, in fact, advocates of a particular treatment publish the work themselves. Some of these treatments are even promoted through multilevel marketing techniques (e.g., the substance God's Recipe). Parent or professional support groups, formed primarily to advocate this particular treatment, then play an important role in publicizing and promoting the treatment. The Feingold Association, advocating dietary intervention as a means of correcting children's behavioral and learning problems, is an example.

These alternative treatments commonly claim effectiveness for a broad range of problems. When pressed for proof, proponents of these treatments are often able to produce large volumes of information, but closer analysis reveals the documentation does not scientifically support the treatment claims. Proponents of controversial treatments often claim to have access to knowledge and information not shared by the medical, mental health, or educational community at large. When their treatments are criticized, they explain that this criticism reflects a conspiracy against them in the scientific community.

In Chapter 5, a number of these issues were discussed from a causal perspective in relation to their hypothesized impact on the development and maintenance of ADHD in childhood. In this chapter, these causes will be reviewed from the perspective of their proposed treatment benefits for ADHD.

Dietary Intervention

Few approaches have generated greater controversy for treating ADHD than those involving special diets. As we discussed in Chapter 5, twenty years ago, physician Benjamin Feingold (1974) reported that children in his practice who were sensitive to aspirin often had adverse behavioral reactions to foods containing salicylates and food coloring. It is important to note that Feingold reported these substances as exerting a toxic rather than allergic effect on the body. Based on his clinical practice over the years, Feingold expanded his elimination diet to include most artificial food flavorings and colorings. Modifications and adjustment of the diet were based on theory rather than scientific assessment. Later proponents of the Feingold diet added the preservatives BHA and BHT to the list of taboo substances. Although Feingold's initial hypothesis related the offending chemicals only to behavior, his theory soon included the claim that these substances were responsible for a broad array of children's learning, behavior, and attention problems.

More recent advocates of the dietary approach (Crook, 1991; Egger, Stolla, & McEwen, 1992; Rapp, 1991) report that problem children, including those with ADHD treated for allergies through dietary control, demonstrate improvements in behavior, attention, schoolwork, and even physical symptoms such as pains. However, Egger, Carter, Graham, Gumley, and Soothill (1985) also concluded that "restricted diets are socially disruptive, expensive and because of nutritional inadequacy may be dangerous if not properly supervised" (p. 1153). Interestingly, Egger et al., (1985) report a high incidence of headache, abdominal pain, and limb aches in their hyperkinetic children treated successfully with diet. This triad has been suggested as having a very strong presentation in psychosomatic disorders (Apley & MacKeith, 1968). Proponents of the dietary approach offer a variety of elimination diets to selectively weed out possible offending foods and substances. In a number of different treatment programs, diet is often combined with other allergy treatments and psychosocial and even medication methods.

Advocates of the Feingold diet, by far the best known of the dietary approaches, have made many dramatic claims (E. Wender, 1986). It is suggested by proponents of the dietary approach that additive-free diets improve most (if not all) of children's learning and attention problems. In the past twenty years, however, dozens of well-controlled studies published in peer review journals have consistently failed to find support for Feingold's approach (for review, see Ingersoll & Goldstein, 1993). Although some studies have reported limited success with a dietary approach (Kaplan et al., 1989), at best the data suggest there may be a very small group of children—primarily hyperactive preschool boys with histories of multiple allergies—who appear somewhat responsive to additive-free diets.

A lack of well-controlled studies is also evident concerning the relationship between treatment of specific allergies and improving ADHD symptoms. Although proponents of this approach acknowledge that careful scientific studies are necessary (Rapp, 1991), such studies have not yet been conducted. Therefore, these proponents are left to provide case studies as their only supporting evidence (Rapp, 1991).

Nearly 100 conditions can present with varying degrees of hypoglycemia. ADHD is not one of them (Sauls, 1974). A number of studies have examined the relationship between sugar and hyperactive behavior, generally finding limited if any significant relationship (Behar, Rapoport, Adams, et al., 1984; Kaplan et al., 1986; Kruesi et al., 1987; Wolraich, Milich, Stumbo, & Schultz, 1985). Of the few studies suggesting some negative effects of sugar on behavior, these effects are minimal and only a small percentage of ADHD children appear vulnerable (for review, see Ingersoll & Goldstein, 1993). Most recently, Proanthocyanidian (pychnogenol), an antioxidant, has been reported to be beneficial for ADHD. Proponents of pychnogenol suggest that it is similar to vitamins C and E, which neutralize unstable, radical oxygen molecules that attack body cells. It is suggested that when these free radical molecules go unchecked, they degrade the tissue-strengthening collagens within the body's joints, skin, and organs, causing problems implicated in disorders ranging from depression and Alzheimer's to diabetes and arthritis. Proponents of pychnogenol market the product with the claim that life expectancy can be increased by 20%.

As Accardo and Whitman (1991b) suggest, ADHD may be influenced by but clearly is not caused by dietary issues. After analyzing the existing evidence, reviewers have consistently concluded that the evidence fails to support a link between modifying diet and improving ADHD symptoms (Barkley, 1990a; Goldstein & Goldstein, 1990; Milich & Pelham, 1986). It is fair to conclude that children with ADHD require a healthy, well-balanced diet, as do all children. There is also reason to believe that a good breakfast is particularly important and that, to be most helpful, breakfast should offer a balance of protein and carbohydrate (Conners, 1989c). Finally, although many children with ADHD are picky eaters or crave certain foods, there is no research to suggest that their dietary habits or cravings are related to their behavior. At this time it has not been demonstrated that dietary intervention offers significant help to children with ADHD. It is, however, an area worthy of continued research.

Megavitamins and Mineral Supplements

The use of very high doses or megadoses of vitamins and minerals to treat ADHD has its roots in the model of orthomolecular psychiatry (Pauling, 1968). According to this school of thought, some people possess a genetic abnormality that results in increased requirements for vitamins and minerals. When these higher-than-normal requirements are not met, various forms of illness result, including ADHD. Thus, it has been proposed that treating ADHD children with very high doses of vitamins will decrease hyperactivity and improve attention and concentration. A variety of related alternative theories have also proposed modifying and controlling various minerals, such as potassium and sodium, as well as trace elements, including zinc and copper. It has been suggested that manganese may be responsible for aggressive and possibly inattentive behavior.

Vitamins are synonymous with health and have intuitive appeal for treating children's problems. Vitamins are considered "natural" substances, giving them an aura of safety reassuring to many parents. Conceptually, the vitamin approach appears reasonable, as it is well-known that vitamin deficiencies can cause an array of serious diseases, such as scurvy, pellagra, and rickets. It does not appear farfetched to hypothesize that vitamin excesses or deficiencies might produce more subtle symptoms such as those related to ADHD. In spite of its intuitive appeal, however, there is no supporting evidence for the orthomolecular approach to treating ADHD (Haslam, Dalby, & Rademaker, 1984; Kershner & Hawke, 1979). Among the studies supporting the megavitamin approach, all suffer from serious methodological flaws (Brenner, 1982; Colgan & Colgan, 1984; Harrell, Capp, & Davis, 1981). Proponents of the orthomolecular approach have been reduced to citing clinical experience or single case studies to support this treatment. More important, it is well-known that vitamin and mineral supplements can be harmful when taken in excessive doses. For example, too much vitamin C has been reported as leading to the formation of kidney stones; high doses of nicotinic acid have been reported as producing skin rashes and liver damage.

In 1973, a task force appointed by the American Psychiatric Association concluded that the use of megavitamins to treat behavioral and learning problems was not justified based on the available research literature; thirteen years later, the American Academy of Pediatrics issued a similar paper. In the past twenty-five years, despite claims made by proponents of these types of treatments, there has not been any well-constructed scientific research to justify altering these conclusions. The absence of supportive data for these treatments, combined with the potential dangers, should alert practitioners to carefully monitor any child whose parents have chosen this type of treatment approach.

The Vestibular System

Two different schools of thought have proposed that an underlying dysfunction in the vestibular system is responsible for ADHD and other learning and behavior problems in children (Ayres, 1965, 1979; H. Levinson, 1990). Ayres viewed the vestibular system as the unifying system of the brain and stated that "when it does not function properly, incoming sensory information is interpreted inconsistently and inaccurately" (Ayres, 1979). Levinson reports that a dysfunction in the cerebellar vestibular system causes a wide range of problems; he hypothesizes that there is a relationship between ADHD and problems with coordination and balance, thought to reflect a dysfunction in the inner ear system because this system plays a major role in balance and coordination.

Levinson's Approach

To treat ADHD, Levinson (1991) proposes a mixed array of medications, include three anti-motion-sickness antihistamines (meclizine, cyclizine, and dimenhydrinate) and three stimulants (pemoline, methylphenidate, and dextroamphetamine). Using a variety of combinations of these medicines at various doses, Levinson claims a success rate in excess of 90% (H. Levinson, 1991). Unfortunately, his proof consists of single case studies.

Levinson's theory and approach are not consistent with what is currently known about ADHD. Although there is a limited body of research supporting a link between the inner ear system and attentional processes, anatomically and physiologically, it does not appear that the inner ear system is involved in causing or maintaining symptoms of ADHD other than, at the very best, in marginal ways.

Levinson's presentation of anecdotal evidence in a series of single case studies is all that has been offered to suggest that this is a proven, effective treatment. Results of the single controlled study of this approach fail to support the inner ear system theory in any way (Fagan, Kaplan, Raymond, & Eddington, 1988). Levinson reports that the combination of medications necessary to help most children makes it difficult if not impossible to provide proof that this is an effective treatment through well-controlled double-blind studies. At best, this response to a lack of scientific analysis is a convenient means of avoiding putting his theory to the test. Further, practitioners need to be cautioned about potential side effects when combinations of stimulants are prescribed in excessive doses.

Ayres's Sensory Integrative Therapy

Sensory integrative therapy was developed by the late occupational therapist, Jean Ayres (1979). Ayres coined the term "sensory integration" to refer to the brain's ability to organize and make use of incoming information from various senses. The vestibular system appears to be the central control function for this process. Sensory integrative therapy consists of exercises encouraging the child to use as many nerve-cell connections as possible. Ayres (1979) reported that this helps children learn how to organize their brains, which in turn makes them better able to learn, behave, and pay attention.

Cermack (1988a, 1988b) argues that children with ADHD respond to sensory integration procedures because improvements in attention "appears to be related to some arousal, regulation and sensory integration treatment which uses sensory input coupled with the demand for adaptive motor responses: This may enhance the effectiveness of the arousal centers and an increase in attention could be related to more effective regulation of arousal" (p. 3 of 1988a). However, even this author notes that this hypothesis requires further testing.

The popularity of this approach can be explained in part by the fact that exercise, like vitamins, appears to be a natural way to treat ADHD symptoms. Further, a large organization boasting over 5,000 members firmly supports and believes this method of treatment (Cermack, 1988a, 1988b). Ayres's theories, however, do not appear to be consistent with what is currently known about the cause or treatment of ADHD. There is insufficient data to suggest that the vestibular system is primarily involved in regulating attention, activity level, or impulse control.

Serious questions have been raised concerning the methodology and statistical analyses used in the studies originally offered by Ayres to support her approach (Cummins, 1991; Polatajko, 1985). The results of two well-controlled studies failed to find support for the effectiveness of sensory integrative training as a treatment for learning or behavior problems (Densem, Nuthall, Bushnell, & Horn, 1989; Humphries, Wright, Snider, & McDougall, 1992). Caplan, Polatajko, Wilson, and Faris (1993) concluded that the effects of sensory integration therapy on learning disabilities is not greater than any other more traditional method of intervention. These authors note that parents and therapists often perceive children improving with sensory integration treatment, yet improvements are often difficult to measure in operational ways. At this time, there is no evidence supporting sensory integration training as a treatment for ADHD (Hoehn & Bauermeister, 1994; for review, see Feldman, 1990 or Ingersoll & Goldstein, 1993). Although there do not appear to be any dangers associated with this treatment, and in fact, the exercises offered might lead to improvements in motor skills (Cammisa, 1994), there are no proven benefits for ADHD symptoms beyond what might be attributed to placebo. However, the scientific literature has not compared benefits for children with ADHD treated with sensory integrative therapy versus other proven treatment methods. (Arnold, 1985). The interested reader is referred to Sensory Integration International (1994) for a review of these types of studies.

Candida Albicans

Candida albicans is a type of yeast living in the human body. It has been demonstrated that candida can overgrow when the immune system is weakened or certain bacteria are killed by antibiotics. This can lead to vaginal yeast infection known as candidiasis and, less commonly, infections of the skin, nails, and mouth. Crook (1986, 1991) has proposed that yeast infections also cause ADHD. According to this theory, toxins produced by the overgrowth of yeast circulate through the body, weaken the immune system, and make the individual susceptible to a frightening array of infections and illnesses, including psychiatric disorders and ADHD.

The Candida albicans program is designed to discourage the growth of Candida in the body. The program frequently consists of the use of antifungal medication such as Nystatin (to kill yeast without harming other bacteria) and a low-sugar diet (because sugar is proposed as stimulating yeast growth in the body). Other aspects of this treatment program include an elimination diet to avoid food allergies and the use of vitamin and mineral supplements. Further, Crook proposes that children with yeast-related problems may be susceptible to chemicals and molds and suggests additional assessment to determine if these offending substances should be avoided as well.

There is consistent medical evidence to demonstrate that Candida can cause infections of the vagina, mouth, and skin; however, there is limited evidence to support the idea that Candida causes other illnesses. Further, in the single controlled study exploring the presumed relationship between Candida in the body and candidiasis hypersensitivity syndrome, it was concluded that the syndrome itself cannot be verified (Dismukes, Wade, Dockery, & Hain, 1990). Thus, not only has a causal relationship not been found, but the treatment model is so obtuse as to make assessment difficult if not impossible. The theory is not consistent with current knowledge concerning ADHD, and there is no evidence from controlled studies supporting the method of treatment; again, only anecdotal evidence and testimonials are provided to support the theory.

EEG Biofeedback

After reviewing forty-four studies, Cobb and Evans (1981) concluded that biofeedback was not particularly effective for a variety of childhood behavioral and learning disorders. Lee (1991) reviewed thirty-six studies in which biofeedback is used as a treatment for hyperactivity; biofeedback treatments alone were not reported to be effectively evaluated, such that methodological problems limited the conclusions that could be drawn from these studies. Table 18–1 contains a summary of the characteristics of these treatment studies. Lee concludes, however, that "most of the research reviewed here is replete with methodological flaws, including small samples, few placebo control groups, diverse criteria for classification of a child as hyperactive and routinely a lack of follow-up. In addition, only two studies used biofeedback separately or independently of other treatment techniques. From a clinical viewpoint in nearly all of these studies, biofeedback was used with additional techniques (e.g., relaxation training, contingent reinforcement) so its effectiveness alone cannot be assessed" (p. 186). It is difficult to understand how others, based on the same review of the literature, can conclude that biofeedback should be considered in the treatment of a wide range of childhood problems (Barowsky, 1991). Interestingly, Electromyogram (EMG) and Galvanic Skin Response (GSR) studies appeared to yield better benefits for specific target symptoms than EEG studies, yet it is EEG biofeedback that has become increasingly touted as beneficial for ADHD.

The EEG biofeedback approach to treating ADHD has become popular and received an increasingly larger share of media attention over the past ten years. Proponents of the EEG biofeedback approach suggest that ADHD can be trained away by increasing the type of brain wave activity associated with sustained attention and decreasing the type of activity associated with daydreaming and distraction (Barowsky, 1991; Lubar, 1991). Although proponents of this approach are not claiming that EEG abnormalities are the cause of ADHD, they suggest that by altering EEG patterns, the manner in which the brain operates can be modified, and that this modification leads to improvements in ADHD symptoms.

Biofeedback is a twentieth-century treatment. Children are attached by wires to machines, which measure various involuntary body functions and provide information to the individual, who uses this feedback to gain voluntary control over these body functions. EEG biofeedback specifically measures levels of electrical activity in various regions of the brain; this information is fed into a computer, which transforms it into a

Table 18–1. Biofeedback treatment for hyperactivity

Classification	Number	Classification	Number
Research Methodology		Additional Techniques	
Case study	3	Stimulant medications	3
Pre-posttest	24	Positive reinforcement	9
A-B designs	8	Progressive relaxation	12
Multiple baseline	1	Autogenic phrases	4
		Visual imagery	10
Training Location		Presession practice	7
Hospital	1	Self-questionnaire	1
School	17	Other rewards	1
Laboratory	6		
Not reported	11	Results	
		Reductions in impulsivity	2
Biofeedback Treatment Modality		Improvements on physiologic	
Actometer/Body movement	5	(biofeedback) indicators	21
EMG	25	Improvement on behavioral	
Skin temperature	4	indicators	10
EEG	6	Improvement on educational	
GSR	4	indicators	7
		Reductions in activity level	7
Subjects' Characteristics		No improvement on behavioral	
Age range, 6 to 16 yr.		observations	4
Mean no. of subjects per study: 22		Improved self-concept	2
Males: 555		No improvement in attention	
Females: 31		span	4
		More internal locus of control	4
Length of Training		No improvement on	
Mean no. sessions: 17;		educational indicators	2
range 3–158		No improvement on locus of	
Mean session length: 34 min.,		control	1
range: 8–120 min.		No improvement on recall	1
Average training time (weeks): 7–8		Increased paired-associate	
range 3–23		memory	1

Source: Lee, S. W. (1991). Biofeedback as a treatment for hyperactivity: A critical review of the literature. *Psychological Reports, 68,* 163–192. Reprinted by permission of the publisher.

signal such as a light or tone. In the case of children, the signal is turned into a video game, and control of the game is based on increasing certain brain waves and decreasing others. Using this signal as feedback, the child is reinforced in the game to modify brain wave activity. Proponents of this treatment suggest that training involves between forty and eighty sessions, each lasting forty minutes or more (Lubar, 1992); sessions are held as often as two to three times per week. The procedures are usually augmented by proven treatments, including behavior management, educational intervention, academic tutorial, and even medication if necessary.

As we discussed in Chapters 2, 5, and 9, the theory underlying EEG biofeedback as a treatment for ADHD is consistent with what is known about low levels of arousal in frontal brain areas in individuals with ADHD (Lou, Henriksen, & Bruhn, 1984;

Zametkin et al., 1990). There has also been documentation that the brain wave patterns of some children with ADHD differ from other children who do not experience ADHD; specifically, ADHD children produce more theta and fewer beta waves, particularly in frontal regions (Mann, Lubar, Zimmerman, Miller, & Muenchen, 1990; Satterfield et al., 1988). However, other studies have failed to support a demonstrable relationship between the brain wave activity of ADHD children and those who do not suffer from ADHD. Halperin et al., (1986), for example, found no relationship among EEG abnormalities, the severity of the ADHD child's symptoms, and responsiveness to medication treatment.

Some studies have suggested dramatic results for EEG biofeedback, but in general, these have been poorly controlled (Potashkin & Beckles, 1990; Tansey, 1985). A better series of studies has been proposed but has still not undergone the rigors of peer review and publication. In all of these studies, children are reported to quickly learn to increase the desired brain wave activity. Dependent measures include parent and teacher ratings, as well as IQ and achievement tests. The claim has also been made that this treatment produces long-lasting permanent results—unlike any other treatment used for ADHD children (Lubar, 1991; Othmer, 1993).

The majority of these positive outcome studies, however, are seriously flawed by the use of small numbers of subjects, ambiguous diagnoses, and poor methodology. They often do not include appropriate controls to allow the determination that it is the EEG biofeedback producing results rather than placebo or some of the ancillary treatments offered. In 1981, when Cobb and Evans reviewed forty-four studies that had investigated the benefits of biofeedback techniques in treating childhood behavioral and learning problems, they concluded that although the research suggested that children can learn to voluntarily control a variety of physical processes, methodological flaws in the majority of them made it impossible to specify the exact mechanisms responsible for change. These authors additionally concluded that the data did not suggest that biofeedback techniques were superior to more conventional treatments for remediating children's learning and behavioral problems. Research since that time does not justify altering these conclusions (Levy, 1994).

Further, the process of EEG biofeedback, when the trappings of technology are removed, simply reinforces a child for paying attention. If in fact brain wave activities are altered when children pay attention, it would be expected that any activity ADHD children engage in that requires them to pay attention and reinforces them for increasing consistent attention would yield the same types of benefits. In a single case study this has been suggested to be the case (Kotwal, Burns, & Montgomery, 1996). Finally, there are data to suggest that a reduction in theta wave activity is causally linked to reduced brain blood flow (increasing risk of ischemic hypoxia), metabolism-impaired neurotransmitter biosynthesis, and numerous types of brain pathology (Fried, 1993). Thus, if one accepts that there are benefits in reducing theta wave activity in the brain, one has to accept also that there are potentially serious liabilities and consequences.

The application of EEG biofeedback technology in the treatment of ADHD at this time must be considered unproven and controversial. Although biofeedback in general as a treatment has not lived up to its promises, it does offer proven documented benefits for pain management and other physical disorders. It is thus an area worthy of continued research. Until that time, it is an expensive approach whose effectiveness for ADHD remains scientifically undemonstrated (Levy, 1994). As Culbert, Kajander, and Reaney (1996) note, "the literature to support its (EEG biofeedback) efficacy suffers from many methodological flaws. This is an area in which clinical practice has outpaced clear, scientific evidence of efficacy" (p. 346).

Auditory Training

Auditory training was developed by French neurologist Guy Berard. It was originally proposed to treat autism. The treatment is based on an auditory training desensitization model (Edelsohn & Waddell, 1992). It has been suggested in the lay press that this treatment may also be beneficial for ADHD. It has been marketed as helpful for a wide range of childhood disorders as well (R. Bender, 1993). However, no controlled studies have been completed for ADHD.

Cognitive Interventions

In the first edition of this text, we offered a chapter touting the potential benefits of cognitive interventions to increase self-regulation in children with ADHD. Since that time, published research necessitates a more conservative stance for the use and potential benefits of cognitive treatments for ADHD. In this edition, we have offered a modified position concerning cognitive interventions, but we believe the interventions still hold an adjunctive place in the treatment of ADHD in childhood. We would be remiss, however, if we did not mention cognitive treatment in this chapter specifically in regard to ADHD.

Recent studies and reviews of the literature have consistently demonstrated that cognitive interventions have failed to provide more than limited positive effects for ADHD (Abikoff, 1991; Fehlings et al., 1991). These studies have suggested that cognitive techniques are more beneficial for normal children or children with other developmental or behavioral problems than for children with ADHD. For children with ADHD, benefits, even when statistically significant, are usually small in comparison to other, less difficult temperament treatments such as behavior management or medication (Barkley, 1990a). Further, most research studies dealing with cognitive interventions are short term and have not demonstrated long-term maintenance or generalization of skills learned.

As noted in Chapter 14, for cognitive behavioral interventions to succeed with ADHD children, the interventions must be taught to primary caregivers, used on a daily basis, and implemented in a variety of settings over the long term (Barkley, 1990a). Further, successful programs utilizing cognitive interventions for ADHD children must establish environmental cues and consequences, which are critical to the use of these skills. Practitioners, however, must be aware that for cognitive interventions to work, all adults involved with the child, from parents to educators to Scout leaders, must play an active role. Parents must also be informed that cognitive intervention for ADHD as a primary, singular treatment will not be effective unless paired with medication or behavior management.

HELPING PARENTS BECOME WISE CONSUMERS

The treatments reviewed in this chapter vary in their theoretical underpinnings, extent of research, and claims for effectiveness. Some merit continued research, some have demonstrated ancillary though proven benefits for ADHD, and others actually could do harm.

Practitioners must be aware that when these treatments are offered in the marketplace, they cross the line from unproven to controversial. Proponents of these treatments can be very convincing that their approach is proven and acceptable despite the fact that little if any data exist to support their claims. Because these treatments are often sold in the marketplace in a manner similar to other products, the trappings and attractiveness of marketing may distract parents—and practitioners, for that matter—from asking important questions. Practitioners must caution parents considering these treatments that time and money, which are often limited resources, might be better spent on treatments with proven track records. As we have summarized, among the most effective methods for treating children with ADHD are the judicious use of medication and behavior management. In addition, when cognitive programs designed to modify the way children think and problem-solve are applied carefully, consistently, and with opportunities for new learning to generalize, they can also be helpful. Finally, as we have emphasized, parent education is an essential component of any effective childhood treatment program.

The practitioner's obligation is to assist parents in obtaining the most appropriate and best treatments for their children. Parents in desperate straits, faced with their children's failure on the playground, at school, and at home, are often at the mercy of the marketing techniques utilized by these controversial treatments. Frequently, they adopt the attitude "How can it hurt to try?" When faced with this approach, practitioners have the ethical responsibility to accurately and thoroughly inform parents, educators, and other professionals concerning the current status of these various treatments.

Accardo and Whitman (1991b) point out that proponents of controversial treatments frequently argue that people should be free to choose whatever they want and that alternative remedies offer a last chance for help. These authors suggest that "irrational" would be a better term than controversial for these treatments. Ingersoll and Goldstein (1993) suggest that parents considering these treatments or any others be advised of the following warning signs:

1. Overstatement and exaggerated claims for certain treatments are red flags. Parents should be suspicious of any product or treatment that is described as "astonishing," "miraculous," or "an amazing breakthrough." Legitimate medical and mental health professionals do not use words like these, nor do they boast of their success in treating huge numbers of patients.

2. Parents should be advised to be suspicious, too, of any therapy that claims to treat a wide variety of ailments. Common sense tells us that the more grandiose the claim, the less likely it is there is any real merit behind it.

3. Parents should not rely on testimonials from people who say they have been helped by the product or treatment: first, legitimate medical and mental health

professionals do not solicit testimonials from their patients; second, testimonials are not substitutes for evidence; third, patient enthusiasm is also not a substitute for scientific evidence. Testimonials in no way prove effectiveness. Choosing treatments for children's attention and impulse problems is not like choosing a mechanic for your car.

4. Parents should request printed information about a treatment they are considering. They should be wary if the bulk of this information is published by the particular practitioner or by a group whose sole purpose is to promote that treatment.

5. Parents must be skeptical about claims that a treatment is being suppressed or unfairly attacked by the medical or mental health establishment. Legitimate medical and mental health professionals eagerly welcome new knowledge and better methods of treatment. They have no reason to suppress or oppose promising new approaches derived from scientifically valid research.

Practitioners are urged to ask the question, How do I know this treatment will really work? Asking this question and having a consistent set of guidelines to evaluate the answers provided for a proposed treatment will prevent overtrust in costly, quick-fix cures. Most important it will ensure that children with ADHD and their parents are informed of the benefits and risks associated with any treatment offered to their children.

SUMMARY

In 1993, Ingersoll and Goldstein, based upon an extensive review of the then available literature concerning hypothesized cause and treatments for ADHD, concluded that many of the alternative, scientifically unproven treatments for ADHD finding their way into the marketplace appeared to be taking advantage of many parents "desperate to help their children but confused about the nature of the problem and the kinds of treatment most likely to help" (p. 210). In the spirit of how can it hurt to try, parents appear to be increasingly tempted to throw caution to the wind, expending time, money, and energy on treatments promising quick cures and miraculous benefits. Many of these treatments deserve continued research. Others do not. In the interim, however, these treatments, marketed beyond their proven worth, must be considered controversial. Practitioners must be knowledgeable about them and willing to ethically accept their responsibility to communicate such knowledge to their patients and families.

Chapter 19 ————————————————————————

CONCLUDING REMARKS

As we prepare to enter the twenty-first century, the advances of the past decade place us at the gateway to a limitless future, one few of us can imagine. At no time in human history have so many and such rapid advances in science, technology, medicine, and education been realized. In a few short years, even the great mysteries of human genetic complexities, including ADHD, will be mapped and defined. Our knowledge of the interaction of psychosocial factors in the presentation of ADHD has also rapidly increased. This should, therefore, also represent the very best of times for our youth. The closing of one century and the opening of another in light of the advances of this past decade suggests that our children will experience lives that many of us could never have imagined. Yet, as the principles of yin and yang dictate, if there is a sunny side of the mountain, there must be a dark side: although it appears to be the best of times for our youth, the beginning of this century may also bring greater challenges and hurdles as our children grow into their adult years. Depression, for example, is increasing at a higher rate among younger people than among older people (Ingersoll & Goldstein, 1995). Are we giving birth to more depressed children than did our grandparents and great-grandparents? The diagnostic rate of ADHD also appears to be increasing. Are we producing more offspring with these qualities? Can we blame the increase in depression, ADHD, and other childhood problems on genetics alone?

Throughout this text, we have emphasized that genetic and multiple environmental factors play a role in explaining the escalating problems our youth are experiencing. As Rutter (1997) has noted, environmentality and heritability are both strong influences on behavior. Poverty, the victimization of children, family dysfunction, and changes in societal expectations all appear to be contributing to an alarming trend of increasing life problems among our children. As Elkind (1981) pointed out seventeen years ago, well-meant efforts to prepare our children for successful adulthood may be backfiring: our intentions, though noble, may be ill-timed, unrealistically demanding, and stress-inducing. The increasingly rapid pace of our technologically complex society may be hurrying our children; we may be exposing them to situations that are beyond their emotional, behavioral, and cognitive capacities. We may be preparing them for later life at a very dear cost.

With this general trend of problems among our youth, it is not surprising that children with developmental and psychiatric problems are further compromised in their ability to cope with the demands in their lives. And it is not surprising that research over the past twenty years have well documented that children with ADHD, perhaps due to their impulsive qualities, experience more comorbid problems than those with any other childhood disorder. As a group, if left to fend for themselves, they develop into adults with serious and significant problems. It is this often tragic outcome that most concerns us. It may not be the case that ADHD qualities in themselves define the "twentieth-century equivalent of the devil." Rather, as we have suggested, qualities of ADHD may be catalytic, placing children with the disorder at greater risk to develop comorbid problems in our current society. A significant percentage of delinquent youth have histories of ADHD; a significant percentage of adults with antisocial, criminal, and substance abuse problems appear to have suffered with ADHD from early childhood as well. It is the fear of what today's ADHD children may become in light of society's current trends that most concerns us.

In a thorough review article, Yoshikawa (1994) discussed the early risk factors for chronic delinquency. Family factors play a powerful role; thus, as we have argued in this text, lack of family and educational support may each represent significant risks for producing later delinquency and ultimately adult antisocial problems in individuals with ADHD. A relatively small group of offenders is responsible for most juvenile offenses: multiple studies have reported that fewer than 10% of adolescents in the juvenile justice system are responsible for over 60% of the crimes (Farrington, 1987; Shannon, 1978; Tracy, Wolfgang, & Figlio, 1990). This group appears to contain a large number of adolescents with ADHD. Farrington (1987) reported that temperament is a significant factor contributing to risk within the child. Practitioners must be aware of the multiple forces that influence children's development: those involving family, such as parenting, quality of attachment, marital conflict, and child abuse; contextual factors such as socioeconomic status; and factors within the child, including genetic vulnerability and perinatal risk. Perhaps more important than anything else we do for youth with ADHD, our goal must be to prevent the progression to delinquency. Ensminger, Kellam, and Rubin (1983) reported that 45% of children demonstrating teacher-rated aggressive behavior in first grade had self-reported delinquency scores at age 15 in the highest range. Children rated by teachers and peers as most troublesome at age 8 to 10 years represented 22% of the entire sample at the time of assessment, but 70% of future chronic offenders (Farrington, 1987). Although early age of onset for delinquency may be characteristic of children without ADHD as well as those with ADHD, the risk is greater for the ADHD group (LeBlanc & Freschette, 1989; McCord, 1980; Tolan & Lorion, 1988).

A cascade of multiple environmental risk factors impacts social and related development (Rutter, 1979; Sameroff & Fiese, 1990). The relationship between genetic vulnerability and later delinquency is strengthened in the presence of early family conflict. The relationship between perinatal risk and later antisocial behavior and delinquency is strengthened by the presence of poverty and family adversity. The relationship between marital discord and later behavior problems is strengthened in the presence of poor parenting. Insecure attachment and later antisocial behavior is strengthened in the presence of poor parenting and negative environmental factors such as life stress and low social support. Poverty increases risk for delinquency, but poverty alone is insufficient to predict delinquency. However, delinquency in the face of poverty appears to be mediated by family factors. Positive child-rearing practices protect against the development of antisocial behavior. Support for parents protects against poor child-rearing practices among high- and low-risk families (Farrington, 1987). Further, the cost of supporting at-risk families has been estimated at approximately 10% of what it costs for each of these families had they required more traditional justice and division of family service interventions (Earle, 1995); resilience, good outcome despite high problem-risk status, sustained competence under stress, and the ability to recover from trauma all appear to explain this phenomenon. As Emmy Werner noted in 1994, even in the most disorganized and impoverished homes, some children develop stable, healthy personalities and function successfully in school and in the community at large. Increasingly, our understanding of what is right about these children points to the quality of their family relationships.

We believe that families faced with raising a child with ADHD, even in the absence of additional risk factors, require comprehensive, intensive, and flexible support throughout the years of raising their children. Such qualities define successful programs, demonstrating good outcome for high-risk children (Schorr, 1988). Embry (1995) suggests that building in protective and resilient factors for at-risk children must be part of a comprehensive plan. Such a plan would include:

- Enhancing everyday parenting competence, beginning at young age of the child.
- Increasing the rates of praise and reward for positive daily behavior and reducing verbal threats in the home and school.
- Teaching children to reduce insults, increase their use of praise, accept feedback, and engage others in a cooperative way.
- Teaching children how to self-monitor their behavior, a quality lacking in children with ADHD.
- Increasing the daily frequency and availability of positive social skills and parenting models in the mass media and school and community settings.
- Disseminating practical, hands-on tools to reduce disruptive aggressive behavior at home, in the community, and at school.
- Disseminating practical tools to help teachers improve the school climate.
- Planning and designing interventions so that they generalize across behaviors, people, settings, and time.

We believe that all of these factors will lead to more efficient and effective personal control. It has been suggested that one of the greatest human fears is losing control (Seligman, 1991), and that one of the strongest motivations of humans is to have control over one's life (Rothbaum & Weiz, 1989). As Shapiro, Schwartz, and Astin (1996) so aptly pointed out in their review of the self-control literature, psychologically normal individuals develop a greater sense of control than do those with problems. Normal individuals tend to overestimate the amount of control they have in a situation, are more optimistic about their ability to achieve control, and believe they have skills to solve their problems. The manner in which children with ADHD attempt to gain and maintain control over their lives, unfortunately, is impulsive and nonthinking. This results in less control and coercively contributes to an increasing pattern of helplessness and for some a subsequent profile of maladaptive efforts to gain and maintain control. Thus, a central goal in our work with youth with ADHD is to help them develop skills to exert and maintain appropriate control over themselves, their lives, and their environment.

As practitioners, we must undertake and accept responsibility for the task of doing a better job of translating what has been demonstrated scientifically into the clinical setting and beyond. We must bring our knowledge to the families, educators, and professionals with whom we work. We must take our expertise into their homes, schools, and communities. Because ADHD is a biopsychosocial disorder, practitioners must possess a thorough knowledge of the developmental course, definition, evaluation, and, most important, proven treatments for the disorder. Effective treatments for ADHD require the interface of medical, mental health, and educational professionals. Each specialty area must possess a working knowledge of all aspects of the diagnosis and treatment of ADHD. Although nonprescribing practitioners are often well aware of psychosocial treatment strategies for children with ADHD, their knowledge of medications, the most effective treatment, as well as their ability to communicate efficiently with treating physicians is often lacking. The corollary is true of physicians, who may possess an excellent working knowledge of symptom targets for medication treatment but are often not in a position to gather the data necessary to demonstrate treatment effectiveness.

The topic of ADHD likely will continue to be the most widely researched and argued area in child development and psychopathology. New ground is broken daily. Research studies are more complex, better controlled, and quicker to be replicated. Increasingly, as Rutter (1997) has pointed out, we are coming to recognize that "nature and nurture do not operate independently of each other, and there needs to be an explicit focus on the interplay between them" (p. 396). The five-year multisite, multimodal treatment ADHD study underway at this time by the National Institute of Mental Health aims to provide even better-defined answers concerning comorbid conditions, gender issues, family history, home environment, and age variables (Richters et al., 1995). This knowledge will impact diagnosis and treatment in the short and long term.

The United Nations Convention on the Rights of the Child (Limber & Flekkly, 1995) has accepted that, as we are an international community, it is the duty of each citizen of each nation to ensure that children's rights to survival, protection, development, and education are fulfilled. Our emphasis on the best interests of children, their rights, and their dignity represents a bright star in our passage into the twenty-first century. As a society, we must understand and deal effectively with the alarming trend of problems among our youth. To practitioners working with children with ADHD and their families, this future trend offers great hope. For, in the end, no matter how effective and efficient our treatments are for ADHD, it is the course of society and the outcome for all children that will best predict and contribute to the successful life outcome for children with ADHD.

APPENDIXES

Appendix 1

Practice Parameters for the Assessment and Treatment
of Attention-Deficit Hyperactivity Disorder

Below is the first set of practice parameters developed by the American Academy of Child and Adolescent Psychiatry. This document was created during approximately one year by the Work Group on Quality Issues, chaired by Steven Jaffe, M.D., with contributions from *many* other Academy members. These practice parameters will be reviewed for revision at least every two years and at shorter intervals if new discoveries are made regarding the assessment and treatment of ADHD.

The recommendation that the Academy begin to set practice parameters was formally made by the original Work Group on Quality Issues, chaired by William Ayres, M.D. In its Final Report published in 1988, the Work Group recommended:

> The Academy should begin setting standards, recognizing that this process will be selective and not all-inclusive. It will have to be an ongoing process, with revisions made as new knowledge becomes available. The standards will not be academic standards but a reflection of accepted mainstream clinical practice.

Council endorsed this recommendation, and a new Work Group began the process of setting practice parameters. The first draft on ADHD was sent to three expert consultants for review and comments and then revised. The resulting draft was sent to the entire Academy membership in June, 1989 and approximately 150 members responded with comments and specific revisions. Most agreed that there was a need for the Academy to develop parameters of practice.

Many suggestions were incorporated into the draft by the Work Group, and another draft was given to all registrants at the Academy's Annual Meeting in New York City, October 11 to 15, 1989. During the Annual Meeting, the Assembly of Regional Organizations of Child and Adolescent Psychiatry unanimously endorsed the Academy's setting of practice parameters. At a 2-hour Member Forum, Academy members had the opportunity to make additional suggestions for the document and discuss the concept of setting practice parameters.

After final revisions by the Work Group, the document was reviewed by Council in early 1990 and approved for publication. Following the parameters is a list of selected references on ADHD.

Introduction

Child and adolescent psychiatrists and adolescents who have specific psychiatric disorders that impair emotional, cognitive, and/or behavioral functioning. The child or

AACAP Official Action (1991). *Journal of the American Academy of Child and Adolescent Psychiatry,* *30*(3), 1–111. Reprinted with permission of the publisher.

adolescent is evaluated in the context of the family, school, community, and culture. When specific signs and symptoms are present, a diagnosis should be made. These signs and symptoms with their associated impairments in developmental function as well as other areas of comorbidity may require and respond to known treatments. The risk/benefit ratio of any treatment should be considered along with the likely course of the disorder without treatment. These parameters are guidelines for the generally accepted level of practice for the assessment and treatment of ADHD as of July, 1990. Periodic revisions will be needed as new assessment procedures and treatment modalities are developed and studied.

These parameters of practice should not be construed as including all proper methods of care or excluding other acceptable methods of care reasonably directed to obtaining the same results. The ultimate judgment regarding any specific clinical procedure or treatment must be made by the physician in light of all the circumstances presented by the patient and the resources particular to the locality or institution.

These parameters of practice were approved as of the date indicated, and they should not be applied to clinical situations occurring before that date.

Practice Parameters for the Assessment and Treatment of ADHD

I. For grade school-aged children (ages 6–12)
  A. Initial evaluation
    1. Diagnostic assessment
      a. Interview with parent(s)
        1) Obtain child's history
          a) Emphasis on developmental history and DSM-III-R target symptoms
          b) Development of symptoms including family, peer and academic problems
          c) Medical history and releases
        2) Obtain family history
          a) ADHD, tics, alcoholism, somatization disorder, and personality disorders
          b) Developmental and learning disorders
          c) Family coping style and resources
      b. School information
        1) Obtain information about school functioning from contact (in person, by phone, or through written reports) with appropriate staff, such as principal, teacher, and/or nurse if release of information is granted by parents
        2) Document the source of the information
      c. Child diagnostic interview
        (Note: Target symptoms of DSM-III-R may not be present during interview with the child)
      d. Standard parent and teacher rating scales of child's behavior may be useful

      e. Consider referral for IQ, psychological, speech and language, and learning disability (high incidence of concurrence) testing if clinically indicated

      f. Physical evaluation of the child

          1) Pediatric examination within 12 months as indicated

          2) Contact and collaboration with family doctor/pediatrician or other health care providers

          3) Vision and hearing check as indicated

          4) Evaluation of other medical and neurological conditions as indicated

2. Identify presence of DSM-III-R target symptoms from preceding information

3. In the assessment of a school-aged child with symptoms suggestive of ADHD, evaluation includes consideration of the following:

      a. Recent onset of biopsychosocial stresses

      b. Educational potential and achievement

      c. Peer, sibling, and family problems

      d. Environmental factors including disorganized home, presence of child abuse/neglect, mental illness in parents, and environmental neurotoxins (e.g., lead intoxication)

4. The following diagnoses should be considered (these may be concurrent or confused with ADHD):

      a. Oppositional/conduct disorder

      b. Specific developmental disorder (e.g., speech, language, and learning)

      c. Mood disorders

      d. Anxiety disorders (including post-traumatic stress disorder)

      e. Borderline personality disorder (in adolescence)

      f. Substance abuse disorders

      g. Tic disorders (including Tourette's disorder)

      h. Mental retardation

      i. Pervasive developmental disorders (cannot be concurrent diagnosis)

      j. Schizophrenic disorder

      k. Medical/neurological primary diagnosis, e.g., hyperthyroidism, seizure disorder (e.g., petit mal), migraine

      l. Medication related, e.g., antiasthmatics, phenobarbital, antihistamines, sympathomimetics, steroids

B. Treatment—*Multimodal* (psychotherapies and psychosocial modalities as well as pharmacological treatments should be considered)

    1. Education and consultation

      a. Educate parents, grandparents, and other significant people about ADHD (symptoms, clinical course, prognosis, etc.) and counsel parents in behavior management techniques

      b. Educate the child about ADHD in an age-appropriate manner, and share observations from clinical assessment engaging the child as observer

     c. Educate/collaborate with the school system personnel as available

     d. Consult with parents and school on appropriate class or school placement and management

  2. Psychotherapies and other psychosocial interventions as indicated

     a. Family psychotherapy for family dysfunction

     b. Individual and/or group psychotherapy for poor self-esteem and/or peer problems

     c. Social skill training for poor social capacities (including promoting capacity for empathy) and cognitive therapies for attention/impulsivity symptoms

     d. Parent behavior training—to develop appropriate, consistent limit-setting abilities and behavior modification programs for behavior problems

  3. Consider medication for symptom relief in school, home, and other settings. Medication may be indicated during weekends and summer in addition to school

     a. Stimulants are usually the medication of first choice. Pulse and blood pressure should be monitored

     b. The antidepressants, i.e., imipramine and desipramine, also may be considered.

        1) Baseline blood pressure and pulse should be recorded before antidepressants are prescribed

        2) An electrocardiogram should be considered if there is a concern about cardiac functioning

        3) Electrocardiogram monitoring should be obtained when dosages exceed 3.5 mg/kg/d

        4) Antidepressant serum levels may be useful when there are concerns about toxicity and/or noncompliance

     c. The risks of neuroleptics usually exceed their possible usefulness in the treatment of ADHD and would require careful consideration before use

     d. If medication is recommended, inform parents of risks and benefits associated with and without medication use. The information should include the following:

        1) Changes to expect

        2) Appropriate dosage and course of administration

        3) Possible side effects

     e. If medication is prescribed, monitor the effects in school, at home, and during the child's activities. Engage the child as an active participant in this process

     f. Other medications are being used and studied but have not achieved the status of accepted parameters

C. Monitor child's progress

  1. Target symptoms of inattention, impulsivity, and hyperactivity (see DSM-III-R)

2. Academic performance and school behavior

3. Emotional growth

4. Peer relationships

5. Leisure time activity

6. Family interactions

7. If the child is on medication, monitor blood pressure and pulse, height and weight, tics, appetite, mood, and side effects

8. If the child is taking stimulant medication for ADHD, consider monitored trials off the medication one or more times per year to ascertain continued need for medication. This should be done with parent/child/teacher collaboration and observation. Similar consideration is indicated for antidepressants, with careful concern for tapered medication withdrawal

II. Preschool children (ages 3–6 years)

Same evaluation and treatment protocol as for grade school-aged children except as follows:

1. Emphasize parent training, collaborative treatment, and specially structured   . preschool

2. If above is not effective, then consider medication

III. Adolescents

Same evaluation and treatment protocol as for school-aged children except as follows:

1. Evaluate especially for signs of coexisting conduct disorder, mood disorders, substance abuse disorders, and personality disorders

2. If conduct disorder and/or substance abuse disorder are present, be cautious of the possibility that the adolescent may abuse or sell prescribed medication. Antidepressants may be the medication of choice.

IV. Special associated issues

A. If academic performance is impaired, the presence of a borderline IQ, mental retardation, or a learning disability should be considered

B. If tics are present in a child or adolescent who is diagnosed with ADHD or if there is a family history of tics, it should be noted that the use of stimulants in children with tics or Tourette's disorder is controversial but not absolutely contraindicated.

V. Other treatments for ADHD are outside the realm of the usual parameters of practice of child and adolescent psychiatry.

Appendix 2

Childhood History Form

Child's Name _____

Birth Date _____ Age _____ Sex _____

Home Address _____
                    Street   City

_____ Home Phone _____
     State   Zip   Area Code

Child's School _____
                Name   Address

Grade _____ Special Placement (if any) _____

Child is presently living with:

_____ Natural Mother _____ Natural Father _____ Stepmother _____ Stepfather

_____ Adoptive Mother_____ Adoptive Father _____ Foster Mother _____ Foster Father
_____ Other Specify _____

Non-residential adults involved with this child on a regular basis:

_____

_____

Source of referral: Name _____
Address _____ Phone _____

Briefly state main problem of this child: _____

_____

_____

_____

PARENTS

    Mother _____

    Occupation _____ Business Phone _____

    Age _____ Age at time of pregnancy with patient _____

    School: Highest grade completed _____

            Learning problems _____

            Attention problems _____

            Behavior problems _____

Medical Problems _____

Have any of your blood relatives experienced problems similar to those your child is experiencing? If so, describe: _____

_____

_____

Father _____

Occupation _____ Business Phone _____

School: Highest grade completed _____

      Learning problems _____

      Attention problems _____

      Behavior problems _____

Medical Problems _____

Have any of your blood relatives experienced problems similar to those your child is experiencing? If so, describe: _____

_____

_____

_____

SIBLINGS

  1. _____

  2. _____

  3. _____

  4. _____

  5. _____

  6. _____

PREGNANCY—Complications

Excessive vomiting _____ hospitalization required _____

Excessive staining/blood loss _____ threatened miscarriage _____

Infection(s) (specify) _____

Toxemia _____ Operation(s) (specify) _____

Other illness(es) (specify) _____

Smoking during pregnancy _____ # cigarettes per day _____

Alcoholic consumption during pregnancy _____

   Describe if beyond an occasional drink _____

Medications taken during pregnancy _____

X-ray studies during pregnancy _____

Duration of pregnancy (weeks) _____

DELIVERY

Type of Labor: Spontaneous _____ Induced _____ Duration (hrs.) _____

Type of Delivery: Normal _____ Breech _____ Caesarean _____

Complications: Cord around neck _____ Hemorrhage _____

Infant injured during delivery _____ Other _____

Birth Weight _____

POST DELIVERY PERIOD

Jaundice _____ Cyanosis (turned blue) _____ Incubator Care ____

Infection (specify) _____

Number of days infant was in the hospital after delivery _____

INFANCY PERIOD

Were any of the following present—to a significant degree—during the first few years of life? If so, describe:

Did not enjoy cuddling _____

Was not calmed by being held or stroked _____

Difficult to comfort _____

Colic _____ Excessive restlessness _____

Excessive irritability _____

Diminished sleep _____

Frequent head banging _____

Difficulty nursing _____

Constantly into everything _____

TEMPERAMENT

Please rate the following behaviors as your child appeared during infancy and toddlerhood:

Activity Level: How active has your child been from an early age? _____

Distractibility: How well did your child pay attention? _____

Adaptability: How well did your child deal with transition and change? _____

Approach/Withdrawal: How well did your child respond to new things (i.e., places, people, food)? _____

Intensity: Whether happy or unhappy, how aware are others of your child's feelings? _____

Mood: What was your child's basic mood? _____

_____

Regularity: How predictable was your child in patterns of sleep, appetite, etc.? __

_____

MEDICAL HISTORY

If your child's medical history includes any of the following, please note the age when the incident or illness occurred and any other pertinent information:

Childhood diseases (describe ages and any complications) _____

_____

Operations _____

Hospitalization for illness _____

_____

Head injuries _____

Convulsions _____ with fever _____ without fever _____

Coma _____

Persistent high fevers _____

Eye problems _____

Tics (i.e., eye blinking, sniffing, any repetitive, non-purposeful movements) _____

_____

Ear problems _____

Allergies or asthma _____

Poisoning _____

Sleep_____

   Does your child settle down to sleep? _____

   Sleep through the night without disruption? _____

   Experience nightmares, night terrors, sleep walking, sleep talking? _____

_____

   Is your child a very restless sleeper? _____

   Does your child snore? _____

Appetite _____

_____

PRESENT MEDICAL STATUS

Height _____ Weight _____

Present Illnesses for which the child is being treated _____

_____

Medications child is taking on ongoing basis? _____

_____

DEVELOPMENTAL MILESTONES

If you can recall, record the age at which your child reached the following developmental milestones. If cannot recall exactly, check item at right:

	Age	Early	Normal	Late
Smiled	_____	_____	_____	_____
Sat without support	_____	_____	_____	_____
Crawled	_____	_____	_____	_____
Stood without support	_____	_____	_____	_____
Walked without assistance	_____	_____	_____	_____
Spoke first words	_____	_____	_____	_____
Said phrases	_____	_____	_____	_____
Said sentences	_____	_____	_____	_____
Bladder trained, day	_____	_____	_____	_____
Bowel trained, night	_____	_____	_____	_____
Rode tricycle	_____	_____	_____	_____
Rode bicycle (without training wheels)	_____	_____	_____	_____
Buttoned clothing	_____	_____	_____	_____
Tied shoelaces	_____	_____	_____	_____
Named colors	_____	_____	_____	_____
Named coins	_____	_____	_____	_____
Said alphabet in order	_____	_____	_____	_____
Began to read	_____	_____	_____	_____

COORDINATION

Rate your child as Good, Average, or Poor on the following skills:

Walking _____

Running _____

Throwing _____

Catching _____

Shoelace tying _____

Buttoning _____

Writing _____

Athletic abilities _____

Excessive number of accidents
   compared to other children _____

COMPREHENSION AND UNDERSTANDING

Do you consider your child to understand directions and situations as well as other children his or her age? _____

If not, why not? _____

_____

How would you rate your child's overall level of intelligence compared to other children?
Below Average _____ Above Average _____ Average _____

SCHOOL HISTORY

Were you concerned about your child's ability to succeed in kindergarten? If so, please explain: _____

_____

Rate your child's school experiences related to academic learning:

Nursery School _____

Kindergarten _____

Current Grade _____

To the best of your knowledge, at what grade level is your child functioning:
Reading _____ Spelling _____ Arithmetic _____

Has your child ever had to repeat a grade? If so, when? _____

_____

Present class placement: Regular Class _____ Special class (if so, specify)

_____

Kinds of special counseling or remedial work your child is currently receiving ____

_____

Describe briefly any academic school problems _____

_____

_____

Rate your child's school experiences related to behavior as Good, Average or Poor:

Nursery school _____

Kindergarten _____

Current grade _____

Does your child's teacher describe any of the following as significant classroom problems?

Doesn't sit still in his or her seat _____

Frequently gets up and walks around the classroom _____

Shouts out. Doesn't wait to be called on _____

Won't wait his or her turn _____

Doesn't cooperate well in group activities _____

Typically does better in a one-to-one relationship _____

Doesn't respect the rights of others _____

Doesn't pay attention during storytelling or show and tell _____

Describe briefly any **other** classroom behavioral problems _____

_____

_____

As best you can recall, please use the following space to provide a general description of your child's school progress in each grade. Use the back of this form if extra space is needed:

_____

_____

_____

_____

_____

_____

PEER RELATIONSHIPS

Does your child seek friendships with peers? _____

Is your child sought by peers for friendship? _____

Does your child play with children primarily his or her own age? _____

Younger? _____ Older? _____

Describe briefly any problems your child may have with peers: _____

_____

_____

_____

HOME BEHAVIOR

All children exhibit, to some degree, the behaviors listed below. Check those that you believe your child exhibits to an excessive or exaggerated degree when compared to other children his or her own age.

Fidgets with hands, feet or squirms in seat _____

Has difficulty remaining seated when required to do so _____

Easily distracted by extraneous stimulation _____

Has difficulty awaiting his turn in games or group situations _____

Blurts out answers to questions before they have been completed _____

Has problems following through with instructions (usually not due to opposition or failure to comprehend) _____

Has difficulty paying attention during tasks or play activities _____

Shifts from one uncompleted activity to another _____

Has difficulty playing quietly _____

Often talks excessively _____

Interrupts or intrudes on others (often not purposeful or planned but impulsive) _____

Does not appear to listen to what is being said _____

Loses things necessary for tasks or activities at home _____

Boundless energy and poor judgment _____

Impulsivity (poor self-control) _____

History of temper tantrums _____

Temper outbursts _____

Frustrates easily _____

Sloppy table manners _____

Sudden outbursts of physical abuse of other children _____

Acts like he or she is driven by a motor _____

Wears out shoes more frequently than siblings _____

Excessive number of accidents _____

Doesn't seem to learn from experience _____

Poor memory _____

A "different child" _____

How well does your child work for a short term reward? _____

How well does your child work for a long term reward? _____

Does your child create more problems, either purposeful or non-purposeful, within the home setting than his or her siblings? _____

_____

Does your child have difficulty benefitting from his experiences? _____

_____

Types of discipline you use with your child _____

_____

_____

Is there a particular form of discipline that has proven effective? _____

_____

Have you participated in a parenting class or obtained other forms of information concerning discipline and behavior management? _____

_____

INTERESTS AND ACCOMPLISHMENTS

What are your child's main hobbies and interests? _____

_____

What are your child's areas of greatest accomplishment? _____

_____

What does your child enjoy doing most? _____

_____

What does your child dislike doing most? _____

_____

What do you like about your child? _____

_____

**LIST NAMES AND ADDRESSES OF ANY OTHER PROFESSIONALS
CONSULTED:** (Including family doctor)

1. _____
2. _____
3. _____
4. _____

ADDITIONAL REMARKS:

Please write any additional remarks you may wish to make regarding your child.

_____

_____

_____

_____

_____

Appendix 3

Parenting Scale

Child's Name: _____ Today's Date: _____

Sex: Boy _____ Girl _____ Child's Birthdate: _____

At one time or another, all children misbehave or do things that could be harmful, that are "wrong," or that parents don't like. Examples include:

hitting someone	whining	throwing food
forgetting homework	not picking up toys	lying
having a tantrum	refusing to go to bed	wanting a cookie before dinner
running into the street	arguing back	coming home late

Parents have many different ways or styles of dealing with these types of problems. Below are items that describe some styles of parenting.

For each item, fill in the circle that best describes your style of parenting during the past two months with the child indicated above.

SAMPLE ITEM

At meal time . . .

I let my child decide how much to eat. ○—○—○—○—○—○—○ I decide how much my child eats.

1. When my child misbehaves . . .

   I do something right away. ○—○—○—○—○—○—○ I do something about it later.

2. Before I do something about a problem . . .

   I give my child several reminders or warnings. ○—○—○—○—○—○—○ I use only one reminder or warning.

3. When I'm upset or under stress . . .

   I am picky and on my child's back. ○—○—○—○—○—○—○ I am no more picky than usual.

4. When I tell my child not to do something . . .

   I say very little. ○—○—○—○—○—○—○ I say alot.

Scale developed by Susan G. O'Leary, David S. Arnold, Lisa S. Wolff & Maureen M. Acker. Psychology Department, State University of New York at Stony Brook. Stony Brook, NY 11794. Used with permission of the authors.

5. When my child pesters me . . .

    I can ignore the pestering. ○—○—○—○—○—○—○ I can't ignore the pestering.

6. When my child misbehaves . . .

    I usually get into a long ○—○—○—○—○—○—○ I don't get into an argument with my child. argument.

7. I threaten to do things that . . .

    I am sure I can carry out. ○—○—○—○—○—○—○ I know I won't actually do.

8. I am the kind of parent that . . .

    sets limits on what my ○—○—○—○—○—○—○ lets my child do child is allowed to do. whatever he or she wants.

9. When my child misbehaves . . .

    I give my child a long ○—○—○—○—○—○—○ I keep my talks short lecture. and to the point.

10. When my child misbehaves . . .

    I raise my voice or yell. ○—○—○—○—○—○—○ I speak to my child calmly.

11. If saying no doesn't work right away . . .

    I take some other kind ○—○—○—○—○—○—○ I keep talking and try to of action. get through to my child.

12. When I want my child to stop doing something . . .

    I firmly tell my child ○—○—○—○—○—○—○ I coax or beg my child to stop. to stop.

13. When my child is out of my sight . . .

    I often don't know ○—○—○—○—○—○—○ I always have a good what my child is doing. idea of what my child is doing.

14. After there's been a problem with my child . . .

    I often hold a grudge. ○—○—○—○—○—○—○ things get back to normal quickly.

15. When we're not at home . . .

    I handle my child the ○—○—○—○—○—○—○ I let my child get away way I do at home. with a lot more.

16. When my child does something I don't like . . .

    I do something about it ○—○—○—○—○—○—○ I often let it go. every time it happens.

17. When there's a problem with my child . . .

    things build up and I do   ○—○—○—○—○—○—○   things don't get out of
    things I don't mean to do.   hand.

18. When my child misbehaves, I spank, slap, grab, or hit my child . . .

    never or rarely.   ○—○—○—○—○—○—○   most of the time.

19. When my child doesn't do what I ask . . .

    I often let it go or end   ○—○—○—○—○—○—○   I take some other action.
    up doing it myself.

20. When I give a fair threat or warning . . .

    I often don't carry it out. ○—○—○—○—○—○—○   I always do what I said.

21. If saying no doesn't work . . .

    I take some other kind   ○—○—○—○—○—○—○   I offer my child
    of action.   something nice so
                                                                 he/she will behave.

22. When my child misbehaves . . .

    I handle it without   ○—○—○—○—○—○—○   I get so frustrated or
    getting upset.   angry that my child can
                                                                 see I'm upset.

23. When my child misbehaves . . .

    I make my child tell me   ○—○—○—○—○—○—○   I say "No" or take some
    why he/she did it.   other action.

24. If my child misbehaves and then acts sorry . . .

    I handle the problem   ○—○—○—○—○—○—○   I let it go that time.
    like I usually would.

25. When my child misbehaves . . .

    I rarely use bad language   ○—○—○—○—○—○—○   I almost always use bad
    or curse.   language.

26. When I say my child can't do something . . .

    I let my child do it   ○—○—○—○—○—○—○   I stick to what I said.
    anyway.

27. When I have to handle a problem . . .

    I tell my child I'm   ○—○—○—○—○—○—○   I don't say I'm sorry.
    sorry about it.

28. When my child does something I don't like, I insult my child, say mean things, or
    call my child names . . .

    never or rarely.   ○—○—○—○—○—○—○   most of the time.

29. If my child talks back or complains when I handle a problem . . .

    I ignore the complaining   ○—○—○—○—○—○—○   I give my child a talk
    and stick to what I said.   about not complaining.

30. If my child gets upset when I say "No," . . .

    I back down and give   ○—○—○—○—○—○—○   I stick to what I said.
    in to my child.

Scoring Instructions for the Parenting Scale

Each item receives a 1–7 score, where 7 is the "ineffective" end of the item. Thus, the following items have 7 on the left side (the others on the right): 2, 3, 6, 9, 10, 13, 14, 17, 19, 20, 23, 26, 27, 30

To compute the total score, average the responses on all items.

To compute a factor score, average the responses on the items on that factor.

Laxness: 7, 8, 12, 15, 16, 19, 20, 21, 24, 26, 30 (11 items)
Overreactivity: 3, 6, 9, 10, 14, 17, 18, 22, 25, 28 (10 items)
Verbosity: 2, 4, 7, 9, 11, 23, 29 (7 items)
items not on a factor: 1, 5, 13, 27 (4 items)

Demographics, Parenting Scale & CBCL Scores
for a Clinic and Control Group

(Standard deviations are in parentheses).

Category	Clinic Group ($n=26$)	Control Group ($n=51$)
Child's age (months)	29.9 (4.5)	28.6 (3.3)
Mother's age (years)	29.6 (6.7)	31.7 (3.9)
Mother's Education (years)	13.6 (1.7)	15.5 (2.6)*
Family Income (thousands)	33.4 (9.3)	33.4 (10.2)
Parenting Scale Scores:		
Total	3.1 (.7)	2.6 (.6)**
Laxness	2.8 (1.0)	2.4 (.8)*
Overreactivity	3.0 (1.0)	2.4 (.7)**
Verbosity	3.4 (1.0)	3.1 (1.0)
CBCL Externalizing Scale		
(T-Score)	58.7 (10.3)	47.7 (8.4)***

  * $p<.05$
 ** $p<.01$
*** $p<.001$

Appendix 4

Overview of
The Community Parent Education (COPE) Program

Charles E. Cunningham
Rebecca Bremner
Margaret Secord

Children with disruptive behavior disorders f(DBD) such as attention-deficit hyperactivity disorder (ADHD), oppositional disorder, or conduct disorder (CD) place an enormous burden on family relationships (Cunningham & Barkley, 1979; Mash & Johnston, 1982), peers (Cunningham & Siegel, 1987; Cunningham, Siegel, & Offord, 1985, 1991), and teachers (Whalen, Henker, & Dotemoto, 1980). The DBD child's behavior elicits a more controlling, less positive parental response (Barkley & Cunningham, 1979; Barkley, Karlsson, Pollard, & Murphy, 1985; Cunningham & Barkley, 1979; Patterson, 1982) which may compound the child's difficulties (Patterson, 1982) and adversely influence longer term adjustment (Earls & Jung, 1987; Weiss & Hechtman, 1986). Parents report a limited sense of control over the child's behavior (Sobol, Ashbourne, Earn, & Cunningham, 1989), low self-esteem (Mash & Johnston, 1982), increased stress (Anastopoulos, Shelton, DuPaul, & Guevremont, 1992), greater social isolation (Cunningham, Benness, & Siegel, 1988), and higher depression scores (Cunningham et al., 1988).

Given the severity of the DBD child's problems, the persistence of these disorders (Barkley, Fischer, Edelbrock, & Smallish, 1990; Offord et al., 1987) and the counterproductive pattern in the management of this population (Barkley, 1990; Dumas, 1989; Kazdin, 1987b). Clinical trials confirm that parent training programs are helpful for families of both ADHD and conduct problem children. With ADHD children, for example, parent training programs improve child management skills (Barkley, Guevremont, Anastopoulos, & Fletcher, 1992; Dubey, O'Leary, & Kaufman, 1983; Freeman, Phillips, & Johnston, 1992; Pisterman, McGrath, Firestone, Goodman, Webster, Mallory, & Goffin, 1992) and improve secondary behavior problems (Anastopoulos et al., 1992; Freeman et al., 1992; Pisterman et al., 1989; Pollard et al., 1983). Participants report increased confidence (Anastopoulos et al., 1992; Pisterman, McGrath, Firestone, Goodman, Webster, Mallory, & Goffin, 1992), reduced stress (Anastopoulos et al., 1992; Pisterman et al., 1992) and improved family relationships (Anastopoulos et al., 1992; Barkley, Guevremont, et al., 1992). Follow-up studies suggest that the effects of parent training are maintained over 6 week (Freeman et al., 1992), 2 month (Anastopoulous et al., 1992), 3 month (Pisterman et al., 1989), and 9 month (Dubey, O'Leary, & Kaufman, 1983) intervals.

Parent training programs are particularly important for families of children with conduct problems (Hinshaw, 1987; Szatmari, Offord, & Boyle, 1989a) who must deal

Cunningham, C., Bremner, R., and Secord, M. (1995). *COPE: The Community Parent Education Program.* Hamilton, Ontario, Canada: McMaster University. Used with permission of the authors and publisher.

with more serious antisocial behaviors and cope with increasing social, psychiatric, and legal problems during adolescence (Barkley et al., 1990; Mannuzza, Gittelman-Klein, Konig, & Giampino, 1989; Satterfield et al., 1982). Parents consider conduct disorders less controllable and respond more negatively to antisocial behavior than primary ADHD symptoms (Johnston & Patenaude, 1994; Johnston, Patenaude, & Inman, 1992). In addition, parents of ADHD/CD children report more personal psychopathology, marital conflict, family dysfunction, and social adversity than those of ADHD without CD (Lahey, Piacentini, et al., 1988; Owing-West & Prinz, 1987; Reeves et al., 1987; Szatmari et. al., 1989a), factors which themselves disrupt parenting and compound child management difficulties (Bond & McMahon, 1984). Outcome studies confirm that parent training improves antisocial behavior among conduct disordered children (Bank, Marlow, Reid, Patterson, & Weinrott, 1991; Forehand & McMahon, 1981; Kazdin, 1987b; Patterson, 1982; Webster-Stratton, 1991) and reduces noncompliant (Pisterman et al., 1989, 1992) and aggressive (Freeman et al., 1992) behavior in ADHD populations.

While promising, the effectiveness of parent training programs is limited by several factors (Whalen & Henker, 1991). First, although DBD children constitute a majority of the referrals to outpatient centers, a considerable percentage of children with significant psychiatric disorders do not receive treatment (Offord et al., 1987).

Secondly, where parent training programs are available, attendance is limited (Cunningham, Boyle, Bremner, & Secord-Gilbert, 1991). Dropouts range from 255 (Forehand, Middlebrook, Rogers, & Steffe, 1983) to 50% (Firestone & Witt, 1982) with economically disadvantaged, socially isolated (Wahler, 1980), single, or depressed parents whose children are at greatest risk most likely to discontinue treatment (Firestone & Witt, 1982; Webster-Stratton & Hammond, 1990). Third, parent training program participants often arrive late, neglect homework, miss appointments, and engage in "resistant" behavior which may compromise outcome (Patterson & Forgatch, 1985).

This chapter summarizes the theoretical rationale, organization, in-session process, and curriculum of a program developed to address a number of limits in the design of more traditional parent training programs.

Improving Availability

First, given long waiting lists, limited professional resources, and financial constrains, this program was designed to increase the availability of parent training programs by shifting from individual or small group models (Cunningham, 1990) to a large group format (Cunningham, Bremner, et al., 1993; Cunningham, Bremner, & Boyle, 1995). Over the last several years, for example, enrollment in our program has averaged 27 participants per group. A combination of small subgroup problem solving and role playing exercises coupled with larger group discussions retains the important components of traditional parent training programs and permits active participation while allowing substantial increases in enrollment and cost efficacy.

Improving Utilization

To improve accessibility, reduce obstacles to attendance, and eliminate the psychological barriers associated with hospital and mental health settings, this program is typically conducted in neighborhood schools, early childhood educational settings, and community centers. As a significant percentage of working parents prefer evening programs, courses are scheduled at both day and evening times. Moreover, as many high risk families are unable to secure reliable child care, the program offers a children's social skills activity group in conjunction with each session of the program.

Improving Parenting Skills

Managing children with challenging behavior is a technically demanding exercise. While most parents deal effectively with problems presented by the average child, the persistence, complexity, and pervasiveness of the problems of unusually challenging children demands more specialized strategies. Moreover, the problems parents confront can erode their confidence, increase conflict, and add an enormous burden of stress to the existing challenges of family life. This program, therefore, develops the more specialized approaches needed to promote positive behavior, improve self-regulation, reduce antisocial behavior, and cope with the child's difficulties more successfully.

Building Problem-Solving Skills and Reducing Resistance

Client resistance may, paradoxically, be a function of the didactic teaching strategies used in many parent training programs (Cunningham et al., 1995; Patterson & Forgatch, 1985). Recent evidence, for example, suggests that, while direct efforts to teach new skills often increases resistance, more facilitative strategies increase adherence and positive participation (Patterson & Forgatch, 1985). To reduce the resistance elicited by more didactic parent training models (Patterson & Forgatch, 1985), this program uses a Coping Modeling Problem Solving approach to skill acquisition (Cunningham, 1990; Cunningham et al., 1995; Cunningham, Davis, Bremner, Rzasa, & Dunn, 1993). In contrast to more didactic parent training models in which leaders teach the correct execution of new skills, Coping Modeling Problem Solving participants formulate their own solution. In this program, participants observe videotapes depicting exaggerated versions of common parenting errors, identify what went wrong, discuss the impact of these errors on child behavior and family relationships, devise alternative strategies, and formulate supporting rationales.

Coping Modeling Problem Solving has several advantages over more didactic approaches to parent training. First, exploring the consequences of both common child management errors and more effective alternative strategies should enhance parents' understanding of their impact on sociodemographic heterogeneity common in large parenting groups, Coping Modeling Problem Solving may yield solutions which are more meaningful to individual participants. Third, formulating and publicly stating solutions enhances attitude, change, and commitment (Greenwald & Albert, 1968; Janis, 1983; Leary & Miller, 1986; Meichenbaum & Turk, 1987). Fourth, (Mash & Johnston, 1982) and control (Sobol et al., 1989) reported by parents of ADHD children than more didactic models (Bandura, 1982; Meichenbaum & Turk, 1987). Finally, Coping Modeling Problem Solving improves adherence and reduces the resistance elicited by more didactic approaches (Cunningham et al., 1995).

Improving Family Functioning

While parent training programs typically focus on the acquisition of parenting skills, a number of investigators have suggested that a more systemic approach addressing contributing influences in the child's family, peer group, and school might enhance outcome (Miller & Prinz, 1990). Links between family dysfunction and antisocial behavior (Szatmari, Offord, & Boyle, 1989b; McGee, Silva, & Williams, 1984; Moffitt, 1990) suggest that improving key domains of family functioning is particularly important (Hinshaw, 1987; Szatmari et al., 1989b).

While simply including fathers in parent training programs does not improve outcome (Adesso & Lipson, 1981; Firestone, Kelly, & Fike, 1980; Martin, 1977) enhancing problem solving, communication, and conflict resolution skills appears to yield better results for discordant families (Dadds, Schwartz, & Sanders, 1987). Moreover, the improvements in management skill, parental confidence, and child behavior accomplished in parent training programs may yield collateral improvements in marital functioning (Anastopoulos et al., 1992; Eyberg & Robinson, 1982). Families which function effectively are more capable of responding to the challenges of a difficult to manage child. This program, therefore, attempts to strengthen several dimensions of family functioning. First, as families of challenging children will inevitably be confronted by a greater number of difficulties, this program focuses on the development of an effective approach to the solution of child management problems. Secondly, in two parent families, the program encourages a more balanced allocation of child care and child management responsibilities. Third, this program encourages supportive communication among partners.

Developing Supportive Personal Networks

Networks of supportive personal contacts play an extremely important role in effective parenting. Contact with parents facing similar difficulties provides families of challenging children with logistical assistance, information, support, and encouragement. Families of DBD children move frequently (Barkley, Fischer, et al., 1990), consider relationships with relatives to be disruptive, and report fewer contacts with extended family members (Cunningham et al., 1988) who may be an important source of direct assistance, child rearing information, and personal support (Cochran & Brassard, 1979; Crnic & Greenberg, 1990). As social isolation may adversely influence child management (Dumas, 1986) and compromise the outcome of parent training programs (Wahler, 1980), this program's neighborhood school based large course format provides an opportunity for parents to develop a network of personal contacts (Miller & Prinz, 1990).

Increasing Utilization of Local Resources

Many parents are unaware of the potentially useful programs, services, activities, and materials available in their local communities. For example, extracurricular programs which engage children in constructive activities during high risk, unsupervised periods, promote skill development, and enhance self-esteem may prevent or reduce the prevalence of conduct problems (Jones & Offord, 1989). In each session of this program, parents are encouraged to exchange information about local resources and share materials which have been helpful.

Organization of the Parenting Program

The organization of the parent training program is summarized below.

Advertising and Recruiting Participants

To increase utilization among higher risk, socially isolated families, this program goes beyond traditional medical, mental health, and educational referral sources to school newsletters, newspapers, radio, and television programs to notify families regarding upcoming courses. Chapter 3 describes a series of meetings designed to inform school representatives regarding the course, enlist their participation in the development of a strategy for actively recruiting parental participation, and solve the logistical details of executing courses in school settings.

Information Session

Parents considering enrolling attend a meeting in which leaders discuss the goals of the course, the format of individual sessions, start times, and optional locations. As many parents unrealistically anticipate short term resolution of chronic child management difficulties, leaders note that improvements should not be anticipated until the course is completed. To enhance commitment to the program, parents are encouraged to discuss personal goals and the benefits participation might offer their family. Given the importance of parental involvement in child management (Webster-Stratton, 1985), leaders encourage participants to consider the potential benefits of active participation by both mothers and fathers, consistent attendance, and homework completion. Finally, since transportation difficulties, baby sitting problems, or work schedules prevent many parents from enrolling, parents consider solutions to obstacles which might limit participation.

Parenting Course

The parenting course is organized into 16 sessions. By combining sessions addressing similar issues or deleting topics, these can be composed into courses varying in length from 8 to 16 sessions.

Children's Social Skills Activity Group

To address the DBD child's social skills deficits (Cunningham & Siegel, 1987) and provide child care for parents who are unable to secure babysitters, children have the option of participating in a social skills activity group scheduled adjacent to the parenting course. The children's group introduces a weekly curriculum of social skills. Children have an opportunity to observe adult models and rehearse new skills in role playing exercises. Leaders prompt children to apply skills during in-session activities, reinforce follow-through, and help children plan homework projects (Cunningham, Clark, Heaven, Durrant, & Cunningham, 1989). This group also allows parents to rehearse the application of newly developed skills during brief activities with their children.

Booster Groups to Support Gains

While improved parenting skills may reduce problems and improve longer term outcome, most parents note continuing problems punctuated by more challenging episodes of extremely difficult behavior. To sustain the gains accomplished in the course, graduates are encouraged to attend monthly booster groups which provide opportunities to renew acquaintances, forge new contracts, share useful strategies, reinstate previously successful approaches, refine skills, formulate solutions to new problems, explore community resources, and invite speakers with expertise on topics of interest.

Format of Parent Training Sessions

Social Networking and Community Resources

Each session begins with a social phase encouraging supportive contacts among parents. Leaders display information regarding professional services, extracurricular activities, books, and videotapes on a resource table. Parents are encouraged to add resources, ask questions, and borrow materials of interest.

Subgrouping

To promote active participation within the context of a large group (average of 27 members), parents are divided into five to seven member subgroups, seated at separate tables, and asked to identify a leader responsible for keeping members on task, encouraging participation, and recording the subgroup's discussions. To accelerate the emergence of cohesive working relationships (MacKenzie, 1990), members are grouped according to important shared characteristics (e.g., age, diagnostic subgroup, family status, etc.) and encouraged to work together for the duration of the program.

Success Oriented Homework Review

To enhance a sense of personal efficacy and counter the low self-esteem common to parents of DBD children (Mash & Johnston, 1982) each subgroup member reviews situations where the preceding sessions' strategies were applied successfully. To minimize unrealistic short term outcome expectations, parents are encouraged to consider the longer term impact of strategies on parent-child relationships, self regulation, or social conduct. Subgroup members are prompted to give supportive feedback regarding their homework efforts and subgroup leaders summarize the examples to the larger group.

Trouble Shooting Videotaped Parenting Errors

According to the program's Coping Modeling Program protocol, parents formulate solutions to videotaped child management errors by identifying mistakes and discussing potential consequences. Subgroup leaders summarize these discussions for the larger group. Next, each subgroup formulates alternative conclusions to the larger group. Leaders complete this phase by summarizing and integrating the conclusions of the respective subgroups.

Modeling Proposed Strategies

To encourage the application of newly formulated strategies to problems of interest, the larger group is asked to suggest several common problems to which the session's strategy might be applied. Leaders prompt the larger group to formulate detailed plans regarding the implementation. The leader then models each solution proposed by the group with a member of the group playing the role of a child.

Brainstorming Application

To encourage a more generalized application of the strategies formulated during Coping Modeling Problem Solving discussions, subgroups spend time generating a range of different situations, behaviors, or problems to which the session's strategy might be applied. Again, subgroup leaders present the ideas suggested by their members to the larger group.

Rehearsing Solutions

To enhance skill acquisition, confidence, and generalized application at home, the group divides into dyads, finds a comfortable location, and rehearses the application of the session's strategy to problems of personal interest in a series of role playing episodes. At the completion of each episode, role playing partners give positive feedback on strategies the role playing parent used effectively. Parents whose children are attending the social skills activity group may be given an opportunity to apply these strategies to a series of structured interactions with their child.

Planning Homework

Parents set goals to apply new strategies at home, post visual reminders of the session's plan, monitor daily follow through in selected high risk situations, and discuss new skills with non-attending spouses. In addition, parents review the skill introduced during the children's social skills activity group, note the skill of the week in schools were a classroom based social skills training program is in place, and consider strategies developed in the program that might be used to prompt and reinforce application at home.

Closing the Session

To enhance participation, leaders close sessions by prompting members to contact participants who were unable to attend and discussing solutions to obstacles which might prevent members from attending next week.

Process of Individual Sessions

The process of this parent training course is based on four hierarchically organized conceptual models: a social learning model of skill acquisition, cognitive-attributional models of attitude change (Leary & Miller, 1986), a systems model of the family's structural and relational environment (Epstein, Bishop, & Levine, 1978), and formulations of the large group process in which skill acquisition and attitude change is embedded (MacKenzie, 1990).

Social Learning Process

Each session's modeling, role playing, and homework exercises contribute to the development of an increasingly complex repertoire of child management skills. Monitoring homework successes, supportive feedback from spouses and group members, self-monitoring, and the successful resolution of child management problems reinforce the sustained application of new skills. Brainstorming exercises, homework projects, and homework sheets prompt the generalized application of new skills to different settings and behaviors.

Cognitive-Attributional Process

Social psychological models suggest an approach to enhancing commitment to new skills, improving adherence, and changing counter-productive attributions regarding child behavior (Leary & Miller, 1986). Accordingly, the opportunity to formulate solutions to child management problems should exert a greater impact on attributions regarding personal control and self-efficacy than solutions suggested by the leader. Secondly, reaching a subgroup consensus regarding general approaches to parenting and publicly stating the advantages of new strategies should contribute to a more stable commitment to new skills than rationales supplied by the group leader (Leary & Miller, 1986; Meichenbaum & Turk, 1987). To maximize the attributional impact of these discussions, leaders respond to proposals regarding new approaches to child management or family relationships by asking the group to consider: (1) what lessons a particular strategy teaches, (2) what message a particular response communicates to the child, spouse, or family, (3) what difference the approach might make (for the child, parent siblings, or family) if applied consistently over a period of years, and (4) whether the effort required to maintain the strategy is justified.

As attributional research suggest that parental beliefs regarding the causes (intentional vs. unintentional) and controllability of their child's behavior influences both emotional and disciplinary responses (Johnston et al., 1992), group discussions provide an important opportunity to correct counter-productive attributions regarding child behavior and formulate cognitive strategies for controlling anger.

Appendix 5

Resource List for Parents

Textbooks

Alexander-Roberts, C. (1995). *A parent's guide to making it through the tough years, ADHD and teens.* (Dallas, TX: Taylor Publishing Co).

Bain, L. J. (1991). *A parent's guide to attention deficit disorders.* (New York: Bantam Doubleday Dell Publishing Group).

Barkley, R. A. (1995). *Taking charge of ADHD: The complete authoritative guide for parents.* (New York: Guilford Press).

Bloomquist, M. (1996). *Skills training for children.* (New York: Guilford Press).

Children and Adults with Attention Deficit Disorder (CH.A.D.D.). (1996). *ADD in adolescence: Strategies for success from CH.A.D.D.* Plantation, FL: Author).

Clark, L. (1986). *SOS: Help for parents.* (Bolling Green, KY: Parent's Press).

Conners, C. K. (1990). *Feeding the brain.* (New York: Plenum Publishers).

Crutsinger, C., & Moore, D. (1997). *ADD quick tips: Practical ways to manage attention deficit disorder successfully.* (Carrollton, TX: Brainworks, Inc.).

Dendy, C. A. Z. (1995). *Teenagers with ADHD: A parent's guide.* (Bethesda, MD: Woodbine House).

Fowler, M. (1990). *Maybe you know my kid: A parent's guide to identifying, understanding and helping your child with attention deficit hyperactivity disorder.* (New York: Birchline Press).

Garber, S. W., Garber, M. D., & Spizman, R. S. (1990). *If your child is hyperactive, inattentive, impulsive and distractable.* (New York: Villard Books).

Goldstein, S., & Goldstein, M. (1992). *Hyperactivity: Why won't my child pay attention?* (New York: John Wiley & Sons, Inc.).

Goldstein, S., & Goldstein, M. (1995). *A teacher's guide: Attention deficit hyperactivity disorders in children, 3rd ed.* (Salt Lake City, UT: Neurology, Learning and Behavior Center).

Goldstein, S., & Goldstein, M. (1997). *A parent's guide: Attention deficit hyperactivity disorders in children, 4th ed.* (Salt Lake City, UT: Neurology, Learning and Behavior Center).

Goldstein, S., & Hinerman, P. (1988). *A parent's guide: Language and behavior problems in children.* (Salt Lake City, UT: Neurology, Learning and Behavior Center.

Gordon, M. (1990). *ADHD/Hyperactivity consumer's guide for parents and teachers.* (DeWitt, NY: GSI Publications).

Greenburg, G. S., & Horne, W. F. (1991). *Attention deficit hyperactivity disorder: Questions and answers for parents.* (Champaign, IL: Research Press).

Ingersoll, B. (1997). *Dare devils and daydreamers: New perspectives on attention deficit hyperactivity disorder.* (New York: Doubleday).

Ingersoll, B., & Goldstein, S. (1993). *Attention deficit disorder and learning disabilities: Myths, realities and controversial treatments.* (New York: Doubleday).

Ingersoll, B., & Goldstein, S. (1995). *Lonely, sad and angry: A parent's guide to depression in children and adolescents.* (New York: Doubleday).

Jones, C. B. (1991). *Sourcebook for children with attention deficit disorder: A guide for early childhood professionals.* (Tucson, AZ: Communication Skill Builders).

Jones, C. B. (1994). *Attention deficit disorder: Strategies for school aged children.* (Tucson, AZ: Communication Skill Builders).

Katz, M. (1997). *On playing a poor hand well: Insights from the lives of those who have overcome childhood risks and adversities.* (New York: W.W. Norton & Co.).

McCarney, S. B., & Johnson, N. W. (1995). *A parent's guide to early childhood attention deficit disorders.* (Columbia, MO: Hawthorne Press).

Parker, H. C. (1988). *The ADD hyperactivity workbook for parents, teachers and kids.* (Plantation, FL: Specialty Press). (Also available in Spanish).

Patterson, G. R., & Forgatch, M. (1988). *Parents and adolescents living together: Part I. The basics; Part II. Family problem solving.* (Eugene, OR: Castalia Press).

Phelan, T. (1984). *1-2-3 Magic.* (Glen Ellyn, IL: Child Management Press).

Phelan, T. W. (1993). *All about attention deficit disorder: A comprehensive guide.* (Glen Ellyn, IL: Child Management, Inc.).

Shure, M. B. (1994). *Raising a thinking child: Helping your young child to resolve everyday conflicts and get along with others.* (New York: Henry Holt & Co.).

Silver, L. B. (1993). *Dr. Larry Silver's advice to parents on attention deficit hyperactivity disorder.* (Washington, DC: American Psychiatric Press, Inc.).

Taylor, J. F. (1990). *Helping your hyperactive child.* (Rocklin, CA: Prima Publishing).

Turecki, S., & Tonner, L. (1985). *The difficult child.* (New York: Bantam Books).

Videos

Barkley, R. A. (1995). *ADHD in the classroom: Strategies for teachers.* (New York, NY: Guilford Press).

Barkley, R. A. (1995). *ADHD: What can we do?* (New York, NY: Guilford Press).

Barkley, R. A. (1995). *ADHD: What do we know?* (New York, NY: Guilford Press).

Brooks, R. (1997). *Look what you've done! Learning disabilities and self esteem: Stories of hope and resilience.* (Washington, DC: Educational Telecommunications Association).

Davis, L., & Sirotowitz, S. with Parker, H. (1997). *Study strategies made easy: A practical plan for school success grades 6–12.* (Plantation, FL: Specialty Press).

Goldstein, S. (1989). *Why won't my child pay attention?* Salt Lake City, UT: Neurology, Learning and Behavior Center. (Also available in European PAL format)

Goldstein, S. (1994). *Why isn't my child happy?* Salt Lake City, UT: Neurology, Learning and Behavior Center. (Also available in European PAL format)

Goldstein, S., & Goldstein, M. (1990). *Educating inattentive children.* Salt Lake City, UT: Neurology, Learning and Behavior Center. (Also available in European PAL format)

Goldstein, S., & Goldstein, M. (1991). *It's just attention disorder: A video guide for kids.* Salt Lake City, UT: Neurology, Learning and Behavior Center. (Also available in European PAL format)

Reif, S. (1997). *How to help your child succeed in school: Strategies for parents of children with ADHD and/or learning disabilities.* (San Diego, CA: Educational Resource Specialists).

Appendix 6

Materials, Information, and Additional Resources

CH.A.D.D.
499 N.W. 70th Avenue, Suite 109
Plantation, Florida 33317
(954) 587-3700

National Attention Deficit Disorders Association (ADDA)
9930 Johnnycake Ridge, Suite 3E
Mentor, Ohio 44060
(216) 350-9595

ADD Warehouse
300 N.W. 70th Avenue, Suite 102
Plantation, Florida 33317
(800) 233-9273

Learning Disabilities Association of America (LDA)
4156 Library Road
Pittsburgh, Pennsylvania 15234

American Psychiatric Association
1400 "K" Street, NW
Washington, DC 20005
(202) 682-6000

American Psychological Association (APA)
750 First Street, NE
Washington, DC 20002-4242
(202) 336-5500

References

American Academy of Child and Adolescent Psychiatry Official Action. (1991). Practice parameters for the assessment and treatment of attention deficit hyperactivity disorder. *Journal of the American Academy of Child and Adolescent Psychiatry, 30*(3), I–III.

Abidin, R. R. (1983). *Parenting stress index.* Charlottesville, VA: Pediatric Psychology Press.

Abikoff, H. (1985). Efficacy of cognitive training interventions in hyperactive children: A critical review [Special issue]. *Clinical Psychology Review, 5,* 479–512.

Abikoff, H. (1987). An evaluation of cognitive behavior therapy for hyperactive children. In B. B. Lahey & A. E. Kazdin (Eds.), *Advances in clinical child psychology* (Vol. 10, pp. 171–216). New York: Plenum Press.

Abikoff, H. (1991). Cognitive training in ADHD children: Less to it than meets the eye. *Journal of Learning Disabilities, 24,* 205–209.

Abikoff, H., Courtney, M., Pelham, W. E., & Koplewicz, H. S. (1993). Teachers' ratings of disruptive behaviors: The influence of halo effects. *Journal of Abnormal Child Psychology, 21,* 519–533.

Abikoff, H., Ganeles, G., Reiter, G., Blum, C., Foley, C., & Klein, R. G. (1988). Cognitive training in academically deficient ADHD boys receiving stimulant medication. *Journal of Abnormal Child Psychology, 16,* 411–432.

Abikoff, H., & Gittelman, R. (1985a). Hyperactive children treated with stimulants: Is cognitive training a useful adjunct? *Archives of General Psychiatry, 42,* 953–961.

Abikoff, H., & Gittelman, R. (1985b). The normalizing effects of methylphenidate on the classroom behavior of ADHD children. *Journal of Abnormal Child Psychology, 13,* 33–44.

Abikoff, H., Gittelman-Klein, R., & Klein, D. F. (1977). Validation of a classroom observation code for hyperactive children. *Journal of Consulting and Clinical Psychology, 45,* 772–783.

Abikoff, H., & Klein, R. G. (1992). Attention deficit hyperactivity and conduct disorder: Comorbidity and implications for treatment. Special Section: Comorbidity and treatment implications. *Journal of Consulting and Clinical Psychology, 60,* 881–892.

Abramowitz, A. J., Eckstrand, D., O'Leary, S. G., & Dulcan, M. K. (1992). ADHD children's responses to stimulant medication and two intensities of a behavioral intervention. Special Issue: Treatment of children with attention deficit hyperactivity disorder (ADHD). *Behavior Modification, 16,* 193–203.

Abramowitz, A. J., & O'Leary, S. G. (1990). Effectiveness of delayed punishment in an applied setting. *Behavior Therapy, 21,* 231–239.

Abramowitz, A. J., & O'Leary, S. G. (1991). Behavior interventions for the classroom: Implications for students with ADHD. *School Psychology Review, 20,* 220–234.

Abramowitz, A. J., O'Leary, S. G., & Futtersak, M. W. (1988). The relative impact of long and short reprimands on children's off-task behavior in the classroom. *Behavior Therapy, 19,* 243–247.

Abramowitz, B., Lieberwitz, M. R., Hollander, E., & Fazzini, E. (1994). Neuropsychiatric and neuropsychological findings in conduct disorder and ADHD. *Journal of Neuropsychiatry and Clinical Neurosciences, 6,* 245–249.

Abravanel, E. (1968). The development of intersensory patterning with regard to selected spatial dimensions. *Monographs of the Society for Research in Child Development, 333,* 527.

Accardo, P. J., Blondis, T. J., & Whitman, B. Y. (1990). Disorders of attention and activity level in a referral population. *Pediatrics, 85,* 426–431.

Accardo, P. J., Tomazic, T., & Morrow, J. (1991). Minor malformations, hyperactivity and learning disabilities. *American Journal of Disabilities in Childhood, 145,* 1184.

Accardo, P. J., Tomazic, T., Morrow, J., & Whitman, B. Y. (1990). Fetal activity level in developmental disabilities [Abstract]. *Pediatric Resources.*

Accardo, P. J., & Whitman, B. Y. (1991a). The misdiagnosis of the hyperactive child. In P. J. Accardo, T. A. Blondis, & B. Y. Whitman (Eds.), *Attention deficit disorders and hyperactivity in children.* New York: Marcel Dekker.

Accardo, P. J., & Whitman, B. Y. (1991b). Other treatments for hyperactivity. In P. J. Accardo, T. A. Blondis & B. Y. Whitman (Eds.). *Attention deficit disorders and hyperactivity in children.* New York: Marcel Dekker.

Achenbach, T. M. (1975). Longitudinal study of relations between association of responding, IQ changes, and school performance from grades 3 to 12. *Developmental Psychology, 11,* 653–654.

Achenbach, T. M. (1978). The child behavior profile: I. Boys aged 6–11. *Journal of Consulting and Clinical Psychology, 46,* 478–488.

Achenbach, T. M. (1984). *Current status of the child behavior checklist and related materials.* Burlington, VT: University Associates in Psychiatry.

Achenbach, T. M. (1985). *Assessment and taxonomy of child and adolescent psychopathology.* Beverly Hills, CA: Sage.

Achenbach, T. M. (1996). Subtyping ADHD: The request for suggestions about relating empirically based assessment to *DSM-IV. The ADHD Report, 4,* 5–9.

Achenbach, T. M., & Edelbrock, C. (1981). Behavioral problems and competencies reported by parents of normal and disturbed children aged 4 through 16. *Monographs of the Society for Research and Child Development, 46*(Serial No. 188).

Achenbach, T. M., & Edelbrock, C. (1983). *Manual for the child behavior checklist and revised child behavior profile.* Burlington, VT: Department of Psychiatry.

Achenbach, T. M., & Edelbrock, C. (1991). *Normative data for the child behavior checklist* (rev.). Burlington, VT: Department of Psychiatry.

Achenbach, T. M., Howell, C. T., McConaughy, S. H., & Stanger, C. (1995). Six-year predictors of problems in a national sample of children and youth: II. Signs of disturbance. *Journal of the American Academy of Child and Adolescent Psychiatry, 34,* 488–498.

Achenbach, T. M., & McConaughy, S. H. (1996). *Empirically based assessment of child and adolescent psychopathology: Practical applications* (2nd ed.). Thousand Oaks, CA: Sage.

Achenbach, T. M., McConaughy, S. H., & Howell, C. T. (1987). Child/adolescent behavioral and emotional problems: Implications of cross-informant correlations for situational specificity. *Psychological Bulletin, 101,* 213–232.

Acker, M. M., & O'Leary, S. G. (1987). Effects of reprimands and praise on appropriate behavior in the classroom. *Journal of Abnormal Child Psychology, 15,* 549–557.

Acker, M. M., & O'Leary, S. G. (1988). Effects of consistent and inconsistent feedback on inappropriate child behavior. *Behavior Therapy, 19,* 619–624.

Ackerman, P. T., Anhalt, J. M., & Dykman, R. A. (1986). Arithmetic automatization failure in children with attention and reading disorders: Associations and sequela. *Journal of Learning Disabilities, 19,* 222–232.

Ackerman, P. T., Dykman, R. A., & Gardner, M. Y. (1990). ADD students with and without dyslexia differ in sensitivity to rhyme and alliteration. *Journal of Learning Disabilities, 23,* 273–289.

Ackerman, P. T., Dykman, R. A., & Oglesby, D. M. (1983). Sex and group differences in reading in attention disordered children with and without hyperkinesis. *Journal of Learning Disabilities, 16,* 407–414.

Ackerman, P. T., Dykman, R. A., & Peters, J. E. (1977). Teenage status of hyperactive and nonhyperactive learning disabled boys. *American Journal of Orthopsychiatry, 47,* 577–596.

Ackerman, P. T., Weir, N. L., Holloway, C. A., & Dykman, R. A. (1995). Adolescents earlier diagnosed as dyslexic show major IQ declines on the WISC-III. *Reading and Writing, 7,* 163–170.

Adalbjarnardottir, S. (1995). How school children propose to negotiate: The role of social withdrawal, social anxiety, and locus of control. *Child Development, 66,* 1739–1751.

Adams, M. J., Buschelia, J., DeSanchez, M., & Swets, J. A. (1986). *Odyssey: A curriculum for thinking—foundations of reasoning.* Watertown, MA: Mastery Education.

Adams, W. V., Robins, P. F., & Sheslow, D. V. (1991). *Memory abilities in children with attention deficit hyperactivity disorder.* Paper presented at the third Florida conference on Child Health Psychology, Gainsville.

Adams, W., & Sheslow, D. (1990). *Wide range assessment of memory and learning (WRAML).* Wilmington, DE: Jastak Wide Range.

Addesman, A. R. (1991). Test and measurement review: The attention deficit disorders evaluation scale. *Developmental and Behavioral Pediatrics, 12,* 65–66.

Addesman, A. R., Altshuler, L. A., Lipkin, P. H., & Walce, G. A. (1990). Otitis media in children with learning disabilities and in children with attention deficit disorder with hyperactivity. *Pediatrics, 85,* 442.

Adesso, V. J., & Lipson, J. W. (1981). Group training of parents as therapists for their children. *Behaviour Therapy, 12,* 625–633.

Adler, L. A., Resnick, S., Kunz, M., & Devinsky, O. (1995). Open-label trial of venlafaxine (effexor) in attention deficit disorder. *Psychopharmacology Bulletin, 31,* 544.

Ager, C. L., & Cole, C. L. (1991). A review of cognitive-behavioral interventions for children and adolescents with behavioral disorders. *Behavior Disorders, 16,* 276–287.

Ahmann, P. A., Waltonen, S. J., Olson, K. A., Theye, F. W., Van Erem, A. J., & LaPlant, R. J. (1993). Placebo-controlled evaluation of ritalin side effects. *Pediatrics, 91,* 1101–1106.

Aicardi, J. (1988). The Lennox-Gastaut syndrome. *International Pediatrics, 3,* 152–157.

Ajibola, O., & Clement, P. W. (1995). Differential effects of methylphenidate and self-reinforcement on attention deficit hyperactivity disorder. *Behavior Modification, 19,* 211–233.

Akiskal, H. S., Downs, J., Jordan, P., Watson, S., Dougherty, D., & Pruitt, D. B. (1985). Affective disorders in referred children and younger siblings of manic depressives. *Archives of General Psychiatry, 42,* 996–1004.

Alberts, E., & van der Meere, J. (1992). Observations of hyperactive behavior during vigilance. *Journal of Child Psychology and Psychiatry in Allied Disciplines, 33,* 1355–1364.

Aldenkamp, A. P., Alpherts, W. C., Dekker, M. J., & Overweg, J. (1990). Neuropsychological aspects of learning disabilities in epilepsy. *Epilepsia, 31,* S9–S20.

Aleman, S. R. (1991). Special education for children with attention deficit disorder: Current issues. *Congressional Research Service Report for Congress, 91,* 862.

Alessandri, S. M. (1992). Attention play on social behavior in ADHD preschoolers. *Journal of Abnormal Child Psychology, 20,* 289–302.

Alessandri, S. M., & Schramm, K. (1991). Effects of dextroamphetamine on the cognitive and social play of a preschooler with ADHD. *Journal of the American Academy of Child and Adolescent Psychiatry, 30,* 768–772.

Alessi, N., Naylor, M. W., Ghaziuddin, M., & Zubieta, J. K. (1994). Update on lithium carbonate therapy in children and adolescents. *Journal of the American Academy of Child and Adolescent Psychiatry, 33,* 291–304.

Alexander, K. L., Entwisle, D. R., & Dauber, S. L. (1993). First grade classroom behavior. Its short and long term consequences for school performance. *Child Development, 64,* 801–814.

Allen, K. E., Henke, L. B., Harris, F. R., Baer, D. M., & Reynolds, N. J. (1967). Control of hyperactivity by social reinforcement of attending behavior. *Journal of Educational Psychology, 58,* 231–237.

Altepeter, T. S., & Breen, M. J. (1989). The home situations questionnaire (HSQ) and the school situations questionnaire (SSQ): Normative data and an evaluation of psychometric properties. *Journal of Psychoeducational Assessment, 7,* 312–322.

Altepeter, T. S., & Breen, M. J. (1992). Situational variation and problem behavior at home and in school and attention deficit disorder with hyperactivity: A factor analytic study. *Journal of Child Psychology and Psychiatry in Allied Disciplines, 33,* 741–748.

Aman, M. G., & Kearn, R. A. (1989). Review of fenfluramine in the treatment of the developmental disabilities. *Journal of the American Academy of Child and Adolescent Psychiatry, 28,* 549–565.

Aman, M. G., Marks, R. E., Turbott, S. H., Wilsher, C. P., & Merry, S. N. (1991). Clinical effects of methylphenidate and thioridazine in intellectually subaverage children. *Journal of the American Academy of Child and Adolescent Psychiatry, 30,* 246–256.

Aman, M. G., Mitchell, E. A., & Turbott, S. H. (1987). The effects of essential fatty acid supplementation by efamol in hyperactive children. *Journal of Abnormal Child Psychology, 15,* 75–90.

Aman, M. G., & Turbott, S. H. (1986). Incidental learning, distraction, and sustained attention in hyperactive and control subjects. *Journal of Abnormal Child Psychology, 14,* 441–455.

Aman, M. G., & Turbott, S. H. (1991). Prediction of clinical response in children taking methylphenidate. *Journal of Autism and Developmental Disorders, 21,* 211–228.

Ambrosini, P. J., Bianchi, M. D., Rabinovich, H., & Elia, J. (1993). Antidepressant treatments in children and adolescents: I. Affective disorders. *Journal of the American Academy of Child and Adolescent Psychiatry, 32,* 1–6.

American Academy of Child and Adolescent Psychiatry. (1997). Practice parameters for the assessment and treatment of children and adolescents with bipolar disorder. *Journal of the American Academy of Child and Adolescent Psychiatry, 36,* 138–157.

American Academy of Pediatrics. (1987). Committee on drugs report: Medication for children with an attention deficit disorder. *Pediatrics, 80,* 5.

American Bar Association Working Group. (1993). *Report of the ABA working group of the United Nations conventions on the rights of the child.* Washington, DC: Author.

American Psychiatric Association. (1968). *Diagnostic and statistical manual of mental disorders* (2nd ed.). Washington, DC: Author.

American Psychiatric Association. (1973). *Megavitamin and orthomolecular therapy in psychiatry* (Task Force Report No. 7). Washington, DC: Author.

American Psychiatric Association. (1980). *Diagnostic and statistical manual of mental disorders* (3rd ed.). Washington, DC: Author.

American Psychiatric Association. (1987). *Diagnostic and statistical manual of psychiatric disorders* (3rd ed., rev.). Washington, DC: Author.

American Psychiatric Association. (1994). *Diagnostic and statistical manual of mental disorders* (4th ed., rev.). Washington, DC: Author.

American Speech and Language Association. (1992). *Central auditory processing deficits.* American Speech and Language Association Adhock Committee on Central Auditory Processing Disorders. Rockville, MD: Author.

Ames, C. (1992). Classrooms: Goals, structures, and student motivation. *Journal of Educational Psychology, 84,* 261–271.

Ames, C., & Ames, R. (1984). *Research on motivation in education* (Vol. 1). San Diego, CA: Academic Press.

Amin, K., Douglas, V., Mendelson, M. J., & Dufresene, J. (1993). Separable/integral classification by hyperactive and normal children. *Development and Psychopathology, 5*(3), 415–431.

Anastasi, A. (1976). *Psychological Testing* (4th ed.). New York: Macmillan.

Anastopoulos, A. D. (1991). Facilitating parental understanding and management of attention-deficit/hyperactivity disorder. In M. A. Reinecke, F. M. Dattilio, & A. Freeman (Eds.), *Cognitive therapy with children and adolescents: A casebook for clinical practice* (pp. 327–343). New York: Guilford Press.

Anastopoulos, A. D. (1993). Assessing ADHD with the child behavior checklist. *The ADHD Report, 3,* 4.

Anastopoulos, A. D., & Barkley, R. A. (1990). Counseling and training parents. In R. A. Barkley (Ed.), *Attention-deficit hyperactivity disorder: A handbook for diagnosis and treatment.* New York: Guilford Press.

Anastopoulos, A. D., Barkley, R. A., & Shelton, T. (1994). The history and diagnosis of attention deficit/hyperactivity disorder. *Therapeutic Care and Education, 3,* 96–110.

Anastopoulos, A. D., DuPaul, G. J., & Barkley, R. A. (1991). Stimulant medication and parent training therapies for attention-deficit hyperactivity disorder. *Journal of Learning Disabilities, 24,* 210–218.

Anastopoulos, A. D., Guevremont, D. C., Shelton, T. L., & DuPaul, G. J. (1992). Parenting stress among families of children with attention deficit hyperactivity disorder. *Journal of Abnormal Child Psychology, 20,* 503–520.

Anastopoulos, A. D., Shelton, T. L., DuPaul, G. J., & Guevremont, D. C. (1993). Parent training for attention-deficit hyperactivity disorder: Its impact on parent functioning. *Journal of Abnormal Child Psychology, 21,* 581–596.

Anastopoulos, A. D., Spisto, M., & Maher, M. C. (1993). The WISC-III, third factor: A preliminary look at its diagnostic utility. *The ADHD Report, 1,* 4–5.

Anastopoulos, A. D., Spisto, M., & Maher, M. C. (1994). The WISC-III freedom from distractibility factor: Its utility in identifying children with attention deficit hyperactivity disorder. *Psychological Assessment, 6,* 368–371.

Anderson, B. W. (1992). Comorbidity of attention deficit hyperactivity disorder with conduct, depressive, anxiety and other disorders: Comment. *American Journal of Psychiatry, 149,* 148–149.

Anderson, E. E., Clement, P. W., & Oettinger, L. (1981). Methylphenidate compared with behavioral self-control in attention deficit disorder. Preliminary report. *Developmental and Behavioral Pediatrics, 4,* 137–141.

Anderson, J. C., Williams, S., McGee, R., & Silva, P. A. (1987). The prevalence of *DSM-III* disorders in a large sample of pre-adolescent children from the general population. *Archives of General Psychiatry, 44,* 69–81.

Anderson, J. C., Williams, S., McGee, R., & Silva, P. (1989). Cognitive and social correlates of *DSM-III* disorders in pre-adolescent children. *Journal of the American Academy of Child and Adolescent Psychiatry, 28,* 842–846.

Anderson, K., Lytton, H., & Romney, D. (1986). Mothers interactions with normal and conduct-disordered boys: Who affects whom? *Developmental Psychology, 22,* 604–609.

Anesko, K. M., Schoiock, G., Ramirez, R., & Levine, F. M. (1987). The homework problem checklist: Assessing children's homework difficulties. *Behavioral Assessment, 9,* 179–185.

Anthony, B. J., Mirsky, A. F., Ahearn, M. B., Kellam, S. G., & Eaton, W. W. (1988). *Structure of attention and epidemiology of its dysfunction in children.* Paper presented at the annual meeting of the American Academy of Child and Adolescent Psychiatry, Seattle, WA.

Applegate, B., Lahey, B. B., Hart, E. L., Biederman, J., Hynd, G. W., Barkley, R. A., Ollendick, T., Frick, P. J., Greenhill, L., McBurnett, K., Newcorn, J. H., Kerdyk, L., Garfinkel,

B., Waldman, I., & Shaffer, D. (1997). Validity of the age-of-onset criterion for ADHD. A report from the *DSM-IV* field trials. *Journal of the American Academy of Child and Adolescent Psychiatry, 36,* 1211–1221.

Apley, J., & MacKeith, R. (1968). *The child and his symptoms: A comprehensive approach.* Philadelphia: Davis.

Archer, A., & Gleason, M. (1989). *Skills for school success (grades 3–6).* North Billerica, MA: Curriculum.

Arcia, E., Ornstein, P. A., & Otto, D. A. (1991). Neurobehavioral evaluation system and school performance. *Journal of School Psychology, 29,* 337–352.

Arcia, E., & Roberts, J. E. (1993). Brief report: Otitis media in early childhood and its association with sustained attention in structured situations. *Developmental and Behavioral Pediatrics, 14,* 181–183.

Arnio, R. (1991). *Parent training for families of children with ADHD.* Unpublished manuscript, Rapid City, ND.

Arnold, D. S., O'Leary, S. G., Wolff, L. S., & Acker, M. M. (1993). The parenting scale: A measure of dysfunctional parenting in discipline situations. *Psychological Assessment, 5,* 137–144.

Arnold, E., Molinoff, P., & Rutledge, C. (1977). The release of endogenous norepinephrine and dopamine from cerebral cortex by amphetamine. *Journal of Pharmacological Experimental Therapy, 202,* 544–557.

Arnold, L. E. (1985). Vestibular and visual rotational stimulation as treatment for attention deficit and hyperactivity. *American Journal of Occupational Therapy, 39,* 84–91.

Arnold, L. E. (1996). Sex differences in ADHD: Conference summary. *Journal of Abnormal Child Psychology, 24,* 555–569.

Arnold, L. E., Votolato, N. A., Kleykamp, D., & Baker, G. B. (1990). Does hair zinc predict amphetamine improvement of ADD/hyperactivity? *International Journal of Neuroscience, 50,* 103–107.

Aronen, E. T., Noam, G. G., & Weinstein, S. R. (1993). Structured diagnostic interviews and clinician's discharge diagnoses in hospitalized adolescents. *Journal of the American Academy of Child and Adolescent Psychiatry, 32,* 647–681.

Aronfreed, J., & Reber, A. (1965). Internalized behavioral suppression and the timing of social punishment. *Journal of Personality and Social Psychology, 1,* 3–16.

Asher, R., & Dodge, R. A. (1986). Identifying children who are rejected by their peers. *Developmental Psychology, 22,* 444–449.

Asher, S. R., & Gottman, J. M. (1981). *The development of children's friendships.* New York: Cambridge University Press.

Astbury, J., Orgill, A. A., & Bajuk, B. (1987). Relationship between two-year behavior and neurodevelopmental outcome at five years of very low birthweight survivors. *Developmental Medicine and Child Neurology, 29,* 370–379.

Astbury, J., Orgill, A. A., Bajuk, B., & Yu, V. Y. (1985). Neonatal and neurodevelopmental significance of behavior in very low birthweight children. *Early Human Development, 1,* 113–121.

Atkins, E., Vetere, A., & Grayson, K. (1995). Sleep disruption in young children. The influence of temperament on the sleep patterns of pre-school children. *Child Care, Health and Development, 21,* 233–246.

Atkins, M. S. (1985). Acting out in children: A review of the literature. *Child and Adolescent Social Work Journal, 2,* 247–257.

Atkins, M. S., & Pelham, W. E. (1991). School-based assessment of attention deficit-hyperactivity disorder. *Journal of Learning Disabilities, 24*(4), 197–204.

Atkins, M. S., Pelham, W. E., & Licht, M. H. (1985). A comparison of objective classroom measures and teacher ratings of attention deficit disorder. *Journal of Abnormal Child Psychology, 13,* 155–167.

Atkins, M. S., & Stoff, D. M. (1993). Instrumental and hostile aggression in childhood disruptive behavior disorders. *Journal of Abnormal Child Psychology, 21,* 165–178.

August, G. J., & Garfinkel, B. D. (1989). Behavioral and cognitive subtypes of ADHD. *Journal of the American Academy of Children and Adolescent Psychiatry, 28,* 739–748.

August, G. J., & Garfinkel, B. D. (1990). Comorbidity of ADHD and reading disability among clinic-referred children. *Journal of Abnormal Child Psychology, 18,* 29–45.

August, G. J., & Garfinkel, B. D. (1993). The nosology of attention-deficit hyperactivity disorder. *Journal of the American Academy of Child and Adolescent Psychiatry, 32,* 155–165.

August, G. J., Ostrander, R., & Bloomquist, M. J. (1992). Attention deficit hyperactivity disorder: An epidemiological screening method. *American Journal of Orthopsychiatry, 62*(3), 387–396.

August, G. J., Realmuto, G. M., Crosby, R. D., & MacDonald, A. W. (1995). Community based multiple-gate screening of children at risk for conduct disorder. *Journal of Abnormal Child Psychology, 23,* 521–544.

August, G. J., Stewart, M. A., & Holmes, C. S. (1983). Four year follow-up of hyperactive boys with and without conduct disorders. *British Journal of Psychiatry, 143,* 192–198.

Ayllon, T., Garber, S., & Pisor, K. (1975). The elimination of discipline problems through a combined school-home motivational system. *Behavior Therapy, 6,* 616–626.

Aylward, E. H., Reiss, A. L., Reader, M. J., Singer, H. S., Brown, J. E., & Denckla, M. B. (1996). Basal ganglia volumes in children with attention deficit hyperactivity disorder. *Journal of Child Neurology, 11,* 112–115.

Aylward, G. P. (1992). Relationship between environmental risk and developmental outcome. *Developmental and Behavioral Pediatrics, 13,* 222–229.

Aylward, G. P., Verhulst, S. J., & Bell, S. (1990). Individual and combined effects of attention deficits and learning disabilities on computerized ADHD assessment. *Journal of Psychoeducational Assessment, 8,* 497–508.

Aylward, G. P., Verhulst, S. J., & Bell, S. (1993, September). *Inter-relationships between measures of attention deficit disorders: Same scores, different reasons.* Paper presented at the meeting of the Society for Behavioral Pediatrics, Providence, RI.

Ayres, A. J. (1965). Patterns of perceptual-motor dysfunction in children: A factor analytic study. *Perceptual and Motor Skills, 20,* 335–368.

Ayres, A. J. (1979). *Sensory integration and the child.* Los Angeles: Western Psychological Services.

Bachman, D. S. (1981). Pemoline-induced Tourette's disorder: A case report. *American Journal of Psychiatry, 138,* 1116–1117.

Baddeley, A. (1992). Working memory. *Science, 255,* 556–559.

Baden, A. D., & Howe, G. W. (1992). Mothers' attributions and expectancies regarding their conduct-disordered children. *Journal of Abnormal Child Psychology, 20,* 467–486.

Badian, M. A. (1983). Arithmetic and non-verbal learning. In H. R. Myklebust (Ed.), *Progress and learning disabilities* (Vol. 5, pp. 253–264). New York: Grune and Stratton.

Baer, R. A., & Nietzel, M. T. (1991). Cognitive and behavioral treatment of impulsivity in children: A meta-analytic review of the outcome literature. *Journal of Clinical Child Psychology, 20,* 400–412.

Bahr, N. W., Fuchs, L. S., Fuchs, D., Ferstrom, P., & Stecker, B. M. (1993). Effectiveness of student versus teacher monitoring during preferential intervention. *Exceptionality, 4,* 17–30.

Bailey, D. P., Jr., & Simeonsson, R. J. (1985). A functional model of social competence. *Topics in Early Childhood, 4,* 20–31.

Baker, D. B. (1994). Parenting stress and ADHD: A comparison of mothers and fathers. *Journal of Emotional and Behavioral Disorders, 2,* 46–50.

Baker, D. B., Taylor, C. J., & Leyva, C. (1995). Continuous performance test: A comparison of modalities. *Journal of Child Psychology, 51,* 548–551.

Baker, H. J., & Leland, B. (1967). *Detroit tests of learning aptitude.* Indianapolis: Bobbs-Merrill.

Baker, L., & Cantwell, D. P. (1987). A prospective psychiatric follow-up of children with speech/language disorders. *Journal of the American Academy of Child Psychiatry, 26,* 546–553.

Baker, L., & Cantwell, D. P. (1992). Attention deficit disorder and speech/language disorders. *Comprehensive Mental Health Care, 2,* 3–16.

Baldwin, M. A. (1976). *Activity level, attention span, and deviance: Hyperactive boys in the classroom.* Unpublished doctoral dissertation, University of Waterloo, Canada.

Ball, J. D., & Koloian, B. (1996). Sleep patterns among ADHD children. *Clinical Psychology Review, 15,* 681–691.

Ballenger, J. C., Reus, V. I., & Post, R. M. (1982). The "atypical" picture of adolescent mania. *American Journal of Psychiatry, 139,* 602–606.

Balthazor, M. J., Wagner, R. K., & Pelham, W. E. (1991). The specificity of the effects of stimulant medication on classroom learning-related measures of cognitive processing for attention deficit disorder children. *Journal of Abnormal Child Psychology, 19,* 35–52.

Bandura, A. (1969). *Principles of behavior modification.* New York: Holt, Rinehart and Winston.

Bandura, A. (1977). *Social learning theory.* Englewood Cliffs, NJ: Prentice-Hall.

Bandura, A. (1982). Self-efficacy mechanism in human agency. *American Psychologist, 37,* 122–147.

Bank, B. J. (1985). Student sex and classroom behavior. In T. Husen & T. N. Postlethwaite (Eds.), *The International Encyclopedia of Education.* Oxford, England: Pergamon Press.

Bank, L., Marlow, H., Reid, J. B., Patterson, G. R., & Weinrott, M. R. (1991). A comparative evaluation of parent-training interventions for families of chronic delinquents. *Journal of Abnormal Child Psychology, 19,* 15–33.

Banks, S. R., Guyer, B. B., & Guyer, K. E. (1995). A study of medical school students and physicians referred for learning disabilities. *Annals of Dyslexia, 45,* 233–245.

Barber, B. K., Olsen, J. E., & Shagle, S. C. (1994). Associations between parental psychological and behavioral control and youth internalized and externalized behaviors. *Child Development, 65,* 1120–1136.

Bar-Joseph, H., Mester, R., & Rothenberg, M. (1995). Delayed detection of attention deficit disorder: A research study. *International Journal of Adolescent Medicine and Health, 8,* 53–64.

Barkley, R. A. (1976). Predicting the response of hyperkinetic children to stimulant drugs: A review. *Journal of Abnormal Child Psychology, 4,* 327–348.

Barkley, R. A. (1977a). A review of stimulant drug research with hyperactive children. *Journal of Child Psychology and Psychiatry, 18,* 137–165.

Barkley, R. A. (1977b). The effects of methylphenidate on various measures of activity level and attention in hyperkinetic children. *Journal of Abnormal Child Psychology, 5,* 351–369.

Barkley, R. A. (1978). Recent developments in research on hyperactive children. *Journal of Pediatric Psychology, 3,* 158–163.

Barkley, R. A. (1981a). *Hyperactive children: A handbook for diagnosis and treatment.* New York: Guilford Press.

Barkley, R. A. (1981b). Hyperactivity. In E. Mash & L. Terdal (Eds.), *Behavioral assessment of childhood disorders.* New York: Guilford Press.

Barkley, R. A. (1982). Guidelines for defining hyperactivity in children. In B. B. Lahey & A. E. Kazdin (Eds.), *Advances in clinical child psychology.* New York: Plenum Press.

Barkley, R. A. (1985). The social behavior of hyperactive children: Developmental changes, drug effects and situational variation. In R. McMahon & R. Peters (Eds.), *Childhood disorders: Behavioral-developmental approaches.* New York: Brunner/Mazel.

Barkley, R. A. (1987a). *Defiant children: A clinician's manual for parent training.* New York: Guilford Press.

Barkley, R. A. (1987b). What is the role of group parent training in the treatment of AD children? In J. Loney (Ed.), *The young hyperactive child: Answers to questions about diagnosis, prognosis, and treatment.* New York: Haworth Press.

Barkley, R. A. (1988a). An alert to a national campaign of disinformation. *Clinical Child Psychology Newsletter,* (Section 1, Division 12), 3.

Barkley, R. A. (1988b). Attention. In M. Tramontana & S. Hooper (Eds.), *Issues in child clinical neuropsychology.* New York: Plenum Press.

Barkley, R. A. (1988c). Attention-deficit hyperactivity disorder. In E. J. Mash & L. G. Terdal (Eds.), *Behavioral assessment of childhood disorders* (2nd ed.). New York: Guilford Press.

Barkley, R. A. (1988d). The effects of methylphenidate on the interactions of preschool ADHD children with their mothers. *Journal of American Academy of Child and Adolescent Psychiatry, 27,* 336–341.

Barkley, R. A. (1989). Placebo "side effects" and Ritalin. *Clinical Child Psychology Newsletter, 3,* 2.

Barkley, R. A. (1990a). *Attention-deficit hyperactivity disorder: A handbook for diagnosis and treatment.* New York: Guilford Press.

Barkley, R. A. (1990b). A critique of current diagnostic criteria for attention deficit hyperactivity disorder: Clinical and research implications. *Journal of Developmental and Behavioral Pediatrics, 11,* 343–352.

Barkley, R. A. (1991a). The ecological validity of laboratory and analogue assessment methods of ADHD symptoms. *Journal of Abnormal Child Psychology, 19,* 149–178.

Barkley, R. A. (1991b). Attention-deficit hyperactivity disorder. *Psychiatric Annals, 21,* 725–733.

Barkley, R. A. (1991c). *Attention-deficit hyperactivity disorder: A clinical workbook.* New York: Guilford Press.

Barkley, R. A. (1991d). Diagnosis and assessment of attention deficit hyperactivity disorder. *Comprehensive Mental Health Care, 1,* 27–43.

Barkley, R. A. (1993a). The latest on *DSM-IV* and the disruptive behavior disorders. *The ADHD Report, 1*(1), 3–5.

Barkley, R. A. (1993b). A new theory of ADHD. *The ADHD Report, 1,* 1–4.

Barkley, R. A. (1993c). Pseudo science in treatments for ADHD. *The ADHD Report, 1,* 1–4.

Barkley, R. A. (1994). What to look for in a school for a child with ADHD. *The ADHD Report, 2,* 1–3.

Barkley, R. A. (1995a). ADHD and I.Q. *The ADHD Report, 3,* 1–3.

Barkley, R. A. (1995b). A closer look at *DSM-IV* criteria for ADHD: Some unresolved issues. *The ADHD Report, 3,* 1–5.

Barkley, R. A. (1996a). Clinical use of the third factor—proceed with caution. *The ADHD Report, 4,* 6–8.

Barkley, R. A. (1996b). Eighteen ways to make token systems more effective for ADHD children and teens. *The ADHD Report, 4,* 1–5.

Barkley, R. A. (1996c). Gender is already implicit in the diagnosis of ADHD: Shouldn't it be explicit? *The ADHD Report, 4*(2), 3–7.

Barkley, R. A. (1997a). Behavioral inhibition, sustained attention, and executive functions: Constructing a unifying theory of ADHD. *Psychological Bulletin, 121,* 65–94.

Barkley, R. A. (1997b). *Defiant children: A clinician's manual for assessment and parent training* (2nd ed.). New York: Guilford Press.

Barkley, R. A. (1997c). *ADHD and the nature of self-control.* New York: Guilford Press.

Barkley, R. A., Anastopoulos, A. D., Guevremont, D. C., & Fletcher, K. E. (1991). Adolescents with ADHD: Patterns of behavioral adjustment, academic functioning and treatment utilization. *Journal of the American Academy of Child and Adolescent Psychiatry, 30,* 752–761.

Barkley, R. A., Anastopoulos, A. D., Guevremont, D. C., & Fletcher, K. E. (1992). Adolescents with attention deficit hyperactivity disorder: Mother-adolescent interactions, family beliefs and conflicts, and maternal psychopathology. *Journal of Abnormal Child Psychology, 20,* 263–288.

Barkley, R. A., Copeland, A. P., & Sivage, C. (1980). A self-controlled classroom for hyperactive children. *Journal of Autism and Developmental Disorders, 10,* 75–89.

Barkley, R. A., & Cunningham, C. E. (1979). The effects of methylphenidate on the mother-child interactions of hyperactive children. *Archives of General Psychiatry, 36,* 201–208.

Barkley, R. A., & Cunningham, C. E. (1980). The parent-child interactions of hyperactive children and their modification by stimulant drugs. In R. N. Knights & D. Bakker (Eds.), *Treatment of hyperactive and learning disordered children.* Baltimore: University Park Press.

Barkley, R. A., DuPaul, G. J., & McMurray, M. B. (1990). A comprehensive evaluation of attention deficit disorder with and without hyperactivity as defined by research criteria. *Journal of Consulting and Clinical Psychology, 58,* 775–789.

Barkley, R. A., DuPaul, G. J., & McMurray, M. B. (1991). Attention deficit disorder with and without hyperactivity: Clinical response to three dose levels of methylphenidate. *Pediatrics, 87,* 519–531.

Barkley, R. A., Fischer, M., Edelbrock, C. S., & Smallish, L. (1990). The adolescent outcome of hyperactive children diagnosed by research criteria: I. An eight-year prospective follow-up study. *Journal of the American Academy of Child and Adolescent Psychiatry, 29,* 546–557.

Barkley, R. A., Fischer, M., Edelbrock, C. S., & Smallish, L. (1991). The adolescent outcome of hyperactive children diagnosed by research criteria: III. Mother-child interactions, family conflicts and maternal psychopathology. *Journal of Child Psychology and Psychiatry and Allied Disciplines, 32,* 233–255.

Barkley, R. A., Fischer, M., Newby, R., & Breen, M. (1988). Development of a multi-method clinical protocol for assessing stimulant drug responses in ADHD children. *Journal of Clinical Child Psychology, 17,* 14–24.

Barkley, R. A., & Grodzinsky, G. M. (1994). Are tests of frontal lobe functions useful in a diagnosis of attention deficit disorders? *Clinical Neuropsychologists, 8,* 121–139.

Barkley, R. A., Grodzinsky, G., & DuPaul, G. J. (1992). Frontal lobe functions and attention deficit disorder with and without hyperactivity. A review and research report. *Journal of Abnormal Child Psychology, 20,* 163–188.

Barkley, R. A., Guevremont, D. C., Anastopoulos, A. D., DuPaul, G. J., & Shelton, T. L. (1993). Driving-related risks and outcomes of attention deficit hyperactivity disorder in adolescents and young adults: A 3- to 5-year follow-up survey. *Pediatrics, 92,* 212–218.

Barkley, R. A., Guevremont, D. C., Anastopoulos, A. D., & Fletcher, K. E. (1992). A comparison of three family therapy programs for treating family conflicts in adolescents with attention deficit hyperactivity disorder. *Journal of Consulting and Clinical Psychology, 60,* 450–462.

Barkley, R. A., Karlsson, J., & Pollard, S. (1985). Effects of age on the mother-child interactions of ADD/H and normal boys. *Journal of Abnormal Child Psychology, 13,* 631–637.

Barkley, R. A., Karlsson, J., Pollard, S., & Murphy, K. (1985). Developmental changes in the mother-child interactions of hyperactive boys: Effects of two doses of Ritalin. *Journal of Child Psychology and Psychiatry, 26,* 705–715.

Barkley, R. A., Karlsson, J., Strzelecki, E., & Murphy, J. V. (1984). Effects of age and Ritalin dosage on the mother-child interactions of hyperactive children. *Journal of Consulting and Clinical Psychology, 52,* 750–758.

Barkley, R. A., McMurray, M. B., Edelbrock, C. S., & Robbins, K. (1989). The response of aggressive and non-aggressive ADHD children to two doses of methylphenidate. *Journal of the American Academy of Child and Adolescent Psychiatry, 28,* 873–881.

Barkley, R. A., McMurray, M. B., Edelbrock, C. S., & Robbins, K. (1990). Side effects of methylphenidate in children with attention deficit hyperactivity disorder: A systemic, placebo-controlled evaluation. *Pediatrics, 86,* 184–192.

Barkley, R. A., & Murphy, J. V. (1991). Pediatric annals: Treating attention-deficit hyperactivity disorder: Medication and behavior management training. *Pediatric Annals, 20,* 256–266.

Barkley, R. A., & Murphy, K. (1993). Differential diagnosis of adult ADHD: Some controversial issues. *The ADHD Report, 1*(4), 1–3.

Barkley, R. A., & Ullman, D. G. (1975). A comparison of objective measures of activity and distractibility in hyperactive and non-hyperactive children. *Journal of Abnormal Child Psychology, 3,* 231–244.

Barlow, D. (Ed.). (1981). *Behavioral assessment of adult disorders.* New York: Guilford Press.

Barnes, G. M., & Welte, J. W. (1986). Patterns and predictors of alcohol use among 7–12th grade students in New York State. *Journal of Studies on Alcohol, 47,* 53–60.

Barowsky, E. (1991). Use of biofeedback in the treatment of disorders of childhood. *Annals of the New York Academy of Sciences, 68,* 221–233.

Barratt, E. S. (1985). Impulsiveness subtraits: Arousal and information processing. In J. T. Spence & C. E. Izard (Eds.), *Motivation, emotion and personality.* Amsterdam, The Netherlands: Elsevier Press.

Barrett, P. M., Rapee, R. M., Dadds, M. M., & Ryan, S. M. (1996). Family enhancement of cognitive style in anxious and aggressive children. *Journal of Abnormal Child Psychology, 24,* 187–203.

Barrickman, L., Noyes, R., Kuperman, S., & Schumacher, E. (1991). Treatment of ADHD with fluoxetine: A preliminary trial. *Journal of the American Academy of Child and Adolescent Psychiatry, 30*(5), 762–767.

Barrickman, L. L., Perry, P. J., Allen, A. J., Kuperman, S., Arndt, S. V., Herrman, K., & Schumacher, E. (1995). Bupropion versus methylphenidate in the treatment of attention-deficit hyperactivity disorder. *Journal of the American Academy of Child and Adolescent Psychiatry, 34,* 649–657.

Barrios, B. A., & Hartmann, D. P. (1988). Fears and anxieties. In E. J. Mash & L. G. Terdal (Eds.), *Behavioral assessment of childhood disorders* (2nd ed., pp. 196–264). New York: Guilford Press.

Barrish, H. H., Saunders, N., & Wolfe, N. D. (1969). Good behavior gain: Effects of individual contingencies for group consequences and disruptive behavior in the classroom. *General Applied Behavioral Analysis, 2,* 119–124.

Bartel, S. S., & Solanto, M. V. (1995). Usefulness of the Rorschach Ink Blot Test: An assessment of attention deficit hyperactivity disorder. *Perceptual and Motor Skills, 80,* 531–541.

Bartels, M. G., Varley, C. K., Mitchell, J., & Stamm, J. (1991). Pediatric cardiovascular effects of imipramine and desipramine. *Journal of the American Academy of Child and Adolescent Psychiatry, 30,* 100–103.

Bash, M. S., & Camp, B. (1985). *Think aloud: Increasing social and cognitive skills: A problem-solving program for children.* Champaign, IL: Research Press.

Bates, J. E. (1987). Temperament in infancy. In J. D. Osofsky (Ed.), *Handbook of infant development* (2nd ed., pp. 1101–1149). New York: Wiley.

Bates, J. E. (1991). *Early temperament and mother-child relationship as interactive factors in the development of behavior problems.* Paper presented at the meeting of the Society for Research in Child and Adolescent Psychopathology, Zandvoort, Holland.

Battle, E. S., & Lacy, B. (1972). A context for hyperactivity in children, over time. *Child Development, 43,* 757–773.

Bauermeister, J. J. (1992). Factor analyses of teacher ratings of attention deficit hyperactivity disorder and oppositional defiant symptoms in children aged four through thirteen years. *Journal of Clinical Child Psychology, 21,* 27–34.

Bauermeister, J. J., Alegria, M., Bird, H. R., Rubio-Stipec, M., & Canino, G. (1992). Are attentional-hyperactivity deficits unidimensional or multi-dimensional syndromes? Empirical findings from a community survey. *Journal of the American Academy of Child and Adolescent Psychiatry, 31,* 423–431.

Bauermeister, J. J., Berrios, V., Jimenez, A. L., & Acevedo, L. (1990). Some issues and instruments for the assessment of attention-deficit hyperactivity disorder in Puerto Rican children. *Journal of Clinical Child Psychology, 19*(1), 9–16.

Baumgaertel, A., Wolraich, M. L., & Dietrich, M. (1995). Attention deficit disorders in German elementary school-age sample. *Journal of the American Academy of Child and Adolescent Psychiatry, 34,* 629–638.

Baumrind, D. (1968). Authoritarian vs. authoritative parental control. *Adolescence, 3,* 255–272.

Bawden, H. N., MacDonald, W., & Shea, S. (1997). Treatment of children with Williams Syndrome with methylphenidate. *Journal of Child Neurology, 12,* 248–252.

Bean, A. W., & Roberts, M. W. (1981). The effects of time-out release contingencies on changes in child non-compliance. *Journal of Abnormal Child Psychology, 9,* 95–105.

Beardslee, W. R., Wright, E., Rothberg, P. C., Salt, P., & Versage, E. (1996). Responsive families to two preventive intervention strategies: Long-term differences in behavior and attitude change. *Journal of the American Academy of Child and Adolescent Psychiatry, 35,* 774–782.

Beck, A. T. (1970). Cognitive therapy: Nature and relation to behavior therapy. *Behavior Therapy, 1,* 184–200.

Beck, J. S. (1996, March 6–7). *Cognitive therapy with depressed patients.* The eleventh annual Treatment Conference, Hilton Head, SC.

Beck, L., Langford, W. S., MacKay, M., & Sum, G. (1975). Childhood chemotherapy and later drug abuse and growth curve: A follow-up study of 30 adolescents. *American Journal of Psychiatry, 132,* 436–438.

Beck, S. J., Young, G. H., & Tarnowski, K. J. (1990). Maternal characteristics and perceptions of pervasive and situational hyperactives and normal controls. *Journal of the American Academy of Child and Adolescent Psychiatry, 29,* 558–565.

Becker, D. F., Doane, J. A., & Wexler, B. E. (1993). Effects of emotion on perceptual asymmetry in adolescent inpatients with attention-deficit hyperactivity disorder. *Journal of the American Academy of Child and Adolescent Psychiatry, 32,* 318–321.

Becker, L. E. (1990). *Comprehensive auditory visual attention assessment system.* Ft. Wayne, IN: Lowell E. Becker.

Becker, W. C. (1971). *Parents are teachers: A child management program.* Champaign, IL: Research Press.

Bedi, G. C., Halperin, J. M., & Sharma, V. (1993). Investigation of modality-specific distractibility in children. *International Journal of Neuroscience, 74,* 79–85.

Befera, M. S., & Barkley, R. A. (1985). Hyperactive and normal girls and boys: Mother-child interaction, parent psychiatric status and child-psychopathology. *Journal of Child Psychology and Psychiatry, 26,* 439–452.

Behar, D., Rapoport, J. L., Adams, A. J., Berg, C. J., & Cornblath, M. (1984). Sugar challenge testing with children considered behaviorally "sugar reactive." *Journal of Nutrition and Behavior, 1,* 277–288.

Behar, D., Rapoport, J. L., Berg, C. J., Denckla, M. B., Mann, L., Cox, C., Fedio, P., Zahn, T., & Wolfman, M. G. (1984). Computerized tomography and neuropsychological test measures in adolescents with obsessive-compulsive disorder. *American Journal of Psychiatry, 141,* 363–369.

Behar, D., & Stewart, M. A. (1984). Aggressive conduct disorder: The influence of social class, sex and age on the clinical picture. *Journal of Child Psychology and Psychiatry, 25,* 191–124.

Behar, L. B. (1977). The preschool behavior questionnaire. *Journal of Abnormal Child Psychology, 5,* 265–295.

Beitchman, J. H. (1987). Language delay and hyperactivity in preschoolers. *Canadian Journal of Psychiatry, 32,* 683–687.

Beitchman, J. H., Hood, J., Rochon, J., & Peterson, M. (1989). Empirical classification of speech/language impairment in children: II. Behavioral characteristics. *Journal of the American Academy of Child and Adolescent Psychiatry, 28,* 118–123.

Beitchman, J. H., & Inglis, A. (1991). The continuum of linguistic dysfunction from pervasive developmental disorders to dyslexia. *Pervasive Developmental Disorders, 14,* 95–111.

Beitchman, J. H., Wilson, B., Brownlie, E. B., Walters, H., & Lancee, W. (1996). Long-term consistency in speech/language profiles: I. Developmental and academic outcomes. *Journal of the American Academy of Child and Adolescent Psychiatry, 35,* 804–811.

Belfiore, P. J., Grskovic, J. A., Murphy, A., & Zentall, S. S. (1996). The effects of antecedent color on reading for students with learning disabilities and co-occurring attention deficit hyperactivity disorder. *Journal of Learning Disabilities, 29,* 432–438.

Bell, C. (1995). Exposure to violence distresses children and may lead to their becoming violent. *Psychiatric News, 15,* 6–8.

Bell, C., & Jenkins, E. J. (1991). Traumatic stress and children. *Journal of Health Care for the Poor and Underserved, 2,* 175–185.

Bellak, L. (Ed.). (1979). *Psychiatric aspects of minimal brain dysfunction in adults.* New York: Grune and Stratton.

Bellak, L. (1992). Comorbidity of attention deficit hyperactivity disorder and other disorders. *American Journal of Psychiatry, 149,* 147–148.

Bellak, L. (1994). The schizophrenic syndrome and attention deficit disorder: Thesis, antithesis, and synthesis? 101st annual convention of the American Psychological Association, 1993, Toronto, Canada. *American Psychologist, 49,* 25–29.

Bellak, L., & Bellak, S. S. (1968). *Children's apperception test.* Los Angeles: Western Psychological Services.

Bell-Dolan, D. J., Foster, S. L., & Sikoria, D. M. (1989). Effects of socio-metric testing on children's behavior and loneliness in school. *Developmental Psychology, 25,* 306–311.

Belsky, J., Woodworth, S., & Crnic, K. (1996). Trouble in the second year: Three questions about family interaction. *Child Development, 67,* 556–578.

Benasich, A. A., & Brooks-Gunn, J. (1996). Maternal attitudes and knowledge of child-rearing: Associations with family and child outcomes. *Child Development, 67,* 1186–1205.

Benasich, A. A., Curtiss, S., & Tallal, P. (1993). Language, learning and behavioral disturbances in childhood: A longitudinal perspective. *Journal of the American Academy of Child and Adolescent Psychiatry, 32,* 585–594.

Bender, B., & Milgrom, H. (1992). Theophylline-induced behavior change in children. An objective evaluation of parents' perceptions. *Journal of the American Medical Association, 267,* 19.

Bender, L. (1942). Post encephalitic behavior disorders in children. In J. B. Neal (Ed.), *Encephalitis: A clinical study.* New York: Grune and Stratton.

Bender, L. (1956). *Psychopathology of children with organic brain disorders.* Springfield, IL: Thomas.

Bender, R. (1993). *Auditory integration training.* Unpublished brochure, Wichita Falls, TX

Benjamin, J., Li, L., Patterson, C., Greenberg, B. D., Murphy, D. L., & Hamer, D. H. (1996). Population and familial association between D4 dopamine receptor gene and measures of novelty seeking. *National Genetics, 12,* 81–84.

Ben-Yishay, Y., Rattok, J., & Diller, L. (1979). *A clinical strategy for the systematic amelioration of attentional disturbances in severe head trauma patients* [Monograph]. New York: New York University Medical Center, Institute of Rehabilitation Medicine.

Bereiter, C., & Anderson, V. (1983). *Willy the wisher and other thinking stories: An Open Court thinking storybook.* LaSalle, IL: Open Court.

Berg, C., Hart, D., Quinn, P., & Rapoport, J. (1978). Newborn minor physical anomalies and prediction of infant behavior. *Journal of Autism and Childhood Schizophrenia, 8,* 427–439.

Berg, C., Quinn, P. O., & Rapoport, J. L. (1978). Clinical evaluation of one-year-old infants: Possible predictors of risk for the "hyperactive syndrome." *Journal of Pediatric Psychology, 3,* 164–167.

Berg, C., Rapoport, J. L., Barkley, L. S., Quinn, P. O., & Timmins, P. (1980). Newborn minor physical anomalies and problem behavior at age three. *Medical Journal of Psychiatry, 137,* 791–796.

Bergan, J. R., & Kratochwill, T. R. (1990). *Behavioral consultation and therapy.* New York: Plenum Press.

Berk, L. E., & Landau, S. (1993). Private speech of learning disabled and normally achieving children in classroom academic and laboratory contexts. *Child Development, 64,* 556–571.

Berk, L. E., & Potts, M. K. (1991). Developmental and functional significance of private speech among attention deficit hyperactivity disordered and normal boys. *Journal of Abnormal Child Psychology, 19,* 357–377.

Bernier, J. C., & Siegel, D. H. (1994). Attention-deficit hyperactivity disorder: A family and ecological systems perspective. *Families in Society, 75,* 142–151.

Bernstein, G. A., Carroll, M. E., Crosby, R. D., Perwien, A. R., Go, F. S., & Benowitz, N. L. (1994). Caffeine effects on learning, performance, and anxiety in normal school-age children. *Journal of the American Academy of Child and Adolescent Psychiatry, 33,* 407–415.

Berry, C. A., Shaywitz, S. E., & Shaywitz, B. A. (1985). Girls with attention deficit disorder: A silent minority? A report on behavioral and cognitive characteristics. *Pediatrics, 76,* 801–809.

Berry, K., & Cook. V. J. (1980). Personality and behavior. In H. Rie & E. D. Rie (Eds.), *Handbook of minimal brain dysfunction.* New York: Wiley.

Bhatia, M. S., Nigam, V. R., Bohra, N., & Malik, S. C. (1991). Attention deficit disorder with hyperactivity among pediatric outpatients. *Journal of Child Psychology and Psychiatry and Allied Disciplines, 32,* 297–306.

Bickett, L., & Milich, R. (1990). First impressions formed of boys with learning disabilities and attention deficit disorder. *Journal of Learning Disabilities, 23,* 253–259.

Biederman, J. (1991). Attention deficit hyperactivity disorder (ADHD). *Annals of Clinical Psychiatry, 3,* 9–22.

Biederman, J., Baldessarini, R. J., Wright, V., Keenan, K., & Faraone, S. (1993). A double-blind placebo controlled study of desipramine in the treatment of ADD: III. Lack of impact of comorbidity and family history factors on clinical response. *Journal of the American Academy of Child and Adolescent Psychiatry, 32,* 199–204.

Biederman, J., Baldessarini, R. J., Wright, V., Knee, D., & Harmatz, J. S. (1989). A double-blind placebo controlled study of desipramine in the treatment of ADD: I. Efficacy. *Journal of the American Academy of Child and Adolescent Psychiatry, 28,* 777–784.

Biederman, J., Baldessarini, R. J., Wright, V., Knee, D., Harmatz, J. S., & Goldblatt, M. D. (1989). A double-blind placebo controlled study of desipramine in the treatment of ADD: II. Serum drug levels and cardiovascular findings. *Journal of the American Academy of Child and Adolescent Psychiatry, 28,* 903–911.

Biederman, J., Faraone, S. V., & Chen, W. J. (1993). Social adjustment inventory for children and adolescents: Concurrent validity in ADHD children. *Journal of the American Academy of Child and Adolescent Psychiatry, 32,* 1059–1064.

Biederman, J., Faraone, S. V., Doyle, A., & Lehman, B. K. (1993). Convergence of the child behavior checklist with structured interview-based psychiatric diagnoses of ADHD children with and without comorbidity. *Journal of Child Psychology and Psychiatry and Allied Disciplines, 34*(7), 1241–1251.

Biederman, J., Faraone, S. V., Keenan, K., & Benjamin, J. (1992). Further evidence for family-genetic risk factors in attention deficit hyperactivity disorder: Patterns of comorbidity in probands and relatives in psychiatrically and pediatrically referred samples. *Archives of General Psychiatry, 49*(9), 728–738.

Biederman, J., Faraone, S. V., Keenan, K., Knee, D., & Tsuang, M. T. (1990). Family-genetic and psychosocial risk factors in *DSM-III* attention deficit disorder. *Journal of the American Academy of Child and Adolescent Psychiatry, 29,* 526–533.

Biederman, J., Faraone, S. V., Keenan, K., Steingard, R., Spencer, T., & Tsuang, M. (1991). Familial association between attention deficit disorder and anxiety disorders. *American Journal of Psychiatry, 148,* 251–256.

Biederman, J., Faraone, S. V., Keenan, K., Steingard, R., & Tsuang, M. T. (1991). Familial association between attention deficit disorder and anxiety disorder. *American Journal of Psychiatry, 148,* 251–256.

Biederman, J., Faraone, S. V., Keenan, K., & Tsuang, M. T. (1991). Evidence of familial association between attention deficit disorder and major affective disorders. *Archives of General Psychiatry, 48,* 633–642.

Biederman, J., Faraone, S. V., Knee, D., & Munir, K. (1990). Retrospective assessment of *DSM-III* attention deficit disorder in non-referred individuals. *Journal of Clinical Psychiatry, 51,* 102–106.

Biederman, J., Faraone, S. V., Mick, E., & Lelon, E. (1995). Psychiatric comorbidity among referred juveniles with major depression: Fact or artifact? *Journal of the American Academy of Child and Adolescent Psychiatry, 34,* 579–590.

Biederman, J., Faraone, S. V., Mick, E., Moore, P., & Lelon, E. (1996). Child behavior checklist findings further support comorbidity between ADHD and major depression in a referred sample. *Journal of the American Academy of Child and Adolescent Psychiatry, 35,* 734–742.

Biederman, J., Faraone, S. V., Mick, E., Wozniak, J., Chen, L., Ouelette, C., Marrs, A., Moore, P., Garcia, J., Mennin, D., & Lelon, E. (1996). Attention deficit hyperactivity disorder in juvenile mania: An overlooked comorbidity? *Journal of the American Academy of Child and Adolescent Psychiatry, 35,* 997–1008.

Biederman, J., Faraone, S. V., Milberger, S., Curtiss, S., Chen, L., Marrs, A., Ouellette, C., Moore, P., & Spencer, T. (1996). Predictors of persistence and remissions of ADHD in adolescence: Results from a four-year prospective follow-up study. *American Journal of Child and Adolescent Psychiatry, 35,* 343–351.

Biederman, J., Faraone, S. V., Milberger, S., & Doyle, A. (1993). Diagnoses of attention-deficit hyperactivity disorder from parent reports predict diagnoses based on teacher reports. *Journal of the American Academy of Child and Adolescent Psychiatry, 32,* 314–317.

Biederman, J., Faraone, S. V., Milberger, S., & Guite, J. (1996). A prospective 4-year follow-up study of attention-deficit and related disorders. *Archives of General Psychiatry, 53,* 437–446.

Biederman, J., Faraone, S. V., Milberger, S., Jetton, J. G., Chen, L., Mick, E., Ross, W., Greene, R. W., & Russell, R. L. (1996). Is childhood oppositional defiant disorder a precursor to adolescent conduct disorder? Findings from a four-year follow-up study of children with ADHD. *Journal of the American Academy of Child and Adolescent Psychiatry, 35,* 1193–1204.

Biederman, J., Faraone, S. V., Spencer, T., & Wilens, T. (1993). Patterns of psychiatric comorbidity, cognition, and psychological functioning in adults with attention deficit hyperactivity disorder. *American Journal of Psychiatry, 150,* 1792–1798.

Biederman, J., Faraone, S. V., Taylor, A., Sienna, M., Williamson, S., & Fine, C. (1997). *Diagnostic continuity between child and adolescent ADHD: Findings from a longitudinal clinical sample.* Paper presented at the 44th annual meeting of the American Academy of Child and Adolescent Psychiatry, Toronto, Canada.

Biederman, J., Faraone, S. V., Weber, B. A., Russell, B. A., Rater, M., & Park, K. (1997). *Correspondence between* DSM III-R *and* DSM-IV *attention deficit hyperactivity disorder.* Paper presented at the annual meeting of the American Academy of Child and Adolescent Psychiatry, Toronto, Canada.

Biederman, J., Keenan, K., & Faraone, S. V. (1990). Parent-based diagnosis of attention deficit disorder predicts a diagnosis based on teacher report. *Journal of the American Academy of Child and Adolescent Psychiatry, 29,* 698–701.

Biederman, J., Milberger, S., & Faraone, S. V. (1995). Impact of adversity on functioning and comorbidity in children with attention-deficit hyperactivity disorder. *Journal of the American Academy of Child and Adolescent Psychiatry, 34,* 1495–1503.

Biederman, J., Milberger, S., Faraone, S. V., Guite, J., & Warbourton, R. (1994). Associations between childhood asthma and ADHD: Issues of psychiatric comorbidity and familiality. *Journal of the American Academy of Child and Adolescent Psychiatry, 33,* 842–848.

Biederman, J., Munir, K., Knee, D., Habelow, W., Armentano, M., Autor, S., & Hoge, S. K. (1986). A family study of patients with attention deficit disorder and normal controls. *Journal of Psychiatric Research, 20,* 263–274.

Biederman, J., Munir, K., Knee, D., Armentano, M., Autor, S., Waternaux, C., & Tsuang, M. (1987). High rate of affective disorder in probands with attention deficit disorder and in their relatives: A controlled family study. *American Journal of Psychiatry, 144,* 330–333.

Biederman, J., Newcorn, J., & Sprich, S. (1991). Comorbidity of attention deficit hyperactivity disorder with conduct, depressive, anxiety and other disorders. *American Journal of Psychiatry, 148,* 564–577.

Biederman, J., Santangelo, S. L., Faraone, S. V., Kiely, K., Guite, J., Mick, E., Reed, E. D., Kraus, I., Jellinek, M., & Perrin, J. (1995). Clinical correlates of enuresis in ADHD and non-ADHD children. *Journal of Child Psychology and Psychiatry and Allied Disciplines, 36,* 865–877.

Biederman, J., Wilens, T., Mick, E., Faraone, S. V., Weber, W., Curtis, S., Thornell, A., Pfister, K., Jetton, J. G., & Storiano, J. (1997). Is ADHD a risk factor for psychoactive substance use disorders? Findings from a four-year prospective follow-up study. *Journal of the American Academy of Child and Adolescent Psychiatry, 36,* 21–29.

Biederman, J., Wozniak, J., Kiely, K., Ablon, S., Faraone, S. V., Mick, E., Mundy, E., & Kraus, I. (1995). CBCL clinical scales discriminate pre-pubertal children with structured interview-derived diagnosis of mania from those with ADHD. *Journal of the American Academy of Child and Adolescent Psychiatry, 34,* 464–471.

Bierman, K. L. (1986). The relationship between social aggression and peer rejection in middle childhood. In R. Prinz (Ed.), *Advances in behavioral assessment of children and families* (Vol. 2, pp. 151–178). Greenwich, CT: JAI Press.

Bierman, K. L., Miller, C. L., & Stabb, S. D. (1987). Improving the social behavior and peer acceptance of rejected boys: Effects of social skill training with instructions and prohibitions. *Journal of Consulting and Clinical Psychology, 55,* 194–200.

Billing, L., Ericksson, M., Jonsson, B., Steneroth, G., & Zetterstrom, R. (1994). The influence of environmental factors on behavioral problems in 8-year-old children exposed to amphetamine during fetal life. *Child Abuse and Neglect, 18,* 3–9.

Bird, H., Canino, G., Rubio-Stipec, M., Gould, M. S., Ribera, J., Sesman, M., Woodbury, M., Huertas-Goldman, S., Pagan, A., Sanchez-Lacey, A., & Moscoso, M. (1988). Estimates of the prevalence of childhood maladjustment in a community survey in Puerto Rico. *Archives of General Psychiatry, 45,* 1120–1126.

Bird, H. R., Gould, M. S., & Staghezza, B. M. (1993). Patterns of diagnostic comorbidity in a community sample of children aged 9 through 16 years. *Journal of the American Academy of Child and Adolescent Psychiatry, 32,* 361–368.

Bird, H. R., Gould, M. S., Yager, T., Staghezza, B., & Canino, G. (1989). Risk factors for maladjustment in Puerto Rican children. *Journal of the American Academy of Child and Adolescent Psychiatry, 28,* 847–850.

Birmaher, B., Greenhill, L. L., Cooper, T. B., Fried, J., & Maminski, B. (1989). Sustained release methylphenidate: Pharmacokinetics studies in ADHD males. *Journal of the American Academy of Child and Adolescent Psychiatry, 28,* 768–772.

Birmaher, B., Quintana, H., & Greenhill, L. L. (1988). Methylphenidate treatment of hyperactive autistic children. *Journal of American Academy of Child and Adolescent Psychiatry, 27,* 248–251.

Black, A. (1994). The drugging of America's children. *Redbook, 50,* 41–44.

Black, M. B., & Sonnenschein, S. (1993). Original articles: Early exposure to otitis media: A preliminary investigation of behavioral outcome. *Developmental and Behavioral Pediatrics, 14,* 150–155.

Blackman, J. A., Westervelt, V. D., Stevenson, R., & Welch, A. (1991). Management of preschool children with attention deficit hyperactivity disorder. *Topics in Early Childhood Special Education, 11,* 91–104.

Blakemore, B., Shindler, S., & Conte, R. (1993). A problem solving training program for parents of children with attention deficit hyperactivity disorder. *Canadian Journal of School Psychology, 9,* 66–85.

Blaney, N. T., Stephan, S., Rosenfield, D., Aronson, E., & Sikes, J. (1977). Interdependence in the classroom: A field study. *Journal of Educational Psychology, 69,* 121–128.

Blick, D. W., & Test, D. W. (1987). Effects of self-recording on high-school students' ontask behavior. *Learning Disability Quarterly, 10,* 203–213.

Bloch, H., Cole, W., & Willwerth, J. (1994, July 18). Behavior: Life in overdrive. *Time Magazine,* 42–50.

Block, J., Block, J. H., & Keyes, S. (1988). Longitudinally foretelling drug usage in adolescence: Early childhood personality and environmental precursors. *Child Development, 59,* 336–355.

Block, J. H. (1977). Hyperactivity: A cultural perspective. *Journal of Learning Disabilities, 10,* 236–240.

Blondis, T. A., Accardo, P. J., & Snow, J. H. (1989). Measures of attention deficit: II. Clinical perspectives and test interpretation. *Clinical Pediatrics, 28*(6), 268–276.

Blondis, T. A., Clippard, D. S., Scroggs, D. J., & Peterson, L. (1991). Multi-disciplinary habilitative prescriptions for the attention deficit hyperactivity disorder child. In P. J. Accardo, T. A. Blondis, & B. Y. Whitman (Eds.), *Attention deficit disorders and hyperactivity in children.* New York: Marcel Dekker.

Blondis, T. A., Snow, J. H., Stein, M., & Roizen, N. J. (1991). Appropriate use of measures of attention and activity for the diagnosis and management of attention deficit hyperactivity disorder. In P. J. Accardo, T. A. Blondis, & B. Y. Whitman (Eds.), *Attention deficit disorders and hyperactivity in children.* New York: Marcel Dekker.

Bloom, A. S., Russell, L. J., Weisskopf, B., & Blackerby, J. L. (1988). Methylphenidate-induced delusional disorder in a child with attention deficit disorder with hyperactivity. *Journal of American Academy of Child and Adolescent Psychiatry, 27,* 88–89.

Bloom, B. S. (1956). *Taxonomy of educational objectives.* New York: Longman.

Bloomquist, M. L. (1996). *Skills training for children with behavior disorders: A parent and therapist guidebook.* New York: Guilford Press.

Bloomquist, M. L., August, G., & Garfinkel, B. D. (1989). *Cognitive-behavioral therapy for attention-deficit hyperactivity disordered children: Additive effects of parent involvement and methylphenidate.* Unpublished manuscript, University of Minnesota.

Bloomquist, M. L., August, G., & Ostrander, R. (1991). Effects of a school-based cognitive-behavioral intervention for ADHD children. *Journal of Abnormal Child Psychology, 19,* 591–605.

Blouin, A. G., Bornstein, M. A., & Trites, R. L. (1978). Teenage alcohol abuse among hyperactive children: A five-year follow-up study. *Journal of Pediatric Psychology, 3,* 188–194.

Blouin, A. G., Conners, K., Seidel, W. T., & Blouin, J. (1989). The independence of hyperactivity from conduct disorder: Methodological considerations. *Canadian Journal of Psychiatry, 34,* 279–282.

Blumstein, A. (1995, August). Violence by young people: Why the deadly nexus? *National Institute of Justice Journal,* 1–9.

Blunden, D., Spring, C., & Greenberg, L. M. (1974). Validation of the Classroom Behavior Inventory. *Journal of Consulting and Clinical Psychology, 42,* 604–608.

Bond, C., & McMahon, R. J. (1984). Relationships between marital distress and child behavior problems, maternal personal adjustment, maternal personality, and maternal parenting behavior. *Journal of Abnormal Psychology, 93,* 348–351.

Bond, E. P., & Partridge, C. E. (1926). Post encephalitic behavior disorders in boys and their management in the hospital. *American Journal of Psychiatry, 6,* 103.

Boone, F. (1992). Comorbidity of attention deficit hyperactivity disorder and other disorders. *American Journal of Psychiatry, 149,* 148–155.

Borcherding, B. G., Keysor, C. S., Rapoport, J. L., Elia, J., & Amass, J. (1990). Motor/vocal tics and compulsive behaviors on stimulant drugs: Is there a common vulnerability? *Psychiatry Research, 33,* 83–94.

Borden, K. A., & Brown, R. T. (1989). Attributional outcomes: The subtle messages of treatments for attention deficit disorder. *Cognitive Therapy and Research, 13,* 147–160.

Borden, K. A., Brown, R. T., Jenkins, P., & Clingerman, S. R. (1987). Achievement attributions and depressive symptoms in attention-deficit disordered and normal children. *Journal of School Psychology, 25,* 399–404.

Borghgraef, M., Fryns, J. P., & van Den Berghe, H. (1990). The female and the Fragile X syndrome: Data on clinical and psychological findings in 7 Fragile X carriers. *Clinical Genetics, 37,* 341–346.

Boris, M., & Mandel, F. S. (1994). Foods and additives are common causes of the attention deficit hyperactivity disorder in children. *Annals of Allergy, 72,* 462–467.

Borland, B. L., & Hechtman, H. K. (1976). Hyperactive boys and their brothers: A 25-year follow-up study. *Archives of General Psychiatry, 33,* 669–675.

Bornstein, P., & Quevillon, R. (1976). The effects of a self-instructional package on overactive preschool boys. *Journal of Applied Behavior Analysis, 9,* 179–188.

Bornstein, R. A., Baker, G. B., Carroll, A., & King, G. (1990). Plasma amino acids in attention deficit disorder. *Psychiatry Research, 33*(3), 301–306.

Bos, C. S., & Vaughn, S. (1991). *Strategies for teaching students with learning and behavior problems* (2nd ed.). Boston: Allyn & Bacon.

Boucugnani, L. L., & Jones, R. W. (1989). Behaviors analogous to frontal lobe dysfunction in children with attention deficit hyperactivity disorder. *Archives of Clinical Neuropsychology, 4,* 161–173.

Boudreault, M., Thievierge, J., Cote, R., Boutin, P., Julien, Y., & Bergerson, S. (1988). Cognitive development and reading achievement in pervasive-ADD, situational ADD and control children. *Journal of Child Psychology and Psychiatry, 29,* 611–619.

Bowers, T., Washburn, S., & Livsay, J. (1986). Predicting neuropsychological impairment by screening instruments and intellectual evaluation indices: Implications for the measuring of Kaufman's Factor III. *Psychological Reports, 59,* 487–493.

Bowers, T. G., Risser, M. G., Suchaneck, J. F., Tinker, D. E., Raemer, J. C., & Domoto, M. (1992). A developmental index using the Wechsler Intelligence Scale for Children. Implications for the diagnosis and nature of ADHD. *Journal of Learning Disabilities, 25,* 179–185.

Bowker, L. H. (1988). On the relationship between wife beating and child abuse. In K. Yllo & M. Bograd (Eds.), *Feminist perspectives on wife abuse.* Newbury Park, CA: Sage.

Bowler, R., Sudia, S., Mergler, D., Perez-Arce, P., Harrison, R., & Cone, J. (1990, August). *Comparison of digit symbol and symbol digit modalities tests.* Paper presented at the American Psychological Association, Boston.

Bowley, B., & Walther, E. (1992). Attention deficit disorders and the role of the elementary school counselor. *Elementary School Guidance and Counseling, 27,* 39–46.

Boyle, M. H., Offord, D. R., Hofmann, H. G., & Catlin, G. P. (1987). Ontario child health study: I. Methodology. *Archives of General Psychiatry, 44*(9), 826–831.

Boyle, M. H., Offord, D. R., Racine, Y. A., & Fleming, J. E. (1993). Evaluation of the revised Ontario child health study scales. *Journal of Child Psychology and Psychiatry and Allied Disciplines, 34*(2), 189–213.

Boyle, M. H., Offord, D. R., Racine, Y., Szatmari, P., Fleming, J. E., & Sanford, M. (1996). Identifying thresholds for classifying childhood psychiatric disorder: Issues and prospects. *Journal of the American Academy of Child and Adolescent Psychiatry, 35,* 1440–1448.

Bradley, C. (1937). The behavior of children receiving benzedrine. *American Journal of Psychiatry, 94,* 577–585.

Bradley, C. (1950). Benzedrine and dexedrine in the treatment of children's behavior disorders. *Pediatrics, 5,* 24–36.

Bradley, C., & Bowen, M. (1940). School performance of children receiving amphetamine (benzedrine) sulfate. *American Journal of Orthopsychiatry, 10,* 787–788.

Bradley, C., & Bowen, M. (1941). Amphetamine (benzedrine) therapy of children's behavior disorders. *American Journal of Orthopsychiatry, 11,* 92–103.

Bradley, R. H., & Caldwell, B. M. (1984). One hundred seventy-four children: A study of the relationship between home environment and cognitive development during the first five years. In A. W. Gottfried (Ed.), *Home environment and early cognitive development: Longitudinal research.* Orlando, FL: Academic Press.

Bradley, R. H., Caldwell, B. M., & Rock, S. L. (1989). Home environment and cognitive development in the first three years of life: A collaborative study involving six sites and three ethnic groups in North America. *Developmental Psychology, 25,* 217–235.

Brand, E. F., Das-Smaal, E. A., & De Jonge, B. F. (1996). Subtypes of children with attention disabilities. *Child Neuropsychology, 2,* 109–122.

Brandon, K. A., Kehle, T. J., Jenson, W. R., & Clark, E. (1990). Regression, practice, and expectation effects on the Revised Conners Teacher Rating Scale. *Journal of Psychoeducational Assessment, 8*(4), 456–466.

Brantner, J. P., & Doherty, M. A. (1983). A review of timeout: A conceptual and methodological analysis. In S. Axelrod & J. Apsche (Eds.), *The effects of punishment on human behavior* (pp. 87–132). New York: Academic Press.

Braswell, L. (1993). Cognitive-behavioral groups for children manifesting ADHD and other disruptive behavior disorders. *Special Services in the Schools, 8,* 91–117.

Braswell, L., August, G., Bloomquist, M. L., Realmuto, G. M., Skare, S., & Crosby, R. (1997). School-based secondary prevention for children with disruptive behavior: Initial outcomes. *Journal of Abnormal Child Psychology, 25,* 197–208.

Braswell, L., & Bloomquist, M. L. (1991). *Cognitive-behavioral therapy with ADHD children: Child, family and school interventions.* New York: Guilford Press.

Braswell, L., & Kendall, P. C. (1988). Cognitive-behavioral methods with children. In K. S. Dobson (Ed.), *Handbook of cognitive behavioral therapies.* New York: Guilford Press.

Braswell, L., Koehler, C., & Kendall, P. C. (1985). Attributions and outcomes in child psychotherapy. *Journal of Social and Clinical Psychology, 3,* 458–465.

Braun, L., Kundert, D. K., Hess, A. W., & May, D. C. (1992). *Attentional profiles of children clinically diagnosed with ADHD and undifferentiated ADD: A neurocognitive approach.* Paper presented at the twelfth annual meeting of the National Academy of Neuropsychology, Pittsburgh.

Braverman, E. R. (1989). Phenylketonuria in an 8-year-old hyperactive child. *Brain Dysfunction, 2*(4), 217–218.

Breen, M. J. (1986). Normative data on the home situations and school situations questionnaires. *ADD/Hyperactivity Newsletter, 3,* 6.

Breen, M. J. (1989). ADHD girls and boys: An analysis of attentional, emotional, cognitive and family variables. *Journal of Child Psychology and Psychiatry, 30,* 711–716.

Breen, M. J., & Altepeter, T. S. (1990). Situational variability in boys and girls identified as ADHD. *Journal of Clinical Psychology, 46,* 486–490.

Breen, M. J., & Barkley, R. A. (1988). Child psychopathology and parenting stress in girls and boys having attention deficit disorder with hyperactivity. *Journal of Pediatric Psychology, 13,* 265–280.

Bregman, J. D. (1991). Current developments in the understanding of mental retardation: Part II. Psychopathology [Special article]. *Journal of the American Academy of Child and Adolescent Psychiatry, 30,* 861–872.

Bregman, J. D., Dykens, E., Watson, M., & Ort, S. I. (1987). Fragile-X syndrome: Variability of phenotypic expression. *Journal of the American Academy of Child and Adolescent Psychiatry, 26*(4), 463–471.

Bregman, J. D., Dykens, E., Watson, M., & Ort, S. I. (1988). Fragile-X syndrome: Variability of phenotypic expression. *Annual Progress in Child Psychiatry and Child Development,* 468–491.

Bregman, J. D., Leckman, J., & Ort, S. (1988). Fragile X syndrome: Genetic predisposition to psychopathology. *Journal of Autism and Developmental Disorders, 18,* 343–354.

Brenner, A. (1982). The effect of megadoses of selected B-complex vitamins on children with hyperkinesis: Controlled studies with long-term follow-up. *Journal of Learning Disabilities, 15,* 258–264.

Brent, D. A., Perper, J. A., Goldstein, C. E., Kolko, D. J., Allan, M. J., & Zelevnak, J. P. (1988). Risk factors for adolescent suicide: A comparison of adolescent suicide victims with suicidal patients. *Archives of General Psychiatry, 45,* 581–588.

Brent, D. A., Perper, J. A., Moritz, G., Allman, C., Friend, A., Roth, C., Schweers, J., Balach, L., & Baugher, M. (1993). Psychiatric risk factors for adolescent suicide: A case-controlled study. *Journal of the American Academy of Child and Adolescent Psychiatry, 32,* 521–529.

Brewin, C. R., Andrews, B., & Furnham, A. (1996). Intergenerational links and positive self-cognitions: Parental correlates of optimism, learned resourcefulness, and self-evaluation. *Cognitive Therapy and Research, 20,* 247–263.

Bridgeman, D. L. (1981). Enhanced role-taking through cooperative interdependence: A field study. *Child Development, 52,* 1231–1238.

Brier, N. (1995). Review article: Predicting antisocial behavior in youngsters displaying poor academic achievement: A review of risk factors. *Developmental and Behavioral Pediatrics, 16,* 271–276.

Brinich, P. (1980). Some potential effects of adoption on self and object representations. In A. Solnit, R. Eissler, A. Freud, M. Kris, & P. Neubauer (Eds.), *The psychoanalytic study of the child.* New Haven, CT: Yale University Press.

British Psychological Society. (1996). *Attention deficit hyperactivity disorder (ADHD): A psychological response to an evolving concept* (Report by a Working Party). Leicester, England: The British Psychological Association.

Broadbent, D. E. (1971). *Decision and stress.* New York: Academic Press.

Broden, M., Hall, R. V., & Mitts, B. (1971). The effect of self-recording on the classroom behavior of two eighth-grade students. *Journal of Applied Behavior Analysis, 4,* 191–199.

Brody, G. H., Stoneman, Z., & Gauger, K. (1996). Parent-child relationships, family problem-solving behavior and sibling relationship quality: The moderating role of sibling temperaments. *Child Development, 67,* 1289–1300.

Brodzinsky, D. M. (1990). A stress and coping model of adoption adjustment. In D. M. Brodzinsky & M. Schechter (Eds.), *The psychology of adoption.* New York: Oxford University Press.

Brodzinsky, D. M. (1993). Long-term outcomes in adoption. *The Future of Children, 3,* 153–166.

Brodzinsky, D. M., Singer, L. M., & Braff, A. M. (1984). Children's understanding of adoption. *Child Development, 55,* 869–878.

Bronfenbrenner, U. (1975). Is early intervention effective? In M. Guttentag & E. Streuning (Eds.), *Handbook of evaluation research* (Vol. 2). Beverly Hills, CA: Sage.

Bronowski, J. (1977). *Human and animal languages. A sense of the future* (pp. 104–131). Cambridge, MA: MIT Press.

Brook, J. S., Nomura, C., & Cohen, P. (1989). A network of influences on adolescent drug involvement: Neighborhood, school, peer and family. *Genetic, Social and General Psychology Monographs, 113,* 125–143.

Brook, J. S., Whiteman, M., Cohen, P., Shapiro, J., & Balka, E. (1995). Longitudinally predicting late adolescent and young adult drug use: Childhood and adolescent precursors. *Journal of the American Academy of Child and Adolescent Psychiatry, 34,* 1230–1238.

Brooks, R. (1993). Enhancing self-esteem in children and adolescents with ADHD. *The ADHD Report, 2,* 8–9.

Brooks, R. (1994). Children at risk: Fostering resilience and hope. *American Journal of Orthopsychiatry, 64,* 545–553.

Brooks, R. B. (1991). *The self-esteem teacher.* Circle Pines, MN: American Guidance Service.

Brooks-Gunn, J., Klebanov, P. K., & Duncan, G. J. (1996). Ethnic differences in children's intelligence test scores: Role of economic deprivation, home environment and maternal characteristics. *Child Development, 67,* 396–408.

Brookshire, B. L., Butler, I. J., Ewing-Cobbs, L., & Fletcher, J. M. (1994). Neuropsychological characteristics of children with Tourette's syndrome: Evidence for a non-verbal learning disability. *Journal of Clinical and Experimental Neuropsychology, 16,* 289–302.

Brophy, J., & Good, T. L. (1974). *Teacher-student relationships. Causes and consequences.* New York: Holt, Rinehart and Winston.

Brown, C. S., Wells, B. G., Cold, J. A., & Froemming, J. H. (1990). Possible influence of carbamazepine on plasma imipramine concentrations in children with attention deficit hyperactivity disorder. *Journal of Clinical Psychopharmacology, 10*(5), 359–362.

Brown, G. L., Hunt, R. D., Ebert, M. H., Bunney, W. E., & Kopin, I. J. (1979). Plasma levels of d-amphetamine in hyperactive children. *Psychopharmacology, 62,* 133–140.

Brown, L., & Hammill, D. D. (1990). *Behavior rating profile* (2nd ed.). Austin, TX: Pro-Ed.

Brown, L., Sherbenou, R. J., & Dollar, S. J. (1983). *Test of non-verbal intelligence.* Austin, TX: Pro-Ed.

Brown, R. T. (1980). Impulsivity and psychoeducational intervention in hyperactive children. *Journal of Learning Disabilities, 13,* 249–254.

Brown, R. T. (1982). A developmental analysis of the visual and auditory sustained attention and reflection-impulsivity in hyperactive and normal children. *Journal of Learning Disabilities, 15,* 353–357.

Brown, R. T. (1985). The validity of teacher ratings in differentiating between two subgroups of attention deficit disordered children with or without hyperactivity. *Educational and Psychological Measurement, 45*(3), 661–669.

Brown, R. T., & Borden, K. A. (1986). Hyperactivity at adolescence: Some misconceptions and new directions. *Journal of Clinical Child Psychology, 15,* 194–209.

Brown, R. T., Borden, K. A., Clingerman, S. R., & Jenkins, P. (1988). Depression in attention deficit disordered and normal children and their parents. *Child Psychiatry and Human Development, 18,* 119–132.

Brown, R. T., Borden, K. A., Spunt, A. L., & Medenis, R. (1985). Depression following pemoline withdrawal in a hyperactive child. *Clinical Pediatrics, 24*(3), 174.

Brown, R. T., Borden, K. A., Wynne, M. E., Schleser, R., & Clingerman, S. R. (1986). Methylphenidate and cognitive therapy with ADD children: A methodological consideration. *Journal of Abnormal Child Psychology, 14,* 481–497.

Brown, R. T., Borden, K. A., Wynne, M. E., & Spunt, A. L. (1988). Patterns of compliance in a treatment program for children with attention deficit disorder. *Journal of Compliance in Health Care, 3*(1), 23–39.

Brown, R. T., Borden, K. A., Wynne, M. E., Spunt, A. L., & Clingerman, S. R. (1987). Compliance with pharmacological and cognitive treatments for attention deficit disorder. *Journal of the American Academy of Child and Adolescent Psychiatry, 26,* 521–526.

Brown, R. T., Coles, C. D., Smith, I. E., & Platzman, K. A. (1991). Effects of prenatal alcohol exposure at school age. *Attention, Behavior, Neurotoxicology and Teratology, 13*(4), 369–376.

Brown, R. T., Ingber, P. S., & Tross, S. (1983). Pemoline and lithium in a patient with attention deficit disorder. *Journal of Clinical Psychiatry, 44,* 146–148.

Brown, R. T., Madan-Swain, A., & Baldwin, K. (1991). Gender differences in a clinic-referred sample of attention-deficit disordered children. *Child Psychiatry and Human Development, 22,* 111–128.

Brown, R. T., & Pacini, J. N. (1989). Perceived family functioning, marital status, and depression in parents of boys with attention deficit disorder. *Journal of Learning Disabilities, 22,* 581–587.

Brown, R. T., & Sexson, S. B. (1989). Effects of methylphenidate on cardiovascular responses in attention deficit hyperactivity disordered adolescents. *Journal of Adolescent Health Care, 10,* 179–183.

Brown, R. T., & Wynne, M. E. (1982). Correlates of teacher ratings, sustained attention, and impulsivity in hyperactive and normal boys. *Journal of Clinical Child Psychology, 11,* 262–267.

Brown, R. T., Wynne, M. E., & Medenis, A. (1985). Methylphenidate in cognitive therapy: A comparison of treatment approaches with hyperactive boys. *Journal of Abnormal Child Psychology, 13,* 69–87.

Brown, T. E. (1995). *Brown attention-deficit disorder scales for adolescents and adults: Brown ADD scales.* San Antonio, TX: The Psychological Corporation.

Brown, V. L., Hammill, D. D., & Wiederholt, J. L. (1995). *Test of reading comprehension* (3rd ed.). Los Angeles: Western Psychological Services.

Brunquell, P., Russman, B. S., & Lerer, T. (1988, September). *The mental status examination by pediatric neurologists in children with learning problems.* Presentation made at the seventeenth national meeting of the Child Neurology Society, Halifax, Canada.

Bryant, L. E., & Budd, K. S. (1984). Teaching behaviorally handicapped preschool children to share. *Journal of Applied Behavioral Analysis, 17,* 45–56.

Buchoff, R. (1990). Attention deficit disorder: Help for the classroom teacher. *Childhood Education, 67,* 86–90.

Buchsbaum, M. S., Haier, R. J., Sostek, A. J., Weingartner, H., Zahn, T. P., Siever, L. J., Murphy, D. L., & Brody, L. (1985). Attention dysfunction and psychopathology in college men. *Archives of General Psychiatry, 42,* 354–360.

Buckley, N. K., & Walker, H. M. (1970). *Modifying classroom behavior.* Champaign, IL: Research Press.

Budd, K. S., Liebowitz, J. M., Riner, L. S., Mindell, C., & Goldfarb, A. L. (1981). Home-based treatment of severe disruptive behaviors: A reinforcement package for preschool and kindergarten children. *Behavior Modification, 5,* 273–298.

Budoff, M., Thormann, J., & Gras, A. (1984). *Microcomputers in special education.* Cambridge, MA: Brookline Books.

Bugental, D. B., Collins, S., Collins, L., & Chaney, L. F. (1978). Attributional and behavioral changes following two behavior management interventions with hyperactive boys: A follow-up study. *Child Development, 49,* 247–250.

Bugental, D. B., & Cortez, V. L. (1988). Physiological reactivity to responsive and unresponsive children as moderated by perceived control. *Child Development, 59,* 686–693.

Bugental, D. B., Whalen, C. K., & Henker, B. (1977). Causal attributions of hyperactive children and motivational assumptions of two-behavior change approaches: Evidence for an interaction as position. *Child Development, 48,* 874–884.

Buhrmester, D., Camparo, L., Christensen, A., & Gonzalez, L. S. (1992). Mothers and fathers interacting in dyads and triads with normal and hyperactive sons. *Developmental Psychology, 28,* 500–509.

Buhrmester, D., Whalen, C. K., Henker, B., & MacDonald, V. (1992). Prosocial behavior in hyperactive boys: Effects of stimulant medication and comparison with normal boys. *Journal of Abnormal Child Psychology, 20,* 103–121.

Buitelaar, J. K., Rutger, J. V. D. G., Swaab-Varneveld, H., & Kuiper, M. (1995). Prediction of clinical response to methylphenidate in children with attention-deficit hyperactivity disorder. *Journal of the American Academy of Child and Adolescent Psychiatry, 34,* 1025–1032.

Buitelaar, J. K., Swinkles, S. H., DiVries, H., van der Gaag, R. J., & van Hoof, J. A. (1994). An ethological study on behavioral differences between hyperactive aggressive, combined hyperactive/aggressive and controlled children. *Journal of Child Psychology and Psychiatry, 45,* 1437–1446.

Buitelaar, J. K., van der Gaag, R. J., Swaab-Varneveld, H., & Kuiper, M. (1996). Pindolol and methylphenidate in children with attention-deficit hyperactivity disorder: Clinical efficacy and side effects. *Journal of Child Psychology and Psychiatry, 37,* 587–595.

Bukstein, O. G., Brent, D. A., & Kaminer, Y. (1989). Comorbidity of substance abuse and other psychiatric disorders in adolescents. *American Journal of Psychiatry, 146,* 1131–1141.

Bunney, B. S., & Aghajanian, C. K. (1976). d-Amphetamine-induced inhibition of central dopaminergic neurons: Mediation by striatonigral feedback pathway. *Science, 192,* 391.

Burcham, B., Carlson, L., & Milich, R. (1993). Promising school-based practices for students with attention deficit disorder: Issues in the education of children with attentional deficit disorder [Special issue]. *Exceptional Children, 60,* 174–180.

Burchard, J. D., & Barrera, F. (1972). An analysis of time-out and response cost in a programmed environment. *Journal of Applied Behavior Analysis, 5,* 271–282.

Burd, L., & Fisher, W. (1986). Central auditory processing disorder or attention deficit disorder? *Developmental and Behavioral Pediatrics, 7,* 215.

Burnley, G. D. (1993). A team approach for identification of an attention deficit hyperactivity disorder child. *School Counselor, 40*(3), 228–230.

Burnowski, J. (1977). *Human and animal languages. A sense of the future.* Cambridge, MA: MIT Press.

Burns, B. (1991). Mental health service use by adolescents in the 1970s and 1980s. *Journal of the American Academy of Child and Adolescent Psychiatry, 30,* 144–150.

Burns, B. J. (1972). *The effect of self-directed verbal commands in arithmetic performance and activity level of urban hyperactive children.* Unpublished doctoral dissertation.

Busch, B. (1993). Attention deficits: Current concepts, controversies, management and approaches to classroom instruction. *Annals of Dyslexia, 43,* 5–25.

Bushell, D. (1973). *Classroom behavior.* Englewood Cliffs, NJ: Prentice-Hall.

Buss, A. H., & Ploman, R. (1975). *A temperament theory of personality development.* New York: Wiley.

Buss, A. H., & Ploman, R. (1984). *Temperament: Early developing personality traits.* Hillsdale, NJ: Erlbaum.

Bussin, R., & Levin, G. M. (1993). Methamphetamine and fluoxetine treatment of a child with attention-deficit hyperactivity disorder and obsessive-compulsive disorder. *Journal of Child and Adolescent Psychopharmacology, 31*(1), 53–58.

Butler, F. S., Arredondo, D. E., & McCloskey, V. (1995). Affective comorbidity in children and adolescents with attention deficit hyperactivity disorder. *Annals of Clinical Psychiatry, 7,* 51–55.

Byers, R. K. (1959). Lead poisoning: Review and report of 45 cases. *Pediatrics, 23,* 585.

Cadoret, R. J., Cunningham, L., Loftus, R., & Edwards, J. (1975). Studies of adoptees from psychiatrically disturbed biologic parents: II. Temperament, hyperactive, antisocial and developmental variables. *Pediatrics, 87,* 301–306.

Cadoret, R. J., & Gath, A. (1980). Biologic correlates of hyperactivity: Evidence for a genetic factor. In S. Sells, R. Crandall, M. Roff, J. Strauss, & W. Pollin (Eds.), *Human functioning in longitudinal perspective* (pp. 103–114). Baltimore: Williams and Wilkins.

Cahn, D. A., & Marcotte, A. C. (1995). Rates of forgetting in attention deficit hyperactivity disorder. *Child Neuropsychology, 1,* 158–163.

Cahn, D. A., Marcotte, A. C., Stern, R. A., Arruda, J. E., Akshoomoff, N. A., & Leshko, I. C. (1996). Boston qualitative scoring system for the Rey-Osterreith Complex Figure: A study of children with ADHD. *Clinical Neuropsychologist, 10,* 397–406.

Calame, A., Fawer, C. L., & Claeys, V. (1986). Neurodevelopmental outcome in school performance of very low birth weight infants at eight years of age. *European Journal of Pediatrics, 145,* 461–466.

Callaghan, M. J., Byrnes, R. Y., Gray, B. H., Harvey, J. M., Mohay, H., Rogers, Y. M., & Tudehope, D. I. (1996). School performance in extremely low birthweight children: A controlled study. *Developmental Medicine and Child Neurology, 38,* 917–926.

Cameron, M. I., & Robinson, V. M. (1980). Effects of cognitive training on academic and on-task behavior of hyperactive children. *Journal of Abnormal Child Psychology, 8,* 405–419.

Cammisa, K. M. (1994). Educational kinesiology with learning disabled children: An efficacy study. *Perceptual Motor Skills, 78,* 105–106.

Camp, B. W. (1996). Adolescent mothers and their children: Changes in maternal characteristics and child developmental and behavioral outcome at school age. *Journal of Developmental and Behavioral Pediatrics, 17,* 162–169.

Camp, B. W., & Bash, M. S. (1981). *Think aloud-increasing social and cognitive skills: A problem-solving program for children.* Champaign, IL: Research Press.

Camp, B. W., & Bash, M. S. (1985). *Think aloud classroom program, grades 5–6.* Champaign, IL: Research Press.

Campbell, J. W., D'Amato, R. C., Roggio, D. J., & Stephens, K. D. (1991). Construct validity of the computerized continuous performance test with measures of intelligence, achievement and behavior. *Journal of School Psychology, 29,* 143–150.

Campbell, M., Anderson, L. T., Meier, M., Cohen, I. L., Small, A. M., Samit, C., & Sachar, E. J. (1978). A comparison of haloperidol and behavior therapy and their interaction in autistic children. *Journal of the American Academy of Child and Adolescent Psychiatry, 17,* 640–645.

Campbell, S. B. (1975). Mother-child interaction: A comparison of hyperactive, learning disabled, and normal boys. *American Journal of Orthopsychiatry, 45,* 51–57.

Campbell, S. B. (1985). Hyperactivity in preschoolers: Correlates and prognostic implications. *Clinical Psychology Review, 5,* 405–428.

Campbell, S. B. (1993). Some issues in identifying problem behaviors in very young children. *The ADHD Report, 1,* 5–6.

Campbell, S. B. (1995). Behavior problems in preschool children: A review of recent research. *Journal of Child Psychology and Psychiatry in Allied Disciplines, 36,* 113–149.

Campbell, S. B., Breaux, A. M., Ewing, L. J., & Szumowski, E. K. (1986). Correlates and predictors of hyperactivity and aggression: A longitudinal study of parent-referred problem preschoolers. *Journal of Abnormal Child Psychology, 14,* 217–234.

Campbell, S. B., Breaux, A. M., Ewing, L. J., Szumowski, E. K., & Pierce, E. W. (1986). Parent-identified problem preschoolers: Mother-child interaction during play at intake and 1-year follow-up. *Journal of Abnormal Child Psychology, 14,* 425–440.

Campbell, S. B., & Cluss, P. (1982). Peer relationships or young children with behavior problems. In K. H. Rubin & H. S. Ross (Eds.), *Peer relationships and social skills in childhood.* New York: Springer-Verlag.

Campbell, S. B., Endman, M. W., & Bernfeld, G. A. (1977). A three-year follow-up of hyperactive preschoolers into elementary school. *Journal of Child Psychology and Psychiatry, 18,* 239–249.

Campbell, S. B., & Ewing, L. J. (1990). Follow-up of hard-to-manage preschoolers: Adjustment at age 9 and predictors of continuing symptoms. *Journal of Child Psychology and Psychiatry, 31,* 871–890.

Campbell, S. B., Ewing, L. J., Breaux, A. M., & Szumowski, E. K. (1986). Parent-referred problem three-year-olds: Follow-up at school entry. *Journal of Child Psychology and Psychiatry and Allied Disciplines, 27,* 473–488.

Campbell, S. B., & Paulauskas, S. (1979). Peer relations in hyperactive children. *Journal of Child Psychology and Psychiatry, 20,* 233–246.

Campbell, S. B., Szumowski, E. K., Ewing, L. J., Gluck, D. S., & Breaux, A. M. (1982). A multi-dimensional assessment of parent-identified behavior problem toddlers. *Journal of Abnormal Child Psychology, 10,* 569–592.

Campbell, S. B., Tamburrino, M. B., Evans, C. L., & Franco, K. N. (1995). Fluoxetine for ADHD in a young child [Letters to the editor]. *Journal of the American Academy of Child and Adolescent Psychiatry, 34,* 10.

Cantor, D. S. (1990). Neurometrics in neuropsychological practice. *Bulletin of the National Academy of Neuropsychologists, 7,* 6–10.

Cantwell, D. P. (1972). Psychiatric illness in the families of hyperactive children. *Archives of General Psychiatry, 27,* 411 417.

Cantwell, D. P. (1975). Genetics of hyperactivity. *Journal of Child Psychology and Psychiatry, 16,* 261–264.

Cantwell, D. P. (1979). The "hyperactive" child. *Hospital Practice, 14,* 65–73.

Cantwell, D. P. (1984). The attention deficit disorder syndrome current knowledge, future needs. *Journal of the American Academy of Child and Adolescent Psychiatry, 23,* 315–318.

Cantwell, D. P. (1985). The attention deficit disorder syndrome: Current knowledge, future needs: Response. *Journal of the American Academy of Child Psychiatry, 24,* 115–116.

Cantwell, D. P. (1993). Effects of emotion on perceptual asymmetry in adolescent inpatients with attention-deficit hyperactivity disorder: Discussion. *Journal of the American Academy of Child and Adolescent Psychiatry, 32,* 322–323.

Cantwell, D. P., & Baker, L. (1977). Psychiatric disorder in children with speech and language retardation. *Archives of General Psychiatry, 34,* 583–591.

Cantwell, D. P., & Baker, L. (1984). The attention deficit disorder syndrome current knowledge, future needs. *Journal of the American Academy of Child Psychiatry, 23,* 315–318.

Cantwell, D. P., & Baker, L. (1985). Psychiatric and learning disorders in children with speech and language disorders: A descriptive analysis. *Advances in Learning and Behavioral Disabilities, 4,* 29–47.

Cantwell, D. P., & Baker, L. (1987). Differential diagnosis of hyperactivity. Response to commentary. *Journal of Developmental Behavioral Pediatrics, 8,* 159–165, 169–170.

Cantwell, D. P., & Baker, L. (1988). Issues in classification of child and adolescent psychopathology. *Journal of the American Academy of Child and Adolescent Psychiatry, 27,* 521–533.

Cantwell, D. P., & Baker, L. (1989). Stability and natural history of *DSM-III* childhood diagnoses. *Journal of the American Academy of Child and Adolescent Psychiatry, 28,* 691–700.

Cantwell, D. P., & Baker, L. (1991). Association between attention-deficit hyperactivity disorder and learning disorders. *Journal of Learning Disabilities, 24*(2), 88–95.

Cantwell, D. P., & Baker, L. (1992). Attention deficit disorder with and without hyperactivity: A review and comparison of matched groups. *Journal of the American Academy of Child and Adolescent Psychiatry, 31,* 432–438.

Cantwell, D. P., Baker, L., & Mattison, R. (1981). Prevalence, type and correlates of psychiatric disorder in 200 children with communication disorder. *Journal of Developmental and Behavioral Pediatrics, 2,* 131–136.

Cantwell, D. P., & Carlson, G. A. (1978). Stimulants. In J. S. Werry (Ed.), *Pediatric psychopharmacology: The use of behavior modifying drugs in children.* New York: Brunner/Mazel.

Cantwell, D. P., Lewinsohn, P. M., Rhode, P., & Seeley, J. (1997). Correspondence between adolescent report and parent report of psychiatric diagnostic data. *Journal of the American Academy of Child and Adolescent Psychiatry, 36,* 610–619.

Cantwell, D. P., & Satterfield, J. H. (1978). The prevalence of academic underachievement in hyperactive children. *Journal of Pediatric Psychology, 3,* 168–171.

Cantwell, D. P., & Swanson, J. M. (1997). Does methylphenidate influence cognitive performance? [Letter to the editor–reply]. *Journal of the American Academy of Child and Adolescent Psychiatry, 36*(10), 1323–1324.

Caplan, V. J., Polatajko, H. J., Wilson, B. N., & Faris, P. D. (1993). Re-examination of sensory integration treatment: A combination of two efficacy studies. *Journal of Learning Disabilities, 26,* 342–347.

Capute, A. J. (1991). The "expanded" Strauss syndrome: MBD revisited. In P. J. Accardo, T. A. Blondis, & B. Y. Whitman (Eds.), *Attention deficit disorders and hyperactivity in children.* New York: Marcel Dekker.

Cardon, L. R., Smith, S. D., Fulker, D. W., Kimberling, W. J., Pennington, B. F., & De Fries, J. C. (1994). Quantitative trait locus for reading disability in chromosome 6. *Science, 266,* 276–279.

Caresia, L., Pugnetti, L., Besana, R., Barteselli, F., Cazzullo, A. G., Musetti, L., & Scarone, S. (1984). EEG and clinical findings during pemoline treatment in children and adults with attention deficit disorder. *Neuropsychobiology, 11,* 158–167.

Carey, W. B. (1970). A simplified method for measuring infant temperament. *Journal of Pediatrics, 77,* 188–194.

Carey, W. B. (1988). A suggested solution to the confusion in attention deficit diagnoses. *Clinical Pediatrics, 27,* 348–349.

Carlson, C. L., Lahey, B. B., Frame, C. L., & Walker, J. (1987). Sociometric status of clinic-referred children with attention deficit disorders with and without hyperactivity. *Journal of Abnormal Child Psychology, 15,* 537–547.

Carlson, C. L., Lahey, B. B., Frame, C. L., Walker, J., & Hynd, G. W. (1989). Sociometric status of clinic-referred children with attention deficit disorders with and without hyperactivity—Errata. *Journal of Abnormal Child Psychology, 17,* 371.

Carlson, C. L., Lahey, B. B., & Neeper, R. (1986). Direct assessment of the cognitive correlates of attention deficit disorders with and without hyperactivity. *Journal of Psychopathology and Behavioral Assessment, 8,* 69–86.

Carlson, C. L., Pelham, W. E., Milich, R., & Dixon, J. (1992). Single and combined effects of methylphenidate and behavior therapy on the classroom performance of children with attention-deficit hyperactivity disorder. *Journal of Abnormal Child Psychology, 20,* 213–232.

Carlson, C. L., Pelham, W. E., Milich, R., & Hoza, B. (1993). ADHD boys' performance and attributions following success and failure: Drug effects and individual differences. *Cognitive Therapy and Research, 17,* 269–287.

Carlson, C. L., Pelham, W. E., Swanson, J. M., & Wagner, J. L. (1991). A divided attention analysis of the effects of methylphenidate on the arithmetic performance of children with attention-deficit hyperactivity disorder. *Journal of Child Psychology and Psychiatry, 32,* 463–471.

Carlson, G. A. (1983). Bipolar affective disorders in childhood and adolescence. In D. P. Cantwell & G. A. Carlson (Eds.), *Affective disorders in childhood and adolescence* (pp. 61–83). New York: Spectrum.

Carlson, G. A., & Cantwell, D. P. (1980). Unmasking masked depression in children and adolescents. *American Journal of Psychiatry, 137,* 4.

Carlson, G. A., Rapport, M. D., Kelly, K. L., & Pataki, C. S. (1992). The effects of methylphenidate and lithium on attention and activity level. *Journal of the American Academy of Child and Adolescent Psychiatry, 31,* 262–270.

Carlson, G. A., & Weintraub, S. (1993). Childhood behavior problems and bipolar disorder: Relationship or coincidence? *Journal of Affective Disorders, 28,* 143–153.

Carney, R. M., Levin, M. E., & Levin, J. R. (1993). Mnemonic strategies: Instructional techniques worth remembering. *Teaching Exceptional Children, 4,* 24–30.

Carnine, D. W. (1976). Effects of two teacher presentation rates on off-task behavior. Answering correctly and participation. *Journal of Applied Behavior Analysis, 9,* 199–206.

Caron, C., & Rutter, M. (1991). Comorbidity in child psychopathology: Concepts, issues and research strategies. *Journal of Child Psychology ad Psychiatry, 32,* 1063–1080.

Carroll, K. M., & Rounsaville, B. J. (1993). History and significance and childhood attention deficit disorder in treatment-seeking cocaine abusers. *Comprehensive Psychiatry, 34,* 75–82.

Carter, B. D., Zelko, F. A., Oas, P. T., & Waltonen, S. (1990). A comparison of ADD/H children and clinical controls on the Kaufman assessment battery for children (K-ABC). *Journal of Psychoeducational Assessment, 8,* 155–164.

Carter, C. M., Urbanowicz, M., Hemsley, L., Mantilla, L., Stroebel, S., Graham, P. J., & Taylor, E. (1993). Effects of a few food diets in attention deficit disorder. *Archives of Disease in Childhood, 69,* 564–568.

Carter, E. N., & Reynolds, J. N. (1976). Imitation in the treatment of a hyperactive child. *Psychotherapy: Theory, Research and Practice, 13,* 160–161.

Carter, J. F. (1993, Spring). Self-management: Education's ultimate goal. *Teaching Exceptional Children,* 28–31.

Cartlege, G., & Milburn, J. F. (1980). *Teaching social skills to children.* New York: Pergamon Press.

Cartlege, G., & Milburn, J. F. (1995). *Teaching social skills to children and youth: Innovative approaches* (3rd ed.). Boston: Allyn & Bacon.

Casat, C. D. (1982). The under- and over-diagnosis of mania in children and adolescents. *Comprehensive Psychiatry, 23,* 552–559.

Casat, C. D., Cherek, C., Van Davelaar, M. J., & Pearson, D. (1994). Methylphenidate effects on a lab aggression paradigm in attention deficit hyperactivity disorder (ADHD). *Psychopharmacology Bulletin, 30,* 658.

Casat, C. D., Pearson, D. A., Van Davelaar, M. J., & Cherek, D. R. (1995). Methylphenidate effects on a laboratory aggression measure in children with ADHD. *Psychopharmacology Bulletin, 31,* 353–356.

Casat, C. D., Pleasants, D. Z., Schroeder, D. H., & Parler, D. W. (1989). Bupropion in children with attention deficit disorder. *Psychopharmacology Bulletin, 25,* 198–201.

Casat, C. D., Pleasants, D. Z., & Van Wyck Fleet, J. (1987). A double blind trial of bupropion in children with attention deficit disorder. *Psychopharmacology Bulletin, 23,* 120–122.

Casey, B. J., Giedd, J., Vauss, Y., Vaituzis, C. K., & Rapoport, J. L. (1992). Selective attention and the anterior cingulate: A developmental neuroanatomical study. *Society of Neuroscience Abstracts, 18,* 332.

Casey, J. E., Rourke, B. B., & Del Dotto, J. E. (1996). Learning disabilities in children with attention deficit disorder with and without hyperactivity. *Child Neuropsychology, 2,* 83–98.

Caspi, A., & Silva, P. A. (1995). Temperamental qualities at age three predict personality traits in young adulthood: Longitudinal evidence from a birth cohort. *Child Development, 66,* 486–498.

Castellanos, F. X., Elia, J., Kruesi, M. J. P., Marsh, W. L., Gulotta, C. S., Potter, W. Z., Ritchie, G. F., Hamburger, S. D., & Rapoport, J. L. (1996). Cerebrospinal fluid homovanillic acid predicts behavioral response to stimulants in 45 boys with attention deficit/hyperactivity disorder. *Neuropsychopharmacology, 14,* 125–137.

Castellanos, F. X., Giedd, J. N., Eckburg, P., Marsh, W., Kozuch, P., King, A., Hamburger, S., Ritchie, G., & Rapoport, J. (1994). Quantitative morphology of the caudate nucleus in attention deficit hyperactivity disorder. *American Journal of Psychiatry, 151,* 1791–1796.

Castellanos, F. X., Giedd, J. N., Marsh, W. L., Hamburger, S. D., Vaituzis, A. C., Dickstein, D. P., Sarfatti, S. E., Vauss, Y. C., Snell, J. W., Rajapakse, J. C., & Rapoport, J. L. (1996). Quantitative brain magnetic resonance imaging in attention-deficit hyperactivity disorder. *Archives of General Psychiatry, 53,* 607–616.

Casti, J. (1989). *Paradigms lost.* New York: Avon Books.

Caufield, J. B., & Rattan, G. (1996). *Empirical evaluation of Barkley's "new theory" of attention deficit hyperactivity disorder employing a computerized version of the Wisconsin card sorting test.* Paper submitted for publication.

Caul, J. D. (1985). Psychological and behavioral development of infants and children. In V. C. Kelley (Ed.), *Practice of pediatrics.* Philadelphia: Harper & Row.

Cavanagh, R., Clifford, J. S., & Gregory, W. L. (1989). The use of bromocriptine for the treatment of attention deficit disorder in two chemically dependent patients. *Journal of Psychoactive Drugs, 21,* 217–220.

Ceaser, L. D. (1986). *Comprehension capers: Main ideas and inferences.* Belmont, CA: David S. Lake.

Center for Human Development. (1996). *Temperament talk: A guide to understanding your child.* LeGrange, OR: Author.

Cermak, S. A. (1988a). The relationship between attention deficit and sensory integration disorders, Part One. *Sensory Integration, Special Interest Section Newsletter, 11*(2), 1–4.

Cermak, S. A. (1988b). The relationship between attention deficit and sensory integration disorders, Part Two. *Sensory Integration, Special Interest Section Newsletter, 11*(3), 1–4.

Chan, D. A., Marcotte, A. C., Stern, R. A., Arruda, J. E., Akshomoff, M. A., & Leshko, I. C. (1995, October). *Qualitative features of visual, constructional performance in children with ADHD.* Paper presented at the meeting of the National Academy of Neuropsychology, San Francisco.

Chandler, M. L., Branhill, J. L., Gualtieri, C. T., & Patterson, D. R. (1989). Letters to the editor. *Journal of Clinical Psychopharmacology, 9,* 69.

Chandola, C. A., Robling, M. R., Peters, T. J., Melville-Thomas, G., & McGuffin, P. (1993). Pre- and perinatal factors and the risk of subsequent referral for hyperactivity. *Journal of Child Psychology and Psychiatry and Allied Disciplines, 33*(6), 1077–1090.

Chappell, P. B., Riddle, M. A., Scahill, L., Lynch, K. A., Schultz, R., Arnsten, A., Leckman, J. F., & Cohen, D. J. (1995). Guanfacine treatment of comorbid attention-deficit hyperactivity disorder and Tourette's syndrome. *Journal of the American Academy of Child and Adolescent Psychiatry, 34,* 1140–1146.

Chappell, P. B., Riddle, M., Scahill, L., Schultz, R., & Leckman, J. (1994). Guanfacine treatment of children with attention deficit hyperactivity disorder (ADHD) and tics: Preliminary clinical experience. *Psychopharmacology Bulletin, 30,* 659.

Charles, L., Schain, R. J., & Zelniker, T. (1981). Optimal dosages of methylphenidate for improving the learning and behavior of hyperactive children. *Behavioral Pediatrics, 2,* 78–81.

Charles, L., Schain, R. J., Zelniker, T., & Guthrie, D. (1979). Effects of methylphenidate on hyperactive children's ability to sustain attention. *Pediatrics, 64,* 412–418.

Chase, S. N., & Clement, P. W. (1985). Effects of self-reinforcement and stimulants on academic performance in children with attention deficit disorder. *Journal of Clinical Child Psychology, 14,* 323–333.

Chase-Lansdell, P. L., Cherlan, A. J., & Kiernan, K. E. (1995). The long-term effects of parental divorce on the mental health of young adults: A developmental perspective. *Child Development, 66,* 1614–1634.

Chee, P., Logan, G., Schachar, R. J., & Lindsay, P. (1989). Effects of event rate and display on time on sustained attention in hyperactive, normal, and control children. *Journal of Abnormal Child Psychology, 17,* 371–391.

Chelune, G. J., Ferguson, W., Koon, R., & Dickey, T. O. (1986). Frontal lobe disinhibition in attention deficit disorder. *Child Psychiatry and Human Development, 16,* 221–232.

Chen, W. J., Faraone, S. V., Biederman, J., & Tsuang, M. T. (1994). Diagnosis accuracy of the child behavior checklist scales for attention-deficit hyperactivity disorder: A receiver-operating characteristic analysis. *Journal of Consulting and Clinical Psychology, 62*(5), 1017–1025.

Chen, Y. C., Wang, Y. F., & Yang, X. L. (1985). An epidemiological investigation of minimal brain dysfunction in six elementary schools in Bejing. *Journal of Child Psychology and Psychiatry, 26,* 777–787.

Cherkes-Julkowski, M., Stolzenberg, J., & Siegal, L. (1991). Prompted cognitive testing as a diagnostic compensation for attentional deficits: The Raven standard progressive matrices and attention deficit disorder. *Learning Disabilities, 2,* 1–7.

Christian, R. E., Frick, P. J., Hill, N. L., Tyler, L., & Frazer, D. R. (1996). Psychopathy and conduct problems in children: II. Implications for subtyping children with conduct problems. *Journal of the American Academy of Child and Adolescent Psychiatry, 36,* 233–241.

Christie, D. J., Hiss, M., & Lozanoff, B. (1984). Modification of inattentive classroom behavior: Hyperactive children's use of self-recording with teacher guidance. *Behavior Modification, 8,* 391–406.

CIBA Geneva Pharmaceuticals. (1996, January). *Letter to doctors.* Summit, NJ: Author.

CIBA Pharmaceuticals. (1974). *NBD compendium* (Vol. 1, pp. 1–12). Summit, NJ: Author.

Cicchetti, D., & Toth, S. L. (1995). A developmental psychopathology perspective on child abuse and neglect. *Journal of the American Academy of Child and Adolescent Psychiatry, 34,* 541–565.

Clampit, M. K., & Silver, S. J. (1989). Distribution of relative attention deficits on the WISC-R by age, sex, social class, and region. *Journal of Learning Disabilities, 22,* 258–259.

Clark, L. (1986). *SOS: Help for parents.* Bowling Green, KY: Parent's Press.

Clark, L., & Elliott, S. (1988). The influence of treatment strength information on knowledgable teachers' pretreatment evaluations of social skills training methods. *Professional School Psychology, 3,* 241–251.

Clark, M. L., Cheyne, J. A., Cunningham, C. E., & Siegel, L. S. (1988). Dyadic peer interaction and task orientation in attention deficit disordered children. *Journal of Abnormal Child Psychology, 16,* 1–15.

Clausen, J. A. (1987). Health and life course: Some personal observations. *Journal of Health and Social Behavior, 28,* 236–344.

Clayton, A. H. (1995). Antidepressant-induced tardive dyskinesia: Review and case report. *Psychopharmacology Bulletin, 31,* 259–264.

Clement, P. W., Anderson, E. E., Arnold, J. H., Butman, R. E., Fantuzzo, J. W., & Mays, R. (1978). Self-observation and self-reinforcement as sources of self-control in children. *Biofeedback Self-Regulation, 3,* 247–267.

Clements, S. D., & Peters, J. E. (1962). Minimal brain dysfunctions in the school-aged child. *Archives of General Psychiatry, 6,* 185–197.

Cleveland, S. (1997). Central auditory processing disorder: When is evaluation referral indicated? *The ADHD Report, 5,* 9–12.

Cobb, D. E., & Evans, J. R. (1981). The use of biofeedback techniques with school-aged children exhibiting behavioral and/or learning problems. *Journal of Abnormal Child Psychology, 9,* 251–281.

Cocciarella, A., Wood, R., & Lowe, K. G. (1995). Brief behavioral treatment for ADHD. *Perceptual Motor Skills, 81,* 225–226.

Cochran, M., & Brassard, J. A. (1979). Child development and personal social networks. *Child Development, 50,* 601–615.

Cococres, J. A., Patel, M. D., Gold, M. S., & Pottash, A. C. (1987). Cocaine abuse, attention deficit disorder and bipolar disorder. *Journal of Nervous and Mental Disease, 175,* 431–432.

Cody, H., Hynd, G. W., & Hall, L. J. (1996, November). *Depression symptomatology as a distinguishing characteristic between ADHD inattentive and combined subtypes.* Paper presented at the National Academy of Neuropsychology annual conference, New Orleans, LA.

Cohen, L. S., & Biederman, J. (1988). Further evidence for an association between affective disorders and anxiety disorders: Review and case reports. *Journal of Clinical Psychiatry, 49,* 313–316.

Cohen, M. (1985). Serum carnosinase deficiency: A non-disabling phenotype? *Journal of Mental Deficiency Research, 29*(4), 383–389.

Cohen, M. (1988). The revised Conners parent rating scale: Factor structure replication with a diversified clinical sample. *Journal of Abnormal Child Psychology, 16*(2), 187–196.

Cohen, M., Becker, M. G., & Campbell, R. (1990). Relationships among four methods of assessment of children with attention deficit hyperactivity disorder. *Journal of School Psychology, 28,* 189–202.

Cohen, M., & Hynd, G. W. (1986). The Conners Teacher's Rating Scale: A different factor structure with special education children. *Psychology in the Schools, 23,* 13–23.

Cohen, M. J., Riccio, C. A., & Gonzalez, J. J. (1994). Methodological differences in the diagnosis of attention-deficit hyperactivity disorder: Impact on prevalence. *Journal of Emotional and Behavioral Disorders, 2*, 31–38.

Cohen, M. J., Sullivan, S., Minde, K. K., Novak, C., & Helwig, C. (1981). Evaluation of the relative effectiveness of methylphenidate and cognitive behavior modification in the treatment of kindergarten-aged hyperactive children. *Journal of Abnormal Child Psychology, 9*, 43–54.

Cohen, N. J., Davine, M., Horodezky, N., Lipsett, L., & Isaacson, L. (1993). Unsuspected language impairment in psychiatrically disturbed children: Prevalence and language and behavioral characteristics. *Journal of the American Academy of Child and Adolescent Psychiatry, 32*, 595–603.

Cohen, N. J., Davine, M., & Meloche-Kelly, M. (1989). Prevalence of unsuspected language disorders in a child psychiatric population. *Journal of the American Academy of Child and Adolescent Psychiatry, 28*, 107–111.

Cohen, N. J., Douglas, V. I., Morgenstern, G. (1971). The effect of methylphenidate on attentive behavior and autonomic activity in hyperactive children. *Psychopharmacology Bulletin, 22*, 282.

Cohen, N. J., Weiss, G., & Minde, K. (1972). Cognitive styles in adolescents previously diagnosed as hyperactive. *Journal of Child Psychology and Psychiatry, 13*, 203–209.

Cohen, P., Cohen, J., & Brook, J. S. (1993). An epidemiological study of disorders in late childhood and adolescence: II. Persistence of disorders. *Journal of Child Psychology and Psychiatry and Allied Disciplines, 34*, 869–877.

Cohen, P., Cohen, J., Kasen, S., Velez, C. (1993). An epidemiological study of disorders in late childhood and adolescence: I. Age- and gender-specific prevalence. *Journal of Child Psychology and Psychiatry and Allied Disciplines, 34*, 851–867.

Cohen, S., & Bromet, E. (1992). Maternal predictors of behavioral disturbance in preschool children: A research note. *Journal of Child Psychology and Psychiatry in Allied Disciplines, 33*, 941–946.

Coie, J. D., Dodge, K. A., & Coppotelli, H. (1982). Dimensions and types of social status: A cross-age perspective. *Developmental Psychology, 18*, 557–570.

Coie, J. D., & Kuperschmidt, J. B. (1983). A behavioral analysis of emerging social status in boys' groups. *Child Development, 54*, 1400–1416.

Coleman, W. S. (1988). *Attention deficit disorders, hyperactivity and associated disorders: A handbook for parents and professionals* (5th ed.). Madison, WI: Calliope Books.

Colgan, M., & Colgan, L. (1984). Do nutrient supplements and dietary changes affect learning and emotional reactions of children with learning difficulties? A controlled series of 16 cases. *Nutrition and Health, 3*, 69–77.

Coll, P. G., & Bland, R. (1979). Manic-depressive illness in adolescence and childhood. *Canadian Journal of Psychiatry, 24*, 255–263.

Collier, C. P., Soldin, S. J., Swanson, J. M., MacLeod, S. M., Weinberg, F., & Rochefort, J. G. (1985). Pemoline pharmacokinetics and long-term therapy in children with attention deficit disorder and hyperactivity. *Clinical Pharmacokinetics, 10*, 269–278.

Collins, B. E., Whalen, C. K., & Henker, B. (1980). Ecological and pharmacological influences on behaviors in the classroom. The hyperkinetic behavioral syndrome. In S. Salzinger, J. Antrobus, & J. Glick (Eds.), *The ecosystem of the "sick" child*. New York: Academic Press.

Colvin, G. T., & Sugai, G. M. (1988). Proactive strategies for managing social behavior problems: An instructional approach. *Education and Treatment of Children, 11*, 341–348.

Comalli, P. E., Wapner, S., & Werner, H. (1962). Interference effects of Stroop color-wood test in childhood, adulthood and aging. *Journal of Genetic Psychology, 100*, 47–52.

Comings, D. E. (1990). *Tourette's syndrome and human behavior*. Duarte, CA: Hope Press.

Comings, D. E. (1994). Genetic factors in substance abuse based on studies of Tourette syndrome and ADHD probands and relatives: I. Drug Abuse. *Drug and Alcohol Dependence, 35*(1), 1–16.

Comings, D. E., & Comings, B. G. (1990). A controlled family history study of Tourette's syndrome: I. Attention-deficit hyperactivity disorder and learning disorders. *Journal of Clinical Psychiatry, 51,* 275–280.

Comings, D. E., Comings, B. G., Tacket, T., & Li, S. (1990). The clonidine patch and behavior problems [Letters to the editor]. *Journal of the American Academy of Child and Adolescent Psychiatry, 29,* 667–668.

Comings, D. E., Wu, S., & Chiu, C. (1996). Polygenic inheritance of Tourette syndrome, stuttering, attention deficit hyperactivity, conduct and oppositional defiant disorder. *American Journal of Medical Genetics (Neuropsychiatric Genetics), 67,* 264–288.

Committee for Children. (1992). *Second step: A violence prevention curriculum (Preschool-kindergarten teacher's guide).* Seattle, WA: Author.

Compas, V. E., Ley, S., & Grant, K. E. (1993). Taxonomy, assessment and diagnosis of depression during adolescence. *Psychological Bulletin, 114,* 323–344.

Condor, A., Anderson, V., & Saling, M. (1995). Do reading disabled children have planning problems? *Developmental Neuropsychology, 11,* 485–502.

Conners, C. K. (1969). A teacher rating scale for use with drug studies with children. *American Journal of Psychiatry, 126,* 885–888.

Conners, C. K. (1970). Symptom patterns in hyperkinetic, neurotic and normal children. *Child Development, 41,* 667–682.

Conners, C. K. (1972). Symposium: Behavior modification of drugs: II. Psychological effects of stimulant drugs in children with minimal brain dysfunction. *Pediatrics, 49,* 702–708.

Conners, C. K. (1973). Rating scales for use in drug studies with children: Pharmacotherapy with children [Special issue]. *Psychopharmacology Bulletin, 2,* 84.

Conners, C. K. (1975a). Minimal brain dysfunction and psychopathology in children. In A. Davids (Ed.), *Child personality and psychopathology: Vol. 2. Current topics.* New York: Wiley.

Conners, C. K. (1975b). Control trial of methylphenidate in preschool children with minimal brain dysfunction. *International Journal of Mental Health, 4,* 61–74.

Conners, C. K. (1980). *Food additives and hyperactive children.* New York: Plenum Press.

Conners, C. K. (1982). Parent and teacher rating forms for the assessment of hyperkinesis in children. In P. A. Keller & L. G. Ritt (Eds.), *Innovations in clinical practice: A sourcebook* (Vol. 1). Sarasota, FL: Professional Resource Exchange.

Conners, C. K. (1987). How is the Teacher Rating Scale used in the diagnosis of attention deficit disorder? In J. Loney (Ed.), *The young hyperactive child: Answers to questions about diagnosis, prognosis and treatment* (p. 142). New York: Haworth Press.

Conners, C. K. (1989a). *Conners' teacher rating scales.* Toronto: Multi-Health Systems.

Conners, C. K. (1989b). *Conners' parent rating scales.* Toronto: Multi-Health Systems.

Conners, C. K. (1989c). *Feeding the brain: How foods affect children.* New York: Plenum Press.

Conners, C. K. (1990, Spring/Summer). How food affects behavior and learning in children. *CH.A.D.D.ER,* 10.

Conners, C. K. (1994). An interview with C. Keith Conners, Ph.D. *Attention, 1,* 7–9.

Conners, C. K. (1995). *Continuous performance test.* North Tonawanda, NY: Multi-Health Systems.

Conners, C. K. (1996). Letter to the editor. *The ADHD Report, 4,* 13.

Conners, C. K. (1997). *Conners rating scales* (Rev.). North Tonawanda, NY: Multi-Health Systems.

Conners, C. K., Eisenberg, L., & Barcai, A. (1967). Effect of dextroamphetamine on children: Studies on subjects with learning disabilities and school behavior problems. *Archives of General Psychiatry, 17,* 478–485.

Conners, C. K., Eisenberg, L., & Sharpe, L. (1964). Effects of methylphenidate (Ritalin) on paired-associate learning and Porteus maze performance in emotionally disturbed children. *Journal of Consulting and Clinical Psychology, 28,* 14–22.

Conners, C. K., Levin, E. D., March, J., Sparrow, E., & Erhard, D. (1995). Neurocognitive and behavioral effects of nicotine in adult attention deficit hyperactivity disorder (ADHD). *Psychopharmacology Bulletin, 31,* 559.

Conners, C. K., Levin, E. D., Sparrow, E., Hinton, S. C., et al. (1996). Nicotine and attention in adult attention deficit hyperactivity disorder. *Psychopharmacology Bulletin, 32,* 67–74.

Conners, C. K., March, J. S., Fiore, C., & Butcher, T. (1993). *Information processing deficits in ADHD: Effects of stimulus rate and methylphenidate.* Paper presented at the 32nd annual meeting of the American College of Neuropsychopharmacology, Honolulu, HI.

Conners, C. K., & Rothchild, G. H. (1968). Drugs and learning in children. In J. Helmuth (Ed.), *Learning disorders* (Vol. 3, pp. 192–223). Seattle, WA: Special Child Publications.

Conners, C. K., & Taylor, E. (1980). Pemoline, methylphenidate and placebo in children with minimal brain dysfunction. *Archives of General Psychiatry, 37,* 922–930.

Conners, C. K., Taylor, E., Meo, G., Kurtz, M. A., & Fournier, M. (1972). Magnesium pemoline and dextroamphetamine: A controlled study in children with minimal brain dysfunction. *Psychopharmocologia, 26,* 321–336.

Conners, C. K., & Wells, K. C. (1985). ADD-H adolescent self-report scale. *Psychopharmacology Bulletin, 21,* 921–922.

Conners, C. K., & Wells, K. C. (1986). *Hyperkinetic children: A neuropsychosocial approach.* Beverly Hills, CA: Sage.

Conners, C. K., & Werry, J. S. (1979). *Psychopathological disorders of childhood* (2nd ed.). New York: Wiley.

Connoloy, A. J., Nachtman, W., & Pritchett, E. M. (1976). *Key math diagnostic arithmetic test.* Circle Pines, MN: American Guidance Service.

Connor, D. F., & Swanson, J. M. (1997). Safety of combined pharmacotherapy [Letter to the editor–reply]. *Journal of the American Academy of Child and Adolescent Psychiatry, 36*(11), 1489–1490.

Constantino, G., Collin-Malgady, G., Malgady, R. G., & Perez, A. (1991). Assessment of attention deficit disorder using a thematic apperception technique. *Journal of Personality Assessment, 57,* 87–95.

Constantino, G., Malgady, R., & Rogler, L. H. (1988). *Tell me a story manual.* Los Angeles, CA: Western Psychological Services.

Cook, E. H., Stein, M. A., & Krasowski, M. D. (1995). Association of attention deficit disorder and the dopamine transporter gene. *American Journal of Human Genetics, 56,* 993–998.

Coombs, R. H., Wellisch, D. K., & Fawzy, F. I. (1985). Drinking patterns and problems among female children and adolescents: A comparison of abstainers, past users and current users. *American Journal of Drug and Alcohol Abuse, 11,* 315–348.

Cooper, L. J., Wacker, D. P., Millard, T., Derby, R., & Mark, K. (1993). Assessing environmental and medication variables in an outpatient setting: A proposed model and preliminary results with ADHD children [Special issue]. *Pharmacotherapy Journal of Developmental and Physical Disabilities, 5,* 71–85.

Copeland, A. P. (1979). Types of private speech produced by hyperactive and nonhyperactive boys. *Journal of Abnormal Child Psychology, 7,* 169–177.

Copeland, L., Wolraich, M., Lindgren, S., Milich, R., & Woolson, R. (1987). Pediatricians' reported practices in the assessment and treatment of attention deficit disorders. *Journal of Developmental and Behavioral Pediatrics, 8,* 191–197.

Corbett, J. A. (1985). Mental retardation: Psychiatric aspects. In M. Rutter & L. Hesov (Eds.), *Child and adolescent psychiatry.* London: Blackwell.

Corkum, P. B., Beig, S., Tannock, R., & Moldofsky, H. (1997). *Comorbidity: The potential link between ADHD and sleep problems.* Paper presented at the annual meeting of the American Academy of Child and Adolescent Psychiatry, Toronto, Canada.

Corkum, P. V., Schachar, R. J., & Siegel, L. S. (1996). Performance on the continuous performance task and the impact of reward. *Journal of Attention Disorders, 1,* 114–121.

Corkum, P. V., & Siegel, L. S. (1993). Is the Continuous Performance Task a valuable research tool for use with children with attention-deficit-hyperactivity disorder? *Journal of Child Psychology and Psychiatry and Allied Disciplines, 34,* 1217–1239.

Cornett-Ruiz, S., & Hendricks, B. (1993). Effects of labeling and ADHD behaviors on peer and teacher judgments. *Journal of Educational Research, 86,* 349–355.

Costello, E. J. (1989a). Child psychiatric disorders and their correlates: A primary care pediatric sample. *Journal of the American Academy of Child and Adolescent Psychiatry, 28,* 851–855.

Costello, E. J. (1989b). Developments in child psychiatric epidemiology. *Journal of the American Academy of Child and Adolescent Psychiatry, 28,* 836–841.

Costello, E. J., Edelbrock, C. S., Dulcan, M. K., & Kalas, R. (1984). *Testing of the NIMH diagnostic interview schedule for children (DISC) in a clinical population: Final report* (Contract No. RFP-DB-81-0027). Rockville, MD: Center for Epidemiological Studies, National Institute for Mental Health.

Costello, E. J., Loeber, R., Stouthamer-Loeber, M. (1991). Pervasive and situational hyperactivity-confounding effect of informant: A research note. *Journal of Child Psychology and Psychiatry and Allied Disciplines, 32*(2), 367–376.

Cotugno, A. J. (1993). The diagnosis of ADHD in community mental health centers: Where and when? *Psychology in the Schools, 30,* 338–344.

Cotugno, A. J. (1995). Personality attributes of attention deficit hyperactivity disorder using the Rorschach ink blot test. *Journal of Clinical Psychology, 5,* 554–562.

Coulton, C. J., Korbin, J. E., Su, M., & Chow, J. (1995). Community level factors and child maltreatment rates. *Child Development, 66,* 1262–1276.

Cousins, L. S., & Weiss, G. (1993). Parent training and social skills training for children with attention-deficit hyperactivity disorder: How can they be combined for greater effectiveness? *Canadian Journal of Psychiatry, 38,* 449–457.

Covey, S. (1989). *The seven habits of highly effective people.* New York: Simon & Schuster.

Cowart, V. S. (1988a). Reply to behavior disorders and the Ritalin controversy. *Journal of the American Medical Association, 260,* 2219.

Cowart, V. S. (1988b). The Ritalin controversy: What's made this drug's opponents hyperactive? *Journal of the American Medical Association, 259,* 2521–2523.

Cowen, E., Pederson, A., Babigan, H., Izzo, L., & Trost, M. (1973). Long-term follow-up of early detected vulnerable children. *Journal of Consulting and Clinical Psychology, 41,* 438–446.

Cox, R. D., & Gunn, W. B. (1980). Interpersonal skills in the schools: Assessment and curriculum development. In D. P. Rathjen & J. P. Foreyt (Eds.), *Social competence: Interventions for children and adults.* New York: Pergamon Press.

Cramond, B. (1994). ADHD and creativity: What is the connection? *Journal of Creative Behavior, 28,* 193–210.

Crinella, F. M., Teixeira, J. L., Wigal, T. L., & Yu, J. (1994). Partitioning neuropsychological deficit in children with attention deficit hyperactivity disorder. *Archives of Clinical Neuropsychology, 9,* 117–118.

Crnic, K. A., & Greenberg, M. T. (1990). Minor parenting stresses with young children. *Child Development, 61,* 1628–1637.

Cromer, B. A., Tarnowski, K. J., Stein, A. M., Harton, P., & Thonton, D. J. (1990). The school breakfast program and cognition in adolescents. *Developmental and Behavioral Pediatrics, 11,* 295–300.

Cronbach, L. J., & Meehl, P. E. (1955). Construct validity in psychological tests. *Psychological Bulletin, 52,* 281–302.

Crook, W. G. (1985). Candida yeasts and behavior [Letters to the editor]. *Pediatrics, 76,* 139.

Crook, W. G. (1986). *The yeast connection: A medical breakthrough.* Jackson, TN: Professional Books.

Crook, W. G. (1991). *Help for your hyperactive child.* Jackson, TN: Professional Books.

Crouch, P. L., Gresham, F. M., & Wright, W. R. (1985). Interdependent and independent contingencies with immediate and delayed reinforcement for controlling classroom behavior. *Journal of School Psychology, 23,* 177–188.

Crouter, A. C., McDermid, S. M., McHale, S. M., & Perry-Jenkins, M. (1990). Parental monitoring and perceptions of children's school performance and conduct in dual- and single-earner families. *Developmental Psychology, 26,* 649–657.

Crowley, T. J., & Riggs, P. D. (1995). Adolescent substance use disorder with conduct disorder, and comorbid conditions. *NIDA Monograph, 156,* 49–111.

Crystal, D. (1987). Concepts of language development: A realistic perspective. In W. Yule & M. Rutter (Eds.), *Language development and disorders.* London: MacKeith Press.

Cueva, J. E., Overall, J. E., Small, A. M., Armenteros, J. G., Perry, R., & Campbell, M. (1996). Carbamazepine in aggressive children with conduct disorder: A double-blind and placebo-controlled study. *Journal of the American Academy of Child and Adolescent Psychiatry, 35,* 480–490.

Cuffe, S. P., McCullough, E. L., & Pumariega, A. J. (1994). Comorbidity of ADHD and post traumatic stress disorder. *Journal of Child and Family Studies, 3,* 327–336.

Culbert, T. P., Banez, G. A., & Reiff, M. I. (1994). Children who have attentional disorders: Interventions. *Pediatrics in Review, 15,* 5–15.

Culbert, T. P., Kajander, R. L., & Reaney, J. B. (1996). Biofeedback with children and adolescents: Clinical observations and patient perspectives. *Developmental and Behavioral Pediatrics, 17,* 342–350.

Cummins, R. A. (1991). Sensory integration and learning disabilities: Ayres' factor analyses reappraised. *Journal of Learning Disabilities, 24,* 160–168.

Cunningham, C. E. (1990). A family systems approach to parent training. In R. A. Barkley (Ed.), *Attention-deficit hyperactivity disorder: A handbook for diagnosis and treatment.* New York: Guilford Press.

Cunningham, C. E., & Barkley, R. A. (1978a). The role of academic failure in hyperactive behavior. *Journal of Learning Disabilities, 11,* 15–21.

Cunningham, C. E., & Barkley, R. A. (1978b). The effects of methylphenidate on the mother-child interaction of hyperactive identical twins. *Developmental Medicine and Child Neurology, 20,* 634–642.

Cunningham, C. E., & Barkley, R. A. (1979). The interactions of hyperactive and normal children with their mothers during free play and structured tasks. *Child Development, 50,* 217–224.

Cunningham, C. E., Benness, B. B., & Siegel, L. S. (1988). Family functioning, time allocation, and parental depression in the families of normal and ADHD children. *Journal of Clinical Child Psychology, 17,* 169–177.

Cunningham, C. E., Boyle, M., Bremner, R., & Secord-Gilbert, M. (1991). Improving the efficacy and accessibility of parent training programs: School based family system's oriented courses for parents of ADHD children. In W. E. Pelham (Chair), *Behavioral interventions for attention-deficit hyperactivity disorder: New directions for a chronic disorder.* Symposium presented at the annual conference of the Association for the Advancement of Behaviour Therapy, New York.

Cunningham, C. E., Bremner, R., & Boyle, M. (1995). A large group community-based parenting programs for families of preschoolers at risk for disruptive behavior disorders: Utilization, cost effectiveness, and outcome. *Journal of Child Psychology and Psychiatry, 36,* 1141–1159.

Cunningham, C. E., Bremner, R., & Secord, M. (1995). *The community parent education program (COPE): A school-based family systems oriented workshop for parents of children with disruptive behavior disorders.* Hamilton, Ontario, Canada.

Cunningham, C. E., Bremner, R., & Secord-Gilbert, M. (1993). Increasing the availability, accessibility, and cost efficacy of services for families of ADHD children: A school-based systems-oriented parenting course [Special issue]. *Canadian Journal of School Psychology, 9,* 1–15.

Cunningham, C. E., Clark, M. L., Heaven, R. F., Durrant, J., & Cunningham, L. J. (1989). The effects of group problem solving and contingency management procedures on the positive and negative interactions of learning disabled and attention deficit disordered children with an autistic peer. *Child and Family Behaviour Therapy, 11,* 89–106.

Cunningham, C. E., & Cunningham, L. J. (1995). Reducing playground aggression: Student-mediated conflict resolution. *The ADHD Report, 3*(4), 9–11.

Cunningham, C. E., Cunningham, L. J., Martorelli, V., Tran, A., Young, J., & Zacharias, R. (1995). *The effects of primary division student-mediated conflict resolution programs on playground aggression.* Unpublished manuscript.

Cunningham, C. E., Davis, J. R., Bremner, R., Dunn, K. W., & Rzasa, T. (1993). Coping modeling, problem solving versus mastery model: Effects on adherence, in-session process, and skill acquisition in the residential parent-training program. *Journal of Consulting and Clinical Psychology, 61,* 871–877.

Cunningham, C. E., & Siegel, L. S. (1987). Peer interactions of normal and attention-deficit disordered boys during free-play, cooperative task, and simulated classroom situations. *Journal of Abnormal Child Psychology, 15,* 247–268.

Cunningham, C. E., Siegel, L. S., & Offord, D. R. (1985). A developmental dose response analysis of the effects of methylphenidate on the peer interactions of attention-deficit disordered boys. *Journal of Child Psychology and Psychiatry, 26,* 955–971.

Cunningham, C. E., Siegel, L. S., & Offord, D. R. (1991). A dose-response analysis of the effects of methylphenidate on the peer interactions and simulated classroom performance of ADD children with and without conduct problems. *Journal of Child Psychology and Psychiatry, 32,* 439–452.

Cutler, M., Little, J. W., & Strauss, A. A. (1940). The effect of benzedrine on mentally deficient children. *American Journal of Mental Deficiency, 45,* 59–65.

Dadds, M. R., Schwartz, S., & Sanders, M. R. (1987). Marital discord and treatment outcome in behavioral treatment of child conduct disorders. *Journal of Consulting and Clinical Psychology, 55,* 396–403.

Dahl, R. E., Pelham, W. E., & Wierson, M. (1991). The role of sleep disturbances in attention deficit disorder symptoms: A case study. *Journal of Pediatric Psychology, 16*(2), 229–239.

Daigneault, S., Braun, C. M. J., & Whitaker, H. A. (1992). An empirical test of two opposing theoretical models of prefrontal function. *Brain and Cognition, 19,* 48–71.

Dailey, E. M., & Rosenberg, M. S. (1994). ADD, computers and learning. *Attention, 1,* 8–10.

Dainer, K. B., Klorman, R., Salzman, L. F., Hess, D. W., Davidson, P. W., & Michael, R. L. (1981). Learning-disordered children's evoked potentials during sustained attention. *Journal of Abnormal Child Psychology, 9,* 79–94.

Dalby, J. T., Kinsbourne, M., & Swanson, J. M. (1989). Self-paced learning in children with attention deficit disorder with hyperactivity. *Journal of Abnormal Child Psychology, 17,* 269–275.

Daly, J. M., & Fritsch, S. L. (1995). Case study: Maternal residual attention deficit disorder associated with failure to thrive in a two month old infant. *Journal of the American Academy of Child and Adolescent Psychiatry, 34,* 55–57.

Danforth, J. S., Barkley, R. A., & Stokes, D. F. (1991). Observations of parent-child interactions with hyperactive children: Research and clinical implications. *Clinical Psychology Review, 11,* 703–727.

Danziger, S., & Danziger, S. (1993). Child poverty and public policy: Toward a comprehensive anti-poverty agenda. *Daedelus, 122,* 57–84.

Das, J. P., & Melnyk, L. (1989). Attention checklist: A rating scale for mildly mentally handicapped adolescents. *Psychological Reports, 64,* 1267–1274.

Daugherty, T. K., & Quay, H. C. (1991). Response perseveration and delayed responding in childhood behavior disorders. *Journal of Child Psychology and Psychiatry, 32,* 453–461.

Daugherty, T. K., Quay, H. C., & Ramos, L. (1993). Response perseveration, inhibitory control, and central dopaminergic activity in childhood behavior disorders. *Journal of Genetic Psychology, 154,* 177–188.

Davids, A. (1971). An objective instrument for assessing hyperkinesis in children. *Journal of Learning Disabilities, 4,* 499–501.

Davila, R. R., Williams, M. L., & MacDonald, J. T. (1991). *Verification of policy to address the needs of children with attention deficit disorder within general and/or special education* [Memorandum]. United States Department of Education, Office of Special Education and Rehabilitation Services.

Davis, L., Sirotowitz, S., & Parker, H. C. (1996). *Study strategies made easy: A practical plan for school success.* Plantation, FL: Specialty Press.

DeBrueys, M. T. (Project Coordinator). (1986). *125 ways to be a better student: A program for study skill success.* Moline, IL: LinguiSystems.

Debus, R. L. (1970). Effects of brief observation of model behavior on conceptual tempo of impulsive children. *Developmental Psychology, 2,* 22–32.

Debus, R. L. (1985). Students' cognitive characteristics and classroom behavior. In T. Husen & T. N. Postlewaite (Eds.), *The international encyclopedia of education* (Vol. 8). Oxford, England: Pergamon Press.

DeFilippis, N. (1979). The historical development of the diagnostic concept of hyperkinesis. *Clinical Neuropsychology, 1,* 15–19.

De Fries, J. C., & Fulker, D. W. (1985). Multiple regression analysis of twin data. *Behavioral Genetics, 15,* 467–473.

De Fries, J. C., & Fulker, D. W. (1988). Multiple regression analysis of twin data: Etiology of deviant scores versus individual differences. *Acta Genet Med Gemmellol (Roma), 37,* 205–216.

deHaas, P. A., & Young, R. D. (1984). Attention styles of hyperactive and normal girls. *Journal of Abnormal Child Psychology, 12,* 531–546.

de la Burde, B., & Choate, M. S. (1975). Early asymptomatic lead exposure and development at school age. *Behavioral Pediatrics, 4,* 638–642.

Delaney-Black, V., Camp, B. W., Lubchenco, L. O., Swanson, C., Roberts, L., Gaherty, P., & Swanson, B. (1989). Neonatal hyperviscosity association with lower achievement and IQ scores at school age. *Pediatrics, 83,* 662–667.

DeLong, R. (1994). Children with autistic spectrum disorder and a family history of affective disorder. *Developmental Medicine and Child Neurology, 36,* 674–688.

Demaray, M. K., Ruffalo, S. L., Carlson, J., Busse, R. T., Olson, A. E., McManus, S. M., & Leventhal, A. (1995). Social skills assessment: A comparative evaluation of six published rating scales. *School Psychology Review, 24,* 648–671.

DeMarco, S., Sunder, T., Batts, C., Fruitiger, A. D., & Levey, B. (1988, September). *The incidence of a developmental right-hemisphere deficit syndrome in dyseidetic children.* Presentation made at the seventeenth national meeting of the Child Neurology Society, Halifax, Canada.

Demont, L. (1933). *A concise dictionary of psychiatry and medical psychology.* Philadelphia: Lippincott.

Denckla, M. B. (1985). Revised neurological examination for subtle signs. *Psychopharmacology Bulletin, 21,* 773–789.

Denckla, M. B. (1992). Commentary: The myth of ADHD. *Journal of Child Neurology, 7,* 458–461.

Denckla, M. B. (1996a). Basal ganglia volumes in children with attention-deficit hyperactivity disorder. *Journal of Child Neurology, 11,* 112–115.

Denckla, M. B. (1996b). Research on executive function in a neurodevelopmental context: Application of clinical measures. *Developmental Neuropsychology, 12,* 5–15.

Denckla, M. B., Bemporad. J. R., & MacKay, M. C. (1976). Tics following methylphenidate administration. *Journal of American Medical Association, 235,* 1349–1351.

Denckla, M. B., LeMay, M., & Chapman, C. A. (1985). Few CT scan abnormalities found even in neurologically impaired learning disabled children. *Journal of Learning Disabilities, 18,* 132–135.

Denckla, M. B., & Rudel, R. G. (1978). Anomalies of motor development in hyperactive boys. *Annals of Neurology, 3,* 231–233.

Denckla, M. B., Rudel, R. G., Chapman, C., & Krieger, J. (1985). Motor proficiency in dyslexic children with and without attentional disorders. *Archives of Neurology, 42,* 228–231.

Dendy, C. A. Z. (1995). *Teenagers with ADHD: A parent's guide.* Bethesda, MD: Woodbine House.

Denhoff, E., Davids, A., & Hawkins, R. (1971). Effects of dexedrine on hyperkinetic children: A controlled double-blind study. *Journal of Learning Disabilities, 4,* 27–34.

Denman, S. B. (1984). *Denman neuropsychology memory scale.* Charleston, SC: Author.

Deno, S. L. (1980). Direct observation approach to measuring classroom behavior. *Exceptional Children, 46,* 396–399.

Densem, J. F., Nuthall, G. A., Bushnell, J., & Horn, J. (1989). Effectiveness of a sensory integrative therapy program for children with perceptual motor deficits. *Journal of Learning Disabilities, 22,* 221–229.

deQuiros, G., Kinsbourne, M., Palmer, R. L., & Roufo, D. T. (1994). Attention deficit disorder in children: Three clinical variants. *Developmental and Behavioral Pediatrics, 15,* 311–319.

Desch, L. W. (1986). High technology for handicapped children: A pediatrician's viewpoint. *Pediatrics, 77,* 71.

Desch, L. W. (1991). Microcomputer software in the treatment of attention deficit hyperactivity disorder. In P. J. Accardo, T. A. Blondis, & B. Y. Whitman (Eds.), *Attention deficit disorders and hyperactivity in children.* New York: Marcel Dekker.

Desgranges, K., Desgranges, L., & Karsky, K. (1995). Attention deficit disorder: Problems with preconceived diagnosis. *Child and Adolescent Social Work Journal, 12,* 3–17.

Desmond, K., Forney, J., Parker-Fisher, S., & Jones, M. (1993). Evaluating and managing attention deficit disorder in children who are deaf or hard of hearing. *American Annals of the Deaf, 138,* 349–357.

deSonnerville, L. M. J., Njiokiktjien, C., & Bos, H. (1994). Methylphenidate and information processing: Part 1. Differentiation between responders and non-responders: Part 2. Efficacy in responders. *Journal of Clinical and Experimental Neuropsychology, 16,* 877–897.

de Unamuno, M. (1984). *The private world: Selections from the diary and selected letters 1890–1936* (p. 151) (A. Kerrigan, A. Lacy, & M. Nozick, Trans.). Princeton, NJ: Princeton University Press.

Deutsch, C. K., Matthysse, S., Swanson, J. M., & Farkas, L. (1990). Genetic latent structure analysis of dysmorphology in attention deficit disorder. *Journal of the American Academy of Child and Adolescent Psychiatry, 29,* 189.

Devers, R., Bradley-Johnson, S., & Johnson, C. M. (1994). The effect of token reinforcement on WISC-R performance for fifth through ninth grade American Indians. *Psychological Record, 44,* 441–449.

DeVries, D. L., Edwards, K. J., & Slavin, R. E. (1978). Biracial learning teams and race relations in the classroom: Four filed experiments on teams-games-tournaments. *Journal of Educational Psychology, 70,* 356–362.

DeVries, D. L., & Slavin, R. E. (1978). Teams-games-tournament: Review of ten classroom experiments. *Journal of Research and Development in Education, 12,* 28–38.

Diamond, B. I., Borison, R. L., Katz, R., & DeVeaugh-Geiss, J. (1989). Rebound withdrawal reactions due to clomipramine. *Psychopharmacology Bulletin, 25,* 209–212.

Diamond, K. E. (1993). The role of parents' observations and concerns in screening for developmental delays in young children. *Topics in Early Childhood Education, 13,* 68–81.

Dickman, S. J. (1990). Functional and dysfunctional impulsivity: Personality and cognitive correlates. *Journal of Personality and Social Psychology, 58,* 95–102.

Dicks, T., & Grusec, J. (1995). Parent attribution processes in the socialization of children. In I. E. Siegel (Ed.), *Parental belief systems* (pp. 201–233). Hillsdale, NJ: Erlbaum.

Dickson, L. R., Heffron, W. M., & Parker, C. (1990). Children from disrupted and adoptive homes on an inpatient unit. *American Journal of Orthopsychiatry, 60,* 594–602.

Dienske, H., de Jonge, G., & Sanders-Woudstra, J. A. (1985). Quantitative criteria for attention and activity in child psychiatric patients. *Journal of Child Psychology and Psychiatry and Allied Disciplines, 26,* 895–915.

Diller, L., & Morrow, R. (1997). The case of the missing methylphenidate [Letter to the editor]. *Pediatrics, 100*(4), 730.

Dinkmeyer, D., & McKay, G. D. (1982). *Systematic training for effective parenting: The parent's handbook.* Circle Pines, MN: American Guidance Service.

Dismukes, W. E., Wade, L., Dockery, R., & Hain, S. (1990). A randomized, double-blind trial of nystatin therapy for the candidiasis hypersensitivity syndrome. *New England Journal of Medicine, 323,* 1717–1723.

DiTraglia, J. (1991). Methylphenidate protocol: Feasibility in a pediatric practice. *Clinical Pediatrics, 30,* 656–660.

Dix, T. H., & Lochman, J. E. (1990). Social cognition and negative reactions to children: A comparison of mothers of aggressive and nonaggressive boys. *Journal of Social and Clinical Psychology, 9,* 418–438.

Dix, T. H., Ruble, D. M., Grusec, J. E., & Nixon, S. (1986). Mothers' implicit theories of discipline: Child effects, parent effects, and the attribution process. *Child Development, 57,* 879–894.

Doberman, F. J. (1993). Family preservation: A key to the development of resilient children and competent adults–work in progress. *LDA Newsbriefs, 23,* 8–9.

Dodge, K. A., McCluskey, C. L., & Feldman, E. (1985). Situational approach to the assessment of social competence in children. *Journal of Consulting and Clinical Psychology, 53,* 344–353.

Donahue, M., Cole, D., & Hartas, D. (1994). Links between language and emotional behavioral disorders. *Education and Treatment of Children, 17,* 244–254.

Donnelly, M., Rapoport, J. L., Potter, W. Z., Oliver, J., Keysor, C. S., & Murphy, D. L. (1989). Fenfluramine and dextroamphetamine treatment of childhood hyperactivity, clinical and biochemical findings. *Archives of General Psychiatry, 46,* 205–212.

Donney, V. K., & Poppen, R. (1989). Teaching parents to conduct behavioral relaxation training with their hyperactive children. *Journal of Behavior Therapy and Experimental Psychiatry, 20,* 319–325.

Doob, L. (1990). *Hesitation: Impulsivity and reflection.* New York: Greenwood Press.

Dorn, M., Mazzocco, M. M., & Hagerman, R. (1994). Behavioral and psychiatric disorders in adult male carriers of fragile X. *Journal of the American Academy of Child and Adolescent Psychiatry, 33,* 256–264.

Dornbusch, S., Ritter, P., Lieberman, P., Roberts, D., & Fraleigh, M. (1987). The relation of parenting style to adolescent school performance. *Child Development, 58,* 1244–1257.

Doubros, S. G., & Daniels, G. J. (1966). An experimental approach to the reduction of overactive behavior. *Behaviour Research and Therapy, 4,* 251–258.

Dougherty, P. M., & Redomski, N. V. (1987). *The cognitive rehabilitation workbook.* Rockville, MD: Aspen.

Douglas, V. I. (1972). Stop, look and listen: The problem of sustained attention and impulse control in hyperactive and normal children. *Canadian Journal of Behavioral Science, 4,* 259–282.

Douglas, V. I. (1974). Sustained attention and impulse control: Implications for the handicapped child. In J. A. Swets & L. L. Elliott (Eds.), *Psychology and the handicapped child* (DHEW Pub. No. OE 73-05000). Washington, DC: U.S. Department of Health, Education and Welfare.

Douglas, V. I. (1980). Treatment and training approaches to hyperactivity: Establishing internal or external control. In C. K. Whalen & B. Henker (Eds.), *Hyperactive children: The social ecology of identification and treatment.* New York: Academic Press.

Douglas, V. I. (1983). Attentional and cognitive problems. In M. Rutter (Ed.), *Developmental neuropsychiatry.* New York: Guilford Press.

Douglas, V. I. (1984). The psychological processes implicated in ADD. In L. M. Bloomingdale (Ed.), *Attention deficit disorder: Diagnostic, cognitive and therapeutic understanding.* New York: Spectrum.

Douglas, V. I. (1985). The response of ADD children to reinforcement: Theoretical and clinical implications. In L. N. Bloomingdale (Ed.), *Attention deficit disorder: Identification, course and rationale.* Jamaica, NY: Spectrum.

Douglas, V. I. (1988). Cognitive deficits in children with attention deficit disorder with hyperactivity. In L. M. Bloomingdale & J. Sergeant (Eds.), *Attention deficit disorder: Criteria, cognition and intervention* (A book supplement to the Journal of Child Psychology and Psychiatry, No. 5). New York: Pergamon Press.

Douglas, V. I., Barr, R. G., Desilets, J., & Sherman, E. (1995). Do high doses of stimulants impair flexible thinking in attention-deficit hyperactivity disorder? *Journal of the American Academy of Child and Adolescent Psychiatry, 34,* 877–885.

Douglas, V. I., Barr, R. G., O'Neil, M. E., & Britton, B. G. (1986). Short-term effects of methylphenidate on the cognitive, learning, and academic performance of children with attention deficit disorder in the laboratory and classroom. *Journal of Child Psychology and Psychiatry, 27,* 191–211.

Douglas, V. I., & Benezra, E. (1990). Supraspan verbal memory in attention deficit disorder with hyperactivity normal and reading disabled boys. *Journal of Abnormal Child Psychology, 18,* 617–638.

Douglas, V. I., & Parry, P. A. (1983). Effects of reward on delayed reaction time task performance of hyperactive children. *Journal of Abnormal Child Psychology, 11,* 313–326.

Douglas, V. I., & Parry, P. A. (1994). Effects of reward and non-reward on frustration and attention in attention deficit disorder. *Journal of Abnormal Child Psychology, 22,* 281–302.

Douglas, V. I., Parry, P., Martin, P., & Garson, C. (1976). Assessment of a cognitive training program for hyperactive children. *Journal of Abnormal Child Psychology, 4,* 389–410.

Douglas, V. I., & Peters, K. G. (1979). Toward a clearer definition of the attentional deficit of hyperactive children. In G. A. Hale & M. Lewis (Eds.), *Attention and the development of cognitive skills.* New York: Plenum Press.

Drabman, R. S., Spitalnik, R., & O'Leary, K. D. (1973). Teaching self-control to disruptive children. *Journal of Abnormal Psychology, 82,* 10–16.

Draeger, S., Prior, M., & Sanson, A. (1986). Visual and auditory attention performance in hyperactive children: Competence or compliance. *Journal of Abnormal Child Psychology, 14,* 411–424.

Driscoll, M. S., & Zecker, S. G. (1991). Attention deficit disorder: Are there subtypes? A review of the literature from 1980–1989. *Learning Disabilities, 2,* 55–64.

Dubey, D. R., O'Leary, S., & Kaufman, K. F. (1983). Training parents of hyperactive children in child management: A Comparative outcome study. *Journal of Abnormal Child Psychology, 11,* 211–246.

Dubois, D. L., Felner, R. D., Brand, S., Adam, A. M., & Evans, E. G. (1992). A prospective study of life stress, social support and adaptation in early adolescence. *Child Development, 63,* 542–557.

Duffy, F. H., Denckla, M. B., Bartels, P. H., Sandini, G., & Kiessling, L. S. (1980a). Dyslexia: Regional differences in brain electrical activity by topographic mapping. *Annals of Neurology, 7,* 412–420.

Duffy, F. H., Denckla, M. B., Bartels, P. H., Sandini, G., & Kiessling, L. S. (1980b). Dyslexia: Automated diagnosis by computerized classification of brain electrical activity. *Annals of Neurology, 7,* 421–428.

Duish, S. S., Adams, W., Sheslow, D., Robins, P., & Luerssen, T. G. (1996, October 30–November 2). *Memory functions in children with reading disorder, attention deficit hyperactivity disorder, and traumatic brain injury: Clinical implications of the WRAML.* Paper presented at the 16th annual meeting of the National Academy of Neuropsychology, New Orleans, LA.

Dumas, J. (1986). Indirect influence of maternal social contacts on mother-child interactions: A setting event analysis. *Journal of Abnormal Child Psychology, 14,* 302–316.

Dumas, J. (1989). Treating antisocial behavior in children: Child approaches. *Clinical Psychology Review, 9,* 197–222.

Dunkin, M. J., & Doenau, S. J. (1985). Student ethnicity and classroom behavior. In T. Husen & T. N. Postelwaite (Eds.), *The international encyclopedia of education* (Vol. 8). Oxford, England: Pergamon Press.

Dunlap, G., Clarke, S., Jackson, M., Wright, S., Ramos, E., & Brinson, S. (1995). Self-monitoring of classroom behaviors with students exhibiting emotional and behavioral challenges. *School Psychology Quarterly, 10,* 165–177.

Dunlap, G., Dyer, L., & Koegel, R. L. (1983). Autistic self-stimulation and intertrial interval duration. *American Journal of Mental Deficiency, 88,* 194–199.

Dunlap, G., & Kern, L. (1996). Modifying instructional activities to promote desirable behavior: A conceptual and practical framework. *School Psychology Quarterly, 11,* 297–312.

Dunlap, G., Kern-Dunlap, L., Clarke, S., & Robbins, F. R. (1991). Functional assessment, curricular revision, and severe behavior problems. *Journal of Applied Behavior Analysis, 24,* 387–397.

Dunn, L. M., & Markwardt, F. C. (1970). *Peabody individual achievement test.* Circle Pines, MN: American Guidance Service.

DuPaul, G. J. (1990). *Academic-performance rating scale and ADHD rating scale.* Worcester: Department of Psychiatry, University of Massachusetts.

DuPaul, G. J. (1991a). Attention-deficit hyperactivity disorder: Classroom intervention strategies. *School Psychology International, 12,* 85–94.

DuPaul, G. J. (1991b). Parent and teacher ratings of ADHD symptoms: Psychometric properties in a community-based sample. *Journal of Clinical Child Psychology, 20,* 245–253.

DuPaul, G. J. (1992). How to assess attention-deficit hyperactivity disorder within school settings. *School Psychology Quarterly, 7,* 60–74.

DuPaul, G. J., Anastopoulos, A. D., Shelton, T. L., Guevremont, D. C., & Metevia, L. (1992). Multimethod assessment of attention-deficit hyperactivity disorder: The diagnostic utility of clinic-based tests. *Journal of Clinical Child Psychology, 21,* 394–402.

DuPaul, G. J., & Barkley, R. A. (1992). Situational variability of attention problems: Psychometric properties of the revised home and school situations questionnaires. *Journal of Clinical Child Psychology, 21*(2), 178–188.

DuPaul, G. J., & Barkley, R. A. (1993). Behavioral contributions to pharmacology: The utility of behavioral methodology in medication treatment of children with attention deficit hyperactivity disorder. *Behavior Therapy, 24,* 47–65.

DuPaul, G. J., Barkley, R. A., & McMurray, M. B. (1994). Response of children with ADHD to methylphenidate: Interaction with internalizing symptoms. *Journal of the American Academy of Child and Adolescent Psychiatry, 33,* 894–903.

DuPaul, G. J., & Eckert, T. L. (1994). The effects of social skills curricula: Now you see them, now you don't. *School Psychology Quarterly, 9,* 113–132.

DuPaul, G. J., & Eckert, T. L. (1997). The effects of school-based interventions for ADHD: A meta-analysis. *School Psychology Review, 26,* 5–27.

DuPaul, G. J., & Ervin, R. A. (1996). Children with ADHD: Linking assessment to treatment. *The ADHD Report, 4,* 9–11.

DuPaul, G. J., Guevremont, D. C., & Barkley, R. A. (1991). Attention deficit hyperactivity disorder in adolescence: Critical assessment parameters. *Clinical Psychological Review, 11,* 231–245.

DuPaul, G. J., Guevremont, D. C., & Barkley, R. A. (1992). Behavioral treatment of attention-deficit hyperactivity disorder in the classroom: The use of the attention training systems. Treatment of children with attention-deficit hyperactivity disorder (ADHD) [Special issues]. *Behavior Modification, 16,* 204–225.

DuPaul, G. J., & Henningson, P. N. (1993). Peer tutoring effects on the classroom performance of children with ADHD. *School Psychology Review, 22,* 134–143.

DuPaul, G. J., & Rapport, M. D. (1993). Does methylphenidate normalize the classroom performance of children with attention deficit disorder? *Journal of the American Academy of Child and Adolescent Psychiatry, 32,* 190–198.

DuPaul, G. J., Rapport, M. D., & Perriello, L. M. (1991). Teacher ratings of academic skills: The development of the academic performance rating scale. *School Psychology Review, 20,* 284–300.

DuPaul, G. J., & Stoner, G. (1994). *ADHD in the schools: Assessment and intervention strategies.* New York: Guilford Press.

DuPaul, G. J., Stoner, G., Tilly, W. D., & Putnam, D. (1991). Interventions for attention problems. In G. Stoner, M. Shinn, & H. Walker (Eds.), *Interventions for achievement and behavior problems.* Silver Springs, MD: National Association of School Psychologists.

Durlak, J. A. (1983). Social problem-solving as a primary prevention strategy. In R. D. Felner, L. A. Jason, J. N. Moritsugu, & S. S. Fanber (Eds.), *Preventive psychology* (pp. 31–48). New York: Pergamon Press.

Durlak, J. A., Fuhrman, T., & Lampman, C. (1991). Effectiveness of cognitive-behavior therapy for maladapting children: A meta-analysis. *Psychological Bulletin, 110,* 204–214.

Dweck, C. S. (1975). The role of expectations and attributions in the alleviation of learned helplessness. *Journal of Personality and Social Psychology, 31,* 674–685.

Dweck, C. S., & Leggett, E. (1988). A social-cognitive approach to motivation and personality. *Psychological Review, 95,* 256–273.

Dykens, E., Leckman, J., Riddle, M., Hardin, M., Schwartz, S., & Cohen, D. (1990). Intellectual, academic, and adaptive functioning of Tourette syndrome children with and without attention deficit disorder. *Journal of Abnormal Child Psychology, 18,* 607–615.

Dykman, R. A., & Ackerman, P. T. (1991). Attention deficit disorder and specific reading disability: Separate but often overlapping disorders. *Journal of Learning Disabilities, 24,* 96–103.

Dykman, R. A., & Ackerman, P. T. (1993). Cluster versus dimensional analysis of attention deficit. In J. L. Matson (Ed.), *Handbook of hyperactivity in children.* Needham Heights, MA: Allyn & Bacon.

Dykman, R. A., Ackerman, P. T., Clements, S. D., & Peters, J. E. (1971). Specific learning disabilities: An attentional deficit syndrome. In H. R. Myklebust (Ed.), *Progress in learning disabilities* (Vol. 2, pp. 56–93). New York: Grune and Stratton.

Dykman, R. A., Ackerman, P. T., & Holcomb, P. J. (1985). Reading disabled and ADD children: Similarities and differences. In D. Gray (Ed.), *Behavioral measures of dyslexia.* Parkton, MD: York Press.

Dykman, R. A., Ackerman, P. T., Holcomb, P. J., & Boudreau, A. Y. (1983). Physiological manifestations of learning disability. *Journal of Learning Disabilities, 16,* 46–53.

Dykman, R. A., McGrew, J., & Ackerman, P. T. (1974). A double-blind chemical study of pemoline on MBD children: Comments on the psychological test results. In C. K. Conners (Ed.), *Clinical use of stimulant drugs in children* (pp. 125–129). Amsterdam, The Netherlands: Excerpta Medica.

Dykman, R. A., McGrew, J., Harris, T. S., Peters, J. E., & Ackerman, P. T. (1976). Two blinded studies of the effects of stimulant drugs on children: Pemoline, methylphenidate and placebo. In R. T. Anderson & C. G. Halcomb (Eds.), *Learning disability/minimal brain dysfunction syndrome* (pp. 217–235). Springfield, IL: Thomas.

D'Zurilla, T. J. (1986). *Problem-solving therapy: A social competence approach to clinical intervention.* New York: Springer.

Earle, R. B. (1995). *Helping to prevent child abuse and future criminal consequences: Hawaii healthy start* (National Institute of Justice Program Focus, NCJ156216). Washington, DC: U.S. Department of Justice.

Earls, F., & Jung, K. G. (1987). Temperament and home environment characteristics as casual factors in the early development of childhood psychopathology. *Journal of the American Academy of Child and Adolescent Psychiatry, 26,* 491–498.

Earls, F., Smith, E., Reich, W., & Jung, K. G. (1988). Investigating psychopathological consequences of a disaster in children: A pilot study incorporating a structured diagnostic interview. *Journal of the American Academy of Child and Adolescent Psychiatry, 27,* 90–95.

Eaves, L. J., Silberg, J. L., & Hewitt, J. K. (1993). Genes, personality and psychopathology: A latent class analysis of liability to symptoms of attention-deficit hyperactivity disorder in twins. In R. Plomin & G. McClean (Eds.), *Nature, nurture and psychology.* Washington, DC: American Psychological Association.

Ebaugh, F. G. (1923). Neuropsychiatric sequelae of acute epidemic encephalitis in children. *American Journal of Diseases of Children, 25,* 89–97.

Ebben, P. A. (1996, October 30–November 2). *Birth order relationships among children with attention deficit hyperactivity disorder and specific learning disabilities.* Poster presented at the 1996 National Academy of Neuropsychology Conference in New Orleans, LA.

Ebstein, R. P., Novick, O., & Umansky, R. (1996). Dopamine D4 receptor (D4DR) exon III polymorphism associated with human personality trait of novelty seeking. *National Genetics, 12,* 78–80.

Edelbrock, C. (1989). *Childhood conduct problems: Developmental considerations and a proposed taxonomy.* Unpublished manuscript, University of Massachusetts Medical Center, Worcester.

Edelbrock, C. (1990). Childhood attention problems (CAP) scale. In R. A. Barkley (Ed.), *Attention-deficit hyperactivity disorder: A handbook for diagnosis and treatment.* New York: Guilford Press.

Edelbrock, C., & Achenbach, T. (1984). The teacher version of the child behavior profile: I. Boys age 6–11. *Journal of Consulting and Clinical Psychology, 52,* 207–217.

Edelbrock, C., Costello, A. J., & Kessler, M. D. (1984). Empirical corroboration of attention deficit disorder. *Journal of the American Academy of Child Psychiatry, 23,* 285–290.

Edelbrock, C., Rende, R., Plomin, R., & Thompson, L. A. (1995). A twin study of competence and problem behavior in childhood and early adolescence. *Journal of Child Psychology and Psychiatry, 36,* 775–785.

Edelsohn, G., Ialongo, N., Werthamer-Larrson, L., Crockett, L., & Kellam, S. (1992). Self-reported depressive symptoms in first-grade children: Developmentally transient phenomenon? *Journal of the American Academy of Child and Adolescent Psychiatry, 31,* 282–290.

Edelsohn, S. M., & Waddell, L. L. (1992). *Auditory training and the auditory training research project.* Newberg, OR: Center for the Study of Autism.

Edley, R. S., & Knopf, I. J. (1987). Sustained attention as a predictor of low academic readiness in preschool children. *Journal of Psychoeducational Assessment, 5,* 340–352.

Edwards, G. (1996). Children's perception of sleep (guest commentary). *The ADHD Report, 4,* 1–2.

Egeland, B., & Weinberg, R. A. (1976). The matching familiar figures test: A look at psychometric credibility. *Child Development, 47,* 483–491.

Egger, J., Carter, C. M., Graham, P. J., Gumley, D., & Soothill, J. F. (1985, March 9). Controlled trial of oligoantigenic treatment in the hyperkinetic syndrome. *Lancet,* 540–545.

Egger, J., Stolla, A., & McEwen, L. M. (1992). Control trial of hyposensitization in children with food-induced hyperkinetic syndrome. *Lancet, 339,* 1150–1153.

Eiraldi, R. B., Power, T. J., & Nezu, C. M. (1997). Patterns of comorbidity associated with subtypes of attention deficit/hyperactivity disorder among six- to twelve-year-old children. *Journal of the American Academy of Child and Adolescent Psychiatry, 36,* 503–514.

Eisenberg, N., Fabes, R. A., Murphy, B., Mazek, P., Smith, M., & Karbon, M. (1995). The role of emotionality and regulation in children's social functioning: A longitudinal study. *Child Development, 66,* 1360–1384.

Eisenberger, R., & Cameron, J. (1996). Detrimental effects of reward: Reality or myth? *Journal of the American Psychological Association, 51,* 1153–1166.

Elardo, P., & Cooper, M. (1977). *AWARE: Activities for social development.* Menlo Park, CA: Addison-Wesley.

Elbert, J. C. (1993). Occurrence and pattern of impaired reading and written language in children with attention deficit disorders. *Annals of Dyslexia, 43,* 26–43.

Elia, J., Borcherding, B. G., Rapoport, J. L., & Keysor, C. S. (1991). Methylphenidate and dextroamphetamine treatments of hyperactivity: Are there true nonresponders? *Psychiatry Research, 36*(2), 141–155.

Elia, J., Gulotta, C., Rose, S. R., Marin, G., & Rapoport, J. L. (1994). Thyroid function and attention-deficit hyperactivity disorder. *Journal of the American Academy of Child and Adolescent Psychiatry, 33,* 169–172.

Elias, M. J., Tobias, S. E., & Friedlander, B. S. (1994). Enhancing skills for every day problem solving, decision making, and conflict resolution in special needs students with the support of computer-based technology. *Special Services in the Schools, 8,* 33–52.

Elkind, D. (1981). *The hurried child: Growing up too fast too soon.* Reading, MA: Addison-Wesley.

Elkins, I. J., McGue, M., & Iacono, W. G. (1997). Genetic and environmental influences on parent-son relationships: Evidence for increasing genetic influence during adolescence. *Developmental Psychology, 33,* 351–363.

Elliason, M. J., & Richmond, L. C. (1988). Behavior and attention in LD children. *Learning Disability Quarterly, 11,* 360–369.

Elliot, E. S., & Dweck, C. S. (1988). Goals: An approach to motivation and achievement. *Journal of Personality and Social Pathology, 54,* 5–12.

Elliot, S. M. (1988). Acceptability of behavioral treatments: Review of variables that influence treatment selection. *Professional Psychology Research and Practice, 19,* 68–80.

Elliott, G. R., & Popper, C. W. (1991). Tricyclic antidepressants: The QT interval and other cardiovascular parameters [Editorial]. *Journal of Child and Adolescent Psychopharmacology, 1,* 187–189.

Elliott, J. (1996). Locus of control in behaviourally disordered children. *British Journal of Educational Psychology, 66,* 47–57.

Elliott, S. N., & Busse, R. T. (1991). Social skills assessment and intervention with children and adolescents: Guidelines for assessment and training procedures. *School Psychology International, 12,* 63–83.

Ellis, A. (1962). *Reason and emotion in psychotherapy.* New York: Stuart.

Ellis, A., & Harper, R. (1975). *A new guide to rational living.* New York: Wilshire Book.

Ellis, A. W. (1985). The cognitive neuropsychology of development (and acquired) dyslexia: A critical survey. *Cognitive Neuropsychology, 2,* 169–205.

Elwood, R. W. (1993). Clinical discriminations and neuropsychological tests: An appeal to Bayes Therom. *Clinical Neuropsychologists, 7,* 24–33.

Embry, D. D. (1995). *Reasons for hope: Creating a climate for change and resiliency* [Invited address]. Urban Child Research Center, Cleveland State University, Cleveland, OH.

Emery, R. E. (1982). Interparental conflict and the children of discord and divorce. *Psychological Bulletin, 92,* 310–330.

Emery, R. E., & O'Leary, K. D. (1982). Children's perceptions of marital discord and behavior problems of boys and girls. *Journal of Abnormal Child Psychology, 10,* 11–24.

Endicott, J., Knee, J., Anderson, N., Clayton, P., Keller, M., & Coryell, W. (1985). Bipolar II: Combine or keep separate? *Journal Affective Disorders, 8,* 17–28.

English, H. (1928). *A student's dictionary of psychological terms.* Yellow Springs, OH: Antioch Press.

Ensminger, M. E., Kellam, S. G., & Rubin, B. R. (1983). School and family origins of delinquency: Comparisons by sex. In K. T. Van Dusen & S. A. Mednick (Eds.), *Prospective studies of crime and delinquency.* Boston: Kluwer-Nijhoff.

Entwisle, D. R. (1990). Schools and adolescents. In S. S. Feldman & G. R. Elliot (Eds.), *At the threshold.* Cambridge, MA: Harvard University Press.

Epstein, L. C., Lasgna, L., Conners, C. K., & Rodriguez, A. (1968). Correlation of dextroamphetamine excretion and drug response in hyperactive children. *Journal of Nervous and Mental Disease, 146*(2), 136–146.

Epstein, M. A., Shaywitz, S. E., Shaywitz, B. A., & Woolston, J. L. (1991). The boundaries of attention deficit disorder. *Journal of Learning Disabilities, 24,* 78–86.

Epstein, N., Schlesinger, S. E., & Dryden, W. (1988). Concepts and methods of cognitive-behavioral family treatment. In N. Epstein, S. E. Schlesinger, & W. Dryden (Eds.), *Cognitive behavioral therapy with families* (pp. 5–48). New York: Brunner/Mazel.

Epstein, N. B., Bishop, D. S., & Levine, S. (1978). The McMaster model of family functioning. *Journal of Marriage and Family Counseling, 4,* 19–31.

Erenberg, G., Cruse, R. P., & Rothmer, A. D. (1985). Gilles de la Tourette's syndrome: Effect of stimulant drugs. *Neurology, 35,* 1346–1348.

Erhardt, D., & Baker, B. L. (1990). The effects of behavioral parent training on families with young hyperactive children. *Journal of Behavior Therapy and Experimental Psychiatry, 2,* 121–132.

Erhardt, D., & Hinshaw, S. P. (1994). Initial sociometric impressions of attention deficit hyperactivity disorder and comparison boys: Prediction from social behaviors and from nonbehavioral variables. *Journal of Consulting and Clinical Psychology, 62,* 833–842.

Erickson, M. F., Sroufe, L. A., & Edgeland, B. (1995). The relationship between quality of attachment and behavior problems in preschool in a high-risk sample. In I. Bretherton & E. Waters (Eds.), Growing points of attachment, theory and research. *Monographs of the Society for Research in Child Development, 50*(1/2, Serial No. 209), 147–166.

Erikson, E. (1963). *Childhood and society* (2nd ed.). New York: Norton.

Ernst, M. (1996). Neuroimaging in attention-deficit/hyperactivity disorder. In G. R. Lyon & J. M. Rumsey (Eds.), *Neuroimaging: A window to the neurological foundations of learning and behavior in children.* Baltimore: Brooks.

Ernst, M., Cohen, R. M., Liebenauer, L. L., Jons, P. H., & Zametkin, A. J. (1997). Cerebral glucose metabolism in adolescent girls with attention-deficit hyperactivity disorder. *Journal of the American Academy of Child and Adolescent Psychiatry, 36,* 1399–1406.

Ernst, M., Liebenauer, L. L., King, A. C., Fitzgerald, G. A., Cohen, R. M., & Zametkin, A. J. (1994). Reduced brain metabolism in hyperactive girls. *Journal of the American Academy of Child and Adolescent Psychiatry, 33,* 858–868.

Ernst, M., Zametkin, A. J., Matochik, J. A., Liebenauer, L., Fitzgerald, G. A., & Cohen, R. M. (1994). Effects of intravenous dextroamphetamine on brain metabolism in adults with attention-deficit hyperactivity disorder (ADHD). Preliminary findings. *Psychopharmacology Bulletin, 30,* 219–225.

Escalona, S. K. (1987). *Critical issues in the early development of premature infants.* New Haven, CT: Yale University Press.

Evans, J. H., Ferre, L., Ford, L. A., & Green, J. L. (1995). Decreasing ADHD symptoms utilizing an automated classroom reinforcement device. *Psychology in the Schools, 32,* 210–219.

Evans, S. W., & Pelham, W. E. (1991). Psychostimulant effects on academic and behavioral measures for ADHD junior high school students in a lecture format classroom. *Journal of Abnormal Child Psychology, 19,* 537–552.

Everett, J., Thomas, J., Cote, F., Levesque, J., & Michaud, D. (1991). Cognitive effects of psychostimulant medication in hyperactive children. *Child Psychiatry and Human Development, 22,* 79–87.

Eyberg, S., & Robinson, E. A. (1982). Parent-child interaction training: Effects on family functioning. *Journal of Clinical Child Psychology, 11,* 130–137.

Eyestone, L. L., & Howell, R. J. (1994). An epidemiological study of ADHD and major depression in a male prison population. *Bulletin of the American Academy of Psychiatry and the Law, 22,* 181–193.

Eysenck, H. J., & Eysenck, M. (1985). *Personality and individual differences.* New York: Plenum Press.

Fagan, J. E., Kaplan, H., Raymond, R., & Eddington, S. (1988). The failure of antimotion sickness medication to improve reading in developmental dyslexia: Results of a randomized trail. *Developmental and Behavioral Pediatrics, 9,* 359–366.

Fagot, B. I. (1984). The consequences of problem behavior in toddler children. *Journal of Abnormal Child Psychology, 12,* 385–396.

Famularo, R., Kinsherff, R., & Fenton, R. (1992). Psychiatric diagnoses of maltreated children: Preliminary findings. *Journal of the American Academy of Child and Adolescent Psychiatry, 31,* 863–867.

Faraone, S. V., Biederman, J., Chen, W. J., & Krifcher, B. (1992). Segregation analysis of attention deficit hyperactivity disorder. *Psychiatric Genetics, 2,* 257–275.

Faraone, S. V., Biederman, J., Keenan, K., & Tsuang, M. T. (1991). A Family-genetic study of girls with *DSM-III* attention deficit disorder. *American Journal of Psychiatry, 148*(1), 112–117.

Faraone, S. V., Biederman, J., Lehman, B., & Spencer, T. (1993). Intellectual performance and school failure in children with attention deficit hyperactivity disorder and in their siblings. *Journal of Abnormal Psychology, 102,* 616–623.

Faraone, S. V., Biederman, J., Mennin, D., Gershon, J., & Tsuang, M. T. (1996). A prospective four-year follow-up study of children at risk for ADHD: Psychiatric, neuropsychological, and psychosocial outcome. *Journal of the American Academy of Child and Adolescent Psychiatry, 35,* 1449–1459.

Faraone, S. V., Biederman, J., Mennin, D., Wozniak, J., & Spencer, T. (1997). Attention-deficit hyperactivity disorder with bipolar disorder. A familial subtype? *Journal of the American Academy of Child and Adolescent Psychiatry, 36,* 1378–1387.

Faraone, S. V., Biederman, J., & Milberger, S. (1995). How reliable are maternal reports of their children's psychopathology? One-year recall of psychiatric diagnoses of ADHD children. *Journal of the American Academy of Child and Adolescent Psychiatry, 34,* 1001–1008.

Faraone, S. V., Biederman, J., Sprich-Buckminster, S., Chen, W., & Tsuang, M. T. (1993). Efficiency of diagnostic criteria for attention deficit disorder. Towards an empirical approach to designing and validating diagnostic algorithms. *Journal of the American Academy of Child and Adolescent Psychiatry, 32,* 166–174.

Farnett, C., Forte, I., & Loss, B. (1976). *Special kid's stuff.* Nashville, TN: Incentive.

Farrington, D. P. (1987). Early precursors of frequent offending. In J. Q. Wilson & G. C. Loury (Eds.), *From children to citizens: Families, schools and delinquency prevention.* New York: Springer-Verlag.

Fee, V. E., & Matson, J. L. (1993). Past development and future trends. In J. L. Matson (Ed.), *Handbook of hyperactivity in children.* Needham Heights, MA: Allyn & Bacon.

Fee, V. E., Matson, J. L., & Benavidez, D. A. (1994). Attention deficit-hyperactivity disorder among mentally retarded children. *Research in Developmental Disabilities, 15,* 67–79.

Feehrer, C. E., & Adams, M. J. (1986). *Odyssey: A curriculum for thinking—decision making.* Watertown, MA: Mastery Education.

Fehlings, D. L., Eriksson, M., Johnsson, B., Steneroth, G., & Zetterstrom, R. (1994). The influence of environmental factors on behavioral problems in eight-year-old children exposed to amphetamine during fetal life. *Child Abuse and Neglect, 18,* 3–9.

Fehlings, D. L., Roberts, W., Humphries, T., & Dawe, G. (1990). An evaluation of the effectiveness of cognitive behavioral therapy to improve home behavior in boys with ADHD [Abstract]. *Journal of Developmental and Behavioral Pediatrics, 11,* 216.

Fehlings, D. L., Roberts, W., Humphries, T., & Dawe, G. (1991). Attention deficit hyperactivity disorder: Does cognitive behavioral therapy improve home behavior? *Journal of Developmental and Behavioral Pediatrics, 12,* 223–228.

Feigin, A., Kurlan, R., McDermott, M. P., Beach, J., Dimitsopoulos, T., Brower, C. A., Chapieski, L., Trinidad, K., Como, P., & Jankovic, J. (1996). A controlled trial of deprenyl in children with Tourette's syndrome and attention deficit hyperactivity disorder. *Neurology, 46,* 965–968.

Feindler, E. L., & Ecton, R. B. (1986). *Adolescent anger control: Cognitive-behavioral techniques.* New York: Pergamon Press.

Feindler, E. L., & Fremouw, W. J. (1983). Stress inoculation training for adolescent anger problems. In D. Meichenbaum & M. E. Jaremko (Eds.), *Stress reduction and prevention.* New York: Plenum Press.

Feingold, B. F. (1974). *Why your child is hyperactive.* New York: Random House.

Feldman, H., Crumrine, P., Handen, B. L., Alvin, R., & Teodori, J. (1989). Methylphenidate in children with seizures and attention-deficit disorder. *American Journal of Diseases in Children, 143,* 1081–1086.

Feldman, M. J., & Drasgow, J. (1981). *The visual-verbal test.* Los Angeles: Western Psychological Services.

Feldman, W. (1990). *Learning disabilities: A review of available treatments.* Springfield, IL: Thomas.

Felton, R. H., & Wood, F. B. (1989). Cognitive deficits in reading disability and attention deficit disorder. *Journal of Learning Disabilities, 22,* 3–13.

Felton, R. H., Wood, F. B., Brown, I. S., Campbell, S. K., & Harter, M. R. (1987). Separate verbal memory and naming deficits in attention deficit disorder and reading disability. *Brain and Language, 31,* 171–184.

Ferdinand, R., & Verhulst, C. (1994). The prediction of poor outcome in young adults. Comparison of the young adult self-report, the general health questionnaire and the symptom checklist. *Actica Psychiatrica Scandinavia, 89,* 405–410.

Ferdinand, R. F., Verhulst, F. C., & Wiznitzer, M. (1995). Continuity and change of self-reported problem behaviors from adolescence into young adulthood. *Journal of the American Academy of Child and Adolescent Psychiatry, 34,* 680–690.

Fergusson, D. M., & Horwood, L. J. (1992). Attention deficit and reading achievement. *Journal of Child Psychology and Psychiatry, 33,* 375–385.

Fergusson, D. M., & Horwood, L. J. (1993). The structure, stability and correlations of the trait components of conduct disorder, attention deficit and anxiety/withdrawal reports. *Journal of Child Psychology and Psychiatry and Allied Disciplines, 34,* 749–766.

Fergusson, D. M., & Horwood, L. J. (1995). Predictive validity of categorically and dimensionally scored measures of disruptive childhood behaviors. *Journal of the American Academy of Child and Adolescent Psychiatry, 34,* 477–496.

Fergusson, D. M., Horwood, L. J., & Lloyd, M. (1991). Confirmatory factor models of attention deficit and conduct disorder. *Journal of Child Psychology and Psychiatry, 32,* 257–274.

Fergusson, D. M., Horwood, L. J., & Lynskey, M. T. (1993). The effects of conduct disorder and attention deficit in middle childhood on offending and scholastic ability at age 13. *Journal of Child Psychology and Psychiatry, 34,* 899–916.

Fergusson, D. M., Horwood, L. J., & Lynskey, M. T. (1994a). Parental separation, adolescent psychopathology and behavior problems. *Journal of the American Academy of Child and Adolescent Psychiatry, 33,* 1122–1131.

Fergusson, D. M., Horwood, L. J., & Lynskey, M. T. (1994b). Structure of *DSM-III-R* criteria for disruptive childhood behaviors: Confirmatory factor models. *Journal of the American Academy of Child and Adolescent Psychiatry, 33,* 1145–1155.

Fergusson, D. M., & Lynskey, M. T. (1993). The effects of maternal depression on child conduct disorder and attention deficit behaviours. *Social Psychiatry and Psychiatric Epidemiology, 28,* 116–123.

Fergusson, D. M., Lynskey, M. T., & Horwood, L. J. (1993). Conduct problems and attention deficit behaviour in middle childhood and cannabis use by age 15. *Australian and New Zealand Journal of Psychiatry, 27*(4), 673–682.

Filipek, P. A., Semrud-Clikeman, M., Steingard, R. J., Renshaw, P. F., Kennedy, D. N., & Biederman, J. (1997). Volumetric MRI analysis comparing subjects having attention-deficit hyperactivity disorder with normal controls. *Neurology, 48,* 589–601.

Finch, A. J., Saylor, C. F., & Edwards, G. L. (1985). Children's depression inventory: Sex and grade norms for normal children. *Journal of Consulting and Clinical Psychology, 53,* 424 425.

Fine, S., & Jewesson, B. (1989). Active drug placebo trial of methylphenidate: A clinical service for children with an attention deficit disorder. *Canadian Journal of Psychiatry, 34,* 447–449.

Fiore, T. A., & Becker, E. A. (1992). *Classroom interventions for students with ADD.* Silver Springs, MD: National Association of School Psychologists.

Fiore, T. A., Becker, E. A., & Nero, R. C. (1993). Educational interventions for students with attention deficit disorder. Issues in the education of children with attentional deficit disorder [Special issue]. *Exceptional Children, 60,* 163–173.

Fiorella, I., Douglas, V. I., & Baker, A. G. (1995). Effects of reward and response costs on inhibition in ADHD children. *Journal of Abnormal Child Psychology, 104,* 232–240.

Firestone, P., Davey, J., Goodman, J. T., & Peters, S. (1978). The effects of caffeine and methylphenidate on hyperactive children. *Journal of the American Academy of Child Psychiatry, 17,* 445–456.

Firestone, P., Kelly, M. J., & Fike, S. (1980). Are fathers necessary in parent training groups? *Journal of Consulting and Clinical Psychology, 10,* 44–77.

Firestone, P., & Witt, J. (1982). Characteristics of families completing and prematurely discontinuing a behavioral parent training program. *Journal of Pediatric Psychology, 7,* 209–221.

Fischer, M. (1990). Parenting stress in the child with attention deficit hyperactivity disorder. *Journal of Clinical Child Psychology, 19,* 337–346.

Fischer, M., Barkley, R. A., Edelbrock, C. S., & Smallish, L. (1990). The adolescent outcome of hyperactive children diagnosed by research criteria: II. Academic, attentional and neuropsychological status. *Journal of Consulting and Clinical Psychology, 58,* 550–588.

Fischer, M., Barkley, R. A., Fletcher, K. E., & Smallish, L. (1993). The adolescent outcome of hyperactive children: Predictors of psychiatric, academic, social, and emotional adjustment. *Journal of the American Academy of Child and Adolescent Psychiatry, 32,* 324–332.

Fischer, N., Newby, R., & Gordon, M. (1995). Who are the false negatives on continuous performance tests? *Journal of Clinical Child Psychology, 24,* 427–433.

Fisk, A. D., & Schneider, W. (1981). Control and automatic processing during tasks requiring sustained attention. *Human Factors, 23,* 737–750.

Fitzgerald, G., Fick, L., & Milich, R. (1986). Computer-assisted instruction for students with attentional difficulties. *Journal of Learning Disabilities, 19,* 376.

Fitzpatrick, P. A., Klorman, R., Brumaghim, J. T., & Bortstedt, A. D. (1992). Effects of sustained-release and standard preparations of methylphenidate on attention deficit disorder. *Journal of the American Academy of Child and Adolescent Psychiatry, 31,* 226–234.

Flavell, J. H., Green, F. L., & Flavell, E. R. (1995). The development of children's knowledge about attentional focus. *Developmental Psychology, 31,* 706–712.

Fleece, L., O'Brien, T., & Drabman, R. (1981). The use of a contingent observation procedure to reduce disruptive behavior in a preschool child. *Journal of Clinical Child Psychology, 10,* 128–130.

Fleischman, M. J., Horne, A. M., & Arthur, J. L. (1983). *Troubled families: A treatment program.* Champaign, IL: Research Press.

Fleming, K., Bigelow, L. B., Weinberger, D. R., & Goldberg, T. E. (1995). Neuropsychological effects of amphetamine may correlate with personality characteristics. *Pharmacology Bulletin, 31,* 357–362.

Fletcher, J. M., Morris, R. D., & Francis, D. J. (1991). Methodological issues in the classification of attention-related disorders. *Journal of Learning Disabilities, 24,* 72–77.

Fletcher, K. (1994). Differential diagnosis of post traumatic stress disorder and ADHD. *The ADHD Report, 2,* 6–7.

Flicek, M. (1992). Social status of boys with both academic problems and attention-deficit hyperactivity disorder. *Journal of Abnormal Child Psychology, 20,* 353–366.

Flynn, N. M., & Rapoport, J. L. (1976). Hyperactivity in open and traditional classroom environments. *Journal of Special Education, 10,* 285–290.

Fonagy, P., Steele, M., Steele, H., Higgitt, A., & Target, M. (1994). The Emmanuel Miller Memorial Lecture, 1992: The theory and practice of resilience. *Journal of Child Psychology and Psychiatry, 35,* 231–257.

Fonagy, P., & Target, M. (1994). The advocacy of psychoanalysis for children with disruptive disorders. *Journal of the American Academy of Child and Adolescent Psychiatry, 33,* 45–55.

Ford, M. J., Poe, V., & Cox, J. (1993). Attending behaviors of ADHD children in math and reading using various types of software. *Journal of Computing in Childhood Education, 4,* 183–196.

Forehand, R., & McMahon, R. (1981). *Helping the non-compliant child: A clinician's guide to parent training.* New York: Guilford Press.

Forehand, R., Middlebrook, J., Rogers, R., & Steffe, M. (1983). Dropping out of parent training. *Behaviour Research and Therapy, 21,* 663–668.

Forehand, R., Wells, K., & Griest, D. (1980). An examination of the social validity of a parent-training program. *Behavior Therapy, 11,* 488–502.

Forehand, R. L., Wierson, M., Frame, C., & Kemptom, T. (1991). Juvenile delinquency entry and persistence: Do attention problems contribute to conduct problems? *Journal of Behavior Therapy and Experimental Psychiatry, 22*(4), 261–264.

Foreyt, J., & Rathjen, D. (Eds.). (1978). *Cognitive behavior therapy: Theory, research, and practice.* New York: Plenum Press.

Fox, N. A. (1989). Psychophysiological correlates of emotional reactivity during the first year of life. *Developmental Psychology, 25,* 364–372.

Foxx, R. M., Faw, G. D., & Weber, G. (1991). Producing generalization of inpatient adolescents' social skills with significant adults in a natural environment. *Behavior Therapy, 22,* 85–99.

Francis, G. (1993). A prevalence study: ADHD in elementary school children [Special issue]. *Canadian Journal of School Psychology, 9,* 16–27.

Frank, Y., & Ben-Nun, Y. (1988). Toward a clinical subgrouping of hyperactive and non-hyperactive attention deficit disorder: Results of a comprehensive neurological and neuropsychological assessment. *Journal of Diseases in Children, 142,* 153–155.

Fraser, C., Belzner, R., & Conte, R. (1992). Attention deficit hyperactivity disorder and self-control: A single case study of the use of a timing device in the development of self-monitoring. *School Psychology International, 13,* 339–345.

Frederick, B. P., & Olmi, D. J. (1994). Children with attention-deficit/hyperactivity disorder: A review of the literature on social skills deficits. *Psychology in the Schools, 31,* 288–296.

Freeman, A., Pretzer, J., Fleming, B., & Simon, K. (1990). *Clinical applications of cognitive therapy.* New York: Plenum Press.

Freeman, W., & Johnston, C. (1992, October). *Predictors of behavioral parent training outcome.* Paper presented at the Children and Adults with Attention Deficit Disorder (CH.A.D.D.) 4th annual meeting, Chicago, IL.

Freeman, W., Phillips, J., & Johnston, C. (1992, June). *Treatment effects on hyperactive and aggressive behaviours in ADHD children.* Paper presented at the meeting of the Canadian Psychological Association, Quebec City.

Freidling, C., & O'Leary, S. G. (1979). Effects of self-instructional training on second and third grade hyperactive children: A failure to replicate. *Journal of Applied Behavior Analysis, 12,* 211–219.

Frick, P. J. (1994). Family dysfunction and the disruptive behavior disorders: A review of recent empirical findings. *Advances in Clinical Child Psychology, 16,* 203–226.

Frick, P. J., Kamphaus, R. W., Lahey, B. B., Loeber, R., Christ, M. G., Hart, E. L., & Tannenbaum, L. E. (1991). Academic underachievement and the disruptive behavior disorders. *Journal of Consulting and Clinical Psychology, 59,* 289–294.

Frick, P. J., & Lahey, B. B. (1991). The nature and characteristics of attention-deficit hyperactivity disorder. *School Psychology Review, 20,* 163–173.

Frick, P. J., Lahey, B. B., Christ, M. A., Loeber, R., & Green, S. (1991). History of childhood behavior problems in biological relatives of boys with attention-deficit hyperactivity disorder and conduct disorder. *Journal of Clinical Child Psychology, 20,* 440–451.

Frick, P. J., Lahey, B. B., Loeber, R., Stouthamer-Loeber, R., Green, S., Hart, E. L., & Christ, M. G. (1991). Oppositional defiant disorder and conduct disorder in boys: Patterns of behavioral covariation. *Journal of Clinical Child Psychology, 20,* 202–208.

Fried, R. (1993). What is theta? *Biofeedback and Self-Regulation, 18,* 53–58.

Friedman, H. S., Tucker, J. S., Schwartz, J. E., Tomlinson-Keasey, C., Martin, L. R., Wingard, D. L., & Criqui, M. H. (1995a). Childhood conscientiousness and longevity: Health behaviors and cause of death. *Journal of Personality and Social Psychology, 68,* 696–703.

Friedman, H. S., Tucker, J. S., Schwartz, J. E., Tomlinson-Keasey, C., Martin, L. R., Wingard, D. L., & Criqui, M. H. (1995b). Psychological and behavioral predictors of longevity: The aging and death of the "Termites." *American Psychologist, 50,* 69–78.

Friedman, J. T., Carr, R., Elders, J., Ringdahal, I., & Roache, A. (1981). Effect on growth in pemoline treated children with attention deficit disorder. *Medical Journal Disabilities in Children, 135,* 329–332.

Friedman, R. J. (1988). *Attention-deficit hyperactivity disorder* [A video tape]. St. Clair Shores, MI.

Friedman, R. J., & Doyal, G. T. (1987). *Attention deficit disorder and hyperactivity* (2nd ed.). Danville, IL: Interstate.

Fristad, M. A., Weller, E. B., & Weller, R. A. (1982). The mania rating scale: Can it be used in children? A preliminary report. *Journal of the American Academy of Adolescent and Child Psychiatry, 31,* 252–257.

Fromm-Auch, D., & Yeudall, L. T. (1983). Normative data for the Halstead-Reitan neuropsychological test. *Journal of Clinical Neuropsychology, 5,* 221–232.

Frost, L. A., Moffitt, T. E., & McGee, R. (1989). Neuropsychological correlates of psychopathology in an unselected cohort of young adolescents. *Journal of Abnormal Child Psychology, 98,* 307–313.

Fuhrman, M. J., & Kendall, P. C. (1986). Cognitive tempo and behavioral adjustment in children. *Cognitive Therapy and Research, 10,* 45–50.

Funk, J. B., & Ruppert, E. S. (1984). Language disorders and behavioral problems in preschool children. *Developmental and Behavioral Pediatrics, 5,* 357–360.

Furman, W., & Gavin, L. A. (1989). Peers' influence on adjustment and development: A view from the intervention literature. In T. T. J. Berndt & G. W. Ladd (Eds.), *Peer relationships in child development* (pp. 319–340). New York: Wiley.

Fuster, J. M. (1989). A theory of prefrontal functions: The prefrontal cortex and the temporal organization of behavior. In J. M. Fuster (Ed.), *The prefrontal cortex: Anatomy, physiology, and neuropsychology of the frontal lobe.* New York: Raven Press.

Futtersak, M. W., O'Leary, S. G., & Abramowitz, A. J. (1989). *The effects of consistently and increasingly strong reprimands in the classroom.* Unpublished manuscript.

Gable, R. A., Hendrickson, J. M., Shores, R. E., & Young, C. D. (1983). Teacher-handicapped child classroom interactions. *Teacher Education and Special Education, 6,* 88–95.

Gabel, S., & Shindledecker, R. (1992). Behavior problems in sons and daughters of substance abusing parents. *Child Psychiatry and Human Development, 23,* 99–115.

Gadow, K. D., & Nolan, E. E. (1993). Practical considerations in conducting school-based medication evaluations for children with hyperactivity. *Journal of Emotional and Behavioral Disorders, 1,* 118–126.

Gadow, K. D., Nolan, E. E., & Sverd, J. (1992). Methylphenidate in hyperactive boys with comorbid tic disorder: II. Short-term behavioral effects in school settings. *Journal of the American Academy of Child and Adolescent Psychiatry, 31,* 462–471.

Gadow, K. D., Nolan, E. E., Sverd, J., Sprafkin, J., & Paolicelli, L. (1990). Methylphenidate in aggressive-hyperactive boys: I. Effects on peer aggression in public school settings. *Journal of the American Academy of Child and Adolescent Psychiatry, 29,* 710–718.

Gadow, K. D., Paolicelli, L. M., Nolan, E. E., & Schwartz, J. (1992). Methylphenidate in aggressive hyperactive boys: II. Indirect effects of medication treatment on peer behavior. *Journal of Child and Adolescent Psychopharmacology, 2,* 49–61.

Gadow, K. D., & Sprafkin, J. (1994). *Child symptom inventories manual.* Stony Brook, NY: Checkmate Plus.

Gadow, K. D., & Sprafkin, J. (1995). *Adolescent supplement to the child symptom inventories manual.* Stony Brook, NY: Checkmate Plus.

Gadow, K. D., & Sprafkin, J. (1997). *ADHD symptom checklist—Manual* (4th ed.). Stony Brook, NY: Checkmate Plus.

Gadow, K. D., & Sverd, J. (1990). Stimulants for ADHD in child patients with Tourette's syndrome: The issue of relative risk. *Developmental and Behavioral Pediatrics, 2,* 269–271.

Gajar, A. H., Schloss, P. J., Schloss, C. N., & Thompson, C. K. (1984). Effects of feedback and self-monitoring on head trauma youths' conversational skills. *Journal of Applied Behavioral Analysis, 17,* 353–358.

Gallucci, F., Bird, H. R., Berardi, C., Gallai, V., Pfanner, S., & Weinberg, W. A. (1993). Symptoms of attention-deficit hyperactivity disorder in an Italian school sample: Findings of a pilot study. *Journal of the American Academy of Child and Adolescent Psychiatry, 32,* 1051–1058.

Gamble, R., & Strain, P. S. (1979). The effects of dependent and interdependent group contingencies on socially appropriate responses in classes for emotionally handicapped children. *Psychology in the Schools, 16,* 253–260.

Gammon, G. D., & Brown, T. E. (1993). Fluoxetine and methylphenidate in combination for treatment of attention deficit disorder and comorbid depressive disorder. *Journal of Child and Adolescent Psychopharmacology, 3,* 1–10.

Gandour, M. J. (1986). Activity level as a dimension of temperament in toddlers: Its relevance for the organismic specificity hypothesis. *Child Development, 60,* 1092–1098.

Garbarino, J. (1992). The meaning of poverty in the world of children. *American Behavioral Scientist, 35,* 220–237.

Gard, G. C., & Berry, K. K. (1986). Oppositional children: Taming tyrant. *Journal of Clinical Child Psychology, 15,* 148–158.

Gardner, F. E. M. (1992). Parent-child interaction and conduct disorder. *Educational Psychology Review, 4,* 135–163.

Gardner, R. A. (1978). *The talking, feeling and doing game.* Cresskill, NJ: Creative Therapeutics.

Gardner, R. A. (1979). *The objective diagnosis of minimal brain dysfunction.* Cresskill, NJ: Creative Therapeutics.

Gardner, R. A. (1982a). *Family evaluation and child custody litigation.* Cresskill, NJ: Creative Therapeutics.

Gardner, R. A. (1982b). *Psychostimulant medication assessment battery.* Unpublished manuscript.

Gardner, R. A., Gardner, A. K., Caemmerer, A., & Broman, M. (1979). An instrument for measuring hyperactivity and other signs of minimal brain dysfunction. *Journal of Clinical Child Psychology, 8,* 173–179.

Gardner, W. I., & Cole, C. (1988). Conduct disorders: Psychological therapies. In J. L. Matson (Ed.), *Handbook of treatment approaches in childhood psychopathology.* New York: Plenum Press.

Garfinkel, B. G. (1989, June). *Recent advances in attention deficit disorder.* Presentation made at the first National Conference on Attention Deficit Disorders, Orlando, FL.

Garfinkel, B. G., & Klee, S. H. (1983). A computerized assessment battery for attention deficits. *Psychiatric Hospitalization, 14,* 163–166.

Garfinkel, B. G., Webster, C. D., & Sloman, L. (1975). Methylphenidate and caffeine in the treatment of children with minimal brain dysfunction. *American Journal of Psychiatry, 132,* 723–728.

Garfinkel, B. G., Wender, P. H., Sloman, L., & O'Neill, I. (1983). Tricyclic antidepressant and methylphenidate treatment of attention deficit disorder in children. *Journal of the American Academy of Child Psychiatry, 22,* 343–348.

Garmezy, N., & Rutter, M. (Eds.). (1983). *Stress coping and development in children.* New York: Aldine de Gruyter.

Garretson, H. B., Fein, D., & Waterhouse, L. (1990). Sustained attention in children with autism. *Journal of Autism and Developmental Disorders, 20,* 101–114.

Gascon, G. G., Johnson, R., & Burd, L. (1986). Central auditory processing and attention deficit disorders. *Journal of Child Neurology, 1,* 27–33.

Gaub, M., & Carlson, C. L. (1997). Gender differences in ADHD: A meta-analysis and critical review. *Journal of the American Academy of Child and Adolescent Psychiatry, 36,* 1036–1045.

Gay, C. T., & Ryan, S. G. (1994). Paroxysmal kinesigenic dystonia after methylphenidate administration. *Journal of Child Neurology, 9,* 45–46.

Gayton, W. F., Bailey, C., Wagner, A., & Hardesty, V. A. (1986). Relationship between childhood hyperactivity and accident proneness. *Perceptual Motor Skills, 63,* 801–802.

Geffner, D. L., Jay, R., & Koch, W. (1996). Evaluation of auditory discrimination in children with ADD and without ADD. *Child Psychiatry and Human Development, 26,* 169–180.

Gerbing, D. W., Ahadi, S. A., & Patton, J. H. (1987). Toward a conceptualization of impulsivity: Components across the behavioral and self-report domains. *Multi-variate Behavioral Research, 22,* 357–379.

Ghaziuddin, M., Tsai, L., & Alessi, N. (1992). ADHD and PDD. *Journal of the American Academy of Child and Adolescent Psychiatry, 31,* 567.

Giambra, L. N. (1989). Task unrelated thought frequency as a function of age: A laboratory study. *Psychology and Aging, 4,* 136–143.

Gibbs, D. P., & Cooper, E. B. (1989). Prevalence of communication disorders in students with learning disabilities. *Journal of Learning Disabilities, 22,* 60–63.

Gibson, E., & Radner, N. (1979). Attention: Perceiver as performer. In G. Hale & M. Lewis (Eds.), *Attention and cognitive development.* New York: Plenum Press.

Giddan, J. J. (1991). Communication issues and attention-deficit hyperactivity disorder. *Child Psychiatry in Human Development, 22,* 45–51.

Giedd, J. N., Castellanos, F. X., Casey, B. J., Kozuch, P., King, A. C., Hamburger, S. D., & Rapoport, J. L. (1994). Quantitative morphology of the corpus callosum in attention deficit hyperactivity disorder. *American Journal of Psychiatry, 151,* 665–669.

Gilger, J. W., Pennington, B. F., & DeFries, J. (1992). A twin study of the etiology of comorbidity: Attention-deficit hyperactivity disorder and dyslexia. *Journal of the American Academy of Child and Adolescent Psychiatry, 31,* 343–348.

Gillberg, C., Carlstrom, G., & Rasmussen, P. (1983). Hyperkinetic disorders in seven-year-old children with perceptual motor and attentional deficits. *Journal of Child Psychology and Psychiatry, 24,* 233–246.

Gillberg, C., Matousek, M., Petersen, I., & Rasmussen, P. (1984). Perceptual, motor and attentional deficits in seven-year-old children. *Paedopsychiatrica, 50,* 243–253.

Gillberg, I. C., Gillberg, C., & Groth, J. (1989). Children with preschool minor neurodevelopmental disorders: V. Neurodevelopmental profiles at age 13. *Developmental Medicine and Child Neurology, 31*(1), 14–24.

Gillis, J. J., Gilger, J. W., Pennington, B. F., & De Fries, J. C. (1992). Attention-deficit disorders in reading disabled twins: Evidence for a genetic etiology. *Journal of Abnormal Child Psychology, 20,* 303–315.

Gilmore, J. N., & Gilmore, E. S. (1968). *Gilmore oral reading test.* New York: Harcourt, Brace, & World.

Gittelman, D. R., Alpert, N. M., Rosslyn, S. M., Daffner, K., Scinto, S., Thompson, W., & Mesulam, M. M. (1996). Functional imaging of human right hemisphere activation for exploratory movements. *Annals of Neurology, 39,* 174–179.

Gittelman, R. (1985). Self-evaluation (teenagers) self-report. *Psychopharmacology Bulletin, 21,* 925–926.

Gittelman, R., Abikoff, H., & Pollack, E. (1980). A controlled trial of behavior modification and methylphenidate in hyperactive children. In C. K. Whalen & B. Henker (Eds.),

Hyperactive children: The social ecology of identification (pp. 221–243). New York: Academic Press.

Gittelman, R., Klein, D. F., & Feingold, I. (1983). Children with reading disorders. Two effects of methylphenidate in combination with reading remediation. *Journal of Child Psychology and Psychiatry, 24,* 193–212.

Gittelman, R., Mannuzza, S., Shenker, R., & Bonagura, N. (1985). Hyperactive boys almost grown up: I. Psychiatric status. *Archives of General Psychiatry, 42,* 937–947.

Gittelman-Klein, R., Abikoff, H., Pollack, E., Klein, D. F., Katz, S., & Mattes, J. (1980). A controlled trial of behavior modification and methylphenidate in hyperactive children. In C. K. Whalen & B. Henker (Eds.), *Hyperactive children: The social ecology of identification and treatment.* New York: Academic Press.

Gittelman-Klein, R., Klein, D. F., Katz, S., Saraf, K., & Pollack, E. (1976). Comparative effects of methylphenidate and thioridazine in hyperkinetic children: I. Clinical results. *Archives of General Psychiatry, 33,* 1217–1231.

Glasser, J. M. (1995). Differential diagnosis of ADHD in bipolar disorder. *The ADHD Report, 3,* 8–10.

Glick, I. D. (1992). Medication and family therapy for schizophrenia and mood disorder. *Psychopharmacology Bulletin, 28,* 223–225.

Glow, R. A., & Glow, P. H. (1980). Peer and self-rating: Children's perception of behavior relevant to hyperkinetic impulse disorder. *Journal of Abnormal Psychology, 8,* 471–490.

Goals 2000. (1993). *General aptitude test battery (GATB).* Washington, DC: U.S. Department of Education.

Goldberg, J. O., & Konstantareas, M. M. (1981). Vigilance in hyperactive and normal children on a self-paced operant task. *Journal of Child Psychology and Psychiatry, 22,* 55–63.

Golden, G. S. (1977). Tourette's syndrome: The pediatric perspective. *American Medical Journal of Diseases in Children, 131,* 531–534.

Golden, G. S. (1987). Tic disorders in childhood. *Pediatrics, 8,* 229–234.

Golden, G. S. (1991). Role of attention deficit hyperactivity disorder in learning disabilities. *Seminars in Neurology, 11.*

Golden, J. (1996). Are tests of working memory and inattention diagnostically useful in children with ADHD? *The ADHD Report, 4,* 6–8.

Golden, M., Montare, A., & Bridger, W. (1977). Verbal control of delay behavior in two-year-old boys as a function of social class. *Child Development, 48,* 1107–1111.

Goldhaber, S. B. (1991). Summer day treatment for children with attention-deficit hyperactivity disorder. *Hospital and Community Psychiatry, 42,* 422–424.

Goldstein, A. P. (1988). *The prepare curriculum. Teaching prosocial competencies.* Champaign, IL: Research Press.

Goldstein, A. P., & McGinnis, E. (1988). *The skill streaming video.* Champaign, IL: Research Press.

Goldstein, A. P., Sprafkin, R. P., Gershaw, N. J., & Klein, P. (1980). *Skill-streaming the adolescent: A structured learning approach to teaching prosocial skills.* Champaign, IL: Research Press.

Goldstein, K. (1942). *After-effects of brain injuries in war.* New York: Grune and Stratton.

Goldstein, S. (1980). *Relationship between maternal self-report and rated behavior in mother-child interactions with clinic and non-clinic subjects.* Unpublished doctoral dissertation.

Goldstein, S. (1987a). *Adolescent school situations questionnaire.* Salt Lake City, UT: Neurology, Learning and Behavior Center.

Goldstein, S. (1987b). *Incomplete sentences form.* Salt Lake City, UT: Neurology, Learning and Behavior Center.

Goldstein, S. (1988a). *Social skills assessment questionnaire.* Salt Lake City, UT: Neurology, Learning and Behavior Center.

Goldstein, S. (1988b). *Teacher observation checklist.* Salt Lake City, UT: Neurology, Learning and Behavior Center.

Goldstein, S. (1989a). *ADHD diagnostic checklist.* Salt Lake City, UT: Neurology, Learning and Behavior Center.

Goldstein, S. (1989b). *Why won't my child pay attention? A video guide for parents.* Salt Lake City, UT: Neurology, Learning and Behavior Center.

Goldstein, S. (1992). *Why won't my child pay attention?* New York: Wiley.

Goldstein, S. (1994). Understanding and assessing ADHD and related educational and behavioral and emotional disorders. *Therapeutic Care and Education, 3,* 111–129.

Goldstein, S. (1995). *Understanding and managing children's classroom behavior.* New York: Wiley.

Goldstein, S. (1996, January/February). Sibling rivalry. *CH.A.D.D.ER Box,* 11–13.

Goldstein, S. (1997a, June). Attention-deficit hyperactivity disorder. *FBI Law Enforcement Bulletin,* 11–16.

Goldstein, S. (1997b). *Managing attention and learning disorders in late adolescence and adulthood: A guide for practitioners.* New York: Wiley.

Goldstein, S., & Goldstein, M. (1985). *The multi-disciplinary evaluation and treatment of attention deficit disorders in children: Symposium handbook.* Salt Lake City, UT: Neurology, Learning and Behavior Center.

Goldstein, S., & Goldstein, M. (1986). *A parent's guide: Attention deficit disorders in children.* Salt Lake City, UT: Neurology, Learning and Behavior Center.

Goldstein, S., & Goldstein, M. (1987). *A teacher's guide: Attention-deficit disorders in children.* Salt Lake City, UT: Neurology, Learning and Behavior Center.

Goldstein, S., & Goldstein, M. (1990a). *Educating inattentive children* [video]. Salt Lake City, UT: Neurology, Learning and Behavior Center.

Goldstein, S., & Goldstein, M. (1990b). *Understanding and managing attention disorders in children: A guide for practitioners.* New York: Wiley.

Goldstein, S., & Goldstein, M. (1991). *It's just attention disorder: A user's manual.* Salt Lake City, UT: Neurology, Learning and Behavior Center.

Goldstein, S., & Goldstein, M. (1992). *Hyperactivity: Why won't my child pay attention?* New York: Wiley.

Goldstein, S., & Goldstein, M. (1993). *Childhood history form.* Salt Lake City, UT: Neurology, Learning and Behavior Center.

Goldstein, S., & Hinerrman, P. (1988). *Language and behavior problems in children.* Salt Lake City, UT: Neurology, Learning and Behavior Center.

Goldstein, S., & Mather, N. (1998). *Overcoming underachieving: An action guide to helping your child succeed in school.* New York: Wiley.

Goldstein, S., & Pollock, E. (1988). *Social skills training for attention deficit children.* Salt Lake City, UT: Neurology, Learning and Behavior Center.

Gomez, K. M., & Cole, C. L. (1991). Attention deficit hyperactivity disorder: A review of treatment alternatives. *Elementary School Guidance and Counseling, 26,* 106–114.

Gomez, R., & Sanson, A. V. (1994). Mother-child interactions and non-compliance in hyperactive boys with and without conduct problems. *Journal of Child Psychology and Psychiatry, 35,* 477–490.

Good, M. I. (1978). Primary affective disorder, aggression, and criminality: A review and clinical study. *Archives of General Psychiatry, 35,* 954–960.

Goodman, G., & Poillion, M. J. (1992). ADD: Acronym for any dysfunction or difficulty. *Journal of Special Education, 26,* 37–56.

Goodman, L. S., & Gilman, A. (Eds.). (1975). *The pharmacological basis of therapeutics* (5th ed.). New York: Macmillan.

Goodman, R., & Stevenson, J. (1989). A twin study of hyperactivity: II. The aetiological role of genes, family relationships and perinatal activity. *Journal of Child Psychology and Psychiatry, 30,* 691–709.

Goodnow, J. J., & Collins, W. A. (1990). *Development according to parents: The nature, sources and consequences of parents' ideas.* London: Erlbaum.

Goodwin, S. E., & Mahoney, M. J. (1975). Modification of aggression through modeling: An experimental probe. *Journal of Behavior Therapy and Experimental Psychiatry, 6,* 200–202.

Goodyear, P., & Hynd, G. (1992). Attention-deficit disorder with (ADD/+H) and without (ADD/–H) hyperactivity: Behavioral and neuropsychological differentiation. *Journal of Clinical Child Psychology, 21,* 273–305.

Gordon, M. (1979). The assessment of impulsivity and mediating behaviors in hyperactive and non-hyperactive boys. *Journal of Abnormal Child Psychology, 7,* 317–326.

Gordon, M. (1986). Norms for the home situations questionnaire and the school situations questionnaire. *ADD/Hyperactivity Newsletter, 6,* 2.

Gordon, M. (1988). *The Gordon diagnostic system.* Dewitt, NY: Gordon Systems.

Gordon, M. (1990). *ADHD profiles based upon a cluster analysis of clinic measures.* Paper presented at the meeting of the Society for Research in Child and Adolescent Psychopathology, Irvine.

Gordon, M. (1991). The relationship between language and behavior. *Developmental Medicine and Child Neurology, 33,* 86–89.

Gordon, M. (1993a). *Clinical and research applications of the Gordon diagnostic system: A survey of users.* DeWitt, NY: Gordon Systems.

Gordon, M. (1993b). Do computerized measures of attention have a legitimate role in ADHD evaluations? *The ADHD Report, 1,* 5–6.

Gordon, M. (1995a). Certainly not a fad, but it can be over-diagnosed. *Attention, 2,* 20–22.

Gordon, M. (1995b). *How to own and operate an ADHD clinic.* DeWitt, NY: Gordon Systems.

Gordon, M. (1996). Must ADHD be an equal opportunity disorder? *The ADHD Report, 4*(2), 1–3.

Gordon, M. (1997). *Gordon diagnostic system* (Promotional materials). DeWitt, NY: Gordon Systems.

Gordon, M., & Aylward, G. P. (1995). Is the delay task a good test of Barkley's new theory of ADHD? *ADHD Hyperactivity Newsletter, 23,* 6–7.

Gordon, M., DiNiro, D., & Mettelman, B. B. (1989). Observations of test behavior, quantitative scores, and teacher ratings. *Journal of Psychoeducational Assessment, 7,* 141–147.

Gordon, M., Mammen, O., DiNiro, D., & Mettelman, B. (1988). Source-dependent subtypes of ADHD. *ADHD-Hyperactivity Newsletter, 10,* 2–5.

Gordon, M., & McClure, F. D. (1983, August). *The objective assessment of attention deficit disorders.* Paper presented at the 91st annual convention of the American Psychological Association, Anaheim, CA.

Gordon, M., & Mettelman, B. B. (1987). *Technical guide to the Gordon diagnostic system.* Syracuse, NY: Gordon Systems.

Gordon, M., & Mettelman, B. B. (1994, Spring/Summer). Gender differences in ADHD referrals: IQ, laboratory measures, and behavior ratings. *Hyperactivity Newsletter, 21,* 7–9.

Gordon, M., Mettelman, B. B., & Irwin, M. (1994). Sustained attention and grade retention. *Perceptual and Motor Skills, 78,* 555–560.

Gordon, M., Mettelman, B., Smith, D., & Irwin, M. (1989). *Cluster analysis of instruments used in the diagnosis of ADHD.* Paper presented at the annual meeting of the American Academy of Child and Adolescent Psychiatry, New York.

Gordon, M., Thomason, D., Cooper, S., & Ivers, C. L. (1991). Nonmedical treatment of ADHD/hyperactivity: The attention training system. *Journal of School Psychology, 29,* 151–159.

Gordon, S. D. (1990). Parenting skills for children with self-control problems. *The CH.A.D.D.ER Box, 3,* 4–5.

Gordon, S. D., & Davidson, N. (1981). Behavioral parent training. In N. German & L. Kriskern (Eds.), *Handbook of family therapy.* New York: Brunner/Mazel.

Gorenstein, E. E., Mamamoto, C. A., & Sandy, J. M. (1989). Performance of inattentive-overactive children on selected measures of prefrontal-type function. *Journal of Clinical Psychology, 45,* 619–632.

Gorenstein, E. E., & Newman, J. P. (1980). Disinhibitory psychopathology: A new perspective and model for research. *Psychology Review, 87,* 301–315.

Gortmaker, S. L., Walker, D. K., Weitzman, M., & Sobel, A. M. (1990). Chronic conditions, socioeconomic risks, and behavioral problems in children and adolescents. *Pediatrics, 85,* 267–276.

Goslin, D. (Ed.). (1969). *Handbook of socialization theory and research.* Chicago, IL: Rand McNally.

Gottfried, A. W., & Gottfried, A. E. (1984). Home environment and cognitive development in young children of middle-socioeconomic status families. In A. W. Gottfried (Ed.), *Home environment and early cognitive development: Longitudinal research.* Orlando, FL: Academic Press.

Gottman, J. M., Gonso, J., & Schuler, P. (1976). Teaching social skills to isolated children. *Journal of Abnormal Child Psychology, 4,* 179–197.

Gottschalk, L. A. (1984). Hyperactive children: A study of the content analysis of their speech. *Psychotherapy and Psychosomatics, 4,* 125–135.

Goulden, K. J., & Shinnar, S. (1988, September). *Epilepsy and behavior disturbance in children with multiple developmental disabilities.* Presentation made at the seventeenth national meeting of the Child Neurology Society, Halifax, Canada.

Goyer, P. F., Davis, G. C., & Rapoport, J. L. (1979). Abuse of prescribed stimulant medication by a 13-year-old hyperactive boy. *Journal of the American Academy of Child Psychiatry, 18,* 170–175.

Goyette, C. H., Conners, C. K., & Ulrich, R. F. (1978). Normative data on the revised Conners parent and teacher rating scales. *Journal of Abnormal Child Psychology, 6,* 221–236.

Graham, S., & Harris, K. (1989). A components analysis of cognitive strategy instruction: Effects on learning disabled students' compositions and self-efficacy. *Journal of Educational Psychology, 81,* 353–361.

Graham, S., Harris, K., & Reid, R. (1992). Developing self-regulated learners. *Focus on Exceptional Children, 24,* 1–16.

Granger, D. A., Whalen, C. K., & Henker, B. (1993a). Malleability of social impressions of hyperactive children. *Journal of Abnormal Child Psychology, 21,* 631–647.

Granger, D. A., Whalen, C. K., & Henker, B. (1993b). Perceptions of methylphenidate effects on hyperactive children's peer interactions. *Journal of Abnormal Child Psychology, 21,* 535.

Granger, D. A., Whalen, C. K., Henker, B., & Cantwell, C. (1996). ADHD boys' behavior during structured classroom social activities: Effects of social demands, teacher proximity and methylphenidate. *Journal of Attention Disorders, 1,* 16–30.

Grant, M. L., Ilai, D., Nussbaum, N. L., & Bigler, E. D. (1990). The relationship between continuous performance tasks and neuropsychological tests in children with attention-deficit hyperactivity disorder. *Perceptual and Motor Skills, 70,* 435–445.

Grant, W. (1991). Attention deficit disorder: What is it? How to help? Prepared by Dr. Wilson Grant, M.D. *Strategies for Success Newsletter.*

Gray, J. W., Dean, R. S., Strom, D. A., Wheeler, T. E., & Brockley, M. (1989). Perinatal complications as predictors of developmental disabilities. *Developmental Neuropsychology, 5,* 105–113.

Gray, W. S. (1967). *Gray oral reading test.* New York: Bobbs-Merrill.

Gray, W. S., & Sime, S. (1989). *Discipline in schools* (the Elton Report). London: HMSO.

Graziano, A. M. (1977). Parents as behavior therapists. In M. Hersen, R. M. Eisler, & P. M. Miller (Eds.), *Progress in behavior modification.* New York: Academic Press.

Graziano, A. M. (1983). Behavioral approaches to child and family systems. *Counseling Psychologist, 11,* 47–56.

Green, L. L. (1992). Pharmacologic treatment of attention deficit hyperactivity disorder. *Psychiatric Clinics of North America, 15,* 1–27.

Green, S. M., Loeber, R., & Lahey, B. B. (1991). Stability of mothers' recall of the age of onset of their child's attention and hyperactivity problems. *Journal of the American Academy of Child and Adolescent Psychiatry, 30,* 135–137.

Greenbaum, P. E., Prange, M. E., Friedman, R. M., & Silver, S. E. (1991). Substance abuse prevalence and comorbidity with other psychiatric disorders among adolescents with severe emotional disturbances. *Journal of the American Academy of Child and Adolescent Psychiatry, 30,* 575–583.

Greenberg, L. (1991). *Test of variables of attention (TOVA).* St. Paul, MN: Attention Technology.

Greenberg, L. (1996). Letter to the editor. *The ADHD Report, 4,* 16.

Greenberg, L. M., & Crosby, R. D. (1992). *Specificity and sensitivity of the test of variables of attention (TOVA).* Manuscript submitted for publication.

Greenberg, L. M., & Waldman, I. D. (1991). *Test of variables of attention (TOVA), developmental normative data.* Submitted to Journal of Child Psychology and Psychiatry, Universal Attention Disorders.

Greene, R. (1993). Hidden factors affecting the education success of ADHD students. *The ADHD Report, 2,* 8–9.

Greenhill, L., Cooper, T., Solomon, M., Fried, J., & Cornblatt, B. (1987). Methylphenidate saliva levels in children. *Psychopharmacology Bulletin, 23,* 115–119.

Greenhill, L. L., & Osman, B. B. (1991). *Ritalin: Theory and patient management.* New York: Liebert.

Greenhill, L. L., Rieder, R. O., & Wender, P. H. (1973). Lithium carbonate in the treatment of hyperactive children. *Archives of General Psychiatry, 28,* 636–645.

Greenwald, A. G., & Albert, R. D. (1968). Acceptance and recall of improvised arguments. *Journal of Personality and Social Psychology, 8,* 31–35.

Gregg, S. (1996). *Preventing anti-social behavior in disabled and at-risk students* [Policy briefs]. Charleston, WV: Appalachian Educational Laboratory.

Gregorich, B., & Armstrong, B. (1985). *Logical logic.* Santa Barbara, CA: The Learning Works.

Gresham, F. M. (1986). Conceptual issues in the assessment of social competence in children. In P. Strain, M. Guralnick, & H. M. Walker (Eds.), *Children's social behavior: Development, assessment and modification.* New York: Academic Press.

Gresham, F. M. (1988). Social skills: Conceptual and applied aspects of assessment, training, and social validation. In J. C. Witt, S. N. Elliott, & F. M. Gresham (Eds.), *Handbook of behavior therapy in education* (pp. 523–546). New York: Plenum Press.

Gresham, F. M. (1991). Conceptualizing behavior disorders in terms of resistance to intervention. *School Psychology Review, 20,* 23–36.

Gresham, F. M. (1995). Best practices in social skills assessment. In A. Thomas & J. Grimes (Eds.), *Best practices in school psychology* (Vol. 3). Washington, DC: National Association of School Psychologists.

Gresham, F. M., & Elliott, S. (1984). Assessment and classification of children's social skills: A review of methods and issues. *School Psychology Review, 13,* 292–300.

Gresham, F. M., & Elliott, S. N. (1990). *Social skills rating system: Manual.* Circle Pines, MN: American Guidance Services.

Gresham, F. M., & Gansle, K. A. (1992). Misguided assumptions of *DSM-III-R:* Implications for school psychological practice. *School Psychology Quarterly, 7,* 79–95.

Gresham, F. M., & Nagle, R. J. (1980). Social skills training with children: Responsiveness to modeling and coaching as a function of peer orientation. *Journal of Consulting and Clinical Psychology, 48,* 718–729.

Gresham, F. M., & Reschly, D. J. (1988). Issues in the conceptualization, classification, and assessment of social skills in the mildly handicapped. In T. R. Kratochwill (Ed.), *Advances in school psychology* (Vol. 6, pp. 203–247). Hillsdale, NJ: Erlbaum.

Greve, K. W., Brooks, J., Crouch, J., Rice, W. J., Cicerone, K., & Rowland, L. (1993). Factorial structure of the Wisconsin card sorting test. *Clinical Neuropsychologist, 7,* 350–351.

Greve, K. W., Williams, M. C., Haas, W. G., Littell, R. R., & Reinoso, R. (1996). The role of attention in Wisconsin card sorting test performance. *Archives of Clinical Neuropsychology, 11,* 215–222.

Grieger, T., Kauffman, J. M., & Grieger, R. M. (1976). Effects of peer reporting on cooperative play and aggression of kindergarten children. *Journal of School Psychology, 14,* 307–313.

Griffith, D. R., Azuma, S. D., & Chasnoff, I. J. (1994). Three-year outcome of children exposed prenatally to drugs. *Journal of the American Academy of Child and Adolescent Psychiatry, 33,* 20–27.

Grignetti, M. C. (1986). *Odyssey: A curriculum for thinking—problem solving.* Watertown, MA: Mastery Education.

Grigoroiu-Serbanescu, M., Christoderescu, D., Jipescu, I., Totoescu, A., Marinescu, E., & Ardeleau, V. (1989). Psychopathology in children aged 10–17 of bipolar parents: Psychopathology rate and correlates of the severity of the psychopathology. *Journal of Affective Disorders, 16,* 167–179.

Grilo, C. M., Becker, D. F., Fehon, D. C., & Edell, W. S. (1996). Conduct disorder, substance use disorders, and co-existing conduct and substance use disorders in adolescent inpatients. *American Journal of Psychiatry, 153,* 914–920.

Grilo, C. M., Becker, D. F., Walker, M. L., Levy, K. N., Edell, W. S., & McGlashan, T. H. (1995). Psychiatric comorbidity in adolescent inpatients with substance use disorders. *Journal of the American Academy of Child and Adolescent Psychiatry, 34,* 1085–1091.

Grimley, L. K. (1993). Academic assessment of ADHD children. In J. L. Matson (Ed.), *Handbook of hyperactivity in children.* Needham Heights, MA: Allyn & Bacon.

Grizenko, N., Papineau, D., & Sayegh, L. (1993). Effectiveness of a multimodal day treatment program for children with disruptive behavior problems. *Journal of the American Academy of Child and Adolescent Psychiatry, 32,* 127–134.

Grizenko, N., & Pawliuk, N. (1994). Risk and protective factors for disruptive behavior disorders in children. *American Journal of Orthopsychiatry, 64,* 534–544.

Grodzinsky, G. M., & Diamond, R. (1992). Frontal lobe functioning in boys with attention-deficit hyperactivity disorder. *Developmental Neuropsychology, 8,* 427–445.

Gross, M. D. (1976). Growth of hyperkinetic children taking methylphenidate, dextroamphetamine or imipramine/desipramine. *Pediatrics, 58,* 423–431.

Gross-Tsur, V., Manor, O., & Shalev, R. S. (1996). Developmental dyscalculia: Prevalence in demographic features. *Developmental Medicine in Child Neurology, 38,* 25–33.

Gross-Tsur, V., Shalev, R. S., Manor, O., & Amir, N. (1995). Development of right hemisphere syndrome. Clinical spectrum of the non-verbal learning disability. *Journal of Learning Disabilities, 28,* 80–86.

Grotevant, H. D., & McRoy, R. G. (1990). Adopted adolescents in residential treatment: The role of the family. In D. Brodzinsky & M. Schechter (Eds.), *The psychology of adoption.* New York: Oxford University Press.

Gualtieri, C. T., & Hicks, R. E. (1985). Neuropharmacology of methylphenidate and a neural substitute for childhood hyperactivity. *Psychiatric Clinics of North America, 8,* 875–892.

Gualtieri, C. T., Hicks, R. E., Patrick, K., Schroeder, S. R., & Breese, G. R. (1984). Clinical correlates of methylphenidate blood levels. *Therapeutic Drug Monitoring, 6,* 379–392.

Gualtieri, C. T., Quade, D., Hicks, R. E., Mayo, J. P., & Schroeder, S. R. (1984). Tardive dyskinesia and other clinical consequences of neuroleptic treatment in children and adolescents. *American Journal Psychiatry, 141,* 20–23.

Guare, R. (1988). *Head injury rehabilitation: Managing attention deficits.* Houston, TX: HDI.

Guerin, D. W., Gottfried, A. W., Oliver, P. H., & Thomas, C. W. (1994). Temperament and school functioning during early adolescence. *Journal of Early Adolescence, 14,* 200–225.

Guevremont, D. C. (1990). Social skills and peer relationship training. In R. A. Barkley (Ed.), *Attention-deficit hyperactivity disorder: A handbook for diagnosis and treatment.* New York: Guilford Press.

Guevremont, D. C. (1993a). Atypical children: Diagnostic and treatment considerations. *The ADHD Report, 2,* 5–6.

Guevremont, D. C. (1993b). Social skills training: A viable treatment of ADHD? *The ADHD Report, 1,* 6–7.

Guevremont, D. C., DuPaul, G. J., & Barkley, R. A. (1990). Diagnosis and assessment of attention deficit hyperactivity disorder in children. *Journal of School Psychology, 28,* 51–78.

Guevremont, D. C., DuPaul, G. J., & Barkley, R. A. (1993). Behavioral assessment of attention deficit hyperactivity disorder. In J. L. Matson (Ed.), *Handbook of hyperactivity in children.* Needham Heights, MA: Allyn & Bacon.

Guffey, D. G. (1992). Ritalin: What educators and parents should know. *Journal of Instructional Psychology, 19,* 167–169.

Gunter, P., Fox, J. J., Brady, M. P., Shores, R. E., & Cavanaugh, K. (1988). Nonhandicapped peers as multiple exemplars: A generalization tactic for promoting autistic students' social skills. *Behavioral Disorders, 13,* 116–126.

Gurainick, M. J., Connor, R. T., Hammond, M. A., Gottman, J. M., & Kinnish, K. (1996). The peer relations of pre-school children with communication disorders. *Child Development, 67,* 471–489.

Guy, W. (1976). *ECDEU assessment manual for psychopharmacology* (pp. 383–406). Rockville, MD: National Institute of Mental Health.

Haake, C. A. (1991). Behavioral markers and intervention strategies for regular and special education teachers. In P. J. Accardo, T. A. Blondis, & B. Y. Whitman (Eds.), *Attention deficit disorders and hyperactivity in children.* New York: Marcel Dekker.

Hack, M., Taylor, H. G., Klein, N., Eiben, R., Schatschneider, C., & Mercuri-Minich, N. (1994). School-age outcomes in children with birth weights under 750 g. *The New England Journal of Medicine, 331,* 753–759.

Hadders-Algra, M., & Touwen, B. C. (1992). Minor neurological dysfunction is more closely related to learning difficulties than to behavioral problems. *Journal of Learning Disabilities, 25,* 649.

Haenlein, M., & Caul, W. F. (1987). Attention deficit disorder with hyperactivity: A specific hypothesis of reward dysfunction. *Journal of the American Academy of Child and Adolescent Psychiatry, 26,* 356–362.

Hagen, J. W., & Hale, G. H. (1973). The development of attention in children. In *Child Psychology* (Vol. 7, p. 117). Minneapolis: University of Minnesota Press.

Hagerman, R. (1991). Organic causes of ADHD. *ADD-VANCE, 3,* 4–6.

Hagerman, R., Amiri, K., & Cronister, A. (1991). Fragile X checklist. *American Journal of Medical Genetics, 38,* 283–287.

Hagerman, R., & Falkenstein, A. R. (1987). An association between recurrent otitis media in infancy and later hyperactivity. *Clinical Pediatrics, 5,* 253–257.

Hagerman, R., Kemper, M., & Hudson, M. (1985). Learning disabilities and attentional problems in boys with fragile-X syndrome. *American Journal of Diseases of Children, 139,* 674–678.

Hagerman, R., & Sobesky, W. (1989). Psychopathology in fragile-X syndrome. *American Journal of Orthopsychiatry, 59,* 142–152.

Hagino, O. R., Weller, E. B., Weller, R. A., Washing, D., Fristad, M. A., & Kontras, S. B. (1995). Untoward effects of lithium treatment in children aged four through six years. *Journal of the American Academy of Child and Adolescent Psychiatry, 34,* 1584–1590.

Hakola, S. (1992). Legal rights of students with attention deficit disorder. *School Psychology Quarterly, 7,* 285–297.

Halikas, J. A., Meller, J., Morse, C., & Lyttle, M. D. (1990). Predicting substance abuse in juvenile offenders: Attention deficit disorder versus aggressivity. *Child Psychiatry and Human Development, 21*(1), 49–55.

Hall, C. W., & Kataria, S. (1992). Effects of two treatment techniques on delay and vigilance tasks with attention deficit hyperactivity disorder (ADHD) children. *Journal of Psychology, 126,* 17–25.

Hall, C. W., & Sudesh, K. (1992). Effects of two treatment techniques on delay and vigilance tasks with ADHD children. *Journal of Psychology, 126,* 17–25.

Hall, L. E., & Kramer, J. R. (1995). Neurological soft signs in childhood do not predict neuropsychological dysfunction in adulthood. *Developmental Neuropsychology, 11,* 223–235.

Hall, S. J., Halperin, J. M., Schwartz, S. T., & Newcorn, J. H. (1997). Behavioral and executive functions in children with attention deficit hyperactivity disorder and reading disability. *Journal of Attention Disorders, 1,* 235–247.

Hallahan, D. P., Lloyd, J. W., Kneedler, R. D., & Marshall, K. J. (1982). A comparison of the effects of self- versus teacher-assessment of on-task behavior. *Behavior Therapy, 12,* 715–723.

Hallahan, D. P., Marshall, K. J., & Lloyd, J. W. (1981). Self-recording during group instruction: Effects on attention to task. *Learning Disability Quarterly, 4,* 407–413.

Hallahan, D. P., & Sapona, R. (1983). Self-monitoring of attention with learning-disabled children: Past research and current issues. *Journal of Learning Disabilities, 16,* 616–620.

Hallowell, E. M., & Ratey, J. J. (1994). *Driven to distraction.* New York: Pantheon Books.

Halperin, J. M. (1991). The clinical assessment of attention. *Journal of Neuroscience, 58,* 171–182.

Halperin, J. M., & Gittelman, R. (1986). Do hyperactive children and their siblings differ in IQ and academic achievement? *Psychiatry Research, 6,* 253–258.

Halperin, J. M., Gittelman, R., Katz, S., & Struve, F. A. (1986). Relationship between stimulant effect, electroencephalogram, and clinical neurological findings in hyperactive children. *Journal of the American Academy of Child Psychiatry, 25,* 820–825.

Halperin, J. M., Gittelman, R., Klein, D. F., & Rudel, R. G. (1984). Reading-disabled hyperactive children: A distinct subgroup of attention deficit disorder with hyperactivity? *Journal of Abnormal Child Psychology, 12,* 1–14.

Halperin, J. M., Matier, K., Bedi, G., Sharma, V., & Newcorn, J. H. (1992). Specificity of inattention, impulsivity and hyperactivity to the diagnosis of attention-deficit hyperactivity disorder. *Journal of American Academy of Child and Adolescent Psychiatry, 31,* 190–196.

Halperin, J. M., Newcorn, J. H., Kopstein, I., McKay, K. E., Schwartz, S. T., Siever, L. J., & Sharma, V. (1997). Serotonin, aggression and parental psychopathology in children with attention-deficit hyperactivity disorder. *Journal of the American Academy of Child and Adolescent Psychiatry, 36,* 1391–1398.

Halperin, J. M., Newcorn, J. H., Matier, K., Bedi, G., Hall, S., & Sharma, V. (1995). Impulsivity and the initiation of fights in children with disruptive behavior disorders. *Journal of Child Psychology and Psychiatry in Allied Disciplines, 36,* 1199–1211.

Halperin, J. M., Newcorn, J. H., Matier, K., Sharma, V., McKay, K. E., & Schwartz, S. (1993). Discriminant validity of attention-deficit hyperactivity disorder. *Journal of the American Academy of Child and Adolescent Psychiatry, 32,* 1038–1043.

Halperin, J. M., Newcorn, J. H., Sharma, V., & Healey, J. M. (1990). Inattentive and noninattentive ADHD children: Do they constitute a unitary group? *Journal of Abnormal Child Psychology, 18,* 437–449.

Halperin, J. M., O'Brien, J. D., & Newcorn, J. H. (1990). Validation of hyperactive, aggressive, and mixed hyperactive/aggressive childhood disorders: A research note. *Journal of Child Psychology and Psychiatry, 31,* 455–459.

Halperin, J. M., Sharma, V., Greenblatt, E., & Schwartz, S. T. (1991). Assessment of the continuous performance test: Reliability and validity in a non-referred sample. *Journal of Child Psychology and Psychiatry, 31,* 455–459.

Hamlett, K. W., Pellegrini, D. S., & Conners, C. K. (1987). An investigation of executive processes in the problem-solving of attention deficit disorder-hyperactive children. *Journal of Pediatric Psychology, 12,* 227–240.

Hammill, D. D. (1985). *Detroit tests of learning aptitude: 2.* Austin, TX: Pro-Ed.

Hammill, D. D., & Larsen, S. C. (1996). *The test of written language: 3.* Austin, TX: Pro-Ed.

Handen, B. L., Breaux, A. M., Gosling, A., Ploor, P. L., & Feldman, H. (1990). Efficacy of methylphenidate among mentally retarded children with attention deficit hyperactivity disorder. *Pediatrics, 86,* 922–930.

Handen, B. L., Breaux, A. M., Janosky, J., McAuliffe, S., Feldman, H., & Gosling, A. (1992). Effects and non-effects of methylphenidate in children with mental retardation and ADHD. *Journal of the American Academy of Child and Adolescent Psychiatry, 31,* 455–461.

Handen, B. L., Feldman, H., Gosling, A., Breaux, A. M., & McAuliffe, S. (1991). Adverse side effects of methylphenidate among mentally retarded children with ADHD. *Journal of the American Academy of Child and Adolescent Psychiatry, 30,* 241–245.

Handen, B. L., Janosky, J., McAuliffe, S., Breaux, A. M., & Feldman, H. (1994). Prediction of response of methylphenidate among children with ADHD and mental retardation. *Journal of the American Academy of Child and Adolescent Psychiatry, 33,* 1185–1193.

Hanf, C. (1978). *Parent training for behaviorally disordered children.* Workshop presented for the psychology staff in Granite School District, Salt Lake City, UT.

Hanna, G. L. (1994). Demographic and clinical features of obsessive-compulsive disorder in children and adolescents. *Journal of the American Academy of Child and Adolescent Psychiatry, 34,* 19–27.

Hansen, D. J., St. Lawrence, J. S., & Christoff, K. A. (1989). Group conversational-skills training with inpatient children and adolescents: Social validation, generalization, and maintenance. *Behavior Modification, 13,* 4–31.

Harcherik, D. F., Cohen, D. J., Ort, S., Paul, R., Shaywitz, B. A., Volkmar, F. R., Rothman, S. L. G., & Leckman, J. F. (1985). Computed tomographic brain scanning in four neuropsychiatric disorders of childhood. *Medical Journal of Psychiatry, 142,* 731–734.

Harman, P. K., & Morton, D. G. (1993). The link between developmental dyslexia, ADD and chemical dependency [Special issue]. *Learning Disability Quarterly: Adults with Learning Disabilities, 16,* 8.

Harrell, R. F., Capp, R., & Davis, S. (1981). Can nutritional supplements help mentally retarded children? An exploratory study. *Proceedings of the National Academy of Science, 78,* 574.

Harris, E. L. (1994). Parents' and caregivers' perceptions of their children's development. *Developmental Medicine and Child Neurology, 36,* 918–923.

Harris, E. L., Singer, H. S., Reader, M. J., Brown, J. E., Cox, C. S., Mohr, J. H., Schuerholz, L. J., Chase, G. A., & Denckla, M. B. (1995). Executive function in children with Tourette's Syndrome and/or ADHD. *Journal of International Neuropsychological Society, 1,* 511–516.

Harris, K. R. (1986). Self-monitoring of attentional behavior versus self-monitoring of productivity: Effects on-task behavior. An academic response rate among learning disabled children. *Journal of Applied Behavior Analysis, 19,* 417–423.

Hart, E. L., Lahey, B. B., Loeber, R., Applegate, B., & Frick, P. (1995). Developmental change in attention-deficit hyperactivity disorder in boys: A four-year longitudinal study. *Journal of Abnormal Child Psychology, 23,* 729–749.

Hart, E. L., Lahey, B. B., Hynd, G. W., & Loeber, R. (1995). Associations of chronic overanxious disorder with atopic rhinitis in boys: A four-year longitudinal study. *Journal of Clinical Psychology, 24,* 332–337.

Harter, M. R., Anllo-Vento, L., Wood, F. B., & Schroeder, M. M. (1988). Separate brain potential characteristics in children with reading disability and attention deficit disorder: II. Color and letter relevance effects. *Brain and Cognition, 7,* 115–140.

Harter, M. R., Diering, S., & Wood, F. B. (1988). Separate brain potential characteristics in children with reading disability and attention deficit disorder: I. Relevance-independent effects. *Brain and Cognition, 7,* 54–86.

Hartmann, T. (1993). *Attention deficit disorder: A different perception.* Novato, CA: Underwood Miller.

Hartsough, C. S., & Lambert, N. M. (1982). Some environmental and familial correlates and antecedents of hyperactivity. *American Journal of Orthopsychiatry, 52,* 272–287.

Hartsough, C. S., & Lambert, N. M. (1985). Medical factors in hyperactive and normal children. *American Journal of Orthopsychiatry, 55,* 190–201.

Hartup, W. (1983). Peer relations. In E. M. Heatherington & P. H. Mussen (Eds.), *Handbook of child psychology: Vol. 4. Socialization, personality and social development* (pp. 103–196). New York: Wiley.

Hartup, W. W. (1996). Presidential address. The company they keep: Friendships and their developmental significance. *Child Development, 67,* 1–13.

Harvey, J. R., & Chernouskas, C. A. (1995, October). *Diagnosis and description of attention deficit hyperactivity disorder with the Woodcock-Johnson psychoeducational battery-revised.* Paper presented at the CH.A.D.D. National Conference, Washington, DC.

Hasher, L. T., & Zaks, R. T. (1988). Working memory, comprehension and aging: A review and a new view. In G. H. Bower (Ed.), *The psychology of learning and motivation: Advances in research and theory* (Vol. 22, pp. 193–222). San Diego: Academic Press.

Haslam, R. H., Dalby, J. T., & Rademaker, A. W. (1984). Effects of megavitamins on children with attention deficit disorder. *Pediatrics, 74,* 103–111.

Hassanyeh, F., & Davidson, K. (1980). Bipolar affective psychosis with onset before age 16 years. Report of ten cases. *British Journal of Psychiatry, 137,* 530–539.

Hatch, T. F. (1988). Encopresis and constipation in children. *Pediatric Clinics of North America, 35,* 257–280.

Hathaway, S. R., & McKinley, J. C. (1989). *Minnesota multiphasic personality inventory: II (MMPI-II).* Circle Pines, MN: NCS Assessments.

Hauser, P., Soler, R., Brucker-Davis, F., & Weintraub, B. D. (1997). Thyroid hormones correlate with symptoms of hyperactivity but not in attention-deficit hyperactivity disorder. *Psychoneuroendocrinology, 22,* 107–114.

Hauser, P., Zametkin, A. J., Martinez, P., Vitiello, B., Matochik, J. A., Mixson, A. J., & Weintraub, B. D. (1993). Attention-deficit hyperactivity disorder in people with generalized resistance to thyroid hormone. *New England Journal of Medicine, 328,* 997.

Haut, J. S., Haut, M. W., Callahan, T. S., & Franzen, N. D. (1992). *Factoral analysis of the wide range assessment of memory and learning scores in a clinical sample.* Paper presented at the twelfth annual meeting of the National Academy of Neuropsychology, Pittsburgh, PA.

Hawkins, J. D., Catalano, R. F., & Miller, J. Y. (1992). Risk and protective factors for alcohol and other drug problems in adolescence and early adulthood Implications for substance abuse prevention. *Psychological Bulletin, 112,* 64–105.

Hayes, S. C., & Nelson, R. O. (1983). Similar reactivity produced by external cues and self-monitoring. *Behavior Modification, 7,* 193–196.

Hayvren, M., & Hymel, S. (1984). Ethical issues in socio-metric testing: The impact of sociometric measures on interaction behavior. *Developmental Psychology, 28,* 844–849.

Hazel, J. S., Bragg-Schumaker, J., Sherman, J. A., & Sheldon-Wildgen, J. (1981). *Asset: A social skills program for adolescents.* Champaign, IL: Research Press.

Healey, J. M., Newcorn, J. H., Halperin, J. M., & Wolf, L. E. (1993). The factor structure of ADHD items in *DSM-III-R:* Internal consistency and external validation. *Journal of Abnormal Child Psychology, 21,* 441–453.

Heaton, R. K. (1981). *Wisconsin card sorting test manual.* Odessa, FL: Psychological Assessment Resources.

Heaton, T. B., & Bigler, E. D. (1991). Neuroimaging techniques in neuropsychological research. *Bulletin of the National Academy of Neuropsychology, 9,* 14.

Hechtman, L. (1981). Families of hyperactives. *Research in Community and Mental Health, 2,* 275–292.

Hechtman, L. (1993a). Aims and methodological problems in multimodal treatment studies. *Canadian Journal of Psychiatry, 38,* 458–464.

Hechtman, L. (1993b). Genetic and neurobiological aspects of attention-deficit hyperactivity disorder: A review. *Journal of Psychiatric Neuroscience, 19,* 193–201.

Hechtman, L., Weiss, G., & Perlman, T. (1980). Hyperactives as young adults: Self-esteem and social skills. *Canadian Journal of Psychiatry, 25,* 478–483.

Hechtman, L., Weiss, G., & Perlman, T. (1984). Young adult outcome of hyperactive children who received long-term stimulant treatment. *Journal of American Academy of Child Psychiatry, 23,* 261–269.

Hechtman, L., Weiss, G., Perlman, T., & Amsel, R. (1984). Hyperactives as young adults: Initial predictors of adult outcome. *Journal of the American Academy of Child and Adolescent Psychiatry, 23,* 250–260.

Heffron, W. M., Martin, C. A., Welsh, R. J., & Perry, P. (1987). Hyperactivity and child abuse. *Canadian Journal of Psychiatry, 32,* 384–386.

Heilman, K. M., Voeller, K. K. S., Nadeau, S. E. (1991). A possible pathophysiological substrate of attention deficit hyperactivity disorder. *Journal of Child Neurology, 6*(Suppl.), S76–S81.

Heinicke, C. M. (1995). Expanding the study of the formation of the child's relationships: Commentary. In E. Waters, B. Vaughn, G. Posada, & K. Kondo-Ikemuria (Eds.), Caregiving, cultural and cognitive perspectives on secure-base behavior and working models: New growing points of attachment, theory and research. *Monographs of the Society for Research in Child Development,* (2/3, Serial No. 244), 300–309.

Heins, E. D., Lloyd, J. W., & Hallahan, D. P. (1986). Cued and non-cued self-recording of attention to task. *Behavior Modification, 10,* 235–254.

Heinze, A., Helsel, W. J., Matson, J. L., & Kapperman, G. (1987). Assessing general psychopathology in children and youth with visual handicaps. *Journal of Developmental Disabilities, 13,* 219.

Hellgren, L., Gillberg, C., Gillberg, I. C., & Enerskog, I. (1993). Children with deficits in attention, motor control and perception (DAMP) almost grown up; General health at 16 years. *Developmental Medicine and Child Neurology, 35,* 881–892.

Helsel, W. J., & Fremer, C. M. (1993). Theory and hyperactivity. In J. L. Matson (Ed.), *Handbook of hyperactivity in children.* Needham Heights, MA: Allyn & Bacon.

Helsel, W. J., Hersen, M., & Lubetsky, M. J. (1989). Stimulant medication and the retarded. *Journal of the American Academy of Child and Adolescent Psychiatry, 28,* 138–139.

Hendrickson, J. M., Strain, P. S., Tremblay, A., & Shores, R. E. (1982). Interactions of behaviorally handicapped children: Functional effects of peer social interactions. *Behavior Modification, 6,* 323–353.

Henker, B., Buhrmester, D., Hinshaw, S. P., Huber, A., & Laski, K. (1989). Does stimulant medication improve the peer status of hyperactive children? *Journal of Consulting and Clinical Psychology, 57,* 545–549.

Henker, B., & Whalen, C. K. (1980). The changing faces of hyperactivity: Retrospect and prospect. In C. K. Whalen & B. Henker (Eds.), *Hyperactive children: The social ecology of identification and treatment.* New York: Academic Press.

Henker, B., & Whalen, C. K. (1989). Hyperactivity and attention deficits. *American Psychologist, 44,* 216–223.

Henker, B., Whalen, C., & Hinshaw, S. (1980). The attributional contexts of cognitive motivational strategies. *Exceptional Educational Quarterly, 1,* 17–30.

Herjanic, B., & Reich, W. (1982). Development of a structured psychiatric interview for children: Agreement between child and parent on individual symptoms. *Journal of Abnormal Child Psychology, 10,* 307–324.

Hern, K. L., & Hynd, G. W. (1992). Clinical differentiation of the attention deficit disorder subtypes: Do sensory motor deficits characterize children with ADD/without hyperactivity. *Archives of Clinical Neuropsychology, 7,* 77–83.

Hernandez, D. J. (1994). Children's changing access to resources: A historical perspective. *Social Policy Report: Society of Research and Child Development, 8*(1).

Hertz-Lazarowitz, R., Sharan, S., & Steinberg, R. (1980). Classroom learning style and cooperative behavior of elementary school children. *Journal of Educational Psychology, 72,* 99–106.

Hier, D., LeMay, M., Rosenberger, P., & Perlo, V. (1978). Developmental dyslexia: Evidence for a subgroup with reversal of cerebral asymmetry. *Archives of Neurology, 35,* 90–92.

Higgenbotham, P., & Bartling, C. (1993). The effects of sensory distractions on short-term recall of children with attention deficit-hyperactivity disorder versus normally achieving children. *Bulletin of the Psychonomic Society, 31,* 507–510.

Hill, R. D., Olympia, D., & Angerbuer, K. C. (1991). A comparison of preference for familial, social and material rewards between hyperactive and non-hyperactive boys. *School Psychology International, 12,* 225–229.

Hilton, D. K., Martin, C. A., Heffron, W. M., Hall, B. D., & Johnson, G. L. (1991). Imipramine treatment of ADHD in a fragile-X child. *Journal of the American Academy of Child and Adolescent Psychiatry, 30,* 831–834.

Hinshaw, S. P. (1987). On the distinction between attention deficits/hyperactivity and conduct problems/aggression in child psychopathology. *Psychological Bulletin, 101,* 443–463.

Hinshaw, S. P. (1992a). Academic underachievement. Attention deficits and aggression: Comorbidity and implications for intervention. *Journal of Consulting and Clinical Psychology, 60,* 893–903.

Hinshaw, S. P. (1992b). Externalizing behavior problems and academic underachievement in childhood and adolescence: Casual relationships and underlying mechanisms. *Psychological Bulletin, 111,* 127–155.

Hinshaw, S. P., Buhrmester, D., & Heller, T. (1989). Anger control in response to verbal provocation: Effects of stimulant medication for boys with ADHD. *Journal of Abnormal Child Psychology, 17,* 393–407.

Hinshaw, S. P., & Erhardt, D. (1991). Attention-deficit hyperactivity disorder. In P. C. Kendall (Ed.), *Child and adolescent therapy: Cognitive-behavioral procedures.* New York: Guilford Press.

Hinshaw, S. P., Heller, T., & McHale, J. P. (1992). Covert antisocial behavior in boys with attention-deficit hyperactivity disorder: External validation and effects of methylphenidate. *Journal of Consulting and Clinical Psychology, 60,* 274–281.

Hinshaw, S. P., Henker, B., & Whalen, C. K. (1984a). Self-control in hyperactive boys and anger-inducing situations: Effects of cognitive-behavioral training and of methylphenidate. *Journal of Abnormal Child Psychology, 12,* 55–78.

Hinshaw, S. P., Henker, B., & Whalen, C. K. (1984b). Cognitive-behavioral and pharmacologic interventions for hyperactive boys: Comparative and combined effects. *Journal of Consulting and Clinical Psychology, 52,* 739–749.

Hinshaw, S. P., Henker, B., Whalen, C. K., Erhardt, D., & Dunnington, R. E. (1989). Aggressive, prosocial, and nonsocial behavior in hyperactive boys: Dose effects of methylphenidate in naturalistic settings. *Journal of Consulting and Clinical Psychology, 57,* 636–643.

Hinshaw, S. P., & Melnick, S. (1992). Self-management therapies and attention-deficit hyperactivity disorder: Reinforced self-evaluation and anger control interventions. *Behavior Modification, 16,* 253–273.

Hinshaw, S. P., Morrison, D. C., Carte, E. T., & Cornsweet, C. (1987). Factorial dimensions of the revised behavior problem checklist: Replication and validation within a kindergarten sample. *Journal of Abnormal Child Psychology, 15,* 309–327.

Hinslie, L., & Shatzky, J. (1940). *Psychiatric dictionary.* New York: Oxford University Press.

Hinton, S. C., Conners, C. K., Levin, E. D., & Meck, W. H. (1995). Nicotine and attention deficit disorder: Effects on temporal generalization. *Psychopharmacology Bulletin, 31,* 579.

Hodges, K., & Craighead, W. E. (1990). Relationship of children's depression inventory factors to diagnosed depression. *Psychological Assessment, 2,* 489–492.

Hodges, K., Kline, J., Stern, L., Cytryn, L., & McKnew, D. (1982). The development of a child assessment interview for research and clinical use. *Journal of Abnormal Child Psychology, 10,* 173–189.

Hoehn, T. B., & Bauermeister, A. A. (1994). A critique of the application of sensory integration therapy to children with learning disabilities. *Journal of Learning Disabilities, 27,* 338–365.

Hoffman, L. W. (1980). The effects of maternal employment on the academic attitudes and performance of school-age children. *School Psychology Review, 9,* 319–335.

Hohman, L. B. (1922). Post-encephalitic behavior disorder in children. *Johns Hopkins Hospital Bulletin, 33,* 372–375.

Holborow, P. L., & Berry, P. S. (1986). Hyperactivity and learning difficulties. *Journal of Learning Disabilities, 19,* 426–431.

Holden, G. W., & Edwards, L. E. (1989). Parental attitudes towards child rearing: Instruments, issues and implications. *Psychological Bulletin, 106,* 29–58.

Holden, N. L. (1991). Adoption and eating disorders: A high-risk group? *British Journal of Psychiatry, 158,* 858–867.

Holdnack, J. A., Noberg, P. J., Arnold, S. E., Gur, R. C., & Gur, R. E. (1995). Speed of processing and verbal learning deficits in adults diagnosed with ADHD. *Neuropsychiatry, Neuropsychology and Behavioral Neurology, 8,* 282–292.

Hollon, S. D., & Beck, A. T. (1978). Psychotherapy and drug therapy: Comparisons and combinations. In S. Garfield & A. Burgan (Eds.), *Handbook of psychotherapy and behavior change. An empirical analysis* (2nd ed.). New York: Wiley.

Holt, B. A., & Lehman, E. B. (1995). Development of children's knowledge and use of strategies for self-control in a resistance-to-distraction task. *Merrill-Palmer Quarterly, 41,* 361–380.

Holt, K. G. (1992). Growth deficits and desipramine. *Journal of the American Academy of Child and Adolescent Psychiatry, 31,* 1167.

Hooper, S. R., Linz, T. D., Tramontana, M. G., & Stein, M. B. (1992). *Utility of the screening index of the wide range assessment of memory and learning for children with and without attention problems.* Paper presented at the twelfth annual meeting of the National Academy of Neuropsychology, Pittsburgh, PA.

Hops, H., & Lewin, L. (1984). Peer sociometric forms. In T. H. Ollendick & M. Hersen (Eds.), *Child behavioral assessment: Principles and procedures.* New York: Pergamon Press.

Hops, H., Walker, H. M., & Greenwood, C. R. (1988). *Procedures for establishing effective relationship skills (PEERS): Manual for consultants.* Delray, FL: Educational Achievement Systems.

Horacek, H. J. (1994). Clonidine extended-release capsules as an alternative to oral tablets and transdermal patches. *Journal of Child and Adolescent Psychopharmacology, 4,* 211–212.

Horder, B. R., & Scheibe, K. E. (197). Prevalence and implications of attention-deficit hyperactivity disorder among adolescents in treatment for substance abuse. *Journal of the American Academy of Child and Adolescent Psychiatry, 36,* 30–36.

Horn, W. (1988). *Parent training program.* Unpublished manuscript.

Horn, W. F., Chatoor, I., & Conners, C. K. (1983). Additive effects of dexedrine and self-control training: A multiple assessment. *Behavior Modification, 7,* 383–402.

Horn, W. F., & Ialongo, N. (1988). Multi-modal treatment of attention deficit hyperactivity disorder in children. In H. Fitzgerald, B. Lester, & M. Yogman (Eds.), *Theory and research in behavioral pediatrics* (Vol. 4). New York: Plenum Press.

Horn, W. F., Ialongo, N., Greenberg, G., Packard, T., & Smith-Winberry, C. (1990). Additive effects of behavioral parent training and self-control therapy with ADHD children. *Journal of Clinical Child Psychology, 19,* 98–110.

Horn, W. F., Ialongo, N. S., Pascoe, J. M., & Greenberg, G. (1991). Additive effects of psychostimulants, parent training, and self-control therapy with ADHD children. *Journal of the American Academy of Child and Adolescent Psychiatry, 30,* 233–240.

Horn, W. F., Ialongo, N., Popovich, S., & Peradotto, D. (1987). Behavioral parent training and cognitive-behavioral self-control therapy with ADD-H children: Comparative and combined effects. *Journal of Clinical Child Psychology, 16,* 57–68.

Horn, W. F., Wagner, A. E., & Ialongo, N. (1989). Sex differences in school-aged children with pervasive attention deficit disorder. *Journal of Abnormal Child Psychology, 17,* 109–125.

Horner, B. R., & Scheive, K. E. (1997). Prevalence and implications of attention-deficit hyperactivity disorder among adolescents in treatment for substance abuse. *Journal of the American Academy of Child and Adolescent Psychiatry, 36,* 30–36.

Horner, R. H., Albin, R. W., & O'Neill, R. E. (1991). *Generalization and maintenance: Lifestyle changes in applied settings.* Baltimore: Brookes.

Horner, R. H., Dunlap, G., & Koegel, R. L. (1988). Supporting students with severe intellectual disabilities and severe challenging behaviors. In G. Stoner, M. R. Shinn, & H. M. Walker (Eds.), *Interventions for achievement and behavior problems.* Silver Springs, MD: National Association of School Psychologists.

Horner, R. H., McDonnell, J. J., & Bellamy, G. G. (1986). Teaching generalized skills: General case instruction in simulation and community settings. In R. H. Horner, L. H. Meyer, & H. D. B. Fredericks (Eds.), *Education of learners with severe handicaps: Exemplary service strategies* (pp. 289–314). Baltimore: Brooks.

Hornig-Rohan, M., & Amsterdam, J. D. (1995). Venlafaxine versus stimulant therapy in patients with dual diagnoses of attention deficit disorder and depression. *Psychopharmacology Bulletin, 31,* 580.

Horrigan, J. P., & Barnhill, L. J. (1995). Guanfacine for treatment of attention-deficit hyperactivity disorder in boys. *Journal of Child and Adolescent Psychopharmacology, 5,* 215–223.

Hovens, J. G., Cantwell, D. P., & Kiriakos, R. (1994). Psychiatric comorbidity in hospitalized adolescent substance abusers. *Journal of the American Academy of Child and Adolescent Psychiatry, 33,* 476–483.

Hoy, E., Weiss, G., Minde, K., & Cohen, N. (1978). The hyperactive child at adolescence: Cognitive, emotional and social functioning. *Journal of Abnormal Child Psychology, 6,* 311–324.

Hoza, B., Pelham, W., Milich, R., Pillow, D., & McBride, K. (1993). The self-perceptions and attributions of ADHD and non-referred boys. *Journal of Abnormal Child Psychology, 21,* 271–286.

Huang, Y. H., & Maas, J. W. (1981). d-Amphetamine at low doses suppresses noradrenergic functions. *European Journal of Pharmacology, 75,* 187.

Hubbard, J. A., & Newcomb, A. F. (1991). Initial dyadic peer interaction of attention deficit hyperactivity disorder and normal boys. *Journal of Abnormal Child Psychology, 19,* 179–195.

Huessy, H. R. (1988). Behavior disorders and the Ritalin controversy. *Journal of the American Medical Association, 260,* 2219.

Huessy, H. R., Metoyer, M., & Townsend, M. (1973). 8–10 year follow-up of children treated in rural Vermont for behavior disorder. *American Journal of Orthopsychiatry, 43,* 236–238.

Huessy, H. R., & Wright, A. I. (1970). The use of imipramine in children's behavior disorders. *Acta Paedopsychiatrica, 37,* 194–199.

Huestis, R. D., Arnold, L. E., & Smeltzer, D. J. (1975). Caffeine versus methylphenidate and d-amphetamine in minimal brain dysfunction: A double-blind comparison. *American Journal of Psychiatry, 132,* 868–870.

Hughes, C. A. (1987). Test-taking skills for handicap students. In C. R. Reynolds & L. Mann (Eds.), *Encyclopedia of special education: A reference for the education of the handicapped and other exceptional children and youth.* New York: Wiley.

Hughes, C. A., & Hendrickson, J. M. (1987). Self-monitoring with at-risk students in the regular class setting. *Education and Treatment of Children, 10,* 236–250.

Huh, K., Meador, K. J., Loring, D. W., Lee, G. P., & Brooks, B. S. (1989). Attentional mechanisms during the intracarotid amobarbital test. *Neurology, 39,* 1183–1186.

Humphrey, L. L. (1982). Children's and teachers' perspectives on children's self-control: The development of two rating scales. *Journal of Consulting and Clinical Psychology, 50,* 624–633.

Humphries, T., Kinsbourne, M., & Swanson, J. (1978). Stimulant effects on cooperation and social interaction between hyperactive children and their mothers. *Journal of Psychology and Psychiatry, 19,* 13–22.

Humphries, T., Koltun, H., Malone, M., & Roberts, W. (1994). Teacher-identified oral language difficulties among boys with attentional problems. *Developmental and Behavioral Pediatrics, 15,* 92–98.

Humphries, T., Wright, N., Snider, L., & McDougall, B. (1992). Comparison of the effectiveness of sensory integrative therapy and perceptual-motor training in treating children with learning disabilities. *Developmental and Behavioral Pediatrics, 13,* 31–40.

Hundert, J. (1976). The effectiveness of reinforcement, response cost, and mixed programs on classroom behaviors. *Journal of Applied Behavior Analysis, 9,* 107.

Hunt, J. V., Tooley, D. H., & Harvin, D. (1982). Learning disabilities in children with birth weights below < 1599 grams. *Seminars in Perinatal, 6,* 280–286.

Hunt, R. D. (1987). Treatment effects of oral and transdermal clonidine in relation to methylphenidate: An open pilot study in ADD-H. *Psychopharmacology Bulletin, 23,* 111–114.

Hunt, R. D., Arnsten, A., & Asbell, M. D. (1994). The use of guanfacine in the treatment of children with attention deficit hyperactivity disorder (ADHD). *Psychopharmacology Bulletin, 30,* 680.

Hunt, R. D., Minderra, R., & Cohen, D. J. (1985). Clonidine benefits children with attention deficit disorder and hyperactivity: Report of a double-blind placebo cross over therapeutic trial. *Journal of the American Academy of Child Adolescent Psychiatry, 24,* 617–629.

Hurley, M. K. (1994). Impediments to parental acceptance of ADHD diagnosis. *The ADHD Report, 2,* 8–9.

Huston, A. C. (1994). Children and poverty: Designing research to affect policy. *Social Policy Report: Society for Research and Child Development, 8*(2).

Hutt, C., Hutt, S. J., & Ounsted, C. (1963). A method for the study of children's behavior. *Developmental Medicine and Child Neurology, 5,* 233.

Hyamns, M. H. (1994). Impulsive behavior: A case for helping children "think" about change. *Educational Psychology and Practice, 10,* 141–148.

Hynd, G. W., Hern, K. L., Novey, E. S., & Eliopulos, D. (1993). Attention-deficit hyperactivity disorder and asymmetry of the caudate nucleus. *Journal of Child Neurology, 8,* 339–347.

Hynd, G. W., Lorys, A. R., Semrud-Clikeman, M., Nieves, N., Huettner, N., & Lahey, B. B. (1991). Attention deficit disorder without hyperactivity: A distinct behavioral and neurocognitive syndrome. *Journal of Child Neurology, 6,* S37–S43.

Hynd, G. W., Morgan, A. E., Edmonds, J. E., Black, K., Riccio, C. A., & Lombardino, L. (1995). *Developmental Neuropsychology, 11,* 311–322.

Hynd, G. W., Nieves, N., Connor, R. T., & Stone, P. (1989). Attention deficit disorder with and without hyperactivity: Reaction time and speed of cognitive processing. *Journal of Learning Disabilities, 22,* 573–580.

Hynd, G. W., Semrud-Clikeman, M., Lorys, A. R., Novey, E. S., Eliopulos, D., & Lyytinen, H. (1990). Brain morphology in developmental dyslexia and attention deficit disorder/hyperactivity. *Archives of Neurology, 47,* 919–926.

Hynd, G. W., Semrud-Clikeman, M., Lorys, A. R., Novey, E. S., Eliopulos, D., & Lyytinen, H. (1991). Corpus callosum morphology in attention-deficit hyperactivity disorder (ADHD): Morphometric analysis of MRI. *Journal of Learning Disabilities, 24,* 141–146.

Ialongo, N. S., Horn, W. F., Pascoe, J. M., Greenberg, G., Packard, T., Lopez, M., Wagner, A., & Puttler, L. (1993). The effects of a multi-modal intervention with attention-deficit hyperactivity disorder children: A 9-month follow-up. *Journal of the American Academy of Child and Adolescent Psychiatry, 32,* 182–189.

Ideus, K. (1994). Cultural foundations of ADHD: A sociological analysis. *Therapeutic Care and Education, 3,* 173–192.

Imber, S. C., Imber, R. D., & Rothstein, C. (1979). Modifying independent work habits: An effective teacher-parent communication program. *Exceptional Children, 45,* 218–221.

Individuals with Disabilities Act. (1977). In P. S. Latham & P. H. Latham (Eds.), *Attention deficit disorder and the law: A guide for advocates.* Washington, DC: JKL Communications.

Individuals with Disabilities Education Act. (1990). IDEA 20 USC § 1400 et seq. In P. S. Latham & P. H. Latham (Eds.), *Attention deficit disorder and the law: A guide for advocates.* Washington, DC: JKL Communications.

Ingersoll, B., & Goldstein, S. (1993). *Attention deficit disorder and learning disabilities: Realities, myths and controversial treatments.* New York: Wiley.

Ingersoll, B., & Goldstein, S. (1995). *Lonely, sad and angry: A parent's guide to depression in children and adolescents.* New York: Doubleday.

Irwin, M., & Mettelman, B. B. (1989). Pitfalls of the continuous performance test. *Journal of Developmental and Behavioral Pediatrics, 10,* 284–286.

Iversen, S. D. (1977). Behavior after neostriatal lesions in animals. In I. Divac & R. G. E. Oberg (Eds.), *The neostriatum.* Elmsford, NY: Pergamon Press.

Iwata, B. A., & Bailey, J. S. (1974). Reward versus cost token systems: An analysis of the effects on students and teachers. *Journal of Applied Behavior Analysis, 7*, 567–576.

Jackson, N. F., Jackson, D. A., & Monroe, C. (1983). *Getting along with others: Teaching social effectiveness to children.* Champaign, IL: Research Press.

Jacob, R. G., O'Leary, K. D., & Rosenblad, C. (1978). Formal and informal classroom settings: Effects on hyperactivity. *Journal of Abnormal Child Psychology, 6*, 47–59.

Jacobsen, N. S., & Truax, P. (1991). Clinical significance: A statistical approach to defining meaningful change in psychotherapy research. *Journal of Consulting and Clinical Psychology, 59*, 12–19.

Jacobson, N. (Ed.). (1987). *Psychotherapists in clinical practice: Cognitive and behavioral perspectives.* New York: Guilford Press.

Jacobvitz, D., & Sroufe, L. A. (1987). The early caregiver child relationship and attention deficit disorder with hyperactivity in kindergarten: A perspective study. *Child Development, 58*, 1496–1504.

Jaffe, P. G., Wolfe, D. A., & Wilson, S. K. (1990). *Children of battered women.* Newbury Park, CA: Sage.

Jaffe, P. G., Wolfe, D. A., Wilson, S. K., & Zak, L. (1986). Similarities in behavioral and social maladjustment among child victims and witnesses to family violence. *American Journal of Orthopsychiatry, 56*, 142–146.

Jaffe, S. L. (1989). Pemoline and liver function. *Journal of the American Academy of Child and Adolescent Psychiatry, 28*, 457–458.

Jaffe, S. L. (1991). Intranasal abuse of prescribed methylphenidate by an alcohol and drug abusing adolescent with ADHD. *Journal of the American Academy of Child and Adolescent Psychiatry, 30*, 773–775.

James, W. (1890). *The principles of psychology.* New York: Holt.

Jan, J. J., Freeman, R. D., & Scott, E. P. (1977). Types of hearing loss in children. In B. F. Jaffe (Ed.), *Hearing loss in children.* Baltimore: University Park Press.

Janis, I. (1983). The role of social support in adherence to stressful decisions. *American Psychologist, 38*, 143–160.

Jankovic, J. (1993). Deprenyl in attention deficit associated with Tourette's syndrome. *Archives of Neurology, 50*, 286–288.

Jaspan, J. B. (1989). Hypoglycemia: Fact or fiction. *Hospital Practice, 24*, 11–14.

Jastak, J. F., Bijou, S. W., & Jastak, S. (1978). *Wide range achievement test.* Wilmington, DE: Jastak Associates.

Jastak, S., & Wilkinson, G. S. (1984). *Wide range achievement test: Administration manual.* Wilmington, DE: Jastak Associates.

Javorsky, J., & Gussin, B. (1994). College students with attention deficit hyperactivity disorder: An overview and description of services. *Journal of College Student Development, 35*, 170–177.

Jensen, J. B., Burke, N., & Garfinkel, B. D. (1988). Depression and symptoms of attention deficit disorder with hyperactivity. *Journal of the American Academy of Child and Adolescent Psychiatry, 27*, 742–747.

Jensen, P. S., Martin, D., & Cantwell, D. P. (1997). Comorbidity in ADHD: Implication for research practice and *DSM-V. Journal of the American Academy of Child and Adolescent Psychiatry, 36*, 1065–1079.

Jensen, P. S., Mrazek, D., Knapp, P. K., Steinberg, L., Pfeffer, C., Schowalter, J., & Shapiro, T. (1997). Evolution and revolution in child psychiatry: ADHD as a disorder of adaptation. *Journal of the American Academy of Child and Adolescent Psychiatry, 36*, 1672–1679.

Jensen, P. S., Shervette, R. E., Xenakis, S. N., & Richters, J. (1993). Anxiety and depressive disorders in attention deficit disorder with hyperactivity: New findings. *American Journal of Psychiatry, 150*, 1203–1209.

Jensen, W . (1982). *Children's behavior therapy unit parenting program.* Unpublished manuscript.

Jiron, C., Sherrill, R., & Chiodo, A. (1995, November). *Is ADHD being overdiagnosed?* Paper presented at the National Academy of Neuropsychology, San Francisco, Ca.

Jody, D., Lieberman, J. A., Geisler, S., Szymanski, S., & Avir, J. J. (1990). Behavioral response to methylphenidate and treatment outcome in first episode schizophrenia. *Psychopharmacology Bulletin, 26,* 224–230.

Johnson, B. D. (1995, August). *Differential performance of ADHD/LD subtypes on a continuous performance test.* Paper presented at the meeting of the American Psychological Association, New York.

Johnson, C. (1997). *Shadow syndromes.* New York: Pantheon Press.

Johnson, D. W., Maruyama, G., Johnson, R., Nelson, D., & Skon, L. (1981). Effects of cooperative, competitive, and individualistic goal structures on achievement: A meta-analysis. *Psychological Bulletin, 89,* 47–62.

Johnson, R. T., Johnson, D. W., & Scott, L. (1978). The effects of cooperative and individualized instruction on student attitudes and achievement. *Journal of Social Psychology, 104,* 207–216.

Johnson, S. M., & Bolstead, O. D. (1973). Methodological issues in naturalistic observation. Some problems and solutions. In L. A. Hamerlynck, L. E. Handy, & E. J. Mash (Eds.), *Behavior change: Methodology, concepts and practice.* Champaign, IL: Research Press.

Johnson, S. M., & White, G. (1971). Self-observation as an agent of behavioral change. *Behavior Therapy, 2,* 488–497.

Johnston, B. D., & Wright, J. A. (1993). Attentional dysfunction in children with encopresis. *Developmental and Behavioral Pediatrics, 14,* 381–385.

Johnston, C., & Behrenz, K. (1993). Child-rearing discussions in families of nonproblem children and ADHD children with higher and lower levels of aggressive-defiant behavior [Special issue]. *Canadian Journal of School Psychology, 9,* 53–65.

Johnston, C., & Fine, S. (1993). Methods of evaluating methylphenidate in children with attention deficit hyperactivity disorder: Acceptability, satisfaction, and compliance: Interventions in pediatric psychology [Special issue]. *Journal of Pediatric Psychology, 18,* 717–730.

Johnston, C., & Patenaude, R. (1994). Parent attributions for inattentive-overactive and oppositional-defiant child behaviors. *Cognitive Therapy and Research, 18,* 261–275.

Johnston, C., Patenaude, R., & Inman, G. (1992). Causal attributions for hyperactive and aggressive child behaviors. *Social Cognition, 10,* 255–270.

Johnston, C., Pelham, W. E., Hoza, J., & Sturges, J. (1988). Psychostimulant rebound in attention deficit disordered boys. *Journal of the American Academy of Child and Adolescent Psychiatry, 27,* 806–810.

Johnston, E., Weinrich, B., & Johnson, A. (1984). *A sourcebook for pragmatic activities.* San Antonio, TX: Communication Skill Builders: A Division of the Psycholgical Corp.

Jones, C. (1989, November/December). Managing the difficult child. *Family Day Caring,* 6–7.

Jones, C. (1991). *Sourcebook on attention disorders: A management guide for early childhood professionals and parents.* San Antonio, TX: Communication Skill Builders: A Division of the Psychological Company.

Jones, C. B. (1994). *Attention deficit disorder: Strategies for school age children.* San Antonio, TX: Communication Skill Builders: A Division of the Psychological Corp.

Jones, M. B., & Offord, D. R. (1989). Reduction of antisocial behavior in poor children by non-school skill development. *Journal of Child Psychology and Psychiatry, 30,* 737–750.

Jones, T. W., Borg, W. P., Boulware, S. D., McCarthy, G., Sherwin, R. S., & Tamborlaine, W. V. (1995). Original articles: Enhanced adrenomedullary response and increased susceptibility to neuroglycopenia: Mechanisms underlying the adverse effects of sugar ingestion in healthy children. *Journal of Pediatrics, 126,* 171–177.

Jones, V. F., & L. S. Jones, (1986). *Comprehensive classroom management: Creating positive learning environments.* Boston: Allyn & Bacon.

Jorm, A. F., Share, D. L., Matthews, R., & Maclean, R. (1986). Behavior problems in specific reading retarded and general reading backward children: A longitudinal study. *Journal of Child Psychology and Psychiatry, 27,* 33–43.

Kafantaris, V., Campbell, M., Padron-Gayol, M. V., Small, A. M., Locascio, J. J., & Rosenberg, C. R. (1992). Carbamazepine in hospitalized aggressive conduct disorder children: An open pilot study. *Psychopharmacology Bulletin, 28,* 193–199.

Kagan, J. (1964). *The matching familiar figures test.* Unpublished manuscript, Harvard University, Cambridge, MA.

Kagan, J. (1989). Temperamental contributions to social behavior. *American Psychologist, 44,* 668–674.

Kagan, J., Lapidus, D., & Moore, M. (1979). Infant antecedents of cognitive functioning: A longitudinal study. *Annual Progress in Child Psychiatry and Child Development,* 46–77.

Kagan, J., Rosman, B. L., Day, D., Albert, J., & Phillips, W. (1964). Information processing in the child: Significance of analytic and reflective attitudes. *Psychological Monographs, 78*(1, Whole No. 578).

Kahl, T. N. (1985). Students' social background and classroom behavior. In T. Husen & T. N. Postlethwaite (Eds.), *The international encyclopedia of education* (Vol. 8). Oxford, England: Pergamon Press.

Kahn, C. A., Kelly, P. C., & Walker W. L. (1995). Lead screening in children with ADHD and developmental delay. *Clinical Pediatrics, 34,* 498–501.

Kahn, E., & Cohen, L. H. (1934). Organic drivenness: A brain stem syndrome and an experience with case reports. *New England Journal of Medicine, 210,* 748–756.

Kahn, N. A., & Hoge, R. D. (1983). A teacher-judgement measure of social competence: Validity data. *Journal of Consulting and Clinical Psychology, 51,* 809–814.

Kalachnik, J. E., Sprague, R. L., Sleator, E. K., Cohen, M. N., & Ullmann, R. K. (1982). Effect of methylphenidate hydrochloride on stature of hyperactive children. *Developmental Medicine Child Neurology, 24,* 586–595.

Kaminer, Y. (1992). Clinical implications of the relationship between attention-deficit hyperactivity disorder and psychoactive substance use disorders. *American Journal of Addictions, 1,* 257–274.

Kanbayashi, Y., Naketa, Y., Fujii, K., & Kita, M. (1994). ADHD related behavior among non-referred children: Parents' ratings of *DSM III-R* symptoms. *Child Psychiatry and Human Development, 25,* 13–29.

Kaneko, M., Hoshino, Y., Hashimoto, S., & Okano, T. (1993). Hypothalamic-pituitary-adrenal axis function in children with attention-deficit hyperactivity disorder. *Journal of Autism and Developmental Disorders, 23*(1), 59–65.

Kanfer, F. H. (1970a). Self-monitoring: Methodological limitations and clinical applications. *Journal of Consulting and Clinical Psychology, 35,* 148–152.

Kanfer, F. H. (1970b). Self-regulation: Research, issues, and speculations. In C. Neuringer & J. L. Michel (Eds.), *Behavior modification in clinical psychology.* New York: Appleton-Century-Crofts.

Kaplan, B. J., McNicol, J., Conte. R. A., & Moghadam, H. K. (1989). Dietary replacement in preschool-aged hyperactive boys. *Pediatrics, 83,* 7–17.

Kaplan, H. K., Wamboldt, F., & Barnhardt, R. D. (1986). Behavioral effects of dietary sucrose in disturbed children. *American Journal of Psychology, 7,* 143.

Kaplan, S. L., Busner, J., Kupietz, S., Wasserman, E., & Segal, B. (1990). Effects of methylphenidate on adolescents with aggressive conduct disorder and ADHD: A preliminary report. *Journal of the American Academy of Child and Adolescent Psychiatry, 29,* 719–723.

Karp, S. A., & Konstadt, N. (1971). *Children's embedded figures test.* Palo Alto, CA: Consulting Psychologist Press.

Kashani, J. H., Beck, N. C., Hoeper, E. W., Fallahi, C., Corcoran, C. M., & McAllister, J. A. (1987). Psychiatric disorders in a community sample of adolescents. *American Journal of Psychiatry, 144,* 584–589.

Kashani, J. H., Chapel, J., & Ellis, J. (1979). Hyperactive girls. *Journal of Operational Psychiatry, 10,* 145–149.

Kashani, J. H., & Orvaschel, H. (1988). Anxiety disorders in mid-adolescence: A community sample of adolescents. *American Journal of Psychiatry, 144,* 584–589.

Kasten, E. F., Coury, D. L., & Heron, T. E. (1992). Educators' knowledge and attitudes regarding stimulants in the treatment of attention deficit hyperactivity disorder. *Developmental and Behavioral Pediatrics, 13,* 215–219.

Kataria, S., Hall, C. W., Wong, M. M., & Keys, G. F. (1992). Learning styles of LD and non-LD ADHD children. *Journal of Clinical Psychology, 48,* 371–378.

Katz, L., Wood, S., & Auchenbach, R. (1994). Utility of current tests in diagnosing ADHD. *Archives of Clinical Neuropsychology, 9,* 146–147.

Katz, M. (1997). *Playing a poor hand well.* New York: Norton.

Kaufman, A. S. (1979). *Intelligence testing with the WISC-R.* New York: Wiley.

Kaufman, A. S., & Kaufman, N. L. (1983). *K-ABC: Kaufman assessment battery for children.* Circle Pines, MN: American Guidance Service.

Kaufman, A. S., & Kaufman, N. L. (1985). *Kaufman test of educational achievement.* Circle Pines, MN: American Guidance Services.

Kaufman, K. F., & O'Leary, K. D. (1972). Reward, cost and self-evaluation procedures for disruptive adolescents in a psychiatric hospital school. *Journal of Applied Behavior Analysis, 5,* 293–309.

Kazdin, A. E. (1975). Recent advances in token economy research. In M. Hersen, R. M. Eisler, & P. M. Miller (Eds.), *Progress in behavior modification* (Vol. 1). New York: Academic Press.

Kazdin, A. E. (1982). The token economy: A decade letter. *Journal of Applied Behavior Analysis, 15,* 431–445.

Kazdin, A. E. (1987a). *Conduct disorder in childhood and adolescence.* Newbury Park, CA: Sage.

Kazdin, A. E. (1987b). Treatment of antisocial behavior in children: Current status and future directions. *Psychological Bulletin, 102,* 187–203.

Kazdin, A. E., & Matson, J. L. (1981). Social validation and mental retardation. *Applied Research in Mental Retardation, 2,* 39–53.

Kazdin, A. E., Mazurieck, J. L., & Siegel, T. C. (1994). Treatment outcome among children with externalizing disorder who terminate prematurely versus those who complete psychotherapy. *Journal of the American Academy of Child and Adolescent Psychiatry, 33,* 549–557.

Kazdin, A. E., Siegel, T. C., & Bass, D. (1992). Cognitive problem-solving skills training and parent management training in the treatment of antisocial behavior in children. *Journal of Consulting and Clinical Psychology, 60,* 733–747.

Kehle, T. J., Clark, E., Jenson, W. R., & Wampold, B. E. (1996). Effectiveness of self-observation with behavior disordered elementary school children. *School Psychology Review, 15,* 289–295.

Keith, R. W. (1994). *The auditory continuous performance test.* San Antonio, TX: Psychological Corporation.

Keith, R. W., & Engineer, P. (1991). Effects of methylphenidate on the auditory processing abilities of children with attention deficit-hyperactivity disorder. *Journal of Learning Disabilities, 24*, 630–636.

Keith, R. W., Rudy, J., Donahue, P. A., & Katbamna, B. (1989). Comparison of SCAN results with other auditory and language measures in a clinical population. *Ear Hear, 10*, 382–386.

Keller, M. B., Lavoi, P. W., Beardslee, W. R., Wunder, J., Schwartz, C. E., Roth, J., & Biederman, J. (1992). The disruptive behavioral disorder in children and adolescents: Comorbidity and clinical course. *Journal of the American Academy of Child and Adolescent Psychiatry, 41*, 204–209.

Kelly, D. P., & Aylward, G. P. (1992). Attention deficit in school-aged children and adolescents. Current issues and practice. *Pediatric Clinics of North America, 39*, 487–512.

Kelly, D. P., Forney, J., Parker-Fisher, S., & Jones, M. (1993a). The challenge of attention deficit disorder in children who are deaf or hard of hearing. *American Annals of the Deaf, 138*, 343–348.

Kelly, D. P., Forney, J., Parker-Fisher, S., & Jones, M. (1993b). Evaluating and managing attention deficit disorder in children who are deaf or hard of hearing. *American Annals of the Deaf, 138*, 349–357.

Kelly, D. P., Kelly, S. J., Jones, M., Moulton, N., Verhulst, S. J., & Bell, S. (1990). Hearing loss and attention deficits: Etiological considerations [abstract]. *American Journal of Disabilities in Children, 144*, 439.

Kelly, J. A., & Drabman, R. S. (1977). The modification of socially detrimental behavior. *Journal of Behavioral Therapy and Experimental Psychiatry, 8*, 101–104.

Kelly, L. M., Sonis, W., Fialkov, J., Kazdin, A., & Matson, J. (1986). Behavioral assessment of methylphenidate in a child with frontal lobe damage. *Journal of Psychopathology and Behavioral Assessment, 8*, 47–54.

Kelly, M. L. (1990). *School-home notes: Promoting children's classroom success.* New York: Guilford Press.

Kelly, P. C., Cohen, M. L., Walker, W. O., Caskey, O. L., & Atkinson, A. W. (1989). Self-esteem in children medically managed for attention deficit disorder. *Pediatrics, 83*, 211–217.

Kelso, J., & Stewart, M. A. (1986). Factors which predict the persistence of aggressive conduct disorder. *Journal of Child Psychology and Psychiatry, 27*, 77–86.

Kendall, P. C. (1988). *Stop and think workbook.* Marion Station, PA: Author.

Kendall, P. C. (1993). Cognitive-behavioral therapies with youth: Guiding theory, current status, and emerging developments. *Journal of Consulting and Clinical Psychology, 61*, 235–247.

Kendall, P. C. (1994). Treating anxiety disorders in youth: Results of a randomized clinical trial. *Journal of Consulting and Clinical Psychology, 62*, 100–110.

Kendall, P. C., & Braswell, L. (1982). Cognitive-behavioral self-control therapy for children: A components analysis. *Journal of Consulting and Clinical Psychology, 50*, 672–689.

Kendall, P. C., & Braswell, L. (1985). *Cognitive-behavioral therapy for impulsive children.* New York: Guilford Press.

Kendall, P. C., & Braswell, L. (1993). *Cognitive-behavioral therapy for impulsive children* (Rev. ed.). New York: Guilford Press.

Kendall, P. C., & Hollon, S. (Eds.). (1979). *Cognitive-behavioral interventions: Theory, research, and procedures.* New York: Academic Press.

Kendall, P. C., Panichelli-Mindel, S. M., & Gerow, M. A. (1995). Cognitive-behavioral therapies with children and adolescents: An integrative overview. In H. van Bilsen, P. C. Kendall, & J. Slavenburg (Eds.), *Behavioral approaches for children and adolescents* (pp. 1–18). New York: Plenum Press.

Kendall, P. C., Stark, K., & Adam, T. (1990). Cognitive distortion or cognitive deficit in childhood depression. *Journal of Abnormal Child Psychology, 18*, 255–270.

Kendall, P. C., & Wilcox, L. E. (1979). Self-control in children: Development of a rating scale. *Journal of Consulting and Clinical Psychology, 47,* 1020–1029.

Kent, J. D., Blader, J. C., Koplewicz, H. S., Abikoff, H., & Foley, C. A. (1995). Effects of late-afternoon methylphenidate administration on behavior and sleep in attention-deficit hyperactivity disorder. *Pediatrics, 96,* 320–325.

Keogh, M. J. (1994). Effects of neuropsychological training on attention and concentration skills in children with attention deficit hyperactivity disorder (ADHD). *Archives of Clinical Neuropsychology, 9,* 149–150.

Keough, B. K. (1971). Hyperactivity and learning disorders: Review and speculation. *Exceptional Child, 38,* 101–109.

Keough, B. K., & Barkett, C. J. (1980). An educational analysis of hyperactive children's achievement problems. In C. K. Whalen & B. Henker (Eds.), *Hyperactive children: The social ecology of identification and treatment.* New York: Academic Press.

Keough, B. K., & Margolis, J. S. (1976). A component analysis of attentional problems of educationally handicapped boys. *Journal of Abnormal Child Psychology, 4,* 349–359.

Kershner, J., & Hawke, W. (1979). Megavitamins and learning disorders: A controlled double-blind experiment. *Journal of Nutrition, 109,* 819–826.

Kestenbaum, C. J. (1979). Children at risk for manic-depressive illness: Possible predictors. *American Journal of Psychiatry, 136,* 1206–1208.

Kewley, G. D., Facer, R., & Scott, M. (1994). *Awareness diagnosis and management of ADD amongst United Kingdom community pediatricians and child psychiatrists.* Unpublished manuscript.

Kiessling, L., Marcotte, A., & Culpepper, S. (1993). Antineuronal antibodies in movement disorders. *Pediatrics, 92,* 20–23.

King, C., & Young, R. D. (1982). Attentional deficits with and without hyperactivity: Teacher and peer perceptions. *Journal of Abnormal Child Psychology, 10,* 483–495.

Kingston, L., & Prior, M. (1995). The development of patterns of stable, transient and school-age onset aggressive behavior in young children. *Journal of the American Academy of Child and Adolescent Psychiatry, 34,* 348–358.

Kinsbourne, M. (1977). The mechanism of hyperactivity. In M. Blaw, I. Rapin, & M. Kinsbourne (Eds.), *Topics of child neurology.* New York: Spectrum.

Kirby, E. A., & Grimley, L. K. (1986). *Understanding and treating attention deficit disorder.* New York: Pergamon Press.

Kirby, E. A., & Horne, A. (1986). A comparison of hyperactive and aggressive children. In E. A. Kirby & L. K. Grimley (Eds.), *Understanding and treating attention deficit disorder.* New York: Pergamon Press.

Kirby, F., & Shields, F. (1972). Modification of arithmetic response rate and attending behavior in a seventh-grade student. *Journal of Applied Behavior Analysis, 5,* 79–84.

Kirk, S. A., McCarthy, J. J., & Kirk, W. D. (1968). *The Illinois test of psycholinguistic abilities* (Rev. ed.). Urbana: University of Illinois Press.

Kirschenbaum, D., & Ordman, A. M. (1984). Preventive intervention for children: Cognitive behavioral perspective. In A. W. Meyers & W. E. Craighead (Eds.), *Cognitive behavior therapy for children* (pp. 397–409). New York: Plenum Press.

Klee, S. H. (1990). *Screening for attention deficit disorder.* Paper presented at the National Academy of Neuropsychology, Washington, DC.

Klee, S. H., & Garfinkel, B. D. (1983). The computerized continuous performance task: A new measure of inattention. *Journal of Abnormal Child Psychology, 11,* 487.

Klein, A. R., & Young, R. D. (1979). Hyperactive boys in their classroom: Assessment of teacher and peer perceptions, interactions and classroom behaviors. *Journal of Abnormal Child Psychology, 7,* 425–442.

Klein, R. D. (1979). Modifying academic performance in the grade school classroom. In M. Hersen, R. M. Eisler, & P. M. Miller (Eds.), *Progress in behavior modification* (Vol. 8, pp. 293–321). New York: Academic Press.

Klein, R. G. (1991). Thioridazine effects on the cognitive performance of children with attention-deficit hyperactivity disorder. *Journal of Child and Adolescent Psychopharmacology, 1,* 263–270.

Klein, R. G., Landa, B., Mattes, J. A., & Klein, D. F. (1988). Methylphenidate and growth in hyperactive children: A controlled withdrawal study. *Archives of General Psychiatry, 45,* 1127–1130.

Klein, R. G., & Mannuzza, S. (1991). Long-term outcome of hyperactive children: A review. *Journal of the American Academy of Child and Adolescent Psychiatry, 30,* 383–387.

Klerman, L. V. (1991). *Alive and well? A research and policy review of health programs for poor young children.* New York: National Center for Children in Proverty, Columbia University School of Public Health.

Klinteberg, B., Anderson, T., Magnusson, D., & Stattin, H. (1993). Hyperactive behavior in childhood as related to subsequent alcohol problems and violent offending: A longitudinal study of male subjects. *Personality and Individual Differences, 15*(4), 381–388.

Klorman, R. (1991). Cognitive event-related potentials in attention deficit disorder: Attention deficit disorder [Special series]. *Journal of Learning Disabilities, 24,* 130–140.

Klorman, R., Bauer, L. O., Coons, H. W., Lewis, D., Peloquin, L. J., Perlmutter, R. A., Ryan, R. M., Salzman, L. F., & Strauss, A. A. (1984). Enhancing effects of methylphenidate on normal young adults' cognitive processes. *Psychopharmacology Bulletin, 20,* 3.

Klorman, R., Brumaghim, J. T., Fitzpatrick, P. A., & Borgstedt, A. D. (1990). Clinical effects of a controlled trial of methylphenidate on adolescents with attention deficit disorder. *Journal of the American Academy of Child and Adolescent Psychiatry, 29,* 702–709.

Klorman, R., Brumaghim, J. T., & Salzman, L. F. (1988). Effects of methylphenidate on AD hyperactivity disorder with and without aggressive/non-compliant features. *Journal of Abnormal Psychology, 97,* 413–422.

Klorman, R., Brumaghim, J. T., Salzman, L. F., Strauss, J., Borgstedt, A. D., McBride, M. C., & Loeb, S. (1989). Comparative effects of methylphenidate on attention deficit hyperactivity disorder with and without aggressive/noncompliant features. *Psychopharmacology Bulletin, 25,* 109–113.

Klorman, R., Salzman, L., Borgstedt, A., & Dainer, K. (1981). Normalizing effects of methylphenidate on hyperactive children's vigilance, performance and evoked potentials. *Psychopharmacology, 6,* 665–667.

Klorman, R., Salzman, L. F., Pass, H. L., Borgstedt, A. D., & Dainer, K. B. (1979). Effects of methylphenidate on hyperactive children's evoked responses during passive and active attention. *Psychophysiology, 16,* 23–29.

Kneedler, R. D., & Hallahan, D. P. (1981). Self-monitoring of on-task behavior with learning-disabled children: Current study and directions. *Exceptional Education Quarterly, 2,* 73–82.

Knell, E. R., & Comings, D. E. (1993). Tourette's syndrome and attention-deficit hyperactivity disorder: Evidence for a genetic relationship. *Journal of Clinical Psychiatry, 54,* 331–337.

Knights, R. N. (1966). *Normative data on tests for evaluating brain damage in children from five to fourteen years of age* (Research Bulletin #20). London, Canada: University of Western Ontario.

Knobel, M., Walman, M. B., & Mason, E. (1959). Hyperkinesis and organicity in children. *Archives of General Psychiatry, 1,* 310–321.

Knobolc, H., & Pasamanick, B. (1959). The syndrome of minimal cerebral damage in infancy. *Journal of the American Medical Association, 70,* 1384–1386.

Kochanska, G. (1991). Socialization and temperament in the development of guilt and conscience. *Child Development, 62,* 1379–1392.

Kochanska, G. (1993). Toward a synthesis of parental socialization and child temperament in early development of conscience. *Child Development, 64,* 325–347.

Kochanska, G., Kuczynski, L., Radke-Yarrow, M., & Darby-Welsh, J. D. (1987). Resolutions of control episodes between well and affectively ill mothers and their young children. *Journal of Abnormal Child Psychology, 15,* 441–456.

Kochanska, G., Murray, K., Jacques, T. Y., Koneig, L. A., & Vandegeest, K. A. (1996). Inhibitory control in young children and its role in emerging internalization. *Child Development, 67,* 490–507.

Koehler-Troy, C., Strober, M., & Malenbaum, R. (1986). Methylphenidate-induced mania in a prepubertal child: A case report. *Journal of Clinical Psychiatry, 47,* 566–567.

Kohn, A. (1989, November). Suffer the restless children. *The Atlantic Monthly,* 90–100.

Koizumi, H. M. (1985). Obsessive-compulsive symptoms following stimulants. *Biological Psychiatry, 20,* 1332–1333.

Kolko, D. J. (1993). Conduct disorder and ADD with hyperactivity in child inpatients: Comparisons on home and hospital measures. *Journal of Emotional and Behavioral Disorders, 1,* 75–86.

Kolko, D. J., Allan, M. J., & Zelevnak, J. P. (1988). Risk factors for adolescent suicide: A comparison of adolescent suicide victims with suicidal inpatients. *Archives of General Psychiatry, 45,* 581–588.

Kolko, D. J., Loar, L. L., & Sturnick, D. (1990). Inpatient social-cognitive skills training groups with conduct disordered and attention deficit disordered children. *Journal of Child Psychology and Psychiatry and Allied Disciplines, 31,* 737–748.

Kollins, S. H., Lane, S. D., & Shapiro, S. K. (1997). Experimental analysis of childhood psychopathology: A laboratory analysis of the behavior of children diagnosed with ADHD. *Psychological Record, 47,* 25–44.

Konstantareas, M. M., & Hermatidis, S. (1983). Effectiveness of cognitive mediation and behavior modification with hospitalized hyperactives. *Canadian Journal of Psychiatry, 28,* 462–470.

Koplewicz, H. S., Abikoff, H., & Foley, C. A. (1995). Effects of late-afternoon methylphenidate administration on behavior and sleep in attention-deficit hyperactivity disorder. *Pediatrics, 96,* 320–325.

Kopp, C. B. (1982). Antecedents of self-regulation: A developmental perspective. *Developmental Psychology, 18,* 199–214.

Kopp, C. B. (1987). The growth of self-regulation: Caregivers and children. In N. Eisenberg (Ed.), *Contemporary topics in developmental psychology.* New York: Wiley.

Koren, P. E., DeChillo, N., & Friesen, B. J. (1992). Measuring empowerment in families whose children have emotional disabilities: A brief questionnaire: Family and disability research: New directions in theory, assessment, and intervention [Special issue]. *Rehabilitation Psychology, 37,* 305–321.

Koriath, U., Gualtieri, T., Van Bourgondien, M. E., Quade, D., & Werry, J. S. (1985). Construct validity of clinical diagnosis in pediatric psychiatry: Relationship among measures. *Journal of the American Academy of Child Psychiatry, 242,* 429–436.

Korkman, M., & Peltomaa, K. (1991). A pattern of test findings predicting attention problems at school. *Journal of Abnormal Child Psychology, 19,* 451–467.

Koscinski, S. T., & Gast, D. L. (1993). Computer-assisted instruction with constant time delay to teach multiplication facts to students with learning disabilities. *Learning Disabilities and Research and Practice, 8,* 157–168.

Koth, G. W. (1991). *Managing attention deficit/hyperactive disorders. A parent education program.* Unpublished manuscript, Baltimore County Public Schools.

Kotwal, D. P., Burns, W. J., & Montgomery, D. D. (1996). Computer-assisted cognitive training for ADHD: A case study. *Behavior Modification, 20,* 85–96.

Kotwal, D., Montgomery, D., & Burns, W. (1994, August). *Computer assisted cognitive training with a pre-adolescent ADHD male.* Paper presented at the annual convention of the American Psychological Association, Los Angeles.

Kounin, J. S. (1970). *Discipline and group management in classrooms.* Melbourne, FL: Krieger.

Kovacs, M. (1983). *The children's depression inventory: A self-rated depression scale for school-aged youngsters.* Unpublished manuscript, University of Pittsburgh.

Kovacs, M. (1996). *Children's depression inventory (CDI).* North Tonawanda, NY: Multi-Health Systems.

Koziol, L. F., & Stout, C. E. (1992). Use of a verbal fluency measure in understanding and evaluating ADHD as an executive function disorder. *Perceptual and Motor Skills, 75,* 1187–1192.

Kramer, J. R. (1987). What are hyperactive children like as young adults? In J. Loney (Ed.), *The young hyperactive child: Answers to question about diagnosis, prognosis and treatment.* New York: Haworth Press.

Kramer, J. R., & Loney, J. (1982). Childhood hyperactivity and substance abuse: A review of the literature. In A. D. Gadow & I. Bailer (Eds.), *Advances in learning and behavioral disabilities* (Vol. 1). Greenwich. CT: JAI Press.

Kratochwill, T. R., Elliott, S. N., & Rotto, P. C. (1990). Best practices and behavioral consultation. In A. Thomas & J. Grimes (Eds.), *Best practices in school psychology* (Vol. 2). Washington, DC: The National Association of School Psychologists.

Krueger, R. F., Caspi, A., Moffitt, T. E., & White, J. (1996). Delay of gratification, psychopathology, and personality: Is low self-control specific to externalizing problems? *Journal of Personality, 64,* 107–129.

Kruesi, M. J. P., Rapoport, J. L., Cummings, E. M., Berg, C. J., Ismond, D. R., Flament, M., Yarrow, M., & Zahn-Waxler, C. (1987). Effects of sugar and aspartame on aggression and activity in children. *American Journal of Psychiatry, 144,* 1487–1490.

Krug, D. A., Arrick, J. R., & Almond, P. J. (1978). *Autism behavior checklist.* Portland, OR: ASIEP.

Krusch, D. A., Klorman, R., Brumaghim, J. T., Fitzpatrick, P. A., Borgstedt, A. D., & Strauss, J. (1996). Methylphenidate slows reactions of children with attention deficit disorder during and after an error. *Journal of Abnormal Child Psychology, 24,* 633–650.

Kubany, E. S., Weiss, L. E., & Sloggett, B. B. (1971). The good behavior clock: A reinforcement/time out procedure for reducing disruptive classroom behavior. *Journal of Behavior Therapy and Experimental Psychiatry, 2,* 173–179.

Kuczynski, L., Kochanska, G., Radke-Yarrow, M., & Girnius-Brown, Q. (1987). A developmental interpretation of young children's non-compliance. *Developmental Psychology, 23,* 799–806.

Kuehne, C. (1985). *A discriminant analysis of behavioral and psychometric measures of attention in children with attention deficit disorder and specific learning disabilities.* Unpublished doctoral dissertation, University of Utah, Salt Lake City.

Kuperman, S., Johnson, B., Arndt, S., Lindgren, S., & Wolraich, N. (1996). Quantitative EEG differences in a non-clinical sample of children with ADHD and undifferentiated ADD. *Journal of the American Academy of Child and Adolescent Psychiatry, 35,* 1009–1017.

Kupietz, S., Winsberg, B., Richardson, E., Maitinsky, S., & Mendell, N. (1988). Effects of methylphenidate dosage on hyperactive reading-disabled children: I. Behavior and cognitive performance effects. *Journal of the American Academy of Child and Adolescent Psychiatry, 27,* 70–77.

Kupke, T., & Lewis, R. (1985). WAIS and neuropsychological tests: Common and unique variance within an epileptic population. *Journal of Clinical and Experimental Neuropsychology, 7,* 353–366.

Kurzweil, S. R. (1992). Developmental reading disorder: Predictors of outcome in adolescents who received early diagnosis and treatment. *Developmental and Behavioral Pediatrics, 13,* 399–404.

L'Abate, L., & Milan, M. (1985). *Handbook of social skills training and research.* New York: Wiley.

Ladd, G. W. (1981). Effectiveness of a social learning method for enhancing children's social interaction and peer acceptance. *Child Development, 52,* 171–178.

Ladd, G. W., Kochenderfer, B. J., & Coleman, C. C. (1996). Friendship quality as a predictor of young children's early school adjustment. *Child Development, 67,* 1103–1118.

la Greca, A. M. (1990). *Through the eyes of the child.* Boston: Allyn & Bacon.

la Greca, A. M., & Stark, P. (1986). Naturalistic observations of children's social behavior. In P. S. Strain, M. J. Guralnick, & H. M. Walker (Eds.), *Children's social behavior: Development, assessment, and modification* (pp. 181–213). New York: Academic Press.

Lahey, B. B., Applegate, B., McBurnett, K., Biederman, J., Greenhill, L., Hynd, G., Barkley, R. A., Newcorn, J., Jensen, P., Richters, J., Garfinkel, B., Kerdyk, L., Frick, P. J., Ollendick, T., Perez, D., Hart, E. L., Waldman, I., & Shaffer, D. (1994). *DSM-IV* field trial for attention deficit/hyperactivity disorder in children and adolescents. *American Journal of Psychiatry, 151,* 1673–1685.

Lahey, B. B., & Carlson, C. L. (1991). Validity of the diagnostic category of attention deficit disorder without hyperactivity: A review of the literature. *Journal of Learning Disabilities, 24,* 110–120.

Lahey, B. B., & Carlson, C. L. (1992). Validity of the diagnostic category of attention deficit disorder without hyperactivity: A review of the literature. In S. E. Shaywitz & B. A. Shaywitz (Eds.), *Attention deficit disorder comes of age: Toward the twenty-first century.* Austin, TX: Pro-Ed.

Lahey, B. B., Loeber, R., Hart, E. L., & Frick, P. J. (1995). Four-year longitudinal study of conduct disorder in boys: Patterns and predictors of persistence. *Journal of Abnormal Child Psychology, 10,* 83–93.

Lahey, B. B., Loeber, R., Stouthamer-Loeber, M., Christ, M. A. G., Green, S., Russo, M. F., Frick, P. J., & Dulcan, M. (1990). Comparison of *DSM-III* and *DSM-III-R* diagnoses for prepubertal children: Changes in prevalence and validity. *Journal of the American Academy of Child and Adolescent Psychiatry, 29,* 620–626.

Lahey, B. B., Pelham, W. E., Schaughency, E. A., Atkins. M. S., Murphy, H. A., Hynd, G., Russo, M., Hartdagen, S., & Lorys-Vernon, A. (1988). Dimensions in types of attention deficit disorder. *Journal of American Academy of Child and Adolescent Psychiatry, 27,* 330–335.

Lahey, B. B., Piacentini, J. C., McBurnett, K., Stone, P., Hartdagen, S., & Hynd, G. (1988). Psychopathology in the parents of children with conduct disorder and hyperactivity. *Journal of the American Academy of Child and Adolescent Psychiatry, 27,* 163–170.

Lahey, B. B., Schaughency, E. A., Frame, C. L., & Strauss, C. C. (1985). Teacher ratings of attention problems in children experimentally classified as exhibiting attention deficit disorders with and without hyperactivity. *Journal of the American Academy of Child and Adolescent Psychiatry, 24,* 613–616.

Lahey, B. B., Schaughency, E. A., Hynd, G. W., Carlson, C. L., & Nieves, N. (1987). Attention deficit disorder with and without hyperactivity: See comparison of behavioral characteristics of clinic-referred children. *Journal of the American Academy of Child and Adolescent Child Psychiatry, 26,* 718–723.

Lahey, B. B., Schaughency, E. A., Strauss, C. C., & Frame, C. L. (1984). Are attention deficit disorders with and without hyperactivity similar or dissimilar disorders? *Journal of the American Academy of Child and Adolescent Psychiatry, 23,* 302–309.

LaHoste, G. J., Swanson, J. M., & Wigal, S. B. (1996). Dopamine D4 receptor gene polymorphism is associated with attention deficit hyperactivity disorder. *Molecular Psychiatry, 1,* 121–124.

Lambert, N. M., & Hartsough, C. S. (1984). Contribution of predispositional factors to the diagnosis of hyperactivity. *American Journal of Orthopsychiatry, 54,* 97–109.

Lambert, N. M., & Hartsough, C. S. (1987). The measurement of attention deficit disorder with behavior ratings of parents. *American Journal of Orthopsychiatry, 57*(3), 361–370.

Lambert, N. M., Hartsough, C. S., Sassone, D., & Sandoval, J. (1987). Persistence of hyperactivity symptoms from childhood to adolescence and associated outcomes. *American Journal of Orthopsychiatry, 57,* 22–32.

Lambert, N. M., & Sandoval, J. (1980). The prevalence of learning disabilities and a sample of children considered hyperactive. *Journal of Abnormal Child Psychology, 8,* 33–50.

Lambert, N. M., Sandoval, J., & Sassone, D. (1978). Prevalence of hyperactivity in elementary school children as a function of social system definers. *American Journal of Orthopsychiatry, 48,* 446–463.

Lambert, N. M., Windmiller, M., Tharinger, D., & Cole, L. J. (1981). *AAMD adaptive behavior scale—School edition.* Monteray, CA: CTB/McGraw-Hill.

Lamborn, S., Mounts, N., Steinberg, L., & Dornbusch, S. (1991). Patterns of competence and adjustment among adolescents from authoritative, authoritarian, indulgent and neglectful homes. *Child Development, 62,* 1049–1065.

Lamminmaki, T., Ahonen, T., Narhi, V., Lyytinen, H., & Todd de Barra, H. (1995). Attention deficit hyperactivity disorder subtypes: Are there differences in academic problems? *Developmental Neuropsychology, 11,* 297–310.

Landau, S., & Milich, R. (1988). Social communication patterns of attention-deficit-disordered boys. *Journal of Abnormal Child Psychology, 16,* 69–81.

Landau, S., Milich, R., & Whitten, P. (1984). A comparison of teacher and peer assessment of social status. *Journal of Clinical Child Psychology, 13,* 44–49.

Landau, S., Milich, R., & Widiger, T. A. (1991). Conditional probabilities of child interview symptoms in the diagnosis of attention deficit disorder. *Journal of Child Psychology and Psychiatry and Allied Disciplines, 32,* 501–513.

Landau, S., & Moore, L. A. (1991). Social skills deficits in children with attention-deficit hyperactivity disorder. *School Psychology Review, 20,* 235–251.

Landrigan, P. J., Whitworth, R. H., Baloh, R. W., Staehling, N. W., Barthel, W. F., & Rosenbloom, B. F. (1975, March 29). Neuropsychological dysfunction in children with chronic low-level lead absorption. *Lancet,* 708–712.

Landrum, T. J., & Lloyd, J. W. (1992). Generalization in social behavior research with children and youth who have emotional or behavioral disorders. *Behavior Modification, 16,* 593–616.

Lang, A. R., Pelham, W. E., Johnston, C., & Gelernter, S. (1989). Levels of adult alcohol consumption induced by interactions with child confederates exhibiting normal versus externalizing behaviors. *Journal of Abnormal Psychology, 98,* 294–299.

Lang, P. J. (1968). Fear reduction and fear behavior: Problems in treating a construct. In J. M. Schleen (Ed.), *Research in psychotherapy.* Washington, DC: American Psychological Association.

Langer, D. H., Rapoport, J. L., Brown, G. L., Ebert, M. H., & Bunney, W. E. (1982). Behavioral effects of cabidopa/levodopa in hyperactive boys. *Journal of the American Academy of Child and Adolescent Psychiatry, 21,* 10–18.

Langhorne, J. E., & Loney, J. (1979). A 4-fold model for subgrouping the hyperkinetic/MBD syndrome. *Child Psychiatry and Human Development, 9,* 153–159.

LaPouse, R., & Monk, M. (1958). An epidemiological study of behavior characteristics in children. *American Journal of Public Health, 48,* 1134–1144.

Larsen, V. (1964). Physical characteristics of disturbed adolescents. *Archives of General Psychiatry, 10,* 55.

Larson, J. (1994). Violence prevention in the schools: A review of selected programs and procedures. *School Psychology Review, 23,* 151–164.

Lasley, T. J. (1986). *Issues in teacher education: Vol. 2. Background papers from the national commission for excellence in teacher education* (Teacher Education Monograph No. 6). Washington, DC: American Association of Colleges for Teacher Education.

Lassiter, K. S., D'Amato, R. C., Raggio, D. J., & Whitten, J. C. (1994). The construct specificity of the continuous performance test: Does inattention relate to behavior and achievement? *Developmental Neuropsychology, 10,* 179–188.

Last, C. G., Hersen, M., Kazdin, A., Orvaschel, H., & Perrin, S. (1991). Anxiety disorders in children and their families. *Archives of General Psychiatry, 48,* 928–934.

Last, C. G., Perrin, S., Hersen, M., & Kazdin, A. E. (1992). *DSM-III-R* anxiety disorders in children: Sociodemographics and clinical characteristics. *Journal of American Academy of Child and Adolescent Psychiatry, 31,* 1070–1076.

Last, C. G., Strauss, C. C., & Francis, G. (1987). Comorbidity among childhood anxiety disorders. *Journal of Nervous and Mental Disorders, 175,* 726–730.

Laszlo, J. I. (1990). Child perceptual-motor development. Normal and abnormal development of skilled behavior. In C. A. Hauert (Ed.), *Developmental psychology: Cognitive, perceptual-motor and neuropsychological perspectives.* North Holland: Elsevier Science.

Latham, P. S., & Latham, P. H. (1994). *Succeeding in the workplace—Attention deficit disorder and learning disabilities in the workplace: A guide for success.* Washington, DC: JKL Communications.

Latham, P. H., & Latham, P. S. (1995). *Documentation disclosure and the law for individuals with learning disabilities and attention deficit disorder.* Cabin John, MD: National Center for Law and Learning Disabilities.

Latham, P. S., & Latham, P. H. (1997). Legal rights. In S. Goldstein (Ed.), *Managing attention and learning disorders in late adolescence and adulthood: A guide for practitioners.* New York: Wiley.

Lathrop, A. (1982). The terrible ten in education programming. *Educational Computers, 20,* 144.

Laub, L., & Braswell, L. (1992). Suggestions for classroom teachers of ADHD elementary school students. In L. Braswell & M. L. Bloomquist (Eds.), *Cognitive-behavioral therapy with ADHD children.* New York: Guilford Press.

Laufer, M. W. (1979). Defining the minimal brain dysfunction syndrome. In E. Denhoff & L. Stern (Eds.), *Minimal brain dysfunction: A developmental approach.* New York: Mason.

Laufer, M. W., & Denhoff, E. (1957). Hyperkinetic behavior syndrome in children. *Journal of Pediatrics, 50,* 463–474.

Lavigne, J. V., Gibbons, R. D., Christoffell, K. K., Arend, R., Rosenbaum, D., Binns, H., Dawson, N., Sobel, H., & Isaacs, C. (1996). Prevalence rates in correlative psychiatric disorders among preschool children. *Journal of the American Academy of Child and Adolescent Psychiatry, 35,* 204–214.

Lavin, M. R., & Rifkin, A. (1993). Diagnosis and pharmacotherapy of conduct disorder. *Progressive Neuro-Psychopharmacology and Biological Psychiatry, 17,* 875–885.

Lavin, P. (1989). *Parenting the over-active child: Alternatives to drug therapy.* Landham, MD: Madison Books.

Lavin, P. (1991). The counselor as consultant-coordinator for children with attention deficit hyperactivity disorder. *Elementary School Guidance and Counseling, 26,* 115–120.

Lavoie, M. E., & Charlebois, P. (1994). The discriminant validity of the Stroop color and word test: Towards a cost-effective strategy to distinguish sub-groups of disruptive pre-adolescents. *Psychology in the Schools, 31*, 98–107.

Leary, M. R., & Miller, R. S. (1986). *Social psychology and dysfunctional behaviour.* New York: Springer-Verlag.

LeBlanc, M., & Freschette, M. (1989). *Male criminal activity from childhood through youth: Multi-level and developmental perspectives.* New York: Springer-Verlag.

Lee, C. L., & Bates, J. E. (1985). Mother-child interaction at age two years and perceived difficult temperament. *Child Developmental, 56*, 1314–1325.

Lee, S. W. (1991). Biofeedback as a treatment for childhood hyperactivity: A critical review of the literature. *Psychological Reports, 68*, 163–192.

Lehtonen, L., Korhonen, T., & Korvenranta, H. (1994). Temperament and sleeping patterns in colicky infants during the first year of life. *Developmental and Behavioral Pediatrics, 15*, 416–420.

Leichtman, H. M. (1993). *Attention deficit disorder subgroups: ADD outcome matrix.* Boston: Wediko Children's Services.

Leimbach, J. (1986). *Primarily logic.* San Luis Obispo, CA: Dandilion.

Lerner, J. W., & Lowenthal, B. (1992). Attention deficit disorders: New responsibilities for the special educator. *Learning Disabilities, 4*, 1–8.

Lester, M. L., & Fishbein, D. H. (1988). Nutrition and childhood neuropsychological disorders. In R. E. Tarter, D. H. Van Thiel, & K. L. Edwards (Eds.), *Medical neuropsychology* (pp. 291–325). New York: Plenum Press.

Leung, P. W., & Connolly, K. J. (1994). Attentional difficulties in hyperactive and conduct-disordered children: A processing deficit. *Journal of Child Psychology and Psychiatry and Allied Disciplines, 35*, 1229–1245.

Leung, P. W., & Connolly, K. J. (1997). Test of two views of impulsivity in hyperactive and conduct-disordered children. *Developmental Medicine and Child Neurology, 39*, 574–582.

Leutwyler, J. (1996). In focus, paying attention. News and analysis. *Scientific America, 12*, 14.

Levin, H. S., & Culhane, K. A. (1991). Developmental changes in performance on tests of reported frontal lobe functions. *Developmental Neuropsychology, 7*, 377–396.

Levine, M. D. (1982). Encopresis: It's potentiation, evaluation and alleviation. *Pediatric Clinics of North America, 29*, 315–330.

Levine, M. D. (1987). Attention deficit: The diversive effects of weak control systems in childhood. *Pediatric Annals, 16*, 117–130.

Levine, M. D. (1992). Commentary: Attentional disorders: Elusive entities and their mistaken identities. *Journal of Child Neurology, 7*, 449–453.

Levinson, H. N. (1990). *Total concentration: How to understand attention deficit disorders with treatment guidelines for you and your doctor.* New York: Evans.

Levinson, H. N. (1991). Dramatic favorable responses of children with learning disabilities or dyslexia and attention deficit disorder to antimotion sickness medications: Four case reports. *Perceptual and Motor Skills, 73*, 723–738.

Levinson, S. (1991). *Simple electronic device to help students and teachers change their behavior.* Thief River Falls, MN: Behavioral Dynamics.

Levy, F. (1994). Neurometrics: Review and comments. *The ADHD Report, 2*, 1–3.

Levy, F., Hay, D. A., McStephen, M., Wood, C., & Waldman, I. (1997). Attention-deficit hyperactivity disorder: A category or a continuum? Genetic analysis of a large scale twin study. *Journal of the American Academy of Child and Adolescent Psychiatry, 36*, 737–744.

Levy, F., & Hobbes, G. (1989). Reading, spelling and vigilance in attention deficit and conduct disorder. *Journal of Abnormal Child Psychology, 17*, 291–298.

Levy, F., Horn, K., & Dalglish, R. (1987). Relation of attention deficit and conduct disorder to vigilance and reading lag. *Australian and New Zealand Journal of Psychiatry, 21*, 242–254.

Lewinsohn, P. M., Gotlieb, I. H., & Seeley, J. R. (1995). Adolescent psychopathology: IV. Specificity of psychosocial risk factors for depression and substance abuse in older adolescents. *Journal of the American Academy of Child and Adolescent Psychiatry, 34*, 1221–1229.

Lewinsohn, P. M., Rhode, P., & Seeley, J. R. (1994). Adolescent psychopathology: III. The clinical consequences of comorbidity. *Journal of the American Academy of Child and Adolescent Psychiatry, 34*, 510–519.

Lewis, K. (1992). Family functioning as perceived by parents of boys with attention deficit disorder. *Issues in Mental Health Nursing, 13*, 369–386.

Lewis, T. J., & Sugai, G. (1993). Teaching communicative alternatives to socially withdrawn behavior: An investigation in maintaining treatment effects. *Journal of Behavioral Education, 3*, 61–75.

Lewis, T. M., & Greenberg, G. D. (1995, August). *ADHD children's performance on visual and auditory continuous performance tests.* Paper presented at the meeting of the American Psychological Association, New York.

Lewis-Abney, K. (1993). Correlates of family functioning when a child has attention deficit disorder. *Issues in Comprehensive Pediatric Nursing, 16*, 175–190.

Lewit, E. M., & Baker, L. S. (1995). School readiness. The future of children. *Critical Issues for Children and Youths, 5*(2), 128–133.

Lezak, M. D. (1983). *Neuropsychological assessment* (2nd ed.). New York: Oxford University Press.

Li, A. K. F., Sauve, R. S., & Creighton, D. E. (1990). Early indicators of learning problems in high risk children. *Developmental and Behavioral Pediatrics, 11*, 1–6.

Liberman, L, (1986). *Special educator's guide.* Weston, MA: Nobb Hill Press.

Licamele, W. L., & Goldberg, R. L. (1989). The concurrent use of lithium and methylphenidate in a child. *Journal of the American Academy of Child and Adolescent Psychiatry, 28*, 785–787.

Licht, B. G., Kistner, J. A., Ozkaragoz, T., Shapiro, S., & Clausen, L. (1985). Causal attributions of learning disabled children: Individual differences and their implications for persistence. *Journal of Educational Psychology, 77*, 208–216.

Lie, N. (1992). Follow-ups of children with attention deficit hyperactivity disorder (ADHD): Review of literature. *Acta Psychiatrica Scandinavica, 85*(Suppl. 368), 40.

Light, J. G., Pennington, B. F., Gilger, J. W., & DeFries, J. C. (1995). Reading disability and hyperactivity disorder: Evidence for a common genetic etiology. *Developmental Neuropsychology, 11*, 323–336.

Limber, S. P., & Flekkly, M. G. (1995). The UN convention on the rights of the child: It's relevance for social scientists. *Social Policy Report: Society for Research and Child Development, 9*(2).

Linden, M., Habid, T., & Radogevic, V. (1992). *Controlled study of EEG biofeedback effects on cognitive and behavioral measures with ADHD and learning disabled children.* Paper presented at the national meeting of Children and Adults with Attention Deficit Hyperactivity Disorder, Washington, DC.

Lindsley, O. R. (1991). From technical jargon to plain English for application. *Journal of Applied Behavior Analysis, 24*, 449–458.

Linn, R. T., & Hodge, G. K. (1982). Locus of control in childhood hyperactivity. *Journal of Consulting and Clinical Psychology, 50*, 592–593.

Lipkin, P. H., Goldstein, I. J., & Addesman, A. R. (1994). Tics and dyskinesias associated with stimulant treatment in attention deficit hyperactivity disorder. *Archives of Pediatric Adolescent Medicine, 148*, 859.

Lipsey, M. W., & Wilson, D. B. (1993). The efficacy of psychological, educational and behavioral treatment. *American Psychologist, 48,* 1181–1209.

Liu, C., Robin, A. L., Brenner, S., & Eastman, J. (1991). Social acceptability of methylphenidate and behavior modification for treating attention deficit hyperactivity disorder. *Pediatrics, 88,* 560.

Livingston, R., Dykman, R. A., & Ackerman, P. T. (1990). The frequency and significance of additional self-reported psychiatric diagnoses in children with attention deficit disorder. *Journal of Abnormal Child Psychology, 18,* 465–478.

Livingston, R., Lawson, L., & Jones, J. G. (1993). Predictors of self-reported psychopathology in children abused repeatedly by a parent. *Journal of the American Academy of Child and Adolescent Psychiatry, 32,* 948–953.

Livsay, J. (1986). Clinical utility of Wechsler deterioration index screening for behavioral impairment. *Perceptual and Motor Skills, 25,* 1191–1194.

Lloyd, J. W., Bateman, D. F., Landrum, T. J., & Hallahan, D. (1989). Self-recording of attention versus productivity. *Journal of Applied Behavior Analysis, 22,* 315–323.

Lloyd, M. E., & Hilliard, A. M. (1989). Accuracy of self-recording as a function of repeated experience with different self-control contingencies. *Child and Family Behavior Therapy, 11,* 1–14.

Lochman, J. E. (1992). Cognitive-behavioral intervention with aggressive boys: Three-year follow-up and preventive effects. *Journal of Consulting and Clinical Psychology, 60,* 426–434.

Lochman, J. E., & Wayland, K. K. (1994). Aggression, social acceptance, and race as predictors of negative adolescent outcomes. *Journal of the American Academy of Child and Adolescent Psychiatry, 33,* 1026–1035.

Loeber, R. (1982). The stability of antisocial and delinquent child behavior: A review. *Child Development, 53,* 1443–1446.

Loeber, R., & Dishion, T. (1983). Early predictors of male delinquency: A review. *Psychological Bulletin, 94,* 68–99.

Loeber, R., Green, S. M., & Keenan, K. (1995). Which boys will fare worse? Early predictors of the onset of conduct disorder in a six-year longitudinal study. *Journal of the American Academy of Child and Adolescent Psychiatry, 34,* 499–509.

Loeber, R., & Keenan, K. (1994). Interaction between conduct disorder and its comorbid conditions: Effects of age and gender. *Clinical Psychology Review, 14,* 497–523.

Loeber, R., Lahey, B. B., & Thomas, C. (1991). Diagnostic conundrum of oppositional defiant disorder and conduct disorder. *Journal of Abnormal Psychology, 100,* 379–390.

Logan, G. D., Cowan, W. B., & Davis, K. A. (1984). The ability to inhibit simple and choice reaction time responses: A model and a method. *Journal of Experimental Psychology: Human Perception and Performance, 10,* 276–291.

Logan, W. J., Farrell, J. E., Malone, M. A., & Taylor, M. J. (1988, September). *Effect of stimulant medications on cerebral event-related potentials.* Presentation made at the seventeenth national meeting of the Child Neurology Society, Halifax, Canada.

Loge, D. V., Staton, R. D., & Beatty, W. W. (1990). Performance of children with ADHD on tests sensitive to frontal lobe dysfunction. *Journal of the American Academy of Child and Adolescent Psychiatry, 29,* 540–545.

Londerville, S., & Main, M. (1981). Security of attachment, compliance, and maternal training methods in the second year of life. *Developmental Psychology, 17,* 289–299.

Loney, J. (1974). The intellectual functioning of hyperactive elementary school boys: A cross sectional investigation. *American Journal of Orthopsychiatry, 44,* 754–762.

Loney, J. (1980a). Hyperkinesis comes of age: What do we know and where should we go? *American Journal of Orthopsychiatry, 50,* 28–42.

Loney, J. (1980b). The Iowa theory of substance abuse among hyperactive adolescents. In D. J. Lettieri, M. Sayers, & H. W. Pearson (Eds.), *Theories on drug abuse: Selective contemporary perspectives* (NIDA Research Monograph 30, March).

Loney, J. (1986). Hyperactivity and aggression in the diagnosis of attention deficit disorder. In B. B. Lahey & A. E. Kazdin (Eds.), *Advances in clinical child psychology.* New York: State University Press.

Loney, J. (Ed.). (1987). *The young hyperactive child: Answers to questions about diagnosis, prognosis and treatment.* New York: Haworth Press.

Loney, J., Kramer, J., & Milich, R. (1981). The hyperkinetic child grownup: Predictors of symptoms, delinquency and achievement at follow-up. In K. D. Gadow & J. Loney (Eds.), *Psychosocial aspects of drug treatment for hyperactivity.* Boulder, CO: Westview Press.

Loney, J., & Milich, R. S. (1981). Hyperactivity, inattention, and aggression in clinical practice. In M. Wolraich & D. K. Routh (Eds.), *Advances in behavioral pediatrics* (Vol. 2). Greenwich, CT: JAI Press.

Loney, J., & Milich, R. (1982). Hyperactivity, inattention, and aggression in clinical practice. *Advances in Developmental and Behavioral Pediatrics, 3,* 113–147.

Lorys, A. R., Hynd, G. W., & Lahey, B. B. (1990). Do neurocognitive measures differentiate attention deficit disorder (ADD) with and without hyperactivity? *Archives of General Neuropsychology, 5,* 119–135.

Lorys-Vernon, A. R., Hynd, G. W., Lyytinen, H., & Hern, K. (1993). Etiology of attention deficit hyperactivity disorder. In J. L. Matson (Ed.), *Handbook of hyperactivity in children.* Needham Heights, MA: Allyn & Bacon.

Lou, H. C., Henriksen, L., & Bruhn, P. (1984). Focal cerebral hypoperfusion in children with dysphasia and/or attention deficit disorder. *Archives of Neurology, 41,* 825–829.

Lou, H. C., Henriksen, L., & Bruhn, P. (1990). Focal cerebral dysfunction in developmental learning disabilities. *Lancet, 335,* 8–11.

Lou, H. C., Henriksen, L., Bruhn, P., Borner, H., & Nielsen, J. B. (1989). Striatal dysfunction in attention deficit and hyperkinetic disorder. *Archives of Neurology, 41,* 825–829.

Love, A. J., & Thompson, M. (1988). Language disorders and attention deficit disorders in young children referred for psychiatric services: Analysis of prevalence and a conceptual synthesis. *American Journal of Orthopsychiatry, 58,* 52–64.

Lovejoy, M. C., & Rasmussen, N. H. (1990). The validity of vigilance tasks in differential diagnosis of children referred for attention and learning problems. *Journal of Abnormal Child Psychology, 18,* 671–681.

Lovitt, T. C. (1973). Self-management projects with children with behavioral disorders. *Journal of Learning Disabilities, 6,* 138–150.

Lovitt, T. C., & Curtiss, K. A. (1969). Academic response rate as a function of teacher and self-imposed contingencies. *Journal of Applied Behavior Analysis, 2,* 49–53.

Lovrich, D., & Stamm, J. S. (1983). Event-related potential and behavioral correlates of attention in reading retardation. *Journal of Clinical Neuropsychology, 5,* 13–37.

Lowe, T. L., Cohen, D. J., Detlor, J., Kremenitzer, M. W., & Shaywitz, B. A. (1982). Stimulant medications precipitate Tourette's syndrome. *Journal of the American Medical Association, 247,* 1729–1731.

Lubar, J. F. (1991). Discourse on the development of EEG diagnostics and biofeedback for ADHD. *Biofeedback and self-regulation, 16,* 201–225.

Lubar, J. F. (1992). *Psychophysiology in biofeedback treatment for ADHD.* Wheatridge, CO: Association of Applied Psychophysiology and Biofeedback.

Lubar, J. F., Mann, C. A., Gross, D. M., & Shively, M. S. (1992). Differences in semantic event-related potentials in learning-disabled, normal, and gifted children. *Biofeedback and Self Regulation, 17,* 41–57.

Lucker, J. R., Geffner, D., & Koch, W. (1996). Reception of loudness in children with ADD and without ADD. *Child Psychiatry and Human Development, 26,* 181–190.

Ludlow, C. L., Cudahy, E. A., Bassich, C., & Brown, G. L. (1983). Auditory processing skills of hyperactive, language impaired and reading disabled boys. In E. Z. Lasky & J. Katz

(Eds.), *Central auditory processing disorders: Problems of speech, language and learning* (pp. 163–184). Boulder, CO: Aspen Press.

Lufi, D., & Cohen, A. (1985). Using the WISC-R to identify attention deficit disorder. *Psychology Schools, 22,* 40–42.

Lufi, D., Cohen, A., & Parrish-Plass, J. (1990). Identify attention deficit hyperactivity disorder with the WISC-R and the Stroop color and word test. *Psychology in the Schools, 27,* 28–34.

Luisada, P. V. (1969). REM deprivation and hyperactivity in children. *Chicago Medical School Quarterly, 28,* 97–108.

Luiselli, J. K. (1991). Assessment-derived treatment of children's disruptive behavior disorders. *Behavior Modification, 18,* 294–309.

Luk, S. (1985). Direct observations studies of hyperactive behaviors. *Journal of the American Academy of Child Psychiatry, 24,* 338–344.

Luk, S. L., Leung, P. W., & Yuen, J. (1991). Clinic observations in the assessment of pervasiveness of childhood hyperactivity. *Journal of Child Psychology and Psychiatry and Allied Disciplines, 32,* 833–850.

Luria, A. R. (1959). The directive function of speech in development. *Word, 15,* 341–352.

Luria, A. R. (1961). *The role of speech and the regulation of normal and abnormal behaviors.* New York: Liveright.

Lynam, D., Moffitt, T., & Strouthamer-Loeber, M. (1993). Explaining the relation between IQ and delinquency: Class, race, test, motivation, school failure, or self-control? *Journal of Abnormal Psychology, 102,* 187–196.

Lynskey, M. T., & Fergusson, D. M. (1995). Childhood conduct problems, attention deficit behaviors, and adolescent alcohol, tobacco, and illicit drug use. *Journal of Abnormal Child Psychology, 23,* 281.

Maag, J. W., & Reid, R. (1994). ADHD: A functional approach to assessment and treatment. *Behavioral Disorders, 20,* 5–23.

MacArdle, P., O'Brien, G., & Kolvin, I. (1995). Hyperactivity: Prevalence and relationship with conduct disorder. *Journal of Child Psychology and Psychiatry in Allied Disciplines, 36,* 279–303.

Maccoby, E. E. (1980). *Social development.* New York: Harcourt Brace Jovanovich.

Maccoby, E. E., & Martin, J. A. (1983). Parent-child interaction. In E. M. Hetherington & P. H. Mussen (Eds.), *Handbook of child psychology: Vol. 4. Socialization, personality and social development.* New York: Wiley.

MacDonald, V. M., & Achenbach, T. M. (1996). Attention problems versus conduct problems as six-year predictors of problem scores in a national sample. *Journal of the American Academy of Child and Adolescent Psychiatry, 35,* 1237–1246.

MacKenzie, K. R. (1990). *Introduction to time limited group psychotherapy.* Washington, DC: American Psychiatric Press.

Mackworth, N. H. (1957). Some factors affecting vigilance. *Advancements in Science, 53,* 389–393.

Madsen, C. H., Becker, W. C., & Thomas, D. R. (1968). Rules, praise and ignoring: Elements of elementary classroom control. *Journal of Applied Behavior Analysis, 1,* 139–150.

Madsen, C. H., Becker, W. C., Thomas, D. R., Koser, L., & Plager, E. (1968). An analysis of the reinforcing function of "sit-down" commands. In R. K. Parker (Ed.), *Readings in educational psychology.* Boston: Allyn & Bacon.

Maehr, M. L., & Nicholls, C. (1980). Culture and achievement motivation: A second look. In N. Warren (Ed.), *Studies in cross-cultural psychology.* New York: Academic Press.

Mahoney, M. J. (1977a). Personal science: A cognitive learning therapy. In A. Ellis & R. Grieger (Eds.), *Handbook of rational psychotherapy* (pp. 352–366). New York: Springer.

Mahoney, M. J. (1977b). Some applied issues in self-monitoring. In J. D. Cone & R. P. Hawkins (Eds.), *Behavioral assessment: New direction in clinical psychology* (pp. 245–254). New York: Brunner/Mazel.

Mainville, F., & Friedman, R. J. (1976). Peer relations of hyperactive children. *Ontario Psychologist, 8,* 17–20.

Malone, R. P., Luebbert, M. D., Pena-Ariet, M., Biesecker, K., & Delaney, M. A. (1994). The overt aggression scale in a study of lithium in aggressive conduct disorder. *Psychopharmacology Bulletin, 30,* 215–218.

Mann, C. A., Lubar, J. F., Zimmerman, B., Miller, K., & Muenchen, A. (1990). Quantitative analysis of EEG in boys with attention deficit hyperactivity disorder: Controlled with clinical implications. *Pediatric Neurology, 8,* 30–36.

Mann, E. M., Ikeda, Y., Mueller, C. W., & Takahshi, A. (1992). Cross cultural differences in rating hyperactive disruptive behaviors in children. *American Journal of Psychiatry, 149,* 1539–1542.

Mannuzza, S., Gittelman-Klein, R., & Addalli, K. A. (1991). Young adult mental status of hyperactive boys and their brothers. A prospective follow-up study. *Journal of the American Academy of Child and Adolescent Psychiatry, 30,* 743–751.

Mannuzza, S., Gittelman-Klein, R., Konig, P. H., & Giampino, T. L. (1989). Hyperactive boys almost grown up: IV. Criminality and its relationship to psychiatric status. *Archives of General Psychiatry, 46,* 1073–1079.

Mannuzza, S., Klein, R. G., Bessler, A., & Malloy, P. (1993). Adult outcome of hyperactive boys: Educational achievement, occupational rank, and psychiatric status. *Archives of General Psychiatry, 50,* 565–576.

Mannuzza, S., Klein, R. G., Bessler, A., Malloy, P., & Hynes, M. E. (1997). Educational and occupational outcome of hyperactive boys grown up. *Journal of the American Academy of Child and Adolescent Psychiatry, 36,* 1222–1227.

Mannuzza, S., Klein, R. G., Bonagura, N., Malloy, P., Giampino, T. L., & Addalli, K. A. (1991). Hyperactive boys almost grown up: V. Replication of psychiatric status. *Archives of General Psychiatry, 48,* 77–83.

Margolin, G. (1995). *The effects of domestic violence on children.* Paper presented at the conference on violence against children in the family and community, Los Angeles.

Margolies, B. (1990). Attention deficit and the Macintosh. *Macintosh Lab Monitor, 9,* 11–13.

Margolis, H. (1990). Relaxation training: A promising approach for helping exceptional learners. *International Journal of Disability, Development and Education, 37,* 215–234.

Margolis, J. S. (1972). *Academic correlates of sustained attention.* Unpublished doctoral dissertation, University of California, Los Angeles.

Mariani, M. A., & Barkley, R. A. (1997). Neuropsychology and academic functioning in preschool boys with attention deficit hyperactivity disorder. *Developmental Neuropsychology, 13,* 111–129.

Marshall, K. J., Lloyd, J. W., & Hallahan, D. (1993). Effects of training to increase self-monitoring accuracy. *Journal of Behavioral Education, 3,* 445–459.

Marshall, P. (1989). Attention deficit disorder and allergy: A neurochemical model of the relation between the illnesses. *Psychological Bulletin, 106,* 434–446.

Marshall, V. G., Longwell, L., Goldstein, M. J., & Swanson, J. M. (1990). Family factors associated with aggressive symptomatology in boys with attention deficit hyperactivity disorder: A research note. *Journal of Child Psychology and Psychiatry and Allied Disciplines, 31,* 629–636.

Martin, B. (1977). Brief family intervention: The effectiveness and importance of including father. *Journal of Consulting and Clinical Psychology, 45,* 1002–1010.

Martin, C. S., Earleywine, M., Blackson, T. C., & Vanyukov, M. M. (1994). Aggressivity, inattention, hyperactivity, and impulsivity in boys at high and low risk for substance abuse. *Journal of Abnormal Psychology, 22,* 177–203.

Martin, D. J., Oren, Z., & Boone, K. (1990). *Major depressive's and dysthymic's performance on the Wisconsin card sorting test.* Unpublished manuscript.

Martin, D. R., Ryan, C., Nakayama, D., & Ramenofsky, M. (1990). Psychiatric sequelae after traumatic injury: The Pittsburgh regatta accident. *Journal of the American Academy of Child and Adolescent Psychiatry, 29,* 70–75.

Martin, G. L. (1993). Assessment procedures for attention deficit disorders in children. *Journal of Psychology and Christianity, 12,* 357–374.

Mash, E. J., & Johnston, C. (1982). A comparison of the mother-child interactions of younger children and older hyperactive and normal children. *Child Development, 53,* 1371–1381.

Mash, E. J., & Johnston, C. (1983a). The prediction of mothers' behavior with their hyperactive children during play and task situations. *Child and Family Behavior Therapy, 5,* 1–14.

Mash, E. J., & Johnston, C. (1983c). Parental perceptions of child behavior problems, parenting self-esteem, and mothers' reported stress in younger and older hyperactive and normal children. *Journal of Consulting and Clinical Psychology, 51,* 68–99.

Mash, E. J., & Johnston, C. (1983b). Sibling interactions of hyperactive and normal children and their relationship to reports of maternal stress and self-esteem. *Journal of Clinical Child Psychology, 12,* 91–99.

Massachusetts Coalition of Battered Women Service Groups. (1995). *Children of domestic violence. Working report on children's working group.* Boston: Author.

Massachusetts Medical Society. (1995). Trends in smoking initiation among adolescents and young adults: United States, 1980–1989. *MMWR: Morbidity, Mortality, Weekly Report, 44,* 521–524.

Massman, P. J., Nussbaum, N. L., & Bigler, E. D. (1988). The mediating effect of age on the relationship between child behavior checklist hyperactivity scores and neuropsychological test performance. *Journal of Abnormal Child Psychology, 16,* 89–95.

Masten, A. S., Morison, P., & Pelligrini, D. S. (1985). A revised class play: Method of peer assessment. *Developmental Psychology, 3,* 523–533.

Mastropieri, M. A., & Scruggs, T. (1991). *Teaching students ways to remember: Strategies for learning mnemonically.* Cambridge, MA: Brookline Books.

Mather, N. (1996). *An instructional guide to the Woodcock-Johnson psychoeducational battery—revised.* New York: Wiley.

Mather, N., & Jaffe, L. (1992). *Woodcock-Johnson psychoeducational battery revised recommendations and reports.* Vermont: Clinical Psychology.

Mather, N., & Roberts, R. (1996). *Informal assessment and instruction in written language.* New York: Wiley.

Mathison, R. R. (1958). *The eternal research: The story of man and his drugs.* New York: Putnam.

Matier, K., Halperin, J. M., Sharma, V., Newcorn, J. H., & Sathaye, N. (1992). Methylphenidate response in aggressive and nonaggressive ADHD children: Distinctions on laboratory measures of symptoms. *Journal of the American Academy of Child and Adolescent Psychiatry, 31,* 219–225.

Matochik, J. A., Liebenauer, L. L., King, A. C., Szymanski, H. V., Cohen, R. M., & Zametkin, A. J. (1994). Cerebral glucose metabolism in adults with attention deficit hyperactivity disorder after chronic stimulant treatment. *American Journal of Psychiatry, 151,* 658–664.

Matochik, J. A., Nordahl, T. E., Gross, M., Semple, W. E., King, A. C., Cohen, R. C., & Zametkin, A. J. (1993). Effects of acute stimulant medication on cerebral metabolism in adults with hyperactivity. *Neuropsychopharmacology, 8,* 377–386.

Matsura, M., Okubo, Y., Toru, M., & Kojima, T. (1993). A cross-national EEG study of children with emotional and behavioral problems: A WHO collaborative study in the Western Pacific region. *Biological Psychiatry, 34,* 59–65.

Mattes, J. A. (1980). The role of frontal lobe dysfunction in childhood hyperkinesis. *Comprehensive Psychiatry, 21,* 358–369.

Maughan, B. (1988). School experiences as risks/protective factors. In M. Rutter (Ed.), *Studies of psychosocial risk* (pp. 200–220). New York: Press Syndicate of the University of Cambridge.

Max, J. E., & Dunisch, D. L. (1997). Traumatic brain injury in a child psychiatry outpatient clinic: A controlled study. *Journal of the American Academy of Child and Adolescent Psychiatry, 36,* 404–411.

Max, J. E., Richards, L., & Hamdan-Allen, G. (1995). Case study: Antimanic effectiveness of dextroamphetamine in a brain-injured adolescent. *Journal of the American Academy of Child and Adolescent Psychiatry, 34,* 472–476.

Maxwell, V. (1989). Diagnosis and treatment of the gifted student with attention deficit disorder: A structure of intellect (SOI) approach. *Journal of Reading, Writing, and Learning Disabilities International, 5,* 247–252.

Mayes, S. D., & Bixler, E. O. (1993). Reliability of global impressions for assessing methylphenidate effects in children with attention deficit hyperactivity disorder. *Perceptual and Motor Skills, 77,* 1215–1218.

Mayes, S. D., Crites, D. L., Bixler, E. O., Humphrey, F. J., & Mattison, R. E. (1994). Methylphenidate and ADHD: Influence of age, IQ and neurodevelopmental status. *Developmental Medicine and Child Neurology, 36,* 1099–1107.

Mayes, S. D., Sanderson, D. L., Bixler, E. O., Humphrey, F. J., & Mattison, R. E. (1993). Influence of age, IQ and other neurodevelopmental disorders on methylphenidate response in children with attention deficit hyperactivity disorder. *Developmental Medicine and Child Neurology, 35*(Suppl.), 20–21.

Maytal, J., Young, M., Shechter, A., & Lipton, R. B. (1997). Pediatric migraine and the international headache society (IHS) criteria. *Neurology, 48,* 602–607.

McBurnett, K., Lahey, B. B., & Pfiffner, L. J. (1993). Diagnosis of attention deficit disorders in DSM-IV: Scientific basis and implications for education: Issues in the education of children with attentional deficit disorder [Special issue]. *Exceptional Children, 60,* 108–117.

McBurnett, K., & Pfiffner, L. J. (1991). Attention deficit hyperactivity disorder: Is it a learning disability or a related disorder? Comment. *Journal of Learning Disabilities, 24,* 258–259.

McCain, A. P., & Kelly, M. L. (1993). Managing the classroom behavior of an ADHD preschooler: The efficacy of a school-home note intervention. *Child and Family Behavior Therapy, 15,* 33–44.

McCarney, S. B. (1989). *Attention deficit disorders evaluation scale; school version rating form; home version rating form.* Columbia, MO: Hawthorne Educational Services.

McCarney, S. B. (1996). *Attention deficit disorders evaluation scale (ADDES).* Columbia, MO: Hawthorne Educational Services.

McClelland, J. M., Rubert, M. P., Reichler, R. J., & Sylvester, C. E. (1989). Attention deficit disorder in children at risk for anxiety and depression. *Journal of the American Academy of Child and Adolescent Psychiatry, 29,* 534–539.

McCloskey, L. A., Figueredo, A. J., & Koss, M. P. (1995). The effects of systemic family violence on children's mental health. *Child Development, 66,* 1239–1261.

McConaughy, S. H., Achenbach, T. M., & Gent, C. L. (1988). Multiaxial empirically based assessment: Parent, teacher, observational, cognitive and personality correlates of child behavior profile types for 6- to 11-year-old boys. *Journal of Abnormal Child Psychology, 16,* 485–509.

McConaughy, S. H., & Skiba, R. J. (1993). Comorbidity of externalizing and internalizing problems. *School Psychology Review, 22,* 421–436.

McConnell, S. R. (1987). Entrapment effects and the generalization and maintenance of social skills training for elementary students with behavioral disorders. *Behavioral Disorders, 13,* 252–263.

McConnell, S., & Odom, S. (1986). Sociometrics: Peer referenced measures and the assessment of social competence. In P. Strain, M. Guralnick, & H. M. Walker (Eds.), *Children's social behavior: Development, assessment and modification.* New York: Academic Press.

McCord, J. (1980). Patterns of deviance. In S. B. Sells, R. Crandall, M. Roff, J. S. Strauss, & W. Pollin (Eds.), *Human functioning in longitudinal perspective: Studies of normal and psychopathic populations.* Baltimore: Williams & Wilkins.

McCord, W., McCord, J., & Howard, A. (1961). Familial correlates of aggression in non-delinquent male children. *Journal of Abnormal and Social Psychology, 62,* 79–93.

McCown, W. G., & DeSimone, P. A. (1993). Impulses, impulsivity, and impulsive behaviors: A historical review of a contemporary use. In W. G. McCown, J. L. Johnson, & M. B. Shure (Eds.), *The impulsive client: Theory, research and treatment.* Washington, DC: American Psychological Association.

McCown, W. G., Johnson, J. L., & Shure, M. B. (1993). *The impulsive client: Theory, research and treatment.* Washington, DC: American Psychological Association.

McDaniel, K. D. (1986). Pharmacologic treatment of psychiatric and neurodevelopmental disorders in children and adolescents (Part 2). *Clinical Pediatrics, 25,* 143–146.

McDaniel, T. (1980). Corporal punishment and teacher liability: Questions teachers ask. *Clearing House, 54,* 10–13.

McDowell, M. J., & Rappaport, L. R. (1992). *Neurodevelopmental comorbidity with attention deficit hyperactivity disorder. A clinical review.* Paper presented at the 10th annual meeting of the Society for Behavioral Pediatrics, St. Louis, MO.

McGee, R., & Feehan, M. (1991). Are girls with problems of attention under recognized? *Journal of Psychopathology and Behavioral Assessment, 13,* 187–198.

McGee, R., Feehan, M., Williams, S., Partridge, F., Silva, P. A., & Kelly, J. (1990). *DSM-III* disorders in a large sample of adolescents. *Journal of the American Academy of Child and Adolescent Psychiatry, 29,* 611–619.

McGee, R., & Share, D. L. (1988). Attention deficit disorder hyperactivity and academic failure: Which comes first and what should be treated? *Journal of the American Academy of Child and Adolescent Psychiatry, 27,* 318–325.

McGee, R., Silva, P. A., & Williams, S. (1984). Behavior problems in a population of seven-year-old children: Prevalence, stability and types of disorder—A research report. *Journal of Child Psychology and Psychiatry, 25,* 251–259.

McGee, R., Stanton, W. R., & Sears, M. R. (1993). Allergic disorders and attention deficit disorder in children. *Journal of Abnormal Child Psychology, 21*(1), 79–88.

McGee, R., Williams, S., Anderson, J., & McKenzie-Parnell, J. M. (1990). Hyperactivity and serum and hair zinc levels in 11-year-old children from the general population. *Biological Psychiatry, 28*(2), 165–168.

McGee, R., Williams, S., & Feehan, M. (1992). Attention deficit disorder and age of onset of problem behaviors. *Journal of Abnormal Child Psychology, 20,* 487–503.

McGee, R., Williams, S., Moffitt, T., & Anderson, J. (1989). A comparison of 13-year-old boys with attention deficit and/or reading disorder on neuropsychological measures. *Journal of Abnormal Child Psychology, 17,* 37–53.

McGee, R., Williams, S., & Silva, P. A. (1984). Background characteristics of aggressive, hyperactive and aggressive hyperactive boys. *Journal of the American Academy of Child and Adolescent Psychiatry, 23,* 280–284.

McGee, R., Williams, S., & Silva, P. A. (1987). A comparison of girls and boys with teacher-identified problems of attention. *Journal of the American Academy of Child and Adolescent Psychiatry, 26,* 711–716.

McGinnis, E., Goldstein, A. P., Sprafkin, R. P., & Gershaw, N. J. (1984). *Skill-streaming the elementary school child: A guide for teaching prosocial skills.* Champaign, IL: Research Press.

McGlashan, T. (1988). Adolescent versus adult onset of mania. *American Journal of Psychiatry, 145,* 221–223.

McKinnery, J. D., Montague, M., & Hocutt, A. M. (1993). *Synthesis of research literature on assessment and identification of children and youth with attention deficit disorder.* First Draft: January 10, 1993.

McLeer, S. V., Callaghan, M., Henry, D., & Wallen, M. W. (1994). Psychiatric disorders in sexually abused children. *Journal of the American Academy of Child and Adolescent Psychiatry, 33,* 313–319.

McLloyd, V. C., & Wilson, L. (1991). The strain of living poor: Parenting, social support and child mental health. In A. C. Huston (Ed.), *Children in poverty: Child development and public policy.* New York: Cambridge University Press.

McMahon, S. A., & Greenberg, L. M. (1977). Serial neurological examination of hyperactive children. *Pediatrics, 59,* 584–587.

McNamara, J. J. (1972). Hyperactivity in the apartment bound child. *Clinical Pediatrics, 11,* 371–372.

McNutt, B., Ballard, J. E., & Boileau, R. (1976). The effects of long-term stimulant medication on growth and body composition of hyperactive children. *Psychopharmocology Bulletin, 12,* 13–14.

McRae, K. M., & Vickar, E. (1991). Simple developmental speech delay: A follow-up study. *Developmental Medicine and Child Neurology, 33,* 868–874.

McRoy, R. G., Grotevant, H. D., & Zurcher, L. A. (1988). *Emotional disturbance in adopted adolescents: Origins and development.* New York: Praeger.

Mealer, C., Morgan, S., & Luscomb, R. (1996). Cognitive functioning of ADHD and non-ADHD boys on the WISC-III and WRAML: An analysis within a memory model. *Journal of Attention Disorders, 1,* 133–147.

Meichenbaum, D. (1975). Self-instructional methods. In F. H. Kanfer & A. P. Goldstein (Eds.), *Helping people change.* New York: Pergamon Press.

Meichenbaum, D. (1976). Cognitive-behavior modification. In J. T. Spence, R. C. Carson, & J. W. Thibaut (Eds.), *Behavioral approaches to therapy.* Morristown, NJ: General Learning Press.

Meichenbaum, D. (1977). *Cognitive-behavior modification.* New York: Plenum Press.

Meichenbaum, D., & Goodman, J. (1969). Reflection-impulsivity and verbal control of motor behavior. *Child Development, 40,* 785–797.

Meichenbaum, D., & Goodman, J. (1971). Training impulsive children to talk to themselves: A means of developing self-control. *Journal of Abnormal Psychology, 77,* 115–126.

Meichenbaum, D., & Turk, D. C. (1987). *Facilitating treatment adherence: A practitioner's guidebook.* New York: Plenum Press.

Melnick, S. M., & Hinshaw, S. P. (1996). What they want and what they get: The social goals of boys with ADHD and comparison boys. *Journal of Abnormal Child Psychology, 24,* 169–185.

Mendelson, W., Johnson, N., & Stewart, M. A. (1971). Hyperactive children as teenagers: A follow-up study. *Journal of Nervous and Mental Disorders, 153,* 273–279.

Mendler, A. N. (1992). *What do I do when . . . ? How to achieve discipline with dignity in the classroom.* Bloomington, IN: National Education Service.

Merrell, K. W. (1990). Teacher ratings of hyperactivity in self-control and learning-disabled boys: A comparison with low achieving and average peers. *Psychology in the Schools, 27,* 289–296.

Merrell, K. W. (1993). *School social behavior scales.* Brandon, VT: Clinical Psychology.

Merry, S. N., & Andrews, M. B. (1994). Psychiatric status of sexually abused children twelve months after disclosure abuse. *Journal of the American Academy of Child and Adolescent Psychiatry, 33,* 939–944.

Messer, S. B. (1976). Reflection-impulsivity. A review. *Psychological Bulletin, 83,* 1026–1052.

Mesulam, M. M. (1985). *Principals of behavioral neurology.* Philadelphia: Davis.

Mesulam, M. M. (1990). Large-scale neurocognitive networks and distributed processing for attention, language, and memory. *Annals of Neurology, 28,* 597–613.

Meyer, M. C., Leonard, H. L., Allen, A. J., Swedo, S. E., Rapoport, J., Richter, D., Hamburger, S. D., & Tucker, E. (1996). TCA Cardiotoxicity: The latest [Letter to the editor–reply]. *Journal of the American Academy of Child and Adolescent Psychiatry, 35,* 701–702.

Mikkelsen, E. J., Brown, G. L., Minichiello, M. D., Millican, F. K., & Rapoport, J. L. (1982). Neurologic status in hyperactive, enuretic, encopretic and normal boys. *Journal of American Academy of Child Psychiatry, 21,* 75–81.

Milberger, S., Biederman, J., Faraone, S. V., Chen, L., & Jones, J. (1997). ADHD as associated with early initiation of cigarette smoking in children and adolescents. *Journal of the American Academy of Child and Adolescent Psychiatry, 36,* 37–44.

Milberger, S., Biederman, J., Faraone, S. V., & Murphy, J. (1995). Attention deficit hyperactivity disorder and comorbid disorder: Issues of overlapping symptoms. *American Journal of Psychiatry, 152,* 1793–1799.

Milberger, S., Biederman, J., Faraone, S. V., Murphy, J., & Tsuang, M. (1994). *Attention deficit hyperactivity disorder and comorbid diagnoses: Problems of overlapping symptomatology.* Presented at the annual meeting of the American Academy of Child and Adolescent Psychiatry.

Milich, R. (1984). Cross-sectional and longitudinal observations of activity level and sustained attention in a normative sample. *Journal of Abnormal Child Psychology, 12,* 261–276.

Milich, R., Carlson, C. L., Pelham, W. E., & Licht, B. G. (1991). Effects of methylphenidate on the persistence of ADHD boys following failure experiences. *Journal of Abnormal Child Psychology, 19,* 519–536.

Milich, R., & Diner, M. B. (1995). The self-perception of children with ADHD: A paradox resolved? *The ADHD Report, 3,* 1–3.

Milich, R., & Kramer, J. (1984). Reflections on impulsivity: An empirical investigation of impulsivity as a construct. In K. Gadow & I. Bialer (Eds.), *Advances in learning and behavioral disabilities* (Vol. 3, pp. 117–150). Greenwich, CT: JAI Press.

Milich, R., & Landau. S. (1981). Socialization and peer relations in the hyperactive child. In K. D. Gadow & I. Bailer (Eds.), *Advances in learning and behavior disabilities* (Vol. 1). Greenwich, CT: JAI Press.

Milich, R., Landau, S., Kilby, G., & Whitten, P. (1982). Preschool peer perceptions of the behavior of hyperactive and aggressive children. *Journal of Abnormal Child Psychology, 10,* 497–510.

Milich, R., Licht, B. G., Murphy, D. A., & Pelham, W. E. (1989). Attention-deficit hyperactivity disordered boys' evaluations of and attributions for task performance on medication versus placebo. *Journal of Abnormal Psychology, 98,* 280–284.

Milich, R., & Loney, J. (1979). The role of hyperactive and aggressive symptomatology in predicting adolescent outcome among hyperactive children. *Journal of Pediatric Psychology, 4,* 93–112.

Milich, R., Loney, J., & Landau, S. (1982). The independent dimensions of hyperactivity and aggression: A validation with playroom observation data. *Journal of Abnormal Psychology, 91,* 183–198.

Milich, R., Loney, J., & Roberts, M. A. (1986). Playroom observations of activity level and sustained attention: Two-year stability. *Journal of Consulting and Clinical Psychology, 54,* 272–274.

Milich, R., & Lorch, E. P. (1994). Television viewing methodology to understand cognitive processing of ADHD children. *Advances in Clinical Child Psychology, 16,* 177–201.

Milich, R., & Okazaki, M. (1991). An examination of learned helplessness among attention deficit hyperactivity disordered boys. *Journal of Abnormal Child Psychology, 19,* 607–623.

Milich, R., & Pelham, W. E. (1986). Effects of sugar ingestion on the classroom and playgroup behavior of attention deficit disordered boys. *Journal of Consulting and Clinical Psychology, 54,* 714–718.

Milich, R., Whidiger, T. A., & Landau, S. (1987). Differential diagnosis of attention deficit and conduct disorders using conditional probabilities. *Journal of Consulting and Clinical Psychology, 55,* 762–767.

Milich, R., Wolraich, M., & Lindgren, S. (1986). Sugar and hyperactivity: A critical review of empirical findings. *Clinical Psychology Review, 6,* 493–513.

Milin, R., Halikas, J. A., Meller, J. E., & Morse, M. (1991). Psychopathology among substance abusing juvenile offenders. *Journal of the American Academy of Child and Adolescent Psychiatry, 30,* 569–574.

Miller, G. E., & Prinz, R. J. (1990). Enhancement of social learning family interventions for childhood conduct disorder. *Psychological Bulletin, 108,* 291–307.

Miller, L. G., & Kraft, I. A. (1992). Sleep disturbances and epileptiform activity in a subpopulation of children with attention deficit hyperactivity disorder (ADHD): A literature review generating an hypothesis with implications for drug therapy. *Behavioral Neurology, 5,* 149–154.

Miller, P., & Bigi, L. (1979). The development of children's understanding and attention. *Merrill-Palmer Quarterly, 25,* 235–250.

Miller, S. A. (1995). Parents' attributions for the children's behavior. *Child Development, 66,* 1557–1584.

Millon, T. (1981). *Disorders of personality: DSM-III: Axis II.* New York: Wiley.

Millon, T., Green, C. J., & Meagher, R. B. (1982). *Millon adolescent personality inventory.* Minneapolis: Minneapolis National Computer Systems.

Minde, K. K., Lewin, D., Weiss, G., Lavigueur, H., Douglas, V., & Sykes, E. (1971). The hyperactive child in elementary school: A five-year controlled follow-up. *Exceptional Children, 38,* 215–221.

Mind Guided Technologists. (1994). *Mindscope.* Meadville, PA: Author.

Minuchin, S. (1974). *Families and family therapy.* Cambridge, MA: Harvard University Press.

Minuchin, S., & Fishman, H. C. (1981). *Family therapy techniques.* Cambridge, MA: Harvard University Press.

Mirskey, A. F., Anthony, B. J., Duncan, C. C., Ahearn, M. B., & Kellam, S. G. (1991). Analysis of the elements of attention: A neuropsychological approach. *Neuropsychology Review, 2,* 109–145.

Mischel, W., Shoda, Y., & Rodriguez, M. L. (1989). Delay of gratification in children. *Science, 244,* 933–938.

Mitchell, E., & Matthews, K. L. (1980). Gilles de la Tourette's disorder associated with pemoline. *American Journal of Psychiatry, 137,* 1618–1619.

Mitchell, W. G., Chavez, J. M., Zhou, Y., & Guzman, B. L. (1988, September). *Relationship of anti-epileptic drugs to reaction time, impulsivity, and attention in children with epilepsy.* Presentation made at the seventeenth national meeting of the Child Neurology Society, Halifax, Canada.

Mize, J. (1995). Coaching preschool children in social skills: A cognitive-social learning curriculum. In G. Cartledge & J. F. Milburn (Eds.), *Teaching social skills to children and youth: Innovative approaches* (3rd ed., pp. 237–261). Boston: Allyn & Bacon.

Moehle, K. A., & Fitzhugh-Bell, K. B. (1989). Factor analysis of the CTRS. *Psychology in Schools, 26,* 118–125.

Moffitt, T. E. (1990). Juvenile delinquency and attention deficit disorder: Developmental trajectories from age 3 to 15. *Child Development, 61,* 893–910.

Moffitt, T. E., & Henry, B. (1989). Neuropsychological assessment of executive functions in self-reported delinquents. *Developmental Psychopathology, 1,* 105–118.

Moffitt, T. E., & Silva, P. A. (1988). Self-reported delinquency, neuropsychological deficit, and history of attention deficit disorder. *Journal of Abnormal Child Psychology, 16,* 553–569.

Molina, L. R. (1990). Adoptees may be at risk for hyperactivity but no one knows why. *Adopted Child, 9,* 1–2.

Molitch, M., & Eccles, A. K. (1937). Effects of benzedrine sulphate on intelligence scores of children. *American Journal of Psychiatry, 94,* 587–590.

Molter, R. (1995, March). *Freedom from distractibility or auditory processing problems: A critical look at the WISC-III factor.* Paper presented at the Learning Disabilities Association Annual Conference, Orlando, FL.

Moore, L. A. (1994). The effects of social skills curricula: Were they apparent initially? *School Psychology Quarterly, 9,* 133–136.

Moore, L. A., Hughes, J. N., & Robinson, M. (1992). A comparison of the social information-processing abilities of rejected and accepted hyperactive children. *Journal of Clinical Child Psychology, 21,* 123–131.

Moos, R. H., & Moos, B. S. (1981). *Family environment scale manual.* Palo Alto, CA: Consulting Psychologists Press.

Moreland, J. R., Schwebel, A. I., Beck, S., & Wells, R. T. (1982). Parents as therapists: A review of the behavior therapy parent training literature, 1975–1981. *Behavior Modification, 6,* 250–276.

Moretti, M. M., Holland, R., & Peterson, S. (1994). Long-term outcome of an attachment-based program for conduct disorder. *Canadian Journal of Psychiatry, 39,* 360–370.

Morgan, A. E., Hynd, G. W., Riccio, C. A., & Hall, J. (1996). Validity of *DSM-IV* ADHD predominantly inattentive and combined types: The relationship to previous DSM diagnoses/subtype differences. *Journal of the American Academy of Child and Adolescent Psychiatry, 35,* 325–333.

Morgan, C. D., & Murray, H. A. (1935). A method for investigating fantasies: The thematic apperception test. *Archives of Neurology and Psychiatry, 34,* 289–307.

Morgan, D. P., & Jenson, W. R. (1988). *Teaching behaviorally disordered students.* New York: Macmillan.

Mori, L., & Peterson, L. (1995). Knowledge of safety of high and low active-impulsive boys: Implications for child injury protection. *Journal of Clinical Child Psychology, 24,* 370–376.

Morris, G. B. (1993). A rational-emotive treatment program with conduct disorder and attention-deficit hyperactivity disorder adolescents. *Journal of Rational-Emotive and Cognitive Behavior Therapy, 11,* 123–134.

Morrison, J., & Stewart, M. (1971). A family study of hyperactive child syndrome. *Biological Psychiatry, 3,* 189–195.

Morrison, J., & Stewart, M. (1973a). Evidence for polygenetic inheritance in the hyperactive child syndrome. *American Journal of Psychiatry, 130,* 791–792.

Morrison, J., & Stewart, M. (1973b). The psychiatric status of legal families of adopted hyperactive children. *Archives of General Psychiatry, 28,* 888–891.

Moss, W. L., & Sheifele, W. A. (1994). Can we differentially diagnose an attention deficit disorder without hyperactivity from a central auditory processing problem? *Child Psychiatry and Human Development, 25,* 85–96.

Mostovsky, D. I. (1970). *Attention: Contemporary theory and analysis.* New York: Appleton-Century-Crofts.

Mulhern, S., Dworkin, P. H., & Bernstein, B. (1994). Do parental concerns predict a diagnosis of attention-deficit hyperactivity disorder? *Journal Developmental and Behavioral Pediatrics, 15,* 348–352.

Munoz-Mallan, R. J., & Casteel, C. R. (1989). Attention-deficit hyperactivity disorder: Recent literature. *Hospital and Community Psychiatry, 48,* 699–707.

Murphy, K., & Barkley, R. (1995). Preliminary normative data on *DSM-IV* criteria for adults. *The ADHD Report, 3*(3), 6–7.

Murphy, K., & Barkley, R. (1996a). Prevalence of *DSM-IV* symptoms of ADD and adult licensed drivers: Implications for clinical diagnosis. *Journal of Attention Disorders, 1,* 147–161.

Murphy, K., & Barkley, R. (1996b). Updated adult norms for the ADHD behavior checklist for adults. *The ADHD Report, 4*(4), 12–16.

Murphy, V., & Hicks-Stewart, I. (1991). Learning disabilities and attention deficit hyperactivity disorder: An interactional perspective. *Journal of Learning Disabilities, 24,* 386–388.

Murray, J. B. (1987). Psychophysiological effects of methylphenidate (Ritalin). *Psychological Reports, 61,* 315–336.

Murray, L., Stanley, C., Hooper, R., King, F., & Fiori-Cowley, A. (1996). The role of infant factors in post natal depression and mother-infant interactions. *Developmental Medicine in Child Neurology, 38,* 109–119.

Musten, L. M., Firestone, P., Pisterman, S., Bennett, S., & Mercer, J. (1997). Effects of methylphenidate on preschool children with ADHD: Cognitive and behavioral functions. *Journal of the American Academy of Child and Adolescent Psychiatry, 36*(10), 1407–1416.

Nada-Raja, S., Langley, J. D., McGee, R., Williams, S. M., Begg, D. J., & Reeder, A. I. (1997). Inattentive and hyperactive behaviors and driving offenses in adolescence. *Journal of the American Academy of Child and Adolescent Psychiatry, 36,* 515–522.

Naglieri, J. A. (1989). Planning, attention, simultaneous, and successive cognitive processes: A summary of recent studies with exceptional samples. *Mental Retardation and Learning Disability Bulletin, 17,* 3–22.

Nall, M., Corbett, M., McLoughlin, J., Petrosko, J., Garcia, D., & Karibo, J. (1992). Impact of short-term oral steroid use upon children's school achievement and behavior. *Annals of Allergy, 69,* 218–220.

Nanson, J. L., & Hiscock, M. (1990). Attention deficits in children exposed to alcohol prenatally. *Clinical and Experimental Research, 14*(5), 656–661.

Napiorkowski, B., Lester, B. M., Freier, M. C., Brunner, S., Dietz, L., Nadra, A., & Oh, W. (1996). Effects of in utero substance exposure on infant neurobehavior. *Pediatrics, 98,* 71–75.

Narhi, V., & Ahonen, T. (1995). Reading disability with or without attention deficit hyperactivity disorder: Do attentional problems make a difference? *Developmental Neuropsychology, 11,* 337–349.

Nass, R., & Ross, G. (1991, September 19–21). *The child with a history of prematurity: A neuroanatomical model for an etiology of ADHD.* Paper presented at the third annual CH.A.D.D. conference, Washington, DC.

Nathan, W. A. (1992). Integrated multimodal therapy of children with attention-deficit hyperactivity disorder. *Bulletin of the Menninger Clinic, 56,* 283–312.

Needleman, H. L., Gunnoe, C., Leviton, A., Reed, R., Peresie, H., Maher, C., & Barrett, P. (1979). Deficits in psychological and classroom performance of children with elevated dentine lead levels. *New England Journal of Medicine, 300,* 689–695.

Needleman, H. L., Riess, J. A., Tobin, M. J., Biesecker, G. E., & Greenhouse, J. B. (1996). Original contributions: Bone lead levels and delinquent behavior. *Journal of the American Medical Association, 275,* 363–370.

Neff, N. A., & Iwata, B. A. (1994). Current research on functional analysis methodologies: An introduction. *Journal of Applied Behavior Analysis, 27,* 211–214.

Nehra, A., Mullick, F., Ishak, K. G., & Zimmerman, H. J. (1990). Pemoline-associated hepatic injury. *Gastroenterology, 99,* 1517–1519.

Neiswroth, J. T., & Smith, R. M. (1983). *Modifying retarded behavior.* Boston: Houghton Mifflin.

Nelson, J. R., Smith, D. J., Young, R. K., & Dodd, J. M. (1991). A review of self-management outcome research conducted with students who exhibit behavioral disorders. *Behavior Disorders, 3,* 169–179.

Nelson, K. B., & Ellenberg, J. H. (1979a). Apgar scores and long-term neurological handicap [Abstract]. *Annals of Neurology, 6.*

Nelson, K. B., & Ellenberg, J. H. (1979b). Neonatal signs as predictors of cerebral palsy. *Pediatrics, 64,* 225–232.

Netter, F. H. (1986). *The CIBA collection of medical illustrations. Nervous system: Part 11. Neurologic and neuromuscular disorders.* West Caldwell, NJ: CIBA.

Newby, R. S., Fischer, M., & Roman, M. A. (1991). Parent training for families of children with ADHD. *School Psychology Review, 20,* 252–265.

Newcorn, J. H., Halperin, J. M., Healey, J. M., O'Brien, J. D., Pascualvaca, D. M., Wolf, L. E., Morganstein, A., Sharma, V., & Young, J. G. (1989). Are ADDH and ADHD the same or different? *Journal of the American Academy of Child and Adolescent Psychiatry, 285,* 734–738.

Newcorn, J. H., Halperin, J. M., Schwartz, S., Pascualvaca, D., Wolf, L., Schmeidler, J., & Sharma, V. (1994). Parent and teacher ratings of attention-deficit hyperactivity disorder symptoms: Implications for case identification. *Developmental and Behavioral Pediatrics, 15,* 86–91.

Newman, J. P., & Wallace, J. F. (1993). Diverse pathways to deficient self-regulation: Implications for disinhibitory psychopathology in children. *Clinical Psychology Review, 13,* 699–720.

Nichamin, S. J. (1972). Recognizing minimum cerebral dysfunction in the infant and toddler. *Clinical Pediatrics, 11,* 255–257.

Nicholi, A. M., Jr. (1978). The adolescent. In A. M. Nicholi, Jr. (Ed.), *The Harvard guide to modern psychiatry.* London: Belnap.

Nicholls, J. G. (1984). Achievement motivation: Conceptions of ability, subjective experience, task choice, and performance. *Psychological Review, 91,* 328–346.

Nieman, G. W., & DeLong, R. (1987). Use of the personality inventory for children as an aid in differentiating children with mania from children with attention deficit disorder with hyperactivity. *Journal of the American Academy of Child and Adolescent Psychiatry, 26,* 381–388.

Nickerson, R. S. (1986). *Odyssey: A curriculum for thinking–verbal reasoning.* Watertown, MA: Mastery Education.

Ninness, H. A. C., Ellis, J., Miller, W. B., Baker, D., & Rutherford, R. (1995). The effect of a self-management training package on the transfer of aggression control procedures in the absence of supervision. *Behavior Modification, 19,* 464–490.

Nixon, S. B. (1969). Increasing task oriented behavior. In J. D. Krumboltz & C. Thoresen (Eds.), *Behavioral counseling cases and techniques* (pp. 207–213). New York: Holt.

Nolan, E. E., & Gadow, K. D. (1994). Relation between ratings and observations of stimulant drug response in hyperactive children. *Journal of Clinical Child Psychology, 23,* 78.

Nolan, E. E., & Gadow, K. D. (1997). Children with ADHD and tic disorder and their classmates: Behavioral normalization with methylphenidate. *Journal of the American Academy of Child and Adolescent Psychiatry, 36,* 597–604.

Norman, D. A. (1969). *Memory and attention.* New York: Wiley.

Northup, J. J., Broussard, C., Jones, K., & George, T. (1995). A preliminary comparison of reinforcer assessment methods for children with ADHD. *Journal of Applied Behavior Analysis, 28,* 99–100.

Nottelmann, E. D., & Jensen, P. S. (1995). Bipolar affective disorder in children and adolescents. *Journal of the American Academy of Child and Adolescent Psychiatry, 34,* 705–708.

Novaco, R. W. (1975). *Anger control: The development and evaluation of an experimental treatment.* Lexington, MA: Lexington Books.

Nowicki, S., & Strickland, B. R. (1973). Locus of control scale for children. *Journal of Consulting and Clinical Psychology, 40,* 1–8.

Nussbaum, N. L., Grant, M. L., & Bigler, E. D. (1990, February 14–17). *A comparison of neuropsychological test performance in boys and girls with attention deficit hyperactivity disorder.* Poster presented at the 18th annual meeting of the International Neuropsychological Society, Kissimmee, FL.

Nussbaum, N. L., Grant, M. L., Roman, M. J., Poole, J. H., & Bigler, E. D. (1990). Attention deficit disorder land the mediating effective of age on academic and behavioral variables. *Developmental and Behavioral Pediatrics, 11,* 22–26.

Nuwer, M. (1997). Assessment of digital EEG, quantitative EEG, and EEG brain mapping: Report of the American Academy of Neurology and the American Clinical Neurophysiology Society (formerly the American Electroencephalographic Society). *Neurology, 49,* 277–292.

Oades, R. D., Dittman-Balcar, A., Schepker, R., Eggers, C., & Zerbin, D. (1996). Auditory event-related potentials (ERPs) and mismatch negativity (MMN) in healthy children and those with attention deficit hyperactivity disorder. *Biological Psychology, 43,* 163–185.

Oberklaid, F., Harris, C., & Keir, E. (1989). Auditory dysfunction in school children. *Clinical Pediatrics, 28,* 397.

O'Brien, J. D., Halperin, J. M., Newcorn, J. H., Sharma, V., Wolf, L., & Morganstein, A. (1992). Psychometric differentiation of conduct disorder and attention deficit disorder with hyperactivity. *Developmental and Behavioral Pediatrics, 13,* 274–277.

O'Callaghan, M., Williams, G. N., Anderson, M. J., Bor, W., & Najaman, J. M. (1996). Social and biological risk factors for mild and borderline impairment of language comprehension in a cohort of five-year-old children. *Developmental Medicine and Child Neurology, 37,* 1051–1061.

O'Connor, R. D. (1969). Modification of social withdrawal through symbolic modeling. *Journal of Applied Behavior Analysis, 2,* 15–22.

O'Connor, R. D. (1972). Relative efficacy of modeling, shaping, and the combined procedures of the modification of social withdrawal. *Journal of Abnormal Psychology, 79,* 327–334.

Oden, S. L., & Asher, S. R. (1977). Coaching children in social skills for friendship making. *Child Development, 48,* 495–506.

Oesterheld, J. (1996). TCA Cardiotoxicity: The latest [Letter to the editor]. *Journal of the American Academy of Child and Adolescent Psychiatry, 35,* 701–702.

Offord, D. R., Aponte, J. F., & Cross, L. A. (1969). Presenting symptomatology of adopted children. *Archives of General Psychiatry, 20,* 110–116.

Offord, D. R., & Bennett, K. J. (1994). Conduct disorder: Long-term outcomes and intervention effectiveness. *Journal of the American Academy of Child and Adolescent Psychiatry, 33,* 1069–1078.

Offord, D. R., Boyle, M., Racine, Y. A., Fleming, J. E., Cadman, D. T., Bloom, H. M., Byrne, C., Links, P. S., Lipman, E. L., Macmillan, H. L., Grant, N. I., Sanford, M. N., Szatmari, P., Thomas, H., & Woodword, C. A. (1992). Outcome, prognosis and risk in a longitudinal follow-up study. *Journal of the American Academy of Child and Adolescent Psychiatry, 5,* 916–923.

Offord, D. R., Boyle, M. H., Racine, Y., Szatmari, P., Fleming, J. E., Sanford, M., & Lipman, E. L. (1996). Integrating assessment data for multiple informants. *Journal of the American Academy of Child and Adolescent Psychiatry, 35,* 1078–1085.

Offord, D. R., Boyle, M. H., Szatmari, P., Rae-Grant, N., Links, P. S., Cadman, D. T., Byles, J. A., Crawford, J. W., Munroe-Blum, H., Byrne, C., Thomas, H., & Woodward, C. (1987). Ontario child health study: II. Six month prevalence of disorder and rates of service utilization. *Archives of General Psychiatry, 44,* 832–836.

Okyere, B. A., & Heron, T. E. (1991). Use of self-correction to improve spelling in regular education classrooms. In G. Stoner, M. R. Shinn, & H. M. Walker (Eds.), *Interventions for achievement and behavior problems.* Silver Springs, MD: National Association for School Psychologists.

O'Leary, K. D., Emery, R., & Porter, B. (1981). *Marital discord and child behavior problems.* Paper presented at the annual meeting of the American Psychological Association, Los Angeles.

O'Leary, K. D., Kaufman, K. F., Kass, R. E., & Drabman, R. S. (1970). The effects of loud and soft reprimands on the behavior of disruptive students. *Exceptional Children, 37,* 145–155.

O'Leary, K. D., & O'Leary, S. G. (1977). *Classroom management: The successful use of behavior modification* (2nd ed.). Elmsford, NY: Pergamon Press.

O'Leary, K. D., Pelham, W. E., Rosenbaum, A., & Price, G. H. (1976). Behavioral treatment of hyperkinetic children: An experimental evaluation of its usefulness. *Clinical Pediatrics, 15,* 510–515.

Olson, G. M. (1976). An information-processing analysis of visual memory and habituation in infants. In R. J. Tighe, R. N. Leaton (Eds.), *Information-processing throughout the life-span.* Hillsdale, NJ: Erlbaum.

Olson, S. L., Bates, J. E., & Bayles, K. (1990). Early antecedents of childhood impulsivity: The role of parent-child interaction, cognitive competence and temperament. *Journal of Abnormal Child Psychology, 18,* 317–334.

Olweus, D. (1979). Stability of aggressive reaction patterns in males: A review. *Psychological Bulletin, 86,* 852–875.

O'Malley, K. D. (1994). Fetal alcohol effect and ADHD [Letters to the editor]. *Journal of the American Academy of Child and Adolescent Psychiatry, 33,* 1060–1061.

O'Malley, K. D. (1997). Safety of combined pharmacotherapy [Letter to the editor]. *Journal of the American Academy of Child and Adolescent Psychiatry, 36*(11), 1489–1490.

O'Neill, M. E., & Douglas, V. I. (1991). Study strategies and story recall on attention deficit disorder and reading disability. *Journal of Abnormal Child Psychology, 19,* 671–692.

O'Neill, M. E., & Douglas, V. I. (1996). Rehearsal strategies and recall performance with boys with and without attention deficit hyperactivity disorder. *Journal of Pediatric Psychology, 21,* 73–88.

Oosterland, J., & Sergeant, J. (1996). Inhibition in ADHD, aggressiveness and anxious children: A biologically based model of child psychopathology. *Journal of Abnormal Child Psychology, 24,* 19–36.

Ornoy, A., Uriel, L., & Tennenbaum, A. (1993). Inattention, hyperactivity and speech delay at two-four years of age as a predictor for ADD-ADHD syndrome. *Israel Journal of Psychiatry and Related Sciences, 30,* 155–163.

Oski, F. A., & Rosenstein, B. J. (1992). The iron status of female adolescents. *Pediatric Currents, 41*(5).

Osofsky, J. D. (1995). Children who witness domestic violence: The invisible victims. *Social Policy Report: Society for Research in Child Development, 9*(3), 1–16.

Osofsky, J. D., Cohen, G., & Drell, M. (1995). The effects of trauma on young children: A case of 2-year-old twins. *International Journal of Psychoanalysis, 76,* 595–607.

Osofsky, J. D., & Feinichel, E. (1994). *Hurt, healing and hope: Caring for infants and toddlers in violent environments.* Arlington, VA: Zero to Three/National Center for Clinical Infant Programs.

Ostrom, N. N., & Jenson, W. R. (1988). Assessment of attention deficits in children. *Professional School Psychology, 3,* 253–269.

Othmer, S. (1993). *EEG biofeedback training: A response to Russell Barkley.* Encino, CA: Unpublished paper.

O'Toole, K., Abramowitz, A., Morris, R., & Dulcan, M. (1997). Effects of methylphenidate on attention and non-verbal learning in children with attention deficit hyperactivity disorder. *Journal of the American Academy of Child and Adolescent Psychiatry, 36,* 531–538.

Ott, D. A., & Lyman, D. (1993). Automatic and effortful memory in children exhibiting attention deficit hyperactivity disorder. *Journal of Clinical Child Psychology, 22,* 420–427.

Ottinger, D., Halpin, B., Miller, M., Durmain, L., & Hanneman, R. (1985). Evaluating drug effectiveness in an office setting for children with attention deficit disorders. *Clinical Pediatrics, 24,* 245–251.

Ouellette, E. M. (1991). Legal issues in the treatment of children with attention deficit hyperactivity disorder. *Journal of Child Neurology, 6* (Suppl.), S68–S75.

Owing-West, N., & Prinz, R. J. (1987). Parental alcoholism and childhood psychopathology. *Psychological Bulletin, 102,* 204–218.

Ozawa, J. P., & Michael, W. B. (1983). The concurrent validity of a behavioral rating scale for assessing attention deficit disorder (*DSM-III*) in learning disabled children. *Educational and Psychological Measurement, 43,* 623–632.

Page, J. G., Bernstein, J. E., Janicki, R. S., & Michelli, F. A. (1974). A multi-clinical trial of pemoline in childhood hyperkinesis. *Excerpta Medica, 48,* 99–124.

Pagelow, M. D. (1984). *Family violence.* New York: Praeger.

Paine, S. C., Ridicchi, J., Rosellini, L. C., Deutchman, L., & Darch, C. B. (1983). *Structuring your classroom for academic success.* Champaign, IL: Research Press.

Palkes, H. S., & Stewart, M. A. (1972). Intellectual ability and performance of hyperactive children. *American Journal of Orthopsychiatry, 42,* 35–39.

Palkes, H. S., Stewart, M. A., & Freedman, J. (1971). Improvement in maze performance of hyperactive boys as a function of verbal-training procedures. *Journal of Special Education, 5,* 337–342.

Palkes, H. S., Stewart, M. A., & Kahana, B. (1968). Porteus maze. Performance of hyperactive boys after training in self-directed verbal commands. *Child Development, 39,* 817–826.

Palm, L., Persson, E., Elmqvist, D., & Blennow, G. (1992). Sleep and wakefulness in preadolescent children with deficits in attention, motor control, and perception. *Acta Paediatrica, 81,* 618–624.

Paniagua, F. A. (1987). Management of hyperactive children through correspondence training procedures: A preliminary study. *Behavioral Residential Treatment, 2,* 1–23.

Paniagua, F. A. (1992). Verbal-nonverbal correspondence training with ADHD children. Treatment of children with attention-deficit hyperactivity disorder (ADHD) [Special issue]. *Behavior Modification, 16,* 226–252.

Paniagua, F. A., & Black, S. A. (1990). Management and prevention of hyperactivity and conduct disorders in 8–10-year-old boys through correspondence training procedures. *Child and Family Behavior Therapy, 12,* 23–56.

Paniagua, F. A., & Black, S. A. (1992). Correspondence training and observational learning in the management of hyperactive children: A preliminary study. *Child and Family Behavior Therapy, 14,* 1–19.

Papazian, O. (1995). The story of fidgety Philip. *International Pediatrics, 10,* 188–190.

Parasuraman, R. (1994). The psychobiology of sustained attention. In J. S. Warm (Ed.), *Sustained attention in human performance* (pp. 61–101). London: Wiley.

Parke, R. D. (1969). Effectiveness of punishment as an interaction of intensity, timing, agent nurturance and cognitive structuring. *Child Development, 40,* 213–235.

Parker, H. C. (1988). *The ADD hyperactivity workbook.* Plantation, FL: Impact.

Parker, H. C. (1989, November). *Education position paper. Children with attention deficit disorder association.* Plantation, FL: Children and Adults with Attention Deficit Disorder (CH.A.D.D.).

Parker, H. C., Davis, L., & Sirotowitz, S. (1996). *Study strategies made easy: A practical plan for school success.* Plantation, FL: Special Press.

Parker, J. D., Bagby, R. M., & Webster, C. D. (1993). Domains of the impulsivity construct: A factor analytic investigation. *Personality and Individual Differences, 15,* 267–274.

Parker, J. D., Sitarenios, G., & Conners, C. K. (1996). Abbreviated Conners' rating scales revisited: A confirmatory factor analytic study. *Journal of Attention Disorders, 1,* 55–62.

Parker, J. G., & Asher, S. R. (1987). Peer relations and later personal adjustment: Are low-accepted children at risk? *Psychological Bulletin, 102,* 357–389.

Parker, V. S., & TenBrooek, N. L. (1987). *Problem solving, planning and organizational tasks: Strategies for retraining.* Tucson, AZ: Communication Skill Builders.

Parry, P., & Douglas, V. I. (1983). Effects of reinforcement on concept identification in hyperactive children. *Journal of Abnormal Psychology, 11,* 327.

Parsons, J. E., Adler, T. F., & Kaczala, C. M. (1982). Socialization of achievement attitudes and beliefs: Parental influences. *Child Development, 53,* 310–321.

Passler, M. A., Isaac, W., & Hynd, G. W. (1995). Neuropsychological development of behaviors attributed to frontal lobe functioning in children. *Developmental Neuropsychology, 1,* 349–370.

Pasuraman, R. (1994). Sustained attention and detection in discrimination. In R. Pasuraman & R. Davies (Eds.), *Varieties of attention.* New York: Academic Press.

Pataki, C. S., Carlson, G. A., Kelly, K. L., Rapport, M. D., & Biancaniello, T. M. (1993). Side effects of methylphenidate and desipramine alone and in combination in children. *Journal of the American Academy of Child and Adolescent Psychiatry, 32*(5), 1065–1072.

Paternite, C. E., & Loney, J. (1980). Childhood hyperkinesis: Relationships between symptomatology and home environment. In C. K. Whalen & B. Henker (Eds.), *Hyperactive children: The social ecology of identification and treatment.* New York: Academic Press.

Paternite, C. E., Loney, J., & Langhorne, J. E. (1976). Relationships between symptomatology and SES-related factors in hyperkinetic/MBD boys. *American Journal of Orthopsychiatry, 46,* 291–301.

Paternite, C. E., Loney, J., & Roberts, M. A. (1996). A preliminary validation of subtypes of *DSM-IV.* Attention-deficit/hyperactivity disorder. *Journal of Attention Disorders, 1,* 70–86.

Patterson, G. R. (1964). An application of conditioning techniques to the control of the hyperactive child. In L. P. Ullmann & L. Krasner (Eds.), *Case studies in behavior modification* (pp. 370–375). New York: Holt, Rinehart and Winston.

Patterson, G. R. (1974). Interventions for boys with conduct problems: Multiple settings, treatments, and criteria. *Journal of Consulting and Clinical Psychology, 42,* 471–481.

Patterson, G. R. (1975). *Families: Applications of social learning to family life.* Champaign, IL: Research Press.

Patterson, G. R. (1976a). The aggressive child: Victim and architect of a coercive system. In E. J. Mash, L. A. Hamerlynck, & L. C. Handy (Eds.), *Behavioral modification and families.* New York: Brunner/Mazel.

Patterson, G. R. (1976b). *Living with children: New methods for parents and teachers.* Eugene, OR: Castalia Press.

Patterson, G. R. (1979). A performance theory for coercive family interaction. In R. B. Cairns (Ed.), *The analysis of social interactions: Methods, issues and illustrations* (pp. 119–162). Hillsdale, NJ: Erlbaum.

Patterson, G. R. (1982). *Coercive family process.* Eugene, OR: Castalia Press.

Patterson, G. R., & Fleishman, M. J. (1979). Maintenance of treatment effects: Some considerations concerning family systems and follow-up data. *Behavior Therapy, 10,* 168–185.

Patterson, G. R., & Forgatch, M. S. (1985). Therapist behavior as a determinant for client noncompliance: A paradox for behavior modification. *Journal of Consulting and Clinical Psychology, 53,* 846–851.

Patterson, G. R., & Forgatch, M. S. (1988). *Parents and adolescents living together. Part 1: The basics. Part 2: Family problem solving.* Eugene, OR: Castalia Press.

Patterson, G. R., Reid, J., & Dishion, T. (1992). *Antisocial boys.* Eugene, OR: Castalia Press.

Paul, R., & James, D. F. (1990). Language delay and parental perceptions. *Journal of the American Academy of Child and Adolescent Psychiatry, 29,* 669–670.

Pauling, L. (1968). Orthomolecular psychiatry. *Science, 160,* 265–271.

Payton, J. B., Burkhart, J. E., Hersen, M., & Helsel, W. J. (1989). Treatment of ADDH in mentally retarded children. *Journal of the American Academy of Child and Adolescent Psychiatry, 28,* 761–767.

Pearson, D. A., & Aman, M. G. (1994). Ratings of hyperactivity and development indices: Should clinicians correct for developmental level? *Journal of Autism and Developmental Disorders, 24*(4), 395–411.

Pearson, D. A., Lane, D. M., & Swanson, J. M. (1991). Auditory attention switching in hyperactive children. *Journal of Abnormal Psychology, 19,* 479–492.

Pearson, D. E., Teicher, M. H., Shaywitz, B. A., Cohen, D. J., Young, J. G., & Anderson, G. M. (1980). Environmental influences on body weight and behavior in developing rats after neonatal 6-hydroxydopal line science. *Science, 209,* 715–717.

Pelham, W. E. (1977). Withdrawal of stimulant drug and concurrent behavioral intervention in the treatment of a hyperactive child. *Behavior Therapy, 8,* 473–479.

Pelham, W. E. (1987). What do we know about the use and effects of CNS stimulants in ADD? In J. Loney (Ed.), *The young hyperactive child: Answers to questions about diagnosis, prognosis and treatment.* New York: Haworth Press.

Pelham, W. E. (1991). ADHD and alcohol problems: Related disorders of childhood and adulthood. *Parents of ADD/Hyperactive Children,* 1st Quarter.

Pelham, W. E., Atkins, M. S., Murphy, H. A., & White, K. S. (1981a). Attention deficit disorder with and without hyperactivity: Definitional issues and correlates. In W. Pelham (Ed.), *DSM-III category of attention deficit disorders: Rationale, operationalization and correlates.* Los Angeles: American Psychological Association.

Pelham, W. E., Atkins, M. S., Murphy, H. A., & White, K. S. (1981b). *Operationalization and validation of attention deficit disorder.* Paper presented at the annual meeting of the Association for Advancement of Behavioral Therapy, Toronto, Canada.

Pelham, W. E., & Bender, M. E. (1982). Peer relationships in hyperactive children. In K. D. Gadow & I. Bialer (Eds.), *Advances in learning and behavioral disabilities* (Vol. 1, pp. 365–436). Greenwich, CT: JAI Press.

Pelham, W. E., Bender, M. E., Caddell, J., Booth, S., & Moorer, S. H. (1985a). V Methylphenidate and children with attention deficit disorder: Dose effects on classroom, academic and social behavior. *Archives of General Psychiatry, 42,* 948–952.

Pelham, W. E., Bender, M. E., Caddell, J., Booth, S., & Moorer, S. H. (1985b). Medication effect on arithmetic learning. *Archives of General Psychiatry, 42,* 948–951.

Pelham, W. E., Carlson, C. L., Sams, S. E., & Vallano, G. (1993). Separate and combined effects of methylphenidate and behavior modification on boys with attention deficit hyperactivity disorder in the classroom. *Journal of Consulting and Clinical Psychology, 61,* 501–513.

Pelham, W. E., & Gnagy, E. (1995). Summer treatment program for children with ADHD. *The ADHD Report, 3,* 6–8.

Pelham, W. E., Gnagy, E., Greenslade, K. E., & Milich, R. (1992). Teacher ratings of *DSM III-R* symptoms for the deceptive behavior disorders. *Journal of the American Academy of Child and Adolescent Psychiatry, 31,* 210–218.

Pelham, W. E., Greenslade, K., & Cunningham, S. L. (1990). Sleep disturbances in children with attention deficit disorder [Abstract]. *Journal of Developmental and Behavioral Pediatrics, 11,* 218.

Pelham, W. E., Greenslade, K. E., Vodde-Hamilton, M., Murphy, D. A., Greenstein, J. J., Gnagy, E. M., Guthrie, K. J., Hoover, M. D., & Dahl, R. E. (1990). Relative efficacy of long-acting stimulants on children with attention deficit-hyperactivity disorder. A comparison of standard methylphenidate, sustained-release methylphenidate, sustained-release dextroamphetamine, and pemoline. *Pediatrics, 86,* 87–93.

Pelham, W. E., & Hoza, J. (1987). Behavioral assessment of psychostimulant effects on ADD children in a summer day treatment program. *Advances in Behavioral Assessment of Children and Families, 3,* 3–34.

Pelham, W. E., McBurnett, K., Harper, G. W., Milich, R., Murphy, D. A., Clinton, J., & Thiele, K. (1990). Methylphenidate and baseball playing in ADHD children: Who's on first? *Journal of Consulting and Clinical Psychology, 58,* 130–133.

Pelham, W. E., & Milich, R. (1984). Peer relations of children with hyperactivity/attention deficit disorder. *Journal of Learning Disabilities, 17,* 560–568.

Pelham, W. E., Milich, R., Cummings, E. M., Murphy, D. A., Schaughency, R., & Greiner, R. (1991). Effects of background anger, provocation, and methylphenidate on emotional arousal and aggressive responding in attention-deficit hyperactivity disordered boys with and without concurrent aggressiveness. *Journal of Abnormal Child Psychology, 19*(4), 407–426.

Pelham, W. E., Milich, R., Murphy, D. A., & Murphy, H. A. (1989). Normative data on the IOWA Conners teacher rating scale. *Journal of Clinical Child Psychology, 18*(3), 259–262.

Pelham, W. E., Milich, R., & Walker, J. L. (1986). Effects of continuous and partial reinforcement and methylphenidate on learning in children with attention deficit disorder. *Journal of Abnormal Child Psychology, 95,* 319–325.

Pelham, W. E., Murphy, D., Vannatta, K., Milich, R., Licht, M. H., Gnagy, E., Greenslade, K. E., Greiner, R., & Vodde-Hamilton, M. (1992). Methylphenidate and attributions in boys with attention-deficit hyperactivity disorder. *Journal of Consulting and Clinical Psychology, 61,* 282–292.

Pelham, W. E., & Murphy, H. A. (1986). Behavioral and pharmacological treatment of hyperactivity and attention-deficit disorders. In M. Herson & S. E. Breuning (Eds.), *Pharmacological and behavioral treatment: An integrative approach.* New York: Wiley.

Pelham, W. E., Schnedler, R. W., Bologna, N., & Contreras, J. A. (1980). Behavioral and stimulant treatment of hyperactive children: A therapy study with methylphenidate probes in a within-subject design. *Journal of Applied Behavior Analysis, 13,* 221–236.

Pelham, W. E., Schnedler, R. W., Miller, J., Ronnei, M., Paluchowski, C., Budrow, M., Marx, D., Nilsson, D., & Bender, M. E. (1986). The combination of behavior therapy and psychostimulant medication in the treatment of hyperactive children: A therapy outcome study. In L. Bloomingdale (Ed.), *Attention deficit disorders.* New York: Spectrum Books.

Pelham, W. E., Sturges, J., Hoza, J., Schmidt, C., Bijlsma, J. J., Milich, R., & Moorer, S. (1987). Sustained release and standard methylphenidate effects on cognitive and social behavior in children with attention deficit disorder. *Pediatrics, 4,* 491–501.

Pelham, W. E., Swanson, J., Bender, M., & Wilson, J. (1980, August). *Effects of pemoline on hyperactivity: Laboratory and classroom measures.* Presented to the annual meeting of the American Psychological Association, Montreal, Canada.

Pelham, W. E., Walker, J. L., Sturges, J., & Hoza, J. (1989). Comparative Effects of methylphenidate on ADD girls and ADD boys. *Journal of the American Academy of Child and Adolescent Psychiatry, 28,* 773–776.

Pellegrini, A. D., & Horvat, M. (1995). A developmental contextualist critique of attention deficit hyperactivity disorder. *Educational Researcher, 24,* 13–18.

Pellock, J. M., Culbert, J. P., Garnett, W. R., Crumrine, P. K., Kaplan, A. M., O'Hara, K. A., Driscoll, S. M., Frost, M. M., Alvin, R., Hamer, R. M., Handen, B., Horowitz, I. W., & Nichols, C. (1988). *Significant differences of cognitive and behavioral effects of anti epileptic drugs in children.* Presentation made at the seventeenth national meeting of the Child Neurology Society, Halifax, Canada.

Pennington, B. F. (1991). *Diagnosing learning disorders: A neuropsychological framework.* New York: Guilford Press.

Pennington, B. F., Bennett, L., McLeer, O., & Roberts, R. (1996). Executive function and working memory: Theoretical and measurement issues. In J. R. Lyon & N. A. Krasnegor (Eds.), *Attention, memory and executive function.* Baltimore: Brookes.

Pennington, B. F., Groisser, D., & Welsh, M. C. (1993). Contrasting cognitive deficits in attention deficit-hyperactivity disorder versus reading disability. *Developmental Psychology, 29,* 511–523.

Perez, E. R., Davidoff, V., Despland, P. A., & Deonna, T. (1993). Mental and behavioral deterioration of children with epilepsy and CSWS: Acquired epileptic frontal syndrome. *Developmental Medicine and Child Neurology, 35,* 661–674.

Perkins, D. N., & Laserna, C. (1986). *Odyssey: A curriculum for thinking–inventive thinking.* Watertown, MA: Mastery Education.

Perrin, S., & Last, C. (1992). Do childhood anxiety measures measure anxiety? *Journal of Abnormal Child Psychology, 20,* 567–578.

Perrin, S., & Last, C. (1996). Relationship between ADHD and anxiety in boys: Results from a family study. *Journal of the American Academy of Child and Adolescent Psychiatry, 35,* 988–996.

Perrino, L. J., Rapoport, J. L., Behar, D., Ismond, D. R., & Bunney, W. E. (1983). A naturalistic assessment of the motor activity of hyperactive boys: II. Stimulant drug effects. *Archives of General Psychiatry, 40,* 688–693.

Persson-Blennow, I., & McNeil, T. F. (1988). Frequencies and stability of temperament types in childhood. *Journal of the American Academy of Child and Adolescent Psychiatry, 27,* 619–622.

Peterson, L., Homer, A. L., & Wunderlich, S. A. (1982). The integrity of independent variables in behavior analysis. *Journal of Applied Behavior Analysis, 15,* 466–492.

Pfeffer, C. R., Klerman, G. L., Hurt, S. W., Lesser, M., Peskin, J. R., & Seifker, C. A. (1991). Suicidal children grown up: Demographic and clinical risk factors for adolescent suicide attempts. *Journal of the American Academy of Child and Adolescent Psychiatry, 30,* 609–616.

Pfiffner, L. J., & Barkley, R. A. (1990). Educational placement and classroom management. In R. A. Barkley (Ed.), *Attention-deficit hyperactivity disorder: A handbook for diagnosis and treatment.* New York: Guilford Press.

Pfiffner, L. J., & O'Leary, S. G. (1987). The efficacy of all-positive management as a function of the prior use of negative consequences. *Journal of Applied Behavior Analysis, 20,* 265–271.

Pfiffner, L. J., & O'Leary, S. G. (1993). School-based psychological treatments. In J. L. Matson (Ed.), *Handbook of hyperactivity in children.* Boston: Allyn & Bacon.

Pfiffner, L. J., O'Leary, S. G., & Rosen, L. A. (1985). The efficacy of an all-positive approach to classroom management. *Journal of Applied Behavior Analysis, 18,* 257–261.

Pfiffner, L. J., O'Leary, S. G., Rosen, L. A., & Sanderson, W. C., Jr. (1985). A comparison of the effects of continuous and intermittent response cost and reprimands in the classroom. *Journal of Clinical Child Psychology, 14,* 348–352.

Phares, D., & Compas, D. E. (1992). The role of fathers in child and adolescent psychopathology: Make room for daddy. *Psychological Bulletin, 111,* 387–412.

Phelan, T. (1985). *1-2-3 Magic: Training your preschoolers and preteens to do what you want.* Glen Ellyn, IL: Child Management Press.

Phelps, L. A. (1995). Exploratory factor analysis of the WRAML with academically at risk students. *Journal of Psychoeducational Assessment, 13,* 384–390.

Phillips, J. S., & Ray, R. S. (1980). Behavioral approaches to childhood disorders: Review and critique. *Behavior Modification, 4,* 3–34.

Physician's Desk Reference. (1997). Oradell, NJ: Medical Economics.

Picano, J. J., Klusman, L. E., Hornbestel, L. K., & Moulton, J. M. (1992). Replication of three-component solution for common measures of attention in HIV seropositive males. *Archives of Clinical Neuropsychology, 7,* 271–274.

Pico della Mirandola, G. (1930). *On the imagination* (H. Caplan, Trans.). New Haven, CT: Yale University Press.

Piers, E. V., & Harris, D. B. (1984). *Piers-Harris children's self-concept scale.* Los Angeles: Western Psychological.

Pike, A., & Plomin, R. (1996). Importance of nonshared environmental factors for childhood and adolescent psychopathology. *Journal of the American Academy of Child and Adolescent Psychiatry, 35,* 560–570.

Pinto, L. P., & Tryon, W. W. (1996). Activity measurements support dimensional assessment. *Behavior Modification, 20,* 243–258.

Pisterman, S., McGrath, P., Firestone, P., Goodman, J. T., Webster, I., & Mallory, R. (1992). The role of parent training in treatment of preschoolers with ADHD. *American Journal of Orthopsychiatry, 62,* 397–408.

Pisterman, S., McGrath, P., Firestone, P., Goodman, J. T., Webster, I., & Mallory, R. (1989). Outcome of parent-mediated treatment of preschoolers with attention deficit disorder with hyperactivity. *Journal of Consulting and Clinical Psychology, 57,* 628–635.

Pisterman, S., McGrath, P., Firestone, P., Goodman, J. T., Webster, I., Mallory, R. & Goffin, B. (1992). The effects of parent training on parenting stress and sense of competence. *Canadian Journal of Behavioral Science, 24,* 41–58.

Platzman, K. A., Stoy, M. R., Brown, R. T., Coles, C. D., Smith, I. E., & Falek, A. (1992). Review of observational methods in attention deficit hyperactivity disorder (ADHD): Implications for diagnosis. *School Psychology Quarterly, 7,* 155–177.

Pleak, R. R. (1995). Adverse effects of chewing methylphenidate. *American Journal of Psychiatry, 152,* 811.

Pleak, R., Birmaher, B., Gavrilescu, A., Abichandini, A., & Williams, D. (1988). Mania and neuropsychiatric excitation following carbamazepine. *Journal of the American Academy of Child and Adolescent Psychiatry, 27,* 500–503.

Plenk, A. (1975). *Plenk storytelling test.* Salt Lake City, UT: The Children's Center.

Pless, I. B., Taylor, H. G., & Arsenault, L. (1995). The relationship between vigilance deficits and traffic injuries involving children. *Pediatrics, 95,* 219–224.

Pliszka, S. R. (1987). Tricyclic antidepressants in the treatment of children with attention deficit disorder. *Journal of the American Academy of Child and Adolescent Psychiatry, 26,* 127–132.

Pliszka, S. R. (1989). Effect of anxiety on cognition, behavior, and stimulant response in ADHD. *Journal of the American Academy of Child and Adolescent Psychiatry, 28,* 882–887.

Pliszka, S. R. (1990). Effect of anxiety on cognition, behavior, and stimulant respose in ADHD. *Annual Progress in Child Psychiatry and Child Development,* 454–466.

Pliszka, S. R. (1992). Comorbidity of attention-deficit hyperactivity disorder and overanxious disorder. *Journal of the American Academy of Child and Adolescent Psychiatry, 31,* 197–203.

Poillion, M. J. (1991). A comparison of characteristics and causes of attention deficit hyperactivity disorder identified by social defining groups. *Dissertation Abstracts International, 52*(5-A), 1695.

Polacco, M., Casella, S., & Condini, A. (1992). Clinical aspects of the rehabilitation of hyperactive children. *Giornale di Neuropsichiatria dell'eta Evolutiva, 12,* 15–23.

Polatajko, H. J. (1985). A critical look at vestibular dysfunction in learning disabled children. *Developmental Medicine and Child Neurology, 27,* 283–292.

Polirstok, S. R. (1987). Training handicapped students in the mainstream to use self-evaluation techniques. *Techniques: A Journal for Remedial Education and Counseling, 3,* 9–18.

Pollard, S., Ward, E. N., & Barkley, R. A. (1983). The effects of parent training and Ritalin on the parent-child interactions of hyperactive boys. *Child and Family Behavior Therapy, 5,* 51–69.

Pomerleau, O., Downey, K., Stelson, F., & Pomerleau, C. (1995). Cigarette smoking in adult patients diagnosed with attention deficit hyperactivity disorder. *Journal of Substance Abuse, 7,* 373–378.

Pomeroy, J. C., Sprafkin, J., & Gadow, K. D. (1988). Minor physical anomalies as a biologic marker for behavior disorders. *Journal of the American Academy of Child and Adolescent Psychiatry, 27,* 466–473.

Pope, A. T., & Bogart, E. H. (1996). Extended attention span training system: Video game neurotherapy for attention deficit disorder. *Child Study Journal, 26,* 39–50.

Pope, L. (1970). Motor activity in brain-injured children. *American Journal of Orthopsychiatry, 40,* 783–794.

Popkin, M. (1986). *Active parenting.* Atlanta, GA: Author.

Porrino, L. J., Lucignani, G., Dow-Edwards, D., & Sokoloff, L. (1984). Dose dependent effects and acute amphetamine administration on functional brain metabolism in rats. *Brain Research, 307,* 311–320.

Porrino, L. J., Rapoport, J. L., Behar, D., Sceery, W., Ismond, D. R., & Bunney, W. E. (1983). A naturalistic assessment of the motor activity of hyperactive boys: I. Comparison with normal controls. *Archives of General Psychiatry, 40,* 681–687.

Posner, M. I. (1987). Selective attention in head injury. In H. S. Levin, J. Grafman, & H. M. Eisenberg (Eds.), *Neurobehavioral recovery from head injury.* New York: Oxford University Press.

Posner, M. I., & Petersen, S. E. (1990). The attention system of the human brain. *Annual Review of Neuroscience, 13,* 25–42.

Posner, M. I., & Raichle, M. E. (1994). Networks of attention. In M. I. Posner & M. E. Raichle (Eds.), *Images of mind.* New York: Scientific American Library.

Posner, M. I., & Snyder, C. R. (1975). Attention and cognitive control. In R. Solso (Ed.), *Information processing and cognition: The Loyola symposium.* Hillsdale, NJ: Erlbaum.

Potashkin, B. D., & Beckles, N. (1990). Relative efficacy of ritalin and biofeedback treatments in the management of hyperactivity. *Biofeedback and Self-Regulation, 15,* 305–315.

Pottick, K., Hansell, S., Gutterman, E., & Raskin-White, H. (1995). Factors associated with inpatient and outpatient treatment for children and adolescents with serious mental illness. *Journal of the American Academy of Child and Adolescent Psychiatry, 34,* 425–433.

Power, T. G., & Chapieski, M. L. (1986). Child rearing and impulse control in toddlers: A naturalistic investigation. *Developmental Psychology, 22,* 272–275.

Power, T. J. (1992). Contextual factors in vigilance testing of children with ADHD. *Journal of Abnormal Child Psychology, 20,* 579–593.

Power, T. J., Hess, L. E., & Bennett, D. S. (1995). The acceptability of interventions for attention-deficit hyperactivity disorder among elementary and middle school teachers. *Developmental and Behavioral Pediatrics, 16,* 238–243.

Prater, M. A., Hogen, S., & Miller, S. R. (1992). Using self-monitoring to improve on task behavior in academic skills in an adolescent with mild handicaps across special and regular education settings. *Education and Treatment of Children, 15,* 43–55.

Prater, M. A., Joy, R., Chilman, B., Temple, J., & Miller, S. R. (1991). Self-monitoring of on-task behavior with adolescents with learning disabilities. *Learning Disability Quarterly, 14,* 164–177.

Preskorn, S. H., Bupp, S. J., Weller, E. B., & Weller, R. A. (1989). Plasma levels of imipramine and metabolites in 68 hospitalized children. *Journal of the American Academy of Child and Adolescent Psychiatry, 28,* 373–375.

Preuss, J., Elia, J., Gulotta, C., Rose, S. R., Marin, G., & Rapoport, J. L. (1994). ADHD and the thyroid. Thyroid function and attention-deficit hyperactivity disorder [Letters to the editor]. *Journal of the American Academy of Child and Adolescent Psychiatry, 33,* 1057–1058.

Price, R. A., Leckman, J. F., Pauls, D. L., Cohen, D. J., & Kidd, K. K. (1986). Gilles de la Tourette's syndrome: Tics and central nervous system stimulants in twins and non-twins. *Neurology, 36,* 232–237.

Prichep, A., Sutton, S., & Hakerm, G. (1976). Evoked potentials in hyperkinetic and normal children under certainty and uncertainty: A placebo and methylphenidate study. *Psychophysiology, 13,* 419–428.

Prifitera, A., & Dersh, J. (1993). Base rates of WISC-III diagnostic subtest patterns among normal, learning disabled and ADHD samples. *Journal of Psychoeducational Assessment: WISC-III Monograph,* 43–55.

Prinz, R. J., Connor, P. A., & Wilson, C. C. (1981). Hyperactive and aggressive behaviors in childhood: Intertwined dimensions. *Journal of Abnormal Psychology, 9,* 191–192.

Prinz, R. J., & Loney, J. (1974). Teacher-rated hyperactive elementary school girls: An exploratory developmental study. *Child Psychiatry in Human Development, 4,* 246–257.

Prinz, R. J., Myers, D. R., Holder, E. W., Tarnowski, K. J., & Roberts, W. A. (1983). Marital disturbance and child problems: A cautionary note regarding hyperactive children. *Journal of Abnormal Child Psychology, 11,* 393–399.

Prior, M., & Sanson, A. (1986). Attention deficit disorder with hyperactivity: A critique. *Journal of Child Psychology and Psychiatry, 27,* 307–320.

Prior, M., & Sanson, A. (1989). Attention deficit disorder with hyperactivity: A reply. *Journal of Child Psychology and Psychiatry, 29,* 223–225.

Puczynski, M. S., Puczynski, S. S., Reich, J., Kaspar, J. C., & Emanuele, M. A. (1990). Mental efficiency and hypoglycemia. *Developmental and Behavioral Pediatrics, 11,* 170–174.

Puig-Antich, J. (1980). Affective disorders in childhood: A review and perspective. *Psychiatric Clinics of North America, 3,* 403–423.

Pulkkinen, L. (1995). Behavioral precursors to accidents and result in physical impairment. *Child Development, 66,* 1660–1679.

Pulkkinen, L., & Tremblay, R. E. (1992). Patterns of boys' social adjustment in two cultures and at different ages: Longitudinal perspective. *International Journal of Behavioral Development, 15,* 527–553.

Purvis, K. L., & Tannock, R. (1997). Language abilities in children with ADHD, reading disabilities and normal controls. *Journal of Abnormal Child Psychology, 25,* 133–144.

Pynoos, R. S. (1993). Traumatic stress and developmental psychopathology in children and adolescents. In J. M. Oldham, M. B. Riba, & A. Tasman (Eds.), *American psychiatric press review of psychiatry* (Vol. 12, pp. 205–238). Washington, DC: American Psychiatric Press.

Quadrel, M. J., Fischoff, B., & Davis, W. (1993). Adolescent (in)vulnerability: Adolescence [Special issue]. Guest Editor: Ruby Takanishi. *American Psychologist, 48*(2), 102.

Quay, H. C. (1979). Classification. In H. C. Quay & J. S. Werry (Eds.), *Psychopathological disorders of childhood* (2nd ed.). New York: Wiley.

Quay, H. C. (1997). Inhibition and attention deficit hyperactivity disorder. *Journal of Abnormal Child Psychology, 25,* 7–13.

Quay, H. C., & Peterson, D. R. (1987). *Manual for the revised behavioral problem checklist.* Miami: Authors.

Quay, H. C., Sprague, R. O., Werry, J. S., & McQueen, M. (1967). Conditioning visual orientation of conduct problem children in the classroom. *Journal of Experimental Child Psychology, 5,* 512–517.

Quinn, P. O., & Rapport, M. D. (1974). Minor physical anomalies and neurologic status in hyperactive boys. *Pediatrics, 53,* 742–747.

Radal, M., Milgrom, P., Cauce, A. M., & Manci, L. (1994). Behavior problems in 5- to 11-year-old children from low-income families. *Journal of the American Academy of Child and Adolescent Psychiatry, 33,* 1017–1025.

Ramey, C. T., & Campbell, F. A. (1991). Poverty, early childhood educational, and academic competence. The Abecedarian experience. In A. C. Huston (Ed.), *Children in poverty: Child development and public policy.* New York: Cambridge University Press.

Rapin, I. (1995). Physicians' testing of children with developmental disabilities. *Journal of Child Neurology, 10*(Suppl. No. 1), S11–S15.

Rapp, D. J. (1991). *Is this your child? Discovering and treating unrecognized allergies.* New York: Morrow.

Rapoport, J. L., & Elia, J. (1991). *Ritalin versus dextroamphetamine in ADHD: Both should be tried.* Bethesda, MD: National Institutes of Mental Health.

Rappaport, J. L., Jenswold, M., & Elkins, R. (1981). Behavioral and cognitive effective caffeine in boys and adult males. *Journal of Mental Disorders, 169,* 726–732.

Rappaport, L., Coffman, H., Guare, R., Fenton, T., DeGraw, C., & Twarog, F. (1989). The effect of theophylline on behavior and learning in children with asthma. *American Journal of Diseases in Children, 3,* 368.

Rapport, M. D. (1987a). Attention-deficit disorder with hyperactivity. In M. Hersen & V. B. Van Hasselt (Eds.), *Behavior therapy with children and adolescents.* New York: Wiley.

Rapport, M. D. (1987b). *The attention training system.* DeWitt, NY: The Gordon Systems.

Rapport, M. D. (1988). Hyperactivity and attention deficits. In M. Hersen & V. B. Van Hasselt (Eds.), *Behavior therapy with children and adolescents.* New York: Wiley.

Rapport, M. D. (1989). The classroom functioning and treatment of children with ADHD: Facts and fictions. *CH.A.D.D.ER, 3,* 4–5.

Rapport, M. D. (1992). Treating children with attention-deficit hyperactivity disorder. *Behavior Modification, 16,* 155–163.

Rapport, M. D., Carlson, G. A., Kelly, K. L., & Pataki, C. (1993). Methylphenidate and desipramine in hospitalized children: I. Separate and combined effects on cognitive function. *Journal of the American Academy of Child and Adolescent Psychiatry, 32*(2), 333–342.

Rapport, M. D., Denny, C., DuPaul, G. J., & Gardner, M. J. (1994). Attention deficit disorder and methylphenidate: Normalization rates, clinical effectiveness, and response prediction in 76 children. *Journal of the American Academy of Child and Adolescent Psychiatry, 33,* 882–893.

Rapport, M. D., DuPaul, G. J., Stoner, G., Birmingham, B. K., & Massey, G. (1985). Attention deficit disorder with hyperactivity. Differential effects of methylphenidate on impulsivity. *Pediatrics, 76,* 938–943.

Rapport, M. D., DuPaul, G. J., Stoner, G., & Jones, T. J. (1986). Comparing classroom and clinic measures of attention deficit disorder: Differential, idiosyncratic and dose response effects of methylphenidate. *Journal of Consulting and Clinical Psychology, 54,* 334–341.

Rapport, M. D., Jones, J. T., DuPaul, G. J., Kelly, K. L., Gardner, M. J., Tucker, S. B., & Shea, M. S. (1987). Attention deficit disorder and methylphenidate: Group and single-subject analyses of dose effects on attention in clinic and classroom settings. *Journal of Clinical Child Psychology, 16,* 329–338.

Rapport, M. D., & Kelly, K. L. (1991). Psychostimulant effects on learning and cognitive function: Findings and implications for children with attention deficit hyperactivity disorder. *Clinical Psychology Review, 11,* 61–92.

Rapport, M. D., Loo, S., & Denney, C. (1995). The paired associate learning task: Is it an externally valid instrument for assessing methylphenidate response in children with attention deficit disorder? *Journal of Psychopathology and Behavioral Assessment, 17*(2), 125–144.

Rapport, M. D., Murphy, H. A., & Bailey, J. S. (1982). Ritalin vs. response cost in the control of hyperactive children: A within-subject comparison. *Journal of Applied Behavior Analysis, 15,* 205–216.

Rapport, M. D., Quinn, S. O., DuPaul, G. J., Quinn, E. P., & Kelly, K. L. (1989). Attention deficit disorder with hyperactivity and methylphenidate: The effects of dose and mastery level on children's learning performance. *Journal of Abnormal Child Psychology, 17,* 669–689.

Rapport, M. D., Stoner, G., DuPaul, G. J., Birmingham, B. K., & Tucker, S. (1985). Methylphenidate in hyperactive children: Differential effects of dose on academic learning and social behavior. *Journal of Abnormal Child Psychology, 13,* 227–244.

Rapport, M. D., Stoner, G., DuPaul, G., Kelly, K. L., Tucker, S. B., & Schoeler, T. (1988). Attention deficit disorder and methylphenidate: A multilevel analysis of dose response effects on children's impulsivity across settings. *American Academy of Child and Adolescent Psychiatry, 27,* 60–69.

Rapport, M. D., Tucker, S. B., DuPaul, G. J., Merlo, M., & Stoner, G. (1986). Hyperactivity and frustration: The influence of size and control over rewards in delaying gratification. *Journal of Abnormal Child Psychology, 14,* 191–204.

Rasanen, P., & Ahonen, T. (1995). Arithmetic disabilities with and without reading difficulties: A comparison of arithmetic errors. *Developmental Neuropsychology, 11,* 269–274.

Raskin, L. A., Shaywitz, S. E., Shaywitz, B. A., Anderson, G. M., & Cohen, D. J. (1984). Neurochemical correlates of attention deficit disorder. *Pediatric Clinics of North America, 54,* 714–718.

Rasmussen, N. H., Colligan, R. C., & Suman, V. J. (1995, November). *An investigation of clinic-based laboratory measures in the differential diagnosis of ADHD versus externalizing disruptive behavior disorder.* Paper presented at the National Academy of Neuropsychology, San Francisco, CA.

Ratey, J. J. (1991, Fall/Winter). Paying attention to attention in adults. *CH.A.D.D.ER Newsletter, 13*–14.

Rattan, G., & Caulfield, J. B. (1996). *Discriminating ADHD and normal children on measures of attention and response latencies using an auditory-visual temporal-spatial task.* Paper submitted for publication.

Reader, M. J., Harris, E. L., Schuerholz, L. J., & Denckla, M. B. (1994). ADHD and executive dysfunction. *Developmental Neuropsychology, 10,* 493–512.

Reardon, S. M., & Naglieri, J. A. (1992). PASS cognitive processing characteristics of normal and ADHD males. *Journal of School Psychology, 30,* 150–163.

Rebok, G. W., Hawkins, W., Krener, P., Mayer, L. S., & Kellam, S. G. (1996). Effective concentration problems on the malleability of children's aggressive and shy behaviors. *Journal of the American Academy of Child and Adolescent Psychiatry, 35,* 193–203.

Redd, W. H., Morris, E. K., & Martin, J. A. (1975). Effects of positive and negative adult-child interactions on children's social preferences. *Journal of Experimental Child Psychology, 19,* 153–164.

Reeve, R. E. (1994). The academic impact of ADD. *Attention, 1,* 8–12.

Reeve, R. E., Spressard, M., Walker, R. A., Welch, A. B., & Wright, J. (1994, April). *Attention deficit disorder: Identification programs and interventions.* Participant's manual, Council for Exceptional Children, Denver, CO.

Reeves, J. C., & Werry, J. S. (1987). Soft signs in hyperactivity. In D. E. Tupper (Ed.), *Soft neurological signs.* Troy, NY: Grune and Stratton.

Reeves, J. C., Werry, S., Elkind, G. S., & Zametkin, A. (1987). Attention deficit, conduct, oppositional and anxiety disorders in children: II. Clinical characteristics. *Journal of the American Academy of Child and Adolescent Psychiatry, 26,* 144–155.

Regier, D. A., Burke, J. D., & Burke, K. C. (1990). Comorbidity of anxiety and affective disorders in the NIMH epidemiological catchment area program. In J. D. Maser & C. R. Cloninger (Eds.), *Comorbidity of mood and anxiety disorders.* Washington, DC: American Psychiatric Press.

Rehabilitation Act of 1973, P.L. 93-112. 20 U.S.C. 1412(2).

Reichenbach, L. C., Halperin, J. M., Sharma, V., & Newcorn, J. H. (1992a). Children's motor activity: Reliability and relationship to attention and behavior. *Developmental Neuropsychology, 8,* 87–97.

Reichenbach, L. C., Halperin, J. M., Sharma, V., & Newcorn, J. H. (1992b). Situational hyperactivity in a U.S. clinical setting. *Journal of Child Psychology and Psychiatry, 27,* 639–646.

Reid, J. B. (1978). *A social learning approach to family intervention: Vol. 2. Observation in home settings.* Eugene, OR: Castalia Press.

Reid, M. K., & Borkowski, J. G. (1987). Causal attributions of hyperactive children: Implications for teaching strategies and self-control. *Journal of Educational Psychology, 79,* 296–307.

Reid, R., & Harris, K. R. (1993). Self-monitoring of attention versus self-monitoring of performance: Effects on attention and academic performance. *Exceptional Children, 59,* 1–13.

Reid, R., Maag, J. W., & Vasa, S. F. (1994). Attention deficit hyperactivity disorder as a disability category: A critique. *Exceptional Children, 60,* 198–214.

Reitan, R. M. (1958). Validity of the trail-making test as an indication of organic brain damage. *Perceptual Motor Skills, 8,* 271–276.

Reitan, R. M. (1987). *Neuropsychological evaluation of children (Workshop training manual).* Tucson, AZ: Neuropsychology Press.

Reitan, R. M., & Wolfson, D. (1985). *The Halstead-Reitan neuropsychological test battery: Theory and clinical interpretation.* Tucson, AZ: Neuropsychology Press.

Reith, H., Bahr, C., Polsgrove, L., Okolo, C., & Eckert, R. (1987). The effects of microcomputers on the secondary special education classroom ecology. *Journal of Special Education Technology, 8,* 36–45.

Reith, H. J., & Semmel, M. I. (1991). Use of computer-assisted instruction in the regular classroom. In G. Stoner, M. R. Shinn, & H. M. Walker (Eds.), *Interventions for achievement and behavior problems.* Silver Springs, MD: National Association of School Psychologists.

Resnick, R. J., & McEvoy, K. (1994). *Attention deficit hyperactivity disorder. Bibliographies in psychology* (Abstracts of the Psychological and Behavioral Literature, 1971–1994, No. 14). Washington, DC: APA.

Restasp, E. J. (1994). Written expression skills in boys with ADHD. *Perceptual Motor Skills, 79,* 1131–1138.

Rey, J. M. (1994). Comorbidity between disruptive disorders and depression in referred adolescents. *Australia and New Zealand Journal of Psychiatry, 28,* 106–113.

Reynolds, C. (1994). *Neuropsychological characteristics of low incidence childhood syndromes.* Presented at the 14th annual conference of the National Academy of Neuropsychology, Orlando, FL.

Reynolds, C. R., & Bigler, E. B. (1994). *Test of memory and learning (TOMAL).* Austin, TX: Pro-Ed.

Reynolds, C. R., & Kamphus, R. W. (1992). *Behavior assessment system for children.* Circle Pines, MN: American Guidance System.

Reynolds, C. R., & Richmond, B. O. (1985). *The revised children's manifest anxiety scale.* Los Angeles, CA: Western Psychological Services.

Reynolds, W. M. (1987). *Reynolds adolescent depression scale.* Odessa, FL: Psychological Assessment Resources.

Reynolds, W. M. (1989). *Reynolds child depression scale.* Odessa, FL: Psychological Assessment Resources.

Rhode, G., Jenson, W. R., & Reavis, H. K. (1992). *The tough kid book.* Longmont, CO: Sopris-West.

Rhode, G., Morgan, D. P., & Young, K. R. (1983). Generalization and maintenance of treatment gains of behaviorally handicapped students from resource rooms to regular classrooms using self-evaluation procedures. *Journal of Applied Behavioral Analysis, 16,* 171–188.

Riccio, C. A., Cohen, M. J., Hynd, G. W., & Keith, R. W. (1994). *Central auditory processing disorder in ADHD: Results of the auditory continuous performance test.* Unpublished manuscript.

Riccio, C. A., Gonzalez, J. J., & Hynd, G. W. (1994). Attention deficit hyperactivity disorder and learning disabilities. *Learning Disability Quarterly, 17,* 311–322.

Riccio, C. A., Hall, J., Morgan, A., & Hynd, G. W. (1995, November). *Relationship of the Wisconsin card sorting test with cognitive ability and behavioral ratings with children.* Paper presented at the National Academy of Neuropsychology, San Francisco, CA.

Riccio, C. A., & Hynd, G. W. (1993). Developmental language disorders in children: Relationship with learning disabilities and attention deficit hyperactivity disorder. *School Psychology Review, 22,* 696–708.

Riccio, C. A., Hynd, G. W., Cohen, M. J., Hall, J., & Molt, L. (1994). Comorbidity of central auditory processing disorder and attention-deficit hyperactivity disorder. *Journal of the American Academy of Child and Adolescent Psychiatry, 33,* 849–857.

Riccio, C. A., Vaughn, M. L., Morgan, A., Hall, J., & Hynd, G. W. (1995). *Auditory processing of children with ADHD.* Presented at the 15th annual meeting of the National Academy of Neuropsychology, San Francisco, CA.

Richards, G. P., Samuels, S. J., Turnure, J. E., & Ysseldyke, J. E. (1990). Sustained and selective attention in children with learning disabilities. *Journal of Learning Disabilities, 23,* 129–136.

Richardson, E., Kupietz, S., & Maitinsky, S. (1986). What is the role of academic intervention in the treatment of hyperactive children with reading disorders? *Journal of Children in Contemporary Society, 19,* 153–167.

Richardson, E., Kupietz, S., & Maitinsky, S. (1987). What is the role of academic intervention in the treatment of hyperactive children with reading disorders? In J. Loney (Ed.), *The young hyperactive child: Answers to questions about diagnosis, prognosis and treatment.* New York: Haworth Press.

Richardson, E., Kupietz, S. S., Winsberg, B. G., Maitinsky, S., & Mendell, N. (1988). Effects of methylphenidate dosage in hyperactive reading-disabled children: II. Reading achievement. *Journal of American Academy of Child and Adolescent Psychiatry, 27,* 78–87.

Richman, N., Stevenson, J. E., & Graham, P. (1982). *Preschool to school: A behavioral study.* London: Academic Press.

Richters, J. E., Arnold, L. E., Jensen, P. S., Abikoff, H., Conners, C. K., Greenhill, L. L., Hechtman, L., Hinshaw, S. P., Pelham, W. E., & Swanson, J. M. (1995). NIMH collaborative multi-site, multi-mode treatment study of children with ADHD: I. Background and rationale. *Journal of the American Academy of Child and Adolescent Psychiatry, 34,* 987–1000.

Richters, J. E., & Martinez, P. (1983). The NIMH community violence project: Children as victims of and witness to violence. In D. Reiss, J. E. Richters, M. Radke-Yarrow, & D. Scharf (Eds.), *Children and violence.* New York: Guilford Press.

Riddle, K. D., & Rapoport, J. L. (1976). A 2-year follow-up of 72 hyperactive boys. Classroom behavior and peer acceptance. *Journal of Nervous and Mental Disease, 162,* 126–134.

Riddle, M. A., Geller, B., & Ryan, N. (1993). Case study: Another sudden death in a child treated with desipramine. *Journal of the American Academy of Child and Adolescent Psychiatry, 32,* 792–797.

Riddle, M. A., Hardin, M. T., Cho, S. C., Woolston, J. L., & Leckman, J. F. (1988). Desipramine treatment of boys with attention deficit hyperactivity disorder and tics: Preliminary clinical experience. *Journal of the American Academy of Child and Adolescent Psychiatry, 27,* 811–814.

Riddle, M. A., King, R. A., Hardin, M. T., Scahill, L., Ort, S. I., Chappell, P., Rasmussen, A., & Leckman, J. F. (1991). Behavioral side effects of fluoxetine in children and adolescents. *Journal of Child and Adolescent Psychopharmacology, 1*(3).

Riddle, M. A., Nelson, J. C., Kleinman, C. S., Rasmussen, A., Leckman, J. F., King, R. A., & Cohen, D. J. (1991). Sudden death in children receiving noripramine: A review of three reported cases and commentary. *Journal of the American Academy of Child and Adolescent Psychiatry, 30,* 104–108.

Rie, H. E. (1980). Definitional problems. In H. E. Rie & E. D. Rie (Eds.), *Handbook of minimal brain dysfunctions: A critical review.* New York: Wiley.

Rief, S. (1993). *How to reach and teach ADD/ADHD children.* West Nyack, NY: The Center for Applied Research in Education.

Rifkin, A. (1992). Pharmacological treatment of conduct disorder. *New Directions for Mental Health Services, 54,* 59–63.

Risser, A. H. (1996, November). *Parenting stress. Normative data and initial examination in families of children with neuropsychological disorders.* Paper presented at the 16th annual meeting of the National Academy of Neuropsychology, New Orleans, LA.

Risser, M. G., & Bowers, T. G. (1993). Cognitive and neuropsychological characteristics of attention deficit hyperactivity disorder children receiving stimulant medications. *Perceptual and Motor Skills, 77,* 1023–1031.

Robaey, P., Breton, F., Dugas, M., & Renault, B. (1992). An event-related potential study of controlled and automatic processes in 6–8-year-old boys with attention deficit hyperactivity disorder. *Electroencephalography and Clinical Neurophysiology, 82,* 330–340.

Roberts, G. E. (1982). *Robert's apperception test for children.* Los Angeles: Western Psychological Services.

Roberts, M. (1979). *A manual for the restricted academic playroom situation.* Iowa City, IA: Author.

Roberts, M. A. (1990). A behavioral observation method for differentiating hyperactive and aggressive boys. *Journal of Abnormal Child Psychology, 18,* 131–142.

Roberts, M. W. (1982). The effects of warned versus unwarned time-out procedures on child noncompliance. *Child and Family Behavior Therapy, 4,* 37–53.

Roberts, M. W. (1988). Enforcing chair timeouts with room timeouts. *Behavior Modification, 12,* 353–370.

Roberts, R. J., & Pennington, B. (1996). An interactive framework for examining pre-frontal cognitive processes. *Developmental Neuropsychology, 12,* 105–126.

Roberts, W., & Strayer, J. (1996). Empathy, emotional expressiveness and pro-social behavior. *Child Development, 67,* 449–470.

Robertson, I. H., Ward, T., Ridgeway, V., & Nimmo-Smith, I. (1996). *The test of every day attention.* Gaylord, MI: National Rehabilitation Services.

Robin, A. (1981). Controlled evaluation of problem-solving communication training with parent-adolescent conflict. *Behavior Therapy, 12,* 593–609.

Robin, A. L. (1979). Problem-solving communication training: A behavioral approach to the treatment of parent-adolescent conflict. *American Journal of Family Therapy, 7,* 69–82.

Robin, A. L. (1990, Summer/Spring). Living in the fast lane: Parenting your ADHD adolescent. *CH.A.D.D.ER,* 12–15.

Robin, A. L., & Foster, S. L. (1989). *Negotiating parent-adolescent conflict.* New York: Guilford Press.

Robin, A. L., & van der May, S. J. (1996). Validation of a measure for adolescent self-report of attention deficit disorder symptoms. *Journal of Developmental and Behavioral Pediatrics, 17,* 211–215.

Robin, A. L., & Weiss, J. (1980). Criterion-related validity of behavioral and self-report measures of problem-solving communication skills in distressed and non-distressed parent-adolescent dyads. *Behavioral Assessment, 2,* 339–352.

Robin, S. S., & Bosco, J. J. (1973). Ritalin for school children: The teachers' perspective. *Journal of School Health, 10,* 624–628.

Robins, L. N. (1979). Follow-up studies. In H. C. Quay & J. S. Werry (Eds.), *Psychopathological disorders of childhood.* New York: Wiley.

Robins, P. (1992). A comparison of behavioral and attentional functioning in children diagnosed as hyperactive or learning-disabled. *Journal of Abnormal Child Psychology, 20,* 608–682.

Robinson, P. W., Newby, T. J., & Ganzell, S. L. (1981). A token system for a class of under-achieving children. *Journal of Applied Behavior Analysis, 14,* 307–315.

Robson, A. L., & Pederson, D. R. (1997). Predictors of individual differences in attention among low birth weight children. *Developmental and Behavioral Pediatrics, 18,* 13–21.

Rodriguez, M. L., Shoda, Y., Mischel, W., & Wright, J. (1989). *Delay of gratification in children's social behavior in natural settings.* Paper presented at a meeting of the Eastern Psychological Association, Boston.

Roehling, P. V., & Robin, A. L. (1986). Development and validation of the family beliefs inventory: A measure of unrealistic beliefs among parents and adolescents. *Journal of Consulting and Clinical Psychology, 54,* 693–697.

Roeltgen, D. P., & Schneider, J. S. (1991). Chronic low-dose MPTP in nonhuman primates: A possible model for attention deficit disorder. *Journal of Child Neurology, 6*(Suppl.), S82–S89.

Rogers, H., & Saklofske, D. H. (1985). Self-concepts, locus of control and performance expectations of learning disabled children. *Journal of Learning Disabilities, 18,* 273–278.

Romanov, K., Hatakka, M., Keskinen, E., Laaksonen, H., Kaprio, J., Rose, R. J., & Koskenvuo, M. (1994). Self-reported hostility and suicidal acts, accidents and accidental deaths: A perspective study of 21,443 adults age twenty-five to fifty-nine. *Psychosomatic Medicine, 56,* 328–336.

Rooney, K. (1990). *Independent strategies for efficient study.* Richmond, VA: J.R. Enterprises.

Rooney, K. J., Hallahan, D. P., & Lloyd, J. W. (1984). Self-recording of attention by learning-disabled students in the regular classroom. *Journal of Learning Disabilities, 17,* 360–364.

Rosen, L. A., O'Leary, S. G., Joyce, S. A., Conway, G., & Pfiffner, L. J. (1984). The importance of prudent negative consequences for maintaining the appropriate behavior of hyperactive students. *Journal of Abnormal Child Psychology, 12,* 581–604.

Rosenbaum, M., & Baker, E. (1984). Self-control behavior in hyperactive and non-hyperactive children. *Journal of Abnormal Child Psychology, 12,* 303–331.

Rosenbaum, M. S., & Drabman, R. S. (1979). Self-control training in the classroom: A review and critique. *Journal of Applied Behavior Analysis, 12,* 467–485.

Rosenberg, D. R., Johnson, K., & Sahl, R. (1992). Evolving mania in an adolescent treated with low-dose fluoxetine. *Journal of Child and Adolescent Psychopharmacology, 2*(4), 299–306.

Rosenberg, L. A., Brown, J., & Singer, H. S. (1995). Behavioral problems and severity of tics. *Journal of Clinical Psychology, 51,* 760–767.

Rosenfeld, G. B., & Bradley, C. (1948). Childhood behavior sequelae of asphyxia in infancy. *Pediatrics, 2,* 74–84.

Rosenthal, N. E. (1995). Syndrome triad in children and adolescents. *American Journal of Psychiatry, 152,* 1402.

Rosenthal, R. H., & Allen, T. W. (1978). An examination of attention, arousal and learning dysfunctions of hyperkinetic children. *Psychological Bulletin, 85,* 689–715.

Ross, D. M., & Ross, S. A. (1976). *Hyperactivity: Research, theory and action.* New York: Wiley.

Ross, D. M., & Ross, S. A. (1982). *Hyperactivity: Current issues, research and theory* (2nd ed.). New York: Wiley.

Rosse, R. B., & Licamele, W. L. (1984). Slow release methylphenidate problems when children chew tablets. *Journal of Clinical Psychiatry, 45,* 525.

Rostain, A. L., Power, T. J., & Atkins, M. S. (1993). Assessing parents' willingness to pursue treating for children with ADHD. *Journal of the American Academy of Child and Adolescent Psychiatry, 32,* 175–181.

Rosvold, H. E., Mirsky, A. F., Sarason, I., Bransome, E. D., & Beck, L. H. (1956). A continuous performance test of brain damage. *Journal of Consulting Psychology, 20,* 343–350.

Roth, N., Beyreiss, J., Schlenzka, K., & Beyer, H. (1991). Coincidence of attention deficit disorder and atopic disorders in children: Empirical findings and hypothetical background. *Journal of Abnormal Child Psychology, 19*(1), 1–13.

Rothbart, M. K. (1989a). Temperament and development. In G. A. Kohnstamm, J. A. Bates, & M. K. Rothbart (Eds.), *Temperament in childhood.* New York: Wiley.

Rothbart, M. K. (1989b). Temperament in childhood: A framework. In G. A. Kohnstamm, J. A. Bates, & M. K. Rothbart (Eds.), *Temperament in childhood.* New York: Wiley.

Rothbart, M. K., & Ahadi, S. A. (1994). Temperament and the development of personality. *Journal of Abnormal Psychology, 103,* 55–66.

Rothbart, M. K., Derryberry, D., & Posner, M. I. (1994). A psychological approach to the development of temperament. In J. E. Bates & T. D. Wachs (Eds.), *Temperament: Individual differences at the interface of biology and behavior.* Washington, DC: American Psychological Association.

Rothbaum, F. M., & Weiz, J. R. (1989). *Child pathology and the quest for control.* Newbury Park, CA: Sage.

Rotter, J. B. (1950). *Incomplete sentences blank–high school form.* New York: The Psychological Corporation.

Rotter, J. B. (1966). Generalized expectations for internal versus external control of reinforcement. *Psychological Monographs, 80,* 1–28.

Rourke, D. K. (1989). *Non-verbal learning disabilities: The syndrome and the model.* New York: Guilford Press.

Routh, D. K. (1978). Hyperactivity. In P. R. Magrab (Ed.), *Psychological management of pediatric problems* (Vol. 2). Baltimore: University Park Press.

Routh, D. K., & Schroeder, C. S. (1976). Standardized playroom measures as indices of hyperactivity. *Journal of Abnormal Child Psychology, 4,* 199–207.

Routh, D. K., Schroeder, C. S., & O'Tauma, L. (1974). Development of activity level in children. *Developmental Psychology, 10,* 163–168.

Rowe, K. J. (1991). The influence of reading activity at home on students' attitudes towards reading, classroom attentiveness and reading achievement: An application of structural equation modeling. *British Journal of Educational Psychology, 61,* 19–35.

Rowe, K. J., & Rowe, K. S. (1992a). The relationship between inattentiveness in the classroom and reading achievement: Part A. Methodological issues. *Journal of the American Academy of Child and Adolescent Psychiatry, 31,* 349–356.

Rowe, K. J., & Rowe, K. S. (1992b). The relationship between inattentiveness in the classroom and reading achievement: Part B. An explanatory study. *Journal of the American Academy of Child and Adolescent Psychiatry, 31,* 357–368.

Rowe, K. S., & Rowe, K. J. (1994). Original articles: Synthetic food coloring and behavior: A dose response effect in a double-blind, placebo-controlled, repeated-measures study. *Journal of Pediatrics, 125*(5), 691–698.

Rubin, K. H. (1985). Socially withdrawn children: An "at risk" population. In B. H. Schneider, K. H. Rubin, & J. E. Ledingham (Eds.), *Children's peer relations: Issues in assessment and intervention* (pp. 125–139). New York: Springer-Verlag.

Rubin, K. H., & Daniels-Bierness, T. (1983). Concurrent and predictive correlates of sociometric status in kindergarten and grade 1 children. *Merrill-Palmer Quarterly, 29,* 337–351.

Rubin, K. H., Xinyin, C., McDougal, P., Bowker, A., & McKinnon, J. (1995). The Waterloo longitudinal project: Predicting internalizing and externalizing problems in adolescence. *Development and Psychopathology, 7,* 751–754.

Rubinstein, S., Silver, L. B., & Licamele, W. L. (1994). Clonidine for stimulant-related sleep problems. *Journal of the American Academy of Child and Adolescent Psychiatry, 33*(2), 281–282.

Rudel, R. G., Denckla, M. B., & Broman, N. (1978). Rapid silent response to repeated target symbols by dyslexic and non-dyslexic children. *Brain and Language, 6,* 52–62.

Ruel, J. M., & Hickey, C. P. (1992). Are too many children being treated with methylphenidate? *Canadian Journal of Psychiatry, 37,* 570–572.

Ruff, H. A., & Lawson, K. R. (1990). Development of sustained focused attention in young children during free play. *Developmental Psychology, 26,* 85–93.

Rumberger, R. W. (1987). High school dropouts: A review of issues and evidence. *Review of Educational Research, 57,* 101–121.

Russell, E. W., & D'Hollosy, M. E. (1992). Memory and attention. *Journal of Clinical Psychology, 48,* 530–538.

Rutherford, R. B., & Nelson, C. M. (1982). Analysis of the response-contingent time-out literature with behaviorally disordered students in classroom settings. In R. B. Rutherford (Ed.), *Severe behavior disorders of children and youth* (Vol. 5). Reston, VA. Council for Children with Behavior Disorders.

Rutter, M. (1978). Diagnostic validity in child psychiatry. *Advances in Biological Psychiatry, 2,* 2–22.

Rutter, M. (1979). Protective factors in children's responses to stress and disadvantage. In M. W. Kent & J. E. Rolf (Eds.), *Primary prevention of psychopathology* (Vol. 3). Hanover, NH: University Press of New England.

Rutter, M. (1985). Resilience in the face of adversity: Protective factors and resistance to psychiatric disturbance. *British Journal of Psychiatry, 147,* 598–611.

Rutter, M. (1987). Psychosocial resilience and protective mechanisms. *American Journal of Orthopsychiatry, 57,* 316–331.

Rutter, M. (1988). *DSM-III-R:* A postscript. In M. Rutter, A. H. Tuma, & I. S. Lann (Eds.), *Assessment and diagnosis in child psychopathology* (pp. 453–464). New York: Guilford Press.

Rutter, M. (1989a). Attention deficit disorder/hyperkinetic syndrome: Conceptual and research issues regarding diagnosis and classification. In T. Sagvolden & T. Archer (Eds.), *Attention deficit disorder: Clinical and basic research.* Hillsdale, NJ: Erlbaum.

Rutter, M. (1989b). Isle of Wight revisited: Twenty-five years of child psychiatric epidemiology. *Journal of the American Academy of Child and Adolescent Psychiatry, 28,* 633–653.

Rutter, M. (1997). Nature–nurture integration: The example of antisocial behavior. *American Psychologist, 52,* 390–398.

Rutter, M., Maughan, N., Mortimore, P., & Ouston, J. (1979). *Fifteen thousand hours: Secondary schools and their effects on children.* Cambridge, MA: Harvard University Press.

Rutter, M., Macdonald, H., LeCoutier, A., Harrington, R., Bolton, P., & Bailey, A. (1990). Genetic factors in child psychiatric disorders: II. Empirical findings. *Journal of Child Psychology and Psychiatry, 31,* 39–83.

Rutter, M., Tizard, J., & Whitmore, K. (1970). *Education health and behaviour.* London: Longmass.

Rydell, A. M., Dahlik, M., & Sundelin, C. (1995). Characteristics of school children who are choosy eaters. *Journal of Genetic Psychology, 156,* 217–229.

Sabatino, D. A., & Vance, H. B. (1994). Is the diagnosis of ADHD meaningful? *Psychology in the Schools, 31,* 188–196.

Sadeh, M., Ariel, R., & Inbar, D. (1996). Rey-Osterrieth and Taylor complex figures: Equivalent measures of visual organization and visual memory in ADHD and normal children. *Child Neuropsychology, 2,* 63–71.

Safer, D. J. (1973). A familial factor in minimal brain dysfunction. *Behavioral Genetics, 3,* 175–186.

Safer, D. J. (1992). Relative cardiovascular safety of psychostimulants used to treat attention-deficit hyperactivity disorder. *Journal of Child and Adolescent Psychopharmacology, 2,* 279–290.

Safer, D. J. (1995). Medication usage trends for ADD. *Attention, 2(2),* 11–15,

Safer, D. J., & Allen, R. P. (1973). Factors influencing the suppressant effects of two stimulant drugs on the growth of hyperactive children. *Pediatrics, 51,* 660–667.

Safer, D. J., & Allen, R. P. (1976). *Hyperactive children: Diagnosis and management.* Baltimore: University Park Press.

Safer, D. J., & Allen, R. P. (1989). Absence of tolerance to the behavioral effects of methylphenidate in hyperactive and inattentive children. *Pediatric Pharmacology and Therapeutics: The Journal of Pediatrics, 115,* 1003–1008.

Safer, D. J., Allen, R. P., & Barr, E. (1972). Depression of growth in hyperactive children on stimulant drugs. *New England Journal of Medicine, 287,* 217–220.

Safer, D. J., & Krager, J. M. (1983). Trends in medication treatment of hyperactive children. *Clinical Pediatrics, 22,* 500–504.

Safer, D. J., & Krager, J. M. (1988). A survey of medication treatment for hyperactive and inattentive students. *Journal of the American Medical Association, 260,* 2256–2258.

Safer, D. J., & Krager, J. M. (1989). Hyperactivity and inattentiveness, school assessment and stimulant treatment. *Clinical Pediatrics, 28,* 216–221.

Safer, D. J., & Krager, J. M. (1992). Effect of a media blitz and a threatened lawsuit on stimulant treatment. *Journal of the American Medical Association, 268,* 1004–1007.

Safer, D. J., & Krager, J. M. (1994). The increased rate of stimulant treatment for hyperactive/inattentive students in secondary schools. *Pediatrics, 94,* 462–464.

Safer, D. J., Zito, J. M., & Fine, E. M. (1996). Increased methylphenidate usage for attention deficit disorder in the 1990s. *Pediatrics, 98,* 1084–1088.

Safer, D. J., Zito, J. M., & Fine, E. M. (1997). The case of the missing methylphenidate [Letter to the editor]. *Pediatrics, 100*(4), 730–731.

Saigal, S., Szatmari, P., & Rosenbaum, P. (1991). Learning disabilities and school problems in a regional cohort of extremely low birth weight (<1000 G) children. *Developmental and Behavioral Pediatrics, 12,* 294–300.

Saklofske, D. H., & Schwean, V. L. (1993). Standardized procedures for measuring the correlates of ADHD in children: A research program [Special issue]. *Canadian Journal of School Psychology, 9,* 28–36.

Salend, S. J., Whittaker, C. R., Raab, S., & Giek, K. (1991). Using a self-evaluation system as a group contingency. *Journal of School Psychology, 29,* 319–329.

Sallee, F. R., Stiller, R. L., & Perel, J. M. (1992). Pharmacodynamics of pemoline in attention deficit disorder with hyperactivity. *Journal of the American Academy of Child and Adolescent Psychiatry, 31,* 244–251.

Sallee, F. R., Stiller, R. L., Perel, J. M., & Bates, T. (1985). Oral pemoline, kinetics and hyperactive children. *Clinical Pharmacology Therapy, 37,* 606–609.

Sallee, F. R., Stiller, R. L., Perel, J. M., & Everett, G. (1989). Pemoline-induced abnormal involuntary movements. *Journal Clinical Psychopharmacology, 9,* 125–129.

Salvia, J., & Ysseldyke, J. E. (1991). *Assessment* (5th ed.). Boston: Houghton Mifflin.

Sameroff, A. J., & Chandler, M. J. (1985). Reproductive risk and the continuum of caretaker causality. In F. D. Horowitz, M. Heatherington, S. Scarr-Salatek, & G. Sigel (Eds.), *Review of child development research* (Vol. 4). Chicago: University of Chicago Press.

Sameroff, A. J., & Fiese, B. H. (1990). Transactional regulation and early intervention. In S. J. Meisels & J. P. Shonkoff (Eds.), *Handbook of early childhood intervention.* Cambridge, England: Cambridge University Press.

Samuel, V. J., Curtis, S., Thornell, A., Taylor, G., Broome, D., Biederman, J., & Faraone, S. V. (1997). The unexplored void of ADHD in African-American research: A review of the literature. *Journal of Attention Disorders, 1,* 197–207.

Sanchez, L. E., Armenteros, J. L., Small, A. M., Campbell, M., & Adams, P. B. (1994). Placebo response in aggressive children with conduct disorder. *Psychopharmacology Bulletin, 30,* 209–213.

Sandberg, S. (1996). Hyperkinetic or attention deficit disorder. *British Journal of Psychiatry, 169,* 10–17.

Sandberg, S. T., Rutter, M., & Taylor, E. (1978). Hyperkinetic disorder in psychiatric clinic attenders. *Developmental Medicine in Child Neurology, 20,* 279–299.

Sandford, J. A. (1994, October). *An analysis of computerized cognitive training and neurofeedback in the treatment of ADHD.* Paper presented at the sixth annual CH.A.D.D. conference, Washington, DC.

Sandler, A., Footo, M., Watson, T. E., Coleman, W. L., Hooper, S. R., & Levine, M. D. (1989, November 9). *Talkative children: Verbal fluency as a marker for social problems in children with attention deficits.* Paper presented at the seventh annual scientific meeting of the Society for Behavioral Pediatrics, Cambridge, MA.

Sandler, A. D., Hooper, S. R., Watson, T. E., & Coleman, W. L. (1993). Talkative children: Verbal fluency as a marker for problematic peer relationships in clinic-referred children with attention deficits. *Perceptual and Motor Skills, 76,* 943–951.

Sanger, M. S., MacLean, W. E., & Van Slyke, D. A. (1992). Relation between maternal characteristics and child behavior ratings. Implications for interpreting behavior checklists. *Clinical Pediatrics, 31,* 461–466.

Sanson, A., Smart, D., Prior, M., & Oberklaid, F. (1993). Precursors of hyperactivity and aggression. *Journal of the American Academy of Child and Adolescent Psychiatry, 32,* 1207–1216.

Santora, D. H., & Hart, L. L. (1992). Clonidine in attention deficit hyperactivity disorder. *Annals of Pharmacotherapy, 26,* 37–39.

Santostefano, S., & Paley, E. (1964). Development of cognitive controls in children. *Journal of Clinical Psychology, 20,* 213–218.

Saraf, K. R., Klein, D. F., Gittelman-Klein, R., & Groff, S. (1974). Imipramine side effects in children. *Psychopharmocologia, 37,* 265–274.

Sarasone, S. B. (1949). *Psychological problems in mental deficiency.* New York: Harper & Row.

Sassone, D., Lambert, N. M., & Sandoval, J. (1982). The adolescent status of boys previously identified as hyperactive. In D. M. Ross & S. A. Ross (Eds.), *Hyperactivity: Current issues, research and theory.* New York: Wiley.

Satin, M. S., Winsberg, B. G., Monetti, C. H., Sverd, J., & Ross, D. A. (1985). A general population screen for attention deficit disorder with hyperactivity. *Journal of the American Academy of Child Psychiatry, 24,* 756–764.

Satterfield, B. (1988). *Multi-modal therapy in treating ADHD conduct disorder.* Presented at the Taboroff Child and Adolescent Child Psychiatry Conference on Conduct Disorders, Snowbird, UT.

Satterfield, J. H., & Bradley, B. W. (1977). Evoked potentials in brain maturation in hyperactive children. *Electroencephalography and Clinical Neurophysiology, 43,* 43–51.

Satterfield, J. H., Cantwell, D., & Satterfield, B. (1974). Pathophysiology of the hyperactive child syndrome. *Archives of General Psychiatry, 31,* 839–844.

Satterfield, J. H., Cantwell, D. P., & Satterfield, B. T. (1979). Multi-modality treatment. *Archives of General Psychiatry, 36,* 965–974.

Satterfield, J. H., Cantwell, D. P., Saul, R. E., Lesser, L. I., & Podosin, R. L. (1973). Response to stimulant drug treatment in hyperactive children: Prediction from EEG and neurological findings. *Autism Childhood Schizophrenia, 3,* 36–48.

Satterfield, J. H., & Dawson, M. E. (1971). Electrodermal correlates of hyperactivity in children. *Psychophysiology, 8,* 191–197.

Satterfield, J. H., Hoppe, C. M., & Schell, A. M. (1982). A perspective study of delinquency in 110 adolescent boys with attention deficit disorder and 88 normal adolescent boys. *American Journal of Psychiatry, 139,* 795–798.

Satterfield, J. H., Satterfield, B. T., & Cantwell, D. P. (1981). Three-year multi-modality treatment study of 100 hyperactive boys. *Journal of Pediatrics, 98,* 650–655.

Satterfield, J. H., Schell, A. M., & Backs, R. W. (1987). Longitudinal study of AERPs in hyperactive and normal children: Relationship to antisocial behavior. *Electroencephalography and Clinical Neurophysiology, 67,* 531–536.

Satterfield, J. H., Schell, A. M., Nicholas, T. W., & Backs, R. W. (1988). Topographic study of auditory event-related potentials in normal boys and boys with attention deficit disorder with hyperactivity. *Psychophysiology, 25,* 591–606.

Satterfield, J. H., Schell, A. M., Nicholas, T. W., & Satterfield, B. T. (1990). Ontogeny of selective attention effects on event-related potentials in attention-deficit hyperactivity disorder and normal boys. *Biological Psychiatry, 28,* 879–903.

Satterfield, J. H., Swanson, J., Schell, A., & Lee, F. (1994). Prediction of antisocial behavior in attention-deficit hyperactivity disorder boys from aggression/defiant scores. *Journal of the American Academy of Child and Adolescent Psychiatry, 33,* 185–190.

Sattler, J. M. (1988). *Assessment of children* (3rd ed.). San Diego, CA: Author.

Saudargas, R. A., & Creed, V. (1980). *State-event classroom observation system.* Knoxville: University of Tennessee, Department of Psychology.

Saudergas, R. A., & Fellers, G. (1986). *State-event classroom observation system.* (Research ed.). Knoxville: University of Tennessee, Department of Psychology.

Sauls, H. S. (1974). Hypoglycemia in infancy and childhood. In P. J. Accardo, T. A. Blondis, & B. Y. Whitman (Eds.), *Attention deficit disorders and hyperactivity in children.* New York: Marcel Dekker.

Sawin, D. B., & Parke, R. D. (1979). Inconsistent discipline of aggression in young boys. *Journal of Experimental Child Psychology, 28,* 525–538.

Scerbo, A., & Kolko, D. J. (1994). Salivary testosterone and cortisol in disruptive children: Relationship to aggressive, hyperactive, and internalizing behaviors. *Journal of the American Academy of Child and Adolescent Psychiatry, 33,* 1174–1184.

Schachar, R., & Logan, G. D. (1990a). Impulsivity and inhibitory control in normal development and childhood psychopathology. *Developmental Psychology, 26,* 710–720.

Schachar, R., & Logan, G. (1990b). Are hyperactive children deficient in attentional capacity? *Journal of Abnormal Child Psychology, 18,* 493–513.

Schachar, R., Logan, G., Wachsmuth, R., & Chajczyk, D. (1988). Attaining and maintaining preparation: A comparison of attention in hyperactive, normal and disturbed control children. *Journal of Abnormal Child Psychology,* 361–378.

Schachar, R., & Tannock, R. (1995). A test of four hypothesis for the comorbidity of attention-deficit hyperactivity disorder and conduct disorder. *Journal of the American Academy of Child and Adolescent Psychiatry, 34,* 639–648.

Schachar, R., Tannock, R., & Logan, G. (1993). Inhibitory control, impulsiveness and attention deficit hyperactivity disorder. Disinhibition disorders in childhood [Special issue]. *Clinical Psychology Review, 13,* 721–739.

Schachar, R., Taylor, E., Wieselberg, M. B., Thorley, G., & Rutter, M. (1987). Changes in family function and relationships in children who respond to methylphenidate. *Journal of the American Academy of Child and Adolescent Psychiatry, 26,* 728–732.

Schachar, R., & Wachsmuth, R. (1991). Family dysfunction and psychosocial adversity: Comparisons of attention deficit disorder, conduct disorder, normal and clinic controls. *Canadian Journal of Behavioural Science, 23,* 332–348.

Schaughency, E. A., & Hynd, G. W. (1989). Attentional control systems and attention deficit disorder. *Learning and Individual Differences, 1,* 423–449.

Schaughency, E. A., Lahey, B. B., Hynd, G. W., Stone, P. A., Piacentini, J. C., & Frick, P. J. (1989). Neuropsychological test performance and the attention deficit disorders: Clinical utility of the Luria-Nebraska neuropsychological battery–children's revision. *Journal of Consulting and Clinical Psychology, 57,* 112–116.

Schaughency, E. A., McGee, R., Raja, S. N., Feehan, M., & Silva, P. A. (1994). Self-reported inattention, impulsivity and hyperactivity at ages fifteen and eighteen years in the general population. *Journal of the American Academy of Child and Adolescent Psychiatry, 33,* 173–184.

Schaughency, E. A., & Rothlind, J. (1991). Assessment and classification of attention deficit hyperactivity disorders. *School Psychology Review, 20,* 187–202.

Schaughency, E. A., Vannatta, K., & Mauro, J. (1993). Parent training. In J. L. Matson (Ed.), *Handbook of hyperactivity in children.* Needham Heights, MA: Allyn & Bacon.

Scheel, M. J., & Rieckmann-James, T. (1996). *Predictors of self-efficacy and empowerment in parents with children identified as psychologically disordered.* Unpublished manuscript.

Schleifer, M., Weiss, G., Cohen, N. J., Elman, M., Cvejic, H., & Kruger, E. (1975). Hyperactivity in preschoolers and the effect of methylphenidate. *American Journal of Orthopsychiatry, 45,* 35–50.

Schleser, R., Meyers, A., & Cohen, R. (1981). Generalization of self-instructions: Effects of general versus specific content, active rehearsal, and cognitive level. *Child Development, 52,* 335–340.

Schlieper, A., Alcock, D., Beaudry, P., Feldman, W., & Leikin, L. (1991, March). Effect of therapeutic plasma concentrations of theophylline on behavior, cognitive processing, and affect in children with asthma. *Pediatric Pharmacology and Therapeutics: The Journal of Pediatrics,* 449–455.

Schloss, P. J., Schloss, C. N., Wood, C. E., & Kiehl, W. S. (1986). A critical review of social skills research with behaviorally disordered students. *Behavioral Disorders, 12,* 1–14.

Schmidt, K., & Freidson, S. (1990). Atypical outcome in attention deficit hyperactivity disorder. *Journal of the American Academy of Child and Adolescent Psychiatry, 29,* 566–570.

Schmidt, M., Trueblood, W., Merwin, M., & Durham, R. L. (1994). How much do attention tests tell us? *Archives of Clinical Neuropsychology, 9,* 583–594.

Schmitz, S., Saudino, K. J., Plormin, R., Fulker, D. W., & de Fries, J. C. (1996). Genetic and environmental influences on temperament in middle childhood: Analyses of teacher and tester ratings. *Child Development, 67,* 409–422.

Schneider, J. W., & Hans, S. L. (1996). Effects of pre-natal exposure to opiodis on focused attention in toddlers during free play. *Journal of Developmental Behavioral Pediatrics, 17,* 240–247.

Schneider, M. (1978). Turtle technique in the classroom. In M. Herbert (Ed.), *Conduct disorders of childhood and adolescents* (p. 119). New York: Wiley.

Schnittjer, C. J., & Hirshoren, A. (1981). Factors of problem behavior in visually impaired children. *Journal of Abnormal Child Psychology, 9,* 517.

Schoenfield, M., & Rosenblatt, J. (1985). *Adventures with logic.* Belmont, CA: David S. Lake.

Scholnick, E. K. (1995, Fall). Knowing and constructing plans. *SRCD Newsletter,* 1–3.

Schonfeld, I. S., Shaffer, D., & Barmack, J. E. (1989). Neurological soft signs and school achievement. The mediating effects of sustained attention. *Journal of Abnormal Child Psychology, 17,* 575–596.

Schopler, E., Reichler, R. J., & Renner, B. R. (1988). *Childhood autism rating scale.* Los Angeles: Western Psychological Services.

Schorr, L. (1988). *Within our reach: Breaking the cycle of disadvantage.* New York: Doubleday-Anchor Press.

Schrag, J. (1991). ADD eligibility. *Education of the Handicapped, 19*(11), 5.

Schrumph, F., Crawford, D., & Usadel, H. C. (1991). *Peer mediation: Conflict resolution in schools.* Champaign, IL: Research Press.

Schubiner, H., Tzelepis, S. A., & Isaacson, S. (1995). The dual diagnoses of attention deficit/hyperactivity disorder and substance abuse: History, reports and literature review. *Journal of Clinical Psychiatry, 56,* 146–165.

Schuckit, M. A., Sweeney, S., & Huey, L. (1987). Hyperactivity and the risk for alcoholism. *Journal of Clinical Psychiatry, 48,* 275–277.

Schulman, J. L., & Reisman, J. M. (1959). An objective measure of hyperactivity. *American Journal of Mental Deficiency, 64,* 455–456.

Schumaker, J. B., Hovell, M. F., & Sherman, J. A. (1977). An analysis of daily report cards and parent-managed privileges in the improvement of adolescents' classroom performance. *Journal of Applied Behavior Analysis, 10,* 449–464.

Schumm, J. S., & Strickler, J. (1993). Guidelines for adapting content area of textbooks: Keeping teachers and students content. *Intervention in School and Clinic, 27,* 79–84.

Schwartz, I. S., & Baer, D. M. (1991). Social validity assessments: Is current practice state of the art? *Journal of Applied Behavior Analysis, 24,* 189–204.

Schwartz, J., Barton-Henry, M., & Pruzinsky, T. (1985). Assessing child-rearing behaviors: A comparison of ratings made by mother, father, child and sibling on the CRPBI. *Child Development, 56,* 462–479.

Schwartz, S. T., Healey, J. M., Wolf, L. E., Pascaulvaca, D. M., Newcorn, J. H., Sharma, V., & Halperin, J. M. (1990, February 17). *Inattention and cognitive flexibility: Implications for understanding the processing deficits of ADHD children.* Presented at the eighteenth annual meeting of the International Neuropsychological Society, New York.

Schwean, V. L., Kowalchuk, S., Quinn, D., & Saklofske, D. H. (1991). Cognitive processing in children with ADHD: Research update. *Child Assessment News, 1,* 3.

Schwean, V. L., Parkinson, M., Francis, G., & Lee, F. (1993). Educating the ADHD child: Debunking the myths [Special issue]. *Canadian Journal of School Psychology, 9,* 37–52.

Schwean, V. L., Saklofske, D. H., Yackulic, R. H., & Quinn, D. (1993). WISC-III performance on ADHD children. *Journal of Psychoeducational Assessment: WISC-III Monograph,* 56–70.

Schworm, R. W., & Birnbaum, R. (1989). Symptom expression in hyperactive children: An analysis of observations. *Journal of Learning Disabilities, 22,* 35–40.

Searcy, J. D., & Hawkins-Searcy, J. (1979). Locus of control research and its implications for child personality. In A. J. Finch & P. C. Kendall (Eds.), *Clinical treatment and research in child psychopathology.* Jamaica, NY: Spectrum.

Seashore, C. E., Lewis, D., & Saetveit, D. L. (1960). *Seashore measures of musical talents* (Rev. ed.). New York: Psychological Corporation.

Sebrechts, M. M., Shaywitz, S. E., Shaywitz, B. A., Jatlow, P., Anderson, G. M., & Cohen, D. J. (1986). Components of attention, methylphenidate dosage and blood levels in children with attention deficit disorder. *Pediatrics, 77,* 222–228.

Seeley, S., Murray, L., & Cooper, V. J. (1996). Health visitor intervention for post natal depression and associated difficulties in the mother-infant relationship. *The Health Visitor.*

Seidel, W. T., & Joschko, M. (1991). Assessment of attention in children. *Clinical Neuropsychologist, 5,* 53–66.

Seidman, L. J., Benedict, K. B., Biederman, J., & Bernstein, J. H. (1995). Performance of children with ADHD on the Rey-Osterrieth Complex Figure: A pilot neuropsychology study. *Journal of Child Psychology and Psychiatry and Allied Disciplines, 36,* 1459–1473.

Seidman, L. J., Biederman, J., & Faraone, S. V. (1995). Effects of family history and comorbidity on the neuropsychological performance of ADHD children: Preliminary findings. *Journal of the American Academy of Child and Adolescent Psychiatry, 34,* 1015–1024.

Seidman, L. J., Biederman, J., Faraone, S. V., & Weber, W. (1997). Toward defining the neuropsychology of attention deficit hyperactivity disorder: Performance of children and adolescents from a large clinically referred sample. *Journal of Consulting and Clinical Psychology, 65,* 150–160.

Seidman, L. J., Biederman, J., Faraone, S. V., Weber, W., Mennin, D., & Jones, J. (1997). A pilot study of neuropsychological functioning in girls with ADHD. *Journal of the American Academy of Child and Adolescent Psychiatry, 36,* 366–373.

Seidman, L. J., Biederman, J., Weber, W., Monuteaux, M., & Faraone, S. (1997). *Neuropsychological findings in ADHD children: Findings from a sample of high risk siblings.* Paper presented at the annual meeting of the American Academy of Child and Adolescent Psychiatry, Toronto, Canada.

Seifer, A. J., Sameroff, A. J., Barrett, L. C., & Krafchuk, E. (1994). Infant temperament measured by multiple observations and mother report. *Child Development, 65,* 1478–1490.

Seligman, M. E. P. (1991). *Learned optimism.* New York: Knopf.

Semrud-Clikeman, M., Biederman, J., Sprich-Buckminster, S., Lehman, B. K., Faraone, S. V., & Norman, D. (1992). Comorbidity between ADDH and learning disability: A review and report on a clinically referred sample. *Journal of the American Academy of Child and Adolescent Psychiatry, 31,* 439–448.

Semrud-Clikeman, M., Filipek, P. A., Biederman, J., Steingard, R., Kennedy, D., Renshaw, P., & Bekken, K. (1994). Attention deficit hyperactivity disorder: Magnetic resonance imaging morphometric analysis of the corpus callosum. *Journal of the American Academy of Child and Adolescent Psychiatry, 33,* 875–881.

Semrud-Clikeman, M., Hynd, G. W., Lorys, A. R., & Lahey, B. B. (1993). Differential diagnosis of children with ADHD and ADHD/with co-occurring conduct disorder. *School Psychology International, 14,* 361–370.

Senf, G. M. (1988). Neurometric brain mapping in the diagnosis and rehabilitation of cognitive dysfunction. *Cognitive Rehabilitation, 6,* 20–37.

Sensory Integration International. (1994). *Reviews of research in sensory integration.* Torrance, CA: Author.

Sentle, S. S., & Smith, Y. N. (1993). Mathematical performance and behavior of children with hyperactivity with or without co-existing aggression. *Behavior Research and Therapy, 31,* 701–710.

Sergeant, J. A., & Scholten, C. A. (1985). On resource strategy limitations in hyperactivity: Cognitive impulsivity reconsidered. *Journal of Abnormal Child Psychology and Psychiatry, 26,* 97–109.

Sergeant, J. A., & van der Meere, J. J. (1988). What happens after a hyperactive commits an error? *Psychiatry Research, 24,* 157–164.

Shaffer, D., & Greenhill, L. (1979). A critical note on the predictive validity of the hyperkinetic syndrome. *Journal of Child Psychology and Psychiatry, 20,* 61–72.

Shaffer, D., & Schonfeld, I. (1984). A critical note on the value of attention deficit as a basis for a clinical syndrome. In L. M. Bloomingdale (Ed.), *Attention deficit disorders: Diagnostic, cognitive, and therapeutic understanding.* Long Island, NY: Spectrum.

Shaffer, D., Schonfeld, I., O'Connor, P. A., Stokman, C., Trautman, P., Shafer, S., & Ng, S. (1985). Neurological soft signs: Their relationship to psychiatric disorder and intelligence in childhood and adolescence. *Archives of General Psychiatry, 42,* 342–351.

Shanahan, J., & Morgan, M. (1989). Television as a diagnostic indicator in child therapy: An exploratory study. *Child and Adolescent Social Work Journal, 6,* 175–191.

Shannon, L. W. (1978). A longitudinal study of delinquency and crime. In C. Wellford (Ed.), *Quantitative studies in criminology.* Beverly Hills, CA: Sage.

Shapiro, D. H., Schwartz, C. E., & Astin, J. A. (1996). Controlling ourselves, controlling our world: Psychology's role in understanding positive and negative consequences of seeking and gaining control. *American Psychologist, 51,* 1213–1230.

Shapiro, E. A. K. (1981). Tic disorders. *Journal of the American Medical Association, 24S,* 1583–1585.

Shapiro, E. S., & Cole, C. L. (1994). *Behavior change in the classroom: Self-management interventions.* New York: Guilford Press.

Shapiro, E. S., & Kratochwill, T. R. (1988). Analogue assessment: Methods for assessing emotional and behavioral problems. In E. S. Shapiro & T. R. Kratochwill (Eds.), *Behavioral assessment in the schools: Conceptual foundations and practical applications* (pp. 290–321). New York: Guilford Press.

Shapiro, S. K., & Garfinkel, B. D. (1986). The occurrence of behavior disorders in children: The interdependence of attention deficit disorder and conduct disorder. *Journal of the American Academy of Child Psychiatry, 25,* 809–819.

Sharan, S. (1980). Cooperative learning in small groups: Recent methods and effects on achievement, attitudes, and ethnic relation. *Review of Educational Research, 50,* 241–271.

Shaw, G. A. (1992). Hyperactivity and creativity: The tacit dimension. *Bulletin of the Psychonomic Society, 30,* 157–160.

Shaw, G. A., & Brown, G. (1990). Laterality and creativity concomitants of attention problems. *Developmental Neuropsychology, 6,* 39–56.

Shaw, G. A., & Giambra, L. (1993). Task-unrelated thoughts of college students diagnosed as hyperactive in childhood. *Developmental Neuropsychology, 9*(1), 17–30.

Shaywitz, B. A., Cohen, D. J., & Bowers, M. B. (1977). CSF monoamine metabolites in children with minimal brain dysfunction: Evidence for alteration of brain dopamine. *Journal of Pediatrics, 1,* 67–71.

Shaywitz, B. A., Fletcher, J., Holahan, J. M., & Shaywitz, S. E. (1992). Discrepancy compared to low achievement definitions of reading disability: Results from the Connecticut longitudinal study. *Journal of Learning Disability, 25,* 639–648.

Shaywitz, B. A., Fletcher, J. M., & Shaywitz, S. E. (1995). Defining and classifying learning disabilities and ADHD. *Journal of Child Neurology, 10*(Suppl. 1), S50–S57.

Shaywitz, B. A., Gordon, J. W., Klopper, J. H., & Zelterman, D. (1977). The effect of 6-hydroxydopamine of habituation and activity in the developing rat pup. *Pharmacology, Biochemistry and Behavior, 6,* 391–396.

Shaywitz, B. A., Klopper, J. H., & Gordon, J. W. (1978). Methylphenidate in 6-hydroxy-dopamine-treated developing rat pups. *Archives of Neurology, 35,* 463–469.

Shaywitz, B. A., & Pearson, D. E. (1978). Effects of phenobarbital on activity and learning in 6-hydroxydopamine-treated rat pups. *Pharmacology, Biochemistry and Behavior, 9,* 173–179.

Shaywitz, B. A., & Shaywitz, S. E. (1991). Comorbidity: A critical issue in attention deficit disorder. *Journal of Child Neurology, 6*(Suppl.), S13–S22.

Shaywitz, B. A., Shaywitz, S. E., Anderson, G. M., Jatlow, P., Gillespie, S. M., Sullivan, B. M., Riddle, M. A., Leckman, J. F., & Cohen, D. J. (1988, September). *D-Amphetamine affects central noradrenergic mechanisms in children with attention deficit hyperactivity disorder.* Presentation made at the seventeenth national meeting of the Child Neurology Society, Halifax, Canada.

Shaywitz, B. A., Shaywitz, S. E., Byrne, T., Cohen, D., & Rothman, S. (1983). Attention deficit disorder: Quantitative analysis of CT. *Neurology, 33,* 1500–1503.

Shaywitz, B. A., Yager, R. D., & Klopper, J. H. (1976). Selective brain dopamine depletion in developing rats: An experimental model of minimal brain dysfunction. *Science, 191,* 305–307.

Shaywitz, S. E. (1986). Prevalence of attentional deficits and an epidemiologic sample of school children (unpublished raw data). In J. F. Kavanaugh & T. J. Truss (Eds.), *Learning disabilities: Proceedings of the 1988 national conference* (p. 457). Parkton, MD: York Press.

Shaywitz, S. E. (1987). *Yale children's inventory.* New Haven, CT: Yale University School of Medicine.

Shaywitz, S. E., Hunt, R. D., Jatlow, P., Cohen, D. J., Young, J. G., Pierce, R. N., Anderson, G. M., & Shaywitz, B. A. (1982). Psychopharmacology of attention deficit disorder: Pharmacokinetic neuroendocrine and behavioral measures following acute and chronic treatment with methylphenidate. *Pediatrics, 69,* 688–694.

Shaywitz, S. E., Schell, C., Shaywitz, B. A., & Towle, V. R. (1986). Yale children's inventory (YCI): An instrument to assess children with attention deficits and learning disabilities: I. Scale development and psychometric properties. *Journal of Abnormal Child Psychology, 14,* 347–364.

Shaywitz, S. E., & Shaywitz, B. A. (1986). Attention deficit disorder: Current perspectives. In J. F. Kavanaugh & T. J. Truss (Eds.), *Learning disabilities: Proceedings of the national conference, 1988* (pp. 369–523). Parkton, MD: York Press.

Shaywitz, S. E., & Shaywitz, B. A. (1988). Increased medication use in attention deficit hyperactivity disorder: Regressive or appropriate? [Editorial]. *Journal of the American Medical Association, 260,* 2270–2272.

Shaywitz, S. E., Shaywitz, B. A., Schnell, C., & Towle, V. R. (1986). Concurrent and predictive validity of the Yale children's inventory: An instrument to assess children with attentional deficits and learning disabilities. *Pediatrics, 81,* 562–571.

Shear, S. M., & Shapiro, E. S. (1993). Effects of using self-recording and self-observation in reducing disruptive behavior. *Journal of School Psychology, 31,* 519–534.

Sheard, M. (1971). Effect of lithium on human aggression. *Nature, 230,* 113–114.

Shekim, W. O., Cantwell, D. P., Kashani, J. H., & Beck, N. (1986). Dimensional and categorical approaches to the diagnosis of attention deficit disorder in children. *Journal of the American Academy of Child Psychiatry, 25,* 653–658.

Shekim, W. O., Dekirmenjian, H., & Chapel, J. L. (1977). Urinary catecholamine metabolites in hyperkinetic boys treated with d-amphetamine. *American Journal of Psychiatry, 11,* 1276–1279.

Shekim, W. O., Dekirmenjian, H., Chapel, J. L., Javaid, J., & Davis, J. M. (1979). Norepinephrine metabolism and clinical response to dextroamphetamine in hyperactive boys. *Journal of Pediatrics, 95,* 389–394.

Shekim, W. O., Sinclair, E., Glaser, R., Horwitz, E., Javaid, J., & Bylund, D. (1987). Norepinephrine and dopamine metabolites and educational variables in boys with attention deficit disorder and hyperactivity. *Journal of Child Neurology, 2,* 50–56.

Shelley, E. M., & Riester, A. (1972). Syndrome of minimal brain damage in young adults. *Diseases of the Nervous System, 33,* 335–338.

Shelton, T. L., & Barkley, R. A. (1990). Clinical developmental and biopsychosocial considerations. In R. A. Barkley (Ed.), *Attention deficit hyperactivity disorder: A handbook for diagnosis and treatment.* New York: Guilford Press.

Shepherd, J. T., Broilier, C. B., & Dandro, W. R. (1994). Play skills of preschool children with speech and language delays. *Physical and Occupational Therapy in Pediatrics, 14,* 1–20.

Sheridan, S. M. (1995a). Building social skills in the classroom. In S. Goldstein (Ed.), *Understanding and managing children's classroom behavior.* New York: Wiley.

Sheridan, S. M. (1995b). *The tough kid social skills book.* Longmont, CO: Sopris West.

Sheridan, S. M. (1998). *Why don't they like me? Helping your child make and keep friends.* Longmont, CO: Sopris West.

Sheridan, S. M., Dee, C. C., Morgan, J., McCormick, M., & Walker. D. (1996). A multimethod intervention for social skills deficits in children with ADHD and their parents. *School Psychology Review, 25,* 57–76.

Sheridan, S. M., & Walker, D. (in press). Social skills in context: Considerations for assessment, intervention, and generalization. In C. R. Reynolds & T. B. Gutkin (Eds.), *The handbook of school psychology* (3rd ed.). New York: Wiley.

Sherman, D. K., Iacono, W. G., & McGue, M. K. (1997). Attention-deficit hyperactivity disorder dimensions: A twin study of inattention and impulsivity-hyperactivity. *Journal of the American Academy of Child and Adolescent Psychiatry, 36,* 745–753.

Sherman, S. (1991). Epidemiology. In R. J. Hagerman & A. C. Cronister (Eds.), *The fragile X syndrome: Diagnosis, treatment and research.* Baltimore: Johns Hopkins University Press.

Shetty, T., & Chase, T. N. (1976). Central monoamines and hyperkinesis to childhood. *Neurology, 26,* 1000–1002.

Shiffrin, R. M., & Atkinson, R. C. (1969). Storage and retrieval processes in long-term memory. *Psychological Review, 76,* 179–193.

Shores, R. E., Jack, S. L., Gunter, P. L., Ellis, D. N., DeBriere, T. J., & Wehby, J. H. (1994). Classroom interactions of children with behavior disorders. *Journal of Emotional and Behavioral Disorders, 1,* 27–39.

Shriver, N. D., & Allen, K. D. (1996). The time-out grid: A guide to effective discipline. *School Psychology Quarterly, 11,* 67–74.

Shum, D. H., MacFarland, K. A., & Bain, J. D. (1990). Construct validity of eight tests of attention: Comparison of normal and closed head injured samples. *Clinical Neuropsychologists, 4,* 151–162.

Shure, M. B. (1981). Social competence as a problem-solving skill. In J. D. Wine & M. D. Smye (Eds.), *Social competence.* New York: Guilford Press.

Shure, M. B., & Spivack, G. (1978). *Problem-solving techniques in child rearing.* San Francisco: Jossey-Bass.

Sieel, L. S., & Ryan, E. B. (1989). The development of working memory in normally achieving and subtypes of learning disabled children. *Child Development, 60,* 973–980.

Siegal, E. (1992, October). *Mothering a child with ADHD: Learned mothering.* Paper presented at the 4th annual CH.A.D.D. Conference, Chicago, IL.

Sierra, J., & Kales, S. (1990). Hypnopoly-graphic alterations in attention deficit disorder (ADD) children. *International Journal of Neuroscience, 53,* 87–101.

Sigman, M., Cohen, S. E., & Beckwith, L. (1981). Social and familial influences on the development of pre-term infants. *Journal of Pediatric Psychology, 6,* 1–13.

Silva, R. R., Ernst, M., & Campbell, M. (1993). Lithium and conduct disorder. *Encephale, 19,* 585–590.

Silva, R. R., Munoz, D. M., & Alpert, M. (1996). Carbamazepine use in children and adolescents with features of attention deficit hyperactivity disorder: A meta-analysis. *Journal of the American Academy of Child and Adolescent Psychiatry, 35,* 352–358.

Silver, L. B. (1980a). *Attention deficit disorders: Booklet for parents.* Summit, NJ: CIBA.

Silver, L. B. (1980b). *Attention deficit disorders: Booklet for the classroom teacher.* Summit, NJ: CIBA.

Silver, L. B. (1981). The relationship between learning disabilities, hyperactivity, distractibility and behavioral problems: A clinical analysis. *Journal of the American Academy of Child Psychiatry, 20,* 385–397.

Silver, L. B. (1989). Frequency of adoption of children and adolescents with learning disabilities. *Journal of Learning Disabilities, 22,* 325–328.

Silver, L. B. (1990). Attention deficit hyperactivity disorder: Is it a learning disability or a related disorder? *Journal of Learning Disabilities, 23,* 394–397.

Silver, L. B. (1991). Attention deficit hyperactivity disorder: Is it a learning disability or a related disorder? Silver's Reply. *Journal of Learning Disabilities, 24,* 259–260.

Silverman, I. W., & Ragusa, D. M. (1992). A short-term longitudinal study of the early development of self-regulation. *Journal of Abnormal Child Psychology, 20,* 415–435.

Silverman, I. W., & Ragusa, D. M. (1993). A short-term longitudinal study of the early development of self-regulation: Erratum. *Journal of Abnormal Child Psychology, 21,* 231.

Silverthorn, P., Frick, P. J., Kuper, K., & Ott, J. (1996). Attention deficit hyperactivity disorder and sex: A test of two etiological models to explain the male predominenanc. *Journal of Clinical Child Psychology, 25,* 52–59.

Simon, N. M., & Senturia, A. G. (1966). Adoption and psychiatric illness. *American Journal of Psychiatry, 122,* 858–868.

Sinclair, K. E. (1985). Students' affective characteristics and classroom behaviour. In T. Husen & T. N. Postlethwaite (Eds.), *The international encyclopedia of education* (Vol. 8). Oxford, England: Pergamon Press.

Singer, H. S., Brown, J., Quaskey, S., Rosenberg, L. A., Mellits, D., & Denckla, M. B. (1995). The treatment of attention-deficit hyperactivity disorder in Tourette's syndrome: A double-blind placebo-controlled study with clonidine and desipramine. *Journal of Pediatric Neurology, 5,* 74–81.

Singh, J. (1995). The readability of educational materials written for parents of children with ADHD. *Journal of Child and Family Studies, 4,* 207–218.

Sisson, L. A., Van Hasselt, V. B., Hersen, M., & Strain, P. S. (1985). Peer interventions: Increasing social behaviors in multihandicapped children. *Behavior Modification, 9,* 293–321.

Skinner, B. F. (1953). *Science and human behavior.* New York: Macmillan.

Slavin, R. E. (1983a). *Cooperative learning.* New York: Longman.

Slavin, R. E. (1983b). When does cooperative learning increase student achievement? *Psychological Bulletin, 94,* 429–445.

Slavin, R. E., & Karweit, N. (1981). Cognitive and affective outcomes of an intensive student team learning experience. *Journal of Experimental Education, 50,* 29–35.

Slavin, R. E., Madden, N. A., & Leavey, M. (1984). The effects of cooperative learning and individualized instruction on mainstream students. *Exceptional Children, 54,* 434–443.

Sleator, E. K. (1982). Office diagnosis of hyperactivity by the physician. In K. D. Gadow & I. Bialer (Eds.), *Advances in learning and behavioral disabilities* (Vol. 1). Greenwich, CT: JAI Press.

Sleator, E. K., Ullmann, R. K., & von Neumann, A. (1982). How do hyperactive children feel about taking stimulants and will they tell their doctor? *Clinical Pediatrics, 21,* 474–479.

Small, J. G. (1990). Anticonvulsants in affective disorders. *Psychopharmacology Bulletin, 26,* 25–36.

Smith, A. (1973). *Symbol digithlodalities test manual.* Los Angeles: Western Psychological Services.

Smith, A. M., & O'Leary, S. G. (1995). Attributions and arousal as predictors of maternal discipline. *Cognitive Therapy and Research, 19,* 459–471.

Smith, D. J., Young, K. R., West, R. P., Morgan, D. P., & Rhode, G. (1988). Reducing the disruptive behavior of junior high school students: A classroom of self-management procedures. *Behavioral Disorders, 13,* 231–239.

Smith, H. F. (1986). The elephant on the fence: Approaches to the psychotherapy of attention deficit disorder children. *American Journal of Psychotherapy, 40,* 252–264.

Smith, L. (1952). *A dictionary of psychiatry for the layman.* London: Maxwell.

Snow, D. J. (1992). Marital therapy with parents to alleviate behavioral disorders in their children. *Research on Social Work Practice, 2,* 172–183.

Snow, J. H. (1990). Investigation of a mental rotation task with school-age children. *Journal of Psychoeducational Assessment, 8,* 538–549.

Snow, J. H., & Cunningham, K. J. (1991). Psychoeducational data. In P. J. Accardo, T. A. Blondis, & B. Y. Whitman (Eds.), *Attention deficit disorders and hyperactivity in children.* New York: Marcel Dekker.

Snyder, S. H., & Meyerhoff, J. L. (1973). How amphetamine acts in minimal brain dysfunction. *Annals New York Academy of Sciences, 205,* 310–319.

Sobol, M. P., Ashbourne, D. T., Earn, B. M., & Cunningham, C. E. (1989). Parents' attributions for achieving compliance from attention deficit disordered children. *Journal of Abnormal Child Psychology, 17,* 359–369.

Sohlberg, M. M., & Mateer, C. A. (1992). *Attention process training.* Puyallup, WA: Good Samaritan Hospital.

Solanto, M. V. (1990). Increasing difficulties with age and ADHD children: Commentary. *Developmental and Behavioral Pediatrics, 11,* 27.

Solanto, M. V. (1997). Does methylphenidate influence cognitive performance? [Letter to the editor]. *Journal of the American Academy of Child and Adolescent Psychiatry, 36*(10), 1323–1324.

Solanto, M. V., & Wender, E. H. (1989). Does methylphenidate constrict cognitive functioning? *Journal of the American Academy of Child and Adolescent Psychiatry, 28,* 897–902.

Solomon, R. W., & Wahler, R. G. (1973). Peer reinforcement control of classroom problem behavior. *Journal of Applied Behavior Analysis, 6,* 49–56.

Soltys, S. M., Kashani, J. H., Dandoy, A. C., & Vaidya, A. F. (1992). Comorbidity for disruptive behavior disorders in psychiatrically hospitalized children. *Child Psychiatry and Human Development, 23,* 87–98.

Sonuga-Barke, E. J., Hulberg, K., & Hall, M. (1994). When is "impulsiveness" not impulsive? The case of hyperactive children's cognitive style. *Journal of Child Psychology and Psychiatry, 35,* 1247–1253.

Sonuga-Barke, E. J., Lamparelli, M., Stevenson, J., Thompson, M., & Henry, A. (1994). Behaviour problems and pre-school intellectual attainment: The associations of hyperactivity and conduct problems. *Journal of Child Psychology and Psychiatry, 35,* 949–960.

Sonuga-Barke, E. J., Taylor, E., Sembi, S., & Smith, J. (1992). Hyperactivity and delay aversion: I. The effective delay on choice. *Journal of Child Psychology and Psychiatry in Allied Disciplines, 33,* 387–398.

Sood, R. K., Kirkwood, C. K., & Sood, B. (1994). MPH and thrombocytosis [Letters to the editor]. *Journal of the American Academy of Child and Adolescent Psychiatry, 33,* 592–593.

Soorani-Lunsing, R. J., Hadders-Algra, M., Loinga, A. A., Huisjes, H. J., & Touwen, B. C. L. (1993). Is minor neurological dysfunction at 12 years related to behaviour and cognition? *Developmental Medicine and Child Neurology, 35,* 321–330.

Sparrow, S., Balla, D., & Cicchetti, D. (1984). *Vineland adaptive behavioral scales.* Circle Pines, MN. American Guidance Service.

Speltz, M. L., Varley, C. K., Peterson, K., & Beilke, R. L. (1988). Effects of dextroamphetamine and contingency management on a preschooler with ADHD and oppositional defiant disorder. *Journal of American Academy of Child Adolescent Psychiatry, 27,* 175–178.

Spence, S. H. (1994). Practitioner review: Cognitive therapy with children and adolescents: From theory to practice. *Journal of Child Psychology and Psychiatry, 27,* 381–386.

Spencer, T. J., & Biederman, J. (1992). Growth deficits and desipramine: Reply. *Journal of the American Academy of Child and Adolescent Psychiatry, 31*(6), 1168.

Spencer, T. J., Biederman, J., Kerman, K., Steingard, R., & Wilens, T. (1993). Desipramine treatment of children with attention-deficit hyperactivity disorder and tic disorder or Tourette's syndrome. *Journal of the American Academy of Child and Adolescent Psychiatry, 32,* 354–360.

Spencer, T. J., Biederman, J., Steingard, R., & Wilens, T. (1993). Bupropion exacerbates tic in children with attention-deficit hyperactivity disorder and Tourette's syndrome. *Journal of the American Academy of Child and Adolescent Psychiatry, 32*(1), 211–214.

Spencer, T. J., Biederman, J., & Wilens, T. (1994). Clinical perspectives: Tricyclic antidepressant treatment of children with ADHD and tic disorders. *Journal of the American Academy of Child and Adolescent Psychiatry, 33,* 1203–1204.

Spencer, T. J., Biederman, J., Wilens, T., Steingard, R., & Geist, D. (1993). Nortriptyline treatment of children with attention deficit hyperactivity disorder and tic disorder or Tourette's syndrome. *Journal of the American Academy of Child and Adolescent Psychiatry, 32,* 205–210.

Spencer, T. J., Biederman, J., Wright, V., & Danon, M. (1992). Growth deficits in children treated with desipramine: A controlled study. *Journal of the American Academy of Child and Adolescent Psychiatry, 31,* 235–243.

Spinelli, C. G. (1997). Accommodating the adolescent with attention deficit disorder: The role of the resource center teacher. *Journal of Attention Disorders, 1,* 209–216.

Spitzer, R. L., Davies, M., & Barkley, R. A. (1990). The *DSM III-R* field trial of disruptive behavior disorders. *Journal of the American Academy of Child and Adolescent Psychiatry, 29,* 690–697.

Spivack, G., Platt, J. J., & Shure, M. B. (1976). *The problem-solving approach to adjustment.* San Francisco: Jossey-Bass.

Spivack, G., & Shure, M. B. (1974). *Social adjustment of young children: A cognitive approach to solving real-life problems.* San Francisco: Jossey-Bass.

Spivack, G., & Shure, M. B. (1982). The cognition of social adjustment: Interpersonal cognitive problem-solving thinking. In B. B. Lahey & A. E. Kazdin (Eds.), *Advances in clinical child psychology* (Vol. 5, pp. 323–372). New York: Plenum Press.

Sprafkin, J., & Gadow, K. (1987). An observational study of emotionally disturbed and learning-disabled children in school settings. *Journal of Abnormal Child Psychology, 15,* 393–408.

Sprafkin, J., & Gadow, K. D. (1993). Four reported cases of methylphenidate induced tic exacerbation: Methodological and clinical doubts. *Journal of Child and Adolescent Psychopharmacology, 3,* 231–244.

Sprafkin, J., & Gadow, K. D. (1996). *Early childhood inventories manual.* Stony Brook, NY: Checkmate Plus.

Sprafkin, J., Grayson, P., Gadow, K. D., Nolan, E. E., & Paolicelli, L. M. (1986). *Code for observing social activity (COSA).* Stony Brook: State University of New York, Department of Psychiatry and Behavioral Science.

Sprafkin, J., Loney, J., & Gadow, K. D. (1982). *SLUG Checklist.* Stony Brook, NY: Department of Psychiatry, State University of New York.

Sprague, R. L., & Sleator, E. K. (1977). Methylphenidate in hyperkinetic children: Differences in dose effects on learning and social behavior. *Science, 198,* 1274–1276.

Sprich-Buckminster, S., Biederman, J., Milberger, S., Faraone, S. V., & Lehman, B. K. (1993). Are perinatal complications relevant to the manifestation of ADD? Issues of comorbidity and familiality. *Journal of the American Academy of Child and Adolescent Psychiatry, 32,* 1032–1037.

Spring, C., Blundin, D., Greenberg, L. M., & Yellin, A. M. (1977). Validity and norms of a hyperactivity rating scale. *Exceptional Children, 11,* 313–321.

Spring, C., Yellin, A. M., & Greenberg, L. M. (1976). Effects of imipramine and methylphenidate on perceptual-motor performance of hyperactive children. *Perceptual and Motor Skills, 43,* 459–470.

Srinivas, N. R., Hubbard, J. W., Quinn, D., & Korchinski, E. D. (1991). Extensive and emantioselective presystemic metabolism of DL-threo-methylphenidate in humans. *Progress in Neuro-Psychopharmacology and Biological Psychiatry, 15,* 213–220.

Stanford, L. D., & Hynd, G. W. (1994). Congruence of behavioral symptomatology in children with ADD/H, ADD/WO, and learning disabilities. *Journal of Learning Disabilities, 27,* 243–253.

Stanford, M. S., & Barratt, E. S. (1992). Impulsivity and the multi-impulsive personality disorder. *Personality and Individual Differences, 13,* 831–834.

Stanton, R. D., & Brumback, R. A. (1981). Non-specificity of motor hyperactivity as a diagnostic criterion. *Perceptual Motor Skills, 52,* 323–332.

Stark, K., & Montel, H. (1973). Involvement of a-receptors in clonidine-induced inhibition of transmitter release from central monoamine neurons. *Neuropharmacology, 12,* 1073–1080.

Stark, K. D. (1990). *Childhood depression: School-based interventions.* New York: Guilford Press.

Stark, K. D., Rouse, L. W., & Livingston, R. (1991). Treatment of depression during childhood and adolescence: Cognitive-behavioral procedures for the individual and family. In P. C. Kendall (Ed.), *Child and adolescent therapy: Cognitive-behavioral procedures* (pp. 165–206). New York: Guilford Press.

Stedman, J. M., Lawlis, G. F., Cortner, R. H., & Achterberg, G. (1978). Relationships between WISC-R factors. Wide-range achievement test scores, and visual-motor maturation in children referred for psychological evaluation. *Journal of Consulting and Clinical Psychology, 46,* 869–872.

Stein, M. (1997). We have tried everything and nothing works: Family-centered pediatrics and clinical problem solving. *Journal of Developmental and Behavioral Pediatrics, 18,* 114–119.

Stein, M. A., Szumowski, E., Blondis, T. A., & Roizen, N. J. (1995). Adaptive skills dysfunction in ADD and ADHD children. *Journal of Child Psychology and Psychiatry and Allied Disciplines, 36,* 663–670.

Stein, M. A., Weiss, R. E., & Refetoff, S. (1995). Neuro-cognitive characteristics of individuals with resistance to thyroid hormone: Comparisons with individuals with ADHD. *Developmental and Behavioral Pediatrics, 16,* 406–411.

Steinberg, G. G., Troshinsky, C., & Steinberg, H. R. (1971). Dextroamphetamine responsive behavior disorder in school children. *American Journal of Psychiatry, 128,* 174–179.

Steinberg, L., Dornbusch, S. M., & Brown, B. B. (1992). Ethnic differences in adolescent achievement. An ecological perspective. *American Psychologist, 47,* 723–729.

Steinberg, L., Elmen, J., & Mounts, N. (1989). Authoritative parenting, psychosocial maturity, and academic success among adolescents. *Child Development, 60,* 1424–1436.

Steinberg, L., Lamborn, S. D., Darling, N., Mounts, N. S., & Dornbusch, S. M. (1994). Overtime changes in adjustment and competence among adolescents from authoritative, authoritarian, indulgent and neglectful families. *Child Development, 65,* 754–770.

Steinberg, L., Mounts, N., Lamborn, S., & Dornbusch, S. (1991). Authoritative parenting and adolescent adjustment across various ecological niches. *Journal of Research on Adolescence, 1,* 19–36.

Steingard, R., Biederman, J., Doyle, A., & Sprich-Buckminster, S. (1992). Psychiatric comorbidity in attention deficit disorder: Impact on the interpretation of child behavior checklist results. *Journal of the American Academy of Child and Adolescent Psychiatry, 31,* 449–454.

Steingard, R., Biederman, J., Spencer, T., Wilens, T., & Gonzalez, R. (1993). Comparison of clonidine response in the treatment of attention-deficit hyperactivity disorder with and without comorbid tic disorders. *Journal of the American Academy of Child and Adolescent Psychiatry, 32,* 350–353.

Steingard, R. J., Goldberg, M., Lee, D., & DeMaso, D. R. (1994). Case study: Adjunctive clonazepam treatment of tic symptoms in children with comorbid tic disorders and ADHD. *Journal of the American Academy of Child and Adolescent Psychiatry, 33,* 394–399.

Steinhausen, H. C., Williams, J., & Spohr, H. L. (1993). Long-term psychopathological and cognitive outcome of children with fetal alcohol syndrome. *Journal of the American Academy of Child and Adolescent Psychiatry, 32,* 990–994.

Stephens, R. S., Pelham, W. E., & Skinner, R. (1984). State-dependent and main effects of methylphenidate and pemoline on paired-associate learning and spelling in hyperactive children. *Journal of Consulting and Clinical Psychology, 52,* 104.

Stephens, T. M. (1981). *Technical manual: Social behavior assessment.* Columbus, OH: Cedars Press.

Stephens, T. M., & Arnold, K. D. (1992). *Social behavior assessment inventory: Professional manual.* Odessa, FL: Psychological Assessment Resources.

Sternbach, H. (1981). Pemoline induced mania. *Biological Psychiatry, 16,* 987–989.

Stevens, T. M., Kupst, M. J., Suran, B. G., & Schulman, J. L. (1978). Activity level: A comparison between actometer scores and observer ratings. *Journal of Abnormal Child Psychology, 6,* 163–173.

Stevenson, J. (1992). Evidence for a genetic etiology in hyperactivity in children. *Behavioral Genetics, 22,* 337–344.

Stevenson, J. (1994). *Genetics of ADHD.* Paper presented at the annual meeting of the Professional Group for ADD and Related Disorders, London.

Stevenson, J., Pennington, B. F., Gilger, J. W., DeFries, J. C., & Gillis, J. J. (1993). Hyperactivity and spelling disability: Testing for shared genetic aetiology. *Journal of Child Psychology and Psychiatry, 34,* 1137–1152.

Stevenson, J., Richman, N., & Graham, P. (1985). Behaviour problems and language abilities at three year and behavioural deviance at eight years. *Journal of Child Psychology and Psychiatry, 26,* 215–230.

Stevenson, R. S., Pelham, W., & Skinner, R. (1984). Dependent and main effects of methylphenidate and pemoline on paired associate learning and spelling in hyperactive children. *Journal of Counseling and Clinical Psychology, 52,* 104–113.

Steward-Pinkman, S. M. (1989). Attention deficit disorder: A toxic response to ambient cadmium air pollution. *International Journal of Biosocial Medical Research, 11*(2), 134–143.

Stewart, K. G., & McLaughlin, T. F. (1992). Self-recording: Effects of reducing off-task behavior with a high school student with an attention deficit hyperactivity disorder. *Child and Family Behavior Therapy, 14,* 53–59.

Stewart, K. G., & McLaughlin, T. F. (1993). Self-recording: Effects of reducing off task behavior with a high school student with an attention deficit hyperactivity disorder: Erratum. *Child and Family Behavior Therapy, 15,* 106.

Stewart, M. A. (1980). Genetic, perinatal, and constitutional factors in minimal brain dysfunction. In H. E. Rie & E. D. Rie (Eds.), *Handbook of minimal brain dysfunctions.* New York: Wiley.

Stewart, M. A., Cummings, C., Singer, S., & DeBlois, C. S. (1981). The overlap between hyperactive and unsocialized aggressive children. *Journal of Child Psychology and Psychiatry, 22,* 35–45.

Stewart, M. A., DeBlois, C. S., & Cummings, C. (1980). Psychiatric disorders in parents of hyperactive boys and those with conduct disorder. *Journal of Child Psychology and Psychiatry, 21,* 283–292.

Stewart, M. A., & Olds, S. W. (1973). *Raising a hyperactive child.* New York: Harper & Row.

Stewart, M. A., Thatch, B. T., & Freidin, M. R. (1970). Accidental poisoning in the hyperactive child syndrome. *Diseases of the Nervous System, 31,* 403–407.

Still, G. F. (1902). The Coulstonian lectures on some abnormal physical conditions in children. *Lancet, 1,* 1008–1012.

Stogdill, R. M. (1936). Experiments in the measurement of attitudes towards children: 1899–1935. *Child Development, 7,* 31–36.

Stokes, T. R., & Baer, D. M. (1977). An implicit technology of generalization. *Journal of Applied Behavior Analysis, 10,* 349–367.

Stokes, T. F., & Osnes, P. G. (1989). An operant pursuit of generalization. *Behavior Therapy, 20,* 337–355.

Stolzenberg, J., & Cherkes-Julkowski, M. (1991). Attention deficit disorder: Is it a learning disability or related disorder? [Comment]. *Journal of Learning Disabilities, 24,* 194–195.

Stoner, G., & Carey, S. P. (1992). Serving students diagnosed with ADD: Avoiding deficits in professional attention. *School Psychology Quarterly, 7,* 302–307.

Stoner, S. B., & Glynn, M. A. (1987). Cognitive styles of school-age children showing attention deficit disorders with hyperactivity. *Psychological Reports, 61,* 119–125.

Storch, D. D. (1997). Safety of combined pharmacotherapy [Letter to the editor]. *Journal of the American Academy of Child and Adolescent Psychiatry, 36*(11), 1489–1490.

Stormont-Spurgin, M., & Zentall, S. S. (1995). Contributing factors in the manifestation of aggression in preschoolers with hyperactivity. *Journal of Child Psychology and Psychiatry in Allied Disciplines, 36,* 491–509.

Stowitschek, J., & Stowitschek, C. (1984). Once more with feeling: The absence of research on teacher use of microcomputers. *Exceptional Educational Quarterly, 4,* 13.

Strain, P., Guralnick, M., & Walker, H. M. (1986). *Children's social behavior.* New York: Academic Press.

Strain, P. S., Kerr, M. A., & Ragland, E. U. (1979). Effects of peer-mediated social initiations and prompting/reinforcement procedures on the social behavior of autistic children. *Journal of Autism and Developmental Disabilities, 9,* 41–54.

Strain, P. S., Lambert, D. L., Kerr, M. M., Stagg, V., & Lenkner, D. A. (1993). Naturalistic assessment of children's compliance to teachers' requests and consequences for compliance. *Journal of Applied Behavior Analysis, 16,* 243–249.

Strain, P. S., Shores, R. E., & Timm, M. A. (1977). Effects of peer social initiations on the behavior of withdrawn preschool children. *Journal of Applied Behavior Analysis, 10,* 289–298.

Strauss, A. A., & Kephart, N. C. (1947). *Psychopathology and education of the brain-injured child* (Vol. 2). New York: Grune and Stratton.

Strauss, A. A., & Kephart, N. C. (1955). *Psychopathology and education of the brain injured child: Vol. 2. Progress in theory and clinic.* New York: Grune and Stratton.

Strauss, A. A., & Lehtinen, L. E. (1947). *Psychopathology and education of the brain injured child.* New York: Grune and Stratton.

Strauss, M. A., & Gelles, R. J. (1990). How violent are American families? Estimates from the National Violence Survey and other studies. In M. A. Strauss & R. J. Gelles (Eds.), *Physical violence in American families.* New Brunswick, NJ: Transaction Books.

Strayhorn, J. M., Rapp, N., Donina, W., & Strain, P. S. (1988). Randomized trial of methylphenidate for an autistic child. *Journal of American Academy of Child and Adolescent Psychiatry, 27,* 244–247.

Strayhorn, J. M., & Weidman, C. S. (1989). Reduction of attention deficit and internalizing symptoms in preschoolers through parent-child interaction training. *Journal of the American Academy of Child and Adolescent Psychiatry, 28,* 888–896.

Strayhorn, J. M., & Weidman, C. S. (1991). Follow-up one year after parent-child interaction training. The effects on behavior of pre-school children. *Journal of the American Academy of Child and Adolescent Psychiatry, 30,* 138–143.

Streissguth, A. P., Bookstein, F. L., Sampson, P. D., & Barr, H. M. (1995). Attention: Prenatal alcohol and continuities of vigilance and attention problems from 4 through 14 years. *Development and Psychopathology, 7,* 419–446.

Strober, M. (1992). Relevance of early age-of-onset in genetic studies of bipolar affective disorder. *Journal of the American Academy of Child and Adolescent Psychiatry, 31,* 606–610.

Stroop, J. R. (1935). Studies of interference in serial verbal reactions. *Journal of Experimental Psychology, 18,* 643–661.

Strub, R. L., & Black, F. W. (1977). *The mental status examination in neurology.* Philadelphia: Davis.

Sullivan, A., Kelso, J., & Stewart, M. A. (1990). Mothers' views on the ages of onset for four childhood disorders. *Child Psychiatry and Human Development, 20,* 269–278.

Sullivan, E. V., Mathalon, D. H., Zipursky, R. B., Kersteen-Tucker, Z., Knight, R. T., & Pfefferbaum, A. (1993). Factors of the Wisconsin card sorting test as measures of frontal lobe function in schizophrenia and in chronic alcoholism. *Psychiatry Research, 46,* 175–199.

Sullivan, M. A., & O'Leary, S. G. (1990). Maintenance following reward and cost token programs. *Behavior Therapy, 21,* 139–149.

Sulzer-Azaroff, B., & Mayer, G. R. (1977). *Applying behavior-analysis procedures with children and youth.* New York: Holt, Rinehart and Winston.

Sulzer-Azaroff, B., & Mayer, G. R. (1991). *Behavior analysis for lasting change.* Fort Worth, TX: Holt, Rinehart and Winston.

Sumner, G. S., Mandoki, M. W., & Matthews-Ferrari, K. (1993). Case study: A psychiatric population of prenatally cocaine-exposed children. *Journal of the American Academy of Child and Adolescent Psychiatry, 32,* 1003–1006.

Sunder, T. R., DeMarco, S., Fruitiger, A. D., & Levey, B. (1988, September). *A developmental right hemisphere deficit syndrome in childhood.* Presentation made at the seventeenth national meeting of the Child Neurology Society, Halifax, Canada.

Svensson, P. W., & Hill, M. A. (1990). Interrater reliability of the Koppitz developmental scoring method in the clinical evaluation of the single case. *Perceptual and Motor Skills, 70,* 615–623.

Swain, A. M., & Zentall, S. S. (1990). Behavioral comparisons of liked and disliked hyperactive children in play contexts and the behavioral accommodations by their classmates. *Journal of Consulting and Clinical Psychology, 58,* 197–209.

Swanson, H. L. (1993). A developmental study of vigilance in learning disabled children. *Journal of Abnormal Psychology, 11,* 415–429.

Swanson, J. M. (1985). Measures of cognitive functioning appropriate use in pediatric psychopharmacological research studies. *Psychopharmacology Bulletin, 21,* 887.

Swanson, J. M. (1988). Discussion. In J. F. Kavanaugh & T. J. Truss (Eds.), *Learning disabilities: Proceedings of the national conference,* (pp. 542–546). Parkton, MD: York Press.

Swanson, J. M. (1997). Hyperkinetic disorders and attention deficit hyperactivity disorders. *Current Opinion in Psychiatry, 10,* 300–305.

Swanson, J. M., Cantwell, D., Lerner, M., McBurnett, K., & Hanna, G. (1991). Effects of stimulant medication on learning in children with ADHD. *Journal of Learning Disabilities, 24,* 219–230.

Swanson, J. M., Flockhart, D., Udrea, D., Cantwell, D., Connor, D., & Williams, L. (1995). Clonidine in the treatment of ADHD: Questions about safety and efficacy [Letter to the editor]. *Journal of Child and Adolescent Psychopharmacology, 5,* 301–304.

Swanson, J. M., & Kinsbourne, M. (1979). The cognitive effects of stimulant drugs on hyperactive children. In G. A. Hale (Ed.), *Attention and cognitive development.* New York: Plenum Press.

Swanson, J. M., & Kinsbourne, M. (1980). Food dyes impair performance of hyperactive children on a laboratory learning test. *Science, 207,* 1485–1487.

Swanson, J. M., Kinsbourne, M., Roberts, W., & Zucker, K. (1978). Time-response analysis of the effect of stimulant medication on the learning ability of children referred for hyperactivity. *Pediatrics, 61,* 21–29.

Swanson, J. M., Lerner, M., & Williams, I. (1995). More frequent diagnosis of attention deficit hyperactivity disorder. *New England Journal of Medicine, 333,* 944.

Swanson, J. M., Sandman, C. A., Deutsch, C., & Baren, M. (1983). Methyphenidate hydrochloride given with or before breakfast: I. Behavioral, cognitive and electrophysiological effects. *Pediatrics, 72,* 49.

Swenson, C. C., & Kennedy, W. A. (1995). Perceived control and treatment outcome with chronic adolescent defenders. *Adolescence, 30,* 565–578.

Sykes, D. H., Douglas, V. I., Weiss, G., & Minde, K. K. (1971). Attention in hyperactive children and the effect of methylphenidate (ritalin). *Journal of Child Psychology and Psychiatry and Allied Disciplines, 12,* 129–139.

Sylvester, C. E., Hyde, T. S., & Reichsler, R. J. (1987). The diagnostic interview schedule for children and personality inventory for children in studies of children at risk for anxiety disorders or depression. *Archives of General Psychiatry, 26,* 676–688.

Szatmari, P., Boyle, M., & Offord, D. R. (1989). ADHD and conduct disorder: Degree of diagnostic overlap and differences among correlates. *Journal of the American Academy of Child and Adolescent Psychiatry, 28,* 865–872.

Szatmari, P., Boyle, M. H., & Offord, D. R. (1993). Familial, aggregation of emotional and behavioral problems of childhood in the general population. *American Journal of Psychiatry, 150,* 1398–1403.

Szatmari, P., Offord, D. R., & Boyle, M. H. (1989a). Ontario child health study: Prevalence of attention deficit disorder with hyperactivity. *Journal of Child Psychology and Psychiatry, 30,* 219–230.

Szatmari, P., Offord, D. R., & Boyle, M. H. (1989b). Correlates, associated impairments and patterns of service utilization of children with attention deficit disorder: Findings from the Ontario child health study. *Journal of Child Psychology and Psychiatry, 30,* 205–217.

Szatmari, P., Offord, D. R., Siegel, L. S., Finlayson, M. A., & Tuff, L. (1990). The clinical significance of neurocognitive impairments among children with psychiatric disorders: Diagnosis and situational specificity. *Journal of Child Psychology and Psychiatry and Allied Disciplines, 31,* 287–299.

Szatmari, P., Saigal, S., Rosenbaum, P., Campbell, D., & King, S. (1990). Psychiatric disorders at five years among children with birth weights <1000g: A regional perspective. *Developmental Medicine and Child Neurology, 32,* 954–962.

Tallmage, J., & Barkley, R. A. (1983). The interactions of hyperactive and normal boys with their fathers and mothers. *Journal of Abnormal Child Psychology, 11,* 565–580.

Tannock, R., Purvis, K. L., & Schachar, R. J. (1993). Narrative abilities in children with attention deficit hyperactivity disorder and normal peers. *Journal of Abnormal Child Psychology, 21,* 103–117.

Tannock, R., & Schachar, R. (1992). Methylphenidate and cognitive preversvation in hyperactive children. *Journal of Child Psychology and Psychiatry and Allied Disciplines, 33,* 1217–1228.

Tannock, R., Schachar, R. J., Carr, R. P., & Logan, G. D. (1989). Dose-response effects of methylphenidate on academic performance and overt behavior in hyperactive children. *Pediatrics, 84,* 648–657.

Tannock, R., Schachar, R. J., & Logan, G. D. (1993). Does methylphenidate induce overfocusing in hyperactive children? *Journal of Clinical Child Psychology, 22,* 28–41.

Tansey, M. A. (1985). Brainwave signatures: An index reflective of the brain's functional neuroanatomy. *International Journal of Psychophysiology, 3,* 89–99.

Tant, J. L., & Douglas, V. I. (1982). Problem solving in hyperactive, normal and reading-disabled boys. *Journal of Abnormal Child Psychology, 10,* 285–306.

Tao, K. T. (1992). Clinical comment: Hyperactivity and attention deficit disorder syndromes in China. *Journal of the American Academy of Child and Adolescent Psychiatry, 31,* 1165–1166.

Tarnowski, K. J., & Nay, S. M. (1989). Locus of control in children with learning disabilities and hyperactivity: A subgroup analysis. *Journal of Learning Disabilities, 22,* 381–399.

Tarnowski, K. J., Prinz, R. J., & Nay, S. M. (1986). Comparative analysis of attentional deficits in hyperactive and learning disabled children. *Journal of Abnormal Psychology, 95,* 341–345.

Tarver-Behring, S., Barkley, R. A., & Karlsson, J. (1985). The mother-child interactions of hyperactive boys and their normal siblings. *American Journal of Orthopsychiatry, 355,* 202–209.

Tawney, J. W., & Gast, D. L. (1984). *Applied behavior analysis for teachers.* Columbus, OH: Merrill.

Taylor, D. C., Szatmari, P., Boyle, M. H., & Offord, D. R. (1996). Somatization and the vocabulary of everyday bodily experiences and concerns: A community study of the adolescents. *Journal of the American Academy of Child and Adolescent Psychiatry, 35,* 491–499.

Taylor, E. (1980). Development of attention. In M. Rutter (Ed.), *Scientific foundations of developmental psychiatry.* London: Heinemann Medical Books.

Taylor, E. (1986). Attention deficit. In E. A. Taylor (Ed.), *The overactive child.* London: MacKeith Press.

Taylor, E. (1989). On the epidemiology of hyperactivity. In T. Sagvold & T. Archer (Eds.), *Attention deficit disorder and hyperkinetic syndrome* (pp. 31–52). Hillsdale, NJ: Erlbaum.

Taylor, E., Chadwick, O., Heptinstall, E., & Danckarets, M. (1996). Hyperactivity and conduct problems as risk factors for adolescent development. *Journal of the American Academy of Child and Adolescent Psychiatry, 35,* 1213–1226.

Taylor, E., Everitt, B., Thorley, G., Schachar, R., Rutter, M., & Wieselberg, M. (1986). Conduct disorder and hyperactivity: II. A cluster analytic approach to the identification of a behaviorally syndrome. *British Journal of Psychology, 149,* 768–777.

Taylor, E., Sandberg, S., Thorley, G., & Giles, S. (1991). *The epidemiology of childhood hyperactivity.* New York: Oxford University Press.

Taylor, E., Schachar, R., Thorley, G., & Wieselberg, M. (1986). Conduct disorder and hyperactivity: I. Separation of hyperactivity and antisocial conduct in British child psychiatric patients. *British Journal of Psychiatry, 149,* 760–767.

Taylor, M. J., Voros, J. G., Logan, W. J., & Malone, M. A. (1993). Changes in event-related potentials with stimulant medication in children with attention deficit hyperactivity disorder. *Biological Psychology, 36,* 139–156.

Teeter, P. A. (1991). Attention deficit hyperactivity disorder: A psychoeducational paradigm. *School Psychology Review, 20,* 266–280.

Teeter, P. A., & Semrud-Clikeman, M. (1995). Integrating neurobiological, psychosocial, and behavioral paradigms: A transactional model for the study of ADHD. *Archives of Clinical Neuropsychology, 10,* 433–461.

Teicher, M. H., Ito, Y., Glod, C. A., & Barber, N. (1996). Objective measurement of hyperactivity and attentional problems in ADHD. *Journal of the American Academy of Child and Adolescent Psychiatry, 35,* 334–342.

Telzrow, C. F., & Speer, B. (1986). Learning disabled children: General instructions for maximizing instruction. *Techniques: A Journal for Remedial Education and Counseling, 2,* 341–352.

Terestman, N. (1980). Mood quality and intensity in nursery school children as predictors of behavior disorder. *American Journal of Orthopsychiatry, 50,* 125–138.

Thapar, A., Hervas, A., & McGuffin, P. (1995). Childhood hyperactivity scores are highly heritable and show sibling competition effects: Twin study evidence. *Behavioral Genetics, 25,* 537–544.

Thares, V. (1992). Where's poppa? The relative lack of attention to the role of fathers in child and adolescent psychopathology. *American Psychologist, 47,* 656–664.

Thomas, A., & Chess, S. (1977). *Temperament and development.* New York: Brunner/Mazel.

Thomas, B. H., Byrne, C., Offord, D. R., & Boyle, N. H. (1991). Prevalence of behavioral symptoms in the relationship of child, parent and family variables in 4- and 5-year-olds: Results from the Ontario child health study. *Developmental and Behavioral Pediatrics, 12,* 177–184.

Thomas, D. R., Becker, W. C., & Armstrong, M. (1968). Production and elimination of disruptive classroom behavior by systematically varying teacher's behavior. *Journal of Applied Behavior Analysis, 1,* 35–45.

Thompson, J., Ross, R., & Horwitz, S. (1980). The role of computed tomography in the study of children with minimal brain dysfunction. *Journal of Learning Disabilities, 13,* 48–51.

Thompson, L. L., Riggs, P. D., Mikulich, S. K., & Crowley, T. J. (1996). Contribution of ADHD symptoms in substance problems and delinquency in conduct-disordered adolescents. *Journal of Abnormal Child Psychology, 24,* 325–347.

Thorley, G. (1984). Review of follow-up and follow-back studies of childhood hyperactivity. *Psychological Bulletin, 96,* 116–132.

Thorndike, R. L., Hagen, E. P., & Satler, J. M. (1986). *Revised Stanford Binet intelligence scale.* Boston: Houghton Mifflin.

Timmermans, S. R., & Christensen, B. (1991). The measurement of attention deficits in TBI children and adolescents. *Cognitive Rehabilitation, 9,* 26–31.

Tingelstad, J. B. (1991). The cardiotoxicity of the tricyclics (clinical comment). *Journal of the American Academy of Child and Adolescent Psychiatry, 30,* 845–846.

Tipper, S. P. (1985). The negative priming effect: Inhibitory priming by ignored objects. *Quarterly Journal of Experimental Psychology, 37,* 571–590.

Tirosh, E., Sadeh, A., Munvez, R., & Lavie, P. (1993). Effects of methylphenidate on sleep in children with attention-deficit hyperactivity disorder: An active monitor study. *American Journal of Diseases in Children, 147,* 1313–1315.

Titchener, E. B. (1924). *A textbook of psychology.* New York: Macmillan.

Tobin, E. K., & Selby, M. J. (1995, November). *Memory functioning in children with learning disorder and ADHD.* Paper presented at the annual meeting of the National Academy of Neuropsychology, San Francisco.

Todd, R., Neuman, R., Geller, B., Fox, L., & Hickok, J. (1993). Genetic studies of affective disorders: Should we be starting with childhood onset probands? *Journal of the American Academy of Child and Adolescent Psychiatry, 32,* 1164–1171.

Tofte-Tipps, S., Mendonca, P., & Peach, R. V. (1982). Training and generalization of social skills: A study with two developmentally handicapped, socially isolated children. *Behavior Modification, 6,* 45–71.

Tolan, P. H., & Lorion, R. P. (1988). Multivariate approaches to the identification of delinquency proneness in adolescent males. *American Journal of Community Psychology, 16,* 547–561.

Tomasson, K., & Kuperman, S. (1990). Bipolar disorder in a prepubescent child. *Journal of the American Academy of Child and Adolescent Psychiatry, 29,* 308–310.

Tomc, S. A., Williamson, N. K., & Pauli, R. M. (1991, Fall). Temperament in Williams Syndrome. *Williams Syndrome Association National Newsletter,* 32–39.

Torgersen, J. K., & Wagner, R. K. (1992). Language abilities, reading acquisition, and developmental dyslexia: Limitations and alternative views. *Journal of Learning Disabilities, 25,* 577–581.

Touwen, B. C. L., & Kalverboer, A. F. (1973). Neurologic and behavioral assessment of children with minimal brain dysfunction. *Seminars in Psychiatry, 5,* 79–94.

Towe, R., & Frame, C. L. (1991, September 18–21). *Six-year predictive validity of attention deficit disorder without hyperactivity (ADD-H).* Paper submitted for poster presentation at the Conference of Children with Attention Deficit Disorders (CH.A.D.D.) in Washington, DC.

Tracy, P. E., Wolfgang, M. E., & Figlio, R. M. (1990). *Delinquency careers in two birth cohorts.* New York: Plenum Press.

Trapani, C., & Gettinger, M. (1996). Treatment of students with learning disabilities. In M. Reineke, F. Dattilio, & A. Freeman (Eds.), *Cognitive therapy with children and adolescents: A casebook for clinical practice* (pp. 251–277). New York: Guilford Press.

Trennery, M. R., Crosson, B., DeBoe, J., & Leber, W. R. (1989). *The Stroop neuropsychological screening test.* Odessa, FL: Psychological Assessment Resources.

Tripp, G., & Luk, S. L. (1997). The identification of pervasive hyperactivity: Is clinic observation necessary? *Journal of Child Psychology and Psychiatry in Allied Disciplines, 38,* 219–234.

Trites, R. (1979). Prevalence in hyperactivity in Ottawa, Canada. In R. Trites (Ed.), *Hyperactivity in children.* Baltimore: University Park Press.

Trites, R. L., Blouin, A. G. A., & Laprade, K. (1982). Factor analysis of the Conners teacher rating scale based on a large normative sample. *Journal of Consulting and Clinical Psychology, 50,* 615–623.

Trites, R. L., & LaPrade, K. (1983). Evidence for an independent syndrome of hyperactivity. *Journal of Child Psychology and Psychiatry, 24,* 573–586.

Trommer, B. L., Bernstein, L. P., Rosenberg, R. S., & Armstrong, K. J. (1988, September). *Topographic mapping of P300 in attention deficit disorder.* Presentation made at the seventeenth national meeting of the Child Neurology Society, Halifax, Canada.

Trommer, B. L., Hoeppner, J. B., Lorber, R., & Armstrong, K. (1988). Pitfalls in the use of a continuous performance test as a diagnostic tool in attention deficit disorder. *Developmental and Behavioral Pediatrics, 9,* 339–346.

Trommer, B. L., Hoeppner, J. B., & Zecker, S. G. (1991). The go-no go test in attention deficit disorder is sensitive to methylphenidate. *Journal of Child Neurology, 6*(Suppl.), S128–S131.

Tronick, E. Z., Frank, D. A., Cabral, H., Mirochnick, M., & Zuckerman, B. (1996). Late dose-response effects of prenatal cocaine exposure on newborn neurobehavioral performance. *Pediatrics, 98,* 76–83.

Trott, G. E., Friese, H. J., Menzel, M., & Nissen, G. (1992). Use of moclobemide in children with attention deficit hyperactivity disorder. *Psychopharmacology, 106,* 134–136.

Tryon, G. S. (1997). The use of activity monitors in the assessment of attention deficit hyperactivity disorder. *School Psychologist, 51,* 1–16.

Tryon, W. W. (1984). Principles and methods of mechanically measuring motor activity. *Behavioral Assessment, 6,* 129–140.

Tryon, W. W. (1993). The role of motor excess and instrumented activity measurement in attention deficit hyperactivity disorder. *Behavior Modification, 17,* 371–406.

Tryon, W. W., & Pinto, L. P. (1994). Comparing activity measurements and ratings. *Behavior Modification, 18,* 251–261.

Tscheann, J. M., Kaiser, P., Chesney, N. A., Alkon, A., & Boyce, W. T. (1996). Resilience and vulnerability among preschool children: Family function, temperament and behavior problems. *Journal of the American Academy of Child and Adolescent Psychiatry, 35,* 184–192.

Tupin, J. R. (1972). Lithium use in non-manic depressive conditions. *Comprehensive Psychiatry, 13,* 209–214.

Turecki, S. (1989). The difficult child center. In W. B. Carey & S. C. McDevitt (Eds.), *Clinical and educational applications of temperament research* (pp. 141–153). Berwin, PA: Swets North American.

Turkewitz, H., O'Leary, K. D., & Ironsmith, M. (1975). Generalization and maintenance of appropriate behavior through self-control. *Journal of Consulting and Clinical Psychology, 43,* 577–583.

Twardosz, S., & Sajwaj, T. (1972). Multiple effects of a procedure to increase sitting in a hyperactive retarded boy. *Journal of Applied Behavior Analysis, 5,* 73–78.

Ullman, D. G., Barkley, R. A., & Brown, H. W. (1978). The behavioral symptoms of hyperkinetic children who successfully responded to stimulant drug treatment. *American Journal of Orthopsychiatry, 48,* 425–437.

Ullmann, R. K., & Sleator, E. (1985). Attention deficit disorder. Children with or without hyperactivity. Which behaviors are helped by stimulants? *Clinical Pediatrics, 24,* 547–551.

Ullmann, R. K., & Sleator, E. (1986). Responders, nonresponders, and placebo responders among children with attention deficit disorder. Importance of blinded placebo evaluation. *Clinical Pediatrics, 25,* 594–599.

Ullmann, R. K., Sleator, E. K., & Sprague, R. K. (1985a). *ADD-H: Comprehensive teacher's rating scale.* Champaign, IL: MetriTech.

Ullmann, R. K., Sleator, E. K., & Sprague, R. K. (1985b). Introduction to the use of ACTeRs. *Psychopharmacological Bulletin, 21,* 915–920.

Ullmann, R. K., Sleator, E. K., & Sprague, R. K. (1988). *ADD-H: Comprehensive teacher's rating scale* (2nd ed.). Champaign, IL: MetriTech.

Ullmann, R. K., Sleator, E. K., & Sprague, R. K. (1991). *ADD-H: Comprehensive teacher's rating scale* (Rev. 2nd ed.). Champaign, IL: MetriTech.

Ullmann, R. K., Sleator, E. K., & Sprague, R. K. (1996). *ACTeRS: parent form*. Champaign, IL: MetriTech.

Ullmann, R. K., Sleator, E. K., & Sprague, R. K. (1997). *ADD-H: Comprehensive teacher's rating scale* (2nd ed.). Champaign, IL: MetriTech.

Ultmann, M. H., & Kelly, D. P. (1991). Attention deficits in children with hearing or visual impairments. In P. J. Accardo, T. A. Blondis, & B. Y. Whitman (Eds.), *Attention deficit disorders and hyperactivity in children*. New York: Marcel Dekker.

United Nations. (1989). *Ewing convention on the rights of the child. Adoption of a convention on the rights of the child* (U.N. Document No. A/44/736). New York: Author.

U.S. Department of Education. (1994). *Strong families, strong schools*. Washington, DC: Author.

Urbain, E. S., & Kendall, P. C. (1980). Review of social-cognitive problem-solving interventions with children. *Psychological Bulletin, 88,* 109–143.

Urdan, T., Turner, J., Park, S.-H., & Midgley, C. (1992, April). *Cognitive and motivational orientations of at-risk elementary students: Implications for practice*. Paper presented at the annual meeting of American Educational Research Association, San Francisco.

Urion, D. K. (1988, September). *Attention deficit hyperactivity disorder: Pharmacological response predicted by neurological subtype*. Presentation made at the seventeenth national meeting of the Child Neurology Society, Halifax, Canada.

van Baar, A., & de Graff, B. M. T. (1994). Cognitive development at preschool-age of infants of drug-dependent mothers. *Developmental Medicine and Child Neurology, 36,* 1063–1075.

van den Boom, D. C. (1994). The influence of temperament and mothering on attachment and exploration: An experimental manipulation of sanative responsiveness among lower-class mothers with irritable infants. *Child Development, 65,* 1457–1477.

van den Broek, M. D., Bradshaw, C. M., & Szabadi, E. (1992). Performance of impulse and non-impulsive subjects on two temporal differentiation tasks. *Personality and Individual Differences, 13,* 169–174.

van den Oord, E. J. C. G., & Rowe, D. C. (1997). Continuity and change in children's social maladjustment: A developmental behavior genetic study. *Developmental Psychology, 33,* 319–332.

van der Meere, J. J., & Sergeant, J. (1987). A divided attention experiment with pervasively hyperactive children. *Journal of Abnormal Child Psychology, 15,* 379–391.

van der Meere, J. J., & Sergeant, J. (1988a). Acquisition of attention skill in pervasively hyperactive children. *Journal of Child Psychology and Psychiatry, 29,* 301–310.

van der Meere, J. J., & Sergeant, J. (1988b). Focused attention in pervasively hyperactive children. *Journal of Abnormal Child Psychology, 16,* 627–639.

van der Meere, J. J., & Sergeant, J. (1988c). Controlled processing and vigilance in hyperactivity: Time will tell. *Journal of Abnormal Child Psychology, 16,* 641–655.

van der Meere, J. J., van Baal, M., & Sergeant, J. (1989). The added effect or model. A differential diagnostic tool hyperactivity and learning disability. *Journal of Abnormal Child Psychology, 17,* 409–422.

van der Meere, J. J., Vreeling, H. J., & Sergeant, J. A. (1992). A motor presetting study in hyperactives, learning disabled and control children. *Journal of Child Psychology and Psychiatry, 34,* 1347–1354.

van Engeland, H. (1993). Pharmacotherapy and behaviour therapy—competition or cooperation? *Acta Paedo Psychiatrica, 56,* 123–127.

Van Houten, R., Nau, P. A., MacKenzie-Keating, S. E., Sameoto, D., & Colavecchia, B. (1982). An analysis of some variables influencing the effectiveness of reprimands. *Journal of Applied Behavior Analysis, 15,* 65–83.

Van Zomeren, A. H. (1981). *Reaction time and attention after closed head injury.* Lisse, Switzerland: Swets & Zeitlinger.

Van Zomeren, A. H., & Brouwer, W. H. (1987). Head injury and concepts of attention. In H. S. Levin, J. Grafman, & H. M. Eisenberg (Eds.), *Neurobehavioral recovery from head injury.* New York: Oxford University Press.

Varley, C. K. (1984). Diet and the behavior of children with attention deficit disorder. *Journal of the American Academy of Child Psychiatry, 23,* 182–185.

Varni, J. W., & Henker, B. (1979). A self-regulation approach to the treatment of three hyperactive boys. *Child Behavior Therapy, 1,* 171–191.

Varni, J. W., & Setoguchi, Y. (1993). Effects of parental adjustment on the adaptation of children with congenital or acquired limb deficiencies. *Developmental and Behavioral Pediatrics, 14,* 13–20.

Vaughn, V. (1969). Growth and development. In W. Nelson (Ed.), *Textbook of pediatrics* (9th ed.). Philadelphia: Saunders.

Velez, C. N., Johnson, J., & Cohen, P. (1989). A longitudinal analysis of selected risk factors for childhood psychopathology. *Journal of the American Academy of Child and Adolescent Psychiatry, 28,* 861–864.

verFaellie, M., & Heilman, K. M. (1987). Response preparation and response inhibition after lesions of the mesial frontal lobe. *Archives of Neurology, 44,* 1265–1271.

Verhulst, F. C., Koot, H. M., & van der Ende, J. (1994). Differential predictive value of parents' and teachers' reports of children's problem behaviors: A longitudinal study. *Journal of Abnormal Child Psychology, 22,* 531–546.

Verhulst, F. C., & van der Ende, J. (1993). Six year stability of problem behavior in an epidemiological sample. *Journal of Abnormal Child Psychology, 21,* 307–324.

Verhulst, F. C., & van der Ende, J. (1995). The eight-year stability of problem behavior in an epidemiological sample. *Pediatric Research, 38,* 612–617.

Vincent, J., Varley, C. K., & Leger, P. (1990). Effects of methylphenidate on early adolescent growth. Clinical and research reports. *American Journal of Psychiatry, 147,* 501–502.

Vincent, J. P., Williams, B. J., Harris, G. E., & Duval, G. C. (1981). Classroom observation of hyperactive children: A multiple validation study. In K. D. Gadow & J. Loney (Eds.), *Psychosocial aspects of drug treatment for hyperactivity.* Boulder, CO: Westview Press.

Virginia Department of Education. (1992). *Attention deficit hyperactivity disorder and the schools: Task force report.* Commonwealth of Virginia.

Virkkunen, M., & Penttinen, H. (1984). Serum cholesterol in aggressive conduct disorder: A preliminary study. *Biological Psychiatry, 19*(3), 435–439.

Vitazro, F., Tremblay, R. E., & Gagnon, C. (1995). Teacher ratings of children's behaviors and teachers' management styles: A research note. *Journal of Child Psychology and Psychiatry and Allied Disciplines, 36,* 887–898.

Vitiello, B., Ricciuti, A. J., Stoff, D. M., Behar, D., & Denckla, M. B. (1989). Reliability of subtle (soft) neurological signs in children. *Journal of the American Academy of Child and Adolescent Psychiatry, 28,* 749–753.

Vitiello, B., & Stoff, D. M. (1997). Subtypes of aggression and their relevance to child psychiatry. *Journal of the American Academy of Child and Adolescent Psychiatry, 36,* 307–315.

Vitiello, B., Stoff, D. M., Atkins, M., & Mahoney, A. (1990). Soft neurological signs and impulsivity in children. *Developmental and Behavioral Pediatrics, 11,* 112–115.

Voelker, S. L., Carter, R. A., Sprague, D. J., Gadowski, C. L., & Lachar, D. (1989). Developmental trends in memory and metamemory in children with attention deficit disorder. *Journal of Pediatric Psychology, 14,* 75–88.

Voelker, S. L., Lachar, D., & Gadowski, C. L. (1983). The personality inventory for children and response to methylphenidate: Preliminary evidence for predictive utility. *Journal of Pediatric Psychology, 8,* 161–169.

Voeller, K. S. (1986). Right-hemisphere deficit syndrome in children. *American Journal of Psychiatry, 153,* 1004–1009.

Voeller, K. S. (1991). Towards a neurobiologic nosology of attention deficit hyperactivity disorder. *Journal of Child Neurology, 6,* S2–S8.

Voeller, K. S., & Heilman, K. M. (1988, September). *Motor impersistence in children with attention deficit hyperactivity disorder: Evidence for right-hemisphere dysfunction.* Presentation made at the seventeenth national meeting of the Child Neurology Society, Halifax, Canada.

Vygotsky, L. (1962). *Thought and language.* New York: Wiley.

Vyse, S. A., & Rapport, M. D. (1989). The effects of methylphenidate on learning in children with ADDH: The stimulus equivalence paradigm. *Journal of Consulting and Clinical Psychology, 57,* 425–435.

Waddell, K. J. (1984). The self-concept and social adaptation of hyperactive children and adolescents. *Journal of Clinical Child Psychology, 13,* 50–55.

Wadsbuy, M., Lindehammar, H., & Eeg-Olofsson, O. (1989). Neurofibromatosis in childhood: Neuropsychological aspects. *Neurofibromatosis, 2,* 251–260.

Wagner, G., Rabkin, J. G., & Rabkin, R. (1995). Psychostimulant treatment for depression and low energy in patients with late stage HIV. *Psychopharmacology Bulletin, 31,* 628.

Wagonseller, B. R., Burnett, M., Salzberg, B., & Burnett, J. (1977). *The art of parenting: A complete training guide.* Champaign, IL: Research Press.

Wagonseller, B. R., & McDowell, R. L. (1979). *You and your child: A common sense approach to successful parenting.* Champaign, IL: Research Press.

Wagonseller, B. R., & McDowell, R. L. (1982). *Teaching involved parenting.* Champaign, IL: Research Press.

Wahler, R. G. (1980). The insular mother: Her problems in parent-child treatment. *Journal of Applied Behavior Analysis, 13,* 207–219.

Waldman, I. D. (1996). Aggressive boys' hostile, perceptual and response of biases: The role of attention and impulsivity. *Child Development, 67,* 1015–1033.

Waldman, I. D., & Lilienfeld, S. O. (1991). Diagnostic efficiency of symptoms for oppositional defiant disorder and attention-deficit hyperactivity disorder. *Journal of Consulting and Clinical Psychology, 59,* 732–738.

Walker, C. J., & Clement, P. W. (1992). Treating inattentive, impulsive, hyperactive children with self-modeling and stress inoculation training. *Child and Family Behavior Therapy, 14,* 75–85.

Walker, H., & McConnell, S. (1988). *Walker-McConnell scale of social competence.* Austin, TX: Pro-Ed.

Walker, H. M., & Buckley, N. K. (1973). Teacher attention to appropriate and inappropriate classroom behavior: An individual case study. *Focus on Exceptional Children, 5,* 5–11.

Walker, H. M., & Severson, H. (1988). *Systematic screening for behavior disorders assessment system.* Longmont, CO: Sopris West.

Walker, H. M., Greenwood, C. R., Hops, H., & Todd, N. M. (1979). Differential effects of reinforcing topographic components of social interaction: Analysis and direct replication. *Behavior Modification, 3,* 291–321.

Walker, H. M., McConnell, S., Holmes, D., Todis, B., Walker, J., & Golden, N. (1983). *The Walker social skills curriculum: The ACCEPTS program.* Austin, TX: Pro-Ed.

Walker, H. M., Todis, B., Holmes, D., & Horton, G. (1988). *The Walker social skills curriculum: The ACCESS program.* Austin, TX: Pro-Ed.

Walker, H. M., & Walker, J. E. (1991). *Coping with non-compliance in the classroom.* Austin, TX: Pro-Ed.

Walker, J. E., & Shea, T. M. (1991). *Behavior management: A practical approach for educators.* New York: Macmillan.

Walker, J. L., Lahey, B. B., Hynd, G. W., & Frame, C. L. (1987). Comparison of specific patterns of antisocial behavior in children with conduct disorder with or without coexisting hyperactivity. *Journal of Consulting and Clinical Psychology, 55,* 910–913.

Walker, M. K., Sprague, R. L., Sleator, E. K., & Ullman, R. K. (1988). Effects of methylphenidate hydrochloride on the subjective reporting of mood in children with attention deficit disorder. *Issues in Mental Health Nursing, 9,* 385.

Walkup, J. T. (1995, September–October). Methylphenidate and clonidine. *AACAP News,* 11–15.

Wallander, J. L., Schroeder, S. R., Michelli, J. A., & Gualitieri, C. T. (1987). Classroom social interactions of attention deficit disorder with hyperactivity children as a function of stimulant medication. *Journal of Pediatric Psychology, 12,* 61–76.

Walsh, B. T., Giardina, E. V., Sloan, R. P., Greenhill, L., & Goldfein, J. (1994). Effects of desipramine on autonomic control of the heart. *Journal of the American Academy of Child and Adolescent Psychiatry, 33,* 191–197.

Walters, A. S., & Barrett, R. P. (1993). The history of hyperactivity. In J. L. Matson (Ed.), *Handbook of hyperactivity in children.* Needham Heights, MA: Allyn & Bacon.

Walther, M., & Beare, P. (1991). The effect of videotape feedback on the on-task behavior of a student with emotional/behavioral disorders. *Education and Treatment of Children, 14,* 53–60.

Waltz, G. (1990). Change in response to pemoline at puberty. *American Journal of Psychiatry, 147*(3), 368.

Wandless, R. L., & Prinz, R. J. (1982). Methodological issues in conceptualizing and treating childhood social isolation. *Psychological Bulletin, 92,* 39–55.

Warren, D. H. (1984). *Blindness and early childhood development* (2nd ed., rev.). New York: American Foundation for the Blind.

Warren, R. P., Odell, J. D., Warren, L. W., Burger, R. A., Maciulis, A., Daniels, W. W., & Torres, A. R. (1995). Reading disability: Attention-deficit hyperactivity disorder and the immune system. *Science, 268,* 786–787.

Warren, S. B. (1992). Lower threshold for referral for psychiatric treatment for adopted adolescents. *Journal of the American Academy of Child and Adolescent Psychiatry, 31,* 512–517.

Wartner, U. G., Grossmann, K., Fremmer-Bomvik, E., & Suess, G. (1994). Attachment patterns at age six in South Germany: Predictability from infancy and implications for preschool behavior. *Child Development, 65,* 1014–1027.

Waslick, B. (1995). Cardiac effects of desipramine [Letters to the editor]. *Journal of the American Academy of Child and Adolescent Psychiatry, 34,* 125.

Wasserman, R. C., Diblasio, C. M., Bond, L. A., Young, P. C., & Colletti, R. B. (1990). Infant temperament and school age behavior: Six year longitudinal study in a pediatric practice. *Pediatrics, 85,* 801–807.

Webb, T. E., & Oski, F. A. (1973). Iron deficiency anemia may affect scholastic achievement in young adolescents. *Journal of Pediatrics, 82,* 827–829.

Webb, T. E., & Oski, F. A. (1974). Behavioral status of young adolescents with iron deficiency anemia. *Journal of Special Education, 2,* 153–156.

Webster, C. D., & Jackson, M. A. (1997). *Impulsivity: Theory, assessment and treatment.* New York: Guilford Press.

Webster-Stratton, C. W. (1985). The effects of father involvement in parent training for conduct problem children. *Journal of Child Psychology and Psychiatry, 26,* 801–810.

Webster-Stratton, C. W. (1991). Strategies for helping families of conduct disordered children. *Journal of Child Psychology and Psychiatry, 32,* 1047–1062.

Webster-Stratton, C. W., & Hammond, M. (1990). Predictors of treatment outcome in parent training for families with conduct problem children. *Behavior Therapy, 21,* 319–337.

Webster-Stratton, C., & Spitzer, A. (1991). Development, reliability and validity of the daily telephone discipline interview. *Behavioral Assessment, 13,* 221–239.

Wechsler, D. (1958). *The measurement and appraisal of adult intelligence* (4th ed.). Baltimore: Williams & Wilkins.

Wechsler, D. (1974). *Wechsler intelligence scale for children* (3rd ed., rev.). New York: Psychological Corporation.

Wechsler, D. (1989). *Wechsler intelligence scale for children* (3rd ed.). San Antonio, TX: Psychological Corporation.

Wehrli, K. (1971). *A self-instruction workbook for visual accuracy.* Worthington, OH: Ann Arbor.

Weinberg, W. A. (1986). *Primary disorder of vigilance.* Dallas, TX: Children's Medical Center, Pediatric Neurology.

Weinberg, W. A., & Brumback, R. A. (1992). The myth of attention-deficit hyperactivity disorder: Symptoms resulting from multiple causes. *Journal of Child Neurology, 7,* 431–445.

Weinberg, W. A., & Emslie, G. H. (1991). Attention deficit hyperactivity disorder: The differential diagnosis. *Journal of Child Neurology, 6*(Suppl.), S23–S36.

Weinberg, W. A., McLean, A., & Snider, R. L. (1989). Depression, learning disability and school behavior problems. *Psychological Report, 64,* 275–283.

Weiner, B. (1979). A theory of motivation for some classroom experiences. *Journal of Educational Psychology, 71,* 3–25.

Weiner, I. B. (1990). Distinguishing healthy from disturbed adolescent development. *Developmental and Behavioral Pediatrics, 11,* 151–154.

Weingartner, H., Rapoport, J. L., Buchsbaum, M. S., Bunney, W., Mikkelson, E. J., & Caine, E. D. (1980). Cognitive processes in normal and hyperactive children and their response to amphetamine treatment. *Journal of Abnormal Psychology, 89,* 25–37.

Weintraub, S., & Mesulam, M. M. (1983). Developmental learning disabilities of the right hemisphere. *Archives of Neurology, 40,* 463–468.

Weiss, B., & Laties, V. G. (1962). Enhancement of human performance by caffeine and the amphetamines. *Pharmacology Review, 14,* 1.

Weiss, G. (1985). Hyperactivity: Overview and new directions. *Psychiatric Clinics of North America, 8,* 737–753.

Weiss, G., & Hechtman, L. (1979). The hyperactive child syndrome. *Science, 205,* 1348–1354.

Weiss, G., & Hechtman, L. (1986). *Hyperactive children grown up.* New York: Guilford Press.

Weiss, G., & Hechtman, L. (1993). *Hyperactive children grown up: ADHD in children, adolescents and adults* (2nd ed.). New York: Guilford Press.

Weiss, G., Hechtman, L., & Perlman, T. (1978). Hyperactives as young adults: Social, employer and self-rating scales obtained during ten-year follow-up evaluation. *American Journal of Orthopsychiatry, 48,* 438–445.

Weiss, G., Kurger, E., Danielson, U., & Elman, M. (1975). Effect of long-term treatment of hyperactive children with methylphenidate. *CMA Journal, 112,* 159–163.

Weiss, G., Minde, K., Werry, J. S., Douglas, V. I., & Nemeth, E. (1971). Studies on the hyperactive child: VII. Five-year follow-up. *Archives of General Psychiatry, 24,* 409–414.

Weissberg, R. P. (1985). Designing effective social problem-solving programs for the classroom. In B. H. Schneider, K. H. Rubin, & J. E. Ledingham (Eds.), *Children's peer relations: Issues in assessment and intervention* (pp. 225–242). New York: Springer-Verlag.

Weissberg, R. P., Caplan, M., & Sivo, P. J. (1989). A new conceptual framework for establishing school-based social competence promotion programs. In L. A. Bond & B. E. Compas (Eds.), *Primary prevention and promotion in schools.* Newbury Park, CA: Sage.

Weissberg, R. P., Ruff, H. A., & Lawson, K. R. (1990). The usefulness of reaction timed tasks in studying attention and organization of behavior in young children. *Developmental and Behavioral Pediatrics, 11,* 59–64.

Weissman, M., Gershorn, E., & Kidd, K. (1984). Psychiatric disorders in relatives of probands with affective disorders. *Archives of General Psychiatry, 41,* 13–21.

Welsch, E. B. (1974, February). You may not know it, but your school probably is deeply into the potentially dangerous business of teaching with drugs. *American School Board Journal,* 41–45.

Welsh, M. C., Pennington, B. F., & Groisser, D. D. (1991). A normative developmental study of executive function. A window on pre-frontal function in children. *Developmental Neuropsychology, 7,* 131–149.

Wendel, M. H., Nelson, W. M., Politano, P. M., Mayhal, C. A., & Finch, A. J. (1988). Differentiating inpatient clinically-diagnosed and normal children using the children's depression inventory. *Child Psychiatry and Human Development, 19,* 98–108.

Wender, E. H. (1986). The food additive-free diet in the treatment of behavior disorders: A review. *Developmental and Behavioral Pediatrics, 7,* 35–42.

Wender, E. H. (1995). Attention deficit hyperactivity disorders in adolescence. *Developmental and Behavioral Pediatrics, 16,* 192–195.

Wender, P. H. (1971). *Minimal brain dysfunction in children.* New York: Wiley.

Wender, P. H. (1972). The minimal brain dysfunction syndrome in children. *Journal of Nervous and Mental Disease, 155,* 55–71.

Wender, P. H. (1975). The minimal brain dysfunction syndrome. *Annual Review of Medicine, 26,* 45–62.

Wender, P. H. (1979). The concept of adult minimal brain dysfunction. In L. Bellak (Ed.), *Psychiatric aspects of minimal brain dysfunction in adults.* New York: Grune and Stratton.

Wender, P. H. (1987a). Differential diagnosis of hyperactivity. *Developmental and Behavioral Pediatrics, 8,* 166–167.

Wender, P. H. (1987b). *The hyperactive child, adolescent and adult.* New York: Oxford University Press.

Wender, P. H., & Solanto, M. V. (1991). Effects of sugar on aggressive and inattentive behavior in children with attention deficit disorder with hyperactivity and normal children. *Pediatrics, 88,* 960–966.

Werner, E. E. (1994). Overcoming the odds. *Developmental and Behavioral Pediatrics, 15,* 131–136.

Werner, E. E., Bierman, J. M., French, F. E., Simonian, K., Connor, A., Smith, R. S., & Campbell, M. (1968). Reproductive and environmental casualties: A report on the 10-year follow up of the children of the Kauai pregnancy study. *Pediatrics, 42,* 112–127.

Werner, E. E., & Smith, R. S. (1977). *Kauai's children come of age.* Honolulu: University of Hawaii Press.

Werner, E. E., & Smith, R. S. (1992). *Overcoming the odds: High risk children from birth to adulthood.* Ithaca, NY: Cornell University Press.

Werry, J. S. (1968). Developmental hyperactivity. *Pediatric Clinics of North America, 15,* 581–599.

Werry, J. S. (1978). Measures in pediatric psychopharmacology. In J. S. Werry (Ed.), *Pediatric psychopharmacology: The use of behavior modifying drugs in children.* New York: Brunner/Mazel.

Werry, J. S. (1988). In memoriam—*DSM-III* [Letter to the editor]. *Journal of the American Academy of Child and Adolescent Psychiatry, 27,* 138–139.

Werry, J. S. (1993). Diagnosis. In J. L. Matson (Ed.), *Handbook of hyperactivity in children.* Needham Heights, MA: Allyn & Bacon.

Werry, J. S., Aman, M. G., & Lampen, E. (1975). Haloperidol and methylphenidate in hyperactive children. *ACTA Paedopsychiatrica, 42,* 26–40.

Werry, J. S., Elkind, G. S., & Reeves, J. C. (1987). Attention deficit, conduct, oppositional and anxiety disorders in children: III. Laboratory differences. *Journal of Abnormal Child Psychology, 15,* 409–428.

Werry, J. S., Minde, K., Guzman, A., Weiss, G., Dogan, K., & Hoy, E. (1972). Studies on the hyperactive child: VII. Neurological status compared with neurotic and normal children. *American Journal of Orthopsychiatry, 42,* 141–149.

Werry, J. S., Reeves, J. C., & Elkind, G. S. (1987). Attention deficit, conduct, oppositional, and anxiety disorders in children: I. A review of research on differentiating characteristics. *Journal of the American Academy of Child and Adolescent Psychiatry, 26,* 133–143.

West, R. P., & Sloan, H. N. (1986). Teacher presentation rate and point delivery rate. *Behavior Modification, 10,* 267–286.

West, S. A., McElroy, S. M., Strakowski, P. E., Keck, B. J., & McConville, B. (1994). The co-occurrence of attention deficit hyperactivity disorder in adolescent mania. *Psychopharmacology Bulletin, 30,* 729.

West, S. A., McElroy, S., Strakowski, S., Keck, P., & McConville, B. (1995). Attention deficit hyperactivity disorder in adolescent mania. *American Journal of Psychiatry, 152,* 271–274.

West, S. A., Sax, J. W., Keck, P. E., Strakowski, S. M., & McElroy, S. L. (1995). Thyroid function studies in acutely manic adolescents with and without attention deficit hyperactivity disorder (ADHD). *Psychopharmacology Bulletin, 31,* 630.

West, S. A., Strakowski, S. M., Sax, J. W., McElroy, S. L., & Keck, P. E. (1995). The comorbidity of attention-deficit hyperactivity disorder in adolescent mania: Potential diagnosis and treatment implications. *Psychopharmacology Bulletin, 31,* 347–351.

Westby, C. E., & Cutler, S. K. (1994). Language and ADHD: Understanding the basis and treatment of self-regulatory deficits. *Topics and Language Disorders, 14,* 58–76.

Westerman, M. A. (1990). Coordination of maternal directives with preschoolers' behavior in compliance problem and healthy dyads. *Developmental Psychology, 26,* 621–630.

Weynandt, L. L. (1995). Reported prevalence of attention difficulties in a general sample of college students. *Journal of Psychopathology and Behavioral Assessment, 17,* 293–304.

Whalen, C. K. (1990). Attention deficit and hyperactivity disorders. In T. H. Ollendick & M. Hersen (Eds.), *Handbook of child and adolescent assessment.* New York: Plenum Press.

Whalen, C. K., Collins, B. E., Henker, B., Alkus, S. R., Adams, D., & Stapp, S. (1978). Behavior observations of hyperactive children and methylphenidate (Ritalin) effects in systematically structured classroom environments: Now you see them, now you don't. *Journal of Pediatric Psychology, 3,* 177–184.

Whalen, C. K., & Henker, B. (1976). Psychostimulants and children: A review and analysis. *Psychological Bulletin, 83,* 1113–1130.

Whalen, C. K., & Henker, B. (1980). The social ecology of psychostimulant treatment: A model for conceptual and empirical analysis. In C. K. Whalen & B. Henker (Eds.), *Hyperactive children: The social ecology of identification and treatment.* New York: Academic Press.

Whalen, C. K., & Henker, B. (1985). The social worlds of hyperactive (ADDH) children. *Clinical Psychology Review, 5,* 447–478.

Whalen, C. K., & Henker, B. (1991). Therapies for hyperactive children: Comparisons, combinations and compromises. *Journal of Consulting and Clinical Psychology, 59,* 126–137.

Whalen, C. K., Henker, B., Buhrmester, D., Hinshaw, S. P., Huber, A., & Laski, K. (1989). Does stimulant medication improve the peer status of hyperactive children? *Journal of Consulting and Clinical Psychology, 57,* 545–549.

Whalen, C. K., Henker, B., Castro, J., & Granger, D. (1987). Peer perceptions of hyperactivity and medication effects. *Child Development, 58,* 816–828.

Whalen, C. K., Henker, B., Collins, B. E., Finck, D., & Dotemoto, S. (1979). A social ecology of hyperactive boys: Medication effects in structured classroom environments. *Journal of Applied Behavior Analysis, 12,* 65–81.

Whalen, C. K., Henker, B., Collins, B., McAuliffe, S., & Vaux, A. (1979). Peer interaction in a structured communication task: Comparisons of normal and hyperactive boys and of methylphenidate (Ritalin) and placebo effects. *Child Development, 50,* 388–401.

Whalen, C. K., Henker, B., & Dotemoto, S. (1980). Methylphenidate and hyperactivity: Effects on teacher behavior. *Science, 13,* 1280–1282.

Whalen, C. K., Henker, B., & Dotemoto, S. (1981). Teacher response to methylphenidate (Ritalin) versus placebo status of hyperactive boys in the classroom. *Child Development, 52,* 1005–1014.

Whalen, C. K., Henker, B., & Granger, D. A. (1990). Social judgment processes in hyperactive boys: Effects of methylphenidate and comparisons with normal peers. *Journal of Abnormal Child Psychology, 18,* 297–316.

Whalen, C. K., Henker. B., & Hinshaw, S. P. (1985). Cognitive-behavioral therapies for hyperactive children: Premises, problems and prospects. *Journal of Abnormal Child Psychology, 13,* 391–410.

Whalen, C. K., Henker, B., Hinshaw, S. P., Heller, T., & Huber-Dressler, A. (1991). Messages of medication: Effects of actual versus informed medication status on hyperactive boy's expectancies and self-evaluations. *Journal of Consulting and Clinical Psychology, 59,* 602–606.

Whalen, C. K., Henker, B., Swanson, J. M., Granger, D., Kliewer, W., & Spencer, J. (1987). Natural social behaviors in hyperactive children: Dose effects of methylphenidate. *Journal of Consulting and Clinical Psychology, 55,* 187–193.

Wheeler, J., & Carlson, C. L. (1994). The social functioning of children with ADD with hyperactivity and ADD without hyperactivity: A comparison of their peer relations and social deficits. *Journal of Emotional and Behavioral Disorders, 2,* 2–12.

Wheldall, K., & Larn, Y. Y. (1987). Rows vs. tables: The effects of two classroom seating arrangements on classroom disruption rate, on task behavior and teacher behavior. *Educational Psychology, 7,* 303–312.

Wherry, J. N., Paal, N., Jolly, J. B., & Adam, B. (1993). Concurrent and discriminant validity of the Gordon diagnostic system: A preliminary study. *Psychology in the Schools, 30,* 29–36.

Whimbey, A., & Lochhead, J. (1986). *Problem solving and comprehension.* Hillsdale, NJ: Erlbaum.

White, A. G., & Bailey, J. S. (1990). Reducing disruptive behaviors of elementary physical education students with sit and watch. *Journal of Applied Behavior Analysis, 23,* 353–359.

White, J., Moffit, T. E., Earles, F., Robins, L., & Silva, P. (1990). How early can we tell? Predictors of childhood conduct disorder and adolescent delinquency. *Criminology, 28,* 507–533.

White, M. A. (1975). Natural rates of teacher approval and disapproval in the classroom. *Journal of Applied Behavior Analysis, 8,* 367–372.

Whitehead, P. L., & Clark, L. D. (1970). Effect of lithium carbonate, placebo and thyridizine on hyperactive children. *Medical Journal of Psychiatry, 127,* 824–825.

Whitehill, M. B., Hersen, M., & Bellack, A. S. (1980). Conversational skills training for socially isolated children. *Behavior Research Therapy, 12,* 217–225.

Whitehouse, D., Shah, U., & Palmer, F. B. (1980). Comparison of sustained release and standard methylphenidate in the treatment of minimal brain dysfunction. *Journal of Clinical Psychiatry, 41,* 282–285.

Whitman, B. Y., & Smith, C. (1991). In P. J. Accardo, T. A. Blondis, & B. Y. Whitman (Eds.), *Attention deficit disorders and hyperactivity in children.* New York: Marcel Dekker.

Whitmont, S., & Clark, C. (1996). Kinesthetic acuity and fine motor skills in children with ADHD: A preliminary report. *Developmental Medicine and Child Neuropsychology, 38,* 1091–1098.

Whitmore, E. W., Kramer, J. R., & Knutson, J. F. (1993). The association between punitive childhood experiences and hyperactivity. *Child Abuse and Neglect, 17,* 357–366.

Wiederholt, J. L., & Bryant, B. R. (1992). *Gray oral reading tests revised.* Austin, TX: Pro-Ed.

Wielkiewicz, R. M. (1990). Interpreting low scores on the WISC-R third factor: It's more than distractibility. *Psychological Assessment: A Journal of Consulting and Clinical Psychology, 2,* 91–97.

Wielkiewicz, R. M., & Daood, C. J. (1993). Correlations between WISC-R subtests and scales of the personality inventory for children. *Psychological Report, 73,* 1343–1346.

Wielkiewicz, R. M., & Palmer, C. M. (1996). Can the WISC-R/WISC-III third factor help in understanding ADHD? *The ADHD Report, 4,* 4–6.

Wilens, T. E., & Biederman, J. (1992). The stimulants. *Psychiatric Clinics of North America,* 191–122.

Wilens, T. E., Biederman, J., & Spencer, T. (1994). Clinical perspectives: Clonidine for sleep disturbances associated with attention-deficit hyperactivity disorder. *Journal of the American Academy of Child and Adolescent Psychiatry, 33,* 424–426.

Wilens, T. E., Steingard, R., & Biederman, J. (1992). Clomipramine for comorbid conditions. *Journal of the American Academy of Child and Adolescent Psychiatry, 31*(1), 171.

Wilkenson, D. (1993). *Wide range achievement test* (Rev.). Wilmington, DE: Jastak Associates.

Wilkinson, P. C., Kircher, J. C., McMahon, W. M., & Sloane, H. N. (1995). Effects of methylphenidate on reward strength in boys with attention-deficit hyperactivity disorder. *Journal of the American Academy of Child and Adolescent Psychiatry, 34,* 897–901.

Willerman, L. (1973). Activity level and hyperactivity in twins. *Child Development, 44,* 288–293.

Williams, C. A., & Forehand, R. (1984). An examination of predictor variables for child compliance and non-compliance. *Journal of Abnormal Child Psychology, 12,* 491–504.

Williams, C. D. (1959). The elimination of tantrum behaviors by extinction procedures. *Journal of Abnormal and Social Psychology, 59,* 269–270.

Williams, D. T., Mehl, R., Yudofsky, S., Adams, D., & Roseman, B. (1982). The effect of propranolol on uncontrolled rage outbursts in children and adolescents with organic brain dysfunction. *Journal of the American Academy of Child and Adolescent Psychiatry, 21,* 129–135.

Williams, M. C., Littell, R. R., Reinosos, C., & Greve, K. (1994). Effect of wavelength on performance of attention-discovered and normal children on the Wisconsin card sorting test. *Neuropsychology, 8,* 187–193.

Wilson, J. M., & Kiessling, L. S. (1988). What is measured by the Conners' teacher behavior rating scale? Replication of factor analysis. *Journal of Developmental and Behavioral Pediatrics, 9,* 271–278.

Wilson, J. M., & Marcotte, A. C. (1995, November 3). *Adolescent outcome of childhood diagnosis of ADD as a function of psychostimulant usage.* Poster presented at the 15th annual meeting of the National Academy of Neuropsychologists, San Francisco, CA.

Wilson, L. J., & Jennings, J. N. (1996). Parents' acceptability of alternative treatments for attention-deficit hyperactivity disorder. *Journal of Attention Disorders, 1,* 114–121.

Winnicott, D. W. (1974). *Pediatrics through psychoanalysis: The collective papers of D.W. Winnicott.* New York: Basic Books.

Winokur, G., Coryell, W., Endicott, J., & Akiskal, H. (1993). Further distinction between manic-depressive illness and primary depressive disorder. *American Journal of Psychiatry, 150,* 1176–1181.

Winsberg, B. G., Camp-Bruno, J. A., Vink, J., Timmer, C. J., & Sverd, J. (1987). Mianserin pharmacokinetics and behavior in hyperkinetic children. *Journal of Clinical Psychopharmacology, 7,* 143–147.

Winsberg, B. G., Maitinsky, S., Kupietz, S., & Richardson, E. (1987). Is there dose dependent tolerance associated with chronic methylphenidate therapy in hyperactive children: Oral dose of plasma concentrations. *Psychopharmacology Bulletin, 23,* 107–110.

Winsberg, B. G., Maitinsky, S., Richardson, E., & Kupietz, S. S. (1988). Effects of methylphenidate on achievement in hyperactive children with reading disorders. *Psychopharmacology Bulletin, 24,* 238–241.

Winsberg, D. J., Kupietz, S. S., Sverd, J., Hungdung, B. L., & Young, N. L. (1982). Methylphenidate oral dose plasma concentrations and behavioral response in children. *Psychopharmacology, 76,* 329–332.

Wirt, R. D., Lacher, D., Klinedinst, J. K., & Seat, P. D. (1977). *Multi-dimensional description of child personality: A manual for the personality inventory for children.* Los Angeles: Western Psychological Services.

Witt, J. C., Hannafin, M. J., & Martens, B. K. (1983). Home-based reinforcement: Behavioral covariation between academic performance and inappropriate behavior. *Journal of School Psychology, 21,* 337–348.

Wolff, P. H. (1969). The natural history of crying and other vocalizations in early infancy. In B. M. Foss (Ed.), *Determinants of infant behavior* (Vol. 4). London: Methuen.

Wolraich, M. L., Drummond, T., Salomon, M., O'Brien, M., & Sivage, C. (1978). Effects of methylphenidate alone and in combination with behavior management of hyperactive children. *Journal of Abnormal Child Psychology, 6,* 149–161.

Wolraich, M. L., Hannah, J. N., Pinnock, T. Y., Baumgaertel, A., & Brown, J. (1996). Comparison of diagnostic criteria for attention-deficit hyperactivity disorder in countrywide sample. *Journal of the American Academy of Child and Adolescent Psychiatry, 35,* 319–324.

Wolraich, M. L., Lindgren, S., Stromquist, A., Milich, R., Davis, C., & Watson, D. (1990). Stimulant medication use by primary care physicians in the treatment of attention deficit hyperactivity disorder. *Pediatrics, 86,* 95–101.

Wolraich, M. L., Lindgren, S. D., Stumbo, P. J., Steginik, L. D., Applebaum, M. I., & Kiritsy, M. C. (1994). Journal article reviews: Effects of diets high in sucrose or aspartame on the behavior and cognitive performance of children. *Developmental and Behavioral Pediatrics, 15,* 23–27.

Wolraich, M. L., Milich, R., Stumbo, P., & Schultz, F. (1985). Effects of sucrose ingestion on the behavior of hyperactive boys. *Journal of Pediatrics, 106,* 675–682.

Woltersdorf, M. A. (1992). Videotape self-modeling in the treatment of attention deficit hyperactivity disorder. *Child and Family Behavior Therapy, 14,* 53–73.

Womack, R. L. (1985). *Creating line designs: Books 1–4.* Bothell, WA: Golden Educational Center.

Wong, B. Y. L. (1992). On cognitive process-based instruction: An introduction. *Journal of Learning Disabilities, 25,* 105–115.

Wood, D., Reimherr, F., & Wender, P. H. (1982). Effects of levodopa on attention deficit disorder, residual type. *Psychiatry Research, 6,* 13–20.

Woodcock, R. W. (1973). *Woodcock reading mastery tests.* Circle Pines, MN: American Guidance Service.

Woodcock, R. W. (1987). *Woodcock reading mastery tests* (Rev.). Circle Pines, MN: American Guidance Services.

Woodcock, R. W. (1989). *Woodcock-Johnson psychoeducational battery* (Rev.). Allen, TX: Teaching Resources.

Woodcock, R. W., & Johnson, M. B. (1987). *Woodcock-Johnson psychoeducational battery.* Hingham, MA: Teaching Resources.

Woodside, D. B., Brownstone, D., & Fisman, S. (1987). The dexamethasone suppression test and the children's depression inventory in psychiatric disorders in children. *Canadian Journal of Psychiatry, 32,* 2–4.

Woolston, J. L., Rosenthal, S. L., Riddle, M. A., Sparrow, S. S., Cicchetti, D., & Zimmerman, L. D. (1989). Childhood comorbidity of anxiety/affective disorders and behavior disorders. *Journal of the American Academy of Child and Adolescent Psychiatry, 28,* 707–713.

Wozniak, J., & Biederman, J. (1994). Prepubertal mania exists (and co-exists with ADHD). *The ADHD Report, 2,* 5–6.

Wozniak, J., Biederman, J., Faraone, S. V., Frazier, J., Kim, J., Millstein, R., Gershon, J., Thornell, A., Cha, K., & Snyder, J. B. (1997). Mania in children with pervasive developmental disorder revisited. *Journal of the American Academy of Child and Adolescent Psychiatry, 36,* 1552–1559.

Wozniak, J., Biederman, J., Kiely, K., Ablon, J. S., Faraone, S. V., Mundy, E., & Mennin, D. (1995). Mania-like symptoms suggestive of childhood-onset bipolar disorder in clinically referred children. *Journal of the American Academy of Child and Adolescent Psychiatry, 34,* 867–876.

Wozniak, J., Biederman, J., Mundy, E., Mennin, D., & Faraone, S. V. (1995). A pilot family study of childhood-onset mania. *Journal of the American Academy of Child and Adolescent Psychiatry, 34,* 1577–1583.

Wright, J. C., & Vliestra, A. G. (1975). The development of selective attention: From perceptual exploration to logical search. In H. W. Reese (Ed.), *Advances in child development and behavior.* New York: Academic Press.

Wright, P. F., Sell, S. H., McConnell, K. B., Sitton, A. B., Thompson, J., Vaughn, W. K., & Bess, F. H. (1988). Impact of recurrent otitis media on middle ear function, hearing and language. *Journal of Pediatrics, 113,* 581.

Wyejartz, P. S., Bair, J. P., Besyner, J. K., Hawks, W. M., & Seidenberg, M. (1996). Assessment of attention deficit hyperactivity disorder in adult alcoholics. *Journal of Attention Disorders, 1,* 87–94.

Wyngaarden, J. B. (1988). Adverse effects of low-level lead exposure on infant development. *Journal of the American Medical Association, 259,* 2524.

Xeanah, C. H., Boris, N. W., & Larrieu, J. A. (1997). Infant development and developmental risk: A review of the past ten years. *Journal of the American Academy of Child and Adolescent Psychiatry, 36,* 165–178.

Yanow, M. (1973). Report on the use of behavior modification drugs on elementary school children. In M. Yanow (Ed.), *Observations from the treadmill.* New York: Viking Press.

Yoshikawa, H. (1994). Prevention as cumulative protection: Effects of early family support in education on chronic delinquency and its risks. *Psychological Bulletin, 115,* 28–54.

Younes, R. P., DeLong, G. R., Nieman, G. W., & Rosner, B. (1986). Manic-depressive illness in children: A quantitative retrospective study of treatment with lithium carbonate. *Journal of Child Neurology, 1,* 364–368.

Ysseldyke, J. E., Algozzine, B., & Thurlow, M. L. (1992). *Critical issues in special education.* Boston, MA: Houghton-Mifflin.

Zachman, L., Husingh, R., & Barrett, M. (1988). *Blooming: Language arts.* Moline, IL: LinguiSystems.

Zachman, L., Jorgenson, C., Barrett, M., Husingh, R., & Snedden, M. K. (1982). *Manual of exercises for expressive reasoning.* Moline, IL: LinguiSystems.

Zabar, R., & Bowers, N. (1983). The effect of time of day on problem solving and classroom behavior. *Psychology in the Schools, 20,* 337–345.

Zagar, R., Arbit, J., Hughes, J. R., Busell, R. E., & Busch, K. (1989). Developmental and disruptive behavior disorders among delinquents. *Journal of the American Academy of Child and Adolescent Psychiatry, 28,* 437–440.

Zahn, T. B., Abate, F., Little, B. C., & Wender, P. H. (1975). Minimal brain dysfunction, stimulant drugs and autonomic nervous system activity. *Archives of General Psychiatry, 32,* 381–387.

Zahn-Waxler, C., Schmitz, S., Fulker, D., Robinson, J., & Ende, R. (1996). Behavior problems in five-year-old monozygotic and dizygotic twins: Genetic and environmental influences, patterns of regulation and internationalization of control. *Developmental Psychopathology, 8,* 103–122.

Zametkin, A. J. (1985). The carrot hypothesis. *Journal of the American Academy of Child Psychiatry, 24,* 240–241.

Zametkin, A. J., Karoum, F., & Rapoport, J. L. (1987). Treatment of hyperactive children with d-phenylalanine. *American Journal of Psychiatry, 144,* 792–794.

Zametkin, A. J., Libenauer, L. L., Fitgerald, G. A., King, A. C., Minkunas, D. V., Herscovitch, P., Yamada, E. M., & Cohen, R. M. (1993). Brain metabolism in teenagers with attention-deficit hyperactivity disorder. *Archives of General Psychiatry, 50,* 333–340.

Zametkin, A. J., Nordahl, T. E., & Gross, M. (1990). Cerebral glucose metabolism adults with hyperactivity in childhood onset. *Archives of General Psychiatry, 50,* 333–340.

Zametkin, A. J., Nordahl, T. E., Gross, M., King, A. C., Semple, W. E., Rumsey, J., Hamburger, S., & Cohen, R. M. (1990). Cerebral glucose metabolism in adults with hyperactivity of childhood onset. *New England Journal of Medicine, 323,* 1361–1366.

Zametkin, A. J., & Rapoport, J. L. (1987). Neurobiology of attention deficit disorder with hyperactivity: Where have we come in 50 years? *Journal of American Academy of Child and Adolescent Psychiatry, 26,* 676–686.

Zametkin, A. J., Reeves, J. C., Webster, L., & Werry, J. C. (1986). Promethazine treatment of children with attention deficit disorder and hyperactivity–ineffective and unpleasant. *Journal of the American Academy of Child Psychiatry, 25,* 854–856.

Zamvil, L. S., Wechsler, V., Frank, A., & Docherty, J. P. (1991). *Post-traumatic stress disorder in hospitalized children and adolescents.* Unpublished manuscript, Nashua Brookside Hospital, Nashua, NH.

Zarski, J. J., Cook, R., West, J., & O'Keefe, S. (1987). Attention deficit disorder: Identification and assessment issues. Identifying children and adolescents in need of mental health services [Special issue]. *American Mental Health Counselors Association Journal, 9,* 5–13.

Zelko, F. A. J. (1991). Comparison of parent-completed behavior rating scales: Differentiating boys with ADD from psychiatric and normal controls. *Developmental and Behavioral Pediatrics, 12,* 31–37.

Zentall, S. S. (1975). Optimal stimulation as theoretical basis of hyperactivity. *American Journal of Orthopsychiatry, 4,* 549–653.

Zentall, S. S. (1984). Context effects in the behavioral ratings of hyperactivity. *Journal of Abnormal Child Psychology, 12,* 345–352.

Zentall, S. S. (1985). Stimulus control factors in search performance of hyperactive children. *Journal of Learning Disabilities, 18,* 480–485.

Zentall, S. S. (1988). Production deficiencies in elicited language but not in the spontaneous verbalizations of hyperactive children. *Exceptional Children, 60,* 143–153.

Zentall, S. S. (1989). Attentional cuing and spelling tasks for hyperactive and comparison regular classroom children. *Journal of Special Education, 23,* 83–93.

Zentall, S. S. (1990). Fact-retrieval automatization and math problem solving by learning disabled, attention disordered, and normal adolescents. *Journal of Educational Psychology, 82,* 856–865.

Zentall, S. S. (1991, September). *Outcomes and remediation of ADHD.* Paper presented at the third annual conference of Children and Adults with Attention Deficit Disorder, Washington, DC.

Zentall, S. S. (1993). Research on the educational implications of attention deficit hyperactivity disorder. Issues in the education of children with attentional deficit disorder [Special issue]. *Exceptional Children, 60,* 143–153.

Zentall, S. S. (1995). Modifying classroom tasks and environments. In S. Goldstein (Ed.), *Understanding and managing children's classroom behavior.* New York: Wiley.

Zentall, S. S., & Dwyer, A. M. (1989). Color effects on the impulsivity and activity of hyperactive children. *Journal of School Psychology, 27,* 165–173.

Zentall, S. S., Falkenberg, S. D., & Smith, L. B. (1985). Effects of color stimulation and information on the copying performance of attention-problem adolescents. *Journal of Abnormal Child Psychology, 13,* 501–511.

Zentall, S. S., & Ferkis, M. A. (1993). Mathematical problem solving for youth with ADHD, with and without learning disabilities. *Learning Disability Quarterly, 16,* 6–18.

Zentall, S. S., Harper, G. W., & Stormont-Spurgin, M. (1993). Children with hyperactivity and their organizational abilities. *Journal of Educational Research, 87,* 112–117.

Zentall, S. S., & Kruczek, T. (1988). The attraction of colors for active attention problem children. *Exceptional Children, 54*(4), 357–362.

Zentall, S. S., & Meyer, M. J. (1987). Self-regulation of stimulation of ADD-H children between reading and vigilance task performance. *Journal of Abnormal Child Psychology, 15,* 519–536.

Zentall, S. S., & Smith, Y. N. (1992). Assessment and validation of the learning and behavioral style of hyperactive children. *Learning and Individual Differences, 4,* 25–41.

Zentall, S. S., Smith, Y. N., Lee, Y. B., & Wieczorek, C. (1994). Mathematical outcomes of attention-deficit hyperactivity disorder. *Journal of Learning Disabilities, 27*(8), 510–519.

Zentall, S. S., & Zentall, T. R. (1983). Optimal stimulation: A model of disordered activity and performance in normal and deviant children. *Psychological Bulletin, 94,* 446–471.

Zentall, S. S., Zentall, T. R., & Barrick, R. B. (1978). Distraction as a function of within-task stimulation for hyperactive and normal children. *Journal of Learning Disabilities, 11,* 13–21.

Ziegler, R., & Holden, L. (1988). Family therapy for learning disabled and attention deficit disordered children. *American Journal of Orthopsychiatry, 58,* 196–210.

Zigler, E. F. (1992). Early childhood intervention: The promising preventative for juvenile delinquency. *American Psychologist, 47,* 997–1006.

Zimmerman, M. A., & Arunkumar, R. (1994). Resiliency research: Implications for schools and policy. *Social Policy Report: Society for Research in Child Development, 8*(4).

Zirkel, P. A. (1992). A checklist for determining legal eligibility of ADD/ADHD students. *Special Educator, 8,* 93–97.

Zito, J. M., Safer, D. J., dos Reis, S., Magder, L. S., & Riddle, M. A. (1997). Methylphenidate patterns among medicaid youths. *Psychopharmacology Bulletin, 33,* 143–147.

Zohar, A. H., Ratzoni, G., Pauls, D. L., Apter, A., Bleich, A., Kron, S., Rappaport, M., Weizman, A., & Cohen, D. J. (1992). An epidemiological study of obsessive-compulsive disorder and related disorders in Israeli adolescents. *Journal of the American Academy of Child and Adolescent Psychiatry, 31,* 1057–1061.

Zuckerman, B., Augustyn, M., Groves, B. M., & Parker, S. (1995). Silent victims revisited: The special case of domestic violence. *Pediatrics, 96,* 511–513.

Author Index

Subject Index